TORT LAW
Cases and Economic Analysis

TORT LAW

Cases and Economic Analysis

RICHARD A. POSNER

Judge, United States Court of Appeals for the Seventh Circuit;
Senior Lecturer, University of Chicago Law School

LITTLE, BROWN AND COMPANY
Boston and Toronto

HAL

Published simultaneously in Canada
by Little, Brown & Company (Canada) Limited
Printed in the United States of America

SUMMARY OF CONTENTS

CONTENTS

PART II   UNINTENTIONAL TORTS   195

standard of care —
obj / subj

judge by jury
logis v. Courts
per se rule

**Chapter 11 Is Tort Liability for Accidental Injuries Worth
              Retaining?**   805'

TABLE OF ILLUSTRATIONS

PREFACE

After 10 years of teaching torts, I have come to believe that torts casebooks (1) are too long and (2) fail to reflect adequately the growing interest in economic analysis of torts questions.

The problem with a long casebook is that most of it cannot be covered in a first-year course (and very few students take a second torts course), unless the cases are studied superficially. As a result, coverage in the normal torts course is woefully incomplete. Students often emerge with no knowledge of such important torts as deceit, defamation, invasion of privacy, nuisance, and intentional infliction of emotional distress, and sometimes without having studied assault and battery either.

One solution to this problem is more careful selection and editing of cases and a steadfast refusal to be drawn into issues that, however interesting and important in their own right, are peripheral to the pedagogical function of the first-year torts course. I have tried to do these things, but I have also made organizational changes designed to allow expanded coverage of the central issues while keeping the book short. First, rather than devote separate chapters to those intentional torts rarely reached in a first-year course, such as defamation, I have included a few cases from these fields in the chapter on the prima facie case of intentional tort. This procedure has the incidental advantage of allowing the student to consider early in his or her study of torts something like the full range of interests protected by tort law. The materials on these torts in this book are too brief to constitute anything more than an introduction, but that seems preferable to having lengthy chapters that are never reached during the course.

Damages is another subject too important to skip because of pressure of time — a common result when a separate chapter is devoted to it. In lieu of such a chapter, I have sprinkled Notes on various aspects of tort damages throughout the book. I have done the same thing with such topics as vicarious liability, liability insurance, tort immunities, and workmen's compensation; the reader is warned, however, that the treatment of these topics is less extensive than in most torts casebooks. Finally, cases on land occupiers' tort liability will be found in the chapter on plaintiff's conduct or status as a bar to or limitation on recovery of damages, rather than in a separate chapter. This is in recognition of the similarity between barring recovery on the ground of contributory negligence and barring it because the victim is a trespasser, licensee, or social guest.

With regard to the second novelty in the book, the treatment of economics, I believe it is now widely recognized that law schools should expose students to the tools of economic analysis that are increasingly being used both to explain and to criticize legal doctrines, including those of tort law. There is less agreement on the best way of introducing economics into the law school curriculum. In teaching torts with heavy emphasis on the economic analysis of tort cases and issues, I have become convinced that it is both feasible and desirable to make economics a component of the first-year torts course. This does not mean turning the torts course into a course in economics. It means discussing economic questions as they arise naturally in the examination of cases.

Heretofore I have been hampered in teaching economic analysis of tort law by the absence of a suitable text. In an effort to meet this need, I have included many economic Notes in this casebook. They do not present economic theory in the abstract; they shun the technical apparatus of economics; they presuppose no prior acquaintance with economics. Rather, they seek to elucidate, in the simplest possible terms, the economic concepts inescapably raised by tort cases and questions. A student who reads and studies these Notes faithfully will not learn economics but will acquire a solid base for further and more systematic study of economics, either on his own or in formal courses, including courses in antitrust law and other fields where economics plays a central role in legal thinking. Most important, the student will acquire a better understanding of the nature and purposes of tort law, a better grasp of the interrelationships among tort doctrines, and a better perspective on the intellectual and policy debates which rage today over the merits of tort law and its alternatives.

C. Paul Rogers III has expressed concern about the "seductive power" of economics introduced into first-year law courses:

> Teachers might well be wary of the seductive power of a theory which seems to offer a comprehensive, logical, "right and wrong" explanation of a discipline otherwise frustratingly inconsistent, chaotic and indefinite. Beginning law students, whose consumption of commercial outlines suggests a certain desperation for unequivocal answers and whose familiarity with doctrine and theory is preliminary, would seem especially vulnerable to the attractions of an exclusively economic description of the law. Moreover, even if the use of economics as an analytical tool can be kept in perspective, the appeal and the methodology of the approach may too easily lead the untrained to a much more controversial normative use of the theory. Professors may reasonably fear that first year law students will be unable to discern and discount what many consider the excesses of economics. . . .
>
> Many legal educators now realize that the economic approach to the law has made and promises to continue to make valuable contributions to our understanding of the formulation of doctrine and that, properly presented,

economics can provide beginning law students with a useful tool of analysis as
well as an early familiarity with an important body of literature. But works that
present an exclusively economic perspective . . . must overcome doubt generated by the excesses of the perspective.

Rogers, Book Review (The Economics of Contract Law, by Kronman and
Posner), 93 Harv. L. Rev. 1039, 1044, 1049-1050 (1980). The present book
does not "present an exclusively economic perspective." Despite the title
("and *Economic* Analysis"), the Notes and other materials introduce the
student to historical, philosophical, and other noneconomic approaches to
tort law and to the literature critical of the economic approach. This book
emphasizes the economic approach, though not to the exclusion of other
approaches, because it has received much less attention from casebook editors than it has from scholars and judges. I heartily agree with Rogers that
"properly presented, economics can provide a useful tool of analysis as well as
an early familiarity with an important body of literature." I am certain that
today's law students are sufficiently independent and tough-minded to resist
any improper seductive allure that economics may hold out to them.

I would like to add a final, personal note. This book was completed and
in page proofs before my recent appointment to the U.S. Court of Appeals
for the Seventh Circuit. It should go without saying that any opinions expressed herein are personal and in no way official.

R.A.P.

December 15, 1981

ACKNOWLEDGMENTS

I taught torts for almost 10 years from the Gregory and Kalven torts casebook and its successor, the Gregory, Kalven, and Epstein casebook. See Cases and Materials on Torts (C. O. Gregory & H. Kalven eds., 2d ed. 1969); Cases and Materials on Torts (C. O. Gregory, H. Kalven & R. A. Epstein eds., 3d ed. 1977). My thinking on the teaching of tort law was heavily influenced by these excellent casebooks, and the structure and selection of materials in the present book owe much to them. I particularly want to thank my colleague Professor Epstein for his assistance and graciousness toward a competitor.

A good deal of the economic analysis of tort law presented in this book draws upon my collaboration with Professor William M. Landes, the Clifton R. Musser Professor of Economics at the University of Chicago Law School, on the economics of tort law. This collaboration has produced several articles on the economics of tort law and also a monograph, tentatively entitled The Economic Structure of Tort Law, which is in progress. I want to take this opportunity to thank Professor Landes for allowing me to include in the Notes in this book economic ideas on tort law that he and I have developed jointly.

Jerry Goldman made a number of helpful suggestions on an earlier draft of this book, and Carole Cook, James Finberg, Susan Gray Hanner, and Edward Wahl provided helpful research assistance.

I should also like to thank the following authors and publishers of copyrighted materials for reprint permission:

Baker, An Introduction to English Legal History, 2d ed. Published by Butterworth Law Publishers, London. Copyright © 1979 by Butterworth Law Publishers, London. Reprinted by permission.

Calabresi, The Costs of Accidents: A Legal and Economic Analysis. Published by Yale University Press. Copyright © 1970 by Yale University Press. Reprinted by permission.

Holmes, The Common Law. Published by Little, Brown and Company. Copyright © 1881 by Little, Brown and Company.

Horwitz, The Transformation of American Law, 1780-1860. Published by Harvard University Press. Copyright © 1977 by the President and Fellows of Harvard College. Reprinted by permission.

Prosser, Handbook of the Law of Torts, 4th ed. Published by West Publishing Company. Copyright © 1971 by West Publishing Company. Reprinted by permission of the publisher.

Ross, Settled Out of Court: The Social Process of Insurance Adjustment. Copyright © 1980 by H. Laurence Ross. Reprinted with permission from Settled Out of Court, 2d Edition (New York: Aldine Publishing Company).

White, Tort Law in America: An Intellectual History. Published by Oxford University Press, Inc. Copyright © by Oxford University Press, Inc. Reprinted by permission.

Ames, Law and Morals, 22 Harvard Law Review 97. Copyright © 1908 by the Harvard Law Review Association. Reprinted by permission.

Borgo, Causal Paradigms in Tort Law, 8 Journal of Legal Studies 419. Published by The University of Chicago. Copyright © 1979 by The University of Chicago. Reprinted by permission.

Brenner, Nuisance Law and the Industrial Revolution, 3 Journal of Legal Studies 403. Published by The University of Chicago. Copyright © 1974 by The University of Chicago. Reprinted by permission.

Burnham, Medical Experimentation in Humans, 152 Science (April 22, 1966) 448. Reprinted by permission.

Epstein, A Theory of Strict Liability, 2 Journal of Legal Studies 151. Published by The University of Chicago. Copyright © 1973 by The University of Chicago. Reprinted by permission.

Epstein, Causation and Corrective Justice: A Reply to Two Critics, 8 Journal of Legal Studies 477. Published by The University of Chicago. Copyright © 1979 by The University of Chicago. Reprinted by permission.

Epstein, Nuisance Law: Corrective Justice and Its Utilitarian Constraints, 8 Journal of Legal Studies 49. Published by The University of Chicago. Copyright © 1979 by The University of Chicago. Reprinted by permission.

Gilmore, Products Liability: A Comment, University of Chicago Law Review 103, 107-108. Copyright © 1970 by The University of Chicago Law Review. Reprinted by permission.

Kessel, Transfused Blood, Serum Hepatitis, and the Coase Theorem, 17 Journal of Law and Economics 265. Published by The University of Chicago. Copyright © 1974 by The University of Chicago. Reprinted by permission.

Landes & Posner, Altruism in Law and Economics, 68 American Economic Review (May, No. 2) 417-421. Copyright © 1978 by the American Economic Review. Reprinted by permission of the authors and publisher.

Landes & Posner, Salvors, Finders, Good Samaritans, and Other Rescuers . . ., 7 Journal of Legal Studies 83. Published by The University of Chicago. Copyright © 1978 by The University of Chicago. Reprinted by permission.

Mansfield, Book Review, 73 Harvard Law Review 1243. Copyright © 1960 by the Harvard Law Review Association. Reprinted by permission of the author and the Harvard Law Review.

O'Connell & Beck, An Update of the Surveys on the Operation of No-Fault Auto Laws, The Insurance Law Journal (March 1979) 129-143. Published and copyrighted 1979 by Commerce Clearing House, Inc., Chicago, Illinois. Reprinted with permission of the authors and publisher.

Patten & Stump, Death Related to Informed Consent, 54 Texas Medicine (Dec. 1978) 49-50. Reprinted with permission of the authors and Texas Medicine.

Posner, A Comment on No-Fault Insurance for All Accidents, 13 Osgood Hall Law Journal 471. Copyright © 1975 Osgood Hall Law Journal, Ontario. Reprinted by permission.

Posner, Epstein's Tort Theory: A Critique, 8 Journal of Legal Studies 457. Published by The University of Chicago. Copyright © 1979 by The University of Chicago. Reprinted by permission.

Posner, Some Uses and Abuses of Economics in Law, 46 University of Chicago Law Review 281. Copyright © 1979 by The University of Chicago Law Review. Reprinted by permission.

Schwartz & Komesar, Doctors, Damages and Deterrence: An Economic View of Medical Malpractice, 292 New England Journal of Medicine 1282. Copyright © 1978 by the New England Journal of Medicine. Reprinted by permission.

EDITORIAL AND BIBLIOGRAPHICAL NOTE

Omissions in reprinted materials are indicated in the usual way, with the following exceptions. Footnotes, citations, headings, purely formal order language at the end of opinions (e.g., "Reversed and remanded"), and concurring and dissenting opinions are omitted without indication. Ellipses at the end of a paragraph may indicate omission of subsequent paragraphs as well as of material in the same paragraph. There is occasional reparagraphing of reprinted material without indication, and in a few instances I have corrected obvious typographical errors in the original, or changed italic to roman typeface or vice versa, without indication. Where footnotes are retained, they have *not* been renumbered. My own footnotes are marked by asterisks.

References to the vast secondary literature on tort law — most of it ephemeral, highly specialized, or both — are sparing. Students wishing to consult a treatise on tort law will find W. L. Prosser, A Handbook of the Law of Torts (4th ed. 1971) (hereinafter cited simply as Prosser), lucid and comprehensive, although already outdated in places. Most of the noneconomic questions covered in this casebook can be found in the Prosser index, and that is where the student desirous of additional information and case references should begin his search. Another treatise, more seriously out of date, is F. V. Harper & F. James, Jr., The Law of Torts (3 vols. 1956), though a portion of it was updated in a 1968 Supplement to volume 2. The American Law Institute's Restatements of Torts are also useful references.*

A good book of readings in current intellectual controversies in the tort field is Perspectives on Tort Law (R. Rabin ed. 1976). A brief bibliography of economic writings on tort law appears at the end of Chapter 1 of this book, and selective bibliographical references appear throughout.

---

*American Law Institute, Restatement of Torts (1934-1939) (hereinafter cited as Restatement of Torts); American Law Institute, Restatement of the Law, Second, Torts (1965-1977) (hereinafter cited as Second Restatement of Torts).

TORT LAW
Cases and Economic Analysis

Learned Hand
Photograph by Dan Weiner
Courtesy of Mrs. Jan Weiner

TORT LAW
Cases and Economic Analysis

Learned Hand
Photograph by Dan Weiner
Courtesy of Mrs. Jan Weiner

$p=$

Chapter 1
The Learned Hand Formula for Determining Liability

In United States v. Carroll Towing Co., 159 F.2d 169 (2d Cir. 1947), the question was presented whether it was negligent for the Conners Company, the owner of a barge, to leave it unattended for several hours in a busy harbor. While unattended, the barge broke away from its moorings and collided with another ship. Judge Learned Hand stated for the court (at p. 173):

> there is no general rule to determine when the absence of a bargee or other attendant will make the owner of the barge liable for injuries to other vessels if she breaks away from her moorings. . . . It becomes apparent why there can be no such general rule, when we consider the grounds for such a liability. Since there are occasions when every vessel will break from her moorings, and since, if she does, she becomes a menace to those about her, the owner's duty, as in other similar situations, to provide against resulting injuries is a function of three variables: (1) The probability that she will break away; (2) the gravity of the resulting injury, if she does; (3) the burden of adequate precautions. Possibly it serves to bring this notion into relief to state it in algebraic terms: if the probability be called P; the injury, L; and the burden, B; liability depends upon whether B is less than L multiplied by P: i.e., whether $B < PL$. . . . In the case at bar the bargee left at five o'clock in the afternoon of January 3rd, and the flotilla broke away at about two o'clock in the afternoon of the following day, twenty-one hours afterwards. The bargee had been away all the time, and we hold that his fabricated story was affirmative evidence that he had no excuse for his absence. At the locus in quo — especially during the short January days and in the full tide of war activity — barges were being constantly "drilled" in and out. Certainly it was not beyond reasonable expectation that, with the inevitable haste and bustle, the work might not be done with adequate care. In such circumstances we hold — and it is all that we do hold — that it was a fair requirement that the Conners Company should have a bargee aboard (unless he had some excuse for his absence), during the working hours of daylight.

By redefinition of two terms in the Hand formula it is easy to bring out its economic character. B, the burden of precautions, is the cost of avoiding the accident, while L, the loss if the accident occurs, is the cost of the accident itself. P times L ($P \times L$) — the cost of the accident if it occurs, multiplied (or as is sometimes said, "discounted") by the probability that the accident will

1

occur, is what an economist would call the "expected cost" of the accident. Expected cost is most easily understood as the average cost that will be incurred over a period of time long enough for the predicted number of accidents to be the actual number. For example, if the probability that a certain type of accident will occur is .001 (one in a thousand) and the accident cost if it does occur is $10,000, the expected accident cost is $10 ($10,000 × .001); and this is equivalent to saying that if we observe the activity that gives rise to this type of accident for a long enough period of time we will observe an average accident cost of $10. Suppose the activity in question is automobile trips from point A to point B. If there are 100,000 trips, there will be 100 accidents, assuming that our probability of .001 was correct. The total cost of the 100 accidents will be $1 million ($10,000 × 100). The average cost, which is simply the total cost ($1 million) divided by the total number of trips (100,000), will be $10. This is the same as the expected cost.

Another name for expected accident costs — for P × L, the right-hand side of the Hand formula — is the benefits from accident avoidance. If one incurs B, the burden of precautions or cost of accident avoidance, one produces a benefit — namely, avoidance of the expected accident costs. The Hand formula is simply an application to accidents of the principle of cost-benefit analysis.* Negligence means failing to avoid an accident where the benefits of accident avoidance exceed the costs.

The Hand formula shows that it is possible to think about tort law in economic terms — that, in fact, a famous judge thought about it so. This casebook is premised on the belief that the Hand formula — more broadly, economic analysis — provides a unifying perspective in which to view all of tort law. There are many references to the Hand formula throughout the book; the purpose of this introductory chapter is to explain the formula and to discuss in a preliminary way its relevance to alternative rules of tort liability.

Many questions about the Hand formula will *not* be answered in this chapter. The unanswered questions include: Does the Hand formula provide a good description of what judges and juries do in tort cases in general or negligence cases in particular? Do courts have enough information to apply the formula intelligently? *Should* the courts use either an explicit or implicit economic approach to questions of tort liability, or should noneconomic factors weigh as or more heavily in their decisions? These questions will be considered later; for now, the further explication of the formula will be limited to two rather technical but important qualifications:

1. The relevant cost of accident avoidance is not total cost, but marginal cost. For our purposes, the marginal cost of accident avoidance can be defined as the additional cost that has to be incurred to prevent *this* accident

---

*On the merits of cost-benefit analysis of safety measures see, e.g., M. J. Bailey, Reducing Risks to Life: Measurement of the Benefits 15-27 (Am. Enterprise Inst. 1980); Zeckhauser, Procedures for Valuing Lives, 23 Pub. Policy 427 (1975). For a good introduction to cost-benefit analysis in general see E. J. Mishan, Cost-Benefit Analysis (2d ed. 1976).

(i.e., the accident that imposes a cost of L with a probability of P). Suppose that a person slips on a staircase and is hurt. The probability that he would slip and fall is .001, the cost of the accident is $25,000, and the cost of preventing the accident (say by installing rubber mats on each stair and by providing a guard rail) would be $50. Since $50 is more than $25, the expected accident cost, it might seem that the failure to prevent the accident was not negligent. But this conclusion is not necessarily correct. Suppose that if $10 were spent on just installing rubber mats, the probability of an accident would drop by one half. The expected accident cost would then be $12.50 rather than $25. Thus it is clear that the benefits of the rubber mats in accident avoidance ($12.50) exceed their cost ($10). But once the mats are installed, a guard rail costing $40 would not be worth having since it would avoid only a $12.50 expected accident cost. Thus, to be a correct economic test, the Hand formula must be applied at the margin: the court must examine the incremental benefit in accident avoidance of an incremental expenditure on safety.*

2. An *expected* value (whether cost or benefit) — that is, a value the receipt or expenditure of which is uncertain — may confer less or more utility or disutility than its certain equivalent. Compare a 1 percent chance of winning $100 with a certainty of receiving $1. Are these "worth" the same? They are in the sense that $1 is the expected benefit of a 1 percent chance of obtaining $100. Some people, at least some of the time, are indifferent between the certain amount and its uncertain or expected equivalent. These people are said to be "risk neutral." Many people, however, are "risk averse," meaning that they prefer the certain equivalent; and some are "risk preferring," meaning that they prefer the expected to the certain amount. Gamblers are risk preferring; people who buy insurance are risk averse (can you see why?).

The Hand formula implicitly assumes risk neutrality. That is, it compares a (more or less) certain sum, the cost of accident avoidance, with an uncertain sum, the expected cost of the accident, without adjusting for the fact that one cost is certain and the other uncertain. The formula yields the same result — no negligence — whether B is $2, P 100 percent, and L $1, or B is $2, P is 1 percent and L is $100. However, a strongly risk-averse person might think that a 1 percent chance of incurring a $100 loss was more costly — imposed greater disutility on him — than a certain cost of $2. He might be willing to pay $2 to insure himself against such a loss, and if so this would show that he considered a 1 percent chance of losing $100 to be the equivalent of a 100 percent chance of losing $2. We shall consider later in this book whether application of the Hand formula is likely to yield economically

---

*More technically, since both P and B are functions of expenditures on accident avoidance, the loss from an accident, which is the sum of the expected costs of the accident and the accident-avoidance costs, is minimized by carrying avoidance efforts to the point where the marginal cost of avoidance is equal to the marginal benefit in reduced expected accident costs. Failure to carry accident-avoidance efforts to this point is negligence in an economic sense.

unsound results because it assumes risk neutrality, and we shall also examine in greater detail the sources and nature of attitude toward risk. For now it is enough if the reader understands what it means to say that the Hand formula assumes risk neutrality.

Assuming, though only provisionally, that despite the above qualifications the Hand formula provides a generally sound guide to determining the economically correct investment in care and safety, let us now see how the formula might be used to induce potential injurers (and potential victims) to make that investment: how, in other words, it might be used to shape conduct towards efficient ends.

Let us imagine the world divided strictly into injurers and victims — those who inflict injury (though they are themselves unharmed) and those who are injured. The fact that an individual is sometimes one and sometimes the other — and sometimes both at the same time — will be ignored for now. Let us begin with injurers, and assume for the moment (but just for the moment) that victims are helpless to avoid being injured. Two basic approaches could be taken to the liability of injurers. First, they could be made strictly liable, meaning that if an injury occurs, for whatever reason, and however unavoidable it may have been, the injurer must compensate the victim for the latter's loss. Under strict liability, and assuming that the court assesses damages equal to the loss suffered by the victim, the right-hand side of the Hand formula becomes an expected-damages figure. L is replaced by D (standing for damages) because every time a loss is suffered by an accident victim the injurer must pay for it. P × D is then the expected damages of the injurer if he does not avoid the accident.

In a system of strict liability the injurer must pay the injured victim regardless of the left-hand side of the Hand formula — regardless of whether B is greater than or less than P × L. That is what strict liability means. It does not follow, however, that the Hand formula becomes irrelevant to the level of safety. Although the court will not apply the Hand formula — it will inquire simply whether the accident occurred and not whether the accident could have been prevented at a lower cost than the expected accident cost — rational potential injurers will apply the formula (i.e., use cost-benefit analysis) in order to determine whether to take steps to avoid the accident. And if the cost of avoidance turns out to be greater than the expected accident cost, the rational profit-maximizing (or utility-maximizing) potential injurer will not incur the cost of avoidance. He will prefer a lower expected damages cost to a higher accident-avoidance cost.

A negligence standard differs from strict liability in that under negligence the injurer is liable only for those accidents that he could have avoided at a lower cost than the expected accident cost. This is what Judge Hand suggests in the quotation at the beginning of this chapter. Notice that, at least as a first approximation, the number of accidents is the same under strict liability and negligence. This is because, as just mentioned, a potential injurer in a system of strict liability will not invest in safety beyond the point at which the costs of safety are equal to the benefits in accident avoidance. The difference between strict and negligence liability is that under the former system injurers must pay the losses of victims of accidents that are not worth preventing, whereas under the latter system injurers have no duty to pay victims of such accidents.

The comparison of strict liability and negligence can be clarified by thinking of accidents as falling into two classes: those that can be avoided at a cost lower than the expected accident cost, and those that cannot be avoided at such a cost. The latter are "unavoidable" (in an economic, not necessarily a literal, sense) accidents. Someone who is strictly liable for all accidents he causes will not thereby be induced to avoid those accidents that are unavoidable. By definition, it doesn't pay to avoid them; it is cheaper to compensate the victim. Neither will someone who is liable only if negligent seek to prevent them; he is not liable for his unavoidable accidents and so has no incentive to avoid them.

The fact that negligence and strict liability lead, at least as a rough first approximation, to the same level of accidents may seem to provide an economic argument in favor of negligence. The argument is this: A system of strict liability provides no more (or less) safety than a negligence system. Thus the allocation of resources to safety is unchanged. But strict liability involves more claims than negligence, since under strict liability victims of unavoidable as well as avoidable accidents have claims against their injurers. The additional claims are costly to process, and the added costs confer no benefit in preventing additional accidents: no additional accidents are prevented.

In fact, the economic comparison of negligence and strict liability is more complicated than this. Most of the complications will be postponed but one needs to be considered here. It is as follows. There are two ways of avoiding an accident. One is to conduct the activity giving rise to the accident more carefully; the other is to reduce the amount, or change the nature, of the activity. Suppose that damage to crops from locomotive sparks can be reduced either by installing better spark-arresting equipment (or perhaps maintaining it better) or by running fewer trains. The first alternative relates to the care with which the activity of railroading is conducted, the second to the amount of activity. Under strict liability, the railroad will consider the costs of both alternatives, since both are methods of accident avoidance. What is the situation under negligence? As we shall see in a subsequent chapter, negligence usually (though not always) connotes failure to use the right amount of care rather than failure to reduce the amount of activity to the correct level or change the activity (e.g., from railroading to trucking, or from growing wheat to burning trash). If so, negligence and strict liability may result in a different number of accidents after all. Strict liability will deter certain accidents where the cost of avoiding the accident by reducing the amount of activity is less than the expected accident cost; negligence will not deter such accidents.

However, before concluding that strict liability yields a more efficient allocation of resources to accident avoidance than negligence does, we must consider accident avoidance by victims. We assumed that victims were helpless, but this is not true in general. Suppose that a particular accident, having an expected cost of $100, could be avoided either by the injurer at a cost of $50 or by the victim at a cost of $10. Clearly, it would be more efficient for the victim to avoid than for the injurer to do so. This is a case where we want the victim to bear the full costs of the accident so that he will be induced to avoid it. We want a principle of contributory negligence whereby if the victim could have avoided the accident at a cost lower than the expected accident cost and also lower than the injurer's cost of avoidance, the injurer is not liable for the victim's loss.

It might appear that the easiest way to implement this principle would be simply to apply the Hand formula to victims as well as injurers — to say that if the cost of avoidance to the victim is less than the expected accident cost, he is guilty of contributory negligence (because B is smaller than $P \times L$) and therefore "liable" (i.e., not entitled to recover his damage from the injurer). This approach will yield the economically correct result in many cases, but not in all. The victim might be negligent under the Hand formula because his accident-avoidance cost was lower than the expected accident cost, but at the same time the injurer's accident-avoidance cost might be lower still.* In that event we would want the injurer to be liable after all, even though the victim was contributorily negligent. We shall examine in subsequent chapters the common-law devices by which the economically correct result is achieved notwithstanding the principle that a contributorily negligent victim is barred from recovering damages from his injurer.

Once the possibility of accident avoidance by victims is admitted, the earlier point (that strict liability results in fewer accidents than negligence liability because it induces adjustments in the level of, as well as care taken in, the activity giving rise to the accidents) becomes uncertain. Suppose there is a class of accidents that cannot be avoided by either injurers' or victims' taking more care, but can be avoided — and at lower cost than the expected accident cost — by a reduction in the amount of activity. Under a rule of strict liability potential injurers will reduce their activity because they will be liable for the costs of these accidents; under negligence they will not reduce their activity because they will not be liable for the accident costs. But precisely the reverse is true of potential victims. If injurers are liable only for their negligent accidents, and not for accidents avoidable only by reducing the level of activity, victims will have an incentive to reduce *their* level of activity because they will bear the costs of nonnegligent accidents. If injurers are strictly liable, however, victims will not curtail their activity, because they will be compensated for accidents arising from it.

---

*As would be the case if, for example, PL was $100, B (victim) was $25 and B (injurer) was $10.

To be concrete, under strict liability the railroad in our earlier example will run fewer trains but farmers will plant more crops; under negligence liability, the railroad will run more trains and the farmers plant fewer crops. Because it is impossible to say a priori which is the more efficient adjustment, we cannot conclude that strict liability will generally result in fewer accidents than negligence liability. Of course, if we know that in some particular class of accidents victims or injurers are helpless (in the economic sense that it would cost them more to avoid an accident, whether through more care or less activity, than the expected cost of the accident), that is a reason for preferring strict liability, or negligence liability, or even no liability (when would no liability be optimal?) for that class, depending on which is the helpless group. A recurring question in this book is whether the common law has been sensitive to the factors that sometimes make strict liability, sometimes negligence, and sometimes even no liability the allocatively efficient liability rule.

In comparing strict liability and negligence, we have emphasized possible differences in the allocation of resources to safety. This is one important dimension of efficiency, but another, which should always be kept in mind as well, is administrative cost. Strict liability increases the number of claims but reduces the cost of processing each one by eliminating the issue of negligence; whether the total costs of administering a strict liability system are lower or higher than those of administering a negligence system are unclear. In any event, the optimum liability rule is the one that minimizes the sum of allocative (expected-accident plus accident-avoidance) and administrative costs.

The Hand formula was announced in a negligence case but, it should be clear by now, can be applied to other issues in tort law besides the determination of negligence. It can be used, as we have seen, to answer the question whether a victim is contributorily negligent, or to justify a rule of strict liability in a class of accidents where it is clear that the cost of accident avoidance to injurers is lower than the accident-avoidance cost to victims. The Hand formula can also be used where, unlike the typical accident case, the probability of harm is one. Many pollution cases are of this type, and we shall see in Chapter 10 that they provide particularly clear examples of cost-benefit analysis in tort law since they do not involve the added complication that the accident costs are uncertain.

The Hand formula can be applied even to cases of deliberate injury. Because the injurer in such a case is *trying* to hurt the victim, rather than just hurting him as a by-product of other activity, P tends to be very high in such cases. At the same time, B will often be very low, and even negative, especially if it is interpreted, as it should be, to refer to *social* as distinct from purely *private* costs. What is the social cost of refraining from spitting in someone's face? It is very low — zero or even negative (because it takes an effort to spit, not to avoid spitting).* Although the injury cost is also small, it is higher than

*For example, if it took an effort costing 50¢ to spit at someone, B would be − 50¢.

the social cost of avoidance and is inflicted with a probability close to one. Thus, application of the Hand formula to cases of deliberate harm will typically result in a decision to condemn the defendant's conduct. Nor would a different result be reached by considering the victim's conduct; in most cases of a deliberate or malicious infliction of harm, the injurer is clearly the cheaper harm-avoider than the victim.

Granted that it is possible to derive a system of liability rules from cost-benefit principles as capsulized in the Hand formula, the question remains why common-law judges might want to do so. One reason is that they might want to increase the wealth of society. If an accident having an expected cost of $100 can be avoided at a cost of $60, then a liability rule which induces that expenditure on avoidance will increase the wealth of society by $40. Whether this effect is a good reason in itself for having such a liability rule is a philosophical question that is postponed for later consideration. (For example, quite apart from the question of different attitudes toward risk, a dollar doesn't necessarily confer the same amount of happiness or utility on everyone, in which event imposing a cost of $60 on one person to give another a benefit of $100 may not increase aggregate welfare in the classical utilitarian sense). What should be noted here is that for tort law to increase the wealth of society, liability rules must influence people's behavior, potential injurers' and potential victims' alike. If the threat of liability (or of not being compensated, if a victim) does not deter accidents but only shifts wealth about after the accident occurs, tort law will not increase the wealth of society but will serve only to redistribute the diminished wealth that remains after the accident has occurred; it will not increase efficiency as that term is being used here.

The proposition that liability rules deter is a controversial one. It seems to presuppose not only that people behave rationally with regard to extreme situations of personal danger but that they have sufficient information regarding the principles of tort law and the probabilities of what are often quite remote contingencies (e.g., that a cigar will explode in one's mouth if certain safety precautions in the manufacture of the cigar are not taken), and also that damages are assessed under correct economic principles. The deterrent efficacy of tort law is a matter of fair debate,* which will occupy us throughout this book (above all in Chapter 11). An alternative formulation of the economic theory of torts, however, holds that tort principles express our moral indignation at certain types of invasion of bodily integrity or property rights — an indignation that is rooted, or at least can be expressed, in economic terms. In this view, we are indignant at a negligent injury because our moral natures are offended by economic waste, illustrated by an accident avoidable at a lower cost than the expected accident cost. Thus, even if tort rules operate to provide an outlet for strong emotions rather than to regulate

---

*For a skeptical view, see, e.g., Brown, Deterrence and Accident Compensation Schemes, 17 U.W. Ontario L. Rev. 111 (1979).

conduct (except perhaps insofar as having such an outlet reduces the incidence of violent retaliation), the rules might still have an implicit economic logic.

This completes a brief introduction to the economic theory of torts. The main purpose has been to alert the reader to the fact that an effort will be made throughout this book to provide a unifying perspective to tort law through repeated use of the Hand formula and of the economic concepts that it encapsulates. The reader is asked to suspend judgment regarding the utility of such an approach until he or she has completed the book or the course based on it.

For those who desire to read more widely in the economic approach to torts at this time, the following works are suggested:

Nontechnical:

Coase, The Problem of Social Cost, 3 J. Law & Econ. 1 (1960).
G. Calabresi, The Costs of Accidents: A Legal and Economic Analysis (1970).
R. A. Posner, Economic Analysis of Law, ch. 6 (2d ed. 1977).
_____, A Theory of Negligence, 1 J. Legal Stud. 29 (1972).

Technical:

Brown, Toward an Economic Theory of Liability, 2 J. Legal Stud. 323 (1973).
Diamond, Single Activity Accidents, 3 J. Legal Stud. 107 (1974).
Shavell, Strict Liability versus Negligence, 9 J. Legal Stud. 1 (1980).

General Introductions to Economic Analysis of Common Law:

R. A. Posner, Economic Analysis of Law, pts. I-II (2d ed. 1977).
Symposium on Efficiency as a Legal Concern, 8 Hofstra L. Rev. nos. 3 and 4 (spring and summer 1980).

PART I
INTENTIONAL TORTS

Chapter 2
The Prima Facie Case

I. de S. and Wife v. W. de S.
Y. B. Liber Assisarum, 22 Edw. 3, f. 99, pl. 60 (1348 or 1349)

At the Assizes, coram THORPE, C.J.

I. de S. & M. uxor ejus queruntur De W. de S. de eo quod idem W. anno, &c., vi et armis, &c., apud S., in ipsam M. insultum fecit, et ipsam verberavit, &c. And W. pleaded not guilty. And it was found by verdict of the inquest that the said W. came in the night to the house of the said I., and would have bought some wine, but the door of the tavern was closed; and he struck on the door with a hatchet, which he had in his hand, and the woman plaintiff put her head out at a window and ordered him to stop; and he perceived her and struck with the hatchet, but did not touch the woman. Whereupon the inquest said that it seemed to them that there was no trespass, since there was no harm done. Thorpe, C.J. There is harm, and a trespass for which they shall recover damages, since he made an assault upon the woman, as it is found although he did no other harm. Wherefore tax their damages, &c. And they taxed the damages at half a mark. Thorpe, C.J., awarded that they should recover their damages, &c., and that the other should be taken. Et sic nota, that for an assault the man shall recover damages, &c.

Notes

1. The Latin sentence at the beginning of the case report can be translated into English as follows: "I. of [the town or village of] S. and [his] wife M. complain of W. of S. that the same W. [date] by force and arms [vi et armis], etc., at S. made an assault [insultum] against M. and beat [verberavit] her, etc." The rest of the report, except for the words Et sic nota (and thus note), is translated from "Law French," a kind of pidgin French in which the early English law reports were written.

2. The I. de S. case illustrates the operation of the writ system. Although the system no longer exists (save for certain vestigial remains, as in the writs of

13

certiorari, mandamus, and habeas corpus), some knowledge of it is important to understanding the evolution of tort law.

Civil cases today are commenced by filing in a court of competent jurisdiction a complaint setting forth the basis upon which the plaintiff believes himself entitled to damages or other relief against the defendant. A copy of the complaint is served on the defendant who then files an answer or other responsive pleading. Issue is eventually joined and the case proceeds to trial. If the court awards damages to the plaintiff, either the defendant pays the judgment or, if he fails to do so, the sheriff seizes from the defendant assets out of which the judgment can be paid.

The early English procedure reflected in *I. de S.* was different. To commence a civil action a plaintiff would first procure a writ from the Lord Chancellor of England. The writ would contain a standardized recital of misconduct, and the plaintiff would fill in his name and the defendant's and the date and place of the events complained of. The writ contained a direction to the sheriff to bring the defendant named in the writ before a royal judge at the next Assizes (court session) for a trial. The judge was assisted at the trial by a panel of the local citizenry, the inquest, which later became the jury. The judge could award damages and also mete out a prison sentence, as apparently happened to W. ("Thorpe, C.J., awarded . . . that the other should be taken").

The writ that the plaintiffs in *I. de S.* procured was the writ of trespass vi et armis. Trespass had (and in law continues to have) a much broader meaning than its modern lay meaning of entering another's land without his consent. The writ of trespass vi et armis was originally used to commence an action for battery or wounding — what in modern lay (and criminal law) parlance is usually called "assault and battery." Notice in the first sentence in the case report the reference to the allegation that W. "beat" (verberavit) M. W. did not beat M; he swung at her and missed. Nevertheless, since the writ of trespass vi et armis contained an allegation of beating, and I. and M. were in effect simply filling in the blanks in the writ, they made this allegation.

Why didn't they ask for a writ describing an assault in which the victim was not beaten? Because there was no such writ. The issuance of new types of writ had been frozen in the thirteenth century. The writ closest to the facts of their case was the writ of trespass vi et armis. The royal courts preferred to depart from the literal language of the writ than to decline jurisdiction of a new type of case.

The writ of trespass vi et armis was the vehicle for bringing not only assault cases but also cases involving professional malpractice, collisions and other accidents, and other wrongs far removed from the actual language of the writ. Sometime during the fourteenth century, however, the royal courts stopped requiring that the plaintiff in an accident or malpractice case allege an attack by force and arms. The new form of action became known as "trespass on the case," to distinguish it from the older form, trespass vi et armis, thereafter often called simply "trespass." There were procedural differences between the writs and it became necessary to determine when the one form of action was appropriate and when the other. The following division eventually emerged. Trespass would lie in a case involving direct and immediate application of force, whether intentional or accidental, trespass on the case in cases of indirect or, as it was sometimes called, consequential injury. Thus, if A accidentally ran down B, B would bring action in trespass against A. But if A's servant ran down B, or if A accidentally dropped a log in the road and B ran into it, B could bring an action only in trespass on the case against A. Trespass would not lie because the application of force in these cases was said to be consequential rather than direct. Eventually trespass on the case displaced trespass in all accident cases, and then in the nineteenth century the writ system was abolished in both England and the United States.

This abbreviated and oversimplified history will help you to understand the references to "trespass on the case" or simply "case" in many tort opinions. For a lucid discussion of the writ system see J. H. Baker, An Introduction to English Legal History, ch. 4 (2d ed. 1979); an excerpt from Baker's discussion of the system appears at the beginning of Chapter 4 of this casebook in connection with the historical origins of negligence.

3. What was the source of the disagreement in the *I. de S.* case between the inquest and Chief Justice Thorpe over whether M. was harmed? What is the holding of the case? What is an "assault" in tort law? Is it an attempt to commit a battery?

4. What right or interest of M.'s was invaded by W.'s conduct? And why was M.'s husband a coplaintiff? Had he been harmed?

5. What could the award of damages in the case have been based on? There are three possibilities:

a. M. was frightened, and the damages were designed to compensate her for the fright. Perhaps a half mark was the price she would have demanded to undergo such an experience.

b. M. suffered a serious mental or perhaps even physical injury as a consequence of the fright; it is for these injuries, not mere fright, that she was compensated.

c. M. incurred no mental or physical injury, serious or trivial; the purpose of the damage award was to deter W. and others like him from engaging in such conduct in the future. In this view, the rationale for granting a civil remedy for assault is similar to that for punishing an attempt to commit a crime when no loss or injury is caused by the attempt. But given the criminal law, why is it necessary or appropriate to use the tort law to provide deterrence, as distinct from compensation (which the criminal law does not provide)? Does it make a difference in answering this question whether, historically, tort law is prior or posterior to criminal law? More on the origins of tort law later.

Which of the above damage theories derives the greatest support from economic theory? Which seems closest to the thinking of Chief Justice Thorpe? Is it relevant what a half mark was worth in the middle of the fourteenth century? The half mark had been standardized at 6 shillings and 8 pence, or one third of a pound sterling, in 1344, a few years before the *I. de S.* case was decided. This was a substantial although not enormous sum — it represented about one month's wages for a craftsman and two months' wages for a laborer. It was also the smallest amount awarded as damages by the royal courts.

6. Where did Chief Justice Thorpe get the principle on which he based his judgment that W. had committed an unlawful act?

7. Would the case have been decided differently if M. had not seen W. take a swing at her, but had only found out about it later? How is this question related to question 4 above?

8. Tuberville v. Savage, 1 Mod. Rep. 3, 86 Eng. Rep. 684 (1699), held that it was not an assault for someone to put his hand on his sword and say, "If it were not assize-time, I would not take such language from you." What element of the assault tort was negatived by these words? Suppose he had said instead, "I have a good mind to strike you"; a threatening gesture, in striking distance, accompanied by these words was held to be a criminal assault in State v. Hampton, 63 N.C. 13, 14 (1868). Suppose he had said: "I shall surely kill you before the month is out." Would that be an assault?

9. With *Tuberville* compare Trogden v. Terry, 172 N.C. 540, 90 S.E. 583 (1916), where the following facts were held to establish an assault:

> The defendant admitted that when he learned that the plaintiff was to take dinner in the hotel, he wrote the paper which he called "an apology and retraction," and that then he picked up his walking stick and hung it on his arm, walked down to where the plaintiff was sitting; that he said to the plaintiff, "I want you to read this paper;" that plaintiff read it and asked, "What do you want me to do?" Defendant said, "I want you to sign it." Plaintiff said, "I will think about it." Defendant says, "No; you won't think about it; you are going to sign it now!" Plaintiff said "Suppose I do not sign it?" Defendant says, "I will whip hell out of you!" Plaintiff says, "I have not read it, but I will sign it." Defendant says, "No; you are lying when you say you have not read it; but you can sign it that way." Defendant picked up the paper and read it to plaintiff. Plaintiff signed it. Mr. Lindsay witnessed it. Defendant says: "Trogden, I do not want to ever hear of your writing or saying anything else about me, you damned, contemptible puppy!" There is evidence that while this was going on at the table the defendant had his walking stick on his arm or in his hand, ready for action.

Id. at 541-542, 90 S.E. at 583. See also Keefe v. State, 19 Ark. 190 (1857). Would *Trogden* have been decided differently if defendant had not brandished his walking stick?

Beach v. Hancock
27 N.H. 223 (1853)

. . . [P]laintiff and defendant, being engaged in an angry altercation, the defendant stepped into his office, which was at hand, and brought out a gun, which he aimed at the plaintiff in an excited and threatening manner, the plaintiff being three or four rods distant. The evidence tended to show that the defendant snapped the gun twice at the plaintiff, and that the plaintiff did not know whether the gun was loaded or not, and that, in fact, the gun was not loaded.

GILCHRIST, C.J. . . . Peace and order and domestic happiness, inexpressibly more precious than mere forms of government, cannot be enjoyed without the sense of perfect security. We have a right to live in society without being put in fear of personal harm. But it must be a reasonable fear of which we complain. And it surely is not unreasonable for a person to entertain a fear of personal injury, when a pistol is pointed at him in a threatening manner, when, for aught he knows, it may be loaded, and may occasion his immediate death. The business of the world could not be carried on with comfort, if such things could be done with impunity. . . .

Note

Suppose plaintiff was not frightened; would defendant still be guilty of assault? See Brady v. Schatzel, 1911 Q.S.R. 206. If plaintiff knew the gun was unloaded, but defendant thought it was loaded, would there be an assault?

Degenhardt v. Heller
93 Wis. 662, 68 N.W. 411 (1896)

CASSODAY, C.J. The complaint alleges, in effect, that September 3, 1893, at Milwaukee, the defendant, with force and arms, unlawfully and maliciously assaulted the plaintiff with a revolver, and did then and there, by such unlawful and malicious assault, inflict great and permanent injuries on the plaintiff, in body and mind, whereby he suffered great physical pain, and became hopelessly sick and physically enfeebled, and demands judgment therefor in the sum named. The answer is a general denial. At the close of the trial the jury returned a special verdict to the effect (1) that the defendant on or about September 3, 1893, discharged a revolver in proximity to the plaintiff, (2) at a distance of about sixty feet from him; (3) that the defendant did not aim or present the pistol at the plaintiff at the time the same was discharged; (4) that the defendant did not aim or present the pistol at the plaintiff immediately after the same was discharged; (5) that the defendant, by the discharge of the pistol, did not intend to do any bodily harm to the plaintiff; (6) that the defendant, by threats and the discharge of the pistol, did intend to frighten the plaintiff; (7) that the plaintiff did sustain mental or physical injury, which was proximately caused by the acts of the defendant; (8) that, if the plaintiff is entitled to recover, his damages are assessed at $1,000. From the judgment entered thereon in favor of the plaintiff, the defendant brings this appeal.

The question presented is not whether the plaintiff could maintain an action against the defendant upon the facts found in the special verdict, but whether the verdict sustains the cause of action alleged in the complaint, which was the only cause of action which the defendant was required to defend. The only cause of action so alleged is for an unlawful and malicious assault upon the plaintiff with a revolver. The verdict simply finds that the revolver was not aimed or presented at the plaintiff when discharged, nor immediately thereafter, and that the defendant discharged the same with the intention of frightening the plaintiff, but without intending to do him any bodily harm. . . . "An 'assault' is defined to be an attempt with force or violence to do a corporal injury to another, and may consist of any act tending to such corporal injury, accompanied with such circumstances as denote at the time an intention, coupled with the present ability, of using actual violence against the person." "An assault is an intentional attempt, by violence, to do an injury to another." If there is no such intention, — no present purpose to do such injury, — then there is no assault. Another author says: "An 'assault' is defined to be an inchoate violence to the person of another, with the present means of carrying the intent into effect. Mere threats alone do not constitute the offense. There must be proof of violence actually offered." Such being the law, it is very manifest that the verdict acquits the defendant of committing the assault alleged. . . .

Notes

1. Can *Beach* and *Degenhardt* be reconciled? Did *Beach* involve "an attempt with force or violence to do a corporal injury to another"?

2. In a subsequent case involving facts similar to those in *Beach*, the court stated, "Whether there is an assault in a given case depends more upon the apprehensions created in the mind of the person assaulted than upon what may be the secret intentions of the person committing the assault." Allen v. Hannaford, 138 Wash. 423, 425, 244 P. 700, 701 (1926). What did the court mean? What is the intent requirement in an assault case?

3. In what sense is there a "right to live in society without being put in fear of personal harm," as stated in *Beach*? If a city fails to provide adequate

police protection, and as a result an assault occurs, is the city guilty of assault along with the actual assailant?

Western Union Telegraph Co. v. Hill
25 Ala. App. 540, 150 So. 709 (1933)

SAMFORD, J. . . . . Sapp was the agent of defendant and the manager of its telegraph office in Huntsville. Defendant was under contract with plaintiff to keep in repair and regulated an electric clock in plaintiff's place of business. When the clock needed attention, that fact was to be reported to Sapp, and he in turn would report to a special man, whose duty it was to do the fixing. At 8:13 o'clock P.M. plaintiff's wife reported to Sapp over the phone that the clock needed attention, and, no one coming to attend to the clock, plaintiff's wife went to the office of defendant about 8:30 P.M. There she found Sapp in charge and behind a desk or counter, separating the public from the part of the room in which defendant's operator worked. The counter is four feet and two inches high, and so wide that, Sapp standing on the floor, leaning against the counter and stretching his arm and hand to the full length, the end of his fingers reaches just to the outer edge of the counter. The photographs in evidence show that the counter was as high as Sapp's armpits. Sapp had had two or three drinks and was "still slightly feeling the effects of whisky; I felt all right; I felt good and amiable." When plaintiff's wife came into the office, Sapp came from towards the rear of the room and asked what he could do for her. She replied: "I asked him if he understood over the phone that my clock was out of order and when he was going to fix it. He stood there and looked at me a few minutes and said: 'If you will come back here and let me love and pet you, I will fix your clock.' This he repeated and reached for me with his hand, he extended his hand toward me, he did not put it on me; I jumped back. I was in his reach as I stood there. He reached for me right along here (indicating her left shoulder and arm)." The foregoing is the evidence offered by plaintiff tending to prove an assault. Per contra, aside from the positive denial by Sapp of any effort to touch Mrs. Hill, the physical surroundings as evidenced by the photographs of the locus tend to rebut any evidence going to prove that Sapp could have touched plaintiff's wife across that counter even if he had reached his hand in her direction unless she was leaning against the counter or Sapp should have stood upon something so as to elevate him and allow him to reach beyond the counter. However, there is testimony tending to prove that, notwithstanding the width of the counter and the height of Sapp, Sapp could have reached from six to eighteen inches beyond the desk in an effort to place his hand on Mrs. Hill. The evidence as a whole presents a question for the jury. . . .

The next question is, Was the act of Sapp towards Mrs. Hill, plaintiff's wife, such as to render this defendant liable under the doctrine of respondeat superior? . . .

The defendant is a public service corporation, maintaining open offices for the transaction of its business with the public. In these offices are placed managers, who, within the line and scope of their authority, are the alter ego of the corporation. People entering these offices are entitled to courteous treatment, and if, while transacting the business of the corporation with the agent, an assault is made growing out of, or being related to, the business there in hand, the corporation would be liable. But the assault in this case, if committed, was clearly from a motive or purpose solely and alone to satisfy the sensuous desires of Sapp, and not in furtherance of the business of defendant. In such case the liability rests with the agent and not the master. . . . To our minds, the evidence is conclusive to the effect that, while Sapp was the agent of defendant, in the proposal and technical assault made by him on plaintiff's wife he stepped aside wholly from his master's business to pursue a matter entirely personal. Where this is so, the doctrine of respondeat superior does not apply. The rules of law governing cases of this nature are perfectly clear and well defined. The confusion arises now and then from a failure to keep in mind the distinction between the act done by the servant within the scope of, and the act done during, his employment. The act charged in this case is clearly personal to Sapp and not referable to his employer. . . .

Notes

1. What does the court hold with reference to the elements of an assault?

2. What can you learn from this case about the elements of the tort of battery? How are assault and battery linked?

3. Why does it matter whether Sapp could reach plaintiff's wife, when it was irrelevant in *Beach* that the defendant's gun was not loaded?

4. With *Hill* compare State v. Ingram, 237 N.C. 197, 202-203, 74 S. E.2d 532, 536 (1953):

> The witness said he leered at her as he drove along the highway. This word "leer," according to the dictionary means a look askance, conveying the suggestion of something sly, malign or lustful, but the witness who used the word as descriptive of the defendant's appearance said only it meant "a curious look," without further definition, explanation or demonstration.
>
> That she was frightened is unquestionable, but that fact alone is insufficient to constitute an assault in the absence of a menace of violence of such character, under the circumstances, as was calculated to put a person of ordinary firmness in fear of immediate injury and cause such person to refrain from doing

an act he would otherwise have done, or to do something he would not have done except for the offer or threat of violence.

It is apparent that no assault was committed on her by the defendant as he drove along the highway.

True, the witness thereafter in passing through the small wooded area became frightened by the cessation of the sound of the motor and ran. But the defendant at that time was some distance away and nowhere in sight, and when she came into the open space she reduced her pace to a walk. And then when she saw the defendant walking fast across the cultivated ground and stopping at the cluster of plum bushes, 65 or 70 feet away, she did not accelerate her speed, and continued to walk to the destination she had in view. She said the defendant watched her, but he uttered no sound, made no gesture, did not again leer at her, and then turned and walked back the way he came. There was here no overt act, no threat of violence, no offer or attempt to injure.

It may have been that the defendant had a sinister purpose in stopping his automobile and walking or running the 95 steps across the field. Certainly his stated reason for doing so was rather lame. He may have looked with lustful eyes when he watched her walking along the road, but there was absence of any overt act constituting an offer or attempt to do injury to the person of the witness.

Ingram was a criminal case. Would it have been decided differently if it had been a civil case? If defendant had known that plaintiff was not a person "of ordinary firmness"?

5. Why did plaintiff in *Hill* sue Western Union rather than Sapp? After losing his case against Western Union, could plaintiff have sued Sapp? Could he have sued both?

6. If Sapp had committed an assault in the futherance of his employment, Western Union would have been liable under the doctrine of respondeat superior. What does "in furtherance" mean in this context? When would an intentional tort by an employee be in furtherance of his employer's business?

7. Respondeat superior is a strict liability doctrine. The plaintiff need prove only that the employee's tort was in furtherance of his employment — not that the employer ordered or encouraged the employee to commit the tort, or even that the employer was negligent in hiring the employee in the first place or in failing to prevent him from committing the tort by more careful supervision of his work. Why should the employer be strictly liable in such cases? One explanation stresses the compensatory function of tort law. Employees are typically unable to respond in damages for their torts, so were it not for respondeat superior many tort victims would be uncompensated. But if compensation were in fact the principal goal of tort law, would not the liability standard *always* be strict liability, and with no defenses based on the victim's status or conduct, such as contributory negligence?

The factual premise of the compensation argument for respondeat superior can be used to give an economic explanation of the doctrine. Because employees are typically not answerable in damages for their torts, a threat of tort liability will not deter them from committing wrongful acts. Employers may, however, be able to prevent torts by their employees, either through careful screening of applicants for employment or through careful on-the-job training or monitoring of employees. By making employers liable for the torts of their employees, the law gives them an incentive to screen, train, and monitor their employees carefully. To be sure, this is not an argument for strict liability versus negligence liability, but only for liability versus nonliability. A second consideration, however, suggests that employers' strict liability may make more sense than negligence liability. The tort victim is clearly less able to prevent the employee from behaving negligently than the employer is; the victim is a stranger to the employer's business, and cannot do anything to screen or train or monitor the employer's workers. This asymmetry is a reason for strict liability, as we saw in Chapter 1. But what if the tort victim is not a stranger to the employer's business — what if he is in fact a fellow employee of the employee who injured him? What should the rule of liability be in that case? (See Chapter 5.)

If the economic analysis of respondeat superior is correct, should the employer's liability be limited to employee torts committed in furtherance of his business? Would a better line be between torts committed in the workplace, for whatever purposes, and torts committed elsewhere? How does the analysis apply to an agent who is not an employee but an independent contractor? Suppose you hire a building contractor to build a house for you, and in the course of building he tortiously injures someone. Should you be liable for the tort? An independent contractor differs from an employee in that the principal does not have a right to direct the details of the contractor's work, as the employer does in respect to his employees. Should this make a difference so far as applying respondeat superior is concerned? On these questions, see Calabresi, Some Thoughts on Risk Distribution and the Law of Torts, 70 Yale L.J. 499, 545 (1966); Ira S. Bushey & Sons, Inc. v. United States, 398 F.2d 167 (2d Cir. 1968); Nelson v. United States, 639 F.2d 469 (9th Cir. 1980); Hammond v. Bechtel, Inc., 606 P.2d 1269 (Ala. 1980). For an early example of the application of economic analysis to the independent-contractor exception to respondeat superior, see Douglas, Vicarious Liability and Administration of Risk I, 38 Yale L.J. 584, 601-602 (1929).

Respondeat superior is part of a broader concept in tort law of "vicarious liability." Another important area of vicarious liability concerns the family. At common law a husband was liable for his wife's torts, though this rule has now been abolished by statute in virtually all jurisdictions. Parents were not, however, vicariously liable for the torts of their children, although they would, of course, be liable if their own negligence or other fault contributed to the tort committed by the child. Concerned that most children do not have sufficient assets to pay tort judgments, a number of states have by statute imposed vicarious liability on parents. In many jurisdictions, either by common law decision or by statute, owners of automobiles are vicariously liable for torts committed by family members while driving. A parallel doctrine, now repudiated, "imputed" a parent's contributory negligence to a child hurt in an accident; we shall encounter this doctrine in a subsequent chapter.   *internation*

Can you think of an economic reason for making employees liable for the torts of their employees, but not parents for the torts of their children?

Stearns v. Sampson
59 Me. 568 (1871)

[Defendant purchased a house in which plaintiffs had been living as tenants for more than 20 years and served notice on them to leave. They refused. Defendant sent his assistants to remove the furniture. They removed some of it and also caused the windows of the house to be removed, prevented food from being carried to the house, and removed doors which the plaintiffs had fastened closed. Mrs. Stearns, the female plaintiff, finally left the house and was sick for several weeks.]

APPLETON, C.J. . . . The acts and indignities which from the charge might constitute an assault, were the bursting open a door, which the defendants had no right to fasten, and the inconveniences resulting from taking off the doors and taking out the windows, which made it uncomfortable for the female plaintiff to remain, where remaining, she was a trespasser. So the bringing a bloodhound by the defendant into his house, which is proved to have barked, but not to have bitten, and the making a noise therein, with other similar acts, it was contended, would amount to an assault and trespass. . . . Now such is not the law. An assault and battery is clearly defined thus: "Whoever unlawfully attempts to strike, hit, touch, or do any violence to another, however small, in a wanton, willful, angry, or insulting manner, having an intention, and existing ability, to do some violence to such person, shall be deemed guilty of an assault; and if such attempt is carried into effect, he shall be deemed guilty of an assault and battery." Now the removal of a door or windows, of the owner in possession, would constitute no assault. Indeed, . . . the owner would, in attempting it, have the right to use as much force as was necessary to overcome the resistance of the unlawfully resisting and trespassing tenant. Acts which may embarrass and distress do not necessarily amount to an assault. Indignities may not constitute an assault. Acts aggravating an assault, differ materially from the assault thereby aggravated. Insulting language or conduct may aggravate an assault, but it is not an assault. So the acts of the defendant, in taking out the windows of his own house, in a bleak and cold day, might distress one unlawfully occupying, and illegally refusing to quit his premises, but they could in no sense be regarded as an assault upon her. One may be embarrassed and distressed by acts done "in a wanton, willful, angry, or insulting manner," where there is no "intention, nor existing ability to do some violence" to the person, and yet there be no assault. The instruction on this point is equally at variance with the common law, and the statute of the State. . . .

Notes

1. What is the holding of the *Stearns* case? Is it that the plaintiff failed to make out a prima facie case of assault or battery? Or is it that the defendant had a good defense, based on his right to possess the premises? The distinction between prima facie case and defenses is an important one. A legal rule can be stated in the form of a rule with exceptions, but an alternative approach is to specify the facts that, if shown, enable a plaintiff successfully to resist the defendant's motion for a directed verdict at the close of plaintiff's case. These facts constitute the plaintiff's prima facie case. It does not follow that plaintiff will win the suit. Defendant may have a good defense. That is, even if the facts alleged by plaintiff would, if true, establish a prima facie case of liability, there may be other facts which, if proved by defendant, would negate his liability. There are also defenses to defenses, or rebuttals. The system of common-law pleading is described in Epstein, Pleadings and Presumptions, 40 U. Chi. L. Rev. 556 (1973). Defenses to intentional torts are considered in the next chapter. Can you now state the elements of the prima facie case of assault?

2. Wood v. Young, 20 Ky. L. Rep. 1931, 50 S.W. 541 (1899), affirmed a judgment for plaintiffs on the following facts: Mary and Henry Young, husband and wife, were tenants of appellant's mother. Their term had expired, and although they had promised to vacate the premises by a certain day, they failed to do so. Appellant went to the house and found appellee Mary Young sick in bed. He proceeded to remove the furniture from the house. He did not touch Mary but "tried to smoke her out" by removing a lid from the stove and pouring water on it, and then going out, closing and locking the door, and carrying away the key. What tort? Assault? Battery? Trespass to land? Can the result in the case be reconciled with *Stearns*?

Vosburg v. Putney
80 Wis. 523, 50 N.W. 403 (1891)

. . . At the date of the alleged assault the plaintiff was a little more than 14 years of age, and the defendant a little less than 12 years of age. The injury complained of was caused by a kick inflicted by defendant upon the leg of the plaintiff, a little below the knee. The transaction occurred in a school-room in Waukesha, during school hours, both parties being pupils in the school. A former trial of the cause resulted in a verdict and judgment for the plaintiff for $2,800. The defendant appealed from such judgment to this court, and the same was reversed for error, and a new trial awarded. The case has been again tried in the circuit court, and the trial resulted in a verdict for plaintiff for $2,500. . . . On the last trial the jury found a special verdict, as follows: "(1) Had the plaintiff during the month of January, 1889, received an injury just above the knee, which became inflamed, and produced pus? Answer. Yes. (2) Had such injury on the 20th day of February, 1889, nearly healed at the point of the injury? A. Yes. (3) Was the plaintiff, before said 20th of February, lame, as the result of such injury? A. No. (4) Had the *tibia* in the plaintiff's right leg become inflamed or diseased to some extent before he received the blow or kick from the defendant? A. No. (5) What was the exciting cause of the injury to the plaintiff's leg? A. Kick. (6) Did the defendant, in touching the plaintiff with his foot, intend to do him any harm? A. No. (7) At what sum do you assess the damages of the plaintiff? A. Twenty-five hundred dollars." The defendant moved for judgment in his favor on the verdict, and also for a new trial. The plaintiff moved for judgment on the verdict in his favor. The motions of defendant were overruled, and that of the plaintiff granted. Thereupon judgment for plaintiff, for $2,500 damages and costs of suit, was duly entered. The defendant appeals from the judgment.

LYON, J. . . . The jury having found that the defendant, in touching the plaintiff with his foot, did not intend to do him any harm, counsel for defendant maintain that the plaintiff has no cause of action, and that defendant's motion for judgment on the special verdict should have been granted. In support of this proposition counsel quote the rule that "the intention to do harm is of the essence of an assault." Such is the rule, no doubt, in actions or prosecutions for mere assaults. But this is an action to recover damages for an alleged assault and battery. In such case the rule is correctly stated, in many of the authorities cited by counsel, that plaintiff must show either that the intention was unlawful, or that the defendant is in fault. If the intended act is unlawful, the intention to commit it must necessarily be unlawful. Hence, as applied to this case, if the kicking of the plaintiff by the defendant was an unlawful act, the intention of defendant to kick him was also unlawful. Had the parties been upon the play-grounds of the school, engaged in the usual boyish sports, the defendant being free from malice, wantonness, or negligence, and intending no harm to plaintiff in what he did, we should hesitate to hold the act of the defendant unlawful, or that he could be held liable in this action. Some consideration is due to the implied license of the play-grounds. But it appears that the injury was inflicted in the school, after it had been called to order by the teacher, and after the regular exercises of the school had commenced. Under these circumstances, no implied license to do the act complained of existed, and such act was a violation of the order and decorum of the school, and necessarily unlawful. Hence we are of the opinion that, under the evidence and verdict, the action may be sustained. . . .

Certain questions were proposed on behalf of defendant to be submitted to the jury, founded upon the theory that only such damages could be recovered as the defendant might reasonably be supposed to have contemplated as likely to result from his kicking the plaintiff. The court refused to submit such questions to the jury. The ruling was correct. The rule of damages in actions for torts was held in Brown v. Railway Co. to be that the wrongdoer is liable for all injuries resulting directly from the wrongful act, whether they could or could not have been foreseen by him. The chief justice and the writer of this opinion dissented from the judgment in that case, chiefly because we were of the opinion that the complaint stated a cause of action ex contractu and not ex delicto, and hence that a different rule of damages — the rule here contended for — was applicable. We did not question that the rule in actions for tort was correctly stated. That case rules this on the question of damages. . . .

Notes

1. What is the difference of opinion between the jury and the appellate court regarding the intent required in a battery case? What made defendant's intention unlawful? When might kicking someone not be a prima facie battery?

2. The court states that if the defendant had "intend[ed] no harm to the plaintiff in what he did," he might not have been liable. Is this statement consistent with the court's earlier definition of unlawful intention?

3. Would the case have been decided differently if the school had not yet been called to order?

4. Why should the defendant be liable for the unintended and unforeseeable extent of the injury inflicted by the kick? Wasn't the real cause of the injury the preexisting weakened state of plaintiff's tibia, a state that defendant neither caused nor even knew about? Who was the "cheaper cost avoider" of the accident, plaintiff or defendant?

The principle that a tortfeasor is fully liable for his victim's damages even if the extent of those damages was unforeseeable is well established in tort law. It is often referred to as the "thin skull" or "eggshell skull" rule, and is applied in unintentional as well as intentional tort cases. Some illustrative cases are Watson v. Rhinderknecht, 82 Minn. 235, 84 N.W. 798 (1901); McCahill v. New York Transp. Co., 201 N.Y. 221 (1911); Owen v. Dix, 210 Ark. 562, 196 S.W.2d 913 (1946); Lee v. Augusta Coach Co., 223 Ga. 72, 153 S.E.2d 429 (1967), rev'g 114 Ga. App. 803, 151 S.E.2d 803 (1966); Follett v. Jones, 481 S.W.2d 713 (Ark. 1972). If the tortfeasor were not responsible for the full extent of the damages, there would be underdeterrence. This can be shown by a simple example. Imagine that the average cost of a particular type of accident is $124.30, distributed as follows: in three accidents, the cost per accident is $10 (these are the people with unusually thick skulls); in 22, the cost per accident is $80; in 50 it is $100; in another 22 it is $120; and in three — the eggshell skull cases — it is $1,000. The total accident costs are thus

$12,430, or $124.30 per accident. If the potential injurer is liable to the full extent of any injury he inflicts, he will spend up to $124.30 to avoid an accident. This is true regardless of whom he in fact injures; presumably he does not know in advance whether the victim will have a thin or a thick skull. But now suppose that the rule is that an injurer is not fully liable to the eggshell-skull victims because their damages are deemed unforeseeably severe; if someone who has an eggshell skull is injured, he will be limited to $120, the maximum foreseeable damages. If so, the total liability costs for this type of accident will not be $12,430; it will be only $9,790 ($12,430 − 3 ($1,000 − $120)), because the upper tail of the accident distribution has been cut off. The tortfeasor's expected liability is now only $97.90, so potential injurers will be led to reduce their accident-avoidance efforts below the optimal ($124.30) level.

But why isn't the most efficient way to avoid injury to someone with an eggshell skull for him rather than potential injurers to take precautions? The law can induce him to do so by refusing to compensate him for the full extent of his injury. In *Vosburg*, for example, perhaps plaintiff should have worn a shinguard. But this is not certain: the cost of the shinguard must be compared with the cost to defendant of not kicking plaintiff. The latter cost was presumably low — even negative. (Why?) But is there an argument for reducing plaintiff's damages, though not to the average? See Chapter 8 and the discussion of the *Steinhauser* case.

The question whether the potential accident victim has a duty to protect himself not from the accident itself (the duty imposed by the doctrine of contributory negligence and other doctrines of plaintiff fault), but from the consequences of the accident (the concept of "avoidable consequences"), is discussed in connection with automobile seatbelts in Chapter 5. The question whether the scope of liability is or ought to be broader in intentional than in unintentional tort cases is discussed in Chapter 8.

5. With *Vosburg* compare Matheson v. Pearson, 619 P.2d 321-322 (Utah 1980). Plaintiff was employed as a maintenance man at a junior high school. While unloading supplies outside the school he was struck on the head by a tootsie pop thrown from a second-floor window of the school building by defendant Pearson. Pearson was responding to a dare by defendant Sullivan. "The defendants testified that while they intended to try to hit the plaintiff with the tootsie pop they did not intend to harm him in any way and merely undertook the misadventure as an adolescent prank." Nonetheless, plaintiff was seriously injured and brought suit against defendants, alleging negligence. Defendants argued that his action was really one for battery and hence was barred by the one-year statute of limitations applicable to battery actions. But the court held that defendants were not guilty of battery — rather of "reckless disregard of safety or reckless misconduct," a form of negligence, and the statute of limitations applicable to negligence was four years. The court said that reckless misconduct "results when a person, with no intent to cause harm, intentionally performs an act so unreasonable and dangerous

that he knows or should, it is highly probable that harm will result." If *Matheson* was correctly decided, does it follow that *Vosburg* wasn't really a battery case?

Garratt v. Dailey
46 Wash. 2d 197, 279 P.2d 1091 (1955)

HILL, J.

The liability of an infant for an alleged battery is presented to this court for the first time. Brian Dailey (age five years, nine months) was visiting with Naomi Garratt, an adult and a sister of the plaintiff, Ruth Garratt, likewise an adult, in the back yard of the plaintiff's home, on July 16, 1951. It is plaintiff's contention that she came out into the back yard to talk with Naomi and that, as she started to sit down in a wood and canvas lawn chair, Brian deliberately pulled it out from under her. The only one of the three persons present so testifying was Naomi Garratt. (Ruth Garratt, the plaintiff, did not testify as to how or why she fell.) The trial court, unwilling to accept this testimony, adopted instead Brian Dailey's version of what happened, and made the following findings:

> III. . . . that while Naomi Garratt and Brian Dailey were in the back yard the plaintiff, Ruth Garratt, came out of her house into the back yard. Some time subsequent thereto defendant, Brian Dailey, picked up a lightly built wood and canvas lawn chair which was then and there located in the back yard of the above described premises, moved it sideways a few feet and seated himself therein, at which time he discovered the plaintiff, Ruth Garratt, about to sit down at the place where the lawn chair had formerly been, at which time he hurriedly got up from the chair and attempted to move it toward Ruth Garratt to aid her in sitting down in the chair; that due to the defendant's small size and lack of dexterity he was unable to get the lawn chair under the plaintiff in time to prevent her from falling to the ground. That plaintiff fell to the ground and sustained a fracture of her hip, and other injuries and damages as hereinafter set forth.
>
> IV. That the preponderance of the evidence in this case establishes that when the defendant, Brian Dailey, moved the chair in question *he did not have any wilful or unlawful purpose* in doing so; that *he did not have any intent to injure the plaintiff, or any intent to bring about any unauthorized or offensive contact with her person* or any objects appurtenant thereto; that the circumstances which immediately preceded the fall of the plaintiff established that the defendant, *Brian Dailey, did not have purpose, intent or design to perform a prank or to effect an assault and battery upon the person of the plaintiff.* (Italics ours, for a purpose hereinafter indicated.)

It is conceded that Ruth Garratt's fall resulted in a fractured hip and other painful and serious injuries. To obviate the necessity of a retrial in the event this court determines that she was entitled to a judgment against Brian Dailey, the amount of her damage was found to be $11,000. Plaintiff appeals from a judgment dismissing the action and asks for the entry of a judgment in that amount or a new trial. . . .

We have here the conceded volitional act of Brian, i.e., the moving of a chair. Had the plaintiff proved to the satisfaction of the trial court that Brian moved the chair while she was in the act of sitting down, Brian's action would patently have been for the purpose or with the intent of causing the plaintiff's bodily contact with the ground, and she would be entitled to a judgment against him for the resulting damages.

The plaintiff based her case on that theory, and the trial court held that she failed in her proof and accepted Brian's version of the facts rather than that given by the eyewitness who testified for the plaintiff. After the trial court determined that the plaintiff had not established her theory of a battery (i.e., that Brian had pulled the chair out from under the plaintiff while she was in the act of sitting down), it then became concerned with whether a battery was established under the facts as it found them to be. . . .

A battery would be established if, in addition to plaintiff's fall, it was proved that, when Brian moved the chair, he knew with substantial certainty that the plaintiff would attempt to sit down where the chair had been. If Brian had any of the intents which the trial court found, in the italicized portions of the findings of fact quoted above, that he did not have, he would of course have had the knowledge to which we have referred. The mere absence of any intent to injure the plaintiff or to play a prank on her or to embarrass her, or to commit an assault and battery on her would not absolve him from liability if in fact he had such knowledge. Without such knowledge, there would be nothing wrongful about Brian's act in moving the chair, and, there being no wrongful act, there would be no liability.

While a finding that Brian had no such knowledge can be inferred from the findings made, we believe that before the plaintiff's action in such a case should be dismissed there should be no question but that the trial court had passed upon that issue; hence, the case should be remanded for clarification of the findings to specifically cover the question of Brian's knowledge, because intent could be inferred therefrom. . . .

Garratt v. Dailey
49 Wash. 2d 499, 304 P.2d 681 (1956)

Rosellini, J. . . .

Upon remand for clarification on the issue of the defendant's knowledge, the superior court reviewed the evidence, listened to additional arguments and studied briefs of counsel, and entered a finding to the effect that the defendant knew, with substantial certainty, at the time he removed the chair, that the plaintiff would attempt to sit down where the chair had been, since she was in the act of seating herself when he removed the chair. Judgment was entered for the plaintiff in the amount of eleven thousand dollars, plus costs, and the defendant has appealed. . . .

. . . In order to determine whether the defendant knew that the plaintiff would sit in the place where the chair had been, it was necessary for [the superior-court judge] to consider carefully the time sequence, as he had not done before; and this resulted in his finding that the arthritic woman had begun the slow process of being seated when the defendant quickly removed the chair and seated himself upon it, and that he knew, with substantial certainty, at that time that she would attempt to sit in the place where the chair had been. . . .

The judgment is affirmed.

Madden v. D.C. Transit System, Inc.
307 A.2d 756 (D.C. App. 1973)

PER CURIAM. . . .

. . . [A]ppellant alleged that, while standing first on the traffic island near the northeast corner of 16th and K Streets, N. W. and, shortly thereafter, at the southeast corner of the same intersection, he was assaulted by fumes and offensive oily substances which appellee permitted to spew from two of its buses. Demanding damages in the sum of $70,000, appellant alleged further that appellee was aware that the by-products complained of were regularly discharged from its buses and that for this reason such acts were intentional. . . .

An essential element of the ancient tort of assault is the intentional putting another in *apprehension* of an *immediate* and harmful or offensive conduct. Absent any such allegation of apprehension, the complaint, insofar as it alleged an assault, was clearly deficient.

The complaint was deficient also in respect to the alleged battery. Not only did appellant fail to allege the essential elements of an assault, but he failed also to allege intent — one of the essential elements of the tort of battery. Appellant contends nevertheless that his allegations of wanton and malicious conduct were sufficient to satisfy the requisite intentionality. We disagree. Such allegations were nothing more than legal conclusions which the court was not bound to accept. . . .

Notes

1. What is the difference between Brian Dailey's intent and that of the D.C. Transit System?

2. If the fumes in *Madden* had been lethal, would that have changed the court's result?

3. Did Brian have the mental capacity to form the intent required for assault?

Morgan v. Pistone
25 Utah 2d 63, 475 P.2d 839 (1970)

HENRIOD, J.:

Appeal from a judgment on a jury verdict of no cause of action in an action alleging a battery. Affirmed with costs on appeal to defendant.

The record indicates that the alleged fracas, subject of this action, was the outgrowth of neighborly bad blood, punctuated by verbal pot-shots that pierced the unfenced but psychological barriers existing between the unhappy homesteaders. Plaintiff, a minor female at the time of the alleged terrifying touching, and an adult at the time of the trial, said one thing, and defendant, an adult male, said another, i. e., that he touched simply to call attention by way of explanation that he, a doctor, disliked the degradation attendant on plaintiff's repeated suggestions that his role in society best could be described by the sound of a duck. The doctor took the position of the common-law cool-blood, who, in Tuberville v. Savage, indicated that if it were not assize time he would have run his tormentor through.

On such highly emotional and controversial evidence the jury apparently believed the doctor was put upon with greater force and vigor by the plaintiff's unkind, opprobrious epithets than was the plaintiff by the gentle touching designed only to warn, not to wound. Hence we cannot say that the jury erred in finding that there was not that kind of *intentional* touching amounting to a technical battery. . . .

Notes

1. What is the relevance of plaintiff's "unkind, opprobrious epithets"? Was defendant provoked? Is or should purely verbal provocation be a defense to battery?

2. What is the relevance of *Tuberville*? If defendant had grabbed plaintiff's arm and said, "Shut up or I'll shut you up," would *Tuberville* preclude a finding of a battery?

3. What essential element of the tort of battery was missing here?

Alcorn v. Mitchell
63 Ill. 553 (1872)

MR. JUSTICE SHELDON delivered the opinion of the Court:

The ground mainly relied on for the reversal of the judgment in this case is, that the damages are excessive, being $1,000.

The case presented is this: There was a trial of an action of trespass between the parties, wherein the appellee was defendant, in the circuit court of Jasper county. At the close of the trial the court adjourned, and, immediately upon the adjournment, in the court room, in the presence of a large number of persons, the appellant deliberately spat in the face of the appellee.

So long as damages are allowable in any civil case, by way of punishment or for the sake of example, the present, of all cases, would seem to be a most fit one for the award of such damages. . . .

It is customary to instruct juries that they may give vindictive damages where there are circumstances of malice, wilfulness, wantonness, outrage and indignity attending the wrong complained of. The act in question was wholly made up of such qualities. It was one of pure malignity, done for the mere purpose of insult and indignity.

An exasperated suitor has indulged the gratification of his malignant feelings in this despicable mode. The act was the very refinement of malice. The defendant appears to be a man of wealth; we can not say that he has been made to pay too dearly for the indulgence. . . .

Notes

1. Would it have been proper to award punitive damages in Vosburg v. Putney? Would it have in Garratt v. Dailey? What is the relevance of defendant's wealth in *Alcorn?*

2. "Punishment" can be defined as any sanction, monetary or "afflictive" (e.g., imprisonment), for a wrong other than simple compensation of the victim. A fine in a criminal case is punishment and so are punitive damages in a civil case such as Alcorn v. Mitchell. Since many tortious acts are also crimes, the question arises why punitive damages should be available in addition to criminal penalties. There are two traditional answers. One is that public prosecutors don't have the resources to prosecute minor crimes; the tort action by the victim provides — as in the *I. de S.* case — the only practical opportunity to punish the offender. The other answer is that compensatory damages don't really compensate fully, and punitive damages help close the gap. This is a relevant consideration in a case like *Alcorn*, for how does one monetize the humiliation of being spat upon in anger?

It is also possible, however, to approach the matter from the opposite direction and ask why, given tort law, it is necessary to punish people criminally. There are again two traditional answers. The first is that criminal punishment carries a stigma that a tort judgment, even of punitive damages, does not, and some behavior is so outrageous that we want to stigmatize it. The second answer is that many wrongdoers are not deterrable by purely monetary sanctions because they lack the monetary means to pay a tort judgment. The second answer is more cogent than the first. If criminal punishment stigmatizes, it follows only that the tort award, to impose the same disutility as criminal punishment, must be set higher than if there were no stigma of criminal punishment. Of course, at the equivalence level — the level where the award of punitive damages would have the same deterrent effect as whatever criminal punishment was fixed for the conduct in question — many wrongdoers might not be able to pay. But then we are back to the second objection to placing complete reliance for deterring antisocial behavior on the tort system, the insolvency of many tortfeasors.

In many premodern societies, including many tribal African societies and the Germanic (including Anglo-Saxon) tribes, tort law occupied most of the field of what is now criminal law. If someone killed or injured another, this was regarded as a tort rather than a crime and the injurer had to pay compensation (often according to a fixed schedule) to the victim or his kin. This system, variously called "wergeld," "composition," and "bloodwealth," is discussed in Posner, A Theory of Primitive Society, with Special Reference to Law, 23 J. Law & Econ. 1, 42-51 (1980).

Assume that, for good or bad reasons, punitive damages are available in tort cases, and consider the following question: how should such damages be computed? (Implied is the further question, when should they be awarded at all?) One answer is given by Becker, Crime and Punishment: An Economic Approach, 76 J. Pol. Econ. 169 (1968). (His discussion is of fines, but applies equally to punitive damages in tort cases.) Punitive damages should be so calculated that the total damages awarded — call them D — satisfy the equation $D = C/P_c$, where C is the social cost of the wrong (and let us assume for the moment that C is equal simply to the cost of the injury to the victim) and P_c is the probability that the wrongdoer will be detected, sued, found liable, and forced to pay a judgment of D: call this the probability of collection.

This result is derived from the proposition that optimal deterrence requires — at a minimum (the significance of this qualification will become clear in a moment) — that the expected cost of the judgment to the prospective wrongdoer equal the cost of the injury to the victim. Now even if this condition is satisfied the wrongdoer may not be deterred; he may derive greater benefit than the victim suffers injury. But if this is true, there is a question whether we *want* to deter him. We clearly want to deter him, however, if he derives *less* benefit than the victim suffers harm, for in such a case the injury is not cost-justified, and reduces the wealth of society. That is why optimal deterrence requires, at a minimum, that the expected cost of the judgment to the injurer equal the cost of the victim's injury; otherwise the wrongdoer may not be deterred even if the injury is not cost-justified.

If it is absolutely certain that the wrongdoer will be apprehended, prosecuted, and forced to pay the judgment entered against him, so that P_c equals
1, then the optimal damage judgment, D, will equal the injury to the victim,
C; there will be no punitive damages. But if P_c is less than 1 — if, for example,
there is a chance that the wrongdoer will escape the clutches of the law (a hit-
and-run accident illustrates this possibility*) — then D must be larger than C,
since the prospective wrongdoer will discount (multiply) D by the probability
that he will actually be made to pay it. To offset the effect of this discounting, one simply divides the cost to the victim by the probability that the
damages will be collected. Suppose, for example, that the probability of
collection is .9 and the cost to the victim is $1,800. Then D should be set
equal to $2,000 ($1,800 ÷ .9 = $2,000). In figuring the expected cost of the
tort, the prospective tortfeasor will discount (multiply) the damages by the
probability that he will actually have to pay them, and discounting $2,000 by
.9 yields $1,800 — the cost of the injury to the victim. Thus the expected
damages equal the injury. In this example, the compensatory portion of the
damage award is $1,800, and the punitive portion $200.

Does this analysis explain the award of punitive damages in the *Alcorn*
case? Probably not. There is no suggestion in the case that the tortfeasor tried
to evade apprehension or that the probability of apprehension figured in the
calculation of punitive damages. Why, then, were punitive damages
awarded? An answer is suggested in Calabresi & Melamed, Property Rules,
Liability Rules, and Inalienability: One View of the Cathedral, 85 Harv. L.
Rev. 1089 (1972). The authors point out that in the case where P equals one
and where, therefore, under the formula given above only compensatory
damages would be awarded, an individual considering an act harmful to
another would be indifferent between (1) purchasing the prospective victim's
consent to the act and (2) committing the act and remitting the victim to his
tort remedy. Thus, suppose A covets B's new car. A has a choice of buying the
car from B, or — under a rule that limits damages to compensatory damages if
the tortfeasor does not try to avoid the process of the law — simply taking the
car subject to a lawsuit by B for the value of the car. Even if factors such as
delay and attorney's fees which may make compensatory damages not fully
compensatory are disregarded, we might still want to discourage A from
taking the second route. The second route forces the legal system to value the
car to B, and its judgment is bound to be imperfect even apart from sources of
systematic undercompensation such as the fact that A would have to pay a
lawyer and could not, under the American rule governing allocation of attorney's fees, obtain reimbursement of his attorney's fees from B. An award of
punitive damages would induce A to go the first route.

---

*The hit-and-run possibility also shows that, in principle, punitive damages should be
awarded in some unintentional tort cases. Why, however, is P more likely to be substantially less
than 1 in an intentional than in an unintentional tort case?

This point is easier to grasp in the context of conversion (the tort counterpart to theft) than in the context of the battery involved in the *Alcorn* case. It is difficult to see exactly what the defendant wanted from the plaintiff that he might have obtained in a voluntary negotiation, the counterpart to A's buying B's car. The defendant in *Alcorn* wanted to humiliate the plaintiff rather than to procure a good or service from him. But there is presumably a price at which plaintiff would have been willing to be spat upon by the defendant (it might be a very high price), so in principle at least we can view the award of punitive damages in *Alcorn* as designed to induce the defendant to pay that price rather than impose on the legal system the task of valuing the cost of the spitting to the plaintiff.

If an award of punitive damages can be justified in the *Alcorn* case because we want to encourage the defendant to negotiate with the plaintiff, such awards may be inappropriate in cases where such a negotiation would not be feasible. Take the *Madden* case. The fumes and oily substances emitted by the D.C. Transit System's buses were a source of real if perhaps minor injury to the plaintiff, but do we really want to force the D.C. Transit System to negotiate with everyone who might be injured by its fumes? The costs of such negotiations could be prohibitive. In these circumstances, it would be a mistake to award punitive damages. Notice that the court in *Madden* declined even to characterize the defendant's conduct as an intentional tort. Can you think of cases where classification as an intentional tort is appropriate but punitive damages would be inappropriate?

In a case where we don't want to force the defendant to operate in the voluntary-transaction mode, and the probability that he will be apprehended for the tort and a judgment collected from him (P_c) is one, punitive damages serve no economic function. But is there any social cost of imposing them, beyond that of collecting a larger tort judgment? In particular, will socially desirable activity be deterred? Why should it be? Suppose B is $1, P is .01, and L is $200, so that PL is $2. Then we don't want the defendant to inflict this injury. But does it matter what the damage award is, so long as it exceeds $200? Suppose it's $1,000, or $10,000; what difference will that make? The potential injurer will never have to pay that amount, will he, because so long as he knows that he will have to pay a damage judgment of $200 or more, he will not inflict the injury. Thus, it seems immaterial what the precise size of the award is, so long as it exceeds the injury. In fact, it doesn't have to exceed the injury — it only has to exceed the cost of avoidance divided by the probability of the injury ($1 ÷ .01 = $100, in the last example). If the damage award in the example was $101 rather than $200, the potential injurer would still be deterred, since his expected cost of liability, $1.01, would still exceed the cost of avoidance, which is only $1. Consider another example. Suppose defendant in *Vosburg* derived a benefit from kicking the plaintiff for which defendant would have been willing to pay only $1. Plaintiff, we know, suffered an injury that cost him $2,500. The assumed disparity between the injurer's gain and the plaintiff's loss is plausible because there is no indication that defendant wanted to hurt the plaintiff. In these circumstances, and assuming P_c equals one, defendant would be deterred by any damage award greater than $1 — even one as low as $1.01.

It seems, then, that from a purely deterrent standpoint there is an enormous range of potential damage awards — from a penny more than the defendant's gain to defendant's entire wealth. But is every point within this range equally appropriate in terms of the economic analysis of optimal punishment? The answer is no. If the damage award is set just above the defendant's gain, then in cases like *Vosburg* the expected award may be too small to motivate the victim to sue. If, at the other extreme, the damage award is set equal to the defendant's entire wealth, the legal system will incur costs of collection that will often be disproportionate to the gains in deterrence. Also, since the legal system cannot be expected to operate without occasional errors, the threat of having to pay very large damage awards may induce people to avoid certain perfectly lawful activities because they might mistakenly give rise to liability.

3. Again consider *Alcorn*: what does the case tell you about the nature of the touching required for a battery? If A slaps B on the back in a friendly fashion, and B suffers a serious injury because of a spinal defect unknown to A, is this a prima facie battery with a defense of implied consent, or is it not even a prima facie battery? Suppose A knows that B has an aversion to shaking hands, but nevertheless grabs his hand and shakes it; is this a battery? What does Morgan v. Pistone imply is the answer? (Return to this question after reading the *Berthiaume* case, below.)

4. Battery is a culturally specific wrong: what is deemed an offensive touching is different in different societies. Cf. E. T. Hall, The Hidden Dimension (1966), discussing the "distance zones" at which people interact with each other in different cultures. The following passage from Hall's book (at p. 147) indicates the nature of his analysis and its possible relevance to the concept of battery:

> In the Western world, the person is synonymous with an individual inside a skin. And in northern Europe generally, the skin and even the clothes may be inviolate. You need permission to touch either if you are a stranger. This rule applies in some parts of France, where the mere touching of another person during an argument used to be legally defined as assault. For the Arab the location of the person in relation to the body is quite different. The person exists somewhere down inside the body. The ego is not completely hidden, however, because it can be reached very easily with an insult. It is protected from touch but not from words. The dissociation of the body and the ego may explain why the public amputation of a thief's hand is tolerated as standard punishment in Saudi Arabia.

5. Suppose the defendant in *Alcorn* had spat in the direction of the plaintiff but missed; would he have been guilty of an assault?

6. If the spit had hit a third party, rather than the intended victim, would the third party have had an action against the defendant for battery? He would have, under the fiction of "transferred intent." See, e.g., Alteiri v. Colasso, 168 Conn. 329, 362 A.2d 798 (1975); Lopez v. Surchia, 112 Cal. App. 2d 314, 246 P.2d 111 (1952). Why is this fiction employed?

Wyant v. Crouse
127 Mich. 158, 86 N.W. 527 (1901)

HOOKER, J. The plaintiffs commenced an action by declaration against the defendant to recover damages for the destruction of a blacksmith shop and other property by fire. The declaration stated that he wrongfully broke into the shop, and started a fire in the forge, and the undisputed proof shows that he did so. The declaration purports to be in case, and, after alleging the wrongful entry and building of a fire, alleges negligence in managing it, and a consequent fire a short time after defendant left the shop. It seems to be conceded that, if this was to be treated as a count in trespass quare clausum, the action was barred by the statute of limitations; and the court, acting upon the theory that it was case, directed a verdict, upon the ground that no negligence was shown. The testimony shows that the defendant was a black-smith, who sometimes worked in the shop for plaintiffs' son, who occupied the shop as plaintiffs' tenant; that on this occasion he went to the shop to sharpen some shoes, built a fire in the forge, did his work, and went away. It is in evidence that the wind was blowing, and that about 10 minutes after he went away, the shop was discovered to be on fire, in the southwest corner of the building, the forge being the the northeast corner, and the flames coming out from the roof. The only fire on the floor was that which dropped from above. The forge was connected with the chimney by an old stove pipe, that went up through a ceiling of boards. The defendant stated, the day after the fire, that when he left the shop there was apparently no fire around, but there were some shavings lying around, and he did not know but a spark or piece of hot iron had dropped in the shavings, and that when he went there he found no fire in the shop. The court seems to have considered the wrongful entry as out of the case, and the defendant liable only for a want of ordinary care, after building the fire, in looking after it and keeping it from doing damage. The plaintiffs' counsel insists that the act was wrongful, and might be shown to be so, though it involved a trespass, and that he was liable for the consequences.

We agree with the circuit judge that there is no proof tending to show an absence of ordinary care, but there certainly is proof tending to show that the only fire on the premises came from that started by the defendant. Hence the case is reduced to the question whether trespass quare clausum is the only remedy for an injury resulting to real estate and personal property inadvertently destroyed by a trespasser. Defendant's act, if a trespass, consisted in breaking, entering, and building a fire in the shop. He would have been liable for that in an action of trespass. After he left, the fire burned the shop and adjoining buildings and personal property. There is no doubt that as to the latter, i.e. the personal property, the plaintiff might sue in case, whether they could recover in trespass or not. It is clear that he could not recover in case for the direct damage necessarily done by his trespass to the land. They are not attempting to do so. No claim is made for damages for the mere breaking, entry, or use of the forge, but only for the damage done by the fire. . . .

[I]n Wood v. Railroad Co., Mr. Justice Champlin appears to have recognized that, when damages are consequential, case will lie, for he said: "The injury caused by the trespass in this case was no more indirect and consequential than such as arises in every case of trespass caused by forcible entry and direct injury to plaintiffs' possession and freehold." . . . In the case before us, the defendant intended no such injury, nor did he any act which can be said to have given reason for expecting the consequences. It was a fortuitous consequence of his act, entirely unforeseen. The actual trespass was of little significance compared with this consequential injury. If a wrongdoer, he would be responsible for the damage, if it resulted from the building of a fire by him, regardless of the degree of care used. . . . The liability of the defendant is based upon a wrongful act, and the nature of the act, and not the consequences, determines his liability. He was engaged in an unlawful act, and therefore was liable for all of the consequences, indirect and consequential as well as direct, and there is no occasion to discuss the degree of his negligence in permitting the shop to burn, if the fire was caused by the fire he builded. This accountability for the consequences is not affected by the form of action. The judgment is reversed, and a new trial ordered.

Notes

1. Apart from the statute of limitations, why was trespass quare clausum* an inadequate basis for plaintiff's action? What tort did defendant commit?

2. Is trespass to land a strict analogue to battery? In Dougherty v. Stepp, 18 N.C. 371, 372 (1835), the court stated that from every direct entry on another's land "the law infers some damage; if nothing more, the treading down grass or herbage." Why?

3. What is the required state of mind to commit a trespass? This is a controversial question to which we return in Chapter 7. Consider the view of the court in Hayes v. Bushey, 160 Me. 14, 17, 196 A.2d 823, 824 (1964):

*The full name is trespass quare clausum fregit, the Latin words being translated as "wherefore he broke the close," i.e., entered plaintiff's land without authorization.

It is necessary to keep in mind the distinction between the intention to do *a wrongful act or commit a trespass* and the intention to do *the* act which results in or constitutes the intrusion. One may intend to enter upon the land of another but under the reasonable misapprehension that his entry is lawful. Such a mistake does not avoid his liability for trespass. It is only the intention *to enter* the land of another that is an essential element of trespass and the absence of such an intention or such negligence as will substitute therefor will destroy liability.

4. In the *Wyant* case, if the plaintiff had sustained personal injuries as a result of the fire, would he have been entitled to damages from the defendant? If so, under what tort rubric?

5. For a later case much like *Wyant* see Southern Counties Ice Co. v. RKO Radio Pictures, Inc., 39 F. Supp. 157 (S.D. Cal. 1941); cf. Cleveland Park Club v. Perry, 165 A.2d 485 (D.C. Mun. App. 1960), involving a 9-year-old trespasser.

Koontz v. Keller
52 Ohio App. 265, 3 N.E.2d 694 (1936)

MONTGOMERY, J. . . .

[T]he petition filed by Alverda Koontz avers, that on a certain date defendant's decedent, one Walter B. Robertson, came to the home of the plaintiff and in an outbuilding on said property did willfully, intentionally, and maliciously assault and strike one Jennie Della Crotinger, the sister of the plaintiff, beating her to death; that the blow, so struck by the said Robertson, greatly disfigured said Jennie Della Crotinger; and that the body of the murdered woman was left in plain view and was seen by the plaintiff as she went to and fro between said building and her dwellinghouse. That, unaware of the acts of said Robertson, the plaintiff came upon the body of her sister, in the condition described, causing her great terror and shock so that her nervous system gave way and she suffered great mental and physical pain, as the result of which her health was impaired. . . .

. . . [T]he administratrix defends the sustaining of the demurrer to the petition on the authority of the case of Miller v. B. & O. S. W. R. Co., the purport of which decision is that no liability exists for acts of negligence causing fright or shock, unaccompanied by contemporaneous physical injury, even though subsequent illness results. This holding is in accordance with the general rule in negligence cases. However, it is to be noted that in the *Miller* case the negligent acts complained of were neither willful nor malicious, and the court in its opinion takes care to point out that the petition does not allege intentional or willful negligence on the part of the defendant.

The Supreme Court in the case of Cincinnati Northern Traction Co. v. Rosnagle, distinguishes the case of Miller v. Railroad Co. and concerning its conclusion makes the following observation: "Such a rule is salutary and necessary in negligence cases. But the reasons for the rule do not apply in cases where the act complained of is not only wrongful, but intentional and willful."

Counsel for appellant cite a number of authorities in addition to the *Rosnagle* case, wherein damages may be recovered which ensue as the result of fright or shock, where the act was willful, intentional, or malicious, and they stress particularly the decision of this court in the case of M. J. Rose Co. v. Lowery. In that case the complaint was that the holder of a chattel mortgage on household goods had broken and entered the plaintiff's dwelling house and removed furniture, and that the act was willful, intentional, and wanton. In that case this court held that the buyer "was also entitled to compensatory damages for the humiliation, injury to feelings, and mental suffering which she sustained, resulting naturally and necessarily from the wrongful act."

It is to be observed, however, that in this *Lowery* case, as well as in the other cases relied upon by the appellant, the unlawful act complained of was directed to the person or to the property of the plaintiff seeking damages in the particular instance. They are to be distinguished from the case at bar. Here we have a situation of a plaintiff seeking to recover damages claimed to have been sustained as the result of fright and shock due to an unlawful act committed against the person of another. Counsel have cited no Ohio authority, and we have found none, directly in point. . . .

Courts outside of Ohio in many instances have laid down the rule which seems to us sound and salutary, that one cannot recover for mental suffering resulting from the suffering of another. "There can be no recovery for such mental suffering as merely results from sympathy for another's mental or physical pain, the right of action in such cases being restricted to the person who has directly sustained the injury." . . .

These authorities and the reason back of them seem to us clearly to show that the appellant in the instant case is not entitled to any recovery because of the things of which she complains and, therefore, the court of common pleas was right in sustaining the general demurrer to the petition, and its judgment is affirmed. . . .

Bosley v. Andrews
393 Pa. 161, 142 A.2d 263 (1958)

BELL, J.

Defendant's cattle strayed onto plaintiffs' farm and injured their crops, for which the jury gave plaintiffs a verdict of $179.99. Mrs. Mary Louise Bosley, the wife-plaintiff, sought to recover damages for a heart disability which resulted from her fright and shock upon being chased by a Hereford bull owned by defendant. The bull did not strike or touch plaintiff, and plaintiff suffered no physical injury. The Superior Court sustained the entry of a nonsuit. Considering the record in the light most favorable to plaintiffs, the facts may be thus summarized.

On April 10, 1950, defendant's cattle got through the fence and went on to the plaintiffs' farm. Plaintiffs' daughter and grandson were driving the cattle off plaintiffs' property. Plaintiff, Mrs. Bosley, came out to help them. Plaintiffs' daughter testified as follows:

> As I was driving the cattle, . . . mother was started up towards where I was at to help me and I told her . . . that she didn't need to help me, that they were going all right, so she turned to go up to where my son was and when she turned a bull charged mother out of the herd as she turned and I hollered to her and I told mother then, I says, "Mom, look out, there's a bull after you." As she turned her head to look, the bull was charging her and she started to run and as she started to run, she collapsed.

Mrs. Bosley testified:

> Q. What did you do when your daughter warned you about the bull?
> A. I turned around and looked, and he was coming at me with his head down, and I started to run, but I thought *I could not get my legs to go and I choked up and I collapsed*, and momentarily, I thought he was going to get me, I could just even feel that he was on top of me. . . .

Very fortunately, harassed by a dog, the bull either stopped or was diverted, and the evidence does not show that he got any nearer to Mrs. Bosley than approximately 25 feet. Plaintiff collapsed on the ground and had an attack of coronary insufficiency — shortness of breath, pain in her chest and an insufficiency of blood flowing into the artery into the heart. . . .

Plaintiff's doctors . . . testified that any violent exertion or shock, or sudden death in the family or a near accident while riding in an automobile could have produced the same result.

Plaintiff was a very nervous woman and had on a number of occasions after this episode fainted from coronary or cardiac insufficiency without any outside or known cause. She fainted when she was being examined in 1953 by defendant's doctor, and she also fainted in the courtroom. Dr. Diehl ascribed these fainting spells to a combination of nervousness and cardiac insufficiency.

The rule is long and well established in Pennsylvania that there can be no recovery of damages for injuries resulting from fright or nervous shock or mental or emotional disturbances or distress, unless they are accompanied by physical injury or physical impact. . . .

Plaintiff cites a number of decisions of this Court to support her claim but fails to realize that in those cases where recovery was allowed for nervous shock, *the nervous shock was accompanied by physical injuries*, and that all of her cases recognized and reiterate the above mentioned well settled rule. . . .

To allow recovery for fright, fear, nervous shock, humiliation, mental or emotional distress — with all the disturbances and illnesses which accompany or result therefrom — where there has been no physical injury or impact, would open a Pandora's box. A plaintiff might be driving her car alertly or with her mind preoccupied, when a sudden or unexpected or exceptionally loud noise of an automobile horn behind or parallel with her car, or a sudden loud and unexpected fire engine bell or siren, or a sudden unexpected frightening buzz-sawing noise, or an unexpected explosion from blasting or dynamiting, or an unexpected nerve-wracking noise produced by riveting on a street, or the shrill and unexpected blast of a train at a spot far from a crossing, or the witnessing of a horrifying accident, or the approach of a car near or over the middle line, even though it is withdrawn to its own side in ample time to avoid an accident, or any one of a dozen other everyday events, can cause or aggravate fright or nervous shock or emotional distress or nervous tension or mental disturbance. . . . For every wholly genuine and deserving claim, there would likely be a tremendous number of illusory or imaginative or "faked" ones. . . .

Notes

1. How would the court that decided *Koontz* have decided *Bosley*? How would the court that decided *Wyant* have decided *Bosley*?

2. Why couldn't the doctrine of transferred intent have been used to decide the *Koontz* case in favor of Mrs. Koontz?

3. What was the prima facie tort alleged in *Koontz*? Battery? Trespass to land? Could *Koontz* have been recast as a negligence case? What was the prima facie tort alleged in *Bosley*? Assault? Battery? Trespass to land? If the last, who was the trespasser on the plaintiff's land — the bull or its owner, the defendant? In what sense can an animal be said to commit a tort? (See Chapter 7.)

4. Is it true in general that there can be no recovery for damages caused by fright unaccompanied by physical impact or injury? What would be the implications of such a rule for damages in an assault case?

5. For cases holding that damages for fright occasioned by a trespass to land are recoverable see Newell v. Whitcher, 53 Vt. 589 (1880); Engle v. Simmons, 148 Ala. 92, 41 So. 1023 (1906); Bouillon v. Laclede Gas Light Co., 148 Mo. App. 462, 129 S.W. 401 (1910); May v. Western Union Telegraph Co., 157 N.C. 416, 72 S.E. 1059 (1911).

6. The Pennsylvania "impact" rule applied in *Bosley* was repudiated in Niederman v. Brodsky, 436 Pa. 401, 261 A.2d 84 (1970) — a case, incidentally, that involved shock caused by witnessing an injury to another person, as in

Koontz. On the widening scope of liability for emotional injury in unintentional as well as intentional tort cases (*Niederman* was the former), see Chapter 8.

7. In Davies v. Bennison, 22 Tasmanian L. Rep. 52 (1927), defendant, while in his own yard, apparently deliberately shot and killed plaintiff's cat, which was on the roof of a shed in plaintiff's yard. Plaintiff sued defendant for the value of the cat, for trespass by firing the bullet into her land, and for her shock at witnessing the cat's death. What result?

8. We are about to move on to a class of intentional tort cases where the defendant's conduct causes harm other than, as in the cases discussed so far, through force or fright. Before doing so, some summary reflections and questions seem in order.

a. What exactly does the law mean by intentional conduct? Consider the following possibilities:

(1) *Knowledge of consequences.* Suppose a railroad knows that in the course of a year several travelers will be killed or injured by its trains at railroad crossings. Is the railroad an intentional injurer with regard to these accident victims?

(2) *Intent to injure.* Suppose A, honestly and reasonably believing that V is about to attack him, strikes V in self-defense; in fact, V is not about to attack him. Now suppose the same case, but V really is about to attack A. In either case is the injury to V intentional on A's part?

(3) *Intent to injure wrongfully.* Suppose A, knowing that V is not about to attack him, attacks V because he dislikes him or because he wants to take property from him.

(4) *Recklessness.* Suppose A is driving down a busy street, and closes his eyes because he wants to rest his eyelids. He runs down V. Is A an intentional or merely negligent wrongdoer?

(5) *Intent to injure, with little probability of success.* A, while standing on the top of a tall building, espies his enemy, V, on the ground below. A throws a coin at V, and contrary to the probabilities of the situation hits him. Is A an intentional tortfeasor?

One way to answer these questions would be to examine how the words "intent" and "intentional" are used in everyday language. What are the pros and cons of such an approach? An alternative is to apply the Hand formula to each of the five classes of case listed above; let us see what the results of that approach would be.

In (1), all that is being done in effect is to multiply both sides of the Hand formula, and that should not affect the legal result. To illustrate, suppose the probability that a given train trip will result in an accident is .01, the damage if the accident occurs is $1,000, and the cost of accident avoidance is $20, so that the railroad would not be deemed negligent under the Hand formula. But the railroad makes 100 trips a year (or a month, or a week — the period makes no difference). The expected accident cost is now much higher — $1,000 — and the probability of an accident close to one;* so the railroad knows there will probably be an accident. But since the cost of accident avoidance, viewed over the course of a year, is not $20 but $2,000 dollars, the Hand formula is unaffected. The left-hand side is still greater than the right-hand side. (If B > PL, aB > aPL, where a is some positive number such as 100.) If we want to discourage only accidents that are not cost-justified, we should not deem the railroad an intentional tortfeasor.

In (2), the probability of injury really is high, without having to cumulate low probabilities over a substantial period of time. It is so much higher than in the usual accident case that the law might want to distinguish it from such a case. But B may also be very high — it may easily be as high as L. This is clearest in the second example, the one where V really was about to attack A. What about the first example? What is B in that example? How should mistake be treated in an intentional tort case? Should it be taken into account in deciding whether there is a prima facie case of battery at all, or just in deciding what the appropriate defenses are in battery cases?

Case (3) is simple, is it not? P is high, because (as in case (2)) the defendant desires to bring about the injury; the injury is not the inadvertent by-product of another activity, as in an accident case. B, from a social standpoint, is negative for reasons already discussed.

Case (4) is similar to (3) in that there is a wide gap between the two sides of the Hand formula; B is very low relative to PL. But the gap is not so wide as in case (3). B is positive, although low, because it would take some effort for the defendant to keep his eyes open. P is very high, though lower than in a case where the assailant desires to inflict the injury. But (4) is in conventional thinking a case of recklessness, not intentional wrongdoing. Should this make a difference?

Case (5) differs only in degree from (3). P is lower, and may in fact be quite low. But since B is again negative from a social standpoint, defendant is necessarily liable under the Hand formula.

Cases (3)-(5) are thus clear cases for liability. But is there any reason to classify them differently from ordinary negligence cases, where B is also smaller than PL although the disparity will usually be less pronounced than in these cases? Two reasons come to mind. First, these are cases where the victim's contributory negligence should not be a defense (why not?). Second, they are appropriate cases for punitive damages (why?). On when punitive damages will be awarded in tort cases and on the rules governing such awards see, e.g., Prosser 9-14, 184-186; C. T. McCormick, Handbook on the Law of Damages 275-298 (1935); Morris, Punitive Damages in Tort Cases, 44 Harv. L. Rev. 1173 (1931). On punitive damages in products-liability cases see

---

*It is not exactly 1, however; it is about .86. The probability of avoiding an accident in one trip is $1 - p$, where $p = .01$ in the example. The probability of avoiding an accident in n trips is $(1 - p)^n$ (in our example, n = 100), assuming these are independent events. The probability of having an accident in n trips is therefore $1 - (1 - p)^n$. Can you figure out why the expected accident cost, however, is np rather than $n(1 - (1 - p)^n)$?

Chapter 9. Notice that our analysis makes no distinction between deliberate and reckless wrongdoing. This appears to be the position of the tort law in general except in regard to statute of limitations. See *Matheson*, supra, and the *Hackbart* case in Chapter 3.

(Incidentally, should people be allowed to insure against liability for punitive damages? See, e.g., Cieslewicz v. Mutual Service Casualty Ins. Co., 84 Wis. 2d 91, 267 N.W.2d 595 (1978); Ford Motor Co. v. Home Insurance Co., 172 Cal. Rptr. 59 (Ct. App. 1981). In what circumstances, if any, should a defendant whose liability is based on respondeat superior be liable for punitive damages? See Second Restatement of Torts §909. Should punitive damages ever be awarded in a case where there is no injury to plaintiff?)

Case (1), however, is a simple negligence case. And while case (2) differs from the ordinary accident case by virtue of its higher P, B is not necessarily greatly smaller than PL and could be larger. How does the law treat this case? Would it make more sense to treat it as just another accident case?

b. Professor Epstein has argued that intent should not be relevant at the first stage of pleading in a tort case, that is, in deciding whether the defendant is prima facie liable for the plaintiff's injury. For example, Epstein argues that in Vosburg v. Putney the unauthorized contact between the defendant's foot and the plaintiff's leg was a prima facie battery and it is irrelevant that the defendant intended to bring about such a contact. See Epstein, Intentional Harms, 4 J. Legal Stud. 391 (1975). This approach invites questions such as the following:

(1) If A shakes hands with B, is this a prima facie battery committed by A against B, and perhaps by B against A?

(2) Is a law student a prima facie trespasser on the property of the law school? How about the law professor?

How would Epstein answer these questions? How would an economist answer them?

c. Begin to think about the philosophical foundations of tort liability. At least four basic philosophical approaches (not necessarily mutually exclusive) can be discerned. There is the "responsibility" approach, illustrated by Professor Epstein's views on prima facie liability: causing injury to others, at least in certain ways (Epstein stresses force and fright), creates a moral and legal responsibility to compensate the victim of the injury, at least prima facie. For an elaboration of Epstein's position, see Epstein, A Theory of Strict Liability, 2 J. Legal Stud. 151 (1973). There is the "rights" approach, illustrated by some of Epstein's later work (see, e.g., Epstein, Nuisance Law: Corrective Justice and Its Utilitarian Constraints, 8 J. Legal Stud. 49 (1979)), and by Fletcher, Fairness and Utility in Tort Theory, 85 Harv. L. Rev. 537 (1972). The idea here is that the function of tort law is to redress invasions of rights to bodily integrity and to property, and the key step in determining the scope of liability is therefore the definition of the rights of the plaintiff. There is the "corrective justice" approach, which traces its ancestry to Book V, Chapter 4 of Aristotle's Nicomachean Ethics. Aristotle states that if one man wrongs another, and the wrong causes injury, there is a duty to rectify or redress the wrongful injury, as by payment of damages to the victim by the injurer. See Posner, The Concept of Corrective Justice in Recent Theories of Tort Law, 10 J. Legal Stud. 187 (1981). Finally, there is the economic approach illustrated by this book. To what extent are these really different approaches? Are the first three incompatible with the fourth, the economic approach?

De May v. Roberts
46 Mich. 160, 9 N.W. 146 (1881)

MARSTON, C.J. The declaration in this case in the first count sets forth that the plaintiff was at a time and place named, a poor married woman, and being confined in child-bed and a stranger, employed in a professional capacity defendant De May who was a physician; that defendant visited the plaintiff as such, and against her desire and intending to deceive her wrongfully, etc., introduced and caused to be present at the house and lying-in room of the plaintiff and while she was in the pains of parturition the defendant Scattergood, who intruded upon the privacy of the plaintiff, indecently, wrongfully and unlawfully laid hands upon and assaulted her, the said Scattergood, which was well known to defendant De May, being a young unmarried man, a stranger to the plaintiff and utterly ignorant of the practice of medicine, while the plaintiff believed that he was an assistant physician, a competent and proper person to be present and to aid her in her extremity. . . .

I now quote further from the testimony of Dr. De May as to what took place: "I made an examination of Mrs. Roberts and found no symptoms of labor at all, any more than there was the previous morning. I told them that I had been up several nights and was tired and would like to lie down awhile; previous to this, however, someone spoke about supper, and supper was got and Scattergood and myself ate supper, and then went to bed. I took off my pants and had them hung up by the stove to dry; Scattergood also laid down with his clothes on. We lay there an hour or more, and Scattergood shook me and informed me that they had called and wanted me. Scattergood got my pants and then went and sat down by the stove and placed his feet on a pile of wood that lay beside the stove, with his face towards the wall of the house and his back partially toward the couch on which Mrs. Roberts was lying. I made an examination and found that the lady was having labor pains. Her husband stood at her head to assist her; Mrs. Parks upon one side, and I went to the foot of the couch. During her pains Mrs. Roberts had kicked Mrs. Parks in the pit of the stomach, and Mrs. Parks got up and went out doors, and while away and about the time she was coming in, Mrs. Roberts was subjected to another labor pain and commenced rocking herself and throwing her arms, and I said 'catch her,' to Scattergood, and he jumped right up and came over to her and caught her by the hand and staid there a short time, and then Mrs. Parks came up and took her place again, and Scattergood got up and went and took his place again, back by the stove. In a short time the child was born. Scattergood took no notice of her while sitting by the stove. The child was properly cared for; Mrs. Roberts was properly cared for, dressed and carried and placed in bed. I left some medicine to be given her in case she should suffer from pains."

Dr. De May therefore took an unprofessional young unmarried man with him, introduced and permitted him to remain in the house of the plaintiff, when it was apparent that he could hear at least, if not see all that was said and done, and as the jury must have found, under the instructions given, without either the plaintiff or her husband having any knowledge or reason to believe the true character of such third party. It would be shocking to our sense of right, justice and propriety to doubt even but that for such an act the law would afford an ample remedy. To the plaintiff the occasion was a most sacred one and no one had a right to intrude unless invited or because of some real and pressing necessity which it is not pretended existed in this case. The plaintiff had a legal right to the privacy of her apartment at such a time, and the law secures to her this right by requiring others to observe it, and to abstain from its violation. The fact that at the time, she consented to the presence of Scattergood supposing him to be a physician, does not preclude her from maintaining an action and recovering substantial damages upon afterwards ascertaining his true character. In obtaining admission at such a time and under such circumstances without fully disclosing his true character, both parties were guilty of deceit, and the wrong thus done entitles the injured party to recover the damages afterwards sustained, from shame and mortification upon discovering the true character of the defendants.

Where a wrong has been done another, the law gives a remedy, and although the full extent and character of the injury done may not be ascertained or known until long after, yet in an action brought damages therefore may be fully awarded. This is true both in cases of tort and crime as well as in actions for breach of contract. The charge of the court upon the duty and liability of the defendants and the rights of the plaintiff was full and clear, and meets with our full approval.

It follows therefore that the judgment must be affirmed with costs.

Notes

1. What tort was committed by each defendant in this case? Battery? Trespass to land? Misrepresentation? Intentional infliction of emotional distress? Would the *Bosley* court have affirmed the judgment?

2. *De May* was cited by Warren and Brandeis, in their article on the right of privacy (discussed later in this chapter), for the proposition that the

common law at this early date recognized a tort of invasion of privacy. Do you agree?

3. Suppose a physician has sexual intercourse with a patient, representing that it is part of the treatment for the patient's illness. Is there a battery? See Roy v. Hartogs, 81 Misc. 2d 350, 366 N.Y.S.2d 297 (City Ct. 1975). If A, knowing it is B's firm policy not to shake hands with a Democrat, represents that he is not a Democrat, and B therefore shakes his hand but later discovers that A really is a Democrat, has A committed a battery? Are these better treated as batteries by fraud, or cases where defendant's defense of consent to plaintiff's prima facie case of battery is vitiated by fraud? Does it make any difference? The defense of consent is discussed in the next chapter.

Cucinotti v. Ortmann
399 Pa. 26, 159 A.2d 216 (1960)

COHEN, J.

Plaintiffs instituted an action in trespass in the Court of Common Pleas No. 5 of Philadelphia County against defendants on the following complaint:

> 2. On or about November 20, 1955, and at other divers times, the Defendants threatened the Plaintiffs by threats of violence that unless the Plaintiffs left the premises at 440 East Girard Avenue, Philadelphia, forthwith, that said Defendants would assault the Plaintiffs with great force and violence and would hit, beat and strike the Plaintiffs.
>
> 3. As a result of said assault, the Plaintiffs were put in fear that a battery might be committed against them, and the Plaintiffs did suffer great emotional distress and are so suffering now and may continue so to suffer for a long time in the future. As a result thereof, the Plaintiffs have had to expend sums of money for medicine and medical attention and may continue to have to do so for a long time in the future. . . .

Generally speaking, an assault may be described as *an act* intended to put another person in reasonable apprehension of an immediate battery, and which succeeds in causing an apprehension of such battery. Words in themselves, no matter how threatening, do not constitute an assault; the actor must be in a position to carry out the threat immediately, and he must take some affirmative action to do so. As the lower court correctly pointed out, the allegation in the original complaint amounted to nothing more than threats of violence and was, therefore, legally insufficient to support a cause of action in assault. . . .

Subsequently, the plaintiffs filed the following amended complaint:

> 2.) On or about November 20, 1955, at 440 East Girard Avenue, Philadel-

phia, Pennsylvania, the defendants threatened the plaintiffs with threats of violence that the defendants would commit immediate bodily harm upon the plaintiffs, and would strike the plaintiffs with blackjacks and would otherwise hit them with great force and violence.

3.) At the time as aforesaid, the plaintiffs were put in great fear by the offer of the defendants to commit bodily harm upon them.

4.) As a result of the offers by the defendants to commit immediate bodily harm upon the plaintiffs, the plaintiffs were placed in fear that a battery would be committed against them. . . .

The lower court again sustained preliminary objections brought by the defendant Ulrich, indicating that again no cause of action had been pleaded, but this time the court denied the plaintiffs the right to amend and plead further. From this order the plaintiffs appeal.

As the lower court points out, the only distinction between the two complaints is that in the amended complaint plaintiffs aver that defendants "would commit immediate bodily harm." The amended complaint does not set forth any new facts which would indicate that defendants committed any overt act other than oral threats. Threatening words alone are deemed insufficient in this jurisdiction to put a person in reasonable apprehension of physical injury or offensive touching. We agree that no cause of action in assault was pleaded in the amended complaint.

Plaintiffs would also have us look upon the complaint as stating a cause of action for the intentional infliction of emotional distress. It is the well-settled rule in Pennsylvania that there can be no recovery of damages for unintentional injuries resulting from fright or nervous shock or mental or emotional disturbance or distress, unless they are accompanied by physical injury or physical impact. Bosley v. Andrews. While the rule may be different where the infliction is *intentional*, plaintiffs here plead emotional distress as the consequential result of an alleged offer to inflict bodily harm, which pleadings are legally insufficient to create liability. . . .

In its opinion dismissing the original complaint, the lower court made it clear that plaintiffs would have to allege some affirmative act by defendants in an amended complaint in order to proceed to trial. Plaintiffs cannot, and do not, plead surprise or lack of time to prepare an allegation of this nature. We can only assume, as did the lower court, that plaintiffs are unable to set forth such an allegation.

On this basis alone we would affirm the lower court. We have an additional reason, however, in that the record sets forth plaintiffs' proposed second amended complaint in trespass. The latter differs from the amended complaint before us only in the addition of the following paragraph:

2. On or about November 20, 1955, at 440 East Girard Avenue, Philadelphia, Pennsylvania, the defendants herein did bring into view and show to the plaintiffs that they the defendants were carrying blackjacks.

This additional paragraph in no way cures the defects in the original complaint. There is still no allegation indicating that the blackjacks were produced with such a show of force as to place plaintiffs in immediate fear of harmful bodily contact. Nor is there any indication of a connection in time between the showing of the blackjacks and the asserted threats of violence. The two incidents might very well have occurred at different times on the same day. It simply has not been alleged that defendants have indulged in any act that amounts to an offer to commit a battery. That the defendants had in their possession blackjacks does not convert unactionable words into an actionable trespass unless the blackjacks were displayed and produced in such a manner as to amount to an offer to commit a battery.

Order affirmed.

Notes

1. How is this case distinguishable from *Bosley*?
2. What additional allegations would plaintiffs have had to make in order to state a prima facie case for intentional infliction of emotional distress?

Great Atlantic & Pacific Tea Co. v. Roch
160 Md. 189, 153 A. 22 (1931)

SLOAN, J.

The appellee, Sophia Roch, brought suit against the appellant, the Great Atlantic & Pacific Tea Company, and secured a verdict against it for certain wrongs alleged to have been committed against her by the manager of one of the appellant's grocery stores located on the Belair Road in Baltimore.

The declaration, after describing the nature of the appellant's business and stating that the appellee was one of its customers, went on to say: "On or about the 12th day of July, 1929, the defendant, through a certain Mr. West, its agent, servant and employee and manager of said store premises, caused a package to be prepared in said store premises for delivery to the said plaintiff and caused the delivery boy employed by the said defendant in said store premises to deliver said package to the plaintiff; that under the explicit instructions of the said manager of the said defendant's store the said delivery boy handed said package to the plaintiff at the entrance of her dwelling, 3219 Belair Road, in the City of Baltimore, State of Maryland, and under and by virtue of the explicit directions of the said manager of the said defendant's store, said delivery boy said to the plaintiff then and there, 'Mr. West said you had better open it while I am here'; that the plaintiff then and there opened said package and then and there in said package the plaintiff saw a dead rat; as a result thereof the plaintiff became very sick and ill in body and mind, fainted and fell with great force to the floor, and as a result thereof her nervous system suffered and still is suffering excruciating physical pain and mental anguish and other injuries were then and there sustained by her, and the Plaintiff says that her said injuries were caused by reason of the careless, reckless and negligent act of the defendant, its agents, servants and employees in the premises, in preparing the package aforesaid, causing the same to be delivered to the plaintiff in the manner and form hereinbefore set forth." . . .

The declaration as drawn presents a case against the defendant, popularly known as the "A. and P. Store" for injuries sustained by the plaintiff as a result of a practical joke perpetrated by it. Under the decisions of this court damages may be recovered for physical injuries caused by fright or shock. The declaration as drawn is in accord with the cases cited, and the demurrer was properly overruled. . . .

Buchanan v. Western Union Telegraph Co.
115 S.C. 433, 106 S.E. 159 (1920)

FRASER, J. This is an action for damages. The plaintiff lived, at the time set up in the complaint, in Greenwood, in this state. The plaintiff's husband was working in Columbia, and sent to his wife, through the defendant company, $11.50. The agent of the defendant sent a check for the money to the plaintiff by one of its regular messengers. The messenger found the plaintiff at home alone. While the plaintiff was in the act of signing the receipt the messenger is alleged to have made an indecent proposal to her. There is also evidence that the plaintiff offered to strike the messenger, but the messenger at first advanced towards the plaintiff, and then seized the receipt and ran away. The question is the liability of the defendant for the conduct of its messenger.

At the close of the testimony, the defendant moved for a direction of a verdict in its favor. The presiding judge directed the verdict for the defendant, but said, "I am rather disposed to think that it is a step that the law ought to take, but it hasn't taken yet." The majority of this court think that the principle has been settled. . . .

The judgment appealed from is reversed.

HYDRICK, J. (dissenting) The conduct here complained of was entirely foreign to the master's business, or the purpose for which the boy was employed. It had no connection with or relation to the master's business, but was the boy's own personal escapade, wholly unconnected with the duty for which he was employed; and therefore as to that act he was not defendant's servant. . . .

Notes

1. Does *Roch* hold that a practical joker is responsible for all of the consequences of the joke, however unforeseen they might be? What are the elements of the prima facie tort of intentional infliction of emotional distress? Were they present in *Koontz*?
2. What was the prima facie tort in *Buchanan*?
3. Why was Western Union liable for the messenger's tort in *Buchanan*, but not for Sapp's tort in *Hill*? Could Western Union's liability in the *Buchanan* case possibly be primary rather than derivative? How do you explain A&P's liability for West's prank in the *Roch* case?
4. Illustrative of contemporary expansion in the tort of intentional infliction of emotional distress is Contreras v. Crown Zellerbach Corp., 88 Wash. 2d 735, 565 P.2d 1173 (1977), holding actionable a claim that defendant's employees made racial slurs in the presence of plaintiff, a fellow employee of Mexican descent, causing him severe emotional distress. How would you distinguish this case from the following hypothetical? "A is an otherwise normal girl who is a little overweight, and is quite sensitive about it. Knowing this, B tells A that she looks like a hippopotamus. This causes A to become embarrassed and angry. She broods over the incident, and is made ill. B is not liable to A." Second Restatement of Torts §46, Illus. 13.

National Bond & Investment Co. v. Whithorn
276 Ky. 204, 123 S.W.2d 263 (1938)

FULTON, J.

Appellee, William Whithorn, brought this action for false imprisonment against the appellant, National Bond and Investment Company, in the Jefferson circuit court and on a trial before a jury verdict was rendered in his favor for $700 compensatory damages and $900 punitive damages. Judgment was entered on this verdict and from that judgment this appeal is prosecuted. . . .

The evidence discloses that the appellant had, or at least claimed to have, a conditional sales contract on a car in possession of appellee, and that payments due under this contract had not been made. Appellant desired to repossess the car and assigned its employees, O'Brien and Baer, to this task. . . .

. . . When O'Brien and Baer hailed appellee he thought they were officers and stopped his car, whereupon O'Brien got out of his car, walked up to appellee's car, and invited him to get out and come back and talk to Baer. . . .

. . . [A] wrecker, which had been called by O'Brien, pulled up and one of the appellant's employees motioned for the wrecker to pull in front of appellee's car to hook on, whereupon appellee started the motor in his car for the purpose of driving off, but O'Brien raised the hood of the car and jerked loose the distributor wire. . . .

. . . Baer directed the driver operating the wrecker to hook to appellee's car and pull out with it, but in view of appellee's vehement protest the driver of the wrecker hesitated to act, but after repeated demands by O'Brien finally coupled up with appellee's car and hoisted the front wheels off the ground. Baer then climbed in appellee's car and the wrecker started pulling the car down the street, whereupon appellee put on the emergency brake and threw the car into reverse, thereby managing to stall the wrecker and bring the car to a stop after it had been pulled down the street something like 75 to 100 feet. . . .

If appellant had a valid conditional sales contract on appellee's car, and he was behind in the payments, appellant had the right to repossess the car if it could do so peaceably, but, of course, had no right to create a breach of the peace in doing so, or to put appellee under any kind of restraint, or to use any force directed against him in making the repossession.

Appellant contends the transaction above recited did not amount to false imprisonment, its theory being that appellee was in no wise restrained or impeded, and that he was perfectly at liberty at any time to go his way; that this evidence does not show that O'Brien and Baer prevented him from proceeding in any direction he desired. . . .

It is true, as appellant argues, that appellee was at liberty to depart and these employees were not preventing him from doing so, but the result of his departure would have been an automatic parting with his automobile, which he did not desire to part with, and which he did not have to part with, and which O'Brien and Baer had no right to take over his protests. While he was in this car he was in a place he had a legal right to be, and in which neither O'Brien nor Baer had a legal right to be, by force, and when these men hooked the wrecker on and hoisted the front wheels in the air, forcibly dragging appellee down the street in his car, this was unquestionably a restraint imposed upon him and a detention of his person, such as constitutes a false imprisonment. . . .

Notes

1. If a stickup man points a gun at you and says, "Don't move or I'll shoot," is that false imprisonment?

2. If defendant in *Whithorn* had a right to possess the car, why was the plaintiff, by refusing to leave the car, able to convert his wrongful possession into false imprisonment?

3. Suppose A places a chain across the road in order to prevent B from driving home. What, if any, tort has A committed?

4. Could Whithorn have recovered damages under a battery theory of liability? Could he under a theory of trespass to personal property? How about intentional infliction of emotional distress? To what extent does false imprisonment occupy ground already fully covered by the other torts we have examined?

Griffin v. Clark
55 Idaho 364, 42 P.2d 297 (1935)

BUDGE, J.

On the evening of September 25, 1932, on the highway between Payette and Weiser, a collision occurred between the car of the Griffins and the car of one Ed North, in which Ed North, respondent Marie Williams, and appellants Clark were riding. . . .

. . . On Saturday evening respondent [had] arrived in Payette from Baker to visit appellants. Upon arrival she first saw Ed North, who was acquainted with appellants, and respondent asked him where appellants lived, whereupon he offered to, and did, drive her past appellants' home, but seeing no light North took her to Ontario where she remained the night. In the morning, North called for, and drove, respondent to appellants' home in Payette. The record discloses respondent had to be at work in Baker the following morning, and that North offered to take her there in his car, which proposal respondent refused. About five o'clock respondent called and inquired about train and bus times, and learned the train left Payette about six in the evening and the bus about one o'clock in the morning. It appears that Mrs. Clark "seemed to hesitate" when respondent asked her to take her to the train and that North offered to and took her to the depot about six. A few minutes thereafter, "probably five minutes," North returned to appellants' residence and said: "Grab or take your coats and *we* will go to Weiser and take Marie off the train." Appellants, without argument, immediately acquiesced, and North and appellants proceeded at once to Weiser arriving about the same time as the Portland Rose train on which respondent was riding. It appears that while respondent was looking out the window North boarded the train, grabbed respondent's bag, started to leave the train, and said, "I do not want you to go home on this train." . . .

Appellant Clark testified that respondent as she approached the car at the depot did not seem happy over the situation, and Mrs. Clark likewise stated she did not look happy and smiled "a sickly smile." It further appears from the record that appellant Clark, after the foregoing events occurred, expressed himself as not desiring to make the trip to Baker and the parties then drove some three or four blocks from the depot, stopped at the apartment of Miss Grant where arrangements were made, without the hearing of respondent and without her participation therein, to the effect that North would drive appellants back to Payette, and would then pick up Bill Sodja and a young lady upon his return to Weiser, which couple would accompany respondent and North to Baker. Respondent later learned of this arrangement from Mr. Clark at the time they were starting to Payette. On the trip from Weiser to Payette for the purpose of returning appellants to their home the collision occurred. . . .

. . . There is evidence that there was an intention, known by and entered into by appellants, to take respondent from the train and thence by the North automobile to Baker, and that her removal, while not accomplished by means of physical force or assault, was effected by the removal of her personal property, of which she attempted to regain possession, which means effectively produced the intended result. There is evidence that "in the meantime" the train departed, closing the avenue of travel respondent had chosen and which respondent had previously determined upon as being to her best interest with relation to her employment, and that this was the only means of travel respondent was aware would take her from Weiser to Baker within the time fixed by her to arrive at Baker, other than that provided by the North automobile. She "was not sure whether a bus went through Weiser." Respondent stated, "there was people around there and I did not want to start any commotion," and she therefore, against her will, adopted the means of travel provided. With reference to participation on the part of appellants, in addition to the evidence to the effect that appellants were directed to "grab or take your coats and we will go to Weiser and take Marie off the train," which proposition was immediately accepted and acquiesced in without argument, the record further discloses that one of appellants took the bag from North and put it in the back seat of the automobile. Again, it was through the efforts of appellants that the course of the journey was changed to proceed from Weiser to Payette, rather than to Baker. It was for the jury to determine as a question of fact from the evidence whether respondent was detained as alleged in her cross-complaint [and] whether or not the detention was voluntary or involuntary. . . .

Notes

1. What was defendants' intent?
2. Suppose North had not grabbed Marie's bag. Would he still be guilty of false imprisonment? Would it make a difference if he had grabbed not her bag, but a newspaper she was reading?
3. Was Marie's injury a foreseeable consequence of the false imprisonment? Does it matter? Suppose the probability that the North automobile would be involved in an accident was no greater than that the train would be; would the false imprisonment still be the cause of Marie's injury? Return to this question after reading Chapter 8.

4. Could the action have been maintained on the basis of a trespass to respondent's personal property?

5. North was not named as a defendant. What is the basis of the Clarks' liability?

Barker v. Washburn
200 N.Y. 280, 93 N.E. 958 (1911)

HISCOCK, J. We are led to the consideration of rather unusual facts in this action which was brought for alleged false imprisonment. It was instituted by the respondent as committee of one Sutliff, an incompetent person, to recover for the alleged unlawful removal and restraint of his ward by the appellants. This conduct on the part of the latter is claimed to have been in violation of the will and wishes both of the incompetent himself and of the respondent as his committee, and apparently the real motive involved in this controversy over the possession of the idiot's body is the purpose to reap a profit on his services as a farm laborer. . . .

Robalina v. Armstrong was an action for assault and battery and false imprisonment. The plaintiff was an infant about four years of age and the illegitimate child of one Eliza Gilbert, with whom she had lived since birth. The defendant was the putative father of the child, and had obtained possession of her without the consent of her mother, and refused to restore her to the latter. The court held that the mother and not the father was entitled to the custody of the child, and that, inasmuch as the latter against the will of the mother had wrongfully detained and maintained possession of the infant, an action for false imprisonment would lie in the name of the infant whose rights were violated. In thus ruling in the case of an infant too young to have any volition in the matter the principle was necessarily involved that the unlawful removal of a person having no will by reason of infancy from the custody and possession of the person entitled thereto furnished the basis for an action of false imprisonment. . . .

So far as the principles thus announced are concerned, I see no reason for distinguishing those cases from the present one. There was no objection by the appellants to the theory on which the jury were permitted to find them guilty of false imprisonment because they had violated the wishes and will of the incompetent, if he was possessed of them, but they have expressly and repeatedly argued that the incompetent had no mind or will whose violation could be made the basis of such an action as this. If the jury took that view and concluded that the incompetent like a child of tender years had no such will as would enable him to exercise intelligent and legal volition as to his custody, then the case was brought exactly within the principles of the cases to which reference has been made, and on this theory I think the trial judge committed no error in giving the instructions which have been quoted, but that here as elsewhere with much clearness and fairness he amply protected all the rights of the appellants.

Notes

1. What is the appropriate measure of damages in this case?
2. Evaluate the following proposition: far from awareness of the imprisonment being a necessary element of the tort of false imprisonment, the case where the victim is *not* aware presents the strongest case for recognizing the tort.

Bowden v. Spiegel
96 Cal. App. 2d 793, 216 P.2d 571 (1950)

DOOLING, J.

Plaintiff appeals from an adverse judgment entered after the sustaining of a general demurrer to her first amended complaint without leave to amend.

The allegations of the first amended complaint may be summarized as follows: Defendant Spiegel, Inc., is a corporation operating retail stores under the name of Federal Stores. Defendant First Doe as agent of the corporate defendant on May 28, 1948, telephoned to the home of one Prator at about 11 P.M. and asked for plaintiff. Prator's daughter, who had answered the telephone, asked if it was an emergency call and First Doe replied that it was. The daughter then walked down the street to plaintiff's home and told plaintiff that there was an emergency telephone call for plaintiff at the Prator residence. When plaintiff reached the telephone she asked: "What is the matter?" and First Doe replied: "Please bear up. I know this is going to be a shock; it is as much of a shock to me to have to tell you as it will be to you." Plaintiff answered that she could take the message whereupon First Doe stated: "This is the Federal Outfitting Company — why don't you pay your bill?" Plaintiff attempted to explain that she owed nothing and First Doe replied that he was going to take her to court and that would cost her a lot of money — "unless you come into the Federal Store in Pittsburg tomorrow morning at ten, I am going to cause you a lot of trouble." The entire Prator family listened to plaintiff's end of the conversation. Plaintiff did not owe the company any money. First Doe acted as hereinabove set out maliciously and with intent to vex, harass and annoy plaintiff and with no probable cause. As a result plaintiff is sick and ill and will remain so for an indefinite time.

That the above facts, if true, spell out a cause of action we have no doubt. . . .

The important elements [of the tort of intentional infliction of emotional distress] are that the act is intentional, that it is unreasonable, and that the actor should recognize it as likely to result in illness. Given these elements the modern cases recognize that mere words, oral or written, which result in physical injury to another are actionable. . . .

We entertain no doubt that the intentional use of such an unreasonable method of attempting to collect a debt which proximately results in physical illness is actionable.

The briefs contain much discussion of whether the complaint would support a recovery on the theory of a violation of the right of privacy. Respondent contends that this tort cannot be committed by oral statements. . . . If it were necessary to decide the question we would incline to repudiate this qualification as so broadly stated. The oral dissemination of private matter may be as rapid as the wagging tongue of gossip and as devastating as the printed page; and, to confine the question to the facts in hand, what logical distinction can be found between writing a letter to the Prator family telling them that plaintiff owes defendant a bill and is a deadbeat and summoning her to the telephone before the same family where her spontaneous replies to statements of defendant over the telephone will naturally disclose to the Prator family that she is being dunned for a bill after being summoned from her home at a late hour of the night? It would seem under these circumstances that the oral communication would be more damaging than a written one.

However, since the complaint states a cause of action on the theory first discussed, the decision of the other question becomes unnecessary. . . .

Nader v. General Motors Corp.
25 N.Y.2d 560, 255 N.E.2d 765 (1970)

FULD, C.J. . . .

The plaintiff, an author and lecturer on automotive safety, has, for some years, been an articulate and severe critic of General Motors' products from the standpoint of safety and design. According to the complaint — which, for present purposes, we must assume to be true — the appellant, having learned of the imminent publication of the plaintiff's book Unsafe at any Speed, decided to conduct a campaign of intimidation against him in order to "suppress plaintiff's criticism of and prevent his disclosure of information" about its products. To that end, the appellant authorized and directed the other defendants to engage in a series of activities which, the plaintiff claims in his first two causes of action, violated his right to privacy. . . .

. . . [W]e cannot find any basis for a claim of invasion of privacy . . . in the allegations that the appellant, through its agents or employees, interviewed many persons who knew the plaintiff, asking questions about him and casting aspersions on his character. Although those inquiries may have uncovered information of a personal nature, it is difficult to see how they may be said to have invaded the plaintiff's privacy. Information about the plaintiff which was already known to others could hardly be regarded as private to the plaintiff. Presumably, the plaintiff had previously revealed the information to such other persons, and he would necessarily assume the risk that a friend or acquaintance in whom he had confided might breach the confidence. If, as alleged, the questions tended to disparage the plaintiff's character, his remedy would seem to be by way of an action for defamation, not for breach of his right to privacy.

Nor can we find any actionable invasion of privacy in the allegations that the appellant caused the plaintiff to be accosted by girls with illicit proposals, or that it was responsible for the making of a large number of threatening and harassing telephone calls to the plaintiff's home at odd hours. Neither of these activities, howsoever offensive and disturbing, involved intrusion for the purpose of gathering information of a private and confidential nature.

As already indicated, it is manifestly neither practical nor desirable for the law to provide a remedy against any and all activity which an individual might find annoying. On the other hand, where severe mental pain or anguish is inflicted through a deliberate and malicious campaign of harassment or intimidation, a remedy is available in the form of an action for the intentional infliction of emotional distress — the theory underlying the plaintiff's third cause of action. But the elements of such an action are decidedly different from those governing the tort of invasion of privacy, and just as we have carefully guarded against the use of the prima facie tort doctrine to circumvent the limitations relating to other established tort remedies, we should be wary of any attempt to rely on the tort of invasion of privacy as a means of avoiding the more stringent pleading and proof requirements for an action for infliction of emotional distress.

Apart, however, from the foregoing allegations which we find inadequate to spell out a cause for action for invasion of privacy . . . , the complaint contains allegations concerning other activities by the appellant or its agents which do satisfy the requirements for such a cause of action. The one which most clearly meets those requirements is the charge that the appellant and its codefendants engaged in unauthorized wiretapping and eavesdropping by mechanical and electronic means. . . .

There are additional allegations that the appellant hired people to shadow the plaintiff and keep him under surveillance. In particular, he claims that, on one occasion, one of its agents followed him into a bank, getting sufficiently close to him to see the denomination of the bills he was withdrawing from his account. From what we have already said, it is manifest that the mere observation of the plaintiff in a public place does not amount to an invasion of his privacy. But, under certain circumstances, surveillance may be so "overzealous" as to render it actionable. Whether or not the surveillance in the present case falls into this latter category will depend on the nature of the proof. A person does not automatically make public everything he does merely by being in a public place, and the mere fact that Nader was in a bank did not give anyone the right to try to discover the amount of money he was withdrawing. On the other hand, if the plaintiff acted in such a way as to reveal that fact to any casual observer, then, it may not be said that the appellant intruded into his private sphere. . . .

Notes

1. In an influential article published in 1890, Warren and Brandeis proposed that an appropriate step in the evolution of the common law would be to recognize explicitly a right of privacy protected by tort law. See Warren & Brandeis, The Right to Privacy, 4 Harv. L. Rev. 193 (1890). The particular focus of their concern was the newspaper gossip column.

Beginning with Pavesich v. New England Life Ins. Co., 122 Ga. 190, 50 S.E. 68 (1905), courts began recognizing an explicit common-law right to privacy. (Arguably, De May v. Roberts had recognized an implicit such right.) Over the years, a rather miscellaneous group of wrongs has come to be grouped under the rubric of invasions of the right of privacy. As explained in Prosser, Privacy, 48 Cal. L. Rev. 383 (1960), four separate wrongs are recognized to invade the right: (1) using a person's name or picture in advertising without his consent ("appropriation"); (2) electronic eavesdropping and other intrusive surveillance ("intrusion"); (3) publicizing certain private information about a person ("publicity" or "disclosure"); and (4) publicizing facts about a person that place him in a "false light." The literature on the privacy tort is immense and contentious. For an economic view see Posner, The Right of Privacy, 12 Ga. L. Rev. 393 (1978); for a view highly critical of Posner's see Gavison, Privacy and the Limits of Law, 89 Yale L.J. 421 (1980); and for an eclectic criticism of the tort see Kalven, Privacy in Tort Law — Were Warren and Brandeis Wrong?, 31 Law & Contemp. Prob. 326 (1966).

2. Which of the four wrongs that comprise the privacy tort did Spiegel commit? Is it material that plaintiff didn't in fact owe defendant any money? Would the Nader court have found an invasion of privacy under the facts in Bowden?

3. If Nader had no right to complain about inquiries made of his friends in an effort to elicit private information about him, because he previously had revealed that information to them, why should he be allowed to conceal from General Motors the details of his bank account — details well known to the bank's employees? If privacy connotes selective disclosure rather than total secrecy, was his privacy not invaded by the questioning of his friends and acquaintances?

4. Does the court in Nader have too narrow a conception of privacy? Do not "threatening and harassing telephone calls [made] to the plaintiff's home

at odd hours" invade privacy in a perfectly common sense of that word? In a sense illuminated by Hall's discussion of "distance zones"? In Galella v. Onassis, 487 F.2d 986, 994 (2d Cir. 1973), the court held that the photographer Ron Galella's "frenzied attempts to get . . . pictures" of Jacqueline Kennedy Onassis and her family constituted, among other wrongs, tortious "harassment," which occurs "when, with intent to harass, a person follows another in a public place, inflicts physical contact or engages in any annoying conduct without legitimate cause." Didn't GM harass Ralph Nader in this sense?

In Estate of Berthiaume v. Pratt, 365 A.2d 792, 795 (Me. 1976), it was held to be error to grant defendant's motion for directed verdict on the following facts. Berthiaume was dying of cancer. On the day of, and shortly before, his death, defendant, a physician who was no longer treating Berthiaume, entered his hospital room for the purpose of taking photographs of Berthiaume for Berthiaume's medical records. There was evidence that Berthiaume protested against being photographed, but defendant went ahead and took several pictures. These were placed in Berthiaume's files and were not shown to anyone not having duties in connection with those files. The court held, nevertheless, that if Berthiaume did not consent to being photographed, defendant's action was an invasion of privacy: "an unauthorized intrusion upon a person's physical and mental solitude or seclusion is a tort." Is this approach consistent with *Nader?**

Eckert v. Van Pelt
69 Kan. 357, 76 P. 909 (1904)

SMITH, J. On May 23, 1902, plaintiff in error, who was the editor of the Arkansas City Daily Traveler, printed and published in his newspaper the following: "It is reported that Charlie McIntire may soon take charge of Greer's Supplement in this city. Charlie is all right. In fact anybody would be an improvement on the eunuch who is snorting around in the basement but unable to do anything else." Shortly after this publication, W. W. Van Pelt, plaintiff below, began an action for damages sustained by reason of the alleged libel. The petition alleged that the Traveler was a newspaper of general circulation in Arkansas City and Cowley county; that plaintiff, Van Pelt, was the owner and publisher of a weekly newspaper of general circulation in said city, county, and in Southern Kansas, and that he was of good name, credit, reputation, and social standing, and enjoyed the fellowship, esteem, confidence, and good opinion of many persons of both sexes; and that at the time of said publication he was known and recognized as a man

---

*The court in *Berthiaume* also held that raising Berthiaume's head from the pillow in order to facilitate photographing him was a battery, assuming he did not consent. Is this consistent with Morgan v. Pistone?

possessed of a due amount of potency, virility, and masculinity, and of all the various members and powers which characterize the male portion of the human race, and was a young unmarried man, "in the lusty prime of vigorous youth." . . . Defendant below demurred to the petition on the ground that it did not state facts sufficient to constitute a cause of action. The demurrer was overruled.

It is argued that this ruling of the court was erroneous, for the reason that the newspaper article alleged to be libelous did not contain the name of plaintiff below, and there was no allegation that the public understood the language used to refer to Van Pelt. The averments of the petition expressly charge that defendant published the words "of and concerning the plaintiff." The omission of the name of a libeled person in a publication concerning him does not deprive the matter of its libelous character if it is shown to whom the words used were intended to apply. . . .

Counsel for plaintiff in error further claim that the publication was not libelous per se; that is may be interpreted to mean that the editorial efforts of plaintiff below in his attacks on Mr. Eckert were weak, barren of thought; and that "snorting" may be defined as "loud in roaring sound." Reference is made to the Century Dictionary, where the secondary definition of the word "eunuch" is given as "unproductive, barren," with a quotation from Godwin: "He has a mind wholly eunuch, and unregenerative in matters of literature and taste." The primary and general definition of the word given in all the dictionaries is "a castrated male of the human species." It must be given its usual and ordinary sense as understood in the place where used. We are quite sure that in Arkansas City and vicinity, where the parties resided, the primary signification of the term was conveyed to all persons who read the libelous article in the Daily Traveler. . . . Written words are actionable per se if they tend to render him of whom they are written contemptible or ridiculous. So if they are calculated to produce social ostracism. To say of a woman that she is a hermaphrodite is actionable without alleging special damages. . . . There can be no question or doubt that the publication made was per se libelous. In such cases malice is implied. . . .

Notes

1. If a statement is libelous on its face, i.e., does not depend on facts extrinsic to the statement to make it libelous, plaintiff can recover damages without having to prove an actual pecuniary loss. Such damages, "general damages" as they are called, are to be distinguished from punitive damages, which can also be awarded in an appropriate case. Damages based on proof of an actual pecuniary loss (e.g., lost wages because the defamation induced the employer of the defamed person to discharge him) are "special damages." An example of a statement that is not libelous on its face is the statement that

"Mrs. X gave birth on January 26." An extrinsic fact that would make it libelous would be that Mrs. X got married on January 1 of the same year.

2. Suppose the court in *Eckert* had accepted the defendant's version of the meaning of the word "eunuch": would defendant's statement not have been actionable then? Suppose defendant honestly and reasonably intended "eunuch" to be understood in a nonliteral sense, but readers understood it literally; and suppose further that the nonliteral sense was either nondefamatory or, as applied to plaintiff, true. Would defendant still be guilty of defamation?

3. What was defamatory about the allegation that plaintiff was "snorting"?

4. The court affirmed a judgment of $700 for plaintiff. On what evidence do you think the judgment was based?

5. Could two of the previous cases in this chapter, *Trogden* and *Bowden*, have been brought as defamation cases?

6. B. L. Felknor, Dirty Politics 100 (1966), reports that in the 1950 senatorial primary in Florida Senator Claude Pepper was the victim of a "back-country gossip campaign which suggestively spelled out Pepper's secret vices. He practiced nepotism. He had a sister who was a thespian and a brother who was a practicing homo sapiens. He went to college, where, horror of horrors, he matriculated." Assume that Pepper lost the primary because of this gossip campaign. Put aside any issue of First Amendment privilege. Did Pepper have an action in defamation against the originator of the campaign? Did he against people who repeated the gossip?

Youssoupoff v. Metro-Goldwyn-Mayer Pictures, Ltd.
50 Times L. Rep. 581 (C.A. 1934)

LORD JUSTICE SCRUTTON. An English company called Metro-Goldwyn-Mayer Pictures, Limited, which produces films circulated to the cinemas in this country, . . . produced in this country a film which dealt with the alleged circumstances in which the influence of a man called Rasputin, an alleged monk, on the Czar and Czarina brought about the destruction of Russia. The film also dealt with the undoubted fact that Rasputin was ultimately murdered by persons who conceived him to be the evil genius of Russia.

In the course of that film a lady who had relations of affection with the person represented as the murderer was represented as having also had relations, which might be either relations of seduction or relations of rape, with the man Rasputin, a man of the worst possible character. When the film was produced in this country the plaintiff alleged that reasonable people would understand that she was the woman who was represented as having had these illicit relations. The plaintiff is a member of the Russian Royal House,

Rasputin
Courtesy of the Bettman Archive, Inc.

Princess Irina Alexandrovna of Russia, and she was married after the incidents in question to a man who undoubtedly was one of the persons concerned in the killing of Rasputin. She issued a writ for libel against the English company. The English company declined to stop presenting the film. The action for libel proceeded. It was tried before one of the most experienced Judges on the Bench and a special jury, . . . and, after several days' hearing, and after the jury had twice gone to see the film itself, they returned a verdict for the plaintiff with £25,000 damages. . . .

There have been several formulae for describing what is defamation. The learned Judge at the trial uses the stock formula "calculated to bring into hatred, ridicule, or contempt," and because it has been clearly established some time ago that that is not exhaustive because there may be things which are defamatory which have nothing to do with hatred, ridicule, or contempt he adds the words "or causes them to be shunned or avoided." I, myself, have always preferred the language which Mr. Justice Cave used in Scott v. Sampson (8 Q.B.D. 491), a false statement about a man to his discredit. I think that satisfactorily expresses what has to be found. . . .

. . . I understand the principal thing argued by the defendants is this: "This procedure, as it contains some spoken words, is slander and not libel. Slanders are not as a rule actionable unless you prove special damage. No special damage was proved in this case. Consequently, the plaintiff must get within the exceptions in which slander is actionable without proof of special damage." One of those exceptions is the exception which is amplified in the Slander of Women Act, 1891 — namely, if the slander imports unchastity or adultery to a woman — and this is the argument as I understand it: "To say of a woman that she is raped does not impute unchastity." From that we get to this, which was solemnly put forward, that to say of a woman of good character that she has been ravished by a man of the worst possible character is not defamatory. That argument was solemnly presented to the jury, and I only wish the jury could have expressed, and that we could know, what they thought of it, because it seems to me to be one of the most legal arguments that were ever addressed to, I will not say a business body, but a sensible body. . . .

Then one comes to the third point, and that is the amount of damages. It is the law that in libel, though not in slander, you need not prove any particular damage in order to recover a verdict. What, then, is the position, the jury being the tribunal in libel or no libel, and, following from that, the tribunal as to the damages caused by libel, whose verdict is very rarely interfered with by the Court of Appeal? What have the jury to do? They have to give a verdict of amount without having any proof of actual damage. They need not have any proof of actual damage. They have to consider the nature of the libel as they understand it, the circumstances in which it was published, and the circumstances relating to the person who publishes it, right down to the time when they give their verdict, whether the defence made is true, and, if so, whether that defence has ever been withdrawn — the whole circumstances of the case. It is not the Judge who has to decide the amount. The constitution has thought, and I think there is great advantage in it, that the damages to be paid by a person who says false things about his neighbour are best decided by a jury representing the public, who may state the view of the public as to the action of the man who makes false statements about his neighbour, the plaintiff. . . .

. . . I find it quite impossible to say that the amount of damages here is such that no reasonable jury could have given it. There is the position of the plaintiff, a high position, although the Royal Family of Russia have fallen from their high position. There is the amount of publicity given by circulating the film through a large circle of cinemas to be seen at cheap prices by an enormous number of people. Apparently in this case there were performances for a week in more than 16, possibly 20, cinemas. . . .

LORD JUSTICE GREER. . . . No doubt the damages are very large for a lady who lives in Paris, and who has not lost, so far as we know, a single friend and who has not been able to show that her reputation has in any way suffered from the publication of this unfortunate picture play, but, of course, one must not leave out of account a great many other things. One of them is that it is very difficult to value the reputation of any human being. It is very difficult to put a money figure upon the mental pain and suffering that is necessarily undergone by a good and delicate woman who has been foully libelled in the presence of large numbers of people. . . . [A]nd one is also entitled to take into consideration the fact . . . that the defendants were using the private story of this lady for the purpose of putting money into their pockets, and that they were unwilling to stop using this cinema picture when it was complained of because they said they would lose £40,000 if they did and a great deal more. . . .

LORD JUSTICE SLESSER. This action is one of libel and raises at the outset an interesting and difficult problem which, I believe, to be a novel problem, whether the product of the combined photographic and talking instrument which produces these modern films does, if it throws upon the screen and impresses upon the ear defamatory matter, produce that which can be complained of as libel or as slander.

In my view, this action, as I have said, was properly framed in libel. There can be no doubt that, so far as the photographic part of the exhibition is concerned, that is a permanent matter to be seen by the eye, and is the proper subject of an action for libel, if defamatory. I regard the speech which is synchronized with the photographic reproduction and forms part of one complex, common exhibition as an ancillary circumstance, part of the surroundings explaining that which is to be seen. . . .

Notes

1. Why is it defamatory to say of a woman that she has been raped? Would it be defamatory to say of a person that he was poor? In Katapodis v.

Brooklyn Spectator, Inc., 287 N.Y. 17, 38 N.E.2d 112 (1941), a newspaper article about a traffic accident in which a four-year-old child had been killed was held to defame the child's parents because it stated: "The parents of this youngster are in dire financial straits, and at this writing have no alternative but to let their son go to his final rest in a pauper's grave." But in Grande & Son, Inc. v. Chace, 333 Mass. 166, 129 N.E.2d 898 (1955), it was held not to be defamatory to state that a building contractor had not completed the construction of a school within the time specified in the contract. The court stated:

> Assertion merely of delay in performing a contract does not in itself imply bad management. There might be many reasons which would have made it unavoidable. In the performance of a construction contract, such as this, which was to run substantially for a year, labor and material difficulties might and frequently would be likely to intervene. We think that readers of the published articles would be cognizant of such possibility or probability.

Id. at 169, 129 N.E.2d at 900. Couldn't similarly extenuating circumstances be found for poverty? (Incidentally, plaintiff in *Chace* was a corporation. Should a corporation be allowed to maintain a suit for defamation?) Why should *any* inference regarding character be drawn from the fact that a woman has been raped?

2. As a possible clue to reconciling the above decisions, see the definition of defamation in the Second Restatement of Torts §559: "A communication is defamatory if it tends so to harm the reputation of another as to lower him in the estimation of the community or to deter third persons from associating or dealing with him." Is this one definition or two? Under this definition, would it be defamatory to say of a person that he had a fatal, although not loathsome, disease? See Chuy v. Philadelphia Eagles Football Club, 595 F.2d 1265, 1279-1286 (3d Cir. 1979).

3. An attempt has been made to give "reputation" an economic meaning:

> A person's reputation is other people's valuation of him as a trading, social, marital, or other kind of partner. An asset potentially of great value, it can be damaged both by false and by true defamation. These possibilities are the basis of the individual's incentive both to seek redress against untruthful libels and slanders and to conceal true discrediting information about himself — the former being the domain of the defamation tort and the latter of the privacy tort. . . .
>
> Reputation has an important economic function in a market system (or in any system where voluntary interactions are important). It reduces the search costs of buyers and sellers, makes it easier for the superior producer to increase his sales relative to those of inferior ones, and in these ways helps channel resources into their most valuable employments — a process at the heart of the market system. This role is not limited to explicit markets; it is just as vital to

the functioning of the "marriage market," the market in friends, the political market, and so on.

Posner, Privacy, Secrecy, and Reputation, 28 Buff. L. Rev. 1, 6, 31 (1979). This article contains a general economic analysis of defamation. See id. at 30-41. As the quoted passage suggests, reputation is a device for sorting individuals (or firms) among potential transacting partners, business or social.

4. Is the utterance of a racial slur, as in *Contreras*, actionable as slander?

5. The *Youssoupoff* decision indicates the importance of distinguishing libel from slander — i.e., written from oral defamation (a distinction more difficult to make in the era of movies and television than it formerly was). If a writing is libelous per se — that is, if its libelous character is apparent on the face of the writing — then, as we saw earlier, the plaintiff need not prove special damages; the jury is allowed to award general damages. The rule in slander is different. No damages may be recovered in a slander action unless the plaintiff proves special damages (in which event, however, he can also recover general damages), unless the slander falls into one of the following four per se categories. (Notice that "per se" is being used here in a different sense from its usage in the expression "libel per se," which refers to a writing that is libelous on its face and therefore does not require extrinsic evidence to make it libelous.) The per se slander categories are (1) loathsome disease, (2) crime, (3) unchastity, (4) improper conduct of one's business or trade. If a writing is libelous, but not libelous per se because extrinsic evidence is required to establish the libel, then proof of special damages is required unless the libel falls into one of the four categories of slander per se. By requiring proof of special damages more frequently in slander than in libel cases, the law places a greater burden upon the plaintiff and thus treats one who libels more harshly than one who slanders. Is this difference in treatment justified?

Hartmann v. Winchell
296 N.Y. 296, 73 N.E.2d 30 (1947)

THACHER, J.

The motion to dismiss the amended complaint, pursuant to rule 106 of the Rules of Civil Practice, was denied, and this determination has been affirmed on appeal to the Appellate Division with leave to appeal to this court upon the following certified questions: "1 — Does the utterance of defamatory remarks, read from a script into a radio microphone and broadcast, constitute publication of libel? . . ."

Unless in the case of broadcasting we are prepared to do what Mansfield, C. J., in 1812 declared he could not do in Thorley v. Kerry, namely, abolish the distinction between oral and written defamation, we must hold to the reason for the distinction so well expressed in a single phrase in Ostrowe v.

Lee: "What gives the sting to the writing is its permanence of form." This is true whether or not the writing is seen. Visibility of the writing is without significance and we hold that the defendant's defamatory utterance was libel, not slander. We do not reach the question, which has been much discussed, whether broadcasting defamatory matter which has not been reduced to writing should be held to be libellous because of the potentially harmful and widespread effects of such defamation. . . .

FULD, J. (concurring).

Though I concur in the conclusion reached — that defendant's utterance over the radio is actionable per se, without allegation or proof of special damage — I cannot agree with the court's rationale. It impresses me as unreal to have liability turn upon the circumstance that defendant read from a script when, so far as appears from the complaint before us, none of his listeners saw that script or, indeed, was even aware of its existence. As I see it, liability cannot be determined here without first facing and deciding the basic question whether defamation by radio, either with or without a script, should be held actionable per se because of the likelihood of aggravated injury inherent in such broadcasting. . . .

The common-law action on the case for slander, in its sixteenth-century origin, embraced written as well as oral defamation, and the same rules were applicable to both. Certain classes of words — those charging the commission of a crime, those reflecting on one in his trade or profession, for instance — were held actionable per se, damage being presumed from the nature of the words used. All other defamation was actionable only upon allegation and proof of special damage. The newer tort of libel — adapted by the common-law judges in the latter part of the seventeenth century from the criminal law of libel administered in the Star Chamber — eliminated these refinements as regards written defamation, and made the writing itself presumptive proof of damage.

This emphasis on the form of publication was apparently designed to cope with the new conditions created by the development of the printing press. Another development, another invention — here the radio — invites a similar reappraisal of the old rules. Cf. . . . Yousoupoff v. Metro-Goldwyn-Mayer Pictures, Ltd.

Though some have said that the differentiation between libel and slander is the result of historical accident, without rational basis, this court, disagreeing, has regarded the "schism" as founded upon policy and "not the product of mere accident." If considerations of principle are to control, there is no valid reason why the same consequences should not attach to publication through the medium of radio broadcasting as flow from publication through the medium of writing.

The primary reason assigned by the courts from time to time to justify the imposition of broader liability for libel than for slander has been the greater capacity for harm that a writing is assumed to have because of the wide range of dissemination consequent upon its permanence in form. When account is taken of the vast and far-flung audience reached by radio today — often far greater in number than the readers of the largest metropolitan newspaper — it is evident that the broadcast of scandalous utterances is in general as potentially harmful to the defamed person's reputation as a publication by writing. That defamation by radio, in the absence of a script or transcription, lacks the measure of durability possessed by written libel, in nowise lessens its capacity for harm. Since the element of damage is, historically, the basis of the common-law action for defamation, and since it is as reasonable to presume damage from the nature of the medium employed when a slander is broadcast by radio as when published by writing, both logic and policy point the conclusion that defamation by radio should be actionable per se. . . .

Note

Is there really no difference between defamation in an ad-lib broadcast and defamation in a script read on the radio? The audience may be the same size, and so the costs of defamation (L in the Hand formula) may be the same in the two cases, but what of the costs of avoiding defamation (B)? They are lower in the second case, because writing is a more controlled and deliberate medium of expression than speaking without a script and therefore it is easier in writing to avoid defaming people. Moreover, knowing this, the audience will give greater credence to a written than to a spoken libel — so L may be greater in the second case after all.

Barnes v. Clayton House Motel
435 S.W.2d 616 (Tex. Civ. App. 1968)

WILSON, J.

Summary judgment for defendant was rendered in plaintiff's libel action. Defendant's sole contention concerns the question of whether there was a publication of the asserted libelous letter.

The undisputed facts are as follows: Defendant operates a motel. An unknown person registered under the name of Burne, giving a fictitious address and falsely stating his automobile license number to be that of a vehicle registered in plaintiff's name. This guest left the motel without paying his bill. Motel property was missing from his room.

Defendant's manager traced the automobile registration and wrote a letter on the bottom of an itemized statement addressed to plaintiff at his residence. It stated in effect that plaintiff had registered under the name of Burne, had left without making payment, and had "accidentally packed" listed items of motel property with his own belongings. The letter requested restitution, or suggested plaintiff "contact a lawyer."

The letter was sent as certified mail with return receipt requested. It was received by the maid at plaintiff's residence, who signed the receipt but did not open the letter. The maid delivered the letter to plaintiff's wife, who opened and read it. The wife showed it to the maid and called her husband, who read it. No other person saw the letter.

Defendant's manager did not know plaintiff, and did not know he was married. Plaintiff and his wife had been married more than 20 years. She frequently opened mail addressed to him. . . .

The applicable principle of the law of libel, uniformly recognized, is relatively simple of statement: If one sends a libelous statement through the mails, addressed to the person defamed, with the expectation or intention that it will be read by another person as a matter of course, and such other person so reads it, there is a publication; but where the sender is "not reasonably chargeable with knowledge that a third person might 'intercept' and read the libelous matter before it reached the person allegedly defamed," there is no publication.

The evidence shows that the sender considered it possible that some third person might intercept and read the letter; that some person other than the addressee "might receive" it. This falls far short of a showing he was reasonably chargeable with appreciation or knowledge of likelihood that it would be opened and read by another. It is not sufficient, to constitute publication, that there is a mere conceivable possibility or chance of such eventuality. That chance may nearly always exist when a letter is transmitted through the mails.

Here the sender did not know plaintiff. The sender did not know he was married. There is simply no evidence to show reasonable grounds to anticipate the reading by a third person so as to constitute a publication. Cases relied on by plaintiff rest on special circumstances, as where it is known the letter must be translated, or where the addressee is blind, or where the sender knows of the habit or custom of a third person to open and read the mail. These cases must be distinguished on the facts.

The judgment is affirmed.

Jones v. E. Hulton & Co.
[1909] 2 K.B. 444, aff'd, [1910] A.C. 20 (H.L.)

The plaintiff, Mr. Thomas Artemus Jones, a barrister practising on the North Wales Circuit, brought the action to recover damages for the publication of an alleged libel concerning him contained in an article in the Sunday Chronicle, a newspaper of which the defendants were the printers, proprietors, and publishers. The article, which was written by the Paris correspondent of the paper, purported to describe a motor festival at Dieppe, and the parts chiefly complained of ran thus: "Upon the terrace marches the world, attracted by the motor races — a world immensely pleased with itself, and minded to draw a wealth of inspiration — and, incidentally, of golden cocktails — from any scheme to speed the passing hour. . . . 'Whist! there is Artemus Jones with a woman who is not his wife, who must be, you know — the other thing!' whispers a fair neighbour of mine excitedly into her bosom friend's ear. Really, is it not surprising how certain of our fellow-countrymen behave when they come abroad? Who would suppose, by his goings on, that he was a churchwarden at Peckham? No one, indeed, would assume that Jones in the atmosphere of London would take on so austere a job as the duties of a churchwarden. Here, in the atmosphere of Dieppe, on the French side of the Channel, he is the life and soul of a gay little band that haunts the Casino and turns night into day, besides betraying a most unholy delight in the society of female butterflies." The plaintiff had in fact received the baptismal name of Thomas only, but in his boyhood he had taken, or had been given, the additional name of Artemus, and from that time he had always used, and had been universally known by, the name of Thomas Artemus Jones or Artemus Jones. He had, up to the year 1901, contributed signed articles to the defendants' newspaper. The plaintiff was not a churchwarden, nor did he reside at Peckham. Upon complaint being made by the plaintiff of the publication of the defamatory statements in the article, the defendants published the following in the next issue of their paper: "It seems hardly necessary for us to state that the imaginary Mr. Artemus Jones referred to in our article was not Mr. Thomas Artemus Jones, barrister, but, as he has complained to us, we gladly publish this paragraph in order to remove any possible misunderstanding and to satisfy Mr. Thomas Artemus Jones we had no intention whatsoever of referring to him." The defendants alleged that the name chosen for the purpose of the article was a fictitious one, having no reference to the plaintiff, and chosen as unlikely to be the name of a real person, and they denied that any officer or member of their staff who wrote or printed or published or said before publication the words complained of knew the plaintiff or his name or his profession, or his association with the journal or with the defendants, or that there was any existing person bearing the name of or known as Artemus Jones. They admitted publication, but denied that the words were published of or concerning the plaintiff. On the part of the plaintiff the evidence of the writer of the article and of the editor of the paper that they knew nothing of the plaintiff, and that the article was not intended by them to refer to him, was accepted as true. At the trial witnesses were called for the plaintiff, who said that they had read the article and thought that it referred to the plaintiff. The jury returned a verdict for the plaintiff with £1750 damages, and the learned judge gave judgment for the plaintiff. The defendants appealed.

FARWELL, L.J. . . .

An action for defamation differs from other actions, such for instance as trespass, in that it is of the essence of defamation that the plaintiff should be aimed at or intended by the defendant. The man who throws a squib into a crowd not intending to hit any one is liable for the consequences of his act, whatever his intentions may have been, because the two necessary constituents of tort, namely, a wrongful act by the defendant and actual damage to the plaintiff, are both present. But it is not enough for a plaintiff in libel to show that the defendant has made a libellous statement, and that the plaintiff's friends and acquaintances understand it to be written of him: he must also show that the defendant printed and published it of him; for if the defendant can prove that it was written truly of another person the plaintiff would fail. To this extent I agree with Fletcher Moulton L.J., but we differ as to the meaning of the word "intended." In my opinion the defendant intended the natural meaning of his own words in describing the plaintiff as much as in the innuendo: the inquiry is not what did the defendant mean in his own breast, but what did the words mean having regard to the relevant surrounding circumstances. For example, fraud is proved in an action of deceit not only when a false representation is made knowingly, but also when it is made recklessly, careless whether it be true or false, and although there was no intention to cheat or injure the person to whom the statement was made — and yet the fraudulent intent is of the essence of the action. So the intention to libel the plaintiff may be proved not only when the defendant knows and intends to injure the individuals, but also when he has made a statement concerning a man by a description by which the plaintiff is recognized by his associates, if the description is made recklessly, careless whether it hold up the plaintiff to contempt and ridicule or not. In such a case it is no answer for the defendant to say that he did not intend the plaintiff, because he had never heard of him: he intended to describe some living person: he can suggest no one else; and the plaintiff proves that he is believed by his acquaintances and friends to be the person aimed at, and has suffered damage thereby. The element of intention, which is as essential to an action of defamation as to an action of deceit, can be proved in the same way in both actions. The issue of fact is whether the plaintiff is the person intended by the libeller; but sufficient evidence to prove it may be given, although the defendant had no intention of injuring the plaintiff and had never heard of his existence. The squib thrower is liable for the injury done by his squib to the plaintiff, whether he aimed at or intended to hit him or not: the libeller is not liable to the plaintiff unless it is proved that the libel was aimed at or intended to hit him; the manner of proof being such as I have already stated. If the libel was true of another person and honestly aimed at and intended for him, and not for the plaintiff, the latter has no cause of action, although all his friends and acquaintances may fit the cap on him. If this were not so, no newspaper could ever venture to publish a true statement of A., lest some other person answering the description should suffer thereby. It is said that this would enable several plaintiffs to bring several and distinct actions in respect of one libel, and I think that this is so; but I am unable to see the objection. If the libel consisted in defamation of a number of individuals described generally, that is to say, "as the owners of some of the Irish factories," every member of the class who could satisfy the jury that he was a person aimed at and defamed could recover; and I can see no reason why two or more persons of the name of Artemus Jones who produced evidence from their acquaintances and others in different parts of the kingdom similar to that produced by the plaintiff in this case, the other circumstances being similar, should not recover. . . .

Appeal dismissed.

Notes

1. The *Jones* case brings out an ambiguity in the concept of an "intentional" tort. Did the defendants intend to defame the real Artemus Jones? Suppose I am shooting at a target and unbeknownst to me someone crosses my line of fire and is wounded. Am I guilty of a battery? Holmes, dissenting in a case much like *Jones*, where however the court declined to impose liability, drew this analogy: "This case would be very like firing a gun into a street, and when a man falls, setting up that no one was known to be there." Hanson v. Globe Newspaper Co., 159 Mass. 293, 301 (1893). On this view of the case, is it relevant that Jones is a very common surname? (Refer to the earlier Note on the meaning of "intent" and "intentional" in tort law.)

2. Could the issue in the *Jones* case be recast as whether there is a defense of honest mistake in a defamation case? Can a tort be said to be intentional if no such defense is recognized? Why was mistake a defense in *Barnes* but not in *Jones*? The next chapter discusses the defense of mistake in battery cases.

3. In recent years the Supreme Court, interpreting the First Amendment to the U.S. Constitution, has made substantial inroads into the defamation tort. Strictly speaking, these constitutional decisions do not affect the prima facie case, because the Constitution only provides a defense, based on the First Amendment (freedom of speech and of the press), to the application of state tort law. But they are relevant here because they involve primarily the degree to which newspapers and other media may be held liable for unintentional defamations as in *Jones*. The principal Supreme Court decisions are New York Times Co. v. Sullivan, 376 U.S. 254 (1964), which held that a public official could maintain a defamation action against a newspaper only if he proved the defendant's "actual malice," defined as knowledge of the falsity of the defamatory statement or reckless disregard of whether it was true or false; Curtis Publishing Co. v. Butts, 388 U.S. 130 (1967), which extended the actual-malice rule to suits by public figures as well as public officials; and Gertz v. Robert Welch, Inc., 418 U.S. 323 (1974), which rejected the actual-malice rule for cases not involving public officials or public figures

but held that state courts in such cases could not award recovery of damages without proof of at least the defendant's negligence and, unless the defendant was guilty of actual malice, could not award damages in excess of those required to compensate for actual injury. See also Time, Inc. v. Firestone, 424 U.S. 448 (1976); Comment, In Defense of Fault in Defamation Law, 88 Yale L.J. 1735 (1979). For recent cases allowing "involuntary public figures" to maintain defamation actions without having to prove actual malice see Hutchinson v. Proxmire, 443 U.S. 111 (1979), and Wolston v. Reader's Digest Assn., 443 U.S. 157 (1979). In *Hutchinson* the plaintiff was a scientist who had not sought publicity for his work (ridiculed by defendant, a U.S. Senator) outside of the scientific community. In *Wolston* the plaintiff had been convicted of contempt of Congress 16 years previously but was no longer a public figure.

4. Why is publication an element of the prima facie case of defamation? Can a lie not be just as wounding to the individual about whom it is told if it is communicated only to him? Is the requirement of publication an additional clue to the nature of the interest that is protected by the defamation tort?

5. Why did the court in *Jones* not give any weight to defendant's published retraction of the libel?

6. Group defamation (e.g., "all lawyers are shysters") is not actionable. See, e.g., Talal v. Fanning, 506 F. Supp. 186 (N.D. Cal. 1980). Why not? How is the hypothetical case mentioned in *Jones* of "owners of some of the Irish factories" distinguishable?

7. How would *Jones* have been decided if the court had used the Hand formula? Was P high or low? Was B high or low? What fact mentioned, though not stressed, in the opinion suggests B was very low? How about B to Jones — was it high or low? Could this also be a case where, even if defendant had used due care, he should still have avoided the injury by altering the nature or level of his activity? What is the relevant activity here?

8. For an interesting recent empirical study of defamation suits, finding that few plaintiffs prevail in such suits or obtain good settlements, see Franklin, Winners and Losers and Why: A Study of Defamation Litigation, 1980 Am. Bar Foundation Research J. 487.

Torts Without Damages?

Ordinarily, if the plaintiff in a tort action proves liability but is unable to show that he was damaged, he is entitled only to an award of nominal damages. But defamation seems to be different. Even if the plaintiff cannot prove a monetary or monetizable injury, he is allowed to get substantial "general" damages. This feature has been said to make defamation "an oddity of tort law." Gertz v. Robert Welch, Inc., 418 U.S. 323, 349 (1974). But there is another tort where general damages have traditionally been awarded: deprivation of the right to vote. The leading case is Ashby v. White, 2 Ld. Raym. 938, 92 Eng. Rep. 126 (K.B. 1703). See also Nixon v. Herndon, 273 U.S. 536 (1927); Annot., 153 A.L.R. 109 (1944).

Should general damages be obtainable in all intentional tort cases where no compensatory damages are provable? What light, if any, does economics cast on this question? How do general damages differ from punitive damages? If general damages are awarded, how should they be computed? What should be the respective roles of judge and jury?

For an argument that general damages should be awarded in constitutional tort cases generally see Note, 93 Harv. L. Rev. 966 (1980.

Johnson v. Sampson
167 Minn. 203, 208 N.W. 814 (1926)

LEES, C.J.

... The sole question is whether the complaint states a cause of action. It alleges that on March 25, 1925, the plaintiff was a schoolgirl 15 years of age, residing with her parents in Norman county, attending a public school in that county, and then in good health. On that day the defendants came to the schoolhouse and took her into a separate room, and then and there assaulted her, and committed other wrongs and injuries, "which said assault and other wrongs and injuries consisted of the wrongful and malicious acts hereinafter set forth as follows." The specific acts then set forth are that defendants charged her with having had sexual intercourse with various men. She truthfully denied the charge, whereupon she was told that if she did not confess she would be sent to reform school. By their acts and threats defendants caused her to believe that she would be deprived of her personal liberty and she and her parents disgraced, and put in such fear that she was deprived of her free will and reason. To avoid being imprisoned and disgraced, she admitted the charge, although in truth and in fact it was false. By reason of these acts plaintiff suffered great mental anguish, and received a nervous shock which seriously and permanently impaired her health. . . .

But we think the complaint does state a cause of action for damages for a wrongful invasion of plaintiff's legal rights. In Larson v. Chase, it was said that the law will not furnish redress for a wrong, unless there was an act which took effect upon the person, the property, or some other legal interest of the complainant. But it also said that, wherever there is a wrongful act which infringes on a legal right, even though no physical harm was done or threatened, there may be a recovery, if mental suffering was a proximate result of the act. . . .

The defendants are charged here with having falsely accused plaintiff of fornication.

G.S. 1923, Section 10120, reads in part as follows:

Every person who, in the presence and hearing of another, other than the female slandered, whether she be present or not, shall maliciously speak of or concerning any female of the age of twelve years or upwards . . . any false or defamatory words or language which shall injure or impair the reputation of such female for virtue or chastity, . . . shall be guilty of a misdemeanor. Every slander herein mentioned shall be deemed malicious if no justification therefor be shown. . . .

The complaint alleges that, confronting the plaintiff, the defendants made the charge against her in each other's presence. This was a violation of the statute. If the accusation was false and without justification, there was an invasion of plaintiff's legal right to be secure in her reputation for virtue, and, if, in consequence thereof, she was injured in the manner alleged, there may be a recovery, and an action for slander is not her only remedy. We think that, if everything relative to the alleged assault were stricken from the complaint, enough would remain to state a cause of action. If the facts are as pleaded, defendants' intentional and wrongful acts proximately caused both physical injury and mental suffering. The suddenness and seriousness of the charge would certainly shock a young girl, produce some degree of mental suffering, and would be likely to do harm to her nervous system. An intention to produce the effects alleged to have been produced must be imputed to defendants.

We hold that the complaint states a cause of action, and affirm the order overruling the demurrer.

Notes

1. Why did plaintiff not bring an action for slander?

2. What is the tort in this case? Is it intentional infliction of emotional distress? Is it an invasion of the right of privacy? Is false imprisonment a possibility?

3. Could this be viewed as an action to enforce the statute quoted by the court? We shall see in Chapter 4 that criminal statutes are frequently used as a basis for defining the standard of care in negligence cases.

Melvin v. Reid
112 Cal. App. 285, 297 P. 91 (1931)

[The trial court sustained defendant's demurrer to plaintiff's complaint, one count of which alleged an invasion of her right of privacy, and she appealed.]

MARKS, J. . . .

It is alleged that appellant's maiden name was Gabrielle Darley; that a number of years ago she was a prostitute and was tried for murder, the trial resulting in her acquittal; that during the year 1918, and after her acquittal she abandoned her life of shame and became entirely rehabilitated; that during the year 1919 she married Bernard Melvin and commenced the duties of caring for their home, and thereafter at all times lived an exemplary, virtuous, honorable, and righteous life; that she assumed a place in respectable society and made many friends who were not aware of the incidents of her earlier life; that during the month of July, 1925, the defendants, without her permission, knowledge, or consent, made, photographed, produced, and released a moving picture film entitled "The Red Kimono," and thereafter exhibited it in moving picture houses in California, Arizona, and throughout many other states; that this moving picture was based upon the true story of the past life of appellant, and that her maiden name, Gabrielle Darley, was used therein; that defendants featured and advertised that the plot of the film was the true story of the unsavory incidents in the life of appellant; that Gabrielle Darley was the true name of the principal character; and that Gabrielle Darley was appellant; that by the production and showing of the picture, friends of appellant learned for the first time of the unsavory incidents of her early life. This caused them to scorn and abandon her, and exposed her to obloquy, contempt, and ridicule, causing her grievous mental and physical suffering to her damage in the sum of $50,000. . . .

. . . When the incidents of a life are so public as to be spread upon a public record, they come within the knowledge and into the possession of the public and cease to be private. Had respondents, in the story of "The Red Kimono," stopped with the use of those incidents from the life of appellant which were spread upon the record of her trial, no right of action would have accrued. They went further, and in the formation of the plot used the true maiden name of appellant. If any right of action exists, it arises from the use of this true name in connection with the true incidents from her life together with their advertisements in which they stated that the story of the picture was taken from true incidents in the life of Gabrielle Darley, who was Gabrielle Darley Melvin. . . .

Upon demurrer, the allegations of the complaint must be taken as true. We must therefore conclude that eight years before the production of "The Red Kimono" appellant had abandoned her life of shame, had rehabilitated herself, and had taken her place as a respected and honored member of society. This change having occurred in her life, she should have been permitted to continue its course without having her reputation and social standing destroyed by the publication of the story of her former depravity with no other excuse than the expectation of private gain by the publishers.

One of the major objectives of society as it is now constituted, and of the administration of our penal system, is the rehabilitation of the fallen and the reformation of the criminal. Under these theories of sociology, it is our object to lift up and sustain the unfortunate rather than tear him down. Where a person has by his own efforts rehabilitated himself, we, as right-thinking members of society, should permit him to continue in the path of rectitude rather than throw him back into a life of shame or crime. Even the thief on the cross was permitted to repent during the hours of his final agony.

We believe that the publication by respondents of the unsavory incidents in the past life of appellant after she had reformed, coupled with her true name, was not justified by any standard of morals or ethics known to us, and was a direct invasion of her inalienable right guaranteed to her by our [California] Constitution, to pursue and obtain happiness. Whether we call this a right of privacy or give it any other name is immaterial, because it is a right guaranteed by our Constitution that must not be ruthlessly and needlessly invaded by others. We are of the opinion that the first cause of action of appellant's complaint states facts sufficient to constitute a cause of action against respondents. . . . .

Notes

1. What is the precise holding of this case?

2. Melvin v. Reid has not fared well as a precedent outside California. See, e.g., Rawlins v. Hutchinson Publishing Co., 218 Kan. 295, 543 P.2d 988 (1975). Moreover, a later California case indicates that the right of privacy does not extend to information concerning recent, rather than as in *Melvin* remote, past criminal activity. See Briscoe v. Reader's Digest Assn., 4 Cal. 3d 529, 483 P.2d 34 (1971). The Restatement declines to take a position on whether Melvin v. Reid is still good law. See Second Restatement of Torts §652 D, Illus. 2b.

Two other cases from California illustrate the difficulties that plaintiffs encounter in suits based on Melvin v. Reid. The first case is Cohen v. Marx, 94 Cal. App. 2d 704, 705, 211 P.2d 320, 321 (1950):

> The essential allegations of plaintiff's complaint as amended were that:
> In 1933, he had entered the prize ring as a professional boxer under the name of "Canvasback Cohen"; that he continued this ring career, losing decisions, until about 1939, when he abandoned the prize ring as a career; that on January 12, 1949, defendant Groucho Marx broadcast over a program of the defendant American Broadcast Company on its program "You Bet Your Life", "I once managed a prize-fighter, Canvasback Cohen. I brought him out here, he got knocked out, and I made him walk back to Cleveland."
> The sole question presented for our determination is:
> Did plaintiff, by entering the prize ring, seeking publicity, and becoming widely known as a prize fighter under the name of "Canvasback Cohen" waive his right to privacy?
> This question must be answered in the affirmative. A person who by his accomplishments, fame or mode of life, or by adopting a profession or calling which gives the public a legitimate interest in his doings, affairs, or character, is

said to become a public personage, and thereby relinquishes a part of his right of privacy.

The second case is Smith v. National Broadcasting Co., 138 Cal. App. 2d 807, 292 P.2d 600 (1956). Plaintiff complained about a radio program in the "Dragnet" series that, without naming him, recounted an incident in which he had figured. The incident is described in the complaint as follows:

> . . . [A] number of months ago Plaintiff made a report to the Police Department of the City of Los Angeles, State of California, of the loss, escape or theft of a certain Black Panther animal somewhere within the confines of the City of Los Angeles, which report the Plaintiff, at the time that he made it, believed to be true, and which report was then made in good faith. Plaintiff, in that report, stated to Police that he had placed a Black Panther animal in a motor truck for transport and that the animal was no longer in the truck. The result was a City-wide and later a County-wide search for the animal. The people of the City of Los Angeles became frightened to the point where they would call police and report having seen or heard a Black Panther animal. The people of the City of Los Angeles became frightened and tense and began imagining that they saw and heard things that really did not exist. Many persons called the Police Department and reported seeing or hearing the Panther; in one instance it turned out to be a Black Cat; in another instance it turned out to be children playing games; other times it turned out to be nothing more than the imagination of the caller. Finally, after many days the Police Department came to the conclusion that there probably was no Black Panther loose at all; at about the same time the Plaintiff herein was informed that the animal had actually reached its destination; hence the report was withdrawn, the scare was over, and Los Angeles went back to normal. The Plaintiff was arrested and was caused to be given Psychiatric examination as a result of this report which turned out to be untrue. As a result of the incidents and occurrences above-depicted and above-described the Plaintiff was caused to become nervous and unsteady, and he was subjected to scorn and abandonment by his friends and was exposed to obloquy, contempt, and ridicule resulting in grievous mental and physical suffering.

Id. at 808, 292 P.2d at 601. The court held that there was no invasion of plaintiff's right of privacy:

> On the facts disclosed by the pleadings before the court, it is patent that an essential element of a cause of action is absent in the case at bar, viz., the incident involving plaintiff was not drawn from his private affairs or activities but was known to the public and was a matter not only of public interest and record but of official concern to municipal authorities. . . .
>
> Plaintiff seems to intimate that defendants lost any right they might have had to broadcast their dramatization of the "Black Panther" incident because their broadcast was made three months after the event, which had by then lost any current news value. It is a characteristic of every era, no less than of our contemporary world, that events which have caught the popular imagination or

incidents which have aroused the public interest, have been frequently revivified long after their occurrence in the literature, journalism, or other media of communication of a later day. These events, being embedded in the communal history, are proper material for such recounting. It is well established, therefore, that the mere passage of time does not preclude the publication of such incidents from the life of one formerly in the public eye which are already public property.

Id. at 811-812, 292 P.2d at 603. How can *Cohen* and *Smith* be distinguished from Melvin v. Reid?

3. Did respondents in *Melvin* make a tactical error in demurring to the complaint and thereby conceding, for purposes of the ruling on demurrer and the appeal from that ruling, that the facts alleged in the complaint were true?

4. Why should the law provide assistance to people in trying to conceal their unsavory pasts? How persuasive is the court's repentance rationale? Are concealment and repentance the same thing?

5. Information about an individual's past misconduct is valuable to people who are deciding whether to form or create a social or business relationship with the individual. But a rational person will discount the information by the recency of the misconduct: the more recent it is, the more weight he will assign it; the further in the past it is, the less weight he will assign it. If this is how people in fact behave, was Melvin v. Reid decided correctly?

6. If Melvin v. Reid was decided correctly, does this imply that truth should not be a defense in a defamation action?

Cox Broadcasting Co. v. Cohn
231 Ga. 60, 200 S.E.2d 127 (1973)

GUNTER, J. . . .

On August 18, 1971, the appellee's seventeen-year-old daughter was the victim of the crime of rape. Her death immediately followed. Six young men were subsequently indicted for murder and rape.

The rape and the death of the rape-victim were widely publicized immediately after the occurrence of these events. However, apparently because of a Georgia statute the identity of the female victim was not disclosed by any of the news media. That Georgia statute is as follows: "It shall be unlawful for any news media or any other person to print and publish, broadcast, televise, or disseminate through any other medium of public dissemination or cause to be printed and published, broadcast, televised, or disseminated in any newspaper, magazine, periodical or other publication published in this State or through any radio or television broadcast originating in the State the name or identity of any female who may have been raped or upon whom an assault with intent to commit rape may have been made. Any person or corporation violating the provisions of this section shall, upon conviction, be punished as for a misdemeanor."

Approximately eight months after the commission of the alleged crimes, the six young men were involved in court proceedings pursuant to the indictments returned against them. On the same day of the court proceedings, April 10, 1972, and on the following day, April 11, 1972, the appellant broadcasting company and its agent-reporter originated a telecast from the courthouse which disclosed the identity of the deceased rape-victim.

That telecast in part contained the following: "Six youths went on trial today for the murder-rape of a teenaged girl. The six Sandy Springs high school boys were charged with murder and rape in the death of seventeen year old Cynthia Cohn following a drinking party last August 18. The tragic death of the high school girl shocked the entire Sandy Springs community. Today the six boys had their day in court. There was no jury. The six boys through their lawyers, threw themselves on the mercy of the court . . . and the presiding judge, Sam Phillips McKenzie. The prosecutor, assistant Attorney General John Nuckolls said the girl had apparently drank [sic] a considerable amount of vodka attending a private party. He said the girl was taken to a wooded area and raped. She passed out . . . and the liquids in her stomach were forced upward causing suffocation. The exact cause of death . . . that is whether the rape caused death he said would be difficult to prove. Judge McKenzie dropped the murder charge against all six . . . and proceeded with the charge of rape. The DA told the judge all six defendants wished to plead guilty . . . and not have a jury trial. The DA told the court the girl's family felt that a lenient five year sentence would serve justice and he recommended a five year sentence." . . .

On May 8, 1972, the appellee brought an action for money damages against the broadcasting company and its reporter for having invaded his right to privacy by publishing the identity of his deceased daughter in connection with the circumstances related in the telecast. . . .

The trial court apparently granted summary judgment as to liability against the appellants on the theory that the Georgia statute which prohibits disclosure of the identity of a rape victim gives rise to a civil cause of action in favor of the victim and, in this case, the father of a deceased victim against the party making the disclosure; and there being no question about the disclosure in this case, the trial court determined liability to exist against the disclosing parties as a matter of law.

We disagree with the trial court on this score. This Georgia statute and its predecessor are penal in nature, and while these statutes establish the public policy of this state on this subject, neither of them created a civil cause of action for damages in favor of the victim or anyone else. . . .

Does the father of a deceased minor child have a cause of action in tort by virtue of the public disclosure of the identity of his daughter as the victim of a sex crime and the unpleasant circumstances connected therewith, all of which occurred approximately eight months prior to the public disclosure of his daughter's involvement?

It is clear that the female victim's privacy was not invaded in this case. She had been dead some eight months prior to her identity and involvement being publicly disclosed.

The surviving father of the deceased daughter asserts that the tort was perpetrated directly upon him. He contends that the public disclosure of the identity and involvement of his daughter eight months after the fact invaded his right to privacy and intruded upon his right to be left alone, free from and unconnected with the sad and unpleasant event that had previously occurred. . . .

Although the appellee's complaint in this case stated a claim for relief, the public disclosure, admitted by the appellants, did not establish liability on the part of the appellants as a matter of law. Whether the public disclosure actually invaded the appellee's "zone of privacy," and if so to what extent, are issues to be determined by the fact-finder. And in formulating such an issue for determination by the fact-finder, it is reasonable to require the appellee to prove that the appellants invaded his privacy with wilful or negligent disregard for the fact that reasonable men would find the invasion highly offensive. . . .

Notes

1. In an omitted portion of the opinion, the court held that plaintiff's claim was not barred by the First Amendment. The court relied in part on the Georgia statute making it a crime to disclose the identity of a rape victim in the news media. The court's reasoning was that this statute showed that, in Georgia anyway, the identity of the rape victim was not a matter of such public interest as to override the right of privacy.

The U.S. Supreme Court reversed the *Cox* decision, holding that the Georgia statute was unconstitutional under the First Amendment; the First Amendment creates a privilege to publish any matter contained in public records. 420 U.S. 469 (1975). What is the impact of this ruling on the continued validity of Melvin v. Reid?

Constitutional decisions have made substantial inroads into the tort of invasion of privacy, as they have into the tort of defamation. For a critical discussion of the Supreme Court's decisions dealing with the privacy tort see Posner, The Uncertain Protection of Privacy by the Supreme Court, 1979 Sup. Ct. Rev. 173, 206-208 (Kurland & Casper eds.).

2. Was the case for recognizing a right of privacy stronger in *Cox* or *Reid*? Was the identity of the rape victim a material fact to people contemplating social or business dealings with her parents? How important was it to the news value of the story of the rape trial?

3. What right of action, if any, might the plaintiff in *Cox* have had against the rapists themselves?

4. Do you agree with the Georgia court's view that the Georgia penal statute was not intended to create civil liability?

Sidis v. F-R Publishing Corp.
113 F.2d 806 (2d Cir. 1940)

CLARK, J.

William James Sidis was the unwilling subject of a brief biographical sketch and cartoon printed in The New Yorker weekly magazine for August 14, 1937. Further references were made to him in the issue of December 25, 1937, and in a newspaper advertisement announcing the August 14 issue. He brought an action in the district court against the publisher, F-R Publishing Corporation. . . .

William James Sidis was a famous child prodigy in 1910. His name and prowess were well known to newspaper readers of the period. At the age of eleven, he lectured to distinguished mathematicians on the subject of Four-Dimensional Bodies. When he was sixteen, he was graduated from Harvard College, amid considerable public attention. Since then, his name has appeared in the press only sporadically, and he has sought to live as unobtrusively as possible. Until the articles objected to appeared in The New Yorker, he had apparently succeeded in his endeavor to avoid the public gaze.

Among The New Yorker's features are brief biographical sketches of current and past personalities. In the latter department, which appears haphazardly under the title of "Where Are They Now?" the article on Sidis was printed with a subtitle "April Fool." The author describes his subject's early accomplishments in mathematics and the wide-spread attention he received, then recounts his general breakdown and the revulsion which Sidis thereafter felt for his former life of fame and study. The unfortunate prodigy is traced over the years that followed, through his attempts to conceal his identity, through his chosen career as an insignificant clerk who would not need to employ unusual mathematical talents, and through the bizarre ways in which his genius flowered, as in his enthusiasm for collecting streetcar transfers and in his proficiency with an adding machine. The article closes with an account of an interview with Sidis at his present lodgings, "a hall bedroom of Boston's shabby south end." The untidiness of his room, his curious laugh, his manner of speech, and other personal habits are commented upon at length, as is his present interest in the lore of the Okamakammessett Indians. The subtitle is explained by the closing sentence, quoting Sidis as saying "with a grin" that it was strange, "but, you know, I was born on April Fool's Day." Accompanying the biography is a small cartoon showing the genius of eleven years lecturing to a group of astounded professors.

It is not contended that any of the matter printed is untrue. Nor is the manner of the author unfriendly; Sidis today is described as having "a certain childlike charm." But the article is merciless in its dissection of intimate details of its subject's personal life, and this in company with elaborate accounts of Sidis' passion for privacy and the pitiable lengths to which he has gone in order to avoid public scrutiny. The work possesses great reader interest, for it is both amusing and instructive; but it may be fairly described as a ruthless exposure of a once public character, who has since sought and has now been deprived of the seclusions of private life. . . .

. . . Everyone will agree that at some point the public interest in obtaining information becomes dominant over the individual's desire for privacy. Warren and Brandeis were willing to lift the veil somewhat in the case of public officers. We would go further, though we are not yet prepared to say how far. At least we would permit limited scrutiny of the "private" life of any person who has achieved, or has had thrust upon him, the questionable and indefinable status of a "public figure."

William James Sidis was once a public figure. As a child prodigy, he excited both admiration and curiosity. Of him great deeds were expected. In 1910, he was a person about whom the newspapers might display a legitimate intellectual interest, in the sense meant by Warren and Brandeis, as distinguished from a trivial and unseemly curiosity. But the precise motives of the press we regard as unimportant. And even if Sidis had loathed public attention at that time, we think his uncommon achievements and personality would have made the attention permissible. Since then Sidis has cloaked himself in obscurity, but his subsequent history, containing as it did the answer to the question of whether or not he had fulfilled his early promise, was still a matter of public concern. The article in The New Yorker sketched the life of an unusual personality, and it possessed considerable popular news interest.

We express no comment on whether or not the news worthiness of the matter printed will always constitute a complete defense. Revelations may be so intimate and so unwarranted in view of the victim's position as to outrage the community's notions of decency. But when focused upon public characters, truthful comments upon dress, speech, habits, and the ordinary aspects of personality will usually not transgress this line. Regrettably or not, the misfortunes and frailties of neighbors and "public figures" are subjects of considerable interest and discussion to the rest of the population. And when such are the mores of the community, it would be unwise for a court to bar their expression in the newspapers, books, and magazines of the day. . . .

Notes

1. A defamatory utterance is actionable if it is published to at least one person besides the person defamed; but to be actionable as an invasion of the

right of privacy, a statement must be publicized, i.e., widely disseminated.*
What is the basis of this difference?

2. If Sidis cared so much about his privacy, why did he consent to be
interviewed by the author of the New Yorker article? Was his action in
bringing this lawsuit consistent with his having a high regard for his privacy?

3. Why should Sidis not have been held to have a property right in his
life story, which the New Yorker would have to purchase from him if it
wanted to write an article about his life? Would this approach automatically
balance Sidis's interest in privacy with the public interest in knowing his
interesting life story? In an omitted portion of the opinion in Melvin v. Reid,
the court rejected the plaintiff's alternative contention that she had a property right to her life story.

4. Is *Sidis* distinguishable from Melvin v. Reid? Would it be if *Melvin*
had involved a New Yorker article about Mrs. Melvin's past?

5. Consider the facts of Daily Times Democrat v. Graham, 276 Ala. 380-
381, 162 So. 2d 474-476 (1964), where liability for an invasion of privacy was
upheld:

> Appellee is a woman 44 years of age who has lived in Cullman County,
> Alabama her entire life. She is married and has two sons, ages 10 and 8. The
> family resides in a rural community where her husband is engaged in the
> business of raising chickens. The appellee has led the usual life of a housewife in
> her community, participating in normal church and community affairs.
>
> On 9 October 1961, the Cullman County Fair was in progress. On that day
> the appellee took her two children to the Fair. After going on some of the rides,
> the boys expressed a wish to go through what is called in the record the "Fun
> House." The boys were afraid to enter alone so the appellee accompanied
> them. She testified she had never been through a Fun House before and had no
> knowledge that there was a device that blew jets of air up from the platform of
> the Fun House upon which one exited therefrom.
>
> The appellee entered the Fun House with her two boys and as she was
> leaving her dress was blown up by the air jets and her body was exposed from the
> waist down, with the exception of that portion covered by her "panties."
>
> At this moment the appellant's photographer snapped a picture of the
> appellee in this situation. This was done without the appellee's knowledge or
> consent. Four days later the appellant published this picture on the front page
> of its newspaper.
>
> The appellant publishes about five thousand newspapers daily which are
> delivered to homes, mailed to subscribers, and displayed on racks in various
> locations in the city of Cullman and elsewhere.
>
> On the Sunday following the publication of the picture, the appellee went
> into the city of Cullman. There she saw the appellant's newspaper display with
> her picture on the front page in one of the appellant's newspaper racks, and she
> also saw copies of the said newspaper in other places.

*Is *Berthiaume* consistent with this distinction?

While the appellee's back was largely towards the camera in the picture, her two sons are in the picture and the photograph was recognized as being of her by other people with whom she was acquainted. The matter of her photograph was mentioned to the appellee by others on several occasions. Evidence offered by the appellee during the trial tended to show that the appellee, as a result of the publication of the picture, became embarrassed, self-conscious, upset and was known to cry on occasions.

How is this case distinguishable from *Sidis*? From Melvin v. Reid? Could plaintiff have brought an action for intentional infliction of emotional distress? For defamation? For the "false light" as distinct from "publicity" form of invasion of privacy?

With *Graham* compare Cowan v. Time Inc., 41 Misc. 2d 198-199, 245 N.Y.S.2d 723, 725 (Sup. Ct. 1963):

The action is for damages allegedly resulting from the publication by the defendants in the "Life" magazine of a libelous article. Annexed to and incorporated in the complaint is a copy of the article. Titled "Some Idiots Afloat" the article is composed of about eight pictures of persons using boats, printed commentary concerning each of the pictures, and a brief statement concerning the lack of care by many persons now using boats. No names of the individuals shown in the various pictures are given but the plaintiff claims he is the individual at the tiller of a small boat (in which there are four other persons) on page 64 of the magazine article. Under the picture are the words "Rub-a-dub dub, too many in a tub."

What, if any, tort was committed here?

6. Section 652D of the Second Restatement of Torts states that, "One who gives publicity to a matter concerning the private life of another is subject to liability to the other for invasion of his privacy, if the matter publicized is of a kind that (a) would be highly offensive to a reasonable person, and (b) is not of legitimate concern to the public" — but then warns: "It has not been established with certainty that liability of this nature is consistent with the free-speech and free-press provisions of the First Amendment to the Constitution, as applied to state law through the Fourteenth Amendment."

Chandelor v. Lopus
Cro. Jac. 4, 79 Eng. Rep. 3 (Exch. Ch. 1603)

ACTION UPON THE CASE. Whereas the defendant being a goldsmith, and having skill in jewels and precious stones, had a stone which he affirmed to Lopus to be a bezar-stone, and sold it to him for one hundred pounds; ubi revera it was not a bezar-stone: the defendant pleaded not guilty, and verdict was given and judgment entered for the plaintiff in the king's bench.

But error was thereof brought in the exchequer-chamber; because the declaration contains not matter sufficient to charge the defendant, viz. that he warranted it to be a bezar-stone, or that he knew that it was not a bezar-stone; for it may be, he himself was ignorant whether it were a bezar-stone or not.

And ALL THE JUSTICES AND BARONS (except ANDERSON) held, that for this cause it was error: for the bare affirmation that it was a bezar-stone, without warranting it to be so, is no cause of action: and although he knew it to be no bezar-stone, it is not material; for every one in selling his wares will affirm that his wares are good, or the horse which he sells is sound; yet if he does not warrant them to be so, it is no cause of action, and the warranty ought to be made at the same time of the sale. Wherefore, forasmuch as no warranty is alleged, they held the declaration to be ill.

Gilmore, Products Liability: A Comment
38 U. Chi. L. Rev. 103, 107-108 (1970)

. . . For several hundred years the case [Chandelor v. Lopus] has been cited, with approval or with scorn, as illustrative of the extremely narrow scope of liability which seventeenth century law placed on sellers for the quality of the goods they sold.

The report of the case does not bother to explain what a bezoar was — presumably everyone knew what a bezoar was, just as we all know what a diamond is. It occurred to me one day, in thinking about the case, that I for one had no idea what a bezoar might be. The new Oxford Dictionary proved to be illuminating. A bezoar (or "bezar") was, descriptively, "a calculus or concretion found in the stomachs of some animals, chiefly ruminants, formed of concentric layers of animal matter deposited round some foreign substance, which serves as a nucleus." That explains everything except why a bezoar would have been worth £100 in the early 17th century. The true value of a bezoar, it appears, lay in its magic or, as we should say, medicinal properties: application of the bezoar to a diseased part of the body cured the disease. "Everything that frees the body of any ailment," it was said, "is called the Bezoar of that ailment." And the East India Company had reported in 1618 that: "On the island of Borneo, diamonds, bezoar stones and gold might be obtained."

Now that we know more about bezoars than we did, we may begin to wonder whether our initial reaction to the holding in Chandelor v. Lopus was, historically, correct — or even relevant to the case. It was generally known that there were true, or magic, bezoars. It must also have been a matter of common knowledge that it was extremely difficult, if not impossible, to tell a true bezoar from a false one. And no doubt the attitude of the user counted for something: if I believed in my bezoar it might indeed preserve me from the plague while the same stone in the hands of a skeptical rationalist would be worthless. Under such circumstances a court might hesitate to impose liability on a seller who had merely said that, to the best of his knowledge, he believed (or affirmed) the stone to be a bezoar, but did not warrant it. It may be that the 17th century concept of liability was not as narrow as we have supposed it to be. . . .

Pasley v. Freeman
3 T.R. 51, 100 Eng. Rep. 450 (1789)

[In an action for deceit, plaintiffs alleged that defendant had asserted that one Falch "was a person safely to be trusted and given credit to" in the purchase of goods worth more than £2500, knowing the assertion to be false. Plaintiffs further alleged that defendant had thereby caused them to sell these goods to Falch on credit, and that Falch had failed to pay for the goods. The jury found for plaintiffs. Defendant moved in arrest of judgment. The court held that on these facts an action for deceit could be maintained. An excerpt from CHIEF JUSTICE KENYON'S opinion follows.]

. . . There are many situations in life, and particularly in the commercial world, where a man cannot by any diligence inform himself of the degree of credit which ought to be given to the persons with whom he deals; in which cases he must apply to those whose sources of intelligence enable them to give that information. The law of prudence leads him to apply to them, and the law of morality ought to induce them to give the information required. . . . [T]he plaintiffs had no means of knowing the state of Falch's credit but by an application to his neighbours. The same observation may be made to the cases cited by the defendant's counsel respecting titles to real property. For a person does not have recourse to common conversations to know the title of an estate which he is about to purchase: but he may inspect the title deeds; and he does not use common prudence if he rely on any other security. . . . [I]t was contended here that the action cannot be maintained for telling a naked lie: but that proposition is to be taken sub modo. If, indeed, no injury is occasioned by the lie, it is not actionable: but if it be attended with a damage, it then becomes the subject of an action. As calling a woman a whore, if she sustain no damage by it, is not actionable; but if she loses her marriage by it, then she may recover satisfaction in damages. But in this case the two grounds of the action concur: here are both the damnum et injuria. The plaintiffs applied to the defendant telling him that they were going to deal with Falch, and desiring to be informed of his credit, when the defendant fraudulently, and knowing it to be otherwise, and with a design to deceive the plaintiffs, made the false affirmation which is stated on the record, by which they sustained a considerable damage. Then can a doubt be entertained for a moment but that this is injurious to the plaintiffs? If this be not an injury, I do not know how to define the word. Then as to the loss, this is stated in the declaration, and found by the verdict. Several of the words stated in this declaration, and particularly "fraudulenter," did not occur in several of the cases cited. It is admitted that the defendant's conduct was highly immoral, and detrimental to society. And I am of opinion that the action is maintainable on the grounds of deceit in the defendant, and injury and loss to the plaintiffs. . . .

Swinton v. Whitinsville Savings Bank
311 Mass. 677, 42 N.E.2d 808 (1942)

QUA, J.

The declaration alleges that on or about September 12, 1938, the defendant sold the plaintiff a house in Newton to be occupied by the plaintiff and his family as a dwelling; that at the time of the sale the house "was infested with termites, an insect that is most dangerous and destructive to buildings"; that the defendant knew the house was so infested; that the plaintiff could not readily observe this condition upon inspection; that, "knowing the internal destruction that these insects were creating in said house," the defendant falsely and fraudulently concealed from the plaintiff its true condition; that the plaintiff at the time of his purchase had no knowledge of the termites, exercised due care thereafter, and learned of them about August 30, 1940; and that, because of the destruction that was being done and the dangerous condition that was being created by the termites, the plaintiff was put to great expense for repairs and for the installation of termite control in order to prevent the loss and destruction of said house.

There is no allegation of any false statement or representation, or of the uttering of a half truth which may be tantamount to a falsehood. There is no intimation that the defendant by any means prevented the plaintiff from acquiring information as to the condition of the house. There is nothing to show any fiduciary relation between the parties, or that the plaintiff stood in a position of confidence toward or dependence upon the defendant. So far as appears the parties made a business deal at arm's length. The charge is concealment and nothing more; and it is concealment in the simple sense of mere failure to reveal, with nothing to show any peculiar duty to speak. The characterization of the concealment as false and fraudulent of course adds nothing in the absence of further allegations of fact.

If this defendant is liable on this declaration every seller is liable who fails to disclose any nonapparent defect known to him in the subject of the sale which materially reduces its value and which the buyer fails to discover. Similarly it would seem that every buyer would be liable who fails to disclose any nonapparent virtue known to him in the subject of the purchase which materially enhances its value and of which the seller is ignorant. The law has not yet, we believe, reached the point of imposing upon the frailties of human nature a standard so idealistic as this. That the particular case here stated by the plaintiff possesses a certain appeal to the moral sense is scarcely to be denied. Probably the reason is to be found in the facts that the infestation of buildings by termites has not been common in Massachusetts and constitutes a concealed risk against which buyers are off their guard. But the law cannot provide special rules for termites and can hardly attempt to determine liability according to the varying probabilities of the existence and discovery of different possible defects in the subjects of trade. . . .

Notes

1. The trend is to find deceit in cases of failure to disclose termite infestation, contrary to *Swinton*. See, e.g., Obde v. Schlemeyer, 56 Wash. 2d 449, 353 P.2d 672 (1960); Williams v. Benson, 3 Mich. App. 9, 141 N.W.2d 650 (1966); Miles v. McSwegin, 58 Ohio St. 2d 97, 388 N.E.2d 1367 (1979). Which is the better rule?

2. Was the court in *Swinton* correct in stating that if the seller of property is required to disclose latent defects, the buyer must be required to disclose latent virtues — e.g., that he knows there is oil under the property? Generally, buyers' and sellers' duties to disclose are not treated symmetrically. "The buyer is permitted to reap the advantages which his industry in discovering the facts, and his business acumen, can bring him." Prosser 698. Does this distinction make economic sense? An affirmative answer is given in Kronman, Mistake, Disclosure, Information, and the Law of Contracts, 7 J. Legal Stud. 1 (1978). Kronman argues that a buyer's investment in information about the quality of goods or services that he is buying should be protected by not forcing him to disclose the fruits of that investment to the seller. Protection creates an incentive to make socially valuable investments in information. But where a seller obtains knowledge of a defect in his goods or property without an investment in information, allowing him to conceal his knowledge serves no social purpose.

3. As both *Chandelor* and *Pasley* suggest, an action for deceit will not lie where the information concealed by the defendant is equally accessible to the plaintiff. Is the "equal access" principle intelligible in Hand formula terms? Does it suggest that *Swinton* was decided correctly or incorrectly?

4. Concealment of latent defects is a frequent issue in accident cases. If plaintiff, a guest in defendant's house, falls and is injured when a termite-infested floor gives way, should defendant be liable? Are the considerations the same as they would be if plaintiff were a buyer complaining that defendant had concealed the presence of the termites?

5. Statements of opinion, predictions, and sales "puffery" are rarely actionable. For example, in Finch v. McKee, 18 Cal. App. 2d 90, 62 P.2d 1380 (1936), plaintiffs alleged that defendants had sold them a building and represented among other things that it would withstand earthquake shocks; it was later damaged by an earthquake. The court stated:

> . . . Fraud may not ordinarily be predicated on mere statements of opinion regarding the value, general character or stability of a building, even though such assertions are greatly exaggerated. Since it is difficult to distinguish between expressions of honest convictions respecting the stability, value, or adaptability of property, and false representations of an owner regarding those matters, they are charitably considered mere expressions of opinion which will not afford grounds for suit. Usually a purchaser is charged with knowledge of such excess enthusiasm and human frailty on the part of a vendor, for which he must make due allowance, and he is deemed to accept as true such representations, amounting to mere judgment or opinion, at his own peril.
>
> The mere statement that the building in question was constructed earthquake proof is a matter of pure speculation or prophecy. Every person of common understanding knows it is impossible to estimate the destructive forces of nature accompanying earthquakes, tornadoes, cyclones, storms, or floods. No human being could have prophesied the serious damages which resulted to first-class buildings in San Francisco, Santa Rosa, and San Jose from the earthquake of 1906. Nor could one foretell the damages which resulted to the structures in Long Beach and that vicinity from the earthquake of 1933. Such statements were pure speculations upon which no purchaser had a right to rely. . . .

Id. at 93-94, 62 P.2d at 1382. Is the basis of the court's conclusion the "equal access" principle discussed above?

Derry v. Peek
14 A.C. 337 (H.L. 1889)

[An investor in the Plymouth, Devenport and District Tramways Company brought an action for deceit against the directors of the company, arising from misrepresentations in the prospectus. By a special Act of Parliament, the company was authorized to make tramways. The act provided that the carriages used on the tramways might be moved by animal power and, with the consent of the Board of Trade, by steam or any mechanical power for fixed periods and subject to the regulations of the Board. The prospectus stated:

> One great feature of this undertaking, to which considerable importance should be attached, is, that by the special Act of Parliament obtained, the company has the right to use steam or mechanical motive power, instead of horses, and it is fully expected that by means of this a considerable saving will

result in the working expenses of the line as compared with other tramways worked by horses.

The company proceeded to make tramways, but the Board of Trade refused to consent to the use of steam or mechanical power except on certain portions of the tramways. As a result, the company was wound up. The Court of Appeal, reversing the judgment of the trial court, held that defendants were liable to make good the plaintiff's losses on the shares. They appealed to the House of Lords.]

LORD BRAMWELL:

... The plaintiff's case is that the defendants made an untrue statement, which they knew to be untrue, and likely to influence persons reading it; therefore they were fraudulent. ... The alleged untrue statement is that, "The company has the right to use steam or mechanical power instead of horses," and that a saving would be thereby effected. Now, this is certainly untrue, because it is stated as an absolute right, when in truth it was conditional on the approval of the Board of Trade, and the sanction or consent of two local boards; and a conditional right is not the same as an absolute right. It is also certain that the defendants knew what the truth was, and therefore knew that what they said was untrue. But it does not follow that the statement was fraudulently made. There are various kinds of untruth. There is an absolute untruth, an untruth in itself, that no addition or qualification can make true; as, if a man says a thing he saw was black, when it was white, as he remembers and knows. So, as to *knowing* the truth. A man may know it, and yet it may not be present to his mind at the moment of speaking; or, if the fact is present to his mind, it may not occur to him to be of any use to mention it. For example, suppose a man was asked whether a writing was necessary in a contract for the making and purchase of goods, he might well say "Yes," without adding that payment on receipt of the goods, or part, would suffice. He might well think that the question he was asked was whether a contract for goods to be made required a writing like a contract for goods in existence. If he was writing on the subject he would, of course, state the exception or qualification.

Now, consider the case here. These directors naturally trust to their solicitors to prepare their prospectus. It is prepared and laid before them. They find the statement of their power to use steam without qualification. It does not occur to them to alter it. They swear they had no fraudulent intention. At the very last they cannot see the fraud. There is their oath, their previous character unimpeached, and there is to my mind this further consideration: the truth would have served their purpose as well. "We have power to use steam, etc., of course with the usual conditions of the approval of the Board of Trade and the consent of the local authorities, but we may make sure of these being granted, as the Board of Trade has already allowed the power to be inserted in the Act, and the local authorities have expressed their approbation of the scheme." (See plaintiff's answer, which shows that he would have been content with that statement.) . . .

. . . I think it is most undesirable that actions should be maintainable in respect of statements, made unreasonably perhaps, but honestly. I think it would be disastrous if there was "a right to have true statements only made." This case is an example. I think that in this kind of case, as in some others, Courts of Equity have made the mistake of disregarding a valuable general principle in their desire to effect what is, or is thought to be, justice in a particular instance. It might, perhaps, be well to enact that in prospectuses of public companies there should be a warranty of the truth of all statements except where it was expressly said there was no warranty. The objection is to exceptional legislation, and to the danger of driving respectable and responsible men from being promoters, and of substituting for them those who are neither.

In this particular case I hold that unless fraud in the defendants could be shown, the action is not maintainable. I am satisfied there was no fraud. Further, if an unreasonable misstatement were enough, I hold there was none. Still further, I do not believe that the plaintiff was influenced by the misstatement, though I am entirely satisfied that he was an honest witness.

LORD HERSCHELL. . . .

I turn now to the evidence of the defendants. I will take first that of Mr. Wilde, whose conduct in relation to the promotion of the company is free from suspicion. He is a member of the Bar and a director of one of the London tramway companies. He states that he was aware that the consent of the Board of Trade was necessary, but that he thought that such consent had been practically given, inasmuch as, pursuant to the Standing Orders, the plans had been laid before the Board of Trade with the statement that it was intended to use mechanical as well as horsepower, and no objection having been raised by the Board of Trade, and the Bill obtained, he took it for granted that no objection would be raised afterwards, provided the works were properly carried out. He considered, therefore, that, practically and substantially they had the right to use steam, and that the statement was perfectly true.

Mr. Pethick's evidence is to much the same effect. He thought the Board of Trade had no more right to refuse their consent than they would in the case of a railway; that they might have required additions or alterations, but that on any reasonable requirements being complied with they could not refuse their consent. It never entered his thoughts that after the Board had passed their plans, with the knowledge that it was proposed to use steam, they would refuse their consent.

Mr. Moore states that he was under the impression that the passage in the prospectus represented the effect of sect. 35 of the Act, inasmuch as he understood that the consent was obtained. He so understood from the statements made at the board by the solicitors to the company, to the general effect that everything was in order for the use of steam, that the Act had been obtained subject to the usual restrictions, and that they were starting as a tramway company, with full power to use steam as other companies were doing.

Mr. Wakefield, according to his evidence, believed that the statement in the prospectus was fair; he never had a doubt about it. It never occurred to him to say anything about the consent of the Board of Trade, because as they had got the Act of Parliament for steam he presumed at once that they would get it.

Mr. Derry's evidence is somewhat confused, but I think the fair effect of it is that though he was aware that under the Act the consent of the Board of Trade was necessary, he thought that the company having obtained their Act the Board's consent would follow as a matter of course, and that the question of such consent being necessary never crossed his mind at the time the prospectus was issued. He believed at that time that it was correct to say they had the right to use steam.

As I have said, Stirling J. gave credit to these witnesses, and I see no reason to differ from him. What conclusion ought to be drawn from their evidence? . . . If they believed that the consent of the Board of Trade was practically concluded by the passing of the Act, has the plaintiff made out, which it was for him to do, that they have been guilty of a fraudulent misrepresentation? I think not. I cannot hold it proved as to any one of them that he knowingly made a false statement, or one which he did not believe to be true, or was careless whether what he stated was true or false. In short, I think they honestly believed that what they asserted was true, and I am of opinion that the charge of fraud made against them has not been established. . . .

Notes

1. Was there any doubt that the defendants knew the statement in the prospectus was false? What would they have had to know, in addition to the falsity of the statement, for it to be actionable?

2. Were the defendants or the plaintiff in a better position to discover the falsity of the statement? Do we know enough about conditions in nineteenth-century securities markets to evaluate the court's decision?

3. Derry v. Peek made clear that deceit was an intentional tort. (Is this conclusion consistent with Lord Herschell's suggestion that an action might lie if a defendant was "careless whether what he stated was true or false"?) This circumscribed the utility of the tort in dealing with fraud, perhaps especially in connection with issuance of securities (why "especially"?). Eventually, however, a tort of negligent misrepresentation emerged. See, e.g., Ultramares Corp. v. Touche, 255 N.Y. 170, 174 N.E. 441 (1931); Texas Tunneling Co. v. City of Chattanooga, 329 F.2d 402 (6th Cir. 1964). It will

not be discussed in this book. For an economic analysis see Bishop, Negligent Misrepresentation through Economists' Eyes, 96 L.Q. Rev. 360 (1980). In addition, and more important, the federal securities laws have since the early 1930s imposed stringent disclosure and antifraud duties on issuers of securities. These laws are studied in courses on corporation and securities law.

4. Fraud is frequently available as a ground for rescission of a contract, and the standards for contract fraud are more liberal than those for the tort of deceit. Could Peek have brought an action for breach of contract?

5. Economists distinguish between three types of good, so far as the buyer's information costs are concerned. "Search" or "inspection" goods are those whose qualities can be ascertained at the time of purchase; the ripeness of a cantaloupe is an example. "Experience" goods reveal their qualities only through use; the taste of a breakfast cereal is an example. "Credence" goods are those that do not reliably reveal their qualities through either inspection or use; their qualities are hard to determine. Common examples are auto repairs and vitamin supplements. Does this classification assist you in deciding when the law should grant a remedy for fraud? What kind of good was the bezoar? Falch's credit? The house in *Swinton*? The right of the Plymouth, Devenport and District Tramways Company to use mechanical power?

On the economics of fraud see Darby & Karni, Free Competition and the Optimal Amount of Fraud, 16 J. Law & Econ. 67 (1973); Jordan & Rubin, An Economic Analysis of the Law of False Advertising, 8 J. Legal Stud. 527 (1979); R. A. Posner, Economic Analysis of Law 80-84, 271-276 (2d ed. 1977); Posner, Privacy, Secrecy, and Reputation, 28 Buff. L. Rev. 1, 33 (1979).

6. Could fraud be a basis for collecting damages for emotional distress? For an affirmative answer, in a case involving overbooking by a hotel, see Dold v. Outrigger Hotel, 54 Haw. 18, 501 P.2d 368 (1972).

Morrison v. National Broadcasting Co.
24 App. Div. 2d 284, 266 N.Y.S.2d 406 (1965)

BREITEL, J. . . .

The gist of the claim is that defendants, associated in various ways in television, acting in concert, falsely represented to plaintiff, a young university academic, that they were conducting an authentic and honest contest on television, a "quiz" show, when in fact it was rigged. They made these misrepresentations in order to induce his participation as a contestant. As a result of his innocent participation and the public scandals thereafter occurring, plaintiff sustained harm to his good reputation and in particular was deprived of scholastic fellowships for which he had applied. For purposes of this appeal the description of the promotion and sponsorship of the program must be assumed to be true. As for the harm to plaintiff's reputation and prospects, and his innocent participation in the contest, for the present this too must be assumed to be true. The claim then charges defendants with corrupt purposes, lying to plaintiff to induce his innocent participation in a corrupt enterprise, as a result of which, on public exposure of the enterprise, plaintiff sustained harm to his reputation and academic prospects. In referring to corrupt purposes or enterprises it is not intended to suggest essential illegality but to import necessarily a violation of strong and prevalent moral standards with respect to competitive contests for material awards. The point is that everything that is not illegal is not therefore legitimate or sanctioned conduct.

Notably, each of the ultimate elements of the claim is a recognized element in the law of remedies for one sustaining harms. Nevertheless, defendants contend that there is a failure to state a claim or cause of action because the separate elements do not all fall into any one classic category of tort but are found only in a combination of such categories. If this be right, then once again our jurisprudence would suffer a hardening of its categories making neither for sense nor justice and mark a return to a specious procedural formalism.

In the first place, misplaced speculation about the applicability of "prima facie tort" doctrine to this case should be eliminated. That open-ended, non-category, class or sub-class of tort covers "disinterested malevolence," that is, the intentional malicious injury to another by otherwise lawful means without economic or social justification, but solely to harm the other. The elements in this case are distinguishable and stronger. The means used were not lawful or privileged, in the sense of affirmatively sanctioned conduct, but were intentional falsehood without benevolent purpose uttered to induce action by another to his detriment. The ultimate purpose and the scheme were corrupt, in the sense that no socially useful purpose but only gain by deceit was intended, although perhaps not "illegal." Defendants were engaged in operating a dishonest contest. Innocent contestants were being cheated of the chances for rewards they thought they had. The public was being deceived as to the kind of spectacle it was viewing. Defendants lied to plaintiff to induce his innocent participation. They were engaged in the pursuit of economic gain for themselves. Hence, this is no instance of otherwise lawfully privileged means being made actionable, because without economic or social justification, and because of the exclusive purpose to injure plaintiff, which are the identifying qualities of so-called "prima facie" tort.

Secondly, the claim is not for defamation, as defendants correctly argue, because defendants did not publish in any form anything derogatory to or concerning plaintiff. Instead, they put him in an unduly hazardous position where his reputation might be injured, not because this was their purpose, but because they did not care what happened to him in the pursuit of their purposes for selfish gain. Yet the harm sustained is exactly like that from defamation, albeit induced neither by slander nor libel. Thus, the causative acts are different from those in defamation, but the effect, that is, harm to reputation, is the same.

Thirdly, the acts of defendants are not in deceit although they fit precisely all but one of the several elements of deceit. They fall short with respect to the nature of the harm sustained by plaintiff. There is knowing misrepresentation of fact, for the purpose of inducing plaintiff to act, upon which he relies. But the resulting harm is not the obtaining of plaintiff's property, or even his services; instead, it is the putting him into a hazardous false position, that is, of a cheater or corrupt contestant, to which he would not have consented if he had known the truth. While the harm to plaintiff was never intended, for defendants were gambling that there would be no exposure, the risk of harm to plaintiff's reputation was known or should have been known and therefore completely foreseeable to defendants. In this last respect there is a touch of an element in the law of negligence. But the claim is not for negligence, because while the harm may not have been intended, the act and effect of putting plaintiff into the false position of appearing to be a cheater was. It is not necessary that the intent in tort law be hostile. . . .

The root of the present trouble is that every kind of wrongful conduct, like lying, is not actionable per se. The analysis should not stop short, however, but must continue by examination of the purpose for which one lies, the harm produced by the lie, and whether the harm was foreseeable or the natural consequence of the wrong. The problem may also be looked at conversely. If there be no remedy, then the law would be saying in effect that one is free to lie to another as distinguished from lying about another (which is defamation), for one's private gain, so long as the consequence of the lie is not to take the victim's property (which is deceit), but rather to expose him and his reputation to likely injury.

In passing it should be observed that criminal statutes which must be explicitly directed to conduct forbidden are not involved. Rather this case explores the common law reach in providing a remedy for foreseeable harms resulting from intentional conduct.

In the late nineteenth and early twentieth centuries a great controversy raged over whether there was a law of tort based on general principles or only a law of torts based on specific remedies which could not be rationally correlated but only historically explained. Pollock in England was the chief exponent for the view of a general theory of tort and Salmond was the chief exponent for the contrary view (see Pollock on Torts [15th ed.], pp. 16-17 and Salmond on Torts [12th ed.], pp. 17-19, 20-31; see, also, Advance Music Corp. v. American Tobacco Co., 296 N.Y. 79, 83-84, 70 N.E.2d 401-403). It is significant that the later editors of Salmond retreat from his hard position that "every plaintiff must bring his case under one of the recognized heads of tort." And there is no doubt that the generality of Pollock's position must be a bit restrained, if history is not to be ignored.

But there is no need to join in the overseas controversy. The Court of Appeals in the *Advance Music* case, supra, resolved the dispute for this State.

After discussing the Pollock-Salmond controversy, Chief Judge Loughran had this to say: "This difference over the general principles of liability in tort was composed for us in Opera on Tour, Inc. v. Weber, 285 N.Y. 348, 34 N.E.2d 349, 136 A.L.R. 267. We there adopted from Aikens v. State of Wisconsin [195 U.S. 194, esp. at 204, 25 S. Ct. 3, 49 L. Ed. 154, per Holmes, J.] the declaration that 'prima facie, the intentional infliction of temporal damage is a cause of action, which . . . requires a justification if the defendant is to escape.' "

Then, dropping the commas around the words "prima facie," a new name was created in this State for not such a new tort, the Chief Judge saying: "The above second cause of action alleges such a prima facie tort and, therefore, is sufficient in law on its face."

It is not important to the present analysis that the so-called "prima facie" tort was thus rationalized. It is important that the Court aligned itself with the Holmes-Pollock view that tort concepts of liability did not depend solely upon procedural categories, important as they were, and that intentional harm, without excuse or justification, was actionable, simpliciter. The extension of these principles is well beyond what has been since dubbed the "prima facie" tort. Indeed, the sub-classification of "prima facie" tort has perhaps caused more trouble in understanding than what it was supposed to clarify. . . . What should be clear enough is that "prima facie" tort does not embrace all intentional tort outside the classic categories of intentional torts.

Even before the *Advance Music* case, the Court had no trouble in recognizing as actionable an intentional wrong that did not classify into any of the formal categories. In Gale v. Ryan, 263 App. Div. 76, 31 N.Y.S.2d 732 the complaint charged defendants, for their own tax evasion purposes, and without hostile intention toward plaintiff, with having given false information to the revenue authorities concerning plaintiff's earnings. As a result, plaintiff allegedly was investigated and sustained damage because of these false statements. The Court, recognizing that the claim did not come within any of the classic tort categories, analogized it to various causes of action for injurious falsehood and sustained the complaint. . . .

The present case is similar to the *Gale* case because the harm did not flow directly from the false position as a corrupt contestant into which plaintiff was put, but rather from the public exposure that was likely to follow. In the *Gale* case, although investigation may have been a little more likely than exposure in this case, the harm similarly did not flow directly from the false statements to the revenue officers but only from the ensuing investigation. . . .

It has been assumed by most in the discussion of this case that plaintiff has the burden of alleging special damages. . . . But plaintiff's claim should not depend on the allegation and proof of special damages. The reason is that the harm to reputation alleged here is exactly of the kind for which in the law of defamation recovery is allowed in the way of general damages. . . .

If it be true, as he alleges, that plaintiff, a young academic at the beginning of his professional university career, was tarred as a corrupt conniver with others in a rigged television contest, as a result of defendants' misrepresentations to him, the harm to his professional reputation would be great indeed. Paradoxically, the greater the harm, the less likely would he be able to show future prospects that never materialized because of the scandal associated with his name. Thus the principles implicit in this case associate, as to damages, with those found in the law of defamation, just as in other respects the applicable principles are found in the law of deceit, in the law of injurious falsehood, and in one respect, in the law of negligence. The justification for allowing general damages is the practical recognition that harm normally occurs from a type of conduct even if specific damages are not provable, while general damages are not justified where there is no likelihood or practical presumption that the wrong will result in harm. A bad reason for requiring allegation and proof of special damages is to discourage "new" causes of action. So too, because only "older" forms of action allowed recovery for general damages. . . .

In conclusion, it should be observed that the classical categories of tort were merely classifications, and incomplete ones at that. Omitted were all the law of negligence, the intentional tort committed by lawful means but solely out of malevolence (the "prima facie" tort), and innumerable other remediable wrongs wrought in the later common law years from the formless mold of "action on the case," out of which even the action on assumpsit had to arise because the "contract" categories had hardened into debt, covenant, and the like. This history should create no problems for a modern court but, instead, provides modes of solution, especially so where the claim rests on elements each of which, considered separately, has been recognized as an operative fact in the law of torts. Nor should a slavish formalism apply to the rule of damages any more than to the statement of a substantive claim. In either case, a rule should stand or fall because of its reason or lack of it. . . .

Note

The decision of the Appellate Division was reversed by the Court of Appeals of New York. 19 N.Y.2d 453, 227 N.E.2d 572 (1967). The court held that plaintiff's "cause of action must be deemed to fall within the ambit of tortious injury which sounds in defamation." Id. at 459, 227 N.E.2d at 574. Therefore, the complaint had to be dismissed, plaintiff having failed to allege special damages and to bring his action within the one-year statute of limitations applicable to defamation suits. Do you agree that *Morrison* was a defamation case?

Board of Education v. Farmingdale Classroom Teachers Assn.
38 N.Y.2d 397, 343 N.E.2d 278 (1975)

WACHTLER, J.

This appeal, arising in the context of an apparently bitter dispute between a school district and a teachers' association, concerns the seldom considered tort of abuse of process. The school district contends that the association and its attorney are liable for abusing legal process by subpoenaing, with the intent to harass and to injure, 87 teachers and refusing to stagger their appearances. As a result the school district was compelled to hire substitutes in order to avert a total shutdown. The issue on appeal is whether the complaint states a cause of action.

The controversy began in March, 1972 when a number of teachers employed by the district were absent from their classes on two successive days. The school district considered this illegal and the teachers' association was charged with violating the so-called Taylor law (Civil Service Law, §210, subd. 1) by the Public Employees Relations Board (PERB). The association vehemently denied having engaged in or condoned a strike and the matter was scheduled for a hearing to be held on October 5, 6, 10 and 11.

The complaint contains the following version of the ensuing events. Sometime between September 5, 1972 and October 5, 1972, the attorney for the association prepared and issued judicial subpoenas duces tecum to 87 teachers in order to compel their attendance as witnesses on October 5. The school district learned of these subpoenas on or about October 3, 1972 when the individual teachers requested approved absences from teaching duties in accordance with the collective bargaining agreement. The complaint further alleges that the district's prompt oral request that the majority of teachers be excused from attendance at the initial hearing date was refused by the defendant. Indeed, the defendant refused even to grant the request to stagger the appearances. Consequently all 87 teachers attended the hearing and 77 substitute teachers were hired to replace them. Based on these allegations, the school district asserts three causes of action.

The first alleges an abuse of process in that the defendants wrongfully and maliciously and with intent to injure and harass the plaintiff issued 87 subpoenas with knowledge that all the teachers could not have possibly testified on the initial hearing date. As damages for this cause of action plaintiff seeks the amount expended to engage substitute teachers and an amount representing the aggregate salary of the subpoenaed teachers. The second cause of action reiterates the allegations of the first and prays for punitive damages; while the third alleges defendants' conduct constituted a prima facie tort. Defendants moved to dismiss primarily for failure to state a cause of action. Special Term denied this motion and the Appellate Division affirmed with one Justice dissenting. . . .

Abuse of process, i.e., causing process to issue lawfully but to accomplish some unjustified purpose, is frequently confused with malicious prosecution, i.e., maliciously causing process to issue without justification. Although much of the confusion is dispelled on careful analysis, it must be noted that both torts possess the common element of improper purpose in the use of legal process and both were spawned from the action for trespass on the case in the nature of conspiracy. In order to fully understand the nature of abuse of process a consideration of its origin and evolution is necessary.

Like many causes of action, abuse of process is rooted in the interstices of various common-law concepts. It is important to keep in mind that when a party abuses process his tortious conduct injures not only the intended target but offends the spirit of the legal procedure itself. Insofar as it relates to the harm inflicted on the individual, abuse of process finds its origin in the writ of conspiracy. The earliest meaning ascribed to this writ is extremely vague but refers to improper meddling in a legal dispute. Eventually this writ came to mean several parties allying to procure a false accusation. However, because of its narrow scope, the writ of conspiracy gradually fell ·into disuse.

It was superseded by a more malleable form of action known as an action of case in the nature of conspiracy. This action had a checkered development, due in large measure to the competing policies of seeking to deter false accusers while trying to encourage just ones. Throughout this evolution glimpses of two additional concerns are discernible. The use of process to serve the purposes of oppression or injustice was deemed punishable as contempt and also as giving rise to an action for injury to reputation.

It was at this juncture that the tort of malicious prosecution emerged as a distinct concept and was fully recognized in the case of Savile v. Roberts. There, Lord Holt, C.J., noted that while the existence of such an action was not a question of first impression, it was clear that contriving to injure someone by pretense and color of legal process demanded redress because it resulted in a loss of reputation, anxiety and the expenditure of funds in defense. With *Savile*, malicious prosecution was firmly ensconced in the common law.

The tort of abuse of process makes its first independent appearance in Grainger v. Hill. The plaintiff in that case was the owner and captain of a certain vessel who borrowed a sum of money from Hill and others. Although the loan was secured by a mortgage on the vessel, the defendants were desirous of possessing the ship's register. To accomplish this end they sued Grainger in assumpsit and caused a writ of arrest to issue. Thereafter Grainger, who was wounded and bedridden, was threatened with incarceration unless he delivered the register to defendants. Rather than go to jail he succumbed and relinquished the register. Grainger then sued defendants for procuring the writ of arrest "wrongfully, illegally, and maliciously contriving to injure, harass, and distress the plaintiff, and to compel [him] . . . to give up and relinquish to them . . . a certain register" and certificate of registry to his ship. The court affirmed a judgment in favor of plaintiff. One Judge noted that this was a case of first impression which involved a new species of injury and that a new action must be fashioned according to the particular circumstances. The court held that this action was not for maliciously putting process in force (malicious prosecution) but rather was an action for maliciously abusing the process of the court. It was further held that since process was used to effect an object not within the scope of the process, it was immaterial whether the original suit had been terminated or whether it was founded on probable cause. The employment of process to extort property was, of itself, a sufficient cause of action. These basic principles have been carried forward into modern times and are recognized in this country. . . .

Despite the paucity of New York authority, three essential elements of the tort of abuse of process can be distilled from the preceding history and case law. First, there must be regularly issued process, civil or criminal, compelling the performance or forebearance of some prescribed act. Next, the person activating the process must be moved by a purpose to do harm without that which has been traditionally described as economic or social excuse or justification. Lastly, defendant must be seeking some collateral advantage or corresponding detriment to the plaintiff which is outside the legitimate ends of the process.

. . . The subpoenas here were regularly issued process, defendants were motivated by an intent to harass and to injure, and the refusal to comply with a reasonable request to stagger the appearances was sufficient to support an inference that the process was being perverted to inflict economic harm on the school district. . . .

. . . [O]n its face an allegation that defendants subpoenaed 87 persons with full knowledge that they all could not and would not testify and that this was done maliciously with the intent to injure and to harass plaintiff spells out an abuse of process. Another factor to be weighed at trial is whether the testimony of so many witnesses was material and necessary. As this complaint is framed, it may be inferred that defendants were effecting a not too subtle threat which should be actionable. . . .

. . . [D]efendants contend that the school district cannot bring this action because the alleged abusive process was not issued against them. Although there is support for this proposition we reject it. To hold that the party whom the defendants seek to injure and who has suffered economic injury lacks standing would be to defy reality. Accordingly, the tort of abuse of process will be available to nonrecipients of process provided they are the target and victim of the perversion of that process. . . .

Lastly, we conclude that the third cause of action for prima facie tort is sufficient insofar as it refers to the intentional infliction of economic harm by forcing plaintiff to hire a great many substitutes. It does not matter whether the action is denominated a so-called "prima facie tort" or is called something else. Although in Opera on Tour v. Weber, the court referred to a prima facie tort (with less than an accurate reference to the theory which Mr. Justice Holmes had articulated in Aikens v. Wisconsin) that term is merely an inaccurate mislabel and the plaintiff's right to maintain an action does not hinge on the label used. The operative fact here is that defendants have utilized legal procedure to harass and to oppress the plaintiff who has suffered a grievance which should be cognizable at law. Consequently whenever there is an intentional infliction of economic damage, without excuse or justification, we will eschew formalism and recognize the existence of a cause of action. . . .

Notes

1. Why could defendants not have been found to have committed the tort of malicious prosecution?

2. Are there any defenses open to the association's attorney but not to the association itself?

3. Is the court's treatment of the prima facie tort issue in *Farmingdale* consistent with its treatment of that issue in the *Morrison* case?

4. Aikens v. Wisconsin, 195 U.S. 194 (1904), the source of the concept called in New York the prima facie tort concept, involved an alleged conspiracy by a group of newspapers to refuse to deal with any advertiser who agreed to pay a 25 percent price increase that a competing newspaper had instituted. (Why would they do that?) Defendants were punished under a state criminal statute that forbade "maliciously injuring," which the Court construed to mean injuring with a "malevolent purpose." Id. at 203. The Court held that the statute, so construed, did not violate the Fourteenth Amendment. Can you see why the New York courts have hesitated to classify the kind of conduct involved in *Morrison* and *Farmingdale* under the prima facie tort rubric?

Ely-Norris Safe Co. v. Mosler Safe Co.
7 F.2d 603 (2d Cir. 1925)

HAND, C.J. . . .

American Washboard Co. v. Saginaw Mfg. Co., 103 F. 281 (C.C.A. 6), was . . . a case in substance like that at bar, because there the plaintiff alleged that it had acquired the entire output of sheet aluminum suitable for washboards. It necessarily followed that the plaintiff had a practical monopoly of this metal for the articles in question, and from this it was a fair inference that any customer of the defendant, who was deceived into buying as an aluminum washboard one which was not such, was a presumptive customer of the plaintiff, who had therefore lost a bargain. This was held, however, not to constitute a private wrong, and so the bill was dismissed. . . .

We must concede . . . that on the cases as they stand the law is with the defendant, and the especially high authority of the court which decided American Washboard Co. v. Saginaw Mfg. Co., makes us hesitate to differ from their conclusion. Yet there is no part of the law which is more plastic than unfair competition, and what was not reckoned an actionable wrong 25 years ago may have become such today. We find it impossible to deny the strength of the plaintiff's case on the allegations of its bill. As we view it, the question is, as it always is in such cases, one of fact. While a competitor may, generally speaking, take away all the customers of another that he can, there are means which he must not use. One of these is deceit. The false use of another's name as maker or source of his own goods is deceit, of which the false use of geographical or descriptive terms is only one example. But we conceive that in the end the questions which arise are always two: Has the plaintiff in fact lost customers? And has he lost them by means which the law forbids? The false use of the plaintiff's name is only an instance in which each element is clearly shown.

In the case at bar the means are as plainly unlawful as in the usual case of palming off. It is as unlawful to lie about the quality of one's wares as about their maker; it equally subjects the seller to action by the buyer. . . . The reason, as we think, why such deceits have not been regarded as actionable by a competitor, depends only upon his inability to show any injury for which there is a known remedy. In an open market it is generally impossible to prove that a customer, whom the defendant has secured by falsely describing his goods, would have bought of the plaintiff, if the defendant had been truthful. Without that, the plaintiff, though aggrieved in company with other honest traders, cannot show any ascertainable loss. He may not recover at law, and the equitable remedy is concurrent. The law does not allow him to sue as a vicarious avenger of the defendant's customers.

But, if it be true that the plaintiff has a monopoly of the kind of wares concerned, and if to secure a customer the defendant must represent his own as of that kind, it is a fair inference that the customer wants those and those only. . . .

Yet that is in substance the situation which this bill presents. It says that the plaintiff alone could lawfully make such safes, and that the defendant has sold others to customers who asked for the patented kind. It can make no difference that the defendant sold them as its own. The sale by hypothesis depended upon the structure of the safes, not on their maker. To be satisfied, the customer must in fact have gone to the plaintiff, or the defendant must have infringed. Had he infringed, the plaintiff could have recovered his profit on the sale; had the customer gone to him, he would have made that profit. Any possibilities that the customers might not have gone to the plaintiff, had they been told the truth, are foreclosed by the allegation that the plaintiff in fact lost the sales. . . .

Decree reversed.

Mosler Safe Co. v. Ely-Norris Safe Co.
273 U.S. 132 (1927)

MR. JUSTICE HOLMES delivered the opinion of the Court. . . .

It is consistent with every allegation in the bill and the defendant in argument asserted it to be a fact, that there are other safes with explosion chambers besides that for which the plaintiff has a patent. The defendant is charged only with representing that its safes had an explosion chamber, which, so far as appears, it had a perfect right to do if the representation was true. If on the other hand the representation was false as it is alleged sometimes to háve been, there is nothing to show that customers had they known the facts would have gone to the plaintiff rather than to other competitors in the market, or to lay a foundation for the claim for a loss of sales. The bill is so framed as to seem to invite the decision that was obtained from the Circuit Court of Appeals, but when scrutinized is seen to have so limited its statements as to exclude the right to complain.

Decree reversed.

Notes

1. Would it be sound policy to allow a competitor to sue as "the vicarious avenger of the defendant's customers?" The customers themselves are unlikely to sue, are they not?

2. The Sixth Circuit's decision in *American Washboard* and the Supreme Court's decision in *Mosler* made the tort of deceit of little use in controlling false advertising. Customers would rarely have an incentive to sue (why?) and competitors, who might have an incentive, faced an insurmountable burden of proof under these decisions. Focus shifted to the public remedy provided by the Federal Trade Commission, which has jurisdiction to prevent "unfair or deceptive acts or practices" in interstate commerce. Federal Trade Commission Act, §5, 15 U.S.C. §45. The Commission's performance as a policeman of truth in advertising has been widely criticized, however. See, e.g., R. A. Posner, Regulation of Advertising by the FTC (Am. Enterprise Inst. 1973).

Haelan Laboratories, Inc. v. Topps Chewing Gum, Inc.
202 F.2d 866 (2d Cir. 1953)

FRANK, C.J.

After a trial without a jury, the trial judge dismissed the complaint on the merits. The plaintiff maintains that defendant invaded plaintiff's exclusive right to use the photographs of leading baseball players. . . .

The plaintiff, engaged in selling chewing-gum, made a contract with a ball-player providing that plaintiff for a stated term should have the exclusive right to use the ball-player's photograph in connection with the sales of plaintiff's gum; the ball-player agreed not to grant any other gum manufacturer a similar right during such term; the contract gave plaintiff an option to extend the term for a designated period.

Defendant, a rival chewing-gum manufacturer, knowing of plaintiff's contract, deliberately induced the ball-player to authorize defendant, by a contract with defendant, to use the player's photograph in connection with the sales of defendant's gum either during the original or extended term of plaintiff's contract, and defendant did so use the photograph.

Defendant argues that, even if such facts are proved, they show no actionable wrong, for this reason: The contract with plaintiff was no more than a release by the ball-player to plaintiff of the liability which, absent the release, plaintiff would have incurred in using the ball-player's photograph, because such a use, without his consent, would be an invasion of his right of privacy under Section 50 and Section 51 of the New York Civil Rights Law; this statutory right of privacy is personal, not assignable; therefore, plaintiff's contract vested in plaintiff no "property" right or other legal interest which defendant's conduct invaded. . . .

A majority of this court rejects this contention. We think that, in addition to and independent of that right of privacy (which in New York derives from statute), a man has a right in the publicity value of his photograph, i.e., the right to grant the exclusive privilege of publishing his picture, and that such a grant may validly be made "in gross," i.e., without an accompanying transfer of a business or of anything else. Whether it be labelled a "property" right is immaterial; for here, as often elsewhere, the tag "property" simply symbolizes the fact that courts enforce a claim which has pecuniary worth.

This right might be called a "right of publicity." For it is common knowledge that many prominent persons (especially actors and ball-players), far from having their feelings bruised through public exposure of their likenesses, would feel sorely deprived if they no longer received money for authorizing advertisements, popularizing their countenances, displayed in newspapers, magazines, busses, trains and subways. This right of publicity would usually yield them no money unless it could be made the subject of an exclusive grant which barred any other advertiser from using their pictures. . . .

Notes

1. Could the defendant's conduct invade both the plaintiff's right to privacy and the plaintiff's right to publicity? Can you think of a case in which

the publication of a person's likeness in advertising without his consent really would invade his privacy? See Pavesich v. New England Life Ins. Co., 122 Ga. 190, 50 S.E. 68 (1905).

2. Did defendant invade *plaintiff's* rights? Unless plaintiff was suing merely as the assignee of the ballplayer's (property) right of publicity, what right of plaintiff's was invaded?

American Surety Co. v. Schottenbauer
257 F.2d 6 (8th Cir. 1958)

[Plaintiff, formerly employed by Wabasso Coop Creamery Association, brought suit for actual and punitive damages against American Surety Company, which was the workmen's compensation insurer for Wabasso, and Rohlik, the local agent for the surety company. The jury awarded plaintiff $8,500 (later reduced to $7,000) for wrongful interference with plaintiff's contract of employment. Defendants appealed.]

MATTHES, C.J. . . .

Plaintiff, age 37 at trial time, had lived in Wabasso, Minnesota, all of his life, and had worked continuously for the Wabasso Creamery from 1942 until April, 1956. He worked six days a week, ten hours a day, and an occasional Sunday for an average salary of $365 to $375 per month. He had a high school education, and had been trained for no other type of work. Plaintiff's duties included the making of butter and handling heavy cream cans, and he was required to make frequent trips in and out of a cooler. His hands came in contact with hot and cold water, various chemicals and other liquids. In June, 1955, plaintiff "bumped" the middle finger of his right hand, causing him pain. An open sore or ulcer developed on the finger for which he received treatment from his family physician, Dr. Alcorn, for a period of four or five months. In November, 1955, Dr. Alcorn concluded that plaintiff should undergo an examination at the Mayo Clinic. On December 1, 1955, Dr. Alcorn, by letter, reported to defendant Surety Company the results of his treatment, and on December 28, 1955, again reported to said company. In the latter report, the doctor stated that the "ulcer has healed and remained so in the past two or three weeks," and expressed the opinion the circulation disturbance should be classed as occupational and compensable.

On January 16, 1956, Mayo Clinic reported to the Surety Company, by letter. . . . That institution diagnosed the appellant's condition as a "vaso-spastic disorder with manifestations primarily those of Raynaud's Phenomenon." From other medical evidence it appears that "Raynaud's Phenomenon" is a disease where there is a constriction or a spasm of the small blood vessels of the fingers, which shuts down the supply of the blood. Aside from major surgery, which produces variable results, Raynaud's Phenomenon is incurable, and can be aggravated by sudden temperature changes, trauma or nicotine. Mayo's report stated that it had suggested to plaintiff that it might be advisable for him to change the nature of his job to avoid repeated exposure to cold, the possibility of living in a region with a warm climate on a trial basis, and to discontinue the use of tobacco "because of the vasospastic characteristics of nicotine."

On March 19, 1956, plaintiff was examined by a Dr. Felder on behalf of the defendant Surety Company, and in a report to the company bearing the same date, Dr. Felder stated that since plaintiff's visit to Mayo Clinic in November, 1955, he has had a gradual improvement in his condition; that he had a healed scar on the distal end of right middle finger, and that, "I believe that at the present time he is recovering, but that he still should refrain from the use of tobacco and also should continue to stay away from any work which will repeatedly traumatize the right hand. He informs me that in his present job he is able to do this."

Prior to the examination by Dr. Felder, and on January 16, 1956, Donald L. Barclay, claim manager for the Surety Company, took the Mayo Clinic report to Dr. Orley W. Foster for interpretation. From Dr. Foster, Mr. Barclay learned that Raynaud's Phenomenon was the "contracting or the swelling and contracting of the vessels in the finger, . . ." Following his visit with Dr. Foster, Barclay contacted Mr. John R. Simacek, superintendent of casualty insurance for the Minneapolis Branch Office of the Surety Company, and informed Simacek of the nature of plaintiff's condition. "I told him (Simacek) Raynaud's Phenomenon was a disease in which the vessels in the finger and hand would swell both inwardly and outwardly, causing the circulation to be cut off from the member, . . . I told him, because the circulation could be stopped when the disease is aggravated, that there was a possibility of amputation. I told him that the fingers could easily have this resulting condition and would have to be amputated, and that aggravation of such could even cause the amputation of the hand." Bearing upon the report made by Barclay to Simacek, it should be noted that Dr. Foster, after testifying at some length as to effect of the disease, stated: "If gangrene develops as a result of Raynaud's Phenomenon and amputation is necessary, then the involved area is the distal portion or just a part of the finger or fingers. *It never requires the amputation of a hand.* If Mr. Barclay stressed that thought, he misunderstood or did not understand the medical situation with exact accuracy." . . .

On March 27, 1956, Mr. Simacek wrote the following letter to defendant Rohlik, which is the basis for plaintiff's cause of action:

> We have been advised by our claim department that an employee of yours, Mr. Frank Schottenbauer, went through the Mayo Clinic after [a] recent accident he had while in the employment of the above-captioned insured. The Mayo Clinic diagnosed his case as having Raynaud's Phenomenon, which is a very serious disease and must be taken very close care of. He also was viewed by our company's doctor, Dr. Felder. With this disease, it is felt that our company

could obtain a very serious loss, which the insurance policy is not designed to cover. Therefore, it is our opinion that either this company should immediately terminate this man's employment or else we do feel that we will have no alternative but to cancel the policy.

Under this disease that Mr. Schottenbauer has, by exposure that the Mayo Clinic outlined to him, he would have the possibility of losing one or more of his fingers, or his entire hand, and I am sure you can appreciate that this is a very serious exposure.

We sincerely regret having to take an action such as this, however, we do feel that we have no alternative and we would appreciate your immediate cooperation and your immediate comments. . . .

Following receipt of the letter by Mr. Rohlik, he presented it to the officials of the creamery company; a conference was had with plaintiff in regards to the contents thereof, and plaintiff was discharged on April 14, 1956. . . .

Wrongful interference with a contractual right is actionable in Minnesota, this cause of action being recognized in its various forms; e.g., inducing a breach of an existing contract for broker's fees, inducing a breach of sales and service contracts, leases, etc.; and situations concerning "competitive" motives in inducing an abandonment of preexisting contract[s]. . . .

The courts of Minnesota have ruled that the elements essential to recovery for tortious interference are: (1) the contract; (2) the wrongdoer's knowledge thereof; (3) his intentional procurement of its breach; (4) without justification; and (5) damages resulting therefrom.

Defendants concede the presence of the first two elements, but urgently insist that the evidence failed to establish: . . . (B) Defendants' acts were without justification (i.e., not privileged). . . .

Several reasons are advanced to support contention B. It is argued that since the employment contract between plaintiff and his employer was terminable at will, and plaintiff would have had no right of action against Wabasso Creamery for termination of his employment, plaintiff has no standing to complain of the conduct of defendants, particularly when viewed in light of the relation between the parties.

Regarding the liability of a third person for procuring a breach of contract on the part of another, the general rule is that it is immaterial that the contract is terminable at will . . . , "since until it is terminated the contract is a subsisting relation, of value to the plaintiff, and presumably to continue in effect." . . .

Defendants' principal argument in support of contention B is grounded in the relation existing between the Surety Company and the Wabasso Creamery. More precisely, it is asserted that because of the subsisting contract between those parties (the workmen's compensation insurance policy), the Surety Company could have been exposed to an abnormal risk if plaintiff, suffering from Raynaud's Phenomenon, had been retained as an employee of the creamery. It is said that this situation vested the Surety Company with such an interest in the business of plaintiff's employer, that it was justified, as a matter of law, in interfering as it did, even to the extent of causing plaintiff's discharge. . . .

[T]he issue of justification was one for the jury to resolve. This conclusion is compelled by these aspects of the case: 1. Although defendant Surety Company concededly had the unqualified right to cancel the insurance policy at any time, the question remained as to whether the means it employed (fire plaintiff or we cancel) were proper and fully justified. 2. There was no factual basis for the statement, in the letter to Rohlik, that plaintiff "would have the possibility of losing one or more of his fingers, or his entire hand, and I am sure you can appreciate that this is a very serious exposure." 3. There was meagre evidence to sustain the statement in the letter that "our company could obtain a very serious loss," because plaintiff had Raynaud's Phenomenon. The fact of the matter is, the Surety Company knew that plaintiff's middle finger had been healed for some time when the letter was written. The evidence revealed that his condition had responded satisfactorily to the treatment prescribed; he was performing his duties without difficulty and apparently to the complete satisfaction of his employer. 4. Although defendant Rohlik testified that the Wabasso Creamery could have obtained workmen's compensation insurance from another source without additional cost, this information was not imparted to plaintiff's employer until after plaintiff had been discharged. . . .

Accordingly, the judgment is affirmed.

Notes

1. Since plaintiff's contract with his employer was terminable at will, what right of plaintiff was invaded by the defendant? Is it necessary for a tort plaintiff to show that the defendant's conduct invaded a right of the plaintiff other than the right to be free from tortious injury? For divergent views on this question compare Posner, Epstein's Tort Theory: A Critique, 8 J. Legal Stud. 457, 465-471 (1979), with Epstein, Causation and Corrective Justice: A Reply to Two Critics, 8 J. Legal Stud. 477, 501-502 (1979).

2 In light of this case, what right of plaintiff was invaded in the *Haelan* case?

3. Could Schottenbauer have recovered damages against the surety company for libel?

4. Can the liability of the surety company perhaps be explained on the theory that it was the "cheaper cost avoider," in a Hand formula sense, of an "accident" consisting of erroneously dismissing plaintiff from his employment? For an analysis along these lines see Landes & Posner, Joint and Multiple Tortfeasors: An Economic Analysis, 9 J. Legal Stud. 517, 552-555 (1980). But how well does this analysis apply to other common types of

intentional interference with contract? For example, suppose as in S. C. Posner Co. v. Jackson, 223 N.Y. 325, 119 N.E. 573 (1918), that defendant lures a valued employee away from plaintiff. Why should plaintiff have an action against defendant? Why shouldn't he be limited to his contract rights, if any, against the employee? Are solvency considerations perhaps important here?

5. As the *Haelan* and *Posner* cases illustrate, intentional interference with contract is frequently claimed in a competitive setting. The next group of materials in this chapter deals, very summarily to be sure, with competitive torts not involving fraud or misrepresentation.

Keeble v. Hickeringill
11 East. 574, 103 Eng. Rep. 1127 (K.B. 1706 or 1707)

Action upon the case. Plaintiff declares that he was, 8th November in the second year of the Queen, lawfully possessed of a close of land called Minott's Meadow . . . [in which there was] a decoy pond, to which divers wildfowl used to resort and come: and the plaintiff had at his own costs and charges prepared and procured divers decoy ducks, nets, machines and other engines for the decoying and taking of the wildfowl, and enjoyed the benefit in taking them: the defendant, knowing which, and intending to damnify the plaintiff in his vivary [the duck pond], and to fright and drive away the wildfowl used to resort thither, and deprive him of this profit, did, on the 8th of November, resort to the head of the said pond and vivary, and did discharge six guns laden with gunpowder, and with the noise and stink of the gunpowder did drive away the wildfowl then being in the pond: and on the 11th and 12th days of November the defendant, with design to damnify the plaintiff, and fright away the wildfowl, did place himself with a gun near the vivary, and there did discharge the said gun several times that was then charged with the gunpowder against the said decoy pond, whereby the wildfowl were frighted away, and did forsake the said pond. Upon not guilty pleaded, a verdict was found for £20 damages.

HOLT C.J. I am of opinion that this action doth lie. It seems to be new in its instance, but is not new in the reason or principle of it. For, 1st, this using or making a decoy is lawful. 2dly, this employment of his ground to that use is profitable to the plaintiff, as is the skill and management of that employment. As to the first, every man that hath a property may employ it for his pleasure and profit, as for alluring and procuring decoy ducks to come to his pond. To learn the trade of seducing other ducks to come there in order to be taken is not prohibited either by the law of the land or the moral law; but it is as lawful to use art to seduce them, to catch them, and destroy them for the use of mankind, as to kill and destroy wildfowl or tame cattle. Then when a man useth his art or his skill to take them, to sell and dispose of for his profit;

this is his trade; and he that hinders another in his trade or livelihood is liable to an action for so hindering him. Why otherwise are scandalous words spoken of a man in his profession actionable, when without his profession they are not so? Though they do not affect any damage, yet are they mischievous in themselves; and therefore in their own nature productive of damage; and therefore an action lies against him. Such are all words that are spoken of a man to disparage him in his trade, that may bring damage to him; though they do not charge him with any crime that may make him obnoxious to punishment; as to say a merchant is broken, or that he is failing, or is not able to pay his debts. How much more, when the defendant doth an actual and real damage to another when he is in the very act of receiving profit by his employment. . . . But if a man doth him damage by using the same employment; as if Mr. Hickeringill had set up another decoy on his own ground near the plaintiff's, and that had spoiled the custom of the plaintiff, no action would lie, because he had as much liberty to make and use a decoy as the plaintiff. This is the case of 11 H. 4, 47. One schoolmaster sets up a new school to the damage of an antient school, and thereby the scholars are allured from the old school to come to his new. (The action was held there not to lie.) But suppose Mr. Hickeringill should lie in the way with his guns, and fright the boys from going to school, and their parents would not let them go thither; sure that schoolmaster might have an action for the loss of his scholars. A man hath a market, to which he hath toll for horses sold: a man is bringing his horse to market to sell: a stranger hinders and obstructs him from going thither to the market: an action lies, because it imports damage. Action upon the case lies against one that shall by threats fright away his tenants at will. . . . Now considering the nature of the case, it is not possible to declare of the number [of wildfowl] that were frighted away; because the plaintiff had not possession of them, to count them. Where a man brings trespass for taking his goods, he must declare of the quantity, because he, by having had the possession, may know what he had, and therefore must know what he lost. This is plain by several authorities. Trespass for beating and hindering his servant from taking and collecting his toll: objection that it is not said what quantity of toll he was to take: but that could not be known. Action upon the case because the defendant hindered him from taking toll of divers pieces of wool, and sheweth not how many; yet the declaration was good. . . . The plaintiff in this case brings his action for the apparent injury done him in the use of that employment of his freehold, his art, and skill, that he uses thereby. . . . And when we do know that of long time in the kingdom these artificial contrivances of decoy ponds and decoy ducks have been used for enticing into those ponds wildfowl, in order to be taken for the profit of the owner of the pond, who is at the expence of servants, engines, and other management, whereby the markets of the nation may be furnished; there is great reason to give encouragement thereunto; that the people who are so instrumental by their skill and industry so to furnish the markets should reap the benefit and have their action. But, in short, that which is the true reason is that this action is not brought to recover damage for the loss of the fowl, but for the disturbance. So is the usual and common way of declaring.

Notes

1. What right of plaintiff was invaded by defendant's action? Why would defendant's setting up his own decoy near the plaintiff's not have been actionable? How apposite is the school case mentioned by Chief Justice Holt?

2. Why is competition, as in the school case, not at least prima facie tortious? To change the case slightly, suppose A observes that B has a profitable clothing store on Main Street. A would like to divert some of these profits to himself, so he opens a clothing store just across the street from B. The competition from A reduces B's profits. Here, it would seem, are all the elements of an intentional tort: a deliberate and effective scheme to appropriate an advantage possessed by another, to the injury of that other. Yet, as *Keeble* shows, the common law early held that competition was not a tort. While certain forms of competition have come to be thought of as "unfair" and are actionable under tort law, as illustrated by *Haelan*, the common law rarely afforded relief in competition cases.* How would you distinguish *Haelan* from the hypothetical clothing case? How would you distinguish it from *Keeble*?

For an argument, based on a mixture of "responsibility" and "rights" theories, that competition is not a tort see Epstein, Intentional Harms, 4 J. Legal Stud. 391, 423-441 (1975). The same conclusion can be reached by economic analysis. Suppose B is selling widgets which cost $1 apiece to make (where "cost" includes the opportunity costs of all inputs, including B's time and capital investment) for $1, i.e., at the competitive price. A is more efficient than B; he can make widgets at a total cost of only 80¢ apiece. He enters the market, sells widgets at 90¢, takes the entire market away from B, and then raises price again to $1. Consumers receive the same satisfaction as before, but the total costs of production are 20¢ per widget less. These resources are freed up to produce consumer satisfaction in other markets.

Epstein goes further, arguing that competition is not a tort even when it takes forms, such as predatory pricing, that most economists regard as inefficient. Suppose A sells below cost in an effort to drive B, his only competitor, out of business; B succumbs; A then raises his price to a monopolistic level. Consumers gain in the short run but lose in the long run; B loses money from being forced out of the market. Overall welfare is lower. But Epstein argues that B cannot complain because no right of his is invaded. He has no right to force consumers to pay a higher price to him rather than buy from A at a

---

*A major exception is "passing on" or trademark infringement, where one firm markets its goods in a way that makes consumers believe they are the goods of some other firm.

below-cost price. Further, consumers in the recoupment period (when A, having driven B from the market, raises his price to the monopoly level) cannot complain either, because they have no right to buy from A at the competitive price. The absence of force and fraud in predatory pricing persuades Epstein that there should be no tort liability. Is this an implication of responsibility theory? Rights theory? Corrective justice?

The English common law agreed with Epstein that there was no liability for predatory pricing. See Mogul v. McGregor, 23 Q.B.D. 598 (1889), *aff'd* [1892], A.C. 25. But there is American authority contra. See, e.g., Boggs v. Duncan-Schell Furniture Co., 163 Iowa. 106, 143 N.W. 482 (1913). Beginning with the enactment of the Sherman Act in 1890, an elaborate body of federal (and recently state) antitrust law, enforceable by injured competitors and consumers as well as by public agencies, has evolved; *Aikens*, supra, involved an early example of state legislation in this area. To the extent enforced by private parties, this is a body of tort law (not discussed in this book, however, since it is the subject of separate courses on antitrust law), albeit one based on statute; and tort principles having to do with causation and damages play an important role in private antitrust cases. Predatory pricing is actionable under federal antitrust law. See R. A. Posner & F. H. Easterbrook, Antitrust: Cases, Economic Notes, and Other Materials 680-714 (2d ed. 1981).

3. Why are the doctrines of intentional interference with contract and (in New York) of prima facie tort not adequate vehicles for redressing predatory pricing and other wrongful injuries to competitors?

Other Intentional Torts

The discussion of intentional torts in this chapter is far from complete, quite apart from its emphasis on just the prima facie case (defenses are discussed in the next chapter). Some important torts such as conversion have been mentioned only in passing. The tort counterpart to theft in the criminal law, conversion is an important and highly technical tort that will repay careful study. See Prosser 79-97 for an introduction. The violation of certain statutes may, as in Johnson v. Sampson, give rise to an action for an intentional tort; civil rights laws, and the Constitution itself, are today important sources of tort actions. See Whitman, Constitutional Torts, 79 Mich. L. Rev. 5 (1980), and the *Norton* case in Chapter 3. There is an important tort of false arrest, closely related to false imprisonment, and often conjoined with violations of civil rights statutes. The tort of intentional infliction of emotional distress, or as it was once known the tort of outrage, has many fascinating branches, such as insult by an innkeeper or common carrier and mishandling of dead bodies. On the latter form of outrage see, e.g., Papieres v. Lawrence, 437 Pa. 373, 263 A.2d 118 (1970). Our discussion of business torts has just scratched the surface of a large and important field of intentional torts; statutes are again very important here.

Chapter 3
Defenses in Intentional Tort Cases

Bolen v. Howard
452 S.W.2d 401 (Ky. 1970)

PALMORE, J.

The appellant, Reece Bolen, Administrator of the estate of Alonzo Coburn, deceased, brought this action against the appellee, Ollie Howard, Committee for Lee Howard, an incompetent, seeking compensatory damages for the death of Coburn, who had been shot and killed by Lee Howard. Judgment was entered in accordance with a verdict for the defendant. . . .

The complaint alleges that in January of 1967 Lee Howard "carelessly, negligently, wantonly, maliciously, and not in self-defense" shot and killed Coburn with a shotgun. . . . It is alleged and admitted that at the time of the tragedy Lee Howard was an incompetent whose care, custody and control had been committed by the Veterans' Administration to his brother, the defendant Ollie Howard, serving as committee under appointment of the Knott County Court.

Coburn was a brother of Ollie Howard's wife and had been living in the Howard home for about two years, though he had a wife and children in West Virginia. He was 62 years old and had lost an arm. He drew welfare money of some kind and was not gainfully employed. We do not know Lee's age, but he had been in his brother's custody for 16 years. Neither do we know the details of Lee's mental condition except that he was nervous and easily upset. There was no evidence that he had ever before evinced a disposition to violence.

Lee and the decedent, Coburn, were on good terms and often hunted together. On the occasion in question they and another boarder in the Howard home by the name of Bill Davis were discussing the prospects of going hunting the next day in a certain area of the vicinage. In order to tease Lee, Coburn and Davis told him they were going to take him along but they were not going to let him have a gun. Lee demurred, and said he was not going, because he had hunted in this area when he was younger and there were wild hogs in there. But Coburn and Davis continued in the same vein of conversation until Lee got tired of it and said, "You all better leave me alone." At this point Coburn and Davis desisted, and Coburn retired to his bedroom upstairs. Shortly thereafter Lee went into a back room where a shotgun was kept, took it upstairs and shot Coburn while he was lying in bed reading. The shotgun shell used in the killing was from a box of ammunition Coburn had procured for hunting purposes.

In substance, instruction No. 1 directed the jury to find for the plaintiff if Lee Howard wrongfully and not in self-defense shot and killed Coburn. Instruction No. 2 was to the effect that if Coburn "was contributorily negligent in connection with any threats toward defendant [sic] or he was negligent in making access to the gun or shells, and as a result of said negligence the defendant [sic] shot and killed deceased, then you will find for the defendant."

The liability of an insane person for his torts has been defined as follows: "An insane person is liable civilly for his torts to the same extent as a sane person, except that punitive damages may not be allowed; and such persons are not liable for torts in which the gravamen of the action is malice, such as slander, libel, and malicious prosecution."

Though we gravely doubt the wisdom and justice of this anachronistic approach, since the litigating parties do not question it we shall not undertake to re-examine it at this time.

The evidence established beyond cavil that Lee Howard shot and killed Coburn without legal justification. Without going so far as to say that there can be no case in which recovery would be barred by the victim's own conduct in precipitating the injurious incident, we hold simply that this is not such a case. The two men were on good terms. They had hunted together without untoward incident, leaving no reason to believe that Lee could not be trusted within reach of firearms. There was no indication that he had ever manifested a tendency to do violence, even to the very moment of the fatal shooting. Once it appeared that he was irritated Coburn and Davis ceased their bantering. Clearly, we think, the evidence was not sufficient to support a finding that the tragic consequence was reasonably forseeable.

Despite Coburn's age and non-work status at the time of his death, together with ample defensive testimony that he was not in physical condition to earn a livelihood, there was proof that he had worked in West Virginia shortly before he came to live with the Howards in Kentucky and could have resumed the same work. It will be recalled also that he was able to go hunting, which reflects some degree of physical stamina. He was able to drive a motor vehicle. His earning power may have been minimal, but at the very least his estate is entitled to nominal recovery. Certainly it would not have been proper to direct a verdict for the defendant.

Our conclusion is that under the law as it stands in this case the appellant was entitled to a directed verdict on the issue of liability and that the question of damages should be submitted to a jury. . . .

Notes

1. A defense to a legal action may be defined as a state of facts that, if proved, excuses the defendant from liability, even if all of the facts alleged by plaintiff are true and would, but for the defense, entitle the plaintiff to judgment. The burden of proof (both production of evidence and persuasion of the trier of fact) is on the defendant.

When should a factual issue be a matter of defense, and when a matter to be (dis)proved by the plaintiff? Can this question be answered in terms of legal theory, or has it to do, rather, with relative access to the facts? For example, how should a defendant's alleged mental incapacity be treated in an intentional tort case in which that incapacity is relevant to liability? Should it be treated as a defense, or as a matter to be dealt with in plaintiff's case in chief, alleging that defendant's conduct was intentional?

2. The court's statement in *Bolen* that insanity is not a defense in tort actions except for defamation and malicious prosecution has wide support in the cases. See, e.g., In re Meyer's Guardianship, 218 Wis. 381, 261 N.W. 211 (1935); Shapiro v. Tchernowitz, 3 Misc. 2d 617, 155 N.Y.S.2d 1011 (Sup. Ct. 1956). This result is sometimes explained on the ground, as stated in one of the cases relied on in *Meyer's Guardianship*, that a lunatic "is not a free agent, capable of intelligent, voluntary actions, and therefore is incapable of a guilty intent, which is the very essence of crime; but a civil action, to recover damages for an injury, may be maintained against him, because the intent with which the act is done is not material." 218 Wis. at 386, 261 N.W. at 213. The case in question charged false imprisonment, an intentional tort, so how could it be said that "the intent with which the act is done is not material"? An alternative explanation for the liability of the insane, stated in another case relied on in *Meyer's Guardianship*, is that "where a loss must be borne by one of two innocent persons it should be borne by he who occasioned it." 218 Wis. at 387, 261 N.W. at 213-214. But this is just an argument, which the common law has rejected, for universal strict liability; it is not a justification for imposing liability on the insane person who "intentionally" injures another but not on a driver who, while exercising due care, runs down a pedestrian who is also exercising due care. Is the argument any less applicable to defamation and malicious prosecution?

For a possible clue to the thinking behind the tort law's treatment of insanity see Morriss v. Marsden, [1952] 1 All E.R. 925 (Q.B.D.), which involved a violent battery committed on plaintiff by a defendant described as a catatonic schizophrenic and certifiable lunatic. The court stated (id. at 927-928):

> On the whole, I accept the view that an intention — i.e., a voluntary act, the mind prompting and directing the act which is relied on, as in this case, as the

tortious act — must be averred and proved. For example, I think that, if a person in a condition of complete automatism inflicted grievous injury, that would not be actionable. In the same way, if a sleepwalker inadvertently, without intention or without carelessness, broke a valuable vase, that would not be actionable. . . .

The next matter to consider is whether, granted that the defendant knew the nature and quality of his act, it is a defence in this action that, owing to mental infirmity, he was incapable of knowing that his act was wrong. If the basis of liability be that it depends, not on the injury to the victim, but on the culpability of the wrongdoer, there is considerable force in the argument that it is, but I have come to the conclusion that knowledge of wrongdoing is an immaterial averment, and that, where there is the capacity to know the nature and quality of the act, that is sufficient although the mind directing the hand that did the wrong was diseased. I am fortified in that view by the decision in Astle v. Astle. That was a divorce case, in which cruelty was alleged, and Henn Collins, J., allowed the answer to be amended by inserting the plea that the respondent was of unsound mind and did not know the nature and quality of the act he was committing, but nothing was said about inserting in the amended pleading the other branch of the M'Naghten rules, that he did not know that what he was doing was wrong.

Is the point that the intent requirement in a battery case is so attenuated that defendant's knowledge of the wrongfulness of his act is immaterial? Did Brian Daily know that he was doing wrong? But would the threat of civil liability deter either a 5-year-old or a catatonic schizophrenic? If not, is there any economic argument for liability? Return to this question after reading, in the next chapter, unintentional tort cases where defendant was insane; those cases also cast further light on the "automatism" exception to the liability of the insane discussed in Morriss.

Would or should punitive damages ever be awarded in a case where the defendant is insane?

3. Contributory negligence is not a defense in an intentional tort case (why not?); should provocation be? If plaintiff's decedent in Bolen could reasonably have foreseen the consequences of teasing the defendant, would or should his provocation have been a defense? What was the court's view? Cf. Morgan v. Pistone in Chapter 2.

4. Can there be defenses to defenses?

Damages in Wrongful-Death Cases; Pain and Suffering

1. The award of damages in cases, such as Bolen, where the victim of the tort dies has an interesting history and raises interesting economic questions. As mentioned in the last chapter, in primitive and early legal systems liability for wrongful death was recognized and damages were computed by reference to a fixed schedule or tariff. This approach was followed in Anglo-Saxon

customary law. However, the common law of England, as it evolved after the Norman Conquest, refused to award damages in cases where the victim died; the tort action was said not to survive the victim's death. It was not until 1846 that Parliament, by statute, recognized tort liability in cases where the victim died. Lord Campbell's Act, 9 & 10 Vict., c. 93. The state courts in the U.S. followed the English common law; hence, it was only after states passed wrongful-death statutes modeled on the English law that families of people killed as a result of tortious conduct could obtain damages in American courts.

In thinking about the measurement of damages in death cases, and why the common law refused to award damages in such cases, it is helpful to distinguish between two types of loss in a death case. The first is the loss to the victim. This consists of the utility or satisfaction that the victim would have derived, net of any disutility, over the remaining course of his life. The second is the loss to others: for example, members of his family whom he supported. (Their loss need not, of course, be purely a pecuniary one.)

The first type of loss cannot, strictly speaking, be compensated. No award of damages will restore a dead person to the state of happiness he would have enjoyed but for his death. This is not a compelling argument against awarding damages, provided the purpose of tort damages is deterrent rather than compensatory. The threat of having to pay heavy damages will reduce the incidence of tortious conduct, and so increase social welfare, even though the payment of damages in a case where the victim dies will not compensate him.

But there is an acute problem in measuring this type of loss — in determining the dollar equivalent of the future satisfactions that the victim would have enjoyed had he lived. One might think it could be done by extrapolating from the wage premiums that people demand to work in hazardous occupations. (Such premiums are estimated in R. Thaler & S. Rosen, The Value of Saving a Life: Evidence from the Labor Market, in Household Production and Consumption 265 (Terleckyj ed. 1975).) To illustrate, imagine that in some occupation where there is a risk of being killed of .0001 a year the annual wage is $10 higher than in an otherwise identical occupation involving no risk of death. If workers are willing to accept $10 for a one in ten thousand chance of being killed, perhaps they would demand a wage ten thousand times as great, or $100,000, to accept a 100 percent chance of being killed; if so, we could multiply $100,000 by the number of years by which a worker's life was shortened in order to calculate a damage figure in a wrongful-death case.* But this approach has two serious drawbacks. First, it is impossible even in principle to extrapolate from the premium that a worker demands to take a slight risk of death the price that he would demand to surrender his life

---

*The resulting figure would have to be discounted to present value for purposes of computing the actual damage award. Discounting to present value is discussed in the last note in Chapter 8.

on the spot. That price may be infinite since the worker will not enjoy the wage premium, however great it is, if he is certain to die immediately. Second, risky occupations will naturally attract people who like risk, or at least have less aversion to it than the average person. The premium they demand to take risks may be much smaller than what the average person, including the average tort victim, would demand.

The second problem is solved in Blomquist, Value of Life Saving: Implications of Consumption Activity, 87 J. Pol. Econ. 540 (1979). This article uses the behavior of drivers with respect to use of seat belts to infer the value of life. The driver who does not use his seat belt obtains a (nonpecuniary) cost saving (because use of a seat belt involves some, albeit minor, inconvenience to the user) which plays the same role in Blomquist's analysis that the wage premium for a more risky job played in Thaler and Rosen's. Blomquist's approach yields an estimate of $370,000 for the average present value of a life in 1978 dollars.

For a lucid discussion of the Thaler-Rosen, Blomquist, and other estimates of the value of life see M. J. Bailey, Reducing Risks to Life: Measurement of the Benefits 28-46 (Am. Enterprise Inst. 1980).

The difficulty of determining the value of life to the decedent makes it natural to focus on the second type of loss in a death case, the loss to survivors, as the basis for the damage award. As a first approximation, this loss is the difference between what the victim would have earned during the remainder of his life and what he would have spent on his own consumption; equivalently, it is the sum of what the victim would have given his dependents during his lifetime and what he would have bequeathed to them on his death. This is, to be sure, only the pecuniary dimension of their loss; but monetizing the nonpecuniary dimension would involve the same measurement problems involved in monetizing the utility lost by the victim as a result of being killed.

If measurement problems are thought to limit damages in a death case to the pecuniary loss suffered by the victim's survivors, we may have a clue to why primitive and early societies awarded damages in death cases but our society did not do so until the passage of the wrongful-death statutes in the nineteenth century. In primitive and early societies the family is the basic social unit for purposes both of defense against aggression and insurance against the uncertainties of the harvest and the hunt. See Posner, A Theory of Primitive Society, with Special Reference to Law, 23 J. Law & Econ. 1 (1980). Since the death of an able-bodied family member is a source of substantial loss to the family, we expect, and find, that the family in primitive society is entitled to damages from the wrongdoer. In modern times a different reason supports the award of damages to survivors: the modern working man (or woman) is highly productive and often earns much more than is needed or used for his personal consumption; the difference between what he earns and what he spends on himself becomes a basis for the computation and award of substantial damages in death cases.

In the intermediate period, the period of classical common-law principles, the family was less important than it had been in primitive and early societies, while productivity was not so great that most people produced a substantial surplus over their personal consumption. In this period the damages to survivors would ordinarily have been small; this was a reason against incurring the administrative costs of trying to compute and award such damages in death cases. The reader is warned, however, that this entire analysis is highly conjectural.

There are two approaches today to computing damages in wrongful-death cases. The first and more common, the approach of Lord Campbell's Act itself, is to recognize a right of action in the survivors for the loss of pecuniary benefits to them. Statutes embodying this approach are known as "death" statutes. The second approach, somewhat less common, is simply to provide that the victim's tort right survives his death; becomes, in short, an asset of his estate. Statutes embodying this approach are known as "survival" statutes. Some states have both kinds of statute. Which approach does Kentucky follow? What practical differences, if any, are there between the two approaches? How might damages for pain and suffering before death be treated differently under the two statutes?

2. What would the proper measure of damages have been under either approach, in *Bolen*, assuming that the victim's earning power had been nonexistent, and not just minimal as the court stated? This raises the broader question of the proper measure of damages in death cases involving children, housewives, the old, and others who do not have market income so that there is no pecuniary loss to survivors or to the estate of the decedent. The traditional approach was to award no or merely nominal damages in such cases, but there is growing recognition that nonmarket production is an important, and to some extent a monetizable, source of real although not pecuniary income. Take the case of a child. The modern child does not produce significant market income, but parents would not incur the considerable expenses, pecuniary and nonpecuniary (the latter involving mainly time, which has an opportunity cost because it could be used in some market occupation to generate income), unless the child rendered services (in some intangible, but real, sense) commensurate with those expenses. This suggests that a minimum (why minimum?) estimate of the value of the lost services to the parents from the death of a child is the cost incurred by the parents in raising the child.

Such an approach was taken in Wycko v. Gnodtke, 361 Mich. 331, 105 N.W.2d 118 (1960). Plaintiff's decedent, a 14-year-old boy, was killed in an automobile accident. There was evidence that before his death he helped his father and brother work the family farm. The jury awarded damages of $14,000 plus funeral expenses. The trial court set aside the verdict as excessive. The Michigan wrongful-death statute limited the parents to the "pecuniary loss" caused by the child's death, and the trial judge said that no 14 year old had an earning capacity worth $14,000. The state supreme court reversed and directed that the jury verdict be reinstated, stating in part:

> The pecuniary value of a human life is a compound of many elements. The use of material analogies may be helpful and inoffensive. Just as with respect to a manufacturing plant, or industrial machine, value involves the costs of acquisition emplacement, upkeep, maintenance service, repair, and renovation, so, in our context, we must consider the expenses of birth, of food, of clothing, of medicines, of instruction, of nurture and shelter. Moreover, just as an item of machinery forming part of a functioning industrial plant has a value over and above that of a similar item in a showroom, awaiting purchase, so an individual member of a family has a value to others as part of a functioning social and economic unit. This value is the value of mutual society and protection, in a word, companionship. The human companionship thus afforded has a definite, substantial, and ascertainable pecuniary value and its loss forms a part of the "value" of the life we seek to ascertain. We are, it will be noted, restricting the losses to pecuniary losses, the actual money value of the life of the child, not the sorrow and anguish caused by its death. This is not because these are not suffered and not because they are unreal. The genius of the common law is capable, were it left alone, of ascertaining such damages, but the legislative act creating the remedy forbids. Food, shelter, clothing, and companionship, however, are obtainable on the open market, have an ascertainable money value. Finally if, in some unusual situation, there is in truth, or reasonably forthcoming, a wage-profit capability in the infant (an expectation of an excess of wages over keep, the measure heretofore employed) the loss of such expectation should not be disregarded as one of the pecuniary losses suffered. In such case, however, the assessment is made as a matter of fact and not of fiction. It is true, of course, that there will be uncertainties in all of these proofs, due to the nature of the case, but we are constrained to observe that it is not the privilege of him whose wrongful act caused the loss to hide behind the uncertainties inherent in the very situation his wrong has created.

Id. at 339, 105 N.W.2d at 122. This passage mixes two approaches to assessing damages when the child has no earning capacity. One is based on the cost to the parents of raising the child, the other on the child's (nonpecuniary) value to the parents. (What did the court overlook in attempting to implement the first approach?) The second approach stirred controversy in subsequent cases because of its apparent inconsistency with the "pecuniary loss" language of the Michigan statute, and was repudiated in Breckon v. Franklin Fuel Co., 383 Mich. 251, 268, 174 N.W.2d 836, 842 (1970). But the court in Breckon expressly reaffirmed so much of Wycko as had allowed the parents' pecuniary loss to be measured by their investment in the child, and stated that plaintiff in Wycko was entitled to the following instruction which the trial court had refused to give:

> One who injures another by his negligent act must, under our laws, respond in damages for that injury and the only way that damages can be ordered in our

society is in terms of money retribution. Life cannot be restored but this is not to say that life has no value and a moral jury must not shrink from the assessment of that value. You therefore are to consider the investment of these parents and the dollar and cents cost of the replacement of that investment in their son to the time of his death as the measure of their pecuniary loss.

One year after *Breckon* was decided, the Michigan legislature reinstated *Wycko* in full by amending the wrongful-death statute to eliminate the word "pecuniary" and expressly allow the award of damages for loss of "society and companionship." See Mich. Comp. Laws Ann. §600.2922(2) (1980-1981 Pocket Pt.). For a statistical analysis of damages for loss of society and companionship resulting from the death of a child, see Finkelstein, Pickrel & Glasser, The Death of Children: A Nonparametric Statistical Analysis of Compensation for Anguish, 74 Colum. L. Rev. 884 (1974).

Thus far in the discussion we have assumed that it is infeasible to estimate the earnings that the child would have had when he grew up and went to work. Increasingly, however, courts allow expert testimony to be used to project those lost earnings. See, e.g., Haumersen v. Ford Motor Co., 257 N.W.2d 7 (Iowa 1977); Hughes v. Pender, 391 A.2d 259 (D.C. Ct. App. 1978). Should such damages be considered an addition to or a substitute for damages awarded on a *Wycko* theory?

3. How should the life of a housewife be valued? The conventional answer goes by the name "replacement cost"; the trier of fact tries to estimate the cost of replacing the housewife's services. The great pitfall, which courts sense but have difficulty avoiding, is underestimation through using the prices of market services, such as housekeeping, which are only imperfect substitutes for the services actually rendered by the housewife, to value the housewife's services. An alternative approach has been suggested, the opportunity-cost approach: basing the damage award on what the housewife could have earned if she had worked in the market rather than in "household production." The idea, very similar to that underlying the first approach in *Wycko*, is that the woman would not stay home if her household services were not worth at least as much as she could get in the market. What are the pitfalls in *this* approach? For a good discussion of both approaches see Pottick, Tort Damages for the Injured Homemaker: Opportunity Cost or Replacement Cost?, 50 U. Colo. L. Rev. 59 (1978).

4. Under any of the above approaches to assessing damages in death cases, could plaintiff in *Bolen* have recovered substantial damages? Probably not. Yet if instead of being killed plaintiff's decedent had received a painful wound, he would have been able to recover damages, possibly substantial damages, for his conscious pain and suffering. Thus, tort damages may be greater in a case of nonfatal injury than in an instantaneous-death case. Does this make sense?

5. It has been said of awarding damages for pain and suffering that "pain is a harm, an 'injury,' but neither past pain nor its compensation has any

consistent economic significance." Jaffe, Damages for Personal Injury: The Impact of Insurance, 18 Law & Contemp. Prob. 219, 224 (1953). Is that correct? Or does it confuse "pecuniary" with "economic"? Most people would charge a stiff price to agree to be subjected to pain and suffering (or would pay a stiff price to avoid these things), even if the pain and suffering did not reduce their earnings. Therefore a failure to award damages for pain and suffering would result in a suboptimal allocation of resources to accident avoidance by potential injurers.

6. Should damages be awarded for injuries that are not physically painful or uncomfortable and do not reduce market earnings, but do cause a loss of utility, as by disfiguring the victim, or (otherwise) impairing his or her ability to enjoy leisure? The general answer given by the law is yes. See, e.g., Riddle v. Memorial Hospital, 43 App. Div. 2d 750, 349 N.Y.S.2d 855 (1973) (amateur violinist's ability to play impaired by accident), and for discussion Ogus, Damages for Lost Amenities: For a Foot, a Feeling or a Function?, 35 Mod. L. Rev. 1 (1972); Marth, Loss of Enjoyment of Life—Should It Be a Compensable Element of Personal Injury Damages?, 11 Wake Forest L. Rev. 459 (1975).

For economic analysis of the problem of tort compensation for nonpecuniary losses see Komesar, Toward a General Theory of Personal Injury Loss, 3 J. Legal Stud. 457 (1974); R. A. Posner, Economic Analysis of Law 149-152 (2d ed. 1977). For a good discussion of the many difficult legal questions involved in the administration of wrongful-death statutes see Prosser 901-914.

7. What if the *defendant* dies before the plaintiff can obtain or collect a tort judgment against him? Does the tort cause of action survive the tortfeasor's death? Should it? See Prosser 898-901.

Crowell v. Crowell
180 N.C. 516, 105 S.E. 206 (1920)

CLARK, C.J. . . . Practically, the only point presented by this appeal is whether or not a cause of action is alleged in the complaint.

Paragraph 5 of the complaint alleges:

> That the defendant, by reason of his illicit relations with lewd and profligate women, contracted a venereal disease of a foul and loathsome character, and of a highly infectious and malignant nature, and although he well knew that he was so infected, and well knew the character of said disease and its dangerous and infectious nature, he concealed from the plaintiff the fact that he was so infected with said disease, and, on or about the _____ day of _____ , 1919, committed an assault and trespass upon the person of the plaintiff, and infected her with said foul and loathsome disease, injuring her and damaging as hereinafter set out.

There can be no question in this day that if the defendant had violently assaulted his wife and caused serious bodily injury to her person, and humiliation to her, she could maintain an action for damages against him. Even under the obsolete ruling of the courts (for it was never statutory) that a husband could chastise his wife with immunity, there was an exception that he was liable if he caused her serious bodily harm or permanent injury. . . .

. . . Our Statute, 1913, ch. 13, §1, provides:

> The earnings of a married woman by virtue of any contract for her personal service, and any damages for personal injuries, or other torts sustained by her, can be recovered by her suing alone, and such earnings or recovery shall be her sole and separate property as fully as if she had remained unmarried.

This gives her the right of recovery of damages for any personal injury or other tort sustained by her, and there is no exemption of her husband from liability in an action by her which she is authorized to bring under Rev. §408. As long as the court held that the recovery by the wife of damages for personal injuries was the property of the husband, it was useless for her to sue him under the right given by Rev. §408(2), but the act of 1913, chapter 13, making such damages her property, was promptly passed at the first session of the General Assembly thereafter curing this, and enabled the wife to maintain an action against her husband to recover damages for injuries committed upon her person by him. . . .

As to the suggestion that the defendant could be indicted, that was a matter for the State which has not thus proceeded, and a conviction would be no reparation to the plaintiff. Besides, if the unity does not prevent an indictment why should it prevent a civil action?

At common law neither civil nor criminal actions could be maintained by the wife against the husband, because of the alleged unity of persons of husband and wife, or rather the merger of the wife's existence into the husband's. The real reason was that by marriage the wife became the chattel of the husband (as a reminder of which to this day at a marriage it is asked who "gives this woman away"), and therefore her personal property by the fact of marriage became his, as was the case in this state as to wives until the Constitution of 1868. . . .

It must be remembered that there is not, and never has been, any statute in England or this state declaring that "husband and wife are one, and he is that one." It was an inference drawn by courts in a barbarous age, based on the wife being a chattel, and therefore without any right to property or person. It has always been disregarded by courts of equity. Public opinion and the sentiment of the age, as expressed by all laws and constitutional provisions since, have been against it. The anomalous instances of that conception which still survive in some courts are due to courts construing away the changes made by corrective legislation or restricting their application. . . .

WALKER AND HOKE, JJ. (dissenting).

This case is so distressing and repellent in its details that it is difficult, as it seems, to give it that dispassionate consideration which every case should have. There is not a word of condemnation too severe to be applied to the conduct of the defendant. He has subjected himself to the penalties of the criminal law, but not to prosecution by his wife, and simply because that unity of person, which has always been attributed to the marital relation, still exists, notwithstanding that married women have been endowed with so many property rights, as they should have been, which appear to furnish the only argument for the destruction of that unity so important for the preservation of the peace and happiness of the home. Married women owned, and were constantly acquiring, property by gift, inheritance, and purchase, just as in the case of men, and it was clearly their right to have and possess it freed from the control of their husbands, and this has now become a legal right, with a few certain exceptions. But the Legislature has wisely refused to abolish that legal unity existing between man and wife, which was deemed by it so essential in securing the blessings of the marital union, in which, not only the principles, but society and the community, are so deeply concerned. The privacy of the home is as sacred as it ever was, and it is often better "to draw the curtain, shut out the public gaze, and leave the parties to forget and forgive," and this is done from motives of public policy, in order to preserve the sanctity, as well as the peace and tranquility, of the domestic circle. It concerns too deeply the public welfare that this should be done, for us to change it without a mandate from the Legislature, which makes and controls the public policy of the state, and for the reason we have given, among others, it has withheld its consent to any such amendment of the law. It has been considered so essential to the well-being of the community that this doctrine of the marital unity should continue to be the rule with us that those who have the only power to legislate and abolish it have refrained from doing so. We should not attempt to do that which will effect radical changes in the law by mere construction, for with the policy, wisdom, or justice of the legislation in question this court can have no rightful concern. . . .

Notes

1. What tort did defendant commit? Would there have been a tort if plaintiff had not contracted defendant's venereal disease? Would plaintiff's case in *Crowell* have been stronger or weaker if he had not been married to defendant? How does Roy v. Hartogs in Chapter 2 bear on these issues?

2. What is the relevance of defendant's knowledge that he had a venereal disease? Is it relevant to the prima facie case, to a defense of consent, or to both issues?

3. What do you think of the dissent's argument that interspousal tort immunity and the married woman's incapacity to maintain suit without

joinder by her husband rest on distinct common-law policies, only one of which the statute changed?

4. Does interspousal tort immunity make more or less sense in an intentional tort case than in an accidental tort case? Why? Does it probably increase or reduce the stability of marriages? On the current status of the doctrine see Annot., 92 A.L.R.3d 901 (1979).

O'Brien v. Cunard Steamship Co.
154 Mass. 272, 28 N.E. 266 (1891)

KNOWLTON, J. . . . To sustain the first count, which was for an alleged assault, the plaintiff relied on tha fact that the surgeon who was employed by the defendant vaccinated her on ship-board, while she was on her passage from Queenstown to Boston. On this branch of the case the question is whether there was any evidence that the surgeon used force upon the plaintiff against her will. In determining whether the act was lawful or unlawful, the surgeon's conduct must be considered in connection with the circumstances. If the plaintiff's behavior was such as to indicate consent on her part, he was justified in his act, whatever her unexpressed feelings may have been. In determining whether she consented, he could be guided only by her overt acts and the manifestations of her feelings. It is undisputed that at Boston there are strict quarantine regulations in regard to the examination of immigrants, to see that they are protected from small-pox by vaccination, and that only those persons who hold a certificate from the medical officer of the steam-ship, stating that they are so protected, are permitted to land without detention in quarantine, or vaccination by the port physician. It appears that the defendant is accustomed to have its surgeons vaccinate all immigrants who desire it, and who are not protected by previous vaccination, and give them a certificate which is accepted at quarantine as evidence of their protection. Notices of the regulations at quarantine, and of the willingness of the ship's medical officer to vaccinate such as needed vaccination, were posted about the ship in various languages, and on the day when the operation was performed the surgeon had a right to presume that she and the other women who were vaccinated understood the importance and purpose of vaccination for those who bore no marks to show that they were protected. By the plaintiff's testimony, which, in this particular, is undisputed, it appears that about 200 women passengers were assembled below, and she understood from conversation with them that they were to be vaccinated; that she stood about 15 feet from the surgeon, and saw them form in a line, and pass in turn before him; that he "examined their arms, and, passing some of them by, proceeded to vaccinate those that had no mark"; that she did not hear him say anything to any of them; that upon being passed by they each received a card, and went on deck; that when her turn came she showed him her arm; he looked at it, and said there was no mark, and that she should be vaccinated; that she told him she had been vaccinated before, and it left no mark; "that he then said nothing,that he should vaccinate her again"; that she held up her arm to be vaccinated; that no one touched her; that she did not tell him she did not want to be vaccinated; and that she took the ticket which he gave her, certifying that he had vaccinated her, and used it at quarantine. She was one of a large number of women who were vaccinated on that occasion, without, so far as appears, a word of objection from any of them. They all indicated by their conduct that they desired to avail themselves of the provisions made for their benefit. There was nothing in the conduct of the plaintiff to indicate to the surgeon that she did not wish to obtain a card which would save her from detention at quarantine, and to be vaccinated, if necessary, for that purpose. Viewing his conduct in the light of the circumstances, it was lawful. . . .

Notes

1. Where have we encountered the notion of implied consent to a battery before? To what element of the tort of battery does the doctrine of implied consent relate — plaintiff's state of mind or defendant's? Is the doctrine an example of a legal fiction?

2. Is it realistic to suppose that plaintiff could have refused to be vaccinated? Did the doctor ask her for her consent or did he in effect order her to submit to vaccination?

3. Could defendant have asserted a defense based on the quarantine regulations applicable to immigrants landing at Boston? Alternatively, does the existence of those regulations limit the damages plaintiff could have recovered even if she had proved a battery? Does the answer to this question depend on the nature of the injury that she suffered? (The opinion does not indicate what that injury was.)

4. Mink v. University of Chicago, 460 F. Supp. 713 (N.D. Ill. 1978), was a class action on behalf of more than 1,000 women who had been given diethylstilbestrol (DES) as part of a medical experiment conducted by the defendants, the University of Chicago and Eli Lilly & Company, between 1950 and 1952. The drug was administered to the women during their prenatal care at the University's Lying-In Hospital as part of a double-blind study to determine the value of DES in preventing miscarriages. Plaintiffs alleged that they had not been told either that they were part of an experiment or that the pills administered to them contained DES. On motion to dismiss plaintiff's battery claim, the court held that the facts alleged, if true, made out a prima facie case of battery, and it was a factual question whether plaintiffs' consent to prenatal care embraced the administration of DES to them.

The possible carcinogenic properties of DES were not known at the time of the experiment. Is this relevant to whether there was a prima facie battery? To the defense of consent? To damages?

Plaintiffs alleged that the DES they received had caused certain reproductive-tract abnormalities in them and increased their risk of cancer. Are either of these allegations essential to their battery claim?

Mohr v. Williams
95 Minn. 261, 104 N.W. 12 (1905)

BROWN, J. Defendant is a physician and surgeon of standing and character, making disorders of the ear a specialty, and having an extensive practice in the city of St. Paul. He was consulted by plaintiff, who complained to him of trouble with her right ear, and, at her request, made an examination of that organ for the purpose of ascertaining its condition. He also at the same time examined her left ear, but, owing to foreign substances therein, was unable to make a full and complete diagnosis at that time. The examination of her right ear disclosed a large perforation in the lower portion of the drum membrane, and a large polyp in the middle ear, which indicated that some of the small bones of the middle ear (ossicles) were probably diseased. He informed plaintiff of the result of his examination, and advised an operation for the purpose of removing the polyp and diseased ossicles. After consultation with her family physician, and one or two further consultations with defendant, plaintiff decided to submit to the proposed operation. She was not informed that her left ear was in any way diseased, and understood that the necessity for an operation applied to her right ear only. She repaired to the hospital, and was placed under the influence of anaesthetics; and, after being made unconscious, defendant made a thorough examination of her left ear, and found it in a more serious condition than her right one. A small perforation was discovered high up in the drum membrane, hooded, and with granulated edges, and the bone of the inner wall of the middle ear was diseased and dead. He called this discovery to the attention of Dr. Davis — plaintiff's family physician, who attended the operation at her request — who also examined the ear, and confirmed defendant in his diagnosis. Defendant also further examined the right ear, and found its condition less serious than expected, and finally concluded that the left, instead of the right, should be operated upon; devoting to the right ear other treatment. He then performed the operation of ossiculectomy on plaintiff's left ear; removing a portion of the drum membrane, and scraping away the diseased portion of the inner wall of the ear. The operation was in every way successful and skillfully performed. It is claimed by plaintiff that the operation greatly impaired her hearing, seriously injured her person, and, not having been consented to by her, was wrongful and unlawful, constituting an assault and battery; and she brought this action to recover damages therefor. The trial in the court below resulted in a verdict for plaintiff for $14,322.50. . . .

. . . [I]n all other trades, professions, or occupations, contracts are entered into by the mutual agreement of the interested parties, and are required to be performed in accordance with their letter and spirit. No reason occurs to us why the same rule should not apply between physician and patient. If the physician advises his patient to submit to a particular operation, and the patient weighs the dangers and risks incident to its performance, and finally consents, he thereby, in effect, enters into a contract authorizing his physician to operate to the extent of the consent given, but no further. It is not, however, contended by defendant that under ordinary circumstances consent is unnecessary, but that, under the particular circumstances of this case, consent was implied; that it was an emergency case, such as to authorize the operation without express consent or permission. . . . If a person should be injured to the extent of rendering him unconscious, and his injuries were of such a nature as to require prompt surgical attention, a physician called to attend him would be justified in applying such medical or surgical treatment as might reasonably be necessary for the preservation of his life or limb, and consent on the part of the injured person would be implied. And again, if, in the course of an operation to which the patient consented, the physician should discover conditions not anticipated before the operation was commenced, and which, if not removed, would endanger the life or health of the patient, he would, though no express consent was obtained or given, be justified in extending the operation to remove and overcome them. But such is not the case at bar. The diseased condition of plaintiff's left ear was not discovered in the course of an operation of the right, which was authorized, but upon an independent examination of that organ, made after the authorized operation was found unnecessary. Nor is the evidence such as to justify the court in holding, as a matter of law, that it was such an affection as would result immediately in the serious injury of plaintiff, or such an emergency as to justify proceeding without her consent. She had experienced no particular difficulty with that ear, and the questions as to when its diseased conditions would become alarming or fatal, and whether there was an immediate necessity for an operation, were, under the evidence, questions of fact for the jury.

. . . It is not disputed but that the family physician of plaintiff was present on the occasion of the operation, and at her request. But the purpose of his presence was not that he might participate in the operation, nor does it appear that he was authorized to consent to any change in the one originally proposed to be made. Plaintiff was naturally nervous and fearful of the consequences of being placed under the influence of anaesthetics, and the presence of her family physician was requested under the impression that it would allay and calm her fears. The evidence made the question one of fact for the jury to determine.

The last contention of defendant is that the act complained of did not amount to an assault and battery. This is based upon the theory that, as plaintiff's left ear was in fact diseased, in a condition dangerous and threatening to her health, the operation was necessary, and, having been skillfully performed at a time when plaintiff had requested a like operation on the other ear, the charge of assault and battery cannot be sustained; that, in view of these conditions, and the claim that there was no negligence on the part of defendant, and an entire absence of any evidence tending to show an evil intent, the court should say, as a matter of law, that no assault and battery was committed, even though she did not consent to the operation. . . . We are unable to reach that conclusion, though the contention is not without merit. It would seem to follow from what has been said on the other features of the case that the act of defendant amounted at least to a technical assault and battery. If the operation was performed without plaintiff's consent, and the circumstances were not such as to justify its performance without, it was wrongful; and, if it was wrongful, it was unlawful. . . . [E]very person has a right to complete immunity of his person from physical interference of others, except in so far as contact may be necessary under the general doctrine of privilege; and any unlawful or unauthorized touching of the person of another, except it be in the spirit of pleasantry, constitutes an assault and battery. In the case at bar, as we have already seen, the question whether defendant's act in performing the operation upon plaintiff was authorized was a question for the jury to determine. If it was unauthorized, then it was, within what we have said, unlawful. It was a violent assault, not a mere pleasantry; and, even though no negligence is shown, it was wrongful and unlawful. . . .

The amount of plaintiff's recovery, if she is entitled to recover at all, must depend upon the character and extent of the injury inflicted upon her, in determining which the nature of the malady intended to be healed and the beneficial nature of the operation should be taken into consideration, as well as the good faith of the defendant. . . .

Notes

1. Since the operation was "in every way successful and skillfully performed," how could it — as distinct from the plaintiff's underlying ear condition — have caused damage to her? In an omitted section of the opinion, the court upheld the order of the trial court setting aside the jury verdict on the ground that it was excessive, but did not imply that plaintiff could not recover any damages. What facts not stated in the opinion might support an award of more than merely nominal damages?

2. Is there any reasonable likelihood that plaintiff, if apprised of the true facts, would have refused to undergo an operation on her left rather than her right ear? To answer this question, do we need to know more about the nature of the "trouble with her right ear" of which she complained to defendant?

3. Did the court give sufficient weight to the risks of general anesthesia, which were greater in 1905 than they are today? The court remarks that plaintiff "was naturally nervous and fearful of the consequences of being placed under the influence of anaesthetics. . . ." Suppose that, given the risks of general anesthesia, any rational person in plaintiff's position would, if expressly consulted in advance of the operation, have agreed that if the defendant should decide after she was unconscious that it was advisable to operate on the left ear rather than the right, he was authorized to do so. Would this justify invoking the doctrine of implied consent? Did the court in *Mohr* reject this kind of reasoning, or hold only that it was the province of the jury rather than of the court? Could the Hand formula be used to determine whether plaintiff would probably have consented to the operation on her left ear?

4. Was the court on sound ground in stating that "every person has a right to complete immunity of his person from physical interference of others, except in so far as contact may be necessary under the general doctrine of privilege"? Is this a fair summary of the law of battery? Would it not, if taken literally, amount to strict liability for physical injuries?

5. On remand, the *Mohr* case was again tried and the jury brought in a verdict of $3,500 for plaintiff. The trial court granted defendant's motion for judgment notwithstanding the verdict. The state supreme court again reversed:

> . . . The learned trial court apparently granted the motion [for judgment n.o.v.] upon the ground that the evidence conclusively proved that an emergency existed which called for immediate treatment, and that the operation was justified on that ground, conceding no consent had been given, either expressly or by implication.
>
> Respondent does not question the propositions of law determined on the previous appeal, but insists that the facts elicited at the last trial were more complete and explicit with reference to the condition of appellant's left ear, and demonstrate that he was justified in performing the operation, as the only thing to do under the circumstances to relieve the patient from a critical situation. Appellant concedes that she cannot recover except upon the ground that no authority was granted, express or implied. From an examination of the record we are again of opinion that the evidence does not conclusively establish the fact that the left ear was in such a serious condition as to call for an immediate operation. If the patient placed herself in respondent's care for general ear treatment, why did he not in the first instance make a thorough examination of the left, as well as the right, ear? — is a pertinent inquiry. He testified that he found an obstruction in the left ear which, in itself, was unnatural, and yet he did nothing to ascertain the real condition for nearly three weeks thereafter. If the critical condition discovered at the time of the operation was such as to be reasonably anticipated, then the long delay without attention or treatment is not readily explained, and is suggestive of inattention

and negligence, and has some bearing upon the subsequent conduct of respondent and his explanation of what occurred. Dr. Davis [the family physician referred to in the prior opinion] was not present as the family physician with the right, express or implied, to consent for appellant to an operation on her left ear. The record discloses the fact that Dr. Davis was not appellant's physician, but had treated her sister, and was asked to be present at the operation simply to guard against the effects of the anaesthetic. There is no evidence in the record to justify the conclusion that Dr. Davis had any authority to consult with respondent and speak for the patient as to what might be necessary to do. We do not mean by this that the fact that he was consulted and expressed an opinion may not be given weight in determining the real condition of the left ear, and the good faith of Dr. Williams in operating, but Dr. Davis did not qualify as an expert in that class of diseases, made no personal examination, and simply made the statement that, upon respondent's request to take hold of the probe and detect the presence of dead bone, he did so and found it gave the impression of decayed bone in the ear.

Mohr v. Williams, 98 Minn. 494-496, 108 N.W. 818 (1906). On these facts, do you think the supreme court was right to reverse the trial court?

6. With *Mohr* compare Lloyd v. Kull, 329 F.2d 168-170 (7th Cir. 1964). While repairing a vesicovaginal fistula (described in the court's opinion as "a leak between the bladder and the vagina which permitted urine to flow uncontrolled from the bladder into the vagina") the surgeon also removed a small mole from plaintiff's leg. She sued for battery, and the jury awarded $500 in damages on the ground that the removal of the mole was indeed unauthorized. The defense was that the removal of the mole was authorized by the written permission that plaintiff had given for the fistula operation. The permission stated in pertinent part: "I hereby authorize the physician . . . to administer any treatment . . . and perform such operations as may be deemed necessary or advisable in the diagnosis and treatment of this patient." But the court held that "such written consent does not constitute consent to an operation other than the one to be performed when there is no evidence that a necessity arose during the authorized operation."

a. Did the court in *Lloyd* interpret the written permission correctly? How would you redraft the permission to cover the removal of the mole?

b. Is "necessity" the same standard as was applied in the *Mohr* case? Should the question be whether the operation was necessary or whether in all the circumstances it can fairly be inferred that if the plaintiff had been expressly consulted with regard to the operation he (or she) would have consented to it?

c. Can it be argued that the doctrine of implied consent should be interpreted narrowly in the medical context precisely because of the availability of express contractual arrangements relating to contingencies that may arise after the patient has been placed under a general anesthetic? Could it be said that the law wants the parties themselves, and not judges or juries, to determine the scope of the agreement to operate, and the law induces them to do so by refusing to recognize implied consent in other than the most exigent circumstances? Is this an economic argument?

7. Consider the bearing on the above issues of the famous "Coase theorem." The theorem is that where transaction costs* are zero the law's assignment of a right or liability will not affect the efficiency with which resources are used. See Coase, The Problem of Social Cost, 3 J. Law & Econ. 1 (1960). To illustrate, suppose that a railroad emits locomotive sparks which cause damage to a farmer's crops planted along the right of way, and the question to be decided is whether the farmer should be entitled to obtain damages for, or perhaps enjoin, the destruction of his crops. Assume the cost of the crop damage is $100, the cost to the railroad of avoiding the damage (by running its trains more slowly, or by installing more efficacious spark-arresting equipment) is $110, and the cost to the parties of negotiating an agreement respecting liability or a waiver of liability is zero. Then it makes no difference so far as the efficiency of resource use is concerned whether or not the railroad is liable for the crop damage. If it is liable, it will pay $100 in damage rather than incur a greater cost of avoiding the liability ($110). This is true even if the farmer is entitled to enjoin the railroad, for at any price between $100 and $110 both parties will be better off if the injunction is dissolved than they will be if it is enforced. Thus, the allocation of resources is the same whether or not the railroad is liable. The symmetry is preserved if the numbers are reversed — if the crop damage is $110, and the cost to the railroad of preventing the damage is $100. If the railroad is liable, whether to pay damages or to be enjoined, it will avoid the damage. If the railroad is not liable, the farmer will pay the railroad to avoid the damage anyway, since at any price between $100 and $110 both parties will be made better off by an agreement that requires the railroad to avoid the damage.

Since transaction costs are never zero, the Coase theorem does not, strictly speaking, hold in any real-world setting. Often, however, transaction costs are low, and when this is so we can expect the Coase theorem to hold as an approximation. The operation of the theorem in a real-world setting is illustrated by the written permission in the *Lloyd* case. If the courts interpreted the authorized scope of operations more narrowly than was optimal in an economic sense, doctors and patients would negotiate agreements, analogous to the hypothetical agreements between railroad and farmer in our example, broadening the physician's authority to perform an operation beyond the scope originally contemplated. If such agreements were feasible, cheap, and fairly interpreted and enforced by the courts, it would not matter a great deal whether the courts interpreted the implied-consent doctrine too narrowly or too broadly in cases like *Mohr* and *Lloyd*. The parties would contract around any judicial decision that was nonoptimal, provided that the costs of contracting around were lower than the gains from allocating re-

---

*I.e., the costs of arranging and carrying out a mutually beneficial sale or transfer.

sources more efficiently. It does not follow, however, that the courts have no economic function to perform in making rules for cases where the costs of transacting are low. If the courts assign rights and liabilities efficiently in the first place, they will save parties to future transactions the costs of contracting around inefficient assignments. This is a social saving.

8. The foregoing analysis implies, does it not, that the doctrine of implied consent should (at least to the extent that efficiency considerations are deemed important) be interpreted more broadly in settings where transaction costs are high than in settings where they are low. Some of these are medical settings. Consider the physician who chances upon a stranger unconscious on the street and administers medical aid to him. The physician bills him for his ordinary fee for such treatment, the patient refuses to pay, and the physician sues, seeking payment on a theory of unjust enrichment or "quasi-contract" (a branch of the law of restitution). If the physician's claim is denied, the result will not simply be to induce express transactions, as in the surgery examples we have considered, for there is no actual or feasible preexisting voluntary relationship between the physician and the patient.

The last example is not a part of the law of torts, but it illustrates the general point under consideration. It comes up again later in this book when, in Chapter 6, we consider tort liability for failure to attempt to warn or rescue a person in distress.

Cobbs v. Grant
8 Cal. 3d 229, 502 P.2d 1 (1972)

[Plaintiff was admitted to hospital for treatment of a duodenal ulcer. His family physician recommended surgery and called in defendant, a surgeon, who agreed with this recommendation. Defendant explained the nature of the operation to plaintiff but "did not discuss any of the inherent risks of the surgery." The operation was performed and was a success, but soon plaintiff developed serious complications, involving injury to his spleen and the growth of a gastric ulcer; these were, however, inherent risks of the original operation. Plaintiff sued defendant for medical malpractice based on two theories: negligence in the performance of the operation, and failure to obtain the "informed consent" of plaintiff before performing the operation.]

MOSK, J.

. . . We conclude there was insufficient evidence to support the jury's verdict under the theory that defendant was negligent during the operation. Since there was a general verdict and we are unable to ascertain upon which of the two concepts the jury relied, we must reverse the judgment and remand for a new trial. To assist the trial court upon remand we analyze the doctor's duty to obtain the patient's informed consent and suggest principles for guidance in drafting new instructions on this question. . . .

In giving its instruction [on informed consent] the trial court relied upon Berkey v. Anderson, a case in which it was held that if the defendant failed to make a sufficient disclosure of the risks inherent in the operation, he was guilty of a "technical battery." While a battery instruction may have been warranted under the facts alleged in *Berkey*, in the case before us the instruction should have been framed in terms of negligence.

Where a doctor obtains consent of the patient to perform one type of treatment and subsequently performs a substantially different treatment for which consent was not obtained, there is a clear case of battery. . . . However, when an undisclosed potential complication results, the occurrence of which was not an integral part of the treatment procedure but merely a known risk, the courts are divided on the issue of whether this should be deemed to be a battery or negligence. . . .

Although this is a close question, either prong of which is supportable by authority, the trend appears to be towards categorizing failure to obtain informed consent as negligence. That this result now appears with growing frequency is of more than academic interest; it reflects an appreciation of the several significant consequences of favoring negligence over a battery theory. . . . [M]ost jurisdictions have permitted a doctor in an informed consent action to interpose a defense that the disclosure he omitted to make was not required within his medical community. However, expert opinion as to community standard is not required in a battery count, in which the patient must merely prove failure to give informed consent and a mere touching absent consent. Moreover a doctor could be held liable for punitive damages under a battery count, and if held liable for the intentional tort of battery he might not be covered by his malpractice insurance. Additionally, in some jurisdictions the patient has a longer statute of limitations if he sues in negligence.

We agree with the majority trend. The battery theory should be reserved for those circumstances when a doctor performs an operation to which the patient has not consented. When the patient gives permission to perform one type of treatment and the doctor performs another, the requisite element of deliberate intent to deviate from the consent given is present. However, when the patient consents to certain treatment and the doctor performs that treatment but an undisclosed inherent complication with a low probability occurs, no intentional deviation from the consent given appears; rather, the doctor in obtaining consent may have failed to meet his due care duty to disclose pertinent information. In that situation the action should be pleaded in negligence.

The facts of this case constitute a classic illustration of an action that sounds in negligence. Defendant performed the identical operation to which plaintiff had consented. The spleen injury, development of the gastric ulcer, gastrectomy and internal bleeding as a result of the premature absorption of a suture, were all links in a chain of low probability events inherent in the initial operation. . . .

Notes

1. In holding that failure to obtain informed consent does not make a medical treatment battery, the court in *Cobbs* cited Natanson v. Kline, 186 Kan. 393, 401-402, 350 P.2d 1093, 1100 (1960), where failure to obtain informed consent and battery were distinguished on the following ground:

> What appears to distinguish the case of the unauthorized surgery or treatment from traditional assault and battery cases is the fact that in almost all of the cases the physician is acting in relatively good faith for the benefit of the patient. While it is true that in some cases the results are not in fact beneficial to a patient, the courts have repeatedly stated that doctors are not insurers. The traditional assault and battery involves a defendant who is acting for the most part out of malice or in a manner generally considered as "antisocial." One who commits an assault and battery is not seeking to confer any benefit upon the one assaulted.
>
> The fundamental distinction between assault and battery on the one hand, and negligence such as would constitute malpractice, on the other, is that the former is intentional and the latter unintentional.

Is this reasoning satisfactory? Was the defendant in *Mohr* or *Mink* or *Lloyd* acting out of malice? Is malice an element of the tort of battery? Is not procuring a patient's consent to an operation by failing to disclose the risks inherent in that operation much like the defendant's conduct in the *Crowell* case?

2. In Bang v. Charles T. Miller Hosp., 251 Minn. 427, 88 N.W.2d 186 (1958), plaintiff consented to a prostate resection but was not informed that this procedure involved tying off his sperm ducts; this was held a battery. Can this case be distinguished from *Natanson* and *Cobbs*? In Woolley v. Henderson, 418 A.2d 1123 (Me. 1980), the physician diagnosed a ruptured disc at the L 4,5 vertebral interspace of the spine, but operated at the L 2,3 and L 3,4 interspaces. It was held to be no battery. Is this consistent with *Mohr*?

3. On the contours of the informed-consent requirement in malpractice cases see Chapter 4 of this book; on the validity of waivers of negligence liability, Chapter 5.

Peterson v. Sorlien
299 N.W.2d 123 (Minn. 1980)

SHERAN, C.J.

This action by plaintiff Susan Jungclaus Peterson for false imprisonment . . . arises from an effort by her parents, in conjunction with other individuals named as defendants, to prompt her disaffiliation from an organization known as The Way Ministry.

At trial, the Hennepin County District Court directed a verdict in favor of defendant Paul Sorlien, plaintiff's former minister, finding the evidence proffered against him insufficient as a matter of law. The jury returned a verdict exonerating Mr. and Mrs. Jungclaus and the other remaining defendants of the charge of false imprisonment. . . .

Plaintiff asserts that the trial court erred by failing to grant a judgment notwithstanding the verdict on the claim of false imprisonment. . . .

At the time of the events in question, Susan Jungclaus Peterson was 21 years old. For most of her life, she lived with her family on a farm near Bird Island, Minnesota. In 1973, she graduated with honors from high school, ranking second in her class. She matriculated that fall at Moorhead State College. A dean's list student during her first year, her academic performance declined and her interests narrowed after she joined the local chapter of a group organized internationally and identified locally as The Way of Minnesota, Inc.

The operation of The Way is predicated on the fund-raising activities of its members. The Way's fund-raising strategy centers upon the sale of pre-recorded learning programs. Members are instructed to elicit the interest of a group of ten or twelve people and then play for them, at a charge of $85 per participant, a taped introductory course produced by The Way International. Advanced tape courses are then offered to the participants at additional cost, and training sessions are conducted to more fully acquaint recruits with the orientation of the group and the obligations of membership. Recruits must contribute a minimum of 10 percent of their earnings to the organization; to meet the tithe, student members are expected to obtain part-time employment. Members are also required to purchase books and other materials published by the ministry, and are encouraged to make larger financial contributions and to engage in more sustained efforts at solicitation.

By the end of her freshman year, Susan was devoting many hours to The Way, listening to instructional tapes, soliciting new members and assisting in training sessions. As her sophomore year began, Susan committed herself significantly, selling the car her father had given her and working part-time as a waitress to finance her contributions to The Way. Susan spent the following summer in South Dakota, living in conditions described as appalling and overcrowded, while recruiting, raising money and conducting training sessions for The Way.

As her junior year in college drew to a close, the Jungclauses grew increasingly alarmed by the personality changes they witnessed in their daughter; overly tired, unusually pale, distraught and irritable, she exhibited an increasing alienation from family, diminished interest in education and decline in academic performance. The Jungclauses, versed in the literature of youth cults and based on conversations with former members of The Way, concluded that through a calculated process of manipulation and exploitation Susan had been reduced to a condition of psychological bondage.

On May 24, 1976, defendant Norman Jungclaus, father of plaintiff, arrived at Moorhead to pick up Susan following the end of the third college quarter. Instead of returning to their family home, defendant drove with Susan to Minneapolis to the home of Veronica Morgel. Entering the home of Mrs. Morgel, Susan was greeted by Kathy Mills and several young people who wished to discuss Susan's involvement in the ministry. Each of those present had been in some way touched by the cult phenomenon. Kathy Mills, the leader of the group, had treated a number of former cult members, including Veronica Morgel's son. It was Kathy Mills, a self-styled professional deprogrammer, to whom the Jungclauses turned, and intermittently for the next sixteen days, it was in the home of Veronica Morgel that Susan stayed.

The avowed purpose of deprogramming is to break the hold of the cult over the individual through reason and confrontation. Initially, Susan was unwilling to discuss her involvement; she lay curled in a fetal position, in the downstairs bedroom where she first stayed, plugging her ears and crying while her father pleaded with her to listen to what was being said. This behavior persisted for two days during which she intermittently engaged in conversation, at one point screaming hysterically and flailing at her father. But by Wednesday Susan's demeanor had changed completely; she was friendly and vivacious and that night slept in an upstairs bedroom. Susan spent all day Thursday reading and conversing with her father and on Saturday night went roller-skating. On Sunday she played softball at a nearby park, afterwards enjoying a picnic lunch. The next week Susan spent in Columbus, Ohio, flying there with a former cult member who had shared with her the experiences of the previous week. While in Columbus, she spoke every day by telephone to her fiance who, playing tapes and songs from the ministry's headquarters in Minneapolis, begged that she return to the fold. Susan expressed the desire to extricate her fiance from the dominion of the cult.

Susan returned to Minneapolis on June 9. Unable to arrange a controlled meeting so that Susan could see her fiance outside the presence of other members of the ministry, her parents asked that she sign an agreement releasing them from liability for their past weeks' actions. Refusing to do so, Susan stepped outside the Morgel residence with the puppy she had purchased in Ohio, motioned to a passing police car and shortly thereafter was reunited with her fiance in the Minneapolis headquarters of The Way. Following her return to the ministry, she was directed to counsel and initiated the present action.

Plaintiff seeks a judgment notwithstanding the verdict on the issue of false imprisonment, alleging that defendants unlawfully interfered with her personal liberty by words or acts which induced a reasonable apprehension that force would be used against her if she did not otherwise comply. The jury, instructed that an informed and reasoned consent is a defense to an allegation of false imprisonment and that a nonconsensual detention could be deemed consensual if one's behavior so indicated, exonerated defendants with respect to the false imprisonment claim.

The period in question began on Monday, May 24, 1976, and ceased on Wednesday, June 9, 1976, a period of 16 days. The record clearly demonstrates that Susan willingly remained in the company of defendants for at least 13 of those days. During that time she took many excursions into the public sphere, playing softball and picnicking in a city park, roller-skating at a public rink, flying aboard public aircraft and shopping and swimming while relaxing in Ohio. Had Susan desired, manifold opportunities existed for her to alert the authorities of her allegedly unlawful detention; in Minneapolis, two police officers observed at close range the softball game in which she engaged; en route to Ohio, she passed through the security areas of the Twin Cities and Columbus airports in the presence of security guards and uniformed police; in Columbus she transacted business at a bank, went for walks in solitude and was interviewed by an F.B.I. agent who sought assurances of her safety. At no time during the 13-day period did she complain of her treatment or suggest that defendants were holding her against her will. If one is aware of a reasonable means of escape that does not present a danger of bodily or material harm, a restriction is not total and complete and does not constitute unlawful imprisonment. Damages may not be assessed for any period of detention to which one freely consents.

In his summation to the jury, the trial judge instructed that to deem consent a defense to the charge of false imprisonment for the entire period or for any part therein, a preponderance of the evidence must demonstrate that such plaintiff voluntarily consented. The central issue for the jury, then, was whether Susan voluntarily participated in the activities of the first three days. The jury concluded that her behavior constituted a waiver.

We believe the determination to have been consistent with the evidence. Were the relationship other than that of parent and child, the consent would have less significance.

To determine whether the findings of the jury can be supported upon review, the behavior Susan manifested during the initial three days at issue must be considered in light of her actions in the remainder of the period. Because, it is argued, the cult conditioning process induces dramatic and nonconsensual change giving rise to a new temporary identity on the part of the individuals whose consent is under examination, Susan's volitional capacity prior to treatment may well have been impaired. Following her readjustment, the evidence suggests that Susan was a different person, "like her old self." As such, the question of Susan's consent becomes a function of time. We therefore deem Susan's subsequent affirmation of defendants' actions dispositive. . . .

. . . Although carried out under colorably religious auspices, the method of cult indoctrination, viewed in a light most favorable to the prevailing party, is predicated on a strategy of coercive persuasion that undermines the capacity for informed consent. While we acknowledge that other social institutions may utilize a degree of coercion in promoting their objectives, none do so to the same extent or intend the same consequences. Society, therefore, has a compelling interest favoring intervention. The facts in this case support the conclusion that plaintiff only regained her volitional capacity to consent after engaging in the first three days of the deprogramming process. As such, we hold that when parents, or their agents, acting under the conviction that the judgmental capacity of their adult child is impaired, seek to extricate that child from what they reasonably believe to be a religious or pseudo-religious cult, and the child at some juncture assents to the actions in question, limitations upon the child's mobility do not constitute meaningful deprivations of personal liberty sufficient to support a judgment for false imprisonment.[1] But owing to the threat that deprogramming poses to public order, we do not endorse self-help as a preferred alternative. In fashioning a remedy, the First Amendment requires resort to the least restrictive alternative so as to not impinge upon religious belief.[2] . . .

WAHL, J. (dissenting in part, concurring in part).

I must respectfully dissent. In every generation, parents have viewed their children's religious and political beliefs with alarm and dismay if those beliefs were different from their own. Under the First Amendment, however, adults in our society enjoy freedoms of association and belief. In my view, it is unwise to tamper with those freedoms and with longstanding principles of tort law out of sympathy for parents seeking to help their "misguided" offspring, however well-intentioned and loving their acts may be. Whether or not, as the majority opinion asserts, The Way of Minnesota, Inc. is a "youth-oriented," "pseudo-religious group" which pursues its "fundraising strategy" in such a way as to inflict physical and psychological harm on its members, emphasis on this characterization beclouds the purely legal issues which are presented by this appeal. . . .

The unrebutted evidence shows that defendant Norman Jungclaus, the father of the 21-year-old plaintiff in this case, took his adult daughter, kicking and screaming, to a small bedroom in the basement of the Morgel home on Monday, May 23. Norman Jungclaus admitted that she did not go with him willingly. Plaintiff curled up on the bed, plugged her ears, and cried. Defendant Perkins testified that plaintiff screamed and cried and pleaded with several people to let her go, but her pleas were ignored. This situation continued until 3 A.M. Tuesday. At one point that morning, plaintiff flew at her father, and he held her arms around her from the back, in his words, "for maybe a half an hour, until she calmed down again." Plaintiff testified that defendant Mills told her papers had been drafted to commit her to Anoka

---

1. Plaintiff in her motion for a judgment notwithstanding the verdict stated that she wished to recover only nominal damages against her parents. This court has held that a judgment for defendant will not be reversed on appeal simply to allow a plaintiff to recover nominal damages.

2. While we decline at this time to suggest a particular alternative, we observe that some courts have permitted the creation of temporary guardianships to allow the removal of cult members to therapeutic settings. If the individuals desire, at the end of the conservatorship they may return to the cult. Actions have also been initiated against cult leaders on the basis of criminal liability.

State Hospital if she continued to refuse to cooperate with the "deprogramming."

In its memorandum accompanying the order denying plaintiff's motion for judgment notwithstanding the verdict, the trial court stated:

> It should be noted that there must be considerable room for doubt concerning that portion of the verdict finding that Norman Jungclaus did not participate in a false imprisonment. The evidence is unrebutted that he picked up his 21-year-old daughter Susan and took her into the basement without her permission or consent, and against her will. She remained there several days. However, Plaintiff stated that she was not seeking compensatory damages against her parents, and only $1.00 in punitive damages.
>
> In that light, judgment notwithstanding verdict as to false imprisonment would be of no significance in the matter of compensatory damages. And whether or not Mr. Jungclaus's act was done maliciously or willfully so as to justify $1.00 punitive damages is clearly a matter for determination by the jury; and not the Court. Hence, judgment notwithstanding verdict against Norman Jungclaus as to false imprisonment must be denied. On practical grounds, a new trial will not be ordered for a potential $1.00 recovery in any event.

Thus, the trial court refused to grant judgment against Norman Jungclaus because any damages awarded would be insignificant. However, plaintiff's complaint sought not only money damages but an injunction against further interference with her freedoms of religion, association, and expression. The value to plaintiff of a judgment in her favor, while not monetary, is nevertheless significant. . . .

Certainly, parents who disapprove of or disagree with the religious beliefs of their adult offspring are free to exercise their own First Amendment rights in an attempt, by speech and persuasion without physical restraints, to change their adult children's minds. But parents who engage in tortious conduct in their "deprogramming" attempts do so at the risk that the deprogramming will be unsuccessful and the adult children will pursue tort remedies against their parents. To allow parents' "conviction that the judgmental capacity of their [adult] child is impaired [by her religious indoctrination]" to excuse their tortious conduct sets a dangerous precedent. . . .

Notes

1. Is consent properly regarded as a defense to a false-imprisonment charge, or does the very idea of "false imprisonment" connote a nonconsensual restraint? If the latter, what difference might that have made to the outcome of *Peterson*?

2. What are the outer bounds of the defense recognized by the court?

McNeil v. Mullin
70 Kan. 634, 79 P. 168 (1905)

BURCH, J. The plaintiff sued the defendant for damages resulting from injuries inflicted in a fight. The petition was in the ordinary form for an assault and battery, involving a mayhem. The answer pleaded justification. The evidence given at the trial indicates that insulting words were followed by a mutual stripping of hats and coats, a movement of the defendant toward the plaintiff in an angry manner, mutual challenges of each to whip the other, a statement by the defendant that it would not cost the plaintiff a penny to whip him, a reply by the defendant that he was no more afraid of a dollar than the plaintiff, much vile talk, and then a voluntary separation. Immediately afterward, as the parties were going in the same direction along a public street, the quarrel was renewed. The defendant stopped, alighted from his buggy, tied his horse by the roadside, and removed his hat and coat. The plaintiff stopped his team, left his buggy, and removed his hat and coat. The plaintiff says the defendant approached him in a threatening attitude, and that as soon as they were near enough they clinched and fell. Other testimony is to the effect that they clinched before any blow was struck. The defendant says the plaintiff struck him as soon as he could be reached, thereby delivering the technical "first blow" of the altercation, and his testimony is corroborated in this respect. The succeeding conduct of the parties was characterized by perfect freedom from all hampering conventionalities. . . .

If the parties fought by mutual consent, the circumstance of who committed the first act of violence was immaterial; and, so long as each combatant persisted in his original determination to vanquish his antagonist, the aggressions were mutual. A resistance which has for its real object the securing of an opportunity to mangle the assailant is not legal self-defense. . . .

. . . If the encounter was the result of reciprocal desires to fight, the conduct of each party was criminal. Each one was punishable at least for a breach of the peace and for an assault and battery. . . .

Because it was a criminal enterprise, his consent to participate in the mêlée does not deprive either party of his civil remedy against the other, and each one is entitled to recover from the other all damages resulting from the injuries he received in the fight. Chief Justice Cooley, in his work on Torts, states the law on this subject as follows: "Consent is generally a full and perfect shield, when that is complained of as a civil injury which was consented to. A man cannot complain of a nuisance, the erection of which he concurred in or countenanced. He is not injured by a negligence which is partly chargeable to his own fault. A man may not even complain of the adultery of his wife, which he connived at or assented to. If he concurs in the dishonor of his bed, the law will not give him redress, because he is not wronged. These cases are plain enough, because they are cases in which the questions arise between the parties alone. But in case of a breach of the peace it is different. The state is wronged by this, and forbids it on public grounds. If men fight, the state will punish them. If one is injured, the law will not listen to an excuse based on a breach of the law. There are three parties here; one being the state, which, for its own good, does not suffer the others to deal on a basis of contract with the public peace. The rule of law is therefore clear and unquestionable that consent to an assault is no justification. The exception to this general rule embraces only those cases in which that to which assent is given is a matter of indifference to public order, such as slight batteries in play or lawful games — such unimportant injuries as, even when they constitute technical wrongs, may well be overlooked and excused by the party injured, if not done of deliberate malice. But an injury, even in sport, would be an assault if it went beyond what was admissible in sports of the sort, and was intentional." . . .

There is some natural repugnancy to allowing damages to be recovered by a bullying blackguard who has courted a fight and has been soundly thrashed, but the law can indulge in no sentiment regarding the matter. It can concede no legal effect to his vicious purpose. His consent to fight must be treated as utterly void, and each party must be left to suffer all consequences, civil and criminal, of his reprehensible conduct. . . .

Notes

1. If fights of the sort involved in this case had not been criminal, would the defense of consent have failed?

2. Why did Chief Justice Cooley say that the state is in effect a third party to the suit along with the plaintiff and the defendant? What precisely is the state's interest? An economist might answer that the revenue needs of the state give it an interest in discouraging acts of violence which might impair the ability of a citizen to contribute (directly or indirectly) to the state's tax revenue.

3. Would recognizing a defense of consent advance or retard the public policy of discouraging fights? The minority of courts that allow a defense of consent in mutual-combat cases do so on the ground that the defense discourages fights. See, e.g., Hart v. Geysel, 159 Wash. 632, 294 P. 570 (1930). Are they right? The majority rule (consent not a defense) reduces the expected gains from fighting. The winner must make good the loser's damages, which presumably exceed his own (that is what it means, ordinarily, to win a fight). At the same time, the costs to the loser of fighting are reduced, because he will be compensated. Thus a person who goes into a fight expecting to win will probably be more deterred by the majority than by the minority rule, while the person who goes into a fight expecting to lose will probably be more deterred by the minority rule. But most people who agree to fight expect to win, do they not? If so, the majority rule should have a greater deterrent effect than the minority rule.

4. In Hudson v. Craft, 33 Cal. 2d 654, 204 P.2d 1 (1949), defendant, a carnival operator, conducted a boxing match without the license required by state law; plaintiff, one of the boxers, was injured by his opponent. The court held that regardless of the tort liability of the boxers inter se, the defendant was liable in tort to the plaintiff as a principal. But what tort did defendant commit? Does *McNeil* hold that a boxer injured in a boxing match can obtain damages for a battery? What difference does it make whether the boxing match is licensed? In any event, on what theory is the *promoter* guilty of a battery?

Hackbart v. Cincinnati Bengals, Inc.
601 F.2d 516 (10th Cir. 1979)

DOYLE, J.

The question in this case is whether in a regular season professional football game an injury which is inflicted by one professional football player on an opposing player can give rise to liability in tort where the injury was inflicted by the intentional striking of a blow during the game.

The injury occurred in the course of a game between the Denver Broncos and the Cincinnati Bengals, which game was being played in Denver in 1973. The Broncos' defensive back, Dale Hackbart, was the recipient of the injury and the Bengals' offensive back, Charles "Booby" Clark, inflicted the blow which produced it.

. . . The judge resolved the liability issue in favor of the Cincinnati team and Charles Clark. . . . In essence the trial court's reasons for rejecting plaintiff's claim were that professional football is a species of warfare and that so much physical force is tolerated and the magnitude of the force exerted is so great that it renders injuries not actionable in court; that even intentional batteries are beyond the scope of the judicial process.

Clark was an offensive back and just before the injury he had run a pass pattern to the right side of the Denver Broncos' end zone. The injury flowed indirectly from this play. The pass was intercepted by Billy Thompson, a Denver free safety, who returned it to mid-field. The subject injury occurred as an aftermath of the pass play.

As a consequence of the interception, the roles of Hackbart and Clark suddenly changed. Hackbart, who had been defending, instantaneously became an offensive player. Clark, on the other hand, became a defensive player. Acting as an offensive player, Hackbart attempted to block Clark by throwing his body in front of him. He thereafter remained on the ground. He turned, and with one knee on the ground, watched the play following the interception.

The trial court's finding was that Charles Clark, "acting out of anger and frustration, but without a specific intent to injure . . . stepped forward and struck a blow with his right forearm to the back of the kneeling plaintiff's head and neck with sufficient force to cause both players to fall forward to the ground." Both players, without complaining to the officials or to one another, returned to their respective sidelines since the ball had changed hands and the offensive and defensive teams of each had been substituted. Clark testified at trial that his frustration was brought about by the fact that his team was losing the game.

Due to the failure of the officials to view the incident, a foul was not called. However, the game film showed very clearly what had occurred. Plaintiff did not at the time report the happening to his coaches or to anyone else during the game. However, because of the pain which he experienced he was unable to play golf the next day. He did not seek medical attention, but the continued pain caused him to report this fact and the incident to the Bronco trainer who gave him treatment. Apparently he played on the specialty teams for two successive Sundays, but after that the Broncos released him on waivers. (He was in his thirteenth year as a player.) He sought medical help and it was then that it was discovered by the physician that he had a serious neck fracture injury. . . .

Contrary to the position of the [trial] court . . ., there are no principles of law which allow a court to rule out certain tortious conduct by reason of general roughness of the game or difficulty of administering it.

Indeed, the evidence shows that there are rules of the game which prohibit the intentional striking of blows. Thus, Article 1, Item 1, Subsection C, provides that: "All players are prohibited from striking on the head, face or neck with the heel, back or side of the hand, wrist, forearm, elbow or clasped hands." Thus the very conduct which was present here is expressly prohibited by the rule which is quoted above.

The general customs of football do not approve the intentional punching or striking of others. That this is prohibited was supported by the testimony of all of the witnesses. They testified that the intentional striking of a player in the face or from the rear is prohibited by the playing rules as well as the general customs of the game. Punching or hitting with the arms is prohibited. Undoubtedly these restraints are intended to establish reasonable boundaries so that one football player cannot intentionally inflict a serious injury on another. Therefore, the notion is not correct that all reason has been abandoned, whereby the only possible remedy for the person who has been the victim of an unlawful blow is retaliation. . . .

The Restatement of Torts Second, §500, distinguishes between reckless and negligent misconduct. Reckless misconduct differs from negligence, according to the authors, in that negligence consists of mere inadvertence, lack of skillfulness or failure to take precautions; reckless misconduct, on the other hand, involves a choice or adoption of a course of action either with knowledge of the danger or with knowledge of facts which would disclose this danger to a reasonable man. Recklessness also differs in that it consists of intentionally doing an act with knowledge not only that it contains a risk of harm to others as does negligence, but that it actually involves a risk substantially greater in magnitude than is necessary in the case of negligence. . . .

Subsection (f) also distinguishes between reckless misconduct and intentional wrongdoing. To be reckless the act must have been intended by the actor. At the same time, the actor does not intend to cause the harm which results from it. It is enough that he realized, or from the facts should have realized, that there was a strong probability that harm would result even though he may hope or expect that this conduct will prove harmless. Nevertheless, existence of probability is different from substantial certainty which is an ingredient of intent to cause the harm which results from the act.

Therefore, recklessness exists where a person knows that the act is harmful but fails to realize that it will produce the extreme harm which it did produce. It is in this respect that recklessness and intentional conduct differ in degree.

In the case at bar the defendant Clark admittedly acted impulsively and in the heat of anger, and even though it could be said from the admitted facts that he intended the act, it could also be said that he did not intend to inflict serious injury which resulted from the blow which he struck.

In ruling that recklessness is the appropriate standard and that assault and battery is not the exclusive one, we are saying that these two liability concepts are not necessarily opposed one to the other. Rather, recklessness under §500 of the Restatement might be regarded, for the purpose of analysis at least, a lesser included act.

Assault and battery, having originated in a common law writ, is narrower than recklessness in its scope. In essence, two definitions enter into it. The assault is an attempt coupled with the present ability to commit a violent harm against another. Battery is the unprivileged or unlawful touching of another. Assault and battery then call for an intent, as does recklessness. But in recklessness the intent is to do the act, but without an intent to cause the particular harm. It is enough if the actor knows that there is a strong probability that harm will result. Thus, the definition fits perfectly the fact situation here. Surely, then, no reason exists to compel appellant to employ the assault and battery standard which does not comfortably apply fully in preference to the standard which meets this fact situation.

The appellees contend that Clark was guilty of an assault and battery, if he was guilty of anything; that this is barred by the applicable statute of limitations for a one-year period. Appellant, however, contends that the injury was the result of reckless disregard of the rights of the plaintiff and that the six-year statute provided in Colo. Rev. Stat. Ann. §13-80-110, is applicable. . . .

. . . [I]f the evidence establishes that the injuries were the result of acts of Clark which were in reckless disregard of Hackbart's safety, it can be said that he established a claim which is subject to the six-year statute. . . .

In sum, having concluded that the trial court did not limit the case to a trial of the evidence bearing on defendant's liability but rather determined that as a matter of social policy the game was so violent and unlawful that valid lines could not be drawn, we take the view that this was not a proper issue for determination and that the plaintiff was entitled to have the case tried on an assessment of his rights and whether they had been violated. . . .

Notes

1. Suppose violations of National Football League rules are extremely common; could one infer from this that players in the NFL consent to the type of battery involved in this case? To what type of battery on the football field might they not be presumed to consent?

2. If the court's analysis is correct, was Vosburg v. Putney a case of battery or of recklessness? Does it make a difference other than possibly on the issue of the applicable statute of limitations? Cf. the *Matheson* case in Chapter 2.

3. If Hackbart had not been injured, would he still have had a cause of action in battery against Clark or the Bengals?

4. Should the Bengals be liable for Clark's act under the doctrine of respondeat superior?

5. With *Hackbart*, compare Oswald v. Township High School Dist. No. 214, 84 Ill. App. 3d 723, 406 N.E.2d 157 (1980), holding that "willful and wanton misconduct" must be shown to recover damages for injury resulting to one basketball player from the breach of a safety rule by another. Is this the same standard as in *Hackbart*? Why should a breach of a safety rule not be actionable if the breach is the result of simple negligence? See, generally, Comment, Torts in Sports — Deterring Violence in Professional Athletics, 48 Fordham L. Rev. 764 (1980); R. B. Horrow, Sports Violence: The Interaction between Private Lawmakers and the Criminal Law (1980).

6. Why is the statute of limitations for assault and battery shorter than that for most other torts?

Paxton v. Boyer
67 Ill. 132 (1873)

This was an action of trespass, brought by George W. Boyer against James Paxton, for an assault and battery committed upon his person by the defendant.

. . . A trial was had, and the jury returned the following verdict:

"We, the jury, find the defendant guilty, and assess the plaintiff's damages at $450. We, the jury, find, from the evidence, that the blow complained of was struck by the defendant without malice, and under circumstances which would have led a reasonable man to believe it was necessary to his proper self-defense."

It appeared that the plaintiff's brother and defendant, at the time of the infliction of the injury, had a difficulty, and that defendant was knocked down on the floor. On rising, he struck the plaintiff with a knife, inflicting a wound in his arm. The defendant testified that he thought it was the brother who had knocked him down, and that the plaintiff had hold of him when he got up.

MR. JUSTICE BREESE delivered the opinion of the Court:

. . . The testimony shows the trespass was committed by the defendant against an unoffending party — against one who had given no cause or provocation of any kind.

The defendant asked this instruction, which was refused:

"The defendant can not be found guilty, in an action of this kind, unless, in inflicting the injury complained of, he has been guilty of some wrong, evil intent or want of care; and if you find, from the evidence, he struck the blow without any fault, you will find for the defendant."

On coming in of the verdict, the defendant moved for judgment on the special verdict, which the court denied. This is the first point made by appellant. He insists judgment should have been rendered for the defendant upon the special verdict, as that ignores malice and unlawful intent, and finds that the act was done under circumstances which would have led a reasonable man to believe it was necessary to his proper self-defense.

Appellant's theory is, that he mistook plaintiff for his brother, with whom he was in conflict, and who had felled him to the floor by violence. . . .

Appellant relies, in support of his theory, upon Morris v. Platt and Brown v. Kendall. These cases are fully discussed, and sustain appellant. The facts in both cases are similar to those in this case, and were actions of assault and battery. The principle is announced in those cases, that a person is not liable for an unintentional injury resulting from a lawful act, where neither negligence nor folly is imputable to him who does the act, and that the burden of proving the negligence or folly, where the act is lawful, is upon plaintiff. . . .

. . . The rule is well established that, in an action of assault and battery, the plaintiff must be prepared with evidence to show, either that the intention was unlawful, or that the defendant was in fault.

The jury, by their special finding, have ignored the unlawful intention, and have said the defendant was not in fault. On what principle, then, can he be made chargeable? If a person, doing a lawful act in a lawful manner, with all due care and circumspection, happens to kill another, without any intention of doing so, he is not liable criminally. How, then, can it be said he shall be responsible in a civil case, when, in doing a lawful act with due care, and an injury happens, he shall be deemed in fault, and mulcted in damages?

It is said by appellee the rule is different in civil cases; that the motive, intent or design of the wrongdoer towards the plaintiff is not the criterion as

to the form of the remedy, for when the act occasioning the injury is unlawful, the intent of the wrongdoer is immaterial; but appellant here is no
wrongdoer, as the jury have said by the special verdict.

We do not deny the principle contended for by appellee, that, where a
tort is done, intention is no element to be considered. The special verdict out
of the way, we should not have much difficulty in coming to the conclusion
appellee's counsel have reached, but, with that at the threshold of the case,
we are unable to see the force of them. . . .

The judgment must be reversed, and the cause remanded, with directions to enter judgment for the defendant on the special verdict.

Notes

1. What does it mean to say that to be guilty of battery defendant must
either have an unlawful intention or be in fault? If there is no unlawful
intention, can the defendant be guilty of battery just because he is careless or
otherwise at fault?

2. Could plaintiff be guilty of an assault or battery against defendant
because defendant (as the jury found) reasonably believed that plaintiff was
assailing him? Why not?

3. Notice the court's reliance on Brown v. Kendall, 60 Mass. 292 (1850).
In that case, famous as one of the earliest statements in American law that
the normal standard of liability in an accident case is negligence rather than
strict liability, the defendant, in using his stick in an attempt to separate two
dogs that were fighting, accidentally struck the plaintiff, who was behind him.
But did Paxton strike Boyer accidentally? He *intended* to strike him, did he
not? So what is the relevance of Brown v. Kendall to *Paxton*?

4. Suppose Paxton's mistake about whether Boyer was his attacker was a
careless one, though made in good faith. Would that fact transform his act
into a battery? Or should he be liable only for the unintentional tort of
negligence? Could the Hand formula be used to decide which of the parties
should bear the consequences of the mistake? If Paxton's mistake is analyzed
in Hand formula terms, what is B? P? L?

5. Disagreeing with cases like Paxton v. Boyer, Professor Epstein writes:
"If in the course of activity conducted for his own gain, the defendant had
harmed himself . . . , he would be required to bear that loss himself even if the
expected gains were worth the risk involved, and there is no reason why that
result should not be sought by the legal system as well when the initial harm is
to [another]." Epstein, Intentional Harms, 4 J. Legal Stud. 391, 398 (1975).
But is this a persuasive argument for liability? Suppose a railroad causes spark
damage to crops growing near the tracks. It is true that if the railroad owned
the farm, the damage to the farm would be a cost to the railroad as well. But
by the same token, if the farm owned the railroad, the cost to the railroad of
installing spark-arresting equipment, or running its trains at slower speeds, in

order to reduce the damage to the crops would be a cost to the farm. So if the farmer is fully compensated for his crop damage, he in effect shifts to the railroad a cost (of avoiding the damage) that he would have borne had he owned the railroad.

Likewise, if Paxton and Boyer were somehow the same person, Paxton's mistake would have resulted in a cost to himself that he escapes under the rule of the case, but equally Boyer would have borne the cost (in risk of injury to Paxton = Boyer) of a decision by Paxton not to try to defend himself. So if we compensate Boyer, we in effect shift to Paxton a cost (of self-defense) which Boyer would have borne if he were the same person as Paxton. How should Paxton v. Boyer be decided by a court committed to the view that the function of tort law is to redress invasions of rights rather than to increase wealth or efficiency?

6. What difference (if any) would it have made in *Paxton* if plaintiff had in fact (though unbeknownst to defendant) been trying to protect defendant from plaintiff's brother?

7. In Morris v. Platt, 32 Conn. 75 (1864), also relied on by the court in *Paxton*, the plaintiff alleged that he was a mere bystander. Although it is doubtful on the facts of the case that plaintiff really meant to deny that defendant believed plaintiff was trying to attack him, let us assume this was the case and ask, should it have made a difference? The court in *Morris* held it did not, again citing Brown v. Kendall for the proposition that the liability standard in accident cases is negligence rather than strict liability. Although the plaintiff who is a mere bystander, as in *Morris*, is an even more appealing claimant than the plaintiff who is at least an apparent assailant, as in *Paxton*, the rejection of the bystander's claim is easier, doctrinally, than the rejection of the apparent assailant's — once the principle of Brown v. Kendall is accepted. (Why?)

Nonetheless, the court in *Morris* had some misgivings about its result, stating (32 Conn. at 89-90):

> . . . We are not insensible to the fact that the danger of accidental injury to third persons from the use of fire-arms, even in lawful self-defense, is comparatively very great, that the bearing of these arms is becoming needlessly general and their use in populous places and thoroughfares quite too frequent, and that some further protection to the public from injury by them seems necessary. That protection might be afforded by us perhaps, if we should hold, 1st, the use of fire-arms, even in lawful self-defense, to be attended by so much contingent danger to innocent third persons that accidental injuries by them should be deemed exceptional and wholly inexcusable as matter of law, or inexcusable unless the defendant should show that they were inevitable or absolutely unavoidable; or 2d, that *all* such injuries should be deemed *prima facie* negligent, and that it should be left to the jury to say whether in the particular case the danger of injury to third persons was so slight and improbable that the case was exceptional, and the defendant wholly free from blame, either in having or using the instrument. It is obvious however that if we should thus introduce an

exception into the law to meet new contingencies we should be going beyond the exigencies of this case (there being other errors), and encroaching upon the peculiar duties of the legislative branch of the government; and to that branch, with this statement of the condition of the common law, and suggestion in respect to the importance of a remedy, we must leave the matter.

8. What if Paxton had flung a hand grenade at Boyer, injuring a bystander? Could the bystander recover damages against Paxton?

9. Suppose A assaults B by striking him in an offensive, but not harmful or dangerous, manner, and B responds by trying to kill A. If A kills B to prevent B from killing him, is A entitled to claim self-defense, or is the defense forfeited by reason of his original assault on B? See Brouster v. Fox, 117 Mo. App. 711, 93 S.W. 318 (1906).

Beavers v. Calloway
270 App. Div. 873, 61 N.Y.S.2d 804 (1946)

DICKSTEIN, J.

The defendant is a band leader at Zanzibar Cafe, 1619 Broadway, New York City. On August 14, 1945 ("V J" Day) at about 8:30 P.M. a fracas developed between the defendant and a member of his band. The plaintiff entered the stage while the altercation was in progress and attempted to separate the defendant from the object of his attack, whereupon the defendant turned upon the plaintiff, striking her on the nose and causing her injuries which were described by a physician as a broadening of the bridge of the nose, a widening of the upper part of the septum which is the central partition within the nose which caused obstruction to her breathing and which condition was characterized as permanent.

The defendant maintains that the plaintiff is not entitled to recover any damages in this case, because she deliberately participated in the altercation and was therefore a voluntary participant in the assault and not a party entitled to recover damages for an assault and battery. He cites in support of his contention the well known case of Murphy v. Steeplechase Amusement Co. [infra, Chapter 5 of this casebook], but I cannot see how the holding in that case can help his contention. In that case a visitor to an amusement park after watching the operation of a moving belt which caused many who rose thereon to jump or fall, stepped on the belt and as he did so was thrown to the floor and sustained injuries, the Court refusing him damages because the hazard was invited and foreseen. Clearly a participant in dangerous sports accepts the dangers inherent in the sport and in the language of the Court in the case cited "Volenti non fit injuria." But here the plaintiff cannot be said to have engaged in any "sport," dangerous or otherwise. She merely sought to separate two combatants who were disturbing the peace of the community.

On the question of the assault itself the evidence clearly shows that the assault was unjustified and the defendant does not deny its occurrence. The only excuse offered by the defendant was that he had a couple of drinks before he committed the assault.

On the question of damages, the plaintiff seeks to recover compensatory as well as punitive or exemplary damages. She claims that the defendant's conduct was so reckless as to call for punishment as a deterrent of future acts of like character. But since punitive damages are usually imposed in the case of wilful and malicious assault, I shall award merely compensatory damages, the award of punitive damages being always a matter of discretion and not mandatory in any case. . . .

Notes

1. If plaintiff, in attempting to restrain defendant from attacking the band member, had injured defendant and he had sued her, would she have had a good defense to his battery action, assuming she had acted reasonably?

2. What bearing, if any, do the mutual-combat cases have on this case?

3. Did plaintiff not assume the risk of injury just as much as the participant in a dangerous sport does? Why is this fact irrelevant? Suppose her intervention was foolish — she had no reasonable prospect of protecting the band member from defendant's wrath. Should that affect the outcome of the case?

4. Was the court correct in declining to award punitive damages? What extenuating circumstances other than the excuse offered by the defendant were present? How do they relate to the economic analysis of punitive damages?

Haworth v. Elliott
67 Cal. App. 2d 77, 153 P.2d 804 (1944)

MOORE, J. . . .

On December 18, 1943, plaintiff in company with his wife and some friends entered a barroom operated by defendant Elliott. While there plaintiff became involved in a quarrel with another invitee. Defendants Collier and Symington, bartenders for Elliott, leaped over the bar and began their efforts to eject plaintiff from the room. Collier grabbed him around the neck and with a headlock dragged him to the door and out into the street. In the course of the ejectment plaintiff's little finger and nose were broken and other serious bodily injuries resulted. . . .

. . . The actor is privileged to apply only such force as a reasonable man under the circumstances would believe to be necessary to prevent a further disturbance of the peace within the barroom or to avoid injury to persons or property there. Plaintiff was fighting no one at the time he was seized by Collier and had done no damage to property or person. No justification appears for the "brutal" assault. The force imposed upon plaintiff was unreasonably excessive. . . .

Notes

1. What conduct by plaintiff might have justified "the 'brutal' assault"? What if plaintiff had been asked to leave and had refused? If plaintiff had been about to destroy valuable property? If plaintiff had already destroyed valuable property?

2. What would be an example of "reasonably excessive" force?

Scheufele v. Newman
187 Ore. 263, 210 P.2d 573 (1949)

BELT, J.

This is an action to recover damages for personal injuries resulting from an alleged assault and battery. . . . Defendant is the owner of a summer home near the confluence of Gordon creek and Sandy river about seventeen miles from the city of Portland. It is conceded that he owns land on both sides of Gordon creek and to the ordinary high water mark on Sandy river.

Plaintiff, accompanied by his wife, a few relatives, and friends, went from Portland to Sandy river on a picnic on July 4, 1946. The place chosen for picnic purposes was not on the land of the defendant. Plaintiff decided to go fishing and about eleven o'clock in the morning reached the place in question near the confluence of Gordon creek with Sandy river.

It is plaintiff's contention that he was fishing in Sandy river, below the ordinary high water mark, at the time of the alleged assault and battery and that since Sandy river was a navigable stream — as contended by him — he was not a trespasser. Defendant asserts that plaintiff was fishing in Gordon creek — an admittedly non-navigable stream — and that he was a trespasser on premises owned by him. . . .

Plaintiff testified about seeing the defendant and his son approach and that the defendant shouted that he owned the property and for him to get off. Plaintiff answered that he was not on private property and he "didn't have to get off." As the defendant and his son approached, plaintiff testified that he saw that both of them were armed. The defendant had a regular Army rifle weighing about nine pounds. The son was armed with two revolvers. . . .

Q. Then what happened, if anything?

A. Then Mr. Newman says, "I am a deputy sheriff, and I order you off the river."

Q. Then what happened?

A. Then I told Mr. Newman if he was a deputy to come over and show me his credentials and I would leave.

Q. Then can you tell us in your own words what happened?

A. Well, Mr. Newman had this big gun, and he began to wave it around a little and point it my way a couple of times, and I was getting pretty scared. But he didn't do anything, and then he pointed it into the water and shot again. And then he ordered me off again, and I insisted that he show me his credentials. So after that immediately, why, he came past Mr. Dawson, who was fishing on this little bank there, and waded across Gordon creek and then across this branch over to where I was, so that I was facing just the reverse of what I had been, looking downstream and facing Mr. Newman and he was facing upstream.

When the defendant was two or three feet from the plaintiff:

Q. . . . What was the position of the rifle at that time?

A. He was holding it across his front. I couldn't tell you the exact position, because I wasn't paying close attention to how he held the rifle.

Q. What was the next thing you knew, Mr. Scheufele?

A. Well, I was getting up off the river bank.

Q. Were you in the water?

A. Yes, I had sat down in the water. . . .

Q. Were you in control of your senses? Did you have your faculties about you?

A. Well, enough to insist that he show me his credentials, yes.

Q. Did he show them to you?

A. Yes, he did. . . . After he showed me his card as a deputy sheriff, why, I left, turned around and started walking back down the stream. . . .

[A witness who saw defendant and his son approach plaintiff testified that defendant] "had the rifle about so and let it fall at about so (demonstrating), and caught Mr. Scheufele around his chin and down he went like a gored ox. Two minutes or so later he got up to his feet and picked up his fishing basket which was upset a little way back and started on down the island. . . ."

On this appeal — viewing the record in the light most favorable to the defendant — it will be assumed, although not decided, that plaintiff was a trespasser. It does not follow, however, that the defendant would be justified in using unreasonable force to compel the plaintiff to "get off" the land merely because he was a trespasser. The use of a deadly weapon under such circumstances would be wholly unjustified. The mere fact that plaintiff was a trespasser would not justify the defendant in shooting in front of him or using the heavy gun as a club in an effort to eject him. The rule applicable is stated in Eldred v. Burns, as follows: "A person aggrieved by a trespass may repel the intruder by such force as may be reasonably necessary, short of taking human life or causing great bodily harm; and if, while so doing, the trespasser commits any overt act giving the one aggrieved reasonable ground to believe himself in imminent danger of losing his life or receiving great bodily harm, he may in self-defense use a weapon, even to the extent of taking the life of his assailant, if reasonably necessary." . . .

If the evidence in support of the plaintiff is true, defendant was guilty of a brutal and malicious attack. Defendant was "trigger happy" and had a warped idea of what he could do in defense of his alleged property rights. Had defendant exhibited his deputy sheriff's card before he hit the plaintiff — and not afterwards — this case in all probability would not have resulted. Firing this high-powered Army rifle in front of the plaintiff and in a recreational area was an extremely careless and dangerous thing to do. It manifested an utter disregard not only of the welfare of the plaintiff, but also of other persons who on this Fourth of July might have been picnicking in the immediate vicinity.

Notes

1. What if defendant had shown plaintiff his deputy sheriff's card and plaintiff had still refused to leave? What more could defendant then have lawfully done to induce him to depart?

2. Did defendant commit an assault as well as a battery?

3. The leading American case on the use of force to eject trespassers is M'Ilvoy v. Cockran, 9 Ky. 271 (1820). The complaint alleged that M'Ilvoy "with sticks, clubs, fists, hands and feet, made an assault upon, and beat, wounded and illy treated Cockran, so that his life was greatly despaired of. . . ." M'Ilvoy pleaded that he was trying to prevent Cockran from destroying a fence on his (M'Ilvoy's) property. In the course of holding that M'Ilvoy's plea failed to state a justification for wounding Cockran, the court made three important points:

(1) When the trespasser's entry onto the defendant's land is made without "actual force," the defendant must request the plaintiff to depart before he may lawfully use force to eject him.

(2) But "in cases of *actual force*, as breaking open a gate or door, it is lawful to oppose force with force; and if one breaks down a gate, or comes into a close with force and arms, the possessor need not request him to depart, but may lay hands upon him immediately. . . ." Id. at 275.

(3) In neither case may the defendant wound the plaintiff unless plaintiff assaults him while he is trying to remove plaintiff from, or prevent him from entering, his property. The proper plea in defense of plaintiff's battery

suit is *moliter manus imposuit* ("[the defendant] placed his hand gently [on plaintiff]'").

Why is a request to depart not required in cases of what the court calls "actual force"?

Does M'Ilvoy v. Cockran hold that a wounding is never permissible in defense of property? Or should the case be confined to situations where the defense is of title, or of property of small worth? May not a homeowner lawfully wound to prevent a burglary, even if the burglar does not commit an assault upon or in any way threaten the physical safety of the homeowner or other people in the house? Suppose a person visiting the Louvre attacks the Mona Lisa with a knife, and the only way the destruction of this priceless artistic treasure can be prevented is by wounding, or perhaps even killing, the assailant? Should the right to defend property encompass wounding or killing in *that* case? Cf. Wright v. Haffke, 188 Neb. 270, 274, 196 N.W.2d 176, 179 (1972): "We do not disagree with plaintiff that the law *generally* places a higher value upon human life than mere rights of property." (Emphasis added.)

4. In Hamilton v. Howard, 234 Ky. 321, 323-324, 327-329, 28 S.W.2d 7-10 (1930), the evidence showed the following:

Howard, who was 26 years of age at the time of the trial, and Hamilton who was 29, were both married and lived a few miles from Hartford. Howard was related to Hamilton's wife, and he and Hamilton had been in business together and on friendly terms. There was some talk in the neighborhood concerning the frequency of Hamilton's visits to Howard's home, and the impropriety of the relations between Hamilton and Mrs. Howard. Howard learned of this and claims to have observed that Hamilton was paying undue attention to his wife. He says that Hamilton frequently came to his home, and, instead of joining him, would go around the premises with Mrs. Howard. Hamilton would go to the field where Mrs. Howard was at work, and if she were plowing he would follow her up and down the rows as she plowed while Howard worked in other parts of the field. For a while Hamilton and Howard were engaged in cutting logs together. Howard would go by Hamilton's home and accompany him to work. Though they would start off together Hamilton would return to the Howard home to leave his keys with Mrs. Howard. Though he would generally join the other workmen later, it is claimed that on one occasion he never showed up at all after returning to Mrs. Howard's house under the pretext of taking his keys back to the house. On the day of the shooting Howard said that he found Hamilton's keys at his house on the bed. Howard also said that, if Mrs. Howard was getting breakfast, Hamilton would go to the kitchen where she was; that, if she was milking, he would go out to the cow lot; that, if she were gearing the mules, he would go to the barn where she was engaged. Howard says that at first he was not disturbed by Hamilton's attentions to his wife, but after Hamilton got her picture and went to telling that he was "having fun with that woman," and that he (Howard) was going to live with her only until the child got big enough to work, that caused trouble in his home. Howard then talked to Hamilton on several occasions and told him that the neighbors were talking about the matter. He asked Hamilton to stay away from his house. Hamilton "just laughed," and said he guessed he could. Hamilton did not stay away, but kept up his attentions to Mrs. Howard. Howard again remonstrated and warned him to stay away. After that they would not work together. Howard's father, who had observed Hamilton's attentions to Howard's wife, warned and advised Hamilton to stay away. Howard told Hamilton he was going to hurt him if he did not stay away. Howard describes the difficulty in the following language:

"I had been hauling coal for my brother and got in just a little before sundown and I was coming up the road and I seen my wife get a load of wood and go back in the house and just about that time he come out the same door she went in and he taken up through the woods and orchard circling for E. K. Moseley's, and I went up and got my gun and went toward where he was at, and I walked up and asked him if I hadn't told him to stay away, and talked to him and cried and begged him to stay away, and then I cursed him and told him to stay away, he acknowledged I had, and I told him I had talked every way I could to get him to stay away and I had another remedy I would try to see if that would do.

Q. Did you tell him you were going to kill him?
A. No, sir, I told him I didn't aim to kill him and he need not think it.
Q. What did he say?
A. He didn't say anything.
Q. I mean when you told him you had asked him to stay away?
A. He finally murmured out, after I asked the second time, once.
Q. Did you ask him on more than one occasion to stay away?
A. Several times, more than once.
Q. But he said "once"?
A. Yes, he acknowledged once.
Q. Then you did shoot him?
A. Yes, sir. . . .

Defendant obtained a jury verdict in his favor. Plaintiff appealed from the trial court's action in giving the following instruction requested by defendant:

The defendant had the right to protect his home from intrusion or invasion and if you believe from the evidence that before the occasion on which the plaintiff was shot by defendant, as described to you in evidence, the plaintiff had invaded the defendant's home or had made overtures to the defendant's wife or had sought to ingratiate himself into the affections of defendant's wife or to alienate her affections from the defendant and that the defendant had requested the plaintiff not to go to the defendant's home or to stay away from defendant's home or to desist his attentions to defendant's wife, and if you believe from the evidence plaintiff failed to heed said warnings, if any were given him, and if you believe from the evidence that in shooting and wounding the plaintiff, as described to you in the evidence, the defendant used only such force as was reasonably necessary to prevent the plaintiff from further invading the defendant's home or paying attention to the defendant's wife, then you should find for the defendant.

The appellate court summarized the argument in favor of the instruction as follows:

> ... Hamilton was paying undue and improper attention to Howard's wife, and was endeavoring to win his way into her affections. Though warned by Howard and others to stay away from his home, Hamilton did not stay away, but persisted in his attentions and intrusions. The immediate act of Hamilton in running away from the Howard home was not the cause of the shooting. It was merely the straw that broke the camel's back. It was but one of a long series of oft-repeated and recurring offenses. Patience had ceased to be a virtue. Numerous warnings and commands had proved ineffective. The time had come when Howard was compelled to use some force or stand by and see Hamilton continue to invade his home and impose himself upon his wife. "If there was a drop of red-blooded manhood about Howard; if he cared a whit for his home and family; if he was any part of a man at all, it was time for him to act and to act with force and effectiveness, in the protection of his castle and those in it who were dependent upon him." Whether Howard was trying to prevent Hamilton from stealing his wife's affections, thus breaking up his home, or was trying to protect his wife from undue influence and embarrassment and protect his home from the tongue of evil report and bad repute in the community, he had the right to protect his home against invasion for either purpose, and since the force he used was patently necessary and undeniably effective, and actually resulted in but little temporary damage, the verdict of the jury in favor of Howard should not be set aside.

Do you think this argument persuaded the court? What right of defendant's did plaintiff invade? Should the place where the shooting occurred make any difference? What else could defendant have done to protect his interests against plaintiff? Assuming defendant went too far, could *any* use of force against plaintiff have been justified in the circumstances?

Kent v. Southern Ry. Co.
52 Ga. App. 731, 184 S.E. 638 (1936)

GUERRY, J.

J. G. Kent brought suit against the Southern Railway Company and W. W. Waits. Error is assigned upon the order sustaining a general demurrer to the petition. It was alleged: On September 6, 1934, W. W. Waits was a conductor of the railway company, and brought a train consisting of an engine and three cars to a point about twenty feet from where the company's side track crossed Circle street in the city of Atlanta and near where said side track enters the property of the Exposition Cotton Mills. The plaintiff and about fifty other persons who worked at said mill were gathered along the intersection of Circle street and the side track, blocking the entrance of the train to the mills. Waits advised the plaintiff and the persons with him that it was necessary for him to place some of the cars of his train in the yard of the mill and to take other cars therefrom, and stated to the plaintiff and the others that they were blocking his train and were preventing him from discharging his company's business, and requested them to move off said track that he might proceed with the performance of his duties. Neither the plaintiff nor the other persons moved from their positions, as they were at the time on a strike and picketing the mill. Waits then cursed and swore at said gathering, and threatened their lives and told them he would move them; but they silently maintained their positions. Waits went off and returned in about ten minutes with T. O. Sturdivant, chief of police of the city of Atlanta, who was armed with a gun, and on his arrival counseled, commanded, and ordered T. O. Sturdivant to shoot petitioner and others so gathered as aforesaid, and acting upon and pursuant to said order Sturdivant did shoot petitioner "in the face, mouth and eyes with a large and heavy gun loaded with some form of heavy substance" unknown to petitioner, and "petitioner's eyes were mashed, bruised, burnt, and contused; his mouth and lungs, by reason of said shooting, were scorched, burned, and caused to bleed profusely." After said persons so assembled at, along, and on said crossing were driven and cuffed therefrom, Waits took said train to the mill, left some cars, and removed others. . . .

. . . The plaintiff was engaged, according to the allegations of his petition, in an active, willful, deliberate violation of several penal statutes of this state. The conductor in charge of the train, according to the allegations, had observed every requirement possible to induce the plaintiff to desist from his admitted criminal act, and the plaintiff willfully and purposely continued it. The conductor himself, under these allegations, would have been justified in using such force as was necessary to prevent the continued blocking of the track and train. Peaceful requests, violent and abusive language, and threats of running the train over them had entirely failed to prevent the plaintiff from continuing his criminal enterprise. The means then used to stop the continuation of such action by the plaintiff was not a gun loaded with powder and ball, for it is not so described in the petition (which must be construed most strongly against the pleader), but, from the description, the load was a substance evidently prepared by the police to cause the dispersal of a crowd, without causing death to its members. It is not alleged that such substance was tear gas but the result alleged showed it was somewhat similar. The petition nowhere alleges that the action taken was unnecessary, or that the force used was greater than that required to accomplish the right of removing the plaintiff, which was being carried out by the highest officer in the enforcement of the law in the City of Atlanta. . . .

A distinction is and should be drawn between those cases where the trespass is active and continued after warning to desist, and those that are merely passive. One stealing a ride on a train is a criminal trespasser, and the only duty the company owes him is not to willfully and wantonly injure him after his presence is discovered. When he is discovered and refuses to leave the train on being ordered so to do, and resists by force, the use by the employees of possibly more force than is necessary under the circumstances, in order to put such trespasser off the train, is not negligence imputable to the company. The trespasser by such action puts himself in the position of creating a privilege for the actor to use bodily force without too many fine-drawn distinctions of reasonableness. . . .

Notes

1. If Sturdivant's conduct had been tortious, would defendant have been liable for it under the doctrine of respondeat superior?

2. Was plaintiff a trespasser on defendant's property? Does this depend on who owned the tracks? If there was a trespass to defendant's property, did it involve "actual force" under *M'Ilvoy*? Was plaintiff "wounded" within the meaning of that case?

If plaintiff was not a trespasser, what other tort might he have committed? Could defendant have used force to prevent commission of *that* tort?

3. What is the relevance of the fact that plaintiff was violating the criminal law? Might there be a privilege, distinct from that of defense of property, to prevent crimes? Reconsider this question after reading the spring-gun and defense-of-chattel cases below.

4. Suppose plaintiff had been an innocent bystander, though the police chief reasonably believed that he was one of the crowd blocking the train. Should this change the result in the case?

5. Waits was alleged to have threatened the lives of the strikers. Was this an assault? Might there be a privilege to commit an assault to protect some lawful interest in circumstances where a battery or wounding might not be lawful?

6. In what circumstances is a labor organization liable for the torts of its members—e.g., an assault by a picketer against a person crossing the picket line? See International Assn. of Bridge, Structural & Ornamental Ironworkers, Local 387 v. Moore, 149 Ga. App. 431, 254 S.E.2d 438 (1979); Annot., 36 A.L.R.3d 405 (1971).

Bird v. Holbrook
4 Bing. 628, 130 Eng. Rep. 911 (Com. Pl. 1828)

Before, and at the time of the Plaintiff's sustaining the injury complained of, the Defendant rented and occupied a walled garden in the parish of St. Phillip and Jacob, in the county of Gloucester, in which the Defendant grew valuable flower-roots, and particularly tulips, of the choicest and most expensive description. The garden was at the distance of near a mile from the Defendant's dwelling-house, and above one hundred yards from the road. In it there was a summer-house, consisting of a single room, in which the Defendant and his wife had some considerable time before slept, and intended in a few days after the accident again to have slept, for the greater protection of their property. The garden was surrounded by a wall, by which it was separated on the south from a footway up to some houses, on the east and west from other gardens, and on the north from a field which had no path through it, and was itself fenced against the highway, at a considerable distance from the garden, by a wall. On the north side of the garden the wall adjoining the field was seven or eight feet high. The other walls were somewhat lower. The garden was entered by a door in the wall. The Defendant had been, shortly before the accident, robbed of flowers and roots from his garden to the value of £20 and upwards: in consequence of which, for the protection of his property, with the assistance of another man, he placed in the garden a spring gun, the wires connected with which were made to pass from the doorway of the summer-house to some tulip beds, at the height of about fifteen inches from the ground, and across three or four of the garden paths, which wires were visible from all parts of the garden or the garden wall; but it was admitted by the Defendant, that the Plaintiff had not seen them, and that he had no notice of the spring gun and the wires being there; and that the Plaintiff had gone into the garden for an innocent purpose, to get back a pea-fowl that had strayed.

A witness to whom the Defendant mentioned the fact of his having been robbed, and of having set a spring gun, proved that he had asked the Defendant if he had put up a notice of such gun being set, to which the Defendant answered, that "he did not conceive that there was any law to oblige him to do so," and the Defendant desired such person not to mention to any one that the gun was set, "lest the villain should not be detected." The Defendant stated to the same person that the garden was very secure, and that he and his wife were going to sleep in the summer-house in a few days.

No notice was given of the spring gun being placed in the garden, and before the accident in question occurred, another person to whom the Defendant mentioned the fact of his garden having been robbed of roots to the value of £20, and to whom he stated his intention of setting a spring gun, proved that he had told the Defendant that he considered it proper that a board should be put up.

On the 21st March 1825, between the hours of six and seven in the afternoon, it being then light, a pea-hen belonging to the occupier of a house in the neighbourhood had escaped, and, after flying across the field above mentioned, alighted in the Defendant's garden. A female servant of the owner of the bird was in pursuit of it, and the Plaintiff (a youth of the age of nineteen years), seeing her in distress from the fear of losing the bird, said he would go after it for her: he accordingly got upon the wall at the back of the garden, next to the field, and having called out two or three times to ascertain whether any person was in the garden, and waiting a short space of time without receiving any answer, jumped down into the garden.

The bird took shelter near the summer-house, and the boy's foot coming in contact with one of the wires, close to the spot where the gun was set, it was thereby discharged, and a great part of its contents, consisting of large swan shot, were lodged in and about his knee-joint, and caused a severe wound.

The question for the opinion of the Court was, Whether the Plaintiff was entitled to recover: if so, the verdict was to stand; otherwise a nonsuit was to be entered.

Wilde Serjt. for the Plaintiff. . . . For the protection of property or in defence of possession, it be unlawful to have recourse to desperate violence after the trespass has been committed. Prevention, not punishment, is the foundation of the right. The means lawfully taken to prevent offences, may, and frequently do, operate as punishments: but they are justifiable only in their quality of preventives; and, even then, the degree of force must, in no case, be greater than is necessary to effect the object; and with respect to all the graver degrees of violence, they must not exceed the measure of punishment which the law would have inflicted if the offence had been perpetrated. . . .

Merewether Serjt. for the Defendant. . . . Undoubtedly a man is not allowed to do indirectly what it would be unlawful for him to do directly; but the necessity of protecting property at a distance authorizes the proprietor to resort directly to means, during his absence, which it might be unlawful for him to employ if on the spot. The humanity or inhumanity of a practice, is not a test of its legality; and the law does not exact every line of conduct which benevolence or religion may recommend. It is admitted that a trespasser may be repelled by force, if no more force be employed than is necessary; but, during absence, a man can employ, for the protection of his property, no less and no other force than that of machines, which may repress offenders by the fear of pain or detection; and if they are so employed as not to molest another in the exercise of his rights, there is no violation of the maxim, "Sic utere tuo ut alienum non laedas," which applies to the active invasion of another's rights, and not to the quiet protection of our own. A party present, therefore, cannot justify the shooting [of] a trespasser, because that is a greater degree of violence than the occasion requires; and knowing the trespasser, he should resort to the law, and not take the punishment into his own hands; yet he may well justify placing a gun during his absence, because, by no less degree of probable violence can he deter felons and trespassers. . . .

A clear proof of the legality of the practice, at the time this action commenced, is afforded by the passing of the recent act, against setting spring guns, except in houses and by night. That act is not declaratory, but prohibitory; and when a statute is prohibitory, it is a legislative admission that the act prohibited was not an offence before.

Wilde in reply. The statute is declaratory as to setting guns without notice, and prohibitory as to setting them, even with notice, except in the dwelling-house at night. . . .

No illustration can be drawn from the use of spikes and broken glass on walls, &c. These are mere preventives, obvious to the sight, — unless the trespasser chooses a time of darkness, when no notice could be available, — mere preventives, injurious only to the perservering and determined trespasser, who can calculate at the moment of incurring the danger the amount of suffering he is about to endure, and who will, consequently, desist from his enterprise whenever the anticipated advantage is outweighed by the pain which he must endure to obtain it.

BEST C.J. I am of opinion that this action is maintainable. . . .

It has been argued that the law does not compel every line of conduct which humanity or religion may require; but there is no act which Christianity forbids, that the law will not reach: if it were otherwise, Christianity would not be, as it has always been held to be, part of the law of England. I am, therefore, clearly of opinion that he who sets spring guns, without giving notice, is guilty of an inhuman act, and that, if injurious consequences ensue, he is liable to yield redress to the sufferer. But this case stands on grounds distinct from any that have preceded it. In general, spring guns have been set for the purpose of deterring; the Defendant placed his for the express purpose of doing injury; for, when called on to give notice, he said, "If I give notice, I shall not catch him." He intended, therefore, that the gun should be discharged, and that the contents should be lodged in the body of his victim, for he could not be caught in any other way. On these principles the action is clearly maintainable, and particularly on the latter ground. The only thing which raised any doubt in my mind was the recent act of parliament; and if that had been purely prohibitory, there would be great weight in the argument which has been raised on it; because in a new prohibitory law we have the testimony of the legislature that there was no previous law against the thing prohibited. But the act is declaratory as to part, and prohibitory as to part; declaratory as to the setting of spring guns without notice, and the word "declared" is expressly introduced; prohibitory as to setting spring guns, even with notice, except in dwelling-houses by night. . . .

BURROUGH J. The common understanding of mankind shews, that notice ought to be given when these means of protection are resorted to; and it was formerly the practice upon such occasions to give public notice in market towns. But the present case is of a worse complexion than those which have preceded it; for if the Defendant had proposed merely to protect his property from thieves, he would have set the spring guns only by night. The Plaintiff was only a trespasser: if the Defendant had been present, he would not have been authorised even in taking him into custody, and no man can do indirectly that which he is forbidden to do directly. . . .

Notes

1. Spring guns were something of a cause célèbre in England at the time of the *Bird* decision. The Parliamentary debates preceding the enactment of the statute (7 & 8 George IV, c. 18, §§1, 4 (1827)) mentioned in the decision indicate that the major controversy concerned the use of spring guns by landowners against poachers — a use defended on the ground that it was a cheaper way to defend game than by using armed gamekeepers, especially since poachers had taken to traveling in armed bands. Spring guns were also used by "market gardeners" (what in this country are called truck farmers), such as defendant in the *Bird* case. The market gardeners were located on the outskirts of London and they complained that efficient police protection in central London had driven thieves to the outskirts where police protection was inadequate. (Notice that defendant in *Bird* had recently been a victim of theft from his garden.) In the debates, hostility to the Game Laws and concern with accidents were repeatedly cited as factors warranting statutory prohibition of spring guns, and an effort to carve an exception for the market gardeners failed. See Hansard's Parliamentary Debates, n.s., vols. 12-17 (1825-1827), passim.

2. Suppose Parliament, in requiring that notice be given of the setting of a spring gun, believed that it was prohibiting a practice permitted by the common law. What effect should such a belief have on a court attempting to construe the common law?

3. Why was so much stress laid by the judges and counsel in *Bird* on defendant's intent to catch the thief? Suppose defendant had intended only to deter, and not to wound. Would he then perhaps not have been guilty even of a prima facie battery against the plaintiff? Or is his intent to catch the thief relevant only to his defense-of-property defense? What in any event is the objection to private retribution?

4. Notice Serjeant Wilde's use of an explicit utilitarian calculus to justify the use of spikes and broken glass on walls. He describes them as "mere preventives, injurious only to the persevering and determined trespasser, who can calculate at the moment of incurring the danger the amount of suffering he is about to endure, and who will, consequently, desist from his enterprise whenever the anticipated advantage is outweighed by the pain which he must endure to obtain it." Is the point that the theory of the tort law is deterrence and therefore any self-help remedy for a tort must also be deterrent in nature in order to be lawful? Why was the defendant's conduct in *Bird* not well conceived from a deterrent standpoint?

5. Is it always true that a person may not do indirectly what he would be forbidden to do directly? Suppose a spring gun is set in a home as the only practical way of protecting the life of an invalid, and though it is set only at night — and with notices — a harmless trespasser is killed by it. The home-owner would not be privileged deliberately to kill a harmless trespasser, and let us assume that if he had been manning the gun in person he would have

recognized the trespasser as harmless and would therefore have had no right to shoot him. Does it follow that he would or should be liable if the spring gun injures a harmless trespasser? What would the court in *Bird* have done in such a case?

6. Was the plaintiff in *Bird* in fact a trespasser? Return to this question after reading the private-necessity cases below. Is it important whether or not he was a trespasser?

7. Setting aside the vengeful aspect of the defendant's conduct, we can analyze the case from an economic standpoint as involving a conflict between two legitimate, productive activities: growing tulips and keeping peahens. In order to maximize the value of his tulips, the defendant had to find a cheap method of preventing theft. He had tried sleeping in the summerhouse that was in the garden; do we have any indication whether this was a cheap or an expensive method of protecting the garden? Another alternative would have been to hire a guard to keep watch over the garden; still another was to set a spring gun. The spring gun involved a cost, however, in the form of danger to third parties — the owners of fowl and other animals who might stray into the garden and people such as the plaintiff in *Bird* who might try to recover the animals for their owners — that the alternative methods of protection did not involve. How might this (external) cost of spring guns have been minimized without imposing excessive protection costs on the growers of tulips? Perhaps by setting spring guns only at night. Not only is theft more likely at night than during the day, but the probability that someone would try to recover a lost animal is less at night. Hence, at night, the benefits of the spring gun to tulip growers probably exceeded the costs to peahen owners; during the day, the opposite may have been true. Limiting spring guns to nighttime may therefore have been the optimal solution. Another possibility was to post a notice. Defendant in *Bird* took neither precaution.

Would the court in *Bird* have agreed with this analysis?

8. If there had been no vengeance motive in *Bird*, should the case have been treated as involving an accident rather than an intentional tort, and the issue of liability determined by use of the Hand formula? What reason suggested in Chapter 2 might justify nevertheless classifying the case as an intentional tort case?

9. Suppose the most efficient solution to the problem of conflicting uses in *Bird* would have been increased police protection in defendant's locale; what weight if any should a court give such a fact?

10. Pound, The Economic Interpretation and the Law of Torts, 53 Harv. L. Rev. 365, 371-372 (1940), asks:

> Now who were these judges who [in Bird v. Holbrook] would not uphold land owners in setting spring guns to discourage trespassers? . . . Chief Justice Best, afterward Lord Wynford, was the son of a squire by the daughter of a knight and came into a considerable property before he was called to the bar. He was a member of Parliament before he was appointed to the bench (before the

Reform Act), a Tory, and a friend of George IV. Mr. Justice Burrough was the son of a clergyman of the established church, who, so we are told, was a man of considerable landed property. The judge was a Tory and a protegé of Lord Eldon. Mr. Justice Park was the son of a surgeon, had had a large practice in commercial cases, was a Church of England man, a supporter of the Episcopal Church in Scotland, and a Tory. Mr. Justice Gaselee also was the son of a surgeon (we are told he was an eminent surgeon) and a Tory. Certainly this was not a bench which, according to the realists of today, should have held as it did in Bird v. Holbrook, especially when one reads the vigorous and skilful argument which was made for the defendant, directed to the very ideas of the rights of a land owner which one would have expected to appeal to such a court if it had looked outside of its law books.

Scheuermann v. Scharfenberg
163 Ala. 337, 50 So. 335 (1909)

MAYFIELD, J. This appeal presents but one question, which is as novel as it is difficult. The question is this: Is the owner of a storehouse, in which goods and other valuables are kept by him for sale and in deposit, liable in trespass to a would-be burglar of such store, who is shot by means of a spring gun placed in the store by the owner for the purpose of shooting persons who might attempt to burglarize it — the gun being discharged by the would-be burglar while in the attempt to enter, but after the breaking is completed? We have been unable to find any case exactly like it, and but few kindred ones. . . .

[After reviewing previous spring-gun decisions, the court states:] It will be observed, from these various decisions, that while a man may set spring guns and mantraps upon his own premises to protect them in the nighttime from thieves and burglars, he must see to it that such guns or traps do not inflict injury upon those who go thereon for lawful purposes, and that one has no right to defend his property against mere trespassers by means of such deadly agencies. Liability as to mere trespassers who have no felonious intent depends also upon notice to them of the dangerous agency.

There is another principle of law applicable to this case, which is discussed in these cases cited, and also in others of our own court, which is the right to defend one's property as well as his person against violence and felonies. Mr. Blackstone announced the rule, a long time ago, that where a crime, which is itself punished capitally, is attempted to be committed by force, it may be prevented by force, even to the taking of life. The rule has also been extended to other atrocious and forcible felonies, such as burglary and arson, and this is certainly true where such felony is attempted in the nighttime. . . .

A man's place of business (such as the defendant's store in this case) is pro hac vice his dwelling, and he has the same right to defend it against intrusions, such as burglary, as he has to protect his dwelling. Burglary of a storehouse, such as the one attempted to be burglarized in this case, or in which goods, etc., are kept for sale or in deposit, is by statute made a felony punishable as if it were of a dwelling. Applying these principles of law, we hold that the owner of such a store is not liable in trespass to a would-be burglar thereof, who is shot by means of a spring gun by such owner placed in the store for the purpose of shooting persons who might attempt to burglarize it; the gun being discharged by the would-be burglar in attempting to enter.

Katko v. Briney
183 N.W.2d 657 (Iowa 1971)

MOORE, C.J.

The primary issue presented here is whether an owner may protect personal property in an unoccupied boarded-up farm house against trespassers and thieves by a spring gun capable of inflicting death or serious injury.

We are not here concerned with a man's right to protect his home and members of his family. Defendants' home was several miles from the scene of the incident to which we refer infra.

Plaintiff's action is for damages resulting from serious injury caused by a shot from a 20-gauge spring shotgun set by defendants in a bedroom of an old farm house which had been uninhabited for several years. Plaintiff and his companion, Marvin McDonough, had broken and entered the house to find and steal old bottles and dated fruit jars which they considered antiques.

At defendants' request plaintiff's action was tried to a jury consisting of residents of the community where defendants' property was located. The jury returned a verdict for plaintiff and against defendants for $20,000 actual and $10,000 punitive damages. . . .

Most of the facts are not disputed. In 1957 defendant Bertha L. Briney inherited her parents' farm land in Mahaska and Monroe Counties. Included was an 80-acre tract in southwest Mahaska County where her grandparents and parents had lived. No one occupied the house thereafter. Her husband, Edward, attempted to care for the land. He kept no farm machinery thereon. The outbuildings became dilapidated.

For about 10 years, 1957 to 1967, there occurred a series of trespassing and housebreaking events with loss of some household items, the breaking of windows and "messing up of the property in general." The latest occurred June 8, 1967, prior to the event on July 16, 1967 herein involved.

Defendants through the years boarded up the windows and doors in an attempt to stop the intrusions. They had posted "no trespass" signs on the land several years before 1967. The nearest one was 35 feet from the house. On June 11, 1967 defendants set "a shotgun trap" in the north bedroom.

After Mr. Briney cleaned and oiled his 20-gauge shotgun, the power of which he was well aware, defendants took it to the old house where they secured it to an iron bed with the barrel pointed at the bedroom door. It was rigged with wire from the doorknob to the gun's trigger so it would fire when the door was opened. Briney first pointed the gun so an intruder would be hit in the stomach but at Mrs. Briney's suggestion it was lowered to hit the legs. He admitted he did so "because I was mad and tired of being tormented" but "he did not intend to injure anyone." He gave no explanation of why he used a loaded shell and set it to hit a person already in the house. Tin was nailed over the bedroom window. The spring gun could not be seen from the outside. No warning of its presence was posted.

Plaintiff lived with his wife and worked regularly as a gasoline station attendant in Eddyville, seven miles from the old house. He had observed it for several years while hunting in the area and considered it as being abandoned. He knew it had long been uninhabited. In 1967 the area around the house was covered with high weeds. Prior to July 16, 1967 plaintiff and McDonough had been to the premises and found several old bottles and fruit jars which they took and added to their collection of antiques. On the latter date about 9:30 P.M. they made a second trip to the Briney property. They entered the old house by removing a board from a porch window which was without glass. While McDonough was looking around the kitchen area plaintiff went to another part of the house. As he started to open the north bedroom door the shotgun went off striking him in the right leg above the ankle bone. Much of his leg, including part of the tibia, was blown away. . . .

Plaintiff testified he knew he had no right to break and enter the house with intent to steal bottles and fruit jars therefrom. He further testified he had entered a plea of guilty to larceny in the nighttime of property of less than $20 value from a private building. He stated he had been fined $50 and costs and paroled during good behavior from a 60-day jail sentence. Other than minor traffic charges this was plaintiff's first brush with the law. On this civil case appeal it is not our prerogative to review the disposition made of the criminal charge against him.

The main thrust of defendants' defense in the trial court and on this appeal is that "the law permits use of a spring gun in a dwelling or warehouse for the purpose of preventing the unlawful entry of a burglar or thief." They repeated this contention in their exceptions to the trial court's instructions 2, 5 and 6. They took no exception to the trial court's statement of the issues or to other instructions.

In the statement of issues the trial court stated plaintiff and his companion committed a felony when they broke and entered defendants' house. In instruction 2 the court referred to the early case history of the use of spring guns and stated under the law their use was prohibited except to prevent the commission of felonies of violence and where human life is in danger. The instruction included a statement breaking and entering is not a felony of violence.

Instruction 5 stated: "You are hereby instructed that one may use reasonable force in the protection of his property, but such right is subject to the qualification that one may not use such means of force as will take human life or inflict great bodily injury. Such is the rule even though the injured party is a trespasser and is in violation of the law himself."

Instruction 6 stated: "An owner of premises is prohibited from willfully or intentionally injuring a trespasser by means of force that either takes life or inflicts great bodily injury; and therefore a person owning a premise is prohibited from setting out 'spring guns' and like dangerous devices which will likely take life or inflict great bodily injury, for the purpose of harming trespassers. The fact that the trespasser may be acting in violation of the law does not change the rule. The only time when such conduct of setting a 'spring gun' or a like dangerous device is justified would be when the trespasser was committing a felony of violence or a felony punishable by death, or where the trespasser was endangering human life by his act." . . .

The overwhelming weight of authority, both textbook and case law, supports the trial court's statement of the applicable principles of law. . . .

Notes

1. Can *Katko* be reconciled with *Scheuermann*? Is it relevant that Katko was not convicted of a felony? Can *Katko* be reconciled with *Bird*? What alternative means of protecting their property did the Brineys have that the defendant in *Bird* lacked?

2. What would have been the outcome of the *Scheuermann* case if the plaintiff had been a harmless trespasser rather than a burglar?

3. Should deadly force be privileged if it is necessary to prevent a noncapital felony? According to §143(2) of the Second Restatement of Torts, deadly force is privileged when necessary to prevent a felony "of a type threatening death or serious bodily harm or involving the breaking and entry of a dwelling place." The Restatement takes no position on whether deadly force may be used to prevent breaking into and entering a building, not a dwelling place, "in which property of substantial value is stored if such breaking and entering is by statute made a burglary or tantamount thereto." Wright v. Haffke, supra, was such a case.

4. For recent scholarly discussion of the spring-gun cases see Posner, Killing or Wounding to Protect a Property Interest, 14 J. Law & Econ. 201 (1971); Palmer, The Iowa Spring Gun Case: A Study in American Gothic, 56 Iowa L. Rev. 1219 (1971); Epstein, Intentional Harms, 4 J. Legal Stud. 391, 412-414 (1975).

5. Would a good approach to the spring-gun problem be, perhaps, to deem the use of spring guns an ultrahazardous activity, so that the user would be strictly liable for any injuries caused thereby (see Chapter 7)? Might the user still have a defense in a case like *Scheuermann*?

6. Suppose the Brineys had kept a watch dog in the farmhouse, and the dog bit Katko when he entered the house. What liability? What liability if the dog was trained to kill, and killed Katko?

7. Suppose a landowner puts out poison to kill trespassing cattle. Is this a lawful means of protecting his property? Does it make a difference whether he posts a notice of what he has done? Is this an easier or a harder case than a spring-gun case not involving a vengeance motive? See Johnson v. Patterson, 14 Conn. 1 (1840); Bruister v. Haney, 233 Miss. 527, 102 So. 2d 806 (1958). May a farmer kill a neighbor's dog to prevent it from attacking his cattle? See, e.g., McDonald v. Bauman, 199 Kan. 628, 433 P.2d 437 (1967).

8. In all of the cases discussed, if notices are posted, what defense other than defense of property could defendant invoke, and with what success?

Collyer v. Kress
5 Cal. 2d 175, 54 P.2d 20 (1936)

THOMPSON, J. . . .

. . . [A] customer, the store detective Mrs. E.G. Croswell, and her assistant Sidney Schwartz, saw plaintiff pilfer certain articles from the open counters on which they were displayed and put the articles in his overcoat pockets. He was intercepted at the main exit of the store, just as he was leaving, by Mrs. Croswell and Schwartz, and escorted back into the store to a room on the second floor for the purpose of investigating the matter. The testimony is conflicting as to what actually transpired after they entered the room. However, it appears without dispute that plaintiff was there accused of pilfering, and he denied the accusation, stating he had paid for all the articles in his possession. After considerable difficulty, lasting some twenty minutes, during which an attempt was made by Mrs. Croswell forcibly to search him, it was revealed he had in his possession the articles he was accused of having stolen, and he was asked to sign a statement to the effect that he had taken the articles without paying for them. Still insisting he had paid for the articles, he refused to sign the statement. Meanwhile the police had been summoned, and soon after their arrival, at the request of the store management, the police placed plaintiff under arrest and he was taken to the city prison where he was searched, photographed twice and fingerprinted; and about eight o'clock that night he was released through arrangements made by his nephew with the store management. The day after Christmas Mrs. Croswell swore to a criminal complaint charging plaintiff with petty theft; but a few weeks later a jury found him not guilty. At the time this happened plaintiff was seventy years of age, and until about a year prior thereto he had been for approximately six years a deputy constable and process server in Oakland. There is some evidence tending to show that he had been drinking when he entered the store, but he denied that such was the fact.

There is no substantial conflict in the evidence as to what was said and done on the way to the room to which plaintiff was escorted. Apparently plaintiff made no objection to returning other than to inquire why they wanted him, and in reply Mrs. Croswell told him he knew as well as they. Plaintiff declared, however, he did not know, and just as they were about to ascend the stairway leading to the room he stopped and demanded to know 'what it was all about.' Mrs. Croswell replied, 'Come on, you will learn later,' but plaintiff was not inclined to go further, until Mrs. Croswell threatened to call the police. He then stated she need not do so, that he would go along; and he did without further hesitation. . . .

The cause of action for false imprisonment is predicated upon the twenty minutes or thereabouts between the time the plaintiff was accosted by Mrs. Croswell near the store entrance and the time he was taken into custody by the police officers, during which interval he was detained and questioned by the store employees. . . .

Ordinarily, the owner of property, in the exercise of his inherent right to protect the same, is justified in restraining another who seeks to interfere with or injure it. However, there seems to exist considerable confusion in the cases as to whether probable cause is a defense in false imprisonment cases involving misdemeanors. The broad statement occasionally appears to the effect that probable cause is no defense in actions for false imprisonment. The cited cases involved unlawful arrests under the authority of illegal process issued in civil actions. In such instances, as in all cases involving solely the legality of the process, it is obvious that probable cause is not pertinent to any issue in the case. Because of like irrelevancy, the statement may properly be made in cases of illegal arrests upon suspicion by a private person where, by statutory authority or otherwise, he is permitted to make such an arrest only when the offense is being committed in his presence. However, those authorities which hold, where a person has reasonable grounds to believe that another is stealing his property, as distinguished from those where the offense has been completed, that he is justified in detaining the suspect for a reasonable length of time for the purpose of investigation in a reasonable manner, must necessarily proceed upon the theory that probable cause is a defense. And this is the law because the right to protect one's property from injury has intervened. In an effort to harmonize the individual right to liberty with a reasonable protection to the person or property of the defendant, it should be said in such a charge of false imprisonment, where a defendant had probable cause to believe that the plaintiff was about to injure defendant in his person or property, even though such injury would constitute but a misdemeanor, that probable cause is a defense, provided, of course, that the detention was reasonable. As already indicated, the rule should be different if the offense believed to be in the process of commission relates to the person or property of another. . . .

There yet remains the question of whether the detention was reasonable. The consideration of this problem must be promised by the observation, which must be kept in mind at all times during our examination of the question, that the defendants were entitled to use a reasonable amount of compulsion in order to effect that restraint. In our opinion, the evidence in this case does not disclose an unreasonable compulsion or detention. The respondent was detained for the period of about twenty minutes. The compulsion used was a threat of arrest, which arrest the jury found was not improper. The defendants testified that Mrs. Croswell attempted to take the articles out of his pocket, but that he, by the use of force, prevented that act. . . . The request to sign a statement of his acts was not improper, under the circumstances. In fact, the only way in which defendants could protect their property, if taken, was to ask plaintiff to restore, which if done, in and of itself, amounted to a confession. It nowhere appears, except for the threat of arrest, concerning which we have already commented, that plaintiff might not have left the premises at any time. . . .

Notes

1. The court says the only compulsion used to detain plaintiff was the threat to call the police. Is that enough to constitute an imprisonment? Might plaintiff have had a stronger case of assault and battery than of false imprisonment?

2. How far can one go in defense of one's chattels? According to Estes v. Brewster Cigar Co., 156 Wash. 465, 472, 287 P. 36, 39 (1930),

> it is not a wrong for the manager of a store to pursue a person who has committed a theft in his store and recapture the things stolen. A person whose goods have been stolen may retake them peaceably wherever he may find them. In retaking them from a thief whom he pursues immediately after the theft, he may call persons to his aid and use such force as may be reasonably necessary to accomplish his purpose without liability except for excess of force. But when he pursues an innocent person, under the belief that he has committed a wrong to his property, no matter how strong may be his belief, he is liable for any injury caused the person, whether committed by himself or by the persons he calls to his aid.

Is this the same test as for defense of real property? Should the tests be different for the two kinds of property? In light of this statement, should the court in *Collyer* have given greater weight than it did to the acquittal of plaintiff of the criminal charge of shoplifting?

Girard v. Anderson
219 Iowa 142, 257 N.W. 400 (1934)

KINTZINGER, J.
On the 27th day of August, 1929, the plaintiff purchased a secondhand

piano from the defendant for $125, paying $50 down, the balance to be paid January 1, 1930. Appellant gave his promissory note for the purchase price, and the $50 payment was indorsed thereon. The contract provided that "in case of any default made in the payments . . . it shall be right and lawful for me . . . *to peaceably or forcibly, and without process of law,* enter the premises where said property is . . . and to take . . . procession thereof. . . . And all . . . payments made . . . may be considered as rent for the . . . use of said property."

The evidence shows that the plaintiff-appellant failed to make the payments due on January 1, 1930; it also shows that the defendant accepted further payments on the contract as follows: August 27, 1929, $20; February 25, 1930, $20; March 7, 1931, $10; March 17, 1931, $10; October 29, 1932, $3; a total of $113. Appellee claims that with interest, there is still a balance of $30 due.

The testimony on the part of appellant shows that he and his family left their home to call on relatives at about 11 A.M., Saturday, January 28, 1933, and did not return until about 4:30 that afternoon; that when they left home all the doors were locked. During their absence two employees of the defendant, without appellant's consent, and without notice, broke and entered appellant's home, retook possession of the piano, and returned it to defendant's store. Defendant's employees say that the door through which they entered was not locked, but that they turned the doorknob, opened the door, entered the house, and took the piano. Appellee resold the piano the next Monday morning. Plaintiff's family also testified they kept money in the piano that it contained $27 when taken. On the following Monday, appellant went to defendant's store to inquire about the piano and the money. The appellee said he had resold the piano, and thereupon both he and appellant went to search the piano, but on examination found no money therein. Defendant and his employees say they examined the piano after it was returned to the store Saturday but found no money.

The principal error complained of is the giving of instruction No. 5. In that instruction the court said: "You are instructed that the contract, Exhibit 'A', and all terms and conditions thereof which may be of any materiality in this case are perfectly legal and binding *and fully protect the defendant from any liability in this case,* except the claimed liability of the defendant for the money which plaintiff alleges was stored in the piano. . . . If the terms of the contract, Exhibit 'A,' were not waived by the defendant, *the defendant is in no manner liable* to the plaintiff in this case for the claimed conversion of the piano, because the defendant did no more than the contract as written gave him the legal right to do." Under this instruction the defendant could, without legal process, forcibly break and enter the buyer's home in his absence, for the purpose of repossessing the piano, without being in any manner liable therefor. The question of plaintiff's right to recover any damages therefor was withdrawn from the jury. . . .

. . . Article 1, §8, of the state Constitution provides: "The right of the people to be secure in their persons, houses, papers and effects, against unreasonable seizures and searches shall not be violated." . . . An agreement permitting a family's home to be broken open and entered for the purpose of forcibly taking possession of property therein is contrary to good public policy and void to that extent.

Public policy is that principle of law which provides that parties cannot agree to do anything which has a tendency to be injurious to the public or against the public good. Accordingly it has been held that agreements in violation of constitutional provisions are invalid. . . .

Although a number of cases support the rule that the seller has a right to forcibly retake possession of his property without resort to the courts, under a contract permitting him so to do, the modern view is to the contrary. . . .

The rights of the public are involved in a contract of this nature, because it has a tendency to violate the most sacred right of the home. . . .

We are not willing to adopt a rule that will permit the seller under a contract of this kind to take the law into his own hands by forcibly retaking possession of property sold, where any resistance is offered by the purchaser. The courts are open to him for the protection of his rights in the manner pointed out by statute. In the present day, where innumerable articles of personal property are sold under a conditional sales contract, it would result in too many disturbances of the peace to permit sellers to forcibly retake possession of property in the manner shown in this case. If resort to force must be had, it should be secured through the proper legal outlets. It is our conclusion that the petition in the case is broad enough to include a claim of damages for forcibly breaking and entering into plaintiff's home, and the instruction given withdrawing that issue from the jury was clearly erroneous. . . .

Notes

1. Constitutional rights are normally waivable. For example, by pleading guilty (as you will recall that Katko did) a criminal defendant waives his constitutional right to trial by jury. Why, then, was the court in *Girard* unwilling to enforce the agreement waiving the plaintiff's right to complain about a forcible entry into his home to repossess the piano?

2. What damages is plaintiff entitled to in this case? If the waiver had been enforced, could plaintiff have still recovered the $27 hidden in the piano?

3. What torts did defendant commit? What, if anything, turns on whether the door to plaintiff's house was locked?

4. Suppose that under a conditional-sales contract similar to the one in *Girard,* but involving an automobile rather than a piano, defendant had repossessed plaintiff's auto while it was parked on the street in front of

plaintiff's house. Would defendant be guilty of a tort in that case? Does the *Whithorn* case in Chapter 2 bear on this question?

Mouse's Case
12 Co. Rep. 63, 77 Eng. Rep. 1341 (K.B. 1609)

In an action of trespass brought by Mouse, for a casket, and a hundred and thirteen pounds, taken and carried away, the case was, the ferryman of Gravesend, took forty-seven passengers into his barge, to pass to London, and Mouse was one of them, and the barge being upon the water, a great tempest happened, and a strong wind, so that the barge and all the passengers were in danger to be drowned, if a hogshead of wine and other ponderous things were not cast out, for the safeguard of the lives of the men: it was resolved per totam Curiam, that in case of necessity, for the saving of the lives of the passengers, it was lawful to the defendant, being a passenger, to cast the casket of the plaintiff out of the barge, with the other things in it; . . . and the first day of this term, this issue was tried, and it was proved directly, that if the things had not been cast out of the barge, the passenger had been drowned; and that . . . they were ejected, some by one passenger, and some by another; and upon this the plaintiff was nonsuit. . . .

Ploof v. Putnam
81 Vt. 471, 71 A. 188 (1908)

MUNSON, J. It is alleged as the ground of recovery that on the 13th day of November, 1904, the defendant was the owner of a certain island in Lake Champlain, and of a certain dock attached thereto, which island and dock were then in charge of the defendant's servant; that the plaintiff was then possessed of and sailing upon said lake a certain loaded sloop, on which were the plaintiff and his wife and two minor children; that there then arose a sudden and violent tempest, whereby the sloop and the property and persons therein were placed in great danger of destruction; that, to save these from destruction or injury, the plaintiff was compelled to, and did, moor the sloop to defendant's dock; that the defendant, by his servant, unmoored the sloop, whereupon it was driven upon the shore by the tempest, without the plaintiff's fault; and that the sloop and its contents were thereby destroyed, and the plaintiff and his wife and children cast into the lake and upon the shore, receiving injuries. This claim is set forth in two counts — one in trespass, charging that the defendant by his servant with force and arms willfully and designedly unmoored the sloop; the other in case, alleging that it was the duty of the defendant by his servant to permit the plaintiff to moor his sloop to the dock, and to permit it to remain so moored during the continuance of the tempest, but that the defendant by his servant, in disregard of this duty, negligently, carelessly, and wrongfully unmoored the sloop. Both counts are demurred to generally.

There are many cases in the books which hold that necessity, and an inability to control movements inaugurated in the proper exercise of a strict right, will justify entries upon land and interferences with personal property that would otherwise have been trespasses. A reference to a few of these will be sufficient to illustrate the doctrine. In Miller v. Fandrye, trespass was brought for chasing sheep, and the defendant pleaded that the sheep were trespassing upon his land, and that he with a little dog chased them out, and that, as soon as the sheep were off his land, he called in the dog. It was argued that, although the defendant might lawfully drive the sheep from his own ground with a dog, he had no right to pursue them into the next ground. But the court considered that the defendant might drive the sheep from his land with a dog, and that the nature of a dog is such that he cannot be withdrawn in an instant, and that, as the defendant had done his best to recall the dog, trespass would not lie. . . . A traveler on a highway who finds it obstructed from a sudden and temporary cause may pass upon the adjoining land without becoming a trespasser because of the necessity. . . . In Proctor v. Adams, the defendant went upon the plaintiff's beach for the purpose of saving and restoring to the lawful owner a boat which had been driven ashore, and was in danger of being carried off by the sea; and it was held no trespass. . . .

It is clear that an entry upon the land of another may be justified by necessity, and that the declaration before us discloses a necessity for mooring the sloop. But the defendant questions the sufficiency of the counts because they do not negative the existence of natural objects to which the plaintiff could have moored with equal safety. The allegations are, in substance, that the stress of a sudden and violent tempest compelled the plaintiff to moor to defendant's dock to save his sloop and the people in it. The averment of necessity is complete, for it covers not only the necessity of mooring, but the necessity of mooring to the dock; and the details of the situation which created this necessity, whatever the legal requirements regarding them, are matters of proof, and need not be alleged. It is certain that the rule suggested cannot be held applicable irrespective of circumstance, and the question must be left for adjudication upon proceedings had with reference to the evidence or the charge. . . .

Notes

1. Was there any damage in fact in Mouse's Case?
2. What tort or torts did defendant commit in *Ploof*?

3. Would *Ploof* have been decided the same way if there had been no issue of personal safety, but the entry on defendant's property had been necessary to save property of great value?

4. Does it make any difference whether plaintiff in *Ploof* was a trespasser? Why is M'Ilvoy v. Cockran not compelling authority for plaintiff's position? Cf. Collins v. Lefort, 210 So. 2d 895 (La. App. 1968), where defendant shot a hole in plaintiff's shrimp boat upon plaintiff's refusing to leave a bayou where allegedly he was interfering with defendant's oyster beds. Is *Collins* more like *M'Ilvoy* or *Ploof*?

5. Is it arguable, under the doctrine of necessity, that the plaintiff in Bird v. Holbrook was not a trespasser upon defendant's garden? Cf. Shehyn v. United States, 256 A.2d 404 (D.C. App. 1969), holding that the owner of a cat had a privilege to go peaceably upon appellant's property to retrieve it.

6. For further proceedings in *Ploof*, focusing on the issue of respondeat superior, see Ploof v. Putnam, 83 Vt. 252, 75 A. 277 (1910).

Vincent v. Lake Erie Transp. Co.
109 Minn. 456, 124 N.W. 221 (1910)

O'BRIEN, J. The steamship Reynolds, owned by the defendant, was for the purpose of discharging her cargo on November 27, 1905, moored to plaintiffs' dock in Duluth. While the unloading of the boat was taking place a storm from the northeast developed, which at about 10 o'clock P.M., when the unloading was completed, had so grown in violence that the wind was then moving at 50 miles per hour and continued to increase during the night. There is some evidence that one, and perhaps two, boats were able to enter the harbor that night, but it is plain that navigation was practically suspended from the hour mentioned until the morning of the 29th, when the storm abated, and during that time no master would have been justified in attempting to navigate his vessel, if he could avoid doing so. After the discharge of the cargo the Reynolds signaled for a tug to tow her from the dock, but none could be obtained because of the severity of the storm. If the lines holding the ship to the dock had been cast off, she would doubtless have drifted away; but, instead, the lines were kept fast, and as soon as one parted or chafed it was replaced, sometimes with a larger one. The vessel lay upon the outside of the dock, her bow to the east, the wind and waves striking her starboard quarter with such force that she was constantly being lifted and thrown against the dock, resulting in its damage, as found by the jury, to the amount of $500.

We are satisfied that the character of the storm was such that it would have been highly imprudent for the master of the Reynolds to have attempted to leave the dock or to have permitted his vessel to drift away from it. One witness testified upon the trial that the vessel could have been warped into a slip, and that, if the attempt to bring the ship into the slip had failed, the worst that could have happened would be that the vessel would have been blown ashore upon a soft and muddy bank. The witness was not present in Duluth at the time of the storm, and, while he may have been right in his conclusions, those in charge of the dock and the vessel at the time of the storm were not required to use the highest human intelligence, nor were they required to resort to every possible experiment which could be suggested for the preservation of their property. Nothing more was demanded of them than ordinary prudence and care, and the record in this case fully sustains the contention of the appellant that, in holding the vessel fast to the dock, those in charge of her exercised good judgment and prudent seamanship. . . .

. . . If during the storm the Reynolds had entered the harbor, and while there had become disabled and been thrown against the plaintiffs' dock, the plaintiffs could not have recovered. Again, if while attempting to hold fast to the dock the lines had parted, without any negligence, and the vessel carried against some other boat or dock in the harbor, there would be no liability upon her owner. But here those in charge of the vessel deliberately and by their direct efforts held her in such a position that the damage to the dock resulted, and, having thus preserved the ship at the expense of the dock, it seems to us that her owners are responsible to the dock owners to the extent of the injury inflicted.

In Depue v. Flatau, 100 Minn. 299, 111 N.W. 1, this court held that where the plaintiff, while lawfully in the defendants' house, became so ill that he was incapable of traveling with safety, the defendants were responsible to him in damages for compelling him to leave the premises. If, however, the owner of the premises had furnished the traveler with proper accommodations and medical attendance, would he have been able to defeat an action brought against him for their reasonable worth? . . .

Theologians hold that a starving man may, without moral guilt, take what is necessary to sustain life; but it could hardly be said that the obligation would not be upon such person to pay the value of the property so taken when he became able to do so. And so public necessity, in times of war or peace, may require the taking of private property for public purposes; but under our system of jurisprudence compensation must be made.

Let us imagine in this case that for the better mooring of the vessel those in charge of her had appropriated a valuable cable lying upon the dock. No matter how justifiable such appropriation might have been, it would not be claimed that, because of the overwhelming necessity of the situation, the owner of the cable could not recover its value.

This is not a case where life or property was menaced by any object or thing belonging to the plaintiffs, the destruction of which became necessary to prevent the threatened disaster. Nor is it a case where, because of the act of God, or unavoidable accident, the infliction of the injury was beyond the control of the defendant, but is one where the defendant prudently and advisedly availed itself of the plaintiffs' property for the purpose of preserving its own more valuable property, and the plaintiffs are entitled to compensation for the injury done.

Order affirmed.

LEWIS, J. I dissent. . . .

I am of the opinion that one who constructs a dock to the navigable line of waters, and enters into contractual relations with the owner of a vessel to moor at the same, takes the risk of damage to his dock by a boat caught there by a storm, which event could not have been avoided in the exercise of due care, and further, that the legal status of the parties in such a case is not changed by renewal of cables to keep the boat from being cast adrift at the mercy of the tempest.

Notes

1. What tort did defendant commit? Was it trespass? What other tort could defendant be thought to have committed even if there had been no damage to plaintiff's dock? What result if plaintiff had sued defendant for the value of its use of the dock during the storm? And how should "value" be measured in such a case?

2. In Kank Realty Co. v. Brown, 114 Misc. 357, 187 N.Y.S. 556 (Cty. Ct.), *modified and aff'd,* 198 App. Div. 958, 189 N.Y.S.2d 946 (1921), the limb of a tree on defendant's property was broken by a storm so that it overhung plaintiff's land. Defendant sent an experienced man to remove it. While he was trying to do so, the limb fell (without negligence on his part) and damaged plaintiff's house. Defendant was held not liable for the damage. How is *Kank* distinguishable from *Vincent?*

3. Why isn't the real issue in *Vincent* the implicit terms of the contract between plaintiffs and defendant regarding the mooring of defendant's boat? Would plaintiffs' case be weaker or stronger if there had been no preexisting contractual relationship between the parties — if, as in *Ploof,* the boat had simply moored at the first dock it could find in the storm?

4. Does the award of damages in a case like *Vincent* have any desirable incentive effects, given that under *Ploof* it would have been tortious for plaintiff to have forced defendant's boat to leave during the storm? (Hint: recall the distinction stressed in Chapter 1 between care and activity.)

5. Suppose that in *Vincent* the storm had arisen just after the defendant's boat had left the dock, and the boat's captain had asked the plaintiff to throw him a line. If plaintiff had refused, would he have been liable for any damages to the defendant? Putting aside any question of contract between the parties, the answer is no, as you will see when we reach the "good Samaritan" cases in Chapter 6, where we will also consider more closely restitution as an alternative means to liability of motivating rescue activities.

Whalley v. Lancashire & York R. Co.
13 Q.B.D. 131 (1884)

The defendants were proprietors of a railway which ran from Brecon Station to Southport, and also for some distance from east to west over a flat country on a low embankment by which it was carried a little higher than the adjoining lands, and on each side of which was a ditch for the purpose of draining the railway. The surrounding land declined or sloped from the south-east to the north-west, so that land on the north-west side of the railway embankment at that part was on a lower level than that on the south-east side of it. The plaintiff was a farmer in the occupation of lands on the north-west side of the railway, but separated from it by lands belonging to other persons.

On the 30th of August, 1881, there was an unprecedented storm and rainfall, which blocked up and over-flooded the drains, so that a large quantity of water became dammed up against the south-east side of the railway embankment. This water having afterwards risen so as to expose the embankment to danger, the defendants caused trenches to be made in the embankment, by which the water was enabled to escape to the north-west side of the railway, and from thence to flow into the adjoining land, and ultimately to that of the plaintiff, where it damaged his crops.

The action was brought for the injury which the plaintiff had sustained by the defendants so causing the water to come on his land. . . . [T]he jury found that the defendants cut the trenches and caused the flood-water to flow over the land of the plaintiff, but that the cutting of the trenches was reasonably necessary for the protection of the defendants' property, and that it was not done negligently. They also found that the land of the plaintiff was injured by the water that so came through the trenches to the extent of £130 beyond what it would have been injured if the trenches had not been cut. On these findings the learned judge gave judgment for the plaintiff for £130. . . .

LINDLEY, L.J. . . . This is a case in which the defendants have made an embankment, and against that embankment water from an unusual storm of rain has accumulated to such an extent, and to such a depth, as to endanger the embankment apparently, and to render it reasonable to those who could not foresee how long this storm would last, to get rid of some of the water. Have the defendants a right, in order to save their own embankment, to cut holes through it, and to turn the water from off their land so as to damage their neighbour, and not make him any compensation? Prima facie I take it the defendants should justify what they have done, and it is material that no authority can be found in their favour. . . . It seems to me established . . . that if an extraordinary flood is seen to be coming upon land the owner of such land may fence off and protect his land from it, and so turn it away, without being responsible for the consequences, although his neighbour may be injured by it.... Of course there is a difference between protecting yourself from an injury which is not yet suffered by you, and getting rid of the consequences of an injury which has occurred to you. Then there is the squib case in Scott v. Shepherd, in which Gould, J., says, that if a man throws a squib into a coach, a passenger in the coach may throw it out and not be responsible for the consequences. That is perhaps in point of principle a little nearer to the present case, and there is some little difficulty in seeing a common principle which will explain all cases. We must look at the broad question, which is, whether a landowner on whose land there is a sudden accumulation of water, brought there without any fault or act of his, is at liberty actively to let it off on to the land of his neighbour without making that neighbour any compensation for damages, because the landowner, by doing so, has been able to save his own property from injury? I can see no authority for that, and it appears to me the general rights and duties of landowners are decidedly against it. For these reasons, I agree that ... this appeal must be dismissed....

Notes

1. What tort did defendants commit in this case?

2. Why would there be no liability if defendants had merely blocked the flood and thereby diverted it onto plaintiff's property, as distinct from cutting holes in the embankment?

3. Scott v. Shepherd, 2 Wm. Bl. 892, 96 Eng. Rep. 525 (K.B. 1773), mentioned in the *Whalley* opinion, was an action for injuries caused by the bursting of a squib, a kind of firecracker. Defendant tossed the squib into a marketplace. It landed next to Willis, not a party in the case, who, to protect himself, immediately tossed it away. It then landed next to Ryal (also not a party). He did the same thing. This time the squib hit plaintiff and burst. The court held that defendant was liable for plaintiff's injuries notwithstanding the intermediate actions of Willis and Ryal. The big issue in the case was whether trespass as distinct from case was the correct pleading; a divided court held that it was. But why couldn't plaintiff have recovered damages against Willis or Ryal? Is the squib case more like Vincent v. Lake Erie Transp. Co. or Morris v. Platt? Would there be any problem with intent in an action against Willis or Ryal?

4. Bernard Williams, A Critique of Utilitarianism, in J.J.C. Smart & B. Williams, Utilitarianism, For and Against 77, 98-99 (1967), puts the following hypothetical case: Jim is the guest of an officer in a banana republic who is about to have a group of political prisoners shot. The officer tells Jim that if Jim will shoot one of the prisoners he will release the others. If Jim does so and the rest of the prisoners are released as agreed, does the estate of the prisoner he shot have a good action against him for battery?

Surocco v. Geary
3 Cal. 70 (1853)

MURRAY, C.J., delivered the opinion of the Court. . . .

This was an action, commenced in the court below, to recover damages for blowing up and destroying the plaintiffs' house and property, during the fire of the 24th of December, 1849.

Geary, at that time Alcalde of San Francisco, justified, on the ground that he had authority, by virtue of his office, to destroy said building, and also that it had been blown up by him to stop the progress of the conflagration then raging.

It was in proof, that the fire passed over and burned beyond the building of the plaintiffs, and that at the time said building was destroyed, they were engaged in removing their property, and could, had they not been prevented, have succeeded in removing more, if not all of their goods.

The cause was tried by the court sitting as a jury, and a verdict rendered for the plaintiffs, from which the defendant prosecutes this appeal under the Practice Act of 1850. . . .

The right to destroy property, to prevent the spread of a conflagration, has been traced to the highest law of necessity, and the natural rights of man, independent of society or civil government. "It is referred by moralists and jurists to the same great principle which justifies the exclusive appropriation of a plank in a shipwreck, though the life of another be sacrificed; with the throwing overboard goods in a tempest, for the safety of a vessel; with the trespassing upon the lands of another, to escape death by an enemy. . . ."

The common law adopts the principles of the natural law, and places the justification of an act otherwise tortious precisely on the same ground of necessity.

. . . [T]he instances of tearing down houses to prevent a conflagration, or to raise bulwarks for the defence of a city, are made use of as illustrations, rather than as abstract cases, in which its exercise is permitted. At such times, the individual rights of property give way to the higher laws of impending necessity.

A house on fire, or those in its immediate vicinity, which serve to communicate the flames, becomes a nuisance, which it is lawful to abate, and the private rights of the individual yield to the considerations of general convenience, and the interests of society. Were it otherwise, one stubborn person might involve a whole city in ruin, by refusing to allow the destruction of a building which would cut off the flames and check the progress of the fire, and that, too, when it was perfectly evident that his building must be consumed.

The respondent has invoked the aid of the constitutional provision which prohibits the taking of private property for public use, without just compensation being made therefor. This is not "a taking of private property for public use," within the meaning of the Constitution.

The right of taking individual property for public purposes belongs to the State, by virtue of her right of eminent domain, and is said to be justified on the ground of state necessity; but this is not a taking or a destruction for a public purpose, but a destruction for the benefit of the individual or the city, but not properly of the State.

The counsel for the respondent has asked, who is to judge of the necessity of the destruction of property?

This must, in some instances, be a difficult matter to determine. The necessity of blowing up a house may not exist, or be as apparent to the owner, whose judgment is clouded by interest, and the hope of saving his property, as to others. In all such cases the conduct of the individual must be regulated by his own judgment as to the exigencies of the case. If a building should be torn down without apparent or actual necessity, the parties concerned would undoubtedly be liable in an action of trespass. But in every case the necessity must be clearly shown. It is true, many cases of hardship may grow out of this rule, and property may often in such cases be destroyed, without necessity, by irresponsible persons, but this difficulty would not be obviated by making the parties responsible in every case, whether the necessity existed or not. . . .

The evidence in this case clearly establishes the fact, that the blowing up of the house was necessary, as it would have been consumed had it been left standing. The plaintiffs cannot recover for the value of the goods which they might have saved: they were as much subject to the necessities of the occasion as the house in which they were situate; and if in such cases a party was held liable, it would too frequently happen, that the delay caused by the removal of the goods would render the destruction of the house useless. . . .

Judgment reversed.

Notes

1. This case illustrates the doctrine of "public necessity," where, in contrast to cases of "private necessity" such as *Vincent* and *Whalley*, the person whose property is destroyed has no remedy. As the opinion notes, the issue of public necessity frequently arises in suits for just compensation under the takings clause of the Fifth Amendment or parallel state provisions, rather than in tort suits. (Against whom would such a suit be brought?) Compensation is usually denied, see, e.g., United States v. Caltex, Inc., 344 U.S. 149 (1952), unless authorized by special statute, see, e.g., Mayor of New York v. Lord, 17 Wend. (N.Y.) 285 (1837), and Bowditch v. Boston, 101 U.S. 16 (1879).

2. Was Mouse's Case a case of public or private necessity? Was the necessity public, because many lives were saved, not just the defendant's, or private, because the defendant was actuated by concern for his own safety

rather than, as in *Surocco,* for that of others? What about the *Procter* case mentioned in the *Ploof* opinion?

3. The policy basis of the public necessity doctrine is dramatically illustrated by the events of the Great Fire of London of 1666, which raged for four days and nights, destroying some 13,000 houses and rendering about 100,000 people homeless. The Lord Mayor of London, an inexperienced young man named Thomas Bludworth, refused to order houses taken down in the path of the fire to form a firebreak, stating "who will pay for the damage?" and adding that he "durst not do it without the consent of the owners." The basis of his concern was apparently an old law of the City of London that required anyone destroying another's house to pay for rebuilding it. It is also reported that some barristers of the Inner Temple refused to save the furnishings and law books of their colleagues who were out of London for the summer vacation, on the ground that "it was against the law to break up any man's chambers." Bludworth's refusal to pull down houses is discussed as "a memorable instance of folly" in an early public necessity case, Respublica v. Sparkhawk, 1 U.S. 359 (Pa. Super. Ct. 1788). See also W. G. Bell, The Great Fire of London in 1666 (1920); J. Leasor, The Plague and the Fire (1962).

Is the economist's notion of "externality" perhaps relevant to understanding Bludworth's dilemma? An externality is a cost or benefit that is not taken into account in the decision whether or how much of some good or service to produce. Thus an external cost is a cost that is not borne by the person or persons who cause it and that, because of transaction costs, cannot be brought to bear on their decision processes through the market. A traditional example is pollution. The Coase theorem, presented earlier in this chapter, teaches that an externality will not distort the allocation of resources so long as transaction costs are not prohibitive; but if they are, it will. If Bludworth had ordered houses to be pulled down he would thereby have conferred an external benefit. (Why?)

The issue with regard to the defense of public necessity can thus be stated, in economic terms, as follows: Is cost externalization an appropriate method of encouraging the creation of external benefits?

4. In Allen v. Camp, 14 Ala. App. 341-343, 70 So. 290 (1915),

The evidence without dispute showed that the defendant during the absence of the plaintiff and his family, went to the home of the plaintiff with his (defendant's) son, and entered the house by raising a window and helping his son through the window, by which means an entrance was effected to one of the rooms in plaintiff's home in which the dog was securely fastened by a chain and collar to the furniture or a doorknob; that upon discovering the dog tied in plaintiff's house the defendant shot and killed the animal. The evidence in behalf of the defendant tended to show that the animal was vicious and dangerous, and had bitten the defendant's seven year old daughter a few days previous to the killing; that the defendant had offered to buy the dog for the

purpose of sending its head to the Pasteur Institute at Montgomery for examination for rabies; that the plaintiff had refused to part with the dog; and that
the defendant killed the animal in plaintiff's home under the circumstances
stated, decapitated it, and sent the head to the Pasteur Institute for examination, but ascertained from such examination that it was a healthy specimen.

What is the prima facie tort? Does defendant have a good defense to plaintiff's action for damages?

5. Can the doctrine of necessity ever be used to justify killing a person?
Suppose there are three men in a lifeboat and they must surely starve to
death if one is not killed and eaten by the others. If they draw straws, and kill
and eat the man who draws the short straw, do they have a defense to a'
wrongful-death suit? Is the result different if they kill the weakest, or the one
who has the least earning capacity, or the one likeliest to die first in any
event? Suppose a crew member throws a passenger overboard to lighten a
boat; crew members are spared on the ground that they are needed to
maximize the chances of saving the remaining passengers. Any liability in this
case? Some of these issues have arisen in criminal cases. See United States v.
Holmes, Fed. Cas. No. 15, 383 (Cir. Ct. E.D. Pa. 1842); Regina v. Dudley and
Stevens, 14 Q.B.D. 273 (1884).

M'Dougall v. Claridge
1 Camp. 267, 170 Eng. Rep. 953 (K.B. 1808)

This was an action for a libel on the plaintiff in his profession as a
solicitor. . . .

The libel set out in the declaration was contained in a letter written by
the defendant to Messrs. Wright and Co. bankers at Nottingham, and
charges the plaintiff with improper conduct in the management of their
concerns. It appeared, however, that the letter was intended as a confidential
communication to these gentlemen, and that the defendant was himself
interested in the affairs which he supposed to be mismanaged by the
plaintiff. . . .

LORD ELLENBOROUGH said, if the letter had been written by the
defendant confidentially, and under an impression that its statements were
well founded, he was clearly of opinion that the action could not be maintained. It was impossible to say that the defendant had maliciously published
a libel to aggrieve the plaintiff, if he was acting bona fide, with a view to the
interests of himself and the persons whom he addressed; and if a communication of this sort, which was not meant to go beyond those immediately
interested in it, were the subject of an action for damages, it would be
impossible for the affairs of mankind to be conducted. His Lordship referred
to a case of Cleaver v. Sarraude, where, in an action like the present, it

appeared that the letter had been written confidentially to the Bishop of Durham, who employed the plaintiff as steward to his estates, to inform him of certain supposed malpractices on the part of the plaintiff; upon which the judge who presided declared himself of opinion, that the action was not maintainable, as the defendant had been acting bona fide; and the nonsuit which he directed had been acquiesced in, from a conviction entertained by the plaintiff's counsel of its being founded in law. . . .

Notes

1. If defendant's communication had not been confidential, would he have been liable for defaming plaintiff?

2. The defense of privilege is very important in defamation cases. The *M'Dougall* case illustrates the privilege to defame where the defendant has a legal or moral duty to communicate his view of the plaintiff's character. Another common such case is where the defendant is asked to give a reference for a former employee. See, e.g., Doane v. Grew, 220 Mass. 171, 107 N.E. 620 (1915). What if anything have such cases in common with the public necessity cases? Why wasn't the defense of privilege available in the *Barnes* case (Chapter 2)?

3. The privilege involved in *M'Dougall* and *Doane* is a "conditional privilege," meaning that it is forfeited if defendant does not honestly and reasonably believe that what he is saying is true. Some privileges, for example the privilege of a critic to criticize a book or movie, are absolute. What explains the distinction? For an economic analysis of the privileges in defamation see Posner, Privacy, Secrecy, and Reputation, 28 Buffalo L. Rev. 1, 40-41 (1979). The most important defense in defamation cases is, of course, truth.

Norton v. United States
581 F.2d 390 (4th Cir. 1978)

WINTER, C.J . . .

At approximately eight o'clock on the evening of March 15, 1975, the Alexandria, Virginia, Police Department received an anonymous telephone call advising that the nationally-sought federal fugitive Patricia Hearst was occupying an apartment in the Alexandria area. Federal arrest warrants for her arrest were outstanding. The FBI was immediately notified and, at approximately 9:30 P.M. on the same evening, four FBI agents, together with two local detectives, arrived at the reported address. After surveying the site for approximately thirty minutes, the officers sought entry into the suspect apartment. The officers had been warned that Ms. Hearst should be considered armed and dangerous. No search warrant was either sought or obtained.

The apartment was that of plaintiff who was alone in the apartment. Since it was ten o'clock at night and her door had no peephole for viewing visitors, she refused to admit the agents. Conversation ensued. Unable to prevail upon plaintiff to open the door, the agents began a forcible entry. Plaintiff, fearing that the door would be destroyed, unlatched the lock and the law enforcement officers entered with weapons drawn. A search of the apartment revealed no traces of either Patricia Hearst or her suspected companions. After concluding that the anonymous tip was either a hoax or an attempt by a disgruntled neighbor to harass plaintiff, the officers departed.

Plaintiff subsequently brought this suit for damages against both the law enforcement officers involved and the United States. Suit against the local police officers was brought under 42 U.S.C. §1983, while suit against the federal agents was brought directly under the fourth amendment to the Constitution of the United States. See Bivens v. Six Unknown Named Agents of Federal Bureau of Narcotics, 403 U.S. 388 (1971). Both the local and federal agents defended the suit, inter alia, on the ground that they acted in good faith and with a reasonable belief in the lawfulness of their actions. Damages were claimed against the United States under the Federal Tort Claims Act (FTCA), then recently amended to allow suit against the United States where federal investigative or law enforcement officers commit certain types of intentional torts in the course of conducting searches or making arrests. 28 U.S.C. §2680(h). The United States also defended on the ground, inter alia, of the good faith and reasonable belief in the lawfulness of their actions on the part of its agents. . . .

In this appeal the government does not contest the district court's finding that a violation of plaintiff's fourth amendment rights occurred. Nor does it dispute the applicability of 28 U.S.C. §2680(h), as amended in 1974, to the instant action. The amendment to §2680(h) is clearly intended to waive the federal government's sovereign-immunity defense in suits brought to redress violations of the fourth amendment committed by federal law enforcement officers.

What is the only issue raised by the government in this appeal is the extent of its liability under FTCA. The United States urges that its liability is no greater than that of its employees. It submits that, under both traditional principles of respondeat superior and established FTCA precedent, it is entitled to assert all defenses available to its agents individually, including the defenses of good faith and reasonable belief. Plaintiff, on the other hand, urges that we uphold the district court's more expansive view of governmental liability. We adopt the more limited view of liability urged upon us by the government and hold that the liability of the United States under §2680(h) is coterminous with the liability of its agents under Bivens.

In 1971, the Supreme Court announced a federal damages remedy to redress violations of the fourth amendment by federal law enforcement officers. Bivens v. Six Unknown Named Agents of Federal Bureau of Narcotics. While Bivens created a federal cause of action sounding in tort cognizable in federal courts, it did not delineate the scope of the officer's tort duty. On remand, the Second Circuit concluded that an officer's tort duty under *Bivens* should not be coextensive with his constitutional duty under the fourth amendment. Looking to the traditional doctrine of police-officer liability for common-law torts, the court concluded that an individual officer should escape personal liability if he establishes that he acted "in good faith and [with a] reasonable belief in the validity of the arrest and search and in the necessity for carrying out the arrest and search in the way the arrest was made and the search was conducted." 456 F.2d 1339, 1348 (2d Cir. 1972). This definition of an individual officer's tort duty under *Bivens* has been widely accepted.

While *Bivens* created a federal tort for certain violations of the fourth amendment, it did not (and indeed could not) impose liability on the officer's employer, the federal government. The federal fisc was protected by the traditional doctrine of sovereign immunity.[3] The inability to secure a remedy against the United States severely restricted the effectiveness of the *Bivens* remedy. As Senator Percy remarked after conducting hearings into the much-publicized Collinsville drug raids in which innocent persons suffered not insubstantial abuse at the hands of federal narcotics agents:

> While [*Bivens*] gives victims of abusive tactics some opportunity for relief, their remedy is severely limited by the ease with which agents can usually establish the defense of having acted in good faith and with probable cause. Moreover, causes of action against officials as individuals will, on occasion, be virtually worthless since government employees may be so lacking in funds as to be judgment proof.

Consistent with these remarks, Senator Percy proposed a rider to [a pending bill] "to provide a remedy against the United States for the intentional torts of its investigative and law enforcement officers." Enacted in March, 1974, this legislation amended FTCA so as to create an exception to the intentional-tort exception of 28 U.S.C. §2860(h).

In waiving sovereign immunity with regard to intentional torts committed by federal investigative or law enforcement officers, Congress did not enact a discrete statutory provision; rather, it used as its vehicle the Federal Tort Claims Act, 28 U.S.C. §§1346(b), 2671 et seq. Section 2674, which waives the sovereign immunity of the United States and thus renders it liable for the torts described in the Act, states that the United States "shall be liable . . . *in the same manner and to the same extent as a private individual under like circumstances. . . .*" (Emphasis added.)

---

3. It was reasoned that the tort created by *Bivens* was an intentional tort and that suit against the United States was therefore barred by 28 U.S.C. §2680(h) which, prior to 1974, flatly excepted from FTCA "[a]ny claim arising out of assault, battery, false imprisonment, false arrest, malicious prosecution, abuse of process, libel, slander, misrepresentation, deceit, or interference with contract rights."

. . . Congress did not intend to create substantive federal law in enacting FTCA; it limited the liability of the United States to vicarious liability for the acts or omissions of its employees which, in turn, were tortious under the law of the place where the acts or omissions occurred. Both the precipitating tort and the scope of the government's vicarious liability were to be governed by "the law of the [state] where the act or omission occurred."

It is therefore incongruous that Congress utilized FTCA as the means of waiving sovereign immunity in the *Bivens* context. *Bivens* created a *federal* tort, and the scope of governmental liability under the 1974 amendment presents essentially a question of federal law. Instead of looking to a particular state's doctrine of respondeat superior, as we would in the typical FTCA case, we must seek to determine the scope of liability intended by Congress in enacting the 1974 proviso to §2680(h).

The plain language of the amendment offers no clue as to congressional intent with regard to the scope of the government's liability. . . .

While the legislative history makes clear that the federal government may be sued for *Bivens* torts committed by its agents, the history is not as clear with regard to the intended scope of the government's vicarious liability. It was the district court's view that on balance the legislative history disclosed an intent to impose liability on the government for fourth amendment violations irrespective of any individual defenses that might be asserted. We think not.

Senate Report No. 93-588, which accompanied the amendment to §2680(h), states that the amendment "should be viewed as a counterpart to the *Bivens* case and its progeny, in that it waives the defense of sovereign immunity so as to make the Government independently liable in damages *for the same type of conduct that is alleged to have occurred in* Bivens *(and for which that case imposes liability upon the individual Government officials involved).*" (Emphasis added). We think that this explanation of purpose strongly suggests an intent to allow vicarious liability only in those cases where individual liability would lie under *Bivens.* The district court concluded, however, that this expression of purpose was outweighed by other evidence in the legislative history indicating a more expansive view of governmental liability.

First, the district court concluded that the overall tenor of the Senate Report reflects a concern with providing an effective remedy to individuals whose fourth amendment rights have been violated. As we read that report, however, we think that it shows a concern with providing an effective remedy "for innocent victims of Federal law enforcement *abuses.*" (Emphasis added). It must be remembered that Congress passed this legislation in the wake of the Collinsville drug raids where government officials had engaged in what may fairly be described as outrageous behavior. As the report stresses, it is the *type* of conduct alleged both in *Bivens* and by the victims of the Collinsville raids — intentional and abusive conduct on the part of law enforcement officers — about which Congress was concerned. It was, we think, to remedy these more egregious wrongs that Congress waived sovereign immunity.

Second, the district court thought that other documents in the legislative history — specifically Senator Percy's remarks quoted earlier and a memorandum prepared by the staff of the Senate Government Operations Committee — provide direct support for the conclusion that Congress intended to impose vicarious liability without regard to individual defenses. While we recognize that both of these documents support this conclusion, we do not think that they are entitled to the weight accorded them by the district court. What must guide us is not Senator Percy's intent nor the intent of the committee staff, but rather the intent of Congress. We therefore give most weight to Senate Report No. 93-588, which represents the explanatory remarks of the committee. The Senate Report itself contains none of the clear language found in Senator Percy's remarks or in the staff memorandum. To the contrary, a fair reading of the Report supports the government's position that the remedy against the government under FTCA is inextricably tied to the remedy against the individual officer under *Bivens.*

The decision we reach is also supported by the well-established principle of statutory interpretation that "statutes which waive immunity of the United States from suit are to be construed strictly in favor of the sovereign." While we are mindful of Mr. Justice Frankfurter's admonition not to view ourselves as a "self-constituted guardian of the Treasury [importing] immunity back into a statute designed to limit it," there can be little question but that imposition of liability without regard to the individual officer's defenses of good faith and reasonable belief would be a substantial enough departure from general principles of respondeat superior[13] and would impose a potentially burdensome enough impact on the federal treasury that it should be supported by a clear expression of legislative intent in either the statute itself or in the accompanying legislative history. Because we find no clear statement of a legislative policy to expand the government's vicarious liability beyond the scope of its agents' direct liability, this rule of construction requires that we reverse the decision of the district court and remand this case in order to allow the government to produce evidence of its agents' good faith and reasonable belief in the legality of their conduct.

Notes

1. The Fourth Amendment guarantees the "right of the people to be secure in their persons, houses, papers, and effects, against unreasonable

---

13. As the district court itself noted, employers are generally entitled under traditional principles of respondeat superior to assert all defenses available to their employees. Second Restatement of Agency §219, Comment *c.*

searches and seizures. . . ." What kinds of tort suit under state law might be affected by the Fourth Amendment, and how?

2. 42 U.S.C. §1983 provides damages and injunctive remedies for violations of federal rights under color of law and is a common vehicle for tort suits against state officers based on violation of federal constitutional rights. Such suits have become extremely common in recent years.

3. The immunity of state law-enforcement officers from tort suits is a "qualified" immunity; that is, it is forfeited if the officer is not acting in good faith. It thus resembles conditional privilege in defamation law. What is the basis of this immunity? May the idea be similar to that behind the private-necessity doctrine — the officer is not (not usually, anyway) paid a bonus for successful results achieved through unusual zeal, so neither should he pay for the honest mistakes to which his zeal may occasionally give rise? See Mashaw, Civil Liability of Government Officers: Property Rights and Official Accountability, 42 Law & Contemp. Prob., Winter 1978, at 8, 26-27. (Higher state officers, notably judges and prosecutors, enjoy absolute immunity. Why?) Does this reasoning apply when suit is brought not against the officer himself, but against the agency employing him, under the doctrine of respondeat superior? If not, was *Norton* correctly decided?

4. On sovereign immunity as a defense in tort actions against government agencies (as distinct from government officers), see Note in Chapter 5.

PART II
UNINTENTIONAL TORTS

Chapter 4
The Negligence Standard

A. WHAT IS NEGLIGENCE?

Often an injury is inflicted without intent to injure on the part of the injurer — "by accident," as the layman says. This part of the book deals with the law governing liability for unintentional or accidental injuries. There are two alternative standards for determining such liability. One is the negligence standard, the other strict liability. The question of the relative merits of the two standards, a question touched on briefly in Chapter 1, is of central importance to an understanding of tort law and policy but is postponed to the chapter on strict liability (Chapter 7). In this and the two following chapters, we examine the implementation of the negligence standard, which remains the dominant standard of liability in accident cases. Negligence is also widely used as a standard of civil liability in legal systems outside of, as well as within, the Anglo-American orbit. See, e.g., F. H. Lawson, Negligence in the Civil Law (1950).

J. H. Baker, An Introduction to English Legal History
337-345 (2d ed. 1979)

The word negligenter (negligently), as an adverb designed to indicate wrongful conduct, first appeared in writs of trespass as the antithesis of force and arms. If damage was done in the course of performing carelessly a task undertaken with the plaintiff's consent, it could not be described as having been done vi et armis. If, on the other hand, the wrong was forcible, the complaint was not of mere negligence and so there was no need to mention it in a special case. Negligence and force were thus mutually exclusive.

In all the early cases where negligence was part of the special case in the writ, there was a pre-existing relationship between the parties which precluded an allegation of force against the peace. The relationship arose from some undertaking which brought the defendant into contact with the plaintiff or the plaintiff's property; and, since the plaintiff had consented to this physical contact, the careless defendant who caused harm was liable not for *doing* the act but for doing it *carelessly*.

. . . Actions on the case for negligence were brought against bailees, carriers, surgeons, workmen and tradesmen. They all had a common form: the defendant was alleged to have undertaken to perform some specific task, and to have done it so carelessly that some specified harm resulted. The undertaking was only to do the work, not to use skill or care; so to that extent the obligation to use care was imposed by law rather than by contract. A bailee's undertaking to keep goods "safely" may actually have fixed him with strict liability. The nature of the negligence relied on in these assumpsit actions never clearly emerged in the cases, because the defendant normally pleaded the general issue and the question of negligence was then a question of fact for the jury alone to decide. Whatever it was, it found expression always in negative adverbs, such as negligenter, improvide, inartificialiter, indebite, and so forth. But the adverb always governed a verb of positive action. The best generalization we can make is that a person who embarked upon a service which brought him into contact with the person or property of another was liable if he performed the service with want of care or skill and damage resulted. . . .

Actions on the case were brought in the fourteenth century against innkeepers for the loss of goods belonging to their guests by their "default." The relationship between innkeeper and traveller with respect to luggage was not sufficiently close to be treated as bailment, especially since common innkeepers were bound by law to accept all travellers who wished to stay and for whom there was room. The plaintiff in such an action therefore relied on a "custom of the realm" that all keepers of common inns were bound to accommodate travellers, and to look after their goods so that no harm came to them through their default. The gist of the action was the innkeeper's default in custody, but precisely because there was no liability for negligence without a pre-existing duty of care it was thought necessary to show a custom of the realm which imposed the duty.

By 1400 the custom of the realm approach had been extended to cover liability for fire. Again, it would seem, the necessity for laying such a custom arose from the absence of a pre-existing relationship between the parties. The only relationship was that of being a neighbour. The alleged custom of the realm was therefore stated to be that everyone was bound to keep his fire safe and sound so that it did not injure his neighbour. The operative clause, that the defendant nevertheless kept his fire so negligently that the plaintiff's property was damaged, was borrowed from the action against bailees; but as the complaint was of a default in the custody, not of the plaintiff's goods, but of a dangerous force set in motion by the defendant, it was necessary to allege a customary duty of care and control. . . .

The modern lawyer may see in the so-called customs of the realm the antecedents of the "duty of care"; but there was in fact no continuity between the old doctrine and the new, and the custom of the realm was abandoned as a source of legal development for the simple reason that such a custom could not be other than the common law itself. The legal position until the later seventeenth century, therefore, was that liability for negligence was generally imposed only for default in undertakings, and for breaches of duty by innkeepers or persons who lit fires. No thought was given to liability for negligence as such, and an Elizabethan judge could state without undue conservatism, "Here there is nothing alleged except negligence, and I have never known an action to lie for negligence save where one is retained to do something for someone and does it negligently; and the reason why it lies in that case is because he had undertaken to do it." An obvious explanation for such a restriction would be that the common law could not impose a duty of care on a person who had not undertaken it of his own volition. But the real reason why such a state of affairs was for so long tolerated was the wide scope of trespass vi et armis.

If negligent conduct caused direct physical harm, the appropriate reme- dy, in the absence of an undertaking, was an action of trespass alleging force and arms. Such an action was not based on doing something negligently which would have been lawful if done carefully, but on doing something which there was no right to do at all. The short-sighted archer who shot a passer-by unawares, or the careless driver who ran him down, were just as guilty of battery as if they had injured him deliberately. Negligence in the sense of inadvertence was irrelevant.

A wide range of accidents qualified as battery, but the range was ob- scured by the sameness of the writs and counts. Whatever the real facts, defendants always "assaulted, beat and wounded" the plaintiff "with force and arms, to wit with swords and staves." In the general writ there were no further particulars, and no mention of negligence. The degree of fault of the defendant would only become relevant if he tried to make it so by excusing himself on grounds of accident. Yet, if he did so, he would not usually plead the accident specially, but would plead the general issue "not guilty" and explain the circumstances in evidence to the jury. As a result, the law relating to accident was suppressed for centuries; what happened before the jury was not entered on the record and raised no legal questions for the court in banc. If the short-sighted archer were sued in battery, he might satisfy the jury that the accident was not his fault, and they would then find him not guilty; but the details of his defence would nowhere be set down in writing. It is there- fore an unreal question whether the *law* recognised a defence of accident; the question was treated as being purely of fact. The question only presented itself on the face of the record in one or two exceptional cases where, through mistaken policy by the pleader, accident was raised by a special plea. The plea was regularly rejected, but the cases did not thereby establish that accident was no defence: merely that it could not be pleaded in the manner which had been attempted.

In the Case of Thorns a man was sued for trespassing on his neighbour's land to collect thorns which had fallen there in the process of clipping. He pleaded, as to the trespass by the thorns, that they had fallen against his will (ipso invito); but Choke J held this plea bad because the will was only relevant in felony. It was agreed that if the thorns had been blown by the wind that would not have been the defendant's act, but the act of the wind. Gravity is a more continuous natural phenomenon than wind, and its effects were reasonably predictable even before Newton. A defence that the force of gravity had been overlooked was not a defence consistent with having taken due care. The plea was bad in substance, and so the question of form did not arise.

The problem occurred again in cases arising out of shooting accidents. In Weaver v. Ward the defendant, who had shot the plaintiff during military exercises, pleaded that the wounding was accidental and against his will. The court held the plea bad, but said that if he had shown that the plaintiff ran against his gun as he was firing it, or had shown that the accident was "inevitable" and not his fault, then he might have been excused. Then, in 1682, a defendant adopted this advice and pleaded that as he was firing his pistol the plaintiff accidentally walked across the line of fire and was shot, against the will of the defendant. But even this was held to be a bad plea, "for in trespass the defendant shall not be excused without unavoidable necessity, which is not shewn here." Even if the facts alleged in the plea were true, the defendant might yet have been negligent.

These decisions led subsequent generations to suppose that liability in trespass vi et armis had been strict, and excusable only by "inevitable accident." When examined carefully, the decisions were by no means as sweeping as random dicta suggested. None of the pleas had put the defendant's fault in issue. It did not follow because the damage was accidental (per infortunium) or against the will of the defendant (ipso invito) that the defendant had been without fault. The judges therefore wished to know whether the defendant could have taken steps to avoid the accident; in other words, whether it was "inevitable" — not in the sense of being predestined, but in that there was no reasonable opportunity of prevention. A man who had done wrong could not offer as a defence that he had not wished it to happen. If he had some justification for acting as he did, he could plead by way of confession and avoidance. If he had not done the act at all, if his own act had not caused the accident, or it he had done all he could to prevent it, then his proper course was to plead the general issue and tell his story to the jury.

Thus, although negligence played no formal part in the action of trespass vi et armis, it seems likely that a man was only considered guilty of such a trespass if he had at least been negligent in causing direct, forcible harm. It was not clearly laid down that the standard of liability was exactly the same as in actions on the case until the tort of negligence was established and the forms of action abolished; but there is no reason to suppose it was ever different, since in either action it was for the jury to decide. The writ of trespass vi et armis had been an archaic survival, in that unlike most of the other actions which continued in use its wording almost totally suppressed the real facts. But this formal, procedural distinction between trespass and case was engraved on the heart of the pleader, and it was not until 1959 that a plaintiff complaining of a direct trespass was held obliged to allege negligence as part of his own case.

We now know that the distinction between trespass and case was the result of the jurisdictional accident that the royal courts entertained complaints of forcible wrongs before letting in the rest. There ought, therefore, to have been no substantive gaps between the two. Any wrong which was not forcible ought to have been remediable in case. Harmful carelessness was on the face of it legally wrong, and there was probably no absolute rule to the effect that there could be no duty to take care without an undertaking; it was just that between battery and assumpsit most accidents were provided for. When exceptional cases arose, new actions on the case could be devised. We have already noticed the fourteenth-century device of customs of the realm; but there was no peculiar magic in the two customs, and new duties could be recognised at common law without the use of that label. In 1473 we find an action for putting a pile of firewood near the highway, knowing the danger of its falling, where it did fall on the plaintiff; issue was joined on the negligence. In 1520 we find a mill-keeper sued for breach of his duty ratione officii to control a mill-sluice so that flooding did not occur. In 1530 a person into whose hands the plaintiff's goods had come was successfully sued for negligent keeping, there being no assumpsit or conversion; similar actions were also brought against bailees. And in 1582 an action was brought for damage caused by a spark from a gun, which was a fire accident not covered by the custom of the realm. These cases are few and far between, not because the law had difficulty in recognising the existence of a duty, but because the situations not covered by trespass vi et armis or assumpsit were few and far between. Problems only arose, as elsewhere in the law, when attempts were made to use case instead of an existing remedy. In this sphere the conflict was between case and trespass vi et armis.

The first signs of a tort of negligence, in the more pervasive sense which included forcible wrongs, are found in a long series of running down cases beginning in the seventeenth century. If a man negligently drove his horse and cart or ship into another man or his property, that was a trespass with force. But there could be many disadvantages in bringing trespass. For one thing, the accident might be shown to be the fault of the horse, or of the unpredictable forces of nature, or perhaps partly of the plaintiff himself, and so the jury would be persuaded to find the defendant not guilty of the trespass. Also, for similar reasons, the jury might reduce the damages if the battery turned out to have been unintentional. Moreover, the plaintiff often wished to sue the driver's master, and vicarious liability could only be imposed by an action on the case. And then there was the serious practical danger that recovery of nominal damages in trespass vi et armis carried nominal costs. In all these situations the plaintiff did well to waive the force and sue in an action on the case for negligence. . . .

Mitchil v. Alestree [1676] was an action against a master and servant who had broken in horses in Lincoln's Inn Fields, where many people were walking about, including the plaintiff who was kicked and injured. In his first action the plaintiff alleged that the defendant had negligently permitted the horses to injure the plaintiff; but Hale CJ ruled at the trial that there was no evidence of want of care in controlling the untamed horses. The essence of the wrong was in bringing horses to a public place for breaking in, and so a second action was brought alleging that the defendants had acted improvide, incaute and without consideration of the danger of breaking in horses in a busy place. The action succeeded, even though there was no undertaking, no custom of the realm, and no force and arms. The arguments show that the judges were conscious only of making a slight enlargement of the scienter principle: The negligence was in creating a dangerous situation, rather than in the way the situation was controlled. The new principle was to give some trouble in relation to dogs, which were not normally confined; but as early as 1700 it was contended that the effect was to make a man "answerable for all mischief proceeding from his neglect or his actions, unless they were of unavoidable necessity." Subsequent writers regarded Mitchil v. Alestree as having opened up a new category of actions on the case, and by George II's time a significant chapter headed "Of injuries arising from negligence or folly" had been built around it.

Towards the close of the eighteenth century, numerous problems raised by running down cases vexed the superior courts. Two reasons have been suggested for the glut of these cases in the last three decades of George III's reign. First, there was a heavy increase in the number of driving accidents, as a result of the greater speed and volume of traffic following the improvement of road surfaces by the turnpike trusts and the technical achievements of Telford and Macadam. Stage coaches, driven as often as not by men undistinguished for their sobriety, competed for the fastest journeys; and during such races they not infrequently overturned, collided with other vehicles, or went out of control. Second, the litigation which resulted from busier roads raised numerous legal difficulties, which were accentuated by the rigid insistence of the courts on the artificial boundary between trespass (direct forcible injury) and case (mediate or consequential injury). The metaphysics of directness, as also the problems surrounding vicarious liability, were a constant trouble to courts and practitioners for over thirty years. The solution was found by Tindal CJ, in 1833, when it was laid down that a plaintiff could waive the force and sue in case whenever the injury complained of was not both direct and wilful.

The effect of this decision was that trespass became more and more associated with wilful injuries. Few lawyers today would classify a running down accident as an assault and battery. And since the essence of the action on the case was negligence, the negligence had to be expressly pleaded and proved. The Industrial Revolution and the development of the railway added to the possibilities of frequent, novel and expensive accidents, and litigation about negligence enjoyed a further boom. By the beginning of Victoria's reign, cases on negligence were sufficiently numerous for writers on the law to put them into a separate compartment.

Note

Baker's conclusion that liability for trespass vi et armis was not strict is not universally accepted. For a contrary conclusion, see Arnold, Accident, Mistake, and Rules of Liability in the Fourteenth-Century Law of Torts, 128 U. Pa. L. Rev. 361 (1979). For a view similar to Baker's, see Williams, Transforming American Law: Doubtful Economics Makes Doubtful History, 25 U.C.L.A.L. Rev. 1187, 1188-1193, 1215-1218 (1978).

Brown v. Kendall *is this case sent back for re-trial?*
60 Mass. 292 (1850)

It appeared in evidence, on the trial, . . . that two dogs, belonging to the plaintiff and the defendant, respectively, were fighting in the presence of their masters; that the defendant took a stick about four feet long, and commenced beating the dogs in order to separate them; that the plaintiff was looking on, at the distance of about a rod, and that he advanced a step or two towards the dogs. In their struggle, the dogs approached the place where the plaintiff was standing. The defendant retreated backwards from before the dogs, striking them as he retreated; and as he approached the plaintiff, with his back towards him, in raising his stick over his shoulder, in order to strike the dogs, he accidentally hit the plaintiff in the eye, inflicting upon him a severe injury.

Whether it was necessary or proper for the defendant to interfere in the fight between the dogs; whether the interference, if called for, was in a proper manner, and what degree of care was exercised by each party on the occasion; were the subject of controversy between the parties, upon all the evidence in the case, of which the foregoing is an outline.

The defendant requested the judge to instruct the jury, that "if both the *held* plaintiff and defendant at the time of the blow were using ordinary care, or if at that time the defendant was using ordinary care and the plaintiff was not, or if at that time both plaintiff and defendant were not using ordinary care, then the plaintiff could not recover."

The defendant further requested the judge to instruct the jury, that, "under the circumstances, if the plaintiff was using ordinary care and the defendant was not, the plaintiff could not recover, and that the burden of proof on all these propositions was on the plaintiff."

The judge declined to give the instructions. . . .

SHAW, C.J. This is an action of trespass, vi et armis, brought by George Brown against George K. Kendall, for an assault and battery. . . .

The facts set forth in the bill of exceptions preclude the supposition, that the blow, inflicted by the hand of the defendant upon the person of the plaintiff, was intentional. The whole case proceeds on the assumption, that the damage sustained by the plaintiff, from the stick held by the defendant, was inadvert and unintentional; and the case involves the question how far, and under what qualifications, the party by whose unconscious act the damage was done is responsible for it. . . .

——It appears to us, that some of the confusion in the cases on this subject has grown out of the long-vexed question, under the rule of the common law, whether a party's remedy, where he has one, should be sought in an action of the case, or of trespass. This is very distinguishable from the question, whether in a given case, any action will lie. . . .

In these discussions, it is frequently stated by judges, that when one receives injury from the direct act of another, trespass will lie. But we think this is said in reference to the question, whether trespass and not case will lie, assuming that the facts are such, that some action will lie. These dicta are no authority, we think, for holding, that damage received by a direct act of force from another will be sufficient to maintain an action of trespass, whether the act was lawful or unlawful, and neither wilful, intentional, or careless. In the principal case cited, Leame v. Bray, the damage arose from the act of the defendant, in driving on the wrong side of the road, in a dark night, which was clearly negligent if not unlawful. In the course of the argument of that case, Lawrence, J., said: "There certainly are cases in the books, where, the injury being direct and immediate, trespass has been holden to lie, though the injury was not intentional." The term "injury" implies something more than damage; but, independently of that consideration, the proposition may be true, because though the injury was unintentional, the act may have been unlawful or negligent, and the cases cited by him are perfectly consistent with that supposition. . . .

We think, as the result of all the authorities, the rule is correctly stated by Mr. Greenleaf, that the plaintiff must come prepared with evidence to show either that the *intention* was unlawful, or that the defendant was *in fault*; for if the injury was unavoidable, and the conduct of the defendant was free from blame, he will not be liable. If, in the prosecution of a lawful act, a casualty purely accidental arises, no action can be supported for an injury arising therefrom. In applying these rules to the present case, we can perceive no reason why the instructions asked for by the defendant ought not to have been given; to this effect, that if both plaintiff and defendant at the time of the blow were using ordinary care, or if at that time the defendant was using ordinary care, and the plaintiff was not, or if at that time, both the plaintiff and defendant were not using ordinary care, then the plaintiff could not recover.

In using this term, ordinary care, it may be proper to state, that what *Def.*
constitutes ordinary care will vary with the circumstances of cases. In general,
it means that kind and degree of care, which prudent and cautious men would
use, such as is required by the exigency of the case, and such as is necessary to
guard against probable danger. A man, who should have occasion to discharge
a gun, on an open and extensive marsh, or in a forest, would be required to use
less circumspection and care, than if he were to do the same thing in an
inhabited town, village, or city. To make an accident, or casualty, or as the law
sometimes states it, inevitable accident, it must be such an accident as the
defendant could not have avoided by the use of the kind and degree of care
necessary to the exigency, and in the circumstances in which he was placed.

We are not aware of any circumstances in this case, requiring a distinction between acts which it was lawful and proper to do, and acts of legal duty.
There are cases, undoubtedly, in which officers are bound to act under
process, for the legality of which they are not responsible, and perhaps some
others in which this distinction would be important. We can have no doubt
that the act of the defendant in attempting to part the fighting dogs, one of
which was his own, and for the injurious acts of which he might be responsible, was a lawful and proper act, which he might do by proper and safe means.
If, then, in doing this act, using due care and all proper precautions necessary
to the exigency of the case, to avoid hurt to others, in raising his stick for that
purpose, he accidentally hit the plaintiff in his eye, and wounded him, this
was the result of pure accident, or was involuntary and unavoidable, and
therefore the action would not lie. Or if the defendant was chargeable with
some negligence, and if the plaintiff was also chargeable with negligence, we
think the plaintiff cannot recover without showing that the damage was *H*
caused wholly by the act of the defendant, and that the plaintiff's own
negligence did not contribute as an efficient cause to produce it. . . .

a. Who could have avoided acc. at least too

Notes

1. Does it follow, as the court seems to think, that if defendant is liable
only if negligent, plaintiff's negligence (contributory negligence) necessarily
bars recovery? Should the standard of negligence and of contributory negligence be the same? Should it be the same if, unlike Brown v. Kendall,
defendant is an enterprise and plaintiff is an individual?

Since rightly or wrongly the standards of negligence and of contributory
negligence are in general the same, this chapter will illustrate the negligence
standard from cases involving contributory negligence as well as defendant's
negligence. Questions peculiar to plaintiff conduct in negligence cases are
postponed to the next chapter.

2. The trial court in *Brown* gave the following instruction in lieu of the
instructions requested by defendant:

If the defendant, in beating the dogs, was doing a necessary act, or one which it was his duty under the circumstances of the case to do, and was doing it in a proper way; then he was not responsible in this action, provided he was using ordinary care at the time of the blow. If it was not a necessary act; if he was not in duty bound to attempt to part the dogs, but might with propriety interfere or not as he chose; the defendant was responsible for the consequence of the blow, unless it appeared that he was in the exercise of extraordinary care, so that the accident was inevitable, using the word inevitable not in a strict but a popular sense. *Negligence (to contrib)*

60 Mass. at 293. How great a difference is there between this instruction and those requested by the defendant?

3. Why should the degree of circumspection required of a shooter be greater in the town than in the country? What element in the Hand formula is affected? *P*

4. Is negligence just a synonym for carelessness? Was defendant in Mitchil v. Alestree careless? *No*

O. W. Holmes, Jr., The Common Law
94-96 (1881)

The general principle of our law is that loss from accident must lie where it falls, and this principle is not affected by the fact that a human being is the instrument of misfortune. But relatively to a given human being anything is accident which he could not fairly have been expected to contemplate as possible, and therefore to avoid. In the language of the late Chief Justice Nelson of New York: "No case or principle can be found, or if found can be maintained, subjecting an individual to liability for an act done without fault on his part. . . . All the cases concede that an injury arising from inevitable accident, or, which in law or reason is the same thing, from an act that ordinary human care and foresight are unable to guard against, is but the misfortune of the sufferer, and lays no foundation for legal responsibility." If this were not so, any act would be sufficient, however remote, which set in motion or opened the door for a series of physical sequences ending in damage; such as riding the horse, in the case of the runaway, or even coming to a place where one is seized with a fit and strikes the plaintiff in an unconscious spasm. Nay, why need the defendant have acted at all, and why is it not enough that his existence has been at the expense of the plaintiff? The requirement of an act is the requirement that the defendant should have made a choice. But the only possible purpose of introducing this moral element is to make the power of avoiding the evil complained of a condition of liability. There is no such power where the evil cannot be foreseen. . . .

A man need not, it is true, do this or that act, — the term *act* implies a choice, — but he must act somehow. Furthermore, the public generally prof-

its by individual activity. As action cannot be avoided, and tends to the public good, there is obviously no policy in throwing the hazard of what is at once desirable and inevitable upon the actor.

The state might conceivably make itself a mutual insurance company against accidents, and distribute the burden of its citizens' mishaps among all its members. There might be a pension for paralytics, and state aid for those who suffered in person or estate from tempest or wild beasts. As between individuals it might adopt the mutual insurance principle pro tanto, and divide damages when both were in fault, as in the rusticum judicium of the admiralty, or it might throw all loss upon the actor irrespective of fault. The state does none of these things, however, and the prevailing view is that its cumbrous and expensive machinery ought not to be set in motion unless some clear benefit is to be derived from disturbing the status quo. State interference is an evil, where it cannot be shown to be a good. Universal insurance, if desired, can be better and more cheaply accomplished by private enterprise. The undertaking to redistribute losses simply on the ground that they resulted from the defendant's act would not only be open to these objections, but, as it is hoped the preceding discussion has shown, to the still graver one of offending the sense of justice. Unless my act is of a nature to threaten others, unless under the circumstances a prudent man would have foreseen the possibility of harm, it is no more justifiable to make me indemnify my neighbor against the consequences, than to make me do the same thing if I had fallen upon him in a fit, or to compel me to insure him against lightning. . . .

Notes

1. To adopt a negligence standard is necessarily to reject the principle of strict liability, of "acting at one's peril." The passage from Holmes illustrates the prevalent view in the nineteenth and early twentieth century that negligence liability represented an ethical advance over the era of strict liability which was assumed to have preceded it. "The early law asked simply, 'Did the defendant do the physical act which damaged the plaintiff?' The law of today . . . asks the further question, 'Was the act blameworthy?' The ethical standard of reasonable conduct has replaced the unmoral standard of acting at one's peril." Ames, Law and Morals, 22 Harv. L. Rev. 97, 99 (1908). Questions of ethics to one side, it does seem that strict liability looms larger in primitive and early law than it does in modern law, although negligence never completely swept the field, and in recent decades there has been a resurgence of strict liability in some areas of tort law. Why primitive law places greater emphasis on strict liability, and whether the trend toward negligence really represents an ethical (or any other sort of) advance over strict liability, are questions taken up in Chapter 7 after the student has learned how the negligence and strict liability standards are applied in practice. The passage

from Holmes is included at this point in the book to help the student understand the intellectual atmosphere in which the negligence concept flourished — not to provide adequate materials for a definitive assessment of the merits of negligence relative to the merits of strict liability.

2. Notice Holmes' opposition to strict liability on causal grounds. Reassess his argument after reading Chapter 8.

Blyth v. Birmingham Waterworks Co.
11 Exch. 78, 156 Eng. Rep. 1047 (1856)

. . . The case stated that the defendants were incorporated by stat. 7 Geo. 4, c. cix. for the purpose of supplying Birmingham with water.

By the 84th section of their Act it was enacted, that the company should, upon the laying down of any main-pipe or other pipe in any street, fix, at the time of laying down such pipe, a proper and sufficient fire-plug in each such street. . . . By sect. 87, pipes were to be eighteen inches beneath the surface of the soil. By the 89th section, the mains were at all times to be kept charged with water. The defendants derived no profit from the maintenance of the plugs distinct from the general profits of the whole business, but such maintenance was one of the conditions under which they were permitted to exercise the privileges given by the Act. The main-pipe opposite the house of the plaintiff was more than eighteen inches below the surface. The fire-plug was constructed according to the best known system, and the materials of it were at the time of the accident sound and in good order. The apparatus connected with the fire-plug was as follows:

The lower part of a wooden plug was inserted in a neck, which projected above and formed part of the main. About the neck there was a bed of brickwork puddled in with clay. The plug was also inclosed in a cast iron tube, which was placed upon and fixed to the brickwork. The tube was closed at the top by a moveable iron stopper having a hole in it for the insertion of the key, by which the plug was loosened when occasion required it.

The plug did not fit tight to the tube, but room was left for it to move freely. This space was necessarily left for the purpose of easily and quickly removing the wooden plug to allow the water to flow. On the removal of the wooden plug the pressure upon the main forced the water up through the neck and cap to the surface of the street.

On the 24th of February, a large quantity of water, escaping from the neck of the main, forced its way through the ground into the plaintiff's house. The apparatus had been laid down 25 years, and had worked well during that time. The defendants' engineer stated, that the water might have forced its way through the brickwork round the neck of the main, and that the accident might have been caused by the frost, inasmuch as the expansion of the water would force up the plug out of the neck, and the stopper being encrusted with ice would not suffer the plug to ascend. One of the severest frosts on record set in on the 15th of January, 1855, and continued until after the accident in question. An incrustation of ice and snow had gathered about the stopper, and in the street all round, and also for some inches between the stopper and the plug. The ice had been observed on the surface of the ground for a considerable time before the accident. A short time after the accident, the company's turncock removed the ice from the stopper, took out the plug, and replaced it.

The judge left it to the jury to consider whether the company had used proper care to prevent the accident. He thought that, if the defendants had taken out the ice adhering to the plug, the accident would not have happened, and left it to the jury to say whether they ought to have removed the ice. The jury found a verdict for the plaintiff for the sum claimed.

Field for the appellant. There was no negligence on the part of the defendants. The plug was pushed out by the frost, which was one of the severest ever known.

The Court then called on Kennedy for the respondent. The company omitted to take sufficient precautions. The fire-plug is placed in the neck of the main. In ordinary cases the plug rises and lets the water out; but here there was an incrustation round the stopper, which prevented the escape of the water. This might have been easily removed. . . . It is the defendants' water, therefore they are bound to see that no injury is done to any one by it. . . . [Alderson, B. Is it an accident which any man could have foreseen?] A scientific man could have foreseen it. If no eye could have seen what was going on, the case might have been different; but the company's servants could have seen, and actually did see, the ice which had collected about the plug. It is of the last importance that these plugs, which are fire-plugs, should be kept by the company in working order. The accident cannot be considered as having been caused by the act of God.

ALDERSON, B. I am of opinion that there was no evidence to be left to the jury. The case turns upon the question, whether the facts proved shew that the defendants were guilty of negligence. Negligence is the omission to do something which a reasonable man, guided upon those considerations which ordinarily regulate the conduct of human affairs, would do, or doing something which a prudent and reasonable man would not do. The defendants might have been liable for negligence, if, unintentionally, they omitted to do that which a reasonable person would have done, or did that which a person taking reasonable precautions would not have done. A reasonable man would act with reference to the average circumstances of the temperature in ordinary years. The defendants had provided against such frosts as experience would have led men, acting prudently, to provide against; and they are not guilty of negligence, because their precautions proved insufficient against the effects of the extreme severity of the frost of 1855, which penetrated to a greater depth than any which ordinarily occurs south of the polar regions. Such a state of circumstances constitutes a contingency against which no reasonable man can provide. The result was an accident, for which the defendants cannot be held liable. . . .

BRAMWELL, B. The Act of Parliament directed the defendants to lay down pipes, with plugs in them, as safety-valves, to prevent the bursting of the pipes. The plugs were properly made, and of proper material; but there was an accumulation of ice about this plug, which prevented it from acting properly. The defendants were not bound to keep the plugs clear. It appears to me that the plaintiff was under quite as much obligation to remove the ice and snow which had accumulated, as the defendants. However that may be, it appears to me that it would be monstrous to hold the defendants responsible ✓ because they did not foresee and prevent an accident, the cause of which was so obscure, that it was not discovered until many months after the accident had happened.

Verdict to be entered for the defendants.

Notes

1. How exactly did the accident happen?
2. What is the relevance of the statute to the issue of defendants' negligence?
3. What element of the Hand formula did the court focus on — P, B, or L? (This would be a good time for you to reread Chapter 1 of this book.)
4. How relevant was the unforeseen severity of the frost? The frost set in almost six weeks before the accident; wasn't that time enough for the company to discover and rectify the problem?
5. Is the relevant P in this case the probability of the accident as it appeared before January 15 or after? What is the relevant B? Which judge's reasoning is the more persuasive — Alderson's or Bramwell's?
6. What role, if any, did custom play in the court's decision?

Adams v. Bullock
227 N.Y. 208, 125 N.E. 93 (1919)

CARDOZO, J. The defendant runs a trolley line in the city of Dunkirk, employing the overhead wire system. At one point, the road is crossed by a bridge or culvert which carries the tracks of the Nickle Plate and Pennsylvania Railroads. Pedestrians often use the bridge as a short cut between streets, and children play on it. On April 21, 1916, the plaintiff, a boy of 12 years, came across the bridge, swinging a wire about 8 feet long. In swinging it, he brought it in contact with the defendant's trolley wire, which ran beneath the structure. The side of the bridge was protected by a parapet 18 inches wide. Four feet $7\frac{3}{4}$ inches below the top of the parapet, the trolley wire was strung. The plaintiff was shocked and burned when the wires came together. He had a verdict at Trial Term, which has been affirmed at the Appellate Division by a divided court.

Holding We think the verdict cannot stand. The defendant in using an overhead trolley was in the lawful exercise of its franchise. Negligence, therefore, cannot be imputed to it because it used that system and not another. There was, of course, a duty to adopt all reasonable precautions to minimize the resulting perils. We think there is no evidence that this duty was ignored. The trolley wire was so placed that no one standing on the bridge or even bending over the parapet could reach it. Only some extraordinary casualty, not fairly within the area of ordinary prevision, could make it a thing of danger. Reasonable care in the use of a destructive agency imports a high degree of vigilance. But no vigilance, however alert, unless fortified by the gift of *P* prophecy, could have predicted the point upon the route where such an accident would occur. It might with equal reason have been expected anywhere else. At any point upon the route a mischievous or thoughtless boy might touch the wire with a metal pole, or fling another wire across it. If unable to reach it from the walk, he might stand upon a wagon or climb upon a tree. No special danger at this bridge warned the defendant that there was need of special measures of precaution. No like accident had occurred before. No custom had been disregarded. We think that ordinary caution did not involve forethought of this extraordinary peril. . . . There is, we may add, a *dicta* distinction not to be ignored between electric light and trolley wires. The distinction is that the former may be insulated. Chance of harm, though remote, may betoken negligence, if needless. Facility of protection may impose a duty to protect. With trolley wires, the case is different. Insulation is impossible. Guards here and there are of little value. To avert the possibility of this accident and others like it at one point or another on the route, the *B* defendant must have abandoned the overhead system, and put the wires underground. Neither its power nor its duty to make the change is shown. To hold it liable upon the facts exhibited in this record would be to charge it as an insurer. . . .

Notes

1. Suppose the costs of running the trolley wires underground would have been no greater than the costs of running them overhead, and placing them underground would have eliminated the possibility of accidents such as the one that occurred in this case. Why might defendant still not be adjudged negligent? Is defendant's franchise relevant to this question? *lawful exercise of franchise*

2. What factors discussed in the court's opinion relate to P in the Hand formula, what to B?

Paris v. Stepney Borough Council
1951 A.C. 367 (H.L.)

[A workman employed as a garage hand had, as defendants, his employers, knew, only one good eye. In working on the back axle of a vehicle to remove a U-bolt, which had rusted in, he struck it with a hammer, and a metal chip flew off, seriously injuring his good eye. He was not wearing goggles. He claimed damages against his employers on the ground that they were negligent in failing to provide and require the use of goggles as part of the system of work. The trial court gave judgment for the plaintiff, but this was reversed by the Court of Appeal, and plaintiff appealed to the House of Lords.]

LORD SIMONDS. . . .

My Lords, a study of the evidence leaves me in no doubt that an employer could not be held guilty of negligence if he did not generally provide goggles for the use of his employees engaged in this kind of work. The respondents' public cleansing officer, Mr. Boden, to whom I have already referred, a witness of wide experience, being asked, "Have you seen in work of this kind workmen wearing goggles to do such work?" replied, "Not in my experience. I have never seen any mechanic working in any of the repair shops that I have visited during that thirty-seven years wearing goggles doing that repair work." . . . The appellant himself gave evidence, which, so far as it bears on the obviousness of the risk and corresponding duty, cannot be disregarded. I make nothing of the fact that he did not complain that goggles were not provided, for he might well hesitate to do so. But being asked, "Have you considered as to whether it was dangerous to do this sort of job without eye protection?" he answered, "Well, we were always working through years just doing the same thing. It became natural to get in there without protection." Then he was asked, "You did not think about it?" and answered, "We had been doing it for years and never thought of it." It is true that he added that if goggles had been provided and he had been told to use them, he would have done so. But this does not appear to carry the matter any further. For the appellant, a Captain Paterson said, in answer to the judge, that in the whole of his experience he had about a dozen times seen a man wearing goggles when he was using a hammer to knock a rusted bolt in dismantling a car, adding that that would be when working under a vehicle. It is not clear whether on these occasions the man was wearing goggles for fear of a splinter of metal piercing his eye or of grit or dirt falling into it. . . .

The evidence in regard to practice appears to me overwhelming. But however unlikely such an event may be in such an organized community as ours is today, it is possible that the practice, however widespread, is carried on in disregard of risks that are obvious. Let me then examine this aspect of the evidence. There was undisputed evidence that, when a piece of steel, and particularly of steel corroded with rust, is struck with a steel hammer, chips or splinters of steel may fly off. It could hardly be otherwise. But the question is what is the risk. Captain Paterson, whom I have already mentioned, deposed to having had personal knowledge of about half-a-dozen eye injuries in the course of thirty-two years' experience, the first of them having taken place some six or seven years before. . . .

On this evidence, my Lords, no other conclusion can be reached than that the respondents were not under a duty to provide goggles for their workmen engaged on this work, at least if they were two-eyed men, and the reason why they were under no such duty was because the risk was not one against which a reasonable employer was bound to take precautions. It was from this premise that the inquiry should proceed, whether, nevertheless, in the case of a one-eyed man they were bound to do so. This clearly must depend on whether it should be manifest to the reasonable employer that in the case of a one-eyed workman the possible damage in the event of accident was so much graver than in the case of a two-eyed workman that in the former case he ought to take precautions though in the latter case he need not. I see no justification for such a conclusion. A two-eyed man might, if a splinter struck him in the eye, suffer an injury which in any scale would be considered very grave. He might even suffer injury in both eyes either by immediate damage to both or by the infection of one from the other. The eye which was left to him might have perfect vision or might be defective in a degree varying from the slightest imperfection to almost total blindness. But, however grave, even calamitous, the damage that he suffered by the loss of one eye, the two-eyed man would have no remedy. The question therefore is not of a contrast between damage in the case of one man trivial and in the case of another very grave, but rather of an accident so serious in its consequence to any man, whether one-eyed or two-eyed, that, if the risk of it was appreciable, it would be the clear duty of the employer to provide and enforce the use of proper precautions against it. Yet the risk was not guarded against, for it was regarded, and rightly regarded, as a risk which could reasonably be run. . . . For these reasons I would dismiss this appeal. But as the majority of your lordships are in favour of allowing the appeal, the judgment of Lynskey, J., upon liability must be restored and it will remain for the Court of Appeal to deal with the appellant's appeal upon the quantum of damages.

LORD NORMAND. . . .

The Court of Appeal reversed the judgment for reasons which are very clearly stated by Asquith, L.J.: "The plaintiff's disability could only be relevant to the stringency of the duty owed to him if it increased the risk to which he was exposed. A one-eyed man is no more likely to get a splinter or a chip in his eye than is a two-eyed man. The risk is no greater although the damage may be to a man with only one good eye than to a man with two good eyes. But the quantum of damage is one thing and the scope of duty is another. A greater risk of injury is not the same thing as a risk of greater injury; the first alone is relevant to liability." . . .

. . . The test is what precautions would the ordinary reasonable prudent man take. The relevant considerations include all those facts which could affect the conduct of a reasonable and prudent man and his decision on the precautions to be taken. Would a reasonable and prudent man be influenced, not only by the greater or less probability of an accident occurring, but also by the gravity of the consequences if an accident does occur? In Mackintosh v. Mackintosh Lord Neaves, considering a case of alleged negligence in muir [moor]-burning, said: "It must be observed that in all cases the amount of care which a prudent man will take must vary infinitely according to circumstances. No prudent man in carrying a lighted candle through a powder magazine would fail to take more care than if he was going through a damp cellar. The amount of care will be proportionate to the degree of risk run and to the magnitude of the mischief that may be occasioned." In Northwestern Utilities Ld. v. London Guarantee and Accident Co. Ld. Lord Wright, dealing with the risk of grave damage which may be caused by gas escaping from a main, said: "The degree of care which that duty involves must be proportioned to the degree of risk involved if the duty should not be fulfilled." The learned editor of Salmond on Torts similarly says: "There are two factors in determining the magnitude of a risk — the seriousness of the injury risked, and the likelihood of the injury being in fact caused." These are, in my opinion, accurate statements both of the law and of the ordinary man's conduct in taking precautions for his own safety. "No reasonable man handles a stick of dynamite and a walking-stick in the same way." . . .

The facts on which the judge founded his conclusion, the known risk of metal flying when this sort of work was being done, the position of the workman with his eyes close to the bolt he was hammering and on the same level with it or below it, and the disastrous consequences if a particle of metal flew into his one good eye, taken in isolation, seem to me to justify his conclusion. But even for a two-eyed man the risk of losing one eye is a very grievous risk, not to speak of the foreseeable possibility that both eyes might be simultaneously destroyed, or that the loss of one eye might have as a sequel the destruction of vision in the other. It may be said that, if it is obvious that goggles should have been supplied to a one-eyed workman, it is scarcely less obvious that they should have been supplied to all the workmen, and therefore that the judgment rests on an unreal or insufficient distinction between the gravity of the risk run by a one-eyed man and the gravity of the risk run by a two-eyed man. I recognize that the argument has some force but I do not assent to it. Blindness is so great a calamity that even the loss of one of two good eyes is not comparable; and the risk of blindness from sparks of metal is greater for a one-eyed man than for a two-eyed man, for it is less likely that both eyes should be damaged than that one eye should, and the loss of one eye is not necessarily or even usually followed by blindness in the other. . . .

Notes

1. Defendants originally interposed a plea of contributory negligence, but did not pursue it. Why not?

2. What is the best evidence that failure to supply goggles to two-eyed workmen was not negligent?

3. The *Mackintosh* decision referred to in Lord Normand's opinion was decided in 1864. This is some evidence that the Hand formula was a novel formulation of old principles rather than an announcement of new principles. Also typical of the early judicial analyses of negligence is the following passage from Chicago, B. & Q. R. Co. v. Krayenbuhl, 65 Neb. 889, 903-904, 91 N.W. 880, 882-883 (1902):

> The business of life is better carried forward by the use of dangerous machinery; hence the public good demands its use, although occasionally such use results in the loss of life or limb. It does so because the danger is insignificant, when weighed against the benefits resulting from the use of such machinery, and for the same reason demands its reasonable, most effective, and unrestricted use, up to the point where the benefits resulting from such use no longer outweigh the danger to be anticipated from it. At that point the public good demands restrictions. For example, a turntable is a dangerous contrivance, which facilitates railroading; the general benefits resulting from its use outweigh the occasional injuries inflicted by it; hence the public good demands its use. We may conceive of means by which it might be rendered absolutely safe, but such means would so interfere with its beneficial use that the danger to be anticipated would not justify their adoption; therefore the public good demands its use without them. But the danger incident to its use may be lessened by the use of a lock which would prevent children, attracted to it, from moving it; the interference with the proper use of the turntable occasioned by the use of such lock is so slight that it is outweighed by the danger to be anticipated from an omission to use it; therefore the public good, we think, demands the use of the lock. The public good would not require the owner of a vacant lot on which there is a pond to fill up the pond or inclose the lot with an impassable wall to insure the safety of children resorting to it, because the burden of doing so is out of proportion to the danger to be anticipated from leaving it undone. But where there is an open well on a vacant lot, which is frequented by children, of which the owner of the lot has knowledge, he is liable for injuries, sustained by children falling into the well, because the danger to be anticipated from the open well, under the circumstances, outweighs the slight expense or inconvenience that would be entailed in making it safe.

See also F. V. Harper, A Treatise on the Law of Torts 163-165 (1933).

Nussbaum v. Lacopo
27 N.Y.2d 311, 265 N.E.2d 762 (1970)

BURKE, J.

Plaintiff's home is situate on land abutting the thirteenth hole of the defendant country club. Between plaintiff's patio and the thirteenth fairway are approximately 20 to 30 feet of rough, and located in that golfer's no man's land is a natural barrier of 45- to 60-foot-high trees. Although plaintiff's real property line runs parallel to the thirteenth fairway, the direct and proper line of flight from the tee to the green was at a substantial angle to the right of the property line and the rough. It was thus, as any golfer would know, far to the right of the plaintiff's property line and patio, and it was not a "dog leg."

Facts

On June 30, 1963, defendant Lacopo, a trespasser on the golf course, struck a ball from the thirteenth tee. At that time the rough was dense and the trees were in full foliage. The shot, a high, bad one, "hooked" and crossed over into the area of plaintiff's patio and there allegedly hit the plaintiff. Lacopo did not see plaintiff and did not shout the traditional golfer's warning: "Fore!" . . .

The admission that this was a "bad shot" is not sufficient to warrant submission to a jury. Plaintiff made no effort to show that defendant failed to use due care in striking the ball . . . for example, that defendant aimed so inaccurately as to unreasonably increase the risk of harm. . . . [W]e will not permit an inference of negligence to be drawn merely from the fact that this shot "hooked" sharply.

Golfers are notorious in the tedious preparation they give to a shot. They know that concentration is the key to the game. Yet even the best professional golfers cannot avoid an occasional "hook" or "slice." . . .

One last comment on the lack of foreseeability is necessary. The player, observing the natural barrier between the thirteenth fairway and plaintiff's property, would have less cause than the country club to assume that a golf ball could pass through or over it. The mere fact that a person may have been careless in the performance of an act does not necessarily result in actionable negligence. It is only required that the care be commensurate with the risk and danger. The plaintiff failed to show that the act of this player as to him had possibilities of danger so many and apparent as to entitle him to be protected against the doing of it. His burden of proof required that the act testified to, which he asserts constituted negligence, was not merely possible, but probable. Here, only an extraordinarily misdirected shot attaining great height could possibly drop on plaintiff's property because of the height and density of the protective barrier. Against this kind of unlikely misfortune, the law does not confer protection. Looking back from the alleged injury to the event, we consider it highly exceptional that a player's conduct would have brought about harm. . . .

Notes

1. What weight should the court have given to the fact that defendant was a trespasser on the golf course? Does this not show that B was very low? Is the court's result consistent with Wyant v. Crouse in Chapter 2?   *No*

2. Is the relevant P the probability that this plaintiff would be hit or that

someone — anyone — outside of the golf course would be hit? Compare another of Judge Hand's formulations of the negligence standard, in Conway v. O'Brien, 111 F.2d 611-612 (2d Cir. 1940), *rev'd on other grounds*, 312 U.S. 492 (1941): "The degree of care demanded of a person by an occasion is the resultant of three factors: the likelihood that his conduct will *injure others*, taken with the seriousness of the injury if it happens, and balanced against the interest which he must sacrifice to avoid the risk." (Emphasis added.)

3. Plaintiff in *Nussbaum* also sued the country club that owned the golf course. Analyze the issue of the country club's negligence in terms of the Hand formula.

4. In the celebrated English case of Bolton v. Stone, [1951] A.C. 850 (H.L.), plaintiff, who lived on a street next to a cricket ground, was struck on the head by a cricket ball while stepping from her front yard into the street. The ball was one of the longest that had ever been hit at the cricket ground, but balls had occasionally been hit into that street before — perhaps once every five years. The cricket ground was surrounded by a 12-foot-high fence (which was actually somewhat higher, because of a rise in the ground between the batting area and the street). On these facts, the House of Lords held that the defendants (the owners of the cricket ground) were not negligent. Lord Radcliffe said: "a reasonable man, taking account of the chances against an accident happening, would not have felt himself called upon either to abandon the use of the ground for cricket or to increase the height of his surrounding fences. He would have done what the appellants did: in other words, he would have done nothing." [1951] A.C. at 869.

Why is Bolton v. Stone *not* an appropriate case for strict liability in terms of the analysis in Chapter 1?

Eckert v. Long Island R. Co.
43 N.Y. 502 (1871)

a deceased person

... [Plaintiff's decedent was standing] in conversation with another person about fifty feet from the defendant's track, in East New York, as a train of cars was coming in from Jamaica, at a rate of speed estimated by the plaintiffs' witnesses of from twelve to twenty miles per hour. The plaintiff's witnesses heard no signal either from the whistle or the bell upon the engine. The engine was constructed to run either way without turning, and it was then running backward with the cow-catcher next the train it was drawing, and nothing in front to remove obstacles from the track. The claim of the plaintiff was that the evidence authorized the jury to find that the speed of the train was improper and negligent in that particular place, it being a thickly populated neighborhood, and one of the stations of the road.

The evidence on the part of the plaintiff, also showed, that a child three or four years old, was sitting or standing upon the track of the defendant's road as the train of cars was approaching, and was liable to be run over, if not removed; and the deceased seeing the danger of the child, ran to it, and seizing it, threw it clear of the track on the side opposite to that from which he came; but continuing across the track himself, was struck by the step or some part of the locomotive or tender, thrown down, and received injuries from which he died the same night. . . .

GROVER, J. The important question in this case arises upon the exception taken by the defendant's counsel to the denial of his motion for a nonsuit, made upon the ground that the negligence of the plaintiff's intestate contributed to the injury that caused his death. The evidence showed that the train was approaching in plain view of the deceased, and had he for his own purposes attempted to cross the track, or with a view to save property placed himself voluntarily in a position where he might have received an injury from a collision with the train, his conduct would have been grossly negligent, and no recovery could have been had for such injury. But the evidence further showed that there was a small child upon the track, who, if not rescued, must have been inevitably crushed by the rapidly approaching train. This the deceased saw, and he owed a duty of important obligation to this child to rescue it from its extreme peril, if he could do so without incurring great danger to himself. Negligence implies some act of commission or omission wrongful in itself. Under the circumstances in which the deceased was placed, it was not wrongful in him to make every effort in his power to rescue the child, compatible with a reasonable regard for his own safety. It was his duty to exercise his judgment as to whether he could probably save the child without serious injury to himself. If, from the appearances, he believed that he could, it was not negligence to make an attempt so to do, although believing that possibly he might fail and receive an injury himself. He had no time for deliberation. He must act instantly, if at all, as a moment's delay would have been fatal to the child. The law has so high a regard for human life that it will not impute negligence to an effort to preserve it, unless made under such circumstances as to constitute rashness in the judgment of prudent persons. For a person engaged in his ordinary affairs, or in the mere protection of property, knowingly and voluntarily to place himself in a position where he is liable to receive a serious injury, is negligence, which will preclude a recovery for an injury so received; but when the exposure is for the purpose of saving life, it is not wrongful, and therefore not negligent unless such as to be regarded as either rash or reckless. The jury were warranted in finding the deceased free from negligence under the rule as above stated. The motion for a nonsuit was, therefore, properly denied. . . .

Notes

1. How does one analyze the conduct of plaintiff's decedent in Hand formula terms? What is B? P? L?

2. Suppose Eckert had known he would be killed, but decided to sacrifice himself for the child. Would he be contributorily negligent as a matter of

[handwritten: only if this approaches 100%.]

[handwritten: yes]

law? Does it depend on the probability of his being able to save the child? Or *[handwritten: to save child.]* does it depend on his relationship to the child? *[handwritten: Parent might have duty]*

3. It is in the best interests of the railroad, in the long run, that it be held liable for the damages incurred by prudent rescuers of potential victims of the railroad's negligence. Why?

4. Is it always contributorily negligent to risk life to save property? In Liming v. Illinois Cent. R. Co., 81 Iowa 246, 47 N.W. 66 (1890), plaintiff was injured attempting to rescue a neighbor's horses from a burning barn. The court held that it was a jury question whether he was contributorily negligent in running such a risk.

5. The *Eckert* case is analyzed in Terry, Negligence, 29 Harv. L. Rev. 40, 43-44 (1915) — an article that anticipated the modern economic analysis of negligence — as follows:

> The question was of course whether he [Eckert] had exposed himself to an unreasonably great risk. Here the ... elements of reasonableness were as follows:
>
> (1) The magnitude of the risk was the probability that he would be killed or hurt. That was very great.
>
> (2) The principal object was his own life, which was very valuable.
>
> (3) The collateral object was the child's life, which was also very valuable.
>
> (4) The utility of the risk was the probability that he could save the child. That must have been fairly great, since he in fact succeeded. Had there been no fair chance of saving the child, the conduct would have been unreasonable and negligent.
>
> (5) The necessity of the risk was the probability that the child would not have saved himself by getting off of the track in time.
>
> Here, although the magnitude of the risk was very great and the principal object very valuable, yet the value of the collateral object and the great utility and necessity of the risk counterbalanced those considerations, and made the risk reasonable. The same risk would have been unreasonable, had the creature on the track been a kitten, because the value of the collateral object would have been small.

6. With the Hand formula and Terry's discussion, compare the discussion of the negligence standard in Second Restatement of Torts §298, Comment *b*:

> As in all cases where the reasonable character of the actor's conduct is in question, its utility is to be weighed against the magnitude of the risk which it involves. The amount of attention and caution required varies with the magnitude of the harm likely to be done if care is not exercised, and with the utility of the act. Therefore, if the act has little or no social value and is likely to cause any serious harm, it is reasonable to require close attention and caution. So too, if the act involves a risk of death or serious bodily harm, and particularly if it is capable of causing such results to a number of persons, the highest attention and caution are required even if the act has a very considerable utility. Thus those who deal with firearms, explosives, poisonous drugs, or high tension

electricity are required to exercise the closest attention and the most careful precautions, not only in preparing for their use but in using them. Likewise, a driver approaching a railway crossing is required, for the protection of his passengers, to take precautions to ascertain whether a train is approaching, which would be unduly burdensome at any point where the only danger lay in the possibility of a trivial mishap.

Togstad v. Vesely, Otto, Miller & Keefe
291 N.W.2d 686 (Minn. 1980)

[In this action for legal malpractice, the jury awarded John Togstad and his wife damages of $649,500. Defendants, attorney Jerre Miller and the other members of his law firm, appealed. The case arose out of medical treatment of Mr. Togstad for an aneurism in an artery in his neck. Dr. Paul Blake surgically implanted a Selverstone clamp in Togstad's neck in order gradually to close the artery and thereby relieve pressure on the aneurism. Shortly after the operation a nurse observed that Togstad was unable to speak or move. The nurse called a physician, who did not adjust the clamp. By the time Dr. Blake arrived and opened the clamp, Togstad had suffered severe and permanent brain damage, leading to paralysis and loss of speech.]

PER CURIAM. . . .

About 14 months after her husband's hospitalization began, plaintiff Joan Togstad met with attorney Jerre Miller regarding her husband's condition. Neither she nor her husband was personally acquainted with Miller or his law firm prior to that time. John Togstad's former work supervisor, Ted Bucholz, made the appointment and accompanied Mrs. Togstad to Miller's office. . . .

Mrs. Togstad had become suspicious of the circumstances surrounding her husband's tragic condition due to the conduct and statements of the hospital nurses shortly after the paralysis occurred. One nurse told Mrs. Togstad that she had checked Mr. Togstad at 2 A.M. and he was fine; that when she returned at 3 A.M., by mistake, to give him someone else's medication, he was unable to move or speak; and that if she hadn't accidentally entered the room no one would have discovered his condition until morning. Mrs. Togstad also noticed that the other nurses were upset and crying, and that Mr. Togstad's condition was a topic of conversation.

Mrs. Togstad testified that she told Miller "everything that happened at the hospital," including the nurses' statements and conduct which had raised a question in her mind. She stated that she "believed" she had told Miller "about the procedure and what was undertaken, what was done, and what happened." She brought no records with her. Miller took notes and asked questions during the meeting, which lasted 45 minutes to an hour. At its conclusion, according to Mrs. Togstad, Miller said that "he did not think we had a legal case, however, he was going to discuss this with his partner." She understood that if Miller changed his mind after talking to his partner, he would call her. Mrs. Togstad "gave it" a few days and, since she did not hear from Miller, decided "that they had come to the conclusion that there wasn't a case." No fee arrangements were discussed, no medical authorizations were requested, nor was Mrs. Togstad billed for the interview.

Mrs. Togstad denied that Miller had told her his firm did not have expertise in the medical malpractice field, urged her to see another attorney, or related to her that the statute of limitations for medical malpractice actions was two years. She did not consult another attorney until one year after she talked to Miller. Mrs. Togstad indicated that she did not confer with another attorney earlier because of her reliance on Miller's "legal advice" that they "did not have a case." . . .

Kenneth Green, a Minneapolis attorney, was called as an expert by plaintiffs. He stated that in rendering legal advice regarding a claim of medical malpractice, the "minimum" an attorney should do would be to request medical authorizations from the client, review the hospital records, and consult with an expert in the field. John McNulty, a Minneapolis attorney, and Charles Hvass testified as experts on behalf of the defendants. McNulty stated that when an attorney is consulted as to whether he will take a case, the lawyer's only responsibility in refusing it is to so inform the party. He testified, however, that when a lawyer is asked his legal opinion on the merits of a medical malpractice claim, community standards require that the attorney check hospital records and consult with an expert before rendering his opinion.

. . . Hvass testified that:

> . . . when a person comes in to me about a medical malpractice action, based upon what the individual has told me, I have to make a decision as to whether or not there probably is or probably is not, based upon that information, medical malpractice. And if, in my judgment, based upon what the client has told me, there is not medical malpractice, I will so inform the client.

Hvass stated, however, that he would never render a "categorical" opinion. In addition, Hvass acknowledged that if he were consulted for a "legal opinion" regarding medical malpractice and 14 months had expired since the incident in question, "ordinary care and diligence" would require him to inform the party of the two-year statute of limitations applicable to that type of action.

This case was submitted to the jury by way of a special verdict form. The jury found that Dr. Blake and the hospital were negligent and that Dr. Blake's negligence (but not the hospital's) was a direct cause of the injuries sustained by John Togstad; that there was an attorney-client contractual relationship between Mrs. Togstad and Miller; that Miller was negligent in rendering advice regarding the possible claims of Mr. and Mrs. Togstad; that, but for Miller's negligence, plaintiffs would have been successful in the prosecution of a legal action against Dr. Blake; and that neither Mr. nor Mrs. Togstad was negligent in pursuing their claims against Dr. Blake. . . .

In a legal malpractice action of the type involved here, four elements must be shown: (1) that an attorney-client relationship existed; (2) that defendant acted negligently or in breach of contract; (3) that such acts were the proximate cause of the plaintiffs' damages; (4) that but for defendant's conduct the plaintiffs would have been successful in the prosecution of their medical malpractice claim.

This court first dealt with the element of lawyer-client relationship in the decision of Ryan v. Long, 35 Minn. 394, 29 N.W. 51 (1886). The *Ryan* case involved a claim of legal malpractice and on appeal it was argued that no attorney-client relation existed. This court, without stating whether its conclusion was based on contract principles or a tort theory, disagreed: "[I]t sufficiently appears that plaintiff, for himself, called upon defendant, as an attorney at law, for 'legal advice,' and that defendant assumed to give him a professional opinion in reference to the matter as to which plaintiff consulted him. Upon this state of facts the defendant must be taken to have acted as plaintiff's legal adviser, at plaintiff's request, and so as to establish between them the relation of attorney and client. . . ."

We believe it is unnecessary to decide whether a tort or contract theory is preferable for resolving the attorney-client relationship question raised by this appeal. The tort and contract analyses are very similar in a case such as the instant one,[4] and we conclude that under either theory the evidence shows that a lawyer-client relationship is present here. The thrust of Mrs. Togstad's testimony is that she went to Miller for legal advice, and was told there wasn't a case, and relied upon this advice in failing to pursue the claim for medical malpractice. In addition, according to Mrs. Togstad, Miller did not qualify his legal opinion by urging her to seek advice from another attorney, nor did Miller inform her that he lacked expertise in the medical malpractice area. Assuming this testimony is true, as this court must do, we believe a jury could properly find that Mrs. Togstad sought and received legal advice from Miller under circumstances which made it reasonably foreseeable to Miller that Mrs. Togstad would be injured if the advice were negligently given. Thus, under either a tort or contract analysis, there is sufficient evidence in the record to support the existence of an attorney-client relationship.

4. Under a negligence approach it must essentially be shown that defendant rendered legal advice (not necessarily at someone's request) under circumstances which made it reasonably foreseeable to the attorney that if such advice was rendered negligently, the individual receiving the advice might be injured thereby. Or, stated another way, under a tort theory, "[a]n attorney-client relationship is created whenever an individual seeks and receives legal advice from an attorney in circumstances in which a reasonable person would rely on such advice." A contract analysis requires the rendering of legal advice pursuant to another's request and the reliance factor, in this case, where the advice was not paid for, need be shown in the form of promissory estoppel.

Defendants argue that even if an attorney-client relationship was established the evidence fails to show that Miller acted negligently in assessing the merits of the Togstads' case. They appear to contend that, at most, Miller was guilty of an error in judgment which does not give rise to legal malpractice. However, this case does not involve a mere error of judgment. The gist of plaintiffs' claim is that Miller failed to perform the minimal research that an ordinarily prudent attorney would do before rendering legal advice in a case of this nature. The record, through the testimony of Kenneth Green and John McNulty, contains sufficient evidence to support plaintiffs' position.

In a related contention, defendants assert that a new trial should be awarded on the ground that the trial court erred by refusing to instruct the jury that Miller's failure to inform Mrs. Togstad of the two-year statute of limitations for medical malpractice could not constitute negligence. . . .

The defect in defendants' reasoning is that there is adequate evidence supporting the claim that Miller was also negligent in failing to advise Mrs. Togstad of the two-year medical malpractice limitations period and thus the trial court acted properly in refusing to instruct the jury in the manner urged by defendants. . . .

There is also sufficient evidence in the record establishing that, but for Miller's negligence, plaintiffs would have been successful in prosecuting their medical malpractice claim. Dr. Woods, in no uncertain terms, concluded that Mr. Togstad's injuries were caused by the medical malpractice of Dr. Blake. Defendants' expert testimony to the contrary was obviously not believed by the jury. Thus, the jury reasonably found that had plaintiff's medical malpractice action been properly brought, plaintiffs would have recovered.

Based on the foregoing, we hold that the jury's findings are adequately supported by the record. Accordingly we uphold the trial court's denial of defendants' motion for judgment notwithstanding the jury verdict.

Defendants next argue that they are entitled to a new trial . . . because the $39,000 in damages awarded to Mrs. Togstad for loss of consortium is excessive. In support of this claim defendants refer to the fact that Mr. and Mrs. Togstad were divorced in July 1974 (the dissolution proceeding was commenced in February 1974), and assert that there is "virtually no evidence of the extent of Mrs. Togstad's loss of consortium." . . .

"Consortium" includes rights inherent in the marital relationship, such as comfort, companionship, and most importantly, sexual relationship. Here, the evidence shows that Mr. Togstad became impotent due to the tragic incident which occurred in August 1971. Consequently, Mrs. Togstad was unable to have sexual intercourse with her husband subsequent to that time. The evidence further indicates that the injuries sustained by Mr. Togstad precipitated a dissolution of the marriage. We therefore conclude that the jury's damage award to Mrs. Togstad finds sufficient support in the record. . . .

Affirmed.

Notes

liability, not negligent [handwritten]

1. Suppose the probability that the Togstads would have won a medical malpractice suit if brought before the statute of limitations expired had been low. Would this be relevant to damages or liability in the legal malpractice action? If the latter, to what element in the Hand formula? *P* [handwritten]

No [handwritten]

2. Suppose Miller had simply advised Mrs. Togstad at the outset that his firm did not handle medical malpractice actions; would there have been any basis for a malpractice action against him? Or suppose Mrs. Togstad had met Miller at a party, described the case, and asked him what he thought; and suppose he had told her that he didn't think she had a case. Would he be *No* [handwritten] guilty of malpractice? Return to this question after reading Chapter 6 of this book.

3. Was Mrs. Togstad contributorily negligent? If so, should this bar her *[handwritten: & asked]* husband's action as well as her own? *Yes. she should have called Miller* [handwritten] *If she had a case* [handwritten]

4. Loss of consortium is an important damage item in tort cases. Can you *cost of substitute* [handwritten] think of a way of quantifying such loss objectively?

5. In an omitted part of its opinion, the court refused to deduct the contingent fee that the Togstads would have had to pay a lawyer to bring a medical malpractice suit. Why?

6. For an up-to-date discussion of the practical aspects of legal-malpractice litigation see D. Meiselman, Attorney Malpractice: Law and Procedure (1980).

Quantifying the Hand Formula

The Hand formula is mathematical in form. A person is negligent if B is less than PL. Yet the author of this casebook has found no case where the court attached numbers to each of the three terms in the formula. Sometimes numbers are attached to one of the terms — recall the discussion of the frequency of accidents in the goggle case. And in Hendricks v. Peabody Coal Co., 115 Ill. App. 2d 35, 253 N.E.2d 56 (1969), a case involving alleged negligence in failing to prevent the use of a dangerous water hole by children known to frequent it, the court stated: "The entire body of water could have been closed off with a steel fence for between $12,000 and $14,000. This cost was slight compared to the risk to the children involved." Id. at 45, 253 N.E.2d at 61. Plaintiff, who had broken his neck and as a result had become a quadriplegic, was awarded $200,000 in damages.

Sometimes the probability of an accident can be inferred from past experience. For example, in William Laurie Co. v. McCullough, 174 Ind. 477, 90 N.E. 1014 (1910), a case involving a slip and fall allegedly caused by an oily substance with which defendant store coated its floor (a portion of the opinion is printed later in this chapter), the court stated:

Appellant also had a right to introduce evidence showing the . . . fact, if true, that no prior accidents had occurred from such use. If hundreds or thousands of people had used this floor under similar conditions, in safety and without accident through a term of years, such fact should have some weight as tending to prove that the floor was not unusually dangerous, and that appellant was not lacking in diligence in failing to anticipate and provide against some such accident. . . .

Id. at 487, 90 N.E.2d at 1018. Can the Hand formula yield correct economic results if it is not quantified?

The recent troubles of the Ford Motor Company over the Pinto fuel tank throw a fascinating sidelight on this question. A number of tort actions have been brought against Ford for death or injury resulting from the explosion of the Pinto's fuel tank in low-velocity collisions. (Most of these cases have been decided not under the negligence standard but under principles of strict liability, which most courts today use to decide liability for personal injury caused by defective products. However, the issue whether a product is defective is, as we shall see in Chapter 9, similar to the issue whether conduct is negligent.) Ford had conducted a number of cost-benefit analyses of whether to strengthen the fuel tank. One of these is summarized in the following table:

Benefits $= PL$

Savings —180 burn deaths, 180 serious burn injuries, 2,100 burned vehicles.

Unit Cost —$200,000 per death, $67,000 per injury, $700 per vehicle.

Total Benefit —180 × ($200,000) + 180 × ($67,000) + 2100 × ($700) = $49.5 million.

Costs $= B$

Sales —11 million cars, 1.5 million light trucks.

Unit Cost —$11 per car, $11 per truck.

Total Cost —11,000,000 × ($11) + 1,500,000 × ($11) = $137 million.

(As an exercise, calculate P and do the negligence analysis in strict Hand formula terms.)

Ford's cost-benefit analyses figured prominently in two of the best-known Pinto cases. One was a criminal prosecution of Ford for manslaughter in an Indiana court arising out of a fatal accident to an Indiana resident caused by the rupture of a Pinto fuel tank. The other was a tort action in California where Ford was accused of intentional and willful disregard of safety. Ford was acquitted in the criminal case, but the jury in the tort case awarded the plaintiffs $125 million in punitive damages on top of slightly more than $3.5 million in compensatory damages, for a total of about $128 million; the judge later scaled back the punitive-damage award to $3.5 mil-

lion. So amended, the judgment was affirmed on appeal. Grimshaw v. Ford
Motor Co., 174 Cal. Rptr. 348 (Ct. App. 1981). In both cases, the fact that
Ford had made a deliberate judgment to trade off human safety for cost
savings was used to argue that Ford was an intentional wrongdoer. Was Ford's
conduct intentionally tortious in light of the analysis in Part I of this book?

Ford denied that it had based its decision not to strengthen the fuel tank
on cost-benefit analysis. It claimed that it had been required by the National
Highway Traffic Safety Administration to make the analysis and that the
Administration had supplied it with the figure of $200,000 for the value of a
life and the other damage estimates used in the analysis.

Suppose that if Ford had designed the Pinto properly in the first place it
could have shielded the fuel tank at no extra cost simply by placing the tank
farther forward in the chassis. Would the $10 cost of strengthening the fuel
tank in its actual location then be relevant in applying the Hand formula?
What if the consuming public believed that the Pinto's fuel tank was as safe
as that of other automobiles of its size and price?

For discussions of the Pinto problem, see Ford Ignored Pinto Fire Peril,
Secret Memos Show, Chi. Trib., Oct. 13, 1979, p. 1; Harris, Why the Pinto
Jury Felt Ford Deserved $125 Million Penalty, Wall St. J., Feb. 14, 1978, p. 1;
Epstein, Is Pinto a Criminal?, Regulation, Mar/Apr 1980, p. 15.

G. E. White, Tort Law in America: An Intellectual History
219-221 (1980)

The thrust of recent torts scholarship emphasizing economic theory is
seemingly to return tort law to a deregulated, nondistributional state whose
doctrines are intended to harmonize with and to facilitate private interactions. Richard Posner, for example, has argued that the essential purpose of
late nineteenth-century negligence theory was "to maximize the joint value
of . . . interfering activities," and that, through its use of contributory negligence as an absolute defense, it achieved that purpose rather well. The
prospect of a negligence suit, Posner maintains, created incentives on the part
of enterprises to make their activities safer, up to the point where the cost of
safety did not exceed the cost of satisfying tort claims. Similarly, the defense
of contributory negligence created incentives for enterprises to avoid damage
to their activities, up to the point where the cost of avoidance exceeded the
cost of damage. Thus the activity of enterprise tended to be safer, freer from
damage, and consequently worth more. The "dominant function" of negligence was "to generate rules of liability that [would] bring about . . . the
efficient . . . level of accidents and safety." . . .

Posner's approach is a good example of the subversive effects of neocon-
ceptualist theoretical approaches on traditional doctrinal analysis in tort law.

Under Posner's formulation the only prerequisites for effecting theorizing are acceptance of Posner's assumption that efficiency is an important social value, a rule of tort law that a finding of negligence on the part of an injuring party shifts the costs of his victim's injuries to him, and a rule of tort law that a finding of contributory negligence on the part of the injured party prevents this shift from taking place. With those prerequisites established, Posner can avoid all other doctrinal complexities: the status of the injurer and the injured party, the "duties" imposed on one or another by tort law, questions of "legal" causation, questions of immunity, and so on. The theory is marvelously simple and seemingly cuts through the obscurities of doctrinal analysis.

But for Posner's theory to serve as a standard for assessing tortious conduct the majority of people involved with the tort system have to act as Posner's theory assumes they will. That is, they have to be aware that investments in safety will rebound to their legal advantage and accordingly respond to negligence rules by increasing their investments in safety. They have to make "rational" analyses of the costs of preventing accidents and the costs of injuring or being injured. And they have to be inclined, in the aggregate, to prefer "efficient" interferences to inefficient ones. But while some enterprises are drawn into the system of tort law with sufficient frequency so that they have some realistic basis upon which to weigh the costs of preventing accidents they cause against the costs of paying tort claims, Posner himself concedes that safety advances in industries do not primarily come in response to the rules of tort law.

Moreover, there are numerous tort litigants with no familiarity with negligence or its rules, no consciousness of accident prevention, and perhaps not even any interest in "utility maximization." It seems quixotic to think of such persons as rational planners, weighing the costs of being injured and barred from recovery in a negligence action against the costs of accident prevention. A characteristic of tort law since at least the late nineteenth century has been that its cases involve random interactions between strangers rather than planned interactions between persons with exchange mechanisms. The suggestiveness of Posner's theory is counterbalanced by its highly questionable starting assumptions.

Note

In order to accept the economic approach to negligence, must we accept the proposition that people act rationally in relation to questions of safety? Perhaps one can argue the following alternative:

> Because we do not like to see resources squandered, a judgment of negligence has inescapable overtones of moral disapproval, for it implies that there was a cheaper alternative to the accident. Conversely, there is no moral indignation in the case in which the cost of prevention would have exceeded the cost of

the accident. Where the measures necessary to avert the accident would have consumed excessive resources, there is no occasion to condemn the defendant for not having taken them.

If indignation has its roots in inefficiency, we do not have to decide whether regulation, or compensation, or retribution, or some mixture of these best describes the dominant purpose of negligence law. In any case, the judgment of liability depends ultimately on a weighing of costs and benefits.

Posner, A Theory of Negligence, 1 J. Legal Stud. 29, 33-34 (1972).

Vaughan v. Menlove *Emergence of objective standard of reasonableness*
3 Bing. (N.C.) 468, 132 Eng. Rep. 490 (Com. Pl. 1837).

a stack of hay

. . . At the trial it appeared that the rick in question had been made by the Defendant near the boundary of his own premises; that the hay was in such a state when put together, as to give rise to discussions on the probability of fire: that though there were conflicting opinions on the subject, yet during a period of five weeks, the Defendant was repeatedly warned of his peril; that his stock was insured; and that upon one occasion, being advised to take the rick down to avoid all danger, he said "he would chance it." He made an aperture or chimney through the rick; but in spite, or perhaps in consequence of this precaution, the rick at length burst into flames from the spontaneous heating of its materials; the flames communicated to the Defendant's barn and stables, and thence to the Plaintiff's cottages, which were entirely destroyed. . . .

A verdict having been found for the Plaintiff, a rule nisi for a new trial was obtained on the ground that the jury should have been directed to consider, not, whether the Defendant had been guilty of gross negligence with reference to the standard of ordinary prudence, a standard too uncertain to afford any criterion; but whether he had acted bona fide to the best of his judgment; if he had, he ought not to be responsible for the misfortune of not possessing the highest order of intelligence. . . .

TINDAL C.J. . . . It is contended . . . that the question of negligence was so mixed up with reference to what would be the conduct of a man of ordinary prudence that the jury might have thought the latter the rule by which they were to decide; that such a rule would be too uncertain to act upon; and that the question ought to have been whether the Defendant had acted honestly and bona fide to the best of his own judgment. That, however, would leave so vague a line as to afford no rule at all, the degree of judgment belonging to each individual being infinitely various. . . .

Instead, therefore, of saying that the liability for negligence should be co-extensive with the judgment of each individual, which would be as variable as the length of the foot of each individual, we ought rather to adhere to the

rule which requires in all cases a regard to caution such as a man of ordinary
prudence would observe. That was in substance the criterion presented to the
jury in this case, and therefore the present rule must be discharged. . . .

risk is much greater than cost of avoiding it. B << PL

Notes

1. What is "gross" negligence? Why did plaintiff allege it? How would
you define it in terms of the Hand formula? The "degrees of negligence"
(slight, ordinary, and gross) are relevant principally to plaintiff's rather than
defendant's conduct, and are accordingly reserved for the next chapter.

2. What is the best evidence that defendant was not actually too dumb
to comply with the normal adult standard of care? *bought insurance*

3. Should plaintiff have been awarded punitive damages in this case?
Yess

Fredericks v. Castora
241 Pa. Super. 211, 360 A.2d 696 (1976)

PER CURIAM:

[Plaintiff was injured in an accident in which two trucks and another
vehicle were involved (although it was disputed whether one of the trucks
actually struck the other vehicles). Among the defendants were the two truck
drivers and their employers. These defendants obtained a favorable verdict
from the jury. On appeal, plaintiff argued that the two drivers] should be held
to a higher standard of care than is usually applied to the operator of a motor
vehicle in evaluating both their negligence and the defense of sudden emergency as charged by the trial judge. In support of this position, reference is
made to the evidence that both defendants were professionals who drove
trucks for a living and had done so for over 20 years. . . .

. . . A requirement that experienced truck drivers be subject to a higher
standard of care does not impress us as being a useful concept to infuse into
the law of vehicle negligence. An understanding of the ordinary standard of
due care applicable to the average motorist under the multitude of changing
circumstances likely to confront today's driver is already difficult to grasp and
apply justly. To begin to vary the standard according to the driver's experience would render the application of any reasonably uniform standard
impossible. . . .

The Reasonable-Man Standard

Vaughan and *Fredericks* illustrate the proposition that the standard of
care in negligence cases is defined with reference to the average, not the

atypical, individual. In terms of the Hand formula, the trier of fact is interested in the B (burden of precautions) not of the particular defendant, but of the average individual. (Does this mean that one-half the community is negligent?) Notice that in both cases the court justified this result by reference to the difficulty of determining departures from average accident-avoidance capabilities — in other words, the administrative costs of determining negligence on an individual rather than average basis. Holmes, in what remains the classic discussion of the issue, emphasized a different reason:

> When men live in society, a certain average of conduct, a sacrifice of individual peculiarities going beyond a certain point, is necessary to the general welfare. If, for instance, a man is born hasty and awkward, is always having accidents and hurting himself or his neighbors, no doubt his congenital defects will be allowed for in the courts of Heaven, but his slips are no less troublesome to his neighbors than if they sprang from guilty neglect. His neighbors accordingly require him, at his proper peril, to come up to their standard, and the courts which they establish decline to take his personal equation into account.
>
> The rule that the law does, in general, determine liability by blameworthiness, is subject to the limitation that minute differences of character are not allowed for. The law considers, in other words, what would be blameworthy in the average man, the man of ordinary intelligence and prudence, and determines liability by that. If we fall below the level in those gifts, it is our misfortune; so much as that we must have at our peril, for the reasons just given. But he who is intelligent and prudent does not act at his peril, in theory of law.

O. W. Holmes, Jr., The Common Law 108 (1881).

The repeated reference to acting at one's peril recalls, does it not, that "unmoral" standard — strict liability — of which Ames spoke. If the slips of our neighbors are no less troublesome to us if they spring from innocent rather than guilty neglect, why isn't this an argument for strict liability in general? What does it mean to say that the neighbors require the hasty and awkward man "to come up to their standard"? By definition, he cannot; if he can, but simply fails to do so, that is a clear case of negligence under an individual, as distinct from average, negligence standard. Suppose, for example, that B (for the average person) is $10, P is one percent, and L is $2,000. Then, even though Joe Klutz is hasty and awkward, and his B is $25, nevertheless he will be liable if he is in an accident (because $10 is less than $20). Will he therefore avoid the accident? He will not: the expected cost to him of care, $25, is greater than the expected cost of being made to pay a damages judgment, $20 (.01 times $2,000).

Even more troublesome, one might think, would be the case (not discussed by Holmes, but illustrated by the *Fredericks* case) where the defendant has a greater ability to avoid an accident than the average person but is excused from liability because the average person could not have avoided the accident. In the previous example, B for the average person might be $25, but for the particular defendant only $10. Here, it would seem, the defendant is clearly blameworthy. But he is excused from liability while the defendant disabled by "congenital defects" from avoiding an accident is held liable. What sense does this pattern make?

Economics may help you to answer this question. If the costs of applying a negligence standard on an individual basis were zero (or very low), such a standard would indeed be preferable to an average standard. It would avoid the situation (of the above-average defendant) where an accident that could have been prevented at a lower cost than the expected accident cost is not prevented. It would also avoid converting negligence into strict liability for injurers having below-average ability to avoid accidents. To be sure, the second point is not an objection to the reasonable-man rule if strict liability is always a superior liability principle to negligence. However, as we shall see in Chapter 7, it is not; and if an economically correct decision to subject some area of conduct to a negligence rather than a strict liability standard has been made, then to introduce strict liability by the back door — by applying the reasonable-man standard to people of below-average ability to avoid accidents — is inefficient.

Unfortunately, the costs of applying a negligence standard on an individual rather than average basis are not zero or trivial, but substantial. Apart from the difficulty of measuring departures from the average, there are disincentive effects — a type of cost — that a rule of individualized assessment would create. The incentives of people to improve their safety skills would be reduced, because any improvement would increase their legal duty of care. That is, the private cost of being hasty and awkward would be less if one's hastiness excused one from liability for accidents for which the normal individual would be held liable. Perhaps, in the long run, forcing the hasty and awkward to "act at their peril" really will bring them up to the standard, as Holmes suggested. Furthermore, the fact that a person may not have good reflexes or good eyesight or hearing, or may be clumsy, does not really show that he is incapable at reasonable cost of adhering to the average standard of care. There may be inexpensive methods of correcting or offsetting his deficiency — driving a little more slowly, leaving more space between his car and the car in front, wearing eyeglasses, taking the advice of the better-informed, etc.

These points are variants of the underlying point, which is that the costs of administering an individualized negligence standard may exceed those of the average standard by a great enough margin to offset the benefits of the individualized standard, discussed earlier. To administer an individualized standard sensibly, the trier of fact would have to know a great deal about the technology of safety in order to be confident that a particular deficiency really was irremediable (so that holding the defendant to the normal standard would not lead him to increase his level of safety) or that making a person of above-average safety skills liable for an accident that a person of normal skills could not have avoided would not discourage people from acquiring such skills. One can understand why the courts shy away from such inquiries.

But this analysis also implies, does it not, that where the costs of recognizing an exception to the average standard of care are small, the courts will recognize that exception in order to avoid the inefficient effects of the average standard when applied to the below- or above-average individual. Holmes said:

> When a man has a distinct defect of such a nature that all can recognize it as making certain precautions impossible, he will not be held answerable for not taking them. A blind man is not required to see at his peril; and although he is, no doubt, bound to consider his infirmity in regulating his actions, yet if he properly finds himself in a certain situation, the neglect of precautions requiring eyesight would not prevent his recovering for an injury to himself, and, it may be presumed, would not make him liable for injuring another.

O. W. Holmes, Jr., The Common Law 109 (1881). It is unlikely, to say the least, that someone would neglect measures to prevent or cure blindness merely because the blind are held to a lesser standard of care in tort cases than the sighted; so there is not the kind of disincentive effect we noted earlier. Also, it is much easier (cheaper) to determine whether a person is blind than to determine whether he is below average in intelligence, judgment, or even reflexes. Therefore, another cost of recognizing an exception to the average-person standard is absent — or, rather, attenuated, for there are, of course, borderline cases of blindness. It is true that blind people can and do adopt a variety of precautions to reduce the risk of causing or receiving injury. But these are effective only up to a point: a blind person cannot at reasonable cost become as safe a pedestrian as a sighted person. All of these reasons argue strongly for recognizing a separate standard of care for the blind, and the law does this. See, e.g., Argo v. Goodstein, 438 Pa. 468, 265 A.2d 783 (1970).

What about the professional truck driver in *Fredericks*? Do the same considerations that argue for recognizing a special exception for the blind argue for recognizing a special exception in the opposite direction for the professional driver? In a medical malpractice case, obviously, the standard of care is that of the average physician (or perhaps the average specialist in the relevant area of treatment), not that of the average man in the community, who is not a doctor. Why isn't the same approach used in the case of professional drivers?

Compare Second Restatement of Torts, §298, Comment *d:*

> *d. Necessity that actor employ competence available.* The actor must utilize with reasonable attention and caution not only those qualities and facilities which as a reasonable man he is required to have, but also those superior qualities and facilities which he himself has. Thus a superior vision may enable the actor, if he pays reasonable attention, to perceive dangers which a man possessing only normal vision would not perceive, or his supernormal physical strength may enable him to avoid dangers which a man of normal strength could not avoid.

Is this consistent with *Fredericks?*

Objective standard of Negligence [handwritten]

Goss v. Allen
70 N.J. 442, 360 A.2d 388 (1976)

On February 21, 1972, plaintiff, an experienced skier, was serving as a first aid advisor on the ski patrol at the Mad River Glen ski resort in Vermont. The facility includes a beginners' slope which near its end makes an abrupt left turn. The accident occurred some 60 feet beyond the end of the slope in a flat area where plaintiff and a friend happened to be standing taking pictures. Plaintiff had been working in the first aid room which is adjacent to the area where plaintiff and her friend were standing.

Defendant, then 17 years of age, was a beginning skier who had limited cross-country skiing experience but had never attempted a downhill run. Nor had he ever been to Mad River Glen before. Upon arrival, defendant was sent to the beginners' slope. However, instead of riding the mechanical T-bar lift to the top, defendant confined his first run to the lower portion of the slope. He walked a quarter of the way up the hill and started to ski down, successfully completing the comparatively short run of 30 feet or so until he came to the abrupt left turn. In attempting to negotiate the turn, defendant lost control over his momentum and direction. He saw the two girls ahead of him but because of the short distance remaining, his efforts to regain control and his lack of experience, he did not call out until he was almost upon the girls. Plaintiff attempted to get out of the way but was unable to do so and was struck and knocked down by defendant. . . .

The trial court charged the jury that the standard of care applicable in the case was not the same degree of care required of an adult, but rather that degree of care which a reasonably prudent person of that age (defendant was 17 years of age) would have exercised under the same or similar circumstances. Following a side bar conference, the court supplemented its charge with the following:

> All right. Perhaps I didn't charge as clearly as I had charged with reference to the duty of a 17 year old. I know that I used the term 17-year-old beginner, and that may lead to some confusion. Let me try to straighten it out. The law imposes on a 17 year old that standard of care that a 17 year old with the experience and background that this 17 year old had. It does not impose any higher or any lower degree of care than can reasonably be expected of a 17 year old with respect to the experience and background that Mr. Allen had in this case.

There was no exception taken to the charge. As heretofore noted, the jury in answer to an interrogatory submitted to it found the defendant not negligent.

criteria for objective stand'
• hazardous to others
, what age?

procedure

Plaintiff appealed solely on the ground that the jury verdict was against the weight of the evidence. The Appellate Division, however, sua sponte, raised the issue of plain error in the court's charge on the applicable standard of care. Following briefing of the issue and oral argument thereon, the Appellate Division reversed and remanded for a new trial finding plain error in the charge. In essence, the Appellate Division held that skiing was an adult activity and that where a child engages in an activity which is normally undertaken by adults, such as skiing, he should be held to the standard of adult skill, knowledge and competence, without allowance for his immaturity. The Appellate Division added that had an adult standard of care been imposed, as it should have been, the jury might well have found defendant negligent.

The Appellate Division determination that defendant, in the circumstances presented, should be held to the standard of care required of an adult was premised on its conclusion that skiing is an activity which may be dangerous to others and is normally undertaken only by adults, and for which adult qualifications are required. We find nothing in the record to support this conclusion. We think it judicially noticeable that skiing as a recreational sport, save for limited hazardous skiing activities, is engaged in by persons of all ages. Defendant's attempt to negotiate the lower end of the beginners' slope certainly cannot be characterized as a skiing activity that as a matter of law was hazardous to others and required that he be held to an adult standard of conduct.

We recognize that certain activities engaged in by minors are so potentially hazardous as to require that the minor be held to an adult standard of care. Driving a motor vehicle, operating a motor boat and hunting would ordinarily be so classified. However, as to the activities mentioned, New Jersey law requires that the minor must be licensed and must first demonstrate the requisite degree of adult competence.

We find that the applicable standard of care, correctly charged by the trial court, was that generally applicable to minors. The required standard is that of a reasonable person of like age, intelligence[2] and experience under like circumstances. Among those circumstances, of course, would be the nature of the activity in which the minor was engaged.

Most of the cases which apply this standard have been concerned with the minor's contributory negligence and not primary negligence. It has been suggested that a different standard might well apply where the minor's conduct causes injury to others. . . . We think that a rational basis exists for applying the same standard whether the issue involves a question of contributory negligence of a child, or primary negligence. Moreover, to hold otherwise

---

2. Although the charge to the jury in this case omitted the word intelligence, we do not believe the defendant was thereby prejudiced in the light of the charge as a whole and the facts of the case. There was no objection to the charge based on this omission, nor did the Appellate Division notice it.

would further complicate an already difficult area of tort law. The practicalities of the situation weigh heavily in favor of a single standard.

The Appellate Division, while it decided the case on the ground heretofore discussed, also criticized the trial court's application of the standard applicable to children to a 17-year-old person, pointing out that by N.J.S.A. 9:17B-1 et seq. (eff. January 1, 1973) every person in this State 18 or more years of age is deemed to be an adult. The Appellate Division could see little sense in holding an 18-year-old person to one standard of care and applying a lesser standard to one 17 years of age.

However, this problem will exist no matter where the line is drawn, whether it be at 10, 14 or 18 years. Since it has to be drawn somewhere, it is not unreasonable to fix it at the age of legal maturity — now 18 in this State — holding those under that age and capable of negligence to the standard of care required of a reasonable person of like age, intelligence and experience under like circumstances. This case, though, must be decided on the basis of the law prior to the effective date of the cited statute. Although there is no decided case in New Jersey fixing the age at which the standard of care governing children no longer controls, 18 years would appear to be the age at which a person should be held to adult responsibility in tort matters. Such is already the case with criminal responsibility — 18 being the age at which a person's criminal or anti-social behavior ceases to be regarded as juvenile delinquency and is treated as a criminal or quasi-criminal act, subject to the processes and sanctions normally applicable to adults. The trial court, therefore, charged the jury correctly as to the standard of care applicable to the 17-year-old defendant herein. . . .

SCHREIBER, J. (dissenting). . . .

Presumably the majority is adhering to the principles enunciated in Bush v. N.J. & N.Y. Transit Co., Inc. We held there that a child under age seven was rebuttably presumed to be incapable of negligence and the issue was not to be submitted to the jury in the absence of evidence "from which the jury could infer that the child was capable of understanding and avoiding the danger of injury involved in the circumstances of the case." The party asserting the infant's negligence or contributory negligence bore the burden of proof.

Under the norm adopted this day where the negligence or contributory negligence of an infant between ages 7 and 18 is in issue, his activity or inactivity is to be measured by a reasonable person of the same age, intelligence and experience under similar circumstances unless the activities "are so potentially hazardous as to require that the minor be held to an adult standard of care." There are several inherent difficulties in and inequitable consequences of this rule.

What criteria are to be employed by the jury to ascertain whether an activity is "potentially hazardous"? If a "potentially hazardous" activity is one which results in serious or permanent injury, then almost any activity might fall within that category. The injured person who has lost the sight of an eye resulting from a carelessly thrown dart, or stone, or firecracker, the death caused by a bicycle, or an individual seriously maimed due to an errant skier — all are indisputable proof of "potentially hazardous" activity. The majority prescribes no guideline except to imply that whenever licensing is required, the "potentially hazardous" test is met.[2] But the State does not impose a licensing requirement on all "potentially hazardous" activities and whether one has a license or not is often not relevant in measuring conduct of a reasonably prudent person. Whether the driver of an automobile is licensed, for example, is not relevant in adjudicating if the automobile was being driven in a reasonable prudent manner. In Charbonneau v. MacRury, the New Hampshire Supreme Court pointed out that by licensing drivers the State "has not undertaken to deal with the rule of care at all. It neither expressly or impliedly authorizes the trier of facts to disregard the legally ascertainable defects of the actor when material to the issue of his reasonable conduct, whether he be an adult or a minor. The authorized license is not a certificate of the physical perfection of the adult or of the mental maturity of the eligible minor."

To the injured party, his loss is the same irrespective of the wrongdoer's date of birth and it is inequitable and unjust that a minor should not be expected to exercise the same degree of care as the mythical reasonable and prudent person, at least when engaged in adult activities. The majority's proposition unnecessarily sanctions the imposition of the burden of young people's hazards on innocent victims. Whenever an infant participates in activities in which adults normally engage, the infant should be held to the adult standard of care. Other courts have not hesitated to do so. Minors participating in these activities are mature enough to possess the "discretion and physical capacity consistent with . . . the presumption of adult responsibility. . . ." . . .

Inherent in these approaches, either on the basis of activities or on age well below legal adulthood, is recognition of the realism and justness in applying the adult objective standard. In some measure this is probably due to the expansion of experiences and activity of minors, as well as the protection afforded all members of the family by comprehensive liability insurance policies.[4] Functionally, skiing is as much a sport for people over 18, as under 18. It is no different than golf or cycling. And the hazards to the public whether operating a motor vehicle, power boat, motor scooter, bicycle, tractor or hitting a golf ball, or skiing are self-evident. Third persons may be exposed to serious injury because of the dangers which occur when the activity is not being performed in a reasonably prudent manner by a reasona-

2. No license is required for a motorized bike, but a ten-speed bike can be pedaled at 25 miles per hour on a flat road. The U. S. Consumer Product Safety Commission reports that there are 500 to 1000 fatalities and about 500,000 permanently crippled each year from bicycle mishaps.

4. Payments for child responsibilities are made by adults or insurance companies under policies paid for by adults. . . .

bly prudent person and no sound reason exists for not holding the child defendant to the standard of the reasonably prudent adult.

The 18-year-old line drawn today is contrary to policies enunciated by the legislature in regulating some aspects of the conduct of minors in relation to others. A 16-year-old juvenile may be tried as an adult for a homicide, treason, offense against the person in an aggressive, violent and willful manner, or for sale and distribution of narcotics. At age 16½, a person may obtain a special learner's permit to drive a car so that a driver's license may be obtained at age 17. At age 13 one may be licensed to operate a boat with an outboard motor. Under this Court's rules a 17-year-old infant may file a verified petition. The 18-year-old line is not consonant with the common law rule that at age 14 an infant is presumed to have the capacity to be guilty of criminal intent. . . .

The 18-year demarcation line ignores the earlier mental development of young people. A few comments from experts in the field of child behavior demonstrate the point.

> . . . [T]he middle-years [6 to 12 plus] child's growing mastery of symbols and his ever-broadening fund of general knowledge permit him to think in ways that come to approximate those of adults. Indeed, in some areas, the child may know a great deal more than his less educated parents and so be able to think more rationally than they. . . . [L. Stone and J. Church, Childhood and Adolescence at 412-413 (2d ed. 1968)]. . . .

I would adopt a rule that an infant 16 years or over would be held to an adult standard of care and that an infant between ages 7 and 16 would be rebuttably presumed to have the duty to act, while engaged in an adult activity, that is, one in which adults normally or usually engage, as a reasonably prudent person, but that, upon a showing that adult judgmental capacity for that type of activity is not warranted, the subjective-objective criteria . . . adopted by the majority be applied. Application of this rule recognizes the difference between negligence and contributory negligence since the required judgmental capacity in foreseeing and avoiding the hazards created by others may be substantially greater than that to be comprehended by one's own acts. If the infant between ages 7 and 16 is found not to have been occupied in an adult activity, the . . . rule adopted by the majority would be applicable. As to those 16 or over I would apply the adult standard. . . .

Notes

1. If defendant had been 18, would the fact that he was a beginner have been relevant to his duty of care? *No*

2. What is the relevance of liability insurance to the legal or policy issues in the case? Can a decision on liability be based on whether people carry

liability insurance? Or must the decision whether to carry liability insurance
follow and be guided by the court's decision on liability? Whatever the
answer to these questions, it is indeed true that liability insurance drives a
wedge between L, the loss to the victim of an accident, and the cost that the
negligent injurer must pay in the form of damages. Some think this wedge so
gravely impairs the effectiveness of the tort system as a deterrent that liability
should be abolished, at least in areas like the automobile accident area where
most injurers carry liability insurance or are insolvent (which amounts to the
same thing — why?). An evaluation of this contention is postponed to Chapter 11, which deals with recent legislative activity and proposals regarding "no
fault" compensation for accident victims.

   3. Why is the exception for minors phrased in terms of the care of a
reasonable person of like intelligence and experience, as well as of like age? Is
it because children mature at different rates? By the same token, do not
adults have different mental ages? Does the idea of a *reasonable* 17-year-old
exclude the possibility that the particular defendant might be a 17-year-old of
below- or above-average capacity to take care? Was not the idea that a novice
skier is entitled to take less care than an experienced one implicitly rejected in
the *Fredericks* case? In Dickeson v. Baltimore & Ohio Chicago Terminal R.R.
Co., 42 Ill. 2d 103, 245 N.E.2d 762 (1969), evidence that plaintiff, a 14-year-
old boy who had been injured while climbing a ladder on a moving freight
train, had an I.Q. of only 81 was held admissible on the ground that plaintiff
was entitled to have his intelligence and experience considered in determining the issue of his alleged contributory negligence. Is this result consistent
with Vaughan v. Menlove?

   4. What does it mean to "hold" a minor to the adult standard of care
when he engages in activities, such as driving, that are considered adult
activities because of their hazardous nature? If the minor is incapable in fact
of using the care of an adult, will not the real effect of "holding" a minor to
the adult standard be to make minors strictly liable for their accidents, some
of which are unavoidable by them? There is, however, a slightly different way
of looking at this exception to an exception. To say that an activity is
hazardous is to say that PL, in Hand formula terminology, is high. This means
that the optimal B is also high. One way of taking care is simply not to engage
in an activity; and while it may be costly to forgo an activity, the costs may
well be less than the benefits in accident avoidance if, as assumed, the activity
is a hazardous one. So the exception to the exception may be justifiable on
the ground that the minor who cannot conform his conduct to the adult
standard of care in a hazardous activity ought to refrain from engaging in the
activity — in which event he really can, despite his youth, comply with the
adult standard of care, for one method of compliance is simply to refrain from
the activity that generates the hazards. (Compare the discussion of care and
activity in Chapter 1.) On this basis, can you distinguish (as the dissenting
judge in *Goss* could not) between riding a bicycle and driving an automobile?
Can you see the relevance of licensing in deciding whether an activity is so

potentially hazardous that the adult standard of care should be imposed on minors?

5. Should there be a special standard of care for adult beginners — the new driver, new skier, etc.? If not, should a child's experience be relevant in deciding whether he was acting reasonably?

6. Two drivers, A and B, approach an intersection. A, an adult, recognizes B, whom he knows to be only 17. A does not know how careful or experienced a driver B is. Does A owe B a higher standard of care than he would an adult? Cf. Harrelson v. Whitehead, 236 Ark. 325, 365 S.W.2d 868 (1963).

7. Might the plaintiff in *Goss* have had a tort action against the ski resort? On what theories might she have proceeded?   *Employer*

design of sloe

Buckley & Toronto Transportation Commn. v. Smith Transport Ltd.
[1946] Ont. L. Rep. 798, 4 Dom. L. Rep. 721 (1946)   *INSANITY*

ROACH J.A.: This is an appeal by the defendant from the judgment pronounced by the Honourable Mr. Justice Urquhart on June 16, 1945, awarding damages to the plaintiff Buckley in the sum of $475 and to the plaintiff Commission in the sum of $963.13 and costs.

The plaintiff Buckley is a street car operator employed by the plaintiff Commission. On the night of October 5, 1944, about 9:40 o'clock, he was in charge of one of the Commission's street cars which was proceeding easterly on Queen St. in the City of Toronto; when it was about two car lengths west of Kingston Road, which commences at Queen St. and runs in a northeasterly direction therefrom, Buckley observed a motor transport unit, that is, a tractor with a trailer attached, approaching Queen St. at a speed which he estimated at from 35 to 40 M.P.H. and giving no indication that the driver thereof intended to stop, as he was required to do, before entering Queen St. The course of the transport and its speed spelled danger to traffic on Queen St., and Buckley applied the brakes of the street car and brought it to a stop within about one car-length. The transport continued in its course, without any reduction in its speed, until it was more than half-way across Queen St. and in front of the street car. The operator of the transport, one Taylor, at that point apparently pulled the steering-wheel violently to the right, and due to the speed at which the unit was travelling it "jack-knifed" and came into violent collision with the front of the street car, damaging the street car and injuring the motorman, Buckley.

There is no doubt that the collision was caused solely by the manner in which the transport unit was operated.

The defence, as pleaded and developed in evidence, is that the driver, Taylor, suddenly and without warning, had become insane and was labouring under an insane delusion that the transport unit was under some sort of remote electrical control manipulated from the head office of his employer in the City of Toronto, as a result of which he was unable to control the speed of the vehicle or stop it. Under these alleged circumstances, the defendant pleaded that the collision was an unavoidable accident. Taylor was taken into custody immediately after the collision, and in due course was medically examined and it was found that he was suffering from syphilis of the brain. He died in the Ontario Mental Hospital at Toronto on November 3, 1944, from general paresis. . . .

Supposing a man who was labouring under the insane delusion that his wife was unfaithful to him, but who was otherwise mentally normal, due to the manner in which he operated a motor vehicle on the highway injured some other person on the highway, no one would suggest that he would not be liable in damages simply because of the fact that he had that one particular insane delusion. Then, add to that one delusion the further delusion that his next-door neighbour was conspiring against him to burn down his house, would he still be liable? I entertain no doubt that he might be liable. He might still be a man who . . . would be "in all other respects rational, and capable of transacting the ordinary affairs and fulfilling the duties and obligations incidental to the various relations of life." In particular, notwithstanding those delusions, he might still understand and appreciate the duty which rested upon him to take care. That surely must be the test in all cases where negligence is the basis of the action. If that understanding and appreciation exists in the mind of the individual, and delusions do not otherwise interfere with his ability to take care, he is liable for the breach of that duty. . . . Therefore, the question here, to my mind, is not limited to the bare inquiry whether or not Taylor at the time of the collision was labouring under this particular delusion, but whether or not he understood and appreciated the duty upon him to take care, and whether he was disabled, as a result of any delusion, from discharging that duty.

The delusion or delusions may manifest the fact that due to mental disease the individual's mind has become so deteriorated or dilapidated or disorganized that he has neither the ability to understand the duty nor the power to discharge it. If I have correctly stated the law, as I think I have, then the question is: What was the extent of Taylor's insanity? Did he understand the duty to take care, and was he, by reason of mental disease, unable to discharge that duty? . . .

The day following the collision he was examined by the physician at the Toronto Jail. To that physician he told the story of this remote electrical control having caused the truck to turn off the road at or near Whitby, which is many miles east of the Hunt Club, but did not refer to the fact that he had been, as he thought, stalled at the Hunt Club. That physician found great difficulty in getting facts from him. He did not get a clear story, but as the physician testified, "a few facts could be picked up here and there but he would quite quickly forget the facts and tell us something else, but nothing that was reliable." He said further: "I was able to get some scattered details but I could not make a continued story of it. His answers were slow and poor."

He was seen at the police station the night of the collision by an official of the defendant company, to whom he said: "That machine was under remote control and when you people put the power on I could not do anything." Taylor had a vacant look in his eyes, and his appearance, and the nature of his conversation, were such that that official was frightened.

Having regard to all the evidence, I have reached the conclusion that at *Holding* the time of the collision Taylor's mind was so ravaged by disease that it should be held, as matter of reasonable inference, that he did not understand the duty which rested upon him to take care, and further that if it could be said that he did not understand and appreciate that duty, the particular delusion prevented him from discharging it. Therefore, no liability for the damages which he caused could attach to him. . . .

Notes

1. Why does it matter that Taylor's mind was so "dilapidated" that he had no power to act carefully? Was not the mind of the defendant in Vaughan v. Menlove so dilapidated that he was unable to take elementary precautions? Is the "reasonable man" a lunatic? Can there be a concept of the "reasonable lunatic"?

2. In Bolen v. Howard, in Chapter 3, insanity was rejected as a defense even though the defendant was charged with battery, an intentional tort. How can that result be squared with the result in the *Buckley* case?

3. Suppose defendant, laboring under the insane delusion that his neighbor was conspiring to burn down his house, but otherwise sane, drove at a high rate of speed in an effort to reach his house before it was set on fire. If he had been correct about the existence of such a conspiracy, his speeding would have been considered reasonable. Because he is incorrect as a result of insanity, is his speeding negligent or nonnegligent?

for Mrs. Keith

Breunig v. American Family Insurance Co.
45 Wis. 2d 536, 173 N.W.2d 619 (1970)

[Plaintiff, a truck driver, sued the automobile liability insurer of Erma Veith for injuries sustained when Mrs. Veith drove into the truck driven by plaintiff.]

HALLOWS, C.J. . . .

... The evidence established that Mrs. Veith, while returning home after taking her husband to work, saw a white light on the back of a car ahead of her. She followed this light for three or four blocks. Mrs. Veith did not remember anything else except landing in a field, lying on the side of the road and people talking. She recalled awaking in the hospital.

The psychiatrist testified Mrs. Veith told him she was driving on a road when she believed that God was taking ahold of the steering wheel and was directing her car. She saw the truck coming and stepped on the gas in order to become airborne because she knew she could fly because Batman does it. To her surprise she was not airborne before striking the truck but after the impact she was flying. . . .

The psychiatrist testified Erma Veith was suffering from "schizophrenic reaction, paranoid type, acute."[1] He stated that from the time Mrs. Veith commenced following the car with the white light and ending with the stopping of her vehicle in the cornfield, she was not able to operate the vehicle with her conscious mind and that she had no knowledge or forewarning that such illness or disability would likely occur.

. . . Plaintiff argues there was such evidence of forewarning and also suggests Erma Veith should be liable because insanity should not be a defense in negligence cases. . . .

The case was tried on the theory that some forms of insanity are a defense to and preclude liability for negligence under the doctrine of Theisen v. Milwaukee Automobile Mut. Ins. Co. (1962), 18 Wis. 2d 91, 118 N.W.2d 140, 119 N.W.2d 393.

In *Theisen* we recognized one was not negligent if he was unable to conform his conduct through no fault of his own but held a sleeping driver negligent as a matter of law because one is always given conscious warnings of drowsiness and if a person does not heed such warnings and continues to drive his car, he is negligent for continuing to drive under such conditions. But we distinguished those exceptional cases of loss of consciousness resulting from injury inflicted by an outside force, or fainting, or heart attack, or epileptic seizure, or other illness which suddenly incapacitates the driver of an automobile when the occurrence of such disability is not attended with sufficient warning or should not have been reasonably foreseen. . . .

There are authorities which generally hold insanity is not a defense in tort cases except for intentional torts. These cases rest on the historical view of strict liability without regard to the fault of the individual. . . .

---

1. In layman's language, the doctor explained: "The schizophrenic reaction is a thinking disorder of a severe type usually implying disorientation with the world. Usually implying a break with reality. The paranoid type is a subdivision of the thinking disorder in which one perceives oneself either as a very powerful or being persecuted or being attacked by other people. And acute implies that the rapidity of the onset of the illness, the speed of onset is meant by acute."

Rationale for Holling (handwritten margin note)

The policy basis of holding a permanently insane person liable for his tort is: (1) Where one of two innocent persons must suffer a loss it should be borne by the one who occasioned it; (2) to induce those interested in the estate of the insane person (if he has one) to restrain and control him; and (3) the fear an insanity defense would lead to false claims of insanity to avoid liability. . . .

. . . In Johnson [v. Lombotte, 147 Colo. 203, 363 P.2d 165 (1961)], the defendant was under observation by order of the county court and was being treated in a hospital for "chronic schizophrenic state of paranoid type." On the day in question, she wanted to leave the hospital and escaped therefrom and found an automobile standing on a street with its motor running a few blocks from the hospital. She got into the car and drove off, having little or no control of the car. She soon collided with the plaintiff. Later she was adjudged mentally incompetent and committed to a state hospital. *Johnson* is not a case of sudden mental seizure with no forewarning. The defendant knew she was being treated for a mental disorder and hence would not have come under the nonliability rule herein stated.

We think the statement that insanity is no defense is too broad when it is applied to a negligence case where the driver is suddenly overcome without forewarning by a mental disability or disorder which incapacitates him from conforming his conduct to the standards of a reasonable man under like circumstances. These are rare cases indeed, but their rarity is no reason for overlooking their existence and the justification which is the basis of the whole doctrine of liability for negligence, i.e., that it is unjust to hold a man responsible for his conduct which he is incapable of avoiding and which incapability was unknown to him prior to the accident. . . .

Upheld verdict for ∆ because Mrs. Veith had similar delusions previously—should have been forewarned of the danger that delusions would strike her while driving (handwritten)

Notes

1. How would the court that decided *Breunig* have decided *Buckley*?

2. Is the rule laid down in *Breunig* more consistent with a compensatory or with a deterrent rationale of the law of torts?

3. Is it correct that the rarity of cases "where a driver is suddenly overcome without forewarning of a mental disability or disorder is no reason for overlooking their existence"? Is it necessarily unjust to hold a man responsible for "conduct which he is incapable of avoiding and which incapability was unknown to him prior to the accident"? Why was it important in the *Johnson* case whether the defendant knew that she was mentally ill?

4. Notice the court's explicit reference to the fact that the liability of the insane for their torts is based on the concept of strict liability. Is it not true that whenever someone who is below average in his capacity to avoid accidents is made subject to the standard of care of the average person, he is being made subject, in effect, to strict liability? Are the areas of strict

true (handwritten margin note)

liability created by the reasonable-man rule, as studied thus far, consistent or inconsistent with the economic analysis in Chapter 1 of the choice between negligence and strict liability as standards for regulating conduct?

5. What did the court mean when it said that a sleeping driver is negligent "as a matter of law"?

6. If insanity is sometimes a defense in an unintentional-tort case, what about mental retardation? No case has been found where defendant sought to defend on the ground that he was retarded, but in several cases it has been held that the contributory negligence of a mentally retarded plaintiff is to be determined not by application of the reasonable-man standard but with reference to the plaintiff's actual ability to avoid being injured. See, e.g., Lynch v. Rosenthal, 396 S.W.2d 272 (Mo. App. 1965); Snider v. Callahan, 250 F. Supp. 1022 (W.D. Mo. 1966); Feldman v. Howard, 5 Ohio App. 2d 65, 214 N.E.2d 235 (1966). Are these cases consistent with *Breunig*? With *Buckley*? In Snider v. Callahan, supra, the court acknowledged that it was applying a "double standard" to negligence and contributory negligence in allowing plaintiff's mental capacity to be considered.

The Second Restatement of Torts §464, Comment g, states: "Mental deficiency which falls short of insanity . . . does not excuse conduct which is otherwise contributory negligence." Relying on this passage, the court in Wright v. Tate, 208 Va. 291, 295, 156 S.E.2d 562, 565 (1967), held that "an adult [accident victim] who is of low mentality but not insane is held to the same standard of care as a person of greater intellect." Plaintiff's decedent in *Wright* was mentally slow, but he was not insane, and a guardian had never been appointed to care for either his person or his property.

As a matter of policy:

(a) Should a plaintiff's insanity excuse his negligence in circumstances where it would not excuse the defendant's?

(b) Should severe mental retardation ever excuse either plaintiff's or defendant's negligence?

(c) Should mental deficiency short of severe retardation ever excuse plaintiff's negligence?

7. Insofar as the general effect of the reasonable-man rule is to impose strict liability on the clumsy and the weak-minded and to reduce the tort liability of certain people of superior skill and intelligence (as in *Fredericks*), it probably redistributes wealth from those already worse off than the average to those already better off. One exception to this general tendency should be noted, however. To a person who has high opportunity costs of time by virtue of having a high earned income, the cost of avoiding certain dangerous conduct, such as driving at high speeds, may be higher than the cost to the average person. The reasonable-man standard may therefore have the effect of making the high-income driver liable for certain accidents for which he would be excused if the costs of accident avoidance were assessed on an individual rather than average basis.

8. An important exception to the reasonable-man rule is the locality rule in medical malpractice. That rule is examined in the section on custom later in this chapter.

B.   WHO DECIDES WHAT CONDUCT IS NEGLIGENT, AND ON WHAT BASIS?

Baltimore & Ohio R.R. Co. v. Goodman
275 U.S. 66 (1927)

MR. JUSTICE HOLMES delivered the opinion of the Court.

This is a suit brought by the widow and administratrix of Nathan Goodman against the petitioner for causing his death by running him down at a grade crossing. The defense is that Goodman's own negligence caused the death. At the trial, the defendant asked the Court to direct a verdict for it, but the request, and others looking to the same direction, were refused, and the plaintiff got a verdict and a judgment which was affirmed by the Circuit Court of Appeals.

Goodman was driving an automobile truck in an easterly direction and was killed by a train running southwesterly across the road at a rate of not less than sixty miles an hour. The line was straight, but it is said by the respondent that Goodman "had no practical view" beyond a section house two hundred and forty-three feet north of the crossing until he was about twenty feet from the first rail, or, as the respondent argues, twelve feet from danger, and that then the engine was still obscured by the section house. He had been driving at the rate of ten or twelve miles an hour, but had cut down his rate to five or six miles at about forty feet from the crossing. It is thought that there was an emergency in which, so far as appears, Goodman did all that he could.

We do not go into further details as to Goodman's precise situation, beyond mentioning that it was daylight and that he was familiar with the crossing, for it appears to us plain that nothing is suggested by the evidence to relieve Goodman from responsibility for his own death. When a man goes upon a railroad track he knows that he goes to a place where he will be killed if a train comes upon him before he is clear of the track. He knows that he must stop for the train, not the train stop for him. In such circumstances it seems to us that if a driver cannot be sure otherwise whether a train is dangerously near he must stop and get out of his vehicle, although obviously he will not often be required to do more than to stop and look. It seems to us that if he relies upon not hearing the train or any signal and takes no further precaution he does so at his own risk. If at the last moment Goodman found himself in an emergency it was his own fault that he did not reduce his speed

earlier or come to a stop. It is true ... that the question of due care very
generally is left to the jury. But we are dealing with a standard of conduct,
and when the standard is clear it should be laid down once for all by the
Courts.

O. W. Holmes, Jr., The Common Law
123, 128-129 (1881)

When a case arises in which the standard of conduct, pure and simple, is
submitted to the jury, the explanation is plain. It is that the court, not
entertaining any clear views of public policy applicable to the matter, derives
the rule to be applied from daily experience, as it has been agreed that the
great body of the law of tort has been derived. But the court further feels that
it is not itself possessed of sufficient practical experience to lay down the rule
intelligently. It conceives that twelve men taken from the practical part of
the community can aid its judgment. Therefore it aids its conscience by
taking the opinion of the jury.

But supposing a state of facts often repeated in practice, is it to be
imagined that the court is to go on leaving the standard to the jury forever? Is
it not manifest, on the contrary, that if the jury is, on the whole, as fair a
tribunal as it is represented to be, the lesson which can be got from that
source will be learned? Either the court will find that the fair teaching of
experience is that the conduct complained of usually is or is not blameworthy,
and therefore, unless explained, is or is not a ground of liability; or it will find
the jury oscillating to and fro, and will see the necessity of making up its mind
for itself. There is no reason why any other such question should not be
settled, as well as that of liability for stairs with smooth strips of brass upon
their edges. The exceptions would mainly be found where the standard was
rapidly changing, as, for instance, in some questions of medical treatment. . . .

. . . If the whole evidence in the case was that a party, in full command of
his senses and intellect, stood on a railway track, looking at an approaching
engine until it ran him down, no judge would leave it to the jury to say
whether the conduct was prudent. If the whole evidence was that he attempted to cross a level track, which was visible for half a mile each way, and
on which no engine was in sight, no court would allow a jury to find negligence. Between these extremes are cases which would go to the jury. But it is
obvious that the limit of safety in such cases, supposing no further elements
present, could be determined almost to a foot by mathematical calculation.

The trouble with many cases of negligence is, that they are of a kind not
frequently recurring, so as to enable any given judge to profit by long experience with juries to lay down rules, and that the elements are so complex that
courts are glad to leave the whole matter in a lump for the jury's
determination.

McEvers v. Missouri Pacific R.R. Co.
528 F.2d 220 (7th Cir. 1975)

HOFFMAN, J. . . .

. . . Jurisdiction rests upon diversity of citizenship. . . . Illinois law controls, and establishes that the usual duty of a highway traveler to stop, look, and listen at a railroad crossing may be qualified, or even excused, by the existence of "facts such as obstructions to view or distractions that might mislead" the driver. When such obstructions or misleading conditions appear, "it is for the finder of fact to determine whether he acted prudently."

. . . Plaintiff testified that he stopped his truck some thirty feet from the rear rail of the track. From that point of observation, his view of the tracks to his right, whence the train approached, was impaired by a small signal relay shack, six feet square and eight and one-half feet tall, maintained by the railroad on its right of way some 433 feet from the crossing. Near that point the track curved from the signal shack, heading directly away from the plaintiff's position. With this turn in the tracks according to plaintiff's witnesses, the approaching train was traveling directly toward the signal shack, on a course coinciding with his line of sight toward the shack, so that his view of the head-on train was blocked.

In addition to this evidence of obstructed view, there was some evidence of misleading conditions. Near the point where the track curved, a siding or passing track branched off on plaintiff's side of the track, extending in a straight path, more or less, along the line of the main track as it crossed the highway. Viewed from plaintiff's observation point, this siding was visible while the curved main track was not, and a driver might be misled by these conditions into believing that there was only one track. He might thus be unaware even that his vision was obstructed, and he might be lulled into the belief that he could see clearly the only track on which a train might be approaching.

After stopping, looking, and seeing no train, plaintiff proceeded up the slight grade toward the tracks in lowest gear, at a speed of only about two miles per hour with his load of twenty tons of coal. He did not look again to his right for an estimated ten or twelve seconds, an estimate consistent with the speeds and distances. At that moment his front wheels were on the track, and the locomotive was a little more than 200 feet away. He accelerated but the train collided with the truck at the junction between tractor and trailer. The crossing was guarded only by the conventional fixed wooden crosstrack sign, marked "railroad crossing." There were no gates, flagmen, or warning signals to be actuated by an approaching train. There was evidence that no whistles or bells were sounded from the train until the instant of collision.

Upon this evidence, the District Court ruled that plaintiff was guilty of contributory negligence as a matter of law since he failed to look again to his right during the ten or twelve seconds of his final approach to the track, and since he would have had an unobstructed view of the approaching train at any point within twenty-five feet of the tracks. But Illinois law does not impose a duty to look continuously. While it does not "tolerate the absurdity of permitting a plaintiff to say he looked and did not see the approaching train, when had he looked he would have seen it," Illinois requires that plaintiff's due care must be submitted to the jury when he has offered evidence of obstructions to view or misleading conditions sufficient to "render plausible his assertion that he looked but did not see the train."

Upon this evidence alone, we cannot conclude that no jury finding that plaintiff exercised due care could ever stand. Whether plaintiff could have seen the top of the approaching locomotive over the roof of the signal house, and, if so, whether he was negligent in failing to see it, and whether he was sufficiently familiar with the layout near the crossing so that he could not claim to have been misled, are questions committed to the jury's determination, not ours. It follows that the judgment must be reversed and the case remanded.

Notes

1. *Goodman*, like *McEvers*, was a diversity case. Why did the Court in *Goodman* not refer to any state's law?

2. What is the precise standard of conduct laid down in the *Goodman* case? Is the result in *McEvers* consistent or inconsistent with that standard?

3. In Pokora v. Wabash Ry. Co., 292 U.S. 98 (1934), another railroad crossing accident case decided seven years after *Goodman*, plaintiff's view of the track was obstructed, but he decided to proceed when he heard no bell or whistle announcing the approach of a train. The Supreme Court held that, in the circumstances (which included the fact that the crossing was of a frequented highway in daytime in a populous city, and it was unlikely that defendant would run its train at such a time and place without sounding its bell or whistle as required by state law), it was a jury question whether plaintiff was contributorily negligent. As for *Goodman*, the Court in *Pokora* thought the case had been correctly decided, since *Goodman* had had a clear space of eighteen feet before he reached the track within which the train was visible, and he was traveling slowly enough to stop in that distance. "This," said the Court in *Pokora*, "was decisive of the case. But the Court [in *Goodman*] did not stop there. It added a remark, unnecessary upon the facts before it, which has been a fertile source of controversy. 'In such circumstances it seems to us that if a driver cannot be sure otherwise whether a train is dangerously near he must stop and get out of his vehicle, although obviously he will not often be required to do more than to stop and look.' . . . [The *Goodman* opinion] has been a source of confusion in the federal courts to the extent that it imposes a standard for application by the judge, and has had only wavering support in the courts of the states. We limit it accordingly." 292 U.S. at 103-106. How did the Court limit it?

4. There is no quarrel in general with the proposition that the judge can take the negligence (or contributory negligence) issue away from the jury in a clear case. This follows from the general principles of jury control; it is not a special tort doctrine. Recall the court's remark in *Breunig* that a sleeping driver who has an accident will be deemed negligent per se. This remark illustrates how, by taking the negligence issue away from the jury in appropriate cases, judges create particularized rules of conduct within the overall negligence standard. What was wrong with "stop, look, and listen" as an application of this idea?

5. Holmes in The Common Law seemed to be predicting that over time the negligence standard would become increasingly particularized, a matter of specific rules of conduct, as judges and juries dealt with recurring cases. Surprisingly, this has not occurred; rules such as that the sleeping driver is negligent per se are rare, save when imposed by statute. When there is no statute, most negligence cases continue to be decided under the general negligence standard, applied by the jury to the particular facts of the case. See, e.g., Illinois Pattern Jury Instructions — Civil (1971), passim.

6. The general right to a civil jury trial was abolished by statute in England in 1933, except for cases of fraud, libel, slander, malicious prosecution, false imprisonment, seduction, and breach of promise to marry. Emergency legislation enacted in 1939, during World War II, abolished the civil jury entirely, and, although the legislation was eventually repealed, the civil jury has never returned to England. See Higginbotham, Continuing the Dialogue: Civil Juries and the Allocation of Judicial Power, 56 Tex. L. Rev. 47, 51-52 (1977). Should the U.S. abolish the civil jury? There is growing skepticism concerning the ability of a jury to assimilate the voluminous and complex evidence tendered in large antitrust cases. See, e.g., ILC Peripherals Leasing Corp. v. International Business Machines Corp., 458 F. Supp. 423 (N.D. Cal. 1978). But there is a question how applicable this concern is to the ordinary tort case. (Some tort cases nowadays are, however, highly complex, as we shall see when we come to modern developments in products liability law in Chapter 9.)

An empirical study of automobile accident cases in the province of Ontario showed relatively little difference between jury and nonjury trials. Jury trials took slightly longer (an average of 2.4 days versus 1.9 for nonjury trials), and juries were less likely to award no damages than judges; yet surprisingly, a larger fraction of cases in which damages in excess of $25,000 were awarded were nonjury cases. See Linden & Sommers, The Civil Jury in the Courts in Ontario: A Postscript to the Osgoode Hall Study, 6 Osgoode Hall L.J. 252 (1968). Research on the operation of the civil jury in the U.S. has focused on judges' attitudes toward the jury system. The attitude is generally favorable, but in one study 30 percent of the judges responding favored abolishing the absolute right to jury trial in automobile personal injury suits. See With Love in Their Hearts but Reform on Their Minds: How Trial Judges View the Civil Jury, 4 Colum. J. Law & Soc. Prob. 178, 193 (1968); cf. Kalven, The Dignity of the Civil Jury, 50 Va. L. Rev. 1055 (1964).

statuts

Vaughan v. Taff Vale Ry. Co.
5 H. & N. 679, 157 Eng. Rep. 1351 (Ex. Ch. 1860)

... The defendants are a Company, who, under their special Acts and the General Railway Acts incorporated therewith, are proprietors of, and use and work the Taff Vale Railway with locomotive engines as a passenger and goods line. The plaintiff is the owner of a wood or plantation adjoining the embankment of the railway. On the 14th March, 1856, the plaintiff's wood was discovered to be on fire, and eight acres of it were burnt. The fire may be taken to have originated from a spark or coal from one of the defendants' locomotive engines in the ordinary course of its working. This action was brought by the plaintiff for the damage he sustained by the fire....

From the evidence of the plaintiff and his witnesses it appeared that the fire in the plaintiff's wood was first seen at a place fifty yards from the railway: that there were traces of fire extending continuously all the way between the railway and the wood, and that the railway bank was burning: that the grass on the bank had been cut three or four months before, but that there was grass of a very combustible nature growing on the bank just previous to the fire, and that it was all burned: that there was a great deal of long grass growing in the wood, which was extremely combustible: that the wood was also full of small dry branches, the remains of a former cutting, and was described, by the plaintiff, to be in just about as safe a state as an open barrel of gunpowder would be in the Cyfarthfa rolling-mill.

The wood, however, was in an ordinary and natural condition, and as it had been before and since the railway was made. Whether the injury was caused by the grass on the embankment being first set fire to, or whether by lighted matter being thrown from the locomotive on to the plaintiff's land, was not left to or determined by the jury. The defendants' counsel did not at the trial make any objection on this ground.

On the part of the defendants it was sworn that everything which was practicable had been done to the locomotive to make it safe: that a cap had been put to its chimney: that its ashpan had been secured: that it travelled at the slowest pace consistent with practical utility, and that if its funnel had been more guarded or its ashpan less free, or its pace slower, it could not have been advantageously used; and it must be taken to be the fact that the defendants had taken every precaution and adopted every means in their power, and which science could suggest, to prevent their engines from emitting sparks, but the witness added, "we do occasionally burn our own banks now." ...

COCKBURN, C.J. .... Although it may be true, that if a person keeps an animal of known dangerous propensities, or a dangerous instrument, he will be responsible to those who are thereby injured, independently of any negligence in the mode of dealing with the animal or using the instrument; yet when the legislature has sanctioned and authorized the use of a particular

An 1874 lithograph by W. J. Morgan & Co. showing a spark
arrester on the smokestack and a cowcatcher out front
Courtesy of the Library of Congress

thing, and it is used for the purpose for which it was authorized, and every
precaution has been observed to prevent injury, the sanction of the legislature carries with it this consequence, that if damage results from the use of
such thing independently of negligence, the party using it is not responsible.
It is consistent with policy and justice that it should be so; and for this reason,
so far as regards the first count, I think the judgment of the Court below is
wrong. It is admitted that the defendants used fire for the purpose of propelling locomotive engines, and no doubt they were bound to take proper
precaution to prevent injury to persons through whose lands they passed; but
the mere use of fire in such engines does not make them liable for injury
resulting from such use without any negligence on their part. . . .

Notes

1. There was a strong tendency in the English common law to impose
strict liability for damage caused by fire. Had it not been for the statutes
creating the Taff Vale Railway and authorizing it to engage in the railroad
business, the railway would probably have been strictly liable for any damage
caused by sparks from its locomotives. American common-law judges were
less inclined to impose strict liability for damage caused by fire, both in
general and with specific reference to locomotive sparks. Can you think of an
economic reason for this difference between the English and American common law?

2. But what have the statutes to do with the question of liability for
spark damage? Is there any evidence that the legislature wanted to excuse the
Taff Vale Railway from its common-law tort liabilities?

3. Is the relevance of the statutes perhaps this? The statutes make it
unlikely that the optimal solution to the problem of fire hazard was not to
have the railroad at all; and a principal function of strict liability is to force
the individuals engaged in a dangerous activity to decide whether the activity
is worth carrying on when all of its costs, including accident costs, are weighed
against the benefits. Cf. Adams v. Bullock, supra, and Chapter 7.

4. Is there an argument that plaintiff in *Taff Vale* was contributorily
negligent? Or, alternatively, might a change in the plaintiff's activity have
been as efficient a method of fire prevention as a change in the defendant's
activity? Cf. *LeRoy Fibre* in the next chapter.

Stonehocker v. General Motors Corp.
587 F.2d 151 (4th Cir. 1978)

WIDENER, J.
The plaintiff, Terry Lee Stonehocker, brought this action, charging neg-

ligence, against General Motors Corporation for injuries received when his car, a 1968 Chevrolet Camaro (manufactured by General Motors), rolled over in an accident. Jurisdiction was based on diversity of citizenship and the requisite amount in controversy. The parties agree that General Motors' negligence, if any, did not cause the accident itself, but the plaintiff alleges that General Motors' negligent design of the car's roof and negligent manufacture of the windshield combined to cause injuries which would not otherwise have occurred in an accident of this type or would have been substantially less. At trial, the jury found for the plaintiff and awarded compensatory and punitive damages. . . .

. . . General Motors . . . offered evidence that the Camaro roof structure met and exceeded the requirements of Federal Motor Vehicle Safety Standard 216. 49 C.F.R. §571.216. The district court excluded the evidence of compliance with the safety standard because the standard "was not in force at the time of the automobile's construction or at the time of the accident." . . .

. . . Standard 216 is a federal regulation with force of law promulgated under the Traffic Vehicle and Motor Safety Code of 1966, 15 U.S.C. §1381 et seq. Section 1392(a) directs the Secretary of Transportation to issue "appropriate Federal motor vehicle safety standards." Section 1391(1) defines motor vehicle safety as including "the performance of motor vehicles or motor vehicle equipment in such a manner that the public is protected . . . against unreasonable risk of death or injury to persons in the event accidents do occur, and includes nonoperational safety of such vehicles." Standard 216 in terms "establishes strength requirements for the passenger compartment roof," and gives as its purpose "to reduce deaths and injuries due to the crushing of the roof onto the passenger compartment in rollover accidents." So the statute and the regulation literally address the same subject as a part of the theory upon which this case was brought, that the roof structure of the Camaro was negligently designed. . . .

Not only would a compliance with Standard 216 be relevant to the inquiry at hand according to the terms of the statute and the regulation itself, the congressional history of the statute makes it clear that an object of the statute was to improve the safety of vehicles, and speaks in terms of collision protection, second collision, crashworthiness, etc., which seem to have become words of art as they relate to cases such as the one we have before us. The primary responsibility, says the report of the Senate Committee on Commerce, for regulating the national automotive manufacturing industry must fall squarely upon the federal government.

The statute was enacted in 1966. Standard 216 was last amended in 1973 and was first promulgated in 1971. The automobile involved in the accident was manufactured in 1967 and the accident occurred in 1972. The case was filed in 1974 and terminated in 1976.

It is seen that Standard 216 was not in effect at the time the automobile was manufactured, having been first promulgated some years later. Whether the regulation was in effect at the time of the accident we do not think has any relevance because, the case being based on negligence, the relevant time period involved would be at or prior to the manufacture of the vehicle in 1967. The regulation in terms applies only to motor vehicles the manufacture of which is completed on or after the effective date of the standard.

But we are not here dealing with a claimed violation of the regulation as being either negligence itself or evidence of negligence; we are dealing with the question of whether or not to admit a claimed compliance with the regulation as evidence of due care.

There are many reasons why, if the vehicle manufactured in 1967 did not comply with a regulation later promulgated, as here finally in 1973, that the fact of noncompliance might be inadmissible. In the first place, the time frame of the standard of care must be 1967, not 1973. Further, perfectly valid policy reasons may dictate that such regulations not be made retroactive, and it is well known that retroactive application of statutes in general is not favored. No reason seems apparent to distinguish regulations.

But here General Motors takes the position that in 1967 it, ahead of its time, manufactured a vehicle which complied with safety requirements promulgated from 1971 through 1973. Conceding, as we must, that the statute, 15 U.S.C. §1397(c), would prevent evidence of compliance with the standard from exempting General Motors from negligence for a vehicle subject to the terms of the regulation, nevertheless we believe that a compliance with the standard should have been admitted into evidence as evidence of due care in the design of the vehicle to be considered by the jury with the other evidence in the case. . . .

The plaintiff argues that if the rule would permit General Motors to prove compliance with Standard 216, then the rule should also permit the plaintiff to prove non-compliance with Standard 216, so that, the argument goes, if compliance is evidence of due care, then non-compliance should be evidence of negligence. Quite possibly this might be true in some cases, but it is not necessarily true here, for there is a great deal of difference in failing to comply with a standard several years before it is enacted as tending to show negligence, and designing a car far enough in advance so that it does comply as tending to show due care. The difference is obvious. In all events that question is not now before us and it will have to await another day. . . .

Notes

1. 15 U.S.C. §1397(c), mentioned by the court, provides: "Compliance with any Federal motor vehicle safety standard issued under this subchapter does not exempt any person from any liability under common law." Did the court give adequate weight to this provision in holding that evidence of compliance with Standard 216 was admissible? One could argue, could one not, that if Congress had intended that federal motor vehicle safety standards

should determine the tort standard of care of automobile manufacturers, then compliance with such a standard should be a recognized defense in any tort suit brought under state law; while if not (and §1397(c) implies not), the purposes of the federal standard must be other than prescribing a standard of care, in which event it has no relevance to a tort suit.

2. Is it correct that noncompliance with a future regulation is no evidence of negligence? Does your answer depend on whether technological changes occurred between the design of the automobile and the enactment of the regulation?

3. Does the use of compliance with the standard to show nonnegligence require the jury to construe the federal standard? Is this an appropriate jury function?

4. Should the question of admissibility of the federal standard depend on one's theory of the legislative process? Suppose that statutes, and administrative regulations designed to particularize general legislative standards, are usually or at least commonly the unmoral outcome of a power struggle among interest groups, organized in politically effective coalitions, to get the government to redistribute income and wealth in their favor, directly or indirectly. This "interest group" theory of the political process has been vigorously promoted by political scientists and economists. See, e.g., D. B. Truman, The Government Process: Political Interests and Public Opinion (1951); M. H. Bernstein, Regulating Business by Independent Commission (1955); Stigler, The Theory of Economic Regulation, 2 Bell J. Econ. & Mgmt. Sci. 3 (1971); Jordan, Producer Protection, Prior Market Structure and the Effects of Government Regulation, 15 J. Law & Econ. 151 (1972); Peltzman, Toward a More General Theory of Regulation, 19 J. Law & Econ. 211 (1976). The theory has been applied to an early example of health and safety regulation, Lord Althorp's Factory Act of 1833, 3 & 4 Will. 4, c. 103, regulating child labor in English textile factories. A study of the Act concluded that "this innovation in industrial regulation was not enacted and enforced solely out of compassion for the factory children. It was, instead, an early example of a regulated industry controlling its regulators to further its own interests." Marvel, Factory Regulation: A Reinterpretation of Early English Experience, 20 J. Law & Econ. 379, 402 (1977).

A distinct body of economic literature has found that much health and safety regulation, however motivated, does not increase, but actually reduces, safety. See, e.g., Sands, How Effective Is Safety Legislation?, 11 J. Law & Econ. 165 (1968); Peltzman, An Evaluation of Consumer Protection Legislation: The 1962 Drug Amendments, 81 J. Pol. Econ. 1049 (1973); Peltzman, The Effects of Automobile Safety Regulation, 83 J. Pol. Econ. 677 (1975). The last-cited study found that compulsory seat-belt regulation caused more injuries to pedestrians (because drivers, feeling safer, drove faster) than it averted to drivers. The study is highly controversial, however, and a similar study of Swedish experience with seat-belt requirements produced contrary findings. See Lindgren & Stuart, The Effects of Traffic Safety Regulation in

Sweden, 88 J. Pol. Econ. 412 (1980). Finally, see Linneman, The Effects of Consumer Safety Standards: The 1973 Mattress Flammability Standard, 23 J. Law & Econ. 461 (1980), finding only an insignificant increase in safety due to federal regulation.

The growing scholarly skepticism concerning the effectiveness and public-interest motivation of legislation has implications for the treatment of safety legislation and regulations in tort litigation. If the legislature declares a particular activity safe or unsafe and further declares that its determination shall be controlling in any tort litigation, then, assuming the statute is constitutional, the tort court has no choice but to obey the legislative determination. But often there is uncertainty regarding how much force the legislature intended to give the legislation in tort litigation. When that is so, a judge's attitude is likely to be influenced, consciously or unconsciously, by his opinion on whether the legislature was genuinely and effectively trying to promote the public interest. Moreover, when, as in *Stonehocker*, legislation is introduced as evidence rather than authority concerning the standard of care, the proper weight to be accorded the legislation logically depends on the legislature's actual purpose in enacting it. Is this an argument for exclusion of such evidence?

5. Should skepticism about regulation extend to the regulation of safety by judges and juries interpreting and applying the negligence standard of the common law? Arguably not:

Judicial process

> ... A judge, especially of an appellate court, which is where the most important judge-made rules are fashioned, is unlikely to decide a case on the basis of which of the parties is the "better" person. He knows the parties even less well than the trial judge and ... considerations pertaining to their relative deservedness (wealth, poverty, good breeding, etc.) are suppressed. Moreover, a judgment based on such considerations would be difficult to rationalize in a judicial opinion, or, stated otherwise, to generalize in a rule. Almost by default the judge is compelled to view the parties as representatives of activities — owning land, growing tulips, walking on railroad tracks, driving cars. The methods of judicial compensation and the rules governing conflicts of interest exclude a choice among the competing activities based on the judge's narrowly economic self-interest. In these circumstances, it is natural if not inevitable that he should ask which of the competing activities is more valuable in the economic sense.
>
> The legislative process presents a marked contrast to the judicial. There is no rule against the admission of considerations relating to the relative deservedness of the people affected by proposed legislation. The adversary system, with its comparison of concrete interfering activities that assures that questions of relative costs are always close to the surface of the controversy, is not employed. Also, the legislative tools for redistributing wealth are much more flexible and powerful than the judicial. Ordinarily, the only way a court can redistribute wealth is by means of (in effect) an excise tax on the activity involved in the suit.

Probably more important than any procedural differences in explaining the greater emphasis on distributive considerations in legislative than in judicial lawmaking is the greater reliance on the electoral process for the selection of legislators than for the selection of judges. That process creates a market for legislation in which legislators "sell" legislative protection to those who can help their electoral prospects with money and/or votes. This market is characterized by acute free-rider problems. An individual (or firm) who is within the protective scope of some proposed piece of legislation will benefit from its enactment whether or not he makes any contribution, financial or otherwise, to obtaining its enactment. There is a close analogy to cartelization: the firm that remains outside of the cartel profits more from the cartel than the members, because the nonmember bears none of the costs of cartelization while benefiting equally with the cartel members from the cartel price. The analogy is reinforced by the fact that so much legislation seems designed to facilitate cartel pricing by the regulated firms. And it explains why consumers seem to fare so badly in the legislative process: they are too numerous to organize an effective "cartel" in support of or opposition to existing or proposed legislation.

While the analysis of the factors that predispose an industry to cartelization is thus relevant to predicting who will succeed and who will fail in obtaining legislative protection, there are important differences between the ordinary cartel and the politically effective coalition. In particular, fewness of members seems less critical in the legislative than in the market arena. First, the fewer the competitors in a market, the easier it will be for them to organize a (private) cartel that is unlikely to be detected; hence their demand for legislative protection may be less intense than that of an otherwise similar but more numerous set of competitors. Second, since the antitrust laws do not, and evidently could not constitutionally, forbid competitors to collaborate in influencing legislative action (as distinct from setting price jointly), free-rider problems are more readily overcome in the legislative than in the market arena. Third, to the extent that number of firms is correlated with number of individuals employed by or otherwise economically dependent on the firms, or in cases where it is individuals (for instance, the members of some profession or other occupational group) who are seeking protective legislation, large numbers, while complicating the free-rider problem, may have an offsetting effect by increasing the voting power of the group.

Fourth, large numbers are likely to increase the asymmetry of interests among the members of the group. Protective regulation can take a greater variety of forms (limitation of entry, cash subsidy, tariff, etc.) than a private cartel and where there is asymmetry among the members the choice of form may affect their welfare differently; if so, each will have an incentive to participate so as to influence the choice of form. The foregoing factors may explain why we so often observe monopolistic regulations in areas like agriculture, labor, and the professions where private cartelization would be infeasible because of the large numbers who would have to join any private cartel for it to be effective, and less often in highly concentrated industries such as steel and aluminum.

R. A. Posner, Economic Analysis of Law 404-407 (2d ed. 1977).

Notice how the examples of protectionist legislation in this passage are drawn from statutes that limit competition rather than from statutes designed (ostensibly at least) to promote health or safety. Economists have thus far made little headway in explaining health and safety legislation in interest-group terms.

6. For more on the relationship between federal safety standards and state tort law, see the *Dawson* case in Chapter 9.

White v. Levarn   *Statute*
93 Vt. 218, 108 A. 564 (1918)

[The complaint was in two counts, one for trespass and one for case. Plaintiff and defendant went hunting together on a Sunday. Plaintiff was wearing a cap the color of a gray squirrel, and defendant, mistaking it for a squirrel, shot and injured the plaintiff by accident.]

WATSON, C.J. . . .

Hunting and shooting wild game or other birds or animals, or discharging firearms, on Sunday (with some exceptions not material here), is unlawful by statute. The shooting which injured the plaintiff was therefore an unlawful act voluntarily done by the defendant, and he is answerable, in an action of trespass, for the injury which happened to the plaintiff, either by carelessness or accident.

Against objection and exception, the defendant was permitted to introduce evidence for the purpose of showing contributory negligence by the plaintiff, and facts are found thereon. Without noticing the question of admissibility of such evidence under the count in case, we dispose of the case according to the rights of the parties under the count in trespass. . . . [C]onsent to an assault is no justification, for, since the state is wronged by it, the law forbids it on public grounds. . . . From this it must logically follow that contributory negligence is no defense in an action of trespass for a similar offense in law.

Judgment reversed, and judgment for the plaintiff. Cause remanded for the assessment of damages.

Notes

1. Is the court's result compelled by the logic of McNeil v. Mullin in Chapter 3?   *No*

2. Was the statute designed or likely to make hunting safe? Should this make a difference, or could one argue that because the statute forbade hunting on the day the accident occurred, the *social* cost of avoiding the

accident (B) was zero and hence defendant had to be negligent in a Hand formula sense?

3. Did defendant's violation of the statute "cause" the accident? *No*

4. What kind of implied damage action might the statute in question ? reasonably be thought to have created?

5. On whether the decision is consistent with the modern law on the subject, see Prosser 142-143, and Brown v. Shyne, infra.

Lewis v. City of Miami
127 Fla. 426, 173 So. 150 (1937)

statutory duty

DAVIS, J.

The City of Miami maintains and operates a jail for the incarceration of prisoners who have been convicted of offenses against the ordinances of the city. In this case the City of Miami was sued by one Pat Lewis, a minor, who alleged in his declaration that the municipality aforesaid *knowingly* failed to segregate, from among prisoners whom it confined within its said city jail, one of its prisoners who was known to be then and there infected with a vile and loathsome venereal disease, as a direct and proximate result of which alleged breach of legal duty on the defendant municipality's part, plaintiff, while himself a city prisoner, became exposed to the vile and loathsome venereal disease from which his fellow prisoner was known by the city jail authorities to be suffering, and thereupon became grievously infected in his right eye, which contracted said vile and loathsome venereal infection under the circumstances aforesaid, all to plaintiff's great personal suffering, injury, and damage in the premises.

The case was decided against the plaintiff in the court below on the city's demurrer to plaintiff's declaration. . . .   *Lewis*

At the outset it is conceded by the plaintiff in error that with the exception of our liberalized view of the law as to municipal liability . . . no liability for negligence attaches to a municipality under the strict rule of the common law for the municipality's alleged negligence in the performance of the governmental duty implied in the maintenance of a city lockup or jail for the confinement of persons under arrest, or serving sentences, for the violation of its municipal ordinances.

The common law is in force in this state and were there nothing in the statutes to expressly or impliedly modify the doctrine of nonliability in such cases as that now before the court, we would be bound to affirm the judgment appealed from. . . .

Under sections 3947-3955, C.G.L., chapter 7829, Acts 1919, the public policy of this state has been legislatively declared in favor of the protection of the interest of the inhabitants of this state, as individuals, from exposure to persons known to be afflicted with vile and loathsome communicable infectious, contagious and communicable venereal diseases, such as syphilis, gonorrhea, and chancroid. Under that statute all persons confined or imprisoned in any municipal prison of this state are subject to being examined and treated for venereal diseases by the health authorities or their deputies. And to that end persons found infected with venereal diseases may be compulsorily detained and treated in order to prevent the dissemination of the infection.

An acknowledged rule of the law of actionable negligence is that the violation of a legislative enactment by doing a prohibited act, or by failing to do a required act, makes the actor liable for the invasion of the interest of another where the intent of the statute is to protect the interest of the injured person as an individual, the interest invaded is one the statute was intended to protect, the interest invaded was intended to be protected from the particular hazard, and the violation is a legal cause of the invasion and the other has not so conducted himself as to disable himself from maintaining an action for the violation of the statute.

Section 3947, C.G.L., makes it unlawful for any person infected with venereal disease, contagious, infectious, communicable, and dangerous to the public health, to expose another to infection and its effect is to make the person violating such statutory prohibition subject to both civil and criminal liability under the rule of common-law liability for negligent injuries done through the violation of an express statute, above stated. By necessary implication it is likewise unlawful for the legal custodians or keepers of the persons of individuals known by them to be infected with vile and loathsome communicable venereal disease to knowingly neglect to protect others likewise within their keeping or custody from exposure to such contagious, infectious, communicable and dangerous venereal disease. . . .

There was a time when all municipal functions were governmental and therefore municipal corporations were wholly free from responsibility for torts or civil wrongs, by the common law. This rule of municipal nonliability for torts is still recognized as to all functions whereby the municipality acts simply as an agency of the state for governmental purposes, unless of course a contrary rule be provided by statute. But as to those corporate powers and responsibilities now residing in municipalities that are outside the narrow range of functions heretofore classed by the common law as purely governmental, municipal liability in an action in tort may exist, especially where the wrong and injury is the result of neglecting a positive duty or inhibition enjoined upon the municipality by law.

In municipal corporations of the present day, jails and workhouses are maintained for the detention of persons not only for the simple offences that were within the range of municipal action at common law, but for a multitude of other violations that are purely mala prohibita municipalia and designed to promote the corporate well being of the city and inhabitants more than to advance the performance of its governmental functions. So even in the keeping of jails and workhouses a municipality may be said to be maintaining an institution for its corporate as well as its governmental purposes, under a modern conception of municipal corporations as partly business and partly governmental institutions.

But be that as it may, the liability in this case must rest or fall on the City of Miami's neglect to carry out the mandatory duty enjoined upon it with respect to its inhabitants and its prisoners not to knowingly expose persons in its official custody as jail or workhouse keeper to infection by others known by its authorities in charge to be venereally infected. . . .

. . . [W]e are constrained to hold upon the present appeal that the *Holding* declaration to which demurrer was sustained in this case states a good cause of action for the negligent breach of the statutory duty necessarily resting upon municipal corporations by command of the state law making it unlawful to subject healthy persons to exposure to infection by contagious, infectious, communicable, and dangerous venereal diseases. To hold that municipalities may ignore the provisions of such statute by contributing to the continued spread of the infection through knowing neglect of its prisoners, would be to render frustrate the general intent of the statute in question, which intent, as discerned from its provisions, is, after all is said and done, the law.

Reversed with directions to overrule the demurrer and have such further proceedings as may be according to law.

Notes

1. Was any statute necessary in this case to establish the city's negligence? Conversely, if the city violated a statute, was there any need to decide the immunity issue?

2. Which statutory provision did the City of Miami violate? Is the city's liability primary or vicarious?

3. What is the relevance of the city's "knowing" neglect of its duty to protect prisoners from venereal disease?

4. Is operating a jail not a "governmental" function merely because some of the prisoners are being held for violations of municipal ordinances rather than state statutes? Are not most state statutes designed "to promote the corporate well being of the [state] and inhabitants"?

5. How is an immunity different from the other defenses we have studied?

6. This book will not consider systematically the tangled issue of governmental or sovereign immunity from tort suits (on which see Prosser 970-987 for a good introduction), but the student should have some awareness of the issue. The common-law rule was that a government could not be sued without its consent. In 1946, in the Federal Tort Claims Act (codified in various sections of Title 28 of the United States Code), the federal government waived its immunity from tort suits, with, however, some important exceptions: in particular for intentional torts, and for acts or omissions within the "discretionary function or duty" of any federal agency or employee. Can you

think of any reason for these exceptions? As mentioned in the *Norton* case in Chapter 3, certain intentional torts by law-enforcement personnel are now embraced by the FTCA. All of the states have by statute waived their tort immunity to some, although often a quite limited, extent. Municipalities, such as the City of Miami in *Lewis*, have been treated as a mixed case. The traditional rule was that when a municipality is acting in its "governmental" capacity, as in collecting taxes or enforcing the law, it is immune from tort liability; but when it is acting in its "proprietary" capacity, as in operating a ferry or an airport, or selling gas or electricity, it is not immune. The line has proved difficult to draw in a satisfactory fashion; courts have disagreed over such things as whether maintaining streets and running hospitals are governmental or proprietary. In recent years, there has been a pronounced movement by state courts to abolish the common-law immunity of municipalities, and in some cases of the state itself. A similar judicial movement has largely succeeded in destroying another important common-law tort immunity, that of charitable institutions. See Prosser 992-996. Can you think of an economic reason why it might make sense to grant charitable institutions, but not governmental bodies, tort immunity?

Otto v. Specialties, Inc.
386 F. Supp. 1240 (N.D. Miss. 1974)

KEADY, C.J. . . .
Otto claims damages for his injuries [sustained when he fell off a ladder at defendant's place of business] under both the Mississippi common law of negligence and the Occupational Safety and Health Act of 1970 (OSHA), 29 U.S.C. §651 et seq. Otto's OSHA claim is based on allegations that the ladder from which he fell was structurally deficient, in violation of minimum safety standards issued pursuant to OSHA by the Secretary of Labor.

Defendant contends that OSHA cannot be utilized by Otto in this action, since the Act does not expressly provide any private civil remedy for its violation. Defendant further claims that no private remedy may be implied from the Act and, therefore, plaintiff should be prohibited at trial from referring to the Act or to any of the safety standards promulgated pursuant to it. . . .

The avowed purpose of OSHA, as stated in the initial section of the Act, is to "assure so far as possible every workman and woman in the Nation safe and healthful working conditions." In achieving this goal, OSHA mandates the promulgation of safety and health standards by the Secretary of Labor which have the force of law. Violation of the standards is punishable by specified criminal and civil penalties of considerable severity. Nowhere in the Act or in its legislative history can be found any indication that Congress intended to allow additional civil actions instituted by aggrieved employees

Rationale

injured through violations of OSHA standards. Indeed, 29 U.S.C. §653(b)(4) *Statute*
strongly implies that Congress intended no such remedy should be made
available:

> Nothing in this Act . . . shall be construed to supersede or in any manner *Congress sensitive to need for compensation*
> affect any workmen's compensation law or to enlarge or diminish or affect in
> any other manner the common law or statutory rights, duties, or liabilities of
> employers and employees under any law with respect to injuries, diseases, or
> death of employees arising out of, or in the course of, employment. . . .

. . . In Breitwieser v. KMS Industries, Inc., 467 F.2d 1391 (5th Cir. 1972), *Precedent*
the issue was whether the child labor provisions of the Fair Labor Standards
Act (FLSA), 29 U.S.C. §212, created a private cause of action for damages for
wrongful death. There, as here, violation of the statute was punishable by
criminal and civil sanctions, and the statute did not, on its face, make provision for any civil recovery by aggrieved employees. In rejecting the contentions of plaintiff that the FLSA be read to imply a civil remedy, the Court
adopted a method of analysis which is appropriate here.

"Although federal courts have on occasion implied remedies for infringement of federally conferred rights, . . . they have done so only when the law
creating the right provided for no remedy or for a grossly inadequate remedy.
The courts have thus implied relief when necessary to prevent abrogation of
congressional policies. The instant case presents a very different situation in
that the FLSA, rather than lacking in remedies or providing inadequate
remedies, contains a comprehensive enforcement scheme, . . . including substantial criminal penalties for violations of child labor law." The Court
concluded that the presence of efficacious federal enforcement provisions,
together with an available state remedy, was reason enough not to fashion an
additional cause of action under the FLSA.

We believe this case to be cut from the *Breitwieser* mold. Like the
FLSA, OSHA provides a comprehensive series of criminal and civil penalties
as enforcement mechanisms. Sanctions range from a civil penalty of $1,000
for a first violation not of a serious nature to a $20,000 fine and imprisonment
of one year for repeated, serious violations. These penalties are stringent and
comprehensive. If enforced, they are sufficiently powerful to insure compliance with OSHA and the Safety standards. Further, Mississippi's negligence
law is well-developed and available for Otto's use. No useful purpose related
to Congressional policy goals would be served by tacking on yet another *Holding*
enforcement vehicle. We thus conclude that OSHA permits no civil action
for damages to remedy alleged violations of OSHA safety standards.

Otto's alternative contention, that violation of OSHA standards may be
taken into account in this action as evidence of negligence under Mississippi
negligence law, involves more subtle considerations of federalism. For although it is clear that Specialties is correct in its major premise, i.e., that no
federal civil remedy can be had by a private litigant under OSHA, the effect

of OSHA on the Mississippi common law of torts is another, more perplexing matter.

It has long been the rule in Mississippi, as in most other American jurisdictions, to give effect to regulatory and penal statutes beyond their literal terms, when those statutes are violated and one whom the statute was designed to protect is injured in a manner the statute was designed to prevent. This is the familiar doctrine of negligence per se. . . .

Assuming for the moment an unexcused OSHA violation by Specialties which proximately caused an injury to Otto, can we say with confidence that the Supreme Court of Mississippi would refuse to apply the negligence per se doctrine to this action? . . .

We believe the Supreme Court of Mississippi, if faced with this question, would recognize, as we do, that what is at stake here is a question of judicial buttressing of legislative goals. We believe that with this recognition would come a realization that, before the judiciary undertakes to supplement legislatively designed sanctions it should first inquire whether any supplementation was foreseen or is needed. Such an inquiry into OSHA has been made by the federal courts, which have concluded that no private civil remedy is needed to fulfill the goals established by Congress in its adoption of the statute. That this determination was made in the context of a federal civil remedy and not within the framework of the negligence per se doctrine is to us irrelevant, since both concepts share a common raison d'etre — a judicial addition to statutory penalties thought to be inadequate to the purposes the legislative branch sought to promote. . . .

Therefore, Specialties' motion to pretermit, in the trial of this case, all mention of the Occupational Safety and Health Act and the regulations promulgated pursuant thereto must be sustained.

Notes

1. For other cases holding that there is no private right of action under OSHA, see, e.g., Federal Employees for Non-Smokers' Rights v. United States, 446 F. Supp. 181 (D.D.C. 1978); Horn v. C.L. Osborn Contracting Co., 423 F. Supp. 801 (M.D. Ga. 1976).

2. In several important cases, a federal right to obtain damages for violation of a federal statute has been recognized although the statute made no specific reference to damage actions. For example, in J.I. Case Co. v. Borak, 377 U.S. 426 (1964), the Supreme Court held that an investor could bring a damages action in respect of a proxy statement that contained misleading statements and therefore violated section 14(a) of the Securities Exchange Act of 1934, although the Act contained no reference to such an action. The Court emphasized the practical limitations on the ability of the Securities Exchange Commission to review carefully all of the thousands of proxy statements submitted annually to it, and concluded therefore that

"Private enforcement of the proxy rules provides a necessary supplement to Commission action." 377 U.S. at 432. But in Bivens v. Six Unknown Named Fed. Narcotics Agents, 403 U.S. 388, 397 (1971) (referred to in the *Norton* case in Chapter 3), holding that the Fourth Amendment creates an implied right to damages for an unconstitutional search, the Court denied that the question was "whether the availability of money damages is necessary to enforce the Fourth Amendment." See generally Hazen, Implied Private Remedies under Federal Statutes: Neither a Death Knell nor a Moratorium — Civil Rights, Securities Regulation, and Beyond, 33 Vand. L. Rev. 1333 (1980).

3. Typically, although not invariably, the predicate for invoking the negligence per se doctrine is that the defendants have violated a criminal statute. Why, therefore, should the fact that OSHA provided stringent penalties, including criminal penalties, have persuaded the court in *Otto* not to invoke the doctrine? If a safety statute were enacted without substantial penalties, could not a defendant in a civil case argue that this showed that the legislature was not really serious about enforcement and therefore would not have favored attaching tort sanctions to violations of the statute?

4. Is there any difference between the federal implied right of action doctrine illustrated by *Borak* and *Bivens* and the common-law negligence per se doctrine?

5. Is *Otto* consistent with *Stonehocker*?

Brown v. Shyne   *causal issue*
242 N.Y. 176, 151 N.E. 197 (1926)

LEHMAN, J. The plaintiff employed the defendant to give chiropractic treatment to her for a disease of physical condition. The defendant had no license to practice medicine, yet he held himself out as being able to diagnose and treat disease, and, under the provisions of the Public Health Law he was guilty of a misdemeanor. The plaintiff became paralyzed after she had received nine treatments by the defendant. She claims, and upon this appeal we must assume, that the paralysis was caused by the treatment she received. She has recovered judgment in the sum of $10,000 for the damages caused by said injury.

The plaintiff in her complaint alleges that the injuries were caused by the defendant's negligence. If negligence on the part of the defendant caused the injury, the plaintiff may recover the consequent damages. Though the defendant held himself out, and the plaintiff consulted him, as a chiropractor, and not as a regular physician, he claimed to possess the skill requisite for diagnosis and treatment of disease, and in the performance of what he undertook to do he may be held to the degree of skill and care which he claimed to possess. At the trial the plaintiff gave testimony in regard to the manner in which she was treated. She supplemented this testimony by evidence that the treatment was not in accordance with recognized theory or practice; that it produced the injury which followed; and that a person qualified to treat disease should have foreseen that the treatment might have such result. Though her testimony was contradicted, the jury might well have resolved the conflict in her favor, and, if the only question submitted to the jury had been whether or not this evidence showed that plaintiff's injury was caused by the defendant's negligence, the defendant could not complain of any substantial error at the trial. Indeed, it would seem that in some respects the rulings of the trial judge may have been too favorable to the defendant.

At the close of the plaintiff's case the plaintiff was permitted to amend the complaint to allege "that in so treating the plaintiff the defendant was engaged in the practice of medicine contrary to and in violation of the provisions of the Public Health Law of the state of New York in such case made and provided, he at the time of so treating plaintiff not being a duly licensed physician or surgeon of the state of New York." Thereafter the trial judge charged the jury that they might bring in a verdict in favor of the plaintiff if they found that the evidence established that the treatment given to the plaintiff was not in accordance with the standards of skill and care which prevail among those treating disease. He then continued:

> This is a little different from the ordinary malpractice case, and I am going to allow you, if you think proper under the evidence in the case, to predicate negligence upon another theory. The public health laws of this state prescribe that no person shall practice medicine unless he is licensed so to do by the Board of Regents of this state and registered pursuant to statute.... This statute to which I have referred is a general police regulation. Its violation, and it has been violated by the defendant, is some evidence, more or less cogent, of negligence which you may consider for what it is worth, along with all the other evidence in the case. If the defendant attempted to treat the plaintiff and to adjust the vertebrae in her spine when he did not possess the requisite knowledge and skill as prescribed by the statute to know what was proper and necessary to do under the circumstances, or how to do it, even if he did know what to do, you can find him negligent.

In so charging the jury that from the violation of the statute the jury might infer negligence which produced injury to the plaintiff, the trial justice in my opinion erred.

The provisions of the Public Health Law prohibiting the practice of medicine without a license granted upon proof of preliminary training, and after examination intended to show adequate knowledge, are of course intended for the protection of the general public against injury which unskilled and unlearned practitioners might cause. If violation of the statute by the defendant was the proximate cause of the plaintiff's injury, then the plaintiff may recover upon proof of violation. If violation of the statute has no direct bearing on the injury, proof of the violation becomes irrelevant. For injury caused by neglect of duty imposed by the penal law there is civil remedy; but, of course, the injury must follow from the neglect.

Proper formulation of general standards of preliminary education and proper examination of the particular applicant should serve to raise the standards of skill and care generally possessed by members of the profession in this state; but the license to practice medicine confers no additional skill upon the practitioner, nor does it confer immunity from physical injury upon a patient if the practitioner fails to exercise care. Here, injury may have been caused by lack of skill or care; it would not have been obviated if the defendant had possessed a license yet failed to exercise the skill and care required of one practicing medicine. True, if the defendant had not practiced medicine in this state, he could not have injured the plaintiff, but the protection which the statute was intended to provide was against risk of injury by the unskilled or careless practitioner, and, unless the plaintiff's injury was caused by carelessness or lack of skill, the defendant's failure to obtain a license was not connected with the injury. The plaintiff's cause of action is for negligence or malpractice. The defendant undertook to treat the plaintiff for a physical condition which seemed to require remedy. Under our law such treatment may be given only by a duly qualified practitioner who has obtained a license.

The defendant in offering to treat the plaintiff held himself out as qualified to give treatment. He must meet the professional standards of skill and care prevailing among those who do offer treatment lawfully. If injury follows through failure to meet those standards, the plaintiff may recover. The provisions of the Public Health Law may result in the exclusion from practice of some who are unqualified. Even a skilled and learned practitioner who is not licensed commits an offense against the state; but against such practitioners the statute was not intended to protect, for no protection was needed, and neglect to obtain a license results in no injury to the patient and, therefore, no private wrong. The purpose of the statute is to protect the public against unfounded assumption of skill by one who undertakes to prescribe or treat for disease. In order to show that the plaintiff has been injured by defendant's breach of the statutory duty, proof must be given that defendant in such treatment did not exercise the care and skill which would have been exercised by qualified practitioners within the state, and that such lack of skill and care caused the injury. Failure to obtain a license as required by law gives rise to no remedy if it has caused no injury. No case has been cited where neglect of a statutory duty has given rise to private cause of action where it has not appeared that private injury has been caused by danger against which the statute was intended to afford protection, and which obedience to the statute would have obviated. . . .

It is said that the trial justice did not charge that plaintiff might recover for defendant's failure to obtain a license, but only that failure to obtain a license might be considered "some evidence" of defendant's negligence. Argument is made that, even if neglect of the statutory duty does not itself create liability, it tends to prove that injury was caused by lack of skill or care. That can be true only if logical inference may be drawn from defendant's failure to obtain or perhaps seek a license that he not only lacks the skill and learning which would enable him to diagnose and treat disease generally, but also that he lacks even the skill and learning necessary for the physical manipulation he gave to this plaintiff. Evidence of defendant's training, learning, and skill and the method he used in giving the treatment was produced at the trial, and upon such evidence the jury could base finding either of care or negligence, but the absence of a license does not seem to strengthen inference that might be drawn from such evidence, and a fortiori would not alone be a basis for such inference. . . .

For these reasons the judgments should be reversed, and a new trial granted, with costs to abide the event.

Notes

1. Suppose no evidence had been presented regarding the nature and quality of the medical treatment that plaintiff received from defendant. Would defendant's violation of the statute have been admissible as evidence that defendant had failed to come up to the level of skill which he had represented himself to the plaintiff as possessing?

2. If defendant really did have the skill he represented to plaintiff that he had, then would not plaintiff, if she had gone to a licensed practitioner instead of to defendant, have been just as likely to become paralyzed as a result of the treatment? Is this a reason against liability? If it is, can you see why White v. Levarn was decided incorrectly? Compare Walmsley v. Rural Telephone Assn. of Delphos, 102 Kan. 139, 169 P. 197 (1917). In that case, plaintiff was on a hunting trip and was standing on a wagon carrying a loaded rifle when the wagon was upset because of defendant's telephone wire which was hanging too low across the road. Plaintiff was thrown to the ground and the gun discharged and injured him. He had no hunting license but the court held: "The want of a hunter's license and the breach of the hunter's license law did not contribute in the slightest degree to plaintiff's injuries." 102 Kan. at 142, 169 P. at 199. Do you agree?

3. In Sloan v. Coit Intl., Inc., 292 So. 2d 115 (Fla. 1974), a 14-year-old was injured while working for defendant. Because of the boy's youth, his employment was in violation of the state's child labor law. The court held that the violation was negligence per se. How is the case distinguishable from Brown v. Shyne?

4. On remand in Brown v. Shyne, defendant was found liable and ordered to pay a judgment of $13,029.82. Defendant then filed for bankruptcy. The bankruptcy court held that his judgment debt was dischargeable in bankruptcy since it was not the consequence of a willful or malicious injury.

See In re Shyne, 133 Misc. Rep. 306, 231 N.Y.S. 429 (S. Ct. 1928). Was the court right?

Prosser: this exceedingly narrow Interpretation would be considered unreasonable in recent years.

Mansfield v. Wagner Electric Mfg. Co.
294 Mo. 235, 242 S.W. 400 (1922)

BLAIR, J. . . .

Plaintiff was in the employ of defendant at the time of his injury. He was engaged in polishing a large metal casting with a movable emery wheel. This casting was too heavy to be moved to and held against a stationary emery wheel. The movable emery wheel had no hood connected with a blower or suction fan. Particles flying either from the casting or the wheel by reason of the operation of the rapidly revolving emery wheel entered one of plaintiff's eyes, and caused the injury for which he prayed damages in the sum of $10,000.

While not expressly pleading the statute in terms, plaintiff bases his action upon section 7839, R. S. 1909 (now section 6798, R. S. 1919, as amended by Laws of 1919, page 443). So much of said statute as need be quoted here reads as follows:

> Every person, firm or corporation using any polishing wheel or machine of any character which generates dust, smoke or poisonous gases in its operation, shall provide each and every such wheel or machine with a hood, which shall be connected with a blower or suction fan of sufficient power to carry off said dust, smoke and gases and prevent its inhalation by those employed about said wheel or machine; . . .

Plaintiff cites no decision of this or any other state in support of his contention that the injury sustained by him was of such character as to come within the foregoing statute. Looking to the statute, the hood, connected with the blower or suction fan of sufficient power to carry off dust, smoke, and poisonous gases, is required for the purpose of preventing injury or disease through the inhalation of such smoke, dust or gas by those required to operate polishing wheels or machines. Unless we construe the statute to cover other injuries than those received through inhalation, that is, through breathing such substances into the lungs, plaintiff cannot recover even though defendant may have violated the provisions of said statute. . . .

Respondent quotes in its brief somewhat at length from Gorris v. Scott, 9 L. R. Exchequer 125, an English case. This case strongly supports the contention of respondent. The headnotes set out the meat of the opinion, and we quote therefrom as follows:

"When a statute creates a duty with the object of preventing a mischief of a particular kind, a person who, by reason of another's neglect of the statutory duty, suffers a loss of a different kind, is not entitled to maintain an action in respect of such loss.

"The defendant, a shipowner, undertook to carry the plaintiffs' sheep from a foreign port to England. On the voyage some of the sheep were washed overboard by reason of the defendant's neglect to take a precaution enjoined by an order of Privy Council, which was made under the authority of the Contagious Diseases (Animals) Act, 1869, §75:

"Held, that the object of the statute and the order being to prevent the spread of contagious disease among animals, and not to protect them against perils of the sea, the plaintiffs could not recover."

In his concuring opinion, Pollock, B., said:

"Admit there has been a breach of duty; admit there has been a consequent injury; still the Legislature was not legislating to protect against such an injury, but for an altogether different purpose; its object was not to regulate the duty of the carrier for all purposes, but only for one particular purpose." . . .

. . . The plain purpose of the statute [in this case] is to prevent injury to the health of operators of emery wheels and other polishing wheels, due to the necessity of breathing into their lungs fumes, smoke, dust, and poisonous gases generated by the friction between such polishing wheels and the surface to be polished. The statute was designed to promote the health of employees operating such machines by providing a means of carrying off such smoke, dust, and gas by forced drafts of air or by suction. Following the conclusions reached by Baron Pollock in the *Gorris* case: Admit for the purposes of the case that defendant violated the express provisions of the statute requiring a hood and blower or suction fan; admit that the plaintiff's injury was received in consequence of defendant's failure to install such hood with blower or suction fan; still the Legislature was not legislating to protect employees against the danger of particles flying into their eyes, but for an altogether different purpose; its object was not to regulate the duty of employers for all purposes, but only for one particular purpose, to wit, *to prevent inhalation of smoke, gas and dust* by those employed about such wheels. . . .

Notes

1. Is there any causal issue in this case, as there was in Brown v. Shyne? Did not the violation of the statute increase the probability that plaintiff would injure his eye? Did not the violation of the statute in the *Gorris* case increase the probability that the animals would be washed overboard?

2. The legislature wanted defendant to hood the emery wheel, did it not? Why should it be thought averse to making the defendant pay for any accident that would have been prevented by compliance with the statute, whether or not it was the type of accident that the legislature was trying to prevent? Is it because the additional liability would interfere with the legisla-

ture's perhaps careful calibration of remedies for violation of the statute? But was not such an argument implicitly rejected in the *Otto* case?

3. Larrimore v. American Natl. Ins. Co., 184 Okl. 614, 89 P.2d 340 (1939), involved the following bizarre facts. Defendant, the owner of a hotel, furnished its lessee who operated the coffee shop in the hotel some cans of "Rat Doom" brand rat poison. In lighting the steam table in the coffee shop, the plaintiff, an employee of the lessee, accidentally ignited the rat poison (which was inflammable) lying under the table and was injured in the ensuing explosion. A statute made it a misdemeanor to "lay out strychnine or other poison" except "in a safe place." It was held that plaintiff could not invoke the doctrine of negligence per se because there was no "causal connection" between the violation of the statute and the injury. Is this case like *Mansfield* or *Gorris*? Was the court using the term "causal" in an acceptable sense? Return to these statutory causation questions after reading Chapter 8.

4. A federal regulation forbade flights below an altitude of 1,000 feet over "congested areas of cities, towns, or settlements." Two military aircraft flew less than 1,000 feet above plaintiff's mink ranch, causing the deaths of a number of mink. Fifteen seconds earlier the jets had flown over a town and within a minute after they had flown over the mink ranch they flew over another town — all at an altitude below 1,000 feet. Plaintiff sued the United States under the Federal Tort Claims Act for the damage to its mink. What result? See Wildwood Mink Ranch v. United States, 218 F. Supp. 67 (D. Minn. 1963).

Satterlee v. Orange Glenn School Dist.
29 Cal. 2d 581, 177 P.2d 279 (1947)

EDMONDS, J.

[Plaintiff was injured when his car collided in an intersection with a bus driven by an employee of defendant school district. The evidence was conflicting on who entered the intersection first and at what speed the respective vehicles were traveling. Jury verdict for plaintiff after the trial judge refused to instruct the jury that if it found that the bus had the right of way under the California Vehicle Code and that plaintiff failed to yield the right of way in violation of the Code, plaintiff was guilty of contributory negligence and defendants were therefore entitled to judgment. Instead the judge instructed the jury as follows:]

> Now, with reference to this matter of right of way, I wish to tell you members of the jury that one may have the right of way and yet be negligent. One cannot rely on the right of way arbitrarily and force anyone else off the highway. He cannot barge in and claim the right of way over one whose approach may be a menace to his safety or to the driver of that automobile's

safety. The same test which I have given you originally applies in cases on intersections of highways, regardless of who was in the intersection first, and regardless of which automobile is on the right, if they approached at the same time; that is, what would a reasonably prudent person have done under the same or similar circumstances. That applies to both the drivers colliding, whether they approach the intersection at the same time, enter it at the same time, or one entered the intersection first. In other words, these rules of law are not absolute. They must be considered in connection with what would a reasonably prudent person have done under the same or similar circumstances. . . .

The appellants [defendants] contend that in view of their defense of contributory negligence based upon an asserted violation of section 550 of the Vehicle Code, they were entitled to an unequivocal instruction in the form requested by them. The facts of this case, they insist, do not bring it within the rule that circumstances beyond a plaintiff's control may excuse violation of the statute. The court's instruction to the effect that violation of the statute was of no consequence if the plaintiff acted as a reasonably prudent person would act under similar circumstances is also challenged as erroneous. . . .

The position of the respondent [plaintiff] is that the proposed instruction gives no regard to the circumstances surrounding the accident, such as the speed at which the two vehicles approached the intersection, the attention given by each driver to other traffic, and the respective manner in which the automobile and the bus were operated. Also, the requested instruction does not include as a basis for the jury's consideration circumstances which might properly be considered as excusing violation of the statute. . . .

. . . An act or failure to act below the statutory standard is negligence per se, or negligence as a matter of law. And if the evidence establishes that the plaintiff's or defendant's violation of the statute or ordinance proximately caused the injury and no excuse or justification for violation is shown by the evidence, responsibility may be fixed upon the violator without other proof of failure to exercise due care.

However, in an emergency, or under unusual conditions, it is generally held that circumstances may be shown to excuse the violation. . . . An act which is performed in violation of an ordinance or statute is presumptively an act of negligence, but the presumption is not conclusive and may be rebutted by showing that the act was justifiable or excusable under the circumstances. Until so rebutted, it is conclusive. . . .

Thus in Rath v. Bankston, where an automobile was parked partly on the highway in violation of the statute, the defendant was allowed to show that despite reasonably careful inspection, the gasoline supply became exhausted, and the car stalled. In another case where a collision occurred with a car which had no taillight, evidence that the light was inspected and found in good order a short time before was held admissible to negative the presumption of negligence. . . .

In the application of this rule each violation of a statutory requirement must be considered in connection with the surrounding circumstances. Ordinarily, the excuse relied upon by the violator presents a question of fact for the jury's determination. . . .

In the present case the requested instruction advised the jury that if the school bus entered the intersection before the vehicle operated by Satterlee, his failure to yield the right of way constituted negligence; if the two vehicles entered the intersection at the same time, and the school bus was to the right of the Satterlee vehicle, his failure to yield the right of way constituted negligence; and if Satterlee's violation of these Vehicle Code sections proximately contributed in the slightest degree to the happening of the accident, the verdict must be in favor of the school district and its driver. But an operator of a motor vehicle cannot arbitrarily rely upon the right of way gained as a result of excessive speed or by other negligent act or violation of the law. And although the instruction correctly left the question of fact of violation to the jury, it invaded the province of the trier of fact by not tendering for consideration the issue as to whether the circumstances were such as to excuse violation. From the evidence, the jury reasonably might have found that the bus increased its speed while traveling the 200 feet immediately east of the point of impact. If, as stated by Satterlee, when he observed the bus it was about twice as far from the intersection and traveling at approximately the same speed as his own vehicle, then he reasonably was justified, the jury could have concluded, in assuming that the bus would not dangerously increase its speed in order to enter the intersection first. Certainly by his own act of increasing speed or "racing for the intersection" an automobile driver should not be allowed to charge the operator of the other vehicle in the collision with negligence per se without the right to prove justification for the statutory violation.

Furthermore, the testimony of disinterested witnesses shows that the bus driver, having unimpaired visibility, did not observe the automobile until almost the instant of impact. Under these circumstances it was a question of fact whether Satterlee's violation of the code provisions, if any, was justifiable or excusable. And although judicial discretion may be exercised in the adoption of a standard of care for the purpose of imposing civil liability, the refused instruction did not afford the jury an opportunity to pass upon the question as to whether the circumstances shown by the evidence afforded excuse or justification. For these reasons, to have instructed the jury in the terms proposed by the appellants would have constituted prejudicial error.

The instruction given by the trial judge upon his own motion presents a more difficult question. He refused to adopt the standard of care established by the Legislature and did not instruct the jury that violation of the statutory standard constituted prima facie evidence of negligence which could be rebutted by evidence of justification or excuse. Instead, upon the issue of contributory negligence, the court adopted the reasonable man standard of care exclusively, and allowed the jury to determine what constituted due care under the circumstances.... [T]he jury, in effect, was told that the school district and its driver had the burden of establishing the failure of Satterlee to act as a reasonable man under the circumstances although he had violated a statute and such violation proximately caused the accident. That is not the law. The presumption created by proof of the failure to comply with a statute or ordinance relieves a defendant from the burden of proving that the plaintiff failed to act as a reasonably prudent man. All that the defendant need prove to establish contributory negligence is that plaintiff's violation of the statute in question proximately caused the accident. Therefore, the burden cast upon the defendant where such violation is relied upon, is more easily established than a failure to act as would a reasonably prudent man under similar circumstances. If there was a violation of the applicable statute, the burden of going forward is then cast upon the plaintiff, if the defendant is relying upon contributory negligence, to present evidence justifying an excuse for violation. If the jury does not believe that the evidence is sufficient to excuse violation, it must find for the defendant.

For these reasons the adoption by the trial court of the standard of care imposed by a statute or ordinance becomes an important factor in imposing liability. The instruction given by the court on its own motion had the effect of minimizing, if not completely negativing the code provision. ...

The judgment is reversed.

TRAYNOR, J. (dissenting in part).

I concur in the judgment. I cannot agree, however, with the doctrine set forth in the majority opinion that an act or a failure to act in violation of a statute like the Vehicle Code is merely "presumptive evidence of negligence," which may be rebutted by showing that the act or omission was justifiable or excusable under the circumstances, with the excuse or justification a question of fact for the jury. This doctrine is in effect a modified form of the doctrine that the violation of a statute (herein used to include an ordinance) is merely evidence of negligence. Under the ordinary evidence-of-negligence doctrine the jury, while obliged to consider the statutory standard, is free to substitute a standard of its own. Under the majority opinion it is likewise free to do so, if the one violating the statute offers evidence of excuse or justification. Since it is a question of fact for the jury whether the excuse or justification is sufficient, the result is that one violating the statute need only offer proof that he acted as a reasonably prudent person under the circumstances, and the jury is then free to conclude therefrom that he was justified in violating the statute unless "reasonable men can draw but one inference ... pointing unerringly to ... negligence."

The statement is frequently found in the cases that an act in violation of a statute "is presumptively an act of negligence, and while the defendant is permitted to rebut such presumption by showing that the act was justifiable or excusable under the circumstances, until so rebutted it is conclusive." The vice of such a statement is that it leaves to the jury the determination of the effect of a statute, a question of law that properly belongs to the court.

Presumptions are used in ascertaining what the facts are, not in determining what the law is. If the "presumption" can be rebutted merely by showing that one charged with violating the statute acted as a reasonably prudent person under the circumstances, the controlling standard is no longer the statutory rule, but the view of the jury as to what constitutes reasonable conduct.

The vital question, presented at the outset, is whether the statutory standard is applicable at all. If it is, the conduct of the parties must be measured by that standard, and the jury is not free to determine what a reasonably prudent person would have done under the circumstances. If there is sufficient excuse or justification, there is ordinarily no violation of a statute, and the statutory standard is inapplicable. If a statute is so drawn as not to be susceptible of such a construction, so that it would impose liability without fault, the statutory standard is ordinarily not an appropriate one in a negligence case and should be rejected by the court. It is needlessly circuitous and confusing, and productive of caprice and conflict in decisions, to instruct the jury that they should first determine whether the conduct in question fell below the statutory standard and that they should then determine whether such conduct was justifiable under the circumstances. It is a question of law in each case whether the acts were in violation of the statute, or excepted therefrom, or if not excepted, whether liability without fault would be imposed by adopting the statutory standard. It is of course a question of fact whether the alleged acts occurred.

. . . "[T]o omit, willfully or heedlessly, the safeguards prescribed by law for the benefit of another that he may be preserved in life or limb, is to fall short of the standard of diligence to which those who live in organized society are under a duty to conform. . . . Jurors have no dispensing power, by which they may relax the duty that one traveler on the highway owes under the statute to another. It is error to tell them that they have." Cardozo, J., in Martin v. Herzog, 228 N.Y. 164, 126 N.E. 814. . . .

Extraordinary circumstances may justify conduct that appears to violate the letter of a statute but which is impliedly excepted therefrom, if obedience is substantially impossible or deviation from the letter of the statute is necessary to serve its purpose. "If a criminal statute or ordinance which prohibits a particular act is construed to permit such an act to be done under conditions without criminal responsibility such an act may be done under the same conditions without creating civil liability under the statute or ordinance. Many statutes and ordinances are so worded as apparently to express a universal obligatory rule of conduct. Such enactments, however, may in view of their purpose and spirit be properly construed as intended to apply only to ordinary situations and to be subject to the qualification that the conduct prohibited thereby is not wrongful if, because of an emergency or the like, the circumstances justify an apparent disobedience to the letter of the enactment. Thus, the statutory prohibition against parking an automobile on the traveled part of a highway is not applicable to one which has broken down and is incapable of motion and thus remains on the highway while the driver

is diligently seeking assistance to remove it. . . ." . . . "A classic illustration of
the same general principle is the Bologna ordinance against blood-letting in
the streets, which did not make criminals of surgeons." . . .

A statute regulating traffic must be reasonably construed not only by
limiting its effect to the situations envisaged when it was enacted, but also by
reading such provisions in conjunction with one another and with the rules of
the common law supplementing them. Thus, provisions governing the right
of way at an intersection, by their very nature, apply only to part of the
conduct of each operator of a vehicle. The safety of operators who meet at an
intersection depends also on the conduct of each of them before he reached
the critical juncture. An operator who approaches the intersection at an
improper rate of speed, or suddenly increases his speed before he reaches the
intersection, may be at fault even though he was first at the intersection and
therefore under the letter of the statute entitled to cross it. . . .

Notes

1. Is there any practical difference between interpreting the emergency
exception to the negligence per se principle flexibly — the approach favored
by the majority — and interpreting the statute flexibly — the approach favored by Justice Traynor? Is the issue one of allocation of functions between
judge and jury?

2. Does Traynor ignore the most important question in a statutory
negligence case — whether the legislature desired (or would have, had it
thought about the question) that violators be liable for damages resulting
from the violation?

3. Why does Traynor think the negligence per se doctrine inapplicable if
the criminal statute creates strict liability?

4. Is it true, as suggested by the quotation from Martin v. Herzog, that
the reasonable and prudent man would never violate a safety statute? What
if it were a foolish statute? Does Traynor believe that any statute, properly
construed, could be foolish? In Stevens v. Luther, 105 Neb. 184, 180 N.W. 87
(1920), a statute forbade driving an automobile across an intersection at a
speed exceeding 6 M.P.H. The court stated: "We all know that in the great
majority of cities, many of which in this state have less than 3,000 inhabitants,
to drive across the intersections of streets at 7, 8, 10, or 12 miles an hour is
entirely consistent with the exercise of due care, and therefore, except under
special circumstances, it is not negligence." 105 Neb. at 190, 180 N.W. at 89.
What would Traynor have done with this statute? Suppose the police ticket-
ed someone for violating the statute, in circumstances where the driver was
exercising great care — perhaps even where slowing down to the statutory
limit at an intersection would be careless. Would Traynor construe the
statute as not applying in such a case? Can a criminal statute properly be
construed more broadly in a criminal than in a tort case?

5. In Day v. Pauly, 186 Wis. 189, 202 N.W. 363 (1925), plaintiff was injured in a collision at an intersection when he turned left before reaching the center of the intersection, in violation of state law. His turning was held contributory negligence per se. It was irrelevant that the local authorities had apparently either painted arrows on the street or posted signs indicating that one could or should turn before reaching the intersection.

LEGAL CUSTOM

Warburton v. N.B. Thayer Co.
75 N.H. 592, 72 A. 826 (1909)

Case for negligence. The defendants manufactured shoes at East Rochester. The plaintiff was employed by them as a stitcher, and was injured in consequence of her dress being caught upon a shaft revolving under the bench at which she worked. One ground of negligence was the absence of a skirt guard or board. Subject to exception, the plaintiff was permitted to offer evidence that skirt boards were generally provided in the factory, and that there was none at her bench.

PER CURIAM. Exception overruled.

appellant

William Laurie Co. v. McCullough
174 Ind. 477, 90 N.E. 1014 (1910)

Custom & general usage as a defense against negligence competent, but not conclusive, even

[Plaintiff was injured when she slipped and fell while shopping in defendant's store. Plaintiff alleged that defendant had negligently spread a floor dressing of a greasy and oily nature over the floor.]

MONTGOMERY, J. . . .

Appellant [defendant] by proper questions sought to show that the floor *Proc* dressing to which this accident is attributed was in use in other stores in the city of Indianapolis at and prior to the time appellee received her injury, the experience of appellant in the use of this floor dressing through a term of years, and that no similar accidents had occurred. All such evidence was *LC* excluded. Appellant insists that the proffered testimony was competent as tending to prove that appellant was not lacking in the exercise of ordinary care for the safety of its customers, and was not chargeable with actionable negligence, so long as its conduct measured up to the standard exemplified by the general custom and practice prevailing among persons in like situation and engaged in similar business. . . .

Appellant, as the owner and occupant of the building in question, having *Rationale* induced appellee to enter therein by an implied invitation, owed her the duty of using reasonable or ordinary care to have and keep its premises in safe and suitable condition, so that she would not be unnecessarily or unreasonably

exposed to danger. As a general rule the custom and usages of well-appointed
and managed concerns in the business, or with respect to the particular
matter under investigation, are competent evidence on the question of the
care and diligence required in the proper conduct of such business, or in the
performance of the particular act under consideration. If a person charged
with contributory negligence is shown to have exercised that degree of care
for his own safety which persons of ordinary prudence in like circumstances
are accustomed to use, it may be declared as a matter of law that he is not
guilty of such negligence. The relation of master and servant is contractual,
and the servant is held to an assumption of the ordinary risks and hazards of
the business in which he engages, and the master to the exercise of that
degree of care for the safety of the servant which men of ordinary prudence
engaged in the same line of business commonly employ under like circumstances. In other negligence cases, not founded upon contractual obligations,
in which the use of ordinary care for the safety of others is required, it is
defined in the same general terms as that care which persons of average
prudence ordinarily use in like circumstances, but its application is usually
more difficult by reason of the distinctive circumstances of the particular
case. In such cases, as bearing upon the question of negligence, the custom,
usage, and practice, if any, with respect to the inculpatory act, of other well-
appointed and prudently managed concerns engaged in a similar business, are
clearly competent. A class of tradesmen, for a time, might suffer a negligent
usage or practice to continue, and might not exercise that regard for the
safety of others which would be exacted, but in the end the only standards
known to the law are human, and such as men of reasonable prudence and
care establish. It is apparent that the weight to be accorded to any such
custom or usage must depend upon the extent or the universality of its use
and its age or continuance in time, among other circumstances. Our conclusion is that in this case, and the class of cases to which it belongs, the custom
or usage of using the same and similar floor dressings in other stores and
public buildings was competent, but not conclusive, evidence. . . .

The T.J. Hooper
60 F.2d 737 (2d Cir. 1932)

L. HAND, J.

[Two tugboats owned by petitioner, the "Montrose" and the "Hooper,"
were towing coal barges, owned by Northern Barge Company, along the coast
of New Jersey. A storm came up and the barges sank. The trial court found
the tugs unseaworthy* because they did not carry radio receiving sets in

---

*"Unseaworthiness" is an admiralty doctrine that is the counterpart of the common law's
negligence doctrine. — Ed.

working order; had they done so, they would have gotten word of the change in weather in time to seek shelter in the Delaware Breakwater en route. These radios] were partly a toy, partly a part of the equipment, but neither furnished by the owner, nor supervised by it. It is not fair to say that there was a general custom among coastwise carriers so to equip their tugs. One line alone did it; as for the rest, they relied upon their crews, so far as they can be said to have relied at all. An adequate receiving set suitable for a coastwise tug can now be got at small cost and is reasonably reliable if kept up; obviously it is a source of great protection to their tows. Twice every day they can receive these predictions, based upon the widest possible information, available to every vessel within two or three hundred miles and more. Such a set is the ears of the tug to catch the spoken word, just as the master's binoculars are her eyes to see a storm signal ashore. Whatever may be said as to other vessels, tugs towing heavy coal laden barges, strung out for half a mile, have little power to manoeuvre, and do not, as this case proves, expose themselves to weather which would not turn back stauncher craft. They can have at hand protection against dangers of which they can learn in no other way.

Is it then a final answer that the business had not yet generally adopted receiving sets? There are, no doubt, cases where courts seem to make the general practice of the calling the standard of proper diligence; we have indeed given some currency to the notion ourselves. Indeed in most cases reasonable prudence is in fact common prudence; but strictly it is never its measure; a whole calling may have unduly lagged in the adoption of new and available devices. It never may set its own tests, however persuasive be its usages. Courts must in the end say what is required; there are precautions so imperative that even their universal disregard will not excuse their omission. But here there was no custom at all as to receiving sets; some had them, some did not; the most that can be urged is that they had not yet become general. Certainly in such a case we need not pause; when some have thought a device necessary, at least we may say that they were right, and the others too slack. . . .

Notes

1. Was Judge Hand correct that there was no custom in the trade of equipping seagoing tugs with usable radios? The trial court had found that there was such a custom:

> Captain Powell, master of the Menominee, who was a witness for the tugs, testified that prior to March, 1928, his tug, and all other seagoing tugs of his company, were equipped by the owner with efficient radio sets, and that he regarded a radio as part "of the necessary equipment" of every reasonably well-equipped tug in the coastwise service. He further testified that 90 per cent of the coastwise tugs operating along the coast were so equipped. It is, of course,

true that many of these radio sets were the personal property of the tug master, and not supplied by the owner. This was so with the Mars, Waltham, and Menominee; but, notwithstanding that fact, the use of the radio was shown to be so extensive as to amount almost to a universal practice in the navigation of coastwise tugs along the coast. I think therefore there was a duty on the part of the tug owner to supply effective receiving sets.

The T.J. Hooper, 53 F.2d 107, 111 (S.D.N.Y. 1931). The court of appeals did not overturn this finding. Does it make any difference whether the owner or the master bought and paid for the radio? Certainly to an economist it does not. If the master pays for the radio, the owner will have to compensate him with a higher wage; if the owner pays for the radio, the wage will be lower.

2. The question whether compliance with the customary level of care in a trade should be a defense to a negligence action brings into sharp focus the bearing of the Coase theorem on the law of torts. If the costs of transacting between potential injurers and potential victims are low, then the parties will bargain to the optimal level of safety; the customary level of care will be the optimal level of care. Such was probably the case in The T. J. Hooper. There was an explicit contractual relationship between the owners of the tugs and the owners of the barges they towed and between the owners of the barges and the owners of the cargo carried on the barges. Therefore, if a tug was not equipped with a radio, the natural inference that an economist would draw is that the barge owner had been compensated for the absence of the radio (and hence increased danger of the barge's being damaged) by paying a lower price for towage. By passing on a portion of the savings to the owner of the cargo, the barge owner would compensate the latter for the added risk of damage to his goods. Would it matter to this conclusion what percentage of tugs, short of 100 percent, were equipped with a radio?

Now suppose the safety device in question was one that protected people who were not in any actual or potential contractual relationship with the potential injurer. An example would be a whistle on a train designed to alert travelers at a railroad crossing that the train was approaching. Here it would be improper to conclude that because no trains were equipped with whistles, the failure to have whistles could not be negligence. Since the railroad would not be compensated for the cost of the whistles by the people benefiting from them (or by anyone else for that matter), it would have no incentive to incur this cost unless it was liable for accidents resulting from its failure to do so. In this case, were it not for liability, the accident costs resulting from the failure to take precautions would be external costs of the railroad that it would not consider in making safety decisions unless forced to do so by the legal system, assuming there are too many potential victims to negotiate with over the level of care.

Is *McCullough* more like the tugboat case or more like the whistle case? That is, were transaction costs low or high? Should compliance with the customary standard of care be an absolute defense to tort liability whenever *lack of information, could kill*

No, Strategic behavior, free riders, etc, could keep
parties from reaching optimum in safety agreement

transaction costs are low? Could one reach this conclusion on the basis of the assumption of risk defense? (See Chapter 5.) Finally, suppose defendant in the whistle case proved that although every other railroad in the country had installed a whistle to warn travelers at crossings, it could not afford to do so because it paid higher wages to whistle installers than other railroads did. Is this a good excuse for failing to comply with the customary standard of care? *No*

3. Even in "stranger" (i.e., high transaction cost) cases, where there is no presumption that the customary standard of care is the optimal standard, plaintiffs face an uphill battle in convincing judges and juries that "a whole calling . . . [has] unduly lagged in the adoption of new and available devices." Inevitably in such a case plaintiff's evidence has a somewhat speculative cast. Yet plaintiffs sometimes succeed, as the cases in this section illustrate; and they have had some especially dramatic recent successes in the products liability area, as we shall see in Chapter 9.

Shilkret v. Annapolis Emergency Hospital Assn.
276 Md. 187, 349 A.2d 245 (1975)

LEVINE, J. . . .

. . . [T]he infant plaintiff, Mark Alan Shilkret, was born at the Anne Arundel General Hospital (Anne Arundel) on December 22, 1968, and has been continuously institutionalized since that date because of brain damage that appellants allege resulted from intracranial bleeding caused by negligence at delivery. This was allegedly complicated by subsequent treatment rendered by appellees, the various attending physicians and the hospital. The several physicians who are appellees here include two obstetricians who treated the mother throughout the prenatal stage and then delivered the infant, an anesthesiologist in attendance at birth, and a pediatrician at the hospital who allegedly examined the infant the day after his birth.

At the trial, after excerpts from the depositions of the four defendant-physicians had been admitted in evidence, argument ensued over the applica- — *Issue* — ble standard of care. When the court indicated that it would apply "the strict locality rule," appellants conceded that they could not prove their case against appellees under that standard and requested leave to make a proffer of expert medical testimony which "could meet any other rule in medical negligence cases." They were afforded this opportunity and proceeded with extensive statements of what their two experts, an obstetrician-gynecologist and a neurosurgeon, would say if called as witnesses. Each expert had an impressive curriculum vitae.

The proffered testimony of the obstetrician-gynecologist established that Anne Arundel belongs to the American Hospital Association, one of several members of the accrediting body known as the Joint Commission on Accreditation of Hospitals. It was his opinion that all hospitals belonging to this group meet a national standard in caring for obstetrical patients. At the time of the infant's birth, the witness had been chief of the obstetrical-gynecological services at the U. S. Army Hospital at Aberdeen Proving Ground. He believed that in this branch of medicine, the standards at Anne Arundel were the same as those observed at Aberdeen and at all other accredited hospitals in the United States. Similarly, as a member of the American College of Gynecologists and Obstetricians, and being board certi-fied, he believed that a national standard of care applied to those with the same qualifications. He then detailed how the failure of the four physicians and the hospital to meet the national standards of care applicable to them resulted in the injury to the plaintiff.

The other expert witness whose testimony was proffered would have stated in some detail that he was employed as a neurosurgeon at the National Institutes of Health at Bethesda, Maryland, that a national standard of care is observed in the diagnosis and treatment of neurological diseases, the knowl-edge of which is also possessed by general practitioners, and that each of the defendants had violated what he believed to be a national standard regarding the care of newborn infants.

Following these proffers, the trial judge granted each appellee's motion for a directed verdict. He adhered to his previously pronounced belief that the "strict locality" standard applies in Maryland, rather than the "national" (in which the standard of care is not tied to a particular geographic locality) or "similar locality" (the standard of care observed by physicians of ordinary skill and care in either the defendant-physician's locality or in a similar communi-ty) tests urged by appellants, and therefore ruled that the latter had failed to present a sufficient case for the jury. The Court of Special Appeals affirmed, holding that its own prior cases — and the decisions of this Court — com-pelled this result. For reasons that follow, we reverse. . . .

The earliest traces of the strict locality rule appeared a century ago. It is an exclusive product of the United States; possibly because of the difference in the size of the two countries, the English courts have never developed such a principle. The rule was unquestionably developed to protect the rural and small town practitioner, who was presumed to be less adequately informed and equipped than his big city brother. . . .

> . . . In the smaller towns and country, those who practice medicine and surgery, though often possessing a thorough theoretical knowledge of the high-est elements of the profession do not enjoy so great opportunities of daily observation and practical operations, where the elementary studies are brought into every day use, as those have who reside in the metropolitan towns, and though just as well informed in the elements and literature of their profession, they should not be expected to exercise that high degree of skill and practical knowledge possessed by those having greater facilities for performing and wit-nessing operations, and who are, or may be constantly observing the various accidents and forms of disease. . . .

In short, the rationale underlying the development of the strict locality rule a century ago was grounded in the manifest inequality existing in that day between physicians practicing in large urban centers and those practicing in remote rural areas.

Ultimately, the rule came under sharp attack on two grounds. First, "[i]t effectively immunized from malpractice liability any doctor who happened to be the sole practitioner in his community. He could be treating bone fractures by the application of wet grape leaves and yet remain beyond the criticism of more enlightened practitioners from other communities." Secondly, a "conspiracy of silence" in the plaintiff's locality could effectively preclude any possibility of obtaining expert medical testimony.

Whatever may have justified the strict locality rule fifty or a hundred years ago, it cannot be reconciled with the realities of medical practice today. "New techniques and discoveries are available to all doctors within a short period of time through medical journals, closed circuit television presentations, special radio networks for doctors, tape recorded digests of medical literature, and current correspondence courses." More importantly, the quality of medical school training itself has improved dramatically in the last century. Where early medical education consisted of a course of lectures over a period of six months, which was supplemented by apprenticeships with doctors who had even less formal education, there now exists a national accrediting system which has contributed to the standardization of medical schools throughout the country.

A distinct minority of states, however, cling to the strict locality rule. Nevertheless, recognizing the significant developments which have occurred in the training and practice of medicine, and the population shifts which have marked the increased urbanization of our society, a majority of American courts have now abandoned the strict locality rule as being too narrow. We, too, conclude that it can be sustained no longer given the current state of medical science.

. . . [O]ne of the earliest applications of the similar locality rule occurred in Small v. Howard, where, essentially for the same reasons that have traditionally undergirded the strict locality rule, the court enunciated as the standard: "that skill only which physicians and surgeons of ordinary ability and skill, practising in similar localities, with opportunities for no larger experience, ordinarily possess"; thus the defendant "was not bound to possess that high degree of art and skill possessed by eminent surgeons practising in large cities, and making a specialty of the practice of surgery."

A plurality, if not a majority, of states apply the similar locality rule.

The similar locality rule answers some of the criticism aimed at the strict locality standard by enabling the plaintiff to obtain expert witnesses from different communities, thus reducing the likelihood of their acquaintance with the defendant. It does not, however, effectively alleviate the other potential problem, a low standard of care in some of the smaller communities, because the standard in similar communities is apt to be the same.

Another criticism leveled at the similar locality rule is the difficulty which arises in defining a "similar" locality.[5] For these reasons, the similar locality rule is regarded as no more than a slight improvement over the stricter standard.

These deficiencies in the locality rules and the increasing emphasis on the availability of medical facilities have led some courts to dilute the rules by extending geographical boundaries to include those centers that are readily accessible for appropriate treatment. This expanded rule, expressed in terms of "medical neighborhood" or "medical locality," has paved the way for the national standard. In any event, the trend continues away from standards which rest solely on geographic considerations.

Ever-increasing emphasis on medical specialization has accelerated the erosion of the locality rules and the concomitant emergence of the so-called national standard.[6] Even within the framework of the locality rules, it has been generally accepted that where a physician holds himself out as a specialist, he is held to a higher standard of knowledge and skill than a general practitioner. Some courts, therefore, have abandoned the locality rules for a national standard only as to specialists. This is consistent with the position of the American Law Institute which otherwise adopts the similar locality rule.

Were we to adopt a standard tied to locality for specialists, we would clearly be ignoring the realities of medical life. As we have indicated, the various specialties have established uniform requirements for certification. The national boards dictate the length of residency training, subjects to be covered, and the examinations given to the candidates for certification. Since the medical profession itself recognizes national standards for specialists that are not determined by geography, the law should follow suit.

The courts in another group of cases, however, have gone further, and have adopted this same standard of care — one which is not governed by the locality of the defendant — for all physicians regardless of whether they are specialists or not.

---

5. One standard which has been applied is geographic proximity between communities, which retains much of the "same" locality flavor. Other courts have considered socio-economic factors such as population, type of economy, size of city, and income of inhabitants. Most courts applying this standard, however, have adopted the view that "similar" locality should be defined in terms of medical factors such as the existence of research and laboratory facilities, medical schools, teaching hospitals and modern equipment in the localities to be compared. The commentators agree that this is the most logical application of the rule when measured against a major reason for its adoption — the availability of resources which will enable the physician to maintain the standard of his practice.

6. The editorial board of one law review conducted a survey to determine the extent to which the practice of medicine by certified specialists within each of the 19 specialties recognized by the American Medical Association is similar throughout the country. On the basis of the existence of standarized requirements for certification, subscription to medical specialty journals, specialist societies, and statements from national specialty boards, it was concluded that the practice of medicine by certified specialists within most medical specialties is similar throughout the country.

We agree with these courts that justification for the locality rules no longer exists. The modern physician bears little resemblance to his predecessors. As we have indicated at length, the medical schools of yesterday could not possibly compare with the accredited institutions of today, many of which are associated with teaching hospitals. But the contrast merely begins at that point in the medical career; vastly superior postgraduate training, the dynamic impact of modern communications and transportation, the proliferation of medical literature, frequent seminars and conferences on a variety of professional subjects, and the growing availability of modern clinical facilities are but some of the developments in the medical profession which combine to produce contemporary standards that are not only much higher than they were just a few short years ago, but also are national in scope.

In sum, the traditional locality rules no longer fit the present-day medical malpractice case. *Holding*

Moreover, while a specialist may be held to greater skill and knowledge in his particular field than would be required of a general practitioner under the same or similar circumstances, one standard can be fashioned for all physicians. . . . To that extent, there is no valid basis for distinguishing between general practitioners and specialists in applying standards of care. Although national board certification in the specialties has contributed significantly to standardization on a nationwide scale, all of the other reasons which justify a national standard of care apply with equal validity to general practitioners. . . .

. . . [W]e hold that a physician is under a duty to use that degree of care *Holding* and skill which is expected of a reasonably competent practitioner in the same class to which he belongs, acting in the same or similar circumstances. Under this standard, advances in the profession, availability of facilities, together with all other relevant considerations, are to be taken into account. . . .

. . . Hospitals in general, and Anne Arundel in particular, are accredited by the Joint Commission on Accreditation. This group establishes national standards to which all hospitals seeking accreditation must conform. In addition, hospitals in Maryland are subject to a rigorous regulatory scheme which promotes statewide standards. These factors, together with much of what we said earlier regarding physicians, warrant the adoption of a standard of care for hospitals which conforms to that applied in cases against physicians. . . .

Here, there was evidence that there is a national standard of care for accredited hospitals in the prenatal, intrapartum and perinatal periods of pregnancy. Similarly, the evidence proffered by appellants showed national standards of care for child delivery, infant care, and the treatment of neurological problems generally, and the measure of vital functions specifically, that are observed by specialists and general practitioners alike. Under our holdings here, this evidence was sufficient to take the standard of care issue to the jury as to all of the appellees. . . .

Notes

1. As suggested in the opinion, the strict locality rule made it difficult for plaintiffs in medical malpractice suits to prevail. Only a physician practicing in the locality could give expert evidence concerning the standard of care customary in that locality, and especially in small towns it was difficult to get physicians to testify against a fellow practitioner. (Why is expert testimony regarding the customary standard of care ordinarily an essential part of the plaintiff's evidence in a professional malpractice action?)

2. The locality rules are exceptions to the reasonable-man standard, discussed earlier. Is the rule announced in *Shilkret* a return to that standard? Could abandonment of the locality rules lead to a reduction in the legal standard of care in big cities?

3. Medical malpractice is an area of tort law where, until recently, compliance with the customary standard of care was a complete defense to tort liability. Is this result justified by the technical nature of medical care? Is it justified by the Coase theorem, because the potential injurers and potential victims have a preexisting contractual relationship? In connection with the second question, notice that the market in medical care has characteristics that may prevent it from generating the optimal standard of care without legal intervention: high costs of information, compounded by various legal and professional restrictions on advertising by physicians and hospitals; and prevalence of third-party payment schemes (Medicare, Medicaid, Blue Cross-Blue Shield, etc.) which reduce the incentives of patients to shop carefully among competing providers of health care. How do these factors bear on the appropriateness of recognizing a defense of custom in malpractice cases? How do they bear on the locality-rule question? For economic analysis of medical malpractice, see the essays in The Economics of Medical Malpractice (S. Rottenberg ed. 1978) and the materials in Chapter 11 of this book.

Helling v. Carey
83 Wash. 2d 514, 519 P.2d 981 (1974)

HUNTER, J.

This case arises from a malpractice action instituted by the plaintiff (petitioner), Barbara Helling.

The plaintiff suffers from primary open angle glaucoma. Primary open angle glaucoma is essentially a condition of the eye in which there is an interference in the ease with which the nourishing fluids can flow out of the eye. Such a condition results in pressure gradually rising above the normal level to such an extent that damage is produced to the optic nerve and its fibers with resultant loss in vision. The first loss usually occurs in the periphery of the field of vision. The disease usually has few symptoms and, in the absence of a pressure test, is often undetected until the damage has become extensive and irreversible.

The defendants (respondents), Dr. Thomas F. Carey and Dr. Robert C. Laughlin, are partners who practice the medical specialty of ophthalmology. Ophthalmology involves the diagnosis and treatment of defects and diseases of the eye.

The plaintiff first consulted the defendants for myopia, nearsightedness, *Facts* in 1959. At that time she was fitted with contact lenses. She next consulted the defendants in September, 1963, concerning irritation caused by the contact lenses. Additional consultations occurred in October, 1963; February, 1967; September, 1967; October, 1967; May, 1968; July, 1968; August, 1968; September, 1968; and October, 1968. Until the October 1968 consultation, the defendants considered the plaintiff's visual problems to be related solely to complications associated with her contact lenses. On that occasion, the defendant, Dr. Carey, tested the plaintiff's eye pressure and field of vision for the first time. This test indicated that the plaintiff had glaucoma. The plaintiff, who was then 32 years of age, had essentially lost her peripheral vision and her central vision was reduced to approximately 5 degrees vertical by 10 degrees horizontal.

. . . During trial, the testimony of the medical experts for both the plaintiff and the defendants established that the standards of the profession for that specialty in the same or similar circumstances do not require routine pressure tests for glaucoma upon patients under 40 years of age. The reason the pressure test for glaucoma is not given as a regular practice to patients under the age of 40 is that the disease rarely occurs in this age group. . . .

The defendants argue that the standard of the profession, which does not require the giving of a routine pressure test to persons under the age of 40, is adequate to insulate the defendants from liability for negligence because the risk of glaucoma is so rare in this age group. The testimony of the defendant, Dr. Carey, however, is revealing as follows:

Q.   Now, when was it, actually, the first time any complaint was made to you by her of any field or visual field problem?
A.   Really, the first time that she really complained of a visual field problem was the August 30th date. [1968]
Q.   And how soon before the diagnosis was that?
A.   That was 30 days. We made it on October 1st.
Q.   And in your opinion, how long, as you now have the whole history and analysis and the diagnosis, how long had she had this glaucoma?
A.   I would think she probably had it ten years or longer.
Q.   Now, Doctor, there's been some reference to the matter of taking pressure checks of persons over 40. What is the incidence of glaucoma, the statistics, with persons under 40?

these statistics are entire population, not for people complaining of symptoms compatible with a diagnosis of glaucoma

A.   In the instance of glaucoma under the age of 40, is less than 100 to one per cent. The younger you get, the less the incidence. It is thought to be in the neighborhood of one in 25,000 people or less.

Q.   How about the incidence of glaucoma in people over 40?

A.   Incidence of glaucoma over 40 gets into the two to three per cent category, and hence, that's where there is this great big difference and that's why the standard around the world has been to check pressures from 40 on.

The incidence of glaucoma in one out of 25,000 persons under the age of 40 may appear quite minimal. However, that one person, the plaintiff in this instance, is entitled to the same protection, as afforded persons over 40, essential for timely detection of the evidence of glaucoma where it can be arrested to avoid the grave and devastating result of this disease. The test is a simple pressure test, relatively inexpensive. There is no judgment factor involved, and there is no doubt that by giving the test the evidence of glaucoma can be detected. The giving of the test is harmless if the physical condition of the eye permits. The testimony indicates that although the condition of the plaintiff's eyes might have at times prevented the defendants from administering the pressure test, there is an absence of evidence in the record that the test could not have been timely given. . . .

Holding   Under the facts of this case reasonable prudence required the timely giving of the pressure test to this plaintiff. The precaution of giving this test to detect the incidence of glaucoma to patients under 40 years of age is so imperative that irrespective of its disregard by the standards of the ophthalmology profession, it is the duty of the courts to say what is required to protect patients under 40 from the damaging results of glaucoma.

We therefore hold, as a matter of law, that the reasonable standard that should have been followed under the undisputed facts of this case was the timely giving of this simple, harmless pressure test to this plaintiff and that, in failing to do so, the defendants were negligent, which proximately resulted in the blindness sustained by the plaintiff for which the defendants are liable. . . .

Reasonable standard not always = custom

Notes

1. Despite the statement in the court's opinion regarding the standards of the medical profession, the relevant texts have long urged that the pressure test be administered routinely, regardless of age. "Since elevated intraocular pressure precedes the loss of field [of vision] by a number of years, routine tonometry *on all patients who are old enough to cooperate* is essential if one is to detect early glaucoma. The ophthalmologist has an ideal opportunity and obligation to make such measurements on all patients seen for refractive problems." B. Becker & R. N. Shaffer, Diagnosis and Therapy of the

Glaucomas 183 (2d ed. 1961) (emphasis in original). To similar effect, see L. L. Garner, Tonography and the Glaucomas 384 (1965); Goldwyn, Waltman & Becker, Primary Open-Angle Glaucoma in Adolescents and Young Adults, 84 Archives of Ophthalmology 579, 582 (1970); W. Leydhecker, Glaucoma in Ophthalmic Practice 14-18, 86 (1966).

Nevertheless, the reaction of the medical profession to the *Helling* decision was strongly negative. See, e.g., O'Hern, Medicolegal Rounds: Leading Cases, 230 J. Am. Med. Assn. 1577 (1974). One critic made an interesting technical point: the pressure test is inconclusive. See Bradford, A Unique Decision, 2 J. Legal Medicine 52 (Sept./Oct. 1974). (How would this fact affect a Hand formula analysis of the court's opinion?) He also noted that the test could occasionally cause corneal injury.

2. If the pressure test for people under 40 is as good an idea as the court believed, why don't all ophthalmologists give the test routinely to their under-40 as well as 40-and-over patients? Physicians are in the business of selling medical services — so don't they have a strong self-interest in administering any worthwhile test? Perhaps the answer is that, the court and medical scholars to the contrary notwithstanding, the test is not so worthwhile, at least if evaluated in cost-benefit terms. If only one in 25,000 people under the age of 40 has glaucoma, we must next ask how this incidence is distributed among the different age groups in the under-40 class. Suppose the incidence is evenly distributed among these age groups. This would make the probability that a given individual would get glaucoma in a given year before he reached the age of 40 roughly one in one million (1/25,000 divided by 39 is approximately 1/1,000,000). Hence, if the test is given annually to people in the under-40 class, PL in the Hand formula would be one millionth (P) of the cost (L) in impaired eyesight from failing to detect glaucoma before it has begun to destroy one's peripheral vision. Even if that cost is reckoned to be very high, the time and money costs of the pressure test would have to be very low indeed to make annual testing worthwhile in Hand formula (cost-benefit) terms. However, the possibility of giving the test less frequently, the inconclusiveness of the test, and the fact that the incidence of glaucoma may increase with age even in the under-40 group are considerations that may weaken (or strengthen?) this conclusion.

3. Is there an argument that plaintiff in *Helling* was contributorily negligent?

4. One year after the *Helling* decision, the Washington legislature passed a statute relating to medical malpractice, Wash. Rev. Code §4.24.260 (pocket pt. 1980), which reads in pertinent part as follows:

> In any civil action for damages based on professional negligence against a hospital which is licensed by the state of Washington or against the personnel of any such hospital, or against a member of the healing arts including, but not limited to, a physician . . . the plaintiff in order to prevail shall be required to prove by a preponderance of the evidence that the defendant or defendants

failed to exercise that degree of skill, care and learning possessed by other persons in the same profession and that as a proximate result of such failure the plaintiff suffered damages. . . .

Does the statute overrule *Helling*? See Gates v. Jensen, 20 Wash. App. 81, 579 P.2d 374 (1978).

Cobbs v. Grant
8 Cal. 3d 229, 502 P.2d 1 (1972)

[The facts are set out in the material quoted from this case in Chapter 3, supra.] *p137*

[On the question of informed consent, the judge instructed the jury that the] "physician violates his duty to his patient and subjects himself to liability if he withholds any facts which are necessary to form the basis of an intelligent consent by the patient to the proposed treatment."

Defendant raises two objections to the foregoing instruction. First, he points out that the majority of the California cases have measured the duty to disclose not in terms of an absolute, but as a duty to reveal such information as would be disclosed by a doctor in good standing within the medical community. . . . Defendant's second contention is that this near unanimity reflects strong policy reasons for vesting in the medical community the unquestioned discretion to determine if the withholding of information by a doctor from his patient is justified at the time the patient weighs the risks of the treatment against the risks of refusing treatment. . . .

. . . In many instances, to the physician, whose training and experience enable a self-satisfying evaluation, the particular treatment which should be undertaken may seem evident, but it is the prerogative of the patient, not the physician, to determine for himself the direction in which he believes his interests lie. To enable the patient to chart his course knowledgeably, reasonable familiarity with the therapeutic alternatives and their hazards becomes essential.

Therefore, we hold, as an integral part of the physician's overall obligation to the patient there is a duty of reasonable disclosure of the available choices with respect to proposed therapy and of the dangers inherently and potentially involved in each.

A concomitant issue is the yardstick to be applied in determining reasonableness of disclosure. This defendant and the majority of courts have related the duty to the custom of physicians practicing in the community. The majority rule is needlessly overbroad. Even if there can be said to be a medical community standard as to the disclosure requirement for any prescribed treatment, it appears so nebulous that doctors become, in effect, vested with virtual absolute discretion. . . . Unlimited discretion in the physician is irreconcilable with the basic right of the patient to make the ultimate informed decision regarding the course of treatment to which he knowledgeably consents to be subjected.

A medical doctor, being the expert, appreciates the risks inherent in the procedure he is prescribing, the risks of a decision not to undergo the treatment, and the probability of a successful outcome of the treatment. But once this information has been disclosed, that aspect of the doctor's expert function has been performed. The weighing of these risks against the individual subjective fears and hopes of the patient is not an expert skill. Such evaluation and decision is a nonmedical judgment reserved to the patient alone. A patient should be denied the opportunity to weigh the risks only where it is evident he cannot evaluate the data, as for example, where there is an emergency or the patient is a child or incompetent. . . .

. . . Two qualifications to a requirement of "full disclosure" need little explication. First, the patient's interest in information does not extend to a lengthy polysyllabic discourse on all possible complications. A mini-course in medical science is not required; the patient is concerned with the risk of death or bodily harm, and problems of recuperation. Second, there is no physician's duty to discuss the relatively minor risks inherent in common procedures, when it is common knowledge that such risks inherent in the procedure are of very low incidence.[1] When there is a common procedure a doctor must, of course, make such inquiries as are required to determine if for the particular patient the treatment under consideration is contraindicated — for example, to determine if the patient has had adverse reactions to antibiotics; but no warning beyond such inquiries is required as to the remote possibility of death or serious bodily harm.

However, when there is a more complicated procedure, as the surgery in the case before us, the jury should be instructed that when a given procedure inherently involves a known risk of death or serious bodily harm, a medical doctor has a duty to disclose to his patient the potential of death or serious harm, and to explain in lay terms the complications that might possibly occur. Beyond the foregoing minimal disclosure, a doctor must also reveal to his patient such additional information as a skilled practitioner of good standing would provide under similar circumstances.

In sum, the patient's right of self-decision is the measure of the physician's duty to reveal. That right can be effectively exercised only if the patient possesses adequate information to enable an intelligent choice. The scope of the physician's communications to the patient, then, must be measured by the patient's need, and that need is whatever information is material to the decision. Thus the test for determining whether a potential peril must be divulged is its materiality to the patient's decision. . . .

1. For example, the risks inherent in the simple process of taking a common blood sample are said to include hematoma, dermatitis, cellulitis, abscess, osteomyelitis, septicemia, endocarditis, thrombophlebitis, pulmonary embolism and death, to mention a few. . . .

Whenever appropriate, the court should instruct the jury on the defenses available to a doctor who has failed to make the disclosure required by law. Thus, a medical doctor need not make disclosure of risks when the patient requests that he not be so informed. Such a disclosure need not be made if the procedure is simple and the danger remote and commonly appreciated to be remote. A disclosure need not be made beyond that required within the medical community when a doctor can prove by a preponderance of the evidence he relied upon facts which would demonstrate to a reasonable man the disclosure would have so seriously upset the patient that the patient would not have been able to dispassionately weigh the risks of refusing to undergo the recommended treatment. . . .

Letter from Preston J. Burnham to *SCIENCE* on Medical Experimentation in Humans
152 Sci. 448 (1966)

. . . *Proposed informed-consent form for hernia patient*:

I, _____ , being about to be subjected to a surgical operation said to be for repair of what my doctor thinks is a hernia (rupture or loss of belly stuff — intestines — out of the belly through a hole in the muscles), do hereby give said doctor permission to cut into me and do duly swear that I am giving my informed consent, based upon the following information:

Operative procedure is as follows: The doctor first cuts through the skin by a four-inch gash in the lower abdomen. He then slashes through the other things — fascia (a tough layer over the muscles) and layers of muscle — until he sees the cord (tube that brings the sperm from testicle to outside) with all its arteries and veins. The doctor then tears the hernia (thin sac of bowels and things) from the cord and ties off the sac with a string. He then pushes the testicle back into the scrotum and sews everything together, trying not to sew up the big arteries and veins that nourish the leg.

Possible complications are as follows:

1) Large artery may be cut and I may bleed to death.

2) Large vein may be cut and I may bleed to death.

3) Tube from testicle may be cut, I will then be sterile on that side.

4) Artery or veins to testicles may be cut — same result.

5) Opening around cord in muscles may be made too tight.

6) Clot may develop in these veins which will loosen when I get out of bed and hit my lungs, killing me.

7) Clot may develop in one or both legs which may cripple me, lead to loss of one or both legs, go to my lungs, or make my veins no good for life.

8) I may develop a horrible infection that may kill me.

9) The hernia may come back again after it has been operated on.

10) I may die from general anesthesia.

11) I may be paralyzed if spinal anesthesia is used.

12) If ether is used, it could explode inside me.

13) I may slip in hospital bathroom.

14) I may be run over going to the hospital.

15) The hospital may burn down.

I understand: The anatomy of the body, the pathology of the development of hernia, the surgical technique that will be used to repair the hernia, the physiology of wound healing, the dietetic chemistry of the foods that I must eat to cause healing, the chemistry of body repair, and the course which my physician will take in treating any of the complications that can occur as a sequela of repairing an otherwise simple hernia.

_____
Patient

_____
Lawyer for Patient

_____
Lawyer for Doctor

_____
Lawyer for Hospital

_____
Lawyer for Anesthesiologist

_____
Mother-in-Law

_____
Notary Public

_____
Date

_____
Place

B. M. Patten, Death Related to Informed Consent
72 Tex. Medicine 49 (Dec. 1978)

Recent changes in ethics have altered the patterns of medical practice and medical research in this country. The full impact of the new ethics on medicine has not yet been felt and probably will not be known for some time. Until we see the results of detailed, unbiased studies demonstrating favorable risk-benefit ratios, cost-effectiveness, and lack of significant adverse effects, we should not conclude that the new rules of ethics are necessary, needed, or beneficial. On the contrary, wisdom dictates that customs long established should not be changed for light and transient causes and some physicians have already pointed out possible adverse effects of the new rules. Ingelfinger, for instance, has noted the alarming trend toward dilution and depreciation of the important by a proliferation of the trivial; patients and physicians, deluged with countless releases and consents, may lose sight of, and respect for, the important issues. . . .

The new type of fully informed consent, too, may have adverse effects. Not only is the cost of medical care increased because physicians spend more time explaining medical risks, but also there is danger that complete information may generate uncontrollable fear or irrational rejection of a needed treatment.

The following case reports illustrate possible adverse consequences caused by attempts to obtain fully informed consent.

Case 1: A 52-year-old welder was in excellent health until he was injured in an automobile collision. Following the accident, the patient developed pain in his lumbar region. Muscle relaxants, analgesics, bed rest, bed board, and heating pad gave no lasting relief.

The patient had been a welder for more than 17 years and was proud of his ability and his earnings (more than $17,000 yearly). His main concern, expressed to his physicians many times, was to return to work as soon as possible.

Neurological examination showed weakness of the extensors of the right big toe, decreased ankle jerk, decreased pin perception on the bottom of the right foot, and decreased vibratory sensation on the right big toe.

Roentgenograms of the spine showed six, instead of the normal five, lumbar vertebrae. The myelogram demonstrated extradural defects at L4-5 and L5-6, and nerve conduction tests showed prolongation of distal latency of the right tibial nerve to 8.2 msec, indicating a tarsal tunnel compression.

The plan was to release the tarsal tunnel first and then, if the patient still had symptoms, to do a lumbar laminectomy.

The day before the scheduled operation, the neurosurgeon tried to get truly informed consent by telling the patient that the operation might cause hemorrhage, infection, paralysis, or death. The patient signed himself out of the hospital and wrote the following note to his neurologist: "I decided not to have the operation as Dr. _____ told me it was very dangerous, and couldn't promise me if it would be successful and said there was always a possibility of being paralyzed."

At home, the patient continued to have pain and told his wife that there wasn't much for him to live for because the doctors couldn't help the back pain. One day when pain was particularly severe he put the muzzle of his shotgun in his mouth and pulled the trigger.

Case 2: A 54-year-old lawyer developed substernal crushing chest pain which increased with exercise and decreased with rest or nitroglycerine. Because the chest pains worsened during a three-month period, requiring more nitroglycerine but yielding less benefit, angiocardiograms were performed. They showed segmental occlusion of two coronary arteries. A bypass operation was proposed. In view of the patient's occupation, complete disclosure of risks and possible benefits of surgery and anesthesia was given during a two-hour conference with the patient. Subsequently, he refused surgery. One month later, he suffered a severe myocardial infarction and died en route to the hospital.

The neurosurgeon who tried to get informed consent from patient 1 had had, a few months before, a judgment entered against him for the malpractice of a resident operating under his supervision. His earnest desire to comply with recent legal requirements in order to avoid further litigation probably explains his vivid description of the possible consequences of surgery which, after all, was only a release of the tarsal tunnel. The patient, a man with no medical experience, interpreted the explanation as a sign that the doctor didn't want to do the procedure and that there was no hope that the condition could be corrected. Extinction of hope, according to Beck, is the single most important factor leading to suicide; therefore, the depression caused by physical pain and loss of income, associated with the seeming hopelessness of his situation, probably led to the patient's suicide.

In case 2 it is possible that, if the patient had been an ordinary citizen and not a malpractice lawyer, the minutiae of coronary surgery would not have been covered in the attempt to obtain informed consent, and the patient might have accepted the operation as most patients ordinarily do. The physicians may have erred, for obvious reasons, by overdisclosure of surgical risks so that the patient rejected the procedure which might have saved his life.

Before a drug is released on the market it must undergo pretesting to prove its effectiveness and safety. Similar pretesting should be applied to changes in traditional ethics, especially to the rapidly developing legal concept of informed consent, in order to prove the positive benefit of the changes and to avoid unforeseen adverse effects which can, as illustrated here, be as serious as the most serious side effect of any drug.

Moderation is necessary in deciding how much to tell patients to insure valid consents, and most patients will be better served without overdisclosure—until courts specifically conclude to the contrary.

Notes

1. What is the basis for the court's view in *Cobbs* that disclosure of the risks of minor and common procedures, such as taking blood, is unnecessary even though those risks include death? Can one infer from the fact that a procedure is common that the patient appreciates the risks? Why is the simplicity of the procedure relevant at all?

2. Can an economist help to spell out the materiality requirement imposed by the court by analyzing the requirement in cost-benefit terms? The benefits of disclosure of risks to the patient are related to the gravity of the risks if they materialize and to the probability that they will materialize. The product of probability and magnitude is a measure of the expected risks of the operation, and the greater they are the more likely it is that disclosure would alter the patient's decision to undergo the operation or other treatment in question. Also relevant are the benefits of the operation. These depend on the seriousness of the patient's condition and on the availability of alternative, safer treatments. If the benefits are very great, and the expected risks trivial, the physician can be confident that the patient will consent when the risks are disclosed to him; in these circumstances, the benefits of disclosure are slight. The costs of disclosure include not only the presumably slight time costs involved in explaining the risks to the patient, but also, and more importantly, the disutility to the patient of being forced to think about the dangers he is about to undergo.

3. What damages are appropriate for a failure to obtain the informed consent of the patient? Under the facts of *Cobbs*, what would plaintiff have to show to be entitled to obtain damages for the complications arising from the operation? Is it enough for him to show that if he had been informed of the possibility of such complications, he would not have consented to the operation? How could he prove he would not have consented?

4. In Canterbury v. Spence, 150 U.S. App. D.C. 263, 464 F.2d 772 (1972), plaintiff became paralyzed from the waist down after a laminectomy, which is a surgical procedure for correcting spinal disc problems (cf. Patten article, supra). The evidence showed that paralysis can be expected in about one percent of laminectomies; nevertheless, the surgeon did not inform the plaintiff or his mother (the plaintiff was 19 years of age) of this risk. He gave the following explanation for nondisclosure:

> I think that I always explain to patients the operations are serious, and I feel that any operation is serious. I think that I would not tell patients that they might be paralyzed because of the small percentage, one per cent, that exists. There would be a tremendous percentage of people that would not have surgery and would not therefore be benefited by it, the tremendous percentage that get along very well, 99 per cent.

150 U.S. App. at 285, 465 F.2d at 794. This seems lame (no pun intended). A 1 percent risk of severe and permanent paralysis is unusually high, and laminectomies are declined on just this ground in favor of alternative nonsurgical procedures even by patients with severe disc problems. What would Dr. Patten have done in this case?

To the argument that if a patient wants the physician to disclose to him the risks of a recommended operation or treatment, he should take the initiative by questioning the physician, the court in *Canterbury* replied:

We discard the thought that the patient should ask for information before the physician is required to disclose. Caveat emptor is not the norm for the consumer of medical services. Duty to disclose is more than a call to speak merely on the patient's request, or merely to answer the patient's questions; it is a duty to volunteer, if necessary, the information the patient needs for intelligent decision. The patient may be ignorant, confused, overawed by the physician or frightened by the hospital, or even ashamed to inquire. Perhaps relatively few patients could in any event identify the relevant questions in the absence of prior explanation by the physician. Physicians and hospitals have patients of widely divergent socio-economic backgrounds, and a rule which presumes a degree of sophistication which many members of society lack is likely to breed gross inequities.

Id. at 274, 464 F.2d at 783. A fair point; but if patients are that unsophisticated, how much useful knowledge will they in fact derive from disclosure? Earlier in its opinion the court had stated:

Some doubt has been expressed as to ability of physicians to suitably communicate their evaluations of risks and the advantages of optional treatment, and as to the lay patient's ability to understand what the physician tells him. We do not share these apprehensions. The discussion need not be a disquisition, and surely the physician is not compelled to give his patient a short medical education; the disclosure rule summons the physician only to a reasonable explanation. That means generally informing the patient in nontechnical terms as to what is at stake: the therapy alternatives open to him, the goals expectably to be achieved, and the risks that may ensue from particular treatment and no treatment. So informing the patient hardly taxes the physician, and it must be the exceptional patient who cannot comprehend such an explanation at least in a rough way.

Id. at 273, 464 F.2d at 782. Is the court's view of patient psychology a consistent one? On the general subject of informed consent, see B. Barber, Informed Consent in Medical Therapy and Research (1980).

5. If a patient signs a waiver of his right to be informed of the risks of a recommended medical procedure, is the waiver enforceable? The question of the enforceability of waivers of negligence is taken up in the next chapter. The question is fundamental in the medical malpractice context, where the existence of a preexisting bargaining relationship between potential injurer and potential victim opens up the possibility of wholesale nullification of tort rules by contractual waivers, provided such waivers are enforced. The case for allowing the standard of care in malpractice cases to be set by contract between physician and patient is strongly argued in Epstein, Medical Malpractice: The Case for Contract, 1976 Am. Bar Foundation Research J. 87.

6. A number of states have by statute modified informed-consent requirements imposed by common-law courts as in Cobbs v. Grant. For a list, see 1 S. E. Pegalis & H. F. Wachsman, American Law of Medical Malpractice 107-112 (1980).

Judson v. Giant Powder Co.
107 Cal. 549, 40 P. 1020 (1895)

GAROUTTE, J. Respondents [plaintiffs] recovered judgment for the sum of $41,164.75, as damages for acts of negligence. This appeal is prosecuted from such judgment, and from an order denying a motion for a new trial. The damages to respondents' property were occasioned by an explosion of nitro-glycerine in process of manufacture into dynamite, in appellant's powder factory, situated upon the shore of the Bay of San Francisco. Appellant's factory buildings were arranged around the slope of a hill facing the bay. Nearest to respondents' property was the nitro-glycerine house; next was the washing house; next were the mixing houses; then came the packing houses; and finally the two magazines used for storing dynamite. These various buildings were situated from 50 to 150 feet apart, and a tramway ran in front of them. The explosion occurred in the morning during working hours, and originated in the nitro-glycerine house. There followed, within a few moments of time, in regular order, the explosion of the other buildings, the two magazines coming last; but, though last, they were not least, for their explosion caused the entire downfall and destruction of respondents' factory, residences, and stock on hand. There is no question but what the cause of this series of explosions following the first is directly traceable, by reason of fire or concussion, to the nitro-glycerine explosion. Of the many employes of appellant engaged in and about the nitro-glycerine factory at the time of the disaster, none were left to tell the tale. Hence any positive testimony as to the direct cause of the explosion is not to be had. The witnesses who saw and knew, like all things else around, save the earth itself, were scattered to the four winds. . . . Does the proof of the explosion draw with it a presumption of negligence sufficient to establish a prima facie case for a recovery? . . . All courts agree that, where contractual relations exist between the parties, as in cases of common carriers, proof of the accident carries with it the presumption of negligence, and makes a prima facie case. This proposition is elementary and uncontradicted. Therefore the citation of authority is unnecessary. Yet we know of no sound reason, and have found none stated in the books, why this principle of presumptions should be applicable to cases involving contractual relations, and inapplicable to cases where no contractual relations exist. It is intimated in some Indiana case that the presumption arises upon proof of the accident by reason of the carrier's contract to safely deliver the passenger at his destination, but there is no such contract. The carrier is not an insurer of his passengers. If he were, this presumption of negligence arising from the accident, aside from the act of God, would be conclusive and irrebuttable; but such is not the fact, for it is only prima facie and always disputable. . . . Presumptions arise from the doctrine of probabilities. The future is measured and weighed by the past, and presumptions are created from the experience of the past. What has happened in the past, under the same conditions, will probably happen in the future, and ordinary and probable results will be presumed to take place until the contrary is shown. Based upon the foregoing principles, a rule of law has been formulated, bearing upon a certain class of cases, where damages either to person or property form the foundation of the action. This rule is well declared in Shearman and Redfield on Negligence: "When a thing which causes injury is shown to be under the management of the defendant, and the accident is such as in the ordinary course of things does not happen if those who have the management use proper care, it affords reasonable evidence, in the absence of explanation by the defendant, that the accident arose from the want of care." Tested by this rule, no question of contractual relation could ever form an element in the case....

... In England the authorities are in entire accord. Plaintiff was passing along a highway, under a railroad bridge, when a brick used in the construction of the bridge fell and injured him. Negligence in the railroad was presumed. Kearney v. Railway Co., L.R. 5 Q.B. 411. A barrel of flour rolled out of the window of a warehouse, injuring a person passing upon the street. Negligence in the warehouseman was presumed. Byrne v. Boadle, 2 Hurl. & C. 722. . . . The explosion of a boiler of a steamboat is prima facie evidence of negligence. In the *Rose* case it is said: "In the present case the boiler which exploded was in the control of the employes of the defendant. As boilers do not usually explode when they are in a safe condition and are properly managed, the inference that this boiler was not in a safe condition, or was not properly managed, was justifiable.". . .

There is another class of cases in all essentials fully supporting our views upon this question of negligence. These cases arise in the destruction of property caused by fire escaping from locomotive engines, and, while there is some conflict in the authorities as to the true rule, it is said in Shearman and Redfield on Negligence: "The decided weight of authority and of reason is in favor of holding that, the origin of the fire being fixed upon the railroad company, it is presumptively chargeable with negligence, and must assume the burden of proving that it had used all those precautions for confining sparks and cinders (as the case may be) which have been already mentioned as necessary. This is the common law of England, and the same rule has been followed in New York, Maryland," etc., citing many other states. . . .

In this state the question has never been directly passed upon as to whether or not negligence will be presumed from the fact of sparks escaping from a locomotive engine, and the destruction of grain fields resulting therefrom. In Butcher v. Railroad Co., 67 Cal. 518, 8 Pac. 174, the doctrine is inferentially favored, although in that case the plaintiff placed an expert witness upon the stand, who testified that "a perfect engine, properly equipped and properly run, will not ordinarily throw out sparks sufficient to start a fire." . . . For our purpose it is not necessary to enter into a prolonged investigation to determine why this evidence of the expert strengthened plaintiff's case. But, taking the converse of the proposition, let us assume that defendant's engine was a perfect engine, properly equipped and properly run, and that, notwithstanding such conditions, it would ordinarily when in use throw out sparks of fire, leaving in its wake, as it passed through the country, property destroyed and possibly lives lost. Certainly, this could hardly be tolerated in law. Hence we fail to fully appreciate the importance of this line of evidence. Such conduct upon the part of a railroad company would render it guilty of the commission of a nuisance, and liable in damages for property destroyed. Certainly, it is no answer to such a condition of things to say that the legislative grant to the corporation to do business with the aid of steam locomotives carries with it the right to destroy the property of adjoining owners; but, rather, we must assume that the grant was made only after a prior determination by the same legislative power that a perfect locomotive engine, properly equipped and properly run, will not ordinarily throw out sufficient sparks to destroy adjoining property. It is only upon such a theory that the right to do business by the use of this character of implement was ever granted; and, hence, we again say that it may be considered doubtful if this class of evidence strengthens the plaintiff's case. For it is but proving, as a fact, something of which the courts and possibly all the world take full notice.

In the case at bar, following the lines marked out by the cases last cited, respondents placed before the court expert evidence to the effect that, if the correct process of manufacturing and handling dynamite was carefully carried out, an explosion would not occur. This evidence is stronger than in the smokestack cases, for here it declares as a certainty what there is only stated to be the probable or ordinary result; but, be that as it may, if this character of evidence was relevant and material in the smokestack cases, it is equally relevant and material here. If it was sufficient there to complete and perfect a prima facie case of negligence, it is ample here to do the same. Again, if appellant had the right, under the laws of the state, to manufacture dynamite (which is conceded), and, if by reason of the existence of such right, courts may assume that, if dynamite is properly handled in the process of manufacture, explosions will not probably occur, then respondents' case is doubly proven, for here we have, not only the presumption of the existence of certain conditions, but the evidence of witnesses as to the existence of them. . . .

. . . Appellant was engaged in the manufacture of dynamite. In the ordinary course of things, an explosion does not occur in such manufacture if proper care is exercised. An explosion did occur, ergo, the real cause of the explosion being unexplained, it is probable that it was occasioned by a lack of proper care. . . .

For the foregoing reasons, the judgment and order are affirmed.

Notes

1. Was the expert witness's evidence an alternative to the purely circumstantial evidence — that the accident occurred — or was it essential to the probative value of the circumstantial evidence?

2. Did the plaintiff's expert testify that nitroglycerine never explodes if properly handled? Is this credible? Is it required for an inference of defendant's negligence from the fact of the explosion?

3. If a passenger on a common carrier — a bus, train, airplane, etc. — is injured in an accident, why should it be presumed that the accident is due to negligence? Should it make a difference whether the accident was a collision? If so, whether the collision was with a vehicle owned by the defendant carrier? On these questions see Vogt v. Cincinnati, Newport & Covington St. Ry. Co., 312 Ky. 668, 229 S.W.2d 461 (1950).

4. Is the fact of an accident more likely to give rise to an inference of negligence if the costs of the accident are very great, as in the *Judson* case, or *yes* if they are small? Is the inference more likely if the burden of precautions is great or small?

5. Was it important to the court's analysis of the evidence in the *Judson* case that all of the eyewitnesses were dead? *Yes .·., need circumstantial evidence.*

6. Here is a contemporaneous newspaper account of the Giant Powder disaster, from the New York Times, July 10, 1892, at 1:

MIGHTY FORCE OF POWDER

TERRIFIC EXPLOSIONS IN THE VICINITY OF SAN FRANCISCO.

FIVE WHITE WORKMEN KNOWN TO HAVE BEEN KILLED AND A NUMBER OF CHINESE — SEVEN SHOCKS THAT SHOOK BUILDINGS MILES AWAY AND CAUSED A PANIC.

San Francisco, July 9. — There was a terrific explosion this morning at the works of the Giant Powder Company at West Berkeley, across the bay from San Francisco. Seven distinct shocks were felt, and 300 tons of giant powder brought death and destruction to the immediate neighborhood, and caused great damage in Oakland and San Francisco. People for some moments, in both cities, were panic-stricken.

There were 180 men employed at the works when the explosion occurred, and probably it will never be known how many were killed. The majority of the workmen were Chinese.

Only five white men are known to have been killed. These include John Boe, Charles Gobertig, and Wallace Dickinson.

Eight buildings of the powder works proper, a large boarding house, and a dozen dwelling houses were completely destroyed. The total loss will exceed $500,000. Two giant powder magazines, a nitro-glycerine tank, and an acid tank exploded within a few seconds.

The buildings were principally of brick and stone, although there were also some wooden shops. The group included a nitro-glycerine magazine, packing house, mixing house, capping magazine, storage magazine, and office.

Immediately after the explosion the town of West Berkeley from a distance resembled the site of an actual volcano. Dozens of private houses in the vicinity were partially destroyed, and all along the road from Oakland to West Berkeley Station were damaged buildings.

Near the works lived one of the employes of the name of Borcher. When the first explosion came he made a rush for his home, but his wife had already fled from the falling building. Their son Willie, a lad about ten years old, had been outside playing, and his first thought was to run home to see his mother. He entered the house, and, finding his mother gone, started out, but when he reached the porch it fell upon him. The little fellow's skull was crushed and he lived only two hours.

It was half an hour after the explosion before any one could be found brave enough to enter the ruins. Once a start was made, workmen flocked all over the ground, looking for their missing comrades.

Harry von Proyen was engaged near the magazine, which was open. When the first explosion came he closed and locked the doors and then sought safety in flight. His precaution was of no avail, however, as shortly afterward the magazine blew up.

"What was the explosion like?" He replied, with a look of surprise on his face when questioned, "I can't tell you and I don't think any one else can. There was a roar and then all was over. The first place that blew up was the mixing house. Thirty white men were employed near there. Immediately after the explosion the stampede commenced. Concussion set the glycerine house off and it was there that Dickinson, Gobertig, and Voe lost their lives. I don't think they were in the house, but out on the hill. The explosion of the glycerine house blew them into the bay.

"We had barely reached a place of safety when up went the magazine house. The concussion was something awful, and knocked nearly all the men down. Every one of us is covered from head to foot with powder. When the magazine went off it seemed as though a whole island opened up and let out a gigantic subterranean mine. Flames rushed out and curled over in billows, and then came a shock that made the earth tremble. Such a scene I never expect and never want to see again. Buildings were falling in every direction. We had to move away."

Pandemonium raged about the works and screaming women and children rushed there expecting to see husbands and fathers blown to atoms. Mrs. Painter of West Berkeley, who was sick, was so affected by shock that she is dying.

Willie Schmidt, a brother of Town Marshal Schmidt of Berkeley, was driving to the top of the hill when the first explosion occurred. His face was badly cut and his body bruised. He tied his horse and left the scene as quickly as possible. The horse was subsequently killed when the second explosion came.

The body of a Chinaman was found on the railroad track half a mile from the works. The remains of a boy frightfully mangled were found near the scene.

John Farley, a workman, who was walking near the mixing house, was blown into the bay, but swam out. An old man of the name of Gates was blown from his wagon and badly injured.

Of the white men killed, Dickinson was in charge of the nitro-glycerine house, situated near the wharf, and the other men were in the nitro-glycerine washing house, near by. Their bodies were found in the debris terribly mangled.

Dickinson's arms and legs were broken and twisted and his eyes blown out. The others were badly mutilated. Boe had been married not quite a year, and lived in one of the houses near the mills and chemical works. Dickinson was twenty-five years old and single. Gobertig was also unmarried.

Albert Dibble, ex-President of the Giant Powder Company; J. B. Stetson, one of the Directors and largest stockholders; Julius Bandmann, the general agent of the company, and F. H. Pitman of the Judson Powder Company went to the scene by the first train. Mr. Stetson says it is almost impossible to estimate the loss, but $200,000 will probably be an outside figure for the damage to the powder works. The San Francisco Chemical Works, owned by Egbert Judson and J. L. N. Shepard, were almost completely destroyed, and the loss is not far from $150,000.

The damage to buildings in San Francisco and Oakland will reach $100,000. In this city the scene on the principal streets was one of wild confusion. Men, pale-faced and bareheaded, rushed from business houses and anxiously looked about for some indication of where the explosion had taken place.

All the windows on the west side of the Hopkins-Searles mansion, corner of California and Mason Streets, were broken by the shocks. Other Nob Hill residents suffered considerable loss. One of the largest windows broken was that on the south side of the First National Bank Building. The immense plate glass in front of the Learing House on Samson Street, between Pine and California, was shattered. The Baldwin Hotel was damaged, and windows on several floors were smashed to pieces.

The prisoners confined in the City Prison were in a panic. The shock came like a violent gust of wind that shook the building. Even prison officials were excited, as the rickety old building rocked to and fro from the repeated shocks. When at last the heaviest explosion came, every gas jet in the prison went out, leaving the dismal place in darkness. From without came sounds of crashing glass and cries of excited and frightened people as they ran for places of safety. Prisoners raved, cursed, and prayed in one breath. They begged piteously to be released and then swore terribly at the officials, who were deaf to their entreaties.

In Chinatown the wildest terror prevailed. Frightened Chinese did not stop to find their doors, but dashed head foremost through their windows. Several were badly cut, and one on Bartlett Alley was severely injured by jumping from a veranda on the second floor. About fifty persons sustained slight injuries in this city and in Oakland.

Bollenbach v. Bloomenthal
341 Ill. 539, 173 N.E. 670 (1930)

MR. JUSTICE ORR. . . .

Plaintiff was suffering from a severe toothache on October 30, 1925, and called upon Dr. Honoroff, a dentist, who examined the aching tooth and found it to be infected. It was a dead lower molar, with a large amalgam filling which embraced from one-third to one-half the crown. He advised the extraction of the tooth under a general anesthetic, not believing the condition of the tooth and patient favorable to an extraction under a local anesthetic. Since he did not administer gas in his office, Dr. Honoroff directed plaintiff to defendants, giving her a card on which the tooth to be extracted was marked. Plaintiff then went to the dental offices of defendants, where she met Dr. Bloomenthal, and after some conversation it was agreed that the tooth should be extracted by him under a general anesthetic. The other defendant, Dr. Bennecke, was not present. A prop was placed in patient's mouth to keep it open and the anesthetic administered. According to defendants, a mouth-pack was then inserted in the back part of plaintiff's mouth to make the induction of the anesthetic quicker and to prevent particles of filling or tooth passing down the throat. During the extraction the crown of the tooth fractured into a number of pieces but the roots came out intact. Some pieces of tooth and filling were picked up by Dr. Bloomenthal, while others were rinsed out of patient's mouth into the dental spittoon upon her revival. Dr. Bloomenthal testified that when he saw the roots were out he attempted to assemble the rest of the tooth and filling, but they were so fractured and had scattered so much that there was no way of knowing whether there were any missing fragments. He also testified that during the extraction plaintiff was restless under the anesthetic, several times slumping down in the chair, and the mouth-pack became dislodged and had to be replaced. He further testified that he did not know or suspect that any piece of tooth or filling had gone down plaintiff's throat, and it was almost a year before he heard anything about the matter. After coming out from under the anesthetic, the first thing plaintiff remembered was some one brushing out her mouth, after which she rinsed it and spit several particles of tooth into the basin. After a fifteen minutes' rest she went home. She testified that it was hard for her to get her breath and she felt like a person who had phlegm in his throat. From that time on she suffered with a persistent cough and a condition resembling asthma. In November, 1925, an X-ray disclosed the presence of a small foreign body in her bronchial tube. On January 24, 1926, during a severe coughing spell, she coughed up a small piece of tooth and filling, both of which were introduced in evidence.

The case proceeded to trial on the theory that the facts were sufficient to invoke the doctrine of res ipsa loquitur, and in affirming the judgment the Appellate Court has sustained the application of that doctrine. Defendants seriously contend that the doctrine of res ipsa loquitur is not applicable in this case, and our decision will rest upon the determination of this one question.

The doctrine of res ipsa loquitur is that whenever a thing which produced an injury is shown to have been under the control and management of the defendant and the occurrence is such as in the ordinary course of events does not happen if due care has been exercised, the fact of injury itself will be deemed to afford prima facia evidence to support a recovery in the absence of any explanation by the defendant tending to show that the injury was not due to his want of care. The presumption or inference of negligence raised by the application of this doctrine is not absolute or conclusive but is rebuttable, and vanishes entirely when even slight evidence appears to the contrary. "A presumption is not evidence, and cannot be treated as evidence. It cannot be weighed in the scale against evidence. Presumptions are never indulged in against established facts. They are indulged in only to supply the place of facts. As soon as evidence is produced which is contrary to the presumption which arose before the contrary proof was offered, the presumption vanishes entirely." . . .

. . . Two other reputable and experienced dentists of Chicago testified that Dr. Bloomenthal, in doing plaintiff's work, followed the usual and customary method as approved and employed by extraction experts in Chicago at the time. As to this there is no conflict. No witness, either lay or expert, testified that anything done by Dr. Bloomenthal in extracting plaintiff's tooth was negligent or unskillful, or that he had omitted to do anything which a reasonably careful and skillful dentist would have done under the same or similar circumstances, or that in the exercise of due care and skill he should have known that a fragment of tooth and filling had gone down plaintiff's throat. This explanation by the defendants tending to show that the injury complained of, though unusual, was not due to any lack of care on their part, was sufficient to overcome the prima facie case of the plaintiff and rebut all presumptions of negligence, as such presumptions vanish when contrary evidence is produced. The principle relied upon by plaintiff and contained in many cases cited in her brief is that the doctrine of res ipsa loquitur applies where the defendant was in sole control of the acts, instruments and objects involved. . . . Dr. Bloomenthal did not have complete control of the tooth in question but was seeking to get control of it when the crown fractured into many pieces during the extraction. In extracting a tooth the dentist cannot always produce the most favorable result, as the physical condition of the tooth itself must always be reckoned with. The mouth-pack was likewise shown not to have been under the complete control of Dr. Bloomenthal, as the expert evidence shows that in some manner, either by heavy breathing, nervousness, tendency to vomit, or by an involuntary action of her tongue, the patient may have dislodged it. Thus, to say that Dr. Bloomenthal had complete control over either the tooth or mouth-pack is, under the circumstances, carrying the doctrine of res ipsa loquitur entirely too far.

A mishap, such as the flying of a fragment of tooth or filling into a patient's throat while the tooth is being extracted, is not of itself evidence of negligence or want of skill on the part of the defendant. One of the leading cases in this country on this subject is Ewing v. Goode (C.C.) 78 F. 442, 443, in which the opinion was rendered by the late Chief Justice Taft, then sitting in the United States Circuit Court of Appeals. In that case plaintiff sued a physician to recover damages for an alleged improper treatment of her eyes, her claim being that for his lack of proper care and skill she lost the sight of one eye and part of the sight of the other. In holding there could be no recovery Mr. Justice Taft said: "The naked facts that defendant performed operations upon her eye, that pain followed, and that subsequently the eye was in such a bad condition that it had to be extracted, established neither the neglect and unskillfulness of the treatment, nor the causal connection between it and the unfortunate event. A physician is not a warranter of cures. If the maxim, 'res ipsa loquitur,' were applicable to a case like this, and a failure to cure were held to be evidence, however slight, of negligence on the part of the physician or surgeon causing the bad result, few would be courageous enough to practice the healing art, for they would have to assume financial liability for nearly all the 'ills that flesh is heir to.' " ...

... No case has been cited where the doctrine of res ipsa loquitur has been applied by this court as an aid to recovery in a malpractice suit. ...

Plaintiff's instruction No. 15 as given by the court enunciated the doctrine of res ipsa loquitur by stating, in substance, that if defendants were in sole control of acts, instruments, and objects used in administering the anesthesia and in extracting the tooth, and, as a proximate result of such acts, instruments, and objects a portion of tooth went into the lung of plaintiff through her mouth, and if the jury found "that in the ordinary course of events such an occurrence would not happen if those in control of such acts, instruments and objects use ordinary care, then the occurrence itself may afford reasonable evidence, in the absence of evidence to the contrary of equal weight, if there is such absence, that the occurrence arose from want of ordinary care." This instruction should not have been given. The presumption raised by the doctrine of res ipsa loquitur does not require "evidence to the contrary of equal weight" to overthrow it, for, as above stated, such presumption is not of itself evidence but arises as a rule of evidence and yields to any contrary proof. Presumptions are never indulged in against established facts. They are indulged in only to supply the place of facts, and as soon as any evidence is produced which is contrary to the presumption which arose before the contrary proof was offered, the presumption vanishes entirely. ...

For the above reasons the judgment will be reversed, and the cause remanded.

Notes

1. In reading the cases in this section on the doctrine of res ipsa loquitur, consider the following three possible interpretations of the doctrine.

a. It is simply a principle of circumstantial evidence. Sometimes the fact of an accident is evidence of negligence because it is the kind of accident that is more likely to occur as a result of negligence on the part of the injurer than from other causes. Burden of proof still on Π

b. It is a rule for deciding cases when there is no direct evidence on the issue of negligence; its purpose is to induce the defendant to produce relevant evidence within his control. Burden of persuasion on Δ

c. It establishes a prima facie case of negligence. Π right to directed verdict

2. What are the implications of each of these interpretations for the following issues?

   a. The burden of producing evidence on the negligence question?

   b. The burden of persuasion?

   c. Plaintiff's or defendant's right to a directed verdict?

3. Which interpretation best describes the opinion in *Judson?* Which best describes *Bollenbach?* ↢

4. Do you agree with the court in *Bollenbach* that the presumption of negligence arising from application of the res ipsa loquitur doctrine "vanishes entirely" as soon as contrary evidence is introduced? Does it matter whether the contrary evidence is believed? Do you see an analogy here to Brown v. Shyne, supra? The "vanishes entirely" approach of *Bollenbach* was repudiated in a later Illinois case, Metz v. Central Illinois Electric & Gas Co., 32 Ill. 2d 446, 207 N.E.2d 305 (1965). The court held there that the presumption "remains to be considered with all the other evidence in the case and must be weighed by the jury against the direct evidence offered by the party charged."

5. How should the jury be instructed on res ipsa loquitur in a medical malpractice case? Compare the following two suggested instructions from G. Douthwaite, Alexander's Jury Instructions on Medical Issues 38, 45 (2d ed. 1980). Are they consistent?

2-4 Res ipsa loquitur: shifting of the burden of persuasion.

   If you find that the plaintiff received an injury from some means or instrumentality in the control of the defendant; that the injury was of a kind which does not occur in the absence of negligence on the part of someone; that it occurred under such circumstances that the defendant has the means of determining how it occurred and the cause thereof; and that plaintiff does not have access to this information, then you may infer, from these findings alone, that the situation speaks for itself and that the injury was due to some negligence on the part of the defendant. You are not bound to draw such an inference, but you may do so; and, unless there is evidence satisfactorily showing freedom from negligence, you may return a verdict for the plaintiff on the basis of such an inference of negligence.

2-9 Bad result does not warrant inference of negligence.

   The law does not hold a physician or surgeon liable for every untoward result which may occur in medical practice. The mere fact that the treatment was unsuccessful does not of itself raise any inference of negligence. Ordinarily, therefore, you may not find defendant's conduct to have constituted malpractice without having before you some expert testimony from which you are able to infer that the defendant did not apply the standard of care and skill which was appropriate for the treatment of the patient.

6. Be wary, incidentally, of the following common but careless statement of the res ipsa loquitur principle: "a type of accident that rarely occurs if the potential injurer is careful." This says only that there are few accidents of this

type in which the injurer is not negligent; it does not say how many accidents of this type there are when the injurer is negligent. Suppose there is a one percent chance that nitroglycerine will explode if it is carefully handled; but half of all nitroglycerine explosions are of this type. Then the probability that a given nitroglycerine explosion is due to negligence is only .5. See Kaye, Probability Theory Meets Res Ipsa Loquitur, 77 Mich. L. Rev. 1456 (1979), for an interesting discussion of this point.

Larson v. St. Francis Hotel
83 Cal. App. 2d 210, 188 P.2d 513 (1948)

BRAY, J.

The accident out of which this action arose was apparently the result of the effervescence and ebullition of San Franciscans in their exuberance of joy on V-J Day, August 14, 1945. Plaintiff (who is not included in the above description), while walking on the sidewalk on Post Street adjoining the St. Francis Hotel, just after stepping out from under the marquee, was struck on the head by a heavy, overstuffed arm chair, knocked unconscious, and received injuries for which she is asking damages from the owners of the hotel. Although there were a number of persons in the immediate vicinity, no one appears to have seen from whence the chair came nor to have seen it before it was within a few feet of plaintiff's head, nor was there any identification of the chair as belonging to the hotel. However, it is a reasonable inference that the chair came from some portion of the hotel. For the purposes of this opinion, we will so assume, in view of the rule on nonsuit cases that every favorable inference fairly deducible from the evidence must be drawn in favor of plaintiff, and that all the evidence must be construed most strongly against the defendants.

At the trial, plaintiff, after proving the foregoing facts and the extent of her injuries, rested, relying upon the doctrine of res ipsa loquitur. On motion of defendant the court granted a nonsuit. The main question to be determined is whether under the circumstances shown, the doctrine applies. The trial court correctly held that it did not....

... A hotel does not have exclusive control, either actual or potential, of its furniture. Guests have, at least, partial control. Moreover, it cannot be said that with the hotel using ordinary care "the accident was such that in the ordinary course of events . . . would not have happened." On the contrary, the mishap would quite as likely be due to the fault of a guest or other person as to that of defendants. The most logical inference from the circumstances shown in that the chair was thrown by some such person from a window. It thus appears that this occurrence is not such as ordinarily does not happen without the negligence of the party charged, but, rather, one in which the accident ordinarily might happen despite the fact that the defendants used reasonable care and were totally free from negligence. To keep guests and visitors from throwing furniture out windows would require a guard to be placed in every room in the hotel, and no one would contend that there is any rule of law requiring a hotel to do that. . . .

Connolly v. Nicollet Hotel
254 Minn. 373, 95 N.W.2d 657 (1959)

MURPHY, J.

Action by Marcella A. Connolly against The Nicollet Hotel, a copartnership, and Alice Shmikler, as trustee of Joseph Shmikler, and others, doing business as The Nicollet Hotel, for the loss of the sight of her left eye alleged to have been caused by defendants' negligence.

The accident occurred about midnight June 12, 1953, during the course of the 1953 National Junior Chamber of Commerce Convention which had its headquarters at The Nicollet Hotel in Minneapolis. It was occasioned when plaintiff was struck in her left eye by a substance falling from above her as she walked on a public sidewalk on Nicollet Avenue adjacent to the hotel. . . .

[The] Convention occupied a substantial portion of the hotel at the time of the accident. In connection therewith various delegates and firms maintained hospitality centers there where intoxicants, beer, and milk were served to guests and visitors. Two of such centers were located on the Nicollet Avenue side of the building. . . .

. . . During the course of the convention a mule was stabled in the lobby of the hotel, and a small alligator was kept on the fourth floor. There was firing of guns in the lobby. Broken bottles and broken glass were found on the sidewalk near the garage adjacent to the building so that it was necessary to clean the sidewalk near the garage as frequently as twice a day during the course of the convention. The doorman at the hotel was equipped with a shovel and broom which he used for this sidewalk maintenance. Property of the hotel was damaged on the third, fourth, fifth, sixth, eighth, ninth, tenth, and eleventh floors. The window of the office of the credit manager was broken. From the testimony of the executive housekeeper of the hotel the damage consisted of wet carpets, broken chairs, broken screens, molding torn loose from connecting doors, and walls spotted with liquor and water. The inspection of the building made after the accident indicated that there were three missing window screens, mirrors pulled off the walls in bathrooms, light fixtures were broken, signs were broken, hall lights were broken, exit lights were broken, the bowl in the men's washroom was torn off the wall, holes were drilled through door panels, and 150 face towels had to be removed from service. Broken glass and bottles were found on landings and stair wells, a condition which existed almost every night at all floor levels. It became apparent to the general manager of the hotel on June 11, 1953, the day prior to the accident to the plaintiff, that the disorderly behavior of the hotel guests created a hazard to the defendant's property. He issued the following memorandum to his staff:

> WE HAVE ALMOST ARRIVED AT THE END OF THE MOST HARROWING EXPERIENCE WE HAVE HAD IN THE WAY OF CONVENTIONS, AT LEAST IN MY EXPERIENCE! WHEN WE BECAME INVOLVED AND SAW WHAT THE SITUATION WAS, WE HAD NO ALTERNATIVE BUT TO PROCEED AND 'TURN THE OTHER CHEEK.' HOWEVER, IT INVOLVES CERTAIN EXPENSES THAT I DO NOT PROPOSE TO FOREGO WITHOUT AT LEAST AN ARGUMENT—AND MAYBE LEGAL SUIT.
>
> I, OF COURSE, AM SPEAKING OF ANY DAMAGE, WHICH FOR THE MOST PART WILL BE REPORTED BY THE HOUSEKEEPING DEPARTMENT. HOWEVER, THAT I MAY DRAW UP A COMPREHENSIVE CASE, PLEASE HAVE THE INFORMATION IN MY OFFICE NOT LATER THAN NOON, FRIDAY. WE WILL, INCIDENTALLY, START TO TAKE DOWN ALL SIGNS, ETC., AT 9:00 AM, FRIDAY MORNING. . . .

The defendants contend that the proof is circumstantial and that there is no evidence that the object which struck the plaintiff came from the hotel. The plaintiff was struck in the eye by a mass of moist dirt or earth. The jury could find that this object was not an accumulation of dirt which fell from the structure. The record indicates that periodic inspections were made of the exterior of the building so that there would be no sizeable collection of dirt on it. Nor was it likely that the mass of dirt or earth came from some other building. From the physical location of the place where the accident occurred and the surrounding structures, there was ample evidence from which the jury could find that the place from which the mass of dirt or earth came would be the Nicollet Hotel property. The record before us indicates that the Nicollet Hotel is a 12-story structure. The accident occurred approximately 100 feet from Washington Avenue and 100 feet from the garage entrance south of the hotel. Across the street from the hotel on Nicollet Avenue are two 4-story buildings. Nicollet Avenue is 50 feet in width. There was nothing unusual about the weather conditions and no evidence of a wind which might carry a mass of mud from a distant source. There is no evidence to indicate that the mass of mud came from a vehicle or other pedestrian. We think that under the facts in this case the evidence presents inferences which make the question of where the mass of mud came from one for the jury.

We have said many times that the law does not require every fact and circumstance which make up a case of negligence to be proved by direct and positive evidence or by the testimony of eyewitnesses, and that circumstantial evidence alone may authorize a finding of negligence. Negligence may be inferred from all the facts and surrounding circumstances, and where the evidence of such facts and circumstances is such as to take the case out of the realm of conjecture and into the field of legitimate inference from established facts, a prima facie case is made.

Notes

1. Can *Larson* and *Connolly* be distinguished in terms of the Hand formula?

2. What was the basis for inferring Nicollet Hotel's negligence, *aa Mev/* as distinct from the cause of the accident?

Newing v. Cheatham   *assannyntus c trisk*
15 Cal. 3d 351, 540 P.2d 33 (1975)

SULLIVAN, J.

In this action for damages for wrongful death arising out of the crash of a private airplane, defendant Steven Eugene Cheatham as administrator of the estate of Harold Cheatham (hereafter Cheatham) deceased appeals from a judgment entered upon a jury verdict in favor of plaintiffs and against decedent's estate in the sum of $125,000. Plaintiffs are the surviving wife and children of Richard Newing, an occupant of the plane who died in the crash. Defendant's decedent who also died in the crash was the owner and pilot of the plane.

About 1 P.M. on Sunday, October 25, 1970, Richard Newing, Harold Cheatham, and Ronald Bird departed from Brown Field at Chula Vista, California, aboard a single-engine Cessna 172 aircraft owned and piloted by Cheatham. Neither Newing nor Bird was a licensed pilot. At the time of take-off the weather was clear and the visibility unrestricted. There was no evidence that the plane landed at any other field that afternoon, or that it sent any radio messages. When it failed to return, a search was commenced. On the following day the plane's wreckage was located by a search aircraft in mountainous terrain about 13 miles east of Tijuana, Mexico, and an equal distance southeast of Brown Field. A rescue party found all occupants of the airplane dead. The clock on the instrument panel was stopped at 5:18.

Plaintiffs brought this action for wrongful death alleging that the crash had been caused by Cheatham's negligence. At trial, three theories were advanced in support of plaintiff's case. The first was that Cheatham had negligently permitted the airplane to run out of fuel while in flight. The second was that he had been negligent as a matter of law in that he had violated applicable federal air regulations. Finally, Cheatham's negligence was said to be established by the doctrine of res ipsa loquitur. . . .

After the close of the evidence, the trial judge advised counsel that he would not instruct the jury on the defenses of assumption of risk and contributory negligence. He then granted plaintiffs' motion for a directed verdict on the issue of liability, concluding that the elements of res ipsa loquitur had been established as a matter of law and that the inference of negligence arising from the doctrine had not been rebutted. . . . The jury returned a verdict in favor of plaintiffs in the amount of $125,000. Judgment was entered accordingly. This appeal followed.

We address ourselves at once to defendant's main contention that the trial court committed prejudicial error by directing a verdict on the issue of liability. . . .

It is settled law in this state that the "doctrine of res ipsa loquitur is applicable where the accident is of such a nature that it can be said, in the light of past experience, that it probably was the result of negligence by someone and that the defendant is probably the one responsible." . . .

Whether aircraft accidents are more often than not the result of negligence is a question that has vexed the courts of many jurisdictions for decades. According to Prosser, many early cases took the position that not enough was known about the hazards of flight to permit an inference of negligence to arise from the mere fact of a plane crash. Advances in the safety and frequency of air travel, however, have led to a trend in the opposite direction. Thus, while judicial opinion on the subject is by no means unanimous, res ipsa loquitur, over the years, has been applied to an increasing variety of aircraft mishaps.

It is not fatal to the ruling here under review that the above-cited cases dealt with the application of the doctrine of res ipsa loquitur as a question of fact to be determined by the jury whereas in the case at bench, it was applied by the trial judge to the air crash here involved as a matter of law. Essentially any differences in the manner of establishing the doctrine lie in the state of the evidence and the posture of the case. Although whether any one of the conditions for the application of the doctrine has been met may be usually a question of fact, nevertheless under the particular circumstances of the case, any one of them may exist as a matter of law. . . .

. . . In the instant case, it seems reasonably clear in light of the circumstances surrounding the crash that the accident ordinarily would not have taken place in the absence of negligence. The evidence is uncontradicted that the airplane took off from Chula Vista in clear weather with no restrictions on visibility. There is no evidence that weather conditions contributed in any way to the crash of the plane. Nor was there any evidence that the plane had collided with other aircraft while in flight. Indeed the condition of the plane after the crash was such as to eliminate an air collision. It thus fell to the ground, apparently unaffected by external factors, only a few miles from the airport whence it had departed some hours earlier. Under the circumstances of the present case, "it seems reasonably clear that the accident probably would not have occurred without negligence by someone." The evidence bearing on these circumstances is not only uncontradicted but of such a nature that no issue of fact is raised as to the existence of the first condition for the application of the doctrine of res ipsa loquitur. We conclude that the first condition is established as a matter of law.

The doctrine's second condition, as traditionally formulated, is that the agency or instrumentality causing the accident must have been within the exclusive control or management of the defendant. The purpose of this requirement is to link the defendant with the probability, already established, that the accident was negligently caused.

The facts of this case are such as to satisfy this condition, like the first, as a matter of law. Cheatham was the owner of the aircraft, and there is no dispute that he was at the controls when the plane took off on its final flight. Since neither of his passengers seems to have been a licensed pilot, there is no reason to suppose that anyone other than he operated the plane at any time before the crash. Moreover, Cheatham's ultimate responsibility for all decisions concerning the aircraft's operation was established by an applicable federal air regulation. . . .

Defendant argues, however, that plaintiffs have not negated the possibility that the crash was caused by something other than the manner in which the plane was operated. He states that such crashes commonly occur because of mechanical failures of one kind or another, and cites a considerable array of cases in which such failures were said to have occurred. The short answer is that the record is devoid of evidence of such kind of mechanical failure. Furthermore, if such evidence had been produced, it would have no relevance to the second condition for the application of res ipsa loquitur, namely whether the airplane was within the exclusive control of Cheatham. With respect to the operation and maintenance of the aircraft, the control exercised by Cheatham as owner-pilot was complete. There thus can be no doubt that this element of the doctrine exists as a matter of law.

The third of the traditional conditions for the application of res ipsa loquitur is that the accident must not have been caused by any voluntary action or contribution on the part of the plaintiff. The purpose of this requirement, like that of control by the defendant, is to establish that the defendant is the one probably responsible for the accident. The plaintiff need not show that he was entirely inactive at the time of the accident in order to satisfy this requirement, so long as the evidence is such as to eliminate his conduct as a factor contributing to the occurrence.

Defendant contends that the trial court confused the existence of this third condition with the availability of the defenses of assumption of risk and contributory negligence. It is true that these are separate questions, since the burden of proof with respect to the first rests on the plaintiff as part of his general obligation to establish the defendant's negligence, while the burden of proof as to the latter rests on the defendant. Quite apart from whether or not the trial court's remarks indicate that it confused the above two questions, the uncontradicted evidence shows that the body of plaintiffs' decedent was found by the rescue party in one of the rear seats of the four-seater aircraft. From that position, it is difficult to imagine how he could have interfered physically with the operation of the aircraft in any way. Moreover, as noted above, there is no dispute that Cheatham was the pilot in command of the aircraft, and it must be presumed that he made all decisions concerning its operation and preparation for flight. There is no basis for supposing that Newing exerted any influence with respect to the making of these decisions. Thus the evidence concerning the basic operation of the aircraft is such as to conclusively eliminate Newing's conduct as a potential cause of the accident.

A separate question in this respect, however, is said to arise from the evidence that the three men drank beer together on the day of the crash. Defendant argues that Newing's conduct in drinking with Cheatham may have contributed to the happening of the accident, and that plaintiffs have not carried their burden with respect to negating this possibility. . . . [But] the evidence concerning the beer drinking was too vague to support a finding that Newing contributed by means of it to the happening of the crash. Plaintiffs are not obligated to eliminate entirely speculative causal possibilities involving the conduct of their decedent. It is enough if they rebut those inferences of their decedent's responsibility which are reasonably supported by the evidence. Plaintiffs discharged this burden by introducing evidence from which it must be inferred that Newing did not interfere with Cheatham's operation or command of the aircraft. . . .

Notes

1. Is the third condition stated by the court to be part of the res ipsa loquitur doctrine actually distinct from the second?

2. Suppose evidence were introduced that in 51 percent of airplane accidents of the type involved in this case the cause is the negligence of the pilot, and in the other 49 percent the cause is either culpable mechanical failure or unavoidable accident. Suppose the evidence was uncontradicted, and furthermore was the only evidence that was or could have been introduced on the issue of negligence. Should plaintiff be entitled to a directed verdict on the issue of liability? What if plaintiff were run down by a bus in circumstances indicative of negligence on the part of the bus driver, where 90 percent of the buses on the route in question were defendant's and 10 percent those of another bus company. Would this be a case for res ipsa loquitur? Why not?

3. Suppose the cause of the crash in *Newing* had in fact been traced to a mechanical failure of the aircraft. Could res ipsa loquitur be invoked in a suit by Newing against the manufacturer of the aircraft? Would it make a difference whether the failure occurred in a component of the aircraft that was serviced by the manufacturer or in one that was serviced by an aircraft

maintenance service? Cf. Honea v. Coca Cola Bottling Co., 143 Tex. 272, 183 S.W.2d 968 (1944). On the use of res ipsa loquitur in products-liability cases, see also Chapter 9 of this book.

First medical mal practice case using res insa loquitur
Multiple defendants

Ybarra v. Spangard
25 Cal. 2d 486, 154 P.2d 687 (1944)

GIBSON, C.J.

This is an action for damages for personal injuries alleged to have been inflicted by defendants during the course of a surgical operation. The trial court entered judgments of nonsuit as to all defendants and plaintiff appealed.

On October 28, 1939, plaintiff consulted defendant Dr. Tilley, who *Facts* diagnosed his ailment as appendicitis, and made arrangements for an appendectomy to be performed by defendant Dr. Spangard at a hospital owned and managed by defendant Dr. Swift. Plaintiff entered the hospital, was given a hypodermic injection, slept, and later was awakened by Drs. Tilley and Spangard and wheeled into the operating room by a nurse whom he believed to be defendant Gisler, an employee of Dr. Swift. Defendant Dr. Reser, the anesthetist, also an employee of Dr. Swift, adjusted plaintiff for the operation, pulling his body to the head of the operating table and, according to plaintiff's testimony, laying him back against two hard objects at the top of his shoulders, about an inch below his neck. Dr. Reser then administered the anesthetic and plaintiff lost consciousness. When he awoke early the following morning he was in his hospital room attended by defendant Thompson, the special nurse, and another nurse who was not made a defendant.

Plaintiff testified that prior to the operation he had never had any pain in, or injury to, his right arm or shoulder, but that when he awakened he felt a sharp pain about half way between the neck and the point of the right shoulder. He complained to the nurse, and then to Dr. Tilley, who gave him diathermy treatments while he remained in the hospital. The pain did not cease but spread down to the lower part of his arm, and after his release from the hospital the condition grew worse. He was unable to rotate or lift his arm, and developed paralysis and atrophy of the muscles around the shoulder. He received further treatments from Dr. Tilley until March, 1940, and then returned to work wearing his arm in a splint on the advice of Dr. Spangard.

Plaintiff also consulted Dr. Wilfred Sterling Clark, who had X-ray pictures taken which showed an area of diminished sensation below the shoulder and atrophy and wasting away of the muscles around the shoulder. In the opinion of Dr. Clark, plaintiff's condition was due to trauma of injury by pressure or strain applied between his right shoulder and neck.

Plaintiff was also examined by Dr. Fernando Garduno, who expressed the opinion that plaintiff's injury was a paralysis of traumatic origin, not arising from pathological causes, and not systemic, and that the injury resulted in atrophy, loss of use and restriction of motion of the right arm and shoulder.

Plaintiff's theory is that the foregoing evidence presents a proper case for the application of the doctrine of res ipsa loquitur, and that the inference of negligence arising therefrom makes the granting of a nonsuit improper. Defendants take the position that, assuming that plaintiff's condition was in fact the result of an injury, there is no showing that the act of any particular defendant, nor any particular instrumentality, was the cause thereof. They attack plaintiff's action as an attempt to fix liability "en masse" on various defendants, some of whom were not responsible for the acts of others; and they further point to the failure to show which defendants had control of the instrumentalities that may have been involved. Their main defense may be briefly stated in two propositions: (1) that where there are several defendants and there is a division of responsibility in the use of an instrumentality causing the injury, and the injury might have resulted from the separate act of either one of two or more persons, the rule of res ipsa loquitur cannot be invoked against any one of them; and (2) that where there are several instrumentalities, and no showing is made as to which caused the injury or as to the particular defendant in control of it, the doctrine cannot apply. We are satisfied, however, that these objections are not well taken in the circumstances of this case. . . .

The present case is of a type which comes within the reason and spirit of the doctrine more fully perhaps than any other. The passenger sitting awake in a railroad car at the time of a collision, the pedestrian walking along the street and struck by a falling object or the debris of an explosion, are surely not more entitled to an explanation than the unconscious patient on the operating table. Viewed from this aspect, it is difficult to see how the doctrine can, with any justification, be so restricted in its statement as to become inapplicable to a patient who submits himself to the care and custody of doctors and nurses, is rendered unconscious, and receives some injury from instrumentalities used in his treatment. Without the aid of the doctrine a patient who received permanent injuries of a serious character, obviously the result of someone's negligence, would be entirely unable to recover unless the doctors and nurses in attendance voluntarily chose to disclose the identity of the negligent person and the facts establishing liability. If this were the state of the law of negligence, the courts, to avoid gross injustice, would be forced to invoke the principles of absolute liability, irrespective of negligence, in actions by persons suffering injuries during the course of treatment under anesthesia. But we think this juncture has not yet been reached, and that the doctrine of res ipsa loquitur is properly applicable to the case before us.

The condition that the injury must not have been due to the plaintiff's voluntary action is of course fully satisfied under the evidence produced herein; and the same is true of the condition that the accident must be one which ordinarily does not occur unless someone was negligent. We have here no problem of negligence in treatment, but of distinct injury to a healthy part of the body not the subject of treatment, nor within the area covered by the operation. The decisions in this state make it clear that such circumstances raise the inference of negligence and call upon the defendant to explain the unusual result.

The argument of defendants is simply that plaintiff has not shown an injury caused by an instrumentality under a defendant's control, because he has not shown which of the several instrumentalities that he came in contact with while in the hospital caused the injury; and he has not shown that any one defendant or his servants had exclusive control over any particular instrumentality. Defendants assert that some of them were not the employees of other defendants, that some did not stand in any permanent relationship from which liability in tort would follow, and that in view of the nature of the injury, the number of defendants and the different functions performed by each, they could not all be liable for the wrong, if any.

We have no doubt that in a modern hospital a patient is quite likely to come under the care of a number of persons in different types of contractual and other relationships with each other. For example, in the present case it appears that Drs. Smith, Spangard and Tilley were physicians or surgeons commonly placed in the legal category of independent contractors; and Dr. Reser, the anesthetist, and defendant Thompson, the special nurse, were employees of Dr. Swift and not of the other doctors. But we do not believe that either the number or relationship of the defendants alone determines whether the doctrine of res ipsa loquitur applies. Every defendant in whose custody the plaintiff was placed for any period was bound to exercise ordinary care to see that no unnecessary harm came to him and each would be liable for failure in this regard. Any defendant who negligently injured him, and any defendant charged with his care who so neglected him as to allow injury to occur, would be liable. The defendant employers would be liable for the neglect of their employees; and the doctor in charge of the operation would be liable for the negligence of those who became his temporary servants for the purpose of assisting in the operation.

In this connection, it should be noted that while the assisting physicians and nurses may be employed by the hospital, or engaged by the patient, they normally become the temporary servants or agents of the surgeon in charge while the operation is in progress, and liability may be imposed upon him for their negligent acts under the doctrine of respondeat superior. Thus a surgeon has been held liable for the negligence of an assisting nurse who leaves a sponge or other object inside a patient, and the fact that the duty of seeing that such mistakes do not occur is delegated to others does not absolve the doctor from responsibility for their negligence.

It may appear at the trial that, consistent with the principles outlined above, one or more defendants will be found liable and others absolved, but this should not preclude the application of the rule of res ipsa loquitur. The control at one time or another, of one or more of the various agencies or instrumentalities which might have harmed the plaintiff was in the hands of every defendant or of his employees or temporary servants. This we think, places upon them the burden of initial explanation. Plaintiff was rendered unconscious for the purpose of undergoing surgical treatment by the defendants; it is manifestly unreasonable for them to insist that he identify any one of them as the person who did the alleged negligent act.

The other aspect of the case which defendants so strongly emphasize is that plaintiff has not identified the instrumentality any more than he has the particular guilty defendant. Here, again, there is a misconception which, if carried to the extreme for which defendants contend, would unreasonably limit the application of the res ipsa loquitur rule. It should be enough that the plaintiff can show an ii.jury resulting from an external force applied while he lay unconscious in the hospital; this is as clear a case of identification of the instrumentality as the plaintiff may ever be able to make. . . .

Notes

1. How likely is it that defendant Thompson caused the injury to plaintiff? If another defendant was the cause, could Thompson be liable under some doctrine of vicarious liability? Could she be liable as a coconspirator? Is it important that she be potentially liable for the negligence of the other defendants in the case? See the discussion of joint tortfeasors in Chapter 8.

2. What if defendants on remand discharge their "burden of initial explanation" by testifying that they did not neglect the plaintiff in any way? Should there be directed verdict for defendants, or can the plaintiff still get to the jury? Jaffe, Res Ipsa Loquitur Vindicated, 1 Buffalo L. Rev. 1 (1951), argues that if res ipsa loquitur is invoked for the purpose of inducing defendant to come forward and testify to what he knows about the accident, he does so, and the court is persuaded that he really does not know what caused the accident, defendant is entitled to a directed verdict. Does this mean that if defendants had testified in Ybarra they would have been entitled to a directed verdict unless their testimony showed they were negligent?

On remand from the Supreme Court's decision, the Ybarra case was retried without a jury, there was judgment for the plaintiff, and the judgment was upheld on appeal. The appellate court stated:

> On the first appeal the [Supreme Court] held that proof of the receipt of a traumatic injury during the unconsciousness of anesthesia was sufficient to make a prima facie case against all of the defendants under the rule of res ipsa loquitur. This is the law of the case on the second appeal, and, as well, establishes a rule of law binding upon us as an intermediate appellate court.
>
> The finding that plaintiff suffered a traumatic injury while unconscious although attacked by appellants finds ample support in the record. Respon-

dent's medical experts and an independent expert appointed by the court all testified that in their opinion the injury was traumatic. Respondent testified that prior to the operation he had never had any pain in or injury to the right arm or shoulder and discovered this injury after awakening from the anesthesia. While all of these experts admitted the possibility that respondent's condition might be caused by infection rather than trauma they were strongly of the opinion that the injury was traumatic. Appellants' experts while admitting the possibility of trauma were as strongly of the opinion that the condition was the systemic product of some infection. The resolution of this conflict was for the trial court and we are concluded on appeal by the trial judge's determination on conflicting evidence of medical probabilities.

All of the defendants except the owner of the hospital, who was not personally in attendance upon the respondent, gave evidence and each testified that while he was present he saw nothing occur which could have produced the injury to respondent's arm and shoulder. Upon this evidence appellants insist that the prima facie case made under the res ipsa doctrine was overcome. But it was for the trial judge to weigh the circumstantial evidence which made the prima facie case under the res ipsa rule against the positive testimony of the appellants and to determine whether the prima facie case had been met. There is nothing inherent in direct testimony which compels a trial court to accept it over the contrary inferences which may reasonably be drawn from circumstantial evidence. The view taken of the evidence by the trial judge is illustrated by the following remark made at the hearing of the motion for new trial: "I believe it arose from a traumatic condition. Now, where did it happen? That puts the court right back. Even though their explanations were honest, that there was something they did not appreciate happened in the course of the operation, in the course of handling the patient. That is the way I figured the case and that was my decision." . . .

Appellants argue that since all of them were not present at all times while respondent was unconscious all cannot be held liable except by pure conjecture. . . .

The court having held that the rule of res ipsa loquitur applied in this case, if the defendants had rested without giving any evidence a judgment against all of them would properly have followed. Instead they gave evidence which did not satisfy the court that any of them had met the prima facie case against them. A judgment against all of them as logically resulted.

Ybarra v. Spangard, 93 Cal. App. 2d 43, 45-48, 208 P.2d 445, 447 (1949).

Are you satisfied with this reasoning? The trial judge found that the defendants' explanations for what went on during and after the operation were "honest." If so, how could the injury have been of traumatic origin? How could nurse Thompson conceivably be thought guilty of neglect?

Did the doctrine of res ipsa loquitur play any role, in fact, in the decision on remand?

3. For a decision quite similar to *Ybarra*, see Beaudoin v. Watertown Memorial Hospital, 32 Wis. 2d 132, 145 N.W.2d 166 (1966). Have such decisions been made obsolete by modern liberal rules of pretrial discovery?

4. Samson v. Riesing, 62 Wis. 2d 698, 215 N.W.2d 662 (1974), was an action for negligence, by a lady who attended a luncheon put on by a high school band mothers association, against 11 members of the association for salmonella food poisoning suffered after eating turkey salad at the luncheon. A directed verdict for defendants was affirmed. Although there was evidence that the turkey salad was indeed contaminated with salmonella bacteria,

> nine turkeys were cooked, each by one of nine defendants, but not all of the 11 defendants cooked the turkeys. It does appear, however, that all of them participated in the preparation of the salad. Assuming that, at some stage of the preparation of one or more turkeys, one or more of the 11 ladies were negligent — either by providing inadequate cooking or inadequate refrigeration, or by permitting contamination from external sources—the negligence of any particular defendant remains completely a matter of speculation and conjecture. There was no exclusive control by any of the defendants.

Id. at 708, 215 N.W.2d at 667-668. How if at all is this case distinguishable from *Ybarra*?

Mr. Boyd's Renault

FAIRPLAY FOR MOTORISTS

Dear Sir,—Why should motorists alone be obliged to give warning of their approach at cross roads and corners? The only efficient way to minimize collisions is to insist that all who use the roads should make their advent audible. Horsemen should have a bell or horn affixed to the pummel of their saddles, while pedestrians should have a similar means of signalling attached to the handles of their sticks and umbrellas. The loneliness of the open road, which so often affects the spirits of dwellers in the country, would thus be sensibly mitigated, and the burden of precaution equitably distributed between the tortoises and the hares of modern life.

Yours faithfully,   F.I.A.T. Justitia   The Reeks, Leighton Buzzard

—*Punch*

A Sign of Edwardian Times from Punch
Photograph by Leslie Hamilton Wilson

Chapter 5
Victim's Conduct or Status as a Bar to, or Limitation on, Recovery

In Chapter 4 we saw that under traditional common-law principles the victim's negligence bars his recovery of damages for an injury caused by the negligence of another, provided the victim's negligence contributed to the accident. A closely related doctrine known as "assumption of risk" may also bar an accident victim from obtaining damages for an injury caused by negligence, as may certain types of legal status, such as being a trespasser or being a guest in an automobile. These doctrines have struck many as harsh, and a variety of statutory and common-law mitigating devices have grown up. There is also the economic point made in the first chapter of this book: mechanical application of the Hand formula to the victim's conduct (or status), coupled with the principle that the victim's negligence is a bar to recovery of damages, might sometimes result in inefficient accident prevention. For example, if PL is $100, and the accident could have been avoided at a cost of either $10 to the defendant or $40 to the plaintiff, literal-minded application of the Hand formula to plaintiff's conduct would result in a finding that he was negligent (because $40 is less than $100). If on this ground he is barred from recovery, defendants in similar cases will have no incentive to take precautions. Plaintiffs will have an incentive to take precautions and presumably will do so, but the result will be to spend $30 more than is necessary to avoid each accident ($40 − $10). A recurrent question in this chapter is whether and to what extent doctrines relating to the defenses based on plaintiff's conduct or status solve the economic, as well as the humanitarian, problems raised by these defenses.

LeRoy Fibre Co. v. Chicago, Milwaukee & S.P. Ry. Co.
232 U.S. 340 (1914)

The following questions are certified:
"1. In an action at law by the owner of a natural product of the soil, such as flax straw, which he lawfully stored on his own premises and which was destroyed by fire caused by the negligent operation of a locomotive engine, to

recover the value thereof from the railroad company operating the engine, is it a question for the jury whether the owner was also negligent without other evidence than that the railroad company preceded the owner in the establishment of its business, that the property was inflammable in character and that it was stored near the railroad right of way and track?

"2. Is it a question for the jury whether an owner who lawfully stores his property on his own premises adjacent to a railroad right of way and track is held to the exercise of reasonable care to protect it from fire set by the negligence of the railroad company and not resulting from unavoidable accident or the reasonably careful conduct of its business?

"3. As respects liability for the destruction by fire of property lawfully held on private premises adjacent to a railroad right of way and track, does the owner discharge his full legal duty for its protection if he exercises that care which a reasonably prudent man would exercise under like circumstances to protect it from the dangers incident to the operation of the railroad conducted with reasonable care?" . . .

The evidence at the trial showed the following without dispute: "Some years after defendant had constructed and commenced operating its line of railroad through Grand Meadow, Minnesota, the plaintiff established at the village a factory for the manufacture of tow from flax straw. The plaintiff had adjacent to its factory premises, a tract of ground abutting upon the railroad right of way and approximately 250 by 400 feet in dimension upon which it stored flax straw it purchased for use in its manufacturing business. There were about 230 stacks arranged in two rows parallel with the right of way. Each stack contained from three to three and a half tons of straw. The distance from the center of the railroad track to the fence along the line of the right of way, was fifty feet, from the fence to the nearest row of stacks, twenty or twenty-five feet, and from the fence to the second row of stacks, about thirty-five feet. A wagon road ran between the fence and the first row. On April 2, 1907, during a high wind, a fire started upon one of the stacks in the second row, and as a result all were consumed. The fire did not reach the stack through the intervening growth or refuse but first appeared on the side of the stack above the ground. The flax straw was inflammable in character. It was easily ignited and easily burned.

"There was substantial evidence at the trial tending to show that the fire was started by a locomotive engine of defendant which had just passed and that through the negligent operation of defendant's employés in charge, it emitted large quantities of sparks and live cinders which were carried to the straw stack by a high wind then prevailing. It was contended at the trial by defendant, that plaintiff itself was negligent and that its negligence contributed to the destruction of its property. There was no evidence that plaintiff was negligent save that it had placed its property of an inflammable character upon its own premises so near the railroad tracks, that is to say, the first row of stacks, seventy or seventy-five feet and the second row in which the fire started about eighty-five feet from the center of the railroad track. In other words, the character of the property and its proximity to an operated railroad for which plaintiff was responsible was the sole evidence of plaintiff's contributory negligence.

"The trial court charged the jury that though the destruction of the straw was caused by defendant's negligence, yet if the plaintiff in placing and maintaining two rows of stacks of flax straw within a hundred feet of the center line of the railroad, failed to exercise that ordinary care to avoid danger of firing its straw from sparks from engines passing on the railroad that a person of ordinary prudence would have exercised, under like circumstances and that the failure contributed to cause the accident the plaintiff could not recover. . . ." *what was the holding of the lower court*

MR. JUSTICE MCKENNA, after making the foregoing statement, delivered the opinion of the court.

The questions certified present two facts — (1) The negligence of the railroad was the immediate cause of the destruction of the property. (2) The property was placed by its owner near the right of way of the railroad, but on the owner's own land. *Facts*

. . . That one's uses of his property may be subject to the servitude of the wrongful use by another of his property seems an anomaly. It upsets the presumptions of law and takes from him the assumption and the freedom which comes from the assumption, that the other will obey the law, not violate it. It casts upon him the duty of not only using his own property so as not to injure another, but so to use his own property that it may not be injured by the wrongs of another. How far can this subjection be carried? Or, confining the question to railroads, what limits shall be put upon their immunity from the result of their wrongful operation? In the case at bar, the property destroyed is described as inflammable, but there are degrees of that quality; and how wrongful must be the operation? In this case, large quantities of sparks and "live cinders" were emitted from the passing engine. Houses may be said to be inflammable, and may be, as they have been, set on fire by sparks and cinders from defective or carelessly handled locomotives. Are they to be subject as well as stacks of flax straw, to such lawless operation? And is the use of farms also, the cultivation of which the building of the railroad has preceded? Or is that a use which the railroad must have anticipated and to which it hence owes a duty, which it does not owe to other uses? And why? The question is especially pertinent and immediately shows that the rights of one man in the use of his property cannot be limited by the wrongs of another. The doctrine of contributory negligence is entirely out of place. Depart from the simple requirement of the law, that every one must use his property so as not to injure others, and you pass to refinements and confusing considerations. There is no embarrassment in the principle even to the operation of a railroad. Such operation is a legitimate use of property; other property in its vicinity may suffer inconveniences and be subject to risks by it, but a risk from wrongful operation is not one of them.

maj: RR is liable upon the facts as a matter of law

The legal conception of property is of rights. When you attempt to limit them by wrongs, you venture a solecism. If you declare a right is subject to a wrong you confound the meaning of both. It is difficult to deal with the opposing contention. There are some principles that have axiomatic character. The tangibility of property is in its uses and that the uses by one owner of his property may be limited by the wrongful use of another owner of his, is a contradiction. . . .

MR. JUSTICE HOLMES, partially concurring. . . .

. . . I agree, for the purposes of argument, that as a general proposition people are entitled to assume that their neighbors will conform to the law; that a negligent tort is unlawful in as full a sense as a malicious one, and therefore that they are entitled to assume that their neighbors will not be negligent.

Nevertheless I am not prepared to answer the first question, No, if it is to be answered at all. We are bound to consider that at a trial the case would be presented with more facts — that this case was presented with at least one more fact bearing upon the right to recover — I mean the distance. If a man stacked his flax so near to a railroad that it obviously was likely to be set fire to by a well-managed train, I should say that he could not throw the loss upon the road by the oscillating result of an inquiry by the jury whether the road had used due care. I should say that although of course he had a right to put his flax where he liked upon his own land, the liability of the railroad for a fire was absolutely conditioned upon the stacks being at a reasonably safe distance from the train. . . .

If I am right so far, a very important element in determining the right to recover is whether the plaintiff's flax was so near to the track as to be in danger from even a prudently managed engine. Here certainly, except in a clear case, we should call in the jury. I do not suppose that any one would call it prudent to stack flax within five feet of the engines or imprudent to do it at a distance of half a mile, and it would not be absurd if the law ultimately should formulate an exact measure, as it has tended to in other instances; but at present I take it that if the question I suggest be material we should let the jury decide whether seventy feet was too near by the criterion that I have proposed. Therefore, while the majority answer the first question, No, on the ground that the railroad is liable upon the facts stated as matter of law, I should answer it Yes, with the proviso that it was to be answered No, in case the jury found that the flax although near, was not near enough to the trains to endanger it if the engines were prudently managed, or else I should decline to answer the question because it fails to state the distance of the stacks.

I do not think we need trouble ourselves with the thought that my view depends upon differences of degree. The whole law does so as soon as it is civilized. Negligence is all degree — that of the defendant here degree of the nicest sort; and between the variations according to distance that I suppose to exist and the simple universality of the rules in the Twelve Tables or the Leges Barbarorum, there lies the culture of two thousand years. . . .

Notes

1. Why did the majority think the doctrine of contributory negligence "entirely out of place" in this case? The doctrine limits the freedom of action of a traveler at a railroad crossing; did the majority think that property rights are more important than the right to personal freedom and safety? *No*

2. Justice Holmes thought that if plaintiff had stacked its flax five feet from the railroad track it would have been contributorily negligent as a matter of law. Would the majority have agreed? If so, what is the disagreement between the majority and Holmes? In McKain v. Haynes, 203 S.W.2d 970 (Tex. Civ. App. 1947), plaintiff's filling station was destroyed by a fire that spread from the adjoining lot, where defendants were negligently burning trash. The jury found that plaintiff had been contributorily negligent in failing to cut the dry grass that surrounded the wooden buildings of the filling station, which were saturated with gasoline and oil. Is the result in *McKain* consistent with that in *LeRoy Fibre?* *No*

3. Why did Holmes agree that "as a general proposition people are entitled to assume that their neighbors . . . will not be negligent"? To answer this question requires a distinction between two types of accident — those preventable at least cost by "joint care" and those preventable at least cost by "alternative care." (These concepts are developed in Landes & Posner, Joint and Multiple Tortfeasors: An Economic Analysis, 9 J. Legal Stud. 517 (1980).) In the first type of accident, optimal prevention requires that two or more people do something; in the second, that only one of them do something. Because we are interested in victim conduct, we can assume there are just two people involved and one is the potential victim of the accident and the other the potential injurer. (The extension of the concepts to the case of multiple injurers is discussed in Chapter 8.)

To illustrate joint care, consider the following version of the facts in *LeRoy Fibre*. The expected damage to the flax (PL) is $150 and can be avoided in any of the following ways. First, the railroad can install a super spark arrester that will prevent any sparks or cinders from being spewed on to LeRoy Fibre Company's land, at a cost to the railroad of $100. If the railroad does this, LeRoy Fibre will spend nothing on avoiding damage to its flax since no sparks or cinders will be emitted by the railroad's trains. Second, the railroad can install a good, but not super, spark arrester, which would reduce the emission of sparks and cinders to the point where no flax would be damaged, provided that LeRoy Fibre kept its flax at least five feet from the railroad tracks. Let us assume that the cost of avoiding the damage by this method is $50 to the railroad and $5 to LeRoy Fibre, for a total cost of damage prevention of $55. Finally, if the railroad does not install any sort of spark arrester, LeRoy Fibre can still avoid any damage to its flax by stacking the flax at least 100 feet from the railroad tracks. The cost to LeRoy Fibre of keeping this distance from the tracks is $110; the cost to the railroad is nothing.

Method 2 is obviously the best from a social standpoint, since the total cost of damage prevention under that method is only $55, compared to $100 for Method 1 and $110 for Method 3. However, under a rule of <u>negligence liability</u> with no defense of contributory negligence, Method 1 will be chosen. LeRoy Fibre will stack its flax next to the track because it is compensated for any damage. The railroad will then have an incentive to incur a $100 expense to avoid the accident since it will be deemed negligent if it fails to incur that expense and its expected liability is $150. Under a rule of <u>negligence with contributory negligence</u> interpreted mechanically in accordance with the Hand formula, Method 3 will be chosen. For, knowing that LeRoy Fibre will be deemed contributorily negligent if it fails to keep its flax at least 100 feet from the tracks — because $110 (B to LeRoy Fibre) is less than $150 (PL) — the railroad will not install any spark arrester and LeRoy Fibre will then have an incentive to keep its flax 100 feet from the tracks in order to minimize its damage. If, however, LeRoy Fibre will be deemed contributorily negligent only if it fails to take the precautions that it should take against a potential injurer acting reasonably — i.e., a railroad that installs a good, although not super, spark arrester — LeRoy Fibre will have an incentive to keep its flax five feet away from the tracks, because then, if there is damage, the railroad will be liable for it. At this point the railroad, facing an expected liability of $150, has an incentive to install the good spark arrester and the accident is avoided at minimum social cost — $55. If, under this legal regime, the railroad fails to install any spark arrester *and* LeRoy Fibre fails to keep its flax five feet away from the tracks, the railroad will be deemed negligent but LeRoy Fibre will be unable to recover damages, because it is contributorily negligent. This result is economically correct. Even if the railroad had used due care, the accident would have occurred; therefore, no economic purpose is served by making the railroad liable in this case.

To illustrate <u>alternative care</u> requires only a slight change in the facts of the previous example. Assume that the cost to the railroad of the good but not super spark arrester is not $50 but $90, and the cost to LeRoy Fibre of keeping its flax at least five feet from the tracks is not $5 but $30. Now Method 2, where both parties take some care, is inferior to both Method 1 and Method 3, because the total cost of Method 2 is $120, compared to $100 for Method 1 and $110 for Method 3. Method 1 is best; and it involves care by the railroad but not by LeRoy Fibre. The case is therefore one where alternative rather than joint care is optimal. But again we must be wary of mechanical application of the Hand formula. If LeRoy Fibre is deemed contributorily negligent because its cost of accident avoidance, $110, is less than the expected accident cost, $150, then the accident will be avoided, but at a cost of $10 more than is necessary ($110 − $100). Again the principle that <u>contributory negligence</u> means failure to exercise that care which is optimal, given that the injurer is exercising due care, avoids this result. For here due care requires the railroad to install the super spark arrester, and when this is done the optimal care for LeRoy Fibre is zero.

4. What if the victim of a negligent accident fails to take some measure not to avoid the accident but to limit the damage to him from it? Then a separate doctrine, that of "avoidable consequences," comes into play. If, for example, an accident victim fails to seek medical care, and as a result his injury is more severe than it would otherwise have been, this doctrine will prevent him from collecting damages for the added severity of the injury. Should the doctrine also be used to limit the damages obtainable by an automobile accident victim who fails to fasten his seat belt before the accident occurs? Courts are divided on this question. See Annot., Nonuse of Seat Belt as Failure to Mitigate Damages, 80 A.L.R.3d 1033 (1977). Should nonuse also be deemed contributory negligence?

Alvis v. Ribar
85 Ill. 2d 1, 421 N.E.2d 886 (1981)

MORAN, J. . . .

Plaintiffs ask this court to abolish the doctrine of contributory negligence and to adopt in its place the doctrine of comparative negligence as the law in Illinois. . . .

Generally, under the doctrine of contributory negligence, a plaintiff is barred from recovering compensation for his injuries if his negligence contributed to the accident. The origin of the doctrine can be traced to the case of Butterfield v. Forrester (1809), 11 East 60, 103 Eng. Rep. 926. There defendant had placed a pole across part of a public road. Plaintiff, riding his horse too fast to see the obstruction, rode into the pole and was injured. The concept of contributory negligence was created by the words of Chief Justice Lord Ellenborough: "Two things must concur to support this action, an obstruction in the road by the fault of the defendant, and no want of ordinary care to avoid it on the part of the plaintiff."

The doctrine was swiftly adopted in American jurisprudence, commencing with the case of Smith v. Smith (1824), 19 Mass. (2 Pick.) 621. Legal scholars attribute the swift and universal acceptance of the doctrine to newly formed industry's need for protection "against the ravages which might have been wrought by over-sympathetic juries." Judicial concern was particularly evident in the area of personal injury suits brought by railroad employees against the railroads. The courts realized that, in the pervading public view that saw railroads as "harmful entities with deep pockets," juries' sympathies toward plaintiffs could wreak financial disaster upon that burgeoning industry.

Case law developed the doctrine of contributory negligence in Illinois. In Aurora Branch R.R. Co. v. Grimes (1852), 13 Ill. 585, 587-588, this court followed the Butterfield case and added the requirement that the burden of proof is upon the plaintiff to show not only negligence on the part of the defendant, but also that plaintiff himself exercised proper care and circumspection. In the next few years the decisions involving "last clear chance," degrees of negligence, and proximate cause created confusion. Mr. Justice Breese reviewed these decisions in Galena & Chicago Union R.R. Co. v. Jacobs (1858), 20 Ill. 478, a case which involved a 4½-year-old boy who had been run over by a railroad locomotive. There the court ultimately disagreed with the *Butterfield* holding and adopted a form of comparative negligence in its place. . . . The court concluded that liability does not depend absolutely on the absence of all negligence on the part of the plaintiff but upon the relative degrees of care or want of care manifested by both parties.

"[A]ll care or negligence is at best but relative, the absence of the highest possible degree of care showing the presence of some negligence, slight as it may be. The true doctrine, therefore, we think is, that in proportion to the negligence of the defendant, should be measured the degree of care required of the plaintiff — that is to say, the more gross the negligence manifested by the defendant, the less degree of care will be required of the plaintiff to enable him to recover. Although these cases do not distinctly avow this doctrine in terms, there is a vein of it very perceptible, running through very many of them, as, where there are faults on both sides, the plaintiff shall recover, his fault being to be measured by the defendant's negligence, the plaintiff need not be wholly without fault. . . .

"We say, then, that in this, as in all like cases, the degrees of negligence must be measured and considered, and wherever it shall appear that the plaintiff's negligence is comparatively slight, and that of the defendant gross, he shall not be deprived of his action." . . .

During the next 27 years, the rule stated in *Jacobs* was followed and then abandoned by this court in Calumet Iron & Steel Co. v. Martin (1885), 115 Ill. 358, 368-369, and City of Lanark v. Dougherty (1894), 153 Ill. 163, 165-166, where it unequivocally made any contributory negligence on the part of the plaintiff a complete bar to recovery. Dean Green summarized the reasons for abandonment: the formula was not complete in that the "degrees of negligence" did not mitigate the damages which the plaintiff could recover; the "degrees of negligence" resulted in doctrinal conflict and confusion; and the *Jacobs* case had not overruled the *Grimes* case, so that, during the lifetime of the *Jacobs* decision, courts of appeal could still rely upon the failure of the plaintiff to prove that he had exercised ordinary care in his own behalf before allowing recovery on a comparative negligence basis.

Other jurisdictions found problems in the doctrine of contributory negligence. Criticism of the harshness of the doctrine came as swiftly as did its acceptance into the law, and courts found exceptions to soften that harshness.

The first exception formulated to the rule of contributory negligence was that the negligence of the plaintiff was no defense when the defendant's conduct was "wilful," "wanton," or "reckless." This rule, however, was found to be cumbersome and difficult to apply. Historically, it is of limited importance.

The second exception that developed was limited to cases involving a defendant's violation of a statute designed to protect the plaintiff even against his own improvident acts. Since only a minute number of cases involved such statutes, the exception did little to alleviate the plight of the negligent plaintiff.

Greater relief was found in the creation of a third exception — "last clear chance" — which originated in the 1842 cases of Davies v. Mann (1842), 10 M.&W. 546, 152 Eng. Rep. 588. In *Davies*, the defendant negligently ran into plaintiff's donkey, which plaintiff had left fettered in the highway. The court ruled that plaintiff's negligence in leaving the donkey in the road did not bar his claim for damages against defendant, since defendant had the "last clear chance" to avoid the accident. The basic concept resembles the effect of a superseding event nullifying the negligence of a plaintiff.

The application of the third exception has by no means been uniform. Dean Prosser suggested that "[t]he real explanation would appear to be nothing more than a dislike for the defense of contributory negligence, and a rebellion against its application in a group of cases where its hardship is most apparent." Illinois courts have expressly found the doctrine of "last clear chance" not to be the law of the State. Dean Prosser has stated that although the doctrine has been repudiated in this State, it is nonetheless employed without labeling. See Walldren Express & Van Co. v. Krug (1920), 291 Ill. 472, 477, employing the phrase "conscious indifference to consequences."

Comparative negligence made its first permanent entry into American law in 1908 in the form of the Federal Employers' Liability Act (45 U.S.C. sec. 53). The Act applied to all negligence cases for injuries sustained by railroad employees engaged in interstate commerce, whether such cases were brought in a State or a Federal court. The concept of comparative negligence provided that the contributory negligence of the employee would not act as a bar to recovery, but that recovery would be diminished in proportion to the amount of negligence attributable to him. The introduction of the Federal Employers' Liability Act was the catalyst for a flood of State statutes which established a comparative negligence standard for injuries to laborers, and, especially, for railroad employees. . . .

In 1910, Mississippi became the first State to adopt a comparative negligence statute applicable to negligence cases generally. The statute adopted the "pure" form of comparative negligence under which each responsible party would pay for the injuries sustained according to the relative percentage of his fault. Another form of comparative negligence was enacted by Wisconsin in 1931. This "modified" form allowed a negligent plaintiff to recover for his injuries only if his negligence was "not as great as that of the defendant."

Today, a total of 36 States have adopted comparative negligence. . . . Twenty-three States have adopted the Wisconsin "modified" approach.

Ten States have adopted the Mississippi "pure" comparative negligence approach. Two States, Nebraska and South Dakota, have a system which allows the plaintiff to recover only if his negligence is "slight" and that of defendant is "gross." Georgia has its own unique system. It is important to note that 29 of these 36 States have adopted comparative negligence in the last 12 years.

In England, the birthplace of Butterfield v. Forrester, the concept of contributory negligence was long ago abandoned and replaced by a system of comparative negligence. Similarly, in many jurisdictions outside the United States the rule of contributory negligence has been abandoned in favor of comparative negligence. . . .

The contributory negligence defense has been subject to attack because of its failure to apportion damages according to the fault of the parties. Under a comparative negligence standard, the parties are allowed to recover the proportion of damages not attributable to their own fault. The basic logic and fairness of such apportionment is difficult to dispute. . . .

Defendants contend that the apportionment of relative fault by a jury cannot be scientifically done, as such precise measurement is impossible. The simple and obvious answer to this contention is that in 36 jurisdictions of the United States such apportionment is being accomplished by juries. The Supreme Court of California, in responding to a similar contention, stated: "These inherent difficulties are not, however, insurmountable. Guidelines might be provided the jury which will assist it in keeping focussed upon the true inquiry, and the utilization of special verdicts or jury interrogatories can be of invaluable assistance in assuring that the jury has approached its sensitive and often complex task with proper standards and appropriate reverence." We agree that such guidelines can assist a jury in making apportionment decisions and view the necessary subtle calculations no more difficult or sophisticated for jury determination than others in a jury's purview, such as compensation for pain and suffering. Although it is admitted that percentage allocations of fault are only approximations, the results are far superior to the "all or nothing" results of the contributory negligence rule. "Small imperfections can be disregarded, small inequities tolerated, if the final result is generally satisfactory."

Defendants assert that the contributory negligence rule should be retained in that the comparative negligence doctrine rewards carelessness and ignores the value of requiring prudent behavior. The fallacy of this premise was underscored by Dean Prosser: "[T]he assumption that the speeding motorist is, or should be meditating on the possible failure of a lawsuit for his possible injuries lacks all reality, and it is quite as reasonable to say that the rule promotes accidents by encouraging the negligent defendant." Contrary to defendants' assertion, we believe that the need to deter negligent parties supports the adoption of the comparative negligence doctrine in which each party would be liable for damages in direct proportion to his degree of carelessness.

Defendants claim that the change to comparative negligence will cause administrative difficulties due to an increase in claims, a decrease in settlements, and a resulting overcrowded docket. An Arkansas study showed that, there, the adoption of comparative negligence prompted no drastic change in court burden; that the change increased potential litigation but promoted more pretrial settlements. The report concluded that concern over court congestion should not be a factor in a State's decision to adopt comparative negligence.

In United States v. Reliable Transfer Co. (1975), 421 U.S. 397, wherein the court adopted apportionment of damages over the previous rule of divided damages in admiralty, the court addressed an argument similar to that posited by defendants herein. "[Defendants ask] us to continue the operation of an archaic rule because its facile application out of court yields quick, though inequitable, settlements, and relieves the courts of some litigation. Congestion in the courts cannot justify a legal rule that produces unjust results in litigation simply to encourage speedy out-of-court accommodations." We believe that the defendants' fears concerning the judicial administrative problems attendant upon the adoption of comparative negligence are exaggerated. But were defendants' fears well founded, we could nevertheless not allow the contributory negligence rule to remain the law of this State in the face of overwhelming evidence of its harsh and unjust results.

Defendants claim that the adoption of comparative negligence would escalate insurance rates to an unbearable level. This has not been found to be the case. Effects, in fact, have been found to be minimal.

The amicus curiae brief submitted by the Illinois Defense Counsel suggests that, under the contributory negligence rule, the jury has sufficient flexibility to do substantial justice and that this flexibility negates the necessity for the adoption of comparative negligence. In essence, the Illinois Defense Counsel alludes to the oft-observed phenomenon that, once inside the jury room, juries often ignore the harshness of the contributory negligence rule and, instead, dole out justice by a common sense approach according to the relative culpability of the litigants. We agree that such may be the case and, in fact, find the proclivity of juries to ignore the law to be a compelling reason for the abolition of that law. . . . There is something inherently wrong with a rule of law so repulsive to a jury's common sense of justice that veniremen feel compelled to ignore the law.

It is urged by defendants that the decision to replace the doctrine of contributory negligence with the doctrine of comparative negligence must be made by the legislature, not by this court. In each of the States that have judicially adopted comparative negligence, the court addressed the propriety of judicial versus legislative adoption. In each, the court found that contributory negligence is a judicially created doctrine which can be altered or totally replaced by the court which created it. . . .

The Illinois Defense Counsel has, in its brief, urged that the legislature is better equipped to enact comparative negligence, asserting that "the legislative process . . . involves a broad examination of the entire problem without emphasis on a particular fact situation." The Defense Counsel and defendants claim that judicial adoption of comparative negligence would result in a piecemeal approach that would leave for future cases many ancillary questions. They claim that the law would be left in confusion and turmoil.

An examination of the States from which comparative negligence statutes have emerged reveals that such statutes are very general and brief and do not address collateral issues. Rather, the legislators apparently deemed it wise to leave the solution of collateral issues to the courts. . . .

Defendants urge us to abide by the doctrine of stare decisis and follow the holding in Maki v. Frelk (1968), 40 Ill. 2d 193. They contend that it is crucial to the due administration of justice, especially in a court of last resort, that a question once deliberately examined and decided be closed to further scrutiny. It must first be pointed out that the *Maki* decision, filed 13 years ago, did not, as claimed by defendants, address the merits of the case. On the contrary, the court avoided the merits by holding that the problem was one for the legislature.

It is interesting to observe that if Illinois courts had, in fact, rigidly adhered to the state decisis rule throughout this State's legal history, the comparative standard could not have been adopted in Galena & Chicago Union R.R. Co. v. Jacobs. Similarly, the comparative rule would not have been later discarded in Calumet Iron & Steel Co. v. Martin and City of Lanark v. Dougherty.

The tenets of stare decisis cannot be so rigid as to incapacitate a court in its duty to develop the law. Clearly, the need for stability in law must not be allowed to obscure the changing needs of society or to veil the injustice resulting from a doctrine in need of reevaluation. This court can no longer ignore the fact that Illinois is currently out of step with the majority of States and with the common law countries of the world. We cannot continue to ignore the plight of plaintiffs who, because of some negligence on their part, are forced to bear the entire burden of their injuries. Neither can we condone the policy of allowing defendants to totally escape liability for injuries arising from their own negligence on the pretext that another party's negligence has contributed to such injuries. We therefore hold that in common law cases involving negligence the doctrine of contributory negligence is no longer the law in the State of Illinois, and in those instances where applicable it is replaced by the doctrine of comparative negligence.

There remains the question of the form of comparative negligence to be adopted. Under a "pure" form, the plaintiff's damages are simply reduced by the percentage of fault attributable to him. Under a "modified" form, a negligent plaintiff may recover so long as the percentage of his fault does not exceed 50% of the total.

Defendants argue that should this court decide to adopt comparative negligence, the modified approach should be selected. They point to the basic unfairness of the "pure" system by example: A plaintiff who is 90%

negligent has suffered $100,000 in damages. A defendant who is only 10% negligent has suffered only $10,000 in damages. Defendants here point out the basic unfairness of requiring the 10% negligent defendant to pay $10,000 to a plaintiff who was 90% at fault. The United States Supreme Court answered a similar claim concerning liability under admiralty law. "That a vessel is primarily negligent does not justify its shouldering all responsibility, nor excuse the slightly negligent vessel from bearing any liability at all." The liability of a defendant should not depend upon what damages he sustained but should be determined by the relationship of his fault to the ultimate damages. In a suit under a "pure" form of comparative negligence in which the defendant counterclaims for his own damages, each party must bear the burden of the percentage of damages of all parties in direct proportion to his fault. In the example above, the 90% negligent plaintiff will bear 90% of his own damages as well as 90% of defendant's. On the other hand, the 10% negligent defendant will be made to bear 10% of his own damages as well as 10% of plaintiff's. Neither party is unjustly enriched. Neither party escapes liability resulting from his negligent acts or omissions. It is difficult to see unfairness in such a distribution of liability.

Opponents of the "pure" form of comparative negligence claim that the "modified" form is superior in that it will increase the likelihood of settlement and will keep down insurance costs. However, studies done comparing the effects of the "pure" versus the "modified" forms show the differences in insurance rates to be inconsequential. Fears as to the likelihood of settlement are not supported in fact or logic. It is argued that the negligent plaintiff will refuse to settle knowing that, under the "pure" system he will be able to recover "something" in court. The converse can as easily apply: the defendant may be encouraged to settle knowing that he cannot rely on the "modified" 50% cut-off point to relieve him of liability. A comparison of results under both the "pure" and "modified" forms showed that in Arkansas there was only a slight decrease in number of settlements when the State changed from "pure" to "modified."

Wisconsin's "modified" system has been criticized because a large number of cases appealed focused on the narrow question of whether plaintiff's negligence amounted to 50% or less of the aggregate. This, in fact, caused the Wisconsin Supreme Court to examine the question of whether the "modified" system should be replaced with the "pure" form of comparative negligence. There, as in Maki v. Frelk, the merits of the case were not addressed, for the majority of the court ruled that the determination should be left to the legislature, which had originally adopted the "modified" form by statute. . . .

The "pure" form of comparative negligence is the only system which truly apportions damages according to the relative fault of the parties and, thus, achieves total justice. . . . "[T]he '50 percent' system simply shifts the lottery aspect of the contributory negligence rule to a different ground." There is no better justification for allowing a defendant who is 49% at fault to

completely escape liability than there is to allow a defendant who is 99% at
fault under the old rule to escape liability.

Mindful of the facts stated and that the vast majority of legal scholars
who have studied the area recommend the "pure" approach, we are persuaded that the "pure" form of comparative negligence is preferable, and we
therefore adopt it as the law of Illinois. . . .

Finally, we address the question of the applicability of the rule here
announced. We hold that this opinion shall be applied to the parties before
us on appeal and to all cases in which trial commences on or after June 8,
1981, the date on which the mandate in this case shall issue. This opinion
shall not be applicable to any case in which trial commenced before that date
— except that if any judgment be reversed on appeal for other reasons, this
opinion shall be applicable to any retrial. . . .

Notes

1. Of the 37 states (including Illinois) that have replaced contributory
with comparative negligence, only seven have done so by judicial decision.
Are you persuaded by the court's reasoning on why the matter need not be
left to legislative action? In an omitted portion of the opinion, the court
noted that several bills to replace contributory with comparative negligence
had failed to pass in the Illinois legislature. What weight should the court
have given to this fact? Why did the court take the unusual step of refusing to
make its ruling applicable to trials commenced before its decision?

2. If it is unrealistic to imagine "the speeding motorist . . . meditating on
the possible failure of a lawsuit for his possible injuries," does it follow that
contributory negligence should be replaced by comparative negligence — or
that the victim's negligence should not affect his damage claim at all? In fact,
doesn't the court's point, if correct, argue strongly for abolishing liability for
negligence altogether, at least in automobile cases?

The idea that the existence of a defense of contributory negligence
makes potential accident victims more careful has seemed implausible to
many recent students of tort law. See, e.g., Schwartz, Contributory and
Comparative Negligence: A Reappraisal, 87 Yale L.J. 697 (1978). The c early
writers on the rule thought differently. Thus, Schofield, in Davies v. Mann:
Theory of Contributory Negligence, 3 Harv. L. Rev. 263, 270 (1890), stated
that "the ultimate justification" of the rule lay in "the desire to prevent
accidents by inducing each member of the community to act up to the
standard of due care set by the law. . . . How much influence the rule exerts to
accomplish the object aimed at cannot be known. That it does exert some
influence is sure. A plaintiff who has learned the law of contributory negligence by the hard experience of losing a verdict is likely to be more careful in
future. From his negligence, at least, accidents will be less likely to happen."
On the underlying question whether liability rules add anything to the in-

stinct for self-preservation in inducing people to be careful, see the materials in Chapter 11 of this book.

3. Assuming that the behavior of potential accident victims is affected by their right to recover damages from injurers, does a rule of comparative negligence move the law closer to or further from optimal care, compared to the result under a rule of contributory negligence? Perhaps surprisingly, the victim's incentive to take care is not (or at least should not be) affected by which rule is followed. Recall our first version of the facts in *LeRoy Fibre*, where Method 2 was optimal and involved an expenditure of $50 by the railroad and $5 by LeRoy Fibre on care. If neither party takes care, then under a rule of contributory negligence LeRoy Fibre would be barred from recovering any damages, but under a rule of comparative negligence its damage recovery would merely be reduced by its relative fault. How is relative fault to be measured? A simple method would be to compare the ratio of each party's optimal expenditure on care to the expected accident cost. That ratio is $\frac{1}{3}$ for the railroad and $\frac{1}{30}$ for LeRoy Fibre. The lower the ratio, the more careless the party is (this was the method used in Chapter 2 to compare intentional, reckless, and merely negligent conduct). By this test, LeRoy Fibre is 10 times as negligent as the railroad and should therefore bear 10 times as much of the accident cost as the railroad, implying that LeRoy Fibre could recover only $\frac{1}{11}$ of its damages (in "pure" comparative negligence states; in "modified" comparative negligence states it would recover nothing). If so, does this mean that the railroad will have an inadequate incentive to install the $50 spark arrester? No. It is true that $\frac{1}{11}$ of $150 is less than $50, but the railroad knows that LeRoy Fibre will have an incentive to incur the $5 cost of keeping its flax five feet from the tracks in order to avoid an expected accident cost of $\frac{10}{11}$ of $150, and once LeRoy Fibre does that the railroad will bear the whole cost of the accident. Therefore the railroad will install the $50 spark arrester.

The result is the same under an alternative-care version of the facts in *LeRoy Fibre* so long as neither party is deemed negligent unless it fails to take the precautions that it should have taken if the other party was acting reasonably. If this qualification is ignored, however, and the Hand formula applied mechanically, then comparative negligence can produce a misallocation of resources in one type of alternative care case where a rule of contributory negligence would not. Suppose PL is $1,500 (not $150, as in our original example) and the total cost of Method 1 is $110, of Method 2 $120, and of Method 3 $100, so that Method 3 is optimal. Mechanically applied first to the injurer and then to the victim, the Hand formula would tell us that the railroad is negligent (because $110 is less than $1,500) but LeRoy Fibre contributorily negligent (because $100 also is less than $1,500). Under a rule of contributory negligence, LeRoy Fibre would be barred from recovering damages and thus would have an incentive to avoid the accident at a cost of $100, with the railroad doing nothing; and the optimal result would be achieved. But under a rule of comparative negligence, LeRoy Fibre can expect to recover almost 50 percent of its loss. This means that even if LeRoy Fibre does nothing to prevent the accident, the railroad, rather than having an expected judgment cost of zero, will have an expected judgment cost of almost $750, and this may induce it to incur the $110 cost of the super spark arrester. LeRoy Fibre may do nothing — or, unsure what the railroad will do, may move its flax 100 feet from the tracks. If it does nothing, or if both it and the railroad incur costs of avoiding the accident, there will be a socially excessive expenditure on accident avoidance.

Even if such cases are rare, so that comparative negligence rarely yields worse allocative results than contributory negligence, this is no argument for comparative negligence. In fact, it is an argument against it. Comparative negligence is a more costly standard to administer than contributory negligence, not only because the parties must wrangle over relative fault but also because there will be more cases than when the rule is one of contributory negligence. The added administrative costs are wasted from a social standpoint since they do not lead to an improvement in the allocation of resources to care. From a strictly economic standpoint, then, comparative negligence is unattractive.

What other sources of value should be considered here, besides economics? Does comparative negligence further a just distribution of wealth in the society? Does it carry out our basic ideas of fairness better than contributory negligence? Or is it an example of a short-sighted humanitarianism? Return to these questions after reading Chapter 7, where similar questions are examined in the context of the choice between strict liability and negligence as standards of tort law.

4. The doctrine of "last clear chance" mentioned by the court in *Alvis* is discussed later in this chapter.

Railroad Co. v. Lockwood
84 U.S. 357 (1873)

How is this recencilled this with conse

Lockwood, a drover, was injured whilst travelling on a stock train of the New York Central Railroad Company, proceeding from Buffalo to Albany, and brought this suit to recover damages for the injury. He had cattle in the train, and had been required, at Buffalo, to sign an agreement to attend to the loading, transporting, and unloading of them, and to take all risk of injury to them and of personal injury to himself, or to whomsoever went with the cattle; and he received what is called a drover's pass; that is to say, a pass certifying that he had shipped sufficient stock to pass free to Albany, but declaring that the acceptance of the pass was to be considered a waiver of all claims for damages or injuries received on the train. The agreement stated its consideration to be the carrying of the plaintiff's cattle at less than tariff rates. It was shown on the trial, that these rates were about three times the ordinary rates charged, and that no drover had cattle carried on those terms; but that all signed similar agreements to that which was signed by the plaintiff, and received similar passes. Evidence was given on the trial tending to show that the injury complained of was sustained in consequence of negligence on the part of the defendants or their servants, but they insisted that they were exempted by the terms of the contract from responsibility for all accidents, including those occurring from negligence, at least the ordinary negligence of their servants; and requested the judge so to charge. This he refused, and charged that if the jury were satisfied that the injury occurred without any negligence on the part of the plaintiff, and that the negligence of the defendants caused the injury, they must find for the plaintiff, which they did. Judgment being entered accordingly, the railroad company took this writ of error. . . .

MR. JUSTICE BRADLEY delivered the opinion of the court.

It may be assumed in limine, that the case was one of carriage for hire; for though the pass certifies that the plaintiff was entitled to pass free, yet his passage was one of the mutual terms of the arrangement for carrying his cattle. The question is, therefore, distinctly raised, whether a railroad company carrying passengers for hire, can lawfully stipulate not to be answerable for their own or their servants' negligence in reference to such carriage. . . .

It is a favorite argument in the cases which favor the extension of the carrier's right to contract for exemption from liability, that men must be permitted to make their own agreements, and that it is no concern of the public on what terms an individual chooses to have his goods carried. . . .

Is it true that the public interest is not affected by individual contracts of the kind referred to? Is not the whole business community affected by holding such contracts valid? If held valid, the advantageous position of the companies exercising the business of common carriers is such that it places it in their power to change the law of common carriers in effect, by introducing new rules of obligation.

The carrier and his customer do not stand on a footing of equality. The latter is only one individual of a million. He cannot afford to higgle or stand out and seek redress in the courts. His business will not admit such a course. He prefers, rather, to accept any bill of lading, or sign any paper the carrier presents; often, indeed, without knowing what the one or the other contains. In most cases, he has no alternative but to do this, or abandon his business. In the present case, for example, the freight agent of the company testified that though they made forty or fifty contracts every week like that under consideration, and had carried on the business for years, no other arrangement than this was ever made with any drover. And the reason is obvious enough, — if they did not accept this, they must pay tariff rates. These rates were 70 cents a hundred pounds for carrying from Buffalo to Albany, and each horned animal was rated at 2000 pounds, making a charge of $14 for every animal carried, instead of the usual charge of $70 for a carload; being a difference of three to one. Of course no drover could afford to pay such tariff rates. This fact is adverted to for the purpose of illustrating how completely in the power of the railroad companies parties are; and how necessary it is to stand firmly by those principles of law by which the public interests are protected.

If the customer had any real freedom of choice, if he had a reasonable and practicable alternative, and if the employment of the carrier were not a public one, charging him with the duty of accommodating the public in the line of his employment; then, if the customer chose to assume the risk of negligence, it could with more reason be said to be his private affair, and no concern of the public. But the condition of things is entirely different, and especially so under the modified arrangements which the carrying trade has assumed. The business is mostly concentrated in a few powerful corporations, whose position in the body politic enables them to control it. They do, in fact, control it, and impose such conditions upon travel and transportation as they see fit, which the public is compelled to accept. These circumstances furnish an additional argument, if any were needed, to show that the conditions imposed by common carriers ought not to be adverse (to say the least) to the dictates of public policy and morality. The status and relative position of the parties render any such conditions void. . . .

The defendants endeavor to make a distinction between gross and ordinary negligence, and insist that the judge ought to have charged that the contract was at least effective for excusing the latter.

. . . Strictly speaking, these expressions are indicative rather of the degree of care and diligence which is due from a party and which he fails to perform, than of the amount of inattention, carelessness, or stupidity which he exhibits. If very little care is due from him, and he fails to bestow that little, it is called gross negligence. If very great care is due, and he fails to come up to the mark required, it is called slight negligence. And if ordinary care is due, such as a prudent man would exercise in his own affairs, failure to bestow that amount of care is called ordinary negligence. In each case, the negligence, whatever epithet we give it, is failure to bestow the care and skill which the situation demands; and hence it is more strictly accurate perhaps to call it simply "negligence." . . .

In the case before us, the law, in the absence of special contract, fixes the degree of care and diligence due from the railroad company to the persons carried on its trains. A failure to exercise such care and diligence is negligence. It needs no epithet properly and legally to describe it. If it is against the policy of the law to allow stipulations which will relieve the company from the exercise of that care and diligence, or which, in other words, will excuse them for negligence in the performance of that duty, then the company remains liable for such negligence. The question whether the company was guilty of negligence in this case, which caused the injury sustained by the plaintiff, was fairly left to the jury. It was unnecessary to tell them whether, in the language of law writers, such negligence would be called gross or ordinary. . . .

These conclusions decide the present case, and require a judgment of affirmance. We purposely abstain from expressing any opinion as to what would have been the result of our judgment had we considered the plaintiff a free passenger instead of a passenger for hire.

Notes

1. Is the decision in this case likely to make drovers as a group better off or worse off? They would be better off if the only result of the decision were that railroads would now be liable to them for injuries caused by railroad negligence, but is this likely to be the only result? Suppose the average price that the railroad charges the drover for carrying him and his cattle is $100 and the expected accident cost to the drover is $1. Doesn't this imply that the drover is willing to pay, directly or indirectly, a total of $101 for the trip? If so, won't the consequence of the decision simply be that the railroad will raise its price to $101?

2. Is the decision likely to result in greater care by the railroad, less care, or no change in the level of care? Does the Coase theorem provide an answer to this question?

3. If negligence is calculated according to the Hand formula, why would a potential injurer and a potential victim ever enter into an agreement waiving liability for the injurer's negligence? Negligence implies that the cost of precautions is less than the expected accident cost. Therefore, are not both parties necessarily better off if a cost-justified precaution is taken and negligence thereby avoided? In the above example, suppose the cost to the railroad of preventing a $1 expected accident cost to the drover were 90¢. Then by taking care the railroad could raise its price to $101 (since the expected accident cost to the drover would now be zero), and make an additional profit of 10¢.

4. Quimby v. Boston & M.R. Co., 150 Mass. 365, 23 N.E. 205 (1890), involved the question the Supreme Court had reserved in *Lockwood*. Plaintiff was a railroad passenger who, when injured, "was travelling upon a free pass given him at his own solicitation, and as a pure gratuity." The pass stated on the back that the holder assumed all risk of accident. In the course of holding that this waiver of liability was not contrary to public policy, even if the accident was the result of negligence, the court observed "that in the case at bar the injury occurred through the negligence of defendant's servants, and not through any failure on the part of the corporation to prescribe proper rules or furnish proper appliances of the conduct of its business." 150 Mass. at 372, 23 N.E. at 207. Assuming that in most cases the railroad's liability for negligence would be due to the doctrine of respondeat superior, can you now answer question 3 above? Incidentally, is the result in *Quimby* consistent with that in *Lockwood*?

Yб   Mб

5. Can you distinguish gross from ordinary from slight negligence in Hand formula terms? If defendant is guilty of gross negligence, should it be a defense that plaintiff was guilty of slight or ordinary negligence? The court in *Quimby* described as gross negligence the negligence of a railroad that is not simply derivative from its employees' misconduct. Does this provide a further clue to the answer to question 3 above? Would you expect parties with full information to negotiate a waiver of gross negligence? Railroads and other common carriers are traditionally held to owe a duty of highest care to their passengers and thus to be liable for even slight negligence; but they owe a duty only of ordinary care to their employees and to travelers at crossings and other strangers, and as to them are liable only for ordinary or gross negligence. Does this distinction make economic sense?

6. What is the relevance of the fact that the defendant in *Lockwood* was a common carrier? At common law, providers of certain services — notably innkeepers, ferries, warehousemen, stagecoach companies, and later railroads — were not permitted to pick and choose their customers. They were required to serve all comers at their tariffed (i.e., published) rates, without discrimination. These businesses were said to be "affected with a public interest"; in the case of transportation, they were called "common carriers." (In 1887, the Interstate Commerce Act was passed, subjecting the railroads to regulation by the Interstate Commerce Commission, a federal agency. The original act did little more than codify the traditional common-law duties of a common carrier, but amendments to the act gradually created a comprehensive scheme of regulation of rates and service, a scheme later extended to trucking and now gradually being dismantled as part of the deregulation movement.) Could a waiver of a common carrier's liability for negligence be a method of discriminating against certain shippers, in derogation of the carrier's common-law duties?

7. The Court in *Lockwood* suggested that the defendant had monopoly power over the plaintiff. If so (the fact that the railroad was a common carrier would not necessarily make it a monopolist in an economic sense), is this a reason for declining to enforce a waiver of the railroad's negligence? Why should it be? Is a monopolist likely to be less careful than a competitive firm — or will it simply charge a higher price for whatever level of care its customers desire? Economists have been unable to discover any systematic relationship, positive or negative, between a firm's monopoly power and the quality of the firm's goods or services. See, e.g., Spence, Monopoly, Quality and Regulation, 6 Bell J. Econ. 417 (1975).

McCutcheon v. United Homes Corp.
79 Wash. 2d 443, 486 P.2d 1093 (1971)

STAFFORD, J. . . .
Plaintiff Norma McCutcheon, a tenant of defendant United Homes

Corporation, was injured one evening when she fell down an unlighted flight of stairs leading from her apartment. She alleged the defendant was negligent because the lights at the top and bottom of the stairwell were not operative.

Plaintiff Douglas R. Fuller, also defendant's tenant, was injured as he descended the outside stairs of his apartment on his way to work. A step pulled loose causing him to fall. He, too, alleged negligence on the part of defendant.

Defendant's answer alleged each plaintiff had executed a form "Month to Month Rental Agreement" which contained the following exculpatory clause: "neither the Lessor, nor his Agent, shall be liable for any injury to Lessee, his family, guests or employees or any other person entering the premises or the building of which the demised premises are a part." In each case the trial court granted a summary judgment of dismissal.

The question is one of first impression. The issue is whether the lessor of a residential unit within a multi-family dwelling complex may exculpate itself from liability for personal injuries sustained by a tenant, which injuries result from the lessor's own negligence in maintenance of the approaches, common passageways, stairways and other areas under the lessor's dominion and control, but available for the tenants' use. (Hereinafter called the "common areas.")

Basic to the entire discussion is the common law rule that one who leases a portion of his premises but retains control over the approaches, common passageways, stairways and other areas to be used in common by the owner and tenants, has a duty to use reasonable care to keep them in safe condition for use of the tenant in his enjoyment of the demised premises. The landlord is required to do more than passively refrain from negligent acts. He has a duty of affirmative conduct, an affirmative obligation to exercise reasonable care to inspect and repair the previously mentioned portions of the premises for protection of the lessee.

It is readily apparent that the exculpatory clause was inserted in defendant's form "Month to Month Rental Agreement" to bar its tenants from asserting actions for personal injuries sustained through the landlord's own negligence. It was adopted to negative the result of the lessor's failure to comply with its affirmative duty to the tenants.

The defendant asserts that a lessor may contract, in a rental agreement, to exculpate itself from liability to its lessee, for personal injuries caused by lessor's own negligence. It contends such exculpatory clauses are not contrary to public policy because the landlord-tenant relationship *is not a matter of public interest, but relates exclusively to the private affairs of the parties concerned and that the two parties stand upon equal terms. Thus, there should be full freedom to contract. . . .*

The importance of "freedom of contract" is clear enough. However, the use of such an argument for avoiding the affirmative duty of a landlord to its residential tenant is no longer compelling in light of today's multi-family dwelling complex wherein a tenant merely rents some space with appurtenant rights to make it more usable or livable. Under modern circumstances the tenant is almost wholly dependent upon the landlord to provide reasonably for his safe use of the "common areas" beyond the four walls demised to him.

As early as 1938 Williston recognized that while such exculpatory clauses were recognized as "legal," many courts had shown a reluctance to enforce them. Even then, courts were disposed to interpret them strictly so they would not be effective to discharge liability for the consequences of negligence in making or failing to make repairs. 6 Williston, A Treatise on the Law of Contracts §1751C p. 4968 (Rev. ed. 1938). In §1751B at 4965 the author said:

> A promise not to sue for the future damage caused by simple negligence may be valid. *Such bargains are not favored*, however, and, if possible, bargains are construed not to confer this immunity. (Footnotes omitted. Italics ours.)

The key to our problem is found in Restatement of Contracts §574, p. 1079 (1932) which reads:

> A bargain for exemption from liability for the consequences of negligence *not falling greatly below the standard established by law* for the protection of others against unreasonable risk of harm, is legal. . . . (Italics ours.)

In other words, such an exculpatory clause may be legal, when considered in the abstract. However, when applied to a specific situation, one may be exempt from liability for his own negligence *only when the consequences thereof do not fall greatly below the standard established by law.*

In the landlord-tenant relationship it is extremely meaningful to require that a landlord's attempt to exculpate itself, from liability for the result of its own negligence, *not fall greatly below the standard of negligence set by law.* As indicated earlier, a residential tenant who lives in a modern multi-family dwelling complex is almost wholly dependent upon the landlord for the reasonably safe condition of the "common areas." However, a clause which exculpates the lessor from liability to its lessee, for personal injuries caused by lessor's own acts of negligence, not only lowers the standard imposed by the common law, it effectively *destroys* the landlord's affirmative obligation or duty to keep or maintain the "common areas" in a reasonably safe condition for the tenant's use.

When a lessor is no longer liable for the failure to observe standards of affirmative conduct, or for *any* conduct amounting to negligence, by virtue of an exculpatory clause in a lease, *the standard ceases to exist.* In short, such a clause *destroys* the concept of negligence in the landlord-tenant relationship. Neither the standard nor negligence can exist in abstraction.

It is no answer to argue that the rental agreement relates exclusively to the "personal and private affairs of two parties on equal footing" and thus is "not a matter of public interest." . . .

We no longer live in an era of the occasional rental of rooms in a private home or over the corner grocery. In the relatively short span of 30 years the public's use of rental units in this state has expanded dramatically. In the past 10 years alone, in the state of Washington, there has been an increase of over 77,000 rental units. It takes no imagination to see that a business which once had a minor impact upon the living habits of the citizenry has developed into a major commercial enterprise directly touching the lives of hundreds of thousands of people who depend upon it for shelter.

Thus, we are not faced merely with the theoretical duty of construing a provision in an isolated contract specifically bargained for by *one landlord and one tenant* as a "purely private affair." Considered realistically, we are asked to construe an exculpatory clause, the generalized use of which may have an impact upon thousands of potential tenants.

Under these circumstances it cannot be said that such exculpatory clauses are "purely a private affair" or that they are "not a matter of public interest." The real question is whether we should sanction a technique of immunizing lessors of residential units within a multi-family dwelling complex, from liability for personal injuries sustained by a tenant, which injuries result from the lessor's own negligence in maintaining the "common areas"; particularly when the technique employed destroys the concept of negligence and the standard of affirmative duty imposed upon the landlord for protection of the tenant.

An exculpatory clause of the type here involved contravenes long established common law rules of tort liability that exist in the landlord-tenant relationship. As so employed, it offends the public policy of the state and will not be enforced by the courts. It makes little sense for us to insist, on the one hand, that a workman have a safe place in which to work, but, on the other hand, to deny him a reasonably safe place in which to live.

The trial court is reversed and the cause is remanded for trial.

Notes

1. Does the test of the Restatement of Contracts, quoted by the court, have reference to the degree of negligence of the defendant or to the number of people who would be affected if the defendant (and those like him) were allowed to waive their negligence? Why should courts be suspicious of contracts purporting to waive gross negligence or intentional misconduct?

2. What is the likely effect of the decision on the level of rentals? On the supply of rental housing? Cf. R. A. Posner, Economic Analysis of Law 356-359 (2d ed. 1977).

3. With the approach of the Washington court in *McCutcheon*, compare that of the California court in Tunkl v. Regents of University of California, 60 Cal. 2d 92, 102, 383 P.2d 441, 447 (1963), invalidating an exculpatory clause in an agreement admitting a patient to treatment in a hospital.

> In insisting that the patient accept the provision of waiver in the contract, the hospital certainly exercises a decisive advantage in bargaining. The would-be patient is in no position to reject the proffered agreement, to bargain with the hospital, or in lieu of agreement to find another hospital. The admission room of a hospital contains no bargaining table where, as in a private business transaction, the parties can debate the terms of their contract. As a result, we cannot but conclude that the instant agreement manifested the characteristics of the so-called adhesion contract. Finally, when the patient signed the contract, he completely placed himself in the control of the hospital; he subjected himself to the risk of its carelessness.

At common law, contracts were voidable if procured by duress or fraud. These narrow defenses have blossomed in recent decades into the broad and amorphous concept of "unconscionability," whereby contracts are voidable if the result of the "unequal bargaining power" of the party seeking enforcement. Contracts of "adhesion" — standard printed contracts offered on a take it or leave it basis to the purchaser, with no opportunity to negotiate different terms — are often thought to evidence unequal bargaining power, though they may simply be an effort to reduce transaction costs. For critical discussions of unconscionability and related notions see R. A. Posner, Economic Analysis of Law 84-88 (2d ed. 1977); Epstein, Unconscionability: A Critical Reappraisal, 18 J. Law & Econ. 293 (1975); Schwartz, Seller's Unequal Bargaining Power and the Judicial Process, 49 Ind. L.J. 367 (1974); Trebilcock, The Doctrine of Inequality of Bargaining Power: Post-Benthamite Economics in the House of Lords, 26 U. Toronto L.J. 359 (1976). Would the result in *Tunkl* make better economic sense if the case had involved admission to the emergency room of the hospital? Cf. the *Ploof* case in Chapter 3.

4. What is left of freedom of contract so far as waivers of negligence are concerned? Phillips Home Furnishings, Inc. v. Continental Bank, 231 Pa. Super. 174, 180-182, 331 A.2d 840, 843-844 (1974), contains a useful summary of the current state of the law on this question:

> Generally, a written contract defines the extent of the obligations of contracting parties, and a valid exculpatory clause will preclude recovery. It was recognized long ago that parties may contractually absolve themselves from liability for the consequences of their negligent acts. Maving v. Todd, 4 Camp. 225, 171 Eng. Rep. 72 (1815); see e.g., Dilks v. Flohr Chevrolet, Inc., 411 Pa. 425, 192 A.2d 682 (1963) ("the validity of a contractual provision which exculpates a person from liability for his own acts of negligence is well settled").

However, the law also recognized that lying behind these contracts is a residuum of public policy which is antagonistic to carte blanche exculpation from liability, and thus developed the rule that these provisions would be strictly construed with every intendment against the party seeking their protection. Responding to changes in economic and social necessities, courts then went beyond this rule of construction and found that in certain situations and relations express agreements by which one party assumes the risk of another's conduct could not, in good conscience, be accepted. Where a disparity of bargaining power has grown out of economic necessity for certain goods or services or from a monopolistic position of a seller, courts have found exculpatory agreements inimical to the public interest. Where an agreement does not represent a free choice on the part of the plaintiff, where he is forced to accept the clause by the necessities of his situation, courts have refused to enforce such agreements as contrary to public policy. This rule has been applied broadly in the employer-employee relationship; in situations where one party is charged with a duty of public service [citing cases involving public utilities, common carriers, other carriers, hospitals, and airports]; to agreements which attempt to exculpate one from liability for the violation of a statute or regulation designed to protect human life; and elsewhere, e.g., Uniform Commercial Code §2-719(3), provides that the limitation of consequential damages for injury to the person in the case of consumer goods is prima facie unconscionable.

5. Suppose a wealthy individual — a middle-aged businessman — consults a plastic surgeon with regard to a facelift and the surgeon demands a waiver of negligence before proceeding. Would the waiver be enforced?

6. Suppose the contract in *McCutcheon*, rather than purporting to waive liability for all accidents, had specified the precise safety measures that defendant would take in the common areas and had provided that defendant would not be liable for accidents that could have been prevented by additional safety measures. Would this form of waiver be enforceable if the measures specified fell short of satisfying the tort standard of ordinary care?

Krall v. Royal Inns of America, Inc.
374 F. Supp. 146 (D. Alaska 1973)

PLUMMER, J.

This is an action to recover damages for personal injuries sustained by plaintiff Krall on July 27, 1970, during construction of the Anchorage Royal Inn. Plaintiff sustained injury when he lost his balance while awaiting a hoist on a crossbeam, which was ten stories above the ground and connected the external workmen's hoist to the building, and grabbed a vertical guide of the hoist, the rollers of the hoist coming into contact with his hand. The hoist was erected 14 feet from the building; there were no walkways, guardrails, or toeboards (all required by the Alaska General Safety Code prior to the use of the hoist by workers) between the hoist and the building above the fifth floor.

Plaintiff, an apprentice iron worker employed by Red-E-Steel Co., Inc., a subcontractor of Royal Inns, was working on the installation of the walkways connecting the hoist to the building. The hoist was leased by and in the control of Royal Inns. The court in a previous memorandum and order found Royal Inns' use of the hoist to constitute negligence per se, such negligence being a proximate cause of plaintiff's injury.

This case is presently before the court on motion for summary judgment by plaintiff on the issue of whether contributory negligence affords a defense to negligence per se based upon violation of regulations contained in the Safety Code. . . .

Plaintiff sets forth three reasons for denying the defense: (1) the legislature "clearly intended" to place the "entire responsibility" for injury on the employer; (2) the workman has a limited ability to exercise self-protective care because of economic duress; and (3) employers possess superior ability to bear and distribute the cost of the risk. Defendant asserts that contributory negligence is the general rule in Alaska and argues against the intent and public policy contentions.

To demonstrate the intent of the legislature, plaintiff stresses the Legislative Intent as set forth in A.S. 18.60.010 in force at the time of the accident;[2] Safety Code §300-20 which places a duty upon employers to provide safe working conditions and to use safety devices and safeguards; and Safety Code §§315-01 to 315-61 (concerning hoists and elevators) which delineate specific duties for employers but establish no duties for employees.

Defendant counters that A.S. 18.60.010-18.60.105, comprising the article entitled Accident Prevention provided for penalties as follows: "A person who violates [a provision of this article] is punishable for each offense by a fine . . . or by imprisonment . . . or both." A.S. 18.60.090. No mention is made of tort remedies, nor is mention made concerning the non-availability of contributory negligence. While such statute may be used to establish standards of care for a claim of negligence per se, ordinarily in such instances contributory negligence continues to afford a valid defense. . . .

Plaintiff asserts, however, A.S. 18.60.010-18.60.105 as it existed at the time of the accident had the effect of placing the entire responsibility for harm as occurred upon the employer, and as such constituted one of an unusual type of statute which has been construed as intended to remove contributory negligence as a defense to negligence per se. Plaintiff relies principally upon this court's decision in Vance v. United States, 355 F. Supp. 756 (D. Alaska 1973); Restatement (2d) of Torts, §483; and Koening v.

---

2. (a) The legislature finds that preventable accidents are the leading causes of death in the state, that accidents cause nearly one-fourth of all deaths of the white race in the state and as much as 82 percent of all deaths in certain age groups; that the proportion of accidental deaths to all deaths is three times as high in the state as in other parts of the United States where intensive accident prevention campaigns are conducted, and that an unknown but proportionately as great a rate of nonfatal accidents is sustained in the state.

(b) For these reasons it is found and declared necessary to undertake a program to reduce the incidents of preventable accidents in the state.

Patrick Construction Co., 298 N.Y. 313, 83 N.E.2d 133 (1948). Defendant distinguishes *Vance* and argues §483 is inapplicable. Defendant also contends *Koenig* represents a minority rule and urges against its adoption in Alaska.

In *Vance* the court denied the use of contributory negligence as a defense to defendant's violation of Alaska's Dram Shop Act, A.S. 04.15.020(a), which makes criminal the selling or giving liquor to minors or intoxicated persons. Plaintiff Vance alleged defendant's agent sold him liquor after he had become intoxicated and such act caused the harm. The court cited the following from the Restatement (2d) of Torts:

> 1 . . . Thus a statute which prohibits the sale of firearms to minors may be clearly intended, among other purposes, to protect them against their own inexperience, lack of judgment, and tendency toward negligence, and to make the seller solely responsible for any harm to them resulting from the sale. In such a case the purpose of the statute would be defeated if the contributory negligence of the minor were permitted to bar his recovery. §483, Comment c.

The court then found: "A.S. 04.15.020(a) presents an even more compelling example of a statute intended to place the entire responsibility for resulting harm upon the violator, for it is virtually impossible for the statute to be violated without contributory negligence on the part of the plaintiff-consumer."

The present situation is distinguishable from *Vance* first in that the impairment of judgment in *Vance* was caused by intoxication. Here any impairment of good judgment was caused by economic duress as found in *Koenig*. The court is not persuaded these different kinds of impairment should be afforded the same judicial treatment. Second, in the present situation negligence and contributory negligence can occur independent of one another. Thus, the necessity to construe the statute or regulation as placing the entire responsibility upon one party to effectuate the legislative purpose is much less compelling.

Plaintiff's second reason for eliminating the defense is the worker's limited ability to exercise self-protective care because of economic duress. See *Koenig*, supra. The court concluded above this reason did not persuade the court to construe A.S. 18.60.010-18.60.105 to eliminate the defense. Nor does the argument standing on its own so persuade the court. It might be noted in passing New York alone removes the defense for violations of safety statutes concerning scaffolds, hoists, etc., in the absence of a statutorily-created civil remedy. Other jurisdictions disallowing the defense base their decisions on civil remedy provisions. Most states lacking such statutory direction which have faced the problem retain the defense.

The economic duress argument could be extended to call for "general deterrence" of accidents. See Calabresi, The Costs of Accidents: A Legal and Economic Analysis, 68-94 (1970). In theory requiring employers to bear the full losses of accidents caused by violations of the safety code should sensitize them to the mandates of the code. Obliging employers to internalize fully costs of violation-accidents would aid in the prevention and deterrence of those accidents. Further, theory suggests the employer is primarily a conduit through which accident costs are passed on to consumers. Thus, the removal of the defense would reduce accident costs in two ways: 1) by inducing employers to produce their product by the safest reasonable means, and 2) by increasing the cost and thereby reducing the consumption of high-accident products and services. Since the employer can pass on the costs, whereas the employee can not and the employee is further subject to economic pressure which inhibits his efforts to promote safety, the employer is clearly the better accident avoider. As such, the argument concludes, the employer should be charged with the costs of all accidents caused by violation of the Safety Code.

However, the general deterrence argument not only has theoretical problems, see Calabresi, supra, at 78-88, but it may have practical problems, also, as employers in the construction industry may be insensitive to accident costs regardless of the law's content. Sands, How Effective Is Safety Legislation, 11 J. Law & Econ. 165, 177, 178 (1968). Further, the theory proves too much as the rationale would charge all accident costs to employers. Also, the Unions' increased awareness and assertion of power in the name of safety lessens the economic pressure on workers. Finally, workmen's compensation and tort liability, even with the defense, provide much of the same internalization of accident costs. Thus, the court discerns no compelling reason to deny the defense.

Plaintiff's third reason for denying the defense is that employers possess a superior ability to bear and distribute the cost of the risk. Utilizing this method and reason for shifting the impact of accident costs onto the employer has been referred to as "enterprise liability." See Calabresi, supra, at 50-54. Alaska has examined enterprise liability theory in arriving at a judicial standard in respondeat superior cases. Fruit v. Schreiner, 502 P.2d 133, 141 (Alaska 1972); and Luth v. Rogers and Babler Const. Co., 507 P.2d 761, 763, 764 (Alaska 1973). In *Fruit* the court's modified enterprise theory of respondeat superior called for a jury determination of whether plaintiff was in the scope of his employment at the time of the accident. In *Luth* the Supreme Court reversed the trial court's directed verdict for plaintiff on the scope of employment issue requiring a determination by the finder of fact.

Although *Fruit* and *Luth* engendered the same policy reasons as advocated here for shifting accident losses,[4] the Alaska Supreme Court required

---

4. " . . . it appears more socially desirable for the employer, although faultless itself, to bear the loss than the individual harmed. Insurance is readily available for the employer so that the risk may be distributed among many like insureds paying premiums and the extra cost of doing business may be reflected in the price of the product."

It may be noted the Alaska Court alludes to the general deterrence mechanism in this passage. The reference to the "extra cost of doing business" is another phrase for "internalizing" the costs of accidents. The allusion is almost necessary because shifting losses from the employee to the employer is the mechanism by which both general deterrence and enterprise liability operate.

jury findings on the issue of liability. It may be argued the present case is distinguishable from *Fruit* and *Luth* in that here the employer was negligent, whereas there the employers were not. Such argument confuses the issues of liability based on fault and liability based on enterprise theory. Further, the choice to retain the jury for affixing liability rather than barring the defense of contributory negligence does not reject the policy reasons advocated by plaintiff. The difference is one of degree with the jury accommodating those policy goals a substantial portion of the time.

Fruit and *Luth* weigh against denying the defense of contributory negligence in this case. The existence of workmen's compensation pre-empts part of plaintiff's policy argument by automatically allocating some of the losses to the employer. Finally, reliance upon the finder of fact does not reject the underlying policy. . . .

Notes

1. What do you make of the court's discussion of "economic duress" and "general deterrence"? Consider the following analysis. If a firm is fully liable for the costs of its accidents, it will have an incentive to adopt all cost-justified safety precautions. To the extent that these precautions fail to avert all accidents, the firm's cost of production will include some accident costs and its price therefore will be higher than if it did not bear the costs of its accidents. The higher price will induce substitution of other products and hence lead to a reduction in the output of the firm. Thus, liability will have two effects: greater safety precautions by the firm and a smaller output. Stated differently, liability will cause the firm both to take care and to reduce its activity level (see Chapter 1) and will thereby achieve what Professor Calabresi calls "general deterrence."

This is an economic argument for liability (strict or negligence?) but not for abrogating the defense of contributory negligence. If a potential accident victim can avoid injury at lower cost than the potential injurer, then the social costs of accidents will be minimized by forcing the victim to bear his accident costs. Workers may fear that if they lose their present jobs they will not be able to find other jobs. This seems to be the meaning of "economic duress" in the context of the *Krall* case. Still it is unclear why this fear would prevent them from being careful. That seems reason enough to reject plaintiff's "economic duress" argument in this case; the *Lamson* case, next, presents a more plausible situation of economic duress.

Ignored in the foregoing discussion, as in the court's opinion, is the bearing of the Coase theorem. Although defendant in *Krall* technically was not plaintiff's employer (plaintiff was employed by a subcontractor that defendant had hired to work on the construction of its hotel), there was an indirect contractual relationship between defendant and plaintiff. This implies that the accident costs to plaintiff would be internalized regardless of the rule of liability. If defendant is liable to careless workers, the wage rate will — in principle, at least — be lower, since the worker now receives part of his compensation in the form of insurance against accidents due to his own carelessness. If defendant is not liable, the wage rate will be higher. Defendant's total costs will be the same in either case. On this point see also the Notes following the *Lamson* case.

2. The court's discussion of "enterprise liability" and "risk distribution" is confused and superficial; its conclusion probably is correct. The short answer to plaintiff's argument is that he could have bought insurance against accidents, thereby "distributing" the risk to the other policyholders of the insurance company. It is not obvious that an insurance company is a worse distributor of risk than a firm that distributes risk by charging higher prices to its customers. Again, the discussion ignores the bearing of the Coase theorem, which implies that the risk pool will consist of the workers themselves. (Why?) For more on enterprise liability and risk distribution, see Chapters 7 and 9.

Lamson v. American Axe & Tool Co.
177 Mass. 144, 58 N.E. 585 (1900)

[Directed verdict for defendant. Plaintiff appeals.]

HOLMES, C.J. This is an action for personal injuries caused by the fall of a hatchet from a rack in front of which it was the plaintiff's business to work at painting hatchets, and upon which the hatchets were to be placed to dry when painted. The plaintiff had been in the defendant's employment for many years. About a year before the accident new racks had been substituted for those previously in use, and it may be assumed that they were less safe and were not proper, but were dangerous on account of the liability of the hatchets to fall from the pegs upon the plaintiff when the racks were jarred by the motion of machinery near by. The plaintiff complained to the superintendent that the hatchets were more likely to drop off than when the old racks were in use, and that now they might fall upon him, which they could not have done from the old racks. He was answered in substance that he would have to use the racks or leave. The accident which he feared happened, and he brought this suit.

The plaintiff, on his own evidence, appreciated the danger more than any one else. He perfectly understood what was likely to happen. That likelihood did not depend upon the doing of some negligent act by people in another branch of employment, but solely on the permanent conditions of the racks and their surroundings and the plaintiff's continuing to work where he did. He complained, and was notified that he could go if he would not face the chance. He stayed and took the risk. He did so none the less that the fear of losing his place was one of his motives.

Exceptions overruled.

Notes

[handwritten: negligence more "willful"]

1. Was plaintiff's case stronger or weaker by virtue of his having complained about the new racks? *[handwritten: assumption of risk]*

2. Was defendant negligent? If the cost of replacing the racks with safer *[handwritten: No, not rt]* ones had been less than the expected accident cost to plaintiff and other *[handwritten: the weckandoss so liable]* workmen, wouldn't defendant have replaced them voluntarily? Suppose the expected accident cost was $10 a year, the cost of avoidance (also on a yearly basis) $8, and the annual wage $500. If the defendant replaced the racks, he could lower the wage to $490 and cut his net labor costs by $2 ($500 − $10 + $8). Lamson would be no worse off and the employer would be better off. Transaction costs are low; in these circumstances the Coase theorem implies, does it not, that the employer will replace the dangerous racks. Does his *[handwritten: Not]* failure to do so therefore show that he was not negligent and hence that the assumption of risk doctrine is unintelligible, at least viewed as a defense to a prima facie case of negligence? Before answering yes, consider the following possibilities:

a. The expected accident cost to the *average* workman is $10, but Lamson is above average in his ability to avoid accidents — the expected accident cost to him was only $7.

b. The law had set the standard of care higher than the efficient level.

c. Lamson was a risk preferrer (see discussion in Chapter 1 of risk preference and aversion). He preferred a $10 risk to a certain reduction in his wage of $8.

3. How realistic is it to think that workers demand risk premiums to do dangerous work, and, if the employers refuse, leave for a safer job? The nineteenth-century judicial view was uncompromising. This is what Lord Bramwell, in Smith v. Baker & Sons, [1891] A.C. 325, 344 (H.L.), had to say on the subject:

> The plaintiff here thought the pay worth the risk, and did not bargain for a compensation if hurt: in effect, he undertook the work, with its risks, for his wages and no more. He says so. Suppose he had said, "If I am to run this risk, you must give me 6s. a day and not 5s.," and the master agreed, would he in reason have a claim if he got hurt? Clearly not. What difference is there if the master says, "No; I will only give the 5s."? None. I am ashamed to argue it.

Modern economic scholarship provides some support for the view that workers in dangerous occupations receive a risk premium. See evidence in R. Thaler & S. Rosen, The Value of Saving a Life: Evidence from the Labor Market, in Household Production and Consumption 265, 286-296 (N. E. Terleckyj ed. 1975).

4. Writing in 1906, a torts scholar sought to explain the assumption of risk doctrine in employment cases such as *Lamson* in terms of "economic conditions": "in America as yet there is normally no dearth of work for competent workmen. If one job is dangerous, another can probably be found." Bohlen, Voluntary Assumption of Risk II, 20 Harv. L. Rev. 91, 115 (1906). Suppose the costs to Lamson of finding another job would have been prohibitive ("economic duress"). Would that affect the willingness of his employer to take cost-justified safety measures? Could it affect Lamson's taste for risk?

With the views of Bramwell and Bohlen, compare the more recent evaluation in Friedman & Ladinsky, Social Change and the Law of Industrial Accidents, 67 Colum. L. Rev. 50, 58 (1967): the common law of industrial accidents "socialized the accident costs of building the [rail]roads." Is this plausible? Is it consistent with the Coase theorem? The Friedman and Ladinsky article is a good statement of the prevalent modern view that the common law of industrial accidents was unfair to workers. For a contrasting view, see Croyle, Industrial Accident Liability Policy of the Early Twentieth Century, 7 J. Legal Stud. 279 (1978).

5. Assumption of risk was one of three doctrines that limited the success of injured employees in common law negligence suits against their employers. The other two were contributory negligence and the fellow-servant rule. The latter barred the employee from recovering damages from his employer if the injury was caused by a fellow worker, unless the employer had notice that the worker was negligent. The rule was said to promote safety by encouraging workers to report their negligent coworkers to the employer. See Farwell v. Boston & Worcester Railroad Corp., 45 Mass. 49, 59 (1842); Posner, A Theory of Negligence, 1 J. Legal Stud. 29, 44-45, 67-69 (1972).

The entire area of employers' liability for negligence to their employees is now largely, although not entirely, of historical interest. Beginning in 1910, state after state enacted workmen's compensation laws (today increasingly referred to as "workers' compensation laws," in recognition of the growing participation of women in the industrial work force), whereby the employer's common law liability was replaced by an administrative scheme under which an injured employee could collect compensation for any work-related accident, according to a fixed and modest schedule of payments. Not only did the employee not have to prove the employer's negligence, but assumption of risk, contributory negligence, and the fellow-servant rule were all abolished as defenses. Every state has such a law today, but, since the coverage is not always complete, some room is left for common-law actions. See Prosser 532-534. Because tort damages are larger than workmen's compensation awards, employees themselves sometimes seek ways of bypassing their workmen's compensation remedy. A popular method, examined in Chapter 9, is to sue the manufacturer of any equipment or supplies that contribute to the employee's injury on the job, under a theory of products liability. Cf. *Krall*, supra. However, the employee cannot maintain a common-law suit against his employer if the accident is covered by the state's worker's compensation law.

For detailed studies, theoretical and empirical, of the operation of workmen's compensation laws, see the three-volume Supplemental Studies for the National Commission on State Workmen's Compensation Laws (1973). See also J. R. Chelius, Workplace Safety and Health: The Role of Workers' Compensation (1977).

An important area that remains exempt from workmen's compensation is the railroad industry. The Federal Employers' Liability Act, 45 U.S.C. §§51 et seq., first enacted in 1908 (an earlier act was struck down as unconstitutional), allows railroad employees to bring negligence suits (in either state or federal court, at their election). The act abolished the fellow-servant rule, invalidated waivers of liability, and replaced contributory negligence with comparative negligence; a 1939 amendment to the act abolished assumption of risk. Although the requirement of proving the employer's negligence was retained, the Supreme Court whittled down this requirement to very little by holding that the trial court could not take the negligence issue from the jury unless there was not even a scintilla of evidence of negligence. See, e.g., Rogers v. Missouri Pac. R. Co., 352 U.S. 500 (1957); Gallich v. Baltimore & Ohio R. Co., 372 U.S. 108 (1963). The act covers all railroad activities in or affecting interstate commerce, and within its scope preempts state compensation law. The Jones Act of 1915 and the Merchant Marine Act of 1920 extended the principles of the FELA to seamen. Another complex federal liability statute is the Longshoremen's and Harbor Workers' Compensation Act, on which see, e.g., Rich v. United States, 596 F.2d 541 (3d Cir. 1979).

Would you expect the relaxation of the common-law defenses by workmen's compensation and by FELA and similar statutes to lead to a reduction or an increase in industrial accidents? What does the Coase theorem imply? What does the theory that the common law is efficient imply? A recent statistical study found that industrial accidents declined after and as a consequence of these statutes. See Chelius, Liability for Industrial Accidents: A Comparison of Negligence and Strict Liability Systems, 5 J. Legal Stud. 293 (1976).

Eckert v. Long Island R. Co. p217
43 N.Y. 502 (1871)

[See Chapter 4A supra for the facts and the majority opinion.]

ALLEN, J. (dissenting). The plaintiff's intestate was not placed in the peril from which he received the injury resulting in his death, by any act or omission of duty of the defendants, its servants, or agents. He went upon the

track of the defendant's road in front of an approaching train, voluntarily, in
the exercise of his free will, and while in the full possession of all his faculties,
and with capacity to judge of the danger. His action was the result of his own
choice, and such choice not compulsory. He was not compelled, or apparently
compelled, to take any action to avoid a peril, and harm to himself, from the
negligent or wrongful act of the defendant, or the agents in charge of the
train. . . . [T]he maxim volenti non fit injuria applies. It is a well established
rule, that no one can maintain an action for a wrong, when he consents or
contributes to the act which occasions his loss. One who with liberty of
choice, and knowledge of the hazard of injury, places himself in a position of
danger, does so at his own peril, and must take the consequences of his
act. . . .

The testator had full view of the train and saw, or could have seen, the
manner in which it was made up, and the locomotive attached, and the speed
at which it was approaching, and, if in the exercise of his free will, he chose for
any purpose to attempt the crossing of the track, he must take the consequence of his act. The defendant may have been running the train improperly, and perchance illegally, and so as to create a legal liability in respect to any
one sustaining loss solely from such cause, but the company is not the insurer
of, or liable to those who, of their own choice and with full notice, place
themselves in the path of the train and are injured. . . .

The act of the intestate in attempting to save the child was lawful as well
as meritorious, and he was not a trespasser upon the property of the defendant, but it was not in the performance of any duty imposed by law, or
growing out of his relation to the child, or the result of any necessity. There is
nothing to relieve it from the character of a voluntary act, the performance of
a self-imposed duty, with full knowledge and apprehension of the risk
incurred. . . .

Judson v. Giant Powder Co.
107 Cal. 549, 40 P. 1020 (1895)

[See Chapter 4B supra for the facts of this case.]
GAROUTTE, J. . . .

Respondents [plaintiffs] sold the premises to appellant [defendant] for
the manufacture of dynamite, and it is claimed that the maxim "volenti non
fit injuria" applies, and therefore no recovery can be had. We attach but little
importance to this contention. The grant of these premises for the purposes
of a dynamite factory in no way carried to appellant the right to conduct its
factory as against the grantors in any and every way it might see fit. There is
no principle of law sustaining such a proposition. Let it be conceded that
respondents, by reason of their grant, could not invoke the aid of a court of

equity to prevent the appellant from conducting its business; still that concession proves nothing. This action is not based upon the theory that appellant's business is a nuisance per se, but negligence in the manner in which the business was conducted was alleged in the complaint, and is now insisted upon as having been proved at the trial. In making the grant, respondents had a right to assume that due care would be exercised in the conduct of the business, and certainly they have a right to demand that such care be exercised. It is argued that the explosion of all powder works is a mere matter of time; that such explosions are necessarily contemplated by every one who builds beside such works, or who brings dynamite into his dooryard. It is further contended that appellant gave to respondents actual notice of the dangerous character of its business by a previous explosion, which damaged respondents' property, and that respondents, by still continuing in business after such notice, in a degree assumed and ratified the risk, and cannot now be heard to complain. The only element of strength in this line of argument is its originality. The contention that, in the ordinary course of events, all powder factories explode, conceding such to be the fact, presents an element foreign to the case. The doctrine of fatalism is not here involved. In the ordinary course of events the time for this explosion had not arrived, and appellant had no legal right to hasten that event. . . .

Notes

1. Suppose that plaintiff's intestate in *Eckert* had been trying to rescue not a child, but the child's toy. Would the proper defense in that case be assumption of risk or contributory negligence? Would it make a difference whether, having decided to rescue the toy, the plaintiff's intestate had then exercised all possible care to do so without injury to himself? Suppose the chance of his being hit by the train was so slight that, evaluated under the Hand formula, his decision to rescue the toy would not be adjudged a negligent one even though it turned out fatally for him. Could one nonetheless argue that plaintiff's suit was barred by assumption of risk? Is the difference between assumption of risk and contributory negligence perhaps the difference between level of activity and level of care as methods of accident avoidance?

2. Suppose that in *Judson* the plaintiffs had known at the time they sold defendant the property in question for the manufacture of dynamite that there was a one percent chance that defendant's dynamite factory would some day explode. Would this knowledge support a defense of assumption of risk? Would it make a difference whether the one percent figure included the probability of a negligent as well as nonnegligent explosion? Did the court give enough weight to the previous explosion, or was that irrelevant because it occurred after the sale to the defendant?

assa̱n tio̱ o̱f ri̱sk

Murphy v. Steeplechase Amusement Co.
250 N.Y. 479, 166 N.E. 173 (1929)

CARDOZO, C.J. The defendant, Steeplechase Amusement Company, maintains an amusement park at Coney Island, N. Y. One of the supposed attractions is known as "The Flopper." It is a moving belt, running upward on an inclined plane, on which passengers sit or stand. Many of them are unable to keep their feet because of the movement of the belt, and are thrown backward or aside. The belt runs in a groove, with padded walls on either side to a height of four feet, and with padded flooring beyond the walls at the same angle as the belt. An electric motor, driven by current furnished by the Brooklyn Edison Company, supplies the needed power.

Plaintiff, a vigorous young man, visited the park with friends. One of them, a young woman, now his wife, stepped upon the moving belt. Plaintiff followed and stepped behind her. As he did so, he felt what he describes as a sudden jerk, and was thrown to the floor. His wife in front and also friends behind him were thrown at the same time. Something more was here, as every one understood, than the slowly moving escalator that is common in shops and public places. A fall was foreseen as one of the risks of the adventure. There would have been no point to the whole thing, no adventure about it, if the risk had not been there. The very name, above the gate, "The Flopper," was warning to the timid. If the name was not enough, there was warning more distinct in the experience of others. We are told by the plaintiff's wife that the members of her party stood looking at the sport before joining in it themselves. Some aboard the belt were able, as she viewed them, to sit down with decorum or even to stand and keep their footing; others jumped or fell. The tumbling bodies and the screams and laughter supplied the merriment and fun. "I took a chance," she said when asked whether she thought that a fall might be expected.

Plaintiff took the chance with her, but, less lucky than his companions, suffered a fracture of a knee cap. He states in his complaint that the belt was dangerous to life and limb, in that it stopped and started violently and suddenly and was not properly equipped to prevent injuries to persons who were using it without knowledge of its dangers, and in a bill of particulars he adds that it was operated at a fast and dangerous rate of speed and was not supplied with a proper railing, guard, or other device to prevent a fall therefrom. No other negligence is charged.

We see no adequate basis for a finding that the belt was out of order. It was already in motion when the plaintiff put his foot on it. He cannot help himself to a verdict in such circumstances by the addition of the facile comment that it threw him with a jerk. One who steps upon a moving belt and finds his heels above his head is in no position to discriminate with nicety between the successive stages of the shock, between the jerk which is a cause and the jerk, accompanying the fall, as an instantaneous effect. There is evidence for the defendant that power was transmitted smoothly, and could not be transmitted otherwise. If the movement was spasmodic, it was an unexplained and, it seems, an inexplicable departure from the normal workings of the mechanism. An aberration so extraordinary, if it is to lay the basis for a verdict, should rest on something firmer than a mere descriptive epithet, a summary of the sensations of a tense and crowded moment. But the jerk, if it were established, would add little to the case. Whether the movement of the belt was uniform or irregular, the risk at greatest was a fall. This was the very hazard that was invited and foreseen.

Volenti non fit injuria. One who takes part in such a sport accepts the dangers that inhere in it so far as they are obvious and necessary, just as a fencer accepts the risk of a thrust by his antagonist or a spectator at a ball game the chance of contact with the ball. The antics of the clown are not the paces of the cloistered cleric. The rough and boisterous joke, the horseplay of the crowd, evokes its own guffaws, but they are not the pleasures of tranquillity. The plaintiff was not seeking a retreat for meditation. Visitors were tumbling about the belt to the merriment of onlookers when he made his choice to join them. He took the chance of a like fate, with whatever damage to his body might ensue from such a fall. The timorous may stay at home.

A different case would be here if the dangers inherent in the sport were obscure or unobserved, or so serious as to justify the belief that precautions of some kind must have been taken to avert them. Nothing happened to the plaintiff except what common experience tells us may happen at any time as the consequence of a sudden fall. Many a skater or horseman can rehearse a tale of equal woe. A different case there would also be if the accidents had been so many as to show that the game in its inherent nature was too dangerous to be continued without change. The president of the amusement company says that there had never been such an accident before. A nurse employed at an emergency hospital maintained in connection with the park contradicts him to some extent. She says that on other occasions she had attended patrons of the park who had been injured at the Flopper, how many she could not say. None, however, had been badly injured or had suffered broken bones. Such testimony is not enough to show that the game was a trap for the unwary, too perilous to be endured. According to the defendant's estimate, 250,000 visitors were at the Flopper in a year. Some quota of accidents was to be looked for in so great a mass. One might as well say that a skating rink should be abandoned because skaters sometimes fall. . . .

Notes

1. Did plaintiff make out a prima facie case that defendant was negligent? If not, why did the court bother to discuss assumption of risk?

2. Why would it be a different case "if the accidents had been so many as to show that the game in its inherent nature was too dangerous to be contin-

ued without change"? Certain sports are highly dangerous, such as hang gliding. If the hang glider is aware of the dangers, does it matter, so far as assumption of risk is concerned, how great the dangers are? Cf. Lunsford v. Tucson Aviation Corp., 73 Ariz. 277, 240 P.2d 545 (1952); Weadock v. Eagle Indemnity Co., 15 So. 2d 132 (La. App. 1943). Why then was evidence introduced concerning the number of accidents to people riding on the Flopper?

Wyly v. Burlington Industries, Inc.
452 F.2d 807 (5th Cir. 1971)

RONEY, J.

James W. Wyly was a contestant in "the National Lap Sitting Contest" when a chair proved unable to support him and the 14 co-eds who were sitting on his lap. The chair broke. Wyly was injured. He brought suit against Burlington Industries, Inc., which sponsored the contest. The trial court instructed the jury that defendant was liable for the injuries as a matter of law, and plaintiff won a $13,000 verdict.

Holding that the defendant was entitled to have a jury determine whether the plaintiff voluntarily exposed himself to a known and appreciated danger so as to bar his recovery under the Texas doctrine of volenti non fit injuria, we reverse. . . .

As part of an advertising campaign for wrinkle-resistant slacks, the defendant was promoting "the National Lap Sitting Contest" on college campuses. The object of the contest was to stack co-eds on a contestant's lap with the winner having the lap which holds the most co-eds for a 10 second period. The prize was three or four pairs of slacks and a night on the town. Such a contest was held at the University of Texas at El Paso where plaintiff was a student.

When the plaintiff's turn came to participate, 14 co-eds were placed on his lap, which would have broken the existing record. But the pressure of the contest became too great and the chair collapsed injuring plaintiff. Shortly after the contest began, a different and supposedly less sturdy chair had collapsed under a previous contestant and fewer co-eds. Although the defendant's representative was not present at the time the first chair broke (the students had jumped the starting gun), he was advised of the collapse upon his arrival. The representative then obtained the chair which he had originally asked to have used in the contest. Plaintiff used this chair. While the contest continued, defendant's representative attempted to call a local chair manufacturer to obtain "as good a chair as the company had." The chair used by plaintiff was described as an armless wood office chair with four firm legs, a four inch main supporting piece across the top of the back and four or five one-inch dowels anchored into the seat portion of the chair.

The record contained testimony that when the plaintiff went to the Student Union Building the program had not started; that he was present during the entire program until his accident; that one chair broke under the weight of one man and some girls; that the chair that was used thereafter was a typical wood armless office chair; that plaintiff knew he weighed 240 pounds and intended to hold fourteen girls who weighed about 100 pounds each; that the girls were to be picked up and laid across each other, on his lap, and that the weight was unstable and was ill-distributed; and that he intended to hold the weight, with none of the girls touching the floor, for a period that would be timed.

The dispute in this case involves whether on this evidence the jury could find that plaintiff voluntarily submitted himself to a known and appreciated danger.

Drawing the inference from this evidence most favorable to the defendant, we think that reasonable and fair-minded men could find that the plaintiff knew that such a condition was dangerous. The Texas Supreme Court has stated that the volenti doctrine is a subjective one concerned with the individual plaintiff. A determination of what a particular person knew, appreciated or understood is peculiarly within the province of the jury. No great technical knowledge would be required for a person of plaintiff's intelligence to know that if you put too much weight on a chair it will collapse, that a chair built for the normal use of one person might be in danger of collapse with the weight of 15 people on it, and that the person undergirding the rest would be in danger of injury in such a collapse. The jury could have found that the plaintiff knew the nature and extent of this danger and voluntarily exposed himself to it.

Although plaintiff denied that he knew that the first chair collapsed, he was apparently in the room at the time. His credibility must be determined by the jury. In any event, the importance of the knowledge of the fact, or the lack of such knowledge, was for the jury. . . .

Notes

1. What was the evidence of defendant's negligence?

2. Why was the prior accident relevant in this case, and not in *Judson*? If the prior accident strengthened the defendant's argument for assumption of risk in this case, why did the absence of prior accidents not weaken the assumption of risk defense in *Murphy*?

3. In light of the prior accident, should plaintiff have argued that the defendant was guilty of an intentional tort, because it knew that the winning contestant was bound to break the chair?

4. What is plaintiff's strongest argument against application of the assumption of risk doctrine?

5. How is the *Murphy* case distinguishable from this case?

6. If plaintiff had sued the manufacturer of the chair that broke, would the manufacturer have had an assumption of risk defense? Assumption of risk in products cases is considered in Chapter 9.

Scanlon v. Wedger
156 Mass. 462, 31 N.E. 642 (1892)

ALLEN, J. The several plaintiffs were injured by the explosion of a bomb or shell during a display of fireworks in Broadway Square, which was a public highway in Chelsea. This display was made by the defendant Wedger, who acted under a license from the mayor and alderman of Chelsea for a display of fireworks in Broadway Square on that evening under Pub. St. c. 102, §55. A verdict was returned for the defendant, and the jury made a special finding that the defendant, in firing the bomb, exercised reasonable care. . . .

The plaintiffs apparently were present at the display of fireworks as voluntary spectators, and were of ordinary intelligence. No fact is stated in the report to show the contrary, nor has any suggestion to that effect been made in the argument. The plaintiffs have not rested their claims at all upon the ground that they were merely travelers upon the highway, or that they were unaware of the nature and risk of the display. The report says: "A considerable number of persons were attracted to said square by said meeting, and said bombs and other fireworks which were being exploded there. . . . A portion of the center of the square about 40 by 60 feet was roped off by the police of said Chelsea, and said bombs or shells were fired off within the space so enclosed, and no spectators were allowed to be within said inclosure. . . . The plaintiffs were lawfully in said highway at the time of the explosion of said mortar, and near said ropes, and were in the exercise of due care." The bombs or shells are described in the report, and they were to be thrown from mortars into the air, it being intended that they should explode in the air, and display colored lights. They were apparently a common form of fireworks, such as has long been in use. The ground on which the plaintiffs place their several cases is that Pub. St. c. 102, §55, did not authorize the mayor and aldermen of Chelsea to license the firing of anything but rockets, crackers, squibs, or serpents, and that, therefore, the act of the defendant in firing bombs or shells was unauthorized and unlawful. It is not contended that it was at the time supposed either by the defendant or by anybody else that the license was insufficient to warrant the display which was actually made. The licensee was the chairman of a committee which had a political meeting in charge, and the defendant acted at the request of the committee, and was directed by them as to when and where to fire off the fireworks. Under this state of things, it must be considered that the plaintiffs were content to abide the chance of personal injury not caused by negligence, and that it is immaterial whether there was or was not a valid license for the display. If an ordinary

Assumption of risk

Holding

traveler upon the highway had been injured, different reasons would be applicable. But a voluntary spectator, who is present merely for the purpose of witnessing the display, must be held to consent to it, and he suffers no legal wrong if accidentally injured without negligence on the part of any one, although the show was unauthorized. He takes the risk. In the opinion of a majority of the court, the entry must be, judgments for the defendant.

MORTON, J. I dissent from the opinion of the majority of the court. The majority regard as immaterial the question whether the license was valid or not. It may be treated, therefore, as void, as I think it was. If it was void, then the defendant, Wedger, was using the highway for a purpose that was dangerous, unlawful, wrongful, and unjustifiable as against anybody lawfully in the highway and in the exercise of due care, as it is expressly found that the plaintiffs were, and is liable for any injury caused to them by the explosion, whether they were travelers or not, unless they participated or aided in the display, or contributed by their own conduct to their injuries, or assumed the risk of injury. It is not claimed that there is any evidence that they participated or aided in the display. There is no evidence that they were guilty of contributory negligence. It is said, however, that they assumed the risk. What are the facts? Merely that a political meeting was being held in the square, to which a considerable number of persons had been attracted, and that bombs and other fireworks were being discharged there; and that at the time of the explosion the plaintiffs were near the rope that enclosed the space that had been roped off for discharging the fireworks, but were lawfully there, and in the exercise of due care. There is no evidence that they knew or had any reason to suppose that such mortars were liable to explode and injure bystanders, or that they were familiar with their construction, or the manner in which they were fired, or were aware that the bombs were charged with an explosive more powerful than ordinary gunpowder. There is nothing to show that they had any knowledge or suspicion that they were incurring any risk by being where they were. An inference or a conclusion that they were not unaware of the risk rests, it seems to me, entirely on assumption. The most that can be said of them is that they were voluntary spectators of the display. But before they can be held to have assumed the risk it must appear that they knew all the facts material to the risk, and appreciated and understood it. It is carrying the doctrine of assumption of the risk further than I think it has ever been carried, to say that one who, being lawfully on the highway, and in the exercise of due care, observes as a spectator an unlawful and dangerous exhibition in it, assumes the risk of injury from it. The exhibitor is bound at his peril to see that he has a valid license. If he selects the highway for an unlawful and dangerous display designed or calculated to attract the public, he, and not the spectators, assumes the risk of injury. It is of no consequence that the defendant exercised reasonable care in firing the bomb. It is a contradiction of terms to say of one engaged in an unlawful, dangerous, wrongful, and unjustifiable business that he used due care in it. Due care is predicated of something which a person may lawfully do, but which by his negligent manner of doing it may become injurious to others; not of something which he has no right whatever to do. . . .

Notes

1. Why did the court not invoke the doctrine of negligence per se, as invited to do by the dissent? Was it because the "bombs" were no more dangerous than the "rockets, crackers, squibs, or serpents" that the municipal officials were authorized to license? What case have you read that would make this a relevant ground for not invoking the doctrine? Or is the idea perhaps that the statute was not directed at the defendant?

2. Is this another case where the doctrine of assumption of risk is invoked even though plaintiff failed to make out a prima facie case of defendant's negligence?

3. Why is it relevant that plaintiffs were, so far as appears, of "ordinary intelligence"? Would defendant's duty of care be enlarged if, unbeknownst to him, they were idiots?

4. Suppose plaintiffs had not stopped to watch the fireworks, but had continued on the highway, though aware they were taking a risk, and had been injured by the fireworks. John H. Mansfield, in an interesting article on assumption of risk, suggests that in that case they would have been entitled to recover. See Informed Choice in the Law of Torts, 22 La. L. Rev. 17, 59-61 (1961). Model the difference between these two cases in terms of the Hand formula. (Hint: since PL is unchanged, the difference must be in B.) Which case is *Eckert* closer to?

5. Suppose a foreigner, attending an American baseball game for the first time in his life, is struck by a foul ball hit into the stands and is seriously injured. Does he have a cause of action against the owners of the stadium?

Springrose v. Willmore
292 Minn. 23, 192 N.W.2d 826 (1971)

PETERSON, J.

The central issue for determination is whether the judicially created doctrine of implied assumption of risk, as an absolute defense separate from contributory negligence, should be abolished. It arises out of an injury to a teenage passenger in an automobile negligently operated by its teenage driver — the claim of the injured passenger and her father against the driver and owner of the automobile having been denied solely on the ground that the passenger had assumed the risk of injury.

Assumption of risk has been conceptually distinguished according to its primary or secondary character. Primary assumption of risk, express or im-

plied, relates to the initial issue of whether a defendant was negligent at all —
that is, whether the defendant had any duty to protect the plaintiff from a
risk of harm. It is not, therefore, an affirmative defense. The limited dut[y]
owed . . . patrons of inherently dangerous sporting events [is] illustrative. The
classes of cases involving an implied primary assumption of risk are not many
and, because this is not such a case, we have no occasion to determine the
method by which such issue should be presented to a jury.

Secondary assumption of risk, as an affirmative defense to be proved by a
causally negligent defendant, is the principal issue for our determination
now. The doctrine of implied assumption of risk must, in our view, be recast
as an aspect of contributory negligence, meaning that the plaintiff's assumption of risk must be not only voluntary but, under all the circumstances,
unreasonable. . . . The practical and most important impact of this decision is
to mandate that, like any other form of contributory negligence, assumption
of risk must be apportioned under our comparative negligence statute. . . .

Our retention of the terminology of implied assumption of risk, although only as an element of negligence, may be an unnecessary precaution
in most situations. The only question for submission in the usual case, we
think, will be whether the particular plaintiff was, under the circumstances,
negligent in regard to his own safety, for under that general issue counsel may
fully argue the issue in all its aspects. There may be unusual cases, however,
where contributory negligence and assumption of risk, in any distinctive
aspects, may be separately submitted, subject, of course, to a single apportionment verdict. . . .

The situation in this appeal is not complicated. Plaintiff Mary Springrose, age 16, was a passenger in an automobile owned by defendant Bert
Willmore and driven by his daughter, defendant Margaret Willmore, age 16.
Mary and Margaret attended a school play at Edina High School and thereafter joined a group of about 15 other teenage students to go to a Bridgeman's
restaurant located at Highway No. 100 and Interstate No. 494 in Blooming-
ton. The issues of negligence and assumption of risk arose out of a series of
"drag races" among the drivers of four cars transporting the group to and
from the restaurant, a drag race between Margaret's car and another ultimately resulting in the Willmore automobile overturning and injuring plaintiff Mary.

Defendant Margaret, with plaintiff Mary as a front seat passenger, first
raced with the driver of one of the other automobiles en route to the restaurant, proceeding at speeds approaching 60 miles per hour in a zone posted for
a maximum of 50 miles per hour. They arrived at the restaurant without
incident and remained there for about 45 minutes. Upon leaving the restaurant shortly after 10 P.M. the several automobile drivers raced to be first to
the exit from the restaurant parking lot, Mary having resumed her position as
Margaret's passenger. They drove back in the direction of the Edina High
School. After stopping for a traffic light at the intersection of Highway No.
100 and 66th Street, about a mile from the restaurant, Margaret and the

driver of another automobile raced from that stop and drove at speeds of about 55 miles per hour, in a 40-mile-per-hour zone, a distance of about 3 blocks to and through the intersection of Highway No. 100 and Valley View Road. Margaret, deciding that she had lost the race, began to slow down, but, upon brushing against a dividing curb north of the intersection, lost control of her automobile and overturned upon striking a guard rail on the right hand side of the highway.

Questions as to plaintiff Mary's contributory negligence and assumption of risk were submitted for separate answer by the jury, which found that she was not negligent but that she had assumed the risk. The evidence disclosed that she had consented to driving with defendant Margaret with knowledge of her relative inexperience as a driver and, more importantly, that she had continued as Margaret's passenger after the initial drag racing had demonstrated Margaret's disposition to drive dangerously. It appears that Mary at no time cautioned or protested about Margaret's manner of driving.

Plaintiff's made post-trial motions for an order striking the special verdict question and answer relating to Mary's assumption of risk, for judgment notwithstanding the verdict, and, in the alternative, for a new trial. The trial court denied the motions. . . . This appeal is from the resulting judgment for defendants.

We reverse and remand for a trial limited to the issues of defendant Margaret's negligence and plaintiff Mary's contributory negligence. The issue of damages has been fully determined in the prior trial. We are not unmindful that the jury in the prior trial did find that Margaret was causally negligent and that Mary was not contributorily negligent, but neither finding is of controlling significance now. The finding of Margaret's causal negligence is insufficient to impose liability without the jury's apportionment of it in relation to any contributory negligence of Mary. The finding that Mary was not contributorily negligent is meaningless in view of the jury's finding that she had assumed the risk, now defined as a phase of contributory negligence. The jury necessarily must consider the totality of the evidence on these issues if it is to make a meaningful determination.

Reversed and remanded.

Notes

1. Is, or should, any issue of liability be open on remand?

2. A number of states have abolished "secondary" assumption of risk. The leading case, on which the Minnesota court relied heavily in *Springrose*, is Meistrich v. Casino Arena Attractions, Inc., 31 N.J. 44, 155 A.2d 90 (1959).

3. Consider the effect of abolishing "secondary" assumption of risk on cases such as Le Fleur v. Vergilia, 280 App. Div. 1035, 117 N.Y.S.2d 244 (1952). This case held that a driver who voluntarily accompanies the holder of a learner's permit in the learner's car for the purpose of teaching him to drive

assumes the risk of the learner's inexperience and lack of skill and cannot recover damages for an injury caused by those attributes. The learner whose inexperience or lack of skill results in an accident is negligent under the reasonable-man standard. Is the driving instructor therefore contributorily negligent for accompanying him? Could the case be recast as one of "primary" assumption of risk in a jurisdiction that has abolished "secondary" assumption of risk? Which of the functions of assumption of risk suggested in Note 2 on p. 353 supra was involved in *Le Fleur*? How is it affected by *Springrose*?

4. Did *Wyly* involve primary or secondary assumption of risk? Is it really distinguishable from *Springrose*?

Puchlopek v. Portsmouth Power Co.
82 N.H. 440, 136 A. 259 (1926)

ALLEN, J. The defendant maintained a transformer station at Newmarket on an electric power line. A picket fence enclosed the station. The pickets were nailed from the outside to two rails of two by four lumber. A wire carrying high voltage and fastened to the lower rail on the inside by insulators ran along the fence for some distance to a point where it was turned to a vertical direction and ran upwards as far as or above the upper rail. The fence where the wire was thus attached was on the line of an alley leading from a public highway to land lying between the station and a schoolhouse. The decedent was a school boy. On the day of the accident he went from the schoolhouse to the alley where his arm entered between two pickets of the fence, and he thus came in contact with the live wire in its vertical position between the two rails.

The defendant's claim that because the decedent was a trespasser in the alley he was not entitled to protection from its negligence, cannot be sustained. If he was a trespasser in reaching the alley, there was evidence of his rightful presence there in the testimony of a witness who claimed to own the alley and who testified that without objection from him or the previous owner children had for over 20 years habitually used the alley in going to and from school.

If decedent was a trespasser in the alley, that did not make him one as to the defendant. But as the motion raises only the question of the plaintiff's right to go to the jury on its assigned grounds, not being general, it is unnecessary to consider the defendant's duty to trespassers, not on its own but on adjoining premises. The decedent's rightful presence in the alley could be found, and the defendant's duty if he was a trespasser there is a question not here and now presented.

If the decedent was a trespasser on the defendant's premises, it was in undertaking to commit a wrongful act injurious to the defendant, and there can be no recovery. As such a trespasser he was not "rightfully at the place where he was injured, doing what he had a legal right to do," nor was the situation "such that the defendants ought to have anticipated his presence in a place, where the continued conduct of their business might injure him, in season by reasonable conduct to have prevented such injury." There is no duty to "casual and unknown" trespassers. The record is entirely void of evidence tending to show that the defendant should have foreseen such conduct of the decedent so as to require it to guard him in the depredation of its property or to obstruct his undertaking to that end.

But the evidence was at best inconclusive, and therefore for the jury, in respect to the defendant's claim that the decedent was a trespasser, in that his purpose in going to the alley was to get a piece of wire, and that he put his hand in between the pickets to reach and take away the wire which he took hold of, not knowing that it was charged and dangerous. There was also sufficient evidence to authorize a finding either that his only purpose in going to the alley was to use it as a part of his course in going from the schoolhouse to the highway as his ultimate destination, or that, if he sought a piece of wire, it was in the discarded material placed in the alley by the defendant, and a finding that in carrying out either purpose he slipped and his arm went in between the pickets involuntarily.

Such an involuntary intrusion could not be regarded as a trespass. Whatever the technical and precise definition of a trespass, making it broad enough to include the conduct of infants, and of insane persons, the essential element of force, expressed in the phrase vi et armis, is lacking in such an entrance on another's premises. If the decedent slipped and fell towards the fence, it was a case of force exerted by accident on him and not of force exerted by him. . . .

Notes

1. If plaintiff's decedent was not a trespasser in the alley, because the owner of the alley had not objected to children using it to go to and from school, what was he? Probably he was what is called a "licensee." Traditionally, the duty of a landowner to a licensee is no greater than his duty to a trespasser. For example, in Schreiner v. Great Northern Ry. Co., 86 Minn. 245-247, 90 N.W. 400-401 (1902), where plaintiff was injured while walking on defendant's track, the court had this to say about plaintiff's status and defendant's duty:

> The construction of the complaint most favorable to plaintiff is that he was on the railway tracks in pursuance of a usage by the public, which was permitted without objection from defendant. It does not go further than this. Plaintiff was not passing over the tracks at a crossing which had been adopted or recognized by the railway company, but was simply making use of

its tracks to walk thereon from one place to another, which is a practice adopted by many persons for pleasure or convenience. That such a user is to a certain extent common is well known, but is unquestionably dangerous, and ordinarily regarded as an intrusion upon the legal rights of the railroads, who maintain their tracks and right of way, except at stations and crossings, for the purpose solely of operating their trains thereon. It is not easy to see how such a use by the public could be wholly prevented without force, which would be attended with difficulties that might not be overcome without the imposition of unnecessary burdens upon the railway company, and it may well be doubted whether, upon the allegations of the complaint, the plaintiff was not a trespasser upon the defendant's property at the time he sustained his injury; but it is not necessary to so hold in this case. Conceding, however, that plaintiff had defendant's permission resting upon the usage of the public, to walk upon its tracks, in availing himself of that privilege he was, at best, a mere licensee. His presence thereon was not expressly invited, and was of no advantage to the defendant. Where a licensee, for his own benefit, is upon the property of another, without objection from the owner, such owner owes no duty to guard such licensee or visitor against the obvious risks and dangers which exist thereon. In other words, the licensee or visitor must take care of himself in using the premises as he finds them, and is not entitled to be protected from existing conditions upon the property in their ordinary state. . . .

. . . The plaintiff might, as a mere licensee, have the right to complain of a willful act by defendant in running him down, or of traps and pitfalls, which would be an allurement to unknown danger; but where he has full notice of conditions which are as open and apparent to him as to the railway company itself, he takes the risk of injury therefrom.

Even if a landowner's duty of care is the same to trespassers and to licensees, could it be less to someone who is on his property only by virtue of having trespassed on another's property? This question, reserved by the New Hampshire court in *Puchlopek*, arose a year later in the neighboring state of Vermont. In Humphrey v. Twin State Gas & Elec. Co., 100 Vt. 414, 139 A. 440 (1927), plaintiff, while trespassing on the land of one Thomas for the purpose of hunting, was injured when an electrical wire belonging to defendant fell onto a wire fence from a tree on Thomas's property to which it had been temporarily affixed. The court held that plaintiff's action was not barred by his trespass, since it was not a trespass against defendant, the electrical company. After remarking on the dangerousness of electricity, the court stated:

We deem it of the highest consequence, especially in a rural state like ours where hunters, fishermen, and others roam the woods when lawful, almost at will, and where high-tension electric lines run in every direction, and wire fences are in common and increasing use, that those dealing in such a deadly agency should be accountable to all whose likelihood of injury could reasonably be foreseen.

100 Vt. at 422, 239 A. at 444. Is the decision in *Humphrey* correct? Return to this question after reading the *Herrick* and *Hynes* cases below.

2. The rigor of the traditional "no duty to trespassers" rule is nicely illustrated by Bush v. Brainard, 1 Cow. 78 (N.Y. Sup. Ct. 1823). Bush made maple syrup in an unenclosed piece of woodland 60 or 70 rods from the place where Brainard's cow (no relation to the court reporter) was kept. The cow ran at large in the woods, and Bush knew this. Bush left some buckets of maple syrup under a shed in his sugar works. Brainard's cow came in the night, drank the syrup, and died. A damage judgment in favor of Brainard for the loss of his cow was reversed with the following opinion:

> SAVAGE, C.J. Sic utere tuo, ut non alienum laedas, is a sound as well as an ancient maxim. But in all cases, where damages are sustained by the plaintiff, in consequence of the use which the defendant makes of his own property, it is necessary to inquire, not only whether the defendant has been guilty of culpable negligence on his part, but whether the plaintiff is free from a similar charge. In the case of Blyth v. Topham, the defendant digged a pit in a common, and the plaintiff's mare, *being straying there*, fell into the pit and perished. The Court held that no action lay, because the plaintiff, *shewing no right why his mare should be in the common*, the digging the pit was lawful as against him. His loss was, therefore, damnum absque injuria. Otherwise, had he digged the pit in the highway. In Townsend v. Wathen, the defendant set traps in his unenclosed wood, which was intersected by highways and paths. The plaintiff's dogs were caught in the traps and injured, for which he recovered. Ch. J. Ellenborough places the defendant's liability on the fact, that the traps were set and baited with strong-scented meats, so near the plaintiff's yard, where his dogs were kept, that they might scent the bait without trespassing on the plaintiff's wood. And he asks, what difference there is, in reason, between drawing the animal into the trap, by means of his instinct, which he cannot resist, and putting him there by manual force? . . .
>
> In my opinion, the deduction to be drawn from these decisions is, that although the defendant was guilty of gross negligence, in leaving his syrup where cattle running at large in the woods might have access to it, yet, the plaintiff, having *no right* to permit his cattle to go at large there, has no right of action.

1 Cow. at 78-80. Notice in this passage how trespass is described as a form of "culpable negligence" by plaintiff. What is the difference between setting traps, as in *Townsend*, and leaving maple syrup out where cattle are known to be trespassing, as in *Bush?*

3. Why should a landowner have no duty to avoid negligently injuring trespassers? Is the idea that a trespasser assumes the risk of dangerous conditions in property on which he has no business? Or that there is no negligence in failing to take precautions on behalf of people whom the landowner has no reason to expect on his land since they have no lawful right to enter it? Or does the rule simply recognize that the trespasser can usually avoid being injured at lower cost than the landowner can avoid injuring him, just by not

trespassing? In Hand formula terms, what is B to the potential victim when he is a trespasser?

How is the analysis affected if the victim is a licensee?

4. The "no duty to trespassers" role was never taken literally. Besides the cases in this chapter, what earlier cases establish limitations on the landowner's right to do what he will on his land?

Rossi v. DelDuca
344 Mass. 66, 181 N.E.2d 591 (1962)

SPALDING, J. . . .

In September, 1955, Ida Celia and the plaintiff, both aged eight, were students in the third grade of the Ashford school. In the afternoon of September 26, school having closed, they started walking up Oak Street toward their homes. As they reached the corner of Cambridge Street, they saw the German Weimaraner ahead of them on Oak Street. The dog started to come toward them, and, as the plaintiff testified, "We got frightened so we . . . ran down Cambridge Street . . . [and the dog was] [f]ollowing us." Realizing that Cambridge Street was a dead-end street, the girls left Cambridge Street on the north side, passing around the garage at 70 Cambridge Street and the shed. The dog continued to follow them. After they passed the shed, they ran along a path in the field belonging to the defendant's father. The plaintiff then saw, for the first time, a black great Dane. "[T]he dog was on its hind legs and it was going to jump on her. It did jump on her. She doesn't remember after that, and then she remembers two black dogs on her. She didn't feel anything but they were biting her neck. She shouted for help." The plaintiff's father observed the defendant's great Dane dogs in the field. They "were worrying some object" which he learned was his daughter Patricia who was "crouched down on her knees . . . with her hands on her face." He picked her up and took her to the hospital.

The defendant testified that on September 26, 1955, he owned two "black Dane dogs." The dogs were "trained to stay in the field to the rear of this defendant's home where his equipment was kept. . . . He had a lot of equipment and was concerned about it." The defendant's arrangement with his father regarding this land was that the "defendant could use all of that property for parking his equipment and doing anything he wanted with it in connection with his business. . . . He had full control of the field."

It is clear both from the pleadings and the evidence that the plaintiff seeks to recover under G.L. c. 140, §155, which . . . reads: "If any dog shall do any damage to either the body or property of any person, the owner or keeper, or if the owner or keeper be a minor, the parent or guardian of such minor, shall be liable for such damage, unless such damage shall have been occasioned to the body or property of a person who, at the time such damage was sustained, was committing a trespass or other tort, or was teasing, tormenting or abusing such dog." . . .

The defendant contends that the plaintiff is barred from recovery because on her own testimony — and there is no evidence more favorable to her — she was committing a trespass at the time the defendant's dogs attacked her. . . . A finding was warranted that the plaintiff, an eight year old girl, was frightened by the German Weimaraner dog which was between her and the only means of access to her house; that she turned and ran down a side street; and that because this was a dead-end street she went north across the field in the rear of the defendant's house in order to get home, the Weimaraner following her all the while. This evidence brings the case, we think, within the principle that one is privileged to enter land in the possession of another if it is, or reasonably appears to be, necessary to prevent serious harm to the actor or his property. This privilege not only relieves the intruder from liability for technical trespass . . . but it also destroys the possessor's immunity from liability in resisting the intrusion. Ploof v. Putnam. . . .

Notes

1. Is *Ploof* apposite? Did defendant here commit an intentional tort?
2. What would the outcome of this case have been if there had been no statute? Would it matter whether defendant knew that his dogs had a vicious disposition?

Herrick v. Wixom
121 Mich. 384, 80 N.W. 117 (1899)

MONTGOMERY, J. . . . Defendant was possessed of and managed a tent show or circus, September 18, 1897, which he exhibited from place to place, and on the afternoon of this day at Bancroft. Plaintiff went to the circus grounds on the afternoon of this day in company with his cousin. There is testimony to show that while there he and his cousin were invited by a son of the defendant, who had been selling tickets in the ticket wagon, to enter the tent with him, the entertainment being in progress. This plaintiff did, taking a seat on the lower tier of seats. The testimony on the part of defense tended to show that plaintiff was not invited into the show, and that the son of defendant had no authority to invite him in. There was also evidence that plaintiff had attended a similar exhibition given by defendant the spring before. A part or feature of the entertainment consisted in the ignition and explosion of a giant firecracker attached to a pipe set in an upright position in one of the show rings. This was done by one of the clowns. There is testimony to show that plaintiff sat 30 or 40 feet from the place where the cracker was exploded, but, when the same was exploded a part of the firecracker flew and struck plaintiff in the eye, putting it out, whereby he lost the sight and use of the eye. For this injury action was brought against defendant for damages as a result of defendant's negligence in permitting a dangerous explosive to be used in a dangerous manner, which subjected those present to hazard and risk of injury. Upon the trial of the cause a verdict of no cause of action was rendered, and judgment for the defendant entered accordingly. Plaintiff brings error. . . .

The circuit judge charged the jury as follows: "The negligence charged in this case, gentlemen, is that Mr. Wixom exploded a firecracker, of the dimensions that the plaintiff claims this firecracker was, in the inside of this tent, and in the presence of his audience. They claim that was negligence. And that is the question for you to determine, under the evidence, and under the rules of law that I have given you and that I shall give you hereafter. Now, you must further find, in order that the plaintiff recover, that the plaintiff was in the tent, where he was injured, by the invitation of some person having authority to allow him to go in there. If he was a mere trespasser, who forced his way in, then the defendant owed him no duty that would enable him to recover under the declaration and proofs in this case. . . ." We think this instruction faulty, in so far as it was intended to preclude recovery in any event if the plaintiff was found to be a trespasser. It is true that a trespasser who suffers an injury because of a dangerous condition of premises is without remedy. But, where a trespasser is discovered upon the premises by the owner or occupant, he is not beyond the pale of the law, and any negligence resulting in injury will render the person guilty of negligence liable to respond in damages. In this case the negligent act of the defendant's servant was committed after the audience was made up. The presence of plaintiff was known, and the danger to him from a negligent act was also known. The question of whether a dangerous experiment should be attempted in his presence, or whether an experiment should be conducted with due care and regard to his safety, cannot be made to depend upon whether he had forced himself into the tent. Every instinct of humanity revolts at such a suggestion. For this error the judgment will be reversed, and a new trial ordered.

Notes

1. Why is it relevant that plaintiff, if a trespasser, was a "discovered" trespasser? In some cases, the fact that the trespasser's presence was known could convert an action for negligence into an action for an intentional tort, or something akin to it. This would be the case if, for example, the train engineer refused to slow down, or blow his whistle, after seeing a trespasser on the track who was obviously oblivious to the fact that he was about to be run down. Was *Herrick* such a case? Was Bush v. Brainard?

2. Suppose Herrick had not been sitting in the place where he was injured, and some lawful customer of defendant sitting in that spot sustained the identical injury that Herrick sustained. Would there be an argument that the trespass was not the *cause* of the accident, and so should not operate as a bar to the trespasser's recovery of damages? (Return to this question after studying the materials on causation in Chapter 8.) Was *Humphrey* the same kind of case?

Ehret v. Village of Scarsdale
269 N.Y. 198, 199 N.E. 56 (1935)

LEHMAN, J.

On the morning of December 17, 1931, the dead body of the plaintiff's intestate was found in a vacant house, which had been erected and was still owned by the [defendant] Westchester County Small Estates Corporation. The dead body of the night watchman, employed by the owner, was found there at the same time. Both had been asphyxiated by illuminating gas. The gas did not escape from pipes on the premises. It must have come there from a leak outside. The evidence permits, if, indeed, it does not dictate, the inference that the gas escaped from a leak in a gas main at a point under a village street more than 400 feet from the house. The gas main belonged to the Westchester Lighting Company and had been placed in the street by it. In January, 1931, Westchester County Small Estates Corporation, for the purpose of draining the basements and foundations of houses built by it in that neighborhood, obtained a permit to place a 12-inch tile pipe drain under the surface of the street. At the point in the street where the tile pipe drain crossed the gas main, the Westchester County Small Estates Corporation incased the gas main in its pipe drain. During the night of December 16 it became evident that at that point there was a leak in the gas main. Inevitably gas escaping from the gas main into the pipe drain would find exit into any sewer or drain connected with the pipe drain. After the discovery of the leak, the gas in the gas main was turned off, but too late to prevent escape of the gas from such sewer or drain into the house where the dead bodies of the plaintiff's intestate and of the watchman were found, the next day. An explosion wrecked another house near the same street. . . .

. . . The plaintiff has produced no evidence to explain the presence of the decedent in the defendant's house. . . . We assume upon this appeal that the plaintiff's intestate's death occurred while he was technically a trespasser upon the defendant's property. The question then arises whether through that fact the defendant gains immunity for damages resulting from its lack of care. . . . An owner of land has a right to use his land as he sees fit, at least provided such use causes no danger to others. He may at his pleasure invite or exclude others. If without permission or exclusion, a

stranger unlawfully intrudes upon the land, he voluntarily exposes himself *rationale*
to the risk of unsafe conditions existing thereon or of dangerous activities
conducted there. In the present case the death of the plaintiff's intestate
was due to a wrongful act of the owner of the land performed in a public
street many months before the decedent trespassed upon the land. The
rule that an owner of land is not liable to a trespasser upon his land for
failure to exercise ordinary care should not be extended so far as to confer
immunity upon the defendant for damages caused by his wrong under the
circumstances shown here. . . .

The question is not before us whether an owner of land is liable to a
trespasser for an injury resulting immediately and directly from an act carelessly performed in a public street or other place, where the zone of danger is
confined to persons then upon his land. In this case, . . . the zone of danger
was undefined both in time and space. Injury followed many months after
the defendant's act was completed. Then the result was not only the death of
plaintiff's intestate in a house owned by the defendant, but also the damage
to a house not owned by the defendant. If the death of plaintiff's intestate
had occurred while he was trespassing there, the plaintiff's right to recover
would have been clear. The circumstance that at the time when the defendant's lack of care caused the death of plaintiff's intestate, the vacant house
in which he was a trespasser would still be unsold and unoccupied, could not
have been known to the defendant when it was working in the street. It did
not affect the duty which the defendant then owed to all who might thereafter come within the zone of danger. The act was wrongful at the time it was
performed. Liability for the wrong, it is urged, is escaped because accidentally
it produced injury at a particular point in the zone of danger, and at a
particular time, though liability for the same wrong would have been inevitable if injury had been produced at a different place or time. . . . The construction of a pipe drain in a public street in a manner which created danger to
person or property in nearby houses constituted a wrong. For injury resulting
at any time to any person within the zone of danger, the law gives redress. A
trespasser in a house belonging to the defendant may have assumed the risk
that the defendant's use of its land might endanger persons thereon. He did
not assume the risk that such danger would arise from a condition existing
several hundred feet away in the public street, heedlessly created by the
defendant or any other person. . . .

Notes

1. Could *Herrick* have been decided on the same "zone of danger"
ground?

2. What is the relevance of the court's observation that plaintiff's decedent did not "assume the risk" of being asphyxiated in defendant's unoccupied house? Is the idea behind the "no duty to trespassers" rule akin to that

behind the assumption of risk doctrine? Would the precedential force of *Ehret* be reduced or increased if New York abolished the assumption of risk doctrine?

3. Whose foresight is more important in this case — plaintiff's or defendant's? If the risk of asphyxiation was completely unforeseeable to plaintiff's decedent, could he be expected to weigh it in deciding whether to commit the trespass? Would any economic or deterrent purpose be served by denying trespassers recovery in cases where denial will not affect the decision whether to trespass, because the injury is unforeseeable? Or is the important point, rather, that plaintiff's decedent was no more likely to be asphyxiated while trespassing in defendant's completed, although unsold and unoccupied, house than if he had been sleeping in his own home, or staying in a hotel? Why would that be important? Return to these questions after reading Chapter 8.

4. In Hynes v. New York Cent. R. Co., 231 N.Y. 229, 131 N.E. 898 (1921), a 16-year-old boy was electrocuted when an electric wire belonging to defendant fell on him while he was standing on a springboard that extended from defendant's land over the Harlem River. The boy had gotten on to the springboard from the defendant's land, on which he was, of course, a trespasser. The lower courts held that the springboard was a fixture on defendant's land and hence a part of defendant's property, and that defendant was not liable for the death of the boy since he was trespassing when struck by the falling wire. The court of appeals reversed, in a famous Cardozo opinion that reads in part as follows:

> We assume, without deciding, that the springboard was a fixture, a permanent improvement of the defendant's right of way. Much might be said in favor of another view. We do not press the inquiry for we are persuaded that the rights of bathers do not depend upon these nice distinctions. Liability would not be doubtful, we are told, had the boy been diving from a pole, if the pole had been vertical. The diver in such a situation would have been separated from the defendant's freehold. Liability, it is said has been escaped because the pole was horizontal. The plank when projected lengthwise was an extension of the soil. We are to concentrate our gaze on the private ownership of the board. We are to ignore the public ownership of the circumambient spaces of water and of air. Jumping from a boat or a barrel, the boy would have been a bather in the river. Jumping from the end of a springboard, he was no longer, it is said, a bather, but a trespasser on a right of way.
>
> Rights and duties in systems of living law are not built upon such quicksands.
>
> Bathers in the Harlem River on the day of this disaster were in the enjoyment of a public highway, entitled to reasonable protection against destruction by the defendant's wires. They did not cease to be bathers entitled to the same protection while they were diving from encroaching objects or engaging in the sports that are common among swimmers. Such acts were not equivalent to an abandonment of the highway, a departure

from its proper uses, a withdrawal from the waters, and an entry upon land. A plane of private right had been interposed between the river and the air, but public ownership was unchanged in the space below it and above. The defendant does not deny that it would have owed a duty to this boy if he had been leaning against the springboard with his feet upon the ground. He is said to have forfeited protection as he put his feet upon the plank. Presumably the same result would follow if the plank had been a few inches above the surface of the water instead of a few feet. Duties are thus supposed to arise and to be extinguished in alternate zones or strata. Two boys walking in the country or swimming in a river stop to rest for a moment along the side of the road or the margin of the stream. One of them throws himself beneath the overhanging branches of a tree. The other perches himself on a bough a foot or so above the ground. Both are killed by falling wires. The defendant would have us say that there is a remedy for the representatives of one and none for the representatives of the other. We may be permitted to distrust the logic that leads to such conclusions. . . .

This case is a striking instance of the dangers of "a jurisprudence of conceptions" (Pound, Mechanical Jurisprudence 8 Columbia Law Review, 605, 608, 610), the extension of a maxim or a definition with relentless disregard of consequences to "a dryly logical extreme." The approximate and relative become the definite and absolute. Landowners are not bound to regulate their conduct in contemplation of the presence of trespassers intruding upon private structures. Landowners are bound to regulate their conduct in contemplation of the presence of travelers upon the adjacent public ways. There are times when there is little trouble in marking off the field of exemption and immunity from that of liability and duty. Here structures and ways are so united and commingled, superimposed upon each other, that the fields are brought together. In such circumstances, there is little help in pursuing general maxims to ultimate conclusions. They have been framed alio intuitu. They must be reformulated and readapted to meet exceptional conditions. Rules appropriate to spheres which are conceived of as separate and distinct cannot both be enforced when the spheres become concentric. There must then be readjustment or collision. In one sense, and that a highly technical and artificial one, the diver at the end of the springboard is an intruder on the adjoining lands. In another sense, and one that realists will accept more readily, he is still on public waters in the exercise of public rights. The law must say whether it will subject him to the rule of the one field or of the other, of this sphere or of that. We think that considerations of analogy, of convenience, of policy, and of justice, exclude him from the field of the defendant's immunity and exemption, and place him in the field of liability and duty.

Id. at 233-236, 131 N.E. at 899-900. Is the point that defendant did not own the space above the springboard, where its wire struck the boy? Or is ownership irrelevant? Does it make a difference who affixed the springboard to the shore? Would it make a difference if the *only* access to the river was from defendant's land? How would the case be decided by a court applying the Hand formula to both parties and then comparing the costs of accident avoidance to both?

Keffe v. Milwaukee & St. Paul Ry. Co.
21 Minn. 207 (1875)

[According to the allegations of the complaint, plaintiff, a boy of seven, mangled his leg (so severely as to require amputation) while playing on a turntable owned and operated by defendant on its land. The turntable was so constructed as to be easily made to revolve, and was located in a public place near defendant's passenger depot and within 120 feet of plaintiff's home. The turntable was unlocked, unguarded, and unfenced. Judgment for the defendant on the pleadings, on the ground that plaintiff was a trespasser, and plaintiff appealed.]

YOUNG, J. . . .

To treat the plaintiff as a voluntary trespasser is to ignore the averments of the complaint, that the turn-table, which was situate in a public (by which we understand an open, frequented) place, was, when left unfastened, very attractive, and, when put in motion by them, was dangerous to young children, by whom it could be easily put in motion, and many of whom were in the habit of going upon it to play. The turn-table, being thus attractive, presented to the natural instincts of young children a strong temptation; and such children, following, as they must be expected to follow, those natural instincts, were thus allured into a danger whose nature and extent they, being without judgment or discretion, could neither apprehend nor appreciate, and against which they could not protect themselves. The difference between the plaintiff's position and that of a voluntary trespasser, capable of using care, consists in this, that the plaintiff was induced to come upon the defendant's turn-table by the defendant's own conduct, and that, as to him, the turn-table was a hidden danger, a trap.

While it is held that a mere licensee "must take the permission with its concomitant conditions, it may be perils," yet even such licensee has a right to require that the owner of the land shall not knowingly and carelessly put concealed dangers in his way.

And where one goes upon the land of another, not by mere license, but by invitation from the owner, the latter owes him a larger duty. "The general rule or principle applicable to this class of cases is that an owner or occupant is bound to keep his premises in a safe and suitable condition for those who come upon and pass over them, using due care, if he has held out any inducement, invitation or allurement, either express or implied, by which they have been led to enter thereon." . . .

Now, what an express invitation would be to an adult, the temptation of an attractive plaything is to a child of tender years. If the defendant had left this turn-table unfastened *for the purpose* of attracting young children to play upon it, knowing the danger into which it was thus alluring them, it certainly would be no defence to an action by the plaintiff, who had been attracted upon the turn-table and injured, to say that the plaintiff was a

The Turntable at Embudo, New Mexico
Courtesy of Howell North Pubs., Inc. From the Collection of Otto Perry
Reprinted in Lucius M. Beebe and Charles Clegg, *Narrow Gauge in the Rockies*, 1958

trespasser, and that his childish instincts were no excuse for his trespass. In Townsend v. Wathen, it was held to be unlawful for a man to tempt even his neighbor's dogs into danger, by setting traps on his own land, baited with strong-scented meat, by which the dogs were allured to come upon his land and into his traps. . . .

It is true that the defendant did not leave the turn-table unfastened, *for the purpose* of injuring young children; and if the defendant had no reason to believe that the unfastened turn-table was likely to attract and to injure young children, then the defendant would not be bound to use care to protect from injury the children that it had no good reason to suppose were in any danger. But the complaint states that the defendant knew that the turn-table, when left unfastened, was easily revolved; that, when left unfastened, it was very attractive, and when put in motion by them, dangerous, to young children: and knew also that many children were in the habit of going upon it to play. The defendant therefore knew that by leaving this turn-table unfastened and unguarded, it was not merely inviting young children to come upon the turn-table, but was holding out an allurement, which, acting upon the natural instincts by which such children are controlled, drew them by those instincts into a hidden danger; and having thus knowingly allured them into a place of danger, without their fault, (for it cannot blame them for not resisting the temptation it has set before them,) it was bound to use care to protect them from the danger into which they were thus led, and from which they could not be expected to protect themselves.

We agree with the defendant's counsel that a railroad company is not required to make its land a safe play-ground for children. It has the same right to maintain and use its turn-table that any landowner has to use his property. It is not an insurer of the lives or limbs of young children who play upon its premises. We merely decide that when it sets before young children a temptation which it has reason to believe will lead them into danger, it must use ordinary care to protect them from harm. What would be proper care in any case must, in general, be a question for the jury, upon all the circumstances of the case. . . .

It was not urged upon the argument that the plaintiff was guilty of contributory negligence, and we have assumed that the plaintiff exercised, as he was bound to do, such reasonable care as a child of his age and understanding was capable of using, and that there was no negligence on the part of his parents or guardians, contributing to his injury.

Judgment reversed.

Notes

1. Was it important that the turntable was in a public place?
2. Why is Townsend v. Wathen apposite? Is *Keffe* an intentional-tort case? Is *Keffe* more like Bush v. Brainard? Are the allegations regarding

defendant's knowledge essential or are they just a way of saying that the turntable was really dangerous to children?

3. A series of nineteenth-century cases including *Keffe* in which children were injured playing on railroad turntables — the "turntable cases" — gave rise to what is usually called the "attractive nuisance" doctrine, though it is not a part of the law of nuisance. How does it differ from the "discovered trespasser" doctrine of cases such as *Herrick*? Why was Bush v. Brainard not an attractive-nuisance case, or Hynes v. New York Cent. R. Co.?

4. The doctrine is perhaps best understood in economic terms, as reflecting a comparison of the costs to potential victim and potential injurer of avoiding a serious accident. The presence of allurement establishes that the costs of avoidance to the potential victim are high (and is it practicable to "fence in" a child as one might a cow?). In contrast, the costs of avoidance to the potential injurer are low. At most, the railroad need fence only the area occupied by the turntable, and not its entire property; alternatively, it can put a lock on the turntable or so design it that it will not revolve at the push of a small child.

petitioner

United Zinc & Chem. Co. v. Britt   respondents
258 U.S. 268 (1922)

MR. JUSTICE HOLMES delivered the opinion of the court.

This is a suit brought by the respondents against the petitioner to recover for the death of two children, sons of the respondents. The facts that for the purposes of decision we shall assume to have been proved are these. The petitioner owned a tract of about twenty acres in the outskirts of the town of Iola, Kansas. Formerly it had there a plant for the making of sulphuric acid and zinc spelter. In 1910 it tore the building down but left a basement and cellar, in which in July, 1916, water was accumulated, clear in appearance but in fact dangerously poisoned by sulphuric acid and zinc sulphate that had come in one way or another from the petitioner's works, as the petitioner knew. The respondents had been travelling and encamped at some distance from this place. A travelled way passed within 120 or 100 feet of it. On July 27, 1916, the children, who were eight and eleven years old, came upon the petitioner's land, went into the water, were poisoned and died. The petitioner saved the question whether it could be held liable. At the trial the Judge instructed the jury that if the water looked clear but in fact was poisonous and thus the children were allured to it the petitioner was liable. The respondents got a verdict and judgment, which was affirmed by the Circuit Court of Appeals. . . .

. . . Infants have no greater right to go upon other peoples' land than adults, and the mere fact that they are infants imposes no duty upon landowners to expect them and to prepare for their safety. On the other hand the

[margin handwritten notes: near population area, looked like swamp, hot!]

duty of one who invites another upon his land not to lead him into a trap is well settled, and while it is very plain that temptation is not invitation, it may be held that knowingly to establish and expose, unfenced, to children of an age when they follow a bait as mechanically as a fish, something that is certain to attract them, has the legal effect of an invitation to them although not to an adult. But the principle if accepted must be very cautiously applied. . . .

In the case at bar it is at least doubtful whether the water could be seen from any place where the children lawfully were and there is no evidence that it was what led them to enter the land. But that is necessary to start the supposed duty. There can be no general duty on the part of a landowner to keep his land safe for children, or even free from hidden dangers, if he has not directly or by implication invited or licensed them to come there. . . . It does not appear that children were in the habit of going to the place; so that foundation also fails.

Union Pacific Ry. Co. v. McDonald, 152 U.S. 262, is less in point. There a boy was burned by falling into burning coal slack close by the side of a path on which he was running homeward from other boys who had frightened him. It hardly appears that he was a trespasser and the path suggests an invitation; at all events boys habitually resorted to the place where he was. Also the defendant was under a statutory duty to fence the place sufficiently to keep out cattle. The decision is very far from establishing that the petitioner is liable for poisoned water not bordering a road, not shown to have been the inducement that led the children to trespass, if in any event the law would deem it sufficient to excuse their going there, and not shown to have been the indirect inducement because known to the children to be frequented by others. It is suggested that the roads across the place were invitations. A road is not an invitation to leave it elsewhere than at its end.

Judgment reversed.

Notes

1. The ruling in *Britt* that the attractive nuisance must exercise its allure on the child before he enters the defendant's land follows easily from the reasoning of cases such as *Keffe* and *Townsend*, does it not? Nevertheless, the ruling was roundly criticized, perhaps because of the shocking facts of the case, and most courts have declined to follow it. The ambiguous opinion in Best v. District of Columbia, 291 U.S. 411 (1934), is thought by many to have implicitly overruled *Britt*.

Yet *Britt* has an economic rationale (further confirmation that economics really is the "dismal science"?*). If the pool had been visible to children using the public road alongside defendant's land, and not just to the hardy few who entered and explored though not drawn by the sight of the pool,

*An expression originally inspired by Thomas Malthus's population theory.

more children would have been endangered. Also, the difficulty experienced by a child in resisting the impulse to trespass is greater when there is something especially alluring to a child in the appearance of defendant's property than when there is no such allure. On both counts, P in the Hand formula would have been higher.

In light of this analysis, which of the evidentiary issues in *Britt* was the most important — "whether the water could be seen from any place where the children lawfully were," "what led them to enter the land," or whether the children "were in the habit of going to the place"?

2. One of the most influential efforts of the American Law Institute to restate the principles of tort law is found in §339 of the Second Restatement of Torts. First promulgated in 1934, §339 provides:

§339. Artificial Conditions Highly Dangerous to Trespassing Children

A possessor of land is subject to liability for physical harm to children trespassing thereon caused by an artificial condition upon the land if

(a) the place where the condition exists is one upon which the possessor knows or has reason to know that children are likely to trespass, and

(b) the condition is one of which the possessor knows or has reason to know and which he realizes or should realize will involve an unreasonable risk of death or serious bodily harm to such children, and

(c) the children because of their youth do not discover the condition or realize the risk involved in intermeddling with it or in coming within the area made dangerous by it, and

(d) the utility to the possessor of maintaining the condition and the burden of eliminating the danger are slight as compared with the risk to children involved, and

(e) the possessor fails to exercise reasonable care to eliminate the danger or otherwise to protect the children.

What, if anything, do subsections (a), (b), (c), and (e) add to (d)? How would the *Britt* case have been decided under this standard?

3. Should the attractive nuisance doctrine ever be applicable if the dangerous condition is natural rather than man-made? See Corporation of City of Glasgow v. Taylor, [1922] 1 A.C. 44 (H.L.); Loney v. McPhillips, 268 Or. 378, 521 P.2d 340 (1974). Should it apply if the condition was created by someone other than the owner of the land? See, e.g., Foster v. Lusk, 129 Ark. 1, 194 S.W. 855 (1917); Smith v. Post 212, 241 Minn. 46, 62 N.W.2d 354 (1954). Would the doctrine have been applicable if the plaintiff in *Keffe* had been bitten by a snake while playing on the turntable? Cf. Halloran v. Belt Ry., 25 Ill. App. 2d 114, 166 N.E.2d 98 (1960). Could the doctrine ever be used defensively in a suit *against* a child? See Aetna Insurance Co. v. Stringham, 440 F.2d 103 (6th Cir. 1971). Is there any reason to retain the doctrine in a jurisdiction that has replaced contributory by comparative negligence?

For good law review discussions of the doctrine, see Batson, Trespassing Children: A Study in Expanding Liability, 20 Vand. L. Rev. 139 (1966); Reynolds, Attractive Nuisance: More Nuisance Than Attraction, 26 Okla. L. Rev. 342 (1977).

Kumkumian v. City of New York
305 N.Y. 167, 111 N.E.2d 865 (1953)

FROESSEL, J. . . .

Decedent, thirty-nine years old, was a Western Union messenger in his home city of Philadelphia, using his own automobile in his work. Because it was undergoing repairs, he left his home, without a bag, on January 23, 1945, for a brief "vacation" in Atlantic City. While away, an upstairs neighbor, at the request of his wife who stated he had been sick, listed his name with the local police as a missing person. His wife and cousin testified that each had spoken with him on the telephone on January 25th, when he stated he would come to New York the following day. Nothing further is known of decedent's movements until his body was discovered under the subway train on the following morning as hereinafter set forth.

At about 9:00 A.M. of January 26th, a local subway train, en route to Coney Island from Manhattan on the B.M.T. line in Brooklyn, was being operated between the Prospect Avenue and 25th Street stations. The train was composed of five cars, one a freight car. The only employees thereon were a motorman and a conductor, the latter being stationed in the fourth car. The tunnel between the two stations is about 2,000 feet long and is straight, with a slight downgrade from Prospect Avenue to 25th Street. A "bench walk" forming a narrow (two feet) continuation of the station platforms runs along the tunnel wall between the stations with a handrail next to the wall. Below and adjoining the bench walk are the third rail, then the running rails, and finally a wall separating the local from the express tracks.

The motorman was coasting on the slight grade at a speed of about 12 or 15 miles per hour, when at a point about 1,400 feet from the Prospect Avenue station and 600 feet from the 25th Street station his train came to an emergency stop. This was a "surprise" to him, as it was caused by the automatic emergency equipment, which he testified may be actuated in one of three ways: (1) by the blowing of an electric pneumatic valve; (2) by a passenger pulling the emergency strap, or (3) by the operation of a tripping device under each car indicating that some object or body had come in contact therewith.

When the train had stopped, the motorman made no effort to investigate, but merely reset the brakes by pressing a button in his cab two or three times and proceeded, a matter of a few seconds. He must then have known that the valves were functioning. After proceeding "About a car length" — 67 feet — the train again went into emergency, and again the motorman reset the brakes, and started the train without making any attempt whatsoever to find out what was wrong. The conductor also did nothing, although he knew the first two stops were emergency stops. Again in approximately a car length — the distance between the tripping devices — the emergency brake stopped the train for the third time.

Both motorman and conductor then inspected the valves and found them in order. There was no evidence that anyone had pulled the emergency strap. They thereupon walked through the train, and when they opened the door of the third car they found decedent's body "wedged" between the third rail and the running rail on the right side of the fourth car. Evidence of blood, flesh and clothing was found on the brake rigging of the third and fourth cars on the right side of the wheel trucks. Nowhere else was found any physical evidence of the accident. The motorman stated the body was then "actually steaming."

An inspection of the train disclosed that the tripcock mechanism was in proper order. This is a device which hangs down outside the left front and right rear wheels of each car, about two inches above the track. It is so designed that it will move upon striking any object or body in the roadway and so open a contact causing the brakes to operate. It is returned to the normal operating position when the motorman resets the brakes. It may be noted that apparently there is no prescribed procedure when an emergency stop occurs, for the rule book was produced at the trial but not referred to by either side. The cause of death, according to the medical examiner, was "multiple extreme injuries," the external injuries being multiple amputations and fractures. No alcohol was found in the liver.

The jury and the courts below were clearly right in declining to fasten *L. C.* liability on the theory of ordinary negligence. There is no evidence as to how decedent came into the subway tunnel. Plaintiff's speculation as to how he came into the subway, and from which station he had traveled the long distance into the tunnel, is based wholly on conjecture, or, as the Appellate Division put it, "upon inference heaped upon inference." Any recovery, if at all sustainable, could not be based on ordinary negligence. The indisputable fact remains, even if we accept plaintiff's theory, that decedent left the lighted platform, and walked 1,400 feet (about six or seven city blocks) into the dimly lit tunnel on a narrow walk, the tunnel wall on one side of him and the tracks just below. It is inconceivable that the least perceptive of men would fail to realize the danger of such a course. He had no right to be there. No reasonable man could classify such conduct as anything but negligence, and so we conclude, as the jury must have by failing to find for plaintiff on the theory of ordinary negligence, and as did the Appellate Division in holding that decedent was guilty of contributory negligence as a matter of law.

That leaves for consideration the last clear chance theory upon which *L C* the jury rendered its verdict for plaintiff. We have noted that this doctrine does not apply unless there is present an issue of contributory negligence.

There must be a time sequence — an interval in which plaintiff's act of negligence is complete and in which defendant has an opportunity to avert the disaster. Where defendant thus had a last clear chance to avoid the accident, it may be said that plaintiff's negligence is not the proximate cause of his injury, Bragg v. Central New England Ry. Co., 228 N.Y. 54, 126 N.E. 253.

In the last-cited case, a railroad employee fell asleep close to the rails and was struck by a train. We noted that the railroad could not be held liable merely because the engineer failed to see him in time, or even because he assumed Bragg would get off the tracks when a warning signal was given. "Only, when he discovered that Bragg was inert or unconscious, or for some reason would not or could not safeguard himself, had the engineer any reason to anticipate an accident. Only then should he have sought to avoid it."

Later, in Woloszynowski v. New York Central R.R. Co., 254 N.Y. 206, 208-209, 172 N.E. 471, 472, Chief Judge Cardozo, speaking for the court, summarized the now familiar rule thus: "The doctrine of the last clear chance, however, is never wakened into action unless and until there is brought home to the defendant to be charged with liability a knowledge that another is in a state of present peril, in which event there must be reasonable effort to counteract the peril and avert its consequences. . . . Knowledge may be established by circumstantial evidence, in the face even of professions of ignorance . . . but knowledge there must be, *or negligence so reckless as to betoken indifference to knowledge.*" (Emphasis supplied.) . . .

Surely we cannot say, as a matter of law, under the last clear chance doctrine, that the motorman and conductor were not negligent in *twice* disregarding the emergency equipment, which is not placed in service to be ignored, and were merely chargeable with an error of judgment. At least it became a question of fact as to whether such conduct constitutes "negligence so reckless as to betoken indifference to knowledge." . . . It matters not that they received the warning through a faultless mechanical instrumentality rather than a human agency, so long as they had . . . "the requisite knowledge upon which a reasonably prudent man would act." The jury was entitled to find that lack of knowledge on the part of defendant's employees as to decedent's position of danger did not come about through mere lack of vigilance in observing the tracks, but rather as the result of their own willful indifference to the emergency called to their attention by the automatic equipment, to which clear warning they paid no heed. When they did belatedly carry out their plain duty to investigate, they found decedent, and it may be inferred that they would have seen him had they carried out that duty after the second stop — still belatedly, yet in time to have saved his life. We are of the opinion that plaintiff made out at least a prima facie case under the doctrine of last clear chance. . . .

FULD, J., dissents and votes for affirmance in the following memorandum: This is not, in my view, a case for the application of the doctrine of the last clear chance. Certainly, neither the motorman nor the conductor knew that any person was in peril in time to have prevented his death, and the evidence is insufficient to support the inference that they *should* have known. I would affirm the judgment in defendant's favor.

Notes

1. The last clear chance doctrine is both an exception to the "no duty to trespassers" principle and a defense to contributory negligence. (Plaintiff's decedent in *Kumkumian* was both a trespasser and contributorily negligent.) Could the case have been decided under the discovered-trespasser rationale of *Herrick,* or the intentional-tort rationale of cases like M'Ilvoy v. Cochran and Bird v. Holbrook in Chapter 3?

2. What is the nature of the disagreement between the majority and the dissenting opinions?

3. Let us consider the doctrine, and its application in the *Kumkumian* case, in economic terms. At the moment that the tripcock was tripped by decedent's body, both P and L were very high (though the size of L depends on how serious the injury inflicted when the train first struck him is assumed to have been). B was infinite for plaintiff's decedent — he was helpless. PL was also high as perceived (or perceivable) by the motorman and conductor, since the tripping of the tripcock indicated that there was an object on the tracks which, even if not a body, could have been a source of danger to the passengers and crew of the train. B was trivial for the crew — they had only to get off the train momentarily and look under the cars. They, therefore, were negligent in a Hand formula sense, and since plaintiff's decedent was not, plaintiff should prevail.

But this analysis is perhaps short-sighted. The cost to plaintiff's decedent of avoiding injury *before* he was first struck by the train may have been very low — he had only to avoid trespassing in the tunnel. If trespassers are allowed to recover damages by operation of the last clear chance doctrine, the incentives to avoid trespassing will be reduced and there will be more trespasses and more accidents. Furthermore, if the doctrine is triggered only when the danger is discovered, or clearly discoverable, by the potential injurer, the incentives to install early-warning devices will be reduced. Would the defendant in *Kumkumian* not have been better off, from the standpoint of avoiding liability, if its train had not been equipped with an automatic tripping device?

A third round of the analysis suggests, however, that the decision may be correct after all. The automatic tripping device may have been necessary to discharge the defendant's duty of care to its passengers; in that event, the decision would not lead the defendant to remove the device, and the cost of avoiding the accident by defendant's crew really was close to zero. The cost of avoiding the trespass may have been high to Kumkumian; the statement of facts in the court's opinion suggests, does it not, that he may well have been deranged at the time of the accident.

This analysis is further supported when we remind ourselves that the relationship between taking care and avoiding accidents is probabilistic rather than certain. It does not pay anyone to take such great care not to trespass that the probability of trespassing is reduced to zero. Hence there will be some accidents that cannot reasonably be avoided by taking care not to trespass. The optimal way to avoid these accidents may be for the potential injurer to devote at least modest resources to avoiding injury to trespassers; that is all defendant was asked to do in *Kumkumian*.

Now consider the facts and holding of British Columbia Elec. Ry. Co. v. Loach, [1916] 1 A.C. 719 (P.C. 1915), summarized — and rejected (as by most American jurisdictions) — in Andersen v. Bingham & Garfield Ry. Co., 117 Utah 197, 203, 214 P.2d 607, 610 (1950):

> In the *Loach* case the plaintiff's intestate, one Sands, was a passenger in a wagon approaching the defendant's railway crossing. Apparently neither he nor the driver looked up or down the track until they were so close to the crossing that they could not stop short of it. The motorman of an electric railway car which was about 400 feet away from the crossing appreciated imminent danger and applied his brakes. The brakes were defective and the train did not stop before it passed the crossing, although the evidence indicated that effective brakes would have stopped the car one hundred feet short of the crossing. The jury found that Sands was contributorily negligent, but it was held that the plaintiff's contributory negligence did not disentitle him to recover damages if the defendant, although not committing any negligent act subsequent to the plaintiff's negligence, had incapacitated himself by previous negligence from exercising such care as would have avoided the result of the plaintiff's negligence. "Were it otherwise," the court noted, "the defendant company would be in a better position, when they had supplied a bad brake but a good motorman, than when the motorman was careless but the brake efficient. If the superintendent engineer sent out the car in the morning with a defective brake, which, on seeing Sands, the motorman strove to apply, they would not be liable, but if the motorman failed to apply the brake, which, if applied, would have averted the accident, they would be liable."

Is *Loach* a proper application of the last clear chance doctrine?

4. What happens to the doctrine when a jurisdiction abolishes contributory negligence as a defense and replaces it with comparative negligence? This is the answer given by the California court:

> Although several states which apply comparative negligence concepts retain the last clear chance doctrine, the better reasoned position seems to be that when true comparative negligence is adopted, the need for last clear chance as a palliative of the hardships of the "all-or-nothing" rule disappears and its retention results only in a windfall to the plaintiff in direct contravention of the principle of liability in proportion to fault.

Li v. Yellow Cab Co. of California, 13 Cal. 3d 804, 824, 532 P.2d 1226, 1240 (1975). What would or should be the status of the last clear chance doctrine in California, after *Li*, in a case where the plaintiff is alleged to be a trespasser rather than to be contributorily negligent? (Revisit this question after reading Rowland v. Christian, below.)

Guilford v. Yale University
128 Conn. 449, 23 A.2d 917 (1942)

JENNINGS, J. . . .

The plaintiff had returned to New Haven for the fortieth reunion of his class. On the night in question, at about 12 o'clock, he, accompanied by one of his classmates, proceeded to these premises [the building on the campus that the University had assigned as the reunion headquarters for plaintiff's class] and there met a number of younger men of the class of 1936. After arriving he spent a pleasant period with those gathered there, remaining until about 2 o'clock, at which time it was suggested that the place be closed. Those of the party then remaining left the building and proceeded to the sidewalk in the street where they talked for five or ten minutes. While they were conversing, the plaintiff expressed a desire to urinate and was informed that there was a toilet in the basement. At this time, the lights in the building had been turned out. The plaintiff did not re-enter the building but stepped back upon the premises, crossed the curb between the Trumbull Street walk and the grass plot and proceeded across the grass plot, walking about midway between the side of the building and the stone wall enclosing the property on the Trumbull Street side. There was a tree growing from the lower level beyond the retaining wall at the east of the grass plot. The shape of the tree was such that its top projected above the level of the top of the retaining wall. The plaintiff thought that the top of this tree was a bush growing on the grass plot, and walked towards it. He tripped over the parapet at the top of the retaining wall and fell to its bottom at the lower level. The region generally was well lighted at the time, but the plaintiff claimed that, while he was able to see the street and the sidewalk very well, the ground under his feet was in a dark shadow and that he was walking into the shadow to find a secluded place near the bush to urinate.

If one comes upon the land of another by that other's invitation, he is entitled to the protection of an invitee. An invitation is implied where one person goes upon the land of another for their mutual benefit. Passing both the claim of an express invitation, for which there is some basis in the admissions in the pleadings, and the question of mutual benefit, there is another set of circumstances from which an invitation may be implied. In Sweeny v. Old Colony & Newport R. Co., 92 Mass. 368, 373, Chief Justice Bigelow said this: "The gist of the liability consists in the fact that the person injured did not act merely for his own convenience and pleasure, and from motives to which no act or sign of the owner or occupant contributed, but that he entered the premises because he was led to believe that they were intended to be used by visitors or passengers, and that such use was not only acquiesced in by the owner or person in possession and control of the premises, but that it was in accordance with the intention and design with which the way or place was adapted and prepared or allowed to be so used. The true distinction is this: a mere passive acquiescence by an owner or occupier in a certain use of his land by others involves no liability; but if he directly or by implication induces persons to enter on and pass over his premises, he thereby assumes an obligation that they are in a safe condition, suitable for such use, and for a breach of this obligation he is liable in damages to a person injured thereby." . . . Applying it to the facts of this case it is clear that the jury could have found that plaintiff was on the premises as an invitee. As such the defendant owed him the duty of exercising reasonable care to have its premises safely constructed and maintained and to guard against subjecting him to dangers of which it was cognizant or which it might reasonably have anticipated.

Whether the defendant should have anticipated danger from the particular use made of the premises by the plaintiff presents a close question. An invitee who exceeds the limits of the invitation loses his status as such. Whether the plaintiff has done so in this case depends upon whether his use of the premises was such as the university might reasonably have contemplated. The evidence clearly shows the open house, free and easy hospitality which exists in New Haven at reunion time and existed when this accident occurred. It does not subject the defendant to an undue burden to require that it exercise reasonable care to see that not only the buildings assigned for headquarters but also the surrounding grounds are free from traps dangerous to life and limb. The excellent photographs delineate just such a trap. The jury had the additional advantage of a view of the premises. We cannot say that they could not reasonably have reached the conclusion that the defendant was negligent as alleged, and that the plaintiff was free from contributory negligence, and had not exceeded the limits of his invitation. . . .

Meyer v. Mitchell
248 Minn. 397, 80 N.W.2d 450 (1957)

KNUTSON, J.

Appeal from an order denying plaintiff's motion for a new trial.

Plaintiff, a young man 32 years of age, was employed early in January 1954 as a real estate salesman on a straight commission basis by Fox, Incorporated. Defendant Lenore Mitchell was the secretary and treasurer of Fox, Incorporated, and had charge of closing real estate transactions. On January

12, 1954, at about closing time, defendant Donald Mitchell, Lenore's husband, who was employed elsewhere, came to the office for the purpose of
going home with his wife. One of the other salesmen intended to take the
Mitchells home, but, since it was inconvenient for him to do so, plaintiff
offered to take them home. Plaintiff, with Mr. and Mrs. Mitchell, left the
office between 5:30 and 6 o'clock. It was then dusk or getting dark. When
they reached defendants' home, which was only a few blocks from the office,
plaintiff made a complimentary remark about the house. Lenore Mitchell
thereupon asked him if he would like to come in and see the house. He said
that he would, and they proceeded to enter the house.

The Mitchell home is on a slight hill raised somewhat higher than the
driveway. There is a cement sidewalk from the house to the driveway, which
was not being used at that time because the driveway had been lowered.
Instead, they entered partly by a dirt path which connected with a cement
walk going into the house. They had no difficulty in entering the house.

Mrs. Mitchell showed plaintiff through the house. Two "Highballs"
were served plaintiff. Plaintiff testified that he discussed his previous real
estate work with the Mitchells. There was no discussion of any business
pertaining to his employment.

At about 6:15 or 6:30, plaintiff left defendants' house to go home. He
testified that he usually had his dinner about 6 o'clock. Mrs. Mitchell told her
husband to get a flashlight to assist plaintiff to his car. Plaintiff declined the
help. According to Mitchell's testimony, plaintiff said, "There is no need of
your showing me out. . . . It is light or bright as day," or words to that effect.
The area traversed was lighted from lights which were on the porch and also
from the bedroom. As plaintiff was walking on the dirt path he slipped and
fell, fracturing his leg, for which injury he now seeks to recover. He testified
that the path was icy and that there was snow on the ice where he fell.

The court submitted the case to the jury on the theory that plaintiff was
a gratuitous licensee. The jury returned a verdict for defendants.

It is plaintiff's principal contention that he was a business invitee, or at
least that the jury could find that such relationship existed, and that his right
of recovery is based on the duty of defendants toward him as such.

The authorities are not in harmony as to the test to be applied in
determining who is a business invitee. We have applied the rule adopted by
Restatement, Torts, §332, which reads: "A business visitor is a person who is
invited or permitted to enter or remain on land in the possession of another
for a purpose directly or indirectly connected with business dealings between
them." . . .

Dean Prosser suggests the alternative theory that: " . . . the basis of
liability is not any economic benefit to the occupier, but a representation to
be implied when he encourages others to enter to further a purpose of his
own, that reasonable care has been exercised to make the place safe for those
who come for that purpose." Whether one theory or the other is applied
here, it seems clear that, to be a business invitee, a person must be on the

occupier's premises for some purpose of the invitor that implies an assurance that the premises have been made safe for those who come for such purpose. Under either theory, a mere social visit is not enough.

Plaintiff argues here that he became a business invitee because he, knowing that Mrs. Mitchell was a corporate officer and his superior, did not want to offend her; consequently that the invitation was in the nature of a business command which he could hardly refuse. He argues also that there was a benefit to Mrs. Mitchell in that, in viewing defendants' house, she gave him a valuable demonstration of how a house should be shown to a prospective customer and that they discussed his previous real estate experience. It has not been shown how these things would affect Donald Mitchell, who was not connected with the real estate business. Aside from that, the evidence that the invitation, either expressed or implied, was based on or connected with any purpose even faintly connected with the employer's business is entirely absent. If we were to adopt plaintiff's argument, it would mean that the employee would become a business invitee any time his employer invited him to his home for dinner or cocktails, even though the visit was purely social. Mere desire to be socially polite to an employer can hardly be sufficient to transform a gratuitous licensee into a business invitee. We think that the court correctly determined, under the facts in this case, that plaintiff's visit was purely social and that he was a gratuitous licensee. . . .

Affirmed.

Notes

1. In either *Guilford* or *Meyer*, could defendant have argued that plaintiff was contributorily negligent?

2. Would the *Guilford* court have classified Meyer as a licensee or an invitee? Is there any difference between inviting an alumnus to a reunion and inviting an employee for a cocktail?

3. How is it possible to regard a social guest as a mere licensee rather than as an invitee? Does not the fact of an express invitation confer on the social visitor the status of invitee? Or is "invitee" to be regarded as strictly a term of legal art? If the latter, what is the justification for setting a higher standard of care to those who enter one's premises for business reasons than to those who enter for social reasons? Two economic factors seem pertinent. First, business premises are used more intensively than residences (this is especially clear in the case of retail stores), which means that a given safety precaution is likely to have greater benefits, in terms of accidents avoided, in business premises than in residences. Second, the cost of precautions may be lower to business than residential property owners because of the greater expertise of the former in technical matters including safety.

4. A different economic rationale is possible for the rule, at first glance puzzling, that policemen and firemen who enter a house or building in an

emergency are mere licensees, and not invitees. "A man who climbs in through a basement window in search of a fire or a thief cannot expect any assurance that he will not find a bulldog in the cellar." Prosser 397-398. In Hand formula terms, B is high relative to PL, because the burden of precaution must be borne continuously to make the premises safe for a very infrequent event. And P, as mentioned, is lower than when the premises in question are in continuous use by many visitors, be they customers or employees. Of course, these differences could be taken into account in applying a uniform negligence standard in each case, rather than in setting up a categorical difference between the standard of care due certain public employees and the standard of care due business invitees.

Rowland v. Christian
69 Cal. 2d 108, 443 P.2d 561 (1968)

PETERS, J.

Plaintiff appeals from a summary judgment for defendant Nancy Christian in this personal injury action.

In this complaint plaintiff alleged that about November 1, 1963, Miss Christian told the lessors of her apartment that the knob of the cold water faucet on the bathroom basin was cracked and should be replaced; that on November 30, 1963, plaintiff entered the apartment at the invitation of Miss Christian; that he was injured while using the bathroom fixtures, suffering severed tendons and nerves of his right hand; and that he has incurred medical and hospital expenses. He further alleged that the bathroom fixtures were dangerous, that Miss Christian was aware of the dangerous condition, and that his injuries were proximately caused by the negligence of Miss Christian. Plaintiff sought recovery of his medical and hospital expenses, loss of wages, damage to his clothing, and $100,000 general damages. It does not appear from the complaint whether the crack in the faucet handle was obvious to an ordinary inspection or was concealed.

Miss Christian filed an answer containing a general denial except that she alleged that plaintiff was a social guest and admitted the allegations that she had told the lessors that the faucet was defective and that it should be replaced. Miss Christian also alleged contributory negligence and assumption of the risk. In connection with the defenses, she alleged that plaintiff had failed to use his "eyesight" and knew of the condition of the premises. Apart from these allegations, Miss Christian did not allege whether the crack in the faucet handle was obvious or concealed. . . .

. . . Miss Christian's affidavit and admissions made by plaintiff show that plaintiff was a social guest and that he suffered injury when the faucet handle broke; they do not show that the faucet handle crack was obvious or even nonconcealed. Without in any way contradicting her affidavit or his own admissions, plaintiff at trial could establish that she was aware of the condition and realized or should have realized that it involved an unreasonable risk of harm to him, that defendant should have expected that he would not discover the danger, that she did not exercise reasonable care to eliminate the danger or warn him of it, and that he did not know or have reason to know of the danger. Plaintiff also could establish, without contradicting Miss Christian's affidavit or his admissions, that the crack was not obvious and was concealed. Under the circumstances, a summary judgment is proper in this case only if, after proof of such facts, a judgment would be required as a matter of law for Miss Christian. The record supports no such conclusion. . . .

Without attempting to labor all of the rules relating to the possessor's liability, it is apparent that the classifications of trespasser, licensee, and invitee, the immunities from liability predicated upon those classifications, and the exceptions to those immunities, often do not reflect the major factors which should determine whether immunity should be conferred upon the possessor of land. Some of those factors, including the closeness of the connection between the injury and the defendant's conduct, the moral blame attached to the defendant's conduct, the policy of preventing future harm, and the prevalence and availability of insurance, bear little, if any, relationship to the classifications of trespasser, licensee and invitee and the existing rules conferring immunity.

Although in general there may be a relationship between the remaining factors and the classifications of trespasser, licensee, and invitee, there are many cases in which no such relationship may exist. Thus, although the foreseeability of harm to an invitee would ordinarily seem greater than the foreseeability of harm to a trespasser, in a particular case the opposite may be true. The same may be said of the issue of certainty of injury. The burden to the defendant and consequences to the community of imposing a duty to exercise care with resulting liability for breach may often be greater with respect to trespassers than with respect to invitees, but it by no means follows that this is true in every case. In many situations, the burden will be the same, i.e., the conduct necessary upon the defendant's part to meet the burden of exercising due care as to invitees will also meet his burden with respect to licensees and trespassers. The last of the major factors, the cost of insurance, will, of course, vary depending upon the rules of liability adopted, but there is no persuasive evidence that applying ordinary principles of negligence law to the land occupier's liability will materially reduce the prevalence of insurance due to increased cost or even substantially increase the cost. . . .

A man's life or limb does not become less worthy of protection by the law nor a loss less worthy of compensation under the law because he has come upon the land of another without permission or with permission but without a business purpose. Reasonable people do not ordinarily vary their conduct depending upon such matters, and to focus upon the status of the injured party as a trespasser, licensee, or invitee in order to determine the question whether the landowner has a duty of care, is contrary to our modern social mores and humanitarian values. The common law rules obscure rather than illuminate the proper considerations which should govern determination of the question of duty.

. . . We decline to follow and perpetuate such rigid classifications. The proper test to be applied to the liability of the possessor of land . . . is whether in the management of his property he has acted as a reasonable man in view of the probability of injury to others, and, although the plaintiff's status as a trespasser, licensee or invitee may in the light of the facts giving rise to such status have some bearing on the question of liability, the status is not determinative.

Once the ancient concepts as to the liability of the occupier of land are stripped away, the status of the plaintiff relegated to its proper place in determining such liability, and ordinary principles of negligence applied, the result in the instant case presents no substantial difficulties. As we have seen, when we view the matters presented on the motion for summary judgment as we must, we must assume defendant Miss Christian was aware that the faucet handle was defective and dangerous, that the defect was not obvious, and that plaintiff was about to come in contact with the defective condition, and under the undisputed facts she neither remedied the condition nor warned plaintiff of it. Where the occupier of land is aware of a concealed condition involving in the absence of precautions an unreasonable risk of harm to those coming in contact with it and is aware that a person on the premises is about to come in contact with it, the trier of fact can reasonably conclude that a failure to warn or to repair the condition constitutes negligence. Whether or not a guest has a right to expect that his host will remedy dangerous conditions on his account, he should reasonably be entitled to rely upon a warning of the dangerous condition so that he, like the host, will be in a position to take special precautions when he comes in contact with it. . . .

Notes

1. Would the case have been decided any differently under the traditional rules governing land occupiers' liability, with Rowland classified as a licensee?

2. Does the decision really expand the liability of land occupiers or does it merely replace specific rules governing that liability with a general standard that is essentially compatible with them? Even if the scope of liability is unchanged by the decision, how might plaintiffs, as a practical matter, benefit?

3. A number of states have followed the lead of the California court and abolished the common-law distinctions. See, e.g., Ouellette v. Blanchard, 116 N.H. 552, 364 A.2d 631 (1976), and cases cited therein. Others have declined to follow Rowland. See, e.g., Frazee v. St. Louis-San Francisco Ry. Co., 219 Kan. 661, 549 P.2d 561 (1976).

4. Could the court in *Rowland* have abolished just the distinction between licensees and invitees and continued to apply special rules to trespassers?

Cannon v. Oviatt
520 P.2d 883 (Utah 1974)

CALLISTER, C.J.:

The appeals of the plaintiffs, which arose out of separate and unrelated actions, have been consolidated since they involved one common question of law, namely was Section 41-9-1, U.C.A. 1953,* unconstitutional? Each plaintiff, while a guest in a motor vehicle, moving upon a public highway in this state, sustained personal injuries in a vehicular accident. Each plaintiff initiated an action against his host, the driver of the vehicle, to recover damages for the negligent operation of the vehicle. Each host asserted Section 41-9-1, U.C.A. 1953, as a defense and denied liability. Each plaintiff urged unsuccessfully before the trial court that the Guest Statute, 41-9-1, U.C.A. 153, denied him equal protection of the law under the Constitution of the United States (14th Amendment) and the Constitution of Utah (Article I, Section 24).

On appeal each plaintiff relies on the reasoning set forth in Brown v. Merlo, [8 Cal. 3d 855, 506 P.2d 212 (1973)], wherein the Supreme Court of California held that the proferred justification for that jurisdiction's guest statute did not constitute a rational basis for the differential treatment accorded by the statutory scheme of classification and was therefore a denial of equal protection of the law. The *Brown* decision set forth two distinct justifications for the statute, the protection of hospitality and the prevention of collusive lawsuits. The court found the protection of hospitality rationale fatally defective on the grounds: (1) It failed to explain why the statute accorded differential treatment to automobile guests as distinguished from other guests. (2) In light of recent developments in comparable legal doctrines, the interest in protecting hospitality could not rationally justify the withdrawal of legal protection from guests. (3) It ignored the prevalence of liability insurance coverage today, which undermines any alleged rational connection between prevention of lawsuits and the protection of hospitality. The prevention of collusive lawsuits rationale was determined defective as overinclusive, since it barred valid suits along with the fraudulent claims. The court further found that the classification was aggravated by a series of

---

* "Any person who as a guest accepts a ride in any vehicle, moving upon any of the public highways of the state of Utah, and while so riding as such guest receives or sustains an injury, shall have no right of recovery against the owner or driver or person responsible for the operation of such vehicle.... Nothing in this section shall be construed as relieving the owner or driver or person responsible for the operation of a vehicle from liability for injury to or death of such guest proximately resulting from the intoxication or willful misconduct or such owner, driver or person responsible for the operation of such vehicle." — Ed.

limiting loopholes, which stayed the operation of the statute under a variety of diverse and illogical circumstances. The court explained that the numerous exceptions produced an absurd and illogical pattern which eliminated any rationality which might conceivably be claimed for the statute.

The California court stated that the statute established three distinct levels of classification: (1) The act treated automobile guests differently from paying passengers. (2) It treated automobile guests differently from other social guests and recipients of generosity and withdrew from auto guests the protection from negligently inflicted injuries generally enjoyed by a guest in other contexts. (3) The act distinguished, between subclasses of auto guests, withholding recovery from guests injured while "in a vehicle" "during a ride" "upon a public highway" but permitted recovery by the guest injured under other circumstances. According to the court, the rationality of the tripartite classification scheme must be evaluated in the light of the purposes of the legislation. No other case had adjudicated the constitutional issue on this basis.

The court stated that the hospitality justification provided an inadequate explanation for the differential treatment accorded to automobile guests as distinguished from other guests. Under California law, guests or recipients of hospitality may generally demand that their hosts exercise due care so as not to injure them. In a footnote the court explained that in 1929, the time of enactment, the guest statute had a closer relationship to general tort doctrine, since at that time property owners owed a duty of ordinary care only to invitees (business visitors) and owed only some lesser duty of care to licensees (social guests). Presently, in California, the general duty of ordinary care governs a landowner's duty to all those injured on his property, social guests and business visitors alike. Since the general tort doctrine has been modified [in Rowland v. Christian], the guest statute singles out automobile guests for a special burden and thus creates an arbitrary and unreasonable classification. The court reasoned that no realistic state purpose supported the classification scheme of the statute, since persons situated with respect to the purpose of the law (recipients of hospitality) do not receive like treatment. . . .

The court further explained that the characterization of the guest's lawsuit as an act of ingratitude had been completely eroded by the development of almost universal automobile liability insurance coverage in recent years. Today, the insurance company and not the generous host, was the recipient of the protection of the guest statute. The court was of the opinion that the elimination of the guest doctrine would in most cases shift the burden of loss from the injured individual to the motoring public rather than to the negligent host personally. The court concluded that the discriminatory treatment of automobile guests could not be upheld against the constitutional attack on the basis of the hospitality justification.

Brown v. Merlo is a logical consequence in that jurisdiction stemming from their prior determination to abandon the traditional tort doctrine that the status of a person determined the duty owed to him. In this jurisdiction the distinction between "invitees" or "business visitors" and "licensees" or "social guests" has been preserved. Thus the classification of an automobile guest in Section 41-9-1, U.C.A. 1953, does not single out this one group for treatment different than accorded to other guests. Likewise, the distinction between a paying passenger and an automobile guest has been retained in the correlative distinctions between an invitee and licensee. Thus, in this jurisdiction an automobile guest has not been isolated from all other guests and recipients of generosity and alone denied a duty of due care by his host.

As previously noted, the court in Brown v. Merlo relied extensively on Rowland v. Christian to prove the invalidity of the hospitality justification for the guest statute. This case is cited in 32 A.L.R.3d 513, as part of the general trend in the field of tort laws to eliminate technical status positions, which had the effect of insulating certain classes from liability. In an explanatory footnote, it is stated:

> This movement is probably a result of a general shift in the theory of tort law from the emphasis on the regulation of rights between individuals on the basis of relative fault toward a viewpoint which regards *tort law as a device for social engineering,* primarily concerned with allocation of liability in such a manner as to most satisfactorily protect the social fabric from the impact of such injuries as are a necessary or probable consequence of the complicated organization of society. [Emphasis added.]

Brown v. Merlo, in effect, elevated this device for social engineering to the level of a constitutional doctrine. First, by this device as utilized in Rowland v. Christian, the traditional distinction between invitees and licensees was nullified, resulting in the automobile guest alone being denied the duty of ordinary care by his host. Secondly, to nullify the hospitality justification, the court directly incorporated the underlying rationale of social engineering, namely that there should be an allocation of liability so as to protect the society from the impact of such injuries. The court stated that the widespread use of liability insurance shifted all or part of the burden of loss from the injured individual to the motoring public. Through this process of social engineering a legislative enactment in the area of economics and social welfare was thrust into conflict with the modified tort doctrine promulgated by the court. The court was of the opinion that the statutory classification caused discriminatory treatment to automobile guests and violated the equal protection guarantees of the California and United States Constitutions. . . .

The use of the motor vehicle upon the public highways has been validly subjected to legislative regulation. The presence of the guest in this area would itself create a basis for a distinct classification from other guests located where there was no overwhelming public interest. The motor vehicle exerts a dominant influence in contemporary society and its use creates many economic and social problems. In a state such as Utah a significant portion of

our economic resources must be devoted to the construction and maintenance of highways; the economic burden bears a direct relationship to the
number of vehicles and the total cumulative mileage on the highways each
year. The guest statute encourages hospitality and directly affects the
number of vehicles present on the highways, thus avoiding traffic congestion
and wear to the surfaces of the roadway. The guest statute promotes the
conservation of petroleum and other natural resources consumed in highway
travel. The suggestion that the burden of the injured guest should be borne
by the motoring public through liability insurance is an economic and social
solution that is properly subject to legislative determination. The Legislature
is the proper forum to consider the alternative solutions for the problem of
the injured guest. . . . The suggested simplistic solution that the motoring
public should bear the costs of the injured guests ignores the economic
consequence that increased claims will be reflected in increased insurance
rates, creating an economic hardship on the generous host and chilling
hospitality.

Section 41-9-1, U.C.A. 1953, was enacted to provide some protection to a
generous host, who is sued by his invited guest for ordinary negligence, when
the rider has given no compensation as an inducement for making the trip or
furnishing the carriage for the rider. This act subserved a valid legislative
purpose to encourage hospitality in the use of the public highways. Furthermore, the automobile guest in this jurisdiction is not placed in a distinct
classification, where he alone as a recipient of generosity is deprived of the
duty of due care by his host.

In Brown v. Merlo the court stated that the second justification for the
guest statute was the prevention of collusive lawsuits. The classification in
the statute was allegedly predicated on the concept that a driver who gave a
free ride to a passenger was motivated by his close relationship with his guest,
and the driver might admit liability to assist the guest in collecting from the
insurance company. The court rejected this rationale on the ground that
through prior case law intrafamily tort immunity had been rejected. The
court cited Klein v. Klein wherein it rejected a claim that the possibility of
fraudulent lawsuits between a husband and wife served as a sufficient justification to bar all interspousal negligence actions. In Rubalcava v. Gisseman,
this court held that a wife may not maintain a tort action against her husband
or his estate. This court declined to follow Klein v. Klein and stated that the
legislature and not this court was the proper forum to change this rule. Thus
in Utah the guest statute does not create a distinct classification for automobile guests as compared to others insofar as collusive lawsuits are concerned.

The court stated in Brown v. Merlo that the numerous statutory exceptions had rendered recovery or lack of recovery under the guest statute largely
fortuitous and added another element of irrationality to the statutory
scheme. The court explained that the relationship giving rise to liability
between the driver and occupant might fluctuate during the course of a single
ride, as circumstances brought them within and without the language of the

statute. The court observed that the statute distinguished guests on the basis of (1) whether or not the journey had come to a momentary halt; (2) whether the guest was physically located inside or outside the car; (3) whether the car was on a public highway or private land. The court found that these statutory exceptions operated so illogically as to cause serious inequality and that they did not bear the remotest relation to either the objective of protecting hospitality or preventing collusive lawsuits. The court concluded that under these circumstances, the limiting provisions of the statute constituted further denial of equal protection.

In Andrus v. Allred, this court stated that Section 41-9-1, U.C.A. 1953, should be given a sufficiently practical and reasonable application to cover incidents which occur as an integral part of the ride. This court declined to give the statute such a narrow and literal interpretation as to eliminate incidents which might occur while the vehicle was stopped, however briefly and for any purpose. This court stated: "It is our opinion that a sensible and realistic application of this statute, in conformity with its objective, requires that the protection extend over the entire host-guest relationship in connection with the giving and taking of the ride. . . . the host-guest relationship here must also include getting into the car at the beginning and getting out of it when the ride is completed and any incidents which happen in the course of and arising out of the ride. . . ."

The interpretation of the guest statute by this court has averted the alleged irrationality in the statutory classification which disturbed the court in Brown v. Merlo. Furthermore, the Equal Protection Clause does not compel the State to attack every aspect of a problem or to refrain from any action at all; it is sufficient that the State's action be rationally based and free from invidious discrimination. . . .

Notes

1. Plaintiff in *Cannon* appealed to the U.S. Supreme Court, which dismissed the appeal summarily for want of a substantial federal question. 419 U.S. 810 (1974). Such a dismissal, despite its summary character, is technically a disposition on the merits. On the authority of the dismissal in *Cannon*, a federal court of appeals sustained the Indiana guest statute against equal-protection objections. See Sidle v. Majors, 536 F.2d 1156 (7th Cir. 1976). See also Cory v. Jones, 650 F.2d 803 (5th Cir. 1981). The Supreme Court denied certiorari in *Sidle* over Justice Brennan's vigorous dissent, which argued that, in view of the division among the states on the constitutionality of guest statutes, plenary review of the question was warranted. 429 U.S. 945 (1976). See also Hill v. Garner, 434 U.S. 989 (1977) (White, J., dissenting from denial of certiorari). The states continue to be fiercely divided over the validity of guest statutes as a matter of state constitutional law. Besides

Cannon and *Brown*, see, e.g., Bierkamp v. Rogers, 243 N.W.2d 577 (Iowa 1980); Hydts v. Dixon, 606 P.2d 1303 (Colo. 1980).

2. At common law, a driver was liable toward his guest for "gross negligence" but not for ordinary negligence. About half of the states have, like Utah, a statute essentially codifying the common-law rule. The language of the Utah statute — "intoxication or willful misconduct" — is fairly typical of the standards in the guest statutes. Other common terms are "wanton" and "reckless." These terms have no very clear meaning in tort law. They are perhaps best understood as synonyms for "gross" in the expression "gross negligence" and hence interpreted, in Hand formula terms, as cases in which B is much smaller than PL.

3. Is it true that the insurance companies are the principal beneficiaries of the guest statutes? Will the liability insurance premiums paid by owners of automobiles be higher or lower in a state that has a guest statute than in a state that allows guests to sue their hosts for simple negligence?

4. Looking back over the cases in this chapter, you cannot fail to be struck by the trend toward reducing the scope, theoretical and practical, of defenses based on victim conduct or status. What explains this trend? The following are some conjectures:

a. The rise of the welfare state reflects a declining faith in the ability of the individual to fend for himself; an aspect of this ideological shift is a declining faith in the ability of the individual to protect himself against injury.

b. Judges have simply become more sensitive to the problems of information cost that make it unrealistic to expect workers, travelers, and other potential accident victims to take cost-justified precautions against injury.

c. The relative costs of accident avoidance have shifted over time as between potential victims and potential injurers: it is one thing for a pedestrian to protect himself from an unruly horse, and another for him to protect himself against a speeding automobile.

d. With the growth of both private (especially medical) and social insurance (e.g., social security disability insurance), accident victims no longer bear the full costs of their accidents; a larger part of those costs are shifted to others. This reduces their incentives to take care and may, as a result, increase the importance of care by potential injurers. In other words, if accident victims will not do enough to protect themselves, this argues for a broader liability for injurers, even though, if victims had the proper incentives to take care, the cost to them of accident avoidance would be lower than the costs of care to injurers in many cases.

Return to this question after considering the similar trend toward reduced victim responsibility for accidents in the products-liability area, discussed in Chapter 9.

Chapter 6
The Duty Limitation

Negligence is frequently described as a breach of the duty of care. It may seem to follow that if there is no duty of care toward the particular plaintiff in a case, the mere fact that the defendant can be said to have injured the plaintiff through carelessness will not make him liable under a theory of negligence. In fact, the ground assigned in some cases for denying liability is precisely that the defendant did not owe a duty of care to the plaintiff. The "no duty to trespassers" rule discussed in the last chapter illustrates this use of the duty concept. We shall see in Chapter 8 that sometimes when liability for negligence is denied because the defendant's conduct was not a "proximate cause" of the plaintiff's injury, the courts say the defendant had no duty of care toward the particular plaintiff or with respect to a particular type of injury. This chapter discusses other areas where the duty concept is invoked to deny liability. The areas discussed are: (1) negligent failure to warn, rescue, or otherwise assist someone whose personal safety or property interest is endangered (other than by the anterior negligence of the defendant — those cases are discussed in Chapter 8); (2) negligence arising out of a contract, promise, or representation; (3) negligent damage to something in which plaintiff has an interest but not a right. Aspects of these topics (especially the second and third) are sometimes discussed under the heading of proximate cause, and this chapter may therefore be considered an introduction to the causal issues treated at greater length in Chapter 8.

Ames, Law and Morals
22 Harv. L. Rev. 97 (1908)*

Primitive law regards the word and the act of the individual; it searches not his heart. "The thought of man shall not be tried," said Chief Justice Brian, one of the best of the medieval lawyers, "for the devil himself knoweth not the thought of man."

As a consequence early law is formal and unmoral. Are these adjectives properly to be applied to the English common law at any time within the

*In excerpting this article, I have taken the liberty in one instance of altering the order of the paragraphs. — Ed.

period covered by the reports of litigated cases? To answer this question, let us consider, first, the rule of liability for damage caused to one person by the act of another. Not quite six hundred years ago an action of trespass was brought in the King's Bench for a battery. The jury found that the plaintiff was beaten, but that this was because of his assailing the defendant who had acted purely in self-defense, and that the action was brought out of malice. It was nevertheless adjudged that the plaintiff should recover his damages according to the jury's verdict, and that the defendant should go to prison. The defendant had committed the act of battery; therefore he must make reparation. He was not permitted to justify his act as done in protecting himself from the attack of the plaintiff. That attack rendered the plaintiff liable to a cross action, but did not take away his own action. . . .

There is a certain analogy between the ethical development of the law and that of the individual. As early law is formal and unmoral, so the child or youth is wont to be technical at the expense of fairness. This was brought home to me once by an experience with one of my sons, then about twelve years old. I asked him one day about his plans for the afternoon, and he told me he was to play tennis with his friend John. In the evening, when asked if he had had a good afternoon with John, he said, "Oh, I haven't been with him. I thought I would rather play with Willie." "But didn't John expect you?" "Yes, I suppose he did." "Was it quite right, after you had led him to expect you, to disappoint him?" "Oh, but I didn't promise him that I would come." Remembering Chief Justice Brian, I was lenient with the boy. . . .

. . . [T]oday we may say that the old law has been radically transformed. The early law asked simply, "Did the defendant do the physical act which damaged the plaintiff?" The law of today, except in certain cases based upon public policy, asks the further question, "Was the act blameworthy?" The ethical standard of reasonable conduct has replaced the unmoral standard of acting at one's peril. . . .

. . . The defenses of infancy, statute of frauds, statute of limitations, or that a promise was gratuitous are only too often dishonorable defenses, but their abolition would probably increase rather than diminish injustice. An English judge said from the bench: "You are a harpy, preying on the vitals of the poor." The words were false and spoken for the sole purpose of injuring the person addressed. The latter could maintain no action against the judge. It is believed to be for the public interest that no judge should be called to account in a civil action for words spoken while on the bench.

The law is utilitarian. It exists for the realization of the reasonable needs of the community. If the interest of an individual runs counter to this chief object of the law, it must be sacrificed. That is why, in the cases just considered and others that will occur to you, the innocent suffer and the wicked go unpunished.

But unless exempted from liability by considerations of enlightened public policy, I can see no reason why he who has by his act wilfully caused damage to another should not in all cases make either specific reparation or pecuniary compensation to his victim. . . .

. . . It remains to consider whether the law should ever go so far as to give compensation or to inflict punishment for damage which would not have happened but for the wilful inaction of another. I exclude cases in which, by reason of some relation between the parties like that of father and child, nurse and invalid, master and servant and others, there is a recognized legal duty to act. In the case supposed the only relation between the parties is that both are human beings. As I am walking over a bridge a man falls into the water. He cannot swim and calls for help. I am strong and a good swimmer, or, if you please, there is a rope on the bridge, and I might easily throw him an end and pull him ashore. I neither jump in nor throw him the rope, but see him drown. Or, again, I see a child on the railroad track too young to appreciate the danger of the approaching train. I might easily save the child, but do nothing, and the child, though it lives, loses both legs. Am I guilty of a crime, and must I make compensation to the widow and children of the man drowned and to the wounded child? Macaulay, in commenting upon his Indian Criminal Code, puts the case of a surgeon refusing to go from Calcutta to Meerut to perform an operation, although it should be absolutely certain that this surgeon was the only person in India who could perform it, and that, if it were not performed, the person who required it would die.

We may suppose again that the situation of imminent danger of death was created by the act, but the innocent act, of the person who refuses to prevent the death. The man, for example, whose eye was penetrated by the glancing shot of the careful pheasant hunter, stunned by the shot, fell face downward into a shallow pool by which he was standing. The hunter might easily save him, but lets him drown.

In the first three illustrations, however revolting the conduct of the man who declined to interfere, he was in no way responsible for the perilous situation, he did not increase the peril, he took away nothing from the person in jeopardy, he simply failed to confer a benefit upon a stranger. As the law stands today there would be no legal liability, either civilly or criminally, in any of these cases. The law does not compel active benevolence between man and man. It is left to one's conscience whether he shall be the good Samaritan or not.

But ought the law to remain in this condition? Of course any statutory duty to be benevolent would have to be exceptional. The practical difficulty in such legislation would be in drawing the line. But that difficulty has continually to be faced in the law. We should all be better satisfied if the man who refuses to throw a rope to a drowning man or to save a helpless child on the railroad track could be punished and be made to compensate the widow of the man drowned and the wounded child. We should not think it advisable to penalize the surgeon who refused to make the journey. These illustrations suggest a possible working rule. One who fails to interfere to save another from impending death or great bodily harm, when he might do so with little or no inconvenience to himself, and the death or great bodily harm follows as a consequence of his inaction, shall be punished criminally and shall make compensation to the party injured or to his widow and children in case of death. The case of the drowning of the man shot by the hunter differs from the others in that the hunter, although he acted innocently, did bring about the dangerous situation. Here, too, the lawyer who should try to charge the hunter would lead a forlorn hope. But it seems to me that he could make out a strong case against the hunter on common law grounds. By the early law, as we have seen, he would have been liable simply because he shot the other. In modern times the courts have admitted as an affirmative defense the fact that he was not negligent. May not the same cou-ts refuse to allow the defense, if the defendant did not use reasonable means to prevent a calamity after creating the threatening situation? Be that as it may, it is hard to see why such a rule should not be declared by statute, if not by the courts.

It is obvious that the spirit of reform which during the last six hundred years has been bringing our system of law more and more into harmony with moral principles has not yet achieved its perfect work. It is worthwhile to realize the great ethical advance of the English law in the past, if only as an encouragement to effort for future improvement. In this work of the future there is an admirable field for the law professor. The professor has, while the judge and the practicing lawyer have not, the time for systematic and comprehensive study and for becoming familiar with the decisions and legislation of other countries. This systematic study and the knowledge of what is going on in other countries are indispensable if we would make our system of law the best possible instrument of justice. The training of students must always be the chief object of the law school, but this work should be supplemented by solid contributions of their professors to the improvement of the law.

Epstein, A Theory of Strict Liability
2 J. Legal Stud. 151, 198-203 (1973)

. . . The general use of the cost-benefit analysis required under the economic interpretation of negligence does not permit a person to act on the assumption that he may as of right attach special weight and importance to his own welfare. Under Ames' good Samaritan rule, a defendant in cases of affirmative acts would be required to take only those steps that can be done "with little or no inconvenience." But if the distinction between causing harm and not preventing harm is to be disregarded, why should the difference in standards between the two cases survive the reform of the law? The only explanation is that the two situations are regarded at bottom as raising totally different issues, even for those who insist upon the immateriality of this distinction. Even those who argue, as Ames does, that the law is utilitarian must in the end find some special place for the claims of egoism which are an inseparable byproduct of the belief that individual autonomy — individual liberty — is a good in itself not explainable in terms of its purported social worth. It is one thing to *allow* people to act as they please in the belief that the "invisible hand" will provide the happy congruence of the individual and the social good. Such a theory, however, at bottom must regard individual autonomy as but a means to some social end. It takes a great deal more to assert that men are *entitled* to act as they choose (within the limits of strict liability) even though it is certain that there will be cases where individual welfare will be in conflict with the social good. Only then is it clear that even freedom has its costs: costs revealed in the acceptance of the good Samaritan doctrine.

But are the alternatives more attractive? Once one decides that as a matter of statutory or common law duty, an individual is required under some circumstances to act at his own cost for the exclusive benefit of another, then it is very hard to set out in a principled manner the limits of social interference with individual liberty. Suppose one claims, as Ames does, that his proposed rule applies only in the "obvious" cases where everyone (or almost everyone) would admit that the duty was appropriate: to the case of the man upon the bridge who refuses to throw a rope to a stranger drowning in the waters below. Even if the rule starts out with such modest ambitions, it is difficult to confine it to those limits. Take a simple case first. X as a representative of a private charity asks you for $10 in order to save the life of some starving child in a country ravaged by war. There are other donors available but the number of needy children exceeds that number. The money means "nothing" to you. Are you under a legal obligation to give the $10? Or to lend it interest-free? Does $10 amount to a substantial cost or inconvenience within the meaning of Ames' rule? It is true that the relationship between the gift to charity and the survival of an unidentified child is not so apparent as is the relationship between the man upon the bridge and the swimmer caught in the swirling seas. But lest the physical imagery govern, it is clear in both cases that someone will die as a consequence of your inaction in both cases. Is there a duty to give, or is the contribution a matter of charity?

Consider yet another example where services, not cash, are in issue. Ames insists that his rule would not require the only surgeon in India capable of saving the life of a person with a given affliction to travel across the subcontinent to perform an operation, presumably because the inconvenience and cost would be substantial. But how would he treat the case if some third person were willing to pay him for all of his efforts? If the payment is sufficient to induce the surgeon to act, then there is no need for the good Samaritan doctrine at all. But if it is not, then it is again necessary to compare the costs of the physician with the benefits to his prospective patient. It is hard to know whether Ames would require the forced exchange under these circumstances. But it is at least arguable that under his theory forced exchanges should be required, since the payment might reduce the surgeon's net inconvenience to the point where it was trivial.

Once forced exchanges, regardless of the levels of payment, are accepted, it will no longer be possible to delineate the sphere of activities in which contracts (or charity) will be required in order to procure desired benefits and the sphere of activity in which those benefits can be procured as of right. Where tests of "reasonableness" — stated with such confidence, and applied with such difficulty — dominate the law of tort, it becomes impossible to tell where liberty ends and obligation begins; where contract ends, and tort begins. In each case, it will be possible for some judge or jury to decide that there was something else which the defendant should have done, and he will decide that on the strength of some cost-benefit formula that is difficult indeed to apply. These remarks are conclusive, I think, against the adoption of Ames' rule by judicial innovation, and they bear heavily on the desirability of the abandonment of the good Samaritan rule by legislation as well. . . .

In addition, the incentive effects created by the absence of a good Samaritan rule must be examined in the context of other rules of substantive law. Thus it is critical to ask about the incentives which are created by rules which permit a rescuer to bring an action against the person he saved on quasi-contractual theories. It is also important to ask what modifications of behavior could be expected if the scope of this kind were expanded, and important, too, to know about the possible effects of systems of public honors and awards for good Samaritans. None of these arguments is designed to show that the common law approach can be justified on economic grounds, but they do show how perilous it is to attempt to justify legal rules by the incentives that they create. . . .

W. M. Landes & R. A. Posner, Economics of Rescue Law*

The peril that invites rescue provides a perfect example of external benefits: A sees a flowerpot about to fall on B's (a stranger's) head; if he shouts, B will be saved. Thus A has it in his power to confer a considerable benefit on B. However, it is infeasible for A and B to contract for the rescue because of the lack of time for negotiation.

A standard reaction to a situation in which there are substantial potential external benefits and high transaction costs is to propose legal intervention. In the example put, this would mean giving A the right to either a public or private (i.e., presumably from B) reward for the service he renders in saving B or punishing A if he fails to save B. Either form of intervention, however, is apt to be quite costly. Where, as in the example given, the rescuer is not

*Excerpted, with some interpolations of connective material, from Landes & Posner, Altruism in Law and Economics, 68 Am. Econ. Rev. Papers & Proceedings 417 (May 1978), and Landes & Posner, Salvors, Finders, Good Samaritans, and Other Rescuers: An Economic Study of Law and Altruism, 7 J. Legal Stud. 83 (1978).

engaged in the business of rescue, the appropriate reward, which from the standpoint of economics depends on the opportunity costs of A's time and the expected costs resulting from the dangerousness to him of the rescue, would be costly to compute. And if the optimal reward was low (because the rescue entailed little cost to A), the costs of computation and enforcement of A's legal claim would be high relative to the pure reward component, resulting in potentially serious misallocative effects.[1]

The costs of legal intervention are in one important respect reduced under a system of liability for nonrescue (as distinct from a reward for rescue): damages need to be computed only in cases where the rule of liability is violated (or alleged to be violated), and these occasions may be few if compliance with the rule is widespread. The reward approach, in contrast, would require compensation in every case in which a rescue was made successfully. However the liability approach creates another cost: it operates as a tax on activities in which a person may be called upon to attempt a rescue, and like any tax will cause people to substitute away from those activities. This could result in too few potential rescuers, leading to excessive safety precautions by potential rescuees.

The foregoing objections to using the law to internalize the external benefits of a rescue would be much less imposing were it not for altruism, a factor ignored in most discussion of externalities. Altruism may be an inexpensive substitute for costly legal methods of internalizing external benefits — though this depends, of course, on the degree to which altruism will actually motivate rescue.

The economic analysis of altruistic giving emphasizes wealth disparities between the donor and donee. This emphasis follows from the principle of diminishing marginal rates of substitution; that is, the greater the donor's wealth relative to the donee, the greater the amount the donor is willing to give up at the margin in exchange for a dollar increase in the donee's wealth. The rescue setting presents a dramatic example of wealth disparities. At the moment when the flowerpot is about to crash down on B's head and possibly kill him, A, though he presumably does not know what B's wealth was before the flowerpot toppled over, does know that B's expected wealth is now very small and that his own wealth, however slight, is almost certainly much greater than B's. Moreover, if the cost to A of effecting the rescue is very small (the cost of a shout), A can transfer wealth to B at a very low cost to himself. Thus, even though, because they are strangers, A presumably values a dollar to himself much more highly than he values a dollar to B, the rescue may still be a "profitable" transaction for A. Suppose that A considers a dollar to be worth a dollar in his own possession but only one cent in B's

1. If, for example, the gain to B from rescue was $10 and the optimal reward was $1, but the cost of computation was $100 and was borne by B, B might be led to adopt excessively costly safety precautions to avoid being in the position of having to reward A for rescuing him. Placing the cost on the taxpayer would have different, but not necessarily less serious, misallocative effects.

possession (though if it were not a rescue setting, i.e., if their wealth were more equal, A might value a dollar in B's possession at only .01 cent instead of one cent). Nonetheless, if A can save B's life at a cost of a dollar and thereby confer a benefit on B that A can guess is worth several hundred thousand dollars to B, the transfer will increase A's utility though he receives no compensation from B or anyone else. The "leverage" that A obtains by being able to increase B's wealth very greatly at little cost to himself is the counterpart to the matching grant in the conventional charity context, which reduces the cost of a gift to the donor below the dollar amount received by the donee.

The above analysis does not explain, however, why A derives *any* utility from the welfare of a complete stranger. The biologists have done more work on this question than the economists. They have shown that altruism may increase the likelihood of the altruist's genes surviving in the competition among populations. If insect A saves B from peril, this means that B will be alive to save A should he find himself in danger. This "reciprocal altruism" may enhance the survivorship of the group to which A and B belong relative to that of some nonaltruistic insect group. A closely related concept (call it "gene survival") comes into play where, say, A in our example dies while saving B; A and B may share some of the same genes and B's survival may contribute more to the chances for the survival of their common genetic endowment than A's.

Reciprocal altruism may explain some, but surely today only a very small, fraction of rescues of strangers. In small communities, the person one rescues, even if a stranger, may indeed be a potential rescuer. In modern urban communities the probability that one is saving someone who will someday reciprocate will often be very close to zero — if he is indeed a stranger. To be sure, the stranger may be carrying some of the rescuer's genes, but this possibility will often be as remote as the possibility that he will someday rescue you. Thus the likelihood that the nonaltruist will be "weeded out" in the competition within or among modern societies is slight.

If we emphasize simply the large discount that the potential rescuer will apply to a stranger's welfare in deciding how much cost to incur in rescuing him, the biological analysis of altruism is helpful. However the analysis seems to imply not only that the discount will be large but that normally it will be so large that only a small fraction of cost-justified rescues (i.e., where the costs to the rescuer are less than the benefits to the victim) would be attempted.

A possible alternative to the biological approach is to emphasize the *recognition* factor in rescues. The fact that most charitable donations are not anonymous and, indeed, that many donors seem quite avid to obtain publicity for their gifts (as where a university chair is named after the donor) suggests that the desire for publicity or recognition is an important factor in charitable giving. Rescuers, too, get their names in the newspapers and this may be the "real" reason why they rescue complete strangers.

This analysis may appear merely to push the inquiry back one step: why do donors, whether of money or services, receive favorable public recognition? Presumably, this results from a public sense, however dim, of altruism as an economizing force (i.e., a low-cost method of internalizing external benefits, compared to legal intervention). Notice that this analysis does not require that *anyone* be in fact altruistic in the sense that he derives utility from making a transfer to a stranger. Conceivably everyone who makes such a transfer does so not out of true altruism but to obtain a reward which consists of favorable publicity.

The importance attached to the recognition factor is relevant to shaping public policy toward rescues. If it is deemed a substantial motivating force in rescues, this would argue against creating liability for failure to rescue. One effect of liability is that the successful rescuer will no longer receive as much favorable public attention, because the public will assume he acted simply out of fear of liability. This increases the tax effect of the liability approach in discouraging potential rescuers.

Although the basis for altruistic impulses toward strangers in peril is obscure, the existence of the impulse is verified by the numerous instances in which rescues have occurred where neither reciprocal altruism nor gene survival could provide a plausible motivation. The *fragility* of such impulses — a clear implication of the biological analysis — has also been recognized by the law. Generally the law does not rely on altruism to internalize external benefits where the costs to the rescuer are great. For if the rate at which the potential rescuer equates his costs to the benefits to the person saved is low (for example, it takes $100 in benefits to the person saved to compensate the rescuer for incurring a cost of 1¢), then altruistic rescues are unlikely to occur in cases where the costs of rescue are large.

Two examples will illustrate the law's recognition of this point. Although the ordinary rescuer is entitled to no reward, the professional (normally a physician) is entitled to collect his standard fee from the person rescued in the high-transaction-costs setting (for example, no negotiation is possible because the victim is unconscious). Not only is the physician's opportunity cost of time higher than that of the average nonprofessional rescuer, but, because of his greater knowledge of medical treatment, he is expected to spend more time with the rescued person (treating him, as distinct from simply calling an ambulance). Thus the total costs of rescue to the physician are apt to be higher than those borne by the nonprofessional. (To some extent, however, the greater benefit normally conferred by the professional rescuer's more extensive services may offset the added cost.) The costs of computing the reward, moreover, are relatively slight because the physician's fees for similar services are readily discoverable.

The second example is rescue at sea. Normally this is undertaken by commercial operators (especially in cases where the vessel or its cargo, rather than just passengers and crew, are salvaged) at substantial cost. One is not surprised that a successful rescue at sea entitles the rescuer to a reward — and that the rescuer's right is most firmly established where it is property rather than lives that is rescued: the cost of pure life salvage is normally less than that of property salvage, and the normally greater value of lives versus property increases the likelihood of an altruistically motivated rescue of lives.

Given that legal intervention and altruism are substitute methods of encouraging the internalization of the external benefits of rescues in emergency situations, the question naturally arises whether studying the pattern of legal intervention in rescues might provide a clue to variations over time or across societies in the level of altruism. Many foreign countries, and a single state, impose liability for failure to rescue. It may be significant that no law imposing liability for nonrescue has been found prior to 1867. This may reflect the fact that in a pre-urban society reciprocal altruism may provide an adequate substitute for legal coercion to rescue. Another suggestive feature is the predominance of fascist and communist states among the early adopters of liability for nonrescue. Liability for failure to rescue is a form of conscription for social service which would seem congenial to a state that already regards its citizens' time as public rather than private property. It may not be accidental that the first (and thus far only) state to impose liability for nonrescue is Vermont, which has the third highest tax rate (after Alaska and New York) in the United States.

The imposition of liability for failure to rescue may or may not be efficient; but it is noteworthy that the jurisdictions which impose such liability do so in a way apparently designed to minimize the costs. Specifically, the foreign statutes in this area contain two economizing features. First, liability is not imposed where the cost of the rescue would exceed its value. Second, it is generally confined to cases where the costs of rescue are trivial; this seems calculated to insure that the net social benefits of liability (deducting the costs of operating the legal system) will be positive. A third feature is more questionable: the successful rescuer is entitled to a reward for the rescue. By eliminating (or by reducing) the tax effect of liability, the entitlement to a reward should reduce the number of rescuers substituting away from hazardous activities; but for reasons explored earlier the administrative costs are apt to be quite high. Fourth, the reward permitted under Continental law is not equal to the full consumer surplus generated by the rescue. It is generally limited to reimbursement of out-of-pocket expenses. Since this is an inadequate reward to stimulate rescues by nonaltruists, it is understandable that it is coupled with liability.

The economic analysis of liability for failure to rescue does not come to a definite conclusion regarding the soundness of such liability. It does, however, provide a decisive argument against such liability in just that case where Professor Epstein seems most concerned about the implications of liability for failure to rescue. This is the case where the surgeon refuses to travel across India to save someone's life even though a third person is willing to defray his travel costs. Since transaction costs are low, there is no economic basis for forcing the surgeon to act. The patient (or third party) need but meet his price. Ames's rule is implictly limited to the high-transaction-cost case. It is only here that the economic analysis is indecisive.

Incidentally, limited to the high-transaction-cost case Ames's rule is at once innocuous and, in all likelihood, unnecessary. Since the rule applies only where the cost to the rescuer is small, the tax effect of liability will be small. On the other hand, since the cost *is* small and the benefit great, altruism should be sufficient to motivate rescue without legal intervention. In Epstein's case, where a third party reimburses the surgeon for the costs (including opportunity costs?) of the trip, it is difficult to believe that the surgeon would refuse. But if he did, it would be because his price had not been met, and absent some monopoly or externality element not suggested by the hypothetical, there would be no economic ground for legal intervention. It is thus incorrect that an economic approach to common law rights and liabilities leads to socialism.

Lastly we address the question why, if altruism is a possible substitute for law in internalizing external benefits, it is not equally a substitute for law in internalizing external costs. If we do not need a law to compel rescues, why do we need, for example, a law to compel drivers to avoid running down pedestrians?

The reason would appear to lie in the significant discount the driver is likely to attach to pedestrians' benefits and the high cost of accident avoidance (for example, damage to one's car and personal injury, or the cost of altering one's behavior at an earlier stage, such as driving at a slower speed, to avoid situations in which an accident is imminent). To be sure, when these costs are low, even a relatively slight amount of altruism will be sufficient to induce the driver to avoid the accident. When these costs are substantial, though not so large as the benefits to the pedestrian, altruism is unlikely to be an adequate method of internalizing the pedestrian's losses and hence a liability rule will be required to generate optimal accident avoidance.

Why, therefore, does not society impose liability *only* when the costs of avoidance are high (though still less than the victim's benefits) and rely on altruism alone to prevent low-avoidance-cost accidents? This approach would be symmetrical to the treatment of compensation in the rescue setting. However, the principal objections to compensation in the low-cost rescue case — the cost of computing the reward, the cost of transacting between the parties, and the possible use of costly legal proceedings to enforce one's right to a reward — are not present when the question is whether to impose liability in the low-avoidance-cost accident situation. Here a liability rule, if effective, will be relatively cheap because the accident will usually be deterred.

Notes

1. The right of the maritime rescuer (called a "salvor") to compensation from those whose lives or property he rescues is governed by the law of salvage, which is a part of the law of admiralty. For a discussion of the rules of salvage, see G. Gilmore & C. L. Black, Jr., The Law of Admiralty 532-585 (2d

ed. 1975). The right of compensation in nonmaritime rescue settings is much more limited; such as it is, it is governed by the law of restitution, on which see R. Goff & G. Jones, The Law of Restitution 263-279 (2d ed. 1978); G. E. Palmer, The Law of Restitution §§10.3-10.4 (1978); and Restatement of Restitution, Quasi Contracts and Constructive Trusts 461-491 (1937). The Continental approach to nonmaritime rescues is sharply different from that of the common law: it combines criminal penalties for failure to render emergency assistance with a right of compensation for those who do. For an illuminating discussion of the Continental approach see Dawson, Negotiorum Gestio: The Altruistic Intermeddler, 74 Harv. L. Rev. 1073, 1099-1127 (1961). For economic analysis of both maritime and nonmaritime rescue law see Landes & Posner, Salvors, Finders, Good Samaritans, and Other Rescuers: An Economic Study of Law and Altruism, 7 J. Legal Stud. 83 (1978). Salvage and restitution are not, of course, tort doctrines, but any responsible evaluation of the merits of imposing liability for failure to rescue must consider both altruism and compensation of rescuers as alternative methods to liability of encouraging rescue.

2. The materials excerpted above deal with the economic issues in rescue law. There are also ethical and political issues, discussed in the exchange between Professors Epstein and Posner that follows, and in Weinrib, The Case for a Duty to Rescue, 90 Yale L.J. 247 (1980).

Epstein, A Theory of Strict Liability
2 J. Legal Stud. 151, 165-169, 189-204 (1973)

... The pages that follow are designed to show that the concept of causation, as it applies to cases of physical injury, can be analyzed in a manner that both renders it internally coherent and relevant to the ultimate question who shall bear the loss.

There will be no attempt to give a single semantic equivalent to the concept of causation. Instead, the paper will consider in succession each of four distinct paradigm cases covered by the proposition "A caused B harm." These paradigms are not the only way in which we can talk about torts cases. They do, however, provide modes of description which best capture the ordinary use of causal language. Briefly put, they are based upon notions of force, fright, compulsion and dangerous conditions. The first of them will be the simplest to analyze. Each of the subsequent paradigms will introduce further problems to be resolved before the judgment on the causal issue can be made. Nonetheless, despite the internal differences, it can, I believe, be demonstrated that each of these paradigms, when understood, exhibits the features that render it relevant to the question of legal responsibility.

Force. We begin with the simplest instance of causation: the application of force to a person or thing. In a physical sense, the consequences of the application of force may be quite varied. In some cases the object acted upon will move; in others it will be transformed; in still others it will be damaged. It is this last case that will be of exclusive concern here, because it is accepted without question that the minimum condition of tort liability is damage to the person or property of the plaintiff.

The identification of causation with force does not of itself complete the first instance of the proposition "A caused harm to B." It is still necessary to show that the force in question was applied by human and not natural agencies, and thus to tie the concept of force to that of human volition. The term "volition" is a primitive in the language whose function is to mark off the class of human acts from the class of events; to distinguish between "I raised my arm," and "my arm went up." . . .

The combination of force and volition is expressed in the simple transitive sentence, A hit B. It is true that this proposition as stated is consistent with the assertion that A did not harm B. But in many contexts the implication of harm follows fairly from the assertion, as anyone hit by a car will admit. Where the issue is in doubt, the verb can be changed, even as the form of the proposition remains constant, to bring the element of harm more sharply into relief. Thus instead of "A hit B," another proposition of the requisite form could be "A pummeled B," or "A beat B." But since the specifics of the harm go only to the measure of damages and not to the issue of liability, the proposition "A hit B" will serve as the model of the class of propositions to be considered.

The grammatical structure of the proposition "A hit B" is crucial to analysis of the problem of causation because it describes a situation both where the parties are *linked* to each other and where their respective roles are still *differentiated*. When causation is defined in this manner, the roles of the parties . . . are not reciprocal. The proposition that "A hit B" cannot be treated as synonymous with the proposition that "B hit A." Each of these propositions is complete without reference to either further acts, whether or not voluntary, or to natural events, whether or not abnormal. . . .

Once this simple causal paradigm is accepted, its relationship to the question of responsibility for the harm so caused must be clarified. Briefly put, the argument is that proof of the proposition A hit B should be sufficient to establish a prima facie case of liability. I do not argue that proof of causation is equivalent to a conclusive demonstration of responsibility. Both the modern and classical systems of law are based upon the development of prima facie cases and defenses thereto. They differ not in their use of presumptions but in the elements needed to create the initial presumption in favor of the plaintiff. The doctrine of strict liability holds that proof that the defendant caused harm creates that presumption because proof of the nonreciprocal source of the harm is sufficient to upset the balance where one person must win and the other must lose. There is no room to consider, as part of the prima facie case, allegations that the defendant intended to harm the plaintiff, or could have avoided the harm he caused by the use of reasonable care. The choice is plaintiff or defendant, and the analysis of causation is the tool which, prima facie, fastens responsibility upon the defendant. Indeed for most persons, the difficult question is often not whether these causal assertions create the presumption, but whether there are in fact any means to distinguish between causation and responsibility, so close is the connection between what a man does and what he is answerable for. . . .

[In an omitted portion of the article, Professor Epstein argues that injuries caused by fright, compulsion, and the creation of dangerous conditions can be analyzed as appropriate extensions of the "A hit B" causal paradigm.]

. . . The theories of strict liability explain and justify, as the rules of reasonableness cannot, the common law's refusal to extend liability in tort to cases where the defendant has not harmed the plaintiff by his affirmative action. The problem arises in its starkest form in the case of the good Samaritan. A finds himself in a perilous situation which was not created by B, as when A is overwhelmed by cramps while swimming alone in a surging sea. B, moreover, is in a position where he could, without any danger of injury to himself, come to A's assistance with some simple and well-nigh costless steps, such as throwing a rope to the plaintiff. The traditional common law position has been that there is no cause of action against B solely because B, in effect, permitted A to drown. . . .

. . . [I]f one considers the low costs of prevention to B of rescuing A, and the serious, if not deadly, harm that A will suffer if B chooses not to rescue him, there is no reason why the *Carroll Towing* formula or the general rules of negligence should not require, under pain of liability, the defendant to come to the aid of the plaintiff. Nonetheless, the good Samaritan problem receives special treatment even under the modern law of torts. The reasons for the special position of this problem are clear once the theories of strict liability are systematically applied. Under these rules, the act requirement has to be satisfied in order to show that the defendant in a given lawsuit caused harm to the plaintiff. Once that is done, the private predicament of the defendant, his ability to take precautions against the given risk, and the general economic rationality of his conduct are all beside the point. Only the issue of causation, of what *the defendant did,* is material to the statement of the prima facie case. The theory is not utilitarian. It looks not to the consequences of alternate course of conduct but to what was done. When that theory with its justification is applied to the problem of the good Samaritan, it follows in the case just put that A should not be able to recover from B for his injuries. No matter how the facts are manipulated, it is not possible to argue that B caused A harm in any of the senses of causation which were developed in the earlier portions of this article when he failed to render assistance to A in his time of need. In typical negligence cases, all the talk of avoidance and reasonable care may shift attention from the causation requirement, which the general "but for" test distorts beyond recognition. But its importance is revealed by its absence in the good Samaritan cases where the presence of all those elements immaterial to tortious liability cannot, even in combination, persuade judges who accept the negligence theory to apply it in the decisive case.

The principles of strict liability do more than explain the reasons behind the general common law refusal to require men to be good Samaritans. They also explain why it is that in some cases there are strong arguments to support apparent exceptions to the common law position. The point is best illustrated by two cases. The first case is put by Ames:

> We may suppose again that the situation of imminent danger of death was created by the act, but the innocent act, of the person who refuses to prevent the death. The man, for example, whose eye was penetrated by the glancing shot of the careful pheasant hunter, stunned by the shot, fell face downward into a shallow pool by which he was standing. The hunter might easily save him, but lets him drown.

The second situation, that of Montgomery v. National C. & T., [186 S.C. 167, 195 S.E. 247 (1938),] is described by Gregory as follows:

> Consider this situation. Two of defendant's trucks, due to no fault of the drivers, became stalled on a narrow road, completely blocking the highway. Also, without fault, the men were unable to get the trucks started again. This was at the foot of a short hill, which obscured the view of approaching drivers. Moreover, the hill was somewhat icy. Plaintiff came driving along at a normal speed. By the time he saw the stalled trucks, he was unable to stop and crashed into them. Had one of defendant's truck drivers climbed the hill and posted a warning, this accident would not have happened.

The first of these cases was not the subject of a judicial decision, but Ames was of the opinion that under the modern law "a lawyer who should try to charge the hunter would lead a forlorn hope," because the defendant "simply failed to confer a benefit upon a stranger." In the second case, however, the South Carolina court found that the defendant could be held liable on account of the actionable negligence of its employees in the course of their employment, because on the facts of the case the employees had both the opportunity and the means to place warnings in some form at the top of the hill which would have enabled the plaintiff to avoid the crash in question. The court insisted that this duty rested upon the defendant's employees even though two propositions are settled: first, that no passerby would have been charged with that duty, even if he had the time and means to have taken those steps; and second, that the defendant's employees would have been under no duty to place those warnings if the road had been blocked, say, by a falling tree. In effect, the position of the court is that simply because the defendant's employees blocked the road, they were under a duty to take those precautions reasonably calculated to prevent possible injury to other users of the highway.

Under the theories of strict liability neither of these defendants could take advantage of the good Samaritan doctrine. The hunter should be liable in a trespass action because he shot the plaintiff. Once negligence is no longer regarded as the lynchpin of the law, it should not matter that after the shooting the defendant was in a position to give aid to the plaintiff. He would be held liable even if he were not. The case no longer raises the problem of the good Samaritan; it is a simple case of trespass governed by the rules of strict liability set out above.

The second case is subject to a similar analysis, only here the appropriate theory of causation is the theory of dangerous conditions. The defendant is liable because harm resulted when the plaintiff's car ran into its truck after his employees blocked the road. It is immaterial that the defendant's employees had an opportunity to place warnings at the top of the hill, because the theory of dangerous conditions, too, is a theory of strict liability. Once it is shown that the plaintiff's conduct (he hit the defendant's truck) only serves to complete the prima facie case, the liability follows, because the facts do not even suggest the basis for an affirmative defense. . . .

. . . Compensation for harm caused can be demanded in accordance with the principles of strict liability. Failure to aid those in need can invoke at most moral censure on the ground that the person so accused did not voluntarily conform his conduct to some "universal" principle of justice. . . .

. . . It could be argued that the defendant should be held liable because if the parties had the opportunity to contract between themselves, they doubtless would have agreed that the defendant should assume the obligation to save the plaintiff in his time of distress. Thus one could argue that (in the absence of externalities) an agreement between two persons can only have favorable welfare effects since each person will be better off on account of the voluntary exchange. On this view the function of the law of tort is to anticipate those contractual arrangements which parties would have made had the transactions costs been low enough to permit direct negotiations.

This position, however, is subject to objections. The courts have struggled for years to determine the content of incomplete and ambiguous contracts which were actually negotiated by the parties. There at least they could look to, among other things, the language of the relevant documents, the custom of the trade, and the history of the prior negotiations. In the good Samaritan context, there are no documents, no customs, and no prior negotiations. The courts have only the observation that the parties would have contracted to advance their mutual interests. Given the infinite variation in terms (what price? what services?) that we could expect to find in such contracts, it is difficult to believe that that theoretical observation could enable us to determine or even approximate any bargain which the parties might have made if circumstances had permitted. It is for good reason that the courts have always refused to make contracts for the parties.

But there is a further point. We are concerned with the enforcement of a contract by private action when one of the parties objects to its performance.

It no longer seems possible to argue that both parties are better off on account of the contract since one party has indicated his desire to repudiate it. Even though the theory of the underlying action is shifted from tort to some extended form of contract, the difficulties raised by the rule that forbids interpersonal comparison of utilities still remain. At the time of the enforcement, one party argues not for an *exchange* which makes both parties better off, but for a *transfer* of wealth which makes him better off. Again we must find some way — some theory of fairness — which can explain which of them is to be made better off....

... The arguments made here suggest that the first task of the law of torts is to define the boundaries of individual liberty. To this question the rules of strict liability based upon the twin notions of causation and volition provide a better answer than the alternative theories based upon the notion of negligence, whether explicated in moral or economic terms. In effect, the principles of strict liability say that the liberty of one person ends when he causes harm to another. Until that point he is free to act as he chooses, and need not take into account the welfare of others.

Posner, Epstein's Tort Theory: A Critique
8 J. Legal Stud. 457, 460-462 (1979)

... Suppose that if all of the members of society could somehow be assembled they would agree unanimously that, as a reasonable measure of mutual protection, anyone who can warn or rescue someone in distress at negligible cost to himself (in time, danger, or whatever) should be required to do so. These mutual promises of assistance would create a contract that Epstein would presumably enforce since he considers the right to make binding contracts a fundamental one. However, there are technical obstacles — in this case insurmountable ones — to the formation of an actual contract among so many people. Transaction costs are prohibitive. If, moved by these circumstances, a court were to impose tort liability on a bystander who failed to assist a person in distress, such liability would be a means of carrying out the original desires of the parties just as if it were an express contract that was being enforced.

The point of this example is that tort duties can sometimes (perhaps, as we shall see, generally) be viewed as devices for vindicating the principles that underlie freedom of contract. It may be argued, however, that the contract analogy is inapplicable because the bystander would not be compensated for coming to the rescue of the person in distress. But this argument overlooks the fact that the consideration for the rescue is not payment when the rescue is effected but a commitment to reciprocate should the roles of the parties some day be reversed. Liability would create a mutual protective arrangement under which everyone was obliged to attempt a rescue when circumstances dictated and, in exchange, was entitled to the assistance of anyone who might be able to help him should he ever find himself in a position of peril.

I have suggested that a tort obligation is like a contract obligation, but one can approach the matter from the other direction and show that a contract obligation is like a tort obligation. The essence of contract is that the parties bind themselves to refrain from certain types of action (e.g., abandoning performance because of a rise in costs). The parties are thereby enabled to do things that they might not otherwise dare to do (like completing performance before payment, or vice versa) because each would be afraid that the other party would take advantage of him. A good Samaritan tort obligation would perform the same enabling function. I could take greater risks knowing that other people would assist me in danger and they likewise could take greater risks knowing that I (or others) would come to their assistance. Yet in the absence of a legal obligation — an obligation that, because of transaction costs, must be a tort rather than a contract obligation — it would be in everyone's interest *not* to help others (because there would be no obligation to reciprocate), and the scope for advantageous risk-taking activity would be reduced.

One can of course object that a tort duty is never identical to a contract duty because it is not founded on an explicit agreement. To state this point differently, my initial assumption that the members of society would agree *unanimously* to accept a good Samaritan duty is unrealistic. This point is valid but not fundamental; at least, Epstein does not seem to regard it as fundamental. He is willing to allow a rescuer a right to claim a reward from the rescued person under the law of restitution, and this amounts to enforcing a purely hypothetical contract. So far as the question whether it is ever proper to force people to perform (or pay for) services not actually (though perhaps hypothetically) contracted for is concerned, there is no difference between giving the rescuer a right to demand payment from an unconscious or otherwise unconsenting recipient of his services and imposing a tort duty on potential rescuers, although there are important practical (or economic) differences between these approaches. Even in cases involving explicit contracts, courts are frequently called upon to determine how the parties would have resolved a contingency they did not foresee or provide for, and Epstein has no quarrel with this procedure. Of course there are differences of degree between interpreting explicit contracts to effectuate the (unknown) intentions of the parties and creating tort duties based on purely hypothetical contracts — and one can debate where in this spectrum the "quasi-contract" illustrated by the physician's right to claim his fee from an unconscious stranger falls — but they are just that: differences of degree rather than of kind.

Epstein concedes at one point that the good Samaritan question could be viewed as one of interpreting an implied contract of rescue, but concludes that the courts are incapable of filling in the contractual terms, remarking:

"It is for good reason that the courts have always refused to make contracts for the parties." But that is precisely what the courts do when they award the physician his fee for treating someone whom he finds lying unconscious in the street. Epstein also argues that, once the good Samaritan case is in court, the plaintiff is arguing "not for an *exchange* which makes both parties better off, but for a *transfer* of wealth which makes him better off." Again, the same thing is true in a lawsuit over an express contract, where the plaintiff will be asking for a transfer of wealth (damages) which will make him better off rather than for an exchange which will make both parties better off.

Epstein's clinching argument against a good Samaritan duty is that tort law should be viewed in terms of its "political function. . . . [T]he liberty of one person ends when he causes harm to another. Until that point is reached he is free to act as he chooses, and need not take into account the welfare of others." But this argument would seem equally to require rejection of the principles of the law of restitution for benefits conferred without express consent. The man who faints in the street and is treated by a physician who happens to be passing by has not caused harm to another. Yet the law of restitution will force him to pay the physician's fee — for services, and at a price, that he may not have desired and certainly did not agree to buy.

If Epstein had argued merely that restitution was a more efficient approach to the rescue question than tort, I would have no basis for alleging an inconsistency in his theory. The inconsistency lies in the fact that he defends the no-tort-duty rule on personal-autonomy grounds that seem logically incompatible with his willingness to accept the restitution approach. . . .

Epstein, Causation and Corrective Justice: A Reply to Two Critics
8 J. Legal Stud. 477, 490-492 (1979)

. . . There is no difference between restitution and good Samaritan obligations if the *only* concern is the vindication of individual liberty. I do, however, give uneasy endorsement to the restitution obligation because I am *not* an uncompromising libertarian. To my mind there is a crucial distinction between the two cases: the restitution obligation satisfies appropriate conditions for forced exchanges. The tort obligation does not. The differences cannot be found in the transaction costs before suit. But the other criteria are decisive.

Considering first administrative costs, both restitution and tort obligations involve the expense of an additional cause of action, but of extremely different dimensions. In restitution cases the litigable issues are these: the victim's condition of necessity, the provision of services, the intention to collect compensation, and the amount to be collected. The first two questions are simple enough. The third, the intention to collect, can usually be resolved by a presumption that a professional expects a fee for his services while the casual rescuer does not. The fee then can usually be set by looking at customary charges, complicated by an occasional case of price discrimination and the need to make individualized price determinations for professional salvors.

The proposed good Samaritan course of action presents a wholly different picture. First, *which* persons are subject to the obligation? This is of course not a sticking point in the usual tort case, as causation principles quickly identify the relevant actors; nor is it a sticking point in the usual restitution case because it is easy enough to pick out the person who in fact provided the services. Yet with rescue cases it is uncertain how wide to cast the net. To all persons who are in the vicinity (how defined?) of the victim? To all persons who have the means and ability to rescue him? To all persons who see the problem which they then avoid? The point is by no means trivial because it could well be that many *separate* individuals can be brought into the suit for the losses suffered by a given victim. Joint negative causation is no small puzzle.

Second, what *standard* of liability should be imposed upon persons exposed to judicial sanction? Here a strict liability standard is clearly absurd. Everyone is liable, for if costs are irrelevant then *anybody* might have rescued the victim. A negligence test might seem more inviting, but there is a real reluctance, shared by both Ames and Posner, to impose reasonable-man standards upon individuals who are required to rescue in circumstances not of their own making. And what do we do with insanity and the like, which are often defenses, even in a negligence system? A standard of "little inconvenience or cost" is often proposed, which is more than a de minimis standard yet falls short of the usual Hand formulation of the negligence rule. It has no obvious efficiency appeal and raises questions of degree in individual cases.

Third, what of *causation*? It is true that we cannot talk of the use of force, but it is still necessary to ask whether the rescue could have prevented the loss in question. The whole issue is counterfactual, and in the end demands that we know just *how much* effort should have been expended in the rescue effort.

Fourth, what is the role of the *plaintiff's conduct*? Do we allow some defense based upon the plaintiff's conduct to bar or diminish recovery? If we do not, then we place the defendant in a good Samaritan case in a worse position than the defendant in the ordinary tort action. If we do, then we have to litigate each of the elements of the defense when the original burdens are hard to set and the evidence hard to evaluate.

We can quickly deal with the compensation question. Restitution actions, as noted, involve only small payments in wealth while the tort actions involve enormous ones. In the restitution case there is a strong probability that *both* parties to the transaction *are better off* if the forced exchange is allowed to take place. It is here that imitating the market makes some sense, at least with professionals in one-to-one situations. Although the exchange is forced, it is beneficial to both parties ex ante, and, where services are success-ful, ex post as well. The proposed tort obligation is a different matter, because the only possible compensation is implicit, with each rescuer having the right to demand rescue from his victim in the event that he is faced by imminent peril. It seems highly improbable that the rescuer today will be rescued by his victim tomorrow. Indeed given the variations in aptitudes, strengths, habits, and the like, the differential wealth impact of a uniform rescue obligation is apt to be enormous. We have a "mutual protective arrangement" to be sure, but one on very unfair terms given the uneven distribution of benefits and burdens. There is no case within my framework then for allowing the tort obligation to be imposed. The differences between restitution and tort may be "differences in degree" but so in a sense are the differences between murder and petty theft. All violations of the autonomy principle are not equally severe or deserving of the same response. . . .

Hurley v. Eddingfield
156 Ind. 416, 59 N.E. 1058 (1901)

BAKER, J. The appellant sued appellee for $10,000 damages for wrong-fully causing the death of his intestate. The court sustained appellee's demur-rer to the complaint, and this ruling is assigned as error.

The material facts alleged may be summarized thus: At and for years before decedent's death appellee was a practicing physician at Mace, in Montgomery county, duly licensed under the laws of the state. He held himself out to the public as a general practitioner of medicine. He had been decedent's family physician. Decedent became dangerously ill, and sent for appellee. The messenger informed appellee of decedent's violent sickness, tendered him his fee for his services, and stated to him that no other physi-cian was procurable in time, and that decedent relied on him for attention. No other physician was procurable in time to be of any use, and decedent did rely on appellee for medical assistance. Without any reason whatever, appel-lee refused to render aid to decedent. No other patients were requiring appellee's immediate service, and he could have gone to the relief of dece-dent if he had been willing to do so. Death ensued, without decedent's fault, and wholly from appellee's wrongful act. The alleged wrongful act was appel-lee's refusal to enter into a contract of employment. Counsel do not contend that, before the enactment of the law regulating the practice of medicine, physicians were bound to render professional service to every one who ap-plied. The act regulating the practice of medicine provides for a board of examiners, standards of qualification, examinations, licenses to those found qualified, and penalties for practicing without license. The act is a preventive, not a compulsive, measure. In obtaining the state's license (permission) to practice medicine, the state does not require, and the licensee does not engage, that he will practice at all or on other terms than he may choose to accept. Counsel's analogies, drawn from the obligations to the public on the part of innkeepers, common carriers, and the like, are beside the mark. Judgment affirmed.

Notes

1. Did the court in *Hurley* give sufficient weight to the allegation that plaintiff's decedent had relied on defendant's being willing to treat him for the tendered fee under the circumstances alleged? If defendant induced this reliance, would plaintiff have had a cause of action for breach of contract under modern contract law? See §90(1) of the Second Restatement of Contracts (promissory estoppel).* What damages would be obtainable in such an action?

2. Is the number of doctors in Mace, Indiana a relevant fact?

3. Did defendant violate the Hippocratic Oath? A bit archaic, but still administered to graduating students at most medical schools, the Hipprocatic Oath reads as follows:

> I will look upon him who shall have taught me this Art even as one of my parents. I will share my substance with him, and I will supply his necessities, if he be in need. I will regard his offspring even as my own brethren, and I will teach them this Art, if they would learn it, without fee or covenant. I will impart this Art by precept, by lecture and by every mode of teaching, not only to my own sons but to the sons of him who has taught me, and to disciples bound by covenant and oath, according to the Law of Medicine.
>
> The regimen I adopt shall be for the benefit of my patients according to my ability and judgment, and not for their hurt or for any wrong. I will give no deadly drug to any, though it be asked of me, nor will I counsel such, and especially I will not aid a woman to procure abortion. Whatsoever house I enter, there will I go for the benefit of the sick, refraining from all wrongdoing or corruption, and especially from any act of seduction, of male or female, of bond or free. Whatsoever things I see or hear concerning the life of men, in my attendance on the sick or even apart therefrom, which ought not to be noised abroad, I will keep silence thereon, counting such things to be as sacred secrets.

4. In Wilmington General Hospital v. Manlove, 54 Del. 15, 174 A.2d 135 (1961), plaintiff's decedent, a four-month-old child, died after being refused admission to the emergency room at defendant's hospital. The court stated that although the hospital (which was private) was under no legal obligation to maintain an emergency ward,

*Section 90(1) provides: "A promise which the promisor should reasonably expect to induce action or forbearance on the part of the promisee or a third person and which does induce such action or forbearance is binding if injustice can be avoided only by enforcement of the promise. The remedy granted for the breach may by limited as justice requires."

the maintenance of such a ward to render first-aid to injured persons has become a well-established adjunct to the main business of a hospital. If a person, seriously hurt, applies for such aid at an emergency ward, relying on the established custom to render it, is it still the right of the hospital to turn him away without any reason? In such a case, it seems to us, such a refusal might well result in worsening the condition of the injured person, because of the time lost in a useless attempt to obtain medical aid.

Id. at 23, 174 A.2d at 139. The court held, however, that the duty to admit was limited to cases of "unmistakable emergency" and remanded to the trial court for determination whether this was such a case. See also Guerrero v. Copper Queen Hospital, 112 Ariz. 104, 537 P.2d 1329 (1975).

What is likely to be the effect of *Manlove* on the number of hospital emergency rooms?

4. Could the established-custom approach of *Manlove* have been used in *Hurley* to decide the case in plaintiff's favor?

Randolph's Admr. v. Snyder
139 Ky. 159, 129 S.W. 562 (1910)

HOBSON, J. William Randolph brought this suit on December 16, 1908, against Dr. S. B. Snyder, alleging in his petition that he was a miner in the service of the Cook Jellico Coal mine; and, in connection with the other miners, had made a contract on April 21, 1908, with the defendant by which in consideration of $1 a month paid by each of them through the company's office the defendant agreed to treat each of them and his family as a physician, and would come when called for or send another physician instead; that when the contract was in force on September 29, 1908, his infant child Walter Randolph fell into the fire and got seriously burned, and he called upon the defendant to visit the child, and this he failed and refused to do, or to send another physician in his stead; that by reason of this his child suffered and finally died to his damage in the sum of $10,000, for which he prayed judgment. The defendant filed a motion that the plaintiff be required to elect which cause of action set up in his petition he would prosecute. . . . The plaintiff elected to prosecute the action for the tort. The court then allowed the amended petition to be filed. In the amended petition the plaintiff alleged that . . . when the child was hurt the injuries were painful, but were with proper treatment and care on the part of the physician by no means mortal; that he immediately sent for the doctor and he came and undertook to treat the child; that the child lingered and suffered much agony, and that the defendant treated the injuries in a negligent and unskillful manner and so caused the child to die. . . .

If the defendant made a contract with the plaintiff to treat him and his family as alleged in the petition and amended petition, and simply broke the contract by refusing to come when sent for or to undertake the case, the right of action would be simply for the breach of the contract, and there would be no right of action in tort. But if the physician came and undertook the case and having undertaken it, was negligent in his treatment, then a cause of action in tort may be maintained for the nonperformance of the duty which the law cast upon him when he undertook to treat the case. The rule has often been applied in the case of innkeepers, carriers, attorneys, physicians, etc. They all rest upon the same ground. The plaintiff having elected to sue in tort must recover, if at all, on the latter ground. . . .

Notes

1. Why did plaintiff decide to pursue his tort rather than his contract remedy? Assuming the contract required defendant to treat plaintiff's decedent competently, could plaintiff have obtained the same damages as in a tort action for negligent treatment?

2. Go back a step: Why was plaintiff required to choose between his tort and contract remedies? Why could he not have pursued both remedies, so long as he did not receive duplicate damages?

Prosser has a good summary of the considerations bearing on whether to elect one's tort or one's contract remedy, and the limitations on one's freedom to elect in cases where the facts might support either kind of action.

> Where on the facts either an action in contract or one in tort is open to the plaintiff, his choice may have important consequences. Some considerations may lead the plaintiff to prefer action on the contract. A contract may lead to strict liability for failure to perform, as in the case of a physician's undertaking to cure his patient, where the tort action would require proof of negligence or some other wrongful conduct. A shorter statute of limitations may bar the tort action, or it may not survive the death of one of the parties. Some immunities, such as those of municipal corporations or charities, may prevent recovery in tort, but not in contract. The damages recoverable on the contract may sometimes be greater, to the extent that they give the plaintiff the benefit of the bargain made, rather than compensation for a loss. A contract claim may be assignable where a tort claim is not, or an inferior court may have jurisdiction over it, or the venue may offer more latitude, or the contract suit may open the way to remedies such as attachment or summary judgment, or be available as a set-off or counterclaim, where the other remedy would not. Finally, the plaintiff may by his own conduct so far have accepted and affirmed the contract as to be bound by it, to the exclusion of tort remedies he might otherwise have had.
>
> Generally speaking, the tort remedy is likely to be more advantageous to the injured party in the greater number of cases, if only because it will so often permit the recovery of greater damages. Under the rule of Hadley v. Baxendale,

the damages recoverable for breach of contract are limited to those within the contemplation of the defendant at the time the contract was made, and in some jurisdictions, at least, to those for which the defendant has tacitly agreed to assume responsibility. They may be further limited by the contract itself, where a tort action might avoid the limitation. In contract actions, other than those for breach of promise to marry, punitive damages are not allowed, and there can ordinarily be no recovery for mental suffering. In the tort action the only limitations are those of "proximate cause," and the policy which denies recovery to certain types of interests themselves.

The tort action may offer other advantages. It may permit recovery for wrongful death, for which a contract action normally will not lie. It may be open where the contract fails for lack of proof, for uncertainty, for illegality, for want of consideration, or because of the statute of frauds or the parol evidence rule. It may sometimes avoid some defenses, such as infancy or a discharge in bankruptcy; and it may avoid some counterclaims. It may avoid the necessity of joining several defendants, or permit successive actions for multiple breaches of a single contract, or the application of a favorable rule under the conflict of laws.

Frequently, where either tort or contract will lie and inconsistent rules of law apply to the two actions, the question arises whether the plaintiff may elect freely which he will bring, or whether the court must itself decide that on the facts pleaded and proved the "gist" or "gravamen" of his cause of action is one or the other. As to this the decisions are in considerable confusion, and it is difficult to generalize.

Where the particular point at issue is one of adjective law only, affecting the suit or its procedure, but not the merits of the cause of action, the courts have tended to be quite liberal in giving the plaintiff his freedom of choice, and have upheld his action of tort or contract as he has seen fit to bring it. Likewise where the point is one affecting substantive rights, but the claim is one for damages to property or to pecuniary interests only, the tendency has been, with some occasional dissent, to allow the election. But when the claim is one for personal injury, the decision usually has been that the gravamen of the action is the misconduct and the damage, and that it is essentially one of tort, which the plaintiff cannot alter by his pleading. This has the odd result that the negligence of an attorney will survive the death of his client, while that of a physician is oft interred with his patient's bones.

Prosser 618-622 (footnotes omitted).

3. Suppose a doctor is having dinner in a restaurant when someone at a neighboring table begins to choke. The doctor rushes to his assistance, treats him, and is later sued for having done so negligently. Is the doctor liable for negligence in these circumstances? The general answer is yes, the rationale being that the negligent good Samaritan deprives the person he assists of the opportunity to be helped instead by a careful good Samaritan. See, e.g., Farwell v. Keaton, 396 Mich. 281, 240 N.W.2d 217 (1976). This reasoning has seemed artificial where, as is often the case, there is no other good Samaritan in position to assist the injured person. But in such a case, if the good Samaritan's carelessness does not make the injured person any worse off than

if he had not tried to help him in the first place, ordinary principles of causation should protect the good Samaritan from liability. The law is unclear on this point, however. For example, "it is possible that a court may hold that one who has thrown rope to a drowning man, pulled him half way to shore, and then unreasonably abandoned the effort and left him to drown, is liable even though there were no other possible sources of aid, and the situation is made no worse than it was." Second Restatement of Torts §323, Comment e.'

A number of states have passed laws, called "good Samaritan" laws, exempting the physician or other health professional who renders emergency assistance from liability for ordinary negligence. Are these laws a good thing? Are they necessary given the right of the professional who renders emergency assistance to a stranger to be compensated under principles of restitution? Do you see any resemblance to the public-necessity doctrine in the law of intentional torts discussed in Chapter 3?

Turbeville v. Mobile Light & R. Co.
221 Ala. 91, 127 So. 519 (1930)

Count 10A, to which a demurrer was sustained, to construe it most strongly against the pleader, as must be done on demurrer, alleges that plaintiff's intestate was upon the defendant's track upon which the defendant through its servants was operating a street car; that said car, without negligence on the part of the defendant's servants, was brought to a stop upon or against the body of said intestate, and "the safety guard attached to said car fell across the body of the said Earl Y. Turbeville with heavy pressure and was suffocating him; that said servants of the defendant in charge of said car having knowledge of the perilous situation of plaintiff's intestate under said car, as aforesaid, and while acting within the line and scope of their employment, negligently failed to back said car from or to lift the front end of said car off of the body of the said Earl Y. Turbeville, although there was ample time to have done so and saved the life of the said Earl Y. Turbeville; and that as a proximate consequence of said negligence the said Earl Y. Turbeville was killed."

These averments put plaintiff's intestate in the attitude of a trespasser who through his own negligence is placed in a position of imminent peril, without fault or negligence on the part of the defendant or its servants.

While it may be conceded that these circumstances imposed on those present the duty, from the standpoint of common humanity, to use their best judgment in doing what they could to relieve the unfortunate victim from his peril, we know of no principle of municipal law that imposed on the defendant or its servants a legal duty to relieve him by backing the car off his body or lifting it up so as to relieve his peril. It certainly could not be said that such duty rested on a mere bystander who witnessed his misfortune and who was in no way legally responsible for his predicament. If this be so, what reason can be found in the law to say that the defendant or its servants were under duty to act, when they were guilty of no wrong or negligence in producing or bringing about the unfortunate situation? . . .

While it must be conceded that the defendant's servants in charge of the street car were under duty to the defendant to remove the plaintiff's intestate from the track so that they might proceed, if this could be done without inflicting further injury on him, and in doing so would be acting within the line and scope of their employment, if, in discharging this duty, they negligently caused or accelerated the death of plaintiff's intestate, the company would be liable.

But mere failure of the servants of the defendant in charge of the street car, after it had been stopped by them, to take prompt steps to extricate plaintiff's intestate from his perilous situation under the safety guard, brought about solely by his own negligence, and without negligence on the part of defendant's servants, there being no legal duty on the part of the defendant to so extricate him, was, as a matter of law, not an act or omission within the line and scope of their employment. . . .

[In also holding that the facts of the case did not bring it within the scope of the "discovered trespasser" doctrine, the court mentioned these additional facts.]

Though it was not material to the issues formed by the pleadings, the evidence further shows, that defendant's servants, with the aid of others, took prompt steps to remove plaintiff's intestate from under the safety guard, requiring from five to fifteen minutes to do so. The only physical evidence of injury was that there were some slight scratches or bruises on his face and chest. He expired shortly after he was taken from under the car, only breathed once or twice after his removal.

There was no evidence tending to show that said intestate was in any way injured in removing his body from under the safety guard. . . .

Notes

1. What difference should it make whether the defendant's employees injured plaintiff's decedent while removing him from under the safety guard? Suppose that instead of taking prompt steps to remove him they had blocked other people from removing him. Would that have been actionable negligence?

2. Can the result in *Turbeville* be distinguished from the result in the *Montgomery* case discussed by Professor Epstein? How would he have decided *Turbeville*?

3. Turbeville had been a passenger on the streetcar until 15-30 minutes before the accident. He had boarded in an obviously drunken condition, and

when he left the car he "manifested his drunken condition by standing in the way of the car until he was requested by the motorman to move, and by other acts of indecent behavior." 223 Ala. at 94, 127 So. at 522. He must afterward have stumbled back onto the tracks because he was lying there, at the place he had left the car, when the streetcar came back on its return trip. Compare Fagg's Admr. v. Louisville & N.R. Co., 111 Ky. 30, 63 S.W. 580 (1901), where defendant was held liable for the death of a drunken trespasser whom it ejected from its freight train at a point where it knew that a passenger train was due to pass over the same track soon; the passenger train came and ran over him. The court remarked (id. at 40, 63 S.W. at 583):

> It would be a strange doctrine of ethics and of law if an unfortunate man, on a dark, cold night, in a drunken and helpless condition, is on the track of a railway company in a deep cut, and that fact is known to the superintendent, together with the knowledge that a passenger train will soon pass over the track through the tunnel, and will probably kill him, that the company is not responsible if its superintendent could have avoided the injury by the exercise of ordinary care, and failed to do so.

Is *Fagg's Admr.* consistent with *Turbeville*?

4. Why couldn't the plaintiff in *Turbeville* have argued that the defendant had the "last clear chance" to avoid or at least reduce the injury to him? Is the case distinguishable from *Kumkumian* in Chapter 5? What about the doctrine of avoidable consequences mentioned in that chapter in connection with the seat-belt cases?

5. The tendency of the modern law is to require one who creates, even if nonnegligently, a peril to another to render assistance to him. See, e.g., South v. National Railroad Passenger Corp., 290 N.W.2d 819 (N. D. 1980); Prosser 342-343; Second Restatement of Torts, §322. Criminal statutes in several states require the driver of a car involved in an accident to aid anyone injured in the accident, even if the accident was not the result of negligence on the part of the driver; violation of the statute may expose the driver to tort liability. See, e.g., Brooks v. E.J. Willig Truck Transp. Co., 40, Cal. 2d 669, 255 P.2d 802 (1953). Are these exceptions to the common-law "no duty to rescue" rule economically defensible?

Yania v. Bigan
397 Pa. 316, 155 A.2d 343 (1959)

JONES, J.

A bizarre and most unusual circumstance provides the background of this appeal [from dismissal of the complaint].

On September 25, 1957 John E. Bigan was engaged in a coal strip-mining operation in Shade Township, Somerset County. On the property being stripped were large cuts or trenches created by Bigan when he removed the earthen overburden for the purpose of removing the coal underneath. One cut contained water 8 to 10 feet in depth with side walls or embankments 16 to 18 feet in height; at this cut Bigan had installed a pump to remove the water.

At approximately 4 P.M. on that date, Joseph F. Yania, the operator of another coal strip-mining operation, and one Boyd M. Ross went upon Bigan's property for the purpose of discussing a business matter with Bigan, and, while there, were asked by Bigan to aid him in starting the pump. Ross and Bigan entered the cut and stood at the point where the pump was located. Yania stood at the top of one of the cut's side walls and then jumped from the side wall — a height of 16 to 18 feet — into the water and was drowned. . . .

. . . Bigan stands charged with three-fold negligence: (1) by urging, enticing, taunting and inveigling Yania to jump into the water; (2) by failing to warn Yania of a dangerous condition on the land, i.e. the cut wherein lay 8 to 10 feet of water; (3) by failing to go to Yania's rescue after he had jumped into the water.[1] . . .

Appellant initially contends that Yania's descent from the high embankment into the water and the resulting death were caused "entirely" by the spoken words and blandishments of Bigan delivered at a distance from Yania. The complaint does not allege that Yania slipped or that he was pushed or that Bigan made any *physical* impact upon Yania. On the contrary, the only inference deducible from the facts alleged in the complaint is that Bigan, by the employment of cajolery and inveiglement, caused such a *mental* impact on Yania that the latter was deprived of his volition and freedom of choice and placed under a compulsion to jump into the water. Had Yania been a child of tender years or a person mentally deficient then it is conceivable that taunting and enticement could constitute actionable negligence if it resulted in harm. However, to contend that such conduct directed to an adult in possession of all his mental faculties constitutes actionable negligence is not only without precedent but completely without merit. . . .

Appellant next urges that Bigan, as the possessor of the land, violated a duty owed to Yania in that his land contained a dangerous condition, i.e. the waterfilled cut or trench, and he failed to warn Yania of such condition. Yania was a business invitee. . . .

The *only* condition on Bigan's land which could possibly have contributed in any manner to Yania's death was the waterfilled cut with its high embankment. . . . If this cut possessed any potentiality of danger, such a condition was as obvious and apparent to Yania as to Bigan, both coal strip-

---

1. So far as the record is concerned we must treat the 33 year old Yania as in full possession of his mental faculties at the time he jumped.

mine operators. Under the circumstances herein depicted Bigan could not be held liable in this respect.

Lastly, it is urged that Bigan failed to take the necessary steps to rescue Yania from the water. The mere fact that Bigan saw Yania in a position of peril in the water imposed upon him no legal, although a moral, obligation or duty to go to his rescue unless Bigan was legally responsible, in whole or in part, for placing Yania in the perilous position.... The complaint does not aver any facts which impose upon Bigan legal responsibility for placing Yania in the dangerous position in the water and, absent such legal responsibility, the law imposes on Bigan no duty of rescue.... Yania, a reasonable and prudent adult in full possession of all his mental faculties, undertook to perform an act which he knew or should have known was attended with more or less peril and it was the performance of that act and not any conduct upon Bigan's part which caused his unfortunate death.

Order affirmed.

Notes

1. Don't the allegations of the complaint suggest that Yania was not a "reasonable and prudent adult in full possession of all his mental faculties"? Suppose Bigan taunted Yania to jump, knowing that Yania was excitable and foolhardy and desiring Yania to drown. Would Bigan then be guilty of an intentional tort? Of which intentional tort would he be guilty?

2. Even if Bigan was not culpable for having induced Yania to jump and place himself in peril, wasn't Bigan at least a cause of that peril and hence obliged under §322 of the Restatement to render aid to him, at least if he could do so without serious danger to himself? How would Professor Epstein answer this question?

3. Notice that plaintiff did not join Ross as a defendant, though presumably Ross was also in a position to render aid to Yania after he jumped into the water. The fact that Ross was not sued is some evidence that the principle that a pure bystander has no duty to rescue is well established in the common law. All of the cases involve efforts to show that the defendant was more than a pure bystander. However, as mentioned in an earlier reading in this chapter, Vermont has a statute imposing a general duty to rescue. Passed in 1967, this statute, Vt. Stat. Ann. §519(a) (1973), reads as follows:

> A person who knows that another is exposed to grave physical harm shall, to the extent that the same can be rendered without danger or peril to himself or without interference with important duties to others, give reasonable assistance to the exposed person unless that assistance or care is being provided by others.

Section 519(c) provides a maximum fine of $100 for willful violation of subsection (a). No tort cases have been reported under these provisions. See generally Franklin, Vermont Requires Rescue: A Comment, 25 Stan. L. Rev. 51 (1972). Interestingly, §519(b) provides:

> A person who provides reasonable assistance in compliance with subsection (a) of this section shall not be liable in civil damages unless his acts constitute gross negligence or unless he will receive or expects to receive remuneration. Nothing contained in this subsection shall alter existing law with respect to tort liability of a practitioner of the healing arts for acts committed in the ordinary course of his practice.

Is the first sentence of subsection (b) necessary or appropriate from an incentive standpoint? What is the purpose and force of the second sentence?

4. In Thomas v. Casey, 49 Wash. 2d 14, 297 P.2d 614 (1956), defendant Foster had run his car into a ditch; defendants Casey and Callahan, who were driving by in their pickup truck, offered to help him. There was no request for aid by Foster, and no offer of compensation; the offer of assistance was a purely voluntary gesture. In attempting to tow Foster's car out of the ditch, Casey and Callahan blocked the westbound traffic lane of the highway with their truck and failed to warn adequately the oncoming westbound traffic. Plaintiff's truck was part of that traffic and collided with the Casey truck. Casey and Callahan were held negligent as a matter of law. The hard question was whether Foster was also negligent although (because) he did nothing. The court held that he was negligent too.

> We cannot agree that, under the circumstances, Foster owed no duty to the plaintiffs and other users of the highway. The highway was being obstructed in his presence and for his benefit, with no flares, fuses, or other adequate method of warning oncoming traffic in the blocked traffic lane. Whether, under such circumstances, he could have delegated the performance of his duty to safeguard other users of the highway to Casey and Callahan had they in fact been independent contractors, is likewise not a matter for our present concern. They were not independent contractors; they were but volunteers. *Foster at all times had possession and control of his car.* He could have, and admitted that he would have, stopped Casey and Callahan from doing anything that threatened to damage his car. He testified that he watched carefully to make certain that Callahan did not back the truck into his car. He could have and should have refused to permit them to use methods which he knew to be negligent and unlawful in the attempt to remove his car from the ditch. . . . In the light of his testimony that he was doing nothing useful except during the actual attempt at towing, he could at least have gone eastward and signalled approaching traffic with a flashlight. Doing nothing when action is demanded can constitute negligence. We do not hold that this would have absolved him from negligence in permitting Casey and Callahan to proceed as they were doing, but it might have prevented the collision. We mention the fact that he did not give a warning merely to emphasize the lack of any attempt on his part to warn westbound traffic of a dangerous situation, which it was clearly his duty to do, particularly

if, as he insists, he rendered no "substantial assistance" to Casey and Callahan by remaining where he was.

49 Wash. 2d at 18-19, 297 P.2d at 617. Could plaintiff in *Yania* have relied on this case?

Osterlind v. Hill
263 Mass. 73, 160 N.E. 301 (1928)

BRALEY, J. This is an action of tort, brought by the plaintiff as administrator of the estate of Albert T. Osterlind to recover damages for the conscious suffering and death of his intestate. . . . The first count of the original declaration alleges that, on or about July 4, 1925, the defendant was engaged in the business of letting for hire pleasure boats and canoes to be used on Lake Quannapowitt in the town of Wakefield; that it was the duty of the defendant to have a reasonable regard for the safety of the persons to whom he let boats and canoes; that the defendant, in the early morning of July 4, 1925, in willful, wanton, or reckless disregard of the natural and probable consequences, let for hire, to the intestate and one Ryan, a frail and dangerous canoe, well knowing that the intestate and Ryan were then intoxicated, and were then manifestly unfit to go upon the lake in the canoe; that, in consequence of the defendant's willful, wanton, or reckless disregard of his duties, the intestate and Ryan went out in the canoe, which shortly afterwards was overturned and the intestate, after hanging to it for approximately one-half hour, and making loud calls for assistance, which calls the defendant heard and utterly ignored, was obliged to release his hold, and was drowned; that in consequence of the defendant's willful, wanton, or reckless conduct the intestate endured great conscious mental anguish and great conscious physical suffering from suffocation and drowning. Count 2 differs materially from count 1 only in so far as negligent conduct is alleged as distinguished from willful, wanton, or reckless conduct. In count 3 the acts of the defendant set forth in the previous counts are relied upon as stating a cause of action for death as a result of the defendant's willful, wanton, or reckless conduct. The amended declaration adds allegations to the effect that the plaintiff's intestate and Ryan were intoxicated and incapacitated to enter into any valid contract or to exercise any care for their own safety and that the condition of the intestate was involuntary and induced through no fault of his own.

The trial court sustained demurrers to both the original and amended declarations and reported the case for the determination of this court. . . .

. . . The declaration must set forth facts which, if proved, establish the breach of a legal duty owed by the defendant to the intestate. The plaintiff relies on Black v. New York, New Haven & Hartford Railroad, 193 Mass. 448, 79 N.E. 797, as here establishing such a duty on the part of the defendant. In that case the jury would have been justified in finding that the plaintiff was "so intoxicated as to be incapable of standing or walking or caring for himself in any way. . . ." There was testimony to the effect that, "when he fell, he did not seize hold of anything, his arms were at his side." The defendant's employees placed a helpless man, a man impotent to protect himself, in a dangerous position.

In the case at bar, however, it is alleged in every count of the original and amended declaration that after the canoe was overturned the intestate hung to the canoe for approximately one-half hour and made loud calls for assistance. On the facts stated in the declaration the intestate was not in a helpless condition. He was able to take steps to protect himself. The defendant violated no legal duty in renting a canoe to a man in the condition of the intestate. The allegation appearing in each count of the amended declaration that the intestate was incapacitated to enter into any valid contract states merely a legal conclusion. The allegations, therefore, in the counts of the amended declaration to the effect that the intestate was incapable of exercising any care for his own safety is controlled by the allegations in the same counts that he hung to the side of the canoe for approximately one-half hour, calling for assistance.

In view of the absence of any duty to refrain from renting a canoe to a person in the condition of the intestate, the allegations of involuntary intoxication relating as they do to the issues of contributory negligence become immaterial. The allegations of willful, wanton or reckless conduct also add nothing to the plaintiff's case. The failure of the defendant to respond to the intestate's outcries is immaterial. No legal right of the intestate was infringed. The allegation common to both declarations that the canoe was "frail and dangerous" appears to be a general characterization of canoes. It is not alleged that the canoe was out of repair and unsafe.

It follows that the order sustaining each demurrer is affirmed.

Notes

1. Could it not be argued that there was an implicit contract, based on custom, that the proprietor would assist his customer in such an emergency, at least if he could do so without risk to himself? Does the economist's point, that potential liability may deter people from embarking on activities where they could be called upon to attempt rescues, apply when there is a business relationship of the kind involved in this case?

2. Compare the facts of Allen v. Hixson, 111 Ga. 460, 36 S.E. 810 (1900). The plaintiff was a young woman employed to operate a machine appropriately called a "mangle" in defendant's laundry. Noticing that the machine was not working properly, she called over her superintendent. In the course of showing him what was wrong she caught her hand and wrist in the mangle, allegedly because of a hidden defect in it. She further alleged that defendant

Hotel Mangle.

Indispensable to the economical management of any hotel or public institution.

No. 16750. These are our heavy machines, and are especially adapted for use in hotels, laundries and institutes. They are built to sustain great pressure and are reinforced in all parts exposed to wear or strain. They are double geared, making the action of the rolls positive, and, being fitted with our combination driving gears, are very light running. The machines are mounted on casters, and can be easily moved from place to place, and when not in use are readily set out of the way, occupying but little more room than a sewing machine.

The gears are covered with a handsome guard, preventing the possibility of any danger to the operator.

Our patent automatic table adjustment (furnished only with our mangles) is a very desirable feature in a machine of this kind, being convenient and secure for shipping, and makes the machines always ready for use. The tables, being permanently attached to the machine, are not knocked about and marred or misplaced when needed.

For use it is only necessary to raise the tables parallel with the rolls, and our device automatically secures them firmly into that position. In lowering them they are raised about ten degrees, which releases the lock and they can be lowered to the side of the machine.

Made in Two Sizes.

	Floor space.	Shipping weight.	Price.
Rolls 28 in. long, 6 in. diam.	23x34 in.	275 lbs.	$37.50
Rolls 24 in. long, 6 in. diam.	23x30 in.	260 lbs.	31.50

We can furnish these machines with tight and loose pulleys for power in place of hand wheel if desired at $12.00 extra. Power machines bolted to the floor.

Courtesy of Chelsea House Publishers
Reprinted from the *1897 Sears Roebuck Catalogue,* 1968

negligently allowed her hand and wrist to remain in the machine for half an hour, thereby aggravating her injury. The court held she was not entitled to damages for either the original injury or the aggravation thereof.

> [T]he master was under no duty of protecting her against injuries received while she was, as a mere volunteer, endeavoring to accomplish something entirely outside the scope of her employment. The act which caused her injury was certainly one of this kind; for, in taking hold of the unwrapped cloth for the purpose of showing the superintendent the condition of the machine, she volunteered to perform a service not required of her, and therefore necessarily acted upon her own responsibility and at her own risk. It makes no difference that the machine had a defective part of which she was ignorant, for its existence could not, on the occasion referred to in her petition, have been the source of injury to her, if she had confined herself to the performance of the duties pertaining to the service for which she was employed. As will have been seen, the plaintiff was an adult, and actually knew when she first approached the machine that it was out of order. Recognizing the danger of attempting to operate it in that condition, she prudently refrained from so doing, and made a prompt report to the superintendent in regard to the matter. Unfortunately, however, she did not continue to exercise the same degree of prudence when she went outside the scope of her duties, and, without any direction or request on his part, volunteered to assist him in ascertaining precisely the extent and character of the derangement which had brought about the condition in which she had found the machine.
>
> As to so much of the petition as claims damages because the "defendant negligently allowed petitioner's hand and wrist to remain between said roller and bar," or because of the defendant's "negligently failing . . . to effect her release," we do not think a good cause of action is set forth. When an employe, without fault on the master's part, becomes placed in a dangerous or painful situation, the master is under no positive legal duty of exercising all reasonable care and diligence to effect such employe's speedy release. Being in no way responsible for the unfortunate occurrence, the master cannot be said to be guilty of a tort if he does not promptly take active steps in coming to the rescue. The only duty arising under such circumstances is one of humanity, and for a breach thereof the law does not, so far as we are informed, impose any liability.

Id. at 463, 36 S.E. at 810. In Carey v. Davis, 190 Iowa 720, 180 N.W. 889 (1921), plaintiff had a sunstroke while employed by defendants in excavating a gravel pit, and defendants allegedly "caused him to be removed and laid in a wagon box at or near the place where he had been at work and left there in an even more exposed condition, unattended and without care or protection, for a period of four hours or more." The court held that an action would lie for his employers' failure to care for him, stating:

> There is no allegation or claim that the faintness or prostration of the plaintiff was caused or in any manner produced by the neglect or misconduct of the defendants. So far as the pleading goes, the cause of his ailment is entirely

unknown, a misfortune for which damages are recoverable from no one. If there be any failure of legal duty alleged, it is in the charge that plaintiff being stricken down and rendered helpless while in the defendants' service, and upon their premises and in their presence, it became their duty to render him the needed aid and relief. Did such legal duty arise under the alleged circumstances? It is unquestionably the well-settled general rule that, in the absence of any agreement or contract therefor, the master is under no legal duty to care for a sick or injured servant for whose illness or injury he is not at fault. Though not unjust in principle, this rule, if carried unflinchingly and without exception to its logical extreme, is sometimes productive of shocking results. To avoid this criticism there is a tendency of the courts to hold that, where in the course of his employment a servant suffers serious injury or is suddenly stricken down in a manner indicating the immediate and emergent need of aid to save him from death or serious harm, the master, if present, is in duty bound to take such reasonable measures or make such reasonable effort as may be practicable to relieve him, even though such master be not chargeable with fault in bringing about the emergency.

Id. at 722, 180 N.W. at 890. Is this a rejection of *Allen*, or can the cases be distinguished? In either case, could plaintiff have argued that defendant did not merely fail to render aid, but made his (her) injury worse? Is *Carey* consistent with *Osterlind*? Is *Allen* consistent with Eckert v. Long Island R. Co.?

3. The court in *Carey* relied on DePue v. Flateau, 100 Minn. 299, 111 N.W. 1 (1907), which it summarized as follows:

plaintiff called at the home of the defendant on a business errand and accepted an invitation to dinner. As evening came on, he was suddenly taken sick and requested the privilege to remain overnight; but this was refused. Defendant thereupon helped the plaintiff into his cutter and started him in the direction of his home. Plaintiff had ridden but a short distance when he fell from his vehicle into the snow, where he lay all night before he was rescued in a badly frozen condition. Having brought suit for damages, it was contended for defense that defendant was under no duty to entertain or keep the plaintiff in his own home, and the obligation he was under, if any, was moral only, and for a breach thereof no action would lie. This contention was overruled and plaintiff allowed to recover. The court there says:

"The case falls within 'the more comprehensive principle that whenever a person is placed in such a position with regard to another that it is obvious that, if he does not use due care in his own conduct, he will cause injury to that person, the duty at once arises to exercise care commensurate with the situation in which he thus finds himself ... to avoid such danger, and a negligent failure to perform the duty renders him liable for the consequences of his negligence.'"

Now it is true that the cited case does not involve the relation of master and servant — nor was there any other business relation in which either owed a legal duty to the other — but the plaintiff was rightfully in the defendant's home as a temporary guest, a privilege which ordinarily the defendant could terminate at a moment's notice. The fact, however, that he became suddenly ill and in a condition rendering it unsafe for him to take the road introduced a new factor into the situation charging the defendant with the duty not to expose the sick man to the hazard of perishing in the winter storm.

190 Iowa at 723, 180 N.W. at 891. *Carey* in turn was cited in Hutchinson v. Dickie, 162 F.2d 103 (6th Cir. 1947), where a guest fell over the side of a cabin cruiser and drowned. The court stated (id. at 106):

> We take no stock in appellant's contention that he was under no legal obligation to rescue decedent. Dickie was an invited guest upon appellant's cruiser. When appellant heard the cry "Man Overboard" . . . we think it was his duty to use reasonable care to rescue him. This was certainly a moral duty, universally recognized and acted upon. Dickie was drowning and appellant's cruiser was the only instrumentality by which he might be rescued.

4. In Meador v. Hotel Grover, 193 Miss. 392, 9 So. 2d 782 (1942), plaintiff's decedent (Meador) sustained fatal injuries in an accident that occurred while he was a passenger in defendant's elevator. The complaint had three counts. Count one complained that defendant had maintained the elevator in a defective condition. Count two complained of the alleged wanton and wilful negligence of the elevator operator in failing to stop the elevator promptly when he discovered that Meador had fallen at a place where he was likely to be crushed. Count three was "based upon the humanitarian doctrine that after the injury to decedent the hotel company and its servant, the elevator operator, were under a duty to provide necessary and proper ministration to the injured man by giving or procuring medical aid and comfort, all of which the defendants wilfully and wantonly neglected to do." Id. at 401, 9 So. 2d at 784. The entire court thought that the third count stated a cause of action:

> It was the duty of the hotel company to use reasonable care to see that one injured on its premises and by the operation of its business receives prompt and proper care and treatment to the end that his injuries, however occasioned, may not be aggravated by unnecessary and avoidable delay or inattention.

Id. at 403-404, 9 So. 2d at 785. Two of the judges, however, believed that the first count was insufficient because plaintiff's decedent had gone to the hotel for an unlawful purpose, namely to patronize prostitutes. What cases have you read that indicate the dissenting judges were wrong to dissent on this point? Why did they not also dissent regarding counts two and three?

5. How would you generalize the rule of *Carey, Depue, Hutchinson,* and *Meador*? Are these decisions consistent with *Osterlind*? With *Yania*? With *Allen* and *Turbeville*?

Giles v. Walker
24 Q.B.D. 656 (1890)

Appeal from the Leicester County Court.

The defendant, a farmer, occupied land which had originally been forest land, but which had some years prior to 1883, when the defendant's occupation of it commenced, been brought into cultivation by the then occupier. The forest land prior to cultivation did not bear thistles; but immediately upon its being cultivated thistles sprang up all over it. The defendant neglected to mow the thistles periodically so as to prevent them from seeding, and in the years 1887 and 1888 there were thousands of thistles on his land in full seed. The consequence was that the thistle seeds were blown by the wind in large quantities on to the adjoining land of the plaintiff, where they took root and did damage. The plaintiff sued the defendant for such damage in the county court. The judge left to the jury the question whether the defendant in not cutting the thistles had been guilty of negligence. The jury found that he was negligent, and judgment was accordingly entered for the plaintiff. The defendant appealed.

LORD COLERIDGE, C.J. I never heard of such an action as this. There can be no duty as between adjoining occupiers to cut the thistles, which are the natural growth of the soil. The appeal must be allowed.

LORD ESHER, M.R. I am of the same opinion.

Appeal allowed.

Notes

1. If defendant had dumped his thistles on plaintiff's land, he would presumably have been liable for the damage to plaintiff. Why should it make any difference that he brought about the same result simply by failing to mow them? Was he not the cheaper cost avoider in a Hand formula sense?

2. Whatever its merits, the rule in *Giles*, that there is no liability for damage to one's neighbors caused by natural conditions on one's land, has proved remarkably durable, though some courts now refuse to apply the rule in urban areas. See Prosser 354-356; Mahurin v. Lockhart, 71 Ill. App. 3d 691, 390 N.E.2d 523 (1979). But see Lichtman v. Nadler, 74 App. Div. 2d 66, 426 N.Y.S.2d 628 (1980). Incidentally, was the rule correctly applied in *Giles* itself?

3. Is the basis of *Giles* simply a reluctance to impose liability for nonfeasance as distinct from misfeasance? In this connection, compare Fitzwater v. Sunset Empire, Inc., 263 Or. 276, 502 P.2d 214 (1972). Plaintiff sustained injuries when he slipped and fell on ice on the public sidewalk in front of defendant's restaurant. The court held that defendant owed plaintiff no

common-law duty (even though he was a business invitee) to clear the side-walk. Further, although the defendant was in violation of a municipal ordinance requiring abutting landowners to keep the public sidewalk free of ice and snow, the court held that unlike other municipal safety regulations this one was not intended to create a private action for damages. This is the usual result in such cases. Do Professor Epstein's libertarian grounds for opposing a duty of rescue support the court's decision?

Erie R. Co. v. Stewart
40 F.2d 855 (6th Cir. 1930)

HICKENLOOPER, J.

Stewart, plaintiff below, was a passenger in an automobile truck, sitting on the front seat to the right of the driver, a fellow employee of the East Ohio Gas Company. He recovered a judgment in the District Court for injuries received when the truck was struck by one of the defendant's trains at the 123d Street crossing in the city of Cleveland. Defendant maintained a watchman at this crossing, which was admittedly heavily traveled, but the watchman was either within the shanty or just outside of it as the train approached, and he gave no warning until too late to avoid the accident. . . .

. . . Where the voluntary employment of a watchman was unknown to the traveler upon the highway, the mere absence of such watchman could probably not be considered as negligence toward him as a matter of law, for in such case there is neither an established duty positively owing to such traveler as a member of the general public, nor had he been led into reliance upon the custom. The question would remain simply whether the circumstances demanded such employment. But where the practice is known to the traveler upon the highway, and such traveler has been educated into reliance upon it, some positive duty must rest upon the railway with reference thereto. . . . The company has established for itself a standard of due care while operating its trains across the highway, and, having led the traveler into reliance upon such standard, it should not be permitted thereafter to say that no duty required, arose from or attached to these precautions.

This duty has been recognized as not only actual and positive, but as absolute, in the sense that the practice may not be discontinued without exercising reasonable care to give warning of such discontinuance, although the company may thereafter do all that would otherwise be reasonably necessary. Conceding for the purposes of this opinion that, in cases where a watchman is voluntarily employed by the railway in an abundance of precaution, the duty is not absolute, in the same sense as where it is imposed by statute, still, if there be some duty, it cannot be less than that the company must use reasonable care to see that reliance by members of the educated public upon its representation of safety is not converted into a trap. Responsibility for injury will arise if the service be negligently performed or abandoned without other notice of that fact. If this issue of negligent performance be disputed, the question would still be for the jury under the present concession. But if the evidence in the case justifies only the conclusion of lack of due care, or if the absence of the watchman or the failure to give other notice of his withdrawal be wholly unexplained, so that but one inference may be drawn therefrom, the court is warranted in instructing the jury that, in that particular case, negligence appears as a matter of law.

So, in the present case, the evidence conclusively establishes the voluntary employment of a watchman, knowledge of this fact and reliance upon it by the plaintiff, a duty, therefore, that the company, through the watchman, will exercise reasonable care in warning such travelers as plaintiff, the presence of the watchman thereabouts, and no explanation of the failure to warn. Therefore, even though the duty be considered as qualified, rather than absolute, a prima facie case was established by plaintiff, requiring the defendant to go forward with evidence to rebut the presumption of negligence thus raised, or else suffer a verdict against it on this point. . . . No such evidence was introduced by defendant. No other inference than that of negligence could therefore be drawn from the evidence. . . .

Notes

. 1. If the Erie Railroad would not have been negligent had it never posted a watchman at the crossing where plaintiff was injured, why did it bother to have a watchman? Was it being altruistic? Why is its action in posting a watchman not the strongest possible evidence that failure to have one would have been negligent? If so, is plaintiff's reliance relevant to any issue other than his contributory negligence?

2. Indian Towing Co. v. United States, 350 U.S. 61 (1955), is a clear case where the safety precaution was not required in the first instance to fulfill the defendant's duty of care. This was a suit for damages to a tug and barge that ran aground when, through negligent operation by the Coast Guard of one of its lighthouses, the light was extinguished and no warning was given that the light was not operating properly. The Court held (id. at 69):

> The Coast Guard need not undertake the lighthouse service. But once it exercised its discretion to operate a light on Chandeleur Island and engendered reliance on the guidance afforded by the light, it was obligated to use due care to make certain that the light was kept in good working order; and, if the light did become extinguished, then the Coast Guard was further obligated to use due care to discover this fact and to repair the light or give warning that it was not functioning. If the Coast Guard failed in its duty and damage was thereby caused to petitioners, the United States is liable under the Tort Claims Act.

3. In both *Stewart* and *Indian Towing* the failure to give a customary warning was due to negligence. Is that important? Would the cases have been decided differently if the watchman had had a heart attack right before Stewart reached the crossing, or if the light had been knocked out by lightning just before the tug and barge came on the scene? If not, what do these cases add to the principle that if a volunteer begins a rescue he must carry it through in a nonnegligent manner?

4. Is *Stewart* a joint-care case or an alternative-care case? Does it matter?

Marsalis v. La Salle
94 So. 2d 120 (La. App. 1957)

McBRIDE, J.

Plaintiffs bring this suit for damages against Shelby P. LaSalle, the defendant, as a result of Mrs. Marsalis' having been bitten or scratched by a Siamese cat on January 12, 1953, in a store in Jefferson Parish, of which the defendant is proprietor, the occurrence having taken place while Mrs. Marsalis, who was accompanied by her husband, was shopping. The cat is the pet of defendant's minor son. Mrs. Marsalis is asserting her claim for personal injuries and her husband is seeking reimbursement of the costs of the medical treatment of his wife. From a judgment in favor of plaintiffs, defendant appeals.

While the testimony on that point is in conflict, we believe that it preponderates to the effect that after Mrs. Marsalis sustained her injury, Marsalis requested defendant to keep the cat under observation for fourteen days until it could be determined whether the animal was rabid and what medical precautions Mrs. Marsalis should take against being infected by rabies. We quote Marsalis' words: "Then I asked Mr. LaSalle to lock the cat up for 14 days, and we had a little discussion about the time element relative to keeping a cat up that had bitten someone to note its condition after that period of time, and I asked him to be sure and lock it up, because I didn't want my wife to take rabies treatment because there were numerous cats in the neighborhood that were reported rabid in the Jefferson Herald and Times, and a number of the papers, and there was quite an incident. . . .

"I asked him to keep the cat up, to lock it up, and he said he would. . . ."

The defendant denies there had been any such conversation regarding the restraining of the cat for the purpose of observation, and his testimony is that neither Mr. nor Mrs. Marsalis considered the injury dangerous. He quoted Mrs. Marsalis as having said: "Oh, it is nothing; don't worry about it." We do not doubt that the defendant and his wife, she having been present in the store when the incident occurred, well knew of the serious consequences that could arise from the bite of an animal, nor do we doubt that they agreed to be cooperative in the matter by observing the state of health of the cat during the period of incubation of rabies. At one point we find Mrs. LaSalle let slip this significant statement: "Well, I think my husband notified me not to let it out and I have got that much sense to know that if a cat ever scratches anybody — ."

According to her statement the cat stayed " . . . indoors where we always kept it on the opposite side of the grocery, it's a basement house, and part of the basement is the store and the opposite side is our domicile and that's where he was. He was supposed to be at all times."

At any rate, on the evening of the fourth or fifth day after the episode in the grocery store the cat escaped and the only explanation given is by Mrs. LaSalle, who testified that this occurred as she and some friends were making their exit via the basement door. The cat was gone for about a month, and in the meantime its whereabouts was not known. Upon returning home the animal gave no evidence whatever of being infected.

Two days after she had sustained the injuries, Mrs. Marsalis sought advice from her friend and neighbor, Dr. Homer Kirgis, whose specialty is in the medical field of neurosurgery. He thought Mrs. Marsalis should first determine whether the cat had been inoculated and then consult her family physician. When it was learned a few days later that the animal had strayed from defendant's premises, Dr. Kirgis urged Mrs. Marsalis to see her family doctor and admonished her to contact the Pasteur Treatment Ward of the Charity Hospital in New Orleans. However, Dr. Kirgis subsequently undertook to administer the Pasteur treatment himself at his home, the first injection being made about January 23, 1953. This treatment consists of a number of injections of a prophylactic vaccine for rabies and we are informed that some persons are extremely allergic to the serum. Mrs. Marsalis was evidently in this category as she suffered a noxious reaction to the serum which brought about some ill effects. . . .

It is uncontroverted that there is no liability in defendant merely because the cat bit or scratched Mrs. Marsalis. Never before had the animal exhibited any vicious traits or tendencies and it had been, as the court found, a gentle and well-behaved pet and defendant was guilty of no negligence in allowing it to frequent his premises. . . . *

. . . Perhaps the defendant, LaSalle, initially owed no duty whatever to Mrs. Marsalis, but when he once agreed to restrain and keep the cat under observation, he was bound to use reasonable care and prudence in doing so and to assume and exercise reasonable care and common humanity. It may be that Mrs. Marsalis had open to her some other course by which she could have had the cat incarcerated and examined in order to determine if it was rabid, but she unquestionably and in good faith relied upon defendant to carry out the agreement which he voluntarily made, thus foregoing such other possible available protection. It was of extreme importance to know if the cat had rabies so she could regulate her course of conduct with reference to the

---

*On the legal standard of liability for animal bites, see the cases in Chapter 7. — Ed.

injury. We do not doubt for one moment that both defendant and his wife were fully cognizant that such injuries could be quite serious and exceedingly dangerous in the event the offending animal was infected with rabies. In fact we feel sure of our ground in saying this because of the statement of Mrs. LaSalle: "I have got that much sense to know that if a cat ever scratches anybody — ."

LaSalle's liability would then depend on whether he used reasonable care with reference to keeping the cat, for as it developed later the Pasteur treatment was entirely unnecessary and the escape of the cat was the direct and proximate cause of the necessity for the injections and the ill effects which Mrs. Marsalis suffered as a result thereof.

Neither defendant nor his wife took any especial steps or means to prevent the cat from straying from their premises. The cat, which was three years old, had always been kept in the basement and was allowed access to the yard from time to time. No change whatever in the animal's usual routine was undertaken and we must hold that defendant failed to use ordinary or reasonable care to see to it that the animal was kept secure, and, hence, defendant is liable unto plaintiffs for whatever damages they sustained as a result of such lack of care. . . .

Notes

1. Is it enough that Mrs. Marsalis "may" have had open to her some other course by which she could have had the cat incarcerated and examined? Should she not have had to prove it? Otherwise how could she have been harmed by relying on LaSalle's promise to keep the cat locked up?

2. Notice that the case was brought as a tort rather than a contract action. According to the quotation from Prosser in an earlier note, a suit for personal injuries normally is maintainable only as a tort action. But does this make sense in a case like *Marsalis*, where the issues of liability are primarily contractual in nature — whether there was a promise, its terms, whether plaintiffs relied, and the reasonableness of their reliance? One liability issue in *Marsalis* that was tortious in character was whether defendants used reasonable care to prevent the cat from escaping. Should this have been an issue at all? If defendants promised plaintiff to keep the cat confined, does it make any difference whether the cat escaped because of defendants' carelessness?

3. Was there an enforceable contract under §90(1) of the Second Restatement of Contracts? If so, does it follow that *Hurley* was incorrectly decided?

4. Could *Marsalis* have been decided on the alternative ground that defendant breached a duty to assist a business invitee injured on his premises, as in *Meador*?

H.R. Moch Co. v. Rensselaer Water Co.
247 N.Y. 160, 159 N.E. 896 (1928)

CARDOZO, C.J. The defendant, a water works company under the laws of this state, made a contract with the city of Rensselaer for the supply of water during a term of years. Water was to be furnished to the city for sewer flushing and street sprinkling; for service to schools and public buildings; and for service at fire hydrants, the latter service at the rate of $42.50 a year for each hydrant. Water was to be furnished to private takers within the city at their homes and factories and other industries at reasonable rates, not exceeding a stated schedule. While this contract was in force, a building caught fire. The flames, spreading to the plaintiff's warehouse near by, destroyed it and its contents. The defendant, according to the complaint, was promptly notified of the fire, "but omitted and neglected after such notice, to supply or furnish sufficient or adequate quantity of water, with adequate pressure to stay, suppress, or extinguish the fire before it reached the warehouse of the plaintiff, although the pressure and supply which the defendant was equipped to supply and furnish, and had agreed by said contract to supply and furnish, was adequate and sufficient to prevent the spread of the fire to and the destruction of the plaintiff's warehouse and its contents." By reason of the failure of the defendant to "fulfill the provisions of the contract between it and the city of Rensselaer," the plaintiff is said to have suffered damage, for which judgment is demanded....

. . . The complaint, we are told, is to be viewed as stating: (1) A cause of action for breach of contract . . . ; (2) a cause of action for a common-law tort. . . .

We think the action is not maintainable as one for breach of contract.

. . . In a broad sense it is true that every city contract, not improvident or wasteful, is for the benefit of the public. More than this, however, must be shown to give a right of action to a member of the public not formally a party. The benefit, as it is sometimes said, must be one that is not merely incidental and secondary. It must be primary and immediate in such a sense and to such a degree as to bespeak the assumption of a duty to make reparation directly to the individual members of the public if the benefit is lost. The field of obligation would be expanded beyond reasonable limits if less than this were to be demanded as a condition of liability. A promisor undertakes to supply fuel for heating a public building. He is not liable for breach of contract to a visitor who finds the building without fuel, and thus contracts a cold. The list of illustrations can be indefinitely extended. The carrier of the mails under contract with the government is not answerable to the merchant who has lost the benefit of a bargain through negligent delay. The householder is without a remedy against manufacturers of hose and engines, though prompt performance of their contracts would have stayed the ravages of fire. "The law does not spread its protection so far."

So with the case at hand. By the vast preponderance of authority, a contract between a city and a water company to furnish water at the city hydrants has in view a benefit to the public that is incidental rather than immediate, an assumption of duty to the city and not to its inhabitants. . . . An intention to assume an obligation of indefinite extension to every member of the public is seen to be the more improbable when we recall the crushing burden that the obligation would impose. . . . If the plaintiff is to prevail, one who negligently omits to supply sufficient pressure to extinguish a fire started by another assumes an obligation to pay the ensuing damage, though the whole city is laid low. A promisor will not be deemed to have had in mind the assumption of a risk so overwhelming for any trivial reward. . . .

We think the action is not maintainable as one for a common-law tort. . . .

The plaintiff would have us hold that the defendant, when once it entered upon the performance of its contract with the city, was brought into such a relation with every one who might potentially be benefited through the supply of water at the hydrants as to give to negligent performance, without reasonable notice of a refusal to continue, the quality of a tort. . . . We are satisfied that liability would be unduly and indeed indefinitely extended by this enlargement of the zone of duty. The dealer in coal who is to supply fuel for a shop must then answer to the customers if fuel is lacking. The manufacturer of goods, who enters upon the performance of his contract, must answer, in that view, not only to the buyer, but to those who to his knowledge are looking to the buyer for their own sources of supply. Every one making a promise having the quality of a contract will be under a duty to the promisee by virtue of the promise, but under another duty, apart from contract, to an indefinite number of potential beneficiaries when performance has begun. The assumption of one relation will mean the involuntary assumption of a series of new relations, inescapably hooked together. . . . "The law does not spread its protection so far." . . .

Notes

1. Once plaintiff's contract claim is rejected, should the contract play any further role in the case? If we forget about the contract and simply test defendant's conduct under the standard laid down in cases like *Stewart* and *Indian Towing*, is defendant's failure to keep up the pressure in the hydrants — on which plaintiff must have relied in deciding what type of fire prevention measures to adopt for his warehouse — not actionable negligence? Or is the concern that the potential liability of the water company for failure to keep the pressure up would be too uncertain if the principle of those cases were applied? How would the water company measure its potential liability? Does it know the value of the house and other buildings in Rensselaer? Does it know what kind of fire protection the city has apart from hydrants? Does it

know what the contents of plaintiff's warehouse are worth? Reexamine these questions after reading the *Ryan* case in Chapter 8.

2. In the court's emphasis on foreseeability, is there perhaps an echo of the famous contract case of Hadley v. Baxendale, 9 Ex. 341, 156 Eng. Rep. 145 (1854)? In that case the engine shaft in plaintiffs' corn mill broke, shutting down the mill. Plaintiffs hired defendant's transportation company to carry the shaft to the firm that was to repair it. As a result of a breach of contract of carriage, the shipment of the shaft to the repair firm was delayed, and hence the mill remained shut down longer than would have been the case if the contract had not been breached. Plaintiffs sued defendant for the lost profits of the mill during this period, but the court held that these damages were unforeseeable and plaintiffs could not recover them. One interpretation of this result is that plaintiffs were the cheaper cost avoiders of the injury to their business than defendant: they should have had a spare shaft. Is there an analogy to the situation in *Moch?*

3. Suppose there is a city-wide electrical blackout caused by the negligence of the electric company. Have businesses that lose profits because of the blackout a cause of action against the electric company? See Lee v. Consolidated Edison Co. of New York, 95 Misc. 2d 120, 407 N.Y.S.2d 777 (City Ct.), rev'd on other grounds, 98 Misc. 2d 304, 413 N.Y.S.2d 826 (Sup. Ct., App. Term, 1978).

Schuster v. City of New York
5 N.Y.2d 75, 154 N.E.2d 534 (1958)

VAN VOORHIS, J.

Plaintiff's intestate supplied information to the Police Department of the City of New York leading to the arrest of a dangerous fugitive from justice known as Willie Sutton, a criminal of national reputation. Schuster's part in Sutton's capture was widely publicized. Schuster immediately received communications threatening his life, of which he notified the police. Three weeks later Schuster was shot and killed while approaching his home in the evening. There is no suggestion that Schuster was an underworld character. On the contrary, he appears to have been a public spirited young man who had studied Sutton's picture on an FBI flyer that had been posted in his father's dry-goods store, asking for Sutton's whereabouts.

The complaint is drawn upon the theory that Schuster was shot in consequence of the information about Sutton supplied by Schuster to the police, and that the City of New York owes a special duty under the circumstances alleged to protect persons who have thus co-operated in law enforcement. It is alleged that the city failed to exercise reasonable care in supplying Schuster with police protection upon demand, that Schuster's death was due to negligence of the city in recklessly exposing him to danger, in advising him that the threats upon his life were not seriously made, in failing to supply him with a bodyguard and in heedlessly imparting to him a false impression of safety and lack of danger. The action is not based on any absolute liability claimed to exist on the part of the city, but upon its alleged failure to use ordinary or reasonable care for his security. . . .

The single issue now presented is whether a municipality is under any duty to exercise reasonable care for the protection of a person in Schuster's situation. Predictions of dire financial consequences to municipalities are waved in our faces if Schuster's estate is allowed to recover for his death. An array of authorities is cited on the proposition that there is no liability to the general public from failure of police or fire protection. Moch Co. v. Rensselaer Water Co. One might think that the floodgates of liability have been opened in negligence and compensation cases against municipalities and other defendants where the liability is less clear than it is under the allegations of this complaint. In our view the public (acting in this instance through the City of New York) owes a special duty to use reasonable care for the protection of persons who have collaborated with it in the arrest or prosecution of criminals, once it reasonably appears that they are in danger due to their collaboration. If it were otherwise, it might well become difficult to convince the citizen to aid and co-operate with the law enforcement officers. To uphold such a liability does not mean that municipalities are called upon to answer in damages for every loss caused by outlaws or by fire. Such a duty to Schuster bespeaks no obligation enforcible in the courts to exercise the police powers of government for the protection of every member of the general public. Nevertheless, where persons actually have aided in the apprehension or prosecution of enemies of society under the criminal law, a reciprocal duty arises on the part of society to use reasonable care for their police protection, at least where reasonably demanded or sought. Such a duty would be performed by the regular organs of government, in this instance, by the City of New York. The duty of everyone to aid in the enforcement of the law, which is as old as history, begets an answering duty on the part of government, under the circumstances of contemporary life, reasonably to protect those who have come to its assistance in this manner. . . .

. . . In McCrink v. City of New York, 296 N.Y. 99, 71 N.E.2d 419, a city was held liable for negligently having omitted to discharge a police officer by whom plaintiff's intestate was shot. In Meistinsky v. City of New York, 309 N.Y. 998, 132 N.E.2d 900, the estate of a hold-up victim recovered who had been killed by an untrained officer's bullets. Negligence of the city was found in its omission to use reasonable care in training the police officer so that he could shoot straight and hit the criminal instead of his victim. . . . [I]n each of . . . [these actions — McCrink, Meistinsky, and others discussed in an omitted part of the court's opinion] liability arose from negligence of a city in the exercise of the police power, and in at least two of them the negligence consisted in nonfeasance rather than in misfeasance (McCrink; Meistinsky).

That distinction at best furnishes an incomplete formula, as the opinion of the court by Chief Judge Cardozo says in Moch Co. v. Rensselaer Water Co. The opinion in the *Moch* case states: "If conduct has gone forward to such a stage that inaction would commonly result, not negatively merely in withholding a benefit, but positively or actively in working an injury, there exists a relation out of which arises a duty to go forward."

In a situation like the present, government is not merely passive; it is active in calling upon persons "in possession of any information regarding the whereabouts of" Sutton, quoting from the FBI flyer, to communicate such information in aid of law enforcement. Where that has happened, as here, or where the public authorities have made active use of a private citizen in some other capacity in the arrest or prosecution of a criminal, it would be a misuse of language to say that the law enforcement authorities are merely passive. They are active in calling upon the citizen for help, and in utilizing his help when it is rendered. They have gone forward to such a stage, paraphrasing the opinion in the *Moch* case, that inaction in furnishing police protection to such persons would commonly result, not negatively merely in withholding a benefit, but positively or actively in working an injury. Under such circumstances, we there said "there exists a relation out of which arises a duty to go forward." Such a relationship existed here. . . .

Notes

1. In what sense did defendant "cause" Schuster's death? What right of Schuster did defendant invade? How would Professor Epstein have decided this case? How would an economist have decided it? For legal developments since *Schuster*, see Note, Police Liability for Negligent Failure to Prevent Crime, 94 Harv. L. Rev. 821 (1981). Cf. Kline v. 1500 Massachusetts Avenue Apartment Corp., 439 F.2d 477 (D.C. Cir. 1970), applying the principle of *Schuster* in a suit by a tenant against her landlord seeking damages for injuries sustained in a criminal assault in the common hallway of defendant's apartment house.

2. In Tarasoff v. Regents of University of California, 17 Cal. 3d 425, 551 P.2d 334 (1976), one Prosenjit Poddar confided to a psychologist employed by a hospital at the University of California at Berkeley that he intended to kill plaintiffs' decedent. No one warned decedent or her parents, and Poddar in fact killed her. The court held that the relationship between a doctor (or psychotherapist) and his patient creates a duty to protect others from dangers emanating from the patient's illness. Is this result consistent with the duty-to-rescue cases earlier in this chapter?

3. Is there any liability if a social host negligently fails to protect his guest from the criminal assault of another? See Parish v. Truman, 124 Ariz. 228, 603 P.2d 120 (Ct. App. 1979).

Winterbottom v. Wright
10 M.&W. 109, 152 Eng. Rep. 402 (Ex. 1842)

[Action in case. The declaration (complaint) alleged the following facts. Defendant was a contractor for the supply of mail coaches, and had contracted with the Postmaster-General to provide the mail coach to convey the mail from Hartford to Holyhead. Defendant agreed in the contract to keep the coach "in a fit, proper, safe, and secure state and condition" and to have "the sole and exclusive duty, charge, care, and burden of the repairs, state, and condition" of the coach. Plaintiff was a coachman employed by Atkinson, who had a contract to convey the mail from Hartford to Holyhead using the coach provided by the Postmaster-General — defendant's coach. Plaintiff had gone to work for Atkinson "trusting to and confiding in the contract made between the defendant and the Postmaster-General, and believing that the said coach was in a fit, safe, secure, and proper state and condition." While driving the coach, plaintiff was injured when the coach "gave way and broke down" because of latent defects in it.]

LORD ABINGER, C.B. I am clearly of opinion that the defendant is entitled to our judgment. We ought not to permit a doubt to rest upon this subject, for our doing so might be the means of letting in upon us an infinity of actions. . . . Here the action is brought simply because the defendant was a contractor with a third person; and it is contended that thereupon he became liable to every body who might use the carriage. If there had been any ground for such an action, there certainly would have been some precedent of it; but with the exception of actions against innkeepers, and some few other persons, no case of a similar nature has occurred in practice. That is a strong circumstance, and is of itself a great authority against its maintenance. It is however contended, that this contract being made on the behalf of the public by the Postmaster-General, no action could be maintained against him, and therefore the plaintiff must have a remedy against the defendant. But that is by no means a necessary consequence — he may be remediless altogether. There is no privity of contract between these parties; and if the plaintiff can sue, every passenger, or even any person passing along the road, who was injured by the upsetting of the coach, might bring a similar action. Unless we confine the operation of such contracts as this to the parties who entered into them, the most absurd and outrageous consequences, to which I can see no limit, would ensue. Where a party becomes responsible to the public, by undertaking a public duty, he is liable, though the injury may have arisen from the negligence of his servant or agent. So, in cases of public nuisances, whether the act was done by the party as a servant, or in any other capacity, you are liable to an action at the suit of any person who suffers. Those, however, are cases where the real ground of the liability is the public duty, or the commission of the public nuisance. There is also a class of cases in which the law permits a contract to be turned into a tort; but unless there has been some public duty undertaken, or public nuisance committed, they are all cases in which an action might have been maintained upon the contract. Thus, a carrier may be sued either in assumpsit or case; but there is no instance in which a party, who was not privy to the contract entered into with him, can maintain any such action. The plaintiff in this case could not have brought an action on the contract; if he could have done so, what would have been his situation, supposing the Postmaster-General had released the defendant? That would, at all events, have defeated his claim altogether. By permitting this action, we should be working this injustice, that after the defendant had done everything to the satisfaction of his employer, and after all matters between them had been adjusted, and all accounts settled on the footing of their contract, we should subject them to be ripped open by this action of tort being brought against him.

ALDERSON, B. I am of the same opinion. The contract in this case was made with the Postmaster-General alone; and the case is just the same as if he had come to the defendant and ordered a carriage, and handed it at once over to Atkinson. If we were to hold that the plaintiff could sue in such a case, there is no point at which such actions would stop. The only safe rule is to confine the right to recover to those who enter into the contract: if we go one step beyond that, there is no reason why we should not go fifty. The only real argument in favour of the action is, that this is a case of hardship; but that might have been obviated, if the plaintiff had made himself a party to the contract. . . .

ROLFE, B. The breach of the defendant's duty, stated in this declaration, i[s] his omission to keep the carriage in a safe condition. . . . The duty . . . is shewn to have arisen solely from the contract; and the fallacy consists in the use of that word "duty." If a duty to the Postmaster-General be meant, that is true; but if a duty to the plaintiff be intended (and in that sense the word is evidently used), there was none. This is one of those unfortunate cases in which there certainly has been damnum, but it is damnum absque injuria; it is, no doubt, a hardship upon the plaintiff to be without a remedy, but by that consideration we ought not to be influenced. Hard cases, it has been frequently observed, are apt to introduce bad law.

Judgment for the defendant.

Notes

1. Why should the existence of the contract act as a bar to plaintiff's tort action? If defendant maintained the coach negligently, was it not foreseeable that the driver might be hurt?

2. What result if plaintiff had sued the manufacturer of the coach?

3. Can the result in *Winterbottom* perhaps be defended by reference to the doctrine of governmental immunity? If the Postmaster-General had supplied the coach to Atkinson, plaintiff would have had no remedy. Unless

the supplier is immune, the Postmaster-General will have an incentive to take over the supply function himself — since he will have to compensate the supplier for the latter's costs of performing the contract, including any potential liability costs — even if an independent contractor would be more efficient.

4. Is there not a considerable element of paradox in using the absence of privity of contract between injurer and victim as a ground for denying liability? Is not tort law centrally concerned with preventing injuries by strangers? Contract law could, in principle at least, protect people from injuries arising out of contracts to which they are parties, could it not?

MacPherson v. Buick Motor Co.
217 N.Y. 382, 111 N.E. 1050 (1916)

CARDOZO, J. The defendant is a manufacturer of automobiles. It sold an automobile to a retail dealer. The retail dealer resold to the plaintiff. While the plaintiff was in the car it suddenly collapsed. He was thrown out and injured. One of the wheels was made of defective wood, and its spokes crumbled into fragments. The wheel was not made by the defendant; it was bought from another manufacturer. There is evidence, however, that its defects could have been discovered by reasonable inspection, and that inspection was omitted. . . . The question to be determined is whether the defendant owed a duty of care and vigilance to any one but the immediate purchaser.

The foundations of this branch of the law, at least in this state, were laid in Thomas v. Winchester, 6 N.Y. 397. A poison was falsely labeled. The sale was made to a druggist, who in turn sold to a customer. The customer recovered damages from the seller who affixed the label. "The defendant's negligence," it was said, "put human life in imminent danger." A poison, falsely labeled, is likely to injure any one who gets it. Because the danger is to be foreseen, there is a duty to avoid the injury. Cases were cited by way of illustration in which manufacturers were not subject to any duty irrespective of contract. The distinction was said to be that their conduct, though negligent, was not likely to result in injury to any one except the purchaser. We are not required to say whether the chance of injury was always as remote as the distinction assumes. Some of the illustrations might be rejected today. The *principle* of the distinction is, for present purposes, the important thing. Thomas v. Winchester became quickly a landmark of the law. In the application of its principle there may, at times, have been uncertainty or even error. There has never in this state been doubt or disavowal of the principle itself. . . .

The early cases [following *Thomas*] suggest a narrow construction of the rule. Later cases, however, evince a more liberal spirit. First in importance is

Devlin v. Smith, 89 N.Y. 470. The defendant, a contractor, built a scaffold for a painter. The painter's servants were injured. The contractor was held liable. He knew that the scaffold, if improperly constructed, was a most dangerous trap. He knew that it was to be used by the workmen. He was building it for that very purpose. Building it for their use, he owed them a duty, irrespective of his contract with their master, to build it with care.

From Devlin v. Smith we pass over intermediate cases and turn to the latest case in this court in which Thomas v. Winchester was followed. That case is Statler v. Ray Mfg. Co., 195 N.Y. 478, 88 N.E. 1005. The defendant manufactured a large coffee urn. It was installed in a restaurant. When heated, the urn exploded and injured the plaintiff. We held that the manufacturer was liable. We said that the urn "was of such a character inherently that, when applied to the purposes for which it was designed, it was liable to become a source of great danger to many people if not carefully and properly constructed."

It may be that Devlin v. Smith and Statler v. Ray Mfg. Co. have extended the rule of Thomas v. Winchester. If so, this court is committed to the extension. The defendant argues that things imminently dangerous to life are poisons, explosives, deadly weapons — things whose normal function it is to injure or destroy. But whatever the rule in Thomas v. Winchester may once have been, it has no longer that restricted meaning. A scaffold (Devlin v. Smith) is not inherently a destructive instrument. It becomes destructive only if imperfectly constructed. A large coffee urn (Statler v. Ray Mfg. Co.) may have within itself, if negligently made, the potency of danger, yet no one thinks of it as an implement whose normal function is destruction. . . .

We hold, then, that the principle of Thomas v. Winchester is not limited to poisons, explosives, and things of like nature, to things which in their normal operation are implements of destruction. If the nature of a thing is such that it is reasonably certain to place life and limb in peril when negligently made, it is then a thing of danger. Its nature gives warning of the consequences to be expected. If to the element of danger there is added knowledge that the thing will be used by persons other than the purchaser, and used without new tests, then, irrespective of contract, the manufacturer of this thing of danger is under a duty to make it carefully. That is as far as we are required to go for the decision of this case. There must be knowledge of a danger, not merely possible, but probable. It is possible to use almost anything in a way that will make it dangerous if defective. That is not enough to charge the manufacturer with a duty independent of his contract. Whether a given thing is dangerous may be sometimes a question for the court and sometimes a question for the jury. There must also be knowledge that in the usual course of events the danger will be shared by others than the buyer. Such knowledge may often be inferred from the nature of the transaction. But it is possible that even knowledge of the danger and of the use will not always be enough. The proximity or remoteness of the relation is a factor to be considered. We are dealing now with the liability of the manufacturer of the finished product, who puts it on the market to be used without inspection by his customers. If he is negligent, where danger is to be foreseen, a liability will follow. We are not required, at this time, to say that it is legitimate to go back of the manufacturer of the finished product and hold the manufacturers of the component parts. To make their negligence a cause of imminent danger, an independent cause must often intervene; the manufacturer of the finished product must also fail in *his* duty of inspection. It may be that in those circumstances the negligence of the earlier members of the series is too remote to constitute, as to the ultimate user, an actionable wrong. We leave that question open. . . .

From this survey of the decisions, there thus emerges a definition of the duty of a manufacturer which enables us to measure this defendant's liability. Beyond all question, the nature of an automobile gives warning of probable danger if its construction is defective. This automobile was designed to go 50 miles an hour. Unless its wheels were sound and strong, injury was almost certain. It was as much a thing of danger as a defective engine for a railroad. The defendant knew the danger. It knew also that the car would be used by persons other than the buyer. This was apparent from its size; there were seats for three persons. It was apparent also from the fact that the buyer was a dealer in cars, who bought to resell. The maker of this car supplied it for the use of purchasers from the dealer just as plainly as the contractor in Devlin v. Smith supplied the scaffold for use by the servants of the owner. The dealer was indeed the one person of whom it might be said with some approach to certainty that by him the car would not be used. Yet the defendant would have us say that he was the one person whom it was under a legal duty to protect. The law does not lead us to so inconsequent a conclusion. Precedents drawn from the days of travel by stagecoach do not fit the conditions of travel today. The principle that the danger must be imminent does not change, but the things subject to the principle do change. They are whatever the needs of life in a developing civilization require them to be. . . .

In England the limits of the rule [of Thomas v. Winchester] are still unsettled. Winterbottom v. Wright is often cited. The defendant undertook to provide a mail coach to carry the mail bags. The coach broke down from latent defects in its construction. The defendant, however, was not the manufacturer. The court held that he was not liable for injuries to a passenger. The case was decided on a demurrer to the declaration. . . . [T]he form of the declaration was subject to criticism. It did not fairly suggest the existence of a duty aside from the special contract which was the plaintiff's main reliance. . . . In Elliot v. Hall, 15 Q.B.D. 315, the defendant sent out a defective truck laden with goods which he had sold. The buyer's servants unloaded it, and were injured because of the defects. It was held that the defendant was under a duty "not to be guilty of negligence with regard to the state and condition of the truck." There seems to have been a return to the doctrine of Winterbottom v. Wright in Earl v. Lubbock, [1905] 1 K.B. 253. In that case, however, as in the earlier one, the defendant was not the manufacturer. He had merely made a contract to keep the van in repair. A later case (White v. Steadman, [1913] 3 K.B. 340, 348) emphasizes that element. A livery stable keeper who sent out a vicious horse was held liable, not merely to his customer, but also to another occupant of the carriage, and Thomas v. Winchester was cited and followed. . . .

We think the defendant was not absolved from a duty of inspection because it bought the wheels from a reputable manufacturer. It was not merely a dealer in automobiles. It was a manufacturer of automobiles. It was responsible for the finished product. It was not at liberty to put the finished product on the market without subjecting the component parts to ordinary and simple tests. . . .

BARTLETT, C.J., dissenting. . . .

The theory upon which the case was submitted to the jury by the learned judge who presided at the trial was that, although an automobile is not an inherently dangerous vehicle, it may become such if equipped with a weak wheel; and that if the motor car in question, when it was put upon the market was in itself inherently dangerous by reason of its being equipped with a weak wheel, the defendant was chargeable with a knowledge of the defect so far as it might be discovered by a reasonable inspection and the application of reasonable tests. This liability, it was further held, was not limited to the original vendee, but extended to a subvendee like the plaintiff, who was not a party to the original contract of sale.

I think that these rulings, which have been approved by the Appellate Division, extend the liability of the vendor of a manufactured article further than any case which has yet received the sanction of this court. It has heretofore been held in this state that the liability of the vendor of a manufactured article for negligence arising out of the existence of defects therein does not extend to strangers injured in consequence of such defects, but is confined to the immediate vendee. The exceptions to this general rule which have thus far been recognized in New York are cases in which the article sold was of such a character that danger to life or limb was involved in the ordinary use thereof; in other words, where the article sold was inherently dangerous. As has already been pointed out, the learned trial judge instructed the jury that an automobile is not an inherently dangerous vehicle.

The late Chief Justice Cooley of Michigan, one of the most learned and accurate of American law writers, states the general rule thus:

"The general rule is that a contractor, manufacturer, vendor or furnisher of an article is not liable to third parties who have no contractual relations with him, for negligence in the construction, manufacture, or sale of such article." 2 Cooley on Torts (3d Ed.), 1486.

The leading English authority in support of this rule, to which all the later cases on the same subject refer, is Winterbottom v. Wright. . . .

The doctrine of that decision was recognized as the law of this state by the leading New York case of Thomas v. Winchester, which, however, involved an exception to the general rule. There the defendant, who was a dealer in medicines, sold to a druggist a quantity of belladonna, which is a deadly poison, negligently labeled as extract of dandelion. The druggist in good faith used the poison in filling a prescription calling for the harmless dandelion extract, and the plaintiff for whom the prescription was put up was poisoned by the belladonna. This court held that the original vendor was liable for the injuries suffered by the patient. Chief Judge Ruggles, who delivered the opinion of the court, distinguished between an act of negligence imminently dangerous to the lives of others and one that is not so, saying: "If A. build a wagon and sell it to B., who sells it to C., and C. hires it to D., who in consequence of the gross negligence of A. in building the wagon is overturned and injured, D. cannot recover damages against A., the builder. A.'s obligation to build the wagon faithfully arises solely out of his contract with B. The public have nothing to do with it. . . . So, for the same reason, if a horse be defectively shod by a smith, and a person hiring the horse from the owner is thrown and injured in consequence of the smith's negligence in shoeing, the smith is not liable for the injury." . . .

I do not see how we can uphold the judgment in the present case without overruling what has been so often said by this court and other courts of like authority in reference to the absence of any liability for negligence on the part of the original vendor of an ordinary carriage to any one except his immediate vendee. The absence of such liability was the very point actually decided in the English case of Winterbottom v. Wright, and the illustration quoted from the opinion of Chief Judge Ruggles in Thomas v. Winchester, assumes that the law on the subject was so plain that the statement would be accepted almost as a matter of course. In the case at bar the defective wheel on an automobile, moving only eight miles an hour, was not any more dangerous to the occupants of the car than a similarly defective wheel would be to the occupants of a carriage drawn by a horse at the same speed; and yet unless the courts have been all wrong on this question up to the present time, there would be no liability to strangers to the original sale in the case of the horsedrawn carriage.

Notes

1. Which opinion — the majority or the dissent — has the better of the argument in terms of the precedents? Was Judge Cardozo disingenuous in treating Thomas v. Winchester as the rule and Winterbottom v. Wright as the exception? For an interesting discussion of Cardozo's judicial technique in *MacPherson*, see E. H. Levi, An Introduction to Legal Reasoning 20-25 (1948).

2. Could MacPherson have sued the dealer for breach of warranty, and could the dealer in turn have sued the defendant for breach of its warranty to him for any damages he was forced to pay MacPherson in the latter's warranty action against him? If the answer to these questions is yes, then the

decision can be defended simply on grounds of judicial economy. The role of
implied warranties in the development of the modern law of products liability is considered in Chapter 9.

3. In the *Moch* case, decided after *MacPherson*, Cardozo cited the
earlier case but did not attempt to distinguish it specifically. Are the cases
distinguishable? Did one involve nonfeasance and the other misfeasance?
Was the scope of potential liability more certain in one than in the other?

4. *MacPherson* has been superseded in those states that, in recent years,
have replaced negligence liability for injuries caused by defective products
with strict liability for such injuries. Modern products liability law is taken up
in Chapter 9. What difference does strict liability make if the plaintiff must
still prove that the product was defective? Do the facts of *MacPherson*
answer this question?

Union Oil Co. v. Oppen
501 F.2d 558 (9th Cir. 1974)

SNEED, J.

This is another case growing out of the Santa Barbara oil spill of 1969.
The plaintiffs are commercial fishermen. Each of their complaints alleges
that the cause of action has been brought under the provisions of the Outer
Continental Shelf Lands Act of 1953, 43 U.S.C. §1331 et seq.; that the
defendants joined in an enterprise, the day-to-day operation of which was
within the control and under the management of defendant Union Oil
Company, to drill for oil in the waters of the Santa Barbara Channel; that
during the period commencing on or about January 28, 1969, vast quantities
of raw crude oil were released and subsequently carried by wind, wave and
tidal currents over vast stretches of the coastal waters of Southern California;
and that as a consequence the plaintiffs have suffered various injuries for
which damages are sought. . . .

On May 1, 1970, counsel for all parties to this suit entered into a
Stipulation which was approved by the district court. . . . The relevant portion of the Stipulation relating to the facts reads as follows:

> On or about January 28, 1969, oil began to escape under and near Union Oil
> Company of California's Platform "A" located on the Outer Continental Shelf
> of the United States in the Santa Barbara Channel. The undersigned agree that
> the following is a fair statement of the facts with respect to the Santa Barbara
> Channel occurrence (hereinafter "occurrence"):
>
>   A. Certain operations conducted on Platform "A" resulted in the release
> of unascertained amounts of crude oil from the ocean floor underneath and
> near Platform "A"

B. Such crude oil release was carried by natural forces of winds and tides to various areas of the ocean's surface and towards and in some instances to the adjacent coast lines.

C. An unascertained amount of damage has resulted from said occurrence.

Paragraph 3 of the Stipulation, which sets out the defendants' undertaking to pay damages, provides as follows:

> In order to provide a basis for the disposition of the above referenced claims it is agreed by the undersigned defendants that they will pay to the above referenced persons and/or plaintiffs who are, or who by reason of subsequent joinder herein become, parties hereto, *all legally compensable damages arising from a legally cognizable injury* caused by the aforementioned occurrence as such damages are determined pursuant to the following provisions; *provided however, that the payment assumed hereby will not exceed such amount and such claim as said defendants or their contractors would be responsible for in the case of negligence.* . . . (emphasis added).

In May of 1972, the defendants moved for partial summary judgment before the special masters to strike from plaintiffs' prayers "that item of damage usually denominated as 'ecological damage.' " More specifically, the defendants sought to eliminate from the prayers any element of damages consisting of profits lost as a result of the reduction in the commercial fishing potential of the Santa Barbara Channel which may have been caused by the occurrence. According to the defendants, such long-term ecological damage is not compensable under the law and thus is not within their undertaking as set forth in the Stipulation. . . .

Defendants support their motion for partial summary judgment by pointing to the widely recognized principle that no cause of action lies against a defendant whose negligence prevents the plaintiff from obtaining a prospective pecuniary advantage. As the defendants see it, any diminution of the sea life in the Santa Barbara Channel caused by the occurrence which, it must be remembered, is attributable to the defendants' negligence by reason of the parties' Stipulation, consists of no more than the loss of an economic advantage which is not a "legally cognizable injury" and thus not "legally compensable."

Their argument has strength. It rests upon the proposition that a contrary rule, which would allow compensation for all losses of economic advantages caused by defendant's negligence, would subject the defendant to claims based upon remote and speculative injuries which he could not foresee in any practical sense of the term. Accordingly, in some cases it has been stated as the general rule that the negligent defendant owes no duty to plaintiffs seeking compensation for such injuries. In other of the cases, the courts have invoked the doctrine of proximate cause to reach the same result; and in yet a third class of cases the "remoteness" of the economic loss is relied upon directly to deny recovery. . . .

The general rule has been applied in a wide variety of situations. Thus, the negligent destruction of a bridge connecting the mainland with an island, which caused a loss of business to the plaintiff who was a merchant on the island, has been held not to be actionable. Rickards v. Sun Oil Company, 41 A.2d 267, 23 N.J. Misc. 89 (1945). A plaintiff engaged in commercial printing has been held unable to recover against a negligent contractor who, while engaged in excavation pursuant to a contract with a third party, cut the power line upon which the plaintiff's presses depended. Byrd v. English, 117 Ga. 191, 43 S.E. 419 (1903). A defendant who negligently injures a third person entitled to life-care medical services by the plaintiff is liable to the third person but not to the plaintiff. Fifield Manor v. Finston, 54 Cal. 2d 632, 7 Cal. Rptr. 377, 354 P.2d 1073 (1960). . . . The operators of a dry dock are not liable in admiralty to charterers of a ship, placed by its owners in the dry dock, for negligent injury to the ship's propeller where the injury deprived the charterer of the use of the ship. Robins Dry Dock & Repair Company v. Flint, 275 U.S. 303 (1927). Mr. Justice Holmes, in writing this opinion, observed that ". . . a tort to the person or property of one man does not make the tortfeasor liable to another merely because the injured person was under a contract with that other, unknown to the doer of the wrong." . . .

Prosser recognizes that a recovery for pure economic losses in negligence has been permitted in instances in which there exists "some special relation between the parties." The failure of the plaintiff to obtain a contract because of a telegraph company's negligent transmission of a message has been held to be legally cognizable, and is cited as an example of the "special relationship" qualification. . . .

A more recent development in California law involves the right to recover, absent privity, from a defendant whose negligent failure to obtain a proper attestation of the will of a third party has deprived the plaintiff of a bequest which had been granted in the improperly attested will. Biakanja v. Irving, 49 Cal. 2d 647, 320 P.2d 16 (1958). . . .

The approach adopted by the California Supreme Court in *Biakanja* is particularly instructive. After stating that the question before it was "whether defendant was under a duty to exercise due care to protect plaintiff from injury and was liable for damages caused plaintiff by his negligence even though they were not in privity of contract," the court stated: "The determination whether in a specific case the defendant will be held liable to a third person not in privity is a matter of policy and involves the balancing of various factors, among which are the extent to which the transaction was intended to affect the plaintiff, the foreseeability of harm to him, the degree of certainty that the plaintiff suffered injury, the closeness of the connection between the defendant's conduct and the injury suffered, the moral blame attached to the defendant's conduct, and the policy of preventing future harm." It is thus obvious that California does not blindly follow the general rule upon which the defendants here rely. . . .

... [W]e can not escape the conclusion that under California law the presence of a duty on the part of the defendants in this case would turn substantially on foreseeability. That being the crucial determinant, the question must be asked whether the defendants could reasonably have foreseen that negligently conducted drilling operations might diminish aquatic life and thus injure the business of commercial fishermen. We believe the answer is yes. The dangers of pollution were and are known even by school children. The defendants understood the risks of their business and should reasonably have foreseen the scope of its responsibilities. To assert that the defendants were unable to foresee that negligent conduct resulting in a substantial oil spill could diminish aquatic life and thus injure the plaintiffs is to suppose a degree of general ignorance of the effects of oil pollution not in accord with good sense.

An examination of the other factors mentioned in *Biakanja* only strengthens our conclusion that the defendants in this case owed a duty to the plaintiffs. Thus, the fact that the injury flows directly from the action of escaping oil on the life in the sea, the public's deep disapproval of injuries to the environment and the strong policy of preventing such injuries, all point to existence of a required duty.

The same conclusion is reached when the issue before us is approached from the standpoint of economics. Recently a number of scholars have suggested that liability for losses occasioned by torts should be apportioned in a manner that will best contribute to the achievement of an optimum allocation of resources. See e.g., Calabresi, The Cost of Accidents, 69-73 (1970) (hereinafter Calabresi); Coase, The Problem of Social Cost, 3 J.L. & Econ. 1 (1960). This optimum, in theory, would be that which would be achieved by a perfect market system. In determining whether the cost of an accident should be borne by the injured party or be shifted, in whole or in part, this approach requires the court to fix the identity of the party who can avoid the costs most cheaply. Once fixed, this determination then controls liability.

It turns out, however, that fixing the identity of the best or cheapest cost-avoider is more difficult than might be imagined. In order to facilitate this determination, Calabresi suggests several helpful guidelines. The first of these would require a rough calculation designed to exclude as potential cost-avoiders those groups/activities which could avoid accident costs only at an extremely high expense. Calabresi at 140-43. While not easy to apply in any concrete sense, this guideline does suggest that the imposition of oil spill costs directly upon such groups as the consumers of staple groceries is not a sensible solution. Under this guideline, potential liability becomes resolved into a choice between, on an ultimate level, the consumers of fish and those of products derived from the defendants' total operations.

To refine this choice, Calabresi goes on to provide additional guidelines which, in this instance, have proven none too helpful. For example, he suggests an evaluation of the administrative costs which each party would be forced to bear in order to avoid the accident costs. Calabresi at 143-44. He also states that an attempt should be made to avoid an allocation which will impose some costs on those groups or activities which neither consume fish nor utilize those products of the defendants derived from their operations in the Santa Barbara Channel. Calabresi at 144-50. On the record before us, we have no way of evaluating the relative administrative costs involved. However, we do recognize that it is probable that by imposing liability on the defendants some portion of the accident costs in this case may be borne by those who neither eat fish nor use the petroleum products derived from the defendants' operations in Santa Barbara.

Calabresi's final guideline, however, unmistakably points to the defendants as the best cost-avoider. Under this guideline, the loss should be allocated to that party who can best correct any error in allocation, if such there be, by acquiring the activity to which the party has been made liable. Calabresi at 150-52. The capacity "to buy out" the plaintiffs if the burden is too great is, in essence, the real focus of Calabresi's approach. On this basis there is no contest — the defendants' capacity is superior. . . .

Finally, it must be understood that our holding in this case does not open the door to claims that may be asserted by those, other than commercial fishermen, whose economic or personal affairs were discommoded by the oil spill of January 28, 1969. The general rule urged upon us by defendants has a legitimate sphere within which to operate. Nothing said in this opinion is intended to suggest, for example, that every decline in the general commercial activity of every business in the Santa Barbara area following the occurrences of 1969 constitutes a legally cognizable injury for which the defendants may be responsible. The plaintiffs in the present action lawfully and directly make use of a resource of the sea, viz. its fish, in the ordinary course of their business. This type of use is entitled to protection from negligent conduct by the defendants in their drilling operations. Both the plaintiffs and defendants conduct their business operations away from land and in, on and under the sea. Both must carry on their commercial enterprises in a reasonably prudent manner. Neither should be permitted negligently to inflict commercial injury on the other. We decide no more than this.

Affirmed.

Posner, Some Uses and Abuses of Economics in Law
46 U. Chi. L. Rev. 281, 298-300 (1979)

Oppen concerned a suit by commercial fishermen whose livelihood was impaired as a result of the Santa Barbara oil spill in 1969. . . . The only issue was whether an injury to a business expectancy as distinct from a vested property right was compensable under the applicable tort law. The Ninth

Circuit, in an opinion by Judge Sneed, held that it was compensable. He bolstered this conclusion by reference to Professor Calabresi's book on the costs of accidents. The court's discussion . . . evinces a misunderstanding of the applicable economics.

Judge Sneed begins by noting that the economic approach requires the court to identify "the party who can avoid the costs more cheaply." But he shies away from applying this criterion, on the ground that "fixing the identity of the best or cheapest cost-avoider is more difficult than might be imagined." This is a curious observation in the setting of the case. The court interpreted the defendants' stipulation as a confession of their negligence, which means, at least as an approximation, that they had not thought it worth trying to show that they were not, in Calabresi's terms, the cheapest cost-avoiders. Why then should Judge Sneed have wondered whether the defendants could more cheaply have avoided the harm caused by the Santa Barbara oil spill, especially in the absence of any allegation that the plaintiffs had been contributorily negligent? In any event, it seems obvious that the fishermen were in no position (by breeding a species of oil-resistant fish, or otherwise) to avoid the damage; the oil companies were the cheaper cost-avoiders in Calabresi's sense.

What follows in the opinion — an attempt to apply Calabresi's detailed guidelines designed for cases in which the identity of the cheaper cost-avoider is in serious doubt — is thus superfluous. It is also confused. This part of the opinion begins with the suggestion that "the imposition of oil spill costs directly upon such groups as the consumers of staple groceries is not a sensible solution." I assume that by "staple groceries" Judge Sneed has in mind a product in which neither fish nor oil is a significant input. The relevance of such an example is obscure, since there is no tort mechanism by which the manufacturers, sellers, or consumers of staple groceries could be made to bear the costs of the Santa Barbara oil spill. Continuing with his discussion of Calabresi's detailed guidelines, Judge Sneed next states that an effort should be made to "avoid an allocation which will impose some costs on those groups or activities which neither consume fish nor utilize those products of the defendants derived from their operations in the Santa Barbara Channel." We are back to the staple groceries, an example of an activity unrelated to the accident. Judge Sneed then states that it is probable that imposing liability on the defendants will result, at least partially, in just such an externalization. It is not clear why this should be so, and he gives no reasons for his conclusion.

Having wandered among Calabresian guidelines that he does not find particularly helpful, Judge Sneed finally lights on a helpful one: "[T]he loss should be allocated to that party who can best correct any error in allocation, if such there be, by acquiring the activity to which the party has been made liable. . . . On this basis there is no contest — the defendants' capacity [i.e., to buy out the other party to the accident] is superior." There are some settings where the merger of the interfering activities may be the correct solution to an externalities problem,[71] but it is improbable that the correct solution to the problem of oil spills is to merge the commercial fishing industry and the oil industry into one giant firm. And it is impossible to defend placing liability on the oil companies on the ground that liability would give those companies an incentive to acquire the fishing industry.

With respect, it must be said that Judge Sneed's attempt to apply Professor Calabresi's economic guidelines to the issue of liability in this case is not a success. The judge's conclusion that the oil companies should be liable for the loss to the commercial fishermen even though the fishermen had no property right in fish they had not yet caught seems correct as a matter of economics: only the oil companies can take efficient measures to prevent or limit oil damage to the fish, and making them liable to the fishermen will give the oil companies the correct incentives to take those measures. But Judge Sneed's effort to articulate his reasoning in economic terms was disastrous.

Epstein, Nuisance Law: Corrective Justice and Its Utilitarian Constraints
8 J. Legal Stud. 49, 51-52 (1979)

Nowhere in its analysis . . . did the Court [in *Oppen*] ask who owned the fish. If the fish were owned by the plaintiffs, the case would hardly be complex, either in terms of traditional negligence law or in terms of its modern economic reformulation. "You poisoned my fish," states ownership and causal connection, while the allegations of negligence (assuming they are required) have already been made.

Alternatively, the fish might have been owned by no one, in which event the appropriate precedents are not drawn from tort theory but from cases concerned with the capture of wild animals, like Pierson v. Post.[7] Such cases have held that a person in hot pursuit of an animal is not entitled to complain if someone else captures it first. Presumably he could not therefore complain if his adversary, having achieved capture, mistreats the animal, neglects it, or simply kills it. And so it is with unowned fish in *Oppen*. The plaintiffs who do not own the fish cannot complain if the Union Oil Company captures them. As they cannot complain of capture, they cannot complain of destruction after capture. As they cannot complain of destruction after capture, they cannot complain of it before capture. No theory of tortious liability can make up the plaintiffs' deficit attributable to their want of ownership.

Lastly, assume that the fish are not owned by the plaintiffs but by some third party, X. X can of course maintain his cause of action for the property

71. See Professor Baxter's interesting proposal for forcing airports to condemn the land within the airport's primary noise contour. Baxter & Altree, Legal Aspects of Airport Noise, 15 J.L. & Econ. 1, 69-82 (1972).

7. Pierson v. Post, 3 Cai. R. (N.Y.) 175, 2 Am. Dec. 264 (1805).

loss. The question is, should these plaintiffs be allowed separate actions for
their own economic loss as well? Such actions are difficult to accept if the
plaintiff's own conduct is tortious against X, except on the theory that the
plaintiff should be allowed to steal the fish before the defendant destroys
them. They become more tenable on the assumption that the plaintiff has a
license (whether or not exclusive) to catch the fish, even if the current law is
in a most unsatisfactory state on the question of interference with relational
interests. Whatever the rule, it seems preferable to resolve this matter with X
in the courtroom, especially if X happens to be the government. In any event
the ownership question remains insistent, and it can be answered only with
recourse to treaties, statutes, ordinances, custom, and grants. No general
theory of tort law, however powerful or profound, can tell us who owns what
at the outset. The result in Union Oil v. Oppen may in fact be correct. Yet its
method of analysis, spurred on by a commendable distaste for pollution, is
fatally flawed.

Tort law then presupposes some prior, independent method for defining
and recognizing property rights both in the person and in external objects. . . .

Posner, Epstein's Tort Theory: A Critique
8 J. Legal Stud. 457, 467-468 (1979)

Epstein does not ask why the common law took the position it did on
rights to wild animals or why that position should be thought to control the
oil-spill case. Let me take a stab at these questions. Property rights do not
make economic sense if the value of the right would be less than the cost of
enforcing it. This was probably the case with respect to most wild animals
during the formative years of the common law. The animals were plentiful
relative to the demand and their market value was therefore low, whereas the
cost of establishing property rights by fencing their habitats would have been
high. But growing scarcity might at some point justify recognizing property
rights in some species of wild animals; and with regard to the commercial
fishing industry, that point was reached some time ago. Over-fishing is a
serious problem today. So, potentially at least, is the excessive destruction of
fish by oil spills — excessive in the sense that, when the value of the fish killed
is added to the other losses from the spill, the total losses exceed the costs
that would have been required to prevent the spill from occurring. One way
of preventing oil companies from ignoring the effects of oil spills on fish is to
make the companies liable to the fishermen for the value of the lost catch.
Tort liability would do this.

But Epstein's insistence that the first step in every tort case is to identify
the property right that has been infringed, and that no tort action can be
maintained unless a property right has been infringed, frustrates this simple
and sensible solution. For it is probably impracticable to vest the fishermen

with a property right, as that term is ordinarily understood, in the fish in the Santa Barbara Channel. However abstractly desirable the vesting of such rights might be from a resource-conservation viewpoint, the practical difficulties of tracking schools of fish or fencing or otherwise establishing exclusive fishing "territories" seem insuperable. But why should the impracticability of giving fishermen a property right preclude giving them a tort right? To be sure, some torts, notably trespass to land, are created in order to enforce property rights. But others, clearly, are not (e.g., defamation). Recognizing a tort right in an *Oppen*-type case serves to reduce the divergence between private and social costs that is created when oil companies do not take into account the effects of oil spills on fish.

Epstein, Causation and Corrective Justice: A Reply to Two Critics
8 J. Legal Stud. 477, 502 (1957)

. . . Posner urges that the absence of property rights should be no stumbling block to the plaintiff's action. In his view, it may make good sense to recognize tort actions even in the admitted absence of ownership rights, if only to prevent overexploitation of the common pool. Posner claims that even legislation may be unable to establish property rights in individual fish (though surely not mussels or clams) or in territorial waters given that fish freely migrate from habitat to habitat. "Tort rights" in his view might be appropriate to close the gap. Even if his objection is valid, it only applies to a very tiny proportion of the cases in which property rights are not well established, as with wild animals. It does not, for example, apply to injuries to the person nor to real property.

I quite agree with Posner that it is always an unfortunate situation whenever potentially valuable resources are not the subject of exclusive rights. There are by definition no property rights in this case, yet the constraints of a system of corrective justice do not prevent the creation of suitable systems of public control to reduce if not eliminate the problem. The solution in *Oppen* of sanctioning tort actions by the fishermen does however raise at least three problems.

First, the courts cannot simply designate by whim certain individuals as owners or holders of franchises or profits. It is not clear that they can assign certain individuals mere tort rights, which constitute but a fraction of ownership or franchise rights.

Second, it is not clear that Posner has chosen the proper plaintiff to deal with the concern of overconsumption. Vesting the action in the fishermen only gives them further incentive to engage in the very activities responsible for overconsumption. It may be better therefore to vest the action in an environmental group (which indeed might be allowed to sue the fishermen

Chapter 6   The Duty Limitation

for catching the fish not destroyed by pollution) or in the government with its
control over large bodies of water.

Third, the case illustrates the difficulty of using the judicial forum to
intervene where there are many possible claimants for the allocation of
unowned things. The absence of property rights removes most, if not all, of
the eminent-domain problems from the area. It is a case in which intelligent
legislation or administrative action is required to deal with all the possible
claims that might be raised. The institutional and economic aspects of the
situation only reinforce the corrective-justice arguments for the judicial denial of a private cause of action.

Notes

1. Arguably the *Rickards* case, cited by the court in *Oppen*, can be
distinguished on the following ground: Any damage in lost business to
merchants on the island was probably offset by gains to other merchants to
whom customers of the island merchants switched when the bridge was down.
If so, the lost business did not reflect a net social loss.

Economists distinguish between "technical" and "pecuniary" diseconomies (or externalities), the former resulting from an action that denies someone the use of some scarce resource, the latter resulting from a change in
demand that affects the distribution of wealth in the society rather than the
total amount of wealth. By destroying the fish, defendant in *Oppen* imposed
a technical diseconomy. But if for example a manufacturer relocated from A
to B, the demand for land in A and hence the price of land might fall, but this
fall would be offset by an increase in land values in B resulting from the
increased demand for land there. There would be no net social loss. *Rickards*
is similar. The destruction of the bridge was a real social loss, but the shift in
business from one group of merchants to another was a purely pecuniary
transfer.

As a further illustration of this point, suppose that as a result of damage
to the beaches at Santa Barbara caused by the oil spill, the Biltmore Hotel in
Santa Barbara had lost profitable business — but the Fontainebleau Hotel in
Miami Beach had gained an equivalent amount of business as travelers
switched their vacation plans from Santa Barbara to Miami Beach. Assume
the Biltmore's lost profits were $2 million, the Fontainebleau's additional
profits $2 million, the loss to the commercial fishermen $1 million, and no
one else was affected by the spill. Then the spill would have produced total
losses of $3 million ($1 million to the fishermen, $2 million to the Biltmore)
and total gains of $2 million (to the Fontainebleau), for a net loss of $1
million. If only the fishermen are allowed to obtain damages, the right
amount of deterrence is obtained from an economic standpoint, since the
fishermen's damages equal the net social cost of the oil spill. If the Biltmore is
allowed to sue as well, then there is overdeterrence unless Union Oil Compa-

ny is somehow able to recover the $2 million windfall gain that the spill conferred on the Fontainebleau. But if the Biltmore is not allowed to recover damages, then the victim of a tortious wrong is being denied compensation. What theories of tort law support such a result?

2. In Stevenson v. East Ohio Gas Co., 47 Ohio L. Abs. 586, 73 N.E.2d 200 (App. 1946), liquefied natural gas stored on defendant's premises exploded, allegedly because of defendant's negligence, causing a conflagration that prevented plaintiff from working at his place of employment, which was in the vicinity of defendant's plant. He sued defendant for his lost wages during the period (more than a week) in which he was prevented from working. The court invoked the "economic loss" principle mentioned in *Oppen* and denied recovery. But in Mineral Industries, Inc. v. George, 44 Misc. 2d 764, 255 N.Y.S.2d 114 (Sup. Ct. 1965), where a key employee of plaintiff was injured in an automobile accident through the negligence of defendants (the owner and the operator of the other vehicle in the collision), plaintiff was allowed to recover damages from defendants for the value of the employee's services to plaintiff which plaintiff lost as a result of the accident. Are these decisions consistent with each other? With *Rickards* and *Oppen*?

The right of the master to recover damages for the loss of the servant's services as a result of negligent injury to the servant is very old, but there have been few modern actions and some courts have rejected the right. Thus, for example, in Myrurgia Perfumes, Inc. v. American Airlines, Inc., 68 Misc. 2d 712-713, 327 N.Y.S.2d 861-862 (Cty. Ct. 1971), the court said, "talking of property rights in the sweat of a man's brow falls on my ears like an alien language. It may have been meet in the early days of the crafts in England when a servant lived almost as a member of the master's household and was maintained by the master. It is an absurdity in today's urban world." Other cases are collected in Annot., Employer's Right of Action for Loss of Services or the Like Against Third Person Tortiously Killing or Injuring Employee, 4 A.L.R.4th 504 (1981).

3. A factor that may explain some of the cases in this chapter is judicial concern with the administrative costs of allowing everyone harmed by a negligent act to recover damages. (This is true even in "bad Samaritan" cases. Can you see why?) Consider Petition of Kinsman Transit Co., 388 F.2d 821 (2d Cir. 1968). Like *Rickards*, this was a case where a bridge collapsed because of defendant's negligence. As a result of the disruption of river transportation which followed, a ship carrying plaintiff Cargill's wheat to Cargill's grain elevators could not unload the wheat, and to honor contractual obligations to its customers Cargill was required to secure replacement wheat, incurring transportation and storage charges which it sought to recover from defendant. The trial court disallowed Cargill's claim (and a similar claim of another shipper) on the ground that negligent interference with contractual relations is not actionable. The court of appeals affirmed but on a different ground. It was not satisfied that contractual rights should be treated differently from other rights protected by tort law but thought that the loss to Cargill and the

other shipper was too remote. The court frankly placed its decision on grounds of "expediency," conceding that the injury to the shipper was foreseeable and noting in an interesting footnote:

> Although to reason by example is often merely to restate the problem, the following illustration may be an aid in explaining our result. To anyone familiar with N.Y. traffic there can be no doubt that a foreseeable result of an accident in the Brooklyn Battery Tunnel during rush hour is that thousands of people will be delayed. A driver who negligently caused such an accident would certainly be held accountable to those physically injured in the crash. But we doubt that damages would be recoverable against the negligent driver in favor of truckers or contract carriers who suffered provable losses because of the delay or to the wage earner who was forced to "clock in" an hour late. And yet it was surely foreseeable that among the many who would be delayed would be truckers and wage earners.

Id. at 825 n.8.

Can the court's result be justified on the ground that Cargill's loss represented a mere pecuniary externality? Did it? Or is it that Cargill had no legally protected right that was infringed by defendant's negligence? But if that is so, what is the basis for the tort of intentional interference with contract, discussed in Chapter 2?

To the extent that the cases in this chapter turn on ideas of remoteness or uncertainty of damage, you should reexamine them after reading Chapter 8, which deals with causation and scope of liability. For interesting efforts to explain the economic-loss cases in economic terms see Bishop, Economic Loss in Tort, forthcoming in Oxford J. Legal Stud; Rizzo, A Theory of Economic Loss in the Law of Torts, forthcoming in J. Legal Stud.

Chapter 7
Strict Liability

In the last chapter James Barr Ames characterized strict liability — the principle that a man acts at his peril and must therefore compensate anyone whom he injures by his acts — as an "unmoral" principle that was giving way to the principle that a man is liable for inflicting injury only when he is at fault, that is, only when the injury is deliberate or negligent. Yet even in the heyday of the negligence principle, some activities were governed by strict liability; those activities are considered in this chapter. The domain of strict liability has expanded in this century, first through the replacement of negligence by workmen's compensation to govern injuries to employees, and second through the growing trend toward substituting strict liability for negligence in cases involving injuries caused by defective products. The discussion of modern products liability law, however, is postponed to a subsequent chapter (Chapter 9). The present chapter not only reviews the traditional areas of strict liability but also offers at the end some summary appraisals of the relative merits of negligence and strict liability. The reader should also bear in mind the pockets of strict liability encountered in previous chapters — for example, in defamation and trespass (additional materials on the law of trespass are presented in this chapter).

Behrens v. Bertram Mills Circus Ltd.
[1957] 2 Q.B. 1

The plaintiffs, husband and wife, were both midgets and during the Christmas season beginning in December, 1953, were on exhibition in a booth in the funfair adjoining the defendants' circus at Olympia, which they and their manager occupied under licence from the defendants. At the far end of the funfair the defendants kept six female Burmese elephants which performed in the circus. The plaintiffs' booth was in a passageway leading from the funfair to the circus ring along which the elephants, escorted by their trainer and grooms, passed several times a day on their way to and from the circus ring. On January 2, 1954, the plaintiffs' manager [Whitehead] had in the pay box of their booth a small dog which had been introduced into the premises contrary to the defendants' rules. As the elephants were passing the booth, the dog ran out barking and snapping at one of them. The elephant [named Bullu] turned and went after the dog, followed by some of the other elephants, and the plaintiffs' booth was knocked down, the female plaintiff being seriously injured by falling parts of the booth. None of the elephants directly attacked either of the plaintiffs. . . .

DEVLIN, J. read the following judgment: . . .

A person who keeps an animal with knowledge (scienter-retinuit) of its tendency to do harm is strictly liable for damage it does if it escapes; he is under an absolute duty to confine or control it so that it shall not do injury to others. All animals ferae naturae, that is, all animals which are not by nature harmless, such as a rabbit, or have not been tamed by man and domesticated, such as a horse, are conclusively presumed to have such a tendency, so that the scienter need not in their case be proved. All animals in the second class mansuetae naturae are conclusively presumed to be harmless until they have manifested a savage or vicious propensity; proof of such a manifestation is proof of scienter and serves to transfer the animal, so to speak, out of its natural class into the class of ferae naturae. . . . Four years ago a committee appointed by the Lord Chancellor and presided over by Lord Goddard C.J. recommended that the scienter action should be abolished and that liability for harm done by an animal should be the same as in the case of any other chattel; it should depend on the failure to exercise the appropriate degree of care; which might in the case of very dangerous animals be "so stringent as to amount practically to a guarantee of safety." I wish to express the hope that Parliament may find time to consider this recommendation, for this branch of the law is badly in need of simplification.

The particular rigidity in the scienter action which is involved in this case — there are many others which are not — is the rule that requires the harmfulness of the offending animal to be judged not by reference to its particular training and habits, but by reference to the general habits of the species to which it belongs. The law ignores the world of difference between the wild elephant in the jungle and the trained elephant in the circus. The elephant Bullu is in fact no more dangerous than a cow; she reacted in the same way as a cow would do to the irritation of a small dog; if perhaps her bulk made her capable of doing more damage, her higher training enabled her to be more swiftly checked. But I am compelled to assess the defendants' liability in this case in just the same way as I would assess it if they had loosed a wild elephant into the funfair. This is a branch of the law, which, as Lord Goddard C.J. . . . said recently has been settled by authority rather than by reason. . . .

The defendants submit five answers to the scienter action. They are: First, that elephants are not ferae naturae within the meaning of the rule. Secondly, that the rule does not impose liability for every act that an animal does if it escapes control, but only for those acts which are vicious and savage, which the action of Bullu was not. Thirdly, that the plaintiffs' injuries were caused by their own fault. Fourthly, that the maxim volenti non fit injuria — that is that the plaintiffs accepted the risk — applies to them. Fifthly, that it is a good defence to liability under the rule if the action of the animal is caused by the wrongful act of a third party, in this case Whitehead and his dog.

The first submission is, in my judgment, concluded so far as this court is concerned by the decision of the Court of Appeal in Filburn v. People's Palace and Aquarium Co. Ltd., [[1890] 25 Q.B.D. 258,] which held that as a matter of law an elephant is an animal ferae naturae. [Counsel] has sought to distinguish this case on the ground that the elephants belonging to the defendants are Burmese elephants and he submits that it is open to me to hold that while elephants generally are ferae naturae, Burmese elephants are not. In my judgment, it is not open to me to consider this submission. It is not stated in Filburn v. People's Palace what the nationality of the elephant was with which the court was there dealing, and the case must be regarded as an authority for the legal proposition that all elephants are dangerous. The reason why this is a question of law and not a question of fact is because it is a matter of which judicial notice has to be taken. The doctrine has from its formulation proceeded upon the supposition that the knowledge of what kinds of animals are tame and what are savage is common knowledge. Evidence is receivable, if at all, only on the basis that the judge may wish to inform himself. . . . Common knowledge about the ordinary course of nature will extend to a knowledge of the propensities of animals according to their different genera, but cannot be supposed to extend to the manner of behaviour of animals of the same genus in different parts of the world. Nor can one begin a process of inquiry which might lead in many directions (for example, I am told that female elephants are more docile than male, and that that is why circus elephants are usually female) and be productive of minute subdivisions which would destroy the generality of the rule.

The defendants' second contention raises a point of doubt and difficulty. It may be approached in this way. The reason for imposing a specially stringent degree of liability upon the keeper of a savage animal is that such an animal has a propensity to attack mankind and, if left unrestrained, would be likely to do so. The keeper has, therefore, "an absolute duty to confine or control it so that it shall not do injury." But if it escapes from his control, is he liable (subject, of course, to the rules on remoteness of damage) for any injury which it causes, or only for such injury as flows naturally from its vicious or savage propensity?

[Counsel] submits that it is the latter part of this question which suggests the correct answer and that the rule of absolute liability applies only when an animal is acting savagely and attacking human beings. On the facts of this case, he submits that Bullu was not acting viciously but out of fright; she was seeking to drive off the small dog rather than to attack it; maybe she or another elephant trampled on the dog (there is no conclusive evidence of that, and it might have been crushed by falling timber) but there is nothing to show that she trampled on it deliberately. Certainly she never attacked Mrs. Behrens who was injured only indirectly. In short, if Bullu could be treated as a human being, her conduct would not be described as vicious but as quite excusable.

It does not, to my mind, necessarily follow that the scope of the rule is co-extensive with the reason for making it. It may equally well be argued that once the rule is made, the reason for making it is dissolved and all that then matters are the terms of the rule. That would certainly be the right approach in the case of any statutory rule of absolute liability. Is it so in the case of this rule of common law? There appears to be no authority directly in point. [Counsel] derives the chief support for his contention from an argument which may be summarized as follows. If an animal mansuetae naturae manifests a vicious tendency, the scienter rule applies to it as if it were ferae naturae. . . . How is the principle applied? Suppose a large dog collides with a child and knocks him down, that is an accident and not a manifestation of a vicious propensity and the scienter rule does not apply at all; if it bites a child, it becomes ferae naturae, and the strict rule thereafter applies. But it would seem to be unreasonable that the strict rule should require it to be kept under complete restraint. Suppose that its keeper muzzles it and that while muzzled it playfully or accidentally knocks a child down, ought the keeper to be liable? There is a good deal of authority . . . to show that the keeper is not liable. . . .

This is an impressive argument. But it does not seem to me that the logic of the matter necessarily requires that an animal that is savage by disposition should be put on exactly the same footing as one that is savage by nature. Certainly practical considerations would seem to demand that they should be treated differently. It may be unreasonable to hold the owner of a biting dog responsible thereafter for everything it does; but it may also be unreasonable to limit the liability for a tiger. If a person wakes up in the middle of the night and finds an escaping tiger on top of his bed and suffers a heart attack, it would be nothing to the point that the intentions of the tiger were quite amiable. If a tiger is let loose in a funfair, it seems to me to be irrelevant whether a person is injured as the result of a direct attack or because on seeing it he runs away and falls over. The feature of this present case which is constantly arising to blur the reasoning is the fact that this particular elephant Bullu was tame. But that, as I have said, is a fact which must be ignored. She is to be treated as if she were a wild elephant; and if a wild elephant were let loose in the funfair and stampeding around, I do not think there would be much difficulty in holding that a person who was injured by falling timber had a right of redress. It is not, in my judgment, practicable to introduce conceptions of mens rea and malevolence in the case of animals. . . .

It follows that, subject to any special defence, the defendants are liable for any injury done while the elephant was out of control. It does not follow (I say this because of a point that was raised in the argument) that if an elephant slips or stumbles, its keeper is responsible for the consequences. There must be a failure of control. But here there was such a failure, albeit a very temporary one. . . .

The third point taken by the defence is that the injuries were due to the plaintiffs' own fault. This defence is of a nature well recognized in this class of case and there are many cases in which liability has been successfully contested on the ground that the savage animal was teased or provoked by the plaintiff. I see no reason why the same sort of defence should not prevail where the fault of the plaintiff does not amount to recklessness of this sort, but is failure of due diligence to look after his own safety. The facts said to constitute the defence in this case are pleaded in paragraph 6A of the re-amended defence: "Further or in the alternative the matters complained of were caused or contributed to by the negligence of the plaintiffs and each of them in that they permitted the said dog to be in or near to the said booth well knowing that dogs were not permitted upon the circus premises and/or that dogs were likely to alarm or excite the elephants." In my judgment, this plea breaks down completely upon the allegation that the plaintiffs permitted the dog to be in or near the booth. Even if I were to assume that the plaintiffs knew of the presence of the dog and to assume likewise the other allegations in the paragraph, there is nothing at all to sustain the allegation of permission. Whitehead was not in their employ and they had no power to control him in any way. Conceivably, it might be said that if the presence of the dog amounted to an obvious danger, anyone who knew of it, whether he had power to order it off or not, ought in the interests of his own safety to have reported it to someone who had the necessary authority. But no one puts the danger as high as that.

The fourth contention of the defence is a plea of volenti non fit injuria based on the allegation that the plaintiffs accepted any risk inherent in the passage of elephants past their booth. There is no evidence that either the plaintiffs or Whitehead knew or had any reason to suspect when the licence was granted that the elephants would come anywhere near their booth. [Counsel], however, submits that the time when the licence was entered into is not the decisive time, or not the only decisive time. He submits that when the plaintiffs discovered, as of course they did at the beginning, that the elephants passed the booth, their decision to remain amounted to an assumption of the risk. The situation at this later point of time raises quite different considerations. The plaintiffs had not then to decide, in the light of their knowledge of the conditions under which it would have to be exercised, whether they would acquire a right; but whether they would continue to exercise a right for which they had already paid. It is not per se a defence that the plaintiffs were engaged in exercising a right. The pursuit of one's own rights may sometimes be so foolhardy that the reasonable man should desist and seek another remedy. If a man is on the highway and he sees elephants approaching in procession, the law does not require him to elect between turning down a side street or accepting the risk of their misbehaviour if he goes on; but if he sees them stampeding and remains where he is because he considers that he has as much right to the highway as they have, he might fail to recover. . . . It cannot here be contended that the passing of the elephants created an obvious danger; indeed, the case as pleaded for the defence is that the risk was very small. This plea fails.

The last of the defendants' contentions is that they are freed from liability by the wrongful act of a third party. This point appears to be concluded against them by the decision of the Court of Appeal in Baker v. Snell, in which it was held by a majority that the intervening act of a third party was no defence. . . .

Notes

1. Putting to one side the question whether a tame elephant should be classified as ferae naturae, a rule of strict liability for injuries caused by keeping a dangerous wild animal may be justifiable by the following reasoning.

The expected accident costs of keeping such animals are high, which implies that the optimal costs of precautions are also high. Yet as even the facts of Behrens suggest, it is difficult, merely by taking care, to prevent such animals from doing considerable damage. But there is an alternative to taking care, and that is not keeping such animals at all, or keeping fewer of them. In other words, the keeping of dangerous wild animals is an activity where reducing the level of the activity, just as increasing the care used in it, is an important variable in accident avoidance. This is clearest where the animal is kept for a trivial purpose, as where a man keeps a tiger in his house as a conversation piece or to ward off intruders. While the animal may be highly dangerous even if great care is taken with it, the costs of avoiding the danger by getting rid of the animal may be slight. Those costs are the benefits the owner derives from having the animal, and if the benefits are slight so are the costs of getting rid of it.

Sometimes the negligence standard is interpreted broadly enough to require a change in the level of an activity and not just greater care in a narrow sense of "care." Thus a man who ran into a burning building to retrieve his hat would be deemed contributorily negligent even though he exercised all due care after he entered the building. Usually, however, courts applying a negligence standard do not consider a reduction in the level of an activity as a method of accident avoidance that may be optimal. If a driver exercising due care collides with another driver, the court does not inquire whether the injurer should perhaps not have been taking that particular trip because the benefits to him were less than the total (social) costs when expected accident costs are included. Perhaps he was driving on a minor errand that easily could have been consolidated with another errand, thereby avoiding one trip and the expected accident costs associated with it. Perhaps he should have taken a bus or train instead — alternative transportation modes that may have lower expected accident costs. Because the concept of the optimal level of an activity is less intuitive than that of acting carefully, courts would find it difficult to work activity level into the negligence calculus, and they generally do not try to do so.

A rule of strict liability automatically induces potential injurers to consider activity changes as a method, alternative to greater care, of reducing expected accident costs. Under strict liability the injurer is liable for the consequences of any injury he inflicts, whether or not it could have been avoided by some cost-justified precaution. Therefore, the vehicle driver who is subject to a strict-liability standard will consider every possible way of minimizing his expected accident costs; one way is to drive less. To be sure, he will drive less only if, at the margin, the benefits of driving are less than the expected accident costs. But the driver subject only to a negligence standard will not even make the comparison, because he will assume that negligence is only a matter of care and not of activity level as well.

This analysis may appear to demonstrate that strict liability is allocatively superior to negligence, but this is only because we have ignored the potential victim's activity level. An accident may be avoidable at lower cost by a change in his activity level than by a change in the potential injurer's activity level. Recall the facts of *LeRoy Fibre* in Chapter 5. The damage to the plaintiff's flax could have been avoided by the railroad's running fewer trains or none at all, or by the plaintiff's not stacking its flax so near the track or perhaps by plaintiff's using its land for a different, less fire-sensitive purpose than stacking flax. There is no a priori basis for assuming that potential injurers are in general more likely to be cheaper cost avoiders than potential victims.

The analysis may seem too inconclusive to help in understanding the animal cases. But the coexistence of two facts makes those cases apt ones, under the above analysis, for preferring strict liability to negligence as the liability rule. First, in the case of dangerous wild animals, a change in activity level is often at least as promising a method of accident avoidance as using greater care in controlling them. These animals are normally kept for sport or entertainment. This implies that the benefits of keeping them — and hence the costs of not keeping them — will often be modest relative to either the expected accident costs, which are considerable, or the costs of greater care, which may also be considerable. Second, in these cases a change in the potential injurer's activity level is usually a much more promising method of accident prevention than a change in the potential victim's accident level. The optimal solution to the safety problem created by the homeowner who keeps a tiger in his backyard to scare off intruders is not for all his neighbors to move away or build cages around their houses to keep the tiger out. If we are confident that changing the potential injurer's activity level is the best way of preventing some class of accidents, it makes sense to subject the class to a rule of strict liability rather than to one of negligence.

The following table illustrates the analysis. B, the burden of precautions in the Hand formula, is separated into two components, B_c and B_a. B_c is the burden of preventing the accident by using greater care, B_a the burden of preventing the accident by reducing the activity level. Either party is assumed able to avoid the accident (but at different costs) by either using greater care or reducing activity level. In the hypothetical example illustrated in the table, the optimal precaution is achieved by a rule of strict liability. Negligence would be suboptimal — assuming that courts applying a negligence standard interpret care narrowly.

	Injurer	*Victim*
B_c	180	110
B_a	10	140

$$PL = 100$$

How, if at all, is the analysis affected if B_a to the victim is 40 instead of 140? If B_c to the injurer is 80 instead of 180?

For further discussion of the activity-level argument for strict liability in some cases see R. A. Posner, Economic Analysis of Law 139-141 (2d ed. 1977); Shavell, Strict Liability versus Negligence, 9 J. Legal Stud. 1 (1980).

2. How does the result in *Behrens* square with the above analysis? How should the liability of a public zoo be treated under the analysis?

Here are some other questions about *Behrens:*

a. Was Bullu really no more dangerous than a cow? In what sense was Lord Devlin using the term "dangerous"? Was it the relevant sense? Just how tame was Bullu?

b. Why would there have been no liability if the elephant had merely stumbled?

c. Would Bullu have been ferae naturae in Burma?

d. Was defendant or Whitehead the cheaper cost avoider of the accident?

3. The court in *Behrens* relied on Baker v. Snell, [1908] 2 K.B. 352, in rejecting the argument that Whitehead's bringing the dog into plaintiffs' booth caused the elephants to stampede and thereby excused defendant from liability. In *Baker*, defendant owned a dog known by him to be savage. Defendant's potman (a serving man employed by defendant in his pub) had custody of the dog. One day he brought the dog into the kitchen where plaintiff, a housemaid employed by defendant, was having breakfast. She said, "I will bet the dog will not bite any one in the room," whereupon the potman let the dog go, saying, "Go it, Bob." The dog then attacked plaintiff and bit her. The court held that defendant was liable, even if the potman so far exceeded his authority that the principle of respondeat superior was inapplicable. Can this result be justified by the economic analysis in Note 1 above?

4. On the wonderfully intricate English common law of tort liability for damage caused by animals see G. L. Williams, Liability for Animals (1939).

5. Must strict liability always be understood as liability for an injury inflicted without fault? Could negligence per se (see Chapter 4) be regarded as a strict liability doctrine?

Rolen v. Maryland Casualty Co.
240 So. 2d 42 (La. App. 1970)

BOLIN, J.

Plaintiff, the father of Vickie Lea Rolen, appeals from a judgment rejecting his demands against Maryland Casualty Company for damages for injuries inflicted upon his daughter by a dog owned by defendant's insured. The suit was instituted by plaintiff, individually and as administrator of his minor daughter, against defendant as insurer of Mr. Jones, owner of the dog, under a homeowner's policy in which the company agreed to pay on behalf of Jones any damages for which Jones should be held liable because of bodily injury or property damage.

The Jones family and the Rolen family had been next-door neighbors for more than three years. Approximately one and one-half years prior to the accident on April 21, 1968, Jones purchased the six-weeks-old German Shepherd dog, Shawn, which is concededly the culprit in this case. Although there were no eye witnesses to the occurrence, it is not denied that the dog inflicted a severe wound on Vickie's head and forehead.

Mr. and Mrs. Jones and Mr. and Mrs. Rolen all testified at the trial that their children had played together, either in one or the other's front yard, from the time the Rolens moved next door to the Jones family. Additionally, Mr. Jones testified all the neighborhood children had played with the dog, Shawn, from the time Jones purchased him until the date of the accident, approximately one and one-half years later. Jones said he maintained a fenced backyard and the dog was kept in this enclosure; that there were double gates for entering the carport; that on the day and at the time of the accident one of these gates was open; that he had been carrying trash from the backyard to the front and was entering and leaving by this gate; that his wife called him to the phone while he was thus occupied and he did not close the gate before entering the house to answer the phone.

Although Jones admitted the dog had previously either bitten or scratched one of his own sons and the wound necessitated stitches, nevertheless he denied he considered the dog vicious or dangerous. No other positive evidence was adduced tending to indicate any vicious tendencies on the part of the dog.

The dog was fed in a bowl near the back door leading onto the carport immediately adjacent the open gate. Mr. Jones testified he had fed the dog about 45 minutes prior to the accident. There was no evidence available as to

the reason for or the circumstances surrounding the attack and the child was
evidently unable to explain what had happened. . . .

The logic behind the common law [of liability for animals] . . . is based
upon the premise that animals occupy two categories. The first category
embraces wild or undomesticated animals such as bears, tigers, wolves, et
cetera. These animals are considered inherently dangerous and, therefore,
anyone who owns one does so at his own peril and is absolutely liable for all
injuries caused by it.

The second category includes animals which have become domesticated
by man, such as horses, cows, dogs, et cetera. These animals are regarded as
inherently safe. However, even this type animal may become vicious and the
owner becomes liable for any injury it causes if the animal has a previous
history of a vicious temperament, or if the owner knew or had reason to know
of a dangerous propensity in the animal.

The record does not support appellant's claim that the dog, Shawn, was
inherently dangerous. As previously pointed out, animals usually placed in
this category are wild rather than domesticated. Plaintiff, however, attempted to show the breed classified as German Shepherd is vicious by
nature. Dr. Franks, a Shreveport veterinarian, testified this type of animal
may be either vicious or gentle according to its training. He noted the army
has trained this breed of dog to be vicious and has utilized it for sentry or
guard duty. On the other hand, this same breed has been trained to lead the
blind and, after such training, is very obedient and tame. Dr. Franks' testimony is best summarized when he said, "You can't say, in my way of thinking,
that a shepherd is a bad dog. There are good ones and there are bad ones. It
involves things on a personal dog-situation and you can't say in generalizations that they are all bad dogs." We find appellant has failed to establish
Shawn was inherently dangerous. . . .

The most serious effort made by plaintiff to show Jones knew or should
have known of the vicious nature of Shawn related to the incident involving
one of the Jones children which occurred several months prior to the injury
made the basis of this suit. On that occasion Mr. and Mrs. Rolen were visiting
the Joneses. The children were in the backyard playing with the dog. During
the course of play one of the Jones children received an injury to his forehead.
All of the parties who were present or had any knowledge of this incident
testified it was of a minor nature and no one attached any significance to it
insofar as an indication of the dog's nature. Mr. and Mrs. Rolen were present
and said they did not believe at that time the dog was vicious or dangerous.
The Rolens continued to allow their children to play with Shawn after this
incident occurred.

A single incident does not necessarily place the owner on notice the
animal is dangerous or vicious. The test is whether the incident was of such a
nature as to lead a reasonable person to believe the dog was sufficiently
dangerous as to be likely to cause injury to a person at a later date. The tenor
of the entire record leads us to conclude neither Mr. and Mrs. Rolen nor the

Joneses had any reason to believe Shawn possessed any dangerous propensities.

We conclude plaintiff has failed to establish either that the dog was vicious or that the owner had any reason to believe he had dangerous propensities. . . .

Notes

1. As *Rolen* shows, the widespread popular belief that "every dog is entitled to one bite" is only the crudest approximation of the common-law position. That a dog has bitten before is not conclusive proof that the dog is known by his owner to have a vicious disposition. By the same token, if the dog's viciousness is evidenced by other behavior, his owner may be liable for its first bite.

2. Whitefield v. Stewart, 577 P.2d 1295 (Okla. 1978), was a suit to recover damages for injuries sustained by a six-year-old girl who was allegedly bitten by defendant's pet woolly monkey. The court noted that an "increasing number of jurisdictions . . . are imposing absolute liability on owners of domesticated animals, such as dogs." Continuing, the court stated:

> In 1947 our Legislature enacted a modified version of absolute liability for owners of dogs, 4 O.S. 1971, §42.1, which provides: "The owner or owners of any dog which shall, without provocation, bite or injure any person while such person is in or on a public place, or lawfully in or upon the private property of the owner or owners of such dog, shall be liable for damages to any person bitten or injured by such dog to the full amount of the injury sustained."
>
> Under this statute a dog owner is only liable where without provocation the animal bites or injures a person. If a tame animal that is domesticated, such as a dog, makes its owner absolutely liable under the statute, then it appears to us that at least the same responsibility and liability would be applicable to the owners of a tamed wild animal.
>
> 1 Okl. L. Rev. 111, "Torts: Statutory Liability of Dog Owner," which deals with §42.1 notes the Legislature came very near to imposing absolute liability on the owner of a dog for any injuries inflicted by the dog. It further reflects the struggle between applying the common law rule while keeping the application in line with a desirable public policy. It states there is a feeling on the part of the public generally that one who chooses to harbor a dog on his premises should be responsible for the acts of the animal; and, in the absence of provocation by the victim, the public looks to the owner for redress. We think this philosophy directly applicable to the case at bar involving a tamed wild animal, such as a monkey, and hold that one who chooses to harbor a monkey on his premises is responsible for the acts of the animal to the same extent as provided in §42.1 in the case of owners of dogs. Thus, if in the case at bar the monkey bit Kimberly without provocation by Kimberly, then Appellee would be liable for damages for the full amount of the injury sustained.

577 P.2d at 1298-1299. Is this a proper use of statutes? Why should a statute addressed to the liability of dog owners be thought to change the common law applicable to other tame animals? Where have you seen such a statute before?

There was expert testimony in *Whitefield* "that the woolly monkey belongs to a class of new world monkeys which are very popular pets, but that they were not domesticated because domestication is a genetic problem." Also, while "the woolly monkey is gentle and trusting and can be tamed," it could "without provocation bite a young child. . . . [T]his is the reason primates go to the zoo as they approach adulthood." Id. at 1297. There is no reference to any testimony concerning the size of the monkey. How would the court in *Behrens* have classified Stewart's pet monkey? Would it have found it ferae naturae, on the ground that gorillas and other wild apes are clearly ferae naturae? Or would it have distinguished between monkeys and great apes? What economic reasons can be offered for distinguishing between a tame monkey and a dog or a cat?

3. Both the statute in *Whitefield* and the common-law principles discussed in *Behrens* recognize a defense of provocation in animal cases. Is this defense consistent with the economic analysis of strict liability? Should a broader defense of contributory negligence be recognized?

4. In what circumstances might the owner of an animal known to have a vicious disposition be liable for an intentional tort?

5. What if a fierce animal is stolen from its owner, and while in the hands of the thief bites someone because the thief fails to restrain it? Is the owner liable for the bite? See Note, Domestic Animal Liability in Missouri: Jaws, Paws and Claws, 45 U. Mo.-K.C.L. Rev. 280, 281-284 (1976).

Vaughan v. Miller Bros. "101" Ranch Wild West Show
109 W. Va. 170, 153 S.E. 289 (1930)

HATCHER, J. . . .

The plaintiff's demand in brief is this: He attended a circus, and a vicious ape on exhibition there bit off his finger. There is no allegation of negligence. The plaintiff takes the position that none is requisite; that the gravamen of the action is not in the negligent keeping of a vicious animal, but in keeping it at all. Much authority supports his position. . . . May v. Burdett, 9 Q.B. 101, 115 E.R. 1213, decided in 1846, is the leading English case. Lord Denman, in delivering the judgment of the court said: "The precedents, both ancient and modern, with scarcely an exception, merely state the ferocity of the animal and the knowledge of the defendant without any allegation of negligence or want of care. . . . The conclusion to be drawn from an examination of all the authorities appears to us to be this: That a person keeping a mischievous animal with knowledge of its propensities is bound to keep it secure at his peril, and that, if it does mischief, negligence is presumed, without express averment." Troubled because his position could not be reconciled with the maxim so deeply ingrained in English jurisprudence, "He who suffers a damage by his own fault, is not considered as suffering damage," Lord Denman stated that, if the injury was occasioned solely by the willfulness of the plaintiff, it might be a defense; but on this he did not commit himself. Bramwell, J., in Nichols v. Marsland, L. R. 10 Ex. 255, attempting to bolster Lord Denman's position, said: "I am by no means sure that if a man kept a tiger, and lightning broke his chain, and he got loose and did mischief, that the man who kept him would not be liable." In his enthusiasm, Judge Bramwell overlooked the probable mollifying effect of the lightning on the tiger as well as another maxim, "An act of God does injury to no one."

Based on the pronouncement in May v. Burdett, judicial dicta followed that the owner of animals ferae naturae "is an insurer for," "is liable under all circumstances for," and "is absolutely liable for" all injuries done by them.

The common law accorded to the owner of wild animals (in possession) practically the same property rights therein as in those domesticated. The keeping of a menagerie was not forbidden or deemed in any way blameworthy. If, at common law, the ownership of wild animals was recognized and protected as lawful, how could judges consistently presume such ownership wrongful and negligent? An anomaly indeed! It is true that animals ferae naturae constantly seek to escape confinement, and, if successful, become a menace to mankind. But the tiger, unrestrained, is no more dangerous than fire, water, electricity, or gas uncontrolled. The liability of the owner of these has never been declared absolute, nor his negligence presumed from mere ownership. Why discriminate against the owner of the animate menace? . . . Before the law can redress an injury, "there must be an act which under the circumstances is wrongful." For if the injury "is the result of a lawful act done in a lawful manner, without any carelessness or negligence, there may be no legal injury, and no tort giving rise to an action for damages."

Despite the fallacy of May v. Burdett, the English courts have continued to render it lip service. Not a single adjudication, however, have I found against an owner, based solely on possession, in which arose the question of vis major or contributory negligence. And in Marlor v. Ball, 16 R.L.R. 239, Eng. Rep. Ann. for the year 1900, p. 2585, it was held that the defendant who had zebras on exhibition was without negligence and not liable for the resultant injury to plaintiff, who had stroked a zebra. So by an English court do we find the English doctrine of absolute liability absolutely ignored.

Immediately following the decision in May v. Burdett, it became quite the vogue in the United States to proclaim (by way of dictum) its doctrine. But the principle of absolute liability has no more been enforced here than in England. The Supreme Court of Massachusetts . . . limited the risk of exhibitors of wild animals to "keeping them so as not to injure invitees who are in exercise of due care." . . . Absolute liability on the part of the keeper of a ferocious animal was advocated theoretically in 1862 by the New York court in Scribner v. Kelley, 38 Barb. 14. But in 1878 that theory was discarded in the case of one who with knowledge of an animal's ferocity unnecessarily assumed a position of danger. "In such a case it cannot be said, in a legal sense, that the keeping of the animal, which is the gravamen of the offense, produced the injury." . . . Guzzi v. N.Y. Zoological Society, 192 App. Div. 263, 182 N.Y.S. 257, 260, decided in 1920, indicates a permanent rupture with May v. Burdett, saying: "The cases seem to be unanimous that no recovery can be had where the injured party unnecessarily and voluntarily puts herself in the way to be hurt, knowing the probable consequences of her act." . . .

In this country the right to exhibit wild animals is judicially recognized. "The conducting of shows for the exhibition of wild . . . animals is a lawful business." Such exhibitions are licensed everywhere. Municipalities frequently maintain zoos for the benefit of the public. The idea is no longer indulged that it is prima facie negligent to keep or exhibit wild animals. . . . Hence the gist of modern actions against exhibitors cannot be the mere keeping of savage animals, but must be neglect to restrain them. "Latterly, however, there seems to be a disposition upon the part of the authorities to hold the more reasonable rule, that all that should be required of the keeper of such animals is that he should take that superior caution to prevent their doing mischief which their propensities in that direction justly demand of him."

Hence, if a right of action in such case depends on neglect to restrain, negligence must be alleged. . . .

Notes

1. Did the court state the English position correctly? The English courts recognized a defense of provocation — albeit not of supervening force (or vis major) as in the hypothetical case where the tiger is released from his chains by a bolt of lightning or under the actual facts of *Behrens* and *Baker*, where a third party provoked the animal. Is there an economic reason for distinguishing between provocation by the plaintiff and by a third party? For the defense of supervening force in negligence cases, see the next chapter in this book.

2. Is it possible to distinguish on economic grounds between an exhibitor of animals to the public and an individual who owns a wild animal for personal amusement or defense, so far as the appropriate liability rule is concerned? For a clue, see Cowden v. Bear Country, Ind., 382 F. Supp. 1321, 1326 (D.S.D. 1974), holding that South Dakota law does not impose strict liability on keepers of wild animals:

> a private business for profit that keeps wild animals that are by their nature vicious, unpredictable and dangerous, and invites the public for a fee to enter their premises where these animals are contained, owes their patrons a very high degree of care in the manner and place of keeping such animals. The keeping of

wild animals for exhibition has come to be recognized as proper and useful and is therefore not prima facie negligent. Although the owning and exhibiting of wild animals of a fierce, dangerous, and unpredictable nature is not in and of itself unlawful, the owner is under a duty to exercise the highest degree of care to protect patrons from them. The gist of an action by a patron for injury sustained on the exhibitor's premises is failure to perform the high duty owed to patrons. The owner and exhibitor of wild animals is held to that duty and standard of care commensurate with the high degree of risk of injury to patrons presented by such animals. The owner and exhibitor is held to know of the natural propensity of such animals to attack swiftly without warning and produce serious injury and risk to human life. It is for the jury to decide whether the owner of such animals demonstrated superior caution and a very high standard of care in the manner in which the wild animals were confined and restrained from doing injury to the patrons.

To say that "the keeping of wild animals for exhibition has come to be recognized as proper and useful" is another way of saying, is it not, that the costs of avoiding accidents by eliminating or curtailing the underlying activity, i.e., the exhibition of wild animals, would be substantial relative to the benefits in accident avoidance. The keeping of a wild animal as a pet does not carry with it the same presumption of substantial benefits.

Compare the distinction drawn by the court in City and County of Denver v. Kennedy, 29 Colo. App. 15, 476 P.2d 762-763 (1970), between the liability of an individual who keeps a coyote on his property and that of a city zoo:

> This jurisdiction has adopted the general rule that "one who harbors a wild animal, which by its very nature is vicious and unpredictable, does so at his peril, and liability for injuries inflicted by such animal is absolute." Collins v. Otto, 149 Colo. 489, 369 P.2d 564.
>
> The *Collins* case involved a situation where a coyote kept by the defendants on their property inflicted injury upon a four-year-old child. The rationale upon which absolute liability was predicated by our Supreme Court in that case was that, in keeping a vicious and dangerous animal, the defendants had acted wrongfully and unjustifiably. This is the rationale upon which the rule of absolute liability is imposed by most jurisdictions against one who harbors a wild animal. Under that rationale the act of keeping or harboring the animal is viewed, by itself, as an unreasonable act done in defiance of the safety and desires of the surrounding society, and consequently the one who performs it becomes an insurer as to that society.
>
> Considering such rationale, we do not think the rule in *Collins* extends to, nor was intended to extend to, a situation where a municipality maintains and operates a zoo for the benefit of the public and in response to the public's obvious desires. In such instance the keeping and displaying of animals which are commonly wild in nature is not an unreasonable or unjustified act.
>
> Nor, in our opinion, does the rationale sometimes given for the rule in wild animal cases that one who exposes the public to the risk of a very dangerous thing is absolutely responsible make the rule applicable to a municipally owned

and operated zoo. In the context of today's society and present zoological techniques, it would be unrealistic to hold, as a matter of law, that the operation of a zoo by a municipality exposes the public to an inordinate risk.

Isaacs v. Powell
267 So. 2d 864 (Fla. App. 1972)

McNULTY, J. . . .
Plaintiff-appellant Scott Isaacs was two years and seven months old at the times material herein. His father had taken him to defendants-appellees' monkey farm where, upon purchasing an admission ticket, and as was usual and encouraged by appellees, he also purchased some food to feed the animals. While Scott was feeding a chimpanzee named Valerie she grabbed his arm and inflicted serious injury.

The exact details of how Valerie was able to grab Scott's arm are in dispute. Appellees contend that Scott's father lifted the boy above reasonably sufficient protective barriers to within Valerie's reach, while appellants counter that the barriers and other protective measures were insufficient. But in any case, appellants do not now, nor did they below, rely on any fault of appellees. Rather, they rely solely on the . . . generally accepted strict or, as it is sometimes called, absolute liability doctrine under which negligence or fault on the part of the owner or keeper of an animal ferae naturae is irrelevant. Appellees, on the other hand, suggest that we should adopt the emerging, though yet minority, view that liability should depend upon negligence, i.e., a breach of the duty of care reasonably called for taking into account the nature and species of the animal involved. We will consider this aspect of the problem first and will hereinafter discuss available defenses under the theory we adopt. . . .

. . . [W]e are of the view that the older and general rule of strict liability, which obviates the issue of the owner's negligence, is more suited to the fast growing, populous and activity-oriented society of Florida. Indeed, our society imposes more than enough risks upon its members now, and we are reluctant to encourage the addition of one more particularly when that one more is increasingly contributed by those who, for profit, would exercise their "right" to harbor wild animals and increase exposure to the dangers thereof by luring advertising. . . .

Additionally, we observe that Florida has enacted §767.04, F.S.A.,[5] relating to dogs, which abrogates the permissive "one bite" rule of the common

---

5. This section provides, in pertinent part: "The owners of any dog which shall bite any person, while such person is on or in a public place, or lawfully on or in a private place, including the property of the owner of such dogs, shall be liable for such damages as may be suffered by persons bitten, *regardless of the former viciousness of such dog or the owners' knowledge of such viciousness* . . .; Provided, however, no owner of any dog shall be liable for any damages to any person or his property when such person shall mischievously or carelessly provoke or aggravate

law. That rule posited that an owner of a dog is liable to one bitten by such dog only if he is chargeable with "scienter," i.e., prior knowledge of the viciousness of the dog. Necessarily, of course, the cause of action therefor was predicated on the negligence of the owner in failing to take proper precautions with knowledge of the dog's vicious propensities. Our statute, however, has in effect imposed strict liability on a dog owner (from which he can absolve himself only by complying with the warning proviso of the statute). It would result in a curious anomaly, then, if we were to adopt the negligence concept as a basis for liability of an owner or keeper of a tiger, while §764.04 imposed potential strict liability upon him if he should trade the tiger for a dog. We are compelled to adopt, therefore, the strict liability rule in these cases.

Concerning, now, available defenses under this rule we share the view, and emphasize, that "strict or absolute liability" does not mean the owner or keeper of a wild animal is an absolute insurer in the sense that he is liable regardless of any fault on the part of the victim. Moreover, we do not think it means he is liable notwithstanding an intervening, efficient independent fault which *solely* causes the result, as was possibly the case here if fault on the part of Scott's father were the sole efficient cause.

As to the fault of the victim himself, since the owner or keeper of a wild animal is held to a rigorous rule of liability on account of the danger inherent in harboring such animal, it has generally been held that the owner ought not be relieved from such liability by slight negligence or want of ordinary care on the part of the person injured. The latter's acts must be such as would establish that, with knowledge of the danger, he voluntarily brought the calamity upon himself. This general rule supports the Restatement of Torts, §515,[8] which we now adopt and set forth as follows:

(1) A plaintiff is not barred from recovery by his failure to exercise reasonable care to observe the propinquity of a wild animal or an abnormally dangerous domestic animal or to avoid harm to his person, land or chattels threatened by it.

(2) A plaintiff is barred from recovery by *intentionally and unreasonably* subjecting himself to the risk that a wild animal or an abnormally dangerous domestic animal will do harm to his person, land or chattels. (Italics supplied)

With regard to an intervening fault bringing about the result we have no hesitancy in expanding the foregoing rule to include as a defense the willful or intentional fault of a third party provided such fault is of itself an efficient

---

the dog inflicting such damage; nor shall any such owner be so liable if at the time of any such injury he had displayed in a prominent place on his premises a sign easily readable including the words 'Bad Dog.' " (Italics supplied.)

8. This rule is duplicated in §484, Restatement, Torts 2d, which states that the plaintiff's contributory negligence is not a defense to the strict liability of the possessor of an animal, except where such contributory negligence consists in voluntarily and unreasonably subjecting himself to the risk of harm from the animal.

cause and is the sole cause. If a jury were to decide in this case, therefore, that the *sole* efficient cause of Scott's injury was the intentional assumption of the apparent risks on the part of the boy's father and his placing of the boy within reach of the danger, it would be a defense available to appellees. Clearly, though, this defense would be related only to causation and is not dependent upon any theory of imputation of the father's fault to the son, which is now irrelevant in view of the extent of strict liability in these cases and the limited defenses available thereunder.

The judgment is reversed and the cause is remanded for a new trial on the theory of strict liability, and the defenses thereto, as enunciated above.

Notes

1. What is the relevance to the choice between strict liability and negligence of the features of Florida's society mentioned by the court?

2. Could one argue that the Florida dog-bite statute was even less relevant in *Isaacs* to the question of defendant's liability than the dog-bite statute in *Whitefield*? If it was relevant, why did the court not use its defenses, which included careless provocation? In Donner v. Arkwright-Boston Manufacturers Mutual Insurance Co., 358 So. 2d 21 (Fla. 1978), the Supreme Court of Florida criticized *Isaacs* and other intermediate appellate opinions that had suggested that assumption of risk was a valid defense under the Florida dog-bite law. "However, a careful reading of those cases will show that the defenses asserted, liberally labelled an assumption of risk, were in reality based upon provocation or aggravation of the animal." Id. at 24. A dog owner sued under the statute "has available to him only the defenses expressed in the statute." Id. at 26. But is there any difference between (common-law) assumption of risk and (statutory) provocation? The court thought so. "One can knowingly and voluntarily expose himself to the danger of a vicious dog without necessarily provoking or aggravating him maliciously or carelessly." Id. at 24 n.5. Do you agree? If one knows a dog is vicious, does it not follow that to walk within range of him is to carelessly provoke an attack?

3. Are you satisfied with the analysis in *Isaacs* of causation? How could plaintiff's father have been the "*sole* efficient cause" of the accident? Anyway, does not the court's discussion of causation simply reintroduce contributory negligence by another name? Is there any argument that the causal holding of *Isaacs* survives the ruling in *Donner* that the only defenses to a statutory dog-bite action are statutory defenses?

There used to be a rule, "of a particularly hideous character" (Prosser 490), imputing the negligence of a parent in failing to look after his or her child to the child in the latter's negligence action against an injurer, if the injury could have been prevented by the parent's exercising due care. This rule is said to have been repudiated (id.) — but has it been? Besides *Isaacs*, see, e.g., Selfe v. Smith, 397 So. 2d 348 (Fla. App. 1981), where the court reserved the question whether a parent's failure to fasten her child's seat belt might be grounds for reducing the defendant's damages. What is this but a form of imputed contributory negligence?

4. Is there any economic ground on which to distinguish between the liability of a municipal zoo and the liability of the monkey farm in *Isaacs?*

5. What should be the federal government's liability for injuries inflicted by bears and other wild animals at national parks? What would the court in *Isaacs* have said? The court in *Behrens?* See Rubenstein v. United States, 338 F. Supp. 654 (N.D. Cal. 1972), *aff'd*, 488 F.2d 1071 (9th Cir. 1973).

6. Keyser v. Phillips Petroleum Co., 287 So. 2d 364 (Fla. App. 1973), applied the standard prescribed in the *Isaacs* case for a defense based on plaintiff's conduct. In *Keyser*, plaintiff sued a service station dealer who kept a collection of snakes for public display, for injuries caused when a rattlesnake bit plaintiff. The court held that whether he was barred from recovering damages by having put his hand in the unlocked box of snakes was a jury question, since plaintiff alleged that in putting his hand in the box he "did not realize the dangers involved." Is this result correct?

7. Vaclavicek v. Olejarz, 61 N.J. 581-583, 297 A.2d 3-4 (1972), arose on the following facts:

> Defendant's farm abuts a highway on which the speed limit is 50 M.P.H. He trains quarter horses as a hobby. On the evening in question he placed two horses in a corral so that he might clean their stalls in the barn. Defendant himself built the corral, erecting a fence made of wooden posts and boards with some strands of barbed wire. For reasons unknown, the horses broke through the fence. They raced onto the highway, veering toward plaintiffs' car. The headlights picked up one onrushing animal, which the driver managed to avoid, but the second horse jumped into the windshield, causing the damages and injuries complained of. The second horse, a three-year-old stud, had been acquired by defendant about three weeks before the accident.

Should the applicable standard be strict liability or negligence?

Wenndt v. Latare
200 N.W.2d 862 (Iowa 1972)

MASON, J. . . .

On September 10, 1968, and all times material hereto, plaintiffs and defendant each kept stock cows and an Angus herd sire in adjoining west and east pastures, respectively, separated by a fence line running north and south. That day, however, plaintiffs discovered their bull panting and lathered up in a mud hole near their farm buildings. Simultaneously, plaintiffs also found defendant's bull in their pasture and a hole in defendant's half of the dividing fence. Defendant was summoned by telephone and together plaintiffs and defendant managed to return defendant's bull to defendant's pasture through the newly discovered opening in the fence.

Subsequent examination and treatment by plaintiffs' veterinarian revealed plaintiffs' bull suffered from a severely herniated scrotum. The testicles were badly damaged; all breeding services of the bull were lost. Plaintiffs' bull was otherwise restored to health and sold for scrap to Wilson and Company.

Plaintiffs had alleged in paragraph 4 of their petition filed July 25, 1969 "that the defendant was negligent in failing to restrain his bull from running at large in violation of section 188.2 of the 1966 Code of Iowa."

May 26, 1970, they amended their petition by adding to paragraph 4 the following: "That the defendant's breeding bull came into and trespassed upon lands where plaintiffs' bull and cows were maintained, which lands were lawfully fenced insofar as plaintiffs' portion of the partition line fence was concerned, in violation of section 188.3 of the Iowa Code." . . .

The statutes referred to in plaintiffs' petition as amended provide:

"188.2 Restraint of animals. All animals shall be restrained by the owners thereof from running at large."

"188.3 Trespass on lawfully fenced land. Any animal trespassing upon land, fenced as provided by law, may be distrained by the owner of such land, and held for all damages done thereon by it, unless it escaped from adjoining land in consequence of the neglect of such landowner to maintain his part of a lawful partition fence." . . .

Plaintiffs argue the assignments of error in three divisions. In the first division they argue those errors relating to the court's refusal and omission to give their requested instructions concerning the theory of strict liability in livestock trespass or incorporate such theory in those instructions given. . . .

This court has held in certain factual situations violation of section 188.2 is prima facie evidence of negligence and not negligence as a matter of law.

Hansen v. Kemmish, 201 Iowa 1008, 208 N.W. 277, dealt with the claim of a motorist for injuries resulting from a collision with defendant's boar running at large on the highway in violation of sections 2312 and 2313, The Code, 1897. Plaintiff contended defendant was required to restrain the boar at his peril. This court concluded that with respect to highway accidents the fact the animal was running at large on the highway constituted mere prima facie negligence, defendant having the right to show, if he could, that he exercised reasonable care in restraining the animal. . . .

Examination of the authorities cited, as well as many others, compels the conclusion the proper rule of law in actions seeking damages for injuries to persons or their property alleged to have been proximately caused by trespassing animals dictates that proof of the owner's failure to restrain his animals in violation of section 188.2, The Code, constitutes prima facie evidence of negligence, not negligence per se, and proof of such violation does not impose strict liability on the owner. Such prima facie evidence of negligence may be rebutted by evidence the owner exercised reasonable and ordinary care in restraining his animals.

The court did not err in refusing to submit the issue of strict liability as a result of plaintiffs' pleading and proof defendant was in violation of section 188.2, The Code.

There remains to be considered plaintiffs' contention that by reason of their May 26, 1970 amendment set out, supra, and the evidence adduced in support thereof, a jury question was generated on the issue of strict liability.

By the common law of England, an owner of domestic animals was held strictly liable for their trespasses upon the land of others irrespective of the keeper's negligence. It is clear however, in the early days of the United States many courts, including Iowa, rejected entirely the common-law rule of strict liability for animal trespasses, as contrary to established custom where cattle were allowed to graze at large on the range.

". . . But as the country has become more closely settled, the tendency has been to restore the common law rule, either by statute or by decision. The matter is now very largely governed by statutory provisions. The first legislation to be adopted consisted of 'fencing out' statutes, which provided that if the plaintiff properly fenced his land there was strict liability when the animals broke through the fence, but otherwise there was liability only when the owner was at fault. As the country became more settled the conflict between the grazing and the agricultural interests resulted in many states in 'fencing in' statutes, which required the owner of the animals to fence or otherwise restrain them, and made him strictly liable if he did not do so. . . ."

Section 188.2 may thus be properly described as a "fencing in" statute, section 188.3 as a "fencing out" statute.

Historically, there have grown three distinct areas of liability. A first basis of liability is negligence. Application of the negligence doctrine has classically arisen when the animal is lawfully in the place where the injury occurs. In Iowa, however, liability based on negligence may also arise in certain trespass situations. Typically, violation of the restraint statute, section 188.2, is involved and it constitutes prima facie evidence of negligence; it does not invoke strict liability. . . .

A second gender of liability is strict liability, the basis for recovery in common law for the trespass of animals. Strict liability lies in principle between liability based on negligence and absolute liability. While it may apply in the absence of fault, it becomes operative only upon the satisfaction of certain criteria in a fact situation. Grounded upon section 188.3, strict liability attaches only where the animal has trespassed upon land enclosed by a fence as provided by law. It is in this regard that it is said, ". . . Nevertheless, since the livestock owner is not absolutely liable, he may avoid liability in some situations. It is a valid excuse, for example, if the animal has escaped through plaintiff's portion of a partition fence; it has always been held that the owner is not liable when he is driving livestock along the highway, using reasonable care to control them, and one of them wanders out of his control onto another's land. . . ." . . .

A third basis of liability stems from situations involving wild beasts or dangerous animals, such as lions, tigers, bears, wolves, elephants and the like, and here the owner traditionally is absolutely liable for damages or injury caused by such an animal. This category also presumably includes domestic animals which the owner knew, or should have known, to have dangerous propensities.

Reconciling these principles with relevant statutes, an action based only on the violation of the restraint statute, section 188.2, is founded on the negligence theory alone. An action based on section 188.3 opens the door for liability based on strict liability; the plaintiff need not show defendant's conduct amounted to negligence. Owners of dangerous animals or domestic animals with dangerous propensities, actually or constructively known, presumably may be found absolutely liable. . . .

[The court held that plaintiffs had failed to prove that their part of the fence was lawful under section 188.3, and affirmed the judgment for defendant.]

Notes

1. Why was the court unwilling to infer strict liability from the "fencing in" statute? Which statute is closer to the common-law rule applicable to domestic animals?

2. Was not defendant's bull a dangerous animal? Could plaintiffs therefore have invoked the third theory of liability discussed by the court?

3. Does the reception within the U.S. of the English common-law principles relating to damage caused by straying domestic animals provide evidence for an economic interpretation of the common law? England had long been densely cultivated and the damage from straying animals is typically greatest in cultivated areas. Also, the higher the ratio of cultivated land is to pasture land, the higher the cost of fencing out relative to that of fencing in. A rule of strict liability for damages caused by straying animals gave the owners of such animals an incentive to fence them in or otherwise restrain them from straying and causing damage. A negligence rule would have done the same but strict liability gave the owners an incentive also to consider limiting herd sizes or relocating herds to remote areas. These are important methods of limiting damage because sheep and cattle are difficult to fence in securely. Is it surprising that the western states, where the ratio of pasture to cultivated land was very high, should have rejected the common-law rule? But as cultivation grew relative to grazing, states began passing statutes, similar to section 188.3 of the Iowa Code, providing that if a person fenced his land in the manner prescribed by law the owners of animals who strayed onto his land and caused damage would be strictly liable for that damage. Such statutes

recognize the importance of changes in activity level in limiting damage from straying animals, but also the lower cost of fencing out relative to fencing in when cultivated land is still a relatively minor land use. As the country has become more and more densely cultivated (or densely settled in other ways that could be upset by straying animals), there has been a tendency to return to the common-law rules, either by statute or by decision. But notice the Iowa court's refusal to interpret Iowa's fencing-in statute as restoring the common-law rule of strict liability.

4. What if your gentle dog wanders onto a neighbor's property and causes property damage? Are you liable? Are you liable if he bites the neighbor on the neighbor's property? See Prosser 497. How would an economist answer these questions?

5. In Chapters 2 and 3, we examined the tort of trespass under the heading of intentional torts. But liability for trespassing animals is not based on an intentional tort theory, and this raises the question whether trespass is not a strict-liability rather than an intentional tort. This question is examined in the next case.

General Telephone Co. of Southwest v. Bi-Co Pavers, Inc.
514 S.W.2d 168 (Tex. Civ. App. 1974)

GUITTARD, J.

In this suit by a telephone company against a paving contractor for severing a telephone cable buried in conduit under a public street, the jury found no negligence on the part of the defendant contractor and also found that plaintiff's negligence contributed to the occurrence. On these findings the trial court rendered judgment for defendant, and plaintiff appeals on the ground that other findings of the jury establish a trespass, to which contributory negligence is no defense. We affirm on the ground that no trespass or other ground of liability has been established.

The findings which plaintiff asserts as establishing a trespass are that plaintiff did not give defendant permission to enter its conduit and that defendant cut the conduit in the right-of-way granted to plaintiff by franchise from the city. There was no evidence that defendant intended to cut the cable or intrude into the space where it was maintained, and no issue was submitted on this question.

Plaintiff contends that these findings establish defendant's liability for trespass under Mountain States Tel. & Tel. Co. v. Vowell Construction Co., 161 Tex. 432, 341 S.W.2d 148 (1960). In that case the Supreme Court of Texas held that a paving contractor's act of severing a telephone cable lawfully in place under a street was a violation of a property right and, consequently,

gave rise to a cause of action without proof of negligence or intent to interfere
with the cable. . . .

In *Vowell* the contractor's employee intended to make a cut in the street
down to a level below that at which he struck and severed the telephone
cable. No similar intent appears here. Defendant's contract with the city
required it to stabilize the soil by mixing it with lime down to a depth of six
inches below the surface grade, and for that purpose defendant used a heavy
machine known as a "pulvamixer," which crushed the conduit and severed
the cable. Admittedly, the telephone conduit was more than six inches below
the surface at the point of severance. Before the occurrence a city engineer
had measured the depth of the conduit at a location within twenty feet of the
point where the cable was later severed and had found it to be more than
eleven inches below the surface. After the occurrence, the contractor's engineer found the conduit at the point of the severance to be more than four
inches below the lime work. Thus the evidence, unlike that in *Vowell*, fails to
show that defendant intended to intrude into the space where plaintiff was
lawfully maintaining its cable.

Plaintiff insists that a trespass is established because operation of the
"pulvamixer" was an intentional act which resulted in violation of plaintiff's
property right. Even though defendant intended to operate the machine, its
operation as intended would not necessarily have violated plaintiff's right. A
trespass is usually regarded as an intentional tort in the sense that it involves
an intent to commit an act which violates a property right, or would be
practically certain to have that effect, although the actor may not know that
the act he intends to commit is such a violation. If the act intended would
necessarily violate a property right, whether or not the actor knows it to be a
violation, he is nevertheless liable, and that liability may extend to unintended consequences. However, unless the intended act would violate a property
right, the actor's liability for unintended consequences ordinarily depends
upon proof of negligence. Otherwise, the defense of contributory negligence
could be avoided in any case of an intentional act with unintended consequences by treating the act as an intentional tort.

Since the present case contains no finding and no evidence that defendant's employee intended to operate the "pulvamixer" at the depth where he
severed the cable, it is not like the case of the innocent trespasser who intends
to make excavations on certain land in the mistaken belief that he has a right
to do so, and is liable without proof of negligence. It is more like the case of a
motorist who intends to keep on the road and inadvertently runs over adjacent land. In such a case, liability depends on proof of negligence. Consequently we hold that no trespass, in the sense of an intentional tort is
established.

We recognize that the scope of the *Vowell* decision may not be limited
to the intentional tort theory above discussed. Although in *Vowell* Justice
Norvell uses the term "trespass," he indicates doubt concerning propriety of
that term by observing: "The particular appellation or classification to be

given the particular act is not of controlling effect." Since in *Vowell* the contractor did not know the exact position of the cable, and did not intend to make contact with it, the "trespass" in that case does not fall within the concept of "trespass to personalty" as defined by such authorities as Restatement (Second) of Torts §217, Comment b at 417 (1965). However, the tort recognized in *Vowell* may rest upon the broader concept that one who digs in a public street has a strict duty to avoid disturbing public utility lines buried in it and is liable for any damage to them caused by his digging, whether or not he actually intends to dig into the area where the lines are maintained. . . . Consequently, we must consider the extent of such strict liability and determine whether it applies in this case.

The *Vowell* opinion itself limits the tort recognized in that case to a situation in which the public utility company has no notice of the danger to its lines. Justice Norvell points out that in that case no request had been made to the telephone company to check its lines and lower them if necessary before paving operations were undertaken, and he adds:

> The owner of conduit lines lawfully in a street or alley can hardly be expected to know that their existing location is unsatisfactory in view of contemplated street surfacing or other improvements *unless notified to that effect.* [Emphasis added.] . . .

[I]f the contractor has a strict duty to avoid striking a public utility line in the street, that duty continues only until the owner has had notice that protective action is required. In the present case the undisputed evidence shows that plaintiff telephone company had such a notice. It was fully advised concerning the city's plans, and had actually lowered its conduit in locations where it had determined that the work described in the plans would endanger its cables. Plaintiff's inspector was on the scene from time to time during the work to advise defendant's employees where the conduit was laid and to determine whether other sections of the line should be lowered. This evidence overcomes any prima-facie case of strict liability established by proof that defendant, without plaintiff's consent, cut plaintiff's cable lawfully maintained in the street. . . .

The significance of notice to the owner of the line is that it gives the owner an opportunity to avoid the loss. Of course, that opportunity requires some period of time for action after receiving the notice. Here plaintiff had that opportunity and failed to use it, according to both the undisputed evidence recited above and the findings of the jury. . . .

This concept of opportunity to avoid loss is basic to the theory of tort law. It applies whether the tort under consideration is classed as intentional, negligent, or in breach of a strict duty, and is also relevant to the defenses to each of these classes of torts. A person who intends to commit a wrongful act obviously has the best opportunity to avoid the ensuing loss by refraining from the act. He is liable for the loss, unless the injured party consented, and in that case it may be assumed that the injured party had an equal opportunity. A negligent tort-feasor can avoid the loss by using ordinary foresight and care, and is liable unless the injured party could also have avoided it by using comparable foresight and care. One whose activities are accompanied by an extraordinary risk, such as a user of explosives, a keeper of dangerous animals, or a manufacturer of products which are dangerous if defective, has a better opportunity to avoid loss than a potential victim. Accordingly, he is subject to strict liability regardless of negligence or intention. Such strict liability should not be imposed for the benefit of one who had an equal or better opportunity to avoid the loss and has not availed himself of that opportunity. More particularly, a contractor who digs in the public street has a better opportunity than the owner to prevent damage to utility lines buried there until the owner has had notice of the work to be done and an opportunity to take protective action. When that notice and opportunity is shown, as in this case, no basis for strict liability exists.

Since this record fails to establish either an intentional tort or a basis for strict liability on the part of defendant contractor, the trial court's judgment for defendant on the verdict was correct.

Notes

1. Why should one who digs in the street have a strict duty to avoid disturbing public utility lines buried in it?

2. How is the court's suggested defense of equal or superior loss-avoidance opportunity different from the traditional contributory-negligence defense? Which is more in keeping with the economic theory of tort liability: the traditional rule or the court's reformulation?

3. The view that trespass to land really is an intentional tort is now firmly established. See Prosser 65-66. Some of the older cases took a different view. In Louisville R. Co. v. Sweeney, 157 Ky. 620, 163 S.W. 739 (1914), for example, defendant's street car jumped the tracks and entered plaintiff's property, knocking down a pole which hit a gate which struck plaintiff. Although the entry was unintentional, the court held that defendant was a trespasser and plaintiff could therefore recover damages without proof of negligence. But if the street car in jumping the tracks had hit a pedestrian the applicable standard would have been negligence. This difference has seemed absurd to most commentators, but it is not entirely absurd — at least to an economist. While there is little if anything that an adjacent landowner can do to avoid damage from a street car that jumps the tracks, a pedestrian is less helpless. The case is not like *LeRoy Fibre*. There the danger from locomotive sparks was evident, and the plaintiff could either have altered its activity or taken greater care in an effort to minimize the danger. But the probability that a street car will jump its tracks at a particular point on the line is too remote to justify self-protective measures by adjacent landowners, whether

through a change in activity level or through taking greater care. So there is an argument for strict liability — but one that few if any courts would find convincing today. *Sweeney* itself was overruled in Randall v. Shelton, 293 S.W.2d 559 (Ky. 1956).

If trespass really is an intentional tort, how is one to explain the straying-animal cases? Perhaps it is best to say that while trespass to land is an intentional tort, certain activities that cause damage to a landowner's interests are governed by a rule of strict liability. Sometimes in such cases the courts will speak of trespass, as in the animal cases, but this is to be understood as a synonym for strict liability. It is just another example of ambiguous usage of the word "trespass" in tort law, an ambiguity that can be traced back to the writ system. For a useful discussion see Zimmer v. Stephenson, 66 Wash. 2d 477, 403 P.2d 343 (1965).

Guille v. Swan
19 Johns. (N.Y.) 381, 10 Am. Dec. 234 (1822)

In error, on certiorari, to the Justices' Court in the city of New-York. Swan sued Guille in the Justices' Court, in an action of trespass, for entering his close, and treading down his roots and vegetables, &c. in a garden in the city of New-York. The facts were, that Guille ascended in a balloon in the vicinity of Swan's garden, and descended into his garden. When he descended, his body was hanging out of the car of the balloon in a very perilous situation, and he called to a person at work in Swan's field, to help him, in a voice audible to the pursuing crowd. After the balloon descended, it dragged along over potatoes and radishes, about thirty feet, when Guille was taken out. The balloon was carried to a barn at the farther end of the premises. When the balloon descended, more than two hundred persons broke into Swan's garden through the fences, and came on his premises, beating down his vegetables and flowers. The damage done by Guille, with his balloon, was about fifteen dollars, but the crowd did much more. The plaintiff's damages, in all, amounted to ninety dollars. It was contended before the Justice, that Guille was answerable only for the damage done by himself, and not for the damage done by the crowd. The Justice was of the opinion, and so instructed the jury, that the defendant was answerable for all the damages done to the plaintiff. The jury, accordingly, found a verdict for him, for 90 dollars, on which the judgment was given, and for costs. . . .

SPENCER, J. delivered the opinion of the Court. . . .

I will not say that ascending in a balloon is an unlawful act, for it is not so; but, it is certain, that the Aeronaut has no control over its motion horizontally; he is at the sport of the winds, and is to descend when and how he can; his reaching the earth is a matter of hazard. He did descend on the premises of the plaintiff below, at a short distance from the place where he ascended. Now, if his descent, under such circumstances, would, ordinarily and naturally, draw a crowd of people about him, either from curiosity, or for the purpose of rescuing him from a perilous situation; all this he ought to have foreseen, and must be responsible for. Whether the crowd heard him call for help, or not, is immaterial; he had put himself in a situation to invite help, and they rushed forward, impelled, perhaps, by the double motive of rendering aid, and gratifying a curiosity which he had excited. Can it be doubted, that if the plaintiff in error had beckoned to the crowd to come to his assistance, that he would be liable for their trespass in entering the enclosure? I think not. In that case, they would have been co-trespassers, and we must consider the situation in which he placed himself, voluntarily and designedly, as equivalent to a direct request to the crowd to follow him. In the present case, he did call for help and may have been heard by the crowd; he is, therefore, undoubtedly, liable for all the injury sustained.

Judgment affirmed.

Notes

1. Was defendant a trespasser?

2. *Guille* is an excellent illustration of the difference between care and activity adjustment as methods of accident prevention. Defendant could not control the balloon, so his descent onto plaintiff's property was not a result of carelessness. But he did not have to ascend in a balloon in the first place; and he could have done it elsewhere than in New York City. If ballooning, whether generally or in New York City, had substantial social value in the early nineteenth century, there is no indication of this in the opinion. Maybe the cheapest way to minimize all relevant costs was for defendant not to ascend in the first place, or to do so in a rural area; in either case a rule of strict liability would create the proper incentives, and a rule of negligence liability would not. Does this suggest that strict liability may be the appropriate rule to govern hazardous new activities in general? Why limit the rule just to hazardous activities?

Rylands v. Fletcher
L.R. 3 H.L. 330 (1868)

In November, 1861, Fletcher brought an action against Ryland & Horrocks, to recover damages for an injury caused to his mines by water overflowing into them from a reservoir which the Defendants had constructed. The declaration contained three counts, and each count alleged negligence on the part of the Defendants, but in this House the case was ultimately treated upon the principle of determining the relative rights of the parties independently of any question of personal negligence by the Defendants in the exercise of them. . . .

. . . The Plaintiff was the lessee of certain coal mines known as the Red House Colliery, under the Earl of Wilton. He had also obtained from two other persons, Mr. Hulton and Mr. Whitehead, leave to work for coal under their lands. The positions of the various properties were these: — There was a turnpike road . . . which formed a southern boundary to the properties of these different persons. A parish road . . . formed their northern boundary. These roads might be described as forming two sides of a square, of which the other two sides were formed by the lands of Mr. Whitehead on the east and Lord Wilton on the west. The Defendants' grounds lay along the turnpike road, or southern boundary, stretching from its centre westward. On these grounds were a mill and a small old reservoir. The proper grounds of the Red House Colliery also lay, in part, along the southern boundary, stretching from its centre eastward. Immediately north of the Defendants' land lay the land of Mr. Hulton, and still farther north that of Lord Wilton. On this land of Lord Wilton the Defendants, in 1860, constructed (with his Lordship's permission) a new reservoir, the water from which would pass almost in a southerly direction across a part of the land of Lord Wilton and the land of Mr. Hulton, and so reach the Defendant's mill. The line of direction from this new reservoir to the Red Colliery mine was nearly south-east.

The Plaintiff, under his lease from Lord Wilton, and under his agreements with Messrs. Hulton and Whitehead, worked the mines under their respective lands. In the course of doing so, he came upon old shafts and passages of mines formerly worked, but of which the workings had long ceased; the origin and the existence of these shafts and passages were unknown. The shafts were vertical, the passages horizontal, and the former especially seemed filled with marl and rubbish. Defendants employed for the purpose of constructing their new reservoir persons who were admitted to be competent as engineers and contractors to perform the work. . . . But in the course of excavating the bed of the new reservoir, five old shafts, running vertically downwards, were met with in the portion of the land selected for its site. The case found that "on the part of the Defendants there was no personal negligence or default whatever in or about, or in relation to, the selection of the said site, or in or about the planning or construction of the said reservoir; but, in point of fact, reasonable and proper care and skill were not exercised by, or on the part of, the persons so employed by them, with reference to the shafts so met with as aforesaid, to provide for the sufficiency of the said reservoir to bear the pressure of water which, when filled to the height proposed, it would have to bear."

The reservoir was completed at the beginning of December, 1860, and on the morning of the 11th of that month the reservoir, being then partially filled with water, one of the aforesaid vertical shafts gave way, and burst downwards, in consequence of which the water of the reservoir flowed into the old passages and coal-workings underneath, and by means of the underground communications then existing between them and the Plaintiff's workings in the Red House Colliery, the colliery was flooded and the workings thereof stopped.

The question for the opinion of the Court was whether the Plaintiff was entitled to recover damages by reason of the matters hereinbefore stated. The Court of Exchequer, Mr. Baron Bramwell dissenting, gave judgment for the Defendants. That judgment was afterwards reversed in the Court of Exchequer Chamber. The case was then brought on Error to this House.

THE LORD CHANCELLOR (LORD CAIRNS): . . .

My Lords, the principles on which this case must be determined appear to me to be extremely simple. The Defendants, treating them as the owners or occupiers of the close on which the reservoir was constructed, might lawfully have used that close for any purpose for which it might in the ordinary course of the enjoyment of land be used; and if, in what I may term the natural use of that land, there had been any accumulation of water, either on the surface or underground, and if, by the operation of the laws of nature, that accumulation of water had passed off into the close occupied by the Plaintiff, the Plaintiff could not have complained that that result had taken place. If he had desired to guard himself against it, it would have lain upon him to have done so, by leaving, or by interposing, some barrier between his close and the close of the Defendants in order to have prevented that operation of the laws of nature. . . .

On the other hand if the Defendants, not stopping at the natural use of their close, had desired to use it for any purpose which I may term a non-natural use, for the purpose of introducing into the close that which in its natural condition was not in or upon it, for the purpose of introducing water either above or below ground in quantities and in a manner not the result of any work or operation on or under the land, — and if in consequence of their doing so, or in consequence of any imperfection in the mode of their doing so, the water came to escape and to pass off into the close of the Plaintiff, then it appears to me that that which the Defendants were doing they were doing at their own peril; and, if in the course of their doing it, the evil arose to which I have referred, the evil, namely, of the escape of the water and its passing away to the close of the Plaintiff and injuring the Plaintiff, then for the consequence of that, in my opinion, the Defendants would be liable. . . .

The same result is arrived at on the principles referred to by Mr. Justice Blackburn in his judgment, in the Court of Exchequer Chamber, where he states the opinion of that Court as to the law in these words: "We think that the true rule of law is, that the person who, for his own purposes, brings on his land and collects and keeps there anything likely to do mischief if it escapes, must keep it in at his peril; and if he does not do so, is primâ facie answerable for all the damage which is the natural consequence of its escape. He can excuse himself by shewing that the escape was owing to the Plaintiff's default; or, perhaps, that the escape was the consequence of vis major, or the act of God; but as nothing of this sort exists here, it is unnecessary to inquire what excuse would be sufficient. The general rule, as above stated, seems on principle just. The person whose grass or corn is eaten down by the escaping cattle of his neighbour, or whose mine is flooded by the water from his neighbour's reservoir, or whose cellar is invaded by the filth of his neighbour's privy, or whose habitation is made unhealthy by the fumes and noisome vapours of his neighbour's alkali works, is damnified without any fault of his own; and it seems but reasonable and just that the neighbour who has brought something on his own property (which was not naturally there), harmless to others so long as it is confined to his own property, but which he knows will be mischievous if it gets on his neighbour's, should be obliged to make good the damage which ensues if he does not succeed in confining it to his own property. But for his act in bringing it there no mischief could have accrued, and it seems but just that he should at his peril keep it there, so that no mischief may accrue, or answer for the natural and anticipated consequence. And upon authority this we think is established to be the law, whether the things so brought be beasts, or water, or filth, or stenches."

My Lords, in that opinion, I must say I entirely concur. Therefore, I have to move your Lordships that the judgment of the Court of Exchequer Chamber be affirmed, and that the present appeal be dismissed with costs.

LORD CRANWORTH:

My Lords, I concur with my noble and learned friend in thinking that the rule of law was correctly stated by Mr. Justice Blackburn in delivering the opinion of the Exchequer Chamber. If a person brings, or accumulates, on his land anything which, if it should escape, may cause damage to his neighbour, he does so at his peril. If it does escape, and cause damage, he is responsible, however careful he may have been, and whatever precautions he may have taken to prevent the damage. . . .

The doctrine appears to me to be well illustrated by the two modern cases in the Court of Common Pleas referred to by my noble and learned friend. I allude to the two cases of Smith v. Kenrick and Baird v. Williamson. In the former the owner of a coal mine on the higher level worked out the whole of his coal, leaving no barrier between his mine and the mine on the lower level, so that the water percolating through the upper mine flowed into the lower mine, and obstructed the owner of it in getting his coal. It was held that the owner of the lower mine had no ground of complaint. The Defendant, the owner of the upper mine, had a right to remove all his coal. The damage sustained by the Plaintiff was occasioned by the natural flow or percolation of water from the upper strata. There was no obligation on the Defendant to protect the Plaintiff against this. It was his business to erect or leave a sufficient barrier to keep out the water, or to adopt proper means for so conducting the water as that it should not impede him in his workings. The water, in that case, was only left by the Defendant to flow in its natural course.

But in the later case of Baird v. Williamson the Defendant, the owner of the upper mine, did not merely suffer the water to flow through his mine without leaving a barrier between it and the mine below, but in order to work his own mine beneficially he pumped up quantities of water which passed into the Plaintiff's mine in addition to that which would have naturally reached it, and so occasioned him damage. Though this was done without negligence, and in the due working of his own mine, yet he was held to be responsible for the damage so occasioned. It was in consequence of his act whether skilfully or unskilfully performed, that the Plaintiff had been damaged, and he was therefore held liable for the consequences. The damage in the former case may be treated as having arisen from the act of God; in the latter, from the act of the Defendant. . . .

Losee v. Buchanan
51 N.Y. 476 (1873)

[Action to recover damages caused by the explosion of a steam boiler owned and used by defendant Saratoga Paper Company in its mill in Schuylerville. The explosion flung pieces of the boiler onto plaintiff's premises, damaging them.]

EARL, J. . . . The plaintiff claimed . . . that the defendants were liable without the proof of any negligence, and requested the justice so to rule, and the refusal of the justice to comply with this request raises the principal question for our consideration upon this appeal. . . .

I do not believe this claim to be well founded, and I will briefly examine the authorities upon which mainly an attempt is made to sustain it. . . .

. . . In Hay v. The Cohoes Company, the defendant, a corporation, dug a canal upon its own land for the purposes authorized by its charter. In so doing it was necessary to blast rocks with gunpowder, and the fragments were thrown against and injured the plaintiff's dwelling upon lands adjoining. It was held that the defendant was liable for the injury, although no negligence or want of skill in executing the work was alleged or proved. This decision was well supported by the clearest principles. The acts of the defendant in casting the rocks upon plaintiff's premises were direct and immediate. The damage was the necessary consequence of just what the defendant was doing, and it was just as much liable as if it had caused the rocks to be taken by hand, or any other means, and thrown directly upon plaintiff's land. This is far from an authority for holding that the defendants, who placed a steam boiler upon their lands, and operated the same with care and skill, should be liable for the damages caused by the explosion, without their fault or any direct or immediate act of theirs. It is true that Judge Gardner, in writing the opinion of the court, lays down broadly the principle that "every individual is entitled to the undisturbed possession and lawful enjoyment of his own property," citing the maxim sic utero tuo, etc. But this principle, as well as the maxim, as will be seen, has many exceptions and limitations, made necessary by the exigencies of business and society. . . .

. . . We are also cited to a class of cases holding the owners of animals responsible for injuries done by them. . . . As to all animals, the owner can usually restrain and keep them under control, and if he will keep them he must do so. If he does not, he is responsible for any damage which their well-known disposition leads them to commit. I believe the liability to be based upon the fault which the law attributes to him, and no further actual negligence need be proved than the fact that they are at large unrestrained. But if I am mistaken as to the true basis of liability in such cases, the body of laws in reference to live animals, which is supposed to be just and wise, considering the nature of the animals and the mutual rights and interests of the owners and others, does not furnish analogies absolutely controlling in reference to inanimate property.

Blackstone says, "that whenever an act is directly and immediately injurious to the person or property of another, and therefore necessarily accompanied with some force, an action of trespass vi et armis will lie;" for "the right of meum and tuum or property in lands being once established, it follows as a necessary consequence that this right must be exclusive; that is, that the owner may retain to himself the sole use and occupation of his soil. Every entry, therefore, thereon without the owner's leave, and especially contrary to his express order, is a trespass or transgression." The learned author was here laying down the distinction between an action of trespass and trespass on the case, and asserting the rule that in the former action the injury must be direct and immediate, and accompanied with some force, whereas in the latter action it could be indirect and consequential. He was also manifestly speaking of a direct entrance by one upon the lands of another. He was laying down a general rule that every unauthorized entrance upon the land of another is a trespass. This was sufficiently accurate for the enunciation of a general rule. Judges and legal writers do not always find it convenient, practicable or important, in laying down general rules, to specify all the limitations and exceptions to such rules. The rule, as thus announced, has many exceptions, even when one makes a personal entry upon the lands of another. I may enter my neighbor's close to succor his beast whose life is in danger; to prevent his beasts from being stolen or to prevent his grain from being consumed or spoiled by cattle; or to carry away my tree which has been blown down upon his land, or to pick up my apples which have fallen from my trees upon his land, or to take my personal property which another has wrongfully taken and placed there, or to escape from one who threatens my life. . . .

By becoming a member of civilized society, I am compelled to give up many of my natural rights, but I receive more than a compensation from the surrender by every other man of the same rights, and the security, advantage and protection which the laws give me. So, too, the general rules that I may have the exclusive and undisturbed use and possession of my real estate, and that I must so use my real estate as not to injure my neighbor, are much modified by the exigencies of the social state. We must have factories, machinery, dams, canals and railroads. They are demanded by the manifold wants of mankind, and lay at the basis of all our civilization. If I have any of these upon my lands, and they are not a nuisance and are not so managed as to become such, I am not responsible for any damage they accidentally and unavoidably do my neighbor. He receives his compensation for such damage by the general good, in which he shares, and the right which he has to place the same things upon his lands. I may not place or keep a nuisance upon my land to the damage of my neighbor, and I have my compensation for the surrender of this right to use my own as I will by the similar restriction imposed upon my neighbor for my benefit. I hold my property subject to the risk that it may be unavoidably or accidentally injured by those who live near me; and as I move about upon the public highways and in all places where other persons may lawfully be, I take the risk of being accidentally injured in my person by them without fault on their part. Most of the rights of property, as well as of person, in the social state, are not absolute but relative, and they must be so arranged and modified, not unnecessarily infringing upon natural rights, as upon the whole to promote the general welfare.

I have so far found no authorities and no principles which fairly sustain the broad claim made by the plaintiff, that the defendants are liable in this action without fault or negligence on their part to which the explosion of the boiler could be attributed.

But our attention is called to a recent English case, decided in the Exchequer Chamber, which seems to uphold the claim made [Fletcher v. Rylands]. . . . It was held, reversing the judgment of the Court of Exchequer, that the defendants were liable for the damage so caused, upon the broad doctrine that one who, for his own purposes, brings upon his land, and collects and keeps there, anything likely to do mischief if it escapes, must keep it at his peril, and, if he does not do so, is prima facie answerable for all the damage which is the natural consequence of its escape. . . . This conclusion is reached . . . mainly by applying to the case the same rule of liability to which owners are subjected by the escape of their live animals. As I have shown above, the rules of law applicable to live animals should not be applied to inanimate property. That case was appealed to the House of Lords and affirmed. . . .

It is sufficient, however, to say that the law, as laid down in those cases, is in direct conflict with the law as settled in this country. Here, if one builds a dam upon his own premises and thus holds back and accumulates the water for his benefit, or if he brings water upon his premises into a reservoir, in case the dam or the banks of the reservoir give away and the lands of a neighbor are thus flooded, he is not liable for the damage without proof of some fault or negligence on his part. . . .

In conflict with the rule as laid down in the English cases is a class of cases in reference to damage from fire communicated from the adjoining premises. Fire, like water or steam, is likely to produce mischief if it escapes and goes beyond control; and yet it has never been held in this country that one building a fire upon his own premises can be made liable if it escapes upon his neighbor's premises and does him damage without proof of negligence. . . .

This examination has gone far enough to show that the rule is, at least in this country, a universal one, which, so far as I can discern, has no exceptions or limitations, that no one can be made liable for injuries to the person or property of another without some fault or negligence on his part.

In this case the defendants had the right to place the steam boiler upon their premises. It was in no sense a nuisance, and the jury have found that they were not guilty of any negligence. The judgment in their favor should, therefore, have been affirmed at the General Term. . . .

Notes

1. Rylands v. Fletcher is one of the most famous decisions in the history of tort law. There is a large literature about it. It has been variously described as a resurgence of the medieval idea that a man acts at his peril, a mandate for a general principle of strict liability in tort, a reflection of English landowners' distaste for the encroachments of industry, and a forerunner of the modern idea of "enterprise liability" (considered later in this chapter). For a good introduction to the literature see Fridman, The Rise and Fall of Rylands v. Fletcher, 34 Can. Bar Rev. 810 (1956).

2. Did Lord Cairns really "entirely concur" in Justice Blackburn's opinion in the Exchequer Chamber (quoted in Cairns' opinion)? Is there any suggestion of Cairns' "natural-nonnatural" distinction in Blackburn's opinion? Notice that the court in Losee referred to Blackburn's opinion rather than to any of the opinions in the House of Lords; Blackburn's is the best known opinion in the case. What must a plaintiff show to establish liability under Blackburn's analysis?

3. Why weren't the defendants in Rylands liable under the doctrine of respondeat superior for the negligence of the engineers and contractors who built the reservoir?

4. Were defendants really the cheapest cost avoiders in Rylands v. Fletcher? Rylands knew, did he not, about the network of disused mine shafts. Should he not have investigated where they led?

Was Lord Wilton perhaps the cheapest cost avoider? The reservoir was built on his land, and plaintiff had leased coal rights under adjacent lands from Lord Wilton. Should Wilton not have warned the parties about the interlocking network of disused mine shafts? According to the report of the case in the Court of Exchequer, 3 H.&C. 774 (1865), however, the mining of the coal beneath the reservoir site had been done "beyond living memory," so perhaps neither Lord Wilton nor plaintiff was at fault in failing to warn defendants of the danger posed by the reservoir.

There may be another theory on which to hold Lord Wilton liable. Evidently defendants did not actually lease the land on which they had the reservoir built; they acted with Lord Wilton's permission, of course, but pursuant only to an "arrangement" with him the nature of which is not indicated in the opinions. If Wilton remained in possession of the land on which the reservoir was built, why was the nonnatural use of the land not *his* nonnatural use? Is there a clue in the materials in Chapter 6 of this book?

5. Could (or did) Rylands base his action against defendants on a theory of trespass? Could the action have been based on a theory of nuisance? On the latter question, see Chapter 10; Mowrer v. Ashland Oil & Refining Co., 518 F.2d 659 (7th Cir. 1975).

6. *Losee* is typical of a number of cases in which American courts have "rejected" the doctrine of Rylands v. Fletcher. But what exactly are they rejecting? The doctrine of strict liability applied across the board to any activity that causes harm? The doctrine applied to any *dangerous* activity that causes harm? Strict liability for "nonnatural" uses of land? For damage caused by the collapse, bursting, or overflowing of a reservoir?

7. What does "nonnatural" mean? Lord Cranworth's discussion of Smith v. Kenrick is relevant to this question. In *Smith*, the defendant, in mining the coal in his mine, removed coal that constituted a barrier to the percolation of water through the ground to plaintiff's mine, which was below defendant's. What was "natural" about the damage in this case? Percolation is a natural phenomenon, but so was the movement of the water out of the collapsed reservoir in *Rylands*. The percolation was caused by the act of the defendant in mining coal, just as the flood in *Rylands* was caused by the act of the defendants in having the reservoir built. What is more natural about mining coal than about building a reservoir? Should nonnatural be equated with unusual, as suggested by the facts of *Guille*? Would this enable *Losee* to be distinguished?

Consider, in this connection, the analysis of the court in Turner v. Big Lake Oil Co., 128 Tex. 155, 164-166, 96 S.W.2d 221, 225-226 (1936), where salt water overflowed from an artificial pond used by defendants in the operation of their oil wells and damaged a pasture:

> In Rylands v. Fletcher the court predicated the absolute liability of the defendants on the proposition that the use of land for the artificial storage of water was not a natural use, and that, therefore, the landowner was bound at his peril to keep the waters on his own land. This basis of the English rule is to be found in the meteorological conditions which obtain there. England is a pluvial country, where constant streams and abundant rains make the storage of water unnecessary for ordinary or general purposes. When the court said in Rylands v. Fletcher that the use of land for storage of water was an unnatural use, it meant such use was not a general or an ordinary one; not one within the contemplation of the parties to the original grant of the land involved, nor of the grantor and grantees of adjacent lands, but was a special or extraordinary use, and for that reason applied the rule of absolute liability. This conclusion is supported by the

fact that those jurisdictions which adhere to the rule in Rylands v. Fletcher do not apply that rule to dams or reservoirs constructed in rivers and streams, which they say is a natural use, but apply the principle of negligence. In other words, the impounding of water in stream-ways, being an obvious and natural use, was necessarily within the contemplation of the parties to the original and adjacent grants, and damages must be predicated upon negligent use of a granted right and power; while things not within the contemplation of the parties to the original grants, such as unnatural uses of the land, the landowner may do only at his peril. As to what use of land is or may be a natural use, one within the contemplation of the parties to the original grant of land, necessarily depends upon the attendant circumstances and conditions which obtain in the territory of the original grants, or the initial terms of those grants.

In Texas we have conditions very different from those which obtain in England. A large portion of Texas is an arid or semi-arid region. West of the 98th meridian of longitude, where the rainfall is approximately 30 inches, the rainfall decreases until finally, in the extreme western part of the state, it is only about 10 inches. This land of decreasing rainfall is the great ranch or livestock region of the state, water for which is stored in thousands of ponds, tanks, and lakes on the surface of the ground. The country is almost without streams; and without the storage of water from rainfall in basins constructed for the purpose, or to hold waters pumped from the earth, the great livestock industry of West Texas must perish. No such condition obtains in England. With us the storage of water is a natural or necessary and common use of the land, necessarily within the contemplation of the state and its grantees when grants were made, and obviously the rule announced in Rylands v. Fletcher, predicated upon different conditions, can have no application here.

Again, in England there are no oil wells, no necessity for using surface storage facilities for impounding and evaporating salt waters therefrom. In Texas the situation is different. Texas has many great oil fields, tens of thousands of wells in almost every part of the state. Producing oil is one of our major industries. One of the by-products of oil production is salt water, which must be disposed of without injury to property or the pollution of streams. The construction of basins or ponds to hold this salt water is a necessary part of the oil business. In Texas much of our land was granted without mineral reservation to the state, and where minerals were reserved, provision has usually been made for leasing and operating. It follows, therefore, that as to these grants and leases the right to mine in the usual and appropriate way, as, for example, by the construction and maintenance of salt water pools such as here involved, incident to the production of oil, was contemplated by the state and all its grantees and mineral lessees, that being a use of the surface incident and necessary to the right to produce oil.

From the foregoing it is apparent that we decline to follow and apply in this case the rule of absolute liability laid down in Rylands v. Fletcher. . . .

What version of the doctrine of Rylands v. Fletcher is rejected here? How would you analyze the court's discussion in economic terms?

8. Are you satisfied with the attempt in *Losee* to distinguish the animal cases? Are you satisfied with the attempt to distinguish the *Hay* case? What

relationship if any do cases like *Vincent* and *Whalley* in Chapter 3 have to *Rylands* and Smith v. Kenrick?

Cities Service Co. v. State
312 So. 2d 799 (Fla. App. 1975)

GRIMES, J. . . .

The appellant, Cities Service Company (Cities Service), operates a phosphate rock mine in Polk County. On December 3, 1971, a dam break occurred in one of Cities Service's settling ponds. As a result, approximately one billion gallons of phosphate slimes contained therein escaped into Whidden Creek and thence into the Peace River, thereby killing countless numbers of fish and inflicting other damage.

Appellee, The State of Florida (State), filed suit against Cities Service seeking injunctive relief as well as compensatory and punitive damages arising out of the dam break. The court granted an injunction for a limited period of time and struck the claim for punitive damages. Neither of these points are raised on this appeal. Later the court entered an order granting the State's motion for partial summary judgment on liability. The premise for this order was that Cities Service was liable without regard to negligence or fault for the damage occurring by reason of the escape of the phosphatic wastes into the public waters of the State of Florida.

The determination of this appeal necessarily requires the consideration of the doctrine of strict liability for the hazardous use of one's land which was first announced in Rylands v. Fletcher. . . .

. . . Most of the early American decisions rejected the doctrine. However, the pendulum has now decidedly swung toward its acceptance. According to Prosser, by 1971 the doctrine had been approved in principle by thirty jurisdictions with only seven states still rejecting the principle. . . .

In early days it was important to encourage persons to use their land by whatever means were available for the purpose of commercial and industrial development. In a frontier society there was little likelihood that a dangerous use of land could cause damage to one's neighbor. Today our life has become more complex. Many areas are overcrowded, and even the non-negligent use of one's land can cause extensive damages to a neighbor's property. Though there are still many hazardous activities which are socially desirable, it now seems reasonable that they pay their own way. It is too much to ask an innocent neighbor to bear the burden thrust upon him as a consequence of an abnormal use of the land next door. The doctrine of Rylands v. Fletcher should be applied in Florida.

There remains, however, the serious question of whether the impounding of phosphate slime by Cities Service in connection with its mining operations is a non-natural use of the land. In opposition to the State's motion, Cities Service filed an affidavit of the manager of the plant where the dam break occurred. The affidavit points out that the property is peculiarly suitable for the mining of phosphate and that the central Florida area of which Polk County is the hub is the largest producer of phosphate rock in Florida. It further appears that Florida produced over 80% of the nation's marketable phosphate rock and one-third of the world production thereof in 1973. The affidavit goes on to explain that the storing of phosphate slimes in diked settling ponds is an essential part of the traditional method of mining phosphate rock. Hence, Cities Service argues that its mining operations were a natural and intended use of this particular land.

There have been many American cases which have passed upon the question of whether a particular use of the land was natural or non-natural for the purpose of applying the Rylands v. Fletcher doctrine. Thus, Prosser states:

> The conditions and activities to which the rule has been applied have followed the English pattern. They include water collected in quantity in a dangerous place, or allowed to percolate; explosives or inflammable liquids stored in quantity in the midst of a city; blasting; pile driving; crop dusting; the fumigation of part of a building with cyanide gas; drilling oil wells or operating refineries in thickly settled communities; an excavation letting in the sea; factories emitting smoke, dust or noxious gases in the midst of a town; roofs so constructed as to shed snow into a highway; and a dangerous party wall.
>
> On the other hand the conditions and activities to which the American courts have refused to apply Rylands v. Fletcher, whether they purport to accept or to reject the case in principle, have been with few exceptions what the English courts would regard as a "natural" use of land, and not within the rule at all. They include water in household pipes, the tank of a humidity system or authorized utility mains; gas in a meter, electric wiring in a machine shop, and gasoline in a filling station; a dam in the natural bed of a stream; ordinary steam boilers; an ordinary fire in a factory; an automobile; Bermuda grass on a railroad right of way; a small quantity of dynamite kept for sale in a Texas hardware store; barnyard spray in a farmhouse; a division fence; the wall of a house left standing after a fire; coal mining operations regarded as usual and normal; vibrations from ordinary building construction; earth moving operations in grading a hillside; the construction of a railroad tunnel; and even a runaway horse. There remain a few cases, including such things as water reservoirs or irrigation ditches in dry country, or properly conducted oil wells in Texas or Oklahoma, which are undoubtedly best explained upon the basis of a different community view which makes such things "natural" to the particular locality. *The conclusion is, in short, that the American decisions, like the English ones, have applied the principle of Rylands v. Fletcher only to the thing out of place, the abnormally dangerous condition or activity which is not a "natural" one where it is.* (Emphasis supplied)

The American Law Institute has considered this question in §§519 and 520 of the Restatement of the Law of Torts (1938). These sections state:

§519. MISCARRIAGE OF ULTRAHAZARDOUS ACTIVITIES CAREFULLY
    CARRIED ON
    . . . [O]ne who carries on an ultrahazardous activity is liable to another
whose person, land or chattels the actor should recognize as likely to be harmed
by the unpreventable miscarriage of the activity for harm resulting thereto from
that which makes the activity ultrahazardous, although the utmost care is
exercised to prevent the harm.

§520. DEFINITION OF ULTRAHAZARDOUS ACTIVITY
    An activity is ultrahazardous if it
    (a) necessarily involves a risk of serious harm to the person, land or chattels
of others which cannot be eliminated by the exercise of the utmost care, and
    (b) is not a matter of common usage.

Recognizing the evolving nature of the law in this area, the American Law
Institute published Tentative Draft No. 10 in 1964 in which certain changes
were recommended for §§519 and 520. Thus, in §519 and §520 the substitution of the words "abnormally dangerous" is suggested in place of the word
"ultrahazardous." In §520, the following factors are said to be pertinent in
determining whether an activity is abnormally dangerous:

    (a) Whether the activity involves a high degree of risk of some harm to the
person, land or chattels of others;
    (b) Whether the harm which may result from it is likely to be great;
    (c) Whether the risk cannot be eliminated by the exercise of reasonable
care;
    (d) Whether the activity is not a matter of common usage;
    (e) Whether the activity is inappropriate to the place where it is carried on;
and
    (f) The value of the activity to the community. . . .

    In the final analysis, we are impressed by the magnitude of the activity
and the attendant risk of enormous damage. The impounding of billions of
gallons of phosphatic slimes behind earthen walls which are subject to breaking even with the exercise of the best of care strikes us as being both "ultrahazardous" and "abnormally dangerous," as the case may be. This is not
clear water which is being impounded. Here, Cities Service introduced water
into its mining operation which when combined with phosphatic wastes
produced a phosphatic slime which had a high potential for damage to the
environment. If a break occurred, it was to be expected that extensive damage would be visited upon property many miles away. In this case, the
damage, in fact, extended almost to the mouth of the Peace River, which is
far beyond the phosphate mining area described in the Cities Service affidavit. We conclude that the Cities Service slime reservoir constituted a non-
natural use of the land such as to invoke the doctrine of strict liability.

... The occurrence of the calamity because of an act of God has always been recognized as an exception to the strict liability doctrine of Rylands v. Fletcher. But Cities Service has made no contention that the break in its dam was caused by an act of God. From the transcript of the testimony taken in connection with the injunction proceedings, it is evident that despite the best of care, earthen dams enclosing phosphate settling ponds do give way from time to time without explanation. All of the assertions of Cities Service relative to the need to maintain settling ponds in its mining operations, the suitability of the land for this purpose and the importance of phosphate to the community as well as to the world at large may be accepted at face value. Admitting the desirability of phosphate and the necessity of mining in this manner, the rights of adjoining landowners and the interests of the public in our environment require the imposition of a doctrine which places the burden upon the parties whose activity made it possible for the damages to occur.

Affirmed.

Notes

1. In the final draft of the Second Restatement of Torts (1977), the wording of §520 was changed slightly from the language of Tentative Draft No. 10, quoted by the court, to read as follows:

§520. ABNORMALLY DANGEROUS ACTIVITIES
   In determining whether an activity is abnormally dangerous, the following factors are to be considered:
   (a) existence of a high degree of risk of some harm to the person, land or chattels of others;
   (b) likelihood that the harm that results from it will be great;
   (c) inability to eliminate the risk by the exercise of reasonable care;
   (d) extent to which the activity is not a matter of common usage;
   (e) inappropriateness of the activity to the place where it is carried on; and
   (f) extent to which its value to the community is outweighed by its dangerous attributes.

Notice the congruence between the Restatement's formulation and the economic analysis of strict liability in this chapter. Subsections (a) and (b) relate to the magnitude of the expected loss. Subsections (d)-(f) relate to the costs of reducing the expected loss through curtailing the activity. And subsection (c) posits the unavailability of greater care as a feasible method of accident avoidance. If the expected loss from some type of accident is great, and the loss cannot reasonably be averted by taking greater care but can by an adjustment in the activity level, an economic case for strict liability is made out. For a perceptive judicial analysis in this vein, see Lubin v. City of Iowa City, 396 Mich. 281, 240 N.W.2d 217 (1976).

2. Did the court in *Cities Service* competently apply the Restatement test to the facts? The expected accident loss from the storage of substantial quantities of phosphatic limes behind earthen walls was probably substantial and greater care would probably have been unavailing. What about the feasibility of avoiding or reducing the risk of an accident by a change in activity? Might one feasible change of activity have been not to build an *earthen* dam?

3. Should an act of God that destroyed the dam excuse defendant from liability? What would the *Behrens* court have thought? What would an economist think?

Siegler v. Kuhlman
81 Wash. 2d 448, 502 P.2d 1181 (1972)

HALE, J.

Seventeen-year-old Carol J. House died in the flames of a gasoline explosion when her car encountered a pool of thousands of gallons of spilled gasoline. She was driving home from her after-school job in the early evening of November 22, 1967, along Capitol Lake Drive in Olympia; it was dark but dry; her car's headlamps were burning. There was a slight impact with some object, a muffled explosion, and then searing flames from gasoline pouring out of an overturned trailer tank engulfed her car. The result of the explosion is clear, but the real causes of what happened will remain something of an eternal mystery.

Aaron L. Kuhlman had been a truck driver for nearly 11 years after he completed the tenth grade in high school and after he had worked at other jobs for a few years. He had been driving for Pacific Intermountain Express for about 4 months, usually the night shift out of the Texaco bulk plant in Tumwater. That evening of November 22nd, he was scheduled to drive a gasoline truck and trailer unit, fully loaded with gasoline, from Tumwater to Port Angeles. Before leaving the Texaco plant, he inspected the trailer, checking the lights, hitch, air hoses and tires. Finding nothing wrong, he then set out, driving the fully loaded truck tank and trailer tank, stopping briefly at the Trail's End Cafe for a cup of coffee. It was just a few minutes after 6 P.M., and dark, but the roads were dry when he started the drive to deliver his cargo — 3,800 gallons of gasoline in the truck tank and 4,800 gallons of gasoline in the trailer tank. With all vehicle and trailer running lights on, he drove the truck and trailer onto Interstate Highway 5, proceeded north on that freeway at about 50 miles per hour, he said, and took the offramp about 1 mile later to enter Highway 101 at the Capitol Lake interchange. Running downgrade on the offramp, he felt a jerk, looked into his left-hand mirror and then his right-hand mirror to see that the trailer lights were not in place. The trailer was still moving but leaning over hard, he observed, onto its right side. The trailer then came loose. Realizing that the tank trailer had disengaged from his tank truck, he stopped the truck without skidding its tires. He got out and ran back to see that the tank trailer had crashed through a chain-link highway fence and had come to rest upside down on Capitol Lake Drive below. He heard a sound, he said, "like somebody kicking an empty fifty-gallon drum and that is when the fire started." The fire spread, he thought, about 100 feet down the road.

The trailer was owned by defendant Pacific Intermountain Express. It had traveled about 329,000 miles prior to November 22, 1967, and had been driven by Mr. Kuhlman without incident down the particular underpass above Capitol Lake Drive about 50 times. When the trailer landed upside down on Capitol Lake Drive its lights were out, and it was unilluminated when Carol House's car in one way or another ignited the spilled gasoline.

Carol House was burned to death in the flames. There was no evidence of impact on the vehicle she had driven, Kuhlman said, except that the left front headlight was broken.

Why the tank trailer disengaged and catapulted off the freeway down through a chain-like fence to land upside down on Capitol Lake Drive below remains a mystery. What caused it to separate from the truck towing it, despite many theories offered in explanation, is still an enigma. Various theories as to the facts and case were advanced in the trial. Plaintiff sought to prove both negligence on the part of the driver and owner of the vehicle and to bring the proven circumstances within the res ipsa loquitur doctrine. Defendants sought to obviate all inferences of negligence and the circumstances leading to the application of res ipsa loquitur by showing due care in inspection, maintenance and operation. . . .

The jury apparently found that defendants had met and overcome the charges of negligence. . . . There was evidence obtained at the site of the fire that both of the mainsprings above the tank trailer's front wheels had broken as a result of stress, not fatigue — from a kind of stress that could not be predicted by inspection — and finally there was no negligence on the driver's part.

Defendants also presented some evidence of contributory negligence. . . .

In the Court of Appeals, the principal claim of error was directed to the trial court's refusal to give an instruction on res ipsa loquitur, and we think that claim of error well taken. . . .

But there exists here an even more impelling basis for liability in this case than its derivation by allowable inference of fact under the res ipsa loquitur doctrine, and that is the proposition of strict liability arising as a matter of law from all of the circumstances of the event.

Strict liability is not a novel concept; it is at least as old as Fletcher v. Rylands. . . .

All of the Justices in Fletcher v. Rylands did not draw a distinction between the natural and nonnatural use of land but such a distinction would, we think, be irrelevant to the transportation of gasoline. The basic principles supporting the *Fletcher* doctrine, we think, control the transportation of gasoline as freight along the public highways the same as it does the impounding of waters and for largely the same reasons.

In many respects, hauling gasoline as freight is no more unusual, but more dangerous, than collecting water. When gasoline is carried as cargo — as distinguished from fuel for the carrier vehicle — it takes on uniquely hazardous characteristics, as does water impounded in large quantities. Dangerous in itself, gasoline develops even greater potential for harm when carried as freight — extraordinary dangers deriving from sheer quantity, bulk and weight, which enormously multiply its hazardous properties. And the very hazards inhering from the size of the load, its bulk or quantity and its movement along the highways presents another reason for application of the Fletcher v. Rylands rule not present in the impounding of large quantities of water — the likely destruction of cogent evidence from which negligence or want of it may be proved or disproved. It is quite probable that the most important ingredients of proof will be lost in a gasoline explosion and fire. Gasoline is always dangerous whether kept in large or small quantities because of its volatility, inflammability and explosiveness. But when several thousand gallons of it are allowed to spill across a public highway — that is, if, while in transit as freight, it is not kept impounded — the hazards to third persons are so great as to be almost beyond calculation. As a consequence of its escape from impoundment and subsequent explosion and ignition, the evidence in a very high percentage of instances will be destroyed, and the reasons for and causes contributing to its escape will quite likely be lost in the searing flames and explosions. . . .

The rule of strict liability rests not only upon the ultimate idea of rectifying a wrong and putting the burden where it should belong as a matter of abstract justice, that is, upon the one of the two innocent parties whose acts instigated or made the harm possible, but it also rests on problems of proof:

> . . . [T]he disasters caused by those who engage in abnormally dangerous or extra-hazardous activities frequently destroy all evidence of what in fact occurred, other than that the activity was being carried on. Certainly this is true with explosions of dynamite, large quantities of gasoline, or other explosives. It frequently is the case with falling aircraft. . . .

Transporting gasoline as freight by truck along the public highways and streets is obviously an activity involving a high degree of risk; it is a risk of great harm and injury; it creates dangers that cannot be eliminated by the exercise of reasonable care. That gasoline cannot be practicably transported except upon the public highways does not decrease the abnormally high risk arising from its transportation. Nor will the exercise of due and reasonable care assure protection to the public from the disastrous consequences of concealed or latent mechanical or metallurgical defects in the carrier's equipment, from the negligence of third parties, from latent defects in the highways and streets, and from all of the other hazards not generally disclosed or guarded against by reasonable care, prudence and foresight. Hauling gasoline in great quantities as freight, we think, is an activity that calls for the application of principles of strict liability.

The case is therefore reversed and remanded to the trial court for trial to the jury on the sole issue of damages.

ROSELLINI, J. (concurring).

I agree with the majority that the transporting of highly volatile and flammable substances upon the public highways in commercial quantities and for commercial purposes is an activity which carries with it such a great risk of harm to defenseless users of the highway, if it is not kept contained, that the common-law principles of strict liability should apply. In my opinion, a good reason to apply these principles, which is not mentioned in the majority opinion, is that the commercial transporter can spread the loss among his customers — who benefit from this extrahazardous use of the highways. Also, if the defect which caused the substance to escape was one of manufacture, the owner is in the best position to hold the manufacturer to account. . . .

Notes

1. The question whether an activity is "ultrahazardous," or in the newer formulation "abnormally hazardous," so as to trigger application of the strict liability standard, is one of law for the court to decide rather than a question of fact for the jury. Nevertheless, it is difficult to compile from the cases a dependable list of abnormally dangerous activities. The Restatement standard is a general and flexible one, and an activity that in one era or one area may be classified as abnormally hazardous may in another era or area be classified differently. For example, at one time damage to land caused by airplane crashes was governed by strict liability (*Guille* was a precursor of this view); now, most courts consider negligence the appropriate standard, just as in airplane collisions. See, e.g., Southern California Edison Co. v. Coleman, 150 Cal. App. 2d 829, 310 P.2d 504 (1957). But does it follow that liability damage caused by sonic booms from the Concorde (the supersonic transport plane) should not be strict? Suppose, as appears to be the case, that such damage cannot be appreciably reduced by flying more carefully, but only by flying more slowly or avoiding populated areas; victims are helpless to prevent or reduce damage from sonic booms; and the Concorde is commercially marginal. This combination of circumstances provides a strong argument for strict versus negligence liability,

does it not? Cf. Baxter, The SST: From Watts to Harlem in Two Hours, 21 Stan. L. Rev. 1 (1968).

Blasting with explosives is a traditional example of an activity that is subject to strict liability (remember *Hay*). But blasting in an isolated area may not be. Merely storing explosives, or operating a gunpowder factory, is not. Does this pattern make economic sense?

For a good recent effort to catalog the heads of strict liability based on ultrahazardousness, see Comment, 1978 Ariz. St. L.J. 99.

2. Thus far, our economic analysis of the choice between strict liability and negligence has focused on the difference between curtailing an activity and using greater care in carrying on the activity as methods of accident avoidance. We have suggested that strict liability is the appropriate regime, other things being equal, if the best way of reducing accident costs is for the potential injurer to reduce or change his activity rather than for him to take greater care or for the victim to reduce or change his activity or take greater care himself. (By this analysis, when is no liability the appropriate legal regime?) This seems to be the approach taken by the Restatement, which was, in turn, an effort to state the doctrine of Rylands v. Fletcher as it had been interpreted and applied in the United States. But Justice Rosellini, concurring in *Siegler*, suggested a distinct ground for strict liability — "that the commercial transporter can spread the loss among his customers — who benefit from this extrahazardous use of the highways." The idea of "loss spreading" as a ground for assigning liability to one or another party to an accident has been much discussed in recent years, especially as a basis for respondeat superior and for strict liability in defective-product cases (discussed in Chapter 9).

Among many other cases referring to loss-spreading considerations as a basis for classifying an activity as ultrahazardous is Smith v. Lockheed Propulsion Co., 247 Cal. App. 2d 774, 56 Cal. Rptr. 128 (1967). This was a suit for damages caused by ground tremors due to the testing of a rocket motor. The court stated: "Defendant, who is engaged in the enterprise for profit, is in a position best able to administer the loss so that it will ultimately be borne by the public." Id. at 785, 56 Cal. Rptr. at 137. The court relied in part on a similar case, Berg v. Reaction Motors Division, 37 N.J. 396, 410, 181 A.2d 487, 494 (1962), where the New Jersey court had said: "If damage does occur, it should in all fairness be absorbed as an operating business expense, for the enterprise may not reasonably expect its wholly innocent neighbor to shoulder the loss."

Also noteworthy is the statement of the court in Chavez v. Southern Pacific Transp. Co., 413 F. Supp. 1203, 1209 (E.D. Cal. 1976), in holding defendant liable for damage caused when 18 of its boxcars carrying bombs exploded:

> By indirectly imposing liability on those that benefit from the dangerous activity, risk distribution benefits the social-economic body in two ways: (1) the

adverse impact of any particular misfortune is lessened by spreading its cost over a greater population and over a larger time period, and (2) social and economic resources can be more efficiently allocated when the actual costs of goods and services (including the losses they entail) are reflected in their price to the consumer.

This formulation is useful in making explicit that loss spreading, or, as it is sometimes called, "risk distribution," comprises two distinct ideas; both are economic or can be given an economic interpretation. The first idea is that a concentrated large loss is more painful than the same loss divided up among a large group, each of whose members sustains a small loss. This idea derives ultimately from the concept of diminishing marginal utility of income, which means simply that as one gets more and more dollars, the utility of one's last dollar becomes less and less. Total utility rises but marginal utility — the utility of the last dollar — falls. ("Utility" here means simply subjective satisfaction.) It makes intuitive sense that one's first dollar would be worth more, in a subjective sense, than one's last. The first enables one to satisfy basic and imperative wants; the last dollar — at least for a reasonably affluent person — enables the purchase of some luxury that one could forgo without suffering a tremendous loss of satisfaction.

Someone who experiences diminishing marginal utility of income will be unwilling to gamble his existing wealth to obtain new increments of wealth; he will be risk averse (see Chapter 1). Suppose one has a total wealth of $100,000 and is asked to stake that wealth on a fair gamble — say a gamble that carries a 50 percent chance of producing a $200,000 payoff. The expected value of the gamble is $100,000. But since we know that every dollar the person has generates more subjective satisfaction than every dollar he would gain if he won the bet, it is a losing bet in an expected-utility sense. He is putting up $100,000 for a 50 percent chance of a payoff that will yield less than twice the satisfaction of the $100,000 he is staking.

Even if everyone experiences diminishing marginal utility of income (and the existence of gambling suggests that not everyone does, at least not all the time), it does not follow that taking a dollar from a rich man and giving it to a poor man will increase total utility on the theory that the diminution of the rich man's subjective satisfactions must be less than the augmentation of the poor man's. For we do not know the height of the two men's marginal utility functions. If the functions are of different heights, it is possible that a point far down the marginal utility function of the rich man will still be above a point far up the marginal utility function of the poor man. Therefore, there is an element of conjecture involved in supposing that taking a concentrated loss off the back of a victim of some accident and dividing it up into many small losses to customers or shareholders will increase total utility.

Another objection to using loss-spreading notions to shape the rules of tort liability is that there is an alternative and not obviously inferior method of loss spreading available to potential victims besides strict liability: They can buy insurance (a point made by Holmes in a passage from The Common Law reprinted in Chapter 4). In discussing tort liability as a method of loss spreading, modern courts tend to forget that potential victims can buy first-party, or accident, insurance. Most people have at least some insurance (including social insurance, as through the social security disability program) against loss from accidental injury. Therefore, unless tort liability is a cheaper method of insurance than ordinary accident insurance, there is no economic basis for using the concept of diminishing marginal utility of income, or risk aversion, as a guide to assigning tort liability.* Surprisingly, there have been no studies of the costs of insurance to potential injurers via tort liability relative to the costs of the insurance that potential accident victims can buy in the accident-insurance market. What would you expect such a study to find?

The court in *Chavez* suggested a second reason for loss spreading — or perhaps more accurately in this context, loss shifting — via strict liability: to increase allocative efficiency by making an enterprise pay the full social costs of its activity, which include the costs of accidents that the activity produces. The economics of the matter are more complicated. It is true that if an enterprise or industry is allowed to shift costs from itself to others and there is no market or legal mechanism for shifting them back, there may be too much of the activity from a social standpoint. Suppose that the market will pay $3 a widget when the total output of widgets is 1 million and $2 a widget when the total output is 2 million (the reason for the lower price at the higher output is that consumers must be given an inducement to give up some of what they have been buying instead of widgets). Suppose that the social marginal cost of widgets (at any level of output) is $3, composed of $2 in production costs and $1 in pollution costs. ·If the producers are made to bear the full costs of making widgets, they will produce only 1 million widgets; but if they do not bear the pollution costs, they will (assuming they are competitive) expand output to 2 million, and there will be twice as many widgets produced and sold as is socially optimal.

But this analysis assumes rather than establishes that the optimal method of dealing with the pollution is to impose a cost of $1 per widget on the manufacturer. It may not be the optimal method even if $1 is a correct estimate of the pollution costs generated by each widget produced. The optimal method of dealing with the pollution may be for the victims of pollution to move out of the vicinity of the widget factory — in which event 2 million may be the right number of widgets after all. *There is no presumption that changing the potential injurers' activity level is the economically most efficient method of internalizing some external cost* — a key point of this book.

---

*Question: should the cost of accident insurance be figured as part of the accident cost in deciding whether B < PL in the Hand formula? If so, how should that cost be calculated?

Where the optimal method of accident avoidance *is* to curtail the activity of potential injurers — to scale back the output of widgets from 2 million to 1 million, for example — then strict liability is a sensible rule. This is the thrust of the Restatement formulation and of the economic analysis of activity versus care. But it does not follow that strict liability is always or generally preferable to negligence liability or no liability on allocative-efficiency grounds. Strict liability would give us too little of the potential injurers' activity in any case where the optimal method of accident or pollution cost avoidance was for potential victims to curtail *their* activity. Allocative-efficiency arguments do not always favor strict liability.

3. Under what theory, if any, should Kuhlman himself, as distinct from his employer, have been held strictly liable?

M. J. Horwitz, The Transformation of American Law, 1780-1860
99-101 (1977)

The subversion of the expanding public law principle of just compensation by the increasingly ruthless application of the private law negligence principle must be seen as a phenomenon of industrialization. It is not surprising, therefore, that the negligence standard rose earliest in New York, Pennsylvania, and Massachusetts, to challenge the assumption of strict liability, for there was a relatively advanced level of economic development in these states. Indeed, the rise of the negligence principle was only part of a more general attempt to limit the scope of application of the principle of just compensation. This effort in turn was intimately associated with the need to reduce the crushing burden of damage judgments that a system of strict liability (or just compensation) entailed.

As it developed in the course of the nineteenth century, one legal commentator later observed, the American attitude toward legal liability was based on the assumption that the "quiet citizen must keep out of the way of the exuberantly active one." Indeed, the law of negligence became a leading means by which the dynamic and growing forces in American society were able to challenge and eventually overwhelm the weak and relatively powerless segments of the American economy. After 1840 the principle that one could not be held liable for socially useful activity exercised with due care became a commonplace of American law. In the process, the conception of property gradually changed from the eighteenth century view that dominion over land above all conferred the power to prevent others from interfering with one's quiet enjoyment of property to the nineteenth century assumption that the essential attribute of property ownership was the power to develop one's property regardless of the injurious consequences to others.

One of the most striking aspects of legal change during the antebellum period is the extent to which common law doctrines were transformed to create immunities from legal liability and thereby to provide substantial subsidies for those who undertook schemes of economic development. This pattern of subsidization raises several important questions concerning the relationship between legal and economic change in the period. Was legal subsidization socially efficient? Did it encourage investment in areas in which, as the welfare economist would put it, social benefits exceeded social costs even though private costs were greater than private benefits? Or did it in fact promote overinvestment in technology, which might be inferred from the strikingly low contribution to the gross national product that Robert Fogel has claimed railroads, for example, actually made? Because of the difficulties in accurately determining the indirect benefits that flowed from a particular technology, any conclusions about the social efficiency of subsidization must be advanced quite hesitantly.

Perhaps a more basic and manageable question for the historian is the need to explain why there developed so clear a pattern of subsidization through the use not of the tax system but of the legal system. One of the most consistent features of state economic policy during the first several decades of the nineteenth century was the pattern of extraordinarily low state budgetary expenditures. In Massachusetts, for example, where the state budget between 1795 and 1820 remained constant at roughly $133,000, the Handlins have identified a clear pattern of state use of legal instruments such as monopolies and franchises as an alternative to cash outlays. Even states like New York, which amassed an enormous debt in building its canal system, regarded these financial arrangements as involving profitable investments and not as cash subsidies out of the tax system. Indeed, despite a geometrical increase in its debt during the 1820s and 1830s, New York did not impose a general property tax until 1843. "Taxation played a very unimportant role during the first fifty years of the state's existence." Pennsylvania also was "unwilling to embark upon effective taxation" until 1842, when "a vigorous tax program was finally initiated." Investment in canals had simply "supplemented [a] strong anti-tax bias" with "the idea of a positive profit-making state — a state in which taxes were abolished." In short, every bit as significant as overt forms of direct legislative financial encouragement of enterprise were the enormous, but hidden, legal subsidies and resulting redistributions of wealth brought about through changes in common law doctrines.

What factors led antebellum statesmen generally to turn to subsidization through the legal, rather than through the tax, system? One explanation seems fairly clear. Change brought about through technical legal doctrine can more easily disguise underlying political choices. Subsidy through the tax system, by contrast, inevitably involves greater dangers of political conflict. Beyond these general observations about the consequences of choosing between seemingly nonpolitical as opposed to overtly political forms of subsidization, however, can we in addition say anything about the specific redistributive consequences of the one as opposed to the other? Until we know much more about the potential redistributive effects of state tax systems in this period, it would be dangerous to make any firm comparisons. Nevertheless, it does seem fairly clear that the tendency of subsidy through legal change during this period was dramatically to throw the burden of economic development on the weakest and least active elements in the population. By contrast, it seems plausible to suppose that in a period when the property tax provided the major share of potential state revenue, the burdens of subsidy through taxation would have fallen disproportionately on the wealthier segments of the population.

There is reason to suppose, therefore, that the choice of subsidization through the legal system was not simply an abstract effort to avoid political contention but that it entailed more conscious decisions about who would bear the burdens of economic growth. It does seem likely, moreover, that regardless of the actual distributional effects of resorting to the existing tax system, a more general fear of the redistributional potential of taxation played an important role in determining the view that encouragement of economic growth should occur not through the tax system, but through the legal system. It is, after all, quite striking that a dramatic upsurge of explicit laissez-faire ideology in America can be correlated with a dramatic increase in state taxation during the 1840s. One clear result of this ideological change was that state judges during the 1840s and 1850s began to restrict the scope of redistributive legal doctrines like eminent domain, which formerly had been aggressively used to promote economic development. Thus, whether or not legal subsidies to enterprise were optimally efficient or instead encouraged overinvestment in technology, it does seem quite likely that they did contribute to an increase in inequality by throwing a disproportionate share of the burdens of economic growth on the weakest and least organized groups in American society.

Notes

1. The question whether and to what extent the tort liability standard changed from strict liability to negligence is a much debated one. Professor Baker's analysis in Chapter 4 suggests that the shift may have been less pronounced than Professor Horwitz believes. However, some shift away from strict liability probably occurred. Ames, in the excerpt in Chapter 6, seems to have hit pretty close to the mark when he said there had been a long historical trend away from strict liability (though the trend may have been reversed, after Ames wrote, by the growth of workmen's compensation and of strict liability in products cases). Could there be an economic reason for this trend? One relevant factor may be a change in the costs of information. The use of a negligence standard to determine liability requires more information than the use of a strict liability standard; for the latter, all the court has to know is

that the defendant caused the plaintiff's injury. It is possible that only in comparatively recent times have courts had the capacity to answer the difficult factual questions that arise in applying a negligence standard. (This analysis is developed, in the context of primitive and ancient law, in Posner, A Theory of Primitive Society, with Special Reference to Law, 23 J. Law & Econ. 1, 49-50 (1980).) But this suggests why we might be surprised to find negligence concepts in a primitive legal system — not why we find them in an advanced system. To explain the latter point, we need to consider another economic facet of the strict liability-negligence trade-off, and that will be done below.

2. Assuming Horwitz is correct about the basic shift from strict liability to negligence effected by nineteenth-century tort law, the question remains whether this shift is helpfully described as a shift toward using tort law to "subsidize" activities that give rise to accidents. It is true that, by making an activity pay for even those accidents that are unavoidable in a Hand formula sense, strict liability tends to reduce the level of the activity, as in our widget example. But if there is no economic reason for making an activity strictly liable, the substitution of negligence for strict liability is not the conferral of an unjustified benefit. By using such words as "subversion" and "ruthless," and by describing the movement to negligence as the creation of "immunities from legal liabilities," but above all by the use of the word "subsidy," Horwitz creates the impression that strict liability is the natural, fair, and efficient standard of liability, while negligence results in externalizing accident costs and hence can be justified only if there are external benefits (as in the "public necessity" cases in Chapter 3). But there is no basis in economics for regarding strict liability as inherently more efficient than negligence — or vice versa; it all depends on the nature of the activity in question.

3. Would strict liability have led to a "crushing burden of damage judgments"? An enterprise would be crushed by a system of strict liability only if the optimal level of the activity were zero (which might have been true, for example, of balloon travel over New York City in the early nineteenth century). It is hard to believe that strict liability would have crushed the railroads, the principal inflicters of personal injuries in nineteenth-century tort cases. Did the court in *Losee* share Horwitz's misconception? On the question of "crushing liability," see also the *Duke Power* case, below.

4. To complete our economic analysis of the choice between strict liability and negligence, we need to consider the possible differences in the costs of administering the tort system. As a first approximation, these costs are the product of (1) the number of legal claims filed and (2) the cost of disposing of each claim. Assume to begin with that the number of accidents is unaffected by the choice between strict liability and negligence as the liability rule. Then the number of claims will be higher under strict liability, because all accidents in which someone is injured will give rise to a claim for damages, not just those accidents where the injurer is negligent and the victim nonnegligent. But the cost of disposing of each claim will be higher under negligence than

under strict liability, because a negligence case involves an extra issue — the negligence issue itself. So we have offsetting factors — more claims under strict liability, but a higher cost per claim under negligence. We should also count as a cost of deciding claims the misallocation that occurs when an issue is decided incorrectly — a big factor in the *Siegler* case. (Can you see why?) A further complication is the higher cost of disposing of a claim by means of a trial than by means of a pretrial settlement. Hence an important determinant of the average cost of disposing a claim is the ratio of trials to settlements. This ratio is apt to be higher in a negligence system, because the extra issue injects uncertainty and uncertainty breeds litigation. (For a simple exposition of the economic model of the choice to litigate, and an application of the model to the issue under discussion here, see R. A. Posner, Economic Analysis of Law 434-439, 441-442 (2d ed. 1977).)

To complete our analysis of the effect of the choice between negligence and strict liability on the costs of administering the tort system, we have to consider the effect of that choice on the accident rate, since the number of claims filed — an important determinant of those costs — is a function in part of the accident rate. In cases where adopting strict liability leads to a sharp reduction in the accident rate (because potential injurers are led to curtail their activity), the number of claims may actually drop — even though all accidents that do occur and cause injury give rise to claims — compared to the situation under a negligence system. In such a case, both administrative and allocative cost considerations would favor strict liability. But in an area where most accidents are unavoidable by either care or activity adjustments, the effect of strict liability in increasing the number of claims may dominate all other considerations and indicate that negligence is a superior system on administrative-cost grounds.

A couple of numerical examples will summarize the analysis. First, suppose there is an activity which, in the absence of any liability rule at all, would generate 100 accidents, and the expected accident cost would be $100 per accident. Ten of the accidents are avoidable at a cost of $50 apiece; the other 90 could be avoided, whether by greater care or less activity, at a minimum cost of $120 apiece. The cost of processing a legal claim is $10 under a negligence system and $8 under strict liability. If the rule is negligence, 10 accidents will be deterred, resulting in a net social saving of $500 (10 × $100 − 10 × $50). There is no administrative cost, because that cost is incurred only if a case is brought, and none are brought. Now let strict liability be substituted for negligence. The allocative saving is the same, $500, because the same 10 accidents are deterred. The other 90 are not deterred because the potential injurers prefer $100 in expected judgment costs to $120 in costs of preventing the accidents. But there is a cost to processing the claims in these cases; the cost is $720 (90 × $8). Strict liability is more costly than negligence when administrative costs are figured in.

Change the facts: suppose that while the 90 "unavoidable" accidents are indeed unavoidable *by taking greater care*, 50 of them could be avoided by reducing the activity that generates them, at a cost of only $80 per accident. Under a rule of negligence, the results are just as before. These 50 accidents are not deterred, because the costs of care exceed the expected accident costs. But if we switch to strict liability, 50 more accidents will be deterred, at a social saving, in allocative terms, of $1,000 (50 × $100 − 50 × $80). The administrative costs are $320 ($8 × 40, the latter being the number of accidents that are not deterred because the costs both of greater care and of less activity are greater than the expected accident costs). Hence, in this case, adopting strict liability will generate a net social benefit of $680.

These examples are oversimplified in various ways. In particular, all negligent accidents are assumed to be deterred; and no account is taken of the possible insurance benefits that strict liability offers compared to negligence. Nevertheless, the examples suggest that strict liability is not always and everywhere economically preferable to negligence liability. If this is correct, there can be no presumption that a general movement from strict liability to negligence in the nineteenth century was a movement away from efficiency, procured by powerful business interests. It may conceivably have reflected a fall in the costs of information involved in administering a negligence standard, and also a fall in the costs of safety technology which may have made care relatively more cost-effective than activity changes as a method of controlling accidents. But this is conjecture; the question has yet to be studied in depth.

5. There is an extensive literature on the relative merits of strict liability and negligence. The "enterprise liability" school, which favors strict liability (at least for business enterprises), on "risk distribution" grounds, is described succinctly in C. Morris & C. R. Morris, Jr., Morris on Torts 232-237 (2d ed. 1980). Strict liability is also favored in the pathbreaking book by G. Calabresi, The Costs of Accidents: A Legal and Economic Analysis (1970), the first extended economic analysis of alternative liability rules. Calabresi proposes that a liability rule be chosen with a view to minimizing the sum of three types of cost — "primary" (the allocative costs of accidents), "secondary" (the disutility resulting from failing to spread losses), and "tertiary" (the costs of administering the legal system). Calabresi believes that strict liability is the liability rule most likely to minimize the sum of these costs. Besides its loss-spreading attributes, Calabresi stresses the fact that strict liability forces the potential injurer to make a cost-benefit analysis of alternative methods of accident avoidance, rather than making the legal system do so as under negligence. Calabresi neglects, however, the symmetry between injurers and victims stressed in this chapter. No liability would have the same effect on the victim's incentive to conduct a comprehensive cost-benefit analysis of his safety options as strict liability would have on the injurer's. (Calabresi dismisses the possibility of loss spreading through victim insurance by asserting that people are psychologically incapable of foreseeing the possibility of being injured and taking adequate measures to insure themselves against the risk.) Calabresi gives short shrift to the proposition that the existing tort system,

with its mixture of negligence and strict liability, may actually be the optimal system. For criticism of Calabresi's The Costs of Accidents from an economic standpoint, see Posner, Book Review, 37 U. Chi. L. Rev. 636 (1970); for a later formulation of Calabresi's views on strict liability, see Calabresi & Hirschoff, Toward a Test for Strict Liability in Torts, 81 Yale L.J. 1055 (1972); and for more criticism, see Posner, Strict Liability: A Comment, 2 J. Legal Stud. 205 (1973). The case for strict liability over negligence is also vigorously argued, primarily from an economic standpoint, in Rodgers, Negligence Reconsidered: The Role of Rationality in Tort Theory, 54 S. Cal. L. Rev. 1 (1980).

Klemme, The Enterprise Liability Theory of Torts, 47 U. Colo. L. Rev. 153 (1976), is a detailed analysis of the strict-liability cases, heavily influenced by Calabresi's work. Other economic analyses of the choice between liability rules include Brown, Toward an Economic Theory of Liability, 2 J. Legal Stud. 323 (1973); R. A. Posner, Economic Analysis of Law 137-142 (2d ed. 1977); and Shavell, Strict Liability versus Negligence, 9 J. Legal Stud. 1 (1980). The economic literature on products liability (often strict) is discussed in Chapter 9. Various noneconomic theories of liability are discussed next.

6. Horwitz suggests that the real issue in the movement from strict liability to negligence in the nineteenth century was not efficiency but the distribution of wealth. Negligence made certain business interests wealthier at the expense of the poor and powerless segments of the society. Horwitz presents no evidence of this, however. His analysis is conjectural, and none too plausible. It is true that substituting negligence for strict liability reduces the costs of activities that give rise to the types of accident that cannot be avoided simply by taking greater care. In the nineteenth century these activities were primarily railroads, streetcars, mines, mills, factories, and to a lesser extent electric power companies. However, many of the injuries these enterprises inflicted were inflicted on their employees rather than on strangers, and the Coase theorem implies that the choice of liability rules is unlikely to affect the safety level in factories and other industrial establishments, or the real incomes of workers. But pass this point and assume that the common law of industrial accidents did reduce the real cost of employing workers in dangerous jobs, compared with strict liability. If so, the prices of the goods produced by industry would be lower. This would increase the wealth of consumers, including workers in their capacity as consumers. Since most consumers were workers or members of workers' families, it is unclear how moving to a negligence system would harm the working class as a whole.

Railroads are perhaps the major example of a nineteenth-century industry that caused substantial damage to strangers to the enterprise (spark damage to crops planted along railroad rights of way, personal injuries to travelers at crossings, etc.). Anything that increased the cost of railroading, however, including strict liability, would increase the prices of the commodities shipped by railroads, such as food, so that the effect of strict liability again would be that of an excise tax. An excise tax is usually regarded as a regressive form of taxation.

The whole question of the incidence of a tax — and strict liability is the equivalent of a tax on the activities subject to it, except that it does not generate revenue for the government — is a complex one. It is unclear what the distributive effect would be of changing from strict liability to negligence or vice versa across a broad range of industries.

7. The court in *Siegler*, in discussing the grounds for imposing strict liability, mentioned the "idea of rectifying a wrong and putting the burden where it should belong as a matter of abstract justice, that is upon the one of the two innocent parties whose acts instigated or made the harm possible." The idea that there should be rectification of an injury as a matter not of economic efficiency but of justice can be traced back to the Aristotelian concept of "corrective justice." Several recent torts scholars have argued that strict liability is required by the principle of corrective justice. This argument, together with a related argument drawn from Kant rather than Aristotle, is examined in the next note.

Does Corrective Justice Require Strict Liability?*

In Book V, Chapter 4, of the Nicomachean Ethics, Aristotle develops the concept of corrective justice. He discussed distributive justice — that is, justice in the distribution by the state of money, honors, and other things of value — in Chapter 3, saying that such awards should be made according to merit. Chapter 4 discusses a contrasting concept of justice, the rectificatory or corrective (*diorthōtikos* — literally "making straight"), which he says applies to transactions both voluntary and involuntary; the distinction is roughly that between contracts and torts. The crucial passage in Chapter 4 is the following:

> . . . it makes no difference [from a corrective justice standpoint] whether a good man has defrauded a bad man or a bad man a good one, nor whether it is a good or a bad man that has committed adultery; the law looks only to the distinctive character of the injury, and treats the parties as equal, if one is in the wrong and the other is being wronged, and if one inflicted injury and the other has received it.

As far as remedy is concerned, Aristotle says that

> the judge tries to equalize things by means of the penalty, taking away from the gain of the assailant. For the term "gain" is applied generally to such cases —

*This note is adapted from two recent articles: Posner, The Concept of Corrective Justice in Recent Theories of Tort Law, 10 J. Legal Stud. 187 (1981); and Posner, The Ethical and Political Basis of the Efficiency Norm in Common Law Adjudication, 8 Hofstra L. Rev. 487 (1980).

even if it be not a term appropriate to certain cases, e.g. to the person who inflicts a wound — and "loss" to the sufferer; at all events, when the suffering has been estimated, the one is called loss and the other gain. . . . Therefore the just . . . consists in having an equal amount before and after the transaction.

Three points should be noted about Aristotle's concept of corrective justice.

1. The duty to rectify is based not on the fact of injury but on the conjunction of injury and wrongdoing. The injurer must do wrong as well as do harm, and the victim must be wronged as well as harmed. Not all departures from distributive justice call for correction. Someone who voluntarily makes a bad bargain may end up worse off than the principles of distributive justice would, but for the bad bargain, dictate. But he has not been wronged and is not entitled to rectification. Moreover, what is wrongful or unjust is not defined in Chapter 4; it is assumed. In Chapter 8 of Book V we learn that "Whether an act is or is not one of injustice (or of justice) is determined by its voluntariness or involuntariness." But even within the class of voluntary acts, only those that are deliberate can be acts of injustice. Those done by misadventure (where "the injury takes place contrary to reasonable expectation") or by mistake (where, for example, "he threw not with intent to wound but only to prick") are not.

2. The idea that distributive considerations do not count in a setting of corrective justice ("it makes no difference whether a good man has defrauded a bad man or a bad man a good one . . .") is a procedural principle. It is not equivalent to saying that distributive notions should not affect the definition of rights or even that they should not enter into the determination of what sorts of acts are unjust or wrongful. The point, rather, is that the judge is interested only in the character — whether it is wrongful — of the injury, rather than in the character of the parties apart from that of the injury: "the moral worth of persons . . . is ignored."

3. Aristotle was writing against the background of the Athenian legal system of his day, where even suits to redress crimes were (with rare exceptions) instituted and prosecuted by private individuals, the victim or a member of his family, rather than by the state. So he naturally assumed that redress for wrongful injuries was by means of private actions. But there is no indication in Chapter 4 that he thought there could be only one mode of rectification consistent with the concept of corrective justice — namely, a tort action, in which the judge orders the wrongdoer to pay a damages judgment to the victim. In fact, as we shall see, it is not even certain that Aristotle required that rectification involve full compensation of the victim.

To summarize, the main point in Chapter 4 is that if someone injures another wrongfully, he has behaved unjustly irrespective of his merit, relative to the victim's, evaluated apart from the wrongful injury itself. Chaper 4 is thus a corollary to Chapter 3, which discusses distributive justice. Chapter 4 makes clear that the rights of the superior individual do not include the right to injure an inferior person through wrongful conduct. This idea is important, but it is more limited than the corrective justice concepts of recent tort scholars.

Professor George Fletcher analyzes tort law under two competing "paradigms" — the "paradigm of reciprocity" and the "paradigm of reasonableness." Fletcher, Fairness and Utility in Tort Theory, 85 Harv. L. Rev. 537, 540-542 (1972). The former is derived from notions of corrective justice that Fletcher locates in Book V, Chapter 4 of the Nicomachean Ethics, and the latter from utilitarian ideas. The paradigm of reasonableness corresponds in a rough way to the negligence standard. Under the paradigm of reciprocity, in contrast, "a victim has a right to recover for injuries caused by a risk greater in degree and different in order from those created by the victim and imposed on the defendant" (85 Harv. L. Rev. at 542) irrespective of the social value of the defendant's or the plaintiff's activity giving rise to the injury. The choice between the two paradigms depends on "whether judges should look solely at the claims and interests of the parties before the court . . . without looking beyond the case at hand" (as corrective justice requires, according to Fletcher) — in which event they should choose the paradigm of reciprocity — or whether judges should "resolve seemingly private disputes in a way that serves the interests of the community as a whole," in which event they should choose the paradigm of reasonableness. (Id. at 540.)

Fletcher's suggested rule of reciprocity has no basis in the concept of corrective justice expounded by Aristotle, the only authority on corrective justice to whom Fletcher refers. Nowhere does Aristotle suggest that the concept of wrongful or unjust conduct excludes consideration of the social value of conduct. To be sure, the Aristotelian judge is not to look "beyond the case at hand," but only in the sense that he is not to consider whether the defendant is a better man than the plaintiff, evaluated apart from the character of the injury; it does not follow that the social utility of the defendant's conduct that gave rise to the injury is irrelevant to whether the injury was wrongful. There is no basis in the Aristotelian concept of corrective justice for Fletcher's conclusion that negligence is an inappropriate standard when the victim's conduct is less dangerous to the injurer than the injurer's is to the victim.

Richard Epstein's first article on tort law, excerpted in the preceding chapter of this book, did not mention corrective justice, except for a critical footnote reference to Fletcher. But his subsequent articles used the term repeatedly, and by 1979 Epstein was describing his "basic . . . framework" or "conceptual . . . ideal" as one based on the "principles of corrective justice: rendering to each person whatever redress is required because of the violation of his rights by another." Epstein, Nuisance Law: Corrective Justice and Its Utilitarian Constraints, 8 J. Legal Stud. 49, 50, 99 (1979). Since Epstein does not cite Aristotle, it is not clear that he is trying to invoke the Aristotelian concept; he may be using corrective justice in a different sense. The definition just quoted, however, is an acceptable paraphrase of the Aristotelian notion. But reading further, one realizes that corrective justice means something different to Epstein from what it meant to Aristotle. Epstein speaks of "the distribution of vested rights demanded by a corrective justice theory" and says that "corrective justice principles still help us decide who is a wrongdoer and who is an innocent driver," and again that "corrective justice arguments identify the wrongdoer." (Id. at 77, 101.) But the Aristotelian concept of corrective justice does not tell us who is a wrongdoer or who has vested rights; all it tells us is that a wrongful injury is not excused by the moral superiority of the injurer to the victim. More recently, Epstein has described his conceptual ideas as "straight corrective justice-libertarian theory." Epstein Causation and Corrective Justice: A Reply to Two Critics, 8 J. Legal Stud. 477, 496 (1979). But unless the Aristotelian notion is to be abandoned completely, "corrective justice" and "libertarian" cannot be yoked in this way — the former referring as it does to the rectification of a wrong, the latter to a particular theory of wrongful conduct.

Epstein seems to associate two fundamental ideas with corrective justice. The first is that the victim of wrongdoing has a right to be compensated by the wrongdoer for injury resulting from the invasion. The second is that the fact of injury "permits the plaintiff to show that the initial balance between the two parties is in need of redress because of the defendant's conduct." Epstein, Defenses and Subsequent Pleas in a System of Strict Liability, 3 J. Legal Stud. 165, 167-168 (1974). The first idea, that of the wrongdoer's duty to compensate the victim of wrong, is certainly found in Book V, Chapter 4 of the Nicomachean Ethics but more as background than as a central principle of corrective justice. If one had said to Aristotle, "the best way to deal with wrongful conduct is to deter it through a heavy criminal penalty, rather than to allow private damage actions," there is no evidence that he would have regarded such a substitution as unjust. As to the second point, while the ideas of balance and redress are part of Aristotle's concept of corrective justice, Epstein's idea that the balance is disturbed by injury alone is not. Aristotle requires, as the predicate for redress under a corrective justice theory, that the injurer be acting wrongfully *and* that the victim be harmed. These are two distinct requirements in Aristotle, not one as in Epstein.

Professor John Borgo builds his analysis of corrective justice on Epstein's. Borgo describes Epstein's concept of corrective justice as "the notion that when one man harms another the victim has a moral right to demand, and the injurer a moral duty to pay him, compensation for the harm," and Borgo accepts this as a correct statement of the Aristotelian concept, citing Book V, Chapter 4 of the Nicomachean Ethics. Borgo, Causal Paradigms in Tort Law, 8 J. Legal Stud. 419-420 (1979). But Aristotle does not suggest that a duty to compensate arises from the fact of harm; he states explicitly that the harm must be wrongful.

Borgo's mistake warps his entire analysis. Having defined the idea of corrective justice as requiring compensation paid for harm done, Borgo must do handsprings to come up with an idea of causation that will carry the moral freight that he associates with the idea of corrective justice. He states: "the linchpin of a system of corrective justice is a nonorthodox doctrine of causation. Such a doctrine makes it possible to focus analysis on the causal relation between the defendant's conduct and the plaintiff's harm. That relation in turn provides the basis for ascribing moral, and therefore legal, responsibility for harm." Id. at 454. If causation is defined as moral responsibility, so that the idea of harm is equated to the idea of wrongful harm, the Aristotelian concept is obtained. But this extraordinarily indirect route to the correct conclusion is necessary only because Borgo misreads Aristotle.

It is easy to see how Borgo was inveigled into taking this path by Professor Epstein, who uses the term corrective justice repeatedly, states that corrective-justice principles require that a person be prima facie liable for any injury that he causes, and then, through the idea of "causal paradigms," imposes limitations on the meaning of "cause." In Epstein's view, as we saw in Chapter 6 of this book, the basic meaning of cause is captured in the paradigmatic example "A hit B." To be considered causal, a relationship must resemble closely this example. Using this method, Epstein can show, for example, that competition is not a tort, because the way in which harm occurs when one rival offers a lower price or superior product than another does not involve the use of force or anything enough like force to be assimilated to the A-hit-B example. (See last Note in Chapter 2 of this book.)

Epstein's idea of causation is an unusual one, for there is no linguistic or conceptual difficulty in regarding a successful competitor as having "caused" the business losses of his less successful rival. This idea is also an unnecessary one. Corrective justice does not imply that competition is a tort merely because it causes injury. But because Borgo thinks Epstein has defined the Aristotelian notion of corrective justice correctly, and hence that merely causing harm *does* entitle the victim to redress, Borgo must find some other, non-Epsteinian method of limiting the idea of cause, in order to avoid unacceptable results such as liability in the competition case. Borgo's method is to equate causation in tort law to moral or legal responsibility. It is as curious a way of limiting the idea of causation as Epstein's. It is true that conclusions about causation are frequently influenced by normative considerations: that we may single out one necessary condition from all the others as "the cause" because it is the thing we want to change. But causation and responsibility are not synonyms. The competition example shows this. The successful competitor has indeed "caused" his rival's business losses, but no moral opprobrium, or legal liability, attaches to this injury, because social welfare is enhanced by competition. Only a misreading of Aristotle could make Borgo think it important to pour the idea of moral responsibility into the idea of causation in order to avoid unacceptable results.

Another way to read Epstein is that he believes the duty of corrective justice is triggered not by causing harm but by causing harm through the use of physical force or some closely related modality such as fraud. In this reading, Aristotle's distinction between the wrong and the injury is preserved, and the wrong is the use of force or fraud. But in not making this distinction explicit Epstein merges the issues of wrong and injury, with the result that the ethical basis of his system is unclear.* Early Epstein is a "responsibility" theorist, as is Borgo; later Epstein and Fletcher are "rights" theorists.† Although Epstein has used the term "corrective justice" to describe both stages of his thought, neither responsibility theories nor rights theories are theories of corrective justice. They are theories about the holdings or entitlements that people can legitimately claim. They belong to distributive rather than corrective justice.

Frederick Sharp has written an article applying "the ethical categories of Aristotle" to the question whether tort law should adopt "enterprise liability," defined as "liability without fault imposed on enterprises." Sharp, Aristotle, Justice and Enterprise Liability in the Law of Torts, 34 U. Toronto Faculty L. Rev. 84 and n.1 (1976). Corrective justice is one of these categories, but Sharp realizes that the Aristotelian concept of justice is not exhausted by the discussion of corrective justice in Chapter 4 of Book V.

Sharp's discussion of Rylands v. Fletcher illustrates his method and its shortcomings. He begins by suggesting that there is a problem in applying the Aristotelian categories to the case because, he says, the injury involved a loss to the victim but no gain to the injurer. This is an economic error. The injurer gains by saving the cost of avoiding the injury. Sharp notes, however, that Aristotle said that there is a duty of corrective justice even in cases where there is no apparent gain to the injurer. But Sharp faces another problem: "although the defendant [in Rylands v. Fletcher] inflicted injury on the plaintiff, he did not do so 'wrongfully' since [according to Book V, Chapter 8 of the Nicomachean Ethics] this requires knowledge." Id. at 89.

Sharp nevertheless concludes that corrective justice supports the result in Rylands v. Fletcher:

> Between all citizens there is proportionality, which is altered when one suffers injury. It is unjust to suffer injury at the hands of another, and thus important that the injury be recompensed. But what to do if no one has gained by the injury? Mr. Justice Blackburn justified imposing liability on the defendant by the nature of his activity; "anything likely to do mischief if it escapes." Put in extended Aristotelian terms, anyone who carries on a hazardous activity which alters the social proportion of benefits by inflicting injury must bear the burden, because the nature of the activity has brought "gain" to the enterpriser.

---

*As Joseph Steiner has said of Epstein's tort theory, "The physical descriptions which constitute the paradigms of causation either have no normative content and cannot lead to normative conclusions or they employ words with implicit normative content thereby incorporating unstated, independent, normative premises which are the very principles we are seeking. In neither case do the paradigms, per se, give guidance on the assignment of rights." Steiner, Economics, Morality, and the Law of Torts, 26 U. Toronto L.J. 227, 246 (1976).

†On Epstein, see Posner, Epstein's Tort Theory: A Critique, 8 J. Legal Stud. 457, 465-471 (1979); on Fletcher, see Coleman, Justice and Reciprocity in Tort Theory, 14 W. Ontario L. Rev. 105, 117-118 (1975), explaining and criticizing Fletcher's derivation of the paradigm of reciprocity from a "security principle" analogous to one of John Rawls's principles of distributive justice.

This is corrective justice in the sense that hazardous enterprises can cause injury disproportionate to the expectations of citizens living together by agreement in a commonwealth. A "gain" is imputed to the defendant in this case, since he departed from the restrictive standard of conduct owing to one's neighbours, and so potentially violated the social proportionality from the moment he embarked on the dangerous activity. It is thus that I argue Aristotle's support for the doctrine of enterprise liability for ultrahazardous activities, on the basis that industry must pay its own way. [Id. at 90 (footnotes omitted).]

The key idea is that of proportion. There is indeed much discussion in Book V of the Nicomachean Ethics of proportion, balance, mean, and related terms. In particular, Aristotle makes a distinction between what he calls the "geometrical mean" and the "arithmetical mean," relating the first concept to distributive justice and the second to corrective justice.* If there is some amount of money or of honors to be distributed by the state, it should be distributed in proportion to the relative merits of the citizens. Thus if A is twice as virtuous as B, and virtue is the standard of merit in the society, A should receive two-thirds of the distribution. This is the "geometrical mean." But if A steals a drachma from B, B is entitled to the return of the drachma — not just to one-third of a drachma. This is the "arithmetic mean."

In short, corrective justice requires annulling a departure from the preexisting distribution of money or honors in accordance with merit, but only when the departure is the result of *an act of injustice,* causing injury. Sharp omits this qualification. When he states, "It is unjust to suffer injury at the hands of another, and thus important that the injury be recompensed," he departs from the Aristotelian concept of corrective justice by failing to distinguish injury from wrong. The problem is not that the defendants in Rylands v. Fletcher did not gain from the injury — they did, at least in an economic analysis. The problem is that there is no basis in Aristotelian thought for regarding an injury that occurs without fault as unjust, and therefore as triggering a duty of corrective justice. So we have a paradox: Epstein and Sharp (and also Fletcher) invoke corrective justice in support of enlarging the scope of strict liability as a principle of tort law, but if anything the Aristotelian concept suggests narrowing it, because the concept requires wrongful conduct as well as harmful result.

To all this it may be replied that even if Aristotle's discussion of corrective justice does not support a preference for strict over negligence liability, there is something unfair about a world in which people can inflict injuries without having to compensate the victim. Maybe a duty to compensate cannot be extracted from Aristotle, but if so that may just show the limitations of Aristotelian thinking. The merits of this position are examined briefly at the end of this note. A more interesting point, however, is that even if the position is accepted, it may not lead to a preference for strict liability in

---

*By "mean," he apparently does not mean average, which is the mathematical meaning; his meaning is in fact unclear.

cases where negligence is, on balance, the more efficient method of accident control. Potential victims might actually prefer a system of negligence to one of strict liability, if the former were the more efficient system.

The argument turns on the economic concept of ex ante compensation, i.e., being compensated in advance. Suppose you buy a lottery ticket and then lose the lottery. So long as there is no element of fraud or duress, you may be said to have consented, or at least waived any objections to, your loss. You were compensated for that loss in advance, by the expectation that you might win. There is a kind of assumption of risk, which is the counterpart in unintentional torts to the defense of consent in intentional torts.

Many of the involuntary, uncompensated losses experienced in the market, or tolerated by the institutions that take the place of the market where the market cannot be made to work effectively, are fully compensated ex ante and hence are consented to. Suppose some entrepreneur loses money because a competitor develops a superior product. Since the return to entrepreneurial activity will include a premium to cover the risk of losses due to competition, the entrepreneur is compensated for those losses ex ante. But in what sense may the driver injured by another driver in an accident, in which neither was at fault, be said to have consented to the injury so as not to be entitled, under a negligence system, to compensation?

To answer this question, we must consider the effect on the costs of driving of insisting on ex post compensation, as under a system of strict liability. By hypothesis they would be higher; otherwise the negligence system would not be the most efficient system. Would drivers be willing to incur higher costs of driving in order to preserve the principle of ex post compensation? They would not. Any driver who wanted to be assured of compensation in the event of an accident regardless of whether he was at fault need only buy first-party, or accident, insurance, by hypothesis at lower cost than he could obtain compensation ex post through a system of strict liability.

This can be most easily visualized by imagining that everyone involved in a traffic accident is identical — everyone is the same age, drives the same amount, and so on. In these circumstances everyone will pay the same rate for both liability insurance and accident insurance. The difference between negligence and strict liability will be that under negligence, liability insurance rates will be lower and accident insurance rates higher, because fewer accidents will give rise to liability, while under strict liability the reverse will be true. But if, as assumed, negligence is the more efficient system, the *sum* of the liability and accident insurance premiums will be lower under negligence,* and everyone will prefer this.

Some may object to the above analysis on the ground that the type of consent used in the analysis to justify an institution such as the negligence

---

*This assumes that all accident costs are reflected in insurance rates. Most accident-prevention costs (e.g., the value of time lost in driving more slowly) are not. Presumably these costs would also be higher under strict liability if that is indeed the less efficient liability rule.

system is fictitious because no one has given his *express* consent. It would indeed be naive to regard the political survival of negligence in the automobile accident arena as evidence of such consent; the radical imperfections of the political system in registering preferences are the subject of a vast literature in social choice and in the economic theory of legislation. Nevertheless, the objection founders precisely on the unavailability of a practical method of eliciting express consent, not so much to individual market transactions — though even there the consent of third parties affected by those transactions often cannot feasibly be elicited — as to *institutions,* such as the negligence system or indeed the market itself. If there is no reliable mechanism for eliciting express consent, it follows not that we should abandon the principle of consent but that we should look for implied consent, as by trying to answer the hypothetical question whether, if transaction costs were zero, the affected parties would have agreed to the institution. This procedure for inferring consent resembles a judge's imputing the intent of parties to a contract that fails to provide expressly for some contingency. Although the task of imputation is easier in the contract case, that case is still significant in showing that implicit consent is a meaningful form of consent. The absence of an underlying contract is relevant to the confidence with which an inference of implicit consent can be drawn rather than to the propriety of drawing such inferences.

To be sure, "[a] proposal is not legislation simply because all the members of the legislature are in favor of it." Epstein, Causation and Corrective Justice: A Reply to Two Critics, 8 J. Legal Stud. 477, 496 (1979). But this is because there is a mechanism by which legislators can express actual consent to a proposal. Sometimes the mechanism is inoperative, as when a question arises as to the scope or meaning of a past legislative enactment, and then we allow the courts to infer the legislative intent. This is an example of implicit but meaningful consent.

Another objection to using consent to justify institutions which maximize wealth or efficiency is that the consent will rarely be unanimous. Contrary to our earlier assumption, people are not identical ex ante. Even if the costs of driving would be higher under a system of strict liability than under a negligence system, why should nondrivers prefer the negligence system? To the extent that groups of this sort could actually be identified, one might grant them the protection of a strict liability system if one placed a higher value on compensation per se than Aristotle did. This is essentially Professor Fletcher's approach, mentioned earlier in this note. But this may not be required by the principle of consent. Most people who do not drive do not stay at home either; they use other modes of transportation — taxis, buses, or subways, to name a few — whose costs would by assumption be higher under a system of strict liability. Those costs, or a large fraction of them at least, would be borne by the users. Even the nondrivers might therefore consent to a negligence system of liability for transport accidents if it were cheaper than a system of strict liability. No institution, of course, will command the implicit consent of everyone. But only a fanatic would insist that absolute unanimity is required to legitimize a social institution such as the negligence system.

The above argument concedes that there is a moral basis for requiring an injurer to compensate a victim, even if the injurer was not at fault, but argues that compensation can be ex ante; and that the negligence system, applied for example to automobile accidents, if it is a more efficient system, may be justifiable on that basis. But the more fundamental question is why there should be a duty to compensate the victim of an accident when the injurer was not at fault. Such a duty cannot be derived from the Aristotelian idea of corrective justice, as we have seen. Can it perhaps be derived from the idea, fundamental to Kantian ethics, that people should always use other people as ends, not as means? If a driver runs down a pedestrian and does not compensate him, is not the driver using the pedestrian as a means, and not an end?

The problem with this argument is the symmetry, mentioned repeatedly in this chapter, between potential injurers and potential victims when neither injurer nor victim is at fault. If the farmer can stack his hay near the railroad track and demand compensation if any of it is damaged by locomotive sparks, he is using the railroad as a means to an end. If pedestrians can force drivers to act at their peril, they are using drivers as a means rather than an end. One could argue that people have a right to go about their activities without the threat of uncompensated personal injury hanging over them (of course, they can insure, but then they bear the cost of compensation, rather than the potential injurer). Equally one could argue that people have a right not to be hampered in their activities by being held liable for accidents that they could not have prevented at reasonable cost. Cf. C. Fried, An Anatomy of Values: Problems of Personal and Social Choice 187-189 (1970). No liability seems to deny the full personal autonomy of the victim; strict liability, the full personal autonomy of the injurer. To differentiate the two when neither is at fault is a daunting task.

Duke Power Co. v. Carolina Environmental Study Group, Inc.
438 U.S. 59 (1978)

[Suit by environmental groups for a declaratory judgment that the Price-Anderson Act is unconstitutional.]

MR. CHIEF JUSTICE BURGER delivered the opinion of the Court. . . .

When Congress passed the Atomic Energy Act of 1946, it contemplated that the development of nuclear power would be a Government monopoly. Within a decade, however, Congress concluded that the national interest would be best served if the Government encouraged the private sector to become involved in the development of atomic energy for peaceful purposes under a program of federal regulation and licensing. The Atomic Energy Act of 1954 implemented this policy decision, providing for licensing of private construction, ownership, and operation of commercial nuclear power reactors for energy production under strict supervision by the Atomic Energy Commission (AEC).

Private industry responded to the Atomic Energy Act of 1954 with the development of an experimental power plant constructed under the auspices of a consortium of interested companies. It soon became apparent that profits from the private exploitation of atomic energy were uncertain and the accompanying risks substantial. Although the AEC offered incentives to encourage investment, there remained in the path of the private nuclear power industry various problems — the risk of potentially vast liability in the event of a nuclear accident of a sizable magnitude being the major obstacle. Notwithstanding comprehensive testing and study, the uniqueness of this form of energy production made it impossible totally to rule out the risk of a major nuclear accident resulting in extensive damage. Private industry and the AEC were confident that such a disaster would not occur, but the very uniqueness of nuclear power meant that the possibility remained, and the potential liability dwarfed the ability of the industry and private insurance companies to absorb the risk. Thus, while repeatedly stressing that the risk of a major nuclear accident was extremely remote, spokesmen for the private sector informed Congress that they would be forced to withdraw from the field if their liability were not limited by appropriate legislation.

Congress responded in 1957 by passing the Price-Anderson Act, 71 Stat. 576, 42 U.S.C. §2210 (1970 ed. and Supp. V). The Act had the dual purpose of "protect[ing] the public and . . . encourag[ing] the development of the atomic energy industry." In its original form, the Act limited the aggregate liability for a single nuclear incident[2] to $500 million plus the amount of liability insurance available on the private market — some $60 million in 1957. The nuclear industry was required to purchase the maximum available amount of privately underwritten public liability insurance, and the Act provided that if damages from a nuclear disaster exceeded the amount of that private insurance coverage, the Federal Government would indemnify the licensee and other "persons indemnified" in an amount not to exceed $500 million. Thus, the actual ceiling on liability was the amount of private insurance coverage plus the Government's indemnification obligation which totaled $560 million.

Since its enactment, the Act has been twice amended, the first occasion being on the eve of its expiration in 1966. These amendments extended the basic liability limitation provisions for another 10 years, and added a provision which had the effect of requiring those indemnified under the Act to

2. A "nuclear incident" is defined as "any occurrence . . . within the United States causing, within or outside the United States, bodily injury, sickness, disease, or death, or loss of or damage to property, or loss of use of property, arising out of or resulting from the radioactive, toxic, explosive, or other hazardous properties of source, special nuclear, or by-product material. . . ."

waive all legal defenses in the event of a substantial nuclear accident.[5] This provision was based on a congressional concern that state tort law dealing with liability for nuclear incidents was generally unsettled and that some way of insuring a common standard of responsibility for all jurisdictions — strict liability — was needed. A waiver of defenses was thought to be the preferable approach since it entailed less interference with state tort law than would the enactment of a federal statute prescribing strict liability.

In 1975, Congress again extended the Act's coverage until 1987, and continued the $560 million limitation on liability. However a new provision was added requiring, in the event of a nuclear incident, each of the 60 or more reactor owners to contribute between $2 and $5 million toward the cost of compensating victims. Since the liability ceiling remained at the same level, the effect of the "deferred premium" provision was to reduce the Federal Government's contribution to the liability pool.[8] In its amendments to the Act in 1975, Congress also explicitly provided that "in the event of a nuclear incident involving damages in excess of [the] amount of aggregate liability, the Congress will thoroughly review the particular incident and will take whatever action is deemed necessary and appropriate to protect the public from the consequences of a disaster of such magnitude. . . ."

Under the Price-Anderson Act as it presently stands, liability in the event of a nuclear incident causing damages of $560 million or more would be spread as follows: $315 million would be paid from contributions by the licensees of the 63 private operating nuclear power plants; $140 million would come from private insurance (the maximum now available); the remainder of $105 million would be borne by the Federal Government.[9] . . .

The District Court held that the Price-Anderson Act contravened the Due Process Clause [of the Fifth Amendment] because "[t]he amount of recovery is not rationally related to the potential losses"; because "[t]he Act tends to encourage irresponsibility in matters of safety and environmental protection . . ."; and finally because "[t]here is no quid pro quo" for the liability limitations. . . .

As we read the Act and its legislative history, it is clear that Congress' purpose was to remove the economic impediments in order to stimulate the

5. The waiver provision is incorporated in the indemnity agreement. The defenses of negligence, contributory negligence, charitable or governmental immunity and assumption of risk all are waived in the event of an extraordinary nuclear occurrence, as are, to a limited degree, defenses based on certain short state statutes of limitations.

8. As the number of reactors increases, the $5 million deferred premium in itself will yield a fund exceeding the present liability ceiling. For example, it is predicted that by 1985 there will be a maximum of 138 reactors operating, which would produce $690 million in addition to whatever insurance is available from the private insurance market. Under the Act, the liability ceiling automatically increases to a level equal to the amount of primary and secondary (deferred premium) insurance coverage when the amount of such coverage exceeds the $560 million figure.

9. Appellees' expert witness on insurance testified in the District Court that homeowners were unable to purchase insurance against nuclear catastrophes because "the nuclear industry has essentially absorbed the entire capacity of the private insurance markets in their need for property and liability insurance."

private development of electric energy by nuclear power while simultaneously providing the public compensation in the event of a catastrophic nuclear
incident. The liability-limitation provision thus emerges as a classic example
of an economic regulation — a legislative effort to structure and accommodate "the burdens and benefits of economic life." "It is by now well established that [such] legislative Acts . . . come to the Court with a presumption
of constitutionality, and that the burden is on one complaining of a due
process violation to establish that the legislature has acted in an arbitrary and
irrational way." . . .

When examined in light of this standard of review, the Price-Anderson
Act, in our view, passes constitutional muster. The record before us fully
supports the need for the imposition of a statutory limit on liability to
encourage private industry participation and hence bears a rational relationship to Congress' concern for stimulating the involvement of private enterprise in the production of electric energy through the use of atomic power;
nor do we understand appellees or the District Court to be of a different
view. Rather their challenge is to the alleged arbitrariness of the *particular
figure* of $560 million, which is the statutory ceiling on liability. The District
Court aptly summarized its position: "The amount of recovery is not rationally related to the potential losses. Abundant evidence in the record shows
that although major catastrophe in any particular place is not certain and
may not be extremely likely, nevertheless, in the territory where these plants
are located, damage to life and property for this and future generations could
well be many, many times the limit which the law places on liability."

Assuming, *arguendo*, that the $560 million fund would not insure full
recovery in all conceivable circumstances — and the hard truth is that no one
can ever know — it does not by any means follow that the liability limitation
is therefore irrational and violative of due process. The legislative history
clearly indicates that the $560 million figure was not arrived at on the
supposition that it alone would necessarily be sufficient to guarantee full
compensation in the event of a nuclear incident. Instead, it was conceived of
as a "starting point" or a working hypothesis. The reasonableness of the
statute's assumed ceiling on liability was predicated on two corollary considerations — expert appraisals of the exceedingly small risk of a nuclear incident
involving claims in excess of $560 million, and the recognition that in the
event of such an incident, Congress would likely enact extraordinary relief
provisions to provide additional relief, in accord with prior practice. . . .

Given our conclusion that in general limiting liability is an acceptable
method for Congress to utilize in encouraging the private development of
electric energy by atomic power, candor requires acknowledgment that whatever ceiling figure is selected will, of necessity, be arbitrary in the sense that
any choice of a figure based on imponderables like those at issue here can
always be so characterized. This is not, however, the kind of arbitrariness
which flaws otherwise constitutional action. When appraised in terms of
both the extremely remote possibility of an accident where liability would

exceed the limitation and Congress' own statutory commitment to "take whatever action is deemed necessary and appropriate to protect the public from the consequences of" any such disaster, we hold the congressional decision to fix a $560 million ceiling, at this stage in the private development and production of electric energy by nuclear power, to be within permissible limits and not violative of due process.

This District Court's further conclusion that the Price-Anderson Act "tends to encourage irresponsibility . . . on the part of builders and owners" of the nuclear power plants simply cannot withstand careful scrutiny. We recently outlined the multitude of detailed steps involved in the review of any application for a license to construct or to operate a nuclear power plant; nothing in the liability-limitation provision undermines or alters in any respect the rigor and integrity of that process. Moreover, in the event of a nuclear accident the utility itself would suffer perhaps the largest damages. While obviously not to be compared with the loss of human life and injury to health, the risk of financial loss and possible bankruptcy to the utility is in itself no small incentive to avoid the kind of irresponsible and cavalier conduct implicitly attributed to licensees by the District Court.

The remaining due process objection to the liability-limitation provision is that it fails to provide those injured by a nuclear accident with a satisfactory quid pro quo for the common-law rights of recovery which the Act abrogates. Initially, it is not at all clear that the Due Process Clause in fact requires that a legislatively enacted compensation scheme either duplicate the recovery at common law or provide a reasonable substitute remedy.[32] However, we need not resolve this question here since the Price-Anderson Act does, in our view, provide a reasonably just substitute for the common-law or state tort law remedies it replaces.

The legislative history of the liability-limitation provisions and the accompanying compensation mechanism reflects Congress' determination that reliance on state tort law remedies and state-court procedures was an unsatisfactory approach to assuring public compensation for nuclear accidents, while at the same time providing the necessary incentives for private development of nuclear-produced energy. The remarks of Chairman Anders of the NRC before the Joint Committee on Atomic Energy during the 1975 hearings on the need for renewal of the Price-Anderson Act are illustrative of this concern and of the expectation that the Act would provide a more efficient and certain vehicle for assuring compensation in the unlikely event of a nuclear incident:

---

32. Our cases have clearly established that "[a] person has no property, no vested interest, in any rule of the common law." Second Employers' Liability Cases, 223 U.S. 1, 50 (1912), quoting Munn v. Illinois, 94 U.S. 113, 134 (1877). The "Constitution does not forbid the creation of new rights, or the abolition of old ones recognized by the common law, to attain a permissible legislative object," Silver v. Silver, 280 U.S. 117, 122 (1929), despite the fact that "otherwise settled expectations" may be upset thereby. Indeed, statutes limiting liability are relatively commonplace and have consistently been enforced by the courts. . . .

The primary defect of this alternative [nonrenewal of the Act], however, is its failure to afford the public either a secure source of funds or a firm basis for legal liability with respect to new plants. While in theory no legal limit would be placed on liability, as a practical matter the public would be less assured of obtaining compensation than under Price-Anderson. Establishing liability would depend in each case on state tort law and procedures, and these might or might not provide for no-fault liability, let alone the multiple other protections now embodied in Price-Anderson. The present assurance of prompt and equitable compensation under a pre-structured and nationally applicable protective system would give way to uncertainties, variations and potentially lengthy delays in recovery. It should be emphasized, moreover, that it is collecting a judgment, not filing a lawsuit, that counts. Even if defenses are waived under state law, a defendant with theoretically "unlimited" liability may be unable to pay a judgment once obtained. When the defendant's assets are exahusted by earlier judgments, subsequent claimants would be left with uncollectable awards. The prospect of inequitable distribution would produce a race to the courthouse door in contrast to the present system of assured orderly and equitable compensation.

Appellees, like the District Court, differ with this appraisal on several grounds. They argue, inter alia, that recovery under the Act would not be greater than without it, that the waiver of defenses required by the Act is an idle gesture since those involved in the development of nuclear energy would likely be held strictly liable under common-law principles;[34] that the claim-administration procedure under the Act delays rather than expedites individual recovery; and finally that recovery of even limited compensation is uncertain since the liability ceiling does not vary with the number of persons injured or amount of property damaged. . . .

We disagree. We view the congressional *assurance* of a $560 million fund for recovery, accompanied by an express statutory commitment, to "take whatever action is deemed necessary and appropriate to protect the public from the consequences of" a nuclear accident, to be a fair and reasonable substitute for the uncertain recovery of damages of this magnitude from a utility or component manufacturer, whose resources might well be exhausted at an early stage. The record in this case raises serious questions about the ability of a utility or component manufacturer to satisfy a judgment approaching $560 million — the amount guaranteed under the Price-Anderson Act.[36] Nor are we persuaded that the mandatory waiver of defenses required by the Act is of no benefit to potential claimants. Since there has never been,

34. See Rylands v. Fletcher. . . .

36. The expert testimony before the District Court indicated that Duke Power, one of the largest utilities in the country, could not be expected to accumulate more than $200 million for damages claims without reaching the point of insolvency. This amount, even when coupled with the amount of available private insurance, would be less than the $560 million provided by the Act. Moreover, if the liability were of sufficient magnitude to force the utility or component manufacturer into bankruptcy or reorganization, recovery would likely be further reduced and delayed.

to our knowledge, a case arising out of a nuclear incident like those covered by the Price-Anderson Act, any discussion of the standard of liability that state courts will apply is necessarily speculative. At the minimum, the statutorily mandated waiver of defenses establishes at the threshold the right of injured parties to compensation without proof of fault and eliminates the burden of delay and uncertainty which would follow from the need to litigate the question of liability after an accident. Further, even if strict liability were routinely applied, the common-law doctrine is subject to exceptions for acts of God or of third parties — two of the very factors which appellees emphasized in the District Court in the course of arguing that the risks of a nuclear accident are greater than generally admitted. All of these considerations belie the suggestion that the Act leaves the potential victims of a nuclear disaster in a more disadvantageous position than they would be in if left to their common-law remedies — not known in modern times for either their speed or economy. . . .

Notes

1. Would the owner of a nuclear reactor be strictly liable under common-law principles for any personal injury or property damage caused by a reactor accident? Is it relevant to your answer that there are competing methods of generating electricity?

2. Do you think it is true that private industry would have refused to invest in nuclear power without a cap on its potential tort liability? If the chance of a nuclear-reactor catastrophe is as remote as the sponsors of the Price-Anderson Act thought, why would investors be unwilling to risk it? Any investment carries with it a finite chance of being wiped out by business adversity, however caused.

3. Is the Price-Anderson Act an example of what Horwitz feared — subsidizing industry by allowing it to externalize the costs of its accidents? Suppose a reactor explodes because of the negligence of its owner and causes damages of $560 million. The reactor owner would have to pay only $2-5 million of these damages; the rest would be divided up among other reactor owners, liability insurers, and the federal taxpayer. To be sure, to the extent the negligent owner had liability insurance, he would pay, albeit indirectly, for more of the damages caused by his negligence than the $2-5 million that the Act requires him to contribute out of his own funds. But according to the Court's opinion it is impossible to purchase more than $140 million in liability insurance for a single reactor accident. This leaves a big gap between the cost of an accident to society — $560 million, in our example — and the cost to the reactor owner and its insurer — $145 million at most. To be sure, there is no added deterrent effect from making a firm liable for damages over and above its net worth. But suppose a utility that owned a nuclear reactor had a net worth of $200 million, as the Court implied was true of Duke Power.

Then common-law liability would have a greater effect on its incentive to take care (or reduce its activity level) than the Price-Anderson Act. This is particularly true if, as is frequently alleged (an allegation examined in Chapter 11 of this book), liability insurance eliminates, or at least greatly impairs, the incentive to take care or otherwise avoid injuring others. Given insurance, the maximum exposure of a nuclear reactor owner in the event of an accident is only $5 million under the Price-Anderson Act, but under the common law it would be his entire net worth if the damages from the accident equaled or exceeded the sum of his net worth and his insurance coverage.

Why then did the Court say that "in the event of a nuclear accident the utility itself would suffer perhaps the largest damages"?

On the operation of the nuclear insurance pools, see Long & Long, The Price-Anderson Act and Nuclear Insurance, 1979 Ins. L.J. 367.

4. The Court in *Duke Power* pointed to federal safety regulation as a reason for not worrying that impairing financial incentives might result in reactor safety falling below the optimal level. In the wake of the Three Mile Island reactor accident, which occurred after the Court's decision, public confidence in the efficacy of federal regulation of reactor safety has been shaken. If there were strict liability for nuclear reactor accidents, and no limitation on liability, reactor owners would have an incentive to estimate the costs and benefits of alternative safety measures (including substitution of alternative energy sources) and to adopt those that minimized net expected accident costs. Yet there would still be an argument for supplementing tort liability with direct regulation of safety. Can you think what it is?

Also consider in this connection the serious problems with proving injury in many radiation cases. These problems are discussed in the next chapter. They must be weighed carefully in any responsible assessment of the relative roles of tort liability and direct regulation in bringing about the efficient level of reactor safety.

Chapter 8
Causation and Joint Tortfeasors

Weeks v. McNulty
101 Tenn. 495, 48 S.W. 809 (1898)

[Plaintiff's decedent was killed in a fire in defendant's hotel. Plaintiff brought a negligence action alleging inter alia that defendant had violated a municipal ordinance requiring hotel owners to erect fire escapes. After a jury verdict and judgment for defendant, plaintiff appealed.]

MCALISTER, J. . . .

After a very attentive reading of the record in this cause, we have failed to discover any causal connection between the death of plaintiff's intestate and the failure of defendants in error to erect fire escapes, as required by the ordinance. It is not shown that deceased was at a window, or in any position where a fire escape would have afforded him any benefit whatever. There is evidence tending to show that deceased had locked himself in his room, and was heard beating on his door, trying to make his escape. It is shown that one of the windows of his room overlooked the Third National Bank Building, and that deceased could, and with entire safety to himself, have escaped by leaping to the roof of that building, as many others similarly situated successfully did escape. As already stated, it is not shown that deceased knew of this avenue of escape, and we cannot perceive how he would have been benefited by fire escapes under the circumstances surrounding him. We are, therefore, of opinion that if the contention of counsel for plaintiff in error in respect of the proper construction of this ordinance were correct, and that its breach would constitute actionable negligence, these questions are mere abstractions in this case, since no causal connection between the violation of the ordinance and the injuries sustained by the plaintiff is shown. . . .

Notes

1. It may seem obvious that if the accident would have happened anyway — if the defendant's failure to obey the ordinance was not a necessary condition, or "but for" cause, of Weeks's death — defendant should not be held liable. It is correct, but not obvious. If the defendant was negligent, this

means we want to deter him and others like him from engaging in such conduct in the future. We therefore want to make his negligence as costly to him as possible, and one way to do this is to make him liable for Weeks' death. To be sure, if Weeks was not hurt by the defendant's negligence, because he would have been killed in any event, his actual damages are zero. But if we thought it sensible on deterrent grounds to make defendant pay, we could waive the requirement of proving causation and say that, although an award of damages to plaintiff was a windfall, it was a socially useful windfall because it increased deterrence. This is the approach taken in awarding punitive damages in certain tort cases.

There is, however, an economic objection to the suggested approach; it is explained in Shavell, An Analysis of Causation and the Scope of Liability in the Law of Torts, 9 J. Legal Stud. 463 (1980). Suppose that the negligence standard, as applied, sometimes results in a defendant's being held liable even though the cost to him of avoiding the accident was greater than the expected accident cost. There are three reasons why this might be so.

(1) Judges and juries — or legislatures — might make errors in defining or applying the negligence standard. What feature of the *Weeks* case makes this a distinct possibility?

(2) The application of the reasonable-man standard, examined in Chapter 4, may result in the imposition of liability on someone who, because he is below average in his capacity to take care, cannot conform his behavior to the requirements of the negligence standard at a cost less than the expected accident cost.

(3) Care has a random element. People do not have perfect control over themselves or their instruments (automobiles or whatever); by taking care they reduce the probability of inflicting (or receiving) an injury, but not to zero. Occasionally, therefore, a person will be found negligent although he could not have avoided *that* accident at reasonable cost. For example, if someone strays across the center line of the highway and hits an oncoming car, he is apt to be deemed negligent even though that particular swerve would have been avoided only if the driver always kept to the extreme right-hand side of the highway, which might not be a cost-justified strategy.

For any of these reasons, a person may be deemed negligent although B in the Hand formula was greater than PL. This will not in itself cause potential injurers to overinvest in safety. We know from the last chapter that where B is larger than PL, as in the case of unavoidable accidents under a strict-liability standard, potential injurers will ignore the standard, preferring to pay judgment costs that, by hypothesis, are lower than precaution costs. But if for some reason the expected judgment costs exceed the expected accident costs, as they would if injurers were liable for injuries that would have occurred regardless of their behavior, an incentive to overinvest in safety may be created. Suppose, for example, that the cost of the fire escape to McNulty (B) would have been $50, and the expected accident cost that the fire escape would have averted (PL) was $40, but that McNulty would also have been liable for accidents, as to Weeks, that the fire escape could not have avoided, and this extra liability raises McNulty's expected judgment costs to $60. Now he will have an incentive to spend $50 for the fire escapes, since by doing so he will avoid expected judgment costs of $60. But the social costs of his failure to have a fire escape are actually only $40.

This problem would not arise if the applicable legal standard were strict liability rather than negligence. Why not? Can you see why the objection to imposing liability in negligence cases for accidents not caused by the injurer is equally an objection to awarding punitive damages in such cases?

Despite frequent use of the word "cause," we have not defined the term. The above analysis should not be read to imply that "cause" means "necessary condition," or even that defendant's conduct must be a necessary condition of plaintiff's injury for liability to attach. On the latter point, consider the following hypothetical: A and B shoot C simultaneously, and either shot would have been fatal, so neither shot is a necessary condition of C's death. Should A and B therefore be excused from liability? On the former point, bear in mind that it does not follow that because a cause is usually a necessary condition (but not always, as the A-B example indicates), a necessary condition is usually a cause. It clearly is not. We would not say that Columbus was the "cause" of Weeks' death, although if Columbus had not discovered America, Weeks probably would not have been staying at McNulty's hotel.

2. Do you agree with the court that there was no causal connection between Weeks's death and the violation of the fire-escape ordinance? It is unlikely that the presence of a fire escape would have saved him; but is it totally out of the question? Maybe Weeks had noticed there was no fire escape but had not noticed the roof of the bank building and therefore did not think of trying to escape through the window. Does it make a difference what floor he was on? (It was the third floor.) Could defendant have argued that Weeks was contributorily negligent? Consider 'the possible bearing on either the causal or the contributory-negligence issue of the so-called emergency doctrine. A person faced with an emergency is not expected to react with supreme cool-headedness; he will be deemed negligent only if his behavior is below the norm for people confronting such an emergency. See Prosser 168-170.

Suppose the court had found there was a 95 percent chance that Weeks would have lost his life even if there had been a fire escape, and a 5 percent chance that he would have been saved. Would not the correct result in such a case be to give the plaintiff 5 percent of whatever damages are assessed, rather than zero? Compare the approach of the court in Steinhauser v. Hertz Corp., 421 F.2d 1169 (2d Cir. 1970). The issue was whether a slight automobile accident, which had not resulted in any bodily injuries, had caused Cynthia Steinhauser's schizophrenia. Remanding for a new trial, the court (Judge Friendly) stated (id. at 1173-1174):

Although the fact that Cynthia had latent psychotic tendencies would not defeat recovery if the accident was a precipitating cause of schizophrenia, this may have a significant bearing on the amount of damages. The defendants are entitled to explore the probability that the child might have developed schizophrenia in any event. While the evidence does not demonstrate that Cynthia already had the disease, it does suggest that she was a good prospect. . . . "[I]t is easily seen that the probability of later death from existing causes for which a defendant was not responsible would probably be an important element in fixing damages, but it is not a defense." . . . [I]f a defendant "succeeds in establishing that the plaintiff's pre-existing condition was bound to worsen . . . an appropriate discount should be made for the damages that would have been suffered even in the absence of the defendant's negligence."

The problem in *Steinhauser* is endemic to "eggshell skull" cases (see Note following Vosburg v. Putney in Chapter 2). If plaintiff is highly vulnerable to illness or injury because of a preexisting condition, then probably he would have sustained the same loss that defendant inflicted upon him, but from some other, nonliable cause, and damages should be discounted accordingly. It seems virtually certain that if Cynthia had not been in an accident, some other equally minor incident would soon have triggered her latent schizophrenia. See Birkey & Brown, Crises and Life Changes Preceding the Onset or Relapse of Acute Schizophrenia: Clinical Aspects, in The Schizophrenia Syndrome: An Ann. Rev. 1971, at 293 (R. Cancro ed.); Weiner, Schizophrenia: Etiology, in 2 Comprehensive Textbook of Psychiatry 1123 (H. Kaplan, A. Freedman & B. Sadock eds., 3d ed. 1979); Harrison's Principles of Internal Medicine 150-151 (G.W. Thorn et al. eds., 9th ed. 1980).

How, if at all, does *Weeks* differ from *Steinhauser* and other "eggshell skull" cases? Is *Steinhauser* consistent with Vosburg v. Putney? Could defendant in *Vosburg* have argued successfully for discounting plaintiff's damages by the probability that plaintiff would not have sustained the same injury from some nonculpable cause?

As a variant on *Steinhauser*, consider the facts in Dillon v. Twin State Gas & Electric Co., 85 N.H. 449, 163 A. 111 (1932). A boy, while playing on a bridge, lost his balance and clutched at defendant's power line which ran near the girder from which he fell. The wire was uninsulated, and the boy was electrocuted. The defendant was negligent but what was the extent of its liability?

> The circumstances of the decedent's death give rise to an unusual issue of its cause. In leaning over from the girder and losing his balance he was entitled to no protection from the defendant to keep from falling. Its only liability was in exposing him to the danger of charged wires. If but for the current in the wires he would have fallen down on the floor of the bridge or into the river, he would without doubt have been either killed or seriously injured. Although he died from electrocution, yet, if by reason of his preceding loss of balance he was bound to fall except for the intervention of the current, he either did not have

long to live or was to be maimed. In such an outcome of his loss of balance, the defendant deprived him, not of a life of normal expectancy, but of one too short to be given pecuniary allowance, in one alternative and not of normal, but of limited, earning capacity, in the other.

If it were found that he would have thus fallen with death probably resulting, the defendant would not be liable, unless for conscious suffering found to have been sustained from the shock. In that situation his life or earning capacity had no value. To constitute actionable negligence there must be damage, and damage is limited to those elements the statute prescribes.

If it should be found that but for the current he would have fallen with serious injury, then the loss of life or earning capacity resulting from the electrocution would be measured by its value in such injured condition. Evidence that he would be crippled would be taken into account in the same manner as though he had already been crippled.

His probable future but for the current thus bears on liability as well as damages. Whether the shock from the current threw him back on the girder or whether he would have recovered his balance, with or without the aid of the wire he took hold of, if it had not been charged, are issues of fact, as to which the evidence as it stands may lead to different conclusions.

Id. at 456-457, 163 A. at 114-115.

Haft v. Lone Palm Hotel
3 Cal. 3d 756, 478 P.2d 465 (1970)

[A man and his five-year-old son drowned in a motel swimming pool. No one was present when they drowned. The motel had violated a statute which required that either lifeguard service be provided or a sign be posted clearly indicating that there was no lifeguard present. Jury verdict and judgment for defendants; plaintiffs appealed.]

TOBRINER, J. . . .

Defendant's failure to provide lifeguard service is of course only of consequence if such negligence was a "proximate cause" of either or both of the drownings at issue in the instant case. In view of the absence of any direct evidence on the actual events which resulted in the deaths of the father and son, the problem of "causation" has loomed large in this case from the very outset.

In analyzing this "causation" issue, we must preliminarily reject defendants' contention that the alleged negligence of Mr. Haft could properly be considered as an "intervening" and "superseding" cause which "broke the chain of proximate causation" with respect to the deaths of father or son. Without doubt, one of the principal dangers in swimming pools that the statutory lifeguard requirement sought to control, was the danger to careless swimming novices who might negligently overrate their aquatic skills. . . .

[S]uch negligence could not properly be designated as a "superseding cause" which would automatically relieve defendant of all liability.[14]

The fallacy of defendants' contention as to "superseding cause" is perhaps most clearly illuminated by its application to the cause of action relating to the death of five-year-old Mark. In that context the claim that defendants' responsibility to Mark was "cut off" by Mr. Haft's alleged negligence is in reality no more than an attempt to resurrect the doctrine of "imputed contributory negligence" between a minor and his parent, a theory which the California courts have long repudiated. The "imputed contributory negligence" formula transferred the negligence of a parent (in not carefully supervising his child, for example) to a plaintiff child so as to bar the child's recovery against an admittedly negligent defendant; defendants seek to obtain a like dispensation through the jury's application (in reality, misapplication) of the nebulous "superseding cause" doctrine. This argument has no more merit phrased in "superseding cause" terms than it had in the context of "imputed contributory negligence."

Our rejection of defendants' "superseding cause" theory, however, does not in itself resolve the question of whether, on the basis of the facts adduced at trial, the absence of a lifeguard was a proximate cause of the deaths as a matter of law. The troublesome problems concerning the causation issue in the instant case of course arise out of the total lack of direct evidence as to the precise manner in which the drownings occurred. Although the paucity of evidence on causation is normally one of the burdens that must be shouldered by a plaintiff in proving his case, the evidentiary void in the instant action results primarily from defendants' failure to provide a lifeguard to observe occurrences within the pool area. The main purpose of the lifeguard requirement is undoubtedly to aid those in danger, but an attentive guard does serve the subsidiary function of witnessing those accidents that do occur. The absence of such a lifeguard in the instant case thus not only stripped decedents of a significant degree of protection to which they were entitled, but also deprived the present plaintiffs of a means of definitively establishing the facts leading to the drownings.

Clearly, the failure to provide a lifeguard greatly enhanced the chances of the occurrence of the instant drownings. In proving (1) that defendants were negligent in this respect, and (2) that the available facts, at the very least, strongly suggest that a competent lifeguard, exercising reasonable care, would have prevented the deaths,[18] plaintiffs have gone as far as they possibly

14. This reasoning is not to imply, however, that Mr. Haft's negligence, if any, could not be considered a bar to his recovery under a contributory negligence defense. . . .

18. Uncontradicted evidence at trial established that the pool in which decedents drowned was a relatively small motel pool. Mr. Haft and Mark were the only two persons in the entire pool area and thus a reasonably attentive lifeguard would without doubt have been aware of their activities at the moment that the instant emergency arose. Under these facts, the chances of a successful rescue appear to be very high; indeed, in our view this record comes very close to, and may well succeed in, establishing that the absence of a lifeguard was an actual cause of the deaths as a matter of law even without a shift in the burden of proof. . . .

can under the circumstances in proving the requisite causal link between defendants' negligence and the accidents. To require plaintiffs to establish "proximate causation" to a greater certainty than they have in the instant case, would permit defendants to gain the advantage of the lack of proof inherent in the lifeguardless situation which they have created. Under these circumstances the burden of proof on the issue of causation should be shifted to defendants to absolve themselves if they can.... [Reversed and remanded.]

Notes

1. What is the difference between treating contributory negligence as a defense in itself, or as something that breaks the causal chain between the defendant's conduct and the plaintiff's injury? Does it depend on whether the jurisdiction has substituted comparative for contributory negligence?

2. Is the doctrine of imputed contributory negligence unsound from an economic standpoint? Is it not just a way of placing the legal responsibility for an accident on the cheapest cost avoider, here, surely, Mr. Haft? Cf. Isaacs v. Powell in Chapter 7.

3. The defendants could have complied with their statutory obligation by posting a sign clearly indicating the absence of a lifeguard. Would such a sign have significantly reduced the probability that Haft and his son would enter the pool and drown? Since no one else was in the pool area, was it not obvious to Haft that there was no lifeguard? Why is the father's action not barred by assumption of risk, and the son's by lack of a causal connection between defendant's negligence and the child's death? Do you see a possible analogy to the *Siegler* case in Chapter 7?

4. What is the disagreement, if any, between the *Weeks* and *Haft* courts?

Keegan v. Minneapolis & St. L. R. Co.
76 Minn. 90, 78 N.W. 965 (1899)

MITCHELL, J. This was an action to recover damages for the death of plaintiff's decedent, alleged to have been caused by defendant's negligence. On March 30, 1897, the deceased, a passenger on defendant's road, when alighting from the train, stepped into a hole in the station platform, and sprained his left ankle. He was subsequently attacked by articular, or, as commonly known, "inflammatory," rheumatism, and on August 16, 1897, died of what is known in medical parlance as "endocarditis," which means inflammation of the lining membrane of the cavities of the heart. The evidence is conclusive that the rheumatism was the direct and proximate cause of the endocarditis. It would perhaps be more proper to say that the latter is merely a name for the former, when it reaches the membranes surrounding the heart.

It is conceded that the verdict of the jury (which was in favor of the plaintiff) is conclusive that the injury to the ankle of the deceased was caused by the negligence of the defendant. Hence it is liable, if this injury was the proximate cause of the death. In accordance with the decisions of this, as well as of most, if not all, other courts, if the injury proximately caused the rheumatism, then the injury was a proximate cause of the death. The fact that the deceased might have been, for any reason, predisposed to rheumatism, would be immaterial, provided that but for the injury that disease would not have resulted. And, if the negligence of the defendant was the proximate cause of the injury, the fact that it could not have reasonably anticipated the particular result which followed, viz. that the injury might produce rheumatism, causing death, is also immaterial. Consequences which follow in an unbroken sequence, without an intervening efficient cause, from the original negligent act, are natural and proximate; and for such consequences the original wrongdoer is responsible, even though he could not have foreseen the particular results which did in fact follow. . . .

The precise question presented on this appeal is whether there was legally sufficient evidence to justify the jury in finding that the rheumatism of which the deceased died was directly and proximately caused by the injury to his ankle. The evidence shows that the deceased was 34 years of age; was in good health at the time of the injury; that he had never been sick, at least during his married life of nearly seven years immediately preceding the accident, except for a short time with the grippe, four years previously; that he had never been troubled with anything like rheumatism until after he received this injury; that his father died at the age of between 60 and 70 of what was supposed to be dyspepsia; that his mother was still living at the age of about 70, and had always been in good health, except that she had suffered somewhat from rheumatism during the last year and a half; also that all of his brothers and sisters were living and in good health. The evidence also tends to show that the injury was quite a severe one, producing severe pain, and causing quite serious swelling of the foot and ankle. A physician was called, who at first bandaged the ankle and applied liniment, but subsequently put it into a plaster of Paris cast, in which it was kept for about 10 days. During this time the deceased could not, or at least did not, use his injured foot in walking, but moved about the house on crutches. Some time in April — the exact date does not appear, but apparently in the latter part of the month — articular rheumatism developed itself in the swelling of his right foot and ankle, and soon afterwards of his right hand and wrist, and then of the right elbow, and by the middle of May the swelling sometimes reached to his knees. The disease gradually advanced, until finally, along about the latter part of June, he was compelled to take to his bed, where he remained until his death, on August 16th. The evidence does not disclose any apparent cause of the disease, unless it is the injury to his ankle. . . .

Seven physicians were examined as medical experts, two of whom had attended to deceased professionally during his illness; but it is not apparent that on the subjects as to which they were called to testify the latter had any advantage over those who did not attend deceased, but who heard the testimony as to the nature of the injury and history of the appearance and progress of the disease. All seemed to agree that articular or inflammatory rheumatism is a blood disease, and is caused by the presence of poison in the blood. Three of them testified that traumatism (which means a bodily injury) is one of the causes of articular rheumatism; that the injury to deceased's ankle was a sufficient cause to produce the disease; and that, in their opinion, it was the cause of it in this case. Two of these accepted or favored the "germ theory" as to the cause of articular rheumatism. They admitted that this theory had never been demonstrated, and that the germ had never been discovered or isolated; that there had been great difference of opinion as to the exact cause of the disease, and that there was still some difference of opinion on the subject, but that the general trend of modern opinion was in favor of the germ theory, as being more consonant with the pathological evidences of the disease itself; that traumatism was generally laid down by the standard medical authorities as one of the common causes of the disease, and that they contained numerous well-authenticated instances where traumatism had been followed by articular rheumatism where there was no apparent cause for the disease other than the injury; and that this accorded with their own professional experience. The third agreed with the other two, except that he adhered to the "lactic-acid" theory as to the origin of the disease, but claimed that germs originated from, and were multiplied by, "the fermentation that causes lactic acid"; which was a combination of two theories, not approved of by any other witness on either side. The theory of the two who accepted the "germ theory" was that the injury did not introduce the germs into the system, but that the dead or injured tissue, resulting from the injury, incited the rapid increase of germs from the seed already in the system. On the other side, four expert witnesses testified that, in their opinion, there was no connection between the injury and the rheumatism of which the deceased died. None of them testified that traumatism might not cause articular rheumatism, or that it was not given by medical authorities as one of the causes of the disease, but they testified that they had never seen it given by the authorities as one of the causes, and that they had never met with a case in their practice where the disease had followed an injury, except in the case of the deceased. One of them gave it as his opinion that the most frequent exciting cause of the disease was exposure to cold and dampness, but when asked, on cross-examination, "Suppose a man has never had rheumatism before, and suppose he receives a personal injury, and you knew of no other cause, and there follows, after the injury, acute articular rheumatism, would you not believe that the injury was the cause of the attack of rheumatism?"

answered, "If I could not find any other cause, I probably should." Two of the four admitted that "the weight of authority" or "the bulk of the evidence" supported and favored "the germ theory." One of the four favored the "metabolic theory" as to the origin of the disease, by which he meant a derangement of the digestive organs, where elimination and assimilation were not properly carried on, and as a consequence poisonous matter accumulated in the system and entered into the blood. He admitted, however, that, if the "germ theory" was true, he could see how the injury might have produced rheumatism. The fourth, while of the opinion that the disease is caused by an infectious poison in the blood, "did not know about the germ theory," but could not see how the injury could cause the disease, unless it became infected with pus. He admitted, however, that traumatism was given by the authorities as one of the causes of articular rheumatism.

From this general outline of the evidence, it is apparent that much of the expert testimony as to the origin of the disease, and as to the particular way by which, if at all, an injury produces articular rheumatism, consists, not of demonstrated or discovered facts, but mainly of mere theory or opinion, approaching very nearly to mere speculation. The unsatisfactory, as well as dangerous, character of this kind of evidence, is well known. Experts are nowadays often the mere paid advocates or partisans of those who employ and pay them, as much so as the attorneys who conduct the suit. There is hardly anything, not palpably absurd on its face, that cannot now be proved by some so-called "experts." And, in these "personal injury cases," so-called "medical experts" can be found who will testify that almost any disease or ailment to which human flesh is heir was, in their opinion, caused by the injury. This evil has become so great in the administration of justice as to attract the serious consideration of courts and legislatures. These suggestions are general, and not made with reference to anything peculiar in the present case.

But, conceding that all the expert testimony as to the "germ theory," or any other theory, and as to the precise manner a bodily injury produces articular rheumatism, should be disregarded, yet we think the evidence in this case, based upon both the medical authorities and upon the professional experience of some of the witnesses, is sufficient to justify the conclusion that articular rheumatism so often follows personal injuries that this is not a mere coincidence, but that oftentimes the injury is the exciting cause of the disease. When this is reinforced by the evidence that the deceased was never previously attacked by the disease; that it developed in such a severe form so soon after the injury, without any other apparent cause, — we think that the jury was justified in concluding that the latter was the cause of the former, regardless of the truth or falsity of many of the particular theories of the experts. At least, we do not think that we would be justified in holding that the evidence, although by no means of the most satisfactory or convincing character, did not justify the verdict. . . .

Note

Did the court reach a correct result on the facts? According to the entry for Arthritis in the McGraw-Hill Encyclopedia of Science and Technology (1977), arthritis (called "rheumatism" in the nineteenth century) is

> a general term which refers to any inflammatory process affecting joints or their component tissues. . . .
> Several types of arthritis are recognized by their clinical course or pathologic appearance; non-specific arthritis of undetermined cause is the term reserved for the occasional case in which no etiologic agent can be justifiably named.
> Several kinds of infections including gonorrheal, streptococcal, and staphylococcal invasion may produce arthritis. These usually result from a generalized infection but may appear following local spread or after trauma. The outcome varies considerably with the patient's age and resistance, adequacy of the treatment, and the nature of the organism. . . .
> Rheumatic fever is commonly accompanied by a migratory arthritis that may involve several joints in succession. . . .
> Rheumatoid arthritis is the most common variety of joint inflammation in younger and middle-aged persons. The etiology is unknown, but hypersensitivity, protein derangements, endocrine imbalances, infection, and psychic disturbances have all been incriminated along with lesser factors. This systemic disease is commonly ushered in by some physical or emotional stress and follows a variable but slowly progressive course, marked by spontaneous remissions. The finger joints are often first involved symmetrically, with the hands, wrists, feet, and other smaller joints later becoming affected. Joint destruction is common with advancing disease, so that the incidence of disability is high.

(For more technical discussions, see Bisno, Rheumatic Fever, in Principles and Practice of Infectious Diseases 1574 (G. Mandell, R. G. Douglas & J. E. Bennett eds. 1979); Smith, Infectious Arthritis, in id. at 933; Gilliland & Mannik, Rheumatoid Arthritis, in Harrison's Principles of Internal Medicine 2050 (G. W. Thorn et al. eds., 8th ed. 1977).) Rheumatic fever can of course lead to fatal heart complications; so can rheumatoid arthritis, although this is rare. What ailment did plaintiff's decedent in *Keegan* probably have? What role did the injury to his ankle probably play in his death?

McGrath v. Irving
24 App. Div. 236, 265 N.Y.S.2d 376 (1965)

HERLIHY, J. . . . [In this negligence suit arising from an automobile accident] plaintiff contends, inter alia, that she received an injury to her throat by striking the side of the car and swallowed glass which allegedly caused an epidermoid carcinoma of the larynx resulting eventually in a total laryngectomy.

At the trial a doctor associated with the Chevalier Jackson Clinic, and the Department of Laryngology-bronchoesophagology at Temple University testified. He stated that the Clinic was engaged in the research and treatment of diseases of the larynx, tumors of the larynx, foreign bodies of the larynx and the tracheobronchial tree, and diseases of the bronchial tree, the lungs and the esophagus. He further testified that he was familiar with the history of the plaintiff's injury, the subsequent events and from his own observation, having performed the operation, in answer to a hypothetical question, he said: "My opinion, the events, the accident, the inhalation of glass were a cause of accelerated development or growth of Mrs. McGrath's cancer."

The defendant produced medical testimony that there was no causal relationship between the accident and the resulting carcinoma.

This, of course, presented a sharp medical issue of fact, but we find the resolution of the jury in favor of the plaintiff is supported by a preponderance of the evidence. It would be difficult to conceive a better qualified physician than the plaintiff's expert as to this particular phase of medicine. It is generally conceded by the medical profession that the origin and cause of cancer cells are unknown. It is likewise a fact that medicine is not an exact science but in the legalistic sense when a doctor in circumstances such as here expresses an opinion based upon a fair and accurate hypothetical question and establishes relationship between the accident and the injury, it is acceptable and the only reasonable basis on which to predicate the right to recover. It is for this reason that the courts have come to permit the injection of words such as "possible" and "probable" by the medical profession in expressing an opinion, providing, of course, there is a reasonable basis in fact for such a permit....

Notes

1. In *Keegan* and *McGrath*, and many like cases, the uncertainty regarding causation stems not from a lack of eyewitnesses, as in *Weeks* and *Haft*, but from a lack of consensus in the scientific community over the cause of certain illnesses. Here expert testimony is indispensable; but the problem of experts who act as "mere paid advocates or partisans" and are willing to testify on behalf of any position "not palpably absurd on its face" that will help the party paying them is as serious today as it was when *Keegan* was decided in 1899. The deeper problem is a jury system that sets people of often very limited education and understanding in judgment on issues of scientific fact.

2. What is the tort plaintiff's burden of proof on the issue of causation? Must he prove that it is more likely than not that he would have received the injury complained of if the defendant had not been negligent? Plaintiff's expert in *McGrath* testified only that the accident "accelerated" the devel-

opment or growth of plaintiff's cancer. Was this a case where the "discount" approach of *Steinhauser* should have been utilized? Was it an "eggshell skull" case?

Consider in this connection the entry for Oncology in the McGraw-Hill Encyclopedia, supra:

> ... Chronic irritation and infections are agents which occasionally are associated with the onset of cancer. The site in the urinary bladder where the flatworm parasite Schistosoma hematobium infects is often the site of cancer formation. Lung cancers occasionally originate in the walls of old tuberculous lesions. In Kashmir, people who keep warm by carrying a kangri, a wicker basket containing an earthenware pot filled with smoldering leaves, against their abdominal skin frequently develop skin cancer at this site. Though continuous or intermittent irritation for many years has been associated with the onset of cancer, there is virtually no evidence that single physical trauma such as a bruise or contusion brings about cancerous change. The reported cases, after careful documentation, prove that the trauma merely called attention to a preexisting cancer.

For a fuller treatment see Johnston, Trauma and Cancer, in 3A R. N. Gray, Attorneys' Textbook of Medicine, ch. 72 (1974); and Origins of Human Cancer: Book A, Incidence of Cancer in Humans (H. H. Hiatt, J. D. Watson & J. A. Winston eds. 1977) — the latter a comprehensive symposium on causal agents in cancer that, perhaps significantly, contains no discussion of trauma. Cases involving alleged traumatic cancer are collected in Annot., Sufficiency of Proof that Cancer Resulted from Accident or Incident in Suit Rather Than from Pre-Existing Condition, 2 A.L.R.3d 384 (1961).

3. In Kimball v. Scors, 59 App. Div. 984, 399 N.Y.S.2d 350 (1977), where plaintiffs' decedent died of lung cancer, the negligence alleged was the failure of the defendant surgeon to order a chest X-ray before operating on the decedent for a gallstone condition. The operation took place in August 1969. In 1970 decedent returned to the hospital. A chest X-ray taken at that time indicated a tumor in the lung, which turned out to be cancerous and metastatic; surgery failed to extract it successfully. On January 28, 1971, the decedent died from lung cancer. From a jury verdict for defendants, plaintiffs appealed, alleging among other things

> that it was reversible error for the court to refuse to charge, as requested, that "[t]he jury need only decide whether or not Mr. Kimball could have had a chance to survive had the malpractice not taken place." We disagree ... that a jury need only determine that defendants' malpractice deprived a decedent of a chance of survival, regardless of how small that chance might be. Such a charge is implicit with danger in that it could reasonably be construed by jurors as judicial restraint on their obligation to find that the malpractice proximately caused the death. The ultimate finding cannot be whether the deceased would have a certain percentage chance of recovery; rather, it must be whether there

was a substantial possibility the decedent would have recovered but for the malpractice. If the proof is ambivalent as to the question of whether the deceased would have died regardless of the malpractice, a pure factual issue is raised, as here, and such an issue can only be resolved by a jury determination of whether the malpractice proximately deprived the deceased of that substantial possibility.

Id. at 984-985, 399 N.Y.S.2d at 351. Notice the court's emphasis on the dichotomous nature of the required causation finding: either the alleged negligence deprived decedent of "a substantial possibility" of recovering, or it did not. In the first case there is liability to the full extent of plaintiff's damages; in the second case there is none. But suppose it were shown that if his lung cancer had been diagnosed earlier, Mr. Kimball would have had a 10 percent probability of recovery. Is this a "substantial possibility"? If it is, does it justify a full award of damages, or should a discount factor be applied as suggested in *Steinhauser*? If a discount factor is applied, should it make any difference whether a 10 percent chance of recovery is deemed a "substantial possibility" or not?

4. The recent accident involving the nuclear power station at Three Mile Island (see Report of the President's Commission on the Accident at Three Mile Island (1979)) illustrates the dilemma that confronts the tort system when injury from tortious conduct is probabilistic rather than certain. The release of radiation into the surrounding region created an increased risk of cancer in the exposed population. Scientists do not agree on how great the increased risk is or even whether it is significant; perhaps that is reason enough for a court to throw out any cancer cases brought against the owners of the reactor. Let us assume, however, that the increased risk is known with certainty. Specifically, let us assume that the radioactivity released by the accident at Three Mile Island will cause a doubling in the cancer rates in children whose mothers are exposed to the radioactivity during pregnancy.*Then if someone in the exposed population gets cancer and tries to sue the reactor owners, we know there is only a 50 percent chance that the accident really was the cause of his cancer. Is this enough to satisfy a "substantial possibility" test? If so, and if everybody who gets cancer in the exposed population sues, the liability of the reactor owners will be twice the actual costs imposed by the accident. If, on this ground, no one is allowed to recover

---

*This is the reported estimate of the Dean of the School of Public Health at the University of Illinois. See Kotulak & Van, Only Time Will Tell Casualties of A-Plant Accident, Chicago Tribune, March 31, 1979 at p. 5. It may be much too high. "The maximum radiation dose that any member of the public is estimated to have received from the accident — less than 100 mrem — is smaller than the dose normally received each year from natural background radiation. . . . Estimates of the number of people in the population who may ultimately experience any such effects [i.e., increased risks of cancer, birth defects, and genetic abnormalities] range from 0.4 to 10, in comparison with hundreds of thousands in the same population who can be expected to develop cancer, birth defects, or genetic abnormalities through natural causes." Upton, Health Impact of the Three Mile Island Accident, 365 Annals of the N.Y. Academy of Sciences 63, 68-69 (Moss & Sills eds. 1981).

for his cancer damages, then the reactor owners will have escaped liability for the entire consequences of their negligence. (The applicable standard might not be negligence; it might be strict liability. Would this affect the analysis?)

The economist has a solution. Let each cancer patient sue, but let him recover only 50 percent of his damages, because that is the expected cost of the accident to him. Would this approach be consistent with the discount-factor approach of *Steinhauser*?

The suggested solution may break down when the incremental probability is small — say 2 percent instead of 50 percent — for then the damages may be insufficient to motivate many, or any, of the victims to sue. In that event, we would be back to no liability. Perhaps the problem can be overcome by the class-action device, studied in courses on civil procedure. But courts have been reluctant to allow class actions in personal-injury matters. See, e.g., Morrissey v. Eli Lilly & Co., 76 Ill. App. 3d 753, 394 N.E.2d 1369 (1979); Ryan v. Eli Lilly & Co., 84 F.R.D. 230 (D.S.C. 1979) (both DES cases).

Not surprisingly, there have been relatively few cases involving low-level radiation injuries. See, for an example of such a case, Mahoney v. United States, 220 F. Supp. 823 (E.D. Tenn. 1963), aff'd mem., 339 F.2d 605 (6th Cir. 1964); and for an interesting discussion of the subject, Keyes & Howarth, Approaches to Liability for Remote Causes: The Low-Level Radiation Example, 56 Iowa L. Rev. 531 (1971). A bizarre recent case is Silkwood v. Kerr-McGee Corp., 485 F. Supp. 566 (W.D. Okla. 1979). Besides the problem of proving causation, there are often serious statute of limitations problems. See, e.g., Garrett v. Raytheon Co., 368 So. 2d 516 (Ala. 1979). We return to these problems in the next chapter.

Low-level radiation cases are somewhat more common under workmen's compensation law, where the requirements for proving causation are more relaxed than in the tort law. Cf. McAllister v. Workmen's Compensation Appeals Board, 69 Cal. 2d 408, 416-419, 445 P.2d 313, 317-319 (1968), where the question was whether decedent's death from lung cancer could be said to arise out of his 32 years of employment as a fireman, even though he had been smoking cigarettes for 42 years:

> Dr. Benioff stated that it was "probable" that the smoke inhaled contained carcinogens, and that it was "reasonable" that decedent's prolonged occupational exposure could lead to lung cancer. We have held "reasonable" or "probable" causal connection will suffice; it is to be distinguished from the merely "possible." . . . [I]ntellectual candor may at times require expert testimony in terms of mere probability. For that reason alone we cannot demand that experts be more certain, particularly when industrial causation itself need not be certain, but only "reasonably probable." Similarly it would be a rare case in which further information would not be of value to the expert; to limit expert testimony to such unique situations would be virtually to abolish it. . . .
>
> Respondents urge us to deny the application in view of decedent's history as a smoker. They note that decedent smoked about a pack of cigarettes a day

for some 42 years, although they admit that during at least part of that period he did not inhale. Respondents further point out the statistical correlation between smoking and lung cancer. The board, however, although well aware of these facts, declined to rely upon them as the basis of its decision.

We cannot doubt that the more smoke decedent inhaled — from whatever source — the greater the danger of his contracting lung cancer. His smoking increased that danger, just as did his employment. Given the present state of medical knowledge, we cannot say whether it was the employment or the cigarettes which "actually" caused the disease; we can only recognize that both contributed substantially to the likelihood of his contracting lung cancer. As we noted, however, in Employers, etc., Ins. Co. of Wis. v. Industrial Acc. Comm., (1953), 41 Cal. 2d 676, 680, 263 P.2d 4, the decedent's employment need only be a "contributing cause" of his injury. And in Bethlehem Steel Co. v. Industrial Acc. Comm., 21 Cal. 2d 742, 744, 135 P.2d 153, 154, we pointed out a particular instance of this principle when we stated that it was enough that "the employee's risk of contracting the disease by virtue of the employment must be materially greater than that of the general public." Thus in *Bethlehem* we allowed an award to an employee who contracted a contagious eye disease, since he had shown that the disease was more common at his place of employment than among the public.

Although decedent's smoking may have been inadvisable, respondents offer no reason to believe that the likelihood of contracting lung cancer from the smoking was so great that the danger could not have been materially increased by exposure to the smoke produced by burning buildings.

Workmen's compensation awards are typically smaller than common-law tort awards. Can an economic argument be made that this difference justifies a more relaxed standard of causation in workmen's compensation than in common-law tort cases?

Berry v. Sugar Notch Borough
191 Pa. 345, 43 A. 240 (1899)

FELL, J. The plaintiff was a motorman in the employ of the Wilkes-Barre & Wyoming Valley Traction Company, on its line running from Wilkes-Barre to the borough of Sugar Notch. The ordinance by virtue of which the company was permitted to lay its track and operate its cars in the borough of Sugar Notch contained a provision that the speed of the cars while on the streets of the borough should not exceed eight miles an hour. On the line of the road, and within the borough limits, there was a large chestnut tree, as to the condition of which there was some dispute at the trial. The question of the negligence of the borough in permitting it to remain must, however, be considered as set at rest by the verdict. On the day of the accident the plaintiff was running his car on the borough street in a violent windstorm, and as he passed under the tree it was blown down, crushing the roof of the car, and causing the plaintiff's injury. There is some conflict of testimony as to the speed at which the car was running, but it seems to be fairly well established that it was considerably in excess of the rate permitted by the borough ordinance. We do not think that the fact that the plaintiff was running his car at a higher rate of speed than eight miles an hour affects his right to recover. It may be that in doing so he violated the ordinance by virtue of which the company was permitted to operate its cars in the streets of the borough, but he certainly was not, for that reason, without rights upon the streets. Nor can it be said that the speed was the cause of the accident, or contributed to it. It might have been otherwise if the tree had fallen before the car reached it, for in that case a high rate of speed might have rendered it impossible for the plaintiff to avoid a collision which he either foresaw or should have foreseen. Even in that case the ground for denying him the right to recover would be that he had been guilty of contributory negligence, and not that he had violated a borough ordinance. The testimony, however, shows that the tree fell upon the car as it passed beneath. With this phase of the case in view, it was urged on behalf of the appellant that the speed was the immediate cause of the plaintiff's injury, inasmuch as it was the particular speed at which he was running which brought the car to the place of the accident at the moment when the tree blew down. This argument, while we cannot deny its ingenuity, strikes us, to say the least, as being somewhat sophistical. That his speed brought him to the place of the accident at the moment of the accident was the merest chance, and a thing which no fore-sight could have predicted. The same thing might as readily have happened to a car running slowly, or it might have been that a high speed alone would have carried him beyond the tree to a place of safety. It was also argued by the appellant's counsel that, even if the speed was not the sole efficient cause of the accident, it at least contributed to its severity, and materially increased the damage. It may be that it did. But what basis could a jury have for finding such to be the case? and, should they so find, what guide could be given them for differentiating between the injury done this man and the injury which would have been done a man in a similar accident on a car running at a speed of eight miles an hour or less? The judgment is affirmed.

Notes

1. Plaintiff's speeding in violation of the ordinance was a necessary condition of the accident's occurring, was it not? Why, therefore, was it not a cause of the accident and hence, under the doctrine of negligence per se, a bar to plaintiff's recovering damages? The reference in the court's opinion to "merest chance" supplies a clue to the answer. Plaintiff's speeding did not

increase the probability that he would be injured by a falling tree. P in the Hand formula was therefore zero.

To explain, P in the Hand formula is really the difference between P_n, the probability that the accident will occur if defendant is negligent, and P_c, the probability that the accident will occur even if due care is taken. For example, if the probability that the accident will occur if defendant is negligent is .10, and the precaution would reduce that probability to zero, then

$$P = P_n - P_c = .10$$

In the *Berry* case, suppose the probability of being injured by a falling tree while driving a streetcar is .0001, and the cost of the injury if it occurs is $1,000, so that the expected accident cost is 10¢. Suppose further that the cost to the motorman of driving within the speed limit is trivial — 1¢. Thus P_n is .0001, L is $1,000, and B is 1¢. But before we can apply the Hand formula to his conduct we must know P_c, the probability that an accident of this sort would have occurred if due care had been taken, i.e., if the motorman had driven more slowly. By hypothesis that probability is .0001; such an accident is no more likely to occur if one is speeding than if one is driving slowly. Therefore, $P_n = P_c$, so P is zero. There is no liability under the Hand formula.

Notice what we have done. Instead of asking whether or in what sense the motorman's negligence "caused" the accident, we have applied the Hand formula to determine whether the motorman should be held liable (i.e., denied damages). He should not be. He is not "really" negligent. Why not?

Notice also that in this analysis *Berry* is identical to a case like *Weeks*, where it is assumed that due care would have been ineffective. In both cases P is zero. Yet how can these really be the same cases? In *Weeks*, if one accepts the court's view of the facts, the failure to exercise due care was not a necessary condition of Weeks' death — he would have died anyway. But in *Berry* the motorman's failure to observe the speed limit was a necessary condition of his injury; he would not have been injured had he been driving more slowly (or for that matter faster). The point, however, is that observing the speed limit will not in general reduce damage from falling objects. On average, there will be just as many accidents of the type that occurred in *Berry* whether motormen drive slowly or fast. Driving slowly will therefore not yield any benefit on average in avoiding injuries from falling objects, and should not be encouraged — at least on that ground.

We can view this analysis as a substitute for causal analysis, but alternatively as a clue to the meaning (at least the legal meaning) of causation. Causation means increasing the risk of injury; a causal connection is established if and only if P_n is greater than P_c. See Calabresi, Concerning Cause and the Law of Torts, 43 U. Chi. L. Rev. 69 (1975); Shavell, An Analysis of Causation and the Scope of Liability in the Law of Torts, 9 J. Legal Stud. 463

(1980). Can you think of any earlier cases in this book whose outcomes can be explained by this notion of causation? How much greater must P_n be than P_c for liability to attach?

The suggested approach enables us not only to treat cases like *Berry* and *Weeks* in a unified framework but also to place cases like *Steinhauser* and *Dillon* in the same framework. To see this, rewrite the Hand formula first as B $< (P_n - P_c)L$ and then as $P_nL - P_cL$. (These transformations follow directly from our earlier point that P in the Hand formula is really the difference between P_n and P_c — i.e., $P = P_n - P_c$.) In the special case where P_c is zero, i.e., where taking due care eliminates all possibility of injury, L is the correct measure of the plaintiff's injury if the defendant fails to take due care. But where P_c is positive, the plaintiff's injury actually caused by the defendant is $L - P_cL$ or equivalently $(1 - P_c)L$ — the injury discounted by the probability it really would have been averted by due care. So in the *Steinhauser* case, supposing Cynthia's loss from becoming schizophrenic was $100,000 and the probability that she would have become schizophrenic anyway from some nonliable cause if defendant had not collided with the car in which she was riding was 40 percent, the proper measure of her loss due to the defendant's negligence was $60,000 (60 percent × $100,000). This ignores complications created by the fact that the accident must at least have accelerated her schizophrenia. How would you adjust for this fact? How would you apply this analysis to the *Dillon* case? (Hint for answering both of these questions: view L as the sum of a series of different losses.) Would it make any difference if in *Steinhauser* P_c was 90 percent rather than 40 percent? Does this discussion suggest that the tort law treats eggshell-skull cases and cases like *Weeks* inconsistently?

2. In each of the following cases, the court held that plaintiff had failed to establish that defendant's negligence caused the injury complained of. Were these cases correctly decided on the "probability-enhancement" theory of causation set out above? If not, are there alternative grounds for the decision?

Fowlks v. Southern Ry. Co., 96 Va. 742, 32 S.E. 464 (1899). Plaintiff purchased a ticket from defendant's agent to ride to Skinquarter, on the agent's representation that she could make a close connection with the train to Skinquarter when she reached Mosely Junction. There was no close connection; the representation was negligent.

> It seems that she was pregnant; that the day was hot and sultry, and a storm was brewing, when she got off of the train. The Southern road had no depot there, and she failed to see a small ticket office of the Farmville & Powhatan Railroad, which had been recently constructed. She walked 300 or 400 yards from the place where the train stopped to a store, where she received such accommodations as it afforded. The Southern Railway having made no provision for getting her to her destination, she endeavored to find the means of private conveyance.

After waiting in the store for about four hours, and suffering great anxiety, she succeeded in hiring a team, and set out for her father's home. It was raining at the time, but the owner of the team would not let it wait, and, as it was getting late, she thought best to start. The road was very rough, and she was greatly jolted. Several hard showers came up during the drive, and she was wet through, and her baggage was also damaged. She was perfectly well when she got on the train at Richmond and when she got off at Moseley Junction. When she got to her father's house, she was suffering with abdominal pains and hemorrhage, from the womb. These pains continued till August 23, 1896, when she suffered a miscarriage. Since that time she has been in bad health, and has had another miscarriage.

Id. at 743-744, 32 S.E. at 464.

Doss v. Town of Big Stone Gap, 145 Va. 520, 134 S.E. 563 (1926). This was an action against an airplane pilot and a town to recover damages for the alleged negligent killing of plaintiff's decedent. It was alleged that the town had, through negligence, allowed the only street that provided access to a park on which it permitted planes to land to become impassable. The town permitted traffic to detour around the impassable stretch. The detour ran across the end of the park. While using the detour, plaintiff's decedent was struck by a plane attempting to land. The court held that the pilot's negligence was the sole cause of the accident.

Mahoney v. Beatman, 110 Conn. 184, 147 A. 762 (1929). This was an action for damages to plaintiff's Rolls Royce sustained in a collision with a car driven by defendant. Plaintiff was speeding, as in *Berry*. On the issue whether his contributory negligence was a proximate cause of the damage the court stated:

The damage to the Rolls Royce which occurred when the car struck the tree and stone wall and rolled over is found to have been due to plaintiff's driver's inability to control or stop the car after the collision because of the speed at which he was proceeding and that this speed did materially hamper the driver in controlling the car. The court further finds that the speed of the plaintiff's car, though unreasonable, did not contribute to cause the collision, which was due entirely to the negligence of the defendant. The theory of the court in ascertaining the extent of the damages was that one driving a car at an unreasonable speed when negligently run into by another car cannot recover for any of the injury to his car, after the collision, which could have been avoided by controlling or stopping his car had it not been driven at an unreasonable speed. The car was being driven at the same rate of speed after as before the collision. No negligence on the part of the driver is found. There was no new cause intervening after the collision wholly independent of it which itself caused the further injury. The intervening cause must have diverted the force of the impact, or else the force of the impact must have become spent or exhausted so that the intervening cause became the substantial factor causing these injuries; this does not appear to have been true in this case. Even though these injuries were produced through an intervening agency, if the force of the collision resulting from the defendant's negligence was still a substantial factor in the production of these injuries, the intervening agency would be ineffective to relieve the defendant from liability for the injuries. It is not found specifically that the impact caused the car to veer to the west; but upon the facts as found, especially when read in the light of the trial court's memorandum, it is a necessary inference of fact, which we are required to draw, that this was the cause of the veering. The court's theory was that after the car had veered there would have been an opportunity for the driver to have regained control of the car, or to have stopped it before these injuries occurred. If the facts in evidence had justified the court in finding that after the collision the driver was negligent and his negligence was the cause of the subsequent injuries, a different proposition would have been presented. But the court did not so find. There is no substantial factor standing as a causal connection between the negligent act of the defendant and these injuries except the impact of the collision. The negligent act to which the plaintiff has not materially contributed is responsible for all the injurious consequences and is a substantial factor in producing them. These consequences follow in true causal relation until the negligent act has become spent or exhausted, or some intervening agency has come into existence after the negligent act and diverted the results of the negligent act to "some new and different end."

Id. at 198-199, 147 A. at 768. For criticism, see East Hampton Dewitt Corp. v. State Farm Mutual Automobile Ins. Co., 490 F.2d 1234, 1238-1240 (2d Cir. 1973).

City of Okmulgee v. Hemphill, 183 Okla. 450, 83 P.2d 189 (1938). Plaintiff was struck by a car driven by defendant Hess, who was speeding, driving without lights, and violating several city ordinances. Plaintiff alleged that the city had been negligent in allowing a pool of water to collect in the path of pedestrians; it was while walking on the street to avoid the pool that plaintiff was struck. The court stated:

the question whether the city would be liable should it force a pedestrian into a crowded, dangerous traffic area, the pedestrian being forced there because he had no other choice, is not before us. . . . The evidence reveals that in the instant case the automobile which struck plaintiff was the only car in sight, in any direction. Under the circumstances of the case the most that can be said is that the pool of water caused the plaintiff to take a course where he would be more likely to be struck than if he were on the sidewalk. And when this is said, then all that has been said is that the pool of water constituted merely "a condition" by which the injury was made possible. . . .

It might be said that but for the presence of the water the defendant would have been on the sidewalk and on his way, before Hess's car reached that point; that, therefore, but for the pool the accident would not have occurred. It could with equal logic be said that had not the plaintiff stopped and discussed the weather with some acquaintance down the street, he likewise would not have been struck. It must be borne in mind that when we say that "but for" the pool of water he would not have been struck, it does not follow that the pool of water caused the injury, or even helped cause it. In order truthfully to say that proximate cause exists, there must be some actual causal connection between the negligence and the injury. Had plaintiff gotten stuck in the water or mud, if any, or had he slipped and the automobile struck him there, or had the car skidded in the water and resultingly veered into the plaintiff, the two acts of negligence, that of the city and that of Hess, would possibly be joined; there would be something to "tie them together" in the common result which they both had concurrently caused.

Negligence, to render a person liable, need not be the sole cause of an injury. Where several causes combine to produce an injury a defendant is not relieved from liability because he is responsible for only one of them. It is sufficient if his negligence is an efficient cause, without which the injury would not have resulted. Where several causes producing injury are concurrent and each is an efficient cause without which the injury would not have happened, the injury may be attributed to all or any of the causes.

But what *are* "concurrent" causes? Concurrent causes are causes acting contemporaneously and which together cause the injury, which injury would not have resulted in the absence of either. It is important to distinguish between concurrent cause and a mere condition. For the former a defendant is liable, for producing the latter he is not, as a general rule. It may be stated generally that in order for causes to be concurrent they must join with each other in some manner to produce the injury. If two distinct causes are successive and unrelated in operation they cannot be concurrent; one of them must be the proximate and the other the remote cause. However, an exception exists where the creator of one cause should reasonably have anticipated the occurrence of the other cause, which is not the case here, as will be seen below.

The present situation is similar to cases where a sidewalk has been obstructed in some manner by the city, or by the city's permission. There are several instances of record where persons in walking around such obstructions have been struck while in the street, and in every case we have found on the subject . . . it has been held that such was merely a condition making the injury possible, as distinguished from a concurrent cause. . . .

Our appraisal of the foregoing authorities and the reasoning therein is favorable. We believe that under the prevailing rule, which is consonant with good reasoning, the fact that there was water in the street was not the proximate cause of plaintiff's injuries, nor a concurring cause within the meaning of the law, but that the intervening independent act of the defendant Hess in the operation of his automobile was the proximate cause thereof.

Id. at 452-454, 83 P.2d at 190-192. For an apparently contrary result, see Grainy v. Campbell, 425 A.2d 379 (Pa. 1981).

Notice that the courts use a variety of terms to explain their results in these cases. They speak of "foresight," "conditions," "intervening causes," "concurrent causes," "efficient causes," "proximate cause." Are any of these terms helpful? Would it be better if the courts simply asked whether defendant's conduct increased the risk of the type of accident that occurred? See Prosser 275, where the "risk increase" approach, the counterpart to the economist's approach of "probability enhancement," is discussed with reference to a number of cases. How great a probability enhancement should be required?

Bibb Broom Corn Co. v. Atchison, T. & S. F. Ry. Co.
94 Minn. 269, 102 N.W. 709 (1905)

[Action for damage to plaintiff's corn. Plaintiff delivered the corn to defendant for transportation to Minneapolis via Kansas City. Defendant's line ended at Kansas City, and it was supposed to forward the car containing plaintiff's corn to another railroad. It negligently failed to do so, and as a result the corn was sitting in defendant's yards in Kansas City when a few days later there was a great flood which substantially destroyed the corn.]

BROWN, J. . . .

. . . The rule that permits a carrier to excuse his negligence by an act of God overtaking him while thus in fault seems to us unsound. It is based on too strict an application of the rule of proximate cause. It is the duty of a common carrier to whom goods are delivered for transportation promptly and without unreasonable delay to forward them to their destination, and such was defendant's duty in the case at bar. This it failed to do, and its negligence in this respect is not seriously controverted. The car arrived at its yards in Kansas City on the 23d of May, and was permitted to remain there without proper effort to forward it until it was overtaken by the flood. It could have been moved from defendant's yards on any day after its arrival prior to the 29th of May, and, had this been done, the corn would not have been damaged. If defendant had acted as required by the terms of its contract, and as enjoined by law, the car would have been forwarded, and would have arrived at its destination prior to the flood. That defendant's neglect concurred and mingled with the act of God seems the only reasonable conclusion the facts will warrant, and we feel safe in applying the general rule that an act of of God is not in such cases a defense. Every reason in equity and justice relieves a carrier from the performance of his contract and from liability for injuries to property in his custody for transportation, resulting exclusively from an act of God, or other inevitable accident or cause over which he has no control, and could not reasonably anticipate or guard against. But reasons of that nature lose their force and persuasive powers when applied to a carrier who violates his contract, and by his unreasonable delay and procrastination is overtaken by an overpowering cause, even though of a nature not reasonably to be anticipated or foreseen. . . .

Notes

1. Is there any difference between this case and *Berry*? Suppose the defendant's negligence had resulted in delaying the arrival of plaintiff's corn in Kansas City, and but for that negligence the corn would have arrived just in time to be damaged by the flood. Would defendant have had an action against plaintiff in restitution for having saved the corn through its negli-

gence? If not, doesn't this imply that *Bibb* was decided incorrectly? Or is the point that *any* delay in transit would increase the risk of damage to the corn?

2. There is a division of authority over the result in *Bibb*. Some jurisdictions hold that there is no liability if a carrier causes goods to be delayed in transit and they are then damaged by an act of God. See, e.g., Seaboard Air Line Ry. v. Mullin, 70 Fla. 450, 70 So. 467 (1915), and discussion in Prosser 285-286.

Cook v. Minneapolis, St. P. & S. S. M. Ry. Co.
98 Wis. 624, 74 N.W. 561 (1898)

. . . As to the origin of the fire which destroyed the plaintiffs' property, there was evidence tending to show that, about 9 o'clock on the morning of the 20th of May, 1893, a fire was started in some way by a passing engine, in combustible material on the defendant's right of way near Boom Hill, a mile and a quarter southwest of Corliss, where plaintiffs' property was located; that the wind at that time was blowing from the south and southwest; that the fire spread for a time in a northerly and northeasterly direction, carried by the wind blowing from the south and southwest; that towards noon the wind changed to the west; that between twelve and one o'clock the wind changed so as to blow from a northwesterly direction, and increased to a gale; that at the time the fire was spreading north from Boom Hill as stated, there was a fire some distance northwest of plaintiffs' property, which, as the wind changed to the west and northwest and increased to a gale, was carried southeasterly and easterly to the vicinity of such property, so as to meet the line of fire from the southwest before that reached said property; thereafter and about 1 o'clock, carried by the strong gale of wind aforesaid, fire swept down from the west and northwest, to and into said property, and caused the destruction complained of. . . .

MARSHALL, J. . . .

. . . [W]here an injury accrues to a person, by the concurrence of two causes, one traceable to another person under such circumstances as to render him liable as a wrongdoer, and the other not traceable to any responsible origin, but of such efficient or superior force that it would produce the injury regardless of the responsible cause, there is no legal liability. No damage in such circumstances can be traced, with reasonable certainty, to wrongdoing as a producing cause. The one traceable to the wrongdoer is superseded by the other cause or condition, which takes the place of it and becomes, in a physical sense, the proximate antecedent of what follows.

From the foregoing the conclusion is easily reached that the defendant in this case is not liable for the fire loss from the facts found by the jury. Its negligence, even if operating up to about the instant the fire entered the plaintiff's property, was there superseded by the independent northwest fire.

Whether it can be said that after the two fires became one, the element attributable to the defendant continued, though its identity was lost in the combination and it was superseded by the fire that swept down upon the property from the northwest, it cannot be said that the result which followed would not have occurred but for such responsible element. On the contrary it stands as a verity in the case that it would have occurred just the same, regardless of the negligent fire. . . .

Anderson v. Minneapolis, St. P. & S. S. M. Ry. Co.
146 Minn. 430, 179 N.W. 45 (1920)

LEES, J. . . .

Plaintiff's case in chief was directed to proving that in August, 1918, one of the defendant's engines started a fire in a bog near the west side of plaintiff's land; that it smoldered there until October 12, 1918, when it flared up and burned his property, shortly before it was reached by one of the great fires which swept through Northeastern Minnesota at the close of that day. Defendant introduced evidence to show that on and prior to October 12th fires were burning west and northwest of, and were swept by the winds toward, plaintiff's premises. It did not show how such fires originated, neither did it clearly and certainly trace the destruction of plaintiff's property to them. . . .

Defendant requested the court to instruct that the extraordinary and unusual wind and weather conditions on October 12, 1918, were such an efficient and independent cause of plaintiff's damage as to relieve defendant from liability. The refusal so to instruct is assigned as error. Defendant relies on the rule that a wrongdoer may escape liability by showing that a new cause of plaintiff's injury intervened between the wrongful act and the final injurious result thereof, provided such intervening cause was not under the wrongdoer's control, could not by the exercise of reasonable diligence be anticipated as likely to occur, and except for which the injury would not have been done to plaintiff.

We are of the opinion that the rule does not apply to the facts in this case. There was a drought in Northern Minnesota throughout the summer and fall of 1918. It was protracted and severe. There was a high wind on October 12th. Towards evening and for a short time it reached a velocity of 76 miles an hour. The fire or fires which destroyed plaintiff's property had been burning a long time. Defendant was bound to know that, the greater the drought, the greater danger of the spread of a fire. Strong winds are not uncommon in Minnesota. The evidence showed that a fire, when sufficiently extensive, will create air currents as the heated air rises and cooler air rushes in to take its place. The operation of this natural law tends to increase the violence of any wind that may be blowing in a region of fires.

The court was justified in refusing to give the requested instruction for another reason. Neither the drought nor the wind would or could have destroyed plaintiff's property without the fire. The result was one which might reasonably be anticipated as a natural consequence of setting a fire and permitting it to burn for days in a country abnormally dry. Hence, if it can be said that an extraordinary wind coupled with an unusual drought were proximate causes of the injury, still the fire was a material concurring cause, without which there would have been no damage to plaintiff, and defendant is liable under the established rules of law. . . .

The following proposition is stated in defendant's brief and relied on for a reversal: "If plaintiff's property was damaged by a number of fires combining, one . . . being the fire pleaded . . . and the others being of no responsible origin, but of such sufficient or superior force that they would have produced the damage to plaintiff's property, regardless of the fire pleaded, the defendant was not liable."

This proposition is based upon Cook v. M. St. P. & S. S. M. Ry. Co. . . . If the Cook case merely decides that one who negligently sets a fire is not liable if another's property is damaged, unless it is made to appear that the fire was a material element in the destruction of the property, there can be no question about the soundness of the decision. But if it decides that if such fire combines with another of no responsible origin, and after the union of the two fires they destroy the property and either fire independently of the other would have destroyed it, then, irrespective of whether the first fire was or was not a materal factor in the destruction of the property, there is no liability, we are not prepared to adopt the doctrine as the law of this state. . . .

Notes

1. *Cook* is criticized in the following passage from 1 S. D. Thompson, Commentaries on the Law of Negligence in All Relations 678 (1901):

> [T]he conclusion is so clearly wrong as not to deserve discussion. It is just as though two wrong-doers, not acting in concert, or simultaneously, fire shots from different directions at the same person, each shot inflicting a mortal wound. Either wound being sufficient to cause death, it would be a childish casuistry that would engage in a debate as to which of the wrong-doers was innocent on the ground that the other was guilty. If, in the case above stated, the fire set by the defendant would have, proceeding alone, and did, after mingling with the other fire, cause the damage, then the plaintiff was liable upon plain principles. . . .

Thompson is correct that it would be unsound to excuse the two wrongdoers in his example on the ground that the conduct of neither was a necesary condition of the injury, though the conduct of each was a sufficient condition. But the court in *Cook* stated that the fire to the northwest of plaintiffs' property, which joined with the fire caused by defendant's negligence and swept down and destroyed his property, was "not traceable to any responsible origin." Suppose the northwest fire was due to a bolt of lightning. Then plaintiffs' property would have been destroyed even if defendant had not set its fire. In that event, how would the case be different from *Weeks*?

Is the objection to *Cook* that we do not know what caused the northwest fire? It may have been due not to a bolt of lightning but to someone's negligence, someone not before the court. In a subsequent case, Kingston v. Chicago & N. W. R. Co., 191 Wis. 610, 211 N.W. 913 (1927), the Wisconsin court held that it was the defendant's burden to prove that the other fire had no responsible origin. The courts outside of Wisconsin follow *Anderson* and make no distinction regarding the origin of the other fire. See Prosser 239 n.24.

2. What relevance, if any, did the "extraordinary and unusual wind and weather conditions" on the day of the fire in *Anderson* have to the causal question? The other fire aside, did the wind and weather conditions make P in the Hand formula zero? Does the presence of oxygen in the atmosphere make it more or less likely that careless use of matches will result in fire damage?

Sindell v. Abbott Laboratories
26 Cal. 3d 588, 607 P.2d 924 (1980)

MOSK, J. . . .

Plaintiff Judith Sindell brought an action against eleven drug companies and Does 1 through 100, on behalf of herself and other women similarly situated. The complaint alleges as follows:

Between 1941 and 1971, defendants were engaged in the business of manufacturing, promoting, and marketing diethylstilbesterol (DES), a drug which is a synthetic compound of the female hormone estrogen. The drug was administered to plaintiff's mother and the mothers of the class she represents,[1] for the purpose of preventing miscarriage. In 1947, the Food and Drug Administration authorized the marketing of DES as a miscarriage preventative, but only on an experimental basis, with a requirement that the drug contain a warning label to that effect.

DES may cause cancerous vaginal and cervical growths in the daughters exposed to it before birth, because their mothers took the drug during pregnancy. The form of cancer from which these daughters suffer is known as

1. The plaintiff class alleged consists of "girls and women who are residents of California and who have been exposed to DES before birth and who may or may not know that fact or the dangers" to which they were exposed. Defendants are also sued as representatives of a class of drug manufacturers which sold DES after 1941.

adenocarcinoma, and it manifests itself after a minimum latent period of 10 or 12 years. It is a fast-spreading and deadly disease, and radical surgery is required to prevent it from spreading. DES also causes adenosis, precancerous vaginal and cervical growths which may spread to other areas of the body. The treatment for adenosis is cauterization, surgery, or cryosurgery. Women who suffer from this condition must be monitored by biopsy or colposcopic examination twice a year, a painful and expensive procedure. Thousands of women whose mothers received DES during pregnancy are unaware of the effects of the drug.

In 1971, the Food and Drug Administration ordered defendants to cease marketing and promoting DES for the purpose of preventing miscarriages, and to warn physicians and the public that the drug should not be used by pregnant women because of the danger to their unborn children.

During the period defendants marketed DES, they knew or should have know that it was a carcinogenic substance, that there was a grave danger after varying periods of latency it would cause cancerous and precancerous growths in the daughters of the mothers who took it, and that it was ineffective to prevent miscarriage. Nevertheless, defendants continued to advertise and market the drug as a miscarriage preventative. They failed to test DES for efficacy and safety; the tests performed by others, upon which they relied, indicated that it was not safe or effective. In violation of the authorization of the Food and Drug Administration, defendants marketed DES on an unlimited basis rather than as an experimental drug, and they failed to warn of its potential danger.

Because of defendant's advertised assurances that DES was safe and effective to prevent miscarriage, plaintiff was exposed to the drug prior to her birth. She became aware of the danger from such exposure within one year of the time she filed her complaint. As a result of the DES ingested by her mother, plaintiff developed a malignant bladder tumor which was removed by surgery. She suffers from adenosis and must constantly be monitored by biopsy or colposcopy to insure early warning of further malignancy.

The first cause of action alleges that defendants were jointly and individually negligent in that they manufactured, marketed and promoted DES as a safe and efficacious drug to prevent miscarriage, without adequate testing or warning, and without monitoring or reporting its effects.

A separate cause of action alleges that defendants are jointly liable regardless of which particular brand of DES was ingested by plaintiff's mother because defendants collaborated in marketing, promoting and testing the drug, relied upon each other's tests, and adhered to an industry-wide safety standard. DES was produced from a common and mutually agreed upon formula as a fungible drug interchangeable with other brands of the same product; defendants knew or should have known that it was customary for doctors to prescribe the drug by its generic rather than its brand name and that pharmacists filled prescriptions from whatever brand of the drug happened to be in stock.

Other causes of action are based upon theories of strict liability, violation of express and implied warranties, false and fraudulent representations, misbranding of drugs in violation of federal law, conspiracy and "lack of consent."

Each cause of action alleges that defendants are jointly liable because they acted in concert, on the basis of express and implied agreements, and in reliance upon and ratification and exploitation of each other's testing and marketing methods. . . .

Defendants demurred to the complaint. While the complaint did not expressly allege that plaintiff could not identify the manufacturer of the precise drug ingested by her mother, she stated in her points and authorities in opposition to the demurrers filed by some of the defendants that she was unable to make the identification, and the trial court sustained the demurrers of these defendants without leave to amend on the ground that plaintiff did not and stated she could not identify which defendant had manufactured the drug responsible for her injuries. Thereupon, the court dismissed the action. . . .

. . . In [Summers v. Tice, 33 Cal. 2d 80, 199 P.2d 1 (1948)], the plaintiff was injured when two hunters negligently shot in his direction. It could not be determined which of them had fired the shot that actually caused the injury to the plaintiff's eye, but both defendants were nevertheless held jointly and severally liable for the whole of the damages. We reasoned that both were wrongdoers, both were negligent toward the plaintiff, and that it would be unfair to require plaintiff to isolate the defendant responsible, because if the one pointed out were to escape liability, the other might also, and the plaintiff-victim would be shorn of any remedy. In these circumstances, we held, the burden of proof shifted to the defendants, "each to absolve himself if he can." We stated that under these or similar circumstances a defendant is ordinarily in a "far better position" to offer evidence to determine whether he or another defendant caused the injury. . . .

Plaintiff does not claim that defendants are in a better position than she to identify the manufacturer of the drug taken by her mother or, indeed, that they have the ability to do so at all, but argues, rather, that *Summers* does not impose such a requirement as a condition to the shifting of the burden of proof. In this respect we believe plaintiff is correct.

In *Summers*, the circumstances of the accident themselves precluded an explanation of its cause. To be sure, *Summers* states that defendants are "[o]rdinarily . . . in a far better position to offer evidence to determine which one caused the injury" than a plaintiff, but the decision does not determine that this "ordinary" situation was present. Neither the facts nor the language of the opinion indicate that the two defendants, simultaneously shooting in the same direction, were in a better position than the plaintiff to ascertain whose shot caused the injury. As the opinion acknowledges, it was impossible for the trial court to determine whether the shot which entered the plaintiff's eye came from the gun of one defendant or the other. Nevertheless, burden of proof was shifted to the defendants.

Here, as in *Summers*, the circumstances of the injury appear to render identification of the manufacturer of the drug ingested by plaintiff's mother impossible by either plaintiff or defendants, and it cannot reasonably be said that one is in a better position than the other to make the identification. Because many years elapsed between the time the drug was taken and the manifestation of plaintiff's injuries she, and many other daughters of mothers who took DES, are unable to make such identification. Certainly there can be no implication that plaintiff is at fault in failing to do so — the event occurred while plaintiff was in utero, a generation ago.

On the other hand, it cannot be said with assurance that defendants have the means to make the identification. In this connection, they point out that drug manufacturers ordinarily have no direct contact with the patients who take a drug prescribed by their doctors. Defendants sell to wholesalers, who in turn supply the product to physicians and pharmacies. Manufacturers do not maintain records of the persons who take the drugs they produce, and the selection of the medication is made by the physician rather than the manufacturer. Nor do we conclude that the absence of evidence on this subject is due to the fault of defendants. While it is alleged that they produced a defective product with delayed effects and without adequate warnings, the difficulty or impossibility of identification results primarily from the passage of time rather than from their allegedly negligent acts of failing to provide adequate warnings. Thus Haft v. Lone Palm Hotel, upon which plaintiff relies, is distinguishable.

It is important to observe, however, that while defendants do not have means superior to plaintiff to identify the maker of the precise drug taken by her mother, they may in some instances be able to prove that they did not manufacture the injury-causing substance. In the present case, for example, one of the original defendants was dismissed from the action upon proof that it did not manufacture DES until after plaintiff was born.

Thus we conclude that the fact defendants do not have greater access to information which might establish the identity of the manufacturer of the DES which injured plaintiff does not per se prevent application of the *Summers* rule.

Nevertheless, plaintiff may not prevail in her claim that the *Summers* rationale should be employed to fix the whole liability for her injuries upon defendants, at least as those principles have previously been applied. There is an important difference between the situation involved in *Summers* and the present case. There, all the parties who were or could have been responsible for the harm to the plaintiff were joined as defendants. Here, by contrast, there are approximately 200 drug companies which made DES, any of which might have manufactured the injury-producing drug.

Defendants maintain that, while in *Summers* there was a 50 percent chance that one of the two defendants was responsible for the plaintiff's injuries, here since any one of 200 companies which manufactured DES might have made the product that harmed plaintiff, there is no rational basis upon which to infer that any defendant in this action caused plaintiff's injuries, nor even a reasonable possibility that they were responsible.

These arguments are persuasive if we measure the chance that any one of the defendants supplied the injury-causing drug by the number of possible tortfeasors. In such a context, the possibility that any of the five defendants supplied the DES to plaintiff's mother is so remote that it would be unfair to require each defendant to exonerate itself. There may be a substantial likelihood that none of the five defendants joined in the action made the DES which caused the injury, and that the offending producer not named would escape liability altogether. While we propose, infra, an adaptation of the rule in *Summers* which will substantially overcome these difficulties, defendants appear to be correct that the rule, as previously applied, cannot relieve plaintiff of the burden of proving the identity of the manufacturer which made the drug causing her injuries. . . .

The most persuasive reason for finding plaintiff states a cause of action is that advanced in *Summers:* as between an innocent plaintiff and negligent defendants, the latter should bear the cost of the injury. Here, as in *Summers*, plaintiff is not at fault in failing to provide evidence of causation, and although the absence of such evidence is not attributable to the defendants either, their conduct in marketing a drug the effects of which are delayed for many years played a significant role in creating the unavailability of proof.

From a broader policy standpoint, defendants are better able to bear the cost of injury resulting from the manufacture of a defective product. . . . The manufacturer is in the best position to discover and guard against defects in its products and to warn of harmful effects; thus, holding it liable for defects and failure to warn of harmful effects will provide an incentive to product safety. These considerations are particularly significant where medication is involved, for the consumer is virtually helpless to protect himself from serious, sometimes permanent, sometimes fatal, injuries caused by deleterious drugs.

. . . [W]e hold it to be reasonable in the present context to measure the likelihood that any of the defendants supplied the product which allegedly injured plaintiff by the percentage which the DES sold by each of them for the purpose of preventing miscarriage bears to the entire production of the drug sold by all for that purpose. Plaintiff asserts in her briefs that Eli Lilly and Company and 5 or 6 other companies produced 90 percent of the DES marketed. If at trial this is established to be the fact, then there is a corresponding likelihood that this comparative handful of producers manufactured the DES which caused plaintiff's injuries, and only a 10 percent likelihood that the offending producer would escape liability.

If plaintiff joins in the action the manufacturers of a substantial share of the DES which her mother might have taken, the injustice of shifting the burden of proof to defendants to demonstrate that they could not have made the substance which injured plaintiff is significantly diminished. While 75 to 80 percent of the market is suggested as the requirement . . . , we hold only that a substantial percentage is required.

The presence in the action of a substantial share of the appropriate market also provides a ready means to apportion damages among the defendants. Each defendant will be held liable for the proportion of the judgment represented by its share of that market unless it demonstrates that it could not have made the product which caused plaintiff's injuries. . . .

Notes

1. For background on the DES litigation, see Note, 46 Fordham L. Rev. 963 (1978); Note, 94 Harv. L. Rev. 668 (1981); and the *Mink* case in Chapter 7. Cf. Hardy v. Johns-Manville Sales Corp., 509 F. Supp. 1353 (E.D. Tex. 1981), applying the approach of *Sindell* to an asbestosis case (see Chapter 9).

2. How does Summers v. Tice differ from Ybarra v. Spangard? How does it differ from *Cook* and *Anderson*?

3. Is *Sindell* consistent with Smith v. Rapid Transit Inc., 317 Mass. 469, 58 N.E.2d 754 (1945)? In *Smith*,

These facts could have been found: While the plaintiff at about 1:00 A.M. on February 6, 1941, was driving an automobile on Main Street, Winthrop, in an easterly direction toward Winthrop Highlands, she observed a bus coming toward her which she described as a "great big, long, wide affair." The bus, which was proceeding at about forty miles an hour, "forced her to turn to the right," and her automobile collided with a "parked car." The plaintiff was coming from Dorchester. The department of public utilities had issued a certificate of public convenience or necessity to the defendant for three routes in Winthrop, one of which included Main Street, and this was in effect in February, 1941. "There was another bus line in operation in Winthrop at that time but not on Main Street." According to the defendant's time-table, buses were scheduled to leave Winthrop Highlands for Maverick Square via Main Street at 12:10 A.M., 12:45 A.M., 1:15 A.M., and 2:15 A.M. The running time for this trip at that time of night was thirty minutes.

The direction of a verdict for the defendant was right. The ownership of the bus was a matter of conjecture. While the defendant had the sole franchise for operating a bus line on Main Street, Winthrop, this did not preclude private or chartered buses from using this street; the bus in question could very well have been one operated by someone other than the defendant. . . . [I]t is "not enough that mathematically the chances somewhat favor a proposition to be proved; for example, the fact that colored automobiles made in the current year outnumber black ones would not warrant a finding that an undescribed automobile of the current year is colored and not black, nor would the fact that only a minority of men die of cancer warrant a finding that a particular man did not die of cancer." The most that can be said of the evidence in the instant case is that perhaps the mathematical chances somewhat favor the proposition that a bus of the defendant caused the accident. This was not enough. A "proposition is proved by a preponderance of the evidence if it is made to appear more likely or probable in the sense that actual belief in its truth, derived from the evidence, exists in the mind or minds of the tribunal notwithstanding any doubts that may still linger there."

Id. at 469-470, 58 N.E.2d at 754-755.

4. Try to summarize the economic approach to causation. Then compare your summary with Professor Borgo's philosophical analysis of causation, which follows.

Borgo, Causal Paradigms in Tort Law
8 J. Legal Stud. 419, 432-440 (1979)

. . . [S]uppose that a locomotive throws a spark into a field of corn and a fire is started. There were many conditions, in addition to the spark, that had to be met in order for the fire to occur. Just a few of the more obvious ones are the wind and weather conditions, the presence of the corn, its particular degree of dryness, and the presence of oxygen in the air. All of these factors are necessary conditions for the production of the fire. But as a matter of ordinary language, they are not all its causes. Thus we would certainly not describe the sequence of events by saying that the presence of oxygen in the air caused the fire. But it would be quite natural to say that the spark caused it. The point is not that oxygen and the spark are both causes but that the latter is in some sense the more important of the two. Nor is it that both are part of the same cause. It is rather that oxygen simply is not the cause of the fire, although it is a necessary condition for its production. There is a difference in meaning between "cause" and "necessary condition" that is manifested in ordinary language by our decision to grant causal status to the spark and to refuse it to the presence of oxygen.[33]

This example shows that we do not choose just any antecedent factor as the cause of a particular effect. We are guided in our choice of causes by certain principles of selection, and these principles regulate the ordinary use of the concept of cause. In order to understand the meaning of that concept, we must examine the principles of of selection more closely.

---

33. This is not to say that there is some feature of oxygen that makes it unsuitable to be the cause of a fire. . . . [Consider] the case in which oxygen is accidentally introduced into a manufacturing process from which it is normally excluded because of the danger of fire. If a fire occurs, it is naturally described as having been caused by the presence of oxygen. Nor would we necessarily choose a spark as the cause of a fire whenever one falls into combustible material and a fire is started. Suppose that a workman, despite specific instructions to the contrary, deposits a highly inflammable substance near a machine that produces sparks as part of its normal operation. We would say that the resulting fire was caused by the presence of the substance in a dangerous location.

The first step in elucidating the principles is to ask how the concept of cause is used in our language. The most fundamental role of causal judgments in everyday discourse is explanatory in character. We look for causes when we are confronted with events or states of affairs whose occurrence we are unable to understand and for which we want an explanation. Ordinary causal judgments perform this function by identifying the factor that brought about the occurrence of the effect. It is true that they have other functions. They are used, for example, as the basis of predictions. If called upon to defend my prediction that B will occur, I might say that A has occurred and that A causes B. But the predictive function presupposes an explanatory function. If identifying A as the cause of B did not explain the occurrence of B, I would not have succeeded in defending my prediction. It is precisely because it does explain it that I have good reason, upon observing A, to expect that it will be followed by B. Thus, although explanation is not the only function of causal judgments, it is their most fundamental one.

The explanatory role of ordinary causal judgments suggests an important characteristic of the principles of selection embedded in the concept of cause. The chief requirement imposed by the principles is that we select as the cause of a particular effect a factor that provides a satisfactory causal explanation of its occurrence: that is, an explanation of how the effect was brought about. And this in turn suggests an account of the distinction between cause and necessary condition and of the fact, noted above, that in making causal judgments we do not treat all of the factors necessary for the production of an effect as equally entitled to the status of its cause. When we say that the spark caused the fire in the cornfield and deny that the presence of oxygen in the air did, we do so because the spark explains how the fire occurred and the presence of oxygen does not. The spark has, as it were, an explanatory power that is lacking in the presence of oxygen.

According to this account, the concepts of cause and explanation are logically related. But this raises a further issue. What does it mean to say that the spark explains the occurrence of the fire? What is it for the spark to have, and the presence of oxygen to lack, explanatory power? . . .

Suppose that you see the fire in the field and ask me to explain how it happened. I answer that I struck a match and touched it to a few plants, thereby starting the fire. . . . [That is,] I tell a simple ad hoc story, using familiar transitive verbs. And the explanation succeeds, since you now understand how the fire was brought about. Why is that so?

It succeeds because I described to you a sequence of acts and events that you are able directly to perceive as a perfectly clear case of something starting a fire: that is, a case in which you know, without need of further inquiry, that a particular act (my touching a burning match to a plant) brought about the fire. That it is a perfectly clear case is shown by the fact that a demand for further explanation would be absurd. If, after hearing my story, you replied, "But is that what started the fire?" I would be at a loss to answer. Your reply suggests that I have not yet explained the fire, that you need to know more in order to understand how it was brought about. But what more can I tell you?

If you do not understand that touching a burning match to a plant starts a fire, surely it is not for lack of sufficient evidence. The explanation is complete as it stands. You do not need to know more, because there is nothing more to be known.

Now compare the perfectly clear case to the following one. I drop a cigarette on the road as I stroll past the corn, and a sudden and unexpected gust of wind blows it into the field. Then a fire occurs. Here we have a doubtful case, since it is possible to disagree about what started the fire. This is because there is no single act or event in the sequence I have described that we are able to perceive intuitively as having brought about the fire. Although it is plausible to say that I started it by dropping the cigarette, it is also plausible to say that I did not, that it was started by the gust of wind blowing the cigarette into the field. How shall we decide which is the proper explanation? The natural way to do this is to compare the doubtful case to the clear one, in order to discover suggestive resemblances and analogies. In making this comparison, we are treating the clear case as a paradigm and the similarities and dissimilarities between the two cases as reasons for and against explaining the doubtful case in some particular way. We look to see which of the two events — my dropping the cigarette and the gust of wind blowing it into the field — is most like my touching a burning match to a plant. Since we are able to perceive my act as starting the fire in the paradigm case, the event in the doubtful case that is most similar to it acquires, by virtue of its similarity, a like explanatory power. If we decide — as I think we would — that the wind blowing the cigarette into the field most clearly resembles my touching a match to a plant, we would explain the fire as having been started by that event.

Let us return to the example of the spark thrown into the field. It should now be clear why the proper explanation of the occurrence of the fire is that the spark started it. When we compare the example to the paradigm case, we see that the roles played in their respective contexts by the spark and my touching a match to a plant closely resemble each other. The resemblance is one of analogy: each of them is, as it were, the active factor in a set of circumstances surrounding the production of a fire. The analogy leads us to organize our understanding of the example in a particular way. We say that the spark started the fire because its resemblance to my deliberate act in the paradigm case enables us to perceive it as bringing the fire about. It is for this reason that we are able to explain the occurrence of the fire without reference to the other antecedent conditions. Although the other conditions were necessary in order for the spark to produce the fire, only the spark produced it. . . .

. . . [T]he theory just developed is a theory of ad hoc causal explanation. It presupposes that a causal explanation succeeds by enabling us to see that the explanandum was brought about by some particular factor. According to the theory, to explain an event or state of affairs is to tell a story of how it was brought about. We are able to understand the story by virtue of its resemblance to the paradigm case, which is itself intuitively intelligible.

The notion of an ad hoc causal explanation enables us to understand the logic of ordinary causal judgments. We select as the cause of an event or state of affairs the antecedent condition that would appear in an ad hoc explanation of its occurrence. . . .

. . . [T]he selection of the cause of an event or state of affairs is strongly influenced by the particulars of the context in which the event or state of affairs occurs. This should not be surprising, since the success of an explanation depends upon the resemblances between the production of the explanandum and a paradigm case. These resemblances are numerous, diverse, and highly context-bound. If the circumstances surrounding the occurrence of the explanandum were different, it is possible that we would perceive a different antecedent condition as having brought it about. If so, we would select that condition as the cause. By varying the circumstances of our example, we can imagine cases in which we would not choose the spark as the cause of the fire.

Suppose that corn is normally fire-resistant and that passing locomotives routinely shower sparks into cornfields without fires breaking out. But it has not rained for several weeks, and parched corn is very combustible. A spark falls into the field and a fire occurs. Given the fact that cornfields usually are not set ablaze when sparks fall into them, the analogy between the spark and my touching a match to a plant becomes much weaker. Although in most circumstances we are able to perceive sparks as bringing about fires, the present circumstances are not of the proper sort. Therefore we do not choose the spark as the cause of the fire. Instead we choose a different factor, namely, the recent lack of rain. Our reason for doing so is that it is the factor that makes the present case different from the usual one in which a fire would not occur. Therefore it resembles my deliberate intervention into the ordinary course of affairs, in the paradigm case, in order to start a fire. Notice that the analogy between my act and a state of affairs persisting through time is far more extended than the one between my act and an episodic event like the spark falling into the field. Nonetheless the latter has been weakened by the circumstances surrounding the fire, and so our causal explanation organizes itself around the state of affairs.

This example shows that our selection of a particular antecedent condition as the cause of an event or state of affairs depends upon the role of the condition in the context in which the event or state of affairs occurs. But the matter is more complicated than that. Our selection is also affected by the purpose for which we choose the cause. Again, this is to be expected, given the relation between causal judgments and causal explanations. For what counts as a satisfactory explanation is in part determined by the purpose for which it is demanded. Thus causal explanations, and therefore our selection of causes, will vary with our purposes in making them.

In order to see this, imagine that corn is not fire-resistant, but that locomotives do not throw off sparks unless improperly operated. A spark lands in the field and a fire occurs. Now if we are interested in the physical process by which the fire was brought about, we select the spark as the cause of the fire. Since we are not concerned with how the spark happened to arrive on the scene, the question of human causal agency does not arise. Therefore the manner in which the engineer operated the locomotive does not matter to us, and our causal explanation will not organize itself around it. If, however, we want to decide whether anyone is responsible for starting the fire, then we select the engineer's conduct as the cause. For we are now interested in whether the fire can be explained by reference to a human agent. Our attention therefore shifts from the physical level to that of human action, and the spark is no longer important. Although it was the means by which the engineer started the fire, the fact remains that the engineer, and not the spark, started it. Suppose, finally, that we are interested in determining the social costs associated with railroading, with a view to regulating the industry. Now we say that the fire was caused by the operation — *not* the *improper* operation — of the locomotive (or, more broadly, the activity of railroading). Given our purpose in selecting a cause, our interest shifts to continuing activities rather than discrete acts. We do not want to know whether human conduct brought about the harm, but whether it was brought about by a factor associated with operating a railroad. Therefore our causal explanation focuses on that activity.

Notes

1. The economic analysis of causation uses the word "cause" in a conclusory fashion: if we want to hold the defendant liable, we say his conduct caused the plaintiff's injury; if we do not want to hold the defendant liable, we say the cause of the plaintiff's injury was an act of God, or of the plaintiff, or of someone else. Is this approach compatible with Professor Borgo's analysis?

2. Does Borgo use the word "paradigm" in the same sense as Professor Epstein?

3. For those wanting to delve more deeply into the philosophical analysis of causation, a good place to start is Causation and Conditionals (E. Sosa ed. 1975). For an influential discussion of causal principles in the law, which combines a philosophical point of view similar to Borgo's with a detailed discussion of cases, see H.L.A. Hart & A.M. Honoré, Causation in the Law (1959).

Palsgraf v. Long Island R. Co.
248 N.Y. 399, 162 N.E. 99 (1928)

CARDOZO, C.J. Plaintiff was standing on a platform of defendant's railroad after buying a ticket to go to Rockaway Beach. A train stopped at the station, bound for another place. Two men ran forward to catch it. One of the men reached the platform of the car without mishap, though the train was already moving. The other man, carrying a package, jumped aboard the car, but seemed unsteady as if about to fall. A guard on the car, who had held the door open, reached forward to help him in, and another guard on the platform pushed him from behind. In this act, the package was dislodged, and fell upon the rails. It was a package of small size, about fifteen inches long, and was covered by a newspaper. In fact it contained fireworks, but there was nothing in its appearance to give notice of its contents. The fireworks when they fell exploded. The shock of the explosion threw down some scales at the other end of the platform many feet away. The scales struck the plaintiff, causing injuries for which she sues.

The conduct of the defendant's guard, if a wrong in its relation to the holder of the package, was not a wrong in its relation to the plaintiff, standing far away. Relatively to her it was not negligence at all. Nothing in the situation gave notice that the falling package had in it the potency of peril to persons thus removed. Negligence is not actionable unless it involves the invasion of a legally protected interest, the violation of a right. "Proof of negligence in the air, so to speak, will not do." . . . The plaintiff, as she stood upon the platform of the station, might claim to be protected against intentional invasion of her bodily security. Such invasion is not charged. She might claim to be protected against unintentional invasion by conduct involving in the thought of reasonable men an unreasonable hazard that such invasion would ensue. These, from the point of view of the law, were the bounds of her immunity, with perhaps some rare exceptions, survivals for the most part of ancient forms of liability, where conduct is held to be at the peril of the actor. If no hazard was apparent to the eye of ordinary vigilance, an act innocent and harmless, at least to outward seeming, with reference to her, did not take to itself the quality of a tort because it happened to be a wrong, though apparently not one involving the risk of bodily insecurity, with reference to some one else. . . . "The ideas of negligence and duty are strictly correlative." The plaintiff sues in her own right for a wrong personal to her, and not as the vicarious beneficiary of a breach of duty to another.

A different conclusion will involve us, and swiftly too, in a maze of contradictions. A guard stumbles over a package which has been left upon a platform. It seems to be a bundle of newspapers. It turns out to be a can of dynamite. To the eye of ordinary vigilance, the bundle is abandoned waste, which may be kicked or trod on with impunity. Is a passenger at the other end of the platform protected by the law against the unsuspected hazard concealed beneath the waste? If not, is the result to be any different, so far as the distant passenger is concerned, when the guard stumbles over a valise which a truckman or a porter has left upon the walk? The passenger far away, if the victim of a wrong at all, has a cause of action, not derivative, but original and primary. His claim to be protected against invasion of his bodily security is neither greater nor less because the act resulting in the invasion is a wrong to another far removed. In this case, the rights that are said to have been violated, the interests said to have been invaded, are not even of the same order. The man was not injured in his person nor even put in danger. The purpose of the act, as well as its effect, was to make his person safe. If there was a wrong to him at all, which may very well be doubted, it was a wrong to a property interest only, the safety of his package. Out of this wrong to property, which threatened injury to nothing else, there has passed, we are told, to the plaintiff by derivation or succession a right of action for the invasion of an interest of another order, the right to bodily security. The diversity of interests emphasizes the futility of the effort to build the plaintiff's right upon the basis of a wrong to some one else. The gain is one of emphasis, for a like result would follow if the interests were the same. Even then, the orbit of the danger as disclosed to the eye of reasonable vigilance would be the orbit of the duty. One who jostles one's neighbor in a crowd does not invade the rights of others standing at the outer fringe when the unintended contact casts a bomb upon the ground. The wrongdoer as to them is the man who carries the bomb, not the one who explodes it without suspicion of the danger. Life will have to be made over, and human nature transformed, before prevision so extravagant can be accepted as the norm of conduct, the customary standard to which behavior must conform.

The argument for the plaintiff is built upon the shifting meanings of such words as "wrong" and "wrongful," and shares their instability. What the plaintiff must show is "a wrong" to herself; i.e., a violation of her own right, and not merely a wrong to some one else, nor conduct "wrongful" because unsocial, but not "a wrong" to any one. We are told that one who drives at reckless speed through a crowded city street is guilty of a negligent act and therefore of a wrongful one, irrespective of the consequences. Negligent the act is, and wrongful in the sense that it is unsocial, but wrongful and unsocial in relation to other travelers, only because the eye of vigilance perceives the risk of damage. If the same act were to be committed on a speedway or a race course, it would lose its wrongful quality. The risk reasonably to be perceived defines the duty to be obeyed, and risk imports relation; it is risk to another or to others within the range of apprehension. . . .

Negligence, like risk, is thus a term of relation. Negligence in the abstract, apart from things related, is surely not a tort, if indeed it is understandable at all. Negligence is not a tort unless it results in the commission of a wrong, and the commission of a wrong imports the violation of a right, in this case, we are told, the right to be protected against interference with one's bodily security. But bodily security is protected, not against all forms of interference or aggression, but only against some. One who seeks redress at law does not make out a cause of action by showing without more that there has been damage to his person. If the harm was not willful, he must show that the act as to him had possibilities of danger so many and apparent as to entitle him to be protected against the doing of it though the harm was unintended. . . .

The law of causation, remote or proximate, is thus foreign to the case before us. The question of liability is always anterior to the question of the measure of the consequences that go with liability. If there is no tort to be redressed, there is no occasion to consider what damage might be recovered if there were a finding of a tort. We may assume, without deciding, that negligence, not at large or in the abstract, but in relation to the plaintiff, would entail liability for any and all consequences, however novel or extraordinary. . . .

The judgment of the Appellate Division and that of the Trial Term should be reversed, and the complaint dismissed, with costs in all courts.

ANDREWS, J. (dissenting). . . .

. . . The result we shall reach depends upon our theory as to the nature of negligence. Is it a relative concept — the breach of some duty owing to a particular person or to particular persons? Or, where there is an act which unreasonably threatens the safety of others, is the doer liable for all its proximate consequences, even where they result in injury to one who would generally be thought to be outside the radius of danger? This is not a mere dispute as to words. We might not believe that to the average mind the dropping of the bundle would seem to involve the probability of harm to the plaintiff standing many feet away whatever might be the case as to the owner or to one so near as to be likely to be struck by its fall. If, however, we adopt the second hypothesis, we have to inquire only as to the relation between cause and effect. We deal in terms of proximate cause, not of negligence. . . .

. . . [W]e are told that "there is no negligence unless there is in the particular case a legal duty to take care, and this duty must be one which is owed to the plaintiff himself and not merely to others." This I think too narrow a conception. Where there is the unreasonable act, and some right that may be affected, there is negligence whether damage does or does not result. That is immaterial. Should we drive down Broadway at a reckless speed, we are negligent whether we strike an approaching car or miss it by an inch. The act itself is wrongful. It is a wrong not only to those who happen to be within the radius of danger, but to all who might have been there — a wrong to the public at large. Such is the language of the street. Such the language of the courts when speaking of contributory negligence. Such again and again their language in speaking of the duty of some defendant and discussing proximate cause in cases where such a discussion is wholly irrelevant on any other theory. . . .

It may well be that there is no such thing as negligence in the abstract. "Proof of negligence in the air, so to speak, will not do." In an empty world negligence would not exist. It does involve a relationship between man and his fellows, but not merely a relationship between man and those whom he might reasonably expect his act would injure; rather, a relationship between him and those whom he does in fact injure. If his act has a tendency to harm some one, it harms him a mile away as surely as it does those on the scene. We now permit children to recover for the negligent killing of the father. It was never prevented on the theory that no duty was owing to them. A husband may be compensated for the loss of his wife's services. To say that the wrongdoer was negligent as to the husband as well as to the wife is merely an attempt to fit facts to theory. An insurance company paying a fire loss recovers its payment of the negligent incendiary. We speak of subrogation — of suing in the right of the insured. Behind the cloud of words is the fact they hide, that the act, wrongful as to the insured, has also injured the company. Even if it be true that the fault of father, wife, or insured will prevent recovery, it is because we consider the original negligence, not the proximate cause of the injury. . . .

. . . Any philosophical doctrine of causation does not help us. A boy throws a stone into a pond. The ripples spread. The water level rises. The history of that pond is altered to all eternity: It will be altered by other causes also. Yet it will be forever the resultant of all causes combined. Each one will have an influence. How great only omniscience can say. You may speak of a chain, or, if you please, a net. An analogy is of little aid. Each cause brings about future events. Without each the future would not be the same. Each is proximate in the sense it is essential. But that is not what we mean by the word. Nor on the other hand do we mean sole cause. There is no such thing.

Should analogy be thought helpful, however, I prefer that of a stream. The spring, starting on its journey, is joined by tributary after tributary. The river, reaching the ocean, comes from a hundred sources. No man may say whence any drop of water is derived. Yet for a time distinction may be possible. Into the clear creek, brown swamp water flows from the left. Later, from the right comes water stained by its clay bed. The three may remain for a space, sharply divided. But at last inevitably no trace of separation remains. They are so commingled that all distinction is lost.

As we have said, we cannot trace the effect of an act to the end, if end there is. Again, however, we may trace it part of the way. A murder at Serajevo may be the necessary antecedent to an assassination in London twenty years hence. An overturned lantern may burn all Chicago. We may follow the fire from the shed to the last building. We rightly say the fire started by the lantern caused its destruction.

A cause, but not the proximate cause. What we do mean by the word "proximate" is that, because of convenience, of public policy, of a rough sense of justice, the law arbitrarily declines to trace a series of events beyond a certain point. This is not logic. It is practical politics. . . .

. . . A chauffeur negligently collides with another car which is filled with dynamite, although he could not know it. An explosion follows. A, walking on the sidewalk nearby, is killed. B, sitting in a window of a building opposite, is cut by flying glass. C, likewise sitting in a window a block away, is similarly injured. And a further illustration: A nursemaid, ten blocks away, startled by the noise, involuntarily drops a baby from her arms to the walk. We are told that C may not recover while A may. As to B it is a question for court or jury. We will all agree that the baby might not. Because, we are again told, the chauffeur had no reason to believe his conduct involved any risk of injuring either C or the baby. As to them he was not negligent.

But the chauffeur being negligent in risking the collision, his belief that the scope of the harm he might do would be limited is immaterial. His act unreasonably jeopardized the safety of any one who might be affected by it. C's injury and that of the baby were directly traceable to the collision. Without that, the injury would not have happened. C had the right to sit in his office, secure from such dangers. The baby was entitled to use the sidewalk with reasonable safety.

The true theory is, it seems to me, that the injury to C, if in truth he is to be denied recovery, and the injury to the baby, is that their several injuries were not the proximate result of the negligence. And here not what the chauffeur had reason to believe would be the result of his conduct, but what the prudent would foresee, may have a bearing — may have some bearing, for the problem of proximate cause is not to be solved by any one consideration. It is all a question of expediency. There are no fixed rules to govern our judgment. There are simply matters of which we may take account. We have in a somewhat different connection spoken of "the stream of events." We have asked whether that stream was deflected — whether it was forced into new and unexpected channels. This is rather rhetoric than law. There is in truth little to guide us other than common sense.

There are some hints that may help us. The proximate cause, involved as it may be with many other causes, must be, at the least, something without which the event would not happen. The court must ask itself whether there was a natural and continuous sequence between cause and effect. Was the one a substantial factor in producing the other? Was there a direct connection between them, without too many intervening causes? Is the effect of cause on result not too attenuated? Is the cause likely, in the usual judgment of mankind, to produce the result? Or, by the exercise of prudent foresight, could the result be foreseen? Is the result too remote from the cause, and here we consider remoteness in time and space. . . . Clearly we must so consider, for the greater the distance either in time or space, the more surely do other causes intervene to affect the result. When a lantern is overturned, the firing of a shed is a fairly direct consequence. Many things contribute to the spread of the conflagration — the force of the wind, the direction and width of streets, the character of intervening structures, other factors. We draw an uncertain and wavering line, but draw it we must as best we can. . . .

. . . The act upon which defendant's liability rests is knocking an apparently harmless package onto the platform. The act was negligent. For its proximate consequences the defendant is liable. . . . We are told by the appellant in his brief, "It cannot be denied that the explosion was the direct cause of the plaintiff's injuries." So it was a substantial factor in producing the result — there was here a natural and continuous sequence — direct connection. The only intervening cause was that, instead of blowing her to the ground, the concussion smashed the weighing machine which in turn fell upon her. There was no remoteness in time, little in space. And surely, given such an explosion as here, it needed no great foresight to predict that the natural result would be to injure one on the platform at no greater distance from its scene than was the plaintiff. Just how no one might be able to predict. Whether by flying fragments, by broken glass, by wreckage of machines or structures no one could say. But injury in some form was most probable.

Under these circumstances I cannot say as a matter of law that the plaintiff's injuries were not the proximate result of the negligence. That is all we have before us. The court refused to so charge. No request was made to submit the matter to the jury as a question of fact, even would that have been proper upon the record before us.

The judgment appealed from should be affirmed, with costs.

Notes

1. A study of the record in the *Palsgraf* case reveals that while Mrs. Palsgraf was indeed struck by the scale when it overturned, the principal injury for which she sought damages was a stammer allegedly induced by the shock; and there is some indication that the stammer may have been induced (or at least prolonged) by the anxiety associated with the litigation itself. See J. T. Noonan, Jr., Persons and Masks of the Law 127 (1976). There is also considerable doubt whether the explosion itself knocked over the scale; it appears more likely that the explosion stampeded the crowd and the crowd knocked over the scale. See id. at 119.

2. If we accept that the explosion knocked over the scale (whether through concussion, or through stampeding the crowd) and that the striking of Mrs. Palsgraf by the scale in turn induced her stammer, is there any basis in the previous materials in this chapter for concluding that defendant's negligence did *not* cause the injury of which plaintiff complained? The negligence increased the probability that Mrs. Palsgraf would be injured, did it not? It was not just a matter of delaying (or accelerating) her arrival at a place where an accident occurred.

To be sure, the probability that she would be injured as a result of defendant's negligence was very small; it was a freak accident. But why should a person not be liable for the freak accidents he causes? Four possibilities come to mind.

(1) If an accident has a very low probability, the optimal burden of precautions against it will also be very low, unless the loss, if the accident does occur, is enormous. A defendant would not be negligent for having failed to take some elaborate precaution against a minute probability of a relatively minor accident. But is this what Cardozo meant? He did say that defendant was not negligent as to Mrs. Palsgraf. But if defendant's guards, in trying to shove the man with the package aboard, had pushed him into another passen-

ger, causing injury to that passenger, would not defendant have been liable to that other passenger? And if defendant thus failed to exercise due care, why should it not be liable for all injuries caused by its failure, in the sense of "cause" developed in the previous materials in this chapter? As the court stated in Petition of Kinsman Transit Co., 338 F.2d 708, 725 (2d Cir. 1964):

> We see no reason why an actor engaging in conduct which entails a large risk of small damage and a small risk of other and greater damage, of the same general sort, from the same forces, and to the same class of persons, should be relieved of responsibility for the latter simply because the chance of its occurrence, if viewed alone, may not have been large enough to require the exercise of care. By hypothesis, the risk of the lesser harm was sufficient to render his disregard of it actionable; the existence of a less likely additional risk that the very forces against whose action he was required to guard would produce other and greater damage than could have been reasonably anticipated should inculpate him further rather than limit his liability.

We can put this point into Hand formula terms. Suppose some precaution will prevent two types of accident. The expected accident costs of type 1 are P_1L_1 and of type 2 are P_2L_2. If $B < P_1L_1$, as in *Palsgraf*, where an accident of type 1 would have been an injury to the passenger carrying the fireworks or to other passengers close by and one of type 2 was the injury to Mrs. Palsgraf, then even if P_2 was very small, P_2L_2 must have been greater than the incremental cost of preventing accident type 2; that incremental cost was zero given that B should have been adopted just to prevent accident type 1. Where have we encountered this situation before?

It might seem that if P_2L_2 is very small because P_2 is very small, the allocative benefits of liability would be offset by the administrative costs of litigating a case in which an accident of type 2 occurs. But this is incorrect, as shown in Shavell, An Analysis of Causation and the Scope of Liability in the Law of Torts, 9 J. Legal Stud. 463 (1980). The administrative costs are incurred only when an accident occurs, and by assumption the accident occurs rarely. Thus, the expected administrative costs are a function of P_2 just as the expected accident costs are.

(2) There are costs of foresight. If a class of accidents is so improbable that no reasonable person would think about it in deciding how much care to take, there will be no effect on behavior — no increase in care — from making the person liable if such an accident does occur. But how is a "class" of accidents to be delimited? Every accident, examined closely enough, is a freak accident. Even in a garden-variety automobile collision case, how likely is it that *this* plaintiff and *this* defendant would have reached *this* intersection at *this* exact moment? If "class" is defined too narrowly, we will have the paradox that a defendant whose behavior was highly dangerous and in fact resulted in an accident will get off scot-free because each type of accident that his conduct made more probable was, nevertheless, highly improbable. But

perhaps we do not even consider conduct dangerous unless we can imagine a class of accidents that is a foreseeable consequence of the conduct. If so, using the concept of foreseeability to limit liability may not be quite the onion-peeling exercise that the above discussion suggests.

(3) A property of some freak accidents is that one is skeptical that they really occurred as described. *Palsgraf*, we intimated, may have been such a case. Perhaps, then, the result of the case can ultimately be explained on the same basis as the result in *Keegan*. There is, however, no support for this conjecture in the opinions in *Palsgraf*.

(4) Suppose injurers are risk-averse. Then the prospect of a small probability of having to pay a large damages judgment might impose greater disutility on potential injurers than simply multiplying L by P might suggest. But is this a good reason for limiting the scope of liability? If injurers are risk-averse, why not victims too? Then limiting the scope of liability will impose a corresponding disutility on victims. Anyway, both injurers and victims can insure, the former by buying liability insurance and the latter by buying accident insurance. Since insurance eliminates risk, it is not clear that considerations of risk aversion provide a powerful reason for any particular liability rule.

3. The difference between a case like *Weeks* and a case like *Palsgraf* (or Gorris v. Scott in Chapter 4) is the difference between what is sometimes called "cause in fact" and what is sometimes called "legal causation." In *Weeks* the violation of the ordinance did not cause the accident, in a sense of "cause" which one does not have to be a lawyer to understand. In *Gorris* the violation of the statute requiring sheep to be penned onboard ship was a cause of the accident. The sheep would not have been washed overboard if the statute had been complied with, and compliance would have reduced the probability of such an accident. Nevertheless, there was no liability. The reasons for limiting liability may be related to concepts of causation, as suggested in Note 2(3) above, but they are not causal grounds.

Unfortunately, the law's analytical framework in this area is less clear than one might hope. Some courts and commentators confine the strictly causal inquiry to the question whether defendant's conduct was a necessary condition of plaintiff's injury, treating this as a threshold requirement; every other issue relating to scope of liability they treat as one of "legal causation" or "policy." This position, sharply criticized by Professor Epstein (see Epstein, A Theory of Strict Liability, 2 J. Legal Stud. 151 (1973), excerpted in Chapter 6 of this book), rests on a misunderstanding of the word "cause," which, as we have seen, is not a synonym for necessary condition. Some causes are not necessary conditions, and many necessary conditions are not causes.

Many courts and commentators use the term "proximate cause" to cover issues of causation in fact, and "duty" or "foreseeability" or "scope of risk" or "remoteness" to denote noncausal grounds for limiting liability. (This would be a good time for the reader to become reacquainted with the duty cases in Chapter 6 of this book; they are closely related to the cases in this part of the present chapter.) Still other courts use the term "proximate cause" to cover both cause in fact and "legal causation." The distinction between factual and legal causation is a useful one, but the reader should recognize that the latter involves a contradiction. Even when "cause" is interpreted in light of the philosophical and economic approaches considered earlier, there are cases where the courts refuse to affix liability for wrongfully causing harm. The courts' refusal may, to repeat, be influenced by causal considerations; but, strictly speaking, a refusal to impose liability for causing some harm cannot be a causal ground of decision.

4. If *Palsgraf* had been a battery rather than a negligence case, could Mrs. Palsgraf have recovered damages under the doctrine of transferred intent? More generally, is the scope of liability broader in intentional than unintentional tort cases? Should it be? Authority on this question is surprisingly sparse. See Derosier v. New England Telephone and Telegraph Co., 81 N.H. 451, 130 A. 145 (1925); Note, The Tie That Binds: Liability of Intentional Tort-feasors for Extended Consequences, 14 Stan. L. Rev. 362 (1962). Perhaps the scope of liability in intentional tort cases only looks broader, in the following sense: intentionally dangerous conduct is usually more dangerous than unintentionally dangerous conduct, and the greater the danger the greater the range of foreseeable injuries.

Firman v. Sacia
7 App. Div. 579, 184 N.Y.S.2d 945 (1959)

GIBSON, J.

In a case of first impression, the Special Term has held legally insufficient a complaint which would relate the infant plaintiff's personal injuries from gunshot wounds inflicted by one Richard Springstead on March 12, 1957 to defendant's negligent operation of his automobile on February 6, 1950, whereby Springstead, then three years old, was struck by the automobile and caused to sustain injuries to his brain. The theory of the casual relationship asserted is amplified in a bill of particulars which states: "3. By reason of the injuries sustained by Richard Springstead as a result of the defendant's negligence, he, at the time of the shooting, was prevented from and unable to realize the nature and consequence of his act, was not able to resist pulling the trigger of the rifle, and was deprived of capacity to govern his conduct in accordance with reason." Springstead's injuries are alleged to have resulted "in brain irritability and epilepsy with psychomotor equivalent of epileptic attacks." A supplemental bill of particulars states: "Medically speaking it will not be claimed that he is or was 'insane' or 'incompetent.'" There follows in this bill, however, an indefinite and conditional suggestion of insanity "in the legal sense." . . .

Assuming, as we must, that defendant's conduct was negligent as it related to the rights of the Springstead child, the fact of negligence was not, of course, thereby established for all purposes or as necessarily definitive of defendant's relationship to others. If, in his conduct, there was no risk of danger to this infant plaintiff "reasonably to be perceived," there was no breach of duty, or negligence, as to him. Palsgraf v. Long Island R.R. Co. In this case, the order and judgment seem to us sustainable on the grounds that, as in *Palsgraf*, the risk was not "within the range of apprehension." Whether the doctrine of foreseeability be regarded as the measure of a duty or as a test of proximate causation seems of little moment as respects the result here. If there is, indeed, a distinction, its academic nature is implicit in the comparatively recent holding that the rule in *Palsgraf* "lends guidance in evaluating the proximate causal factor in a given fact situation" and, at the same time "does suggest the only available co-ordinates — duty and foreseeability." . . . [T]he asserted result in this case, when viewed in retrospect, seems so "highly extraordinary" as to negate any theory of defendant's responsibility.

Although, as we have found, the determination at Special Term was proper under the principle of the *Palsgraf* case, consideration of the problem as one of proximate cause, without recourse to the test of foreseeability as such, as strongly mandates the same result. Even if some basis of causation in the general sense or "cause in fact" be admitted, any reasonable mind would have to account the asserted consequences of defendant's acts as too remote for legal recognition. Reasons of policy, as well as good sense, forbid an illimitable extension of liability for a train of events proceeding into the indefinite future with arguable dependence (usually in decreasing degree) upon the original act. . . .

Notes

1. Did plaintiff sue the wrong party? In general, does crippling a person make him more or less dangerous to others?

2. Although *Palsgraf* is a much-cited case, many jurisdictions do not follow its duty, or scope of the risk, approach, but, like Judge Andrews, prefer the proximate-cause formulation. In these jurisdictions the term "proximate cause" may, as mentioned, comprehend both "cause in fact," discussed in the part of this chapter preceding the *Palsgraf* opinion, and "legal causation," which is to say policy reasons, not strictly causal, for limiting the scope of liability. (Yet the attribution of causal status to an antecedent condition may itself be motivated by policy considerations, may it not?)

3. Which, if any, of the interpretations of *Palsgraf* presented in Note 2 following that case explains the result in *Firman*?

4. Here are some more freak-accident cases. After reading them, ask yourself: Were they correctly decided? Are they consistent with each other? Are they consistent with *Palsgraf*?

In re Polemis & Furness, Withy & Co., [1921] 3 K.B. 560. A longshore-man deemed to be a servant of defendants dropped a plank into one of the holds in plaintiff's ship while unloading. The plank, in hitting the floor of the hold, struck a spark which ignited benzine vapor in the hold. The ship was destroyed in the resulting fire. Defendants were held liable for plaintiff's damages.

Hines v. Morrow, 236 S.W. 183 (Tex. Civ. App. 1921). A traveler's car got stuck in mud. The mud was there because of the defendant railroad's failure to comply with its statutory duty to keep the highways at railroad crossings in proper condition. Plaintiff, a workman employed by one Ball, went with Ball to try to extricate the car from the mud. Plaintiff had an artificial foot. It got stuck in a hidden mudhole at the site. He tried to extricate himself by grabbing for the car that was at that moment pulling the traveler's car out of the mud, but in doing so he got entangled with the rope connecting the two cars, and his good leg was mangled and had to be ampu-tated. Defendant was held liable for plaintiff's injury.

Johnson v. Kosmos Portland Cement Co., 64 F.2d 193 (6th Cir. 1933). Gases collected in the hold of defendant's barge because of defendant's negligence in failing to clear the hold properly. A bolt of lightning struck the barge, causing an explosion that killed the plaintiffs' decedents, who were working on the barge at the time. The trial court gave judgment for the defendant on the ground

> that the striking of the barge by lightning, and the explosion of the gases therein as a result thereof, was not such a natural and probable consequence of leaving the gases in the barge as should have reasonably been anticipated by the respondent [i.e., defendant] at the time it permitted decedents to begin work on the barge. . . .

Id. at 194. The court of appeals disagreed, and reversed. The dissent stated:

> Had the gas exploded spontaneously, there would be an unbroken chain be-tween the negligence and the injury. Had it attracted the lightning, the chain of causation would still be complete. In either case the explosion would be the direct or, as sometimes said, the natural consequence of the defendant's negli-gence, and thus the proximate result. But the factual case is different. The gas was inactive or dormant, and a new outside force intervened and caused the explosion. This seems to me to make the defendant's negligence remote unless it created a situation where there was foreseeable danger of the intervention of the new force. I think the danger was not foreseeable. Thunderstorms, it is true, do come, lightning does strike, and men do take out insurance against these risks. So do men run trains into open switches and automobiles into railway cars standing on highways. Many things happen that reasonable foresight cannot anticipate; and so it is that a foreseeable thing is not that which has happened or may happen again but which "could reasonably have been foreseen in the light

of all the attending circumstances." I think a stroke of lightning is beyond the scope of this expectation.

Id. at 197.

Leoni v. Reinhard, 327 Pa. 391, 194 A. 490 (1937). A piece of unslaked lime fell from defendant's truck onto the highway. Plaintiff, a 12-year-old boy, was walking along the highway when the lime fell, and he picked it up and placed it in a bucket of damp earth and fish worms that he was carrying. The lime exploded because of a chemical reaction with the damp earth, causing serious injury to plaintiff's eyes. Defendant was held not liable. The court explained:

> In our opinion, even extraordinary prevision could not have foreseen the sequence of agencies that combined to injure the plaintiff. Over these agencies the defendant had neither influence nor control. Hence by no exercise of vigilance on his part could he have anticipated or prevented their occurrence. The explosion did not happen from the fact alone that the minor plaintiff picked up a piece of unslaked lime which had fallen from defendant's truck. Nor did it occur because the plaintiff dropped that piece of lime into the bucket he was carrying at the time. It was the contact of the lime with the damp earth in the bucket, and the further fact that the earth possessed sufficient moisture to create hydration (but insufficient liquid to absorb the resultant gases), that caused the explosion. There was nothing in the falling of a piece of lime from a truck onto the highway that made this outcome probable. It was necessary that a succession of new and independent factors intervene before the explosion could occur. Hence the injury to the plaintiff was not the proximate result of driving a truck loaded with lime upon the highway. The hazards that materialized into injury were so remote and unlikely that the defendant was under no duty to anticipate their existence. Accordingly negligence has not been shown by the pleadings.

Id. at 394-395, 194 A. at 491-492. Molliere v. American Insurance Group, 158 So. 2d 279 (La. App. 1963), is a similar case with a similar result. The driver of a truck carrying crabs let one of the crabs fall on the ground; he was negligent in doing so. The crab frightened a child, who ran in front of the truck and was injured. The court held that the driver's negligence was not a proximate cause of the injury.

In re Guardian Casualty Co., 253 App. Div. 360, 2 N.Y.S.2d 232, aff'd, 278 N.Y. 674, 16 N.E.2d 397 (1938). A collision between an automobile and a taxicab caused by the concurrent negligence of both drivers was held the proximate cause of a death that occurred 20 minutes later. A woman on the sidewalk was struck by a stone which fell while the taxicab was being removed from a building against which it had been propelled with such force that parts of the structure had been loosened. For criticism of this decision, see Petition of Kinsman Transit Co., 338 F.2d 708, 724-725 n.10 (2d Cir. 1964).

United Novelty Co. v. Daniels, 42 So. 2d 395 (Miss. 1949). Plaintiff's decedent was fatally burned while cleaning coin-operated machines as an employee of appellant:

> The work was being performed in a room eight by ten feet in area, in which there was a gas heater then lighted with an open flame. The cleaning was being done with gasolene. The testimony yields the unique circumstance that the immediate activating cause of a resultant explosion was the escape of a rat from the machine, and its disappointing attempt to seek sanctuary beneath the heater whereat it overexposed itself and its impregnated coat, and returned in haste and flames to its original hideout. Even though such be a fact, it is not a controlling fact, and serves chiefly to ratify the conclusion that the room was permeated with gasolene vapors. Negligence would be predicated of the juxta-position of the gasolene and the open flame. Under similar circumstances, the particular detonating agency, whether, as here, an animate version of the classic lighted squib, or as in Johnson v. Kosmos Portland Cement Co., a bolt of lightning, was incidental except as illustrating the range of foreseeability.

Id. at 396.

Ferroggiaro v. Bowline, 153 Cal. App. 2d 759, 315 P.2d 446 (1957). Defendant Tipri, while driving, negligently collided with a power pole. The collision knocked out the traffic lights at an intersection nearby. Plaintiff's decedent was killed in a collision with another car at the intersection; both cars were approaching the intersection when the lights went out. Whether the accident was a foreseeable consequence of Tipri's negligence was held to be a jury question.

Crankshaw v. Piedmont Driving Club, 115 Ga. App. 820, 156 S.E.2d 208 (1967). It was held that the following allegations demonstrated as a matter of law that defendant's alleged negligence was not the proximate cause of plaintiff's injury:

> Plaintiff Elizabeth Crankshaw seeks damages against Piedmont Driving Club, Inc. alleging that on January 15, 1966, she in company with R. M. Harris and Miss Arlene Harris patronized the dining room of the defendant; that Miss Harris ordered shrimp and began eating same at which time she noticed a peculiar odor emanating from the shrimp dish causing her to feel nauseated; that Miss Harris excused herself and proceeded toward the rest room; shortly thereafter plaintiff proceeded toward the rest room to give aid and comfort to Miss Harris and as plaintiff entered the rest room she saw Miss Harris leaning over one of the bowls; that "unbeknownst to plaintiff, Miss Harris had vomited just inside the entrance to the rest room" and that as she hurried toward her she "stepped into the vomit, and her feet flew out from under her," causing her to fall and break her hip. The petition alleged negligence of the defendant in selling unwholesome, deleterious food and in failing to clean up the floor of the rest room or to warn plaintiff of the condition of the floor.

Id. at 820, 156 S.E.2d at 209.

Talbert v. Talbert
22 Misc. 2d 782, 199 N.Y.S.2d 212 (1960)

SWEENEY, J.

This is a motion to dismiss the complaint. . . .

Plaintiff alleges that on January 7, 1958, at about 12:30 o'clock in the afternoon he was on defendant's premises by invitation; that defendant's wife apprised plaintiff of the fact that defendant was despondent and emotionally distressed; that plaintiff, at defendant's wife's request, went to look for defendant to bring him to the house for lunch; that plaintiff found defendant in his automobile in the garage, the front doors of which were open; that defendant at that time indicated a desire to do away with himself.

It is further alleged that plaintiff requested defendant to join the family for lunch and that defendant responded "saying he would follow plaintiff into the house and that he would be right in for lunch." It is then alleged that plaintiff returned to the house and when defendant did not follow after a short time had elapsed, plaintiff left the house again to request defendant to come for lunch; that at about 1:00 o'clock plaintiff discovered the open front doors to the garage were closed and locked and plaintiff's attempts to open them were futile; that plaintiff observed defendant sitting in the car slumped over the wheel, the motor of the automobile running and apparently attempting to take his own life.

Then follows the allegation that in an attempt to rescue defendant, plaintiff quickly ran to the rear of the garage and in order to gain access to the building through the rear door thereof smashed the rear door window with his hand and arm and as a result thereof he was injured.

The complaint alleges that the defendant was negligent in disregarding his duty to the plaintiff by causing plaintiff to undertake the rescue. The complaint does not state, but it is a fact that the plaintiff is the son of the defendant.

The plaintiff's action is based on negligence and of necessity involves the legal theory of rescue as developed by the Courts of this State.

The plaintiff here was attempting the rescue of the defendant, his father. A person who is injured while attempting to rescue one put in peril through the negligence of a third party, can recover from the third party. Wagner v. International Railway Company; Eckert v. Long Island Railroad Company.

In order that there may be actionable negligence there must be some legal duty or obligation on the part of the person against whom the claim of negligence is made. Palsgraf v. Long Island Railroad Company.

In the case under consideration, the defendant owed a legal duty to those in the immediate vicinity who might attempt to rescue him from his self-imposed plight. This is no less true because the act was a positive one, an attempted suicide, not a simple act of negligence. . . .

... The defendant, by locking all doors to the garage as he did and by sitting in the car with the motor running, exposed himself to undue risk of injury. This act was wrongful to plaintiff because it caused that undue risk of injury to defendant which consequently brought about the attempt to rescue him to plaintiff's injury.

The defendant further contends in support of the motion that he could not have reasonably foreseen such an attempted rescue by the plaintiff. I cannot agree with this contention either. The plaintiff is the son of the defendant. Just prior to the attempted suicide he talked with the defendant. The defendant knew he was to be in this vicinity and could have easily anticipated that when he did not follow plaintiff to the house defendant would return to the garage. They were undoubtedly friendly and an attempt by a son to preserve the life of his father is most reasonable to believe. It was not necessary that the defendant reasonably foresee the manner in which the attempted rescue was going to be made. It is sufficient that the situation in which defendant placed himself was a dangerous one and invited rescue. The foreseeability of the act, therefore, is a question of fact for the jury. . . .

Notes

1. Wagner v. International Ry Co., 232 N.Y. 176, 133 N.E. 437 (1921), cited by the court in *Talbot*, is another famous Cardozo opinion. In *Wagner*, plaintiff and his cousin were passengers on one of defendant's trains. There was a violent lurch, and the cousin was hurled from the train. Plaintiff, a member of the search party looking for his cousin's body, was hurt when he fell off a bridge while searching. The court held that plaintiff's suit against the railroad was not barred on causal grounds, stating:

> Danger invites rescue. The cry of distress is the summons to relief. The law does not ignore these reactions of the mind in tracing conduct to its consequences. It recognizes them as normal. It places their effects within the range of the natural and probable. The wrong that imperils life is a wrong to the imperiled victim; it is a wrong also to the rescuer. The state that leaves an opening in a bridge is liable to the child that falls into the stream, but liable also to the parent who plunges to its aid. The railroad company whose train approaches without signal is a wrongdoer toward the traveler surprised between the rails, but a wrongdoer also to the bystander who drags him from the path.

Id. at 18, 133 N.E. at 437-438. *Wagner* is a famous leading case. But what precisely does it add to *Eckert*? Suppose in *Wagner* that someone had been injured aiding the plaintiff when he was hurt. Would that person have been able to recover damages from the railroad also?

2. Consider the unusual fact pattern in St. Louis-San Francisco R. Co. v. Ginn, 264 P.2d 351 (Okla. 1953). One of defendant's trains set fire to grass on

the railroad's right of way adjacent to plaintiff's farm. When he discovered the fire, plaintiff got his tractor and plowed furrows along his property line in an attempt to halt the spread of the fire to his farm. He had just completed the last furrow and was driving his tractor to a safe place so that he could return and help extinguish the fire when the tractor struck a root or tree limb, which flew up and hit him in the face, injuring his eye. The court held that plaintiff's suit (based on defendant's violation of a statute imposing strict liability for damage caused by fires set by railroads) was not barred on causal grounds. Is this result consistent with *Wagner?* Is it consistent with *Berry?*

3. A case with a strange mixture of *Wagner* and *Palsgraf* elements is Atchison, Topeka & Santa Fe Ry. Co. v. Calhoun, 213 U.S. 1 (1909). Mrs. Calhoun and her son, the plaintiff, a boy a little less than three years old, were passengers on defendant's train. Because of negligence by the trainmen, she was not informed in a timely manner of the train's arrival at her destination. By the time she reached the platform of the car to get off, the train had started up again, and she handed her child to a passenger who had already gotten off and was standing on the station platform. One Jones, whom the passenger erroneously supposed to be an employee of the railroad, took the child out of the passenger's arms and began running with it alongside the ever more rapidly moving train in an effort to return the child to Mrs. Calhoun. Jones ran to the end of the station platform and there collided with a baggage cart, dropping the child under the car, where he was injured. The Court held that Jones' reckless act, and not the negligence of the railroad in failing to give Mrs. Calhoun timely notice of the train's arrival at her destination, was the proximate cause of the accident. Is this result correct?

Leposki v. Railway Express Agency, Inc.
297 F.2d 849 (3d Cir. 1962)

STALEY, J.

In this negligence action for personal injuries and damage to property, a verdict was returned for defendant, and plaintiffs appeal, contending that the district court erroneously charged the jury. Jurisdiction was based on diversity of citizenship, and Pennsylvania law applies.

The facts are not in dispute. On December 5, 1956, a driver making deliveries for the defendant Railway Express Agency, Inc., parked a truck near the curb and against traffic on Righter Street in Philadelphia. The parked truck faced uphill and pitched in towards the curb, with the gasoline tank intake pipe located near the center of the left side. The result was that gasoline dripped out from the top of the pipe into the gutter. While playing nearby, two young boys saw the gasoline and one of them dropped a lighted match into the gutter beneath the pipe, where the gasoline caught fire. After unsuccessfully attempting to extinguish the fire, the driver called the fire department, moved the truck, and stopped in front of plaintiffs' home. Flames and gasoline spread to the house, causing property damage and personal injuries to plaintiffs.

The boys are not parties to this action. One of the defenses raised was that the boy's act in igniting the gasoline constituted an independent intervening act that superseded defendant's negligence. In this regard, the district court charged the jury:

> Assuming, however, you do find that the defendant was negligent, before you can even then arrive at a verdict for the plaintiffs, you next ask yourself the question — should the defendant be excused from liability to the plaintiffs by the intervening act of the boy in igniting the gasoline as he did? Could the defendant reasonably foresee that this might happen? That is, that the children would come along, see the fluid, and light it to see whether it would burn? Could it have been anticipated by the defendant? If you decide that it could, you may find for the plaintiffs. If it could not have been anticipated or foreseen, your verdict should be for the defendant.

We agree with plaintiffs that this part of the charge was incorrect and that their motion for a new trial should have been granted.

In Pennsylvania, an intervening negligent act by a third person does not, in all cases, constitute a superseding cause relieving an antecedent wrongdoer from liability for negligently creating a dangerous condition. The act is superseding only if it was so extraordinary as not to have been reasonably foreseeable. The extraordinary nature of the intervening act is, however, determined by looking back from the harm or injury and tracing the sequence of events by which it was produced . . . i.e., the events are viewed retrospectively and not prospectively.

. . . Whether an intervening act constitutes a superseding cause is a question that is more readily resolved in hindsight, and that which appears to be extraordinary in the abstract may prove to be otherwise when considered in light of surrounding circumstances that existed at the time of the accident. It may be that a particular defendant is unaware of the facts that led to events giving rise to the intervening act, yet the jury, viewing the matter retrospectively, could properly conclude that the act was not extraordinary. Here, the jury was told that defendant would not be liable though found to be negligent unless it could have foreseen and anticipated that the boys would come along, see the gasoline, and ignite it in the manner in which they did, in order to determine whether it would burn. This was a clear direction to the jury to consider the events prospectively. The jury should have been told to consider the fact that Righter Street is in a residential section of Philadelphia, and that the place where the accident happened is near an elementary school. Children played in the area. Also, children while playing find matches, and in satisfying their natural curiosity, will attempt to ignite a fluid to see if it will burn. This is what happened here. The fact that defendant lacked knowledge of the surrounding circumstances when the truck was parked has no bearing on its liability, for the law required it to act in a reasonably prudent manner at all times. That would be particularly true where, as here, the jury could very well find that the intervening act was merely a reaction to a dangerous situation that defendant itself created. Considering the intervening act in light of the circumstances that prevailed at the time defendant parked the truck, can it be said that the boy's act was extraordinary? That is how the jury should have been instructed to view the question. . . .

Notes

1. What is the point of "retrospective foreseeability"? Is it that if we can still describe an accident as "unforeseeable" after the accident is described to us, this must mean we are skeptical whether the defendant's conduct really was the cause of plaintiff's injury?

2. Why should it make a difference whether the area where the truck stopped was near an elementary school? In Watson v. Kentucky & Indiana Bridge & Ry. Co., 137 Ky. 619, 126 S.W. 146 (1910), a tank car was derailed because of defendant's negligence and spilled gasoline. A passerby dropped a lighted match into the pool of gasoline, causing a fire that damaged plaintiff's property. The court stated that if the passerby deliberately dropped the match, defendant would not be liable. But would that case be distinguishable from Leposki? Would it be from Calhoun? Would it be from Aune v. Oregon Trunk Ry., 151 Or. 622, 51 P.2d 663 (1935), where defendant left his boxcars unlocked, hobos congregated there and set a fire that destroyed plaintiff's buildings, and the court held that defendant was not responsible for plaintiff's loss?

Wannebo v. Gates
227 Minn. 194, 34 N.W.2d 695 (1948)

MAGNEY, J. . . .

On July 2, 1947, defendant Frances L. Gates parked a car owned by defendant Elnathan Gates on a public street in a business area in Minneapolis. She went shopping and left the car unattended and the doors and ignition unlocked. The key was not removed from the ignition switch and taken with her. The car was stolen. That night, at about 11:30, the stolen car, negligently operated by a person unknown, collided with plaintiff's automobile, damaging the same and injuring plaintiff. . . .

A part of §11 of an ordinance of Minneapolis, in force at that time, reads as follows: "Every person parking a passenger automobile on any public street or alley in the City shall lock the ignition, remove the key and take the same with him."

In this appeal, there is no question raised as to the negligence of defendants. They deny liability solely on the ground that the damage complained of was not the proximate result of a violation of the ordinance. . . .

. . . [Ross v. Hartman, 139 F.2d 14 (D.C. Cir. 1943),] is the leading case holding an owner liable. In that case, defendant's agent left a truck unattended in a public alley, with the ignition unlocked and the key in the switch. This was in violation of a traffic ordinance. There is nothing in the statement of facts to indicate whether the accident happened while the thief was in flight. All the opinion recites is that "Within two hours an unknown person drove the truck away and negligently ran over the appellant." That would seem to indicate that the thief was still in flight. . . .

In the instant case, it is a fair assumption from the complaint that the thief was no longer in flight when the collision occurred. The accident happened about five miles from the scene of the theft and several hours after the same had taken place. What we might hold if the accident had taken place while the thief was in flight from the scene of his crime is of no importance here, as the thief was no longer in flight. Under our facts, we are one step farther removed from the theft. It has been suggested that a thief, fleeing in a car which he has just stolen, would, while driving, be nervous and full of fear of apprehension, and that these emotions would naturally make him an unsafe driver, which might be anticipated by an owner who left his car doors and ignition unlocked with the key in the ignition switch. But if the accident took place hours, days, or weeks after the flight had terminated, one could hardly say that the owner should anticipate that the thief or his successor in possession would be more likely to have an accident caused by his negligence than the ordinary car operator. The thief in the instant case was not in flight at the time of the accident. We are, of course, not suggesting what our holding might be if the accident had happened through the negligence of the thief while still in flight from the scene of his theft. Here, the nature of the admitted negligent act is such that the criminal act of stealing the car might reasonably have been foreseen. By that criminal act itself, the causal chain may not be broken. The question here, however, is how far that chain may be extended and still hold the original negligent actor liable. Even if one should be of the opinion that the tortious acts of a thief in fleeing in a stolen car from the scene of his crime would be within a foreseeable risk, where a car was left unlocked with the key in the ignition switch on a busy public street, yet it does not follow that the original actor should be held liable for the tortious acts of the thief or his successor in possession of the car if such acts took place hours, days, weeks, or months after the flight from the scene of the theft had terminated. . . .

Notes

1. Does the court's distinction between an accident while the thief is in flight and an accident that occurs later on have anything to do, really, with foreseeability? Doesn't the distinction follow directly from the *Berry* line of cases?

2. A later Minnesota case indicates that the court would have held defendant liable if the accident had occurred in the course of the thief's flight. See State Farm Mutual Automobile Ins. Co. v. Grain Belt Breweries, Inc., 309 Minn. 376, 245 N.W.2d 186 (1976). A majority of states, however, continue to deny liability in "key" cases. See, e.g., Dix v. Motor Market, Inc., 540 S.W.2d 927 (Mo. App. 1976).

3. At least one of the cases upholding liability, Zinck v. Whelan, 120 N.J. Super. 432, 294 A.2d 727 (1972), rejects a categorical distinction between accidents occurring in the course of flight and those occurring later. In *Zinck*, the accident occurred two and one-half days after the theft of the car. Nevertheless, the court stated, a "reasonable jury, in our view, might conclude that the likely potential for disastrous driving by the defendant juvenile incident to his misconduct and inferential inexperience, guilt-consciousness or carefreeness was not fully spent" when the accident occurred. Id. at 450, 294 A.2d at 737. Do you agree? Incidentally, the court mentioned statistics indicating that the accident rate for stolen cars is 200 times that for other cars, and that in a very high percentage of car thefts the owner left his keys in the ignition. These statistics provide powerful support for liability.

4. Perhaps surprisingly, the California court has been reluctant to recognize liability in "key" cases. The leading case is Richards v. Stanley, 43 Cal. 2d 60, 271 P.2d 23 (1954), which was, however, modified in Hergenrether v. East, 61 Cal. 2d 440, 393 P.2d 164 (1964).

Williams v. State of New York
308 N.Y. 548, 127 N.E.2d 545 (1955)

FROESSEL, J. A judgment of $16,826.30 has been awarded to the respondent, executrix of one Albert Williams, who died of a brain hemorrhage brought on by fright when one William Kennedy, a convict, escaped from the Auburn prison farm and induced Williams to drive him to Syracuse in Williams' truck. The Appellate Division has affirmed by a divided court.

Kennedy, prior to the time in question, had been convicted of attempted robbery, third degree, the charge specifying that he "with armed accomplice robbed taxi driver of money and watch at night." The accomplice was his brother, the amount taken $12, and the armed weapon was a toy pistol. He was received at Elmira Reformatory in December, 1948, and paroled in July, 1950. One month later he was returned to prison for violating his parole, and was then transferred to Auburn State Prison late in August. He would have been eligible for parole board consideration again nearly two years later, in July, 1952. In the ensuing eight months at Auburn, he was punished four times (with forfeitures of "good time") for violations of prison discipline. These violations, however, were found to be of a "minor nature," involving horseplay in the dining room, splashing water, wasting four slices of bread, and refusing to co-operate with the guard assigned to awaken prisoners in the morning.

On April 21, 1951, Kennedy, having previously been declared eligible for outside work "in accordance with the administrative rules of the prison," was assigned to the State prison farm at Sennett, about four miles east of Auburn Prison, with a group of other prisoners and guards. The prison farm system is authorized by section 182 of the Correction Law. At the prison farm, prisoners are supervised under conditions of "minimum security." This practice of relaxing security restrictions at prison farms is "proper and approved" in this State, and eligibility for such work is determined by the principal keeper of the prison.

As afore-mentioned, on April 21, 1951, a little over a year before he would again become eligible for parole, Kennedy was among twenty-five prisoners assigned to the farm and was, with seven other prisoners, working under the supervision of one of the two guards on duty there that day. Both guards were unarmed. The prison farm is not fenced and there are no pickets, towers or lookouts. At times the prisoners were allowed to work out of the view of the guards. At about 12:30 P.M. that day, the guard in charge of Kennedy's group went to another part of the farm and remained out of sight for fifteen minutes. When he returned, Kennedy was missing. . . .

The trial court found that, at about 2:00 P.M., the escaped prisoner, "by use of force, threats and duress," compelled Albert Williams, a local farmer, to "drive and transport" him "in attempting to perfect his escape." At about 2:20 P.M., Williams and a man later identified as Kennedy were seen driving easterly in Williams' truck on Route 20 between Williams' home and Skaneateles. They halted for "10, 20 or 30 seconds" in front of a gas station, where a witness, one Donald Clark, could see that Williams "was sort of gesturing with his hands" before they drove on.

At about 2:30 P.M., some ten minutes later, another witness who had known Williams for twenty-five years and had personal knowledge of Williams' ordinary manner of driving his truck, saw that truck going easterly toward Syracuse from Marcellus at a "fast rate of speed" — "probably 45 or 50" — with Williams "hanging onto the wheel." A man was seated beside him whom the witness did not recognize.

At 3:15 P.M., Williams was found in Marcellus sitting on the running board of his truck which was headed in the direction of Skaneateles. He had been vomiting and was apparently very ill. An ambulance was called and he was taken to the hospital. The afore-mentioned "force, threats and duress" and "emotional stress" which Kennedy caused Williams to endure "caused a hemorrhage of his brain" from which he died the next day.

Kennedy was apprehended by a police officer in Syracuse at about 5:30 P.M., the same day of the escape. He was carrying a sweater which Williams had been wearing earlier in the day and a sharp blade, six inches long, which had been part of a farm implement of a type that could have been taken from any of several machines or junk piles on the prison farm.

An autopsy revealed no bruises or other signs of trauma upon Williams' body, and there was no proof that Kennedy had committed any battery upon Williams. The trial court so found, and noted that "the record is devoid of a showing of physical impact contributing to the fright which resulted in Williams' death." It also concluded that "the negligence of the State of New York in permitting Kennedy to escape and in failing diligently to search for him was the proximate cause of the conscious pain and suffering and of the death of Albert Williams."

The courts below have thus found that the State was negligent in *guarding* and *apprehending* Kennedy, and that the latter, by forcing Williams to drive him to Syracuse, frightened Williams and caused his fatal brain hemorrhage. Both the findings of negligence on the part of the State and of Kennedy's responsibility for Williams' death have support in the record before us. Nevertheless, the judgment below must be reversed and the claim dismissed, for, even where negligence and injury are both properly found, the negligent party can be liable only where the negligence charged was the proximate cause of the injury received. The Court of Claims has found proximate causation here, but this, we hold, was error. . . .

The State has frequently been held liable for the consequences of its breach of duty to protect others from the acts of the mentally ill confined to State institutions. In such cases, where the confinement is not in the nature of *punishment*, but rather of *restraint* and, where possible, cure, there is both a duty to the inmate to provide him with reasonable rehabilitational conditions under the circumstances and to the outside public to restrain the dangerous, or potentially dangerous, so that they may not harm others. Between the two "contending interests," it has been said, "A balance must be struck." The risks to be perceived with the mentally ill who are irresponsible defines the State's duty to protect others from them.

Kennedy, by contrast, was not a psychiatric patient; indeed, an examination by the prison psychiatrist in February, 1950, found no indication of psychosis — the worst that could be said of him in that report was that he was "socially maladjusted." Nor was Auburn Prison in any sense a mental institution or hospital. If the jailer owes a duty to the outside world with regard to the same persons who have been placed in his custody for a variety of illegal activities, it is to assure the public that such criminals will remain in his care until, by the course of time or a proper legal determination, they have been declared free of their debts to society. *Restraint* and *punishment* must be distinguished here. In the instant case, the convict who was allowed to escape had been imprisoned for a *toy* pistol holdup, and had a relatively tranquil record while in prison. From nothing in the record and exhibits below can we derive any basis for the foreseeability of his conduct toward Williams.

Despite the Court of Claims' technically accurate description of the original toy pistol robbery as a "crime of violence," it was not, realistically speaking, the act of a desperado inveterately given to assault or violence. At worst, if we study the account of the crime in Kennedy's "Pre-Classification Report" at Elmira Reformatory, it appears to have been the act of an "unemployed and homeless" young man committed after he "had been drinking a great deal." Although these details do not alter the fact that Kennedy committed a crime for which the State was entitled to impose imprisonment, they do indicate that the so-called "crime of violence" for which he was imprisoned could not be said to have foreshadowed Kennedy's alleged assault upon Williams. . . .

. . . It is of some note that the Court of Claims found no fault or negligence in the fact that a man with Kennedy's background was assigned to "minimum security" farm work "in accordance with the administrative rules of the prison," an assignment which is regarded by the prisoners as a "privilege" accorded only those few [here, 25 out of 1,600] whose records merit the lowered security restrictions of the outside work gangs. . . .

But, even beyond the fact that fundamental legal principles will not permit affirmance here, public policy also requires that the State be not held liable. To hold otherwise would impose a heavy responsibility upon the State, or dissuade the wardens and principal keepers of our prison system from continued experimentation with "minimum security" work details — which provide a means for encouraging better-risk prisoners to exercise their senses of responsibility and honor and so prepare themselves for their eventual return to society. Since 1917, the Legislature has expressly provided for out-of-prison work, and its intention should be respected without fostering the reluctance of prison officials to assign eligible men to minimum security work, lest they thereby give rise to costly claims against the State, or indeed inducing the State itself to terminate this "salutary procedure" looking toward rehabilitation. Kennedy was chosen with a small, specially selected group of trusted men, who, in a sense, on the basis of their good records, were given a limited form of liberty, less than parole, under "minimum security," which the trial court found "is a proper and approved prison practice in the State of New York."

Certainly there is no merit to the contention that prisons will become more carelessly guarded by a holding of nonliability here. In view of the duties which the Legislature has imposed upon jailers to apprehend escaped prisoners and the disciplinary measures which careless prison guards must face, such fears are unwarranted.

The State also urges that it cannot be liable for the particular injury here involved — the hemorrhage due to fright — and resulting in death, where, as the courts below have found, there was no showing that Kennedy committed a battery, or otherwise produced an impact, upon the person of Williams. In the absence of any proximate causation between the State's act and Williams' death, we do not reach this question.

The judgment of the Appellate Division and that of the Court of Claims should be reversed and the claim dismissed, without costs.

Notes

1. Is the dispute here really about causation, or about negligence? Was defendant's conduct negligent under the Hand formula? What is the bearing of the court's discussion of public policy on this question?

2. Why should the state have a higher duty of care with regard to injury caused by mental patients?

Dziokonski v. Babineau
375 Mass. 555, 380 N.E.2d 1295 (1978)

WILKINS, J.

These appeals require us to reexamine the question whether a person who negligently causes emotional distress which leads to physical injuries may be liable for those injuries even if the injured person neither was threatened with nor sustained any direct physical injury. At the heart of the plaintiffs' claims is the argument that this court should abandon the so called "impact" rule of Spade v. Lynn & Boston R.R., 168 Mass. 285, 290, 47 N.E. 88 (1897), which denies recovery for physical injuries arising solely from negligently caused mental distress. We agree that the rule of the *Spade* case should be abandoned. Our inquiry does not cease at that point, however, because we must determine what new limits of liability are appropriate and how those limits affect the plaintiffs' decedents, parents of a child alleged to have been injured by the defendants' negligence....

On October 24, 1973, Norma Dziokonski, a minor, alighted from a motor vehicle, used as a school bus, on Route 117 in Lancaster. That motor vehicle was owned by the defendant Pelletier and operated by the defendant Kroll. A motor vehicle owned and operated by the defendant Babineau struck Norma as she was crossing the road. The complaints allege the negligence of each defendant on various grounds.

The complaint filed by the administratrix of the estate of Lorraine Dziokonski (Mrs. Dziokonski) alleges that Mrs. Dziokonski was the mother of Norma and that she "lived in the immediate vicinity of the accident, went to the scene of the accident and witnessed her daughter lying injured on the ground." Mrs. Dziokonski "suffered physical and emotional shock, distress and anguish as a result of the injury to her daughter and died while she was a passenger in the ambulance that was driving her daughter to the hospital." This complaint alleges one count for wrongful death and one count for conscious suffering against each of the three defendants.

The complaint filed by the administratrix of the estate of Anthony Dziokonski (Mr. Dziokonski) alleged the facts previously set forth and added that he was the father of Norma and the husband of Mrs. Dziokonski. Mr. Dziokonski "suffered an aggravated gastric ulcer, a coronary occlusion, physical and emotional shock, distress and anguish as a result of the injury to his daughter and the death of his wife and his death was caused thereby." This complaint similarly alleged a count for wrongful death and one count for conscious suffering against each of the three defendants.[5]

We start with an analysis of *Spade*, which announced a principle of tort law that has been limited and refined by our subsequent decisions but not heretofore abandoned. Margaret Spade had been a passenger on a crowded car of the Lynn & Boston Railroad Company late one Saturday night in February, 1895. She was so frightened by the negligent conduct of an employee of the defendant in removing an unruly passenger from the car that she sustained emotional shock and consequent physical injury. . . .

We acknowledged that fright might cause physical injury and that "it is hard on principle" to say why there should not be recovery even for the mental suffering caused by a defendant's negligence. The court concluded, however, that "in practice it is impossible satisfactorily to administer any other rule." We noted that recovery for fright or distress of mind alone is barred and, that being so, there can be no recovery for physical injuries caused solely by mental disturbance. It was said to be unreasonable to hold persons bound to anticipate and guard against fright and its consequences and thought that a contrary rule would "open a wide door for unjust claims."

In Smith v. Postal Tel. Cable Co., 174 Mass. 576, 55 N.E. 380 (1899), which applied the *Spade* rule to a case involving a claim of gross negligence, Chief Justice Holmes, speaking for the court, said that the point decided in the *Spade* case "is not put as a logical deduction from the general principles of liability in tort, but as a limitation of those principles upon purely practical grounds." Later, he described the *Spade* rule as "an arbitrary exception, based upon a notion of what is practicable."

Consistently and from its inception, the *Spade* rule has not been applied to deny recovery where immediate physical injuries result from negligently induced fright or emotional shock. Thus, recovery has been allowed "[w]hen the fright reasonably induces action which results in external injury." Cameron v. New England Tel. & Tel. Co., 182 Mass. 310, 65 N.E. 385 (1902)

5. Neither complaint involves any claim on behalf of Norma for her own injuries. We do not know whether an action has been brought by or on behalf of Norma. . . .

(defendant's negligent blasting caused the plaintiff to faint and sustain physical harm). . . .

Moreover, recovery for emotionally based physical injuries, sometimes described as "parasitic claims," has been allowed in tort cases founded on traditional negligent impact. Thus, where the plaintiff sustained direct physical injuries as a result of the defendant's negligence and the plaintiff also sustained paralysis, perhaps resulting solely from nervous shock, we did not require the plaintiff to prove that the nervous shock or paralysis was a consequence of the direct physical injuries. We note that allowing recovery for emotionally based physical injuries unrelated to the physical consequences of the negligently caused impact also presents the threat of "unjust claims," or, perhaps more exactly, the threat of exaggerated claims. . . .

We have never applied the *Spade* rule to bar recovery for intentionally caused emotional stress. . . .

Although many industrial States initially required some impact as a basis for liability for physical harm resulting from fright, that rule has been abandoned in more recent times to the point where it has been said that "the courts which deny all remedy in such cases are fighting a rear-guard action." As we have already indicated, we think the *Spade* rule should be abandoned. The threat of fraudulent claims cannot alone justify the denial of recovery in all cases. Whether a plaintiff's injuries were a reasonably foreseeable consequence of the defendant's negligence and whether the defendant caused those injuries are best left to determination in the normal manner before the trier of fact.

The abandonment of the *Spade* rule is only the beginning in the process of determining whether the complaints in these cases state valid claims for relief. The typical case involving physical harm resulting from emotional distress concerns a person who was put in fear for his own safety as a result of alleged negligence of the defendant. Here, neither Mr. nor Mrs. Dziokonski was threatened with direct, contemporaneous injury as a result of the negligence of any defendant. Thus, we must consider the extent to which any defendant in this case may be held liable to the father or the mother, each of whom sustained physical injuries as a result of emotional distress over injuries incurred by their child.

The weight of authority in this country would deny recovery in these cases. . . .

The arguments against imposing liability for a parent's injuries from shock and fear for his child have been stated clearly and forecefully in numerous opinions. See, e.g., Tobin v. Grossman, 24 N.Y.2d 609, 249 N.E. 2d 419 (1969); Amaya v. Home Ice, Fuel & Supply Co., 59 Cal. 2d 295, 379 P.2d 513 (1963); Waube v. Warrington, 216 Wis. 603, 258 N.W. 497 (1935). The reasons advanced for not permitting recovery are principally that (1) there is still a difficulty of proof of causation which has not been mitigated by any change in technology or medical science, (2) no logical justification exists for limiting recovery solely to parents who are affected physically by fear for the safety of an injured child, and (3) the extension of liability will impose an inordinate burden on defendants. In short, under this view, liability should be denied for injuries from shock and fear for another's safety regardless of (a) the relationship of the plaintiff to the accident victim, (b) the plaintiff's proximity to the accident, or (c) whether the plaintiff observed either the accident or its immediate consequences.

Until 1968, the nearly unanimous weight of authority in this country denied recovery for emotionally based physical injuries resulting from concern for the safety of another where the plaintiff was not himself threatened with contemporaneous injury. There was support for recovery where the plaintiff was himself threatened with direct bodily harm because of the defendant's conduct. This rule, known as the zone of danger test, is expressed in Restatement (Second) of Torts §313(2) (1965). It denies recovery for bodily harm "caused by emotional distress arising solely from harm or peril to a third person, unless the negligence of the actor has otherwise created an unreasonable risk of bodily harm to the [plaintiff]." . . .

The "zone of danger" rule has something to commend it as a measure of the limits of liability. It permits a relatively easy determination of the persons who might recover for emotionally caused bodily injury by including only those to whom contemporaneous bodily harm of some sort might reasonably have been foreseen. It is arguably reasonable to impose liability for the physical consequences of emotional distress where the defendant's negligent conduct might have caused physical injury by direct impact but did not. The problem with the zone of danger rule, however, is that it is an inadequate measure of the reasonable foreseeability of the possibility of physical injury resulting from a parent's anxiety arising from harm to his child. The reasonable foreseeability of such a physical injury to a parent does not turn on whether that parent was or was not a reasonable prospect for a contemporaneous injury because of the defendant's negligent conduct. Although the zone of danger rule tends to produce more reasonable results than the *Spade* rule and provides a means of limiting the scope of a defendant's liability, it lacks strong logical support.

In 1968, the Supreme Court of California, by a divided court (four to three), broke the solid ranks, overruled its decision in Amaya v. Home Ice, Fuel & Supply Co., and held that a cause of action was properly stated on behalf of a mother, in no danger herself, who witnessed her minor daughter's death in a motor vehicle accident allegedly caused by the defendant's negligence, and who sustained emotional disturbance and shock to her nervous system which caused her physical and mental pain and suffering. Dillon v. Legg, 68 Cal. 2d 728, 441 P.2d 912 (1968). An intermediate appellate court in California has since applied the reasoning of Dillon v. Legg to permit recovery by a mother who came on the scene of the accident but did not witness it. Archibald v. Braverman, 275 Cal. App. 2d 253, 79 Cal. Rptr. 723 (1969). That court said, "Manifestly, the shock of seeing a child severely injured immediately after the tortious event may be just as profound as that experienced in witnessing the accident itself."[10] . . .

It is not argued seriously here, nor has it been regularly a basis for decisions denying liability, that the threat of fraudulent claims requires the adoption of a rule denying recovery to a parent who sustains physical harm from distress over peril to his child. The facts of cases of this character involve tortious injury to the child and substantial physical consequences to the parent. The tortfeasor is not confronted with the results of a fleeting instance of fear or excitement of which he might be unaware and against which he would be unable to present a defense. The fact that some claims might be manufactured or improperly expanded cannot justify the wholesale rejection of all claims. Of course, there is no suggestion that the physical injuries to Mr. and Mrs. Dziokonski were contrived. We have rejected the idea that tort liability in particular classes of cases must be denied because of the threat of fraud. . . . We have chosen to leave the detection of fraud and collusion to the adversary process.

The fact that the causal connection between a parent's emotional response to peril to his child and the parent's resulting physical injuries is difficult to prove or disprove cannot justify denying all recovery. . . .

Every effort must be made to avoid arbitrary lines which "unnecessarily produce incongruous and indefensible results." The focus should be on underlying principles. In cases of this character, there must be both a substantial physical injury and proof that the injury was caused by the defendant's negligence. Beyond this, the determination whether there should be liability for the injury sustained depends on a number of factors, such as where, when, and how the injury to the third person entered into the consciousness of the claimant, and what degree there was of familial or other relationship between the claimant and the third person. It does not matter in practice whether these factors are regarded as policy considerations imposing limitations on the scope of reasonable foreseeability, or as factors bearing on the determination of reasonable foreseeability itself. . . .

With these considerations in mind, we conclude that the allegations concerning a parent who sustains substantial physical harm as a result of severe mental distress over some peril or harm to his minor child caused by the defendant's negligence state a claim for which relief might be granted, where the parent either witnesses the accident or soon comes on the scene while the child is still there. . . .

---

10. In Krouse v. Graham, 19 Cal. 3d 59, 76, 562 P.2d 1022, 1031 (1977), the California Supreme Court accepted the view of the *Archibald* case, saying "We confirm the propriety of the expression in *Archibald*, supra, that the *Dillon* requirement of 'sensory and contemporaneous observance of the accident' does not require a *visual* perception of the impact causing the death or injury" (emphasis in original).

On this premise, we think it clear that the complaint concerning Mrs. Dziokonski states a claim which withstands a motion to dismiss. The allegations of the complaint concerning Mr. Dziokonski, however, are far more indefinite. We do not know where, when or how Mr. Dziokonski came to know of the injury to his daughter and the death of his wife. We do not have a clear indication of the relationship of his discovery of this information to any mental distress and physical injury he sustained. We cannot say, as matter of law, that, within the scope of the allegations of the complaint concerning Mr. Dziokonski, there are no circumstances which could conceivably justify recovery. Consequently, we conclude that neither of the complaints should be dismissed for failure to state a claim.

Kelley v. Kokua Sales & Supply, Ltd.
56 Hawaii 204, 532 P.2d 673 (1975)

KOBAYASHI, J. . . .

[Plaintiffs appeal from a judgment dismissing, on defendants' motion for summary judgment, plaintiffs' negligence action. The ground for the dismissal was that defendants, as a matter of law, owed no duty to refrain from the negligent infliction of serious mental distress to plaintiffs' decedent, Mr. Kelley. Appellees' vehicle had on August 3, 1971, collided in Honolulu with a vehicle occupied by Frances M. Thomas, who was Mr. Kelley's daughter, and her children Kailani and Kelly.]

Some time between 8:30 and 9:00 P.M. California time on the evening of August 3, 1971, Mr. Kelley's daughter, Laura, called Mr. Kelley by phone from Honolulu and informed him of the accident and the resulting deaths of his daughter, Frances, and his granddaughter, Kailani, and the critical injuries to his other granddaughter, Kelly. Shocked and grieved, he then informed his wife of the tragedy and she became hysterical. Mr. Kelley had planned to take her to a hospital for a sedative, however, he decided first to inform his brothers and sisters of the tragedy. He called his brother-in-law, Mr. Pass, and requested of Mr. Pass to purchase plane tickets to Honolulu for Mr. Kelley and his wife. During the phone conversation, Mr. Kelley complained of chest pains and asked Mr. Pass to come over as quickly as possible. Mr. Kelley apparently died immediately after his conversation with Mr. Pass. Mrs. Kelley discovered him slumped over the telephone and he was pronounced dead upon arrival at the hospital. The cause of death was established as a heart attack. . . .

. . . [I]n the factual context of the instant case, we are of the opinion that merely requiring the proof of serious mental distress, rather than minor mental distress, does not realistically and reasonably limit the liability of the appellees.

Without a reasonable and proper limitation of the scope of the duty of care owed by appellees, appellees would be confronted with an unmanageable, unbearable and totally unpredictable liability. . . .

. . . [N]otwithstanding our sympathies for the appellants for their loss and for the suffering of and death of Mr. Kelley, a reevaluation of the various considerations pertinent to the question of an untrammeled liability of the appellees leads this court to conclude, as a matter of law, that the appellees did not owe a duty to refrain (duty of care) from the negligent infliction of serious mental distress upon Mr. Kelley.

Stated in a different terminology, but reaching the same conclusion as above, we hold that the appellees could not reasonably foresee the consequences to Mr. Kelley. Clearly, Mr. Kelley's location from the scene of the accident was too remote. . . .

Notes

1. One of the influential early decisions refusing to allow damages resulting from shock caused by seeing an accident to another person, Waube v. Warrington, 216 Wis. 603, 258 N.W. 497 (1935), had relied expressly for this result on Cardozo's opinion in *Palsgraf*. The New York courts have been emphatic in adhering to this rule. See Tobin v. Grossman, 24 N.Y.2d 609, 249 N.E.2d 419 (1969). What support does the rule derive from *Palsgraf*?

2. In *Kelley*, could the argument have been made that if Mr. Kelley had such a serious heart condition that the telephone call precipitated a fatal heart attack, the chances are great that he would have died soon in any event? Would this be an argument against allowing recovery, or for discounting his damages in accordance with the principle of *Steinhauser*? In Dulieu v. White & Sons, [1901] 2 K.B. 669, the court held that "a carrier of passengers is not bound to anticipate or to guard against an injurious result which would only happen to a person of peculiar sensitiveness." Could this be the basis for the traditional reluctance to allow recovery for shock caused by seeing an accident to another person? If so, this would be an example of a case where concern over the reliability of a finding of factual causation affected a "legal causation" question.

Might the argument in this note explain why suicide is normally considered an intervening cause? In Lancaster v. Montesi, 216 Tenn. 50, 60, 390 S.W.2d 217, 222 (1955), for example, where defendant was alleged to have hounded plaintiff's decedent into killing herself, the court stated:

> The strongest possible construction of the facts as alleged is that the deceased was tired of her situation in life, and that it had become unendurable to her, and that she wrote a note to her mother in which she said, "Ma Ma, I'm

sorry. Louis has beat me enough." That then, she left her apartment and went to the Memphis-Arkansas bridge, and took her own life.

3. What explains the trend* to broader liability in emotional-distress cases? Are people more sensitive, more loving, or more squeamish today than they used to be? Are courts better able to trace the causal connection between shock and mental distress? Could the increasing use of liability insurance be a factor?

4. Was the court in *Dziokonski* correct that if damages are awarded for emotional distress in cases where there is also a physical impact, they should also be awarded in cases of emotional distress where there is no impact? How can the two types of case be distinguished?

5. Would *Dziokonski* have been decided the same way if Norma had just been scratched?

6. In Johnson v. State, 37 N.Y.2d 378, 334 N.E.2d 590 (1975), a state hospital negligently advised plaintiff that her mother had died. Plaintiff sued for funeral expenses that she incurred in reliance on the misinformation, and also for emotional distress. The court held that she could recover on both claims and that Tobin v. Grossman, where the same court had held that there was no right to recover damages for shock caused by seeing an accident to another, was not a bar. How was *Tobin* distinguishable?

7. What are the outer bounds of liability for negligent infliction of emotional distress? In Jarchow v. Transamerica Title Ins. Co., 48 Cal. App. 3d 917, 122 Cal. Rptr. 470 (1975), plaintiffs alleged that they had suffered emotional distress after discovering clouds on the title to property they were purchasing, defendant title search company having failed to notify them of the clouds before they made the purchase. And in Truestone, Inc. v. Travelers Ins. Co., 55 Cal. App. 3d 165, 127 Cal. Rptr. 386 (1976), shareholders of a closely held corporation sought damages for emotional distress from the corporation's liability insurer for the latter's failure to settle a suit against the corporation within the limits of the insurance policy. In both cases, the court held that damages for the emotional distress could be recovered.

Fent v. Toledo, Peoria & Warsaw Ry. Co.
59 Ill. 349 (1871)

MR. CHIEF JUSTICE LAWRENCE delivered the opinion of the Court:

On the 1st of October, 1867, a locomotive, with a train of freight cars, belonging to the appellee, in passing eastwardly through the village of Fairbury, threw out great quantities of unusually large cinders, and set on fire two buildings and a lumber yard. The weather at the time was very dry, and the

---

*For recent cases in the spirit of *Dziokonski*, see Sinn v. Burd, 404 A.2d 672 (Pa. 1979); Barnhill v. Davis, 300 N.W.2d 104 (Iowa 1981).

wind blowing freely from the south. One of the buildings ignited by the sparks was a warehouse near the track. The heat and flames from this structure speedily set on fire the building of plaintiffs, situated about two hundred feet from the warehouse, and destroyed it and most of its contents. To recover damages for this loss, the plaintiffs have brought this suit.

The defendant in the circuit court demurred to the plaintiffs' evidence, and the court sustained the demurrer. To reverse this judgment, the plaintiffs bring up the record.

The evidence shows great negligence on the part of the defendant, but it is unnecessary to discuss this question. Where a demurrer is interposed to the evidence, the rule is, that the demurrer admits not only all that the plaintiffs' testimony has proved, but all that it tends to prove. In this case, therefore, the defendant's negligence must be regarded as admitted. It is not, indeed, controverted, but the counsel rely for defense solely upon the ground that the plaintiffs' building was not set on fire directly by sparks from the defendant's locomotive, but by the burning of the intermediate warehouse, and that therefore the defendant is to be held harmless, under the maxim "causa proxima, non remota, spectatur." . . .

We now come to the two cases chiefly relied upon by appellee's counsel. They are quite in point, but we are wholly unable to agree with their conclusions. One is Ryan v. The New York Central Railroad Co., 35 N.Y. 214, and the other is Kerr v. The Pennsylvania Railroad Co., decided by the Supreme Court of Pennsylvania, at its May term, 1870. These two cases stand alone, and we believe they are directly in conflict with every English or American case, as yet reported, involving this question.

As we understand these cases, they hold that, where the fire is communicated by the locomotive to the house of A, and thence to the house of B, there can be no recovery by the latter. It is immaterial, according to the doctrine of these cases, how narrow may be the space between the two houses, or whether the destruction of the second would be the natural consequence of the burning of the first. The principle laid down by these authorities and urged by counsel in this case is, that, in order to [obtain] a recovery, the fire which destroys the plaintiff's property must be communicated directly from the railway, and not through the burning of intermediate property. With all our respect for these courts, we can not adopt this principle, and it is admitted by the judges who delivered the opinions to have no precedent for its support, and to be absolutely in conflict with former adjudications. . . .

The Court of Appeals in New York, and the Supreme Court of Pennsylvania, seem, from their opinions, to have attached great weight to an argument urged upon us by the counsel for appellee, and indeed that argument seems to have been the chief reason for announcing a rule which both courts struggle in vain to show is not in conflict with all prior adjudications. That argument is, in brief, that an entire village or town is liable to be burned down by the passing of the fire from house to house, and if the railway company, whose locomotive has emitted the cinders that caused the fire, is to be charged with all the damages, these companies would be in constant danger of bankruptcy, and of being obliged to suspend their operation. We confess ourselves wholly unable to see the overpowering force of this argument. It proceeds upon the assumption that, if a great loss is to be suffered, it had better be distributed among a hundred innocent victims that wholly visited upon the wrong doer.

As a question of law or ethics, the proposition does not commend itself to our reason. We must still cling to the ancient doctrine, that the wanton wrong doer must take the consequences of his own acts, whether measured by a thousand dollars or a hundred thousand.

As to the railroads, however useful they may be to the regions they traverse, they are not operated by their owners for benevolent purposes, or to promote the public welfare. Their object is pecuniary profit. It is a perfectly legitimate object, but we do not see why they should be exempted from the moral duty of indemnification for injuries committed by the careless or wanton spread of fire along their track, because such indemnity may sometimes amount to so large a sum as to sweep away all their profits. The simple question is, whether a loss, that must be borne somewhere, is to be visited on the head of the innocent or the guilty. If, in placing it where it belongs, the consequence will be the bankruptcy of a railway company, we may regret it, but we should not, for that reason, hesitate in the application of a rule of such palpable justice.

But is it true that railroads can not thrive under such a rule? They have now been in operation many years, and extend over very many thousand miles, and we have never yet heard of town or village that has been destroyed by a fire ignited by their locomotives. Improved methods of construction, and a vigilant care in the management of locomotives, have made the probability of loss from this cause so slight that we can not but regard the fears of the disastrous consequences to the railway companies which may follow from an adherence to the ancient rule, as in a large degree chimerical. A case may occur at long intervals in which they will be required to respond in heavy damages; but better this, than that they should be permitted to evade the just responsibilities of their own negligence, under the pretence that the existence of the road may be endangered. It were better that a railway company should be reduced to bankruptcy, and even suspend its operations, than that the courts should establish for its benefit a rule intrinsically unjust, and repugnant not merely to ancient precedent, but to the universal sense of right and wrong. . . .

Notes

1. In Atchison, Topeka & Santa Fe R. Co. v. Stanford, 12 Kan. 354, 379 (1874), the court, agreeing with the decision in *Fent*, added this curious comment:

Railroad companies, however, are not so fearful of paying just claims against them as they are of paying unjust claims. They are really afraid that juries will find that they caused the fires, when in fact they did not cause them; and that juries will find that they were guilty of negligence, when in fact they were not guilty of negligence. In the present case the railroad company was probably not guilty of negligence. But all these fears must necessarily subside as our state grows in population, and as a more general intelligence is diffused among the people, for then better juries may be obtained.

2. In Ryan v. New York Cent. R. Co., 35 N.Y. 210 (1866), referred to by the court in *Fent*, the plaintiff's house was 130 feet from defendant's woodshed. Through defendant's negligence, one of its engines set fire to the woodshed. The fire spread from there to plaintiff's house, and a number of other houses also burned. In deciding that the damage to plaintiff's house was too remote to support his action, the court stated (id. at 216-217):

> To sustain such a claim as the present, and to follow the same to its legitimate consequences, would subject to a liability against which no prudence could guard, and to meet which no private fortune would be adequate. Nearly all fires are caused by negligence, in its extended sense. In a country where wood, coal, gas and oils are universally used, where men are crowded into cities and villages, where servants are employed, and where children find their home in all houses, it is impossible that the most vigilant prudence should guard against the occurrence of accidental or negligent fires. A man may insure his own house or his own furniture, but he cannot insure his neighbor's building or furniture, for the reason that he has no interest in them. To hold that the owner must not only meet his own loss by fire, but that he must guarantee the security of his neighbors on both sides, and to an unlimited extent, would be to create a liability which would be the destruction of all civilized society. No community could long exist, under the operation of such a principle. In a commercial country, each man, to some extent, runs the hazard of his neighbor's conduct, and each, by insurance against such hazards, is enabled to obtain a reasonable security against loss. To neglect such precaution, and to call upon his neighbor, on whose premises a fire originated, to indemnify him instead, would be to award a punishment quite beyond the offense committed. It is to be considered, also, that if the negligent party is liable to the owner of a remote building thus consumed, he would also be liable to the insurance companies who should pay losses to such remote owners. The principle of subrogation would entitle the companies to the benefit of every claim held by the party to whom a loss should be paid.

Notice the confusion in this passage of prevention with insurance. Plaintiff could buy fire insurance, but that would not prevent the fire from occurring or damaging his house; it would merely spread the loss to other potential fire victims. Notice also the analogue between *Ryan* and the Price-Anderson Act, discussed in the last chapter.

3. Prosser (at 256-257 n.75) suggests a possible reconciliation between *Ryan* and *Stanford*:

> New York's prosperity depends upon railroads and heavy industry; its courts have had in mind urban communities in which nearly all property of any value carries fire insurance, and the possibility of a windfall for the insurers in the form of subrogation claims. Kansas has miles of uninsured wheat, and its community attitude toward railroads is by no means the same. Who is to say that each decision is not defensible for the jurisdiction; and what reason is there that both must come to the same conclusion?

How convincing is this suggestion?

a. New York, and for a time Pennsylvania, were the only states to limit liability in the manner of *Ryan;* but they were not the only heavily industrialized and urbanized states. Why should the principle of subrogation result in "windfalls" to insurance companies? Subrogation means that the insurance company, after paying the claim of its insured, steps into the insured's shoes so far as the insured's tort rights are concerned. Where an insurance contract provides for subrogation, the premium received by the insurance company will be lower than if there were no subrogation, since the insurance company will have an expected income from prosecuting the tort claims of its insureds. If, therefore, the insured is compensated in a lower premium for assigning his tort claim to the insurance company, wherein does the latter receive a windfall?*

b. Those miles of uninsured wheat in Kansas presumably were not insured because the expected loss from fire was low; it was higher in a densely urbanized nineteenth-century city or town consisting mostly of wooden buildings. But is the size of the expected loss a reason for limiting the scope of liability?

4. Notice the curious inversion of the loss-spreading idea in *Ryan*. Liability is frequently urged as a method of shifting a concentrated loss from a single victim to the many customers or stockholders of the injurer. The *Ryan* court treated the case as one where a rule of no liability would shift a concentrated loss from a single injurer to a multitude of victims. Was this the right way to look at the facts in the case?

5. Could the result in *Ryan* perhaps be defended by reference to the *uncertainty* of liability? Recall our discussion of the *Moch* case in Chapter 6. Would this be a stronger or a weaker argument if the issue were the scope of liability of nuclear-reactor owners rather than of a railroad?

---

*Does this analysis explain the "collateral source" rule of tort damage law? That is the rule that a plaintiff's compensation for injury from some other source than tort damages — e.g., from the proceeds of an accident-insurance policy — is *not* deducted from the damage award in his tort suit against the injurer. For a sound discussion of the rule, see Rixman v. Somerset Public Schools, 83 Wis. 2d 571, 266 N.W.2d 326 (1978). For economic analysis, see R. A. Posner, Economic Analysis of Law 152-153 (2d ed. 1977).

6. *Ryan* is no longer good law even in New York. See Homac Corp. v. Sun Oil Co., 258 N.Y. 462, 180 N.E. 172 (1932).

Union Stock Yards Co. v. Chicago, Burlington & Quincy R. Co.
196 U.S. 217 (1905)

[Defendant, a railroad, delivered a car with defective brakes to plaintiff, a terminal company. Both companies could by proper inspection have discovered, but did not discover, the defect. An employee of plaintiff was injured as a result of the defective brakes, sued the plaintiff alone, and recovered damages. The present case is a suit by the terminal company against the railroad, seeking the amount which plaintiff paid under judgment to its employee.]

MR. JUSTICE DAY. . . . [T]he general principle of law is well settled that one of several wrongdoers cannot recover against another wrongdoer, although he may have been compelled to pay all the damages for the wrong done. In many instances, however, cases have been taken out of this general rule, and it has been held inoperative in order that the ultimate loss may be visited upon the principal wrongdoer, who is made to respond for all the damages, where one less culpable, although legally liable to third persons, may escape the payment of damages assessed against him by putting the ultimate loss upon the one principally responsible for the injury done. These cases have, perhaps, their principal illustration in that class wherein municipalities have been held responsible for injuries to persons lawfully using the streets in a city, because of defects in the streets or sidewalks caused by the negligence or active fault of a property owner. In such cases, where the municipality has been called upon to respond because of its legal duty to keep public highways open and free from nuisances, a recovery over has been permitted for indemnity against the property owner, the principal wrongdoer, whose negligence was the real cause of the injury. . . .

. . . In the present case there is nothing in the facts as stated to show that any negligence or misconduct of the railroad company caused the defect in the car which resulted in the injury to the brakeman. That company received the car from its owner, the Hammond Packing Company, whether in good order or not the record does not disclose. It is true that a railroad company owes a duty of inspection to its employés as to cars received from other companies as well as to those which it may own. But in the present case the omission of duty for which the railroad company was sought to be held was the failure to inspect the car with such reasonable diligence as would have discovered the defect in it. It may be conceded that the railroad company having a contract with the terminal company, to receive and transport the cars furnished, it was bound to use reasonable diligence to see that the cars were turned over in good order, and a discharge of this duty required an inspection of the cars by the railroad company upon delivery to the terminal company. But . . . the terminal company owed a similar duty to its employés and neglected to perform the same to the injury of an employé. . . .

The case then stands in this wise: The railroad company and the terminal company have been guilty of a like neglect of duty in failing to properly inspect the car before putting it in use by those who might be injured thereby. We do not perceive that, because the duty of inspection was first required from the railroad company, the case is thereby brought within the class which holds the one primarily responsible, as the real cause of the injury, liable to another less culpable, who may have been held to respond for damages for the injury inflicted. It is not like the case of the one who creates a nuisance in the public streets; or who furnishes a defective dock; or the case of the gas company, where it created the condition of unsafety by its own wrongful act; or the case of the defective boiler, which blew out because it would not stand the pressure warranted by the manufacturer. In all these cases the wrongful act of the one held finally liable created the unsafe or dangerous conditions from which the injury resulted. The principal and moving cause, resulting in the injury sustained, was the act of the first wrongdoer, and the other has been held liable to third persons for failing to discover or correct the defect caused by the positive act of the other.

In the present case the negligence of the parties has been of the same character. Both the railroad company and the terminal company failed by proper inspection to discover the defective brake. The terminal company, because of its fault, has been held liable to one sustaining an injury thereby. We do not think the case comes within that exceptional class which permits one wrongdoer who has been mulcted in damages to recover indemnity or contribution from another. . . .

Muth v. Urricelqui
251 Cal. App. 2d 901, 60 Cal. Rptr. 166 (1967)

BROWN, J.

Appellant A. Urricelqui, an excavation and grading contractor, appeals from a judgment entered against him on a verdict in an indemnity action filed by A. Bernard Muth, Leland E. Muth and Albert R. Muth (hereinafter referred to as Muths), general building contractors.

In a prior action Richard and Mary Hackler were awarded judgment against Muths, the general contractors, for damages caused to their (Hacklers') house by reason of landslide and subsidence. Muths in the present action seek to be indemnified, claiming that the subcontractors performed their work in a negligent manner, proximately causing Hacklers' damages. . . .

Muths, licensed building contractors, in 1955 commenced construction of a residential subdivision on a tract of land they owned in Orinda, California. They engaged various subcontractors, including Hersey Inspection Bureau, as soil engineers (hereinafter referred to as Hersey); Riffe, Shipherd & Jones, as civil engineers (hereinafter referred to as Riffe) and appellant, as the grading contractor. Hersey was engaged to make a soils investigation of the natural ground, to issue a preliminary soils report, to make recommendations regarding the natural ground and the slope of the excavated or fill banks, to make tests of the compaction of fill, and to issue reports of the fill compaction tests. As soil engineering specialists, Hersey had charge of the fill area from the inception of the subdivision project. Riffe's duties were to prepare tentative subdivision plans, finished construction plans, and the grading plans for the subdivision.

Muths engaged appellant, a licensed grading contractor, for the fill and grading work. Appellant and Muths entered into a written contract whereby appellant agreed to perform "[I]n a good and workmanlike manner, under the direction of the owner,[2] or his authorized representative, all of the work and improvements set forth below and such work shall be done in accordance with 'Construction Plans' and 'Development Plan' of Tract 2245, Warford Mesa, Unit I, prepared by NORMAN T. RIFFE, CIVIL ENGINEER, a partnership, hereby made a part of this contract, and to the specifications and requirements of the County of Contra Costa. . . . The price paid per cubic yard for earthwork shall include all work necessary to clear the area of debris and trees and grass, excavate, and grade lot and street areas in accordance with F.H.A. Minimum Property Requirements and County requirements to the lines and grades shown on the Construction Plans and Development Plans. . . . The party of the First Part shall hold harmless Albert R. Muth and Sons, the party of the Second Part, for any Public Liability or Property Damage, . . . which may be incurred during completion of this contract."

After the lot involved in this litigation was graded and filled, Muths constructed a house upon the lot, built a driveway and did the finish grading and sloping of the top of the lot so that the surface water would drain to the street. Muths also employed a subcontractor to construct the water and sewer lines.

Respondents sold the completed house and the lot to the Hacklers on June 25, 1956, for a sale price of $20,300. Thereafter substantial damage was caused to the house by reason of the subsiding and sliding of the land. The Hacklers instituted proceedings against Muths and recovered judgment for $22,500 on condition that Hacklers reconvey the lot and house back to Muths. Muths' suit for indemnity and the judgment against appellant followed.

The evidence disclosed that representatives of the Hersey soils engineers were present during the filling operations but, according to good practice, the

_____

2. Muth was both the owner of the tract and the general contractor.

soils engineers were not required to examine and check every truckload of fill prior to its being used at the fill site. It was also accepted practice for soils engineers (a) to make representative tests to determine both the quality and density of the fill, (b) to check the natural land for organic material, and (c) to recommend a maximum slope of 2 feet horizontal to 1 foot vertical. The soils engineers made the necessary tests and advised appellant to remove all grass and brush from the natural ground before placing of fill and, further, in grading not to exceed a maximum slope of 2 feet horizontal and 1 foot vertical.

The lot purchased by the Hacklers was one of many lots in a large subdivision and was the only one that subsided.

An expert witness, John A. Trantina, made an examination of the Hackler property and of the adjacent land after the slide, including test borings and a soil analysis. He testified that the cause of the slide was the failure of appellant to strip the ground of organic material and to remove vegetation and wood debris from the fill. Mr. Trantina also found that the slope of the land as graded by appellant was $1^{1}/_{2}$ feet to 1 foot, which is steeper than the recommended 2 feet to 1 foot, and that the variation in slope was a contributing factor to the settlement of the land. Muths did not direct or supervise Hersey, Riffe or appellant in any of this work. Appellant admitted that Muths did not instruct him in how to strip, excavate or fill the lots but merely informed appellant of the required end result.

Muths, as the owners of the tract and the general contractors, could not escape liability for the damage to the Hacklers by seeking refuge in the defense that the damages were proximately caused by the negligence of one or more of their subcontractors. . . . " '[T]he analogy of MacPherson v. Buick Motor Co. is at last being accepted. Several recent decisions have placed building contractors on the same footing as sellers of goods, and have held them to the general standard of reasonable care for the protection of anyone who may foreseeably be endangered by the negligence, even after acceptance of the work.' . . . There is no reasonable distinction between the owner's inability to escape liability and that of the contractor. The contractor, equally with the owner of the property, has supervision over the entire building and its construction, including the work performed by a subcontractor, and where he negligently creates a condition, either by himself or through a subcontractor, he is primarily[3] responsible for that condition and the consequences that may follow from it. . . ."

Muths, having been held originally responsible to the Hacklers, sought indemnification from the subcontractors alleging that they were actively negligent and created the dangerous condition which proximately caused the Hacklers' loss. . . .

---

3. In indemnity actions this liability is referred to as secondary and the one actively negligent is referred to as primarily responsible.

Muths engaged appellant to do the grading and fill work by written contract wherein appellant agreed to hold Muths harmless from public liability or property damage. This agreement was entered into subsequent to appellant commencing work. It is unnecessary to consider the binding effect of the hold-harmless provision as it fails to provide indemnity for the indemnitee's negligence in clear and explicit language. Muths do not base their claim for indemnity on the agreement but rely upon the doctrine of implied indemnity.

The right to implied indemnity while relatively recent in the law of California is now well established [citing cases]. The import of these cases is that where each of two persons is made responsible by law to an injured party, the one (who is passively negligent) to whom the right of indemnity inures is entitled to shift the entire liability for the loss to the other party (whose active negligence was the proximate immediate cause of the loss). Accordingly a right of implied indemnification may arise as a result of contract or other equitable considerations. The basic theory is not novel. It is a shifting of the risk of loss from one upon whom it falls to the person who in justice should bear it.

" '. . . The right of *indemnity* rests upon a difference between the primary and secondary liability of two persons each of whom is made responsible by the law to an injured party. It is a right which enures to a person who, without active fault on his part, has been compelled by reason of some legal obligation, to pay damages occasioned by the initial negligence of another, and for which he himself is only secondarily liable. The difference between primary and secondary liability is not based on a difference in *degrees* of negligence or on any doctrine of *comparative* negligence — a doctrine which, indeed, is not recognized by the common law; . . . It depends on a difference in the *character* or *kind* of the wrongs which cause the injury and in the nature of the legal obligation owed by each of the wrongdoers to the injured person. . . .' [Emphasis added by the Court.] . . ."

Appellant, although conceding his own negligence, contends that Muths' participation in the final grading just prior to construction of the Hacklers' house and his work in sloping the property for the runoff of surface water constituted active participation in the work with appellant which is fatal to a claim for indemnity. There was no evidence produced to the effect that Muths' actions caused or contributed to the slide. There was ample evidence that appellant's negligence in failing to strip the fill of organic material and in not following the engineers' directions as to sloping the land was the cause of the damage. The extent of the participation of Muths in the affirmative acts of negligence of appellant was a question for the jury. The jury having decided the issue adverse to appellant on substantial evidence, its determination will not be disturbed on appeal. . . .

The fact that Muths had the authority to inspect the work of appellant as it progressed and to specify changes but failed to inspect or advise does not amount to active negligence. . . .

... [A]ppellant concedes that Muths did not supervise the grading or instruct on the method to complete the job. Appellant had been advised by Hersey to remove the vegetation, wood and debris from the fill and from the virgin soil. He also had been advised as to the dimensions of grading. In addition, appellant was an experienced grader who had previously been engaged by Muths on an earlier subdivision. Muths' negligence, if any, was passive and does not foreclose his right to indemnity. . . .

Notes

1. Where an injury is produced by the action of two or more injurers, and each is a tortfeasor with respect to the victim of the injury, and the injury is indivisible from the standpoint of both the injurers and the victim,* the injurers are "joint tortfeasors," with the consequence that each is "jointly and severally liable" for the victim's damages. This means that, as in *Union Stock Yards*, the victim can if he wishes proceed against just one of the injurers and collect his full damages from him. If he prefers he can proceed against more than one and satisfy the judgment partially from the assets of each. But he may not recover in total more than his full damages.

The common law refused to entertain suits by one joint tortfeasor against another for "contribution," i.e., partial reimbursement, of the damages paid out to the victim by the first, even if the plaintiff had been totally capricious or even malicious in the pattern of collection from the joint tortfeasors. *Union Stock Yards* illustrates the operation of this rule too. When that case was decided, the rule of "no contribution among joint tortfeasors" was well established; since then, however, most jurisdictions have abandoned the rule, either by decision or (more commonly) by statute. For a list, see Landes & Posner, Joint and Multiple Tortfeasors: An Economic Analysis, 9 J. Legal Stud. 517, 551 (table A-1) (1980). Generally, however, a distinction is made between intentional and unintentional torts, and the common-law rule of no contribution abrogated only for the latter class. For example, in Texas Industries, Inc. v. Radcliff Materials, Inc., 101 S. Ct. 2061 (1981), the Supreme Court held that there was no right of contribution in private damages actions under the federal antitrust laws. Antitrust violations

---

*On the meaning of "indivisibility," see Note 2 below. Originally, to be held liable as joint tortfeasors injurers had to be involved in some sort of joint activity from which the accident arose. Nowadays, however, if two or more injurers cause a single injury, they are treated as joint tortfeasors even if they acted independently rather than pursuant to some common plan or purpose. For example, in Landers v. French's Ice Cream Co., 98 Ga. App. 317, 106 S.E.2d 325 (1958), defendant's ice cream truck was illegally parked in such a position that two illegally racing drivers could not pass it without hitting plaintiff. The court found the two racing drivers and the ice cream company all to be joint tortfeasors.

Was *Sindell* a case of joint liability? Was Ybarra v. Spangard in Chapter 4? For an influential discussion of joint liability in a *Sindell*-like setting, see Hall v. E. I. du Pont de Nemours & Co., 345 F. Supp. 353, 370-378 (E.D.N.Y. 1972).

are an example of an intentional tort. In unintentional-tort cases governed by federal common law, such as injuries to longshoremen within the federal admiralty jurisdiction, the Supreme Court has followed the trend toward contribution. See, e.g., Cooper Stevedoring Co. v. Fritz Kopke, Inc., 417 U.S. 106 (1974). On the history of contribution in the Supreme Court see Easter-brook, Landes & Posner, Contribution among Antitrust Defendants: A Legal and Economic Analysis, 23 J. Law & Econ. 331, 332-337 (1980).

The economic analysis of the no-contribution rule parallels that of con-tributory negligence, discussed in Chapter 5. The key distinction is again that between joint care and alternative care. Take a case where the optimal method of avoiding an accident is for potential injurer A to spend $5 on care and potential injurer B $10. The expected accident cost to the victim, C, is $20; to make things simpler, assume this is made up of P = 1 and L = $20. Under a rule of no contribution, if an accident occurred, C might decide to sue A for the full $20 and forget about B. You might think this prospect would lead B to take no care; you would be wrong. Facing an expected liability cost of $20 if he fails to take care and an accident results, A has a strong incentive to spend $5 on care, since this will discharge his legal obliga-tion and so get him off the hook if there is an accident. The effect is that now B faces an expected accident cost of $20. So B will spend his $10 on care. Thus the desired result is achieved by the rule of no contribution just as the rule of contributory negligence led to the desired result in joint (injurer-victim) care cases. The no-contribution rule economizes on administrative costs compared to contribution, since there is no subsequent action between injurers to determine how the burden of the tort judgment should be shared in the event deterrence breaks down and an accident occurs. Again the analogy to contrib-utory-comparative negligence is evident.

Consider now an alternative-care case: The accident will be avoided at least cost if either A or B, but not both, take care. As before, the cost to A is $5 and to B $10, and the expected loss is $20. There are two possible approaches here: to make just A liable, because he is the cheaper cost avoider; or to make both A and B liable but allow B to seek reimbursement from A, so that the effect is to shift the liability to the cheaper cost avoider. The second approach may seem unnecessarily circuitous, but the facts of *Muth* suggest otherwise. The Hacklers may not have known who was responsible for the damage to their property, and the subcontractors may not have been fully solvent, in which event making the Muths liable would give them an incen-tive to choose subcontractors more carefully or supervise their work more closely; these may be appropriate second-best solutions given insolvency.*

---

*The problem of the insolvent subcontractor is a serious one, since in many cases the prime contractor will not be liable, because of the independent-contractor exception to respondeat superior (why was that exception not applicable under the facts in *Muth*?). This has led some courts to fashion a "financial-irresponsibility" exception to the exception, which makes the prime contractor liable when the subcontractor is insolvent. See the interesting discussion of this issue in Becker v. Interstate Properties, 569 F.2d 1203 (3d Cir. 1977).

The analogy to respondeat superior should be apparent. Indeed, the torts of employees are another area where the indemnity doctrine is often invoked, allowing an employer who is liable under respondeat superior to recover from the employee who committed the tort (and was thus "primarily" rather than "secondarily" negligent) the damages the employer had to pay to the victim of the tort.

In sum, the much-criticized all-or-nothing approach of the common law — no contribution in some cases, indemnity (equivalent to 100 percent contribution) in others — seems consistent with the economics of the joint-tort problem. Is contribution equally consistent?* It depends on whether the case is one of joint care or alternative care. In a joint-care case, contribution leads to the same allocative result as no contribution. Suppose the principle of contribution is relative fault and is based on relative costs of accident avoidance. A in our first example might therefore be liable for two-thirds of the damages to C on the theory that his optimal investment in safety was only one-half that of B and therefore he is in a sense twice as culpable for having failed to take care. Then B will have an expected damage cost of only $6.67. Since this is more than his optimal expenditure on care, initially he will have no incentive to take care. But if B's expected liability cost is $6.67, A's must be $13.33. A will therefore have a strong incentive to make the investment — only $5 — that gets him off the liability hook. Knowing of this incentive, B will make his $10 investment, for if he does not he will bear the entire $20 expected accident cost. But while the allocative effect of contribution is the same as that of no contribution, the administrative costs are, as mentioned, higher.

In an alternative-care case, contribution, besides being administratively costly, has the bad allocative properties we identified in discussing comparative negligence in alternative-care cases in Chapter 5. Let us change the numbers slightly in our second example to bring out this danger. Let A and B's avoidance costs be $5 and $10 respectively, as before, but now suppose the expected damages to C are $60 rather than $20. Under the relative-fault principle, A will have an expected liability cost of $40, B of $20. As both of these expected losses exceed the costs of care for the respective actors, each may decide to incur those costs. In that event $15 will be spent to avoid an accident that could have been avoided (since it is an alternative-care case) at a cost of only $5. Alternatively, knowing that the other has a strong incentive to incur these costs and that doing so will avoid the accident, each may decide to

---

*We shall not examine the alternative systems of contribution, or the mechanics of contribution litigation, which are complex. Some jurisdictions divide the damages equally among the joint tortfeasors; others use a relative-fault principle, as in comparative negligence. For a discussion of the different systems and their economic properties see Easterbrook, Landes & Posner, Contribution among Antitrust Defendants: A Legal and Economic Analysis, 23 J. Law & Econ. 331 (1980). On the mechanics of contribution litigation, see, e.g., Fleming, Report of the Joint Committee of the California Legislature on Tort Liability on the Problems Associated with American Motorcycle Association v. Superior Court, 30 Hastings L.J. 1464 (1979).

do nothing — in which event the social cost will be $60, rather than $5 if the optimal method of accident avoidance is used.

The upshot of all this is that if the common law is efficient, it will not award indemnity (the only form of "contribution" recognized by the common law) in joint-care cases. The most frequent type of joint-care case is the vehicle collision, because optimal avoidance usually requires both potential injurers to take care (we do not want one to drive carefully and the other to drive with his eyes closed). Here we find that indemnity was almost always denied, even if the joint tortfeasors differed from each other in the degree of their negligence (as arguably was the case in our last example). See, e.g., Warner v. Capital Transit Co., 162 F. Supp. 253 (D.D.C. 1958). Indemnity was allowed, however, in cases where one of the joint tortfeasors had the last clear chance to avoid the accident. Does this exception make good economic sense? *Union Stock Yards* was an alternative-care case, was it not? Why then was indemnity denied?

Test your ability to distinguish a joint-care case from an alternative-care case. A and B shoot C at the same moment; each shot would have been fatal by itself. Is this a joint-care case or an alternative-care case? A drops a match into a pool of gasoline spilled by B. An explosion results, injuring C. Same question.

The analysis presented in this note is somewhat oversimplified. For a more complete economic analysis, and references to the legal literature, see Landes & Posner, supra.

2. We have been speaking of the case where the injury is indivisible from the standpoint of both the injurers and the victims. Sometimes, though there is only one victim, the injuries are divisible. For example, if A shot C in the foot, and B shot C in the arm, and neither wound aggravated the severity of the other, the injuries would be divisible and each injurer would be liable only for the damages attributable to the injury inflicted by him. A subtler type of divisibility occurs where, although the injury remains indivisible from the victim's standpoint, it is divisible from the injurers' standpoint. Suppose A runs down C negligently. B, a physician, fails to administer the proper treatment to C, and as a result he dies; had B treated him properly, C would have lived. There is a single injury, albeit aggravated by B's neglect. But we know from earlier cases that B is liable only for the aggravation due to his neglect. He is not liable for the entire injury to C. What of A's liability? Does it encompass the whole of C's injury, or is it limited to the injury C would have suffered if he had received competent medical treatment? This too is an issue in previous cases in this chapter (which ones?). We know from these cases that A might be held liable for the full extent of C's injury. Does this pattern — broader liability for the first injurer than for the "aggravator" — make economic sense? If stumped, see Landes & Posner, supra, at 548-549.

3. Can *any* of the problems of allocating damages among joint tortfeasors, discussed in Notes 1 and 2 above, be solved by an analysis of

causation? By an economic analysis of causation? By a philosophical analysis à la Borgo? By Epstein's causal paradigms?

Doca v. Marina Mercante Nicaraguense, S.A.
634 F.2d 30 (2d Cir. 1980)

NEWMAN, J.

This appeal from a personal injury award, made pursuant to the Longshoremen's and Harbor Workers' Compensation Act (LHWCA), 33 U.S.C. §§901-950 (1976), primarily requires consideration of the effect of inflation in determining damages for loss of future wages.

Plaintiff Doca was employed as a cargo checker by Hamilton Terminal Company. He was injured when he slipped and fell while carrying out his assigned duties aboard the M. V. Costa Rica. Defendant Marina Mercante Nicaraguense, S. A. ("Marina") is the owner of the ship; it hired defendant Pittston Stevedoring Company ("Pittston") to unload the vessel, and Pittston in turn hired Hamilton to perform certain services in connection with the unloading. Doca went aboard the Costa Rica at the joint request of a Pittston supervisor and a Hamilton supervisor to check the hatches for the presence of some metal pipe. The path to Hatch #4 along the offshore side of the vessel was surrounded by garbage, but there appeared to be a clear route through the center of it, covered with dunnage paper. In fact, there was a turnbuckle underneath the paper; as Doca proceeded toward Hatch #4, he tripped on the turnbuckle and struck his head on the coaming, or rim of the hatch. As a result of this fall, Doca suffered a cerebral concussion and cervical spine injury. This left Doca with a series of neurological symptoms that were found to render him incapable of working, engaging in "most normal recreational activities," or having a normal sexual relationship with his wife.

The District Court for the Southern District of New York found both the shipowner Marina and the stevedoring company Pittston negligent in causing Doca's injury, and, reflecting their relative responsibilities for the injury, found Marina liable for 90% and Pittston liable for 10% of damages totaling $669,127. . . .

. . . The 1972 Amendments to the LHWCA had the effect of applying general tort principles regarding owners and occupiers of land to the duty of a shipowner toward those who come aboard for business reasons. This duty is to maintain the property in a reasonably safe condition in the light of all the circumstances. In the present case, the ship's deck was clearly in an unsafe condition; this was not simply a matter of one turnbuckle being covered by some paper, but of a general obstruction of the walking area by various types of refuse. The ship's crew had created this hazard, and the ship was primarily responsible for it. Moreover, the crew was aware of the hazard, as it had been pointed out to them by Pittston's hatch foreman, who asked them to clean it up. The ship could have contracted with Pittston to clean the deck but it did not do so, and thus retained its basic responsibility. The finding that Marina was 90% responsible for the accident is amply supported.

Pittston's liability is based on a regulation, promulgated by the Occupational Safety and Health Administration, 29 C.F.R. §1918.91(a) (1979), which requires stevedores to keep their work area free of "tripping or stumbling hazards." The District Court held that this regulatory standard created a nondelegable duty to remove the hazard. The fact that the hazard was primarily the ship's responsibility does not excuse the stevedore from fulfilling its regulatory obligation; the stevedore was within its rights in asking the ship's crew to clean the deck, and presumably, it could have obtained monetary compensation for cleaning the deck itself. But since it continued working without making sure the deck was clean, it exposed itself to liability for violation of a statutorily established standard. Pittston's argument that its duty does not run to Doca because Doca was not Pittston's employee cannot be maintained. Since Doca's company, Hamilton, was hired by Pittston, Doca's relationship to Pittston was effectively that of an employee, for purposes of the scope of the duty based on the OSHA regulation, especially since Doca was sent on the mission that led to his injury by a Pittston and a Hamilton supervisor, acting together. . . .

The District Court was also entitled to find that neither of the defendants had established a valid cross-claim for indemnity. Marina's contractual indemnity claim is defeated by the District Court's finding that Pittston's failure to observe the obligation of the OSHA regulation does not establish breach of a warranty of workmanship performance, even though it suffices to establish Pittston's negligence. The District Court also did not err in finding, alternatively, that Marina's own negligence, in the circumstances of this case, was sufficient to preclude an indemnity claim. Finally, the District Court was entitled to reject Pittston's tort theory indemnity claim, apparently predicated on the contention that Marina's negligence was active and Pittston's only passive. The evidence of the omissions of both defendants justified the 90-10 allocation, properly reflecting the relative responsibility of the two tortfeasors, but did not compel a finding that Pittston must be relieved of its share of the damages. . . .

The final and most significant question raised by this appeal is whether and to what extent an award for lost future wages should be adjusted because of inflation. If an adjustment for inflation is to be made, two approaches are available. Under the first method the projection of current wages is increased to reflect the fact that the employee would have received cost of living increases to keep pace with inflation. The sum of those increased annual wage figures is then discounted to present value by the prevailing interest rate. Under the second method the discount rate is decreased below the prevailing interest rate to reflect the estimated rate of inflation. This reduced discount rate is then applied to the sum of the current wages projected to continue for each of the years for which wages will be lost. See Feldman v. Allegheny

Airlines, Inc., 382 F. Supp. 1271 (D. Conn. 1974), aff'd, 524 F.2d 384, 387-388 (2d Cir. 1975). If the same estimated inflation rate is used, the "outcome of the calculation under either approach would be very nearly identical."

In this case the District Court took inflation into account, to an unspecified extent, apparently by using the second approach and adjusting for future inflation by decreasing the present value discount. The Court did not provide a computation for its award for loss of future earnings; however, Judge Duffy stated that he had reached his result by "considering both probability of continued inflation and a discount to present value." Doca infers that Judge Duffy used a discount factor of 1%.[4] Defendants object to this computation for lack of evidence to support an estimate of future inflation and, more fundamentally, on the ground that any adjustment for inflation is impermissible. Since the significance of inflation on damage awards for lost future wages seems to be as persistent a problem as inflation itself, the matter merits some examination. . . .

. . .[R]ecently this Court, in a diversity case, approved District Judge Blumenfeld's use of an "inflation-adjusted discount rate" of 1.5%. Feldman v. Allegheny Airlines, Inc., supra, 524 F.2d at 387. This rate was determined by subtracting the average annual change in the consumer price index over each of several periods of years from the effective annual interest on government bonds held during each of the same periods, and then selecting the average of the rates resulting from these subtractions. The purpose of this method was to determine the " 'real yield' " of money, the portion of interest charged on virtually risk-free investments that represents only the real cost of the money and not the additional cost the lender exacts as a hedge against future inflation. . . .

. . . According to the figures computed by the Bureau of Labor Statistics, United States Department of Labor, inflation has become a constant feature of our modern economy. The Consumer Price Index, perhaps the leading indicator of inflation, has increased in all but two years since the beginning of World War II, and in every year since 1955. This increase was particularly pronounced during the past decade, when the Index increased by five times as much as it had during the previous decade. In 1979, the year in which the District Court decided this case, the average annual Consumer Price Index

---

4. Doca derives this 1% discount rate in the following manner. The difference between the award for lost wages, $352,560, and Doca's projection of future lost wages, $394,861, is $42,301. This difference represents approximately 1% of $352,560, multiplied by the 12 years for which future wages will be lost. Expressed as a formula, the computation would have been $x + (12i)x = w$, where x is the discounted value, i is the interest rate, and w is the projection of total future wages. If the District Court applied a 1% rate in this fashion (and we cannot be certain if the award for lost future wages was determined on this basis), the discount factor was incorrectly applied. The correct method is to apply to the future wages for each year a discount factor of $1/(1 + i)^n$, where i is the interest rate and n is the year for which present value of income is sought. The discounted amounts for each year are then added together to determine the total award. Standard tables are available to avoid the need for calculations.

was 217.4, compared to 100 in 1967, the base year, and 72.1 in 1950.[7] Whether this trend has become an inherent feature of the international economy, irreversible by governmental action, is a subject of spirited debate among economists. But there is broad agreement that our economy, by its very nature, is subject to strong and persistent inflationary pressures, and that the complete elimination of inflation would require Draconian measures, at the very least. In short, courts cannot fail to recognize that inflation is a dominant factor on the current economic scene and, despite episodic recessions, is likely to be so for the foreseeable future.

To be sure, the idea that a person's future income will increase in dollar amount is a prediction, one based largely on our inductive assumption that the future will resemble the past. But using inductive inferences about economic conditions to adjust the value of an award for lost future income is hardly novel. In fact, it underlies the practice of discounting future lost wages to the present value of the right to receive such wages. This practice . . . rests on the inductive inference that interest rates will continue at their present level or above. Discounting to present value determines the amount of money that will produce the lost future wages if the lump sum award (and any interest it earns) is invested at prevailing interest rates. If interest rates decline after the lump sum award is received, the plaintiff will normally fail to realize the full dollar amount of the lost future wages.[8] If it is permissible . . . to make a prediction about interest rates, it seems as reasonable to make a prediction about inflation as well.

In fact, as Judge Blumenfeld demonstrates by the data collected in *Feldman*, there is a fairly constant relationship between interest and inflation rates, so that it is more reasonable to make a prediction about the relation- · ship of both rates than about the level of interest rates alone. Discounting without regard to inflation charges the plaintiff for that portion of the prevailing cost of money that represents the lenders' anticipation of inflation without allowing the plaintiff an offsetting addition for inflation, either by

---

7. Thus, if Doca had received a damage award for twelve years' future wages in 1967, fully discounted to present value at then prevailing interest rates, and had invested this award at those prevailing interest rates with the intention of drawing out one-twelfth each year, his yearly amount, despite the interest, would have declined steadily in purchasing power. For the final year, 1979, the money would have been worth only 42% of what it was worth when the award was made.

8. At a minimum the plaintiff will earn compound interest only at the reduced prevailing interest rate. If the plaintiff invests his lump-sum award (plus earned interest) annually, he will also suffer a decrease of simple interest because of the reduced rates. It is possible for the plaintiff to avoid this latter reduction by investing his lump-sum award in long-term bonds, corresponding to the length of time for which the wages are lost. Yet if the plaintiff makes that type of investment, he takes the risk that if interest rates increase, the market value of his bonds will decrease, and he will suffer a loss each time he sells a bond to meet current needs. One way to avoid that risk is to purchase a series of bonds ranging in maturities from one year up to the number of years for which the wages were lost. That assures that each year's needs will be met from the proceeds of a maturing bond, without the risk of selling a bond at a discount. However, the average rate on such a series of short, medium, and long-term bonds will most likely be less than the rate on long-term bonds, which was used to discount the future wages to present value.

increasing the sum to be discounted or reducing the discount rate. Or, to put it another way, discounting necessarily includes a prediction about inflation (the prediction made by those who determine the interest rate), and it is neither reasonable nor fair to use that prediction only to reduce an award instead of endeavoring to determine an award that approximates the present value of what the future wages would have been. Economics should not be an instrument for the under-compensation of plaintiffs. It should be used to achieve a realistic estimate of future conditions, so that an injured plaintiff can be compensated for his loss as fairly and completely as possible.

The principal argument advanced against taking inflation into account is that it is too speculative. There can be no doubt that predicting next year's inflation rate is at least as hazardous a task as forecasting next year's weather. This concern about speculation persuades us to be rather cautious in determining the way in which inflation should be taken into account, but, for three reasons, is not sufficient to preclude any adjustment for inflation. First, the law of damages frequently recognizes the need to make some predictions about the future, despite the uncertainties of doing so. Estimates of lost future profits are an obvious example. Second, since discounting future lost wages to present value uses an interest rate that reflects inflation, the issue is not whether inflation is too speculative to be considered at all; it is whether inflation, as a component of interest rates, should be considered for the defendant (by discounting at the prevailing interest rate) but ignored for the plaintiff (by rejecting any compensating adjustment for inflation). Finally, and most important, as *Feldman* illustrates, it is entirely feasible to take inflation into account without making any prediction as to the specific level of future inflation rates. All that is needed is a prediction that in the future inflation rates will bear approximately the same relationship to long-term interest rates that they have in the past. Essentially the only premise for that prediction is that over the course of years investors in long-term bonds will demand returns that reflect the prospects of future inflation. They may guess wrong in some years and accept rates that fail to keep pace with inflation. "Yet common sense suggests," as Judge Friendly has pointed out, "that investors will not tolerate such a situation indefinitely." These considerations persuade us that inflation is not too speculative to be taken into account in determining awards for future lost wages.

The next question is how inflation should be considered. Courts have favored various methods, which can generally be divided into two basic categories. In the first category are those methods that submit the question of the inflation rate to the fact-finder, so that a separate determination is made in each case. In this category, one method treats the rate of future inflation as a fact to be proved by evidence, presumably expert opinion. Another method forbids evidence, but permits the fact-finder to apply his own knowledge and prediction in estimating a future inflation rate. A third method permits the fact-finder to apply his own knowledge but also permits expert testimony. In the other basic category are methods that remove the issue from the fact-finder and instead adopt a rule of law that focuses on a constant relationship between inflation and interest rates. Using this approach, the Alaska Supreme Court held that the inflation rate will be assumed to equal the interest rate, thereby eliminating any discount for present value. A somewhat different technique was used in *Feldman*, where it was observed that over a period of years the inflation rate bore a relatively constant relationship to the interest rate, averaging 1.5% less; the Court used this 1.5% rate as a discount rate, reflecting the true cost of money with the effect of inflation removed.

Having considered these alternatives, we are not prepared to require any one particular method by which inflation should be taken into account in estimating lost future wages. Predictive techniques are constantly being refined, as are methods of correctly assessing the immediate past. If litigants prefer to offer evidence as to future rates of both inflation and interest, they are entitled to do so. We note, however, that one virtue of the *Feldman* approach is that it lessens trial disputes concerning the future impact of inflation. The average accident trial should not be converted into a graduate seminar on economic forecasting. The adjusted discount rate approach of *Feldman* avoids all predictions about the level of future inflation, and focuses instead only on the relationship between the inflation rate and the interest rate. Since that relationship is relatively constant in periods of stable inflation, as the historical data set forth in *Feldman* reveal, it may frequently be possible for litigants to agree on an adjusted discount rate, derived from that type of historical data. Without requiring a particular adjusted rate, we suggest that a 2% discount rate would normally be fair to both sides.

A 2% discount rate appears to be the estimate of the true cost of money appropriate for use in a computation whose purpose is to determine the present value of lost future wages. As Judge Blumenfeld recognized in *Feldman*, 2% is the real yield normally attainable during periods of low, stable rates of inflation. It is also a figure that lies within the narrow range bracketed by many economists as representing the true yield of money.[10] *Feldman* used the slightly lower rate of 1.5% to allow "a margin of error to compensate for unexpected increases in the rate of inflation which may depress long term real yields." It may well be that during periods of unusually high inflation rates, interest rates will lag somewhat behind the inflation rate, at least temporarily, with the result that the interest return on a discounted lump sum award will not fully keep pace with inflation. But in such periods of high inflation,

10. Although economists disagree over the validity of the assumption that the real rate of interest is constant and consequently independent of inflation, there is substantial opinion that during periods of stable rates of inflation, the real yield of money, whether constant or slightly fluctuating, is approximately 2%, as estimated in *Feldman*. . . . [A]n appropriate period for determining investor expectations of inflation and real rates of return is 1959-1972, when actual real returns may have been fairly close to expected real returns. For this period the *Feldman* calculation approximates 2%. Moreover, studies by economists, though taking different positions concerning the relation between the real rate and expectations about inflation, have estimated that the real rate of interest was between 1.5% and 3% for a similar time frame. . . .

wages too will not keep pace with inflation. In the only three years since 1947 when the rate of the annual increase in the Consumer Price Index (CPI) exceeded 8%, the annual rate of wage increases (non-farm weekly earnings) has been less than the annual rate of CPI increases by at least 3 percentage points; in all other years since 1947, wages have increased at a rate greater than the rate of increase in the CPI or at least at a rate within 1 percentage point of the CPI percentage increase.[12] Thus, since there is little reason to expect that injured plaintiffs would have received wage increases sufficient to keep pace with unusually high rates of inflation, a present value discount rate normally need not be reduced below 2% just to compensate for unusually high inflation. To do so would ignore the basic objective of selecting a present sum of money that will replace what the future wages would have been.

We emphasize that we are not requiring the use of an adjusted discount rate, nor specifying that when such a rate is used, it must be set at 2%. Litigants are free to account for inflation in other ways, or, if they use the adjusted discount rate approach, to offer evidence of a rate more appropriate than 2%. But in the hope that disputes about the appropriate rate may be minimized, we simply suggest the 2% rate as one that would normally be fair for the parties to agree upon, and we authorize district judges to use such a rate if the parties elect not to offer any evidence on the subject of either inflation or present value discount.

Obviously in this case the District Judge could not have been expected to anticipate this opinion. Nevertheless, his calculation of an award for lost future wages must be reconsidered for two reasons. First, if we assume, as the plaintiff urges, that a 1% discount rate was used, there is nothing in the evidence to support a reduction of the discount rate from prevailing interest rates all the way down to 1%. As indicated, the lowest discount rate we are willing to approve, in the absence of historical data justifying a different rate, is 2%. Second, the District Court to some extent gave duplicative consideration to the impact of inflation. In estimating what Doca's future wages would have been, the Court took into account a post-trial wage increase of 80¢ an hour, specified in Doca's union contract to take effect on October 1, 1979. Having based future lost wages on this cost of living increase, the Court then further reflected the impact of inflation by reducing the discount rate to 1%. When a discount rate is adjusted to reflect inflation, it must be applied to a stream of earnings calculated without regard to inflation, even to a cost of living increase already scheduled to occur. The certainty of such an increase does not lessen the fact that it reflects inflation, which is already accounted for by the reduced discount rate.

We therefore vacate the damage award and remand to the District Court for recomputation of the award for lost future wages in accordance with this opinion. In all other respects the judgment is affirmed. . . .

---

12. For 1974, the annual rate of increase in the CPI was 10.97%, and the annual rate of increase in weekly non-farm wages was 6.44%. For 1975, the comparable figures were 9.14% and 5.67%; for 1979, 11.26% and 7.66%. . . .

Notes

1. Was this a joint-care or alternative-care case? Would Pittston's indemnity claim have succeeded but for the OSHA regulation?

2. Judge Newman's analysis of the computation of lost earnings under conditions of persistent inflation is an admirably lucid discussion and resolution of a complex subject. As the judge explains, because tort courts do not award installment payments, if the victim of a tort is expected to lose wages of X dollars in some future year, it is necessary to compute a present-value equivalent for inclusion in the tort judgment. Even with zero inflation now and in the future, this computation would not be completely straightforward. We would first have to predict what the victim would be earning in each future year for which the tort is expected to disable him in whole or part. His wage 10 years from now may not be the same as his wage today. By studying both the age-earnings profile in his occupation and the earnings trend for the occupation over time, we may be able to derive a reasonable estimate of his wage 10 years from now. (The profile and the trend are two separate inquiries. It may be that in his occupation a 30-year-old is likely to earn 10 percent more than a 20-year-old; but it may also be that wages at all levels in the occupation are rising on average by 3 percent a year. In that event his wage will be almost 50 percent higher in 10 years.) We might then wish to discount (multiply) that figure by the probability that he will still be alive and working 10 years hence. Notice the analogy here to the approach of the *Steinhauser* case.

Assume the figure we derive for the plaintiff's (lost) earnings 10 years hence is $10,000. What is the equivalent of that future sum in present value? Stated differently, what sum, invested today, will, with the interest that it earns, grow to exactly $10,000 in 10 years? This question is answered by multiplying $10,000, the sum we seek, by the formula in Judge Newman's opinion: $1/(1 + i)^n$, where i is the interest rate at which the present sum will be invested over the period and n is the number of years (here 10). Where no inflation is expected, the interest rate will be equal to the real cost of capital, adjusted for risk. Since the tort victim would presumably have received his $10,000, if he continued working, without risk (risks such as death will already have been incorporated in our calculation of the $10,000), we want to use the riskless rate. As Judge Newman noted, this is usually estimated to be between 1 and 3 percent. Let us, like him, use 2 percent. Plugging these values for i and n into the formula yields a present value of $8,203.

The result is clearly very sensitive to the choice of interest rates. If we used not 2 percent but 10 percent, the present value of $10,000 to be received 10 years hence would be not $8,203 but only $3,855. It is here that inflation becomes important. If inflation is anticipated, then even the riskless rate of interest will be high — it will be, in fact, the sum of the inflation-free riskless rate of interest and the inflation rate that is expected over the life of the investment. If the expected inflation rate is 8 percent, then the applicable interest rate will be 10 percent rather than 2 percent.

There is nothing wrong with using the inflation-adjusted, as opposed to the inflation-free, interest rate, so long as we make a corresponding adjustment in the tort victim's estimated future earnings. The inflation will presumably push up his wages — as a first approximation, by the same amount as the rate of inflation. If so, our $10,000 figure will grow by the compound rate of inflation, and when we use the formula with an inflation-adjusted i, but apply it to an inflation-adjusted future wage, the result will be the same present value as when we used inflation-free figures.

For illustrative purposes, we have used only one year's lost wages. When the earnings loss is expected over a series of years, the proper approach is to apply the formula to each year's anticipated (lost) earnings, and sum the results. The sum is the present value to be awarded in the judgment.

For a variety of perspectives on the above issues, see Eden, Estimating Human Life Values, 22 Practical Lawyer, Sept. 1976, at 77; Note, Computation of Lost Future Earnings in Personal Injury and Wrongful Death Actions, 11 Ind. L. Rev. 647 (1978); Note, Considering Inflation in Calculating Lost Future Earnings, 18 Washburn L.J. 499 (1979), Rea, Inflation, Taxation and Damage Assessment, 58 Can. Bar Rev. 280 (1980); Ward, The Economist in Personal Injury and Death Litigation, 15 Trial, Nov. 1979, at 60. See also S. M. Speiser, Recovery for Wrongful Death: Economic Handbook (1970).

Question: How should one go about estimating lost (adult) earnings of a one-year-old child? See Drayton v. Jiffee Chemical Corp., 591 F.2d 352, 367-368 (6th Cir. 1978).

Chapter 9
Modern Products Liability

We concluded our discussion of products liability in Chapter 6 with the *MacPherson* case, which held that a consumer injured by a defective product could recover damages from the manufacturer (provided the latter was negligent) even though he was not in privity of contract with the manufacturer. The rule announced in *MacPherson* was rapidly adopted by the other states, so products liability became a branch of negligence law. Beginning in 1960, however, with the *Henningsen* decision (excerpted later in this chapter), products liability began to diverge from other areas of negligence law. More and more states substituted strict liability for negligence; defenses based on plaintiff conduct shrank; and these and other changes in the law have made products liability a distinct, extremely active, and highly controversial branch of tort law.

We examine the modern law of products liability in this chapter. We begin, however, a little before the modern era, by tracing the development of the implied-warranty concept out of which the modern law of products liability emerged and which still plays a role in product cases in some jurisdictions.

For an excellent and up-to-date treatment of the subject matter of this chapter see R. A. Epstein, Modern Products Liability Law (1980); for a somewhat dated but still useful discussion of the economic issues see Symposium, Products Liability: Economic Analysis and the Law, 38 U. Chi. L. Rev. 1 (1970); for treatise-length treatment see J. E. Beasley, Products Liability and the Unreasonably Dangerous Requirement (1981); and for a brief, eclectic introduction to the field see Schwartz, Foreword: Understanding Products Liability, 67 Cal. L. Rev. 435 (1979).

Chysky v. Drake Bros. Co.
235 N.Y. 468, 139 N.E. 576 (1923)

McLAUGHLIN, J. The plaintiff was employed as a waitress in a lunch room run by one Abraham, for which she was paid $30 a week and furnished board and lodging. On the 4th day of May, 1918, she received from her employer, as part of her lunch, a piece of cake which had been made and sold to him by defendant. While she was eating it, a nail, baked into the cake in such a way that it could not be discovered by inspection, stuck in her gum, which became so infected as to necessitate the removal of three of her teeth. She brought this action against the maker of the cake to recover the damages alleged to have been sustained, upon the theory it was liable to her, since it had impliedly warranted, when the cake was sold, that it was fit for human consumption, and that such implied warranty inured to her benefit. . . . She had a verdict, and the judgment entered thereon was unanimously affirmed by the Appellate Division. Appeal to this court followed.

In Race v. Krum, 222 N.Y. 410, 118 N.E. 853, we held that accompanying all sales by a retail dealer of articles of food for immediate use there is an implied warranty that the same is fit for human consumption. We did not consider or pass upon, as will appear from the opinion, whether such a warranty existed in the case of hotel proprietors or those engaged in a similar business. The cause of action arose before section 96 of the Personal Property Law took effect. In the present case the cause of action arose after the section took effect. This section provides that

> There is no implied warranty or condition as to the quality or fitness for any particular purpose of goods supplied under a contract to sell or a sale, except as follows:
> 1. Where the buyer, expressly or by implication, makes known to the seller the particular purpose for which the goods are required, and it appears that the buyer relies on the seller's skill or judgment (whether he be the grower or manufacturer or not), there is an implied warranty that the goods shall be reasonably fit for such purpose.

If there be any liability, therefore, it must be under this section, and the jury was so instructed.

In Rinaldi v. Mohican, 225 N.Y. 70, 121 N.E. 471, where the cause of action arose after the section of the Personal Property Law quoted took effect, we held: "That the mere purchase by a customer from a retail dealer in foods of an article ordinarily used for human consumption does by implication make known to the vendor the purpose for which the article is required. Such a transaction standing by itself permits no contrary inferences."

Under the section of the Personal Property Law referred to in the *Rinaldi* case, an action may be maintained to recover damages caused by the breach of an implied warranty in the sale of food to a consumer for immediate consumption. Whether this warranty extends to a wholesaler was expressly reserved in the *Rinaldi* case, but is now squarely presented.

The plaintiff received the cake from her employer. By reason of its condition it was not fit for human consumption. Her employer bought the cake from the defendant. Is it liable to the plaintiff for the injury sustained? We do not think so. If there were an implied warranty which inured to the benefit of the plaintiff it must be because there was some contractual relation between her and the defendant, and there was no such contract. She never saw the defendant, and, so far as appears, did not know from whom her employer purchased the cake. The general rule is that a manufacturer or seller of food, or other articles of personal property, is not liable to third persons, under an implied warranty, who have no contractual relations with him. The reason for this rule is that privity of contract does not exist between the seller and such third persons, and unless there be privity of contract, there can be no implied warranty. The benefit of a warranty, either express or implied, does not run with a chattel on its resale, and in this respect is unlike a covenant running with the land so as to give a subsequent purchaser a right of action against the original seller on a warranty.

It may be assumed that under certain facts and conditions the manufacturer of an article would be liable to a third person, even though no contractual relation existed between them, if the article sold were negligently prepared or manufactured. MacPherson v. Buick Motor Co. But the recovery in the present case was not based upon the negligence of the defendant. Plaintiff limited her right to recover to a breach of warranty....

The judgments appealed from, therefore, should be reversed, and the complaint dismissed, with costs in all courts.

Notes

1. Could plaintiff have sued defendent on a theory of negligence under *MacPherson*? Could she have sued Abraham under any theory?

2. What is the economic basis of the implied warranty of fitness of food for human consumption? A warranty is a promise, and a breach is actionable whether or not it is the result of negligence or other fault on the part of the warrantor. Therefore, the effect of the implied-warranty theory is to make the seller of food strictly liable if the food turns out not to be fit for human consumption. What is the basis for this application of the strict-liability concept? Might it be the fact that potential victims can rarely avoid food poisoning or other food-related injuries by changes in either their activities or care level?

3. Section 96 of the New York Personal Property Law was intended to limit the effect of the court's holding in *Race*, was it not? But does Section 96 exclude the specific implied-warranty claim in *Chysky*?

Greenberg v. Lorenz
9 N.Y.2d 195, 173 N.E.2d 773 (1961)

[Action under Section 96 by a 15-year-old girl and her father against defendant, who sold a can of salmon to the father. The can contained some pieces of metal which injured the daughter's teeth and mouth.]
DESMOND, C.J. . . .

... The Appellate Division ... decided (nonunanimously) that the *Chysky* case is still law and that it forbids a recovery on warranty breach to anyone except the purchaser. As the case comes to us, the father has a judgment for his expenses but the child's own suit has been dismissed for lack of privity.

... A wife buying food for her husband may be considered his agent so as to allow a recovery by him (Ryan v. Progressive Grocery Stores, [255 N.Y. 388, 175 N.E. 105]) and she can bring an action of her own if she makes the purchase and suffers from the breach of warranty (Gimenez v. Great A.&P. Tea Co., 264 N.Y. 390, 191 N.E. 27). When two sisters lived in a common household, the one who bought the food was deemed an agent of the other (Bowman v. Great A.&P. Tea Co., 308 N.Y. 780, 125 N.E.2d 165). The same (*Bowman*) theory was expanded to let both husband and wife recover. But a dependent child is not a contracting party and cannot be a warrantee so no damages are due him. ...

The injustice of denying damages to a child because of nonprivity seems too plain for argument. The only real doubt is as to the propriety of changing the rule. ...

The *Ryan, Gimenez* and *Bowman* cases in our court show an increasing tendency to lessen the rigors of the rule. In Blessington v. McCrory Stores Corp., 305 N.Y. 140, 111 N.E.2d 421, we passed on a Statute of Limitations point only but we did not (as we could have under the old cases) dismiss for insufficiency a complaint which demanded damages for an infant's death when the dangerous article had been purchased by the infant's mother. There are a great many well-considered lower court decisions in this State which attest to the prevalent feeling that at least as to injured members of a buyer's family the strict privity rule is unfair and should be revised.

So convincing a showing of injustice and impracticality calls upon us to move but we should be cautious and take one step at a time. To decide the case before us, we should hold that the infant's cause of action should not have been dismissed solely on the ground that the food was purchased not by the child but by the child's father. Today when so much of our food is bought in packages it is not just or sensible to confine the warranty's protection to the individual buyer. At least as to food and household goods, the presumption should be that the purchase was made for all the members of the household. ...

FROESSEL, J. (concurring).

I concur for modification here, but limited to the facts of this case. The infant plaintiff asked for the food purchased, and it was but normal that the father, who was in any event liable for her necessaries, should make the purchase on behalf of both (see Bowman v. Great A.&P. Tea Co.).

The Chief Judge has clearly and succinctly stated the problem before us, and has reviewed the applicable authorities. This is an action in contract based on a statute (Personal Property Law, §96), not for negligence, and it is basic law that unless privity exists there can be no warranty, and where there is no warranty there can be no breach. We may not convert an action in contract into what really amounts to an action in tort.

However much one may think liability should be broadened, that must be left to the Legislature. There are two sides to the problem before us — and one of them is the plight of the seller. It is just as unfair to hold liable a retail groceryman, as here, who is innocent of any negligence or wrong, on the theory of breach of warranty, for some defect in a canned product which he could not inspect and with the production of which he had nothing to do, as it is to deny relief to one who has no relationship to the contract of purchase and sale, though eating at the purchaser's table. As Justice Steuer aptly observed at the Appellate Term, "it may be odd that the purchaser can recover while others cannot, but it is odder still that one without fault has to pay at all." . . .

It is for the Legislature to determine the policy of accommodating those conflicting interests after affording all concerned an opportunity to be heard. Indeed, the Legislature has not been unaware of the problem for, in three separate years — 1943, 1945, 1959 — as noted by the Chief Judge, the New York State Law Revision Commission recommended that the benefits of implied warranties be extended to the buyer's employees and to the members of his household, but the Legislature has declined to act, despite the introduction of legislation. I do not think we should now assume their powers and change the rules, which will undoubtedly affect many cases in which lawyers and litigants understood the law to be otherwise, and governed themselves accordingly.

Notes

1. Why should a retail dealer be liable if he could not inspect the food before he sold it? Is there an argument that he was still the cheaper cost avoider than the plaintiffs?

2. Did the court actually "revise" the strict privity rule? If the father was buying as the girl's agent, would she be in privity with the seller? If the court's interpretation, in *Chysky*, of section 96 was correct, has it the power to revise the strict privity rule?

Goldberg v. Kollsman Instrument Corp.
12 N.Y.2d 432, 191 N.E.2d 81 (1963)

[Plaintiff's intestate was killed in a crash of an American Airlines airplane on which she was a passenger. Plaintiff sued Lockheed Aircraft Corporation, the manufacturer of the plane, and Kollsman Instrument Corporation, the manufacturer of the plane's altimeter, charging breach of their implied warranties of merchantability and fitness, and that the breaches caused the crash. These causes of action were dismissed for failure to state a claim, and plaintiff appealed. The complaint also alleged negligence by American Airlines, Lockheed, and Kollsman, but the negligence cause of action is not involved in this appeal.]

DESMOND, C.J. . . .

. . . A breach of warranty, it is now clear, is not only a violation of the sales contract out of which the warranty arises but is a tortious wrong suable by a noncontracting party whose use of the warranted article is within the reasonable contemplation of the vendor or manufacturer. As to foodstuffs we definitively ruled in Greenberg v. Lorenz that the persons thus protected and eligible to sue include the purchaser's family. We went no further in that case because the facts required no farther reach of the rule.

The concept that as to "things of danger" the manufacturer must answer to intended users for faulty design or manufacture is an old one in this State. The most famous decision is MacPherson v. Buick Motor Co. . . . *MacPherson* and its successors dispelled the idea that a manufacturer was immune from liability in tort for violation of his duty to make his manufactures fit and safe. In *MacPherson's* day enforcement required a suit in negligence. Today, we know from Greenberg v. Lorenz and many another decision in this and other States that, at least where an article is of such a character that when used for the purpose for which it is made it is likely to be a source of danger to several or many people if not properly designed and fashioned, the manufacturer as well as the vendor is liable, for breach of law-implied warranties, to the persons whose use is contemplated. The *MacPherson* holding was an "extension" of existing court-made liability law. In a sense, Greenberg v. Lorenz . . . [was an extension] in favor of noncontracting consumers. But it is no extension at all to include airplanes and the passengers for whose use they are built — and, indeed, decisions are at hand which have upheld complaints, sounding in breach of warranty, against manufacturers of aircraft where passengers lost their lives when the planes crashed. . . .

. . . However, for the present at least we do not think it necessary so to extend this rule as to hold liable the manufacturer (defendant Kollsman) of a component part. Adequate protection is provided for the passengers by casting in liability the airplane manufacturer which put into the market the completed aircraft.

The judgment appealed from should be modified, without costs, so as to provide for the dismissal of the third (Kollsman) cause of action only and, as so modified, affirmed.

BURKE, J. (dissenting). We dissent. . . .

First, we do not find a cause of action stated under the implied warranty provisions of section 96 of the Personal Property Law. Plaintiff[1] purchased no goods; she entered into a contract of carriage with American Airlines. By a

---

1. Edith Feis, for whose death this action is brought, will be referred to herein as plaintiff.

long line of cases in this court, the most recent being Kilberg v. Northeast Airlines, Inc., 9 N.Y.2d 34, 172 N.E.2d 526, it is settled that the measure of American Airlines' duty towards plaintiff was an undertaking of reasonably safe carriage. This duty is, of course, discharged by the use of due care. Crucial is the fact that this duty would be unaffected if American assembled its own planes, even if they contained a latent defect. Why, then, should plaintiff's rights be any greater simply because American chose to contract this work out instead of doing it itself? Absent some equity of direct reliance on the advertised representations of one of the manufacturers, . . . it is no concern of plaintiff how the person with whom she dealt, American, subdivided its responsibility of furnishing the machines and services in discharge of its undertaking of safe carriage.

Of course, plaintiff's right to due care cannot be diminished by American's delegating certain tasks to others. What would be actionable negligence if done by American is not less so because done by another; such a person may be sued by plaintiff, and so may American if the negligence was discoverable by it. By the same token, however, plaintiff's primary right to care from American (and, indeed, all whose actions foreseeably affect her) should not be enlarged to insurance protection simply because American chose to have a certain task performed by another. We note that the argument made in some cases based on the avoidance of a multiplicity of actions is inapplicable here. In such cases, the plaintiff himself is the recipient of a warranty incident to the sale of goods and if the defect is in the manufacture it is at least reasonable to suggest a procedure by which liability may be imposed by the person entitled to the recovery directly against the one who, through a chain of warranties, is ultimately liable. Here, however, plaintiff (or her family, etc.) was not sold the chattel which caused her injury and hence there is no warranty.

It is true we have extended the benefit of an implied warranty beyond the immediate purchaser to those who could be fairly called indirect vendees of the product. (Greenberg v. Lorenz.) Without stressing the weakness of the analogy that plaintiff here is the indirect vendee of the airplane and its parts, or the effect of the interposition between plaintiff and defendants of a federally regulated service industry of dominant economic and legal significance, it must be recognized that the true grounds of decision in a case of this sort lie outside the purpose and policy of the Sales Act and must be evaluated accordingly. Most scholars who have considered this question acknowledge that the warranty rationale is at best a useful fiction. If a strict products or enterprise liability is to be imposed here, this court cannot escape the responsibility of justifying it. We cannot accept the implication of the majority that the difference between warranty and strict products liability is merely one of phrasing.

Inherent in the question of strict products or enterprise liability is the question of the proper enterprise on which to fasten it. Here the majority have imposed this burden on the assembler of the finished product, Lockheed. The principle of selection stated is that the injured passenger needs no more protection. We suggest that this approach to the identification of an appropriate defendant does not answer the question: Which enterprise should be selected if the selection is to be in accord with the rationale upon which the doctrine of strict products liability rests?

The purpose of such liability is not to regulate conduct with a view to eliminating accidents,[2] but rather to remove the economic consequences of accidents from the victim who is unprepared to bear them and place the risk on the enterprise in the course of whose business they arise. The risk, it is said, becomes part of the cost of doing business and can be effectively distributed among the public through insurance or by a direct reflection in the price of the goods or service. As applied to this case we think the enterprise to which accidents such as the present are incident is the carriage of passengers by air — American Airlines. The fact that this accident was due to a defective altimeter should be of no legal significance to plaintiff absent some fault (negligence) on the part of Kollsman or Lockheed. Here, the dominant enterprise and the one with which plaintiff did business and relied upon was the airline.

If the carrier which immediately profited from plaintiff's custom is the proper party on which to fasten whatever enterprise liability the social conscience demands, enterprises which supply the devices with which the carrier conducts its business should not be subject to an action based on this theory. This seems most persuasive where the business that deals directly with the public is not merely a conduit for the distribution of the manufacturer's consumer goods but assumes the responsibility of selecting and using those goods itself as a capital asset in the conduct of a service enterprise such as common carriage. In such a case the relationship between the assembler of these goods and the air traveller is minimal as compared to that obtaining between the traveller and the carrier. In a theory of liability based, not on the regulation of conduct, but on economic considerations of distributing the risk of accidents that occur through no one's neglect, the enterprise most strategically placed to perform this function — the carrier, rather than the enterprise that supplies an assembled chattel thereto, is the logical subject of the liability, if liability there is to be.

Whatever conclusions may flow from the fact that the accident was caused by a defective altimeter should be merged in whatever responsibility the law may place on the airline with which plaintiff did business. To extend warranty law to allow plaintiff to select a defendant from a multiplicity of enterprises in a case such as this would not comport with the rationale of

2. In view of the ease with which lack of care can be brought to light through devices such as res ipsa loquitur, any marginal increase in the stimulus to care would be clearly outweighed by the harshness of the means used to achieve it — the removal of due care as a defense. Apparently the majority agree since Kollsman, the actual manufacturer of the chattel that allegedly caused the accident, is not held liable.

enterprise liability and would only have the effect of destroying whatever rights that exist among the potential defendants by virtue of agreement among themselves. If, on the other hand, plaintiff's maximum rights lie against the carrier, the rules of warranty can perform their real function of adjusting the rights of the parties to the agreements through which the airline acquired the chattel that caused the accident. If, as we maintain in this case, the true theory relied on by plaintiff is enterprise liability, then the rights of those from whom compensation is sought, no less than of those who seek it, "ought not to be made to depend upon the intricacies of the law of sales."

We are therefore of the opinion that any claim in respect of an airplane accident that is grounded in strict enterprise liability should be fixed on the airline or none at all. Only in this way do we meet and resolve, one way or another, the anomaly presented by the reasoning of the majority, which, through reliance on warranty incident to sales, grants a recovery to a passenger injured through a nonnegligent failure of equipment but denies it to one injured through a nonnegligent failure of maintenance or operation. . . . [A]s long as our law holds a carrier chargeable only with negligence, what part of reason is it to hold to a greater duty an enterprise which supplied an assembled aircraft which was certified for commercial service by the Federal Aviation Agency?

Our reluctance to hold an air carrier to strict liability for the inevitable toll of injury incident to its enterprise is only the counsel of prudence. Aside from the responsibility imposed on us to be slow to cast aside well-established law in deference to a theory of social planning that is still much in dispute, there remains the inquiry whether the facts fit the theory. It is easy, in a completely free economy, to envision the unimpeded distribution of risk by an enterprise on which it is imposed; but how well will such a scheme work in an industry which is closely regulated by Federal agencies? In consideration of international competition and other factors weighed by those responsible for rate regulation, how likely is it that rate scales will rise in reflection of increased liability? In turn, how likely is it that the additional risk will be effectively distributed as a cost of doing business? Such questions can be intelligently resolved only by analysis of facts and figures compiled after hearings in which all interested groups have an opportunity to present economic arguments. These matters, which are the factual cornerstones supporting the theory adopted by the majority, aside from our view that they apply it to the wrong enterprise, are classically within the special competence of the Legislature to ascertain. For a court to assume them in order to support a theory that displaces much of the law of negligence from its ancestral environment involves an omniscience not shared by us. For a court to apply them, not to the enterprise with which plaintiff dealt and relied upon, or to the enterprise which manufactured the alleged defective part, but to the assembler of the aircraft used by the carrier, involves a principle of selection which is purely arbitrary.

Notes

1. Suppose Kollsman was negligent in the design or construction of the altimeter; could Lockheed, under the principles discussed in Chapter 8, obtain indemnity from Kollsman for any damages it was forced to pay plaintiff?

2. Can the decision in this case be squared with *Chysky*? Is it supported by *Greenberg*?

3. Notice the dissent's explicit rejection of any notion that strict liability reduces the accident rate. Is this correct?

a. As a first approximation, imposing strict liability in place of negligence should have no effect on the accident rate where, as here, there is a preexisting voluntary relationship (no matter how indirect) between the potential injurers (American Airlines, Lockheed, and Kollsman) and the potential victims. See, e.g., Hamada, Liability Rules and Income Distribution in Product Liability, 66 Am. Econ. Rev. 228 (1976). This is simply an application of the Coase theorem. There is some combination of safety and price that is preferred by consumers. American Airlines will be led to offer this combination to its customers. In turn, it will demand from its suppliers — Lockheed and other aircraft manufacturers — a level of care that enables it to provide the desired level of safety to its customers. Its suppliers will demand the same from their suppliers, such as Kollsman. The only concern of the law is to enforce the contractually determined level of care at each stage in the production-distribution chain.

This does not mean the law should be indifferent to the standard of care in products cases. If it adopts the standard of care that seller and buyer want, it will save them the expense of contracting around the legal standard of care. If, moreover, waivers of liability are disfavored in this area (we shall see that they are), more than transaction costs will be affected by whether the law succeeds in approximating the standard of care desired by seller and buyer, that is, by the market. If the law sets a level of care higher than the market wants, and waivers of liability are unenforceable so that it is impossible to contract around the legal standard, airline passengers will get more safety, at a higher price, than they want.

What is the standard of care that airlines and their passengers desire? It seems unlikely that they would want American Airlines to be strictly liable. The defect was in the altimeter; unless American Airlines had some reason to suspect the altimeter was defective (in which event American would have been negligent), it is hard to see what it could have done to reduce the probability of the accident. (Is this conclusion consistent with the analysis of *Greenberg* in Note 1 following that case?) The argument for Lockheed's strict liability is a bit stronger. True, if Lockheed failed to make an adequate inspection of the altimeter when it installed the instrument in its aircraft, it would be liable for negligence. But strict liability might affect its incentives, in choosing among altimeter suppliers and in deciding what kind of additional safety equipment to install, in ways that might escape the attention of a negligence inquiry. As for Kollsman, the choice between strict liability and negligence is pretty academic; a defective altimeter is a dangerous thing and Kollsman's failure to discover the defect was surely negligent. In sum, the court's result may be reasonable; it may allocate liability among the parties in the way they would have explicitly agreed if they had negotiated over the issue in advance.

b. The analysis is altered if we assume that potential victims are ignorant of many of the risks posed by defective products and that the costs to sellers of informing them of these risks are substantial. Suppose American Airlines could reduce expected accident costs by $10 per passenger per flight if it paid $5 for additional inspections of altimeters. It might nevertheless be unable to convince its passengers that they should be willing on this ground to pay $5.01 (the 1¢ is to make the offer attractive to American) more per ticket. If so, the market will not provide the optimal level of care, and the choice of the liability rule becomes critical. The same conclusion is reached by a slightly different route as well. If the market is not trusted to work effectively, waivers of liability are unlikely to be enforced. The reasoning will be that when Eastern Airlines offers a $5 fare reduction in exchange for limiting its liability for negligence, thereby undercutting American, passengers will find it difficult to evaluate the offer intelligently. If waivers are not enforced, the market will not be able to alter the liability rule if it is nonoptimal; the choice of that rule is again critical.

c. We have ignored the insurance element in strict liability. Could it affect the accident rate indirectly? With strict liability, the purchaser is forced, in effect, to buy an insurance policy with each purchase of a good; after *Goldberg*, when someone flies on American Airlines, he pays for flight insurance in the ticket price. (Lockheed's liability raises the price of its planes and hence American Airlines' costs. Lockheed is the insurer, American its agent.) Some people do not want insurance in this form; in fact, we can assume most do not, or else American would have voluntarily offered it as part of the contract of carriage. (The fact that it did not undermines the analysis in the dissenting opinion, does it not?) With airlines forced to offer an unwanted package of carriage and insurance, the demand for airline service will fall (or grow less rapidly), though doubtless the effect will be slight. If demand falls, so will the number of accidents; the accident rate, however, will be unaffected.

This analysis assumes, as is plausible in the airline example, that the potential victims can do nothing to alter the probability or severity of the accident. If they can, the analysis is more complicated. We take up such cases later.

4. The dissenting opinion in *Goldberg* advocates strict liability in products cases on the basis of a risk-distribution rationale. We discussed risk distribution in Chapter 7. We noted that it had two aspects: "internalizing" accident costs and transforming a single large loss into a multitude of small

losses ("loss spreading"). The first of these is not applicable where, as in most products cases, the injured person is a customer, directly or indirectly, of the injurer (as distinct from a pure bystander — e.g., someone hit on the ground when the plane crashed). This is most easily seen by imagining a product that costs $10 to produce and distribute and involves an expected accident cost to the consumer of 10¢. Under a rule of no liability, the latter cost is nominally borne by the customer. Suppose the value of the product to the consumer, net of any costs which he must incur to use it (and let us assume that the only such cost is the expected accident cost), is $12. Then under a rule of no liability he will pay at most (why "at most"?) only $11.90 for the product. The manufacturer will make a profit of $1.90. This is the same profit he makes under a rule of strict liability, whereby the expected accident cost is explicitly shifted to him. To be sure, under strict liability he can raise his price to the consumer to $12; but his own costs have risen to $10.10. This example shows that the manufacturer gains nothing by a rule of no liability. There is no cost externalization.

The second aspect of "risk distribution" is loss spreading, that is, insurance in one form or another. As mentioned in Note 3 above, the case for using the tort system as an insurance mechanism is weaker in the usual products case than in the cases discussed in Chapter 7. In the products case the potential injurer and potential victim are already in a direct or indirect contractual relationship with each other. If injurer insurance is optimal, potential injurers will expressly warrant the safety of their products to the consumer. If they fail to do so, this is evidence (but not conclusive evidence — why?) that it is not an optimal form of insurance.

There is an extensive economic literature on products liability, much of it rather technical, however. Besides the Hamada piece cited earlier, see, e.g., Buchanan, In Defense of Caveat Emptor, 38 U. Chi. L. Rev. 64 (1970); Eppel & Raviv, Product Safety: Liability Rules, Market Structure, and Imperfect Information, 68 Am. Econ. Rev. 80 (1978); Goldberg, The Economics of Product Safety and Imperfect Information, 5 Bell J. Econ. & Mgmt. Sci. 683 (1974); McKean, Products Liability: Implications of Some Changing Property Rights, 84 Q.J. Econ. 611 (1970); Oi, The Economics of Product Safety, 4 Bell J. Econ. & Mgmt. Sci. 3 (1973); Ordover, Products Liability in Markets with Heterogeneous Consumers, 8 J. Legal Stud. 505 (1979); Simon, Imperfect Information, Costly Litigation, and Product Quality, 12 Bell J. Econ. & Mgmt. Sci. 171 (1981); Spence, Consumer Misperceptions, Product Failure and Producer Liability, 44 Rev. Econ. Stud. 561 (1977).

5. The approach of the dissent in *Goldberg* is the one favored by most jurisdictions: explicit strict liability divorced from any concept of implied warranty. Some states, however, have not adopted explicit strict products liability; in them, implied warranty, with whatever privity requirement the state chooses to impose, continues to be important. See, e.g., Blankenship v. Morrison Machine Co., 255 Md. 241, 257 A.2d 430 (1969).

6. Once the privity requirement is overcome, an implied-warranty case involving personal injury may be hard to distinguish from an ordinary tort case. Consider Guarino v. Mine Safety Appliance Co., 25 N.Y.2d 460, 255 N.E.2d 173 (1969). This was an action for deaths and injuries to members of a sewer repair crew in attempting to rescue a city employee whose oxygen mask, manufactured by defendant, malfunctioned. The court held that the "danger invites rescue" doctrine of *Wagner* was applicable and hence that defendant was liable for the harm to the rescuers. The residual differences between tort and warranty personal-injury cases are discussed later.

7. How far can the warranty idea be pressed in the personal-injury context? Suppose, as in Rowland v. Christian in Chapter 5, a social guest is injured by a defective faucet in his host's bathroom. Is the manufacturer of the faucet liable on an implied-warranty theory? Cf. Schipper v. Levitt & Sons, Inc., 44 N.J. 70, 207 A.2d 314 (1965). How about the host? In Whitmer v. Schneble, 29 Ill. App. 3d 659, 331 N.E.2d 115 (1975), the Schnebles' Doberman Pinscher bit a child. The Schnebles were sued and filed a third-party complaint against the House of Hoyt, from which they had bought the dog, alleging among other things that the House of Hoyt had represented to them that the dog was a "docile dobe." Hoyt was held not liable. Even if there was an express warranty (and not just "sales talk"), it was not a warranty that the dog would never bite, so it was not breached.

8. Another way around the privity requirement, of some contemporary significance as we shall see, is illustrated by the leading case of Baxter v. Ford Motor Co., 168 Wash. 456, 12 P.2d 409 (1932). Plaintiff bought a Model A Ford from St. John Motors, a Ford dealer which had purchased the car from Ford Motor Company. While plaintiff was driving the car, a pebble from a passing car struck the windshield, which shattered, injuring his eyes. Plaintiff based his action against Ford on a claim that Ford had represented in its advertising that the windshield was made of shatterproof glass. The court stated:

> Respondent Ford Motor Company contends that there can be no implied or express warranty without privity of contract, and warranties as to personal property do not attach themselves to, and run with, the article sold.
>
> Mazetti v. Armour & Co., 75 Wash. 622, 135 P. 633, was a case brought against Armour & Co. by proprietors of a restaurant. The complaint alleged that in the course of their business they purchased from the Seattle Grocery Company a carton of cooked tongue, relying upon the representations of Armour & Co. that its goods were pure, wholesome, and fit food for human beings; that in the center of the carton was a foul, filthy, nauseating, and poisonous substance. . . .
>
> The vital principle present in the case of Mazetti v. Armour & Co. confronts us in the case at bar. In the case cited the court recognized the right of a purchaser to a remedy against the manufacturer because of damages suffered by reason of a failure of goods to comply with the manufacturer's representations as to the existence of qualities which they did not in fact possess, when the

absence of such qualities was not readily discoverable, even though there was no privity of contract between the purchaser and the manufacturer.

Since the rule of caveat emptor was first formulated, vast changes have taken place in the economic structures of the English speaking peoples. Methods of doing business have undergone a great transition. Radio, billboards, and the products of the printing press have become the means of creating a large part of the demand that causes goods to depart from factories to the ultimate consumer. It would be unjust to recognize a rule that would permit manufacturers of goods to create a demand for their products by representing that they possess qualities which they, in fact, do not possess, and then, because there is no privity of contract existing between the consumer and the manufacturer, deny the consumer the right to recover if damages result from the absence of those qualities, when such absence is not readily noticeable. . . .

We hold that the catalogues and printed matter furnished by respondent Ford Motor Company for distribution and assistance in sales were improperly excluded from evidence, because they set forth representations by the manufacturer that the windshield of the car which appellant bought contained Triplex non-shatterable glass which would not fly or shatter. The nature of non-shatterable glass is such that the falsity of the representations with reference to the glass would not be readily detected by a person of ordinary experience and reasonable prudence. Appellant, under the circumstances shown in this case, had the right to rely upon the representations made by respondent Ford Motor Company relative to qualities possessed by its products, even though there was no privity of contract between appellant and respondent Ford Motor Company.

Id. at 460, 462-463, 12 P.2d at 411-412. What was the basis of Baxter's action against Ford? Was it breach of implied warranty? Was it breach of express warranty? Was it fraud? Was it negligent misrepresentation? Was it reliance, as in the *Stewart* and *Marsalis* cases in Chapter 6?

Henningsen v. Bloomfield Motors, Inc.
32 N.J. 358, 161 A.2d 69 (1960)

FRANCIS, J.

Plaintiff Claus H. Henningsen purchased a Plymouth automobile, manufactured by defendant Chrysler Corporation, from defendant Bloomfield Motors, Inc. His wife, plaintiff Helen Henningsen, was injured while driving it and instituted suit against both defendants to recover damages on account of her injuries. Her husband joined in the action seeking compensation for his consequential losses. The complaint was predicated upon breach of express and implied warranties and upon negligence. At the trial the negligence counts were dismissed by the court and the cause was submitted to the jury for determination solely on the issues of implied warranty of merchantability.

Verdicts were returned against both defendants and in favor of the plaintiffs. . . .

. . . The record indicates that Mr. Henningsen intended the car as a Mother's Day gift to his wife. He said the intention was communicated to the dealer. When the purchase order or contract was prepared and presented, the husband executed it alone. His wife did not join as a party.

The purchase order was a printed form of one page. . . . The smallest type on the page appears in the two paragraphs, one of two and one-quarter lines and the second of one and one-half lines, on which great stress is laid by the defense in the case. These two paragraphs are the least legible and the most difficult to read in the instrument, but they are most important in the evaluation of the rights of the contesting parties. They do not attract attention and there is nothing about the format which would draw the reader's eye to them. In fact, a studied and concentrated effort would have to be made to read them. De-emphasis seems the motif rather than emphasis. . . .

The two paragraphs are:

> The front and back of this Order comprise the entire agreement affecting this purchase and no other agreement or understanding of any nature concerning same has been made or entered into, or will be recognized. I hereby certify that no credit has been extended to me for the purchase of this motor vehicle except as appears in writing on the face of this agreement.
>
> I have read the matter printed on the back hereof and agree to it as a part of this order the same as if it were printed above my signature. I certify that I am 21 years of age, or older, and hereby acknowledge receipt of a copy of this order. . . .

The testimony of Claus Henningsen justifies the conclusion that he did not read the two fine print paragraphs referring to the back of the purchase contract. And it is uncontradicted that no one made any reference to them, or called them to his attention. With respect to the matter appearing on the back, it is likewise uncontradicted that he did not read it and that no one called it to his attention.

The reverse side of the contract contains $8\frac{1}{2}$ inches of fine print. It is not as small, however, as the two critical paragraphs described above. . . . In the seventh paragraph, about two-thirds of the way down the page, the warranty, which is the focal point of the case, is set forth. It is as follows:

> 7. It is expressly agreed that there are no warranties, express or implied, *made* by either the dealer or the manufacturer on the motor vehicle, chassis, or parts furnished hereunder except as follows.
>
> "The manufacturer warrants each new motor vehicle (including original equipment placed thereon by the manufacturer except tires), chassis or parts manufactured by it to be free from defects in material or workmanship under normal use and service. Its obligation under this warranty being limited to making good at its factory any part or parts thereof which shall, within ninety

(90) days after delivery of such vehicle *to the original purchaser* or before such vehicle has been driven 4,000 miles, whichever event shall first occur, be returned to it with transportation charges prepaid and which its examination shall disclose to its satisfaction to have been thus defective; *this warranty being expressly in lieu of all other warranties expressed or implied, and all other obligations or liabilities on its part,* and it neither assumes nor authorizes any other person to assume for it any other liability in connection with the sale of its vehicles. . . ." (Emphasis ours.) . . .

The insurance carrier's inspector and appraiser of damaged cars, with 11 years of experience, advanced the opinion, based on the history and his examination, that something definitely went "wrong from the steering wheel down to the front wheels" and that the untoward happening [the steering wheel spun in Mrs. Henningsen's hands and the car veered out of control] must have been due to mechanical defect or failure. . . .

As has been indicated, the trial court felt that the proof was not sufficient to make out a prima facie case as to the negligence of either the manufacturer or the dealer. The case was given to the jury, therefore, solely on the warranty theory, with results favorable to the plaintiffs against both defendants.

. . . Under the broad terms of the Uniform Sale of Goods Law any affirmation of fact relating to the goods is an express warranty if the natural tendency of the statement is to induce the buyer to make the purchase. And over the years since the almost universal adoption of the act, a growing awareness of the tremendous development of modern business methods has prompted the courts to administer that provision with a liberal hand. Solicitude toward the buyer plainly harmonizes with the intention of the Legislature. That fact is manifested further by the later section of the act which preserves and continues any permissible implied warranty, despite an express warranty, unless the two are inconsistent.

The uniform act codified, extended and liberalized the common law of sales. The motivation in part was to ameliorate the harsh doctrine of caveat emptor, and in some measure to impose a reciprocal obligation on the seller to beware. The transcendent value of the legislation, particularly with respect to implied warranties, rests in the fact that obligations on the part of the seller were imposed by operation of law, and did not depend for their existence upon express agreement of the parties. And of tremendous significance in a rapidly expanding commercial society was the recognition of the right to recover damages on account of personal injuries arising from a breach of warranty. The particular importance of this advance resides in the fact that under such circumstances strict liability is imposed upon the maker or seller of the product. Recovery of damages does not depend upon proof of negligence or knowledge of the defect.

As the Sales Act and its liberal interpretation by the courts threw this protective cloak about the buyer, the decisions in various jurisdictions revealed beyond doubt that many manufacturers took steps to avoid these ever increasing warranty obligations. Realizing that the act governed the relationship of buyer and seller, they undertook to withdraw from actual and direct contractual contact with the buyer. They ceased selling products to the consuming public through their own employees and making contracts of sale in their own names. Instead, a system of independent dealers was established; their products were sold to dealers who in turn dealt with the buying public, ostensibly solely in their own personal capacity as sellers. In the past in many instances, manufacturers were able to transfer to the dealers burdens imposed by the act and thus achieved a large measure of immunity for themselves. But, as will be noted in more detail hereafter, such marketing practices, coupled with the advent of large scale advertising by manufacturers to promote the purchase of these goods from dealers by members of the public, provided a basis upon which the existence of express or implied warranties was predicated, even though the manufacturer was not a party to the contract of sale.

    . . . It must be noted, however, that the sections of the Sales Act, to which reference has been made, do not impose warranties in terms of unalterable absolutes. [The Act] provides in general terms that an applicable warranty may be negatived or varied by express agreement. As to disclaimers or limitations of the obligations that normally attend a sale, it seems sufficient at this juncture to say they are not favored, and that they are strictly construed against the seller.

    With these considerations in mind, we come to a study of the express warranty on the reverse side of the purchase order signed by Claus Henningsen. At the outset we take notice that it was made only by the manufacturer and that by its terms it runs directly to Claus Henningsen. On the facts detailed above, it was to be extended to him by the dealer as the agent of Chrysler Corporation. . . . The evidence is overwhelming that the dealer acted for Chrysler in including the warranty in the purchase contract.

    The terms of the warranty are a sad commentary upon the automobile manufacturers' marketing practices. Warranties developed in the law in the interest of and to protect the ordinary consumer who cannot be expected to have the knowledge or capacity or even the opportunity to make adequate inspection of mechanical instrumentalities, like automobiles, and to decide for himself whether they are reasonably fit for the designed purpose. But the ingenuity of the Automobile Manufacturers Association, by means of its standardized form, has metamorphosed the warranty into a device to limit the maker's liability. . . .

    The manufacturer agrees to replace defective parts for 90 days after the sale or until the car has been driven 4,000 miles, whichever is first to occur, *if the part is sent to the factory, transportation charges prepaid, and if examination discloses to its satisfaction that the part is defective.* It is difficult to imagine a greater burden on the consumer, or less satisfactory remedy. Aside from imposing on the buyer the trouble of removing and shipping the part, the maker has sought to retain the uncontrolled discretion to decide the issue of defectiveness. . . . Also suppose, as in this case, a defective part or parts caused an accident and that the car was so damaged as to render it impossible to discover the precise part or parts responsible, although the circumstances clearly pointed to such fact as the cause of the mishap. Can it be said that the impossibility of performance deprived the buyer of the benefit of the warranty?

Moreover, the guaranty is against defective workmanship. That condition may arise from good parts improperly assembled. There being no defective parts to return to the maker, is all remedy to be denied? . . .

The matters referred to represent only a small part of the illusory character of the security presented by the warranty. Thus far the analysis has dealt only with the remedy provided in the case of a defective part. What relief is provided when the breach of the warranty results in personal injury to the buyer? . . . [T]he law is clear that such damages are recoverable under an ordinary warranty. The right exists whether the warranty sued on is express or implied. And, of course, it has long since been settled that where the buyer or a member of his family driving with his permission suffers injuries because of negligent manufacture or construction of the vehicle, the manufacturer's liability exists. But in this instance, after reciting that defective parts will be replaced at the factory, the alleged agreement relied upon by Chrysler provides that the manufacturer's "obligation under this warranty" is limited to that undertaking; further, that such remedy is "in lieu of all other warranties, express or implied, and all other obligations or liabilities on its part." The contention has been raised that such language bars any claim for personal injuries which may emanate from a breach of the warranty. . . .

Putting aside for the time being the problem of the efficacy of the disclaimer provisions contained in the express warranty, a question of first importance to be decided is whether an implied warranty of merchantability by Chrysler Corporation accompanied the sale of the automobile to Claus Henningsen.

Preliminarily, it may be said that the express warranty against defective parts and workmanship is not inconsistent with an implied warranty of merchantability. Such warranty cannot be excluded for that reason.

Chrysler points out that an implied warranty of merchantability is an incident of a contract of sale. It concedes, of course, the making of the original sale to Bloomfield Motors, Inc., but maintains that this transaction marked the terminal point of its contractual connection with the car. Then Chrysler urges that since it was not a party to the sale by the dealer to Henningsen, there is no privity of contract between it and the plaintiffs, and the absence of this privity eliminates any such implied warranty.

There is no doubt that under early common-law concepts of contractual liability only those persons who were parties to the bargain could sue for a breach of it. In more recent times a noticeable disposition has appeared in a number of jurisdictions to break through the narrow barrier of privity when dealing with sales of goods in order to give realistic recognition to a universally accepted fact. The fact is that the dealer and the ordinary buyer do not, and are not expected to, buy goods, whether they be foodstuffs or automobiles, exclusively for their own consumption or use. Makers and manufacturers know this and advertise and market their products on that assumption; witness, the "family" car, the baby foods, etc. The limitations of privity in contracts for the sale of goods developed their place in the law when marketing conditions were simple, when maker and buyer frequently met face to face on an equal bargaining plane and when many of the products were relatively uncomplicated and conducive to inspection by a buyer competent to evaluate their quality. With the advent of mass marketing, the manufacturer became remote from the purchaser, sales were accomplished through intermediaries, and the demand for the product was created by advertising media. In such an economy it became obvious that the consumer was the person being cultivated. Manifestly, the connotation of "consumer" was broader than that of "buyer." He signified such a person who, in the reasonable contemplation of the parties to the sale, might be expected to use the product. Thus, where the commodities sold are such that if defectively manufactured they will be dangerous to life or limb, then society's interests can only be protected by eliminating the requirement of privity between the maker and his dealers and the reasonably expected ultimate consumer. In that way the burden of losses consequent upon use of defective articles is borne by those who are in a position to either control the danger or make an equitable distribution of the losses when they do occur. . . .

Although only a minority of jurisdictions have thus far departed from the requirement of privity, the movement in that direction is most certainly gathering momentum. Liability to the ultimate consumer in the absence of direct contractual connection has been predicated upon a variety of theories. Some courts hold that the warranty runs with the article like a covenant running with land; others recognize a third-party beneficiary thesis; still others rest their decision on the ground that public policy requires recognition of a warranty made directly to the consumer. . . .

Most of the cases where lack of privity has not been permitted to interfere with recovery have involved food and drugs. In fact, the rule as to such products has been characterized as an exception to the general doctrine. . . .

We see no rational doctrinal basis for differentiating between a fly in a bottle of beverage and a defective automobile. The unwholesome beverage may bring illness to one person, the defective car, with its great potentiality for harm to the driver, occupants, and others, demands even less adherence to the narrow barrier of privity. . . .

Under modern conditions the ordinary layman, on responding to the importuning of colorful advertising, has neither the opportunity nor the capacity to inspect or to determine the fitness of an automobile for use; he must rely on the manufacturer who has control of its construction, and to some degree on the dealer who, to the limited extent called for by the manufacturer's instructions, inspects and services it before delivery. In such a marketing milieu his remedies and those of persons who properly claim through him should not depend "upon the intricacies of the law of sales. The obligation of the manufacturer should not be based alone on privity of contract. It should rest, as was once said, upon 'the demands of social justice.' " "If privity of contract is required," then, under the circumstances of modern merchandising, "privity of contract exists in the consciousness and understanding of all right-thinking persons."

Accordingly, we hold that under modern marketing conditions, when a manufacturer puts a new automobile in the stream of trade and promotes its purchase by the public, an implied warranty that it is reasonably suitable for use as such accompanies it into the hands of the ultimate purchaser. Absence of agency between the manufacturer and the dealer who makes the ultimate sale is immaterial. . . .

. . . [W]hat effect should be given to the express warranty in question which seeks to limit the manufacturer's liability to replacement of defective parts, and which disclaims all other warranties, express or implied? In assessing its significance we must keep in mind the general principle that, in the absence of fraud, one who does not choose to read a contract before signing it, cannot later relieve himself of its burdens. And in applying that principle, the basic tenet of freedom of competent parties to contract is a factor of importance. But in the framework of modern commercial life and business practices, such rules cannot be applied on a strict, doctrinal basis. The conflicting interests of the buyer and seller must be evaluated realistically and justly, giving due weight to the social policy evinced by the Uniform Sales Act, the progressive decisions of the courts engaged in administering it, the mass production methods of manufacture and distribution to the public, and the bargaining position occupied by the ordinary consumer in such an economy. . . .

The traditional contract is the result of free bargaining of parties who are brought together by the play of the market, and who meet each other on a footing of approximate economic equality. In such a society there is no danger that freedom of contract will be a threat to the social order as a whole. But in present-day commercial life the standardized mass contract has appeared. It is used primarily by enterprises with strong bargaining power and position. "The weaker party, in need of the goods or services, is frequently not in a position to shop around for better terms, either because the author of the standard contract has a monopoly (natural or artificial) or because all competitors use the same clauses. His contractual intention is but a subjection more or less voluntary to terms dictated by the stronger party, terms whose consequences are often understood in a vague way, if at all." . . .

The warranty before us is a standardized form designed for mass use. It is imposed upon the automobile consumer. He takes it or leaves it, and he must take it to buy an automobile. No bargaining is engaged in with respect to it.

In fact, the dealer through whom it comes to the buyer is without authority to alter it; his function is ministerial — simply to deliver it. The form warranty is not only standard with Chrysler but, as mentioned above, it is the uniform warranty of the Automobile Manufacturers Association. Members of the Association are: General Motors, Inc., Ford, Chrysler, Studebaker-Packard, American Motors (Rambler), Willys Motors, Checker Motors Corp., and International Harvester Company. Of these companies, the "Big Three" (General Motors, Ford, and Chrysler) represented 93.5% of the passenger-car production for 1958 and the independents 6.5%. And for the same year the "Big Three" had 86.72% of the total passenger vehicle registrations.

The gross inequality of bargaining position occupied by the consumer in the automobile industry is thus apparent. There is no competition among the car makers in the area of the express warranty. Where can the buyer go to negotiate for better protection? Such control and limitation of his remedies are inimical to the public welfare and, at the very least, call for great care by the courts to avoid injustice through application of strict common-law principles of freedom of contract. Because there is no competition among the motor vehicle manufacturers with respect to the scope of protection guaranteed to the buyer, there is no incentive on their part to stimulate good will in that field of public relations. Thus, there is lacking a factor existing in more competitive fields, one which tends to guarantee the safe construction of the article sold. Since all competitors operate in the same way, the urge to be careful is not so pressing. . . .

The task of the judiciary is to administer the spirit as well as the letter of the law. On issues such as the present one, part of that burden is to protect the ordinary man against the loss of important rights through what, in effect, is the unilateral act of the manufacturer. The status of the automobile industry is unique. Manufacturers are few in number and strong in bargaining position. In the matter of warranties on the sale of their products, the Automotive Manufacturers Association has enabled them to present a united front. From the standpoint of the purchaser, there can be no arms length negotiating on the subject. Because his capacity for bargaining is so grossly unequal, the inexorable conclusion which follows is that he is not permitted to bargain at all. He must take or leave the automobile on the warranty terms dictated by the maker. He cannot turn to a competitor for better security.

Public policy is a term not easily defined. Its significance varies as the habits and needs of a people may vary. It is not static and the field of application is an ever increasing one. A contract, or a particular provision therein, valid in one era may be wholly opposed to the public policy of another. Courts keep in mind the principle that the best interests of society demand that persons should not be unnecessarily restricted in their freedom to contract. But they do not hesitate to declare void as against public policy contractual provisions which clearly tend to the injury of the public in some way.

Public policy at a given time finds expression in the Constitution, the statutory law and in judicial decisions. In the area of sale of goods, the legislative will has imposed an implied warranty of merchantability as a general incident of sale of an automobile by description. The warranty does not depend upon the affirmative intention of the parties. It is a child of the law; it annexes itself to the contract because of the very nature of the transaction. The judicial process has recognized a right to recover damages for personal injuries arising from a breach of that warranty. The disclaimer of the implied warranty and exclusion of all obligations except those specifically assumed by the express warranty signify a studied effort to frustrate that protection. True, the Sales Act authorizes agreements between buyer and seller qualifying the warranty obligations. But quite obviously the Legislature contemplated lawful stipulations (which are determined by the circumstances of a particular case) arrived at freely by parties of relatively equal bargaining strength. The lawmakers did not authorize the automobile manufacturer to use its grossly disproportionate bargaining power to relieve itself from liability and to impose on the ordinary buyer, who in effect has no real freedom of choice, the grave danger of injury to himself and others that attends the sale of such a dangerous instrumentality as a defectively made automobile. In the framework of this case, illuminated as it is by the facts and the many decisions noted, we are of the opinion that Chrysler's attempted disclaimer of an implied warranty of merchantability and of the obligations arising therefrom is so inimical to the public good as to compel an adjudication of its invalidity. . . .

Both defendants contend that since there was no privity of contract between them and Mrs. Henningsen, she cannot recover for breach of any warranty made by either of them. On the facts, as they were developed, we agree that she was not a party to the purchase agreement. Her right to maintain the action, therefore, depends upon whether she occupies such legal status thereunder as to permit her to take advantage of a breach of defendants' implied warranties.

For the most part the cases that have been considered dealt with the right of the buyer or consumer to maintain an action against the manufacturer where the contract of sale was with a dealer and the buyer had no contractual relationship with the manufacturer. In the present matter, the basic contractual relationship is between Claus Henningsen, Chrysler, and Bloomfield Motors, Inc. The precise issue presented is whether Mrs. Henningsen, who is not a party to their respective warranties, may claim under them. In our judgment, the principles of those cases and the supporting texts are just as proximately applicable to her situation. We are convinced that the cause of justice in this area of the law can be served only by recognizing that she is such a person who, in the reasonable contemplation of the parties to the warranty, might be expected to become a user of the automobile. Accordingly, her lack of privity does not stand in the way of prosecution of the injury suit against the defendant Chrysler. . . .

It is important to express the right of Mrs. Henningsen to maintain her action in terms of a general principle. To what extent may lack of privity be disregarded in suits on such warranties? . . . [I]t is our opinion that an implied warranty of merchantability chargeable to either an automobile manufacturer or a dealer extends to the purchaser of the car, members of his family, and to other persons occupying or using it with his consent. It would be wholly opposed to reality to say that use by such persons is not within the anticipation of parties to such a warranty of reasonable suitability of an automobile for ordinary highway operation. Those persons must be considered within the distributive chain.

Harper and James suggest that this remedy ought to run to members of the public, bystanders, for example, who are in the path of harm from a defective automobile. Section 2-318 of the Uniform Commercial Code proposes that the warranty be extended to "any natural person who is in the family or household of his buyer or who is a guest in his home if it is reasonable to expect that such person may use, consume or be affected by the goods and who is injured in person by breach of the warranty." And the section provides also that "A seller may not exclude or limit the operation" of the extension. A footnote thereto says that beyond this provision "the section is neutral and is not intended to enlarge or restrict the developing case law on whether the seller's warranties, given to his buyer, who resells, extend to other persons in the distributive chain."

It is not necessary in this case to establish the outside limits of the warranty protection. For present purposes, with respect to automobiles, it suffices to promulgate the principle set forth above. . . .

[Affirmed.]

Notes

1. Is the attempt of the automobile industry to disclaim liability for personal injuries resulting from breach of an implied-in-law warranty of fitness or merchantability so shocking as the court thought? The industry was not attempting to disclaim liability for negligent design or manufacture of automobiles. Even if the industry was acting in effect as a monopolist, why would a monopolist want to offer consumers less safety than they desire, rather than offer them the desired level of safety but charge a monopoly price? Refer again to the discussion in Chapter 5 of disclaimers of negligence liability.

2. Ordover, Products Liability in Markets with Heterogeneous Consumers, 8 J. Legal Stud. 505 (1979), offers an interesting defense of nonwaivability of products liability. Suppose consumers differ in their ability to avoid being injured by defective products. Manufacturers will offer low-risk consumers an opportunity to waive the manufacturer's strict liability in exchange for a lower price. This will be an attractive deal for them. They create a below-

average risk for the manufacturer, and hence do not want to pay as part of the price for the product a risk premium based on the average, and therefore higher, risks faced by consumers of this product as a group. But, by opting out in this way, the low-risk consumers increase the risk premium that the manufacturer must charge to the remaining consumers, for the average risk has increased as a result of the withdrawal of the low-risk consumers, who kept the average down before. High-risk consumers are thus hurt by the waivers. Is this a good argument for refusing to enforce such waivers?

3. After *Henningsen*, what if anything is left of the contractual origins of an action for personal injuries arising from breach of an implied warranty of fitness or merchantability? What would be the procedural consequences of jettisoning the implied-warranty concept in personal-injury cases altogether and treating them as strict-liability tort cases?

4. Why did the trial court hold that plaintiff had failed to make out a prima facie case of Chrysler's negligence? Was there not adequate evidence that the car was defective? In fact, is proof of a product defect not a threshold requirement of plaintiff's implied-warranty action? If a manufacturer produces a car with defective steering, is he not negligent, given the very high probability of a serious accident that such a defect creates? (There were only 468 miles on the odometer of the Henningsens' car at the time of the accident, no signs of trouble before the accident, and no evidence of any cause of the accident other than the defect.) Apart from procedural differences between tort and contract actions (see Chapter 6, and below in this chapter), is not the principal difference between a negligence action and an implied-warranty action that in the latter action a manufacturer may be liable for a defect in a component that, as in the *Goldberg* case, he could not have discovered by a reasonable inspection?

Greenman v. Yuba Power Products, Inc.
59 Cal. 2d 57, 377 P.2d 897 (1962)

TRAYNOR, J.

Plaintiff brought this action for damages against the retailer and the manufacturer of a Shopsmith, a combination power tool that could be used as a saw, drill, and wood lathe. He saw a Shopsmith demonstrated by the retailer and studied a brochure prepared by the manufacturer. He decided he wanted a Shopsmith for his home workshop, and his wife bought and gave him one for Christmas in 1955. In 1957 he bought the necessary attachments to use the Shopsmith as a lathe for turning a large piece of wood he wished to make into a chalice. After he had worked on the piece of wood several times without difficulty, it suddenly flew out of the machine and struck him on the forehead, inflicting serious injuries. About ten and a half months later, he gave the retailer and the manufacturer written notice of claimed breaches of warranties and filed a complaint against them alleging such breaches and negligence.

After a trial before a jury, the court ruled that there was no evidence that the retailer was negligent or had breached any express warranty and that the manufacturer was not liable for the breach of any implied warranty. Accordingly, it submitted to the jury only the cause of action alleging breach of implied warranties against the retailer and the causes of action alleging negligence and breach of express warranties against the manufacturer. The jury returned a verdict for the retailer against plaintiff and for plaintiff against the manufacturer in the amount of $65,000. The trial court denied the manufacturer's motion for a new trial and entered judgment on the verdict. . . .

Plaintiff introduced substantial evidence that his injuries were caused by defective design and construction of the Shopsmith. His expert witnesses testified that inadequate set screws were used to hold parts of the machine together so that normal vibration caused the tailstock of the lathe to move away from the piece of wood being turned permitting it to fly out of the lathe. They also testified that there were other more positive ways of fastening the parts of the machine together, the use of which would have prevented the accident. The jury could therefore reasonably have concluded that the manufacturer negligently constructed the Shopsmith. The jury could also reasonably have concluded that statements in the manufacturer's brochure were untrue, that they constituted express warranties,[1] and that plaintiff's injuries were caused by their breach.

The manufacturer contends, however, that plaintiff did not give it notice of breach of warranty within a reasonable time and that therefore his cause of action for breach of warranty is barred by section 1796 of the Civil Code. Since it cannot be determined whether the verdict against it was based on the negligence or warranty cause of action or both, the manufacturer concludes that the error in presenting the warranty cause of action to the jury was prejudicial.

Section 1796 of the Civil Code provides: "In the absence of express or implied agreement of the parties, acceptance of the goods by the buyer shall not discharge the seller from liability in damages or other legal remedy for breach of any promise or warranty in the contract to sell or the sale. But, if, after acceptance of the goods, the buyer fails to give notice to the seller of the breach of any promise or warranty within a reasonable time after the buyer knows, or ought to know of such breach, the seller shall not be liable therefor."

---

1. In this respect the trial court limited the jury to a consideration of two statements in the manufacturer's brochure. (1) "WHEN SHOPSMITH IS IN HORIZONTAL POSITION — Rugged construction of frame provides rigid support from end to end. Heavy centerless-ground steel tubing insures perfect alignment of components." (2) "SHOPSMITH maintains its accuracy because every component has positive locks that hold adjustments through rough or precision work."

Like other provisions of the uniform sales act, section 1769 deals with the rights of the parties to a contract of sale or a sale. It does not provide that notice must be given of the breach of a warranty that arises independently of a contract of sale between the parties. Such warranties are not imposed by the sales act, but are the product of common-law decisions that have recognized them in a variety of situations. It is true that in many of these situations the court has invoked the sales act definitions of warranties in defining the defendant's liability, but it has done so, not because the statutes so required, but because they provided appropriate standards for the court to adopt under the circumstances presented.

The notice requirement of section 1769, however, is not an appropriate one for the court to adopt in actions by injured consumers against manufacturers with whom they have not dealt. "As between the immediate parties to the sale [the notice requirement] is a sound commercial rule, designed to protect the seller against unduly delayed claims for damages. As applied to personal injuries, and notice to a remote seller, it becomes a booby-trap for the unwary. . . ."

Moreover, to impose strict liability on the manufacturer under the circumstances of this case, it was not necessary for plaintiff to establish an express warranty. . . . A manufacturer is strictly liable in tort when an article he places on the market, knowing that it is to be used without inspection for defects, proves to have a defect that causes injury to a human being. Recognized first in the case of unwholesome food products, such liability has now been extended to a variety of other products that create as great or greater hazards if defective.

Although in these cases strict liability has usually been based on the theory of an express or implied warranty running from the manufacturer to the plaintiff, the abandonment of the requirement of a contract between them, the recognition that the liability is not assumed by agreement but imposed by law, and the refusal to permit the manufacturer to define the scope of its own responsibility for defective products make clear that the liability is not one governed by the law of contract warranties but by the law of strict liability in tort. Accordingly, rules defining and governing warranties that were developed to meet the needs of commercial transactions cannot properly be invoked to govern the manufacturer's liability to those injured by their defective products unless those rules also serve the purposes for which such liability is imposed.

We need not recanvass the reasons for imposing strict liability on the manufacturer. . . . The purpose of such liability is to insure that the costs of injuries resulting from defective products are borne by the manufacturers that put such products on the market rather than by the injured persons who are powerless to protect themselves. Sales warranties serve this purpose fitfully at best. In the present case, for example, plaintiff was able to plead and prove an express warranty only because he read and relied on the representations of the Shopsmith's ruggedness contained in the manufacturer's brochure. Implicit in the machine's presence on the market, however, was a representation that it would safely do the jobs for which it was built. Under these circumstances, it should not be controlling whether plaintiff selected the machine because of the statements in the brochure, or because of the machine's own appearance of excellence that belied the defect lurking beneath the surface, or because he merely assumed that it would safely do the jobs it was built to do. It should not be controlling whether the details of the sales from manufacturer to retailer and from retailer to plaintiff's wife were such that one or more of the implied warranties of the sales act arose. "The remedies of injured consumers ought not to be made to depend upon the intricacies of the law of sales." To establish the manufacturer's liability it was sufficient that plaintiff proved that he was injured while using the Shopsmith in a way it was intended to be used as a result of a defect in design and manufacture of which plaintiff was not aware that made the Shopsmith unsafe for its intended use. . . .

Notes

1. Two years after *Greenman*, the American Law Institute published §402A of the Second Restatement of Torts, which reads as follows:

§402A. SPECIAL LIABILITY OF SELLER OF PRODUCT FOR PHYSICAL HARM
   TO USER OR CONSUMER
(1) One who sells any product in a defective condition unreasonably dangerous to the user or consumer or to his property is subject to liability for physical harm thereby caused to the ultimate user or consumer, or to his property, if
   (a) the seller is engaged in the business of selling such a product, and
   (b) it is expected to and does reach the user or consumer without substantial change in the condition in which it is sold.
(2) The rule stated in Subsection (1) applies although
   (a) the seller has exercised all possible care in the preparation and sale of his product, and
   (b) the user or consumer has not bought the product from or entered into any contractual relation with the seller.

CAVEAT:
   The Institute expresses no opinion as to whether the rules stated in this Section may not apply
   (1) to harm to persons other than users or consumers;
   (2) to the seller of a product expected to be processed or otherwise substantially changed before it reaches the user or consumer; or
   (3) to the seller of a component part of a product to be assembled.

Is the standard of §402A identical to that of the *Greenman* case? If in doubt, see Morningstar v. Black & Decker Mfg. Co., 253 S.E.2d 666 (W. Va. 1979).

2. What is the difference between strict tort liability according to *Green-man* and §402A and implied-warranty liability according to *Goldberg* or *Henningsen?* This question is discussed in Phipps v. General Motors Corp., 278 Md. 337, 349-350, 363 A.2d 955, 961-962 (1976):

> One of the more significant differences between the two theories is the right of the seller to disclaim or limit remedies for breach of warranty. Although the Maryland Legislature has eliminated the right of sellers to disclaim or limit warranties arising from the sale of *consumer* goods, there is no similar limitation on the right to exclude warranties where the goods involved are not consumer goods as defined in §9-109 [of Maryland's version of the Uniform Commercial Code]. Under §402 A of the Restatement, a limitation or exclusion of warranties is irrelevant to the question of the seller's liability for injury caused by defective goods regardless of the classification of the goods (Comment m). The notice requirement of §2-607 of the Uniform Commercial Code may also prove to be an obstacle to recovery. Although we have recently held that a third party beneficiary of a seller's warranties is not required to give notice of breach as a precondition to maintaining a breach of warranty action, an actual buyer is still required by §2-607(3) to give notice or be barred from any recovery for breach of warranty. There is no similar notice requirement for bringing an action based on strict liability in tort. Also, an action for breach of warranty is governed by the limitations period contained in §2-725 of the Uniform Commercial Code, which provides that an action must be brought within four years of the time it accrues. A cause of action in a warranty case accrues "when tender of delivery is made." An action under the theory of strict liability in tort, however, would be governed by the general tort limitations period, Maryland Code (1974), which is three years but may begin to run at a later time. These are examples of significant differences between actions based upon contract and strict liability in tort.

3. Is there any reason why a plaintiff might still want to bring a negligence action for an injury caused by a defective product? Ward v. Hobart Mfg. Co., 450 F.2d 1176 (5th Cir. 1971), was such a case. The court noted:

> The essential difference in strict liability and negligent design is that in the former it is only necessary to prove that the product was defective when it left the manufacturer's hands — negligence need not be proved. However, in strict liability cases it must be proved that there was no substantial change in the product from the time of manufacture until it reached the consumer.
>
> The complaint in the instant case contained a count in strict liability. The district court, however noted that Mrs. Ward did not pursue that theory. Consequently, the present case was decided solely on negligence principles.

Id. at 1180 n.7. But if there was a "substantial change in the product from the time of manufacture until it reached the consumer," would this not be as much of an obstacle to recovery on a negligence theory as on a strict liability theory? What, for example, would be the effect of such a change on plaintiff's ability to use the doctrine of res ipsa loquitur?

Tillman v. Vance Equipment Co.
286 Or. 747, 596 P.2d 1299 (1979)

DENECKE, C.J.

Plaintiff brought this action based upon the theory of strict liability in tort to recover for personal injuries caused by a 24-year-old crane sold by defendant, a used equipment dealer, to plaintiff's employer, Durametal. The court tried the case without a jury and found for the defendant. The plaintiff appeals and we affirm.

Durametal asked the defendant to locate a crane for purchase by Durametal. Defendant found one that looked suitable; Durametal inspected and approved it. The defendant purchased the crane and immediately resold it to Durametal. Defendant prepared documents making the sale "as is."

Durametal assigned plaintiff to operate the crane, including greasing it. Plaintiff believed the greasing of the gears could not be done properly without removing the gear cover and applying the grease while the gears were moving. While he was so greasing the gears, plaintiff's hand was drawn into them and he was injured.

Plaintiff alleged the defendant seller was liable because the crane was defectively designed in that it could not be properly greased without removing the protective gear covering and for failing to provide warnings of the danger. The trial court found for the defendant because the crane was a used piece of equipment and sold "as is."

The parties disagree about the effect of the "as is" disclaimer in the documents of sale. The issues raised include whether that disclaimer has any effect in an action of strict liability in tort, and whether, if so, it is effective to disclaim liability for a design defect as distinguished from a defect in the condition of the individual product. We do not answer these questions because we conclude that the trial court was correct in holding that a seller of used goods is not strictly liable in tort for a defect in a used crane when that defect was created by the manufacturer. . . .

Because of the impediments accompanying a contractual remedy, including the requirement of privity, we envolved the tort of strict liability. Strict liability could be imposed upon a party with whom the plaintiff was not in privity. For this reason the manufacturer who created the defect could be sued directly. The injured party could usually obtain personal jurisdiction over the the manufacturer by the use of the long-arm statutes. Because of the circumstances, there was no longer any urgent necessity to continue a cause of action against the seller who had not created the defect.

Nevertheless, courts did impose strict liability on the nonmanufacturer sellers of new goods as summarized in a recent study:

> Over time most courts extended the rationale of these cases to both retailers and distributors. . . . Courts extended strict liability to retailers and distributors, in part, on the assumption that these groups would place pressure on the manufacturer to produce safe products. Courts also believed that retailers and distributors might be more accessible to suit than manufacturers.

As Mr. Justice Traynor said in Vandermark v. Ford Motor Company, 61 Cal. 2d 256, 391 P.2d 168 (1964): "Retailers like manufacturers are engaged in the business of distributing goods to the public. They are an integral part of the overall producing and marketing enterprise that should bear the cost of injuries resulting from defective products. In some cases the retailer may be the only member of that enterprise reasonably available to the injured plaintiff. In other cases the retailer himself may play a substantial part in insuring that the product is safe or may be in a position to exert pressure on the manufacturer to that end; the retailer's strict liability thus serves as an added incentive to safety. . . ." . . .

Moreover, if a jurisdiction has adopted the principle of strict liability on the basis of enterprise liability, the liability of the seller of either a new or used product would logically follow. A judge of the Superior Court of New Jersey in a case involving a used truck explained the reasoning: "We will first consider whether this is the type of case for the application of strict liability in tort. An economic analysis of enterprise liability, which includes direct as well as indirect costs, would charge those in the business of selling a defective product with responsibility for all harms, physical and economic, which result from its use. To a considerable extent — with respect to *new* goods — the manufacturer bases the cost of his product on his expenses, which include damages caused by the product and insurance to cover those damages. This cost is spread among all the customers for that product; it reflects the justifiable expectations of customers regarding safety, quality and durability of new goods. Sellers of used goods may similarly distribute their costs of doing business which, in turn, will reflect what is considered by the public to be justifiable expectations regarding safety, quality and durability of used goods." . . .

This court has never been willing to rely on enterprise liability alone as a justification for strict liability for defective products. Instead, we have identified three justifications for the doctrine: ". . . [C]ompensation (ability to spread risk), satisfaction of the reasonable expectations of the purchaser or user (implied representational aspect), and over-all risk reduction (the impetus to manufacture a better product) . . ."

While dealers in used goods are, as a class, capable like other businesses of providing for the compensation of injured parties and the allocation of the cost of injuries caused by the products they sell, we are not convinced that the other two considerations . . . weigh sufficiently in this class of cases to justify imposing liability on sellers of used goods generally. . . .

We conclude that holding every dealer in used goods responsible regardless of fault for injuries caused by defects in his goods would not only affect the prices of used goods; it would work a significant change in the very nature of used goods markets. Those markets, generally speaking, operate on the apparent understanding that the seller, even though he is in the business of selling such goods, makes no particular representation about their quality simply by offering them for sale. If the buyer wants some assurance of quality, he typically either bargains for it in the specific transaction or seeks out a dealer who routinely offers it (by, for example, providing a guarantee, limiting his stock of goods to those of a particular quality, advertising that his used goods are specially selected, or in some other fashion). The flexibility of this kind of market appears to serve legitimate interests of buyers as well as sellers. . . .

As to the risk-reduction aspect of strict products liability, the position of the used-goods dealer is normally entirely outside the original chain of distribution of the product. As a consequence, we conclude, any risk reduction which would be accomplished by imposing strict liability on the dealer in used goods would not be significant enough to justify our taking that step. The dealer in used goods generally has no direct relationship with either manufacturers or distributors. Thus, there is no ready channel of communication by which the dealer and the manufacturer can exchange information about possible dangerous defects in particular product lines or about actual and potential liability claims.

In theory, a dealer in used goods who is held liable for injuries caused by a design defect or manufacturing flaw could obtain indemnity from the manufacturer. This possibility supports the argument that permitting strict liability claims against dealers in used goods will add to the financial incentive for manufacturers to design and build safe products. We believe, however, that the influence of this possibility as a practical factor in risk prevention is considerably diluted where used goods are involved due to such problems as statutes of limitation and the increasing difficulty as time passes of locating a still existing and solvent manufacturer. . . .

For the reasons we have discussed, we have concluded that the relevant policy considerations do not justify imposing strict liability for defective products on dealers in used goods, at least in the absence of some representation of quality beyond the sale itself or of a special position vis-à-vis the original manufacturer or others in the chain of original distribution.

We have suggested, although we have never had occasion to rule on the question, that those who are in the business of leasing products to others may be strictly liable for injuries caused by defective products on the same basis as sellers of new products. It has been urged that recognizing such a liability on the part of lessors while refusing to hold sellers of used goods liable would be logically inconsistent, because most leased goods are used when they reach the lessee. We see no such inconsistency when the focus of analysis is not on the status of the product but on that of the potential defendant. The lessor chooses the products which he offers in a significantly different way than does the typical dealer in used goods; the fact that he offers them repeatedly to different users as products he has selected may constitute a representation as to their quality; and it may well be that he has purchased them, either new or used, from a dealer who is directly related to the original distribution chain. Our rationale in the present case leaves the question of a lessor's strict liability an open one in this jurisdiction. . . .

Affirmed.

Note

If the dealer in used goods has "increasing difficulty as time passes of locating a still existing and solvent manufacturer," won't the injured consumer have even greater difficulty? Will not all the purposes of strict tort liability therefore be defeated if the dealer is not subject to strict liability?

However, Henderson, Extending the Boundaries of Strict Products Liability: Implications of the Theory of the Second Best, 128 U. Pa. L. Rev. 1036 (1980), argues against imposing strict liability on dealers in used goods on the following economic ground: If such dealers are liable, their costs will rise, and they will seek to pass on at least some of these costs to consumers in a higher price of the goods they sell. When they do so, substitute goods will become more attractive to the consumer. One particularly good substitute for a used good sold by a dealer is the same used good sold by another consumer. It is not proposed to make a consumer who sells some good that he owns strictly liable for injuries caused by a defect in that good. Therefore, the principal result of imposing strict liability on dealers in used goods might be to shift sales of used goods from dealers to consumers rather than to increase the safety of the goods. When two goods are excellent substitutes, imposing a tax on one — and liability operates like a tax in this respect — will simply shift purchasers from the taxed to the untaxed good. The Henderson article is of considerable interest because it offers a nonarbitrary method of setting some outer boundaries to the strict liability of sellers of goods and services.

Barker v. Lull Engineering Co.
20 Cal. 3d 413, 573 P.2d 443 (1978)

TOBRINER, C.J.

In August 1970, plaintiff Ray Barker was injured at a construction site at the University of California at Santa Cruz while operating a high-lift loader manufactured by defendant Lull Engineering Co. and leased to plaintiff's employer by defendant George M. Philpott Co., Inc. Claiming that his injuries were proximately caused, inter alia, by the alleged defective design of the loader, Barker instituted the present tort action seeking to recover damages for his injuries. The jury returned a verdict in favor of defendants, and plaintiff appeals from the judgment entered upon that verdict, contending primarily that in view of this court's decision in Cronin v. J.B.E. Olson Corp. (1972) 8 Cal. 3d 121, 501 P.2d 1153, the trial court erred in instructing the jury "that strict liability for a defect in design of a product is based on a finding that the product was unreasonably dangerous for its intended use. . . ." . . .

Plaintiff Barker sustained serious injuries as a result of an accident which occurred while he was operating a Lull High-Lift Loader at a construction site. The loader, manufactured in 1967, is a piece of heavy construction equipment designed to lift loads of up to 5,000 pounds to a maximum height of 32 feet. The loader is 23 feet long, 8 feet wide and weighs 17,050 pounds; it sits on four large rubber tires which are about the height of a person's chest, and is equipped with four-wheel drive, an automatic transmission with no park position and a hand brake. Loads are lifted by forks similar to the forks of a forklift.

The loader is designed so that the load can be kept level even when the loader is being operated on sloping terrain. The leveling of the load is controlled by a lever located near the steering column, and positioned between the operator's legs. The lever is equipped with a manual lock that can be engaged to prevent accidental slipping of the load level during lifting.

The loader was not equipped with seat belts or a roll bar. A wire and pipe cage over the driver's seat afforded the driver some protection from falling objects. The cab of the loader was located at least nine feet behind the lifting forks.

On the day of the accident the regular operator of the loader, Bill Dalton, did not report for work, and plaintiff, who had received only limited instruction on the operation of the loader from Dalton and who had operated the loader on only a few occasions, was assigned to run the loader in Dalton's place. The accident occurred while plaintiff was attempting to lift a load of lumber to a height of approximately 18 to 20 feet and to place the load on the second story of a building under construction. The lift was a particularly difficult one because the terrain on which the loader rested sloped sharply in several directions.

Witnesses testified that plaintiff approached the structure with the loader, leveled the forks to compensate for the sloping ground and lifted the load to a height variously estimated between 10 and 18 feet. During the course of the lift plaintiff felt some vibration, and, when it appeared to several coworkers that the load was beginning to tip, the workers shouted to plaintiff to jump from the loader. Plaintiff heeded these warnings and leaped from the loader, but while scrambling away he was struck by a piece of falling lumber and suffered serious injury.

Although the above facts were generally not in dispute, the parties differed markedly in identifying the responsible causes for the accident. Plaintiff contended, inter alia, that the accident was attributable to one or more design defects of the loader. Defendant, in turn, denied that the loader was defective in any respect, and claimed that the accident resulted either from plaintiff's lack of skill or from his misuse of its product. We briefly review the conflicting evidence.

Plaintiff's principal expert witness initially testified that by reason of its relatively narrow base the loader was unstable and had a tendency to roll over when lifting loads to considerable heights; the witness surmised that this instability caused the load to tip in the instant case. The expert declared that to compensate for its instability, the loader should have been equipped with "outriggers," mechanical arms extending out from the sides of the machine, two in front and two in back, each of which could be operated independently and placed on the ground to lend stability to the loader. Evidence at trial revealed that cranes and some high lift loader models are either regularly equipped with outriggers or offer outriggers as optional equipment. Plaintiff's expert testified that the availability of outriggers would probably have averted the present accident.

The expert additionally testified that the loader was defective in that it was not equipped with a roll bar or seat belts. He stated that such safety devices were essential to protect the operator in the event that the machine rolled over. Plaintiff theorized that the lack of such safety equipment was a proximate cause of his injuries because in the absence of such devices he had no reasonable choice but to leap from the loader as it began to tip. If a seat belt and roll bar had been provided, plaintiff argued, he could have remained in the loader and would not have been struck by the falling lumber.

In addition, plaintiff's witnesses suggested that the accident may have been caused by the defective design of the loader's leveling mechanism. Several witnesses testified that both the absence of an automatic locking device on the leveling lever, and the placement of the leveling lever in a position in which it was extremely vulnerable to inadvertent bumping by the operator of the loader in the course of a lift, were defects which may have produced the accident and injuries in question. Finally, plaintiff's experts testified that the absence of a "park" position on the loader's transmission, that could have been utilized to avoid the possibility of the loader's movement during a lift, constituted a further defect in design which may have caused the accident.

Defendants, in response, presented evidence which attempted to refute plaintiff's claims that the loader was defective or that the loader's condition was the cause of the accident. Defendants' experts testified that the loader was not unstable when utilized on the terrain for which it was intended, and that if the accident did occur because of the tipping of the loader it was only because plaintiff had misused the equipment by operating it on steep terrain for which the loader was unsuited.[2] In answer to the claim that the high-lift loader was defective because of a lack of outriggers, defendants' expert testified that outriggers were not necessary when the loader was used for its intended purpose and that no competitive loaders with similar height lifting capacity were equipped with outriggers; the expert conceded, however, that a competitor did offer outriggers as optional equipment on a high-lift loader which was capable of lifting loads to 40, as compared to 32, feet. The expert also testified that the addition of outriggers would simply have given the loader the functional capability of a crane, which was designed for use on all terrain, and that an experienced user of a high-lift loader should recognize that such a loader was not intended as a substitute for a crane.

The defense experts further testified that a roll bar was unnecessary because in view of the bulk of the loader it would not roll completely over. The witnesses also maintained that seat belts would have increased the danger of the loader by impairing the operator's ability to leave the vehicle quickly in case of an emergency. With respect to the claimed defects of the leveling device, the defense experts testified that the positioning of the lever was the safest and most convenient for the operator and that the manual lock on the leveling device provided completely adequate protection. Finally, defendants asserted that the absence of a "park" position on the transmission should not be considered a defect because none of the transmissions that were manufactured for this type of vehicle included a park position.

In addition to disputing plaintiff's contention as to the defectiveness of the loader, defendants' witnesses testified that the accident probably was caused by the plaintiff's own inexperience and consequent dangerous actions. Defendants maintained that if the lumber had begun to fall during the lift it did so only because plaintiff had failed to lock the leveling device prior to the lift. Defendants alternatively suggested that although the workers thought they saw the lumber begin to tip during the lift, this tipping was actually only the plaintiff's leveling of the load during the lift. Defendants hypothesized that the lumber actually fell off the loader only after plaintiff had leaped from the machine and that plaintiff was responsible for his own injuries because he had failed to set the hand brake, thereby permitting the loader to roll backwards.

After considering the sharply conflicting testimony reviewed above, the jury by a 10 to 2 vote returned a general verdict in favor of defendants. Plaintiff appeals from the judgment entered upon that verdict. . . .

2. In support of this claim, defendants presented the testimony of Bill Dalton, the regular operator of the loader, who testified that he called in sick on the day of the accident because he knew that the loader was not designed to make the lifts scheduled for that day, and he was frightened to make lifts in the area where the accidents occurred because of the danger involved. Dalton testified that he informed his supervisor that a crane, rather than a high-lift loader, was required for lifts on such sloping ground, but that the supervisor had not agreed to obtain a crane for such lifts.

In general, a manufacturing or production defect is readily identifiable because a defective product is one that differs from the manufacturer's intended result or from other ostensibly identical units of the same product line. For example, when a product comes off the assembly line in a substandard condition it has incurred a manufacturing defect. A design defect, by contrast, cannot be identified simply by comparing the injury-producing product with the manufacturer's plans or with other units of the same product line, since by definition the plans and all such units will reflect the same design. Rather than applying any sort of deviation-from-the-norm test in determining whether a product is defective in design for strict liability purposes, our cases have employed two alternative criteria in ascertaining, in Justice Traynor's words, whether there is something "wrong, if not in the manufacturer's manner of production, at least in his product."

First, our cases establish that a product may be found defective in design if the plaintiff demonstrates that the product failed to perform as safely as an ordinary consumer would expect when used in an intended or reasonably foreseeable manner. This initial standard, somewhat analogous to the Uniform Commercial Code's warranty of fitness and merchantability, reflects the warranty heritage upon which California product liability doctrine in part rests. . . .

As Professor Wade has pointed out, however, the expectations of the ordinary consumer cannot be viewed as the exclusive yardstick for evaluating design defectiveness because "[i]n many situations . . . the consumer would not know what to expect, because he would have no idea how safe the product could be made." Numerous California decisions have implicitly recognized this fact and have made clear, through varying linguistic formulations, that a product may be found defective in design, even if it satisfies ordinary consumer expectations, if through hindsight the jury determines that the product's design embodies "excessive preventable danger," or, in other words, if the jury finds that the risk of danger inherent in the challenged design outweighs the benefits of such design.

A review of past cases indicates that in evaluating the adequacy of a product's design pursuant to this latter standard, a jury may consider, among other relevant factors, the gravity of the danger posed by the challenged design, the likelihood that such danger would occur, the mechanical feasibility of a safer alternative design, the financial cost of an improved design, and the adverse consequences to the product and to the consumer that would result from an alternative design.

Although our cases have thus recognized a variety of considerations that may be relevant to the determination of the adequacy of a product's design, past authorities have generally not devoted much attention to the appropriate allocation of the burden of proof with respect to these matters. The allocation of such burden is particularly significant in this context inasmuch as this court's product liability decisions, from *Greenman* to *Cronin*, have repeatedly emphasized that one of the principal purposes behind the strict product liability doctrine is to relieve an injured plaintiff of many of the onerous evidentiary burdens inherent in a negligence cause of action. Because most of the evidentiary matters which may be relevant to the determination of the adequacy of a product's design under the "risk-benefit" standard — e.g., the feasibility and cost of alternative designs — are similar to issues typically presented in a negligent design case and involve technical matters peculiarly within the knowledge of the manufacturer, we conclude that once the plaintiff makes a prima facie showing that the injury was proximately caused by the product's design, the burden should appropriately shift to the defendant to prove, in light of the relevant factors, that the product is not defective. Moreover, inasmuch as this conclusion flows from our determination that the fundamental public policies embraced in *Greenman* dictate that a manufacturer who seeks to escape liability for an injury proximately caused by its product's design on a risk-benefit theory should bear the burden of persuading the trier of fact that its product should not be judged defective, the defendant's burden is one affecting the burden of proof, rather than simply the burden of producing evidence.

Thus, to reiterate, a product may be found defective in design, so as to subject a manufacturer to strict liability for resulting injuries, under either of two alternative tests. First, a product may be found defective in design if the plaintiff establishes that the product failed to perform as safely as an ordinary consumer would expect when used in an intended or reasonably foreseeable manner. Second, a product may alternatively be found defective in design if the plaintiff demonstrates that the product's design proximately caused his injury and the defendant fails to establish, in light of the relevant factors, that, on balance, the benefits of the challenged design outweigh the risk of danger inherent in such design. . . .

. . . [A]n instruction which advises the jury that it may evaluate the adequacy of a product's design by weighing the benefits of the challenged design against the risk of danger inherent in such design is not simply the equivalent of an instruction which requires the jury to determine whether the manufacturer was negligent in designing the product. It is true, of course, that in many cases proof that a product is defective in design may also demonstrate that the manufacturer was negligent in choosing such a design. As we have indicated, however, in a strict liability case, as contrasted with a negligent design action, the jury's focus is properly directed to the condition of the product itself, and not to the reasonableness of the manufacturer's conduct.

Thus, the fact that the manufacturer took reasonable precautions in an attempt to design a safe product or otherwise acted as a reasonably prudent manufacturer would have under the circumstances, while perhaps absolving the manufacturer of liability under a negligence theory, will not preclude the imposition of liability under strict liability principles if, upon hindsight, the trier of fact concludes that the product's design is unsafe to consumers, users, or bystanders. . . .

[Judgment reversed, since it was error under *Cronin* to instruct that the jury must find that the loader was "unreasonably dangerous" as well as defective.]

Notes

1. The test announced by the court for determining whether a design is defective closely resembles the Hand formula. Why, then, does the court think that a negligence test might come out differently?

2. Should the Hand formula be used at all when the alleged "defect" is known to the purchaser, although not necessarily to the user? In such a case, presumably, the purchase price was lower than it would have been if it were not defective. The lower price compensates the purchaser in advance for bearing the risk of an accident caused by the defect; should he, therefore, be heard to complain if an accident occurs? Does it make a difference that in *Barker* the user was not the purchaser, but an employee? Should his rights be greater than those of his employer? If they are, does that not mean that products liability law is being used to circumvent the limitations on compensation for industrial accidents imposed by workmen's compensation law?

3. What does it mean to say that the design of the loader "caused" the injury? Suppose an automobile is demolished and its occupants injured when it collides with a brick wall at a speed of 100 M.P.H. Is the design of the car the cause of the accident because the car could have been designed to withstand impacts at that speed? In this regard, the California court's refusal to adopt the Restatement's "unreasonably dangerous" requirement in design-defect cases is significant. That requirement limits the scope of liability in design cases to failure to adopt safeguards against unreasonably high risks of injury. Under the California court's approach, once the design is shown to have caused the injury, the burden shifts to defendant to prove that no safer design would have been cost-justified. Is this an appropriate burden to place on the manufacturer? Does it give too much power to juries? What would be an appropriate means of jury control in this area?

Owens v. Allis-Chalmers Corp.
83 Mich. App. 74, 268 N.W.2d 291 (1978)

BASHARA, J.

This is an appeal by plaintiff from a directed verdict granted to defendant at the conclusion of plaintiff's proofs. On a theory of products liability, plaintiff sought recovery for the death of her husband, who was killed when the forklift truck he was operating for his employer overturned, crushing his skull with the overhead, protective guard.

No one witnessed the occurrence. Decedent reported to his job and was instructed to drive a forklift to another plant on his employer's property. Moments after he left, other employees, en route over the same roadway to the same location, discovered decedent pinned under the overhead guard of the forklift. As it then appeared, the forklift had traveled off the roadway, struck a concrete-filled post, and turned over onto its side.

The forklift was manufactured by defendant and sold with other forklift vehicles to the decedent's employer by one of defendant's dealers. Plaintiff alleged that defendant was negligent in the design of the forklift, that the defective design constituted a breach of warranty, and that defendant was liable under the doctrine of strict liability in tort. Design defect allegations were predicated principally upon the absence of driver restraints on the vehicle, such as seat belts or a protective enclosure.

At trial, plaintiff's expert witness testified at length about the inadequacy of the static stability tests utilized by the forklift manufacturers, generally. His opinion was that dynamic stability tests were essential to ascertain the true handling characteristics of forklift vehicles so that proper design technology could be developed.

He also testified as to the risks of injury created by the absence of some driver restraint apparatus in forklifts equipped with an overhead guard. He opined that, given the unstable handling qualities of a forklift and the concomitant high probability of rollovers, some form of driver restraint system was necessary for a properly designed forklift. Notably, on cross-examination, the expert witness was unable to specify any industry standard, legislative enactment, or government regulation requiring the installation of a driver restraint device on forklifts or establishing dynamic stability testing requirements.

The trial court concluded there was no evidence to show that defendant was negligent in failing to adhere to some standard for testing or designing its forklifts. Further, the trial court found the evidence presented did not establish that any defect in the forklift was causally related to the decedent's death.

Plaintiff claims that the question of whether the forklift was defectively designed should have been submitted to the jury. She urges that the expert testimony, stating that a driver restraint device would have prevented the decedent's death, is itself sufficient to raise a question of fact as to the defective design.

Our discussion of this case may be narrowed by making a number of observations. This Court has recognized that the requisite elements for a cause of action based upon strict liability in tort are congruent to those for breach of warranty. Therefore, the strict liability count is a mere redundancy, since recovery is equally available by the action for breach of warranty.

Further, we have carefully reviewed the evidence presented by plaintiff on the claim of negligence and defective design, especially the extensive testimony of plaintiff's expert witness. That evidence showed that forklifts are, by their nature, unstable vehicles. There is nothing to show how the vehicles' stability may be enhanced, given the design characteristics mandated by the vehicles' intended uses. Merely because an injury results from the use of a machine does not ipso facto mean that the machine is defective. Manufacturers are not required to make mechanical devices "accident-proof."

At the commencement of this discussion, we deem it important to emphasize that this litigation does not involve a claim that the fatal injury resulted from some machine part that malfunctioned as a result of a defect in its manufacture. The responsibility of the trier of fact for finding a defect and injury causation as a matter of fact is well-established in that context.

When courts are confronted with claims of product design defects, there is a geometric increase in the complexity of the issues. Product design choices are multi-faceted, or as one legal writer has termed it, polycentric.[1] That is, design choices involve such considerations as the intended use and utility of the product, cost constraints dictated by the marketplace and the manufacturer's competitive position, safety standards established by the industry or government regulation and the feasibility of alternative designs, to name only a few.[2] To the extent that another coordinate branch of government has not determined the degree to which public policy shall govern design choices, the task devolves upon the judiciary.

Considering the nature of the design process, we find that adjudication must necessarily play a limited role in setting design standards. Without some extrajudicially established guidelines, the adjudicatory standard-setting process would resort to an assessment of conflicting expert testimony by those not possessed of the requisite expertise to adequately evaluate the interrelated and interdependent design choice criteria. Additionally, this evaluation would be made within an atmosphere susceptible to influence by sympathy for an injured plaintiff, instead of an abstract concern for the desirable effect that public policy should play in governing a manufacturer's design choices. Inevitably, this would lead to varying standards from jury to jury or trial court to trial court.

We are merely recognizing from the foregoing considerations that triers of fact are not formulators of public policy and that trial courts are inappropriate for the task in the area of product design choices. This is not to say that plaintiffs have no means by which they can seek recovery for injuries resulting from the conscious design choices of manufacturers where extrajudicial design guidelines are absent.

---

1. See Henderson, Judicial Review of Manufacturers' Conscious Design Choices: The Limits of Adjudication, 73 Colum. L. Rev. 1531 (1973), Henderson, Design Defect Litigation Revisited, 61 Cornell L. Rev. 541 (1976), Henderson, Expanding the Negligence Concept: Retreat from the Rule of Law, 51 Ind. L.J. 467 (1976).

2. The role of the adjudication process, as it pertains to affecting the design choices of manufacturers, is perceptively explicated in Henderson, Judicial Review of Manufacturers' Conscious Design Choices: The Limits of Adjudication, 73 Colum. L. Rev. 1531 (1973).

There remains a duty of manufacturers to provide adequate warnings to potential users of their products of the latent risks of injury created by their selection of product design. The adequacy of the warning under the particular circumstances of a given case, is a question for resolution by the trier of fact.

Consequently, we conclude that for a plaintiff to establish a question of fact as to a manufacturer's breach of duty in design defect products liability litigation, evidence of the following must be presented: (1) That the particular design was not in conformity with industry design standards, design guidelines established by an authoritative voluntary association, *or* design criteria set by legislative or other governmental regulation; *or* (2) That the design choice of the manufacturer carries with it a *latent* risk of injury *and* the manufacturer has *not* adequately communicated the nature of that risk to potential users of the product.

In determining the propriety of the directed verdict in this case, we must review the evidence presented in a light most favorable to the plaintiff. From our review of the plaintiff's evidence, we conclude that no question was raised as to any fact that would impose liability upon defendant. The evidence raised neither a question of design conformity with established standards nor a risk of injury that would not be readily perceived by decedent, who plaintiff's proofs showed was an experienced forklift operator, familiar with the machine's intrinsic characteristics.[6] . . .

Note

In effect, *Owens* makes compliance with industry custom a defense in a defective-design case, does it not? The court could have cited the Coase theorem in support of this result. Since manufacturers and consumers are in a contractual relationship, direct or indirect, manufacturers have an incentive to provide that design which maximizes consumer benefits, weighing safety considerations and everything else that consumers value. If a manufacturer's design complies with the standard of the industry, a consumer injured because the design was not so safe as it could have been made has no cause to complain. If consumers as a group had wanted a safer design (and been willing to pay for it), presumably the industry would have supplied it; and the

6. Decedent's foreman testified that decedent had been operating forklifts for at least three years. He also testified that every forklift operator, including decedent, had to pass a qualifications examination before being permitted to operate a forklift. This was the only position requiring such an examination.

The safety director for decedent's employer testified that a similar accident happened about a year before this occurrence. As a consequence, pertinent job safety manuals were reviewed with all operators to emphasize the need for caution in operating the forklifts.

Plaintiff testified that decedent had been operating forklifts for approximately four to five years.

industry's failure to respond to idiosyncratic safety preferences does not make its design choice culpable in any reasonable sense.

Should the court have gone even further and confined liability to cases where the defendant flunks the second prong of its two-prong test? If a defect is not latent, how can the consumer complain about it? He must by definition have known of it when he bought the product and been compensated accordingly. Under this approach, the only duty on the manufacturer would be one of notice, since notice transforms a latent into a patent defect, for which, as just argued, there is an economic case for no liability. Are there any problems with this reasoning?

Dawson v. Chrysler Corp.
630 F.2d 950 (3d Cir. 1980)

ADAMS, J.

This appeal from a jury verdict and entry of judgment in favor of the plaintiffs arises out of a New Jersey automobile accident in which a police officer was seriously injured. The legal questions in this diversity action, that are governed by New Jersey law, are relatively straight-forward. The public policy questions, however, which are beyond the competence of this Court to resolve and with which Congress ultimately must grapple, are complex and implicate national economic and social concerns. . . .

On September 7, 1974, Richard F. Dawson, while in the employ of the Pennsauken Police Department, was seriously injured as a result of an automobile accident that occurred in Pennsauken, New Jersey. As Dawson was driving on a rain-soaked highway, responding to a burglar alarm, he lost control of his patrol car — a 1974 Dodge Monaco. The car slid off the highway, over a curb, through a small sign, and into an unyielding steel pole that was fifteen inches in diameter. The car struck the pole in a backwards direction at a forty-five degree angle on the left side of the vehicle; the point of impact was the left rear wheel well. As a result of the force of the collision, the vehicle literally wrapped itself around the pole. The pole ripped through the body of the car and crushed Dawson between the seat and the "header" area of the roof, located just above the windshield. The so-called "secondary collision" of Dawson with the interior of the automobile dislocated Dawson's left hip and ruptured his fifth and sixth cervical vertebrae. As a result of the injuries, Dawson is now a quadriplegic. He has no control over his body from the neck down, and requires constant medical attention.

. . . The plaintiffs' claims were based on theories of strict products liability and breach of implied warranty of fitness. They alleged that the patrol car was defective because it did not have a full, continuous steel frame extending through the door panels, and a cross-member running through the floor board between the posts located between the front and rear doors of the vehicle.

Had the vehicle been so designed, the Dawsons alleged, it would have "bounced" off the pole following relatively slight penetration by the pole into the passenger space.

Expert testimony was introduced by the Dawsons to prove that the existing frame of the patrol car was unable to withstand side impacts at relatively low speed, and that the inadequacy of the frame permitted the pole to enter the passenger area and to injure Dawson. The same experts testified that the improvements in the design of the frame that the plaintiffs proposed were feasible and would have prevented Dawson from being injured as he was. According to plaintiffs' expert witnesses, a continuous frame and cross-member would have deflected the patrol car away from the pole after a minimal intrusion into the passenger area and, they declared, Dawson likely would have emerged from the accident with only a slight injury.

In response, Chrysler argued that it had no duty to produce a "crash-proof" vehicle, and that, in any event, the patrol car was not defective. Expert testimony for Chrysler established that the design and construction of the 1974 Dodge Monaco complied with all federal vehicle safety standards, and that deformation[3] of the body of the vehicle is desirable in most crashes because it absorbs the impact of the crash and decreases the rate of deceleration on the occupants of the vehicle. Thus, Chrysler's experts asserted that, for most types of automobile accidents, the design offered by the Dawsons would be less safe than the existing design. They also estimated that the steel parts that would be required in the model suggested by the Dawsons would have added between 200 and 250 pounds to the weight, and approximately $300 to the price of the vehicle. It was also established that the 1974 Dodge Monaco's unibody construction was stronger than comparable Ford and Chevrolet vehicles.

After all testimony had been introduced, Chrysler moved for a directed verdict, which the district judge denied. The jury thereupon returned a verdict in favor of the plaintiffs. In answers to a series of special interrogatories, the jurors concluded that (1) the body structure of the 1974 Dodge Monaco was defective and unreasonably dangerous; (2) Chrysler breached its implied warranty that the vehicle would be fit for use as a police car; (3) as a result of the defective design and the breach of warranty, Dawson sustained more severe injuries than he would have incurred had Chrysler used the alternative design proposed by Dawsons expert witnesses; (4) the defective design was the proximate cause of Dawson's enhanced injuries; and (5) Dawson's failure to use a seatbelt was not a proximate cause of his injuries. The jury awarded Mr. Dawson $2,064,863.19 for his expenses, disability, and pain and suffering, and granted Mrs. Dawson $60,000.00 for loss of consortium and loss of services. . . .

---

3. Deformation is a term used in this context to describe the collapsing of the body and frame of a vehicle upon impact with a stationary object.

ISSUE

... [T]he controlling issue in the case is whether the jury could be permitted to find, under the law of New Jersey, that the patrol car was defective. In Suter [v. San Angelo Foundry & Machine Co., 81 N.J. 150, 406 A.2d 140 (1979)], the New Jersey Supreme Court summarized its state's law of strict liability as follows: If at the time the seller distributes a product, it is not reasonably fit, suitable and safe for its intended or reasonably foreseeable purposes so that users or others who may be expected to come in contact with the product are injured as a result thereof, then the seller shall be responsible for the ensuing damages. The court, in adopting this test, specifically rejected the requirement of the Restatement (Second) of Torts §402A that the defect must cause the product to be "unreasonably dangerous to the user or consumer." In the court's view, "the Restatement language may lead a jury astray for '[i]t may suggest an idea like ultra-hazardous, or abnormally dangerous, and thus give rise to the impression that the plaintiff must prove that the product was unusually or extremely dangerous.'"

The determination whether a product is "reasonably fit, suitable and safe for its intended or reasonably foreseeable purposes" is to be informed by what the New Jersey Supreme Court has termed a "risk/utility analysis." Under this approach, a product is defective if "a reasonable person would conclude that the magnitude of the scientifically perceivable danger *as it is proved to be at the time of trial* outweighed the benefits of the way the product was so designed and marketed." The court ... identified seven factors that might be relevant to this balancing process:

> (1) The usefulness and desirability of the product — its utility to the user and to the public as a whole.
> (2) The safety aspects of the product — the likelihood that it will cause injury, and the probable seriousness of the injury.
> (3) The availability of a substitute product which would meet the same need and not be as unsafe.
> (4) The manufacturer's ability to eliminate the unsafe character of the product without impairing its usefulness or making it too expensive to maintain its utility.
> (5) The user's ability to avoid danger by the exercise of care in the use of the product.
> (6) The user's anticipated awareness of the dangers inherent in the product and their avoidability, because of general public knowledge of the obvious condition of the product, or of the existence of suitable warnings or instructions.
> (7) The feasibility, on the part of the manufacturer, of spreading the loss by setting the price of the product or carrying liability insurance....

Chrysler maintains that, under these standards, the district court erred in submitting the case to the jury because the Dawsons failed, as a matter of law, to prove that the patrol car was defective. Specifically, it insists that the Dawsons did not present sufficient evidence from which the jury reasonably might infer that the alternative design that they proffered would be safer than the existing design, or that it would be cost effective, practical, or marketable. In short, Chrysler urges that the substitute design would be less socially beneficial than was the actual design of the patrol car. In support of its argument, Chrysler emphasizes that the design of the 1974 Dodge Monaco complied with all of the standards authorized by Congress in the National Traffic and Motor Vehicle Safety Act of 1966, and set forth in accompanying regulations.

Compliance with the safety standards promulgated pursuant to the National Traffic and Motor Vehicle Safety Act, however, does not relieve Chrysler of liability in this action. For, in authorizing the Secretary of Transportation to enact these standards, Congress explicitly provided, "Compliance with any Federal motor vehicle safety standard issued under this subchapter does not exempt any person from any liability under common law." 15 U.S.C. §1397(c) (1976). Thus, consonant with this congressional directive, we must review Chrysler's appeal on the question of the existence of a defect under the common law of New Jersey that is set forth above.

Our examination of the record persuades us that the district court did not err in denying Chrysler's motion for judgment notwithstanding the verdict. The Dawsons demonstrated that the frame of the 1974 Dodge Monaco was noncontinuous — that is, it consisted of a front portion that extended from the front of the car to the middle of the front passenger seat, and a rear portion that ran from the middle of the rear passenger seat to the back end of the vehicle. Thus, there was a gap in the seventeen-inch side area of the frame between the front and rear seats. The plaintiffs also proved that, after colliding with the pole, the car slid along the left-side portion of the rear frame until it reached the gap in the frame. At that point, the pole tore through the body of the vehicle into the passenger area and proceeded to push Dawson into the header area above the windshield.

Three experts — a design analyst, a mechanical engineer, and a biochemical engineer — also testified on behalf of the Dawsons. These witnesses had examined the patrol car and concluded that it was inadequate to withstand side impacts. They testified that there was an alternative design available which, had it been employed in the 1974 Monaco, would have prevented Dawson from sustaining serious injuries. The substitute design called for a continuous frame with an additional cross member running between the so-called B-posts — the vertical posts located at the side of the car between the front and rear seats. According to these witnesses, this design was known in the industry well before the accident and had been tested by a number of independent testing centers in 1969 and in 1973.

The mechanical engineer conducted a number of studies in order to ascertain the extent to which the alternative design would have withstood the crash. On the basis of these calculations, he testified that the pole would have penetrated only 9.9 inches into the passenger space, and thus would not have crushed Dawson. Instead, the engineer stated, the car would have deflected off the pole and back into the highway. Under these circumstances, according to the biochemical engineer, Dawson would have been able to "walk away from the accident" with but a bruised shoulder.

Also introduced by the Dawsons were reports of tests conducted for the United States Department of Transportation, which indicated that, in side collisions with a fixed pole at twenty-one miles per hour,[7] frame improvements similar to those proposed by the experts presented by the Dawsons reduced intrusion into the passenger area by fifty percent, from sixteen inches to eight inches. The study concluded that the improvements, "in conjunction with interior alterations, demonstrated a dramatic increase in occupant protection." There was no suggestion at trial that the alternative design recommended by the Dawsons would not comply with federal safety standards. On cross-examination, Chrysler's attorney did get the Dawsons' expert witnesses to acknowledge that the alternative design would add between 200 and 250 pounds to the vehicle and would cost an additional $300 per car. The Dawsons' experts also conceded that the heavier and more rigid an automobile, the less able it is to absorb energy upon impact with a fixed object, and therefore the major force of an accident might be transmitted to the passengers. Moreover, an expert for Chrysler testified that, even if the frame of the patrol car had been designed in conformity with the plaintiffs' proposals, Dawson would have sustained injuries equivalent to those he actually incurred. Chrysler's witness reasoned that Dawson was injured, not by the intrusion of the pole into the passenger space, but as a result of being thrown into the header area of the roof by the vehicle's initial contact with the pole — that is, prior to the impact of the pole against the driver's seat.

On the basis of the foregoing recitation of the evidence presented respectively by the Dawsons and by Chrysler, we conclude that the record is sufficient to sustain the jury's determination, in response to the interrogatory, that the design of the 1974 Monaco was defective. . . .

Although we affirm the judgment of the district court, we do so with uneasiness regarding the consequences of our decision and of the decisions of other courts throughout the country in cases of this kind.

As we observed earlier, Congress, in enacting the National Traffic and Motor Vehicle Safety Act, provided that compliance with the Act does not exempt any person from liability under the common law of the state of injury. The effect of this provision is that the states are free, not only to create various standards of liability for automobile manufacturers with respect to design and structure, but also to delegate to the triers of fact in civil cases arising out of automobile accidents the power to determine whether a particular product conforms to such standards. In the present situation, for example, the New Jersey Supreme Court has instituted a strict liability

7. Eyewitness as well as expert testimony was introduced to show that the speed of the car at the time of impact was between twenty-four and twenty-six miles per hour.

standard for cases involving defective products, has defined the term "defective product" to mean any such item that is not "reasonably fit, suitable and safe for its intended or reasonably foreseeable purposes," and has left to the jury the task of determining whether the product at issue measures up to this standard.

The result of such arrangement is that while the jury found Chrysler liable for not producing a rigid enough vehicular frame, a factfinder in another case might well hold the manufacturer liable for producing a frame that is too rigid. Yet, as pointed out at trial, in certain types of accidents — head-on collisions — it is desirable to have a car designed to collapse upon impact because the deformation would absorb much of the shock of the collision, and divert the force of deceleration away from the vehicle's passengers. In effect, this permits individual juries applying varying laws in different jurisdictions to set nationwide automobile safety standards and to impose on automobile manufacturers conflicting requirements. It would be difficult for members of the industry to alter their design and production behavior in response to jury verdicts in such cases, because their response might well be at variance with what some other jury decides is a defective design. Under these circumstances, the law imposes on the industry the responsibility of insuring vast numbers of persons involved in automobile accidents.

Equally serious is the impact on other national social and economic goals of the existing case-by-case system of establishing automobile safety requirements. As we have become more dependent on foreign sources of energy, and as the price of that energy has increased, the attention of the federal government has been drawn to a search to find alternative supplies and the means of conserving energy. More recently, the domestic automobile industry has been struggling to compete with foreign manufacturers which have stressed smaller, more fuel-efficient cars. Yet, during this same period, Congress has permitted a system of regulation by ad hoc adjudications under which a jury can hold an automobile manufacturer culpable for not producing a car that is considerably heavier, and likely to have less fuel efficiency.

In sum, this appeal has brought to our attention an important conflict that implicates broad national concerns. Although it is important that society devise a proper system for compensating those injured in automobile collisions, it is not at all clear that the present arrangement of permitting individual juries, under varying standards of liability, to impose this obligation on manufacturers is fair or efficient. Inasmuch as it was the Congress that designed this system, and because Congress is the body best suited to evaluate and, if appropriate, to change that system, we decline today to do anything in this regard except to bring the problem to the attention of the legislative branch.

Bound as we are to adjudicate this appeal according to the substantive law of New Jersey, and because we find no basis in that law to overturn the jury's verdict, the judgment of the district court will be affirmed.

Notes

1. On the role of federal motor vehicle safety standards in tort litigation see also the *Stonehocker* case in Chapter 4.

2. What effect, if any, are decisions like *Dawson* likely to have on competition between domestic and foreign automobiles in the U.S.? How will they affect the design choices of manufacturers? What does the Coase theorem imply on the latter question?

3. Notice that the issue in all of our design-defect cases is what is called crashworthiness or enhanced injury; that is, the alleged defect does not cause the accident itself but only increases the severity of the accident victim's injuries. Would it be reasonable to take the position that the manufacturer's duty of nondefective design is limited to the intended use of the product and that the intended use does not include collisions? Compare Evans v. General Motors Corp., 359 F.2d 822 (7th Cir. 1966), with Huff v. White Motor Corp., 565 F.2d 104 (7th Cir. 1977).

4. Suppose a product is unreasonably dangerous, but not defective. An example is cigarettes. The danger is not that the cigarette is adulterated as in the usual implied-warranty or strict-liability food case; a perfectly well-made, nondefective cigarette is dangerous to health. On this ground, strict products liability has been held inapplicable where a smoker complains that smoking defendant's brand of cigarettes caused lung cancer. See Green v. American Tobacco Co., 409 F.2d 1166 (5th Cir. 1969), adopting Judge Simpson's dissenting views in Green v. American Tobacco Co., 391 F.2d 97 (5th Cir. 1968). Other cases take a somewhat more liberal view yet still uphold judgments for defendants in cigarette cancer cases. See Ross v. Philip Morris & Co., 328 F.2d 3 (8th Cir. 1964); Lartigue v. R.J. Reynolds Tobacco Co., 317 F.2d 19 (5th Cir. 1963). What other obstacles do plaintiffs in such cases face besides having to prove a defect?

Brody v. Overlook Hospital
121 N.J. Super. 299, 296 A.2d 668 (Law Div. 1972)

STEINBRUGGE, J.

This is an action by Sarah Brody, individually and as executrix of the estate of Eugene Brody, against a hospital, two blood banks, two doctors and a medical technician, to recover damages for the death, by serum hepatitis infection of the blood, of plaintiff's late husband, Eugene Brody. The essential facts are not in dispute. Eugene Brody was duly admitted as a paying patient to Overlook Hospital and there received, upon the advice of his physician Cavallaro, a number of blood transfusions. It is alleged that Brody subsequently developed hepatitis; it is uncontroverted that he shortly thereafter expired. . . .

The case at bar presents in starkest relief the issue of what measurement of liability should attach to a hospital when hepatitis-infected blood is transfused to a patient under the hospital's care and supervision. The question usually is seen to turn on whether the blood is perceived to be a "product" or "good" sold to the patient, or whether the blood is merely part and parcel of the "services" supplied by the hospital to the patient. If blood is considered a "product" then, under the Uniform Commercial Code, theories of breach of the warranties of merchantability and of fitness for particular use are applicable. Equally as applicable is the theory of strict tort liability, i.e, liability on the part of the supplier whether or not the supplier was at fault, as expressed in Restatement 2d, Torts, §402A. . . . On the other hand, if the hospital's provision of infected blood is considered a "service," then a negligence action alone against the hospital will be maintainable. . . .

. . . Cunningham v. MacNeal Memorial Hospital, 266 N.E.2d 897 (Ill. Sup. Ct. 1970) held that blood is a "product" to which the doctrine of strict tort liability is applicable when supplied by a hospital for treatment of a patient's condition. . . . In doing so, the Illinois Supreme Court adopted the views that (1) blood *is* a "product" within the meaning of Restatement 2d, Torts, §402A; (2) the product was "*sold*," and (3) the blood *was* "in a defective condition unreasonably dangerous to the user." The court rejected the notion that the imposition of strict liability would hamper a hospital's performance of its primary function: "We do not believe in this present day and age, when the operation of eleemosynary hospitals constitutes one of the biggest businesses in this country, that hospital immunity can be justified on the protection-of-the-funds theory."

However, neither *Perlmutter, Hoffman,** nor *Cunningham* addressed themselves to any sound *policy* reasons for extending the doctrine of strict liability to hepatitis cases. *Perlmutter* dealt only with the semantic question of whether the transaction (the blood transfusion) was a "sale" or a "service"; *Hoffman* recognized the problem; *Cunningham* dealt only with the verbal formula of §402A.

But policy considerations are of the utmost importance. . . . "Even if there is no negligence, however, public policy demands that responsibility be fixed wherever it will most effectively reduce the hazards to life and health inherent in defective products that reach the market. It is evident that the manufacturer can anticipate some hazards and guard against the recurrence of others, as the public cannot."

This theory has the effect of forcing the entity that markets the product to consider the "accident costs" of the product when deciding whether and from where to procure it. In the case of blood, the "safety rationale" emphatically applies to hospitals because, as a general rule, each hospital has a choice of several blood banks as potential suppliers. The blood banks stand in the same position to the hospital as the manufacturer of a product does to a

---

*Earlier decisions dealing with the issue of hospital liability for serum hepatitis. — Ed.

distributor — as supplier to marketer. It can be anticipated that adoption of the strict liability standard for the State of New Jersey will have the beneficial effect of forcing hospitals to deal only with those blood banks which have good safety records, thus decreasing the risk of a patient's becoming infected with hepatitis as a result of a transfusion.

Even in the comparatively low number of cases in which the hospital has recourse to only a single blood bank, imposition of strict tort liability may well spur the hospital to take a more active role in influencing the bank's collection processes, i.e., more careful screening of donors. Most importantly, the imposition of strict liability cannot help but force the hospitals both to supervise more carefully their own use of blood, and to encourage medical research to develop either a more satisfactory test for hepatitis or an immunization vaccine to be given against the disease to a patient about to undergo a transfusion.

The court is not impressed with the argument that a hospital faced with strict liability will only pass along its increased costs to its patients, thus negating the safety incentive. Insurers will not write liability policies unless satisfied with the level of care exercised by the hospital. And, even if the cost to each patient *is* marginally increased, public policy dictates the imposition of strict tort liability.

Another important policy justification for strict liability is that of "loss spreading." If the hospital bears the loss resulting from hepatitis-infected blood, it will tend to spread the loss among all parties, i.e., donors, blood-banks, perhaps its patients. This "allocative effect" will be felt if hospitals allocate their hepatitis costs as a charge on each unit of blood actually used: physicians will automatically more carefully weigh the risks of surgery and transfusions.

This court is mindful of the fact that only nine states still regulate liability for transfusion-associated hepatitis under the common law, while the other 41 have enacted statutes to limit such liability to negligence. No such statute has been enacted in New Jersey. . . .

Public policy dictates the imposition of strict tort liability on blood banks [as well as hospitals], if for no other reason than to discourage carelessness in the selection of donors. If the analogy to traditional products-liability law be followed, a blood bank would appear to stand, not in the shoes of a "manufacturer," but in that of a "supplier": it must decide which donors among many (the real "manufacturers") it will buy from. Goldberg v. Kollsman Instrument Corp. presented a case where the New York Court of Appeals imposed strict liability on a "final assembler" which received its products from many suppliers. The products arrived in sealed containers that could not be opened for inspection without destroying their utility — just as a blood bank receives phials of donated blood, unopenable for inspection. . . .

A blood bank may hold a monopoly in a given area, or it may "compete" with other banks. If the monopoly bank is a volunteer blood bank, it will not be able to pass along too much of the increased cost inevitably associated with strict liability, because too great a price hike will lead to the emergence of commercial blood banks, or to hospitals themselves operating a blood bank. On the other hand, where the monopolistic blood bank is a commercial one, it will even more acutely risk competition if it raises its rates. In those instances where blood banks "compete," the imposition of strict liability will force them to intensify (or in some cases commence) their efforts to find "safe" donors: blood banks with poor safety records will have to charge higher prices, and thus will lose customers.

Where a volunteer blood bank holds a monopoly, strict liability will not end its operations. The blood bank will simply increase its charges, the way all monopolists do when faced with increased costs. Where the volunteer bank is faced with competition, the court believes that the bank would still pass on any cost increases resulting from the imposition of strict liability, because volunteer blood banks have kept their fees lower than what the open market would bring. Should a volunteer blood bank cease operations, this will further insure that less of hepatitis-infected blood will be delivered to hospitals and ultimately to patients.

The "allocative effect" rationale applies to blood banks as well as to hospitals. Where a community has more than one blood bank, strict liability will cause the blood bank with the poorer safety record to charge higher fees. Since hospitals patronize the bank charging the lowest fee, there will be greater demand for blood from the bank with the better safety record. The incidence of hepatitis infection must thus be reduced. . . .

Notes

1. The Appellate Division of the Superior Court of New Jersey reversed *Brody*. See 127 N.J. Super. 331, 317 A.2d 392 (1974). Since "it has been unequivocally established that in 1966 there was no known test available to ascertain the presence of viral hepatitis in the blood," and since "it was not disputed that, at the time, the incidences of this disease being present in the blood were very slight," the court concluded "that the blood transfused to decedent herein falls within the category of an 'unavoidably unsafe product' and thus was not 'unreasonably' dangerous." Id. at 339, 317 A.2d at 397. The court took note of legislative actions in Illinois and other states overruling decisions such as *Cunningham* on which the Law Division had relied. The Supreme Court of New Jersey affirmed the Appellate Division. See 66 N.J. 448, 332 A.2d 596 (1975). The court stated: "There are indications that subsequent to 1966 tests may have become available for discovering the viral infection but for present purposes we need not consider the adequacy of these tests or whether their present availability would hereafter result in accountability under the theory of strict liability in tort." Id. at 450, 332 A.2d at 597. Should the unavailability of tests have played so decisive a role in the thinking of the Appellate Division and Supreme Court?

2. Is the Law Division's second rationale for strict liability — what it called "loss spreading" — in fact distinct from the first? Was the court talking about loss spreading in its usual sense of insurance?

3. Why is it relevant whether or not a blood bank in a particular area faces competition, actual or potential? Even if it faces fierce competition, will it not be able to pass on at least a portion of any higher cost due to strict liability so long as its competitors face the same higher cost? On the simple economics of passing on costs, see R. A. Posner, Economic Analysis of Law 59-60 (2d ed. 1977), and for fuller discussions, see Landes & Posner, Should Indirect Purchasers Have Standing to Sue under the Antitrust Laws? An Economic Analysis of the Rule of *Illinois Brick*, 46 U. Chi. L. Rev. 602, 615-620 (1979); R. A. Musgrave & P. B. Musgrave, Public Finance in Theory and Practice 440-458 (2d ed. 1976).

Kessel, Transfused Blood, Serum Hepatitis, and the Coase Theorem
17 J. Law & Econ. 265, 276-287 (1974)

... Clearly the opposition [by the medical establishment] is not to commercialism per se in the acquisition of blood for transfusions, but only a certain aspect of commercialism — the payment for blood intermediated by money. The opposition to commercialism intermediated by monetary transactions can be rationalized if one accepts the premise that this type of transaction is a proxy for the acquisition of tainted blood and a finer discrimination against tainted blood would cost more than its benefits. (It is also important that there be no easy transference from one category of commercialism to another.)

It is difficult to accept this explanation because there seems to be no reason why drug addicts, derelicts, prisoners and others with a high a priori probability of having hepatitis cannot be screened out directly. Furthermore, the evidence provided by the Mayo Clinic and the Iowa City Blood Bank shows that they can be screened out easily. What then is the explanation for the almost uniform opposition to the acquisition of blood by direct payment?

It is the thesis of this paper that avoiding liability for transfusion hepatitis by the medical establishment explains the opposition to "commercialism" in acquiring blood to be transfused. Eliminating commercialism in blood acquisition is an important plank in the program of the medical establishment for eliminating strict liability in tort for blood.

The recent history of litigation and legislation in Illinois constitutes a piece of evidence in support of the foregoing thesis. In Cunningham v. MacNeal Memorial Hospital, the State Supreme Court upheld a decision of a lower court that strict liability in tort held in the case of a patient, Francis Cunningham, who had contracted serum hepatitis as a result of a transfusion received at MacNeal Memorial which left the patient with permanent disabilities.

As a result of this decision, organized medicine in Illinois, in particular the hospitals, medical societies and blood suppliers, lobbied for and won from the State Legislature exemption from strict liability in tort for blood. Part of the legislative package won by organized medicine is a blood labeling law. This law burdens physicians transfusing commercial blood. (Explanations of why commercial blood was used must be provided in medical records.) As a result of the blood labeling law, commercial blood is now only rarely used in Illinois, and its use occurs only when noncommercial blood is unavailable. Most states have laws exempting the medical establishment from strict liability for transfusion hepatitis and those that do not are contemplating such laws. The State of Washington provides for strict liability for transfused blood only if the donor is compensated, that is, paid with money, and Idaho provides for liability if the donor is compensated or if the blood bank is a for-profit organization.

This legislation, whose enactment runs counter to the trend towards greater product liability declares that the commercial standards of supplier responsibility typically observed in the product market are inoperative for blood. Although caveat emptor is dying in product markets, particularly those served by profit seeking organizations, it is experiencing a renaissance in the blood market. Some of the reasons advanced for this legislation, which is supported by the Red Cross in addition to the medical establishment, is that strict liability for tort will raise the price of blood. But this should not, of course, determine policy; what matters are the full costs of treatment including the costs associated with serum hepatitis. This position can have merit only if the increased price of blood exceeds the reduction in costs of those (a) unfortunate enough to contract transfusion hepatitis and (b) who avoid contracting hepatitis as a result of strict liability.

An argument advanced in support of exemption is the absence of any way of being sure that any particular unit of blood is hepatitis-free. The Illinois Supreme Court rejected this argument in the *Cunningham* case. The Court held that the same defense applies to typhoid bacilli in clams sold commercially; there is no way of being sure they are not present. Nevertheless, it shall be argued here, they correctly upheld the applicability of the strict liability doctrine. . . .

In the abstract zero transactions cost world that Coase investigates . . .* it is irrelevant where liability is placed because one can costlessly contract out of any initial legal position. The choice of the initial position does not affect the allocation of resources. If liability for serum hepatitis is placed on the physician, then his fees to patients being transfused will be sufficiently higher to pay for the expected costs of the liabilities being incurred. If liability is placed on the patient, then the physician's fees will be lower and the differ-

*See note on the Coase theorem in Chapter 3. — Ed.

ence in physician fees in these two instances will pay for the expected costs of
the risks of hepatitis that are assumed. Similar analysis is relevant and probably more appropriate for hospitals and blood suppliers. (The defendants in
the Illinois, Pennsylvania, Florida and Washington cases were either hospitals, blood suppliers, or both.) It is on a par with buying a car with the choice
of a one or a two year warranty with appropriate differences in price. If one
buys a car with a one year warranty, then liability for the second year is borne
by the owner. By contrast, buying a car with a two year warranty implies the
seller bears the liability in the second year.

Where liability in the foregoing world is placed is an accounting detail.
It is very hard to believe this full knowledge, transaction-cost free world is a
prototype for the blood market. The costs incurred by the medical establishment in escaping from liability for tainted blood — there is no free legislation
— suggests that they have a strong stake, presumably financial, in avoiding
liability for hepatitis. . . .

Consider a situation in which liability is placed on a patient and he buys
and pays for blood with three chances in one thousand of incurring hepatitis
per unit purchased. Further assume that he subsequently contracts transfusion hepatitis. It is very difficult ex post to determine whether or not he
bought three chances in one thousand blood or three chances in one hundred.
He has an expensive and virtually insurmountable gap in knowledge to
overcome, particularly in a world in which data on the incidence of hepatitis
is not easy to come by, in finding out whether or not the product purchased is
in fact the product delivered. Hence, civil remedies are virtually precluded
unless strict liability exists.

Moreover, it must not be forgotten that not all blood is transfused as a
result of elective surgery or other elective procedures. A non-trivial fraction of
all blood is transfused to patients that are found in trauma as a result of
accidents and are in no position to weigh alternatives in the blood market.
Under such circumstances, it is somewhat ludicrous to expect patients to take
responsibility for the quality of the blood they receive; whatever virtues
caveat emptor may have in other contexts, it is difficult to argue that it
should prevail here.

Both the physician and the hospital can more cheaply obtain the knowledge required to determine whether the quality of blood ordered for a
patient is in fact received. They are in a better position, as compared with the
patient, to obtain the information relevant for evaluating the medical experiences of all patients transfused with blood from a particular supplier. Hence,
if liability is placed with either the hospital or the physician, which almost
surely will involve some subsequent transference to the blood supplier, those
who have the cheapest access to the relevant information will be making the
choice and evaluating the performance of blood suppliers. This information
will be used in setting fees and hospital charges to the patient who in turn will
be in a better position to evaluate alternatives in the medical care market
than he would be if he were self-insured.

The case for placing liability directly on the physician rather than on the hospital or the blood supplier rests on the fact that he chooses among alternative modes of treatment. Hence he is in the best position to evaluate whether blood or blood substitutes ought to be used, and in what quantities, and to evaluate the risks to specific patients. Therefore, he can, at a lower cost than anyone else, obtain the information relevant for decisions involving the risks of hepatitis and compare them with other medical risks. . . .

. . . Why have not hospitals developed better sources of blood? After all, both physicians and hospitals are concerned with the welfare of their patients. A large part of the answer to this question must be that the dangers of transfusion hepatitis are relatively new on the medical scene and neither patients nor physicians are as alert to this problem currently as they will be when more experience with this complication of transfusions is accumulated. Hence, one can argue that in the long run, the Coase theorem will hold. Under this interpretation, suppliers of blood should be currently moving in the direction of improving blood quality.

A role of strict liability, given the foregoing interpretation, is to influence the pace at which the medical establishment adjusts to the relatively recently developed knowledge about the relationship of blood sources to the transmission of transfusion hepatitis. Currently whether or not a hospital develops good sources seems to be relatively insensitive to pressures from either patients or physicians. . . .

Because of the absence of advertising competition among hospitals, the fact that some hospitals are alert to the dangers of hepatitis to their patients and obtain low risk blood does not force other hospitals to find sources of blood of equal quality in order to remain economically viable. Hence the claims and litigation arising out of the existence of strict liability are especially important in this particular market as a means of exerting pressure on the prime figures in the medical hierarchy of hospitals to obtain low risk blood. Strict liability would reduce the survival properties of hospitals with a medical hierarchy that was insensitive to or ignorant of the risks of hepatitis for their patients. Consequently, they would move faster towards providing the quality of blood their patients want.

In the absence of strict liability, the pace at which the medical establishment will move towards providing low risk blood for patients will be much slower. Eventually enough information is generated by the experience of relatives and friends, by articles and books, by radio and TV, and by newspapers so that both the public and physicians, both sides of the market, will become informed of the risks and only low risk blood will be used. This is a more expensive way of disseminating the relevant information, hence the movement towards long-run equilibrium will be slower than it would be if strict liability existed.

The desire to avoid product liability explains the inconsistency between the opposition to commercialism in blood procurement on the one hand and the promotion of barter as a means of providing blood on the other. In order to avoid product liability, the patient is induced to provide his own blood via blood assurance programs and the hospital provides transfusion services. For the same reason medical insurors controlled by the medical establishment, such as Blue Cross and Blue Shield, do not provide coverage of blood costs, nor do many pre-paid groups, that is the so-called health maintenance organizations. They all wish to establish that the provision of blood is a service and not a product. . . .

The additional financial incentives of strict liability will mobilize the resources of the market to find and utilize economical supplies of high quality blood. Probably a thoroughgoing system of professional blood donors will develop, professionals being usually better than amateurs. The analysis presented implies that voluntarism in blood procurement is a deus ex machina which makes possible the anomalous rule of liability for blood that currently prevails. Hence imposing strict liability for blood would eliminate voluntarism and explains the hostility towards commercial blood procurement by voluntary agencies.

The fact that the Mayo Clinic pays for blood is suggestive of the direction of the medical establishment would move in a world of strict liability. Moreover, more screening by social class, absence or presence of slum background, and medical history would occur. Implicit prices would become explicit; the price of the blood supplied by a given donor would rise as the number of trouble-free units previously supplied increased. Professional donors would have incentives to stay healthy and blood banks would have incentives to weed unsatisfactory donors out of their pools. Moreover, more thought would go into designing programs for administering transfusions that would make it easy and hence less expensive to detect donors of tainted blood. . . .

Notes

1. What market imperfection leads Professor Kessel to his conclusion that a rule of no liability would result in lower-quality blood than a rule of strict liability? To what extent do other markets involved in the cases in this chapter contain similar imperfections? Is the imperfection identified by Professor Kessel a long-run or a short-run phenomenon?

2. Is there not a simpler route to the conclusion that the liability rule in serum hepatitis cases should be strict liability rather than negligence — the distinction between activity and care? Neither the blood bank nor the hospital can reduce the incidence of serum hepatitis merely by more careful handling of the blood they buy and sell. What is required is greater screening of donors or greater use of plasma in place of whole blood or (though Kessel disagrees with this point) a greater reliance on unpaid rather than paid donors. A negligence inquiry might treat these as activity rather than care points, especially the second and third.

Jackson v. Coast Paint & Lacquer Co.
499 F.2d 809 (9th Cir. 1974)

MERRILL, J. . . .

In 1964 plaintiff, a citizen of Utah, was a journeymen painter employed by a Utah painting contractor. His employer entered into a contract with a Montana manufacturing company to paint some railroad tank cars that were to be used for the shipment of bulk quantities of honey. Plaintiff was sent by his employer to Billings, Montana, to do the work.

The paint used to coat the inside of the tank cars, "Copon EA9," was manufactured and sold by defendant Reliance Universal, Inc., a Texas manufacturer of industrial paints and coatings. It is an epoxy paint which is highly flammable. While plaintiff was spray painting the inside of one of the tanks a fire occurred and he was very severely burned. The fuel of the fire consisted of the paint fumes which had accumulated in the tank. The cause of ignition is uncertain and was a disputed issue at trial. There was some evidence that it was caused by breakage of a light bulb used by plaintiff in the tank. This is the theory favored by defendant. There was other evidence, mainly expert testimony including an experiment-demonstration, to the effect that the fire could have been touched off by static electricity, perhaps generated by the friction of the rubber soles of plaintiff's shoes on the tank floor. This is the theory favored by plaintiff.

An officer of Reliance testified that Reliance was aware of the fact that Copon EA9 is hazardous if not properly used under proper conditions. Two hazards are recognized to be associated with use of the paint: breathing the toxic vapors, and fire.

The label on the paint used by plaintiff was introduced into evidence. It contains a warning which first refers to the toxicity of the paint if ingested, and then states:

> Keep away from heat, sparks, and open flame. USE WITH ADEQUATE VENTILATION. Avoid prolonged contact with skin and breathing of spray mist. Close container after each use. KEEP OUT OF REACH OF CHILDREN.

Plaintiff testified that he and other painters of his acquaintance understood the warning regarding adequate ventilation to refer only to the danger of breathing toxic vapors. While painting the tanks he had contrived and used a tube and mask which enabled him to breathe fresh air from outside the tank. Otherwise plaintiff took no precautions in the nature of "ventilation." He testified that he had been unaware of the possibility that flammable vapors permitted to accumulate in a closed, inadequately ventilated area could be touched off by spark resulting in a fire or explosion. There was, however, other evidence that some persons in plaintiff's company were aware that such a danger existed. . . .

It is not essential to strict liability that the product be defective in the sense that it was not properly manufactured. If the product is unreasonably dangerous that is enough. A product may be perfectly manufactured and meet every requirement for its designed utility and still be rendered unreasonably dangerous through failure to warn of its dangerous characteristics. . . .

The district court's instructions to the jury included the following:

> [D]efendant has a duty to supply plaintiff or his employer with proper and adequate directions for the use of the paint and proper and adequate warnings concerning the dangers inherent in the paint. . . .
> If the defendant had reason to believe that plaintiff or his employer knew or would discover the hazards inherent in the paint, then defendant had no duty to warn plaintiff or his employer of these dangers.

In our judgment this instruction was erroneous in three respects.

First. It suggests that liability is based on negligence rather than strict liability. . . . In strict liability it is of no moment what defendant "had reason to believe." Liability arises from "sell[ing] any product in a defective condition unreasonably dangerous to the user or consumer." It is the unreasonableness of the condition of the product, not of the conduct of the defendant, that creates liability.

Second. Plaintiff has contended that a more specific warning of the fire hazard ought to have been given, namely, that accumulated fumes or vapors in an inadequately ventilated area may be ignited by a spark resulting in a violent fire or explosion. His position is that the absence of such a specific warning rendered the paint as marketed by the defendant "unreasonably dangerous to the user or consumer"; in other words, that there was a "duty to warn" of the particular hazard. Defendant contends, in this regard, that it had no duty to warn of this particular hazard because . . . "the danger, or potentiality of danger, is generally known and recognized."

On the evidence presented, this was an issue for the jury. The challenged instruction, however, presents the wrong issue. It is not the knowledge actually possessed by the plaintiff, individually, that determines whether the absence of warning renders a product unreasonably dangerous. The subjective knowledge of the plaintiff becomes relevant upon the issue of contributory negligence, as we explain below. On the issue of duty to warn, however, the question to be put to the jury is whether "the danger, or potentiality of danger, is *generally* known and recognized"; whether the product as sold was "dangerous to an extent beyond that which would be contemplated by the ordinary consumer who purchases it, with *the ordinary knowledge common to the community* as to its characteristics." (Emphasis added.)

Third. The most serious error in the challenged instruction is the statement that knowledge of the hazard on the part of plaintiff's *employer* would obviate any duty to warn plaintiff. Besides improperly focusing on the knowledge of an individual rather than general or common knowledge, this erroneously conceives the "community" whose common knowledge the jury is to ascertain. The seller's duty under §402A [of the Second Restatement of Torts] is to "the ultimate user or consumer." At least in the case of paint sold in labeled containers, the adequacy of warnings must be measured according to whatever knowledge and understanding may be common to painters who will actually open the containers and use the paints; the possibly superior knowledge and understanding of painting contractors is irrelevant. . . .

In Jacobson [v. Colorado Fuel & Iron Corp., 409 F.2d 1263 (9th Cir. 1969),] plaintiff's decedent was killed when steel strand manufactured by the defendant broke during a procedure in the manufacture of prestressed concrete by the decedent's employer. Plaintiff contended that the defendant had inadequately warned the decedent of the particular danger of overstressing the strand. The decedent had been a foreman, whose work was done under the supervision and direction of several superiors. One of them, the production coordinator, admitted knowledge of the relevant danger. There was testimony of other experts in the field that the danger was well known. . . . We adopted the trial court's conclusions of law: " 'Where a supplier furnishes chattels, *the use of which is to be directed by technicians or engineers*, it is sufficient to insulate the supplier from liability for failure to warn if the warnings given are sufficient to apprise the engineers or technicians of the dangers involved, or if the technicians have knowledge of the dangers involved. There is no duty to warn *those who simply follow the directions of the engineers or technicians.* . . .' " (Emphasis added.)

There are important distinctions between . . . the steel strand in *Jacobson* and the paint involved here. Paint is not a product "the use of which is to be directed by technicians or engineers." Further it is a product so dispensed that warning to the ultimate consumer can readily be given. . . .

The district court's instructions on contributory negligence included the following:

> If the plaintiff or his employer had knowledge and was aware of the fact that the paint in question was potentially hazardous and nevertheless proceeded unreasonably to make use of the product, or made an improper use of the product, and was injured as a result, he is barred from recovery.

Here again the court erred in according significance to knowledge of plaintiff's employer. There can be contributory negligence which bars recovery only if plaintiff, the "user or consumer," was aware of and unreasonably embraced the danger. It is manifest not only in the passage quoted but also from all other parts of the Restatement dealing with contributory fault that "the form of contributory negligence which . . . commonly passes under the name of assumption of risk" must be subjective, conscious, and personal to the plaintiff. Such negligence plainly cannot be "imputed" to the plaintiff from another. Therefore any knowledge plaintiff's employer may have had concerning the hazard which resulted in plaintiff's injury is irrelevant, where the employer did not in fact communicate any superior knowledge to plaintiff prior to the accident. This would be true even if the employer himself had an independent legal duty to warn plaintiff. . . .

Karjala v. Johns-Manville Products Corp.
523 F.2d 155 (8th Cir. 1975)

WEBSTER, J.

Appellant Johns-Manville Products Corporation appeals from an adverse judgment in a jury trial in which John A. Karjala, the plaintiff below, was awarded $200,000 for damages sustained as a result of contracting asbestosis from the use of appellant's asbestos products. We affirm the judgment upon the narrow grounds discussed below.

John A. Karjala began working as an installer of asbestos insulation in 1948. Between then and June, 1966, when he quit his job, Karjala was exposed to great quantities of asbestos dust. In 1959, Karjala began to feel a shortness of breath, congestion, a loss of appetite, and general weakness. Suspecting that he might have tuberculosis, he had his chest x-rayed. The x-ray showed no evidence of tuberculosis; Karjala did not see a doctor at that time, but did remain absent from his job for one week. On a later visit to the sanatorium where the x-ray was taken, he noticed that his record showed "possible asbestosis." His shortness of breath grew worse throughout this period. . . .

After coughing up blood in June, 1966, Karajala visited his doctor. Following an examination of his body and of x-ray photographs taken of his lungs, Karjala was told that he had asbestosis and that he should quit his job. He did so, but his health steadily declined.

Karjala filed this action in 1971 against several manufacturers of asbestos insulation, charging that their products were unreasonably dangerous and that they failed to warn him of the products' defective condition. All defendants except Johns-Manville were subsequently dismissed by stipulation.

At trial, in addition to its affirmative defense that Karjala's action was barred by the statute of limitations, Johns-Manville contended principally that since it could not in the exercise of reasonable care have forseen the dangers to insulation installers now known to be associated with its product, it could not be held responsible for the injury to Karjala's health. In support of its contention, Johns-Manville introduced into evidence two scholarly reports, written nineteen years apart. In the first [1946], the authors concluded that inferences drawn from other asbestos industries (i.e., that people who work with asbestos are presented with a health hazard) could not be applied to the asbestos pipe covering industry on board naval vessels and that covering pipes with asbestos insulation was not a dangerous occupation. The authors of the second study [1965] concluded that "asbestosis and its complications are significant hazards among insulation workers in the United States at this time." Johns-Manville contended that it could not be charged with notice of the hazard until after the publication of the second report.

Evidence was also adduced which showed that Johns-Manville knew by at least the 1930's that persons who worked at plants where asbestos products were manufactured were exposed to a substantial health hazard. Also introduced into evidence was testimony concerning several other pre-1950 articles in which some suggestion was made of a connection between asbestosis and those who work with asbestos fibers. . . .

Under Minnesota law, a manufacturer has a duty to warn users of its products of all dangers associated with those products of which it has actual or constructive knowledge. Failure to provide such warnings will render the product unreasonably dangerous and will subject the manufacturer to liability for damages under strict liability in tort. Asbestos insulation is a product that has been held to be susceptible to this standard.

. . . "[A] product is unreasonably dangerous only when it is 'dangerous to an extent beyond that contemplated by the ordinary consumer who purchases it.' "

Thus, a product may be unreasonably dangerous because the manufacturer has failed to give adequate warnings of known or knowable dangers involved.

Of course, a manufacturer is only required to warn of foreseeable dangers. . . :

> The manufacturer's duty to warn users of the potential danger inherent in its product is commensurate with its actual knowledge of the risk involved to those users or the knowledge constructively imparted to it by available scientific or other medical data. . . . [citations and footnote omitted]

The challenged instruction properly informed the jury that Johns-Manville could be held liable for failing to warn if, while held to the "knowledge and skill of an expert," it did not disclose to the public those dangers inherent in its product "that the application of reasonable foresight would reveal." It emphasized that the jury must decide whether Johns-Manville had the requisite knowledge and reminded the jury that Karjala was an installation worker, not a factory worker. The instruction is in accord with the law of Minnesota. We find no error here.

Appellant asserts that Judge Lord's instruction on the statute of limitations was erroneous because it literally told the jury that the statute did not bar Karjala's claim and because the instruction set the date when the statute would begin to run as the date on which Karjala became disabled. We disagree. When read as a whole, the District Court's instruction on the statute of limitations is in accord with Minnesota law. . . .

The applicable Minnesota statute sets six years as the period within which a cause of action for personal injuries resulting from a defective product must be brought. . . .

. . . [U]nder Minnesota law, an instruction on the statute of limitations must be couched in terms of when damage has resulted from the alleged breach of duty, that is, the time when a claim would be brought in a court of law without dismissal for failure to state a claim; in a personal injury action this occurs when some harm or impairment has manifested itself which can be shown to have been caused by an act or omission for which the defendant would be liable. This is precisely the substance of the challenged instruction. We do not agree with Johns-Manville that the use of "disabled" and "disability" in the instruction implied that Karjala had to be totally incapacitated before the statute of limitations would commence. Rather, those terms were properly used as synonyms for "harm" or "impairment."

As in silicosis cases, there is rarely a magic moment when one exposed to asbestos can be said to have contracted asbestosis; the exposure is more in the nature of a continuing tort. It is when the disease manifests itself in a way which supplies some evidence of causal relationship to the manufactured product that the public interest in limiting the time for asserting a claim attaches and the statute of limitations will begin to run. The time at which Karjala's impairment manifested itself was, of course, for the jury to determine. . . .

The judgment of the District Court is affirmed.

Notes

1. Could a plaintiff employ the theory of *Jackson* or *Karjala* — that a manufacturer is strictly liable for failure to warn of the dangers of an unreasonably dangerous but not defective product — in a jurisdiction that still bases strict liability in products cases on breach of an implied warranty? Would such a theory, for example, have changed the result in Green v. American Tobacco Co.?

2. Is it quite so absurd as the court in *Karjala* thought to impute the employer's knowledge of the risk to the employee? The manufacturer of Copon EA9 was selling to employers, not employees. If the manufacturer adequately warned the employer, but the employer failed to transmit the warning to the employee, why should the manufacturer be held liable for a failure to warn? Stated differently, why is the employer's failure to warn not an intervening cause of the accident?

One way to take care of the problem is through the doctrine of indemnity. Could defendant in *Jackson*, after losing the case, have sued the plaintiff's employer for indemnity on the ground that the employer's failure to warn was the primary cause of the employee's injury, and the defendant's failure to warn secondary? In Dole v. Dow Chemical Co., 30 N.Y.2d 143, 282 N.E.2d

288 (1972), a worker was poisoned by inhaling a chemical supplied to his employer by Dow. After he recovered damages from Dow on the theory that Dow should have warned him personally of the danger, Dow turned around and sued the worker's employer. Dow alleged that the employer had been negligent in failing to comply with its instructions regarding the chemical. The court, relying on the state's contribution statute, held that Dow was entitled to contribution from the employer but not to indemnity. Is this result correct? Was this an alternative-care case or a joint-care case?

Indemnity is traditionally allowed in products cases where the defect is in a component and the final manufacturer is, as in *Goldberg*, liable under strict liability principles. The component manufacturer's liability is said to be primary and the final manufacturer's secondary. Is this the correct result under the economic principles of joint tortfeasor law discussed in Chapter 8? See Landes & Posner, Joint and Multiple Tortfeasors: An Economic Analysis, 9 J. Legal Stud. 517, 534-535 (1980).

3. Suppose plaintiff in *Karjala* had worked with the asbestos insulation of several manufacturers, not just Johns-Manville's; which if any would be liable and how would damages be apportioned? This was an issue in another asbestosis case, Borel v. Fibreboard Paper Products Corp., 493 F.2d 1076 (5th Cir. 1973). Plaintiff there sued 11 manufacturers of asbestos insulation, and the court found it "impossible, as a practical matter, to determine with absolute certainty which particular exposure to asbestos dust resulted in injury to Borel." Id. at 1094. The court held defendants jointly and severally liable for Borel's injury. Is *Borel* a stronger or a weaker case for joint liability than *Sindell* in Chapter 8? Would *Sindell's* market-share method of apportionment make more sense here than joint liability with no contribution?

4. As *Karjala* illustrates, statute of limitations is a crucial issue in many products cases; it is, in fact, the issue as to which the choice between implied-warranty and strict-tort-liability theories of product liability has its greatest practical significance. In implied-warranty cases, which are in this respect faithful to their origins in contract law, the statute of limitations begins to run when the warranty was breached, i.e., when the defective product was delivered to the buyer. See, e.g., Thornton v. Roosevelt Hospital, 47 N.Y.2d 780, 391 N.E.2d 1002 (1979). The tort statute of limitations, in contrast, normally begins to run only when an injury occurs. Thus, is a successful DES suit based on strict products liability conceivable in a jurisdiction that imposes such liability only under an implied-warranty theory? See Diamond v. E.R. Squibb & Sons, Inc., 366 So. 2d 1221 (Fla. App. 1979), and, for a general comparison of the contract and tort statutes of limitations in products cases, Victorson v. Bock Laundry Machine Co., 37 N.Y.2d 395, 335 N.E.2d 275 (1975).

Suppose that, when symptoms of illness first occur, the plaintiff is not sure they are the result of the allegedly defective or unreasonably dangerous product. Does the statute of limitations nonetheless begin to run from the first symptoms? Does it begin to run from the time when the symptoms were correctly diagnosed? Does it from the time when the plaintiff could have determined their origin if he had exercised due diligence? On these questions see, e.g., Dalton v. Dow Chemical Co., 280 Minn. 147, 158 N.W.2d 580 (1968); Ricciuti v. Voltarc Tubes, Inc., 277 F.2d 809 (2d Cir. 1960). On asbestosis litigation — one of the most active areas of tort litigation today — see generally Mansfield, Asbestos: The Cases and the Insurance Problem, 15 Forum 860 (1980).

Reyes v. Wyeth Laboratories
498 F.2d 1264 (5th Cir. 1974)

WISDOM, J. . . .

On May 8, 1970, Anita Reyes was fed two drops of Sabin oral polio vaccine by eye-dropper at the Hidalgo County Department of Health clinic in Mission, Texas. The vaccine was administered to Anita by a registered nurse; there were no doctors present. Mrs. Reyes testified that she was not warned of any possible danger involved in Anita's taking the vaccine. Mrs. Reyes has a seventh grade education, but her primary language is Spanish. She signed a form releasing the State of Texas from "all liability in connection with immunization." The form contained no warning of any sort, and it is apparent from her testimony that she either did not read the form or lacked the linguistic ability to understand its significance. About fourteen days after the vaccine was administered, Anita Reyes became ill. On May 23, 1970, she was admitted to the McAllen (Texas) General Hospital, where her disease was diagnosed as Type I paralytic poliomyelitis. As a result of the polio, at the time of trial Anita was completely paralyzed from the waist down, her left arm had become atrophied, and she was unable to control her bladder or bowel movements.

The vaccine given Anita Reyes in the Mission clinic on May 8, 1970 was part of a "lot," No. 15509, prepared by Wyeth. Lot No. 15509 was trivalent oral polio vaccine that Wyeth had titered (mixed) from Types I, II, and III monovalent vaccine provided by Pfizer, Ltd. In response to an order placed by the Texas State Department of Health on December 23, 1969, Wyeth shipped 3500 vials of Lot No. 15509 vaccine to the State Health Department which in turn transferred 400 vials to the Hidalgo County Health Department. The jury found that vaccine from one of these vials was given to Anita Reyes. Included with every vial, each of which contained ten doses of vaccine, was a "package circular" provided by Wyeth which was intended to warn doctors, hospitals, or other purchasers of potential dangers in ingesting the vaccine. Mrs. Lenore Wiley, the public health nurse who administered the vaccine to Anita Reyes, testified that she had read the directions on this package insert, but that it was not the practice of the nurses at the Mission Health Clinic to pass on the warnings to the vaccinees or to their guardians.

She testified that she gave Mrs. Reyes no warning before she administered the vaccine to Anita. . . .

We begin the inquiry by asking whether the vaccine was unreasonably dangerous, that is, in a defective condition when Anita Reyes received it. It is clear, of course, that the vaccine was not itself defective. Wyeth Vaccine Lot No. 15509 was exactly what its makers and the Texas public health authorities intended it to be: trivalent live-virus Sabin oral polio vaccine. The live virus which the jury concluded caused Anita's poliomyelitis was not inadvertently included in the mixture. Indeed, it is the presence of the living but attenuated Type I, II, and III viruses which makes the Sabin vaccine so effective.

Although the living virus in the vaccine does not make the vaccine defective, it does make it what the Restatement calls an "unavoidably unsafe product," one which cannot be made "safe" no matter how carefully it is manufactured. Such products are not necessarily *unreasonably* dangerous," for as this Court has long recognized in wrestling with product liability questions, many goods possess both utility and danger. Rather, in evaluating the possible liability of a manufacturer for injuries caused by his inevitably hazardous products a two-step analysis is required to determine first, whether the product is so unsafe that marketing it at all is "unreasonably dangerous per se," and, if not, whether the product has been introduced into the stream of commerce without sufficient safeguards and is thereby "unreasonably dangerous as marketed." In either case, the applicable standard, as formulated in the Restatement, is as follows: In terms of the user's interests, a product is "unreasonably dangerous" only when it is "dangerous to an extent beyond that contemplated by the ordinary consumer"; or, to phrase it in terms of the seller's responsibility, ":so dangerous that a reasonable man would not sell the product if he knew the risk involved."

In determining whether placing a commodity on the market is "unreasonably dangerous per se," the reasonable man standard of the Restatement becomes the fulcrum for a balancing process in which the utility of the product properly used is weighed against whatever dangers of harm inhere in its introduction into commerce. Obviously, use of an unavoidably unsafe product always presents at least a minimal danger of harm, but only if the potential harmful effects of the product — both qualitative and quantitative — outweigh the legitimate public interest in its availability will it be declared unreasonably dangerous per se and the person placing it on the market held liable. Applying this standard here, the scales must tip in favor of availability. The evil to be prevented — poliomyelitis and its accompanying paralysis — is great. Although the danger that vaccinees may contract polio is qualitatively .devastating, it is statistically minuscule. On balance then, marketing the vaccine is justified despite the danger.

Since Sabin oral polio vaccine is not "unreasonably dangerous per se," we move to the second step of our analysis to determine whether it is "unreasonably dangerous as marketed," for to conclude that the maker of an unavoidably unsafe product did not act unreasonably in placing it on the market is not to relieve him of the responsibility to market it in such a way as to prevent unreasonable danger. In the case of a product such as Sabin oral polio vaccine, this translates into a duty to provide proper warnings in selling the product. As comment k to Section 402A instructs, an unavoidably unsafe product is neither defective nor *unreasonably* dangerous if such a product is "properly prepared, and is accompanied by proper directions and warning." Consequently, the Restatement requires a seller who has reason to believe that danger may result from a particular use of his product to provide adequate warning of the danger in order that the product's potential for harm may be reduced. Failure to give such a warning when it is required will itself present a "defect" in the product and will, without more, cause the product to be "unreasonably dangerous as marketed." . . .

Wyeth does not deny that its vaccine is "unavoidably unsafe," or contend that it was unaware of the danger. Rather, the appellant contends that if it had a duty to warn at all, that duty was discharged by the warning contained on the package insert which accompanied the vials of vaccine sold to the Texas State Department of Health. This is so, Wyeth asserts, because the Sabin trivalent oral polio vaccine in issue here is a "prescription drug," and those who prepare such drugs are not required to warn the ultimate consumer. If the warning to the dispensing physician or authorities (here the Texas and Hidalgo County Public Health Departments) was adequate, Wyeth is not liable for any harm caused by the vaccine. Resolution of these contentions is crucial; Wyeth concedes in its brief that "[s]ince it is undisputed that Wyeth did not warn Reyes, but only the Texas State Department of Health, a finding that the vaccine was not a prescription drug establishes as a matter of law the defectiveness of the vaccine for purposes of a prima facie case in strict products liability."

We cannot quarrel with the general proposition that where *prescription* drugs are concerned, the manufacturer's duty to warn is limited to an obligation to advise the prescribing physician of any potential dangers that may result from the drug's use. This special standard for prescription drugs is an understandable exception to the Restatement's general rule that one who markets goods must warn foreseeable ultimate users of dangers inherent in his products. Prescription drugs are likely to be complex medicines, esoteric in formula and varied in effect. As a medical expert, the prescribing physician can take into account the propensities of the drug, as well as the susceptibilities of his patient. His is the task of weighing the benefits of any medication against its potential dangers. The choice he makes is an informed one, an individualized medical judgment bottomed on a knowledge of both patient and palliative. Pharmaceutical companies then, who must warn ultimate purchasers of dangers inherent in patent drugs sold over the counter, in selling prescription drugs are required to warn only the prescribing physician, who acts as a "learned intermediary" between manufacturer and consumer.

Although there is no question that Sabin oral vaccine is licensed for sale only as a prescription drug, the district court, in its charge to the jury, noted that the vaccine was not administered as a prescription drug at the Mission Clinic. The court charged: "if you [the jury] find that a warning should have been given, the warning had to be given to Anita and her parents, not to Mrs. Wiley, that Public Health nurse, somebody else. . . . The ultimate consumer is the one that had to be warned." The district court apparently based this instruction on the leading federal case in the area, Davis v. Wyeth Laboratories, 9 Cir. 1968, 399 F.2d 121. In Davis, the plaintiff had allegedly contracted polio from Wyeth oral vaccine distributed at a public clinic. The Ninth Circuit held that where no individualized medical judgment intervenes between the manufacturer of a prescription drug and the ultimate consumer, "it is the responsibility of the manufacturer to see that warnings reach the consumer, either by giving warning itself or by obligating the purchaser to give warning." Where there is no physician to make an "individualized balancing . . . of the risks," the Court reasoned, the very justification for the prescription drug exception evaporates. Thus, as in the case of patent drugs sold over the counter without prescription, the manufacturer of a prescription drug who knows or has reason to know that it will not be dispensed as such a drug must provide the consumer with adequate information so that he can balance the risks and benefits of a given medication himself. Moreover, just as the manufacturer cannot make this choice for its ultimate consumers, it cannot allow its immediate purchaser to choose for them. In sum, then, the manufacturer is required to warn the ultimate consumer, or to see that he is warned.

Wyeth does not resist the Ninth Circuit's holding in Davis, but asserts that the instant case can be distinguished on four grounds. First, the appellant argues, Davis received his vaccine during a mass immunization program, whereas Anita Reyes ingested her vaccine at her parents' request. Second, Wyeth stresses the fact that Davis received his vaccine from a pharmacist, but Reyes' was administered by a public health nurse. Third, Wyeth's active participation in the mass immunization program involved in the Davis case is contrasted to its relatively passive role here. Finally, Wyeth urges that unlike the situation in Davis, here it had no knowledge that the vaccine would not be administered as a prescription drug.

None of these asserted grounds for distinguishing Davis justifies a different result here. The first two arguments are admittedly distinctions between Davis and the instant controversy, but they have no bearing on the rationale of the Davis opinion. Whether vaccine was received during a mass immunization or an on-going program, whether it was administered by nurse or pharmacist, it was, in both these cases, dispensed without the sort of individualized medical balancing of the risks to the vaccinee that is contemplated by the prescription drug exception. The third and fourth asserted bases for distinguishing Davis from this case are essentially the same: Wyeth took no active part in the vaccination process here, and did not know that its vaccine would be dispensed without procedures appropriate for distribution of prescription drugs.

Were we to conclude that Wyeth neither knew nor had reason to know that its vaccine would be dispensed without prescription drug safeguards, we might be required to hold that the *rationale* in *Davis* is inapplicable here. But Wyeth had ample reason to foresee the way in which its vaccine would be distributed. A drug manufacturer is held to the skill of an expert in his field, and is presumed to possess an expert's knowledge of the arts, materials, and processes of the pharmaceutical business. Included in such expertise must be a familiarity with practices and knowledge common in the drug industry as to distribution and administration of pharmaceutical products.

Neal Nathanson, Professor of Epidemiology at the Johns Hopkins University School of Public Health and a witness for Wyeth testified that it was common knowledge in the drug industry that "a great majority" of vaccinees receive their Sabin vaccine in mass administrations or county clinics manned at least in part by volunteers. Moreover, Dr. Nathanson agreed that it was well known that such clinics were stocked primarily by sale of vaccine to state health departments. These clinics, as Wyeth must be presumed to know, dispense Sabin vaccine to all comers in an "assembly line" fashion; there is often neither time nor personnel to make an "individualized medical judgment" of the vaccinee's needs or susceptibilities.

Viewed in this light, the present controversy, however it differs from *Davis* factually, invites application of the *Davis* principles, and the conclusion that Wyeth was under a duty to warn Anita Reyes's parents of the danger inherent in its vaccine. Wyeth knew or had reason to know that the vaccine would not be administered as a prescription drug, and therefore was required to warn foreseeable users, or see that the Texas Department of Health warned them. Wyeth's failure to warn was a breach of its duty and made the vaccine "defective" — hence "unreasonably dangerous" — as marketed. . . .

Somewhat . . . troubling is a line of Texas cases involving unusual allergic reactions to potentially dangerous products sold without a warning. These decisions may be read for the proposition that only if the product, properly prepared, will harm a substantial number of people will the manufacturer be held liable for his failure to warn.

Essentially these are foreseeability cases; the element they would require to invoke strict liability doctrines is foreseeability. In these cases, the manufacturer not only marketed the unavoidably unsafe product without adequate warning and with the knowledge that it was inherently dangerous, but the danger to any individual consumer was sufficiently significant and knowable that (1) the manufacturer was cognizant of a need to warn so as to prevent injury and (2) the consumer might or could have altered his conduct in such a way as to lessen or avoid the danger. This ancipital coin of foreseeability is the currency of these Texas cases. What they seek to avoid is the imposition of liability for "abreactions," hypersensitive allergic reactions so unique that the class of persons *exposed* to the risk is minuscule. In such cases, warnings would be meaningless, since the manufacturer can convey nothing meaningful to the allergic consumer unless the latter knows he has the allergy. Without such knowledge, the consumer is apt to assume that he is not a member of the minute susceptible class and to disregard the warning. Thus with the utility of warning limited and the susceptible class minute, the manufacturer is not required to foresee that anyone will suffer an allergic reaction to his product, and is not held liable.

To the instant analysis, these principles present no dilemma, for the effect of the Sabin oral vaccine upon those who contract polio from it cannot fairly be styled an "abreaction." Although the danger of vaccine-induced polio to any one individual is small, the risk appears to be distributed evenly among that substantial segment of the population that is not naturally immune to polio. This is so because the behavior of polio virus in those who contract the disease seems to suggest more a reversion to virulence by the virus than a sensitivity in the vaccinee. Thus, if an individual is a member of the significant susceptible class, and his case should be one of those rare instances in which the vaccine strain reverts to virulence, he may contract polio. . . . In light of such factors, the Texas "abreaction" cases cannot dilute Wyeth's duty to warn here. . . .

Having concluded that Wyeth had a duty to warn Anita Reyes, and that, dispensed without a warning, the vaccine was unreasonably dangerous, we now turn to Wyeth's objections to the trial court's not instructing the jury and not submitting an interrogatory on the issue of "proximate cause". . . .

. . . Where a consumer, whose injury the manufacturer should have reasonably foreseen, is injured by a product sold without a required warning, a rebuttable presumption will arise that the consumer would have read any warning provided by the manufacturer, and acted so as to minimize the risks. In the absence of evidence rebutting the presumption, a jury finding that the defendant's product was the producing cause of the plaintiff's injury would be sufficient to hold him liable.

Such a test makes sense in this case. The jury found that the defendant's polio vaccine caused Anita Reyes's polio. Testimony by her mother as to what she would have done, had proper warnings been provided, would have been both speculative and self-serving. Thus we turn to the . . . presumption that a warning, had it been given, would have been heeded. Buttressing the presumption that Mrs. Reyes might have taken preventive steps is the testimony of Reyes' expert, Dr. Ramiro Casson, that some pediatricians in Hidalgo County, at least by the time of trial, had begun administering killed-virus vaccine to infants in order to build up their level of antibodies before feeding them the live-virus drug. Tending to rebut the presumption that Mrs. Reyes would have behaved differently had she been warned was the fact that she twice returned to the Mission Clinic for further doses of vaccine, even after Anita contracted polio. Yet it is patent from her testimony that Mrs. Reyes had not, even then, been informed of the danger of the polio vaccine, and did not in fact understand what medication Anita was to receive. The legal presumption . . . thus operates here to provide the final element necessary to hold Wyeth Laboratories liable for Anita Reyes' poliomyelitis. Aware of its unavoidable dangers and cognizant that it foreseeably would not be dispensed as a prescription drug, Wyeth nonetheless failed to warn Mrs. Reyes that its vaccine could cause polio in some few of the millions receiving the medication. Administered without a warning, the vaccine was "defective," hence unreasonably dangerous. According to the test we have distilled above, we must assume in the absence of evidence to the contrary that Anita's parents would have acted on the warning, had it been given. Perhaps this would have prevented her polio. It unquestionably would have avoided Wyeth's liability. . . .

Notes

1. When would a product ever be so dangerous that the manufacturer would be strictly liable to those injured by it, even though he had issued full and adequate warnings of the danger? Is there an echo here of Cardozo's opinion in the *Murphy* case in Chapter 5?

2. Do you agree that the sale of a product without warnings should create strict liability no matter how "statistically minuscule" the endangered group is? Is a product "unreasonably dangerous" because it might injure one in 10 million purchasers of it? Is the court here implicitly defining danger only in terms of the loss if an accident occurs, regardless of the probability that the loss will occur? Is this the approach of §402A of the Restatement?

3. Are you satisfied with the court's effort to distinguish the Texas "abreaction" cases? Suppose the same fraction of (but a different group in) the population that contracts polio from the live virus in the Sabin vaccine has an equally serious allergic reaction to the vaccine. Suppose further that the allergic group, or some of them, know they are allergic. Is the case for requiring a warning any weaker in such cases than it was in *Reyes*? Why is the allergic population's knowledge relevant?

4. Does *Reyes* require sellers of food products to provide information on possible allergic reactions? Does it require disclosure of fat, caloric, and cholesterol content?

5. Are you satisfied with the court's resolution of the causation issue? The problem is similar to that in the informed-consent cases discussed in Chapter 4. How likely is it that Anita or Mrs. Reyes would have refused the vaccine if informed of a statistically minuscule chance of contracting polio from it? What of the danger that someone will be scared off by the warning and later contract polio because he or she was not vaccinated against it? Would the decision in *Reyes* make any sense at all if there were not an alternative polio vaccine that did not contain live polio virus? In this connection it should be noted that the alternative, the inactive vaccine, has a number of disadvantages, including "the need for multiple injections and boosters; relatively high cost; need for stringent production controls to ensure

complete inactivation; failure to elicit secretory immunity in the gut; and, in some vaccine lots, inadequate antigenic potency, leading to poor antibody responses," plus "the hypothetical possibility of Guillain-Barre syndrome complicating parenteral inoculation, as has been reported following influenza immunization." Young, Poliovirus, in Principles and Practices of Infectious Diseases 1091, 1100 (G. Mandell, R. G. Douglas & J. E. Bennett eds. 1979). How do these points affect the analysis of causation?

There is another causation issue in the case. In an omitted portion of the opinion, the court upheld, in part because "the exclusion of his testimony was not so 'clearly and manifestly erroneous' as to constitute reversible error," the trial court's exclusion of testimony by a virologist for Wyeth as to the cause of Anita's disease. 498 F.2d at 1284. The virologist was permitted to testify, however, that he had found a "wild strain" of polio virus in Anita's stool. The live virus in polio vaccine is not a wild strain ("wild" in this context means a nonvaccine strain of the virus). See Young, supra, at 1092. Recently Dr. Sabin has written that "In my judgment, there is no acceptable evidence that the very rare oral poliomyelitis vaccine-associated cases of paralysis are caused by the poliomyletis vaccine strains." Sabin, Evaluation of Some Currently Available and Prospective Vaccines, 246 J. Am. Med. Assn. 236 (1981). He notes that "virulent polioviruses continue to be imported, especially by large numbers of immigrants from Mexico. . . ." Id. at 237. The Reyes opinion notes that Mrs. Reyes' primary language was Spanish; might Anita have contracted polio from someone in her community rather than from the vaccine?

6. With the court's discussion in Reyes of the duty to warn when a drug is dispensed by a physician compare Incollingo v. Ewing, 444 Pa. 263, 282 A.2d 206 (1971). Plaintiff's decedent died as the result of the side effects of an antibiotic manufactured by defendant and dispensed by the decedent's physician. The court held that the manufacturer, "in 'overpromoting' its product, primarily through the use of detail men who minimized the dangers of the drug while emphasizing its effectiveness, wide acceptance and use, and lack of certain objectionable side effects associated with other drugs," could be found to have failed in its duty to give adequate warnings of the possible side effects of the drug. Id. at 291, 282 A.2d at 221. Defendant in Reyes was not guilty of "overpromoting," but the court found that it had failed in its duty to "see" that the Texas Department of Health warned the people to whom the vaccine was dispensed that they might get polio from it. What should defendant have done to discharge this duty?

Moran v. Fabergé, Inc.
273 Md. 538, 332 A.2d 11 (1975)

DIGGES, J. . . .

. . . [On] June 8, 1969, Nancy Moran, then 17 years old, visited the home of Mr. and Mrs. Louis P. Grigsby in Hillcrest Heights, Maryland, to meet with a number of friends, including Randy Williams, a young lady of 15 years, who was residing with the Grigsbys at the time. The group congregated in the basement which was being maintained partly as a family clubroom and partly as a laundry room. After listening to music for some time on that warm summer night (estimated to be 72-73°F.), everyone left the basement, except Nancy and Randy. Apparently these two girls were at a loss for entertainment as eventually they centered their attention on a lit Christmas-tree-shaped candle which was positioned on a shelf behind the couch in the clubroom. Possibly because "the idle mind knows not what it is it wants" the girls began to discuss whether the candle was scented. After agreeing that it was not, Randy, while remarking "Well, let's make it scented," impulsively grabbed a "drip bottle" of Fabergé's Tigress cologne, which had been placed by Mrs. Grigsby in the basement for use as a laundry deodorant, and began to pour its contents onto the lower portion of the candle somewhat below the flame. Instantaneously, a burst of fire sprang out and burned Nancy's neck and breasts as she stood nearby watching but not fully aware of what her friend was doing.

During the trial the petitioner introduced evidence, which was not disputed, tending to show that, though no warning of the fact was attached to the bottle or otherwise given, Fabergé's Tigress cologne was highly flammable and, therefore, inherently dangerous. To demonstrate this the petitioner produced scientific experimental evidence revealing that this cologne, composed of, by volume, 82.06% alcohol, 5.1% perfume and oils, and 12.84% water, is a dangerously combustible product with a flash point of 73° Fahrenheit, approximately room temperature.

Additionally, the petitioner evoked testimony from two Fabergé officials, Carl Mann, its Vice President and Chief Perfumer, and Stephen Shernov, a company aerosol chemist, which indicated that not only was the manufacturer aware of this hazardous quality but also Fabergé foresaw that its product might well be dangerous when placed near flame.

Having produced evidence as to this inherently dangerous characteristic of Tigress cologne, which was known to the company though not to the public generally, as well as the fact that the manufacturer knew it might come in contact with fire and be hazardous in that circumstance, the petitioner contends that a jury question was presented as to whether Fabergé was negligent for failing to warn against its product's latent flammability characteristic. . . .

. . . [T]he duty of the manufacturer to warn of latent dangers inherent in its product goes beyond the precise use contemplated by the producer and extends to all those which are reasonably foreseeable. . . . For example, some courts have ruled that a jury may hold a manufacturer to a duty to warn because it is foreseeable that a baby might consume furniture polish. . . .

. . . [T]he standard for determining whether a given consumer use is reasonably foreseeable by the producer so as to require a warning of latent danger is, to say the least, quite vague. Probably because of development on a case-by-case basis with an eye on achieving a desired result in the individual case, without following logic and applying consistent definitions, the decisions often seem to be thrashing about in a semantic and subjective morass in their attempts to apply negligence concepts in products liability litigation. The reason for this confusion is that many cases have failed to recognize that when a product liability suit sounds in tort, rather than in contract as is frequently permissible, the action is based on a negligent breach of duty owed by the manufacturer to the plaintiff[8] and, consequently the settled principles of law pertaining to negligence, including the terms used in explaining that law and their definitions, are appropriately applicable. When these well-established negligence concepts are applied the dense fog which seems to have surrounded litigation concerning the manufacturer's duty to warn will largely dissipate. . . .

Based on this negligence law we think that in the products liability domain a duty to warn is imposed on a manufacturer if the item it produces has an inherent and hidden danger about which the producer knows, or should know, could be a substantial factor in bringing injury to an individual or his property when the manufacturer's product comes near to or in contact with the elements which are present normally in the environment where the product can reasonably be expected to be brought or used.[10] Under this analysis the unusual and bizarre details of accidents, which human experience shows are far from unlikely, are only significant as background facts to the individual case; it is not necessary that the manufacturer foresee the exact manner in which accidents occur. Thus, in the context of this case, it was not necessary for a cologne manufacturer to foresee that someone would be hurt when a friend poured its product near the flame of a lit candle; it was only necessary that it be foreseeable to the producer that its product, while in its normal environment, may be brought near a catalyst, likely to be found in that environment, which can untie the chattel's inherent danger. For example while seated at a dressing table, a woman might strike a match to light a cigarette close enough to the top of the open cologne bottle so as to cause an explosion, or that while seated in a similar manner she might turn suddenly and accidentally bump the bottle of cologne with her elbow, splashing some cologne on a burning candle placed on the vanity. . . .

In applying this test here, we hold that it was unnecessary, to support a verdict in favor of the petitioner, that there be produced evidence, as demanded by the Court of Special Appeals, "which would tend to show or

---

8. Because strict liability has not as yet been accepted in this State, we do not pursue this possibility.

10. In this connection, although not dispositive of the case, in making its determination it is proper for the trier of fact to consider . . . the prior history of the product (such as the evidence in this case which showed a 27 year accident free history of Tigress cologne). . . .

would support a rational inference that Fabergé foresaw or should have foreseen that its [Tigress] cologne would be used in the manner [(pouring the cologne on the lower portion of a lit candle in an attempt to scent it)] which caused the injuries to Nancy Moran"; rather, it was only necessary that the evidence be sufficient to support the conclusion that Fabergé, knowing or deemed to know that its Tigress cologne was a potentially dangerous flammable product, could reasonably foresee that in the environment of its use, such as the home of the Grigsbys, this cologne might come close enough to a flame to cause an explosion of sufficient intensity to burn property or injure bystanders, such as Nancy. . . .

O'DONNELL, J. (dissenting). . . .

It must be emphasized that upon the record there was no evidence whatsoever of such a use as was here made of the cologne ever having previously occurred; in fact, the use of Tigress cologne had a 27 year accident-free history. The evidence does not establish a general flammability of the cologne vapors, but only when such vapors are positioned within one-quarter inch from an open flame. Cologne is not a new or mysterious product and does not have a multitude of uses or functions. Eau de cologne, sometimes called "toilet water," is defined as a "perfumed, largely alcoholic, liquid for use in or after a bath or as a skin freshener"; it has a limited utility; there is no suggestion historically or otherwise of its use as a product other than as a toilet water or skin freshener. There was no evidence presented in the trial court that the Tigress cologne could ever be dangerous when being put to the uses for which it was supplied.

When a use is made of a product so remote from that intended as to be unforeseeable, the manufacturer is relieved of liability from such use. . . .

Notes

1. Was defendant negligent under a proper application of the Hand formula? Was the probability of the injury not extraordinarily low, as indicated by the product's 27-year accident-free history? How effective would a warning have been in the factual circumstances presented by the case? Would the expected benefit of a warning not in fact have been close to zero, and the costs, although small, not trivial in the aggregate?

2. Is there any argument that Randy's conduct was an intervening cause of the accident? Was Nancy contributorily negligent? Had she assumed the risk? Which if any of these arguments would remain open if the case were decided under a strict-liability standard? See Drayton v. Jiffee Chemical Corp., 591 F.2d 352, 359-362 (6th Cir. 1978).

3. For a similarly bizarre case of unanticipated product use, also decided in plaintiff's favor, see De Santis v. Parker Feeders, Inc., 547 F.2d 357 (7th Cir. 1976).

Pritchard v. Liggett & Myers Tobacco Co.
350 F.2d 479 (3d Cir. 1965)

[Plaintiff brought an action for personal injury alleging that he had contracted lung cancer as a result of having smoked Chesterfield cigarettes for many years. He based the action on alleged warranties contained in advertisements for Chesterfields.]

SMITH, J. . . .

An action for personal injury based upon the breach of an express warranty, although it sounds also in tort, is in substance one for breach of contract. The availability of assumption of risk as a defense in such an action depends upon which of two concepts is adopted. The distinction may be of little importance in an action for personal injury based on negligence but it is important where, as here, an additional basis of liability is the alleged breach of an express warranty.

Assumption of risk in its secondary sense is ordinarily synonymous with contributory negligence and involves a failure to exercise reasonable care for one's own safety. Under this concept recovery is barred because of the plaintiff's departure from the standard of reasonable conduct and notwithstanding the misconduct of the defendant. Assumption of risk in its primary and strict sense involves voluntary exposure to an obvious or known danger which negates liability. Under this concept recovery is barred because the plaintiff is assumed to have relieved the defendant of any duty to protect him. . . .

It has been held by the Superior Court of Pennsylvania, an intermediate court of appeals, that contributory negligence is inapposite as a defense in an action for breach of warranty. We have found, and the parties to this appeal have cited, no other case in point. We are therefore obliged to follow this decision in the absence of persuasive evidence that the highest court of the State would reach a different conclusion. . . .

We are of the view, and so hold, that since contributory negligence is not available as a defense in an action for personal injury based on breach of warranty, assumption of risk in the sense of contributory negligence is likewise not available. However, if a consumer uses a product for a purpose not intended by the manufacturer and suffers an injury as a result, he may not recover because such misuse is beyond the scope of the warranty. . . .

It is the law of Pennsylvania that a person who voluntarily exposes himself to a danger of which he has knowledge, or has had notice, assumes the attendant risk. He may not recover for personal injuries sustained as the result of the exposure, because under the circumstances the person responsible for the danger is relieved of any duty to protect the injured person. It is clear from these cases that assumption of risk, in its primary and strict sense, is available as a defense in an action for personal injuries based upon negligence. It follows as a matter of logic that the same defense is apposite in an action based on breach of express warranty.

The defense of assumption of risk rested solely on the testimony of the plaintiff which, viewed in the light most favorable to the defendant, was clearly insufficient. There was no evidence upon which the jury could have predicated a determination that the plaintiff either knew or had notice of the harmful effects of Chesterfields. Absent such evidence, the defense of assumption of risk failed.

There was overwhelming evidence that many of the defendant's advertisements carried factual affirmations, professedly based on medical research, that Chesterfields were safe and smoking them could have no adverse effect on "the nose, throat and accessory organs." These advertisements were calculated to overcome any fears the potential consumers might have had as to the harmful effects of cigarettes, and particularly Chesterfields. Under the circumstances it is difficult to perceive how the plaintiff, a cabinet-maker with no scientific background, could have been charged with notice or knowledge of a danger, which the defendant, with its professed superior knowledge, extensively advertised did not exist. We should emphasize that the medical researchers engaged by the defendant in 1952, apparently failed to detect the danger. . . .

Notes

1. Although the action in *Pritchard* was based on breach of warranty, courts applying the strict tort liability standard of §402A of the Restatement use the same approach to the question of plaintiff's conduct as a bar to or limitation on recovery.

2. Is it true there is no defense of contributory negligence in a product case not itself based on a negligence theory? What is "misuse" but contributory negligence? What other kind of contributory negligence could the plaintiff in a product case commit?

3. The defense of plaintiff's conduct seems to be more narrowly construed in the recent products liability cases than in other areas of tort law. With the cases in Chapter 5 compare the following products cases:

Bachner v. Pearson, 479 P.2d 319 (Alaska 1970). While piloting a plane leased from defendant, plaintiff was overcome by carbon monoxide, allegedly because of the defective condition of the plane's muffler and exhaust system; the plane crashed, injuring plaintiff and others. Suit was based on negligence and on breach of express and implied warranties. The court held that contributory negligence was not a defense to the warranty claims. Evidence that plaintiff had been negligent in starting the plane in cold weather (which might have speeded the deterioration of the muffler and exhaust system), in failing to discover the defective condition of the system, and in failing to realize that carbon monoxide was entering the cabin of the airplane, was therefore irrelevant. Plaintiff's suit would have been barred, the court held, only if plaintiff "actually knew of the defective condition of the muffler, yet proceeded to fly the plane." Id. at 330.

Messick v. General Motors Corp., 460 F.2d 485 (5th Cir. 1972). Plaintiff was injured when his car ran off the road because of a defective steering and suspension mechanism. Messick was aware of the defects:

> In the repeated attempts to ameliorate the defects the dealer's mechanics found the Oldsmobile to have two warped rear wheels and a warped axle. Replacement of these parts reduced the vibration, but did little for the steering problem which the mechanics were unable to explain or repair. Messick then took the automobile to a private mechanic. After examining the vehicle the mechanic informed Messick that in his opinion, if Messick continued to drive the car in its present condition, it was going to kill him. Messick thereupon made a demand upon General Motors to replace the automobile and he had received no reply at the time the car ran off a fog-shrouded road resulting in the injuries sustained.

Id. at 486. The district court had given the following instructions on assumption of risk:

> ... [T]he defense of voluntary assumption of risk has four essential elements:
>
> First, that the Plaintiff has knowledge of facts constituting a dangerous condition;
>
> Second, that he knows that condition is dangerous;
>
> Third, that he realizes and appreciates the nature or extent of the danger; and
>
> Fourth, that he voluntarily exposes himself to this danger.
>
> In this case the first three elements are undisputed. What is in dispute is whether the Plaintiffs' exposure to the risks of operating this automobile was voluntary. If that exposure was voluntary, then Plaintiffs may not recover on either of their alternative grounds of recovery.
>
> If that exposure was involuntary, the Plaintiffs may recover on either or both of such theories.
>
> In connection with determining whether the Plaintiffs' exposure was voluntary, you are instructed that a person is not at fault in voluntarily exposing himself to a known and appreciated danger, if, under the same or similar circumstances, an ordinarily prudent person would have incurred the risk which such conduct involved. Thus, if there was some reasonable necessity or propriety which justified Plaintiffs in exposing themselves to the known risks involved, or if by the exercise of care proportionate to the danger Plaintiffs might reasonably have expected to have avoided the danger, or if there was no other reasonable course open to them but to make continued use of this automobile, then Plaintiffs cannot be found to have voluntarily exposed themselves to the risk.

Id. at 492-493. The court of appeals approved the instruction, stating:

The plaintiff at bar was entitled to go to the jury with the question of whether his consent was voluntary or was the product of duress of circumstances and reasonable. This was the district court's situation at the time General Motors moved for a directed verdict: Messick had testified that he used his automobile in earning his livelihood and drove approximately 1000 miles a week; he had submitted evidence that the Oldsmobile at issue had been financed at a monthly cost of approximately one-sixth of his income. In these circumstances it was for the jury to determine whether a reasonably prudent man would have purchased another while seeking recourse against General Motors under the law of sales. The jury, properly instructed, concluded in plaintiffs' favor.

Id. at 494.

Messick was a federal case arising under the diversity jurisdiction of the federal courts; the applicable substantive law was that of Texas. In holding that plaintiff's assumption of risk would not bar his action if he was reasonable in assuming the risk, the court in *Messick* was guessing what a Texas court would hold in such circumstances. As later appeared, it guessed wrong. See Henderson v. Ford Motor Co., 519 S.W.2d 87 (Tex. 1974); Weakley v. Fischbach & Moore, Inc., 515 F.2d 1260 (5th Cir. 1975). Under the approach in *Messick*, when can the issue of assumption of risk ever be taken from the jury?

Luque v. McLean, 8 Cal. 3d 136, 501 P.2d 1163 (1972). While cutting grass with a rotary lawnmower, plaintiff noticed a small carton in his path. He left the mower in a stationary position with the motor running and walked over to remove the carton. The grass was wet, he slipped and fell, and his hand went into the unguarded hole of the mower and was lacerated by the rotating blade. The trial court instructed the jury that plantiff had to prove that the defect (the unguarded hole in the mower) was latent and not patent. The supreme court held that this instruction was error: the latent-patent question goes only to the assumption of risk defense, on which defendant has the burden of proof.

Schuh v. Fox River Tractor Co., 63 Wis. 2d 728, 218 N.W.2d 279 (1974). Here the defense of misuse was upheld. Plaintiff fell into the fan of his crop blower from a perch on the narrow rim of the hopper portion of the blower, which was above the fan.

The only credible evidence to support a verdict for the plaintiff is that he pulled the clutch lever and because of its position on the crop blower believed that it disengaged both the fan and the auger, when in fact it only disengaged the auger. While the plaintiff's testimony that he thought the fan had stopped could be taken as true, it is clear from these facts that he should have known the fan continued to operate.

The plaintiff was a farmer and had lived on a farm practically all his life. He was familiar with farm machinery. He had worked with this same machine $2\frac{1}{2}$ days the previous year, and a full day on the day of the incident. He knew that the crop blower was equipped with a fan capable of propelling silage through a nine inch pipe at least far enough to reach the top of a silo. It was essential that the fan continue to operate after the auger stopped in order to clear the pipes, and no machine was manufactured by any manufacturer, in which the clutch stopped both the fan and the auger.

On at least two previous occasions on the day in question, the conveyor belt had come off the sprocket and on each occasion plaintiff disengaged the clutch lever. He never did look to see if the fan was disengaged. His counsel argues that even if he had looked, the fan operates so rapidly, that one looking would be unable to tell whether the fan was operating or not. As the trial court observed, ". . . [T]here is no substance to this [argument], for anyone knows that if a fan is stopped one can see the blades . . . , but if it is running or operating one cannot see them."

On the two previous occasions that day when the conveyor belt malfunctioned, he stood on the ground to replace it. On the third occasion, late in the afternoon, he chose to balance or "perch" himself in the dangerous and precarious position with his feet on the narrow rim of the crop blower, while the tractor which powered it was running. In this position, he was approximately 18 inches from the fan, and he testified he felt some vibration. While so situated, he attempted to balance himself only by the use of his feet and used his body and hands to reach over and down and re-engage the conveyor belt. He slipped and fell into the hopper and this unfortunate accident was the result. He testified that he took this position on the rim of the crop blower because the "grandfather" was standing in the position where the plaintiff had stood on the two previous occasions when he fixed the machine while standing on the ground. He did not ask the "grandfather" to move because he was an old man and "you couldn't tell him much." He had been told by Gordon Kohibeck to have Kiel, the owner of the machine, replace the chain on the sprocket. However, because he had done it twice before on this day, he attempted to do it a third time.

We have considered all of the arguments advanced by the plaintiff on this issue and are of the opinion the order and judgment of the trial court granting the motion of the defendant for a directed verdict should be affirmed.

Id. at 744-745, 218 N.W.2d at 287-288.

Melia v. Ford Motor Co., 534 F.2d 795 (8th Cir. 1976). Plaintiff's decedent was involved in an automobile collision. She was thrown from the car in the crash, allegedly because of a design defect in the door latch assembly, and was killed. Defendant contended that the trial court had erred in excluding evidence that the light was still red when decedent entered the intersection where the collision occurred. The court upheld the judge's action on the ground that contributory negligence is not a defense in a products liability case. The trial court had instructed the jury to consider defendant's defense of assumption of risk, but the court of appeals apparently believed that the defense did not encompass evidence that decedent had run the light:

> Clearly, there is no evidence that the decedent's alleged conduct of entering an intersection on a red light was intentional rather than inadvertent. The

defense of assumption of risk under Nebraska law "applies to *known dangers* and not to those things from which, in possibility, danger may flow."

Id. at 801. Can this ruling perhaps be justified on the ground that, in a second-collision or enhanced-injury case, the cause of the first collision is irrelevant?

Fields v. Volkswagen of America, Inc., 555 P.2d 48 (Okla. 1976). Plaintiff was injured when his car overturned, allegedly because the steering locked while he was turning. He was allegedly both intoxicated and speeding at the time of the accident. But the court stated (id. at 57):

> It is certainly foreseeable by a car manufacturer a person might drive a car over the speed limit or after drinking; but unless this excessive speed or drinking caused the accident, these factors do not bar recovery by the plaintiff even though they may have "contributed" to the accident.
>
> In this case appellants claim that appellee's excessive speed and driving while impaired caused the accident. The instructions included these theories.
>
> If Fields had been drinking or driving too fast, this would not constitute a "misuse" but may be more accurately characterized as "use for a proper purpose, but in a careless manner," i.e., contributory negligence, and thus would not be a defense in this case, unless these factors caused the accident, or recovery is sought in pure negligence.
>
> By this we do not mean to say that drunkenness could never be misuse of a product, but the situation does not arise in the peculiar facts and circumstances of this case. The instructions, although lacking in many respects in this area, were more nearly proper than those offered by the appellants and refused by the court.

The court also held that evidence of plaintiff's failure to use a seat belt was inadmissible either to establish a defense of contributory negligence or to be considered in mitigation of damages. Plaintiff was not required to anticipate defendant's negligence, and the duty to mitigate damages cannot arise before the accident occurs. "At most the failure of the [plaintiff] to use the seat belt merely furnished a condition by which the injury was possible. It did not contribute to or cause the accident." Id. at 62. But does the logic of the enhanced-injury cases not imply that plaintiff, too, had a duty to reduce the impact of a collision by fastening his seat belt?

With *Fields* compare Daly v. General Motors Corp., 20 Cal. 3d 725, 575 P.2d 1162 (1978), which involved similar allegations of plaintiff misconduct. The court held that it was error to allow the jury to consider such evidence as a complete bar to plaintiff's recovery; but, for the future, the comparative-negligence principle of the *Li* case (see Chapter 5) would be applicable, and evidence of drunkenness, failure to fasten the seat belt, and similar conduct would be admissible on the issue of comparative negligence.

A host of issues is raised by this ruling. If contributory negligence is not a defense in a strict products liability case, how can comparative negligence be a defense? What relationship if any has comparative negligence to assumption of risk? Since defendant in a strict liability case is not necessarily at fault, how can his fault be compared to that of the plaintiff in deciding how to apportion damages? The court's opinion in *Daly* addresses some of these questions:

Those counseling against the recognition of comparative fault principles in strict products liability cases vigorously stress, perhaps equally, not only the conceptual, but also the semantic difficulties incident to such a course. The task of merging the two concepts is said to be impossible, that "apples and oranges" cannot be compared, that "oil and water" do not mix, and that strict liability, which is not founded on negligence or fault, is inhospitable to comparative principles. The syllogism runs, contributory negligence was only a defense to negligence, comparative negligence only affects contributory negligence, therefore comparative negligence cannot be a defense to strict liability. While fully recognizing the theoretical and semantic distinctions between the twin principles of strict products liability and traditional negligence, we think they can be blended or accommodated.

The inherent difficulty in the "apples and oranges" argument is its insistence on fixed and precise definitional treatment of legal concepts. In the evolving areas of both products liability and tort defenses, however, there has developed much conceptual overlapping and interweaving in order to attain substantial justice. The concept of strict liability itself, as we have noted, arose from dissatisfaction with the wooden formalisms of traditional tort and contract principles in order to protect the consumer of manufactured goods. Similarly, increasing social awareness of its harsh "all or nothing" consequences led us in *Li* to moderate the impact of traditional contributory negligence in order to accomplish a fairer and more balanced result. We acknowledged an intermixing of defenses of contributory negligence and assumption of risk and formally effected a type of merger. "As for assumption of risk, we have recognized in this state that this defense overlaps that of contributory negligence to some extent. . . ." In *Li*, we further reaffirmed our observation in Grey v. Fibreboard Paper Products Co. (1966) 65 Cal. 2d 240, 245, 418 P.2d 153, " '[T]hat in one kind of situation, to wit, where a plaintiff *unreasonably* undertakes to encounter a specific known risk imposed by a defendant's negligence, plaintiff's conduct, although he may encounter that risk in a prudent manner, is in reality a form of contributory negligence. . . .' " We think it clear that the adoption of a system of comparative negligence should entail the merger of the defense of assumption of risk into the general scheme of assessment of liability in proportion to fault in those particular cases in which the form of assumption of risk involved is no more than a variant of contributory negligence."

Furthermore, the "apples and oranges" argument may be conceptually suspect. It has been suggested that the term "contributory negligence," one of the vital building blocks upon which much of the argument is based, may indeed itself be a misnomer since it lacks the first element of the classical negligence formula, namely, a duty of care owing to another. A highly respected torts authority, Dean William Prosser, has noted this fact by observing, "It is perhaps unfortunate that contributory negligence is called negligence at all.

'Contributory fault' would be a more descriptive term. Negligence as it is commonly understood is conduct which creates an undue risk of harm to others. Contributory negligence is conduct which involves an undue risk of harm to the actor himself. Negligence requires a duty, an obligation of conduct to another person. Contributory negligence involves no duty, unless we are to be so ingenious as to say that the plaintiff is under an obligation to protect the defendant against liability for the consequences of his own negligence."

We think, accordingly, the conclusion may fairly be drawn that the terms "comparative negligence," "contributory negligence" and "assumption of risk" do not, standing alone, lend themselves to the exact measurements of a micrometer-caliper, or to such precise definition as to divert us from otherwise strong and consistent countervailing policy considerations. Fixed semantic consistency at this point is less important than the attainment of a just and equitable result. The interweaving of concept and terminology in this area suggests a judicial posture that is flexible rather than doctrinaire.

We pause at this point to observe that where, as here, a consumer or user sues the manufacturer or designer alone, technically, neither fault nor conduct is really compared functionally. The conduct of one party in combination with the product of another, or perhaps the placing of a defective article in the stream of projected and anticipated use, may produce the ultimate injury. In such a case, as in the situation before us, we think the term "equitable apportionment or allocation of loss" may be more descriptive than "comparative fault." . . .

In passing, we note one important and felicitous result if we apply comparative principles to strict products liability. This arises from the fact that under present law when plaintiff sues in negligence his own contributory negligence, however denominated, may diminish but cannot wholly defeat his recovery. When he sues in strict products liability, however, his "assumption of risk" *completely bars* his recovery. Under *Li*, as we have noted, "assumption of risk" is merged into comparative principles. The consequence is that after *Li* in a negligence action, plaintiff's conduct which amounts to "negligent" assumption of risk no longer defeats plaintiff's recovery. Identical conduct, however, in a strict liability case acts as a complete bar under rules heretofore applicable. Thus, strict products liability, which was developed to free injured consumers from the constraints imposed by traditional negligence and warranty theories, places a consumer plaintiff in a worse position than would be the case were his claim founded on simple negligence. This, in turn, rewards adroit pleading and selection of theories. The application of comparative principles to strict liability obviates this bizarre anomaly by treating alike the defenses to both negligence and strict products liability actions. In each instance the defense, if established, will reduce but not bar plaintiff's claim.

Id. at 734-736, 738, 575 P.2d at 1167-1170.

Daly was followed by the New Hampshire Supreme Court in Thibault v. Sears, Roebuck & Co., 118 N.H. 802, 395 A.2d 843 (1978), and a comment on the case suggests that it may signal a trend toward giving greater weight to plaintiff misconduct in products liability cases. Comment, 13

Suffolk U.L. Rev. 1558 (1979). See also Murray v. Fairbanks Morse, 610 F.2d 149 (3d Cir. 1979). But compare Seay v. Chrysler Corp., 93 Wash. 2d 319, 609 P.2d 1382 (1980). Plaintiff was loading a convoy trailer. While driving defendant's truck chassis onto the trailer, plaintiff was injured when the chassis suddenly accelerated. There was evidence that the accelerator linkage mechanism was defective but also that plaintiff was attempting to load a large chassis into too small a place. The case was submitted to the jury on a theory of strict products liability, but the issue of comparative fault was also submitted to the jury, which returned a verdict for plaintiff but also found that 40 percent of plaintiff's damages were attributable to his own negligence. The state supreme court held that comparative fault was irrelevant in a products liability case; plaintiff was entitled to his full damages. For a position curiously between *Daly* and *Seay*, see Suter v. San Antonio Foundry & Mach. Co., 81 N.J. 150, 406 A.2d 140 (1979), referred to in *Dawson*, supra.

4. Assuming defenses based on plaintiff's misconduct will continue to be narrowly construed in product cases, what effect will this have on the safety of products and the number of accidents, relative to a system where the consumer cannot get damages if he is the cheaper accident cost avoider? Two effects should be considered. One, which is straightforward, is that all insurance carries with it what economists call "moral hazard" — it reduces the incentive to prevent an accident. But the effect may be small, if only because many consumers already carry insurance against accidents, and would carry more if products liability law were interpreted less expansively. Second, and more subtle, is the possible effect of strict liability with little or no defense of plaintiff conduct on the composition of the consumers of a particular product. Where people differ in their ability to use products safely, then, as pointed out in an earlier Note, strict products liability makes the safer consumer subsidize the less safe. This effect can be reduced or eliminated, however, either by enforcing disclaimers of liability or by interpreting the misuse and assumption of risk defenses broadly. The more narrowly the defenses are construed, the more pronounced the subsidy of careless or risk-prone consumers by safe ones. The safe consumers may be induced to leave product markets in which careless consumers abound. If so, there will be a higher accident rate in these markets because the average consumer in them will be more careless. A converse possibility is that risk seekers will exit the market if they are forced to pay for insurance that they do not want, and then the accident rate will fall.

It seems, in fact, that the empirical implications for the accident rate of different standards of products liability are unclear. For discussion of those implications and some empirical findings see Oi, The Economics of Product Safety, 4 Bell J. Econ. & Mgmt. Sci. 3 (1973); Higgins, Producers' Liability and Product-Related Accidents, 7 J. Legal Stud. 299 (1978). For an interesting judicial discussion, see *Murray*, supra.

Robinson v. Reed-Prentice Division of Package Machinery Co.
49 N.Y.2d 471, 403 N.E.2d 440 (1980)

COOKE, C.J.

We hold that a manufacturer of a product may not be cast in damages, either on a strict products liability or negligence cause of action, where, after the product leaves the possession and control of the manufacturer, there is a subsequent modification which substantially alters the product and is the proximate cause of plaintiff's injuries.

Plaintiff Gerald Robinson, then 17, was employed as a plastic molding machine operator by third-party defendant Plastic Jewel Parts Co. A recent arrival to New York from South Carolina where he had been an itinerant farm worker, Robinson had been employed by Plastic Jewel for approximately three weeks. On October 15, 1971, plaintiff suffered severe injuries when his hand was caught between the molds of a plastic molding machine manufactured by defendant Reed-Prentice and sold to Plastic Jewel in 1965, some six and one-half years prior to the accident.

Plaintiff commenced this action against Reed-Prentice which impleaded third-party defendant Plastic Jewel. At the close of proof, causes of action in strict products liability and negligence in the design and manufacture of the machine were submitted to the jury. A sizeable general verdict was returned in favor of plaintiff, the jury apportioning 40% of the liability against Reed-Prentice, the remainder against Plastic Jewel. On appeal, the Appellate Division reversed and ordered a new trial limited to the issue of damages unless plaintiff stipulated to a reduced verdict. Plaintiff so stipulated and the judgment, as amended and reduced, was affirmed. This court then granted Reed-Prentice and Plastic Jewel leave to appeal. We now reverse.

The plastic injection molding machine is designed to melt pelletized plastic inside a heating chamber. From the heating chamber, the liquefied plastic is forced into the mold area by means of a plunger. The mold area itself is composed of two rectangular platens on which the plastic molds are attached. One of the platens moves horizontally to open and close the mold; the other remains stationary. When the operating cycle is begun, hydraulic pressure causes the movable platen to be brought up against the stationary platen, thus forming a completed mold into which the heated plastic is pumped. After the plastic is cured, the movable platen returns to its original position, thereby permitting the operator to manually remove the finished product from its mold.

To protect the operator from the mold area, Reed-Prentice equipped the machine with a safety gate mounted on rollers and connecting interlocks in conformity with the State Industrial Code. Completely covering the mold area, the metal safety gate contained a Plexiglas window allowing the operator to monitor the molding process. Since the gate shielded the mold area, access to the platens was impossible while the machine was operating. Only when the molding sequence was completed could the operator roll the safety gate to the open position, allowing him to reach into the mold area to remove the finished product. The interlocks were connected to electrical switches which activated the hydraulic pump. When the safety gate was closed, the interlocks complete a circuit that activates the hydraulic pump, thereby causing the movable platen to close upon its stationary counterpart. When the safety gate was opened, however, this essential circuit would not be completed and hence the machine would not be activated.

After the machine was delivered by Reed-Prentice, Plastic Jewel discovered that its design did not comport with its production requirements. Plastic Jewel purchased the machine in order to mold beads directly onto a nylon cord. The cord was stored in spools at the back of the machine and fed through the mold where the beads were molded around it. After each molding cycle, the beads were pulled out of the mold and the nylon cord was reset in the mold for the next cycle. To allow the beads to be molded on a continuous line, Plastic Jewel determined that it was necessary to cut a hole of approximately 6 by 14 inches in the Plexiglas portion of the safety gate. The machine, as designed, contracted for and delivered, made no provision for such an aperture. At the end of each cycle, the now corded beads would be pulled through the opening in the gate, the nylon cord would be restrung, and the next cycle would be started by opening and then closing the safety gate without breaking the continuous line of beads. While modification of the safety gate served Plastic Jewel's production needs, it also destroyed the practical utility of the safety features incorporated into the design of the machine for it permitted access into the molding area while the interlocking circuits were completed. Although the record is unclear on this point, plaintiff's hand somehow went through the opening cut into the safety gate and was drawn into the molding area while the interlocks were engaged. The machine went through the molding cycle, causing plaintiff serious injury.

The record contains evidence that Reed-Prentice knew, or should have known, the particular safety gate designed for the machine made it impossible to manufacture beads on strings. During the period immediately prior to the purchase of the machine, Reed-Prentice representatives visited the Plastic Jewel plant and observed two identical machines with holes cut in the Plexiglas portion of their safety gates. At that meeting, Plastic Jewel's plant manager discussed the problem with a Reed-Prentice salesman and asked whether a safety gate compatible with its product needs could be designed. Moreover, a letter sent by Reed-Prentice to Plastic Jewel establishes that the manufacturer knew precisely what its customer was doing to the safety gate and refused to modify its design. However, the letter pointed out that the purchaser had "completely flaunted the safeties built into this machine by removing part of the safety window," and that it had not "held up your end of the purchase when you use the machine differently from its design" and the manufacturer stated "[a]s concerns changes, we will make none in our safety setup or design of safety gates." At trial, plaintiff's expert indicated that there were two modifications to the safety gate which could have been made that would have made it possible to mold beads on a string without rendering the machine unreasonably dangerous. Neither of these modifications were made, or even contemplated, by Reed-Prentice. . . .

Where a product presents an unreasonable risk of harm, notwithstanding that it was meticulously made according to detailed plans and specifications, it is said to be defectively designed. This rule, however, is tempered by the realization that some products, for example knives, must by their very nature be dangerous in order to be functional. Thus, a defectively designed product is one which, at the time it leaves the seller's hands, is in a condition not reasonably contemplated by the ultimate consumer and is unreasonably dangerous for its intended use; that is one whose utility does not outweigh the danger inherent in its introduction into the stream of commerce (Restatement, Torts 2d, §402A). Design defects, then, unlike manufacturing defects, involve products made in the precise manner intended by the manufacturer. Since no product may be completely accident proof, the ultimate question in determining whether an article is defectively designed involves a balancing of the likelihood of harm against the burden of taking precaution against that harm.

But no manufacturer may be automatically held liable for all accidents caused or occasioned by the use of its product. While the manufacturer is under a nondelegable duty to design and produce a product that is not defective, that responsibility is gauged as of the time the product leaves the manufacturer's hands. Substantial modifications of a product from its original condition by a third party which render a safe product defective are not the responsibility of the manufacturer.

At the time Reed-Prentice sold the molding machine, it was not defective. Had the machine been left intact, the safety gate and connecting interlocks would have rendered this tragic industrial accident an impossibility. On closer analysis, then, plaintiff does not seek to premise liability on any defect in the design or manufacture of the machine but on the independent, and presumably foreseeable, act of Plastic Jewel in destroying the functional utility of the safety gate. Principles of foreseeability, however, are inapposite where a third party affirmatively abuses a product by consciously bypassing built-in safety features. While it may be foreseeable that an employer will abuse a product to meet its own self-imposed production needs, responsibility for that willful choice may not fall on the manufacturer. Absent any showing that there was some defect in the design of the safety gate at the time the machine left the practical control of Reed-Prentice (and there has been none here), Reed-Prentice may not be cast in damages for strict products liability.

Nor does the record disclose any basis for a finding of negligence on the part of Reed-Prentice in the design of the machine. Well settled it is that a manufacturer is under a duty to use reasonable care in designing his product when "used in the manner for which the product was intended . . . as well as an unintended yet reasonably foreseeable use." Many products may safely and reasonably be used for purposes other than the one for which they were specifically designed. For example, the manufacturer of a screwdriver must foresee that a consumer will use his product to pry open the lid of a can and is thus under a corresponding duty to design the shank of the product with sufficient strength to accomplish that task. In such a situation, the manufacturer is in a superior position to anticipate the reasonable use to which his product may be put and is obliged to assure that no harm will befall those who use the product in such a manner. It is the manufacturer who must bear the responsibility if its purposeful design choice presents an unreasonable danger to users. A cause of action in negligence will lie where it can be shown that a manufacturer was responsible for a defect that caused injury, and that the manufacturer could have foreseen the injury. Control of the instrumentality at the time of the accident in such a case is irrelevant since the defect arose while the product was in the possession of the manufacturer.

The manufacturer's duty, however, does not extend to designing a product that is impossible to abuse or one whose safety features may not be circumvented. A manufacturer need not incorporate safety features into its product so as to guarantee that no harm will come to every user no matter how careless or even reckless. Nor must he trace his product through every link in the chain of distribution to insure that users will not adapt the product to suit their own unique purposes. The duty of a manufacturer, therefore, is not an open-ended one. It extends to the design and manufacture of a finished product which is safe at the time of sale. Material alterations at the hands of a third party which work a substantial change in the condition in which the product was sold by destroying the functional utility of a key safety feature, however foreseeable that modification may have been, are not within the ambit of a manufacturer's responsibility. Acceptance of plaintiff's concept of duty would expand the scope of a manufacturer's duty beyond all reasonable bounds and would be tantamount to imposing absolute liability on manufacturers for all product-related injuries.

Unfortunately, as this case bears out, it may often be that an injured party, because of the exclusivity of workers' compensation, is barred from commencing an action against the one who exposes him to unreasonable peril by affirmatively rendering a safe product dangerous. However, that an employee may have no remedy in tort against his employer gives the courts no license to thrust upon a third-party manufacturer a duty to insure that its product will not be abused or that its safety features will be callously altered by a purchaser. Where the product is marketed in a condition safe for the purposes for which it is intended or could reasonably be intended, the manufacturer has satisfied its duty.

Accordingly, the judgment appealed from and the order of the Appellate Division brought up for review should be reversed, with costs, and the complaint and third-party complaint dismissed.

Notes

1. Is the court's result consistent with Moran v. Fabergé? Is it consistent with the proximate-cause cases in Chapter 8?

2. If defendant had been found negligent, could it still have prevailed on causal grounds?

Codling v. Paglia
32 N.Y.2d 330, 298 N.E.2d 622 (1973)

[Paglia was driving a Chrysler which swerved, allegedly because of a defect in the steering mechanism, and collided head-on with the Codling car which was traveling in the opposite direction. The jury found that the cause of the accident was Chrysler's breach of its implied warranty of merchantability and fitness. The issue on appeal was whether Chrysler's liability extended to the Codlings, "nonuser innocent bystanders with respect to the vehicle."]

JONES, J. . . .

As we are aware, the erosion of the citadel of privity has been proceeding apace and even more rapidly in other jurisdictions, all with the enthusiastic support of text writers and the authors of law review articles as evidenced by an extensive literature. Once one exception has been made, others have followed as appealing fact situations presented instances in which, in language of result, liability has been imposed to avoid injustice and for the protection of the public. Fact situations where recovery was allowed have shifted from those in which the touchstone was said to be the character of the product manufactured (e.g., dangerous instrumentalities, or household products) to those in which the result turned on the classification of the injured person (e.g., member of the family, employee, user, rescuer).

The dynamic growth of the law in this area has been a testimonial to the adaptability of our judicial system and its resilient capacity to respond to new developments both of economics and of manufacturing and marketing techniques. A developing and more analytical sense of justice, as regards both the economics and the operational aspects of production and distribution has imposed a heavier and heavier burden of responsibility on the manufacturer. It is significant that the Appellate Divisions in three of our four Judicial Departments, the First, Third and Fourth, have now found sifficient encouragement in the decisions and opinions of our court and elsewhere, to extend the liability of the manufacturer of a defective product to a nonuser bystander.

We think that the time has now come when our court, instead of rationalizing broken field running, should lay down a broad principle, eschewing the temptation to devise more proliferating exceptions.

Much of what we have written in extending the liability of the manufacturer to the noncontracting user is equally applicable to the bystander. "The policy of protecting the public from injury physical or pecuniary, resulting from misrepresentations, outweighs allegiance to old and outmoded technical rules of law which, if observed, might be productive of great injustice. The manufacturer . . . unquestionably intends and expects that the product will be purchased and used in reliance upon his express assurance of its quality and, in fact, it is so purchased and used. Having invited and solicited the use, the manufacturer should not be permitted to avoid responsibility, when the expected use leads to injury and loss, by claiming that he made no contract directly with the user." . . .

Today as never before the product in the hands of the consumer is often a most sophisticated and even mysterious article. Not only does it usually emerge as a sealed unit with an alluring exterior rather than as a visible assembly of component parts, but its functional validity and usefulness often depend on the application of electronic, chemical or hydraulic principles far beyond the ken of the average consumer. Advances in the technologies of materials, of processes, of operational means have put it almost entirely out of the reach of the consumer to comprehend why or how the article operates, and thus even farther out of his reach to detect when there may be a defect or a danger present in its design or manufacture. In today's world it is often only the manufacturer who can fairly be said to know and to understand when an article is suitably designed and safely made for its intended purpose. Once floated on the market, many articles in a very real practical sense defy detection of defect, except possibly in the hands of an expert after laborious and perhaps even destructive disassembly. By way of direct illustration, how many automobile purchasers or users have any idea how a power steering mechanism operates or is intended to operate, with its "circulating worm and piston assembly and its cross shaft splined to the Pitman arm"? Further, as has been noted, in all this the bystander, the nonuser, is even worse off than the user — to the point of total exclusion from any opportunity either to choose manufacturers or retailers or to detect defects. We are accordingly persuaded that from the standpoint of justice as regards the operating aspect of today's products, responsibility should be laid on the manufacturer, subject to the limitations we set forth.

Consideration of the economics of production and distribution point in the same direction. We take as a highly desirable objective the widest feasible availability of useful, nondefective products. We know that in many, if not most instances, today this calls for mass production, mass advertising, mass distribution. It is this mass system which makes possible the development and availability of the benefits which may flow from new inventions and new discoveries. Justice and equity would dictate the apportionment across the system of all related costs — of production, of distribution, of postdistribution liability. Obviously, if manufacturers are to be held for financial losses of nonusers, the economic burden will ultimately be passed on in part, if not in whole, to the purchasing users. But considerations of competitive disadvantage will delay or dilute automatic transferral of such added costs. Whatever the total cost it will then be borne by those in the system, the producer, the distributor and the consumer. Pressures will converge on the manufacturer, however, who alone has the practical opportunity, as well as a considerable incentive, to turn out useful, attractive, but safe products. To impose this economic burden on the manufacturer should encourage safety in design and production; and the diffusion of this cost in the purchase price of individual units should be acceptable to the user if thereby he is given added assurance of his own protection. . . .

We accordingly hold that, under a doctrine of strict products liability, the manufacturer of a defective product is liable to any person injured or damaged if the defect was a substantial factor in bringing about his injury or damages; provided: (1) that at the time of the occurrence the product is being used (whether by the person injured or damaged or by a third person) for the purpose and in the manner normally intended, (2) that if the person injured or damaged is himself the user of the product he would not by the exercise of reasonable care have both discovered the defect and perceived its danger, and (3) that by the exercise of reasonable care the person injured or damaged would not otherwise have averted his injury or damages.

In the present case, we conclude that the jury properly found that Chrysler had produced an automobile with a defective steering mechanism; that that defect was a substantial factor in bringing about the accident and thus the injuries to the Codlings; that at the time of the accident Paglia was using the automobile for the purpose and in the manner normally intended; that by the exercise of reasonable care, Paglia would neither have discovered the defective steering mechanism nor perceived its danger; and that, as to the Codlings, the exercise of reasonable care on their part would otherwise not have averted the accident.

Thus, we affirm the judgments in favor of the Codlings against Chrysler. . . .

Notes

1. Notice that New York still clings to the implied-warranty theory of strict products liability. Does breach of implied warranty make any sense, however, with respect to liability to a bystander? As regards a bystander, why should the case not be treated the same as any other automobile accident case, i.e., under a negligence theory? If drivers are not liable in collision cases

unless their negligence is proved, why should manufacturers be strictly liable? Is there a possible analogy to the policy basis for respondeat superior?

2. Liability to bystanders invites the question: What are the outer bounds of the strict products liability concept? In Flippo v. Mode O'Day Frock Shops of Hollywood, 248 Ark. 1, 449 S.W.2d 692 (1970), plaintiff, while trying on a pair of slacks in defendant's shop, suddenly felt a burning sensation in her thigh; she had been bitten by a spider concealed in the slacks. The court found her injuries were caused by the spider, not the pants; defendant therefore had not breached its implied warranty of merchantability. In Hoffman v. Simplot Aviation, Inc., 97 Idaho 32, 539 P.2d 584 (1975), plaintiffs sought damages for injuries sustained when their plane crashed after a visual inspection of it by employees of the defendant, an airplane repair company. The court held that the plaintiffs could not recover on a theory of implied warranty without proving negligence. What explains the results in these two cases? Finally, see Ransome v. Wisconsin Electric Powerboat Co., 87 Wis. 2d 605, 275 N.W.2d 641 (1979), holding that electricity is a product subject to strict products liability.

Gillham v. Admiral Corp.
523 F.2d 102 (6th Cir. 1975)

McCREE, J. . . .

Appellant, Zora Gillham, brought this action in the United States District Court for the Southern District of Ohio against appellee, The Admiral Corporation, seeking compensatory and punitive damages for severe burns and other serious and crippling injuries caused by a fire originating in her Admiral color television set. . . .

The issues of liability and damages were tried separately. . . . At the conclusion of the liability phase of the trial, the jury found Admiral liable for Mrs. Gillham's injuries. Thereafter, the claims for compensatory and punitive damages were tried to the same jury. The court permitted the question of punitive damages to go to the jury despite Admiral's motion for a directed verdict on this issue. . . . The jury awarded compensatory damages of $125,000.00, punitive damages of $100,000.00, and attorneys' fees of $50,000.00.

On January 29, 1974, within a month of the conclusion of the trial, the court granted Admiral's motion for judgment n. o. v., setting aside the award of punitive damages and attorneys' fees. In its order, the court stated that the evidence could

> reasonably be interpreted to indicate that the defendant was negligent and even grossly negligent in its design of the television set, in its subsequent activities, and in its failure to warn customers of the potential fire hazard.

It also concluded that Admiral was guilty of a breach of implied warranty.[1] However, it held that Admiral's conduct was not sufficiently reckless, wanton or outrageous to warrant an award of punitive damages.

The facts are not disputed. Mrs. Gillham purchased an Admiral television set with a 24A2 chassis in June 1964. On the evening of November 19, 1968, she watched a television program in her apartment for about an hour, turned the set off, and observed a blue flash come across the television screen, and left the room. She returned to the room about fifteen minutes later to find the television set on fire with flames rising almost to the ceiling. She attempted to beat out the fire with sofa pillows but when she heard an explosion, she called the fire department. She was severely burned by the flames, which had spread to her doorway by the time she fled the apartment. Burns covered 18.5 percent of her body surface, and 11 percent of her skin was destroyed by third degree burns. . . .

The evidence established that the fire in Mrs. Gillham's television set was caused by ignition of the set's high voltage transformer, a component also commonly called a horizontal output transformer (H.O.T.) or "flyback" transformer; that this transformer was defectively designed; that the design created a fire hazard; and that Admiral's officials and designers knew that the high voltage transformer in her set and in other Admiral color television sets of the same model was fire hazardous. . . .

The high voltage transformer in plaintiff's television set was designed by Carl Olson, Project Manager of Admiral's Deflection Laboratory with the assistance of subordinates. Mr. Olson admitted at trial that at the time that he designed the transformer he had anticipated that it might catch fire in customers' homes. Therefore, he designed what Admiral calls a high voltage cage, a device enclosing the high voltage transformer and some other components of the high voltage section. The cage was intended to contain the expected fires. There was testimony that Admiral made two tests in which the transformer was set on fire with a torch, and when the cage was closed, it contained the flames. There was other evidence, however, indicating that it was unreasonable to expect that the cage would contain a fire for any length of time because there were 38 holes in the lid of the cage, an opening at the bottom of the cage, and plastic rivets fastening the cover.

Shortly after the television sets containing this transformer were marketed, Olson and Admiral learned that the wax insulation was melting and dripping out of the high voltage cages and even dripping out of the sets. Olson admitted that this information indicated that the transformers were operating at temperatures higher than Admiral had anticipated. Admiral also

---

1. As the opinion later discusses, the Ohio Supreme Court has stated in some of its opinions that unlawful conduct is an element of a cause of action wherein an award of punitive damages is sought. The district court apparently found only that Admiral's conduct lacked the element of willfulness necessary for an award of punitive damages, and did not consider the element of unlawfulness. We observe that the requisite unlawfulness may be found where a defect in a product breaches a warranty imposed by law. . . .

learned that fires were originating in its 24A2 chassis caused by the high voltage transformer, and that the fires were not being contained in the cage but were igniting the television sets. In some instances, the resulting fires destroyed home furnishings and dwellings, and caused personal injuries.

As early as October 1964, four customers reported to Admiral that fires had occurred in their Admiral color television sets. All four fires were high voltage fires. Thereafter, Admiral received a steady stream of complaints about fires originating in its color television sets. By November 1968 when plaintiff's fire occurred, at least 91 such fires had been reported to Admiral.

Moreover, in November 1966, two years before the plaintiff's set caught fire, one of Admiral's transformer engineers conducted tests on 16 transformers returned by servicemen to Admiral. Every one of these transformers failed and burned. They all failed and burned in the same manner as the high voltage transformer in Mrs. Gillham's set because the paper and wax insulation failed.

All these transformers were identical in construction and insulation materials to the one in plaintiff's set. The engineer who conducted the tests commented, ". . . the wonder is that more failures did not occur." These tests confirmed customer complaints and demonstrated that many of the fires were caused by the high voltage transformers.

The evidence also disclosed that Admiral could feasibly have reduced this fire hazard substantially, or have eliminated it completely. Materials superior to the paper and wax were available for use as insulation in high voltage transformers long before Admiral designed its transformer in 1963, and these materials were used by other television manufacturers before 1963. Also, Admiral could have installed a fuse in the high voltage circuitry to cut off the electricity in the event of overheating.

The evidence thus demonstrated that when Admiral designed, manufactured and marketed appellant's television set it knew that the set presented a serious fire hazard. Nevertheless, Admiral did not warn prospective purchasers or owners of the danger despite the steady flow of reported fires originating in Admiral color television sets. Nor did Admiral redesign this model or stop marketing it during the period in question.

The evidence also disclosed that the highest officials of Admiral were aware of the fire hazard and its precise source and cause. I. F. Johnston, Admiral's Electronic Service Manager, admitted that he knew that these transformers were the "major source" of fires in Admiral color television sets. Summaries of the claims against Admiral arising from fires were circulated to and read by President Ross Siragusa, Jr., who kept some of them, and threw others away, but took no action of any kind. Moreover, there was evidence that Admiral officials sought to deceive customers about the fire hazard presented by the color television sets. . . .

Admiral, although apparently conceding that its actions were reprehensible, argues that the district court was correct in refusing to permit the award of punitive damages to stand. It contends that in Ohio punitive damages may

not be awarded in the absence of proof that the tortfeasor acted with actual
malice, and that this record contains no evidence of malice on Admiral's part.
Admiral does not suggest that punitive damages may not, as a matter of law,
be awarded in products liability actions, but only that the facts of this case do
not permit the implication that Admiral acted maliciously. . . .

. . . [T]he question before us is whether no reasonable person, viewing
the evidence in the light most favorable to Mrs. Gillham, and drawing all
reasonable inferences in her favor, could find that Admiral's conduct was so
intentional, reckless, wanton, willful, or gross that an inference of malice
could be drawn. We conclude that the evidence, viewed in light of this
standard, was sufficient to permit a reasonable person to conclude that
Admiral knew that its design posed a grave danger to the lives and property of
its customers, and therefore that its failure to redesign the set or warn the
public was conduct sufficiently intentional, reckless, wanton, willful, or gross
to permit a reasonable inference of malice.

The record supports the conclusion that Admiral *knew* that its transformers might catch fire because of improper and dangerous design, and that
it knew or should have known, even before the set was marketed, that the
purported safety device designed to contain the anticipated fires was ineffective. Moreover, the evidence demonstrates that shortly after the set was
distributed to the public, and several years before Mrs. Gillham's injury,
Admiral was informed that its transformers were causing fires that the safety
device was not containing. In spite of this knowledge, and its additional
knowledge that its sets were catching fire even when not in use, Admiral
neither redesigned the set nor informed purchasers and prospective purchasers of the hazard. It not only continued to distribute the sets, but also misled
customers by informing them that the sets were safe. . . .

Notes

1. It is sometimes contended that punitive damages are inappropriate in
products-liability cases. The contention is discussed and rejected in Rinker v.
Ford Motor Co., 567 S.W.2d 655, 668-669 (Mo. App. 1978):

> Appellant advances the argument that punitive damages are "inappropri-
> ate" in a products liability case such as this. As appellant suggests, no case in this
> state relied upon by either party has approved of punitive damages in a prod-
> ucts liability case. However, given the purpose of punitive damages to punish a
> defendant for an aggravated act of misconduct and to deter similar conduct in
> the future by the defendant and others, there is no fundamental reason for
> excluding products liability cases from the cases in which punitive damages may
> be recovered. One writer suggests that punitive damages are particularly appro-
> priate in such cases.
>
> Appellant's primary reliance on this contention is upon Roginsky v. Rich-
> ardson-Merrell, Inc., 378 F.2d 832 (2d Cir. 1967). That case involved a drug

produced by defendant to reduce blood cholesterol level which turned out to have serious side effects, including causing cataracts. Punitive damages were sought based upon the claim that the defendant had deceived the Food and Drug Administration, the medical profession and consumers regarding the safety of the drug. A jury awarded the plaintiff $17,500 actual damages and $100,000 punitive damages. The award of punitive damages was reversed in the Court of Appeals on a 2 to 1 vote.

Judge Friendly, the author of the majority opinion, treated at considerable length questions which he felt were presented by allowing punitive damages in such a case. The court noted that the case "was the first to be tried of some 75 similar cases now pending in the District Court for the Southern District of New York. Several hundred actions have been filed elsewhere. . . ." Judge Friendly expressed the "gravest difficulty in perceiving how claims for punitive damages in such a multiplicity of actions throughout the nation can be so administered as to avoid overkill." He questioned whether or not allowance of punitive damages in such a case would provide a greater deterrent than that found in the federal food and drug requirement. He also noted the possibility that "a sufficiently egregious error as to one product can end the business life of a concern that has wrought much good in the past and might otherwise have continued to do so in the future, with many innocent stockholders suffering extinction of their investments for a single management sin."

However, despite these concerns, Judge Friendly acknowledged that in that diversity action, he could not predict that the New York courts would adopt a rule disallowing punitive damages in such a case and he decided the case on the grounds that plaintiff's evidence had not shown that the "management" of the defendant had authorized, participated in or ratified the conduct relied upon as giving rise to punitive damages. As pointed out, New York adheres to the "complicity rule," holding the corporate master liable for punitive damages "only when superior officers either order, participate in, or ratify outrageous conduct."

Missouri does not follow the "complicity rule." Action of a nature which gives rise to such liability by a corporate agent acting within the scope of his authority is all that is required to impose liability for punitive damages on a corporate employer.

The conduct of the same defendant and involving the same product as in *Roginsky* was held to support an award for punitive damages in Toole v. Richardson-Merrell, Inc., 251 Cal. App. 2d 689, 60 Cal. Rptr. 398 (1967). The jury awarded plaintiff $175,000 actual and $500,000 punitive damages. The punitive damages award was reduced by remittitur to $250,000 and that award was upheld on appeal. The court concluded that the evidence showed the malice required to support an award of punitive damages based upon a showing that the "defendant's wrongful conduct was wilful, intentional, and done in reckless disregard of its possible results." The California court disagreed with Judge Friendly's conclusion that management had not participated in the wrongful conduct. . . .

An award of punitive damages for injuries arising out of a defective television receiving set was upheld in Gillham v. The Admiral Corporation. As pointed out by appellant the conduct of the defendant in that case was much more aggravated than that involved in this case. The manufacturer was aware of the defect when it began producing the set and took no remedial action despite numerous reports that the defect had caused fires.

Appellant's authorities and the argument based thereon are not persuasive that this court should, as a matter of public policy, refuse to permit punitive damages in a case such as this. The problems suggested by appellant will be dealt with as they arise. Means are available to both trial and appellate courts of the state for the control of excessive award of punitive damages. No such relief was sought in this case. (No opinion is expressed as to the amount of the judgment here.)

In *Rinker,* an award of $460,000 in punitive damages (on top of $100,000 in compensatory damages) was upheld (567 S.W.2d at 667):

> The evidence would have permitted the jury to find that Ford's Director of Automotive Safety knew that a limited number of 1968 and 1969 Ford vehicles were equipped with fast idle cams subject to breakage; that a broken fast idle cam could cause the throttle to jam open, hurtling the vehicle forward at a high rate of speed with no effective method of promptly stopping the car; that prior to Ms. Rinker's accident, over a period of four years, 29 reports of incidents involving broken fast idle cams had been received by Ford; that Ford took no steps to warn its dealers or customers of this problem.

Is there any essential incompatibility between the principle of strict products liability and the award of punitive damages where defendant's conduct can fairly be described as reckless? A negative answer is suggested by the facts of the *Gillham* case. The *social* cost of accident avoidance may have been zero (or close to it), since consumers of television sets could presumably have purchased a close substitute for Admiral sets with no fire hazard and at no higher price. If so, the discussion of intentional torts in Chapter 2 suggests this may have been an appropriate case for awarding punitive damages. But was *Rinker* anything more than a simple negligence case? What is the economic significance, if any, of the manufacturer's aggregate damage exposure, a point stressed by Judge Friendly?

The objection to punitive damages in the standard products case goes beyond the point that they are unnecessary; they can bring about a misallocation of resources, in a variety of ways discussed in the Note on punitive damages in Chapter 2. One source of misallocation should be noted in particular. Suppose a product contains some component that is defective, but the product's manufacturer could not have ascertained the defect at reasonable cost. He would still be liable for an injury caused by the defect. This is, indeed, the principal difference between strict products liability and liability for negligence as in *MacPherson.* Suppose the expected accident cost from the defect is $1 and the cost of ascertaining the defect to the manufacturer of the product that incorporates the component is $1.10. Then we would not want him to take steps to ascertain it; the accident would be cost-justified. Although the strict liability principle would make him liable (whereas the negligence principle would not), he will prefer to incur liability than to pay a higher accident-avoidance cost, provided he is liable only for compensatory damages. But if he can expect to have to pay punitive damages sufficiently great to bring his expected liability cost above $1.10, then it will pay him to incur the $1.10 cost of ascertaining the defect, and he will do so, resulting in an expected social loss of 10¢. This particular misallocation would not result if the standard were negligence rather than strict liability (though as we saw in Chapter 2 other misallocations might occur).

2. The rapid expansion of the strict liability concept in products cases, the shriveling of defenses based on plaintiff's conduct, the lack of an effective statute of limitations, and the increasingly frequent award of punitive damages (see the Pinto case discussed in Chapter 4) have combined to make this area of tort law extremely controversial. Manufacturers and their insurers have complained bitterly about increased liability. There is a movement afoot in the states for legislation to limit liability in products cases; more than half the states have passed statutes in this area in recent years. For a discussion of these statutes with special references to one state's approach see Note, Insurance Solution or Tort Reform? Iowa Joins the Nationwide Examination of Proposed Product Liability Legislation, 29 Drake L. Rev. 113 (1979-1980). Many fascinating issues of insurance law have been precipitated by the products liability explosion. See, e.g., Insurance Co. of North America v. Forty-Eight Insulations, Inc., 633 F.2d 1212 (6th Cir. 1980); Emons Industries, Inc. v. Liberty Mut. Fire Ins. Co., 481 F. Supp. 1022 (S.D.N.Y. 1979). But they are outside the scope of this book.

There has been little independent evaluation of modern products liability law, except on purely theoretical grounds. Such an evaluation was attempted, however, by the Carter Administration's Interagency Task Force on Product Liability. Although its report is already somewhat dated, and some bias in favor of plaintiffs is discernible, it is nonetheless a valuable compendium of facts and opinions. An excerpt is printed next. The Task Force also drafted a proposed Draft Uniform Product Liability Law; for text, analysis, and criticism of the proposed law, see Twerski & Weinstein, A Critique of the Uniform Product Liability Law — A Rush to Judgment, 28 Drake L. Rev. 221 (1978-1979), and for a sympathetic view (by the draft law's principal draftsman), see Schwartz, The Uniform Product Liability Act — A Brief Overview, 33 Vand. L. Rev. 579 (1980).

Interagency Task Force on Product Liability, Final Report

U.S. Department of Commerce 1978

The Task Force's Briefing Report identified three principal causes of the product liability problem: liability insurance ratemaking procedures, the tort-litigation system and manufacturing practices. Little has changed in the intervening months to alter our perspective on this issue. Therefore, our discussion of the causes of the product liability problem will closely parallel the Briefing Report. Nevertheless, where new information has come to the attention of the Task Force or its staff, it will be identified. More importantly, unlike the Briefing Report, this document will provide a detailed analysis of remedies that purport to address each of these causes.

We are still unable to rank these causes in a meaningful hierarchical chain. Our data simply do not permit a conclusion that one cause is more important than the other. On this issue, we doubt whether data could be obtained that would accomplish that goal.

Nevertheless, we have observed a tendency for each group that has a special interest in the product liability problem to assert that "the cause" lies in conduct unrelated to their own group. For example, most insurers contend that the dramatic increase in product liability insurance premiums is caused by the tort-litigation system. On the other hand, the plaintiff's bar asserts that the cause lies in insurer ratemaking practices and in the failure of manufacturers to use proper product liability prevention techniques. Some manufacturers, in turn, have asserted that the problem has been caused by an irresponsible plaintiff's bar: it is alleged that plaintiff's attorneys bring frivolous claims and have brought about a system of tort law that makes product liability prevention useless as a means of guarding against lawsuits.

It is our view that the product liability problem is based on a confluence of causes and that it will only be resolved if each cause is properly addressed.

Aside from the three principal causes, there are other causes that may have contributed to the problem. While we have discussed those causes herein, they are generally not matters that can be resolved by the remedial proposals discussed in this report, e.g., inflation and the increase in number and complexity of products.

The Briefing Report identified liability insurance ratemaking practices as a cause of the product liability problem. As our data set forth in Chapters III, V and VI show, there have been very substantial increases in product liability insurance premiums in our target industries during the years 1974-1976. We have received anecdotal data that the same has been true for certain industries that were not included in our study, e.g., ladder manufacturers, manufacturers of sporting goods.

On the other hand, there have been no published data that show a similar nationwide increase in the average size of the verdicts rendered against defendants in those industries. Our data do suggest that there has been a substantial increase in the number of pending claims, and our legal contractor found on the basis of limited data collected in the legal system that the average amount of product liability judgments did increase during the 1970-1975 period. Nevertheless, these increases did not appear to the contractor to be large enough to support insurance company premium increases.

In the overwhelming majority of cases, insurance company sources did not rely on data (either in terms of number or size of claims) to support premium increases that occurred in the 1974-1976 period. Thus, at congressional hearings held to determine the role of insurer ratemaking practices in regard to the product liability problem, James A. Kassel, Vice President of the Hartford Insurance Group stated, "the paucity of information we have been able to report to you is an embarrassment . . ." Mr. John K. Dane, Vice President of Liberty Mutual Company, also indicated that "a large part of products liability insurance had been priced in such a way that no ratemaking or claims data were generated . . ."

This testimony tends to confirm a finding of our insurance contractor: it found that neither insurance company representatives nor the Insurance Services Office (the principal ratemaking organization for the insurance industry) have a significant amount of data on the percentage of "pure" product liability experience losses. For the most part, product liability experience, most of which is composite-rated, loss-rated, or large (a) rated,[12] has not been separately recorded.

Nevertheless, based on the limited statistical information that was available, the insurance contractor concluded that insurance companies in the 1971-1974 period "lost money" on product liability business. The insurance contractor based its finding on a showing that "incurred" losses grew more rapidly than premiums. As Chapter V explains, incurred losses do not equal paid losses; rather, that figure includes paid losses, amounts "reserved" against pending claims and also amounts "reserved" against incurred but not reported claims. As Chapter V shows, insurance industry regulators do not systematically determine whether amounts reserved in incurred loss figures in the area of product liability turn out to be too high. This can occur not only when the reserve estimate is too high, but also when the interest or capital gains that may flow from reserves is substantial. . . .

A number of representatives from the insurance industry have said that its product liability rates were set too low in the 1971 through 1974 period. In that regard, insurance industry spokesmen have frequently observed that product liability insurance was "practically given away" in that period of time as part of a larger insurance package. Consumer groups find this explanation unsatisfactory. They argue that insurance companies aggressively sought product liability business in the late 1960's and early 1970's in order to generate income for investment purposes. When the "bear market" struck in 1973-1974 and the insurance industry took heavy losses, thus reducing policyholder surplus, this (it is argued) caused a shortage in underwriting capacity. Thus, stock market losses, *together with* underwriting losses, led to the considerable increases in product liability premiums.

---

12. Large (a) rated classifications are those for which insufficient data are reported to calculate a rate through actuarial techniques.

On the other hand, insurers argue that in the early 1970's, they were not aware that product liability would become a substantial problem. Nevertheless, our Legal Study shows that strict product liability first came into the law as an important matter with the publication of the Restatement (Second) of Torts Section 402A in 1965. By 1971 and 1972, a number of major states (e.g. California, Illinois, Michigan, New Jersey) had adopted strict product liability theories. Nevertheless, this did not alter the product liability insurer practice of combining product liability coverages in Comprehensive General Liability packages. This practice, along with uncertainties in insurer reserving practices, makes it almost impossible to obtain an accurate profit and loss picture for product liability insurance. As indicated in Chapter V, we have been unable to make a finding as to whether product liability premium increases were, as a whole, justified in the 1974-1976 period. Nevertheless, all of the evidence reviewed by the Task Force confirms suspicions of the director of McKinsey, Co., our insurance contractor, that some insurers engaged in "panic pricing." It also confirmed his observation that product liability rates are "effectively uncontrolled." In spite of all this, a number of insurer sources contend that "notwithstanding the shortcomings of our present data base, for many purposes insurer pricing methodologies and prices for products liability are by no means invalid, useless, or in any way lacking in integrity . . . a better data base will result in more reliable pricing, but the absence of that base does not mean that our insurer pricing is wrong."

The absence of data appears to make it impossible to confirm whether insurer price increases in the area of product liability are justified. As insurers appreciate, product liability premiums cannot be utilized to recoup past losses. Nevertheless, it would appear that some insureds may be paying a higher premium than data would justify, and others may be paying a lower premium. The burden of proof would appear to fall on the insurers to justify increases of 200, 300 or 400% in premiums where they do not have data based on claims experience that would suggest that increases of this type are proper. . . .

As the Briefing Report indicated, a review of 655 appellate cases by our Legal Study produced some evidence that part of the product liability problem stems from the fact that some manufacturers are producing unreasonably unsafe products. These products are mismanufactured — they suffer from defects in construction. The products are not in accord with the manufacturer's own specifications. In that connection, our legal contractor noted that in 140 of the 655 appellate cases it sampled, plaintiff relied solely on the fact that there was a defect in the manufacture of the product that caused the injury. Plaintiff was successful in 58 of those cases, was unsuccessful in 36 and 46 were remanded. A review of the cases strongly suggests that careful product liability prevention techniques in the area of quality control would have eliminated the basis for many of those lawsuits.

The same source showed that plaintiff was less successful when he alleged that it was a defect in design that caused his injury. Here, product liability prevention techniques might have prevented some of the suits or at least rendered them unsuccessful. On the other hand, some cases reflect that juries on occasion are allowed to render a "hindsight judgment" about whether the manufacturer designed his product carefully. Product liability prevention would not have prevented those cases.

Our Industry Survey suggests that a number of manufacturers (especially small businesses) do not have planned product liability loss prevention programs in the basic areas of design research and quality control.

The Legal Study showed that some manufacturers do not provide adequate instruction about the dangers that may spring from their products. Product liability prevention procedures have advanced to a point where consumer product misuses may be anticipated before they occur. Nevertheless, a few courts have applied principles of hindsight in this area and appear to require manufacturers to foresee the unforeseeable.

Our Industry Study suggests that some manufacturers do not see a direct relationship between product liability prevention and insurance premium costs. If they did see this relationship, there would be more incentive to give more attention to product liability prevention. . . .

It has been suggested that insurers be required to provide product liability prevention advice to their insureds. . . .

Finally, it has been suggested that the government might provide additional information, data or actual personnel assistance to manufacturers to aid them in implementing product liability prevention techniques. . . .

It does not appear that industry is becoming less interested in product liability prevention techniques. In point of fact, limited data suggest the opposite conclusion. Nevertheless some companies — especially some smaller ones — are unable to devote adequate resources to product liability prevention programs and do not receive assistance from their insurance companies in regard to this problem. It would appear that the overall product liability problem would be reduced in the long run if improvements could be made in this area.

Insurers and many manufacturers have strongly argued to the Task Force that changes in the tort-litigation system have been the primary cause of the product liability problem. It is alleged that the system has brought about an avalanche of claims, unreasonably high verdicts, and a situation where persons recover damages simply on the basis of showing that a particular product injured them.

Data sources conflict as to whether the number of claims filed has increased substantially in our target industries over the total 1970-1976 period. Our industrial contractor's telephone survey does show that the number of pending claims has increased each year. As has been indicated, our data are much less certain in regard to whether there has been a similar increase in the size of judgments or verdicts. Our Legal Study's review of 655 appellate cases does show an increase. A survey conducted of product liability cases in Cook County Illinois from 1970-1975 does show a substantial increase in the size of awards. It is also relevant to note that our industrial contractor indicated that data collected from public accident reporting mechanisms provide some indication that the number of product-related injuries in most of our target groups has not increased as rapidly as the number of product liability claims.

Limited data show that plaintiffs do not win every litigated case. Our Legal Study's sampling of appellate cases shows that the defendant "won" in approximately 49% of the cases. The Cook County Illinois jury survey of product liability cases from 1970-1975 show that the defendant won in approximately 65% of the cases. Nevertheless, data from the Insurance Services Office suggest that 96% of product liability cases are settled before court verdict. In the majority of cases that are settled, plaintiff receives some award.

Our Legal Study's review of the tort-litigation system suggests that it does not, in general, impose absolute liability on manufacturers of products. In many situations, a jury is asked to balance the economic burden on the manufacturer to produce a safe product against the probability that the product may cause injuries and the severity of those injuries. In light of these factors, the jury is asked to determine whether the product is reasonably safe. Nevertheless, there are cases which appear to approach a system of absolute liability. Some appellate courts do not view product liability law as a means of apportioning responsibility between parties, but as a compensation system. These courts come very close to holding that the tort-litigation system should provide a recovery for persons who prove that they were injured by a product. These courts believe that the defendant is in a better position to "distribute the cost of the risk" than the plaintiff is to bear it.

While these cases appear to be relatively few in number, insurers have regarded them as quite important in their pricing practices. As the Briefing Report observed, insurance company ratemaking is an area where "perceptions of reality become as important as reality itself . . ."

Even if insurer ratemaking practices were substantially improved, the spectre of these cases could still serve as an arguable justification for increasing premiums. If one state court reaches a decision of this type, others could follow in the future. It is almost impossible to predict when courts will change product liability rules and broaden the exposure of insureds.

The instability in product liability law has increased costs apart from verdicts and settlements. It has created a climate where it may be rational for a plaintiff's lawyer to bring a case although existing rules suggest that it cannot be won. It apparently has increased defense and investigation costs. Preliminary data from the Insurance Services Office indicated that for every dollar paid to a claimant, an additional $.42 is expended in defense and other loss adjustment procedures.

Individual state modifications of the tort system may not alleviate this problem. Unlike medical malpractice, attorney malpractice and municipal liability problems, product liability is nationwide in scope. This is because most products are distributed in a broad number of jurisdictions. Thus, product liability insurance rates are made on a nationwide, not a local, basis. Where product liability insurance costs are passed on in the price of a product, consumers in some jurisdictions may pay for legal interpretations that are rendered in others.

Among the primary areas of uncertainty in basic product liability laws are the rules relating to the responsibility of the manufacturer in designing his product and warning about hazards connected with that product. As a practical matter, there is no way a manufacturer can always know "in advance" whether he has designed his product properly or given proper warnings about hazards connected with the product. Also, in most situations there is no strict cut-off point where a manufacturer is no longer subject to liability for an injury caused by a product. Rules are also in flux in regard to the responsibility a product user should bear for his own misconduct.

We have concluded that this cause of the product liability problem can only be addressed by a careful review of product liability law as a whole. One must re-examine the basic standard of responsibility for product users and product liability defendants. One must also examine rules relating to damages and how costs are allocated among multiple defendants. It is also important to discern whether no-fault compensation systems can be utilized in the product liability field. These systems have the potential of providing a means of compensating victims of product-related injuries while reducing overall transaction costs that arise out of such payments. Finally, there is a need to explore suggestions that the product liability injury that occurs in the workplace might be handled differently from consumer product injuries. . . .

There are a number of other causes of the product liability problem that this report does not specifically address. These causes do not appear to be as significant as those identified above. The causes include:

(1) *Inflation.* When a product liability claim is made for loss of wages and medical costs in 1976, it will be higher than a similar claim made in 1970 because of inflation. Also, legal defense and investigation costs have increased in this period. There are no data available that suggest whether the average product liability judgment has risen at a rate that is higher than inflation over the past five years. Some limited surveys suggest that this may be true. We do know that the cost of liability insurance for many companies has risen at a rate that is substantially higher than inflation for the years 1974 through 1976. The causes of and cures for inflation go beyond the scope of this report.

(2) *Consumer and Worker Awareness.* Anecdotal data suggest that both consumers and workers are now more aware of their right to bring a product liability suit than they were ten years ago. In that connection, some of the increases in the number of claims may relate to injuries from defective products that would not have resulted in lawsuits in the past. This is one possible explanation of the apparent increase in the number of product liability claims. No one has suggested that a solution to the product liability problem is to make consumers or workers less aware of their rights. On the other hand, some have asserted that the situation has resulted in some

attorneys "playing upon" consumer awareness. It is alleged that the result is that frivolous claims are brought. We discuss proposed remedies that may thwart the bringing of frivolous claims [elsewhere in the report.]

(3) *Increases in the Number and Complexity of Products.* Anecdotal data suggest that in some product lines there has been an increase in both the number and complexity of items manufactured. Obviously, this will result, in the long run, in an increase in the number of product liability claims. We have been unable to quantify this cause of the product liability problem, and no one has suggested a remedy for it. It would seem, however, that continued emphasis on product liability loss prevention may serve as a counterweight to this particular cause of the product liability problem.

(4) *Product Misuse.* According to a recent survey of large product liability claims by the Alliance of American Insurers, misuse and alteration of products by product users is an important causal factor in product-related accidents. This survey was based upon very limited data; nevertheless, our Legal Study's review of case law reflects that product misuse is a factor in bringing about product-related injuries. Even where a manufacturer makes a reasonable attempt to instruct users about dangers connected with products, instructions are sometimes ignored or unforeseeably misinterpreted. The insurer and manufacturer groups that have brought this matter to our attention suggest that the problem of unreasonable product misuse be dealt with by barring or limiting a plaintiff's claim. . . . Of course, there is no assurance that these approaches would *prevent* unreasonable product misuse. One means whereby this cause might be addressed is through continued consumer education by manufacturers, insurers and government. Nevertheless, in the time allotted for our study, we have not developed specific means whereby this education could be increased or made more effective.

Chapter 10
Nuisance

Bryant v. Lefever
4 C.P.D. 172 (1879)

... The plaintiff and the defendants were occupiers of adjoining houses, which were of about the same height. Before 1876 the plaintiff was able to light a fire in any room of his house without the chimneys smoking; the two houses had remained in the same condition some thirty or forty years. In 1876 the defendants took down their house, and began to rebuild it. They carried up a wall by the side of the plaintiff's chimneys much beyond its original height, and stacked timber on the roof of their own house, and thereby caused the plaintiff's chimneys to smoke whenever he lighted fires. . . .

The jury found in substance that for more than twenty years there had been free access of air to the chimneys of the plaintiff's house, and also that the erection of the defendants' wall sensibly and materially interfered with the comfort of human existence in the plaintiff's premises. They assessed the damages at £40., and Lord Coleridge, C.J., directed judgment to be entered for the plaintiff.

The defendants appealed. . . .

BRAMWELL, L.J. . . .

No doubt there is a nuisance, but it is not of the defendants' causing. They have done nothing in causing the nuisance. Their house and their timber are harmless enough. It is the plaintiff who causes the nuisance by lighting a coal fire in a place the chimney of which is placed so near the defendants' wall, that the smoke does not escape, but comes into the house. Let the plaintiff cease to light his fire, let him move his chimney, let him carry it higher, and there would be no nuisance. Who, then, causes it? It would be very clear that the plaintiff did, if he had built his house or chimney after the defendants had put up the timber on theirs, and it is really the same, though he did so before the timber was there. But (what is in truth the same answer), if the defendants cause the nuisance, they have a right to do so. If the plaintiff has not the right to the passage of air, except subject to the defendants' right to build or put timber on their house, then

737

his right is subject to their right, and though a nuisance follows from the exercise of their right, they are not liable. "Sic utere tuo ut alienum non laedas" is a good maxim, but in our opinion the defendants do not infringe it: the plaintiff would if he succeeded. . . .

Judgment for the defendants.

Notes

1. In an omitted portion of the opinion, Lord Justice Bramwell considered and rejected plaintiff's claim of a prescriptive right to the benefit (egress of smoke) that defendants' action in raising their wall and stacking timber on their roof denied him. Having disposed of this issue, Bramwell then turned to the nuisance question. But if plaintiff had no right to emit smoke from its chimneys, how could defendants' conduct be actionable? Is there any suggestion that defendant either deliberately or negligently interfered with plaintiff's enjoyment of his property?

2. With the court's causal analysis, compare that of Professor Coase:

> The smoke nuisance was caused both by the man who built the wall *and* by the man who lit the fires. Given the fires, there would have been no smoke nuisance without the wall; given the wall, there would have been no smoke nuisance without the fires. Eliminate the wall *or* the fires and smoke nuisance would disappear. On the marginal principle it is clear that *both* were responsible and *both* should be forced to include the loss of amenity due to the smoke as a cost in deciding whether to continue the activity which gives rise to the smoke. And given the possibility of market transactions, this is what would in fact happen. Although the wall-builder was not liable legally for the nuisance, as the man with the smoking chimneys would presumably be willing to pay a sum equal to the monetary worth to him of eliminating the smoke, this sum would therefore become for the wall-builder, a cost of continuing to have the high wall with the timber stacked on the roof.

Coase, The Problem of Social Cost, 3 J. Law & Econ. 1, 13 (1960). According to Coase, it does not matter whether the court analyzed the case correctly or not. Since transaction costs were presumably low (why?), the parties would undo, by a voluntary negotiation, whatever allocative error the court committed. If the cost of the smoke to the plaintiff was greater than the cost to the defendants of avoiding interference with plaintiff's chimneys by, say, removing the timber from their roof, plaintiff would be willing to pay defendants a sum great enough to induce them to remove the timber, and the efficient result would be obtained. This is a straightforward application of the Coase theorem.

Bamford v. Turnley
3 B.&S. 66, 122 Eng. Rep. 27 (Ex. Ch. 1862)

[Plaintiff claimed that defendant was committing a nuisance by using his land, which adjoined plaintiff's, for making bricks.]

POLLOCK C.B. The question in this case is, whether the direction of the Lord Chief Justice, professing to be founded on the decision of the Court of Common Pleas in Hole v. Barlow (4 C.B.N.S. 334) [an earlier nuisance case involving brickmaking, in which defendant prevailed], was right, and in my judgment substantially it was right, viz., taking it to have been as stated in the case, viz., "that if the jury thought that the spot was convenient and proper, and the burning of the bricks was, under the circumstances, a reasonable use by the defendant of his own land, the defendant would be entitled to a verdict." I do not think that the nuisance for which an action will lie is capable of any legal definition which will be applicable to all cases and useful in deciding them. The question so entirely depends on the surrounding circumstances, — the place where, the time when, the alleged nuisance, what, the mode of committing it, how, and the duration of it, whether temporary or permanent, occasional or continual, — as to make it impossible to lay down any rule of law applicable to every case, and which will also be useful in assisting a jury to come to a satisfactory conclusion: — it must at all times be a question of fact with reference to all the circumstances of the case.

Most certainly in my judgment it cannot be laid down as a legal proposition or doctrine, that anything which, under any circumstances, lessens the comfort or endangers the health or safety of a neighbour, must necessarily be an actionable nuisance. That may be a nuisance in Grosvenor Square which would be none in Smithfield Market, that may be a nuisance at midday which would not be so at midnight, that may be a nuisance which is permanent and continual which would be no nuisance if temporary or occasional only. A clock striking the hour, or a bell ringing for some domestic purpose, may be a nuisance, if unreasonably loud and discordant, of which the jury alone must judge; but although not unreasonably loud, if the owner, from some whim or caprice, made the clock strike the hour every ten minutes, or the bell ring continually, I think a jury would be justified in considering it to be a very great nuisance. In general, a kitchen chimney, suitable to the establishment to which it belonged, could not be deemed a nuisance, but if built in an inconvenient place or manner, on purpose to annoy the neighbours, it might, I think, very properly be treated as one. The compromises that belong to social life, and upon which the peace and comfort of it mainly depend, furnish an indefinite number of examples where some apparent natural right is invaded, or some enjoyment abridged, to provide for the more general convenience or necessities of the whole community; and I think the more the details of the question are examined the more clearly it will appear that all that the law can do is to lay down some general and vague proposition which will be no guide to the jury in each particular case that may come before them.

... I think the word "reasonable" cannot be an improper word, and too vague to be used on this occasion, seeing that the question whether a contract has been reasonably performed with reference to time, place and subject matter, is one that is put to a jury almost as often as a jury is assembled. If the act complained of be done in a convenient manner, so as to give no unnecessary annoyance, and be a reasonable exercise of some apparent right, or a reasonable use of the land, house or property of the party under all the circumstances, in which I include the degree of inconvenience it will produce, then I think no action can be sustained, if the jury find that it was reasonable, — as the jury must be taken to have found that it was reasonable that the defendant should be allowed to do what he did, and reasonable that the plaintiff should submit to the inconvenience occasioned by what was done....

... [T]he judgment of the court below [for defendant] ought to be affirmed.

MARTIN B. read the judgment of BRAMWELL B. I am of opinion that this judgment should be reversed. The defendant has done that which, if done wantonly or maliciously, would be actionable as being a nuisance to the plaintiff's habitation by causing a sensible diminution of the comfortable enjoyment of it. This, therefore, calls on the defendant to justify or excuse what he has done. And his justification is this: He says that the nuisance is not to the health of the inhabitants of the plaintiff's house, that it is of a temporary character, and is necessary for the beneficial use of his, the defendant's land, and that the public good requires he should be entitled to do what he claims to do.

The question seems to me to be, Is this a justification in law, — and, in order not to make a verbal mistake, I will say, — a justification for what is done, or a matter which makes what is done no nuisance? It is to be borne in mind, however, that, in fact, the act of the defendant is a nuisance such that it would be actionable if done wantonly or maliciously. The plaintiff, then, has a prima facie case. The defendant has infringed the maxim Sic utere tuo ut alienum non laedas. Then, what principle or rule of law can he rely on to defend himself? It is clear to my mind that there is some exception to the general application of the maxim mentioned. The instances put during the argument, of burning weeds, emptying cesspools, making noises during repairs, and other instances which would be nuisances if done wantonly or maliciously, nevertheless may be lawfully done. It cannot be said that such acts are not nuisances, because, by the hypothesis, they are; and it cannot be doubted that, if a person maliciously and without cause made close to a dwelling-house the same offensive smells as may be made in emptying a cesspool, an action would lie. Nor can these cases be got rid of as extreme cases, because such cases properly test a principle. Nor can it be said that the jury settle such questions by finding there is no nuisance, though there is. For that is to suppose they violate their duty, and that, if they discharged their duty, such matters would be actionable, which I think they could not and ought not to be. There must be, then, some principle on which such cases must be excepted. It seems to me that that principle may be deduced from the character of these cases, and is this, viz., that those acts necessary for the common and ordinary use and occupation of land and houses may be done, if conveniently done, without subjecting those who do them to an action. This principle would comprehend all the cases I have mentioned, but would not comprehend the present, where what has been done was not the using of land in a common and ordinary way, but in an exceptional manner — not unnatural nor unusual, but not the common and ordinary use of land. There is an obvious necessity for such a principle as I have mentioned. It is as much for the advantage of one owner as of another; for the very nuisance the one complains of, as the result of the ordinary use of his neighbour's land, he himself will create in the ordinary use of his own, and the reciprocal nuisances are of a comparatively trifling character. The convenience of such a rule may be indicated by calling it a rule of give and take, live and let live.

Then can this principle be extended to, or is there any other principle which will comprehend, the present case? I know of none: it is for the defendant to shew it. None of the above reasoning is applicable to such a cause of nuisance as the present. It had occurred to me, that any not unnatural use of the land, if of a temporary character, might be justified; but I cannot see why its being of a temporary nature should warrant it. What is temporary, — one, five, or twenty years? If twenty, it would be difficult to say that a brick kiln in the direction of the prevalent wind for twenty years would not be as objectionable as a permanent one in the opposite direction. If temporary in order to build a house on the land, why not temporary in order to exhaust the brick earth? I cannot think then that the nuisance being temporary makes a difference.

But it is said that, temporary or permanent, it is lawful because it is for the public benefit. Now, in the first place, that law to my mind is a bad one which, for the public benefit, inflicts loss on an individual without compensation. But further, with great respect, I think this consideration misapplied in this and in many other cases, The public consists of all the individuals of it, and a thing is only for the public benefit when it is productive of good to those individuals on the balance of loss and gain to all. So that if all the loss and all the gain were borne and received by one individual, he on the whole would be a gainer. But whenever this is the case, — whenever a thing is for the public benefit, properly understood, — the loss to the individuals of the public who lose will bear compensation out of the gains of those who gain. It is for the public benefit there should be railways, but it would not be unless the gain of having the railway was sufficient to compensate the loss occasioned by the use of the land required for its site; and accordingly no one thinks it would be right to take an individual's land without compensation to make a railway. It is for the public benefit that trains should run, but not unless they pay their expenses. If one of those expenses is the burning down of a wood of such value that the railway owners would not run the train and burn down the wood if it were their own, neither is it for the public benefit they should if the wood is not their own. If, though the wood were their own, they still would find it compensated them to run trains at the cost of burning the wood, then they obviously ought to compensate the owner of such wood, not being themselves, if they burn it down in making their gains. So in like way in this case a money value indeed cannot easily be put on the plaintiff's loss, but it is equal to some number of pounds or pence, £10, £50 or what not: unless the defendant's profits are enough to compensate this, I deny that it is for the public benefit he should do what he has done; if they are, he ought to compensate.

The only objection I can see to this reasoning is, that by injunction or by abatement of the nuisance a man who would not accept a pecuniary compensation might put a stop to works of great value, and much more than enough to compensate him. This objection, however, is comparatively of small practical importance; it may be that the law ought to be amended, and some means be provided to legalise such cases, as I believe is the case in some foreign countries on giving compensation; but I am clearly of opinion that, though the present law may be defective, it would be much worse, and be unjust and inexpedient, if it permitted such power of inflicting loss and damage to individuals, without compensation, as is claimed by the argument for the defendant.

Since the decision of Hole v. Barlow, claims have been made to poison and foul rivers, and to burn up and devastate land, on the ground of public benefit. I am aware that case did not decide so much, but I have a difficulty, for the reasons I have mentioned, in saying that what has been so contended for does not follow from the principles enunciated in that case. . . .

In the result, then, I think it should be overruled, — which practically is the question here; and that our judgment should be for the plaintiff.

Judgment reversed, and entered for the plaintiff for 40s.

Notes

1. How different in fact are the standards suggested by Barons Pollock and Bramwell? Notice Pollock's emphasis on the place where the alleged nuisance was committed, and whether the activity alleged to be a nuisance was suitable to that place. How does his position differ from Bramwell's "live and let live" principle? Incidentally, how does Bramwell's concept of "reciprocal nuisances" differ from the concept of ex ante compensation, suggested in Chapter 7 as a possible basis for negligence liability?

2. Bramwell's discussion of nuisance under the assumption that the benefited and harmed land are owned by a single person suggests another way of understanding the Coase theorem. If parcel A derives a net benefit from

being used to make bricks of $1,000, and parcel B derives a net detriment as a result of this use of A of $200, then a single owner of both parcels would go ahead and use A for making bricks. But, by the same token, if A and B are separately owned, the owners know that each can be made better off by agreeing that A may be used to make bricks. At any price between $200 and $1,000 for permission to use A for brickmaking, both owners will be better off if permission is granted. Therefore, if transaction costs are low, permission will be granted, and the optimal use of A attained, regardless of the initial assignment of rights.*

Bramwell apparently thought that compensation was important in such a case for its evidentiary value. If the owner of A is required as a condition of using A for making bricks to pay the damages caused to B, and he does so, we can be confident that making bricks really is the optimal use of A. But Bramwell overlooked the fact that even if A's owner is not required to pay compensation, A will be used for making bricks only if that use is optimal. With transaction costs low, B's owner will have an incentive to pay A's owner not to use A for making bricks if the harm to B is greater than the gain to A.

The same point undermines Bramwell's acknowledgment that his approach might lead to a case where "a man who would not accept a pecuniary compensation might put a stop to works of great value, and much more than enough to compensate him." If the value of the works is greater than the cost to the individual whose land is harmed by them, this means there is an amount of money that will compensate him without being so great that the works are no longer financially viable. If he refuses to accept compensation, this shows only that the harm to him is really greater than the value of the works. It would not matter to an economist that he perceived a harm greater than the market perceived; the market value of a thing is the value to its marginal user, and some users are not marginal and so value the thing more than the market does.

The analysis is more complicated, however, when transaction costs are high, a point to which we shall return. Also, there is in fact a subtle transaction-cost problem in the case put by Bramwell; it is the problem of "bilateral monopoly," which we consider later in the context of cases where a nuisance is adjudged but an injunction is withheld and plaintiff is forced to accept damages instead.

3. On Bramwell's view of nuisance see Atiyah, Liability for Railway Nuisance in the English Common Law: A Historical Footnote, 23 J. Law & Econ. 191 (1980). On the economics of nuisance law, see Ellickson, Alternatives to Zoning: Covenants, Nuisance Rules, and Fines as Land Use Controls, 40 U. Chi. L. Rev. 681 (1973); Ogus & Richardson, Economics and the Environment: A Study of Private Nuisance, 36 Camb. L.J. 284 (1977).

---

*Baxter & Altree, Legal Aspects of Airport Noise, 15 J. Law & Econ. 1 (1972), makes the interesting suggestion that airports be required to acquire all the land within their primary noise contour, as a method of internalizing the costs of airport noise.

St. Helen's Smelting Co. v. Tipping
11 H.L. Cas. 642, 11 Eng. Rep. 1483 (1865)

This was an action brought by the plaintiff to recover from the defendants damages for injuries done to his trees and crops, by their works. The defendants are the directors and shareholders of the St. Helen's Copper Smelting Company (Limited). The plaintiff, in 1860, purchased a large portion of the Bold Hall estate, consisting of the manor house and about 1300 acres of land, within a short distance of which stood the works of the defendants. The declaration alleged that, "the defendants erected, used, and continued to use, certain smelting works upon land near to the said dwelling house and lands of the plaintiff, and caused large quantities of noxious gases, vapours, and other noxious matter, to issue from the said works, and diffuse themselves over the land and premises of the plaintiff, whereby the hedges, trees, shrubs, fruit, and herbage, were greatly injured; the cattle were rendered unhealthy, and the plaintiff was prevented from having so beneficial a use of the said land and premises as he would otherwise have enjoyed, and also the reversionary lands and premises were depreciated in value." The defendants pleaded, not guilty.

The cause was tried before Mr. Justice Mellor at Liverpool in August, 1863, when the plaintiff was examined and spoke distinctly to the damage done to his plantations, and to the very unpleasant nature of the vapour, which, when the wind was in a particular direction, affected persons as well as plants in his grounds. On cross examination, he said he had seen the defendants' chimney before he purchased the estate, but he was not aware whether the works were then in operation. On the part of the defendants, evidence was called to show that the whole neighbourhood was studded with manufactories and tall chimneys, that there were some alkali works close by the defendant's works, that the smoke from one was quite as injurious as the smoke from the other, that the smoke of both sometimes united, and that it was impossible to say to which of the two any particular injury was attributable. The fact that the defendants' works existed before the plaintiff bought the property was also relied on.

The learned Judge told the jury that an actionable injury was one producing sensible discomfort; that every man, unless enjoying rights obtained by prescription or agreement, was bound to use his own property in such a manner as not to injure the property of his neighbours; that there was no prescriptive right in this case; that the law did not regard trifling inconveniences; that everything must be looked at from a reasonable point of view; and therefore, in an action for nuisance to property, arising from noxious vapours, the injury to be actionable must be such as visibly to diminish the value of the property and the comfort and enjoyment of it. That when the jurors came to consider the facts, all the circumstances, including those of time and locality, ought to be taken into consideration; and that with respect to the latter it was clear that in counties where great works had been erected and carried on, persons must not stand on their extreme rights and bring actions in respect of every matter of annoyance, for if so, the business of the whole country would be seriously interfered with.

The defendants' counsel submitted that the three questions which ought to be left to the jury were, "whether it was a necessary trade, whether the place was a suitable place for such a trade, and whether it was carried on in a reasonable manner." The learned Judge did not put the questions in this form, but did ask the jury whether the enjoyment of the plaintiff's property was sensibly diminished, and the answer was in the affirmative. Whether the business there carried on was an ordinary business for smelting copper, and the answer was, "We consider it an ordinary business, and conducted in a proper manner, in as good a manner as possible." But to the question whether the jurors thought that it was carried on in a proper place, the answer was, "We do not." The verdict was therefore entered for the plaintiff, and the damages were assessed at £361 18s. 4$^1/_2$d. A motion was made for a new trial, on the ground of misdirection, but the rule was refused. Leave was however given to appeal, and the case was carried to the Exchequer Chamber, where the judgment was affirmed, Lord Chief Baron Pollock there observing, "My opinion has not always been that which it is now. Acting upon what has been decided in this Court, my brother Mellor's direction is not open to a bill of exception." This appeal was then brought. . . .

The Attorney-General (Sir R. Palmer) and Mr. Webster, for the appellants (defendants in the Court below). — The law on this subject is doubtful, and requires to be settled by the authority of this House. A dictum of Lord Chief Baron Comyns declared that an action on the case will not lie "for a reasonable use of my right, though it be to the annoyance of another; as if a butcher, brewer, etc. use his trade in a convenient place, though it be to the annoyance of his neighbour." That dictum, for which it is admitted no authority is cited, nevertheless lays down the true principle. That principle was adopted in Hole v. Barlow. . . . It was adopted in Bamford v. Turnley in the Court of Queen's Bench, but when that case was heard in the Exchequer Chamber, Hole v. Barlow was expressly dissented from by several of the Judges. Their dissent is not warranted by principle or authority. Our material question is the convenience or fitness of the place where the business is carried on.

In Bamford v. Turnley, it is said by Mr. Justice Williams, "It was therefore treated as a doctrine of law that if the spot should be proved by the jury to be proper or convenient, and the burning of the bricks a reasonable use of the land, these circumstances would constitute a bar to the action," and he then proceeds to argue that they would not do so if the work was carried elsewhere, or if it actually created a nuisance to a neighbour. But a part of the fallacy of the argument lies in this mode of stating the case. An act may be an annoyance without being a nuisance. If only an annoyance, then being performed in a convenient place, for the proper phrase is "convenient," and not "suitable," and performed, as here it was expressly found to be, in a careful way, in "the best manner," it is no nuisance.

And in that case itself Mr. Baron Bramwell really has adopted these principles, for he says, "It is to be borne in mind however, that, in *fact*, the act of the defendant is a nuisance." Now, that shows that even in his opinion the doctrine of nuisance would not be applicable except under a certain condition of fact; and it is clear from the verdict in this case that that condition of fact did not exist. In Cavey v. Leadbitter, Lord Chief Justice Erle distinctly states that he did not differ from the judgment of Mr. Justice Willes in Hole v. Barlow. Now in that case Mr. Justice Willes said, "The right of the owner of a house to have the air unpolluted is subject to this qualification, that necessities may arise for an interference with that right pro bono publico, to this extent, that such interference be in respect of a matter essential to the business of life, and be conducted in a reasonable and proper manner, and in a reasonable and proper place." The nature of the thing, the place where it is used, and the fair and proper use of it, are all circumstances to be considered before a thing can be pronounced a nuisance. When, therefore, by the use of certain manufactures, a neighbourhood is, as it may be said, denaturalized, a person who comes into that neighbourhood cannot complain that what was done before he came there is continued. Under such circumstances the ordinary use of property is really that of its use in the special manner, and such use cannot give rise to a right of action by a person who happens to suffer some annoyance from it; what is done around him assumes then the character of the ordinary and proper use of the property. In the Wanstead Local Board of Health v. Hill, it was decided that under the words of a particular statute (11 & 12 Vict. c. 63), brickmaking was not a "noxious or offensive business," but that case is chiefly remarkable for the declaration of Mr. Justice Willes as to the unsettled state of the law on this matter. That learned Judge says, "It is still, I apprehend, an open question which must one day be determined by the highest tribunal, whether one who carries on a business under reasonable circumstances of place, time, and otherwise, can be said to be guilty of an actionable nuisance." . . .

. . . In Baines v. Baker, Lord Hardwicke refused to grant an injunction to prevent the building of a small-pox hospital near Cold Bath Fields, laying down the principle that in all cases the Court must consider not merely the effect on the neighbouring property, but also the reasonableness of doing the thing in the particular place. The statement to the jury here that the business was actionable if it interfered with the comfort of the plaintiff was therefore a misdirection. That alone would not render it actionable; nor would the fact that it produced injury to the plaintiff's trees and shrubs have that effect. It cannot be asserted as an abstract proposition of law that any act by which a man sends over his neighbour's land that which is noxious and hurtful is actionable, but the jury must be told to take into account the condition of the other property in the neighbourhood, the nature of the locality, and the other circumstances which show the reasonable employment of the property, and even the employment of it in a particular manner in that particular locality. To ask the jury merely whether there has been a sensible injury to the plaintiff's property, or to his enjoyment of it, is not sufficient. . . .

THE LORD CHANCELLOR. My Lords, in matters of this description it appears to me that it is a very desirable thing to mark the difference between an action brought for a nuisance upon the ground that the alleged nuisance produces material injury to the property, and an action brought for a nuisance on the ground that the thing alleged to be a nuisance is productive of sensible personal discomfort. With regard to the latter, namely, the personal inconvenience and interference with one's enjoyment, one's quiet, one's personal freedom, anything that discomposes or injuriously affects the senses or the nerves, whether that may or may not be denominated a nuisance, must undoubtedly depend greatly on the circumstances of the place where the thing complained of actually occurs. If a man lives in a town, it is necessary that he should subject himself to the consequences of those operations of trade which may be carried on in his immediate locality, which are actually necessary for trade and commerce, and also for the enjoyment of property, and for the benefit of the inhabitants of the town and of the public at large. If a man lives in a street where there are numerous shops, and a shop is opened next door to him, which is carried on in a fair and reasonable way, he has no ground for complaint, because to himself individually there may arise much discomfort from the trade carried on in that shop. But when an occupation is carried on by one person in the neighbourhood of another, and the result of that trade, or occupation, or business, is a material injury to property, then thre unquestionably arises a very different consideration. I think, my Lords, that in a case of that description, the submission which is required from persons living in society to that amount of discomfort which may be necessary for the legitimate and free exercise of the trade of their neighbours, would not apply to circumstances the immediate result of which is sensible injury to the value of the property.

Now, in the present case, it appears that the plaintiff purchased a very valuable estate, which lies within a mile and a half from certain large smelting works. . . . Of the effect of the vapours exhaling from those works upon the plaintiff's property, and the injury done to his trees and shrubs, there is abundance of evidence in the case.

My Lords, the action has been brought upon that, and the jurors have found the existence of the injury; and the only ground upon which your Lordships are asked to set aside that verdict, and to direct a new trial, is this, that the whole neighbourhood where these copper-smelting works were carried on, is a neighbourhood more or less devoted to manufacturing purposes of a similar kind, and therefore it is said, that inasmuch as this copper smelting is carried on in what the appellant contends is a fit place, it may be carried on with impunity, although the result may be the utter destruction, or the very considerable diminution, of the value of the plaintiff's property. My Lords, I apprehend that this is not the meaning of the word "suitable," or the meaning of the word "convenient," which has been used as applicable to the subject. The word "suitable" unquestionably cannot carry with it this consequence, that a trade may be carried on in a particular locality, the consequence of which trade may be injury and destruction to the neighbouring property. Of course, my Lords, I except cases where any prescriptive right has been acquired by a lengthened user of the place.

On these grounds . . . I advise your Lordships to affirm the decision of the Court below, and to refuse the new trial, and to dismiss the appeal with costs.

LORD CRANWORTH. My Lords, I entirely concur in opinion with my noble and learned friend on the Woolsack . . . that this has been considered to be the proper mode of directing a jury . . . for at least twenty years; I believe I should have carried it back rather further. In stating what I always understood the proper question to be, I cannot do better than adopt the language of Mr. Justice Mellor. He says, "It must be plain, that persons using a limekiln, or other works which emit noxious vapours, may not do an actionable injury to another, and that any place where such an operation is carried on so that it does occasion an actionable injury to another, is not, in the meaning of the law, a convenient place." I always understood that to be so; but in truth, as was observed in one of the cases by the learned Judges, it is extremely difficult to lay down any actual definition of what constitutes an injury, because it is always a question of compound facts, which must be looked to to see whether or not the mode of carrying on a business did or did not occasion so serious an injury as to interfere with the comfort of life and enjoyment of property.

I perfectly well remember, when I had the honour of being one of the Barons of the Court of Exchequer, trying a case in the county of Durham, where there was an action for injury arising from smoke, in the town of Shields. It was proved incontestably that smoke did come and in some degree interfere with a certain person; but I said, "You must look at it not with a view to the question whether, abstractedly, that quantity of smoke was a nuisance, but whether it was a nuisance to a person living in the town of Shields"; because, if it only added in an infinitesimal degree to the quantity of smoke, I held that the state of the town rendered it altogether impossible to call that an actionable nuisance.

There is nothing of that sort, however, in the present case. It seems to me that the distinction, in matters of fact, was most correctly pointed out by Mr. Justice Mellor, and I do not think he could possibly have stated the law, either abstractedly or with reference to the facts, better than he has done in this case.

LORD WENSLEYDALE. My Lords, I entirely agree in opinion with both my noble and learned friends in this case. In these few sentences I think everything is included: The defendants say, "If you do not mind you will stop the progress of works of this description." I agree that it is so, because, no doubt, in the county of Lancaster above all other counties, where great works have been created and carried on, and are the means of developing the national wealth, you must not stand on extreme rights and allow a person to say, "I will bring an action against you for this and that, and so on." Business could not go on if that were so. Everything must be looked at from a reasonable point of view; therefore the law does not regard trifling and small inconveniences, but only regards sensible inconveniences, injuries which sensibly diminish the comfort, enjoyment or value of the property which is affected.

My Lords, I do not think the question could have been more correctly laid down by any one to the jury, and I entirely concur in the propriety of dismissing this appeal.

Brenner, Nuisance Law and the Industrial Revolution
3 J. Legal Stud. 403, 409-420 (1974)

. . . As long as every alleged annoyance was not remediable at law, a court had to evaluate the plaintiff's complaint by striking a balance between his suffering and the general standard of amenity. A plaintiff, said Vice-Chancellor Bruce in 1851, was not entitled to completely "untainted" and "unpolluted" air, but to "air not rendered to an important degree less compatible, or at least not rendered incompatible, with the physical comfort of human existence. . . ." The defendant's brick kiln interfered with this right of the plaintiff's, and his brick burning was enjoined. Levels of comfort change over time, but the element of reasonableness was always there. The vice-chancellor continued:

> ought this inconvenience to be considered in fact as more than fanciful, more than one of mere delicacy or fastidiousness, as an inconvenience materially interfering with the ordinary comfort physically of human existence, not merely according to elegant or dainty modes and habits of living, but according to plain and sober and simple notions among the English people?[19]

This was the balance traditionally implied by "reasonable." The complaint was weighed against general and minimal standards of comfort.

Another kind of balance was also possible. The reasonableness of the standard of amenity could be evaluated in light of the importance of the offending activity and the manner in which the defendant carried it on. This was the balance struck in the mid-nineteenth century, at least temporarily. The case that introduced the change was Hole v. Barlow in 1858. The Common Pleas ruled that a jury had been properly directed that a nuisance action would not lie if the offending activity was legal, reasonable, and carried

19. Walter v. Selfe, 64 Eng. Rep. 849, 4 De G. & Sm. 315, 321-322 (Ch. 1851).

on in a convenient place. "[I]t is not everybody," Byles, J., had said at the trial,

> whose enjoyment of life and property is rendered uncomfortable by the carrying on of an offensive or noxious trade in the neighbourhood, that can bring an action. If that were so . . . the neighbourhood of Birmingham and Wolverhampton and the other great manufacturing towns of England would be full of persons bringing actions for nuisances arising from the carrying on of noxious or offensive trades in their vicinity, to the great injury of the manufacturing and social interests of the community. I apprehend the law to be this, that no action lies for the use, the reasonable use, of a lawful trade in a convenient and proper place even though some one may suffer annoyance from its being carried on.

The Common Pleas approved this direction. The common law right to clean air, said Willes, J., must be qualified: "necessities may arise for an interference with that right pro bono publico . . . private convenience must yield to public necessity." By comparison with such high-powered legal ammunition, the facts of the case were rather paltry. The plaintiff was the occupant of a house next to the defendant's field. The defendant was going to build some houses on the field and had excavated clay for brick-burning, which was a smelly enterprise because of the lime involved. This was held no nuisance. The right to burn bricks, said Willes, in a moment of fancy, was analogous to the Queen's right to take land compulsorily; both activities were necessary.

Hole v. Barlow was a radical departure from previous law. Part of the decision's logic may have lain in the modern association of nuisance with the action on the case, which was being transformed into an action for negligence. But the doctrine was nonetheless novel. I have found only one earlier instance where an English court was willing to allow the convenience of the offending activity to be the deciding factor in an action, and that was a case of overriding and obvious public interest. Moreover, it was a decision in equity, not law, where an injunction was sought to prevent the building of a hospital for infectious diseases, on the grounds that the neighborhood would be endangered. The injunction was refused because the hospital was a matter of great public need and benefit and because a hospital is of no use to anyone if it is moved out of town.[22]

The necessity of the offense may also be inferred in one other situation. I have seen no case in modern reports — and heard of none in the Year Books or even in manorial court records — where a nuisance action was brought in respect of smoke coming from a *domestic* fire. Until relatively recently, if a person wanted to cook food or to keep warm in winter he had to build a fire. Without fire, and therefore smoke, these essential human activities were impossible, and there was no question of a court's enjoining or penalizing them simply because they made some smoke. Before Hole v. Barlow, in other words, the only times the courts had been willing to weigh the importance of

22. Baines v. Baker, 27 Eng. Rep. 105, Amb. 158 (Ch. 1752).

the offending activity was when that activity was absolutely indispensable to human life and society: medical care, sustenance, heat.

Under Hole v. Barlow, the successful plaintiff would probably have had to show that the defendant had acted unreasonably in doing him damage, and the liability would have come to resemble negligence, as it does in America. As it happened, the courts departed from the case rather quickly, although technicalities were found to avoid for a few years the task, which courts always'find unpleasant, of having to overturn it. In a case from 1861, for instance, arsenic from the works of calico printers was found to be polluting the town reservoir eleven miles downstream. The question put to the jury was whether the defendant's occupation was a lawful trade, necessary or useful to the community, and carried on in a reasonable and proper manner and place. To such a direction the jury could only answer yes. On appeal, however, the Court of Exchequer reversed the decision, in effect ruling that the jury had been misdirected. Yet they declined to overturn Hole v. Barlow, because the defendants had produced no evidence to show that their trade was reasonable and had therefore failed to make out an affirmative defense irrespective of the direction.

In the following year the Exchequer Chamber confronted the problem squarely [in Bamford v. Turnley] and Hole v. Barlow was thrown out — but not without several qualifications and a strenuous dissent by Pollock, C.B. . . . The most succinct statement of the law came from Mellish, Q.C. for the plaintiff, who took care to distinguish private purposes from public benefit. "It may be that for the sake of trade in towns, or for the public benefit," he said, "a nuisance is sometimes justified, such as a tallow chandler's factory; but the nuisance in the present case was created by the defendant for a private purpose, viz., burning bricks for a house for himself, and the extent of the advantage or convenience to the defendant cannot justify the creation of such a nuisance to the plaintiff."

While some if not all the judges were ready to see that persons did not ruin their neighbors' amenity in the name of convenience, they were not willing to extend a similar protection to persons suffering personal discomfort from industrial nuisances. The dearth of reported nuisance actions against factories suggests that this dual standard had been long operating before it was effectively ratified by the House of Lords in St. Helen's Smelting Co. v. Tipping in 1865. This is arguably the most important nuisance case of the era. . . .

The Lords upheld the Exchequer Chamber's ruling that the company was liable for any physical damage it caused, but not for the deterioration of the plaintiff's comfort. . . . By ruling against Tipping on the personal discomfort count, the Lords were making an explicit distinction between nuisance actions for physical injury to property and nuisance actions in respect of personal discomfort. This came perilously close to obscuring the fact that, in either case, nuisance was a remedy for injury to land and that a serious interference with the possessor's comfort was per se such an injury.

St. Helen's made actions in respect of discomfort virtually impossible in the industrial Midlands and in regions such as Swansea and Cardiff. This is not to say that a successful action in respect of discomfort caused by an industrial nuisance was no longer *conceivable* in an industrial town, but the discomfort would have had to be direct, immediate, and obviously physical as in trespass. An eye put out by a cinder would have done, but not severe personal discomfort. As for property damage, the plaintiff had to prove that the *value* of his property had *visibly* diminished, else he could not recover. In other words, a decline in property value would not itself support a nuisance action. There also had to be actual, physical damage. In Tipping's case, his property damage was so severe that he eventually had the copper smelting enjoined,[29] but damage to comfort and health commanded no such protection. In this case, where the physical damage allowed Tipping to recover his lost property value, the distinction may not have been significant — assuming that the declining market value was an accurate reflection of the valued amenity. But in cases where there was no physical damage, the distinction was crucial.

Another factor that tended to make nuisance liability less onerous was the emphasis on locality. Stated abstractly, it might mean no more than that neighbors had to be reasonable and tolerant of one another's activities. This was nothing new. After the 1850s, however, the zoning function of nuisance law became more apparent as the importance of locality came to the fore. It was common to hear a judge say that life in factory towns required more forebearance than life elsewhere; or that an annoyance which was a nuisance on a quiet residential street might not be a nuisance elsewhere. It is difficult to assess the extent to which this aspect of nuisance doctrine has actually changed, for the early reports are fragmentary. But it is certain that the milieu in which the law operated changed radically after 1800, and this change had important consequences. In the thirteenth century, when the worst nuisance in a town might be a brick kiln or a chandler, and in the nineteenth, when whole towns could be built, demographic patterns altered, occupations eliminated and created, and skies blackened, all by factories — in such incomparable circumstances the same law could be greatly different in its import. Somehow we do not associate sociological and environmental metamorphosis with brick kilns, chandlers, and privies, annoying though they may have been to those few close by. It was one thing to close down a smelly tannery and to tell the tanner to move elsewhere or to find another occupation. It was quite another to close down two or three objectionable factories in a Merseyside town, when the consequences could be disastrous for hundreds or even thousands of people. So what the Lords meant when they said that location was a factor to be weighed in evaluating the plaintiff's complaint was that they were going to be more forthright in striking a balance

---

29. Tipping v. St. Helen's, L.R. 1 Ch. 66 (1865). Tipping filed his bill in chancery five days after the Lords upheld the damage award.

between comfort and health on the one hand and economic interests on the other.

What the Lords did in effect in the *St. Helen's* case was not to bury Hole v. Barlow, as they seemed to be doing, but rather to apply it discriminatorily. While they were unwilling to recognize the case as good law and thereby to dilute formal nuisance liability, they were also unwilling to apply the "Every man must so use his own" rule to large industrial concerns as well as to ordinary private persons, except in the most extreme cases. They compromised. Strict nuisance liability would apply to John Doe down the street, but Doe Manufacturing Co., Ltd. would be judged by a more lenient rule. In Lancashire above all, said Lord Wensleydale, "where great works have been created and carried on, and are the means of developing the national wealth, you must not stand on extreme rights and allow a person to say, 'I will bring an action against you for this and that, and so on.' Business could not go on if it were so."

. . . What one would like to know is, how serious was Tipping's allegation that the smelting works had created a substantial interference with his personal comfort and therefore with his rights as a landed proprietor? The reports will not yield up an answer. To find out what the case meant, and what the Lords meant then they chose to regard damage to comfort and amenity as a mere trifling inconvenience, a different kind of evidence is required. It is a stroke of unusual good fortune that such evidence is available, for only one year before Tipping brought his action in 1863, the Lords Select Committee on Noxious Vapours singled out the town of St. Helen's for particular attention.

The picture rendered in their report was one of a wasteland. In the immediate neighborhood of the town were seven or eight alkali works, six or eight large copper smelting works, and a large number of collieries, glass works, and other manufactories. The collieries produced annually two million tons of unusually sulphurous coal, of which 600,000 tons were consumed within the district. Together these works produced an amount of smoke and acidic gases which, given the size of the place, may well have been unique. The area, said the Report, was the scene of "the destruction of trees, by hundreds, in successive years, from the effects of these vapours."

> Farms recently well-wooded, and with hedges in good condition, have now neither tree nor hedge left alive; whole fields of corn are destroyed in a single night, especially when the vapours fall upon them while in bloom; orchards and gardens, of which there were great numbers in the neighbourhood of St. Helens, have not a fruit tree left alive; pastures are so deteriorated that graziers refuse to place stock upon them; and some of the witnesses have attributed to the poisonous nature of the grass the fact that their sheep and cattle have lost their young in considerable numbers.

The most vivid testimony was offered by a land agent named Moubert, who had a long familiarity with the area. He is discussing the eastern side of St. Helen's.

It is one scene of desolation. You might look round for a mile, and not see a tree with any foliage on whatever. I do not mean to say that there are not individual trees within a mile of St. Helens that have not foliage on; but I do not think that there is a tree within a mile of St. Helens that possesses half its natural vigour; and I should think that three-fourths of the trees are totally dead. I may instance one [estate] particularly. There is a very respectable house called Park House, having a little ornamental water, and there is a temple erected on the grounds; the place was beautifully planted up to the road, and about nine or ten years ago, it was with the greatest difficulty you could see the house as you were passing, whether on foot or on horseback, and now there are from 45 to 50 trees standing there which have not had a leaf on them for two years, and scarcely a branch. The trees average in height from 25 to 35 feet, and I dare say there is not a pound of bark upon them at the present time; some have fallen down entirely, and at present lie upon the ground, but the 45 or 50 trees which are left standing look like so many stems, and I think it would be difficult for anybody to say that there is a vestige of vegetation left for anyone to see in the shape of grass or anything else. The property seems to be deserted. . . .

So what was to become of it? It "must be converted into labourers' cottages," reported Mr. Moubert.

The effects of such extreme air pollution on the people who lived and worked in St. Helen's and similar places, and on the animals they kept, were less direct and obvious than was the damage to vegetation; but they were no less real, and they were well known. A Royal Commission on Noxious Vapours reported in 1878 that the evidence as to the ill-effects of industrial vapors on all kinds of crops, on cattle, and on sheep was "distinct and emphatic" and "very similar to that given to the Select Committee of the House of Lords in 1862." Typical of the testimony from land owners was that of Sir Richard Brooke, who reported that all the vegetation on his farm was being destroyed and his cattle ill and dying from poisoned feed. His horses would not eat the grass, so he had to buy hay from elsewhere, and he found himself having to recoup tenants' losses. Good tenants, moreover, were leaving and being replaced by bad ones.

As for the health of the people, the evidence is abundant and conclusive that life expectancy in counties such as Lancashire and Glamorganshire was substantially lower than elsewhere; that coughing, nausea, and prostration from gases were regular features of day-to-day life in factory towns; and that the incidence of serious respiratory diseases in these towns was greater than in the nation at large. The most dangerous industries were alkali and other chemical works, but cotton mills and other dusty places of work seem to have been perhaps as bad. The Vicar of Widnes, who himself had felt ill in church from chemical vapors and who complained of throat afflictions from them, said that the gases "cause people to be constantly sick. I have seen three people vomiting in the streets, in the middle of the day, and the workmen said that it was attributable to the chlorine gas coming upon them." . . .

A Dr. Armstrong from Newcastle-upon-Tyne stated that "patients who suffer from heart disease, asthma, tubercular diseases of the chest, and all chest affections are aggravated very greatly by the effect of these cases [primarily chemical wastes] upon the lungs." And a Liverpool physician said that the incidence of chest diseases was higher in St. Helen's and Widnes than in surrounding areas.

Given our present knowledge of medicine, there can be no doubt that chlorine gas and the gases of hydrochloric, sulphurous, and sulphuric acids can damage human health. But such knowledge is unnecessary to know that pollutants which kill cattle and sheep and trees, and which are capable of wiping out a field of grain overnight, also harm people. . . .

From this evidence alone, I conclude that the law of nuisance as it was known at the beginning of the nineteenth century was not being applied in industrial towns. The man who breathed chlorine gas on the job was not entitled to bring an action in nuisance against his employer. But when he got home at night and found the air was bad there, too, he should have had such a right, as occupier, yet no such actions seem to have been reported. Emphysema, lung diseases, nausea — or even the danger of these things — were not mere trifling inconveniences. We cannot demonstrate directly the precise nature of Mr. Tipping's allegation that the St. Helen's Smelting Co. had significantly impaired his ability to enjoy his property by making him physically uncomfortable. But the circumstantial evidence is strong indeed that his allegation was serious and well founded. That being so, one can only conclude that the common law of nuisance, insofar as it protected the occupier from industrial infringements of his ability to use and enjoy his property, hardly existed.

If a man of substance such as Tipping could not win in nuisance except for actual physical damage of his property, then a lesser man was unlikely to make out at all against an industrial opponent. There were a number of reasons why nuisance law did him no good, some legal, some social. First was the exclusion of nearly all injuries except actual, physical damage to property from legal redress under the obscuring phrase, "trifling inconvenience." Second was the ruling, also from the *St. Helen's* case, that damage to property was not actionable unless it involved visible, actual injury *and* a fall in the property's value. No matter what kinds of damage qualified as legal injuries, the measure of damages was strictly the property's market value. Damage to the occupier's health and comfort was no longer a property injury per se. Since property values in the most contaminated areas often rose rather than fell (though in either case there is no logical connection between the value of the property and the right of its occupier to clean air and water), unhealthy conditions were doubly excluded from the scope of a nuisance remedy. The Royal Commission on Noxious Vapours noted in 1878 that both land values and tenant rents rose in the area of works, "and this increase fully compensated for such damage as was to some extent inevitable." This is a confusing and misleading statement. An occupier did not benefit from an increased land value unless he were also the owner. Tenants certainly did not benefit from having their rents raised. But nuisance is an occupier's remedy. A reversioner cannot bring nuisance unless he can demonstrate a clear and permanent physical injury to the property, and he has no remedy for noise, smoke, or other impermanent irritations, even if they drive away his tenants and reduce his rents. Rising land values and higher rents were no substitute for actions at law.

A third reason why an average British workingman did not bring nuisance actions was simply the prohibitive cost of justice. Taking a local smelting company to court was out of the question for most people.

A fourth reason lay in the requirement that the "state of the neighbourhood" be taken into account in evaluating the nuisance. In one sense it could not be otherwise. But the state of many neighborhoods in factory towns was so bad that the requirement militated against the recognition by the common law of minimum standards of comfort and health. It is not surprising to learn that a specially commissioned investigation into industrial nuisances in 1882 found no correlation between the frequency of complaints and the extent and intensity of nuisances. . . .

Notes

1. Why did the court in *St. Helen's* not base its decision for liability on Rylands v. Fletcher?

2. Did the court hold that Tipping could not recover damages for the injury, if any, to his health? Did it hold that other people in St. Helen's, whether landowners or not, could not recover such damages? If the air pollution in St. Helen's was as serious as described in Brenner's article, would the judges have regarded it as a "trifling and small inconvenience"? Can you think of any reasons other than those mentioned by Brenner why workmen and their families who suffered from the air pollution did not bring nuisance actions against St. Helen's Copper Smelting Company or other industrial polluters in the area?

3. What is the prima facie case of nuisance under English law? What defenses do you think the courts would have recognized? We have met an important defense in an earlier chapter: statutory authorization, discussed in Chapter 4 in connection with the *Taff Railway* case. Brenner, in an omitted portion of his article, emphasizes that this defense prevented many nuisance actions against railways and other publicly chartered companies in nineteenth-century England. Statutory authorization to one side, do you think a farmer whose crops were damaged by smoke and sparks from a nonnegligently operated railroad could obtain damages or an injunction on grounds of nuisance? See McClung v. Louisville & N.R. Co., 255 Ala. 302, 51 So. 2d 371 (1951).

Susquehanna Fertilizer Co. v. Malone
20 A. 900 (Md. 1890)

ROBINSON, J. . . . The plaintiff is the owner of five dwelling-houses on Eighth avenue, in Canton, one of the suburbs of Baltimore city. The corner house is occupied and kept by the plaintiff as a kind of hotel or public house, and the other houses are occupied by tenants. On the adjoining lot is a large fertilizer factory, owned and operated by the defendant, from which the plaintiff alleges noxious gases escape, which not only cause great physical discomfort to himself and his tenants, but also cause material injury to the property itself. The evidence on the part of the plaintiff shows that this factory is used by the defendant for the manufacture of sulphuric acid and commercial fertilizers; that noxious gases escape therefrom, and are driven by the wind upon the premises of the plaintiff, and of his tenants; that they are so offensive and noxious as to affect the health of the plaintiff's family, and at times to oblige them to leave the table, and even to abandon the house. It further shows that these gases injure, materially, his property, discolor and injure clothing hung out to dry, slime the glass in the windows, and even corrode the tin spouting on the houses. The evidence on the part of the defendant is in direct conflict with the evidence offered by the plaintiff; but still, assuming the facts testified to by plaintiff's witnesses to be true, — and this was a question for the jury, — an actionable injury was done to the plaintiff, for which he was entitled to recover. No principle is better settled than that where a trade or business is carried on in such a manner as to interfere with the reasonable and comfortable enjoyment by another of his property, or which occasions material injury to the property itself, a wrong is done to the neighboring owner, for which an action will lie; and this, too, without regard to the locality where such business is carried on; and this, too, although the business may be a lawful business, and one useful to the public, and although the best and most approved appliances and methods may be used in the conduct and management of the business. . . .

We cannot agree with the appellant that the court ought to have directed the jury to find whether the place where this factory was located was a convenient and proper place for the carrying on of the appellant's business, and whether such a use of his property was a reasonable use, and if they should so find the verdict must be for the defendant. It may be convenient to the defendant, and it may be convenient to the public, but, in the eye of the law, no place can be convenient for the carrying on of a business which is a nuisance, and which causes substantial injury to the property of another. Nor can any use of one's own land be said to be a reasonable use, which deprives an adjoining owner of the lawful use and enjoyment of his property. The only case which gives countenance to such a doctrine is Hole v. Barlow, in which it was held that, if the place where the bricks were burnt was a proper and convenient place for the purpose, the defendant was entitled to a verdict, notwithstanding the burning of the bricks may have interfered with the physical comfort of the plaintiff. . . . [The court then discusses the rejection of *Hole* in Bamford v. Turnley.] The question was again fully considered in Tipping v. Smelting Co. . . . So we take the law to be well settled that, in actions of this kind, the question whether the place where the trade or business is carried on is a proper and convenient place for the purpose, or whether the use by the defendant of his own land is, under the circumstances, a reasonable use, are questions which ought not to be submitted to the finding of the jury. We fully agree that, in actions of this kind, the law does not regard trifling inconveniences; that everything must be looked at from a reasonable point of view; that, in determining the question of nuisance in such cases, the locality and all the surrounding circumstances should be taken into consideration; and that, where expensive works have been erected and carried on, which are useful and needful to the public, persons must not stand on extreme rights, and bring actions in respect of every trifling annoyance, otherwise, business could not be carried on in such places. But still, if the result of the trade or business thus carried on is such as to interfere with the physical comfort, by another, of his property, or such as to occasion substantial injury to the property itself, there is wrong to the neighboring owner for which an action will lie. . . .

. . . The law, in cases of this kind, will not undertake to balance the conveniences, or estimate the difference between the injury sustained by the plaintiff and the loss that may result to the defendant from having its trade and business, as now carried on, found to be a nuisance. No one has a right to erect works which are a nuisance to a neighboring owner, and then say he has expended large sums of money in the erection of his works, while the neighboring property is comparatively of little value. The neighboring owner is entitled to the reasonable and comfortable enjoyment of his property, and, if his rights in this respect are invaded, he is entitled to the protection of the law, let the consequences be what they may.

Judgment affirmed.

De Blois v. Bowers
44 F.2d 621 (D. Mass. 1930)

MORTON, J.

This is a bill by property owners in the vicinity of the Wickwire-Spencer Company's steel works in Clinton, Mass., to enjoin the defendants from maintaining a nuisance by the emission of obnoxious fumes and odors from a galvanizing plant forming part of said works. . . .

The plaintiffs are the owners in fee of various residential properties situated on the north side of Sterling street, Clinton, opposite the steel works and the galvanizing plant in question. All these houses were built before the galvanizing plant was established on its present location in 1915. The De Blois house is a three-decker apartment house; of the others some are single houses, and some have more than one tenement. They are all of wood construction, and none of them appeared to be in what I should call good condition for such properties. The assessed value of the De Blois property, which is the nearest to the galvanizing plant, is $3,575; of the Stewart property, which is the next property east belonging to one of the plaintiffs, $3,000; of the Shanbaum property, $3,950; and of the Calcia property, $3,000. The aggregate assessment on all the plaintiffs' property is $22,925. There is no evidence that the presence of the galvanizing plant has diminished their value, nor that they would be more valuable if the steel works were permanently closed down.

The plant of the Wickwire-Spencer Company is assessed for $1,100,000. It employs several hundred persons and has a monthly pay roll running from $60,000 to $90,000. About 60 per cent of its total output is galvanized. If a galvanizing plant cannot be operated in connection with the works, the testimony is that they will have to be shut down. There has been a steel works on this site for about fifty years. Of course, many changes have been made in it during that interval.

In the process of galvanizing, the material to be treated is first dipped in a bath of dilute muriatic acid, a 3 per cent solution in water. It is then drained and drawn through a kettle of molten zinc. The heat vaporizes the acid adhering to the material, and it is thrown off as vapor. There are hoods over each kettle which open into ventilating shafts, or "stacks," rising about twenty-five feet above the roof. Through these the acid vapor is drawn up and discharged into the atmosphere. There are four such kettles and stacks in the defendants' plant, but only two of them are generally in operation; a third is run a few weeks each year. The testimony is that all four are never in operation at the same time. The fumes thus discharged move with the wind, diffusing as they go and, being slightly heavier than air, they tend to settle.

In a concentrated form the fumes would be highly disagreeable and possibly dangerous to life if breathed for a substantial time. They never occur in this form in the defendants' plant. There is only about 1 percent of them in the air directly over the molten metal under the hood. As they rise they are much diluted by the air drawn up with them through the ventilating shafts and are still further diluted as they drift with the wind. The original amount of them is not large, as they come only from the small amount of the acid which adheres to the material after it is drained. As I saw them on a pleasant day with a light breeze, they appeared like a very thin bluish smoke, visible for a certain distance as they drifted with the wind away from the stack, and thereafter invisible in the air. They could be smelt slightly after they had ceased to be visible. They would never be objectionable except to leeward of the stacks. In this connection the evidence is that the prevailing winds in Clinton for most of the year are from the northerly sector. As the plaintiffs' houses are from about three hundred to about five hundred feet distant from the galvanizing plant and on the north side of it, they are most of the time to windward of the fumes. Up to this point the facts are not serious controversy.

As to the intensity of the fumes at the plaintiffs' houses, and the effect of the fumes on persons, on vegetable life, and on buildings, the testimony was much in conflict. The plaintiffs and their witnesses testified that at times the fumes were very disagreeable; that they caused acute illness; that they killed trees and other growing things; and that they injured the paint and nails on the exterior of the houses, and injured or destroyed interior furnishings. Mr. Lawson, a civil engineer, who had been connected with the Clinton superintendent of streets' office, and Mr. Hamilton, who had formerly been chairman of the Clinton board of health, both testified that on occasions they had observed fumes drifting across Sterling street onto the plaintiffs' property; that the fumes were plainly visible and had a disagreeable odor and made one cough. A complaint about the fumes was made by some of these plaintiffs to the board of health a year or more ago; and from little things in the testimony of several of the defendants' witnesses it is evident that for the last three years there has been complaint by the plaintiffs about annoyance from these fumes.

The defendants' contention is that the fumes were so diluted by the time they reached the plaintiffs' houses as never to be seriously disagreeable there. Professor Gill of the Massachusetts Institute of Technology testified to pretty careful tests of the air, which he had made in the neighborhood of the plant on more than one occasion, which showed only minute traces of acid even where the fumes were sufficiently concentrated to be visible. He said that the fumes consisted principally of chlorine gas, which in extremely dilute form is not unwholesome; that it would never give paint a brown stain — of which the plaintiffs complained — nor have any effect on the paint at all; that as to persons, chlorine in such dilution as it reached the plaintiffs' houses would not be unhealthy; that he at no time found fumes nearly as strong as are permitted under the English Factory Act. . . .

The testimony coming from the plaintiffs and their families taken as a whole was greatly exaggerated and unreliable. I believe, however, that occasionally in close, damp weather with a light air from the south, the fumes from the galvanizing plant drift across the properties of certain of the plaintiffs in a very annoying concentration. I think this is true only of the houses which may be regarded as directly opposite the galvanizing plant, i.e. the houses of De Blois, Stewart, Shanbaum, and Calcia. The houses of the other plaintiffs are farther away and so screened by trees that I do not believe they ever get the fumes in a concentration which constitutes a legal nuisance. The occasions referred to are not frequent, but they do occur, and the fumes are then quite sufficient to wake the average person out of a sound sleep and make him or her decidedly uncomfortable. I am not satisfied that the fumes discolor or injure the exterior of the houses or the interior furnishings. Nor am I satisfied that they cause serious illness. . . . The plaintiffs also contend that the fumes killed shade and fruit trees around their houses. . . . It is not easy to say what kills a tree; they were exposed to these fumes only on infrequent occasions; and on all the evidence I am not satisfied that the fumes seriously injured trees, shrubs, or growing plants.

The test by which the question of nuisance is to be determined is well stated in Strachan v. Beacon Oil Co., 251 Mass. 479, 146 N.E. 787, 790: "It is a matter of common knowledge that in thickly settled manufacturing communities, the atmosphere is inevitably impregnated with disagreeable odors and impurities. This is one of the annoyances and inconveniences which every one in such a neighborhood must endure. Mere discomfort caused by such conditions without injury to life or health cannot be ruled as *matter of law* (italics mine) to constitute a nuisance. Each case must depend upon its own facts and no rule can be formulated which will be applicable to all cases." On the question of fact whether the smell, smoke, or fumes of manufacturing establishments were of such character as to constitute nuisances, the decisions indicate great liberality towards industrial establishments. In Tuttle v. Church, Judge Colt found that a fish-rendering plant was not a nuisance; in the *Strachan* case, the master found that an oil works was not; in Fay v. Whitman, a jury found that a slaughterhouse was not; in Wade v. Miller, a master found that a hen yard in a village was not. In the *Strachan* case, it was said that mere discomfort without injury to life or health could not be ruled as a matter of law to constitute a nuisance, though apparently it might have been so found as a matter of fact.

Just where the line should be drawn between, on the one side, the interests of a community in its industrial establishments which give occupation to its inhabitants and revenue in the form of taxes and in other ways, and, on the other side, individuals who are annoyed or rendered uncomfortable by the operation of such establishments, is, as the cases say, not easy to define. The question whether the defendants have done everything reasonably practicable to avoid the cause of offense is important. Reasonable care must be used to prevent annoyance and injury to other persons beyond what the fair necessities of the business require. In the present case there is no convincing evidence that the defendants have done everything commercially practicable to control the fumes. It is suggested by the plaintiffs that the fumes could, at not unreasonable expense, be turned into a tall chimney belonging to the defendants near the galvanizing plant and discharged high in the air, so that they would never float across the intervening land to the plaintiffs' houses in such concentrations as under present conditions occasionally occur. The defendants have made no satisfactory answer to this suggestion. While, as above stated, I am not satisfied that the fumes have caused physical illness, nor injured the plaintiffs' buildings or growing trees and plants, I do believe that at times they cause physical discomfort and inconvenience to an extent beyond what the plaintiffs ought reasonably to be expected to endure, unless everything commercially possible has been done to mitigate them. In other words, the property owner has the right to reasonably pure air; it devolves upon the person contaminating it to justify his action by showing the business necessity for so doing; in this case such justification has not been made out. While there are cases in which the contamination is so serious in its effects on persons or property that no business necessity justifies it, the present case is not of this extreme character. The contamination here is justifiable if unavoidable; but the necessity is not proved. On the facts as above stated I find and rule that the defendants are maintaining a nuisance.

I am, however, very clear that in view of the infrequent occasions on which the plaintiffs suffer from the nuisance, and on account of the great and disproportionate injury to the defendants and to the community which would be caused by an injunction preventing the operation of the steel works, no injunction ought to be granted. The inconvenience and temporary discomfort of the plaintiffs during the few occasions each year when the fumes are oppressive are greatly overbalanced by the benefits which the community receives from the presence of the plant. The plaintiffs recognize this and do not insist upon an injunction.

While the plaintiffs are not entitled to, and do not press for, an injunction against the operation of the galvanizing plant, they are entitled to have the defendants make reasonable efforts to abate the nuisance. If the defendants do not forthwith take all steps reasonably within their power to do so, the plaintiffs may move for a mandatory injunction compelling such action.

As to damages, they should be assessed in this proceeding. The damages of the plaintiffs who are entitled to them, viz., De Blois, Stewart, Shanbaum, and Calcia, appear on the present evidence not to be large in amount and perhaps can be adjusted by the parties. If not, inasmuch as a good deal of the evidence on damages has already gone in on the question of liability, it will be more convenient and less expensive for the parties if I undertake the assessment instead of sending that question to a master. The case may be set down before me for this purpose.

Case to stand for further hearing in accordance with this opinion.

Notes

1. With *Susquehanna* and the English cases, compare Strobel v. Kerr Salt Co., 164 N.Y. 303, 58 N.E. 142 (1900). Defendant, a manufacturer of salt, caused diminution of and pollution to a creek whose waters it used in its manufacturing operations. Plaintiffs, owners of mills downstream on the creek, were injured as a result. The court held that plaintiffs were entitled to an injunction, stating:

> While the courts will not overlook the needs of important manufacturing interests, nor hamper them for trifling causes, they will not permit substantial injury to neighboring property, with a small but long-established business, for the purpose of enabling a new and great industry to flourish. They will not change the law relating to the ownership and use of property in order to

accommodate a great business enterprise. According to the old and familiar rule every man must so use his own property as not to injure that of his neighbor, and the fact that he has invested much money and employs many men in carrying on a lawful and useful business upon his own land, does not change the rule, nor permit him to permanently prevent a material portion of the water of a natural stream from flowing over the land of a lower riparian owner, or to so pollute the rest of the stream as to render it unfit for ordinary use.

Id. at 322, 58 N.E. at 147. The decision may, however, reflect the special rights of riparian owners under the riparian system of water law.

2. With *De Blois* compare Riblet v. Spokane-Portland Cement Co., 41 Wash. 2d 249, 248 P.2d 380 (1952), an action for damages allegedly caused to plaintiffs' home by dust from defendant's cement plant. The court stated:

> Our basic point of inquiry relates to the general theory of the law of nuisance. This appears primarily to be based upon generally accepted ideas of right, equity and justice. The thought is inherent that not even a fee-simple owner has a totality of rights in and with respect to his real property. Insofar as the law of nuisance is concerned, rights as to the usage of land are relative. The general legal principle to be inferred from court action in nuisance cases is that one landowner will not be permitted to use his land so unreasonably as to interfere unreasonably with another landowner's use and enjoyment of his land. The crux of the matter appears to be reasonableness. Admittedly, the term is a flexible one. It has many shades and varieties of meaning. In a nuisance case, the fundamental inquiry always appears to be whether the use of certain land can be considered as reasonable in relation to all the facts and surrounding circumstances. Application of the doctrine of nuisance requires a balancing of rights, interests and convenience. . . .
>
> . . . The general neighborhood and its population were not substantially devoted to industrial activity, that is, the production of cement. There was no industrial or manufacturing town wherein plaintiff's property was located. The property of the Riblets was not clearly benefited in value by the operation of the cement plant; if anything, the contrary seems to be true in the case at bar. In the *Powell* case [Powell v. Superior Portland Cement Co., 15 Wash. 2d 14, 129 P.2d 536 (1942), an earlier case involving cement dust, held not to be an actionable nuisance on the facts] the court characterized the damages as an inseparable part of the manufacturing activity, and apparently was of the view that the cost of a dust-controlling program would be prohibitive under the circumstances involved in that case. In the instant case, substantial sums actually have been expended upon a seemingly highly effective dust-control program, installed for some time and now in operation.
>
> We are convinced that the *Powell* case must be distinguished on the basis of its unique facts and circumstances; that it is not controlling as to the case at bar; and that it was error for the trial court to grant the cement company's motion to dismiss.

Id. at 254-256, 248 P.2d at 382-383.

3. Clearly there are conflicting traditions with regard to the elements of the prima facie case of nuisance. The Restatement of Torts (1939) came down on the side of the approach illustrated by *De Blois* and *Riblet*. Section 822 states that "a non-trespassory invasion of another's interest in the private use and enjoyment of land" is actionable if the invasion is "intentional and unreasonable." Section 826 explains that "An intentional invasion of another's interest in the use and enjoyment of land is unreasonable under the rule stated in §822, unless the utility of the actor's conduct outweighs the gravity of the harm." Section 828 states that in determining the utility of the actor's conduct, "the following factors are important: (a) social value which the law attaches to the primary purpose of the conduct; (b) suitability of the conduct to the character of the locality; (c) impracticability of preventing or avoiding the invasion." Professor Epstein argues that the reasonableness standard of nuisance law requires only that the defendant's invasion of the plaintiff's property interest be substantial. See Epstein, Nuisance Law: Corrective Justice and Its Utilitarian Constraints, 8 J. Legal Stud. 49, 68-69, 82-87 (1979). But substantiality is a separate requirement under the Restatement test. See §822(b). In reaching his conclusion Epstein relies exclusively on English authorities. Prosser suggests that the American cases are consistent with the Restatement's balancing test. See Prosser 596-600. And Coase, in one of the earliest efforts to explain common-law decisions on economic grounds, concludes that both the English and the American cases indicate a sensitivity to the importance, from an economic standpoint, of making a comparison between the utility of the defendant's conduct and the harm produced. See Coase, The Problem of Social Cost, 3 J. Law & Econ. 1, 19-23 (1960). Before making up your own mind what the true legal standard is, read on.

4. Why does the Restatement specify the "private" use and enjoyment of land? Why does it describe the invasion brought about by a nuisance as "intentional" — yet apply the kind of reasonableness or balancing test that one associates with the Hand formula of negligence liability? (How, if at all, does the reasonableness test in nuisance cases differ from the Hand formula?) What sense of "intentional" is being used here? Return to these questions after reading the *Copart* case below.

5. Another point should be noted about the Restatement standard. In referring to the utility of the defendant's conduct and not merely to his care, the Restatement automatically includes activity level as well as care level as a factor in the legal judgment. This is presumably because nuisances can often be eliminated by relocating the defendant's activity to another place. This is an activity point; the defendant may be using all possible care to minimize the harm to the plaintiff.

6. What if defendant honestly but mistakenly believes that his activity will not pollute the air or water or otherwise harm surrounding landowners? Can he still be guilty of a nuisance? What if defendant is deliberately trying to hurt plaintiff — i.e., is being spiteful? How would this case be analyzed under the Restatement? (See Note following the *Everett* case, infra.)

Copart Industries, Inc. v. Consolidated Edison Co.
41 N.Y.2d 564, 362 N.E.2d 968 (1977)

COOKE, J.

"There is perhaps no more impenetrable jungle in the entire law than that which surrounds the word 'nuisance.' It has meant all things to all men" (Prosser, Torts [4th ed.], p. 571). From a point someplace within this oft-noted thicket envisioned by Professor Prosser, this appeal emerges.

Plaintiff leased a portion of the former Brooklyn Navy Yard for a period of five years commencing September 1, 1970. On the demised premises during the ensuing eight or nine months it conducted a storage and new car preparation business, the latter entailing over 50 steps ranging from services such as checking brakes to vehicle cleaning, catering to automobile dealers in the metropolitan area of New York City. Adjacent to the navy yard was defendant's Hudson Avenue plant, engaged in the production of steam and electricity since about 1926. This generating system had five smokestacks and during the time in question its burners were fired with oil having a sulphur content of 1% or less. Prior to 1968, coal had been the fuel employed and the main boiler was equipped with an electrostatic precipitator to remove or control the discharged fly ash. Upon conversion to oil, the precipitator had been deactivated.

Based on allegations that noxious emissions from defendant's nearby stacks caused damage to the exterior of autos stored for its customers such as to require many to be repainted, that reports were received in early 1971 from patrons of paint discoloration and pitting, and that dealers served by plaintiff terminated their business by early May, plaintiff contends that because of said emissions it was caused to cease doing business on May 28, 1971. This action was instituted seeking $1,300,000 for loss of investment and loss of profit, . . . asserting "a deliberate and willful violation of the rights of plaintiff, constituting a nuisance." . . .

The jury found in defendant's favor and judgment was entered dismissing the complaint. . . . On appeal to this court, plaintiff maintains that the trial court erred in charging (1) that plaintiff was required to prove an intent of the defendant to cause damages, and (2) that plaintiff had a burden of proof as to defendant's negligence and plaintiff's freedom from contributory negligence.

Much of the uncertainty and confusion surrounding the use of the term nuisance, which in itself means no more than harm, injury, inconvenience, or annoyance, arises from a series of historical accidents covering the invasion of different kinds of interests and referring to various kinds of conduct on the part of defendants. The word surfaced as early as the twelfth century in the assize of nuisance, which provided redress where the injury was not a disseisin but rather an indirect damage to the land or an interference with its use and enjoyment. Three centuries later the remedy was replaced by the common-law action on the case for nuisance, invoked only for damages upon the invasion of interests in the use and enjoyment of land, as well as of easements and profits. If abatement by judicial process was desired, resort to equity was required. Along with the civil remedy protecting rights in land, there developed a separate principle that an infringement of the right of the crown, or of the general public, was a crime and, in time, this class of offenses was so enlarged as to include any "act not warranted by law, or omission to discharge a legal duty, which inconveniences the public in the exercise of rights common to all Her Majesty's subjects." At first, interference with the rights of the public was confined to the criminal realm but in time an individual who suffered special damages from a public nuisance was accorded a right of action.

A private nuisance threatens one person or a relatively few, an essential feature being an interference with the use or enjoyment of land. It is actionable by the individual person or persons whose rights have been disturbed. A public, or as sometimes termed a common nuisance is an offense against the State and is subject to abatement or prosecution on application of the proper governmental agency. It consists of conduct or omissions which offend, interfere with or cause damage to the public in the exercise of rights common to all, in a manner such as to offend public morals, interfere with use by the public of a public place or endanger or injure the property, health, safety or comfort of a considerable number of persons.

As observed by Professor Prosser, public and private nuisances "have almost nothing in common, except that each causes inconvenience to someone, and it would have been fortunate if they had been called from the beginning by different names." Not only does confusion arise from sameness in denomination and from the lack of it in applicability, but also from the fact that, although an individual cannot institute an action for public nuisance as such, he may maintain an action when he suffers special damage from a public nuisance.

This developmental tracing indicates the erroneous concept under which appellant labors. It also points out that nuisance, as a general term, describes the consequences of conduct, the inconvenience to others, rather than the type of conduct involved. It is a field of tort liability rather than a single type of tortious conduct.

Despite early private nuisance cases, which apparently assumed that the defendant was strictly liable, today it is recognized that one is subject to liability for a private nuisance if his conduct is a legal cause of the invasion of the interest in the private use and enjoyment of land and such invasion is (1) intentional and unreasonable, (2) negligent or reckless, or (3) actionable under the rules governing liability for abnormally dangerous conditions or activities.

In urging that the charge in respect to negligence constituted error, plaintiff's brief opens its discussion with the assertion that "[t]he complaint contained no allegations of negligence and its theory was that of nuisance."

This statement is significant in that not only does it miss the fundamental difference between types of conduct which may result in nuisance and the invasion of interests in land, which is the nuisance, but it also overlooks the firmly established principle that negligence is merely one type of conduct which may give rise to a nuisance. A nuisance, either public or private, based on negligence and whether characterized as either negligence or nuisance, is but a single wrong, and "whenever a nuisance has its origin in negligence," negligence must be proven and a plaintiff "may not avert the consequences of his [or her] own contributory negligence by affixing to the negligence of the wrong-doer the label of a nuisance." Although during trial an issue as to causation developed, whether the deleterious substances reaching the customers' vehicles in plaintiff's custody had their origin at defendant's Hudson Avenue property or elsewhere, plaintiff introduced the testimony of different witnesses in support of its contention that defendant operated its plant in a negligent manner. While plaintiff offered expert proof to the effect that it was the general custom or usage in the power plant industry, during the period in question, to use collectors or precipitators, or both, on oil-fired boilers and also to use magnesium as a fuel oil additive to reduce the formation of acid bearing particulates, defendant submitted testimony from similar sources that mechanical and electrostatic precipitators are not commonly utilized on oil-fired burners and that defendant actually was using manganese as an additive.

Besides liability for nuisance arising out of negligence and apart from consideration of a nuisance resulting from abnormally dangerous or ultrahazardous conduct or conditions, the latter of which obviously is not applicable here, one may be liable for a private nuisance where the wrongful invasion of the use and enjoyment of another's land is intentional and unreasonable. It is distinguished from trespass which involves the invasion of a person's interest in the exclusive possession of land. The elements of such a private nuisance, as charged in effect by the Trial Justice, are: (1) an interference substantial in nature, (2) intentional in origin, (3) unreasonable in character, (4) with a person's property right to use and enjoy land, (5) caused by another's conduct in acting or failure to act (Restatement, Torts, §822). Thus, plaintiff's exception that "defendant's intent . . . is not . . . an essential element of the cause of action of nuisance" and its criticism of the charge, which was to the effect that as to the private nuisance plaintiff was required to prove that defendant's conduct was intentional, are not well taken. "An invasion of another's interest in the use and enjoyment of land is intentional when the actor (a) acts for the purpose of causing it; or (b) knows that it is resulting or is substantially certain to result from his conduct."

Negligence and nuisance were explained to the jury at considerable length and its attention was explicitly directed to the two categories of nuisance, that based on negligence and that dependent upon intentional conduct. . . . [T]he trial court properly charged that contributory negligence may be a defense where the nuisance is based on negligent conduct. As to

nuisance involving a willful or intentional invasion of plaintiff's rights, the
jury was instructed that contributory negligence was not a defense and, in this
respect, plaintiff was not prejudiced and has no right to complain. . . .

The order of the Appellate Division should be affirmed, with costs.

FUCHSBERG, J. (dissenting). . . .

Nuisance traditionally requires that, after a balancing of the risk-utility
considerations, the gravity of harm to a plaintiff be found to outweigh the
social usefulness of a defendant's activity. For no matter whether an act is
intentional or unintentional, there should be no liability unless the social
balance of the activity leads to the conclusion that it is unreasonable.

Interestingly, sections 826 and 829A of the Restatement of Torts 2d
(Tent. Draft Nos. 17, 18) have now given recognition to developments in the
law of torts by moving past the traditional rule to favor recovery for nuisance
even when a defendant's conduct is not unreasonable. To be exact, section
826 (Tent. Draft No. 18, pp. 3-4) reads: "An intentional invasion of another's
interest in the use and enjoyment of land is unreasonable under the rule
stated in section 822, if (a) the gravity of the harm outweighs the utility of the
actor's conduct, or (b) the harm caused by the conduct is substantial and the
financial burden of compensating for this and other harms does not render
infeasible the continuation of the conduct." . . .

On the basis of these principles, it follows that, on reversal the plaintiff
in this case should be permitted to sustain its action for damages on proof
that the harm is substantial and that the financial burden of compensating
for the harm does not render "infeasible" the continuation of the defendant's
business activity.

Notes

1. As the court explains, a "public" nuisance is a land use that violates
some law, usually a criminal law. Examples of public nuisances range from
obstructing a highway or water course to keeping a brothel. A public nuisance, as such, unlike a private nuisance, is not actionable in a private suit.
But if the public nuisance inflicts special damage on some individual, i.e.,
damage different in kind from what it inflicts on the community as a whole,
then it is actionable as a private nuisance. Thus, an obstruction of the
highway that caused inconvenience to numerous people would not be actionable as a private nuisance by any of them; but if the obstruction prevented
someone from ingress into or egress from his property, it might well be. Can
you think of an economic reason for this distinction? For a good discussion of
the conditions under which private tort actions can be maintained in respect
of public nuisances, see Prosser 583-591.

2. Why did the majority in *Copart* not refer to §826 in the revised form
proposed by the draftsmen of the Second Restatement of Torts? Would
defendant's conduct be actionable under subsection (b) of the revised sec-

tion? Does subsection (b) have any possible economic rationale? Incidentally, as finally promulgated in 1977 §826 of the Second Restatement of Torts differs only slightly from the tentative draft quoted in *Copart*. It reads:

> An intentional invasion of another's interest in the use and enjoyment of land is unreasonable if
>   (a) the gravity of the harm outweighs the utility of the actor's conduct, or
>   (b) the harm caused by the conduct is serious and the financial burden of compensating for this and similar harm to others would not make the continuation of the conduct not feasible.

3. Section 822(b) of the Second Restatement provides that an invasion of an interest in the private use and enjoyment of land, even if not intentional and unreasonable, is actionable if "unintentional and otherwise actionable under the rules controlling liability for negligent or reckless conduct, or for abnormally dangerous conditions or activities." But is not negligence included in the concept of unreasonableness? Why does the Restatement not make invasions of an interest in the private use and enjoyment of land actionable if they are unreasonable, period? The following cases may cast some light on these questions.

Power v. Village of Hibbing, 182 Minn. 66, 233 N.W. 597 (1930). An owner of real estate and her tenant brought suit to recover damages incurred when water and sewage backed up in defendant's sewer and entered plaintiffs' premises. The court held that this flooding was not a nuisance for which defendant was liable:

> Could the plaintiff, under the evidence in this case, recover on the ground of trespass or of nuisance? We think not. Negligence is not necessarily one of the material elements of trespass or nuisance. Trespass is often used as the equivalent of tort or wrong. It was apparently so used in this case to characterize the resulting consequence of the alleged negligence of the defendant in maintaining this sewer. Defendant's liability here was no greater than would have been that of a private individual in the same situation. Assuming that an adjoining landowner had constructed a drain on his own land past plaintiff's premises, and that this drain was properly constructed and of sufficient capacity to carry all water that could come into it from any maximum rainfall ever known or reasonably to be anticipated and a cloud-burst like that of June 9th came and overflowed the drain and thereby inundated plaintiff's premises, calling the resulting inundation a trespass or nuisance would not impose liability on the owner of the adjacent property. The care required of municipalities in the construction and maintenance of sewers is ordinary or reasonable care and diligence, and the municipality is not liable for injury caused by extraordinary occurrences which could not reasonably be anticipated. . . .
> If there was in our present case no liability of the village for damages on account of the extraordinary rainfall which caused the damage plaintiff seeks to recover, then we cannot see how any recovery could be had on the theory of trespass or nuisance.

In the well-considered case of Uggla v. Brokaw, 117 App. Div. 586, 102 N.Y.S. 857, it is stated that, while courts have often held that it is unnecessary to prove negligence where an action is brought for a nuisance, that rule only applies when the nuisance is the result of an unauthorized or unlawful and wrongful act. Judge Scott, in his concurring opinion, states: "A skylight upon the roof of a building is not per se unreasonable, unlawful, or unwarrantable, and it cannot, therefore, be considered a nuisance, . . . unless there be proof of negligence either in its construction or maintenance" — citing Losee v. Buchanan, 51 N.Y. 476. The same statement may be made as to the sewer here in question.

Plaintiff cites numerous cases involving negligence, trespass, and nuisance. In none of the cases was there any extraordinary occurrence such as could not be reasonably anticipated or guarded against. There was either negligence or some direct invasion of the complainant's property, or both, or the storing up of water or other substances by the defendant in such a situation that, if it escaped, it was bound to invade complainant's premises and cause damage; in other words, a dangerous situation.

182 Minn. at 70-72, 233 N.W. at 598-599.

Rose v. Socony-Vacuum Corp., 54 R.I. 411, 173 A. 627 (1934). Plaintiff, a farmer, complained that defendant's oil refinery had polluted subterranean waters that fed a well and stream on plaintiff's land, causing damage to his farming operation. The court stated:

> It will be observed that in jurisdictions holding that, even though there is no negligence, there is liability for the pollution of subterranean waters, the predominating economic interest is agricultural.
>
> Defendant's refinery is located at the head of Narragansett Bay, a natural waterway for commerce. This plant is situated in the heart of a region highly developed industrially. Here it prepares for use and distributes a product which has become one of the prime necessities of modern life. It is an unavoidable incident of the growth of population and its segregation in restricted areas that individual rights recognized in a sparsely settled state have to be surrendered for the benefit of the community as it develops and expands. If, in the process of refining petroleum, injury is occasioned to those in the vicinity, not through negligence or lack of skill or the invasion of a recognized legal right, but by the contamination of percolating waters whose courses are not known, we think that public policy justifies a determination that such harm is damnum absque injuria.

Id. at 421, 173 A. at 631-632.

Demarest v. Hardham
34 N.J. Eq. 469 (1881)

VAN FLEET, V.C.

This suit is brought to restrain a nuisance. The complainants and defendant occupy adjacent buildings on the north side of Market street, in the city of Newark. The complainants manufacture harness in theirs, and the defendant carries on the printing and book-binding business in his. The complainants are copartners. Each building stands as close up to the line dividing the lots on which they are built as the walls could well be built, and consequently the west wall of the complainants' building, in some places, comes in contact with the east wall of the defendant's building. The defendant has possession of the second, third and fourth floors of the building he occupies, and generates and expends the steam power he uses on the third floor. He has there a twelve-horse power engine with boiler attached, and six printing presses — four operated by steam, and two by hand. This machinery is so placed that its power is exerted in lines running east and west, in other words, across the building, and not longitudinally, and consequently the west wall of the complainants' building is compelled to receive whatever shock is produced by its force.

The bill alleges that the force which the machinery expends against the complainants' building is so great that it causes an oscillation of a quarter of an inch, and that the shaking and jarring thus produced has caused the east wall to crack, and to deflect from its original position to such an extent as to weaken the whole building and endanger its safety and stability. It is also alleged that the motion of the machinery produces a vibration in the complainants' building so constant and serious as to materially obstruct and interfere with them in the prosecution of their business. All their workmen, it is charged, are more or less affected by it. To some it gives headache, and in others it produces sickness at the stomach, and it prevents all from doing their work in comfort and quiet. . . .

The important question presented by the case is, does the manner in which the defendant conducts his business interfere with or injure the business of the complainants to such an extent as to create a nuisance which it is the duty of a court of equity to enjoin? The defendant's business is not only lawful, but necessary. It is carried on in a part of the city of Newark devoted almost exclusively to manufacturing and business purposes. No objection can therefore be made to it on the ground that its location is not a fit one. It is not necessarily or inherently noxious, offensive or injurious. It should not, therefore, be enjoined except under a stern necessity. The complainants ask that it be absolutely interdicted, their prayer being that the defendant be restrained from further operating his engine and presses. To grant their prayer is to destroy the defendant's business. Power attended with such disastrous consequences should always be exercised sparingly, and with the utmost caution. All doubts should be resolved against its exercise. Relief by injunction, in such cases, is not a matter or right, but rests in discretion. If the legal right is not clear, or the injury is doubtful, eventual or contingent, equity will give no aid.

And so, too, the court is bound to compare consequences. If the fact of an actionable nuisance is clearly established, then the court is bound to consider whether a greater injury will not be done by granting an injunction, and thus destroying a citizen's property and taking away from him his means of livelihood, than will result from a refusal, and leaving the injured party to his ordinary legal remedy; and if, on thus contrasting consequences, it appears doubtful whether greater injury will not be done by granting than by withholding the injunction, it is the duty of the court to decline to interfere. . . .

No rule can be framed which will accurately define what acts or facts will constitute a nuisance in every possible contingency. Each case must be decided on its own peculiar facts. There can be no doubt that a lawful business, which is not inherently a nuisance on account of its offensive character, may be so conducted as to render it a nuisance which equity will restrain. The maxim sic utere tuo ut alienum non laedas, undoubtedly expresses the general fundamental rule, but it is also true that the law does not regard every trifling injury or annoyance as an actionable nuisance. Things merely disagreeable, which simply displease the eye, or offend the taste, or shock an oversensitive or fastidious nature, no matter how irritating or unpleasant, are not nuisances. No man is under a legal duty to consult the taste or preferences of his neighbor in the use of his property, but he is bound to respect his neighbor's legal rights. He cannot fill his neighbor's house with smoke, nor the air, which his neighbor has a right to breath pure and unpolluted, with nauseous or deleterious odors, nor can he throw soot or cinders into his neighbor's house or door-yard to such an extent as to deprive him of the free and full enjoyment of his property. Nor will equity permit him, in the prosecution of his business, to use machinery of such weight and power as causes a vibration in the premises of his neighbor of such extent and force as to seriously annoy and disturb his neighbor and materially interfere with him in carrying on his business. . . .

The principle to be deduced from the authorities I understand to be this: that an injunction to restrain a lawful business, on the ground that it is so conducted as to render it a nuisance, should never be granted, except the complainant shows an invasion of a clear legal right, resulting in permanent and serious injury, which cannot be adequately redressed by action at law, and that the allowance of the writ will not inflict upon the defendant a more serious injury than the complainant will sustain if the writ is denied and he be left to his ordinary legal remedy. Equity takes cognizance of a nuisance which is permanent in its character, or which produces a constantly recurring grievance, more readily than any other. . . .

The proofs show that the vibration produced in the complainant's building by the defendant's machinery is so great, at times, as actually to render it impossible to do certain kinds of work there. . . . Unless the complainants' witnesses, without exception, have exaggerated the effect of the vibration to such an extent as to render their stories downright falsehoods, it must be taken as an established fact in the case that the vibration very sensibly and materially interferes with the complainants in the prosecution of their business.

My judgment is that the defendant is guilty of a nuisance which it is the duty of this court to redress. But this conclusion does not necessarily involve the destruction of the defendant's business. The injury to the complainants, in my judgment, is caused solely by the position of the machinery. As already stated, it is now placed so that its whole force is expended across the defendant's building and directly against that occupied by the complainants. To me it seems very plain that if it is changed, so that its force shall be expended longitudinally with the building, and not transversely, the injury the complainants now suffer will be remedied, and all cause of complaint removed. That is the unanimous opinion of all the experts who have spoken upon the subject.

A decree will be advised directing the defendant to change the position of his machinery in accordance with the view above indicated, or that an injunction shall issue restraining him from operating any machinery in the building occupied by him to such an extent as shall produce a vibration in the complainants' building sufficient to annoy or disturb them in the conduct of their business. . . .

Notes

1. Heretofore we have not considered the role of the injunction in enforcing tort law. An injunction is not a usual or appropriate remedy in an accident case. The plaintiff has no incentive to seek an injunction in such a case, because the probability that the defendant will injure him again in the future is normally very low. Nor would the issuance of an injunction, disobedience of which is traditionally punished by a heavy fine levied under the contempt power of the court, be appropriate in a simple accident case, where punitive damages would not be awarded. The first point is applicable to the usual intentional tort case as well: The probability that the plaintiff will be attacked again by this defendant is normally slight. There are exceptions. Defamation, for example, is sometimes a continuing tort, as nuisance often is, and injunctions are sometimes granted in defamation cases.

2. The standard formulation of when an injunction will be granted is when plaintiff's damage remedy is inadequate. But as the *Demarest* opinion suggests, injunction is a standard remedy in nuisance cases and courts rarely bother to consider whether the damages remedy is inadequate. Why is this so? The usual reason given is "that a continuing trespass gives ground for injunctive relief to prevent a multiplicity of actions. If the defendant's plant, with its mode of operation, constitutes a nuisance, it gives rise to a new cause of action each day that it is so operated, and the recovery of daily damages is not an adequate remedy for one whose rights of property are continually invaded." Friedman v. Columbia Mach. Works & Malleable Iron Co., 99 App. Div. 504, 506, 91 N.Y. Supp. 129-130 (1904). But would plaintiff have to seek "daily damages"? Why couldn't he sue for the present value of the

future expected damages, i.e., for the diminution in the value of his property due to defendant's activity? Would estimation of damages on this basis be any more difficult than in a personal injury case involving death or disability, where plaintiff's damages are computed by estimating, and then discounting to present value, the wages he would have earned but for the injury? Is the law's readiness to grant injunctions in nuisance cases perhaps just an aspect of equity's traditionally broad role in protecting interests in land?

3. It is natural for the lawyer to think of the damages remedy as primary and the injunctive remedy as secondary: damages is the legal remedy, injunction the equitable remedy, and equitable remedies developed after and as a supplement to legal remedies. The economist's instinct is to reverse the sequence. The legal remedy, damages, requires the court to set a value on the harm to the plaintiff. An injunction forces a negotiation between the parties. If the harm to the plaintiff is less than the cost to the defendant of being enjoined, defendant will offer, and plaintiff will accept, a price to dissolve the injunction and substitute damages (the Coase theorem again). Why then did the court in *Demarest* not simply enjoin the defendant from continuing to harm plaintiff's business?

4. What substantive standard did the court use to decide whether defendant's activity constituted a nuisance? Was it the English standard or the Restatement (1939) standard?

5. The "balance of injury" language in *Demarest* was later repudiated by the New Jersey court. See Hennessey v. Carmony, 50 N.J. Eq. 616, 25 A. 374 (1892). Does this imply that the relief granted in *Demarest* was improper?

Richard's Appeal
57 Pa. 105 (1868)

THOMPSON, C.J. The complainant in this case is the owner of a dwelling-house and cotton factory in the village of Phoenixville, Chester county; and the respondents are owners of very extensive iron works in the same village. The former complains that by reason of the kind of fuel used by the latter in their works, his residence is rendered uncomfortable and unwholesome, and his factory materially injured in the discoloration of his fabrics and deterioration of his machinery. Claiming that he had established this, he asked the court below for a perpetual injunction to restrain the respondents from using the fuel, bituminous and semi-bituminous coal complained of as the cause of the injury to his property in these furnaces. The case was heard on bill and answer, and the court decided against him. . . .

The defendants' works are very extensive, amongst the most so, it is said, of any of the kind in the Commonwealth, consisting of several blast furnaces, some seventy puddling furnaces, and rolling-mills and other machinery. They began on a small scale some forty-nine or fifty years ago, and up to 1840 used bituminous coal exclusively. . . . The extensions made in the works in 1837, 1846 and 1853, constitute the present works, the cost of which alone is represented as exceeding half a million of dollars, and which at the time of taking the testimony, and previously, employed, as the master reports, from eight hundred to one thousand hands.

The plaintiff's dwelling, it appears, is situated on a bluff or hill northwardly from the defendants' works, about seventy feet above the nearest furnace floor, which brings its first story about on a level with the top of the puddling-stacks, and when the wind is towards the plaintiff's house and from the furnace, the consequence is, that it is at times enveloped in a coal-smoke thrown out of the chimneys of the puddling furnaces. It cannot be doubted, I think, that this materially operates to injure the dwelling-house as a dwelling, and consequently to deteriorate its value. The alleged injury to the factory is mainly that the smoke and soot of the furnace blackens the stock and renders the fabrics less saleable. This I can readily understand and believe. The house was erected in 1829, and the factory in 1834, and both have been generally occupied ever since; the factory not doing full work for some time past, as the master reports.

A careful consideration of the testimony satisfies us that the use of semi-bituminous coal, the fuel complained of, is necessary to the successful manufacture of iron fit for axles, cannon and the like, in the manufacture of which the defendants are largely engaged; that the process of manufacture, and fuel used, are generally employed in similar establishments, and that there was neither a negligent nor wilful infliction of injury upon the plaintiff or his property in the defendants' mode of operating their works. Whatever of injury may have, or shall result to, his property from the defendants' works, by reason of the nuisance complained of, is such only as is incident to a lawful business conducted in the ordinary way, and by no unusual means. Still there may be injury to the plaintiff; but this of itself may not entitle him to the remedy he seeks. It may not, if ever so clearly established, be a case in which equity ought to enjoin the defendants in the use of a material necessary to the successful production of an article of such prime necessity as good iron; especially if it be very certain that a greater injury would ensue by enjoining than would result from a refusal to enjoin. If we were able with certainty to say that the use of semi-bituminous coal, in the process of making good iron by the puddling process, was unnecessary, and other fuel was equally good and available, or that by a reasonable expenditure of money on the works, all injury might be avoided, a different case might appear to our minds as chancellors, and we might then say that the cause of injury should cease, and that a decree in terms to meet such a contingency should be made so as to prevent the injury. But we have not such case before us. Bituminous, or at least semi-bituminous coal, we think, from the testimony, is necessary in the manufacture of iron, such as the business of the defendants require, and whose fabrics the public require. Nor are we shown by testimony or reliable tests of any kind, that the smoke produced in the puddling process can be consumed, as it undoubtedly may be in ordinary chimneys, or when produced in furnaces used to propel machinery. I am personally cognisant that this may be done, from observation both in this country and in England; and I have therefore read with satisfaction and entire conviction of the truth, the article from the London Quarterly of 1866, so largely quoted by the learned counsel for the appellants; but I would be very unwilling to act on that conviction or that theory any further than to the extent to which experiment has gone. I would require very clear proof of the practicability of the application of the principle to uses dissimilar, or partially so, as puddling chimneys from common furnace smoke-stacks. The defendants seem willing to test the applicability of smoke consumers to puddling furnaces, and at the same time express their doubts in a practical shape by offering $50,000 for an invention which will consume the smoke of their puddling stacks without impairing the efficiency of the process of manufacturing iron. However this may be, certain it is, we are not able to say from anything shown, that the evil complained of can be remedied by the application of smoke consumers. We do not know what effect their application might have on the process; nor do we think we should visit the defendants, because they might be unwilling to add to the height of their chimneys without knowing what effect it would have, or because they might not be willing to tear down their establishment and reerect it on Seiman's plan or patent. What effect these remedies, or either of them, ought to have on the mind of a chancellor, if feasible, and the injury complained of were absolutely irreparable, we are not called upon to say, for such is evidently not the case here if there be any damage at all, as we shall presently show. . . .

. . . We have no doubt that an action at law will lie for an injury to property for causes similar to those mentioned in this bill, and if so, why will not the remedy be adequate in such case, and thus the injury be repaired in damages? We are not to presume that it will not be. This would be to impugn the justice of our common-law forms without a reason. We think, under the circumstances of the case, that the injunction ought to be refused, and the plaintiff left to his action at law for the recovery of such damages as he may have sustained or may sustain.

An error seems somewhat prevalent in portions, at least, of this Commonwealth, in regard to proceedings in equity to restrain the commission of nuisances. It seems to be supposed that, as at law, whenever a case is made out of wrongful acts on the one side and consequent injury on the other, a decree to restrain the act complained of, must as certainly follow, as a judgment would follow a verdict in a common-law court. This is a mistake. It is elementary law, that in equity a decree is never of right, as a judgment at law is, but of grace. Hence the chancellor will consider whether he would not do a greater injury by enjoining than would result from refusing, and leaving the party to his redress at the hands of a court and jury. If in conscience the former should appear he will refuse to enjoin. We think this is a safe rule, and that the case we are considering is within it. . . . Appeal dismissed at the cost of the appellant.

Notes

1. If the damage to plaintiff's property could not be avoided except at much greater cost, does this not show, at least under the Restatement (1939) test, that defendant's activity did not constitute a nuisance?

2. With Richard's Appeal compare the discussion in Satren v. Hader Co-Operative Cheese Factory, 202 Minn. 553, 557-558, 279 N.W. 361, 363-364 (1938), where a cheese factory polluted a creek, causing harm to plaintiff's farm:

> The main contention is that the injury to plaintiff being insignificant, only $63 a year in diminished rental value of the farm as found, an injunction should not issue which in effect prevents the operation of a large business of great value to the community. Decisions of high authority are cited and relied on by defendant. . . . The Harrisonville case was one where defendant, a city of 2,000 inhabitants, had its only sewer outlet into a small creek, which thereafter passed through a tract of plaintiff's land devoted solely to pasturage. It appeared that the city was not financially able to install an additional unit costing about $25,000 for the treatment of the sewage. The rental value of the land was $500 for five years. The Supreme Court recognized plaintiff's right to an injunction, but considered full redress could be had by the payment of the rental value during the continuance of the pollution and reversed the injunction awarded. . . . Defendant insists that this court is committed to the doctrine that injunctive relief will not be granted to suppress a nuisance where the injury suffered from its continuance is trifling, and the offending party's business will be totally destroyed or very extensively damaged by its abatement, and points to Roukovina v. Island Farm Creamery Co., 160 Minn. 335, 200 N.W. 350; Village of Wadena v. Folkestad, 194 Minn. 146, 260 N.W. 221. In the Roukovina case the nuisance sought to be enjoined was the noise and disturbance created in a village at unreasonable hours by the business of defendant, a creamery. The nuisance was held properly abated insofar as the findings of fact warranted. In the Wadena case it was held the evidence did not establish the defendant's depot to be a nuisance. In both cases the well-known principle is recognized that courts in the use of the injunctive remedy will avoid as far as possible interfering with a legitimate business or lawful use. In respect to the right of a riparian owner to have a stream flowing through his land in its natural purity, he as well as those above and below, are governed by the rule of reasonable use. It appears to us that the findings and the evidence unquestionably warrant the issuing of the injunction restraining defendant from discharging the whey into the creek. . . . [T]his whey became a putrid mass when it was cast upon plaintiff's farm and constituted both a continuing nuisance and a repeated trespass and hence the court should grant injunctive relief.

Can *Satren* be reconciled with Richard's Appeal? With the cases discussed in *Satren?* For a very strong statement of the point of view in *Satren* see American Smelting & Refining Co. v. Godfrey, 158 F. 225 (8th Cir. 1907).

Whalen v. Union Bag & Paper Co.
208 N.Y. 1, 101 N.E. 805 (1913)

WERNER, J. The plaintiff is a lower riparian owner upon Kayaderosseras creek in Saratoga county, and the defendant owns and operates on this stream a pulp mill a few miles above plaintiff's land. This mill represents an investment of more than a million dollars and gives employment to 400 or 500 operatives. It discharges into the waters of the creek large quantities of a liquid effluent containing sulphurous acid, lime, sulphur, and waste material consisting of pulp wood, sawdust, slivers, knots, gums, resins and fibre. The pollution thus created, together with the discharge from other industries located along the stream and its principal tributary, has greatly diminished the purity of the water.

The plaintiff brought this action to restrain the defendant from continuing to pollute the stream. The trial court granted an injunction to take effect one year after the final affirmance of its decision upon appeal, and awarded damages at the rate of $312 a year. The Appellate Division reversed the judgment of the Special Term upon the law and facts, unless the plaintiff should consent to a reduction of damages to the sum of $100 a year, in which event the judgment as modified should be affirmed, and eliminated that part of the trial court's decree granting an injunction. . . .

. . . The defendant conducts a business in which it has invested a large sum of money and employs great numbers of the inhabitants of the locality. . . . The setting aside of the injunction was apparently induced by a consideration of the great loss likely to be inflicted on the defendant by the granting of the injunction as compared with the small injury done to the plaintiff's land by that portion of the pollution which was regarded as attributable to the defendant. Such a balancing of injuries cannot be justified by the circumstances of this case. . . .

One of the troublesome phases of this kind of litigation is the difficulty of deciding when an injunction shall issue in a case where the evidence clearly establishes an unlawful invasion of a plaintiff's rights, but his actual injury from the continuance of the alleged wrong will be small as compared with the great loss which will be caused by the issuance of the injunction. This appeal has been presented as though that question were involved in the case at bar, but we take a different view. Even as reduced at the Appellate Division, the damages to the plaintiff's farm amount to $100 a year. It can hardly be said that this injury is unsubstantial, even if we should leave out of consideration the peculiarly noxious character of the pollution of which the plaintiff complains. The waste from the defendant's mill is very destructive both to vegetable and animal life and tends to deprive the waters with which it is mixed of their purifying qualities. It should be borne in mind also that there is no claim on the part of the defendant that the nuisance may become less injurious in the future. Although the damage to the plaintiff may be slight as compared with the defendant's expense of abating the condition, that is not a good reason for refusing an injunction. Neither courts of equity nor law can be guided by such a rule, for if followed to its logical conclusion it would deprive the poor litigant of his little property by giving it to those already rich. . . .

The judgment of the Appellate Division, in so far as it denied the injunction, should be reversed and the judgment of the Special Term in that respect reinstated, with costs to the appellant.

Boomer v. Atlantic Cement Co.
26 N.Y.2d 219, 257 N.E.2d 870 (1970)

BERGAN, J.

Defendant operates a large cement plant near Albany. These are actions for injunction and damages by neighboring land owners alleging injury to property from dirt, smoke and vibration emanating from the plant. A nuisance has been found after trial, temporary damages have been allowed; but an injunction has been denied.

The public concern with air pollution arising from many sources in industry and in transportation is currently accorded ever wider recognition accompanied by a growing sense of responsibility in State and Federal Governments to control it. Cement plants are obvious sources of air pollution in the neighborhoods where they operate.

But there is now before the court private litigation in which individual property owners have sought specific relief from a single plant operation. The threshold question raised by the division of view on this appeal is whether the court should resolve the litigation between the parties now before it as equitably as seems possible; or whether, seeking promotion of the general public welfare, it should channel private litigation into broad public objectives.

A court performs its essential function when it decides the rights of parties before it. Its decision of private controversies may sometimes greatly affect public issues. Large questions of law are often resolved by the manner in which private litigation is decided. But this is normally an incident to the court's main function to settle controversy. It is a rare exercise of judicial power to use a decision in private litigation as a purposeful mechanism to achieve direct public objectives greatly beyond the rights and interests before the court.

Effective control of air pollution is a problem presently far from solution even with the full public and financial powers of government. In large measure adequate technical procedures are yet to be developed and some that appear possible may be economically impracticable.

It seems apparent that the amelioration of air pollution will depend on technical research in great depth; on a carefully balanced consideration of the economic impact of close regulation; and of the actual effect on public health. It is likely to require massive public expenditure and to demand more than any local community can accomplish and to depend on regional and interstate controls.

A court should not try to do this on its own as a by-product of private litigation and it seems manifest that the judicial establishment is neither equipped in the limited nature of any judgment it can pronounce nor prepared to lay down and implement an effective policy for the elimination of air pollution. This is an area beyond the circumference of one private lawsuit. It is a direct responsibility for government and should not thus be undertaken as an incident to solving a dispute between property owners and a single cement plant — one of many — in the Hudson River valley.

The cement making operations of defendant have been found by the court at Special Term to have damaged the nearby properties of plaintiffs in these two actions. That court, as it has been noted, accordingly found defendant maintained a nuisance and this has been affirmed at the Appellate Division. The total damage to plaintiffs' properties is, however, relatively small in comparison with the value of defendant's operation and with the consequences of the injunction which plaintiffs seek.

The ground for the denial of injunction, notwithstanding the finding both that there is a nuisance and that plaintiffs have been damaged substantially, is the large disparity in economic consequences of the nuisance and of the injunction. This theory cannot, however, be sustained without overruling a doctrine which has been consistently reaffirmed in several leading cases in this court and which has never been disavowed here, namely that where a nuisance has been found and where there has been any substantial damage shown by the party complaining an injunction will be granted. . . .

The problem of disparity in economic consequence was sharply in focus in Whalen v. Union Bag & Paper Co. A pulp mill entailing an investment of more than a million dollars polluted a stream in which plaintiff, who owned a farm, was "a lower riparian owner." The economic loss to plaintiff from this pollution was small. This court, reversing the Appellate Division, reinstated the injunction granted by the Special Term against the argument of the mill owner that in view of "the slight advantage to plaintiff and the great loss that will be inflicted on defendant" an injunction should not be granted. . . .

. . . The rule laid down in that case, then, is that whenever the damage resulting from a nuisance is found not "unsubstantial," viz., $100 a year, injunction would follow. This states a rule that had been followed in this court with marked consistency. . . .

Although the court at Special Term and the Appellate Division held that injunction should be denied, it was found that plaintiffs had been damaged in various specific amounts up to the time of the trial and damages to the respective plaintiffs were awarded for those amounts. The effect of this was, injunction having been denied, plaintiffs could maintain successive actions at law for damages thereafter as further damage was incurred.

The court at Special Term also found the amount of permanent damage attributable to each plaintiff, for the guidance of the parties in the event both sides stipulated to the payment and acceptance of such permanent damage as a settlement of all the controversies among the parties. The total of permanent damages to all plaintiffs thus found was $185,000. This basis of adjustment has not resulted in any stipulation by the parties.

This result at Special Term and at the Appellate Division is a departure from a rule that has become settled; but to follow the rule literally in these cases would be to close down the plant at once. This court is fully agreed to avoid that immediately drastic remedy; the difference in view is how best to avoid it.*

One alternative is to grant the injunction but postpone its effect to a specified future date to give opportunity for technical advances to permit defendant to eliminate the nuisance; another is to grant the injunction conditioned on the payment of permanent damages to plaintiffs which would compensate them for the total economic loss to their property present and future caused by defendant's operations. For reasons which will be developed the court chooses the latter alternative.

If the injunction were to be granted unless within a short period — e.g., 18 months — the nuisance be abated by improved methods, there would be no assurance that any significant technical improvement would occur.

The parties could settle this private litigation at any time if defendant paid enough money and the imminent threat of closing the plant would build up the pressure on defendant. If there were no improved techniques found, there would inevitably be applications to the court at Special Term for extensions of time to perform on showing of good faith efforts to find such techniques.

Moreover, techniques to eliminate dust and other annoying by-products of cement making are unlikely to be developed by any research the defendant can undertake within any short period, but will depend on the total resources of the cement industry nationwide and throughout the world. The problem is universal wherever cement is made.

For obvious reasons the rate of the research is beyond control of defendant. If at the end of 18 months the whole industry has not found a technical solution a court would be hard put to close down this one cement plant if due regard be given to equitable principles.

---

*Respondent's investment in the plant is in excess of $45,000,000. There are over 300 people employed there.

On the other hand, to grant the injunction unless defendant pays plaintiffs such permanent damages as may be fixed by the court seems to do justice between the contending parties. All of the attributions of economic loss to the properties on which plaintiffs' complaints are based will have been redressed.

The nuisance complained of by these plaintiffs may have other public or private consequences, but these particular parties are the only ones who have sought remedies and the judgment proposed will fully redress them. The limitation of relief granted is a limitation only within the four corners of these actions and does not foreclose public health or other public agencies from seeking proper relief in a proper court.

It seems reasonable to think that the risk of being required to pay permanent damages to injured property owners by cement plant owners would itself be a reasonably effective spur to research for improved techniques to minimize nuisance.

The power of the court to condition on equitable grounds the continuance of an injunction on the payment of permanent damages seems undoubted. . . .

There is some parallel to the conditioning of an injunction on the payment of permanent damages in the noted "elevated railway cases" (Pappenheim v. Metropolitan El. Ry. Co., 128 N.Y. 436, 28 N.E. 518 and others which followed). Decisions in these cases were based on the finding that the railways created a nuisance as to adjacent property owners, but in lieu of enjoining their operation, the court allowed permanent damages.

Judge Finch, reviewing these cases in Ferguson v. Village of Hamburg, 272 N.Y. 234, 239-240, 5 N.E.2d 801, 803, said: "The courts decided that the plaintiffs had a valuable right which was being impaired, but did not grant an absolute injunction or require the railway companies to resort to separate condemnation proceedings. Instead they held that a court of equity could ascertain the damages and grant an injunction which was not to be effective unless the defendant failed to pay the amount fixed as damages for the past and permanent injury inflicted."

Thus it seems fair to both sides to grant permanent damages to plaintiffs which will terminate this private litigation. The theory of damage is the "servitude on land" of plaintiffs imposed by defendant's nuisance. . . .

The judgment, by allowance of permanent damages imposing a servitude on land, which is the basis of the actions, would preclude future recovery by plaintiffs or their grantees.

This should be placed beyond debate by a provision of the judgment that the payment by defendant and the acceptance by plaintiffs of permanent damages found by the court shall be in compensation for a servitude on the land. . . .

The orders should be reversed, without costs, and the cases remitted to Supreme Court, Albany County to grant an injunction which shall be vacated upon payment by defendant of such amounts of permanent damage to the respective plaintiffs as shall for this purpose be determined by the court.

JANSEN, J. (dissenting). . . .

The specific problem faced here is known as particulate contamination because of the fine dust particles emanating from defendant's cement plant. The particular type of nuisance is not new, having appeared in many cases for at least the past 60 years. It is interesting to note that cement production has recently been identified as a significant source of particulate contamination in the Hudson Valley. This type of pollution, wherein very small particles escape and stay in the atmosphere, has been denominated as the type of air pollution which produces the greatest hazard to human health. We have thus a nuisance which not only is damaging to the plaintiffs, but also is decidedly harmful to the general public.

I see grave dangers in overruling our long-established rule of granting an injunction where a nuisance results in substantial continuing damage. In permitting the injunction to become inoperative upon the payment of permanent damages, the majority is, in effect, licensing a continuing wrong. It is the same as saying to the cement company, you may continue to do harm to your neighbors so long as you pay a fee for it. Furthermore, once such permanent damages are assessed and paid, the incentive to alleviate the wrong would be eliminated, thereby continuing air pollution of an area without abatement. . . .

This kind of inverse condemnation may not be invoked by a private person or corporation for private gain or advantage. Inverse condemnation should only be permitted when the public is primarily served in the taking or impairment of property. The promotion of the interests of the polluting cement company has, in my opinion, no public use or benefit.

Nor is it constitutionally permissible to impose servitude on land, without consent of the owner, by payment of permanent damages where the continuing impairment of the land is for a private use. This is made clear by the State Constitution which provides that "[p]rivate property shall not be taken for *public use* without just compensation" (emphasis added). It is, of course, significant that the section makes no mention of taking for a *private* use. . . .

I would enjoin the defendant cement company from continuing the discharge of dust particles upon its neighbors' properties unless, within 18 months, the cement company abated this nuisance.

It is not my intention to cause the removal of the cement plant from the Albany area, but to recognize the urgency of the problem stemming from this stationary source of air pollution, and to allow the company a specified period of time to develop a means to alleviate this nuisance.

I am aware that the trial court found that the most modern dust control devices available have been installed in defendant's plant, but, I submit, this does not mean that *better* and more effective dust control devices could not be developed within the time allowed to abate the pollution.

Moreover, I believe it is incumbent upon the defendant to develop such devices, since the cement company, at the time the plant commenced production (1962), was well aware of the plaintiffs' presence in the area, as well as the probable consequences of its contemplated operation. Yet, it still chose to build and operate the plant at this site.

In a day when there is a growing concern for clean air, highly developed industry should not expect acquiescence by the courts, but should, instead, plan its operations to eliminate contamination of our air and damage to its neighbors. . . .

Notes

1. Though not cited in either opinion in *Boomer*, an earlier New York decision, Bentley v. Empire Portland Cement Co., 48 Misc. Rep. 457, 96 N.Y. Supp. 831 (Sup. Ct. 1905), had refused to issue an injunction on facts strikingly similar to those in *Boomer*. Defendant's cement plant, with a capital value of $650,000 (a large sum in 1905), emitted dust and ashes that reduced the annual rental value of plaintiff's premises by about $25. The plant was located in a sparsely settled community and employed "the most improved apparatus." The dust and ashes were held a nuisance, but injunctive relief was denied. The court quoted approvingly a statement in an earlier case that "where an injunction would cause serious injury to an individual or the community at large and a relatively slight benefit to the party asking its interposition, injunctive relief will be denied and the parties left to their remedy at law." Id. at 464, 96 N.Y. Supp. at 835. Other "balancing" cases are collected in 40 A.L.R.3d 601 (1971).

2. Did the court in *Boomer* make any effort to distinguish *Whalen?* Did it overrule the earlier decision, or can the cases be reconciled?

3. The majority describes the relief that it orders as the creation of a "servitude"; the dissent describes it as "inverse condemnation." A servitude is an interest in real property equivalent to an easement. Inverse condemnation refers to the situation where, instead of the condemnor bringing suit to condemn some property interest, the property owner sues alleging that some act of the defendant amounts to condemnation and that plaintiff is therefore entitled to the same compensation he would have received had defendant brought a condemnation proceeding against him. For an application of this principle in an airplane-noise nuisance case, see Thornburg v. Port of Portland, 223 Or. 178, 376 P.2d 100 (1962). Other courts reach the same result under the rubric of "permanent nuisance," i.e., a nuisance they will not abate by injunction, instead remitting the victims of the nuisance to damages. See, e.g., Northern Indiana Public Service Co. v. W.J. & M.S. Vesey, 210 Ind. 338, 200 N.E. 620 (1936). Under any of these approaches, plaintiff is awarded a lump sum representing the present value of his future anticipated damages

from the nuisance; having received this lump sum, he cannot thereafter complain about the nuisance.

This approach is criticized in Baxter & Altree, Legal Aspects of Airport Noise, 15 J. Law & Econ. 1 (1972). The authors point out that once the defendant has acquired a permanent right to pollute, he no longer has any incentive to explore means of reducing or eliminating the pollution. They suggest time-limited rather than permanent easements, to give the polluter an incentive to continue searching for cost-justified methods of pollution abatement. The point is correct, but incomplete. While time-limited easements preserve the polluter's incentives to search for cost-justified methods of pollution abatement, they reduce the pollutee's incentives to do so. He knows that if he discovers some method of reducing the harm to him from the pollution, the payment he is entitled to receive from the polluter will fall in the next period. A permanent easement preserves the victim's incentives. He has been paid in full for the expected harm from the pollution; if he discovers some method of reducing the harm, he keeps the entire benefits of the discovery.

But is not the deeper economic point that it does not matter whether permanent or time-limited easements, daily damages or permanent injunctions, or any other type of remedy is granted? The parties will bargain to an efficient solution of their competing land uses whatever the assignment of rights and remedies. This is not a problem for Baxter and Altree, because they are discussing the problem of airport noise, which involves numerous victims and therefore high transaction costs. In such a case, to grant a broad injunction at the behest of one or a few of the victims could have serious misallocative consequences. To get the injunction dissolved because the cost to the airport was greater than the total costs to the victims of the airport noise, the airport would have to negotiate with every one of the victims, since an injunction in favor of a single victim would as effectively prevent the airport from operating as an injunction in favor of thousands of them. Knowing this, each victim will have an incentive to be the last to settle with the airport, for the last hold-out can be expected to obtain the highest settlement. (In the last negotiation, the airport is faced with the prospect of having nothing to show for all the money it has paid out in previous settlements with the victims of its noise, unless it can induce the last hold-out to settle with it.) With each victim vying to be last, negotiations are apt to break down. The large-number hold-out case is an important source of high transaction costs, rendering the Coase theorem inapplicable.

If we accept the view of the dissenting judge in Boomer regarding the pervasiveness of cement-dust pollution in the Hudson Valley, then even though there were only seven plaintiffs in Boomer it may be that many other people could have sought and obtained injunctions against defendant if the court had followed Whalen. But, interestingly, even if the parties before the court were the only victims of defendant's activity, or the only victims who could sue defendant successfully, the costs of transacting around an injunction would have been high. The problem is what is called in economics "bilateral monopoly." This refers to a case where two parties can deal only with each other. If the court grants an injunction to Boomer (let's simplify the analysis by assuming there was just one plaintiff whose aggregate damages were $185,000) against the Atlantic Cement Company, and negotiations ensue to transfer Boomer's injunctive right to Atlantic, Boomer and Atlantic are the only possible transactors. There is no market in injunctions to which Boomer and Atlantic can resort; no market determines the price at which to transact.

This creates a problem. The injunction is worth a minimum of $185,000 to Boomer; that is the amount of injury to him that it prevents. Therefore he will not agree to lift the injunction for less than $185,000. The value to Atlantic of lifting the injunction is the cost to it if it has to comply with the injunction. Assume that it can comply only by closing the plant, that the market value of the plant is equal to Atlantic's investment in it, said by the court to exceed $45 million (assume it's exactly $45 million), and that the plant has no salvage value if it is closed. Then the most that Atlantic will pay to lift the injunction is $45 million.

There is thus an enormous bargaining range. At any price for lifting the injunction between $185,000 and $45 million, both parties will be better off. It might seem that with such a large range, a settlement that will result in lifting the injunction is inevitable. But the very size of the range makes it possible that the settlement negotiations will break down; more probably, negotiations will be very costly. Each party will want to engross as much as possible of the bargaining range — Boomer by bargaining Atlantic up near $45 million, Atlantic by bargaining Boomer down near $185,000. With the stakes so large, each party can be expected to spend heavily in time and legal and other negotiating expenses to drive the best possible bargain. Transaction costs will not be trivial. An inefficient allocation of resources (i.e., closing the plant) may result.

For a lucid discussion of the relative economic merits of damages and injunctions in nuisance cases, see Polinsky, Resolving Nuisance Disputes: The Simple Economics of Injunctive and Damage Remedies, 32 Stan. L. Rev. 1075 (1980). Polinsky's article also contains extensive references to other economic discussions of these questions.

Rhodes v. Dunbar
57 Pa. 274 (1868)

THOMPSON, C.J. The plaintiffs by their bill seek to enjoin the defendants from re-erecting or reconstructing a planing-mill, late the property of John D. Jones, situate on the west side of Twenty-first street, between Chestnut and Market streets, which was destroyed by fire in the month of May

1867. It is claimed, that if re-erected it will be a nuisance to the property and dwellings of the complainants, impairing their value, and rendering the enjoyment of them uncomfortable and unsafe; and this, it is alleged, will flow from three causes, incident to the structure, and its intended use if it be permitted to go into operation, viz.: . . . 3d, danger from fire. The very general averment in the bill that the mode in which such a factory or mill is worked renders it unsuited to a neighborhood closely built up, and especially to one occupied by handsome buildings used as residences, and will be calculated to prevent the use of the neighboring ground "for such buildings as would in the ordinary course of affairs, and the extension of the city in that direction, be put up," presents for consideration a subject not within our sphere of judicial action. It presents a question of policy whether a part or portion of a city ought to be devoted exclusively to private residences or other special objects; and that is manifestly for the local authorities or the legislature to determine, and not us. That concerns alone the public, and not private parties. With people's *rights* we deal in cases like the present, and not with questions of mere policy, local or general.

No one will for a moment doubt that we are invested with ample powers to restrain the erection of any building or structure intended for a purpose which will be a nuisance per se; such as bone-boiling, horse-boiling establishments, swine-yards, or pig-styes, and other various like establishments. These not only interfere with the health, but, if they do not reach to that, they do to the usual and ordinary enjoyment of the residences of inhabitants coming within the circle of atmosphere tainted by them, and both property and persons may be prejudiced or injured thereby. The right to claim that such establishments shall be prevented, is the right that every citizen has to pure and wholesome air, at least as pure as it may be, consistent with the compact nature of the community in which he lives. The rule is the same in regard to noises which disturb rest and prevent sleep. There are innumerable cases of injunction for such causes. . . .

Danger, or apprehension of danger from fire, is the last point to be noticed, and this seems to have been really the main ground of decision in the mind of the master, as well as our learned brother, in awarding an injunction.

What is apprehension? It is anticipation of danger, not a certainty that it will occur. It may be felt as well when danger is infinitely remote as when it is near, as well when it may never occur as when it may. It is in regard to fire, "speculative, eventual and contingent," and the books say this is never a ground for interference by injunction. The apprehension of danger must, on the theory of this case at least, be very remote, viz.: that the mill when erected may take fire by negligence, accident or by the work of an incendiary; that the fire may not be extinguished — and that it may be communicated to, and burn the property of the plaintiffs and endanger their lives. Every element in all this is "speculative, contingent and eventual." The mill might take fire, but the flames may be extinguished; and it might be burned down without destroying the property of anybody else. It would be a waste of time I think to labor to prove what every one must assent to, that this as a ground to exercise the power to prevent the occupation and enjoyment of property, would be extremely intangible, and once established as to this kind of mill, might be applied to every other building or business in community, described in fire risks, or known as extra-hazardous, and not only planing-mills, but chemical laboratories, carpenter shops, cotton-mills, barns, stables, in short everything that there might be ground to apprehend danger of fire from, would gradually fall into the vortex of chancery power, and might be banished the city altogether, to the great inconvenience of the people. . . .

But it is said that the rate of insurance upon the plaintiffs' property will be increased as a consequence of the re-erection of this mill. If this fact had been found by the master, it would not have established the point of nuisance. It is well known that the existence of extra-hazardous property in a neighborhood, while it draws upon itself a heavier burthen or rate of insurance, does not usually constitute special rates in regard to proximate property belonging to a class with fixed rates. But it is stated very distinctly in Story's Equity Jurisprudence, §925, that mere diminution in the value of property, without irreparable mischief, will not furnish any foundation for equitable relief. . . .

Grant that the species of property in question is extra-hazardous; is subject to fires; this, on the authority of all the cases, would not render it a nuisance. It does not necessarily affect health, comfort or the ordinary uses and enjoyment of property in the neighborhood. If the business be lawful, and carried on reasonably, and does not interfere in either of these ways with the rights of others, it cannot be a nuisance in fact or in anticipation, and, in my opinion, we have no authority whatever to interfere with it.

These observations give no just grounds to draw the inference that a powder magazine, or depot of nitro-glycerine, or other like explosive materials, might not possibly be enjoined even if not prohibited, as they usually are, by ordinance or law. It is not on the ground alone of their liability to fire, primarily or even secondarily, that they may possibly be dealt with as nuisances, but on account of their liability to explosion by contact with the smallest spark of fire, and the utter impossibility to guard against the consequences, or set bounds to the injury which, being instantaneous, extends alike to property and person within its reach. The destructiveness of these agents results from the irrepressible gases once set in motion infinitely more than from fires which might ensue as a consequence. Persons and property in the neighborhood of a burning building, let it burn ever so fiercely, in most cases have a chance of escaping injury. Not so when explosive forces instantly prostrate everything near them, as in the instances of powder, nitro-glycerine, and other chemicals of an explosive or intensely inflammable nature.

It is a difficult matter at all times to strike the true medium between the conflicting interests and tastes of people in a densely populated city. It requires the merchant, mechanic, manufacturer, baker, butcher and laborer, as well as the wealthy and employed or unemployed citizen, to constitute a city. They all have rights, and the only requirement of the law is, that each shall so exercise and enjoy them as to do no injury in that enjoyment to others, or the rights of others, in the sense in which the law regards injury, namely, accompanied by damage. It might be a great injury to the defendants in this case to restrain them from the enjoyment of their property, without being of any benefit to the plaintiffs. The ground claimed in argument to sustain the decree in this case was mainly the danger of fire. The proof is, that these are dangerous establishments, by comparison with others less dangerous — but there is proof that they do not always burn, and may never burn. In this state of the case, the language of Lord Brougham in The Earl of Ripon v. Hobart, is worthy a reference to here: "It is also," said his lordship, "very material to observe, what is indeed strong authority of a negative kind, that no instance can be produced of the intervention by injunction, in the case of what we have been regarding as *eventual* or *contingent* nuisances." We have said enough to indicate our opinion that the fear of fire is of this description, and that this injunction should not have been granted originally, and therefore that the decree must be reversed, and bill dismissed. . . .

Note

Why should not the only issue have been whether rebuilding defendants' mill near plaintiffs' property would reduce the value of plaintiffs' property by more than it increased the value of defendants' property?

Everett v. Paschall
61 Wash. 47, 111 P. 879 (1910)

CHADWICK, J. The findings of the trial judge show that plaintiffs are the owners of, and reside upon, lot 14, block 19, Madison Park addition to the city of Seattle, in King county; that their property is of the value of $2,000. Defendant is the owner of the south half of lots 12 and 13, block 9, upon which a cottage is situated. An alleyway separates plaintiffs' lot from the fractional lots of the defendant. On November 29, 1909, defendant opened, and has since maintained in his cottage, a private sanitarium for the treatment and care of persons afflicted with tuberculosis. The sanitarium has a capacity for accommodating 10 patients, and, since opening, there have been from 4 to 10 patients under treatment. The court found also, that the Madison Park addition is an established residential portion of the city; that the danger zone of tuberculosis is about three feet, beyond which there is no danger of infection or contagion; that pulmonary tuberculosis is a germ disease, thriving only in warmth and darkness, and propagating only in living animals; that the germ is destroyed by exposure to daylight without and suffused light within rooms in from a few minutes to a few hours; that the danger can be reduced to a negligible quantity by proper care of the expectorants and disinfection of the vessels used by the patients, their clothing, and the surroundings; that defendant was conducting his sanitarium with a due regard for the safety of his patients and the public; that there was no danger to persons living in the immediate vicinity; that the sanitarium had been in the past, and would in all probability continue to be, a great benefit to the community. After finding that the best results could be obtained only by locating the sanitarium within easy reach of the attending physicians, and within easy access of markets where proper food could be obtained, the court found also: "That the disease of pulmonary tuberculosis is very prevalent, and that one-seventh of the deaths in the United States are caused by pulmonary tuberculosis; . . . that said sanitarium conducted by the defendant is not a menace to the plaintiffs, or either of them, or to any person living in any building which may hereafter be erected upon the lots owned by the plaintiffs; . . . that the germs of tuberculosis may be carried by house flies from the sputum of consumptives; . . . that there exists a general public dread of tuberculosis, and the maintenance of a tubercular hospital in the vicinity of residences detracts from the comfortable use of such residential property, on account of the dread of contagion therefrom in the minds of persons ignorant of the true nature of the disease and the harmlessness of such sanitaria; . . . that the plaintiff's property will, by the maintenance of said sanitarium, be less salable and lessened in value from $33\frac{1}{3}$ per cent. to 50 per cent. and the other property in said neighborhood will be lessened in value in decreasing ratio, depending upon the distance located from said sanitarium." . . .

[On the basis of these findings, the trial court dismissed the complaint.]

. . . If dread of the disease and fear induced by the proximity of the sanitarium, in fact, disturb the comfortable enjoyment of the property of the appellants, we question our right to say that the fear is unfounded or unreasonable, when it is shared by the whole public to such an extent that property values are diminished. The question is, not whether the fear is founded in science, but whether it exists; not whether it is imaginary, but whether it is real, in that it affects the movements and conduct of men. Such fears are actual, and must be recognized by the courts as other emotions of the human mind. That fear is real in the sense indicated, and is the most essentially human of all emotions, there can be no doubt. . . . Alfred Capus, the psychological playwright, says: "Fear consists in capitulating to the instinct of self-preservation." . . . "Comfortable enjoyment" means mental quiet as well as physical comfort. . . . Regard should be had for the notions of comfort and convenience entertained by persons generally of ordinary tastes and susceptibilities. The nuisance and discomfort must affect the ordinary comfort of human existence as understood by the American people in their present state of enlightenment. The theories and dogmas of scientific men, though provable by scientific reference, cannot be held to be controlling unless shared by the people generally. . . . This principle applies with peculiar force in this case; for aside from the general dread of the disease, as found by the court, it is also shown that the security of the public depends upon proper precautions and sanitation, which may at any time be relaxed by incautious nurses or careless or ignorant patients.

Furthermore, the court found that the bacilla of the disease may be carried by house flies. Thus every house fly that might drone a summer afternoon in the drawing room or nursery is a constant reminder to plaintiffs of their neighbor, tending to disquiet the mind and render the enjoyment of their home uncomfortable. . . .

We therefore conclude that the lower court erred in denying an injunction. The case is remanded with instructions to enter a decree upon the findings in favor of appellant.

Notes

1. Funeral homes in residential areas have frequently been found to be nuisances. See, e.g., Williams v. Montgomery, 184 Miss. 547, 186 So. 302 (1939). Is the funeral-home case a stronger or a weaker case for finding a nuisance than *Everett*? Is *Rhodes* distinguishable from either?

2. In Puritan Holding Co. v. Holloschitz, 82 Misc. 2d 905, 372 N.Y.S.2d 500 (Sup. Ct. 1975), an abandoned building that was being used by derelicts and impairing property values in the neighborhood was held to be a nuisance. But in Fontainebleau Hotel Corp. v. Forty-Five Twenty-Five, Inc., 114 So. 2d 357 (Fla. App. 1959), where defendant built a hotel that cut off the sunlight to the swimming and sunbathing areas of a neighboring hotel, the court held there was no nuisance, even if defendant was motivated by spite. What earlier case in this chapter does *Fontainebleau* resemble? Can it be distinguished from *Williams, Everett,* or *Puritan* on causal grounds? On any other grounds?

Yet some jurisdictions grant relief on nuisance principles for harm caused by "spite fences." In Hutcherson v. Alexander, 264 Cal. App. 126, 70 Cal. Rptr. 366 (1968), for example, defendant, who was a competitor of plaintiffs', raised the fence that divided his property from plaintiffs' in order to hide plaintiffs' premises from view from the public highway; this was held to be a nuisance. See also Sundowner, Inc. v. King, 95 Idaho 367, 509 P.2d 785 (1973); Brittingham v. Robertson, 280 A.2d 741 (Del. Ch. 1971). Can this result be reconciled with that in the *Fontainebleau* case? Could it be predicated on a tort theory other than that of nuisance?

Sturges v. Bridgman
11 Ch. 852 (1879)

THESIGER, L.J. . . .

The Defendant in this case is the occupier, for the purpose of his business as a confectioner, of a house in Wigmore Street. In the rear of the house is a kitchen, and in that kitchen there are now, and have been for over twenty years, two large mortars in which the meat and other materials of the confectionery are pounded. The Plaintiff, who is a physician, is the occupier of a house in Wimpole Street, which until recently had a garden in the rear, the wall of which garden was a party-wall between the Plaintiff's and the Defendant's premises, and formed the back wall of the Defendant's kitchen. The Plaintiff has, however, recently built upon the site of the garden a consulting-room, one of the side walls of which is the wall just described. It has been proved that in the case of the mortars, before and at the time of action brought, a noise was caused which seriously inconvenienced the Plaintiff in the use of his consulting-room, and which, unless the Defendant had acquired a right to impose the inconvenience, would constitute an actionable nuisance. . . .

. . . Prior to the erection of the consulting-room no material annoyance or inconvenience was caused to the Plaintiff or to any previous occupier of the Plaintiff's house by what the Defendant did. . . . [Therefore, the court explains, defendant did not acquire a noise easement by prescription, i.e., by passage of time. Since defendant's noise did not harm plaintiff before the latter build his consulting room, plaintiff could not have taken legal action against the noise. Therefore his consent to the noise could not be presumed from his failure to take such action; and without consent or acquiescence, defendant could not have acquired an easement by prescription.]

It is said that if this principle is applied in cases like the present, and were carried out to its logical consequences, it would result in the most serious practical inconveniences, for a man might go — say into the midst of the tanneries of Bermondsey, or into any other locality devoted to a particular trade or manufacture of a noisy or unsavoury character, and, by building a private residence upon a vacant piece of land, put a stop to such trade or manufacture altogether. The case also is put of a blacksmith's forge built away from all habitations, but to which, in course of time, habitations approach. We do not think that either of these hypothetical cases presents any real difficulty. As regards the first, it may be answered that whether anything is a nuisance or not is a question to be determined, not merely by an abstract consideration of the thing itself, but in reference to its circumstances; what would be a nuisance in Belgrave Square would not necessarily be so in Bermondsey; and where a locality is devoted to a particular trade or manufacture carried on by the traders or manufacturers in a particular and established manner not constituting a public nuisance, Judges and juries would be justified in finding, and may be trusted to find, that the trade or manufacture so carried on in that locality is not a private or actionable wrong. As regards the blacksmith's forge, that is really an idem per idem case with the present. It would be on the one hand in a very high degree unreasonable and undesirable that there should be a right of action for acts which are not in the present condition of the adjoining land, and possibly never will be any annoyance or inconvenience to either its owner or occupier; and it would be on the other hand in an equal degree unjust, and, from a public point of view, inexpedient that the use and value of the adjoining land should, for all time and under all circumstances, be restricted and diminished by reason of the continuance of acts incapable of physical interruption, and which the law gives no power to prevent. The smith in the case supposed might protect himself by taking a sufficient curtilage to ensure what he does from being at any time an annoyance to his neighbour, but the neighbour himself would be powerless in the matter. Individual cases of hardship may occur in the strict carrying out of the principle upon which we found our judgment, but the negation of the principle would lead even more to individual hardship, and would at the same time produce a prejudicial effect upon the development of land for residential purposes. The Master of the Rolls in the Court below took substantially the same view of the matter as ourselves and granted the relief which the Plaintiff prayed for [an injunction], and we are of opinion that his order is right and should be affirmed, and that this appeal should be dismissed with costs.

Notes

1. Most courts, though not all, have agreed with *Sturges* that a plaintiff is not barred from maintaining a nuisance action by the fact that he bought or built after the nuisance; "coming to the nuisance" is not a defense. See Annot., "Coming to Nuisance" as a Defense or Estoppel, 42 A.L.R.3d 344 (1972). This result seems correct on economic grounds (though *Sturges* itself is one of the cases that Coase used to demonstrate the irrelevance of the assignment of liability to the allocation of resources). As Lord Justice Thesiger suggested, any other rule would (assuming high transaction costs) freeze land development in its current uses. See Wittman, First Come, First Served: An Economic Analysis of "Coming to the Nuisance," 9 J. Legal Stud. 557 (1980).

2. Are you worried that plaintiff in *Sturges* may have gotten a windfall? When plaintiff acquired his property, the price he paid presumably contained a discount reflecting the costs, current and anticipated, resulting from defendant's noisy machinery; plaintiff was therefore compensated for bearing those costs. When he gets the noise enjoined, and his property increases in value as a result, he receives double compensation — or does he? If the law of nuisance was well settled, then plaintiff knew when he acquired his property that he could obtain an injunction if he put the property to a noise-sensitive use; he would not have demanded a discount. Are we imputing excessive foresight to the plaintiff?

In light of this analysis, consider the approach to the coming to the nuisance question taken in Spur Industries, Inc. v. Del E. Webb Development Co., 108 Ariz. 178, 494 P.2d 700 (1972). Spur had a cattle feedlot in a rural area. Webb constructed a residential development nearby and sought to enjoin Spur's operation, from which flies and odors were blowing into the development. The court held that Webb was entitled to the injunction sought, but that, "Having brought people to the nuisance to the foreseeable detriment of Spur, Webb must indemnify Spur for a reasonable amount of the cost of moving or shutting down." Id. at 186, 494 P.2d at 708. What is the legal basis for this result? Does the result give Spur a windfall? What is the economic difference, if any, between the court's result and simply refusing to issue the injunction requested by Webb? On these questions compare Michelman, Property, Utility, and Fairness: Comments on the Ethical Foundations of "Just Compensation" Law, 80 Harv. L. Rev. 1165, 1197-1201, 1237-1244 (1967); Michelman, Book Review, 80 Yale L.J. 647 (1971).

Gronn v. Rogers Construction, Inc.
221 Or. 226, 350 P.2d 1086 (1960)

O'CONNELL, J.

The plaintiffs bring this action to recover damages to their mink herd alleged to have been caused by vibrations, concussion and noise resulting from the defendant's operations in connection with the construction of a road. Plaintiffs appeal from a judgment of involuntary nonsuit.

Plaintiffs own and operate a mink ranch near Clatskanie, Oregon. Defendant, under a contract with the State Highway Department, was engaged in highway construction work near plaintiffs' ranch. In connection with this work defendant engaged in blasting operations at a quarry located approximately one-third of a mile from plaintiffs' ranch. The defendant operated rock-crushing equipment at the quarry site and the rock was then hauled by large mobile conveyors to the road under construction. Plaintiffs allege that the discharge of the explosives at the quarry and the noise and vibration from the rock-crushing equipment and trucks frightened and excited the mink as a result of which a large number of mink kittens were stillborn or stunted in growth, and some of the adult mink were rendered less valuable because they became useless for breeding stock and because of the reduction in the quality of the pelts.

It was shown that the nature of the mink is such that loud and unusual noises or concussions at the time of whelping are likely to cause the female mink to produce stillborn kittens and to neglect or abandon those kittens which are born alive.

Plaintiffs allege two causes of action. . . . In the second case of action, based upon the theory of nuisance, it is alleged that the discharge of explosives, the operation of the rock-crushing equipment and hauling operations caused noises and concussions of great violence and frequency which resulted in the alleged damage. . . .

The defendant relies upon the principle stated in Amphitheaters, Inc. v. Portland Meadows, 1948, 184 Or. 336, 198 P.2d 847, that a landowner "cannot increase the liabilities of his neighbor by applying his own property to special and delicate uses, whether for business or pleasure."

In weighing the conflicting interests of persons using land it is certainly appropriate to take into consideration the fact that the plaintiffs' use is sensitive in character. But a sensitive use is entitled to protection if the conduct of the defendant is unreasonable with respect to that sensitive use. It seems obvious, therefore, that the principle stated in terms of sensitivity of use is nothing more than an emphasis upon one aspect of the general weighing process which must be employed to determine where the balance of interests lies. . . .

Both plaintiffs and defendant were engaged in legitimate uses of property. According to the accepted standards of our society defendant's conduct in constructing a public highway would, undoubtedly, be deemed of greater social value than plaintiffs' operation of a mink farm. However, this fact would not give the defendant a license to carry on its project without regard to the character of plaintiffs' business. This is illustrated in two fairly recent cases involving damage to mink as a result of blasting operations by the defendant. In MacGibbon v. Robinson, [1953] 2 D.L.R. 689, the defendant, in clearing his land, blasted out tree trunks with dynamite. He knew that plaintiffs were operating a mink farm near-by, and he also knew of the propensity of mink, if disturbed by loud noises, to harm their kittens. As a result of defendant's blasting operations plaintiffs' mink were harmed. In holding that the defendant was liable the court said: "The evidence shows that there was no occasion for him to fire the shots during the whelping season. . . . The whelping season would only last a month. There was not the slightest necessity for blasting the two stumps in question at the time he did. It was only at this special period that the blasting would injure the plaintiffs' mink."

Here it will be observed the factor of the defendant's ability to avoid the harm tipped the scale in favor of the plaintiffs. Very possibly the court may have considered the economic importance of the mink industry in Canada, but that factor was not expressly relied upon in the opinion.

Another Canadian case with facts very similar to those of the present case is Mason v. Grandel, [1952] 1 D.L.R. 516. There the defendants were employed by the Department of Highways of the province of Saskatchewan to construct a road near plaintiff's mink farm. The work was done with noisy machinery during the whelping period as a result of which some of the females ate their young. Plaintiff had warned the defendants not to continue their operations and the engineer for the highway department instructed the resident engineer to cease construction on the road in front of plaintiff's farm, but through the error of the defendants' workmen the instruction was not followed and the work was carried on close to the plaintiff's mink sheds. The court held that the defendants were negligent in carrying on their operations with knowledge that the plaintiff's mink would be endangered. Here again the evidence established that it was practicable for the defendants to postpone their operations near plaintiff's farm during the whelping period. In other words, the defendants could have avoided the harm.

Considering the case at bar in light of the foregoing cases, particularly with reference to the question of defendant's fault in proceeding with his operations in face of the knowledge of its effect on plaintiffs' mink, we find substantially different circumstances. . . . The normal whelping season ran from the first part of May to May 20 or not later than May 25. Gronn first heard the noise from defendant's blasting in March. On March 15 he went to the resident engineer of the State Highway Department and made inquiry concerning the blasting operations. He was informed that the dynamiting would continue throughout the summer and that within a week or ten days a large charge would be set off. When Gronn asked if the large explosion could be delayed it was suggested that he see the foreman in charge of the blasting job. Gronn went to the quarry and asked the foreman when the charge would be set off. He was told that it would be "some time in the next week," approximately March 25. . . . Gronn requested a delay in setting off the charge until after April 1st and the defendant complied with the request. When plaintiff was notified that the charge would be set off there was no request for further delay. Under those circumstances the defendant would be justified in assuming that it could proceed to set off the charge without objection and without danger to the plaintiffs' operation. There is no evidence of any further warning by plaintiffs, either with respect to the first blast or any subsequent blasts. There is no evidence that any other blasts caused damage to the plaintiffs' mink. Under these circumstances the defendant cannot be charged with either negligence or intentional conduct to make out a case of nuisance. . . .

Judgment affirmed.

Notes

1. Suppose plaintiff had located his mink farm next to an airport, and the noise from the airport caused the mink kittens to be stillborn. Would he be barred from recovering damages by the principle alluded to in the opinion that damage to an abnormally sensitive land use is not actionable? If the answer is yes, how is the hypothetical case distinguishable from *Sturges*?

2. Is the abnormal-sensitivity concept an activity-level point? To say that a land use is abnormally sensitive is to say, is it not, that the cost to the user of relocating to another place is probably lower than the cost to the defendant of altering the use of his land. Suppose, however, that some activity is a conceded nuisance to normal as well as abnormally sensitive users of the surrounding land. Should the abnormally sensitive user be allowed to collect

his full damages from the actor or should his damages be limited to those of a land user of normal sensitivity?

3. In the *Amphitheaters* case referred to in *Gronn*, light from floodlights in a night horse-race track interfered with the proper showing of movies in plaintiff's drive-in theater, but the court invoked the abnormal-sensitivity principle in holding that there was no actionable nuisance. Is the idea of abnormal sensitivity useful in such a case?

4. Is *Gronn* perhaps best explained as a simple case of contributory negligence? On whether contributory negligence or some analogous plaintiff fault concept can be used in a nuisance case not itself based on negligence, see Cardozo's interesting opinion in McFarlane v. City of Niagara Falls, 247 N.Y. 340, 160 N.E. 391 (1928).

Woodland v. Portneuf Marsh Valley Irr. Co.
26 Idaho 789, 146 P. 1106 (1915)

DAVIS, J. In this action the plaintiff, John T. Woodland, sought to recover damages in the sum of $1,500 for loss of his hay crop, alleged to have been caused by the flooding of his land with water from the canal system owned and operated by the Portneuf-Marsh Valley Irrigation Company, a corporation. The jury awarded plaintiff $700 damages, and defendant appeals from the judgment of the lower court in plaintiff's favor for this amount and costs.

It is established by the evidence and admitted by the company that some water from its canals contributed toward the flow that overflowed Woodland's land and injured his hay. In defense it is contended by the company that the evidence does not show that the water wrongfully discharged from the canals or laterals of its irrigation system was sufficient by itself to overflow the channel of the creek through Woodland's land or cause any of the injury to his crops. But this is not a good defense, even though true, because where one contributes as an independent tort-feasor toward causing an injury, he will be liable for the injury done by him, although his acts or negligence alone might not have caused any injury. In this case the evidence tends to prove that there were at least six sources from which the water came that injured Woodland's hay, and it is not contended by him that the company was responsible for more than one. And, while the evidence is very indefinite as to the relative and specific amount of water from each source, it is sufficient to show that considerable water from the company's canals wrongfully ran into the creek that overflowed its banks and flooded Woodland's property. And every one who permits water to waste onto the land of others without right is liable for his proportionate share of the injury caused or the harm resulting therefrom, even though the water allowed to run down by each would do no harm if not combined with that of others, and the injury is caused by the combined flow, wherein the waters of all are mixed and indistinguishable. If the injury follows as the combined result of the wrongful acts of several, acting independently, recovery may be had severally against each of such independent tort-feasors in proportion to the contribution of each to the injury.

The evidence is sufficient to sustain a verdict in plaintiff's favor for the amount of damage caused by the company's waste water, where it appears, by a preponderance of the evidence, that the company wrongfully permitted waste water to mix with other waters and the combined flow spread over Woodland's land to his damage. Exact and definite measurements of such waters are not essential to sustain the verdict of a jury in determining what amount of damages a company should pay under such ciurcumstances as compensation for the injury caused by its part of such waters, although some evidence in that respect is essential. . . .

The judgement of the district court is therefore affirmed. . . .

Notes

1. Why were damages apportioned? Why was defendant not liable for all of plaintiff's damages under the no-contribution principle of joint-tortfeasor law, discussed in Chapter 8?

2. If the six sources of damage to plaintiff experience identical costs of avoiding the damage, and if these costs are constant over the relevant range, then apportionment makes economic sense. To illustrate, suppose each gallon of water from these sources above some limit imposes $1 in damage on plaintiff, and the cost of avoiding this damage is 98¢ per gallon no matter from whom the gallons are taken. Then if each is held liable for $250 in damages to the plaintiff, each will have an incentive to reduce his flow by 250 gallons and the optimal result will be achieved. But suppose one of the six could reduce his flow by the full 1,500 gallons at a total cost of only $100. Then it would clearly be more efficient for him to be liable for the entire damages, rather than for all six to be liable pro rata. How can this result be achieved within a common-law system? Cf. Polinsky, Strict Liability vs. Negligence in a Market Setting, 70 Am. Econ. Rev. (Papers & Proceedings) 363 (1980).

3. As intimated in the *Boomer* case, the general area of land use and pollution control is increasingly occupied by state and federal statutes; these are studied in courses on environmental law. For a good introduction to the economic issues involved in environmental regulation see W. J. Baumol & W. E. Oates, Economics, Environmental Policy, and the Quality of Life (1979). But it would be wrong to conclude that nuisance law is of declining importance in the environmental field; if anything, the opposite is true. Quite apart from the fact that an environmental statute may create an express or implied private right of action, the common law in its heyday did

not play an important role either in zoning (recall the discussion of this in Rhodes v. Dunbar) — other than through enforcement of restrictive covenants, which is not a part of tort law — or in pollution control. The common law traditionally was not very effective in situations where either victims or injurers were numerous and the injury to any one individual small or difficult to prove, though the aggregate damages might be huge. In such situations, the expected gain from suit is usually too small to motivate victims to sue. But modern innovations in procedure, in particular the class action (studied in other courses), have mitigated, if not entirely solved, this problem. For discussions of the class action from an economic standpoint, stressing its limitations, see Dam, Class Actions: Efficiency, Compensation, Deterrence, and Conflict of Interest, 4 J. Legal Stud. 47 (1975); R. A. Posner, Economic Analysis of Law 449-450 (2d ed. 1977). For a recent example of a nuisance class action, see National Sea Clammers Assn. v. City of New York, 616 F.2d 1222 (3d Cir. 1980). Another possibility is suit by a state on behalf of its citizens. See, e.g., State ex rel. Dresser Indus., Inc. v. Ruddy, 592 S.W.2d 789 (Mo. 1980). For a critical discussion of the impact of liberalized notions of standing to complain of public nuisances, as well as of the impact of the class action, on nuisance law, see Henderson, Expanding the Negligence Concept: Retreat from the Rule of Law, 51 Ind. L.J. 467, 495-501 (1976). The Henderson article contains a number of references to the literature on the use of nuisance law by the environmental movement.

Still another important development to be noted is the emergence of a "federal common law" of nuisance applicable to interstate water pollution. See Illinois v. Milwaukee, 406 U.S. 91 (1972). As a result of all these developments — state and federal environmental statutes, the expanded role of the class action, the development of federal common-law principles applicable to nuisance cases — nuisance litigation is increasingly complex, both procedurally and substantively, and is often dominated by issues of federal jurisdiction that are far beyond the scope of a course in tort law. For an example of such litigation, see Commonwealth of Puerto Rico v. S.S. Zoe Colocotroni, 628 F.2d 652 (1st Cir. 1980), a suit brought by the Commonwealth of Puerto Rico alleging ecological damage to a mangrove forest from an oil spill.

4. Another question is the overlap of nuisance with other torts. Noted earlier was the question of locomotive sparks: Are they actionable as a nuisance as well as under negligence and, perhaps, trespass theories? Was the *Oppen* case in Chapter 6 a nuisance or a negligence case, or both? Cf. Borland v. Sanders Lead Co., 369 So. 2d 523 (Ala. 1979), holding that where defendant's emission of lead particulates and sulfur dioxide rendered plaintiff's land unsuitable for raising crops, defendant was guilty of trespass, and not just nuisance. But cf. Ryan v. Emmetsburg, 232 Iowa 600, 4 N.W.2d 435 (1942), holding that an invasion of intangible substances such as noises or odors is a nuisance rather than a trespass. The law is in considerable ferment on this point. See Annot., Recovery in Trespass for Injury to Land Caused by

Airborne Pollutants, 2 A.L.R.4th 1054 (1980). What difference does it make whether a suit is for trespass or for nuisance?

Can the nuisance concept properly be used to avoid some of the causal limitations on negligence actions discussed in Chapter 8? Could it be used, for example, to abate a source of low-level damage, as from radiation, where a suit for damages for harm actually caused might be precluded by the impossibility of tracing a particular plaintiff's illness to the defendant's activity? See Crowther v. Seaborg, 312 F. Supp. 1205 (D. Colo. 1970); United States v. Reserve Mining Co., 380 F. Supp. 11, 16 (D. Minn. 1974), modified and remanded on other grounds sub nom. Reserve Mining Co. v. Environmental Protection Agency, 514 F.2d 492, 532 (8th Cir. 1975). The district court held in *Reserve* that the discharge of asbestos fibers into Lake Superior constituted a common-law nuisance because of the danger to health posed thereby; the court of appeals found it unnecessary to decide this issue. See, generally, Milhollin, Long-Term Liability for Environmental Harm, 41 U. Pitt. L. Rev. 1 (1979).

Orchard View Farms, Inc. v. Martin Marietta Aluminum, Inc.
500 F. Supp. 984 (D. Or. 1980)

BURNS, C.J. . . .

On March 31, 1971, Orchard View Farms, Inc. (Orchard View) filed this trespass action, seeking compensatory and punitive damages for injuries to its orchards between March 31, 1965 and the filing date. These injuries were alleged to have been caused by fluoride emitted from the aluminum reduction plant operated by Martin Marietta Aluminum, Inc. (the company or Martin Marietta). In April and May, 1973, the case was tried to a jury, which awarded Orchard View $103,655 compensatory damages and $250,000 punitive damages. The company appealed this judgment on numerous grounds.

The Ninth Circuit affirmed the award of compensatory damages but reversed and remanded the punitive damages award because in various rulings at the trial I erroneously admitted evidence of certain events that had occurred before the 1965-71 claim period, events which had been insufficiently linked by the evidence to the company's conduct and policies during the claim period. . . .

In a world where all costs of production were borne by the enterprise, determining whether a firm produced a net benefit, or at least not a net detriment, to society would be as simple as examining the company's balance sheet of income and expenses. In the real world the task is more complex, because enterprises can sometimes shift a portion of their costs of production onto others. In the case of an industrial plant emitting pollution, those harmed by the emissions are, in effect, involuntarily bearing some of the firm's production costs.

Our society has not demanded that such externalized costs of production be completely eliminated. Instead, we tolerate externalities such as pollution as long as the enterprise remains productive: that is, producing greater value than the total of its internalized and externalized costs of production. A business that does not achieve net productivity is harmful to society, detracting from the standard of living it is designed to enhance. Because firms can sometimes impose a portion of their production costs upon others, the mere fact that a company continues to operate at a profit is not in itself conclusive evidence that it produces a net benefit to society.

Our system of law attempts to ensure that businesses are, on balance, socially beneficial by requiring that each enterprise bear its total production costs, as accurately as those costs can be ascertained. A fundamental means to this end is the institution of tort liability, which requires that persons harmed by business or other activity be compensated by the perpetrator of the damage. In the context of pollution, however, the tort system does not always operate smoothly to impose liability for compensatory damages. Among the difficulties encountered are: (1) that the harm may be gradual or otherwise difficult to perceive; (2) that the cause of the harm may be difficult to trace to the pollution and from the pollution to its source; and (3) that the harm may be inflicted in small amounts upon a large number of people, none of whom individually suffer sufficient damage to warrant the time and expense of legal action and whose organization into a plaintiff class is hindered by what has come to be known as the tragedy of the commons.[1]

Because of these impediments to smooth operation of the tort system and to ensuring that each enterprise bears its own costs of production, the law imposes upon businesses a societal obligation not to obstruct legal procedures designed to provide compensation to persons harmed by externalized costs of production. Enterprises must cooperate with their neighbors in ascertaining the nature, severity and scope of the harm and in arranging to prevent the damage or to neutralize it through some form of compensation.

A breach of societal obligations justifies the imposition of punitive damages to deter uncooperative behavior that impedes the legal system from ensuring that enterprises produce a net benefit to society. . . .

The company did not fulfill its societal obligation to adopt and maintain reasonable, efficient pollution control measures. Having located the plant in a rich agricultural district, the company did not diligently monitor the plant's

---

1. Organizing a plaintiff class is hindered by the fact that the benefit of a successful lawsuit against the polluter for compensation is not limited to the plaintiffs. Persons damaged by the pollution but not contributing to the legal action also benefit due to the collateral estoppel effects of the initial lawsuit in subsequent actions and because the first plaintiff or group of plaintiffs has already done the work of organizing some relevant evidence and locating experts willing to testify. Thus, each person damaged by the pollution has an economic incentive to let someone else bring the first lawsuit and then to take a "free ride" or at least a discount excursion to obtaining his own compensation.

emissions nor the ambient concentrations of fluoride in the surrounding orchards. Nor did the company implement before or during the 1965-71 claim period efficient available methods for reducing the emissions. In particular, the company did not adopt cell operating procedures to minimize the escape of fumes from the primary collection system until several years after the end of the claim period, did not install wet electrostatic precipitators in the primary treatment system until 1972, and did not utilize a forced-draft secondary collection system until 1971. All of these measures could have been taken prior to the start of the claim period and would have substantially reduced the plant's emissions of fluoride, perhaps by as much as 80% and at least by 40%. In addition, use of tall or high-velocity stacks might have prevented the occasional concentration of emissions beneath the atmospheric inversion layer. The company's sponsorship of calcium chloride spraying of peach trees was laudable but not sufficient to overcome the preponderance of evidence showing that the company faltered in carrying out its social responsibility to control its harmful emissions.

As the court in determining the propriety of a punitive damage award may consider evidence of harm by the defendant's conduct to persons other than the plaintiff, so should the court take note of the defendant's efforts to neutralize that harm by voluntary payment of compensation, even though this compensation did not extend to the damage for which the jury in this case made a compensatory award. . . .

The company's agreement to recognize that the plant's emissions were damaging the orchards and to compensate the orchardists for the damage under an arbitration arrangement is to be complimented, and future such agreements to be encouraged. Such conduct is strong evidence that the company was attempting to fulfill its societal obligations by accounting for the damage its operations were causing to its neighbors. Though laudable, this conduct does not entirely shield the company from punitive damages liability, for it came about after some eight years of the plant's operation and after the company was faced with numerous lawsuits claiming damages. . . .

If the company during the 1965-71 claim period had cooperated fully in ascertaining the harm from the plant's emissions and in effecting some combination of efficient emission control combined with compensation for the remaining harm, I would rule against the plaintiff's request for punitive damages. The company's participation in the arbitration system is certainly indicative of corporate social responsibility but is insufficient to overcome its failure in the other two respects.

I am satisfied by the evidence in this case that an award of punitive damages is appropriate for the earlier portion of the claim period. It is difficult to put a precise date on the watershed of the company's conduct showing a sufficient compliance with societal obligation so as to rule out punitive damages. In this regard, I rely heavily upon the testimony of Barney

McPhillips, who may almost be regarded as the father of Oregon's polluti
control progress. While his testimony was generalized, and did not contai
any particular dates, nonetheless it furnishes more than adequate support for
a finding that midway through the 1965-71 claim period a change occurred in
both the attitude of the company and its efforts to carry out pollution control
measures so as to behave like a good neighbor. One cannot look at a single
event alone, since the attitude of society (both private and governmental)
was in a state of substantial change. And as society's attitude changed, as was
evidenced by the movement toward a more careful attention to the earth
around us and the necessity of its preservation, so also did society's laws and
regulations, and with that the response of its components — both of the
antagonists here, aluminum company and orchardist. I conclude, therefore,
that a punitive damage award is available for the claim years 1965 through
1968. If the claim years here were only 1969-71, I would not award punitive
damages. By this time — the late 60s and early 70s — on the record in this
case, it cannot be said that the company was in sufficient disregard of its
societal obligations so as to be liable for punitive damages. And while, of
course, the only period of time before me in this case is 1965-71, and the only
orchards involved are the ones of this plaintiff, nonetheless it is difficult to
see how any claim for punitive damages would succeed as to any period of
time in and after about 1969, in view of all of the developments during the
1969-71 period and since that time. Indeed, though of course I need not and
do not decide the question, it seems most unlikely that a punitive damage
claim for any period of time after 1971 based on the record in this case would
even go to a jury.

Because the company did not cooperate in ascertaining the nature,
severity and scope of the harm inflicted upon the plaintiff by the plant's
emissions or in arranging to prevent this damage or to neutralize it through
voluntary compensation arrangements, the company is liable to the plaintiff
for an award of punitive damages.

Previous judicial opinions provide little guidance as to the proper
amount of such an award. Courts often state that such an award should be
sufficient to deter continuation or repetition of the offending conduct. In
this case the offending conduct was the company's refusal either to implement economically efficient emission control measures or voluntarily to compensate the plaintiff for the damage caused by the plant's emissions. Thus,
punitive damages should be awarded in an amount that will deter this and
other companies from attempting to impose a portion of their costs of
production upon their neighbors by compelling those damaged by the emissions to resort to the uncertainties of the legal process in order to obtain
compensation.

Under the circumstances here, I believe an appropriate and measured
award for punitive damages is $200,000 for the claim period here through the
year 1968, but none thereafter. . . .

Notes

1. What is the legal basis for the award of punitive damages in this case? Was the basis that defendant was an intentional or reckless tortfeasor? Was defendant such?

2. Do you agree that "A breach of societal obligations justifies the imposition of punitive damages to deter uncooperative behavior"? What is wrong with this formulation?

3. When, if ever, should punitive damages be awarded in a nuisance case?

Chapter 11
Is Tort Liability for Accidental Injuries Worth Retaining?

To the delight of some students, the dismay of others, and the surprise of all, this chapter contains no cases. It is devoted to an issue of public policy, the ultimate such issue in a course on tort law — whether tort liability should be radically curtailed or eliminated, and replaced by a "no fault" system of accident compensation. The chapter excerpts economic, legal, sociological, statutory, and other nonjudicial materials in an effort to introduce the student to the major positions in the policy debate. The focus is on automobile accidents because it is here that the case for no fault has been argued most forcefully and with greatest legislative success. Efforts to limit liability for medical malpractice and other torts are also examined, however. Note that the no-fault movement is limited to unintentional torts and does not propose to eliminate liability for intentional torts.

The chapter also provides a suitable context for an examination of an important issue that has been deliberately suppressed in previous chapters for the sake of simplicity: the impact of liability insurance on the resource-allocation rationale of tort liability emphasized in those chapters.

W. L. Prosser, A Handbook of the Law of Torts
547-555 (4th ed. 1971)

Dedicated advocates of sweeping change, in which liability insurance is to play a predominant part, have sought to buttress their arguments by the contention that such insurance already has revolutionized the law of torts; that it has rendered obsolete the rules of negligence, which have become a mere set of formulae to which the courts still afford lip service, while in fact looking to the insurance; that the change is half made, and therefore should be completed.

While liability insurance undoubtedly has had its effect, it is difficult to escape the impression that all this has been very much overstated. . . . One illustration will suffice. In 1915 it was held in Nebraska, as a matter of law, that the failure of a surgeon dealing with a bone fracture to take X-ray photographs was not negligence, or evidence from which the jury could find negligence. In 1947, in California, the court took judicial notice of the fact that good surgical practice always requires that such photographs be taken, and held that the failure to do so was in itself enough to support a finding of negligence. In the meantime, insurance against liability for medical malpractice, which was available but not prevalent in 1915, had expanded into an enormous business. It would be easy to attribute the change in the law to this alone, and no doubt some of the writers would do so. But this is to ignore the greatly advanced standards of medicine and surgery, the superior medical education, the increased familiarity of all medical men with X-rays, the improvement in the equipment, its lower cost, and its availability in nearly all communities; and above all the demands which the public now makes, and reasonably makes, upon the profession. It would be quite as logical to say that the spread of the malpractice insurance itself is a consequence of the expanded liability, which is rather the result of a multitude of such other factors.

Two of the effects upon the law claimed for liability insurance have been so-called "invisible" ones, which are not reflected by or in any way apparent from the opinions of appellate courts. One of these is the settlement of cases. The insurance companies, engaged in the business for profit, and manned by unsentimental individuals interested only in financial results, customarily settle a substantial portion of their claims without regard to the existence of any liability. In other words, many claims are paid in which it is clear that the defendant was not at fault, or that the plaintiff was; and the result is compensation not based on fault at all, but on the existence of insurance. This is good business, since it retains the good will of both the plaintiff and the defendant, who may buy more insurance, and it helps the reputation of the company as a liberal payer of claims. It is also the cheapest way out in any case in which the "nuisance value" of the suit, which means the probable cost of investigation, preparation and trial, together with the off chance that the plaintiff might after all be able to prove his case, exceeds the amount paid. For obvious reasons, the claims so settled are almost invariably the smaller ones.

All this is certainly true; but its relevance is not so apparent. Contract claims are customarily settled on the same basis; the return of goods to a store by an unsatisfied customer is a familiar example. Yet no one considers that this has had any particular effect upon the law of contracts. Such settlements are simply extra-legal. Habitual defendants, such as railroad companies, always have settled claims on this basis, and so does the ordinary individual if he has any sense. What insurance has done is to put the settlement of a great many such claims into the hands of professional adjusters who know what they are doing, and so are more disposed to settle. Where the amount of the claim exceeds the nuisance value, settlement may still be made; but it is always made on the basis of the prospects of establishing liability under the existing law, which remains unaffected.

The other "invisible" effect is upon the verdict of the jury. It is more or less notorious among lawyers that juries, in general, tend to return verdicts, or larger verdicts, against defendants who have liability insurance, for the simple reason that they are aware that the defendant will not have to pay the judgment, and that the company has been paid a premium for undertaking the liability. In most jurisdictions the jury are not supposed to be told in so many words that there is insurance in the case, unless the evidence is somehow relevant as bearing upon some other issue. Plaintiff's attorneys have, however, become very adroit in managing to convey the information. The most common device is to ask the jurymen, upon voir dire, about their possible interest in or employment by a liability insurance company. By way of emphasis of the idea, a question asked of a witness may produce an "unexpected" and unresponsive mention of insurance, which, whether it is uttered in good faith or not, is virtually impossible to prevent or control. Even where no such information can be conveyed, jurymen are quite likely to assume that any defendant who owns an automobile and is worth suing is probably insured, and treat him accordingly — which in no way operates to the benefit of a defendant who in fact has no insurance. With financial responsibility laws in many states making insurance practically compulsory for every driver, the whole question of disclosure of insurance is no longer the burning issue that it formerly was; and courts in increasing numbers are asserting that the jurors assume anyway that the defendant is insured.

The result of all this is said, and no doubt quite correctly, to be a substantial increase in the proportion of recoveries in some types of cases, as well as larger recoveries, by plaintiffs as a class. This in turn, of course, has had its effect upon liability insurance rates, which undoubtedly have increased at a pace not entirely to be accounted for by the increase in the accident rate itself.

Assuming that all this is true, it adds nothing that is new to the law. For many years railroad companies, public utilities, municipalities, industrial enterprises, and large corporations in general, who among them have made up the majority of all negligence defendants, have been subjected to this treatment at the hands of juries, and against them the recoveries always have run, and still run, quite as high as against insurance companies. All that the insurance has done is to provide, in lieu of many private individuals such as automobile drivers, a large new source of payment in the form of an additional group against whom the jury may give rein to their natural human desire to see compensation made to an injured human being, at the expense of another who, they feel, should be able to pay it without comparable hardship. From the social point of view this development of course has considerable significance; but it has taken place entirely within the framework of the existing law. . . .

Over the last half century there has been a great decrease in the proportion of directed verdicts. Issues are now commonly left to the jury which fifty years ago would have been decided for the defendant by the court. Since juries are well known to favor the injured plaintiff when they are permitted to do so, this works to his advantage. This too has been ascribed to the presence, or availability, of insurance, either as the sole explanation or as the controlling and decisive factor.

Again there is nothing in the opinions to indicate it. Since the judge usually is aware of insurance when it is in the case, if only because he knows who the lawyers' clients are, and since he also cannot fail to be aware that the mere fact that the defendant has been sued is an indication that he has some means of payment, those who are inclined to think that courts always act for unexpressed reasons which they are unwilling to admit can readily assert that this is the ,only explanation. It is an assertion impossible to prove or to disprove. There are, however, other factors to be accounted for.

The tendency of the courts to abdicate control and decision in favor of the jury has not been confined to cases in which there is insurance, or any likelihood of it. It has not been confined to tort cases, but has been general across the law. It appears to have begun in the days of Theodore Roosevelt, when the "judicial oligarchy" was under violent attack, and the courts were subjected to severe criticism for what was called their arrogant assumption of power and authority. The tendency certainly has not been discouraged by the election of judges, who become reluctant to make unpopular decisions, and by the active resentment of the bar against interference from the court. The same judicial retreat has been apparent in the issuance of injunctions, in punishments for contempt, and in the refusal of the judge, in most American jurisdictions, to comment on the evidence even when he is permitted to do so.

The most likely explanation may be simply the same general shift in popular opinion, and in judicial response to it in favor of the plaintiff, which has been going on in all tort law, and which leads the judge quite reasonably to refuse to deprive the injured man of his chance in any case in which a doubtful question can fairly be conjured up. The tendency has been most marked as to the defenses of contributory negligence and assumption of risk, as to both of which directed verdicts have largely disappeared from the scene. Both defenses have been under attack for many years; and the same reasons which have induced the courts to say that they are disfavored, and to develop such halfway measures as the last clear chance, and which have led to the adoption of comparative negligence acts, are in themselves quite adequate explanation. It can scarcely be supposed that insurance has not been something of a factor, if only as a makeweight; but there is no satisfactory indication that it is the whole story.

Some writers have made a great deal of a supposed change in the character of negligence itself. Beginning, along with the criminal law, with a purpose only of "admonition" of the defendant and deterrence of others like him, and hence with an insistence upon moral blame as essential to liability, it is said to have altered in the direction of a primary concern with compensation of the victim, and so to have become negligence "without fault," or "in name only." Thus the man who is only stupid, ignorant, excitable or congenitally clumsy, or otherwise lacking in the capacity to behave as a normal individual, is held liable for negligence even though he is in no way to blame for it. The psychologists have come up with the classification of the "accident prone," who are predisposed to catastrophe and unable to protect themselves or others against it; and whether this is, as might be suspected, merely a matter of innate stupidity, slow reaction time, poor training and bad habits, or, as some of the psychologists would have it, of a "guilt complex" and a "death wish" subconsciously seeking punishment for past misdeeds, it is undoubtedly true that there are such individuals who have a history of repetition, and that, whether they can help it or not, they are held liable. . . .

It may be suggested that much of this, at least, is setting up a straw man to knock him down. The dual purpose of tort law goes back to very ancient times, and moral blame never has been a requisite of legal liability. As long ago as 1616, it was said that a lunatic is liable for his torts, although not for his crimes. At least since tort law finally split away from crime, it has been primarily concerned with compensation. The very first case in which the objective standard of the reasonable man first emerged was Vaughan v. Menlove in 1837, one of a stupid mistake of an ignorant man who honestly used his own bad judgment. These are developments of earlier centuries, and not of the present day. Nor is liability without moral blame the same thing as liability without fault. There is still legal fault, which is a departure from a standard of conduct required by the community. The defendant may not be to blame for being out of line with it, but he is none the less out of line, and it is on that basis that he is held liable. . . .

As has been indicated, there is really, in the opinions in tort cases, astonishingly little mention of insurance as a reason for holding the defendant liable. This is all the more remarkable when one considers the number of cases in which the court has been scrabbling hard for any reason or argument to support a change in the law. The failure even to mention insurance under such conditions suggests rather a determination *not* to take it into account than an important and influential, but unstated, reason. On the other hand, it has been said often enough that liability insurance does not create liability, but only provides a means of indemnity against it once it has arisen; and that it is not to be considered in determining whether anyone is liable in the first instance.

There are, however, a few cases, out of many thousand, in which insurance has received specific mention as a factor. As long ago as Ryan v. New York Central Railroad Co., in 1866, the prevalence of fire insurance among urban property owners was mentioned as one reason for applying a narrower rule of "proximate cause" in fire cases; and this finds a parallel in some of the decisions denying recovery for private fire losses against a water company which has contracted to supply water to a city.

There is a striking recent Wisconsin decision in which the prevalence of liability insurance is given as one reason for a change in the rule that a host is not liable to his automobile guest for defects in the car of which he does not know. There is also a passage from a concurring opinion of Mr. Justice

Traynor of California which has been much quoted, in which the possibility that the manufacturer of a product can insure against liability, and so distribute the risk, is mentioned as one reason, among others, for holding him to strict liability to the injured consumer. The liability for defective products is a field which has been undergoing rapid and spectacular change, with many courts writing long opinions mustering all available reasons for holding manufacturers and sellers liable without negligence; and dissenting opinions, as well as challenges from other sources, have put them upon their mettle and under considerable pressure to ignore no possible justification. In view of this, it appears quite astonishing that, out of a few thousand opinions dealing with products liability, this was for a long time the *only* one in which there was any mention whatever of insurance. On any conceivable basis, it is not easy to account for the fact; but it is at least some indication that the changes in this area of the law have not been due primarily to this one factor.

The chief visible effect of insurance, however, has been in connection with the abrogation of various immunities from liability. All of these have been under attack for many years, as outmoded vestiges of antique law arising out of historical origins that long since have passed away and been forgotten, and as without logical or moral justification. The presence, or availability, of liability insurance has provided an additional argument, since it means that, although the defendant will have to pay an insurance premium, he will not have to pay the judgment against him. In a few instances this has been enough to tip the scale. Thus there were four decisions eliminating the "family" immunity of a parent toward his child, where the child is injured in the course of a business activity of the parent, which is covered by liability insurance. There were, however, two others in which the business activity alone, without the insurance, was held to be sufficient; and a great many more in which the "family" immunity between husband and wife was abrogated, or numerous other exceptions developed to that between parent and child, in which insurance was not a visible factor at all. Where the question arose, the overwhelming majority of the decisions for a long time declared that liability insurance does not create liability, but only provides indemnity against it when it has arisen; that it is not in itself a sufficient reason for any change in the rule, and any such change must be for the legislature; and that the presence of insurance in the particular case makes no difference. There were even several decisions which gave the insurance as a reason for *not* abrogating the immunity, because of the opportunity for fraud and collusion against the insurance company.

Finally, however, when the modern wave of decisions began to engulf the family immunities, the existence or the possibility of liability insurance began to be stated in nearly all of the overruling cases, as one of the primary reasons for the change.

The immunity of charities has had much the same history. Since 1942 it has been in full retreat, and it appears only a question of time before it is to disappear from American law. The visible part which insurance has played in the change has been quite meagre. In some half dozen states, by statute or decision, the immunity is not recognized when the charity in fact has the insurance, on the ground that liability will not deplete trust funds or discourage donors.

There have been two or three opinions in which insurance has received mention as one reason, among others, for the termination of the immunity; but most of the courts which have abrogated it entirely have made no mention of any such reason. And on the other hand, there are a very large number of cases in which it has been declared specifically that the presence or availability of insurance is not a factor to be considered at all in deciding whether any change shall be made in the law. Governmental immunity, which is also under heavy fire, has undergone little specific change that can be traced to insurance. There are a few decisions holding that statutory authorization to take out the insurance constitutes a "waiver" of the immunity, which makes the government liable; but the large majority of the cases have held that such authorization is not a waiver, and the immunity is not affected by the insurance.

Note

It should not be inferred from the above excerpt that Prosser is complacent about the tort system. He states: "The deficiencies of our present system for compensating personal injuries are manifold . . . ." Prosser 556. Like most other writers on the tort system before the explosion of medical malpractice and products liability suits in the 1970s, Prosser's discussion of deficiencies focuses on the automobile accident area. See id. at 556-559. His critique, which draws heavily on the influential Report to the Columbia University Council for Research in the Social Sciences of a Committee to Study Compensation for Automobile Accidents (1932) (the "Columbia Report"), emphasizes two basic points:

First, the tort system is an inadequate system of compensating victims of automobile accidents. Not every driver carries liability insurance, even where required by law to do so; policy limits are often too low for full compensation of the victim; and anyway liability is limited to those cases where the injurer was negligent and the victim free from negligence.

Second, the litigation process is cumbersome, expensive, and inaccurate. Delays abound, forcing plaintiffs to settle for much less than their true loss ("a hungry man cannot afford to litigate," id. at 558); the negligence standard is difficult to implement in practice (negligence being "a wobbly and uncertain standard based upon the supposed mental processes of a hypothetical and non-existent reasonable man," ibid.); the contingent fee deprives the accident victim of full compensation for his injury; and so "The whole picture is one of a fumbling and uncertain process of awarding a judgment upon the basis of unreliable evidence, fraught with ruinous delay, which fails entirely when proof of fault fails, leaves the entire remedy worthless against many defendants who are not financially responsible, and diverts a large share of the money to the plaintiff's attorney even when it can be collected." Id. at 559. For economic support of these criticisms, see Holmes, On the Economic Welfare of Victims of Automobile Accidents, 60 Am. Econ. Rev. 143 (1970).

To what extent are these criticisms pertinent if the primary function of the tort system is viewed as deterrence rather than compensation, in accordance with the emphasis throughout this book?

H. L. Ross, Settled Out of Court: The Social Process of Insurance Claims Adjustment
232-256 (rev. 2d ed. 1980)

The major thesis of this book is that legal relationships cannot be understood as a product of the formal law alone, but must be understood in terms of the interplay between the formal law and aspects of the situation in which the law is applied. The determination of legal rights is in the vast majority of cases undertaken by means of informal procedures, the character of which substantively changes the rights thus processed. Moreover, the changes are not random. Informality does not mean lack of structure. Informal procedures exhibit regularities that result from the goals and purposes of the people involved, and from sociologically comprehensible pressures and strains upon them.

The regularities induced from the observation of the day-to-day working out of legal relationships constitute the law in action. It is these regularities that have to be taken into account by the ordinary man and his attorney when the question of rights and duties becomes concrete. I propose that the legal critic and the social analyst ought to share this perspective.

In this chapter I shall review the settlement process in automobile bodily injury claims, pointing to the structured differences between the law in action and the formal law in this area of legal rights, and suggesting sociological explanations for the differences observed. This review will lead into a discussion of the current critical debate over the inadequacies of the tort law in this area. Much of this debate has ignored the distinction between the formal law and the law in action. Many of the criticisms and suggestions for change seem to be premised on formal concepts that do not reflect what happens in the real world of day-to-day events. I believe that the debate might be less bitter, and certainly more realistic, were were the parties to discuss the real world rather than the world of doctrine. . . .

Traffic laws are simple rules, deliberately so because their purpose is to provide a universal and comprehensible set of guidelines for safe and efficient transportation. Negligence law is complex, its purpose being to decide after the fact whether a driver was unreasonably careless. However, all levels of the insurance company claims department will accept the former rules as generally adequate for the latter purpose. The underlying reason for this is the difficulty if not impossibility of investigating and defending a more complex decision concerning negligence in the context of a mass operation. In the routine case, the stakes are not high enough to warrant the effort, and the effort is not made. The information that a given insured violated a 'specific traffic law and was subsequently involved in an accident will suffice to allocate fault. No attempt is made to analyze why this took place or how. The legal concepts of negligence and fault in action contain no more substance than the simple and mechanical procedures noted here provide.

The law of damages is also simplified in action. Although the measurement of special damages appears rather straightforward even in formal doctrine, some further simplification occurs in action when, for instance, life table calculations are used to compute future earnings. More important, the measurement of pain, suffering, and inconvenience is thoroughly routinized in the ordinary claim. The adjuster generally pays little attention to the claimant's privately experienced discomforts and agonies; I do not recall ever having read recitals of these matters in the statements, which are the key documents in the settlement process and in which all matters considered relevant to the disposition of a claim are recorded. The calculation of general damages is for the most part a matter of multiplying the medical bills by a tacitly but generally accepted arbitrary constant. This practice is justified by claims men on the theory that pain and suffering are very likely to be a function of the amount of medical treatment experienced. There is of course a grain of truth in this theory, but it also contains several sources of error. Types of injury vary considerably in the degree of pain and suffering, the necessity for treatment, and the fees charged for treatment; and the correlations between these elements are low. I believe that the more important reason for the use of the formula is again that all levels of the claims department find it acceptable in justifying payment over and beyond special damages. The formula provides a conventional measurement for phenomena that are so difficult to evaluate as to be almost unmeasurable. It provides a rule by which a rule-oriented organization can proceed, though the rule is never formalized. This simplification also meets the comparable needs of plaintiffs' attorneys and is acceptable to them as well. Because of the mutual acceptability of the formula, attorneys will try to capitalize on it by adding to the use and cost of medical treatment, a procedure known as "building" the file, and adjusters will argue concerning the reasonableness of many items that purport to be medical expenses and thus part of the base to which the formula is applied. The procedure is still far less complicated — and less sensitive — than that envisaged in the formal law. Thus again it appears that, relative to the formal law, the law in action is simple and mechanical. Although more individual consideration occurs in larger cases, the principle of simplification governs to a great degree the entire range of settled claims.

The tort law in action is more liberal than the formal law. The formal law of negligence appears to be very stingy from the victim's point of view; this appearance is not surprising considering the law's development as a means of relieving nineteenth-century industry of charges imposed for accidental injuries by the earlier strict liability doctrine. The doctrine of contributory negligence is of course the main block to recovery in the formal tort law, and it is this doctrine that is most strongly attenuated in action.

The principal evidence of this attenuation is in the large number of claims on which some payment is made. Insurance company procedures create a file for nearly every accident victim involved with an insured car. Any reasonable estimate of the number of cases in which the insured is not negligent plus the number in which the claimant is contributorily negligent suggests that well under half of all claims deserve payment by formal standards. . . . [C]ontrary to formal expectations the majority of claims are paid, and where serious injuries are involved virtually all claimants recover something from someone else's liability insurance. Similar findings have been reported in other studies. It is true that in larger claims particularly, the payments may not equal the economic loss experienced, but they may still exceed the level of payment required by the formal law with its rule of contributory negligence.

In small claims, a fair number of denials are successfully made. The adjuster rationalizes his actions on the basis of formal law and the company is shielded from reprisals by high processing costs for the claimant relative to the amount at stake. The adjuster closes his files by denial when he feels the formal law warrants this and also that the claimant will take his case no farther. When he believes that the formal law favors the claimant, and thus finds himself ethically obliged, or when he believes the claimant is determined to press the claim, a payment can be made of considerable magnitude relative to the economic loss involved, although collateral sources — e.g., Blue Cross and sick pay — are usually deducted from negotiated settlements.

In claims based on large losses, the claimant's threat to litigate becomes more credible, and denial thus becomes more difficult. However, the adjuster uses the uncertainty of the formal process as a tool to secure a discount from the full formal value of the claim. Although processing costs may be disregarded, most claimants seem to prefer a definite settlement for a lower amount of money to the gamble of trial for a higher amount of money. The company — like a casino, which is able to translate a large number of gambles into mathematical certainty — is indifferent between these outcomes and can demand a concession for the definite settlement.

The claimant determined to press a claim that would most likely be thrown out of court and the company determined to obtain a discount on a claim that would most likely prevail are unforeseen in the formal law, but it is in predicaments like this that the law in action develops. The result may correspond to no theory of formal law, but it is none the less comprehensible. The resultant law in action, on the whole, is more liberal than is the formal law. More claims are paid, particularly where the loss is serious, than might be predicted on the basis of the latter. However, the ratio of payment to loss declines as the size of the loss increases.

The tort law in action may also be termed inequitable. It is responsive to a wide variety of influences that are not defined as legitimate by common standards of equity. The interviews and observations I conducted convinced me that the negotiated settlement rewards the sophisticated claimant and penalizes the inexperienced, the naive, the simple, and the indifferent. Translating these terms into social statuses, I believe that the settlement produces relatively more for the affluent, the educated, the white, and the city-dweller. It penalizes the poor, the uneducated, the Negro, and the countryman. It is also responsive to such matters as the appearances and personalities of the parties and witnesses to the accident. Above all, it rewards the man with an attorney, despite the adjuster's honestly held belief that the unrepresented claimant will fare as well. Apart from the discrimination embodied in allowing recovery of different levels of lost income, these differences are unjustified in formal law, yet their effect on negotiated settlements is considerable. . . .

For the past 40 years, critics have raised the question of how well victims of traffic accidents are compensated by automobile insurance. The question itself might appear paradoxical, since the bulk of insurance coverage contained in the automobile insurance package is found in the liability policy, which was never intended directly to serve the needs of claimants. The purpose of the liability policy — as viewed by virtually all insurance personnel — is to protect the policyholder. One of the hazards to which an individual's assets may be exposed is claims from others whom he has injured through his negligent conduct. Just as a man may protect the assets in his home through fire insurance, he may protect his total assets through liability insurance. The proper test of the adequacy of the latter, according to this viewpoint, is whether insureds are protected when claims are in fact made. I am not aware that this matter has ever been systematically investigated, but there seems to be little concern on the part of critics that a person with reasonably high limits of liability insurance in a prudently managed company is poorly served in this respect.

Liability insurance, then, covers liability. Accidental injury may or may not involve liability; in any event, it is a separately insurable hazard, and insurance against injury in virtually any type of accident is easily purchased on the market. A small accident policy paying medical expenses of the driver and passengers in an insured car is a common part of the total package of insurance routinely sold to automobile owners. Accidental injury is also covered in health insurance plans such as Blue Cross and Blue Shield, and a variety of policies specifically concerned with accidental injuries are also available. The proper test of accident insurance is whether adequate benefits are being paid to all such insureds who are injured in accidents. Again, there has been little critical clamor in this matter.

If both accident insurance and liability insurance seem on the whole to be adequately protecting those who purchase the appropriate policies, why do the critics persist in judging liability insurance by accident compensation standards that are manifestly inapplicable? Two principal reasons are evident. First, many of the millions of people injured in automobile accidents every year are not covered by accident insurance. Moreover, accident insurance seldom covers all economic losses experienced by these victims. Second, liability insurance constitutes a pool of funds to which nearly all users of automobiles contribute. The size of this pool is very large. The vast bulk of automobile victims potentially have access to it, regardless of their own insurance, if liability can be proved, and the allowable damages can compensate for all economic losses and for pain and suffering in addition. If the question of liability could be overcome, automobile liability insurance could virtually guarantee adequate compensation for all aspects of loss on the part of victims of automobile accidents. Furthermore, the payment of all victims from such a fund would be in accord with the thesis that motoring inevitably produces accidents, that these are a true economic cost of motoring, and that those who profit from this enterprise ought to pay all the costs that it entails.

The opportunity to use liability funds for compensation purposes has long been recognized informally and even formally in the tort law. Perhaps the best example of formal recognition is the doctrine of respondeat superior by which an innocent employer is held responsible for the negligent acts of his employees when these are done in the course of the job. Although several reasons are offered for this apparently odd doctrine, the most persuasive is that the employer could pay for the damage, whereas the typical employee (as conceived by judges at the time of the evolution of this doctrine) could not.

There is in fact a long history of developments in the tort law that make it easier for the injured party to prove fault on the part of the defendant and thus to recover. Fleming James summarizes this history as follows:

> Except for Workmen's Compensation and an occasional other forward looking statute, the main assault on the citadel of fault has not been a frontal attack but rather a boring from within. The main trends have been concerned with the enlargement of duties, the liberalization of standards of proof; the increasing concern of society to provide a financially responsible defendant and the erosion of contributory negligence, imputation of negligence to the plaintiff, and other doctrines which impede recovery.

As many critics have suggested, the development of liability insurance accelerated these developments, for courts and legislatures realized that payment of damages was done not by another individual, whose rights had to be balanced against those of the injured, but by a financial pool to which each participant had contributed a relatively small sum. Liability insurance could be seen as creating assets rather than protecting them.

The formal law of negligence is an increasingly liberal law. Perhaps the greatest formal liberalization of the law in recent times has been the replacement of the contributory negligence doctrine by that of comparative negligence, which has been accomplished by statute in six states. However, even in comparative negligence states, the fundamental rule remains that of negligence, and it denies access to the pool of liability insurance funds to people whose injuries cannot be related to the fault of some other insured party.

Judged by the criteria of compensation, the automobile liability insurance system does seem rather inadequate. . . . The empirical research does show, however, that payment was relatively common in cases with larger losses, and this picture is confirmed in the present study. . . .

Given the difference in ostensible goals between liability insurance and compensation, I think that the empirical data require a different emphasis from that most often given. I am most impressed by the extent to which the liability insurance system has come to resemble a compensation system. It would not be very much of an exaggeration to say that when serious injuries have been sustained, at least in metropolitan jurisdictions, automobile liability insurance companies are making payments without regard to liability (though the latter may be reflected in the size of the payments). Flat denials are very largely confined to trivial losses, and although the system might not be paying on the average as much as the tort law says ought to be paid to innocent victims of negligent drivers, liability insurance is still paying more than half of total victim recoveries from all sources, far more than any variety of accident insurance is currently yielding. The liability insurance system as it actually operates is very likely better when judged by the standards of compensation than when judged by the standards of formal negligence law.

. . . The present study confirms previous research on [delay]: although the majority of claims are settled within a few months, some of them — particularly the serious ones — drag on for years. Much of the delay is understandable in the light of the necessity to investigate, evaluate, and negotiate claims. The demand of the formal law that settlement cover all damages for once and forever is an important independent source of delay, as no claimant ought to sign a release of liability until he is fairly sure of the extent of his damages, and these may take some time to ascertain fully. Although the amount of delay seems excessive for the needs to which a compensation system is directed, perhaps cases are settled somewhat too expeditiously for the needs to which a liability system is directed. At least, the possibility of undue haste is suggested by the efforts of adjusters to close claims quickly. . . .

In sum, the current automobile liability insurance system can be viewed as functioning surprisingly like a compensation system, although judged by standards appropriate to the latter it contains many inequities and irrationalities and is intolerably slow and expensive. However, judged by its own formal standards it is remarkably improvident with its funds, as well as sloppy and inconsistent in its criteria for distribution. To a great degree these inadequacies are the result of strains on the liability system to play the role of a compensation system.

The law of negligence prescribes payment not for all injured parties, but only for those who are innocently injured as a direct result of another person's negligent conduct. Among the several reasons that can be cited for this restriction, the must fundamental is that the law shares with its concern for the victim an equally important concern for deterrence of faulty behavior. The conventional view is expressed as follows by an insurance company attorney:

> The greatest single deterrent to the reckless disregard of the rights of others is the consequence of the act upon the wrongdoer. The fear of retribution, retaliation, and restitution has been a most determinative factor in keeping people on the "straight and narrow," whether the issue be one involving morals or whether it be one involving the consequences of careless and reckless acts.

The prevention of "careless and reckless" driving is a laudable purpose, and its accomplishment may well warrant restrictions on the compensation of victims, if such is necessary. Indeed, pursuit of this goal may warrant attempts to strengthen the negligence principle, to repair the breaches in the formal law, and to create incentives for adjusters to follow the formal law more closely. However, if we are to believe that the negligence law does in fact deter careless driving, it must be shown that the law contains sanctions that are in fact visited upon improper driving behavior. Moreover, unless the driving we label negligent is shown to cause accidents, its control is of no great importance. These statements put the deterrence issue in the form of empirical questions concerning which some evidence is available.

Are accidents generally the result of negligent driving? Although knowledge concerning traffic accidents is still primitive, most of what is known suggests a negative answer to the question. Careless or reckless driving certainly can and does cause some accidents, but most accidents do not involve driving behavior that can be meaningfully described as faulty or deficient. As claimed by T. Lawrence Jones, president of the American Insurance Association, in presenting a plan for reforming the current handling of automobile insurance:

> It must be remembered that the vast majority of crashes result not from wanton recklessness, as our critics' simplistic arguments would indicate, but rather from the momentary lapses or errors in judgment of ordinary people like you and me.

Mr. Jones' position is supported very generally in the scientific literature concerning accident causation. It has my endorsement based on experience as the behavioral scientist in the most intensive study of traffic accidents ever conducted, the Case Studies of Traffic Accidents project at the Northwestern University Traffic Institute, which spent three years in the study of fewer than 100 accidents. In the course of that study it became clear that run-of-the-mill accidents nearly all involve failure to see an approaching hazard and to predict its course accurately. However, in the context of these accidents such failure can rarely be considered faulty, in the sense of "unreasonably dangerous conduct by one who is free to choose a feasible safe way to carry on his legitimate activity." As any adjuster could testify, the recurrent statement of the accident-involved driver is "I didn't see him until too late." But hazards can come from many directions, and no driver can be looking everywhere at once. Successful prediction of the course of a moving car depends not only on accurate perception, but on the validity of a large number of conventional assumptions, for example, that a vehicle will proceed in the same lane at the same speed unless indications are to the contrary. These expectations are supported with a high degree of confirmation, and all drivers rely on them, yet occasionally they prove to be unfounded. When such failures occur in conjunction with other factors, including aspects of the road and the vehicles, accidents occur. To put the argument another way, a road network filled with cars driven only by the most skilled, reasonable, and prudent drivers will still generate accidents. Furthermore, if it is assumed that this hypothetical road network includes a representative share of high-speed roads, intersections, curves and turns, and hills and bumps, it can be confidently predicted that the system will generate a certain percentage of serious injuries and of deaths without a single reckless or careless driver being on the road. . . .

The analytical viewpoint suggests, thus, that accidents are most likely not the result of deficient driving. Assuming for the sake of argument that there is still reason to try to deter the driving behavior that is labeled negligent, the question must be raised whether the current system in fact applies sanctions to the drivers whose behavior is thus labeled. As Fleming James, among many others, has pointed out, the tort judgment cannot reasonably be a deterrent to an insured defendant who pays no part of the judgment. Since the vast bulk of defendants are insured, they are susceptible in the main only to whatever deterrent effects may be inherent in the possibility of increased rates under a safe driver rating system — whereby insurance rates are increased as a function of the number of claims — and in the possibility of cancellation or nonrenewal of insurance if they experience what the company regards as an excessive number of claims. . . . [I]t seems unreasonable to posit a significant deterrent effect for these residual penalties in the insurance system as compared with the much more powerful sanctions of possible injury on the one hand, and criminal and administrative penalties leading to loss of license on the other. . . .

There is perhaps somewhat more substance to the assumption of a deterrent value in the rule of contributory negligence. The insured defendant, if he is judged at fault, loses nothing directly. The claimant, if he is judged at fault, may lose whatever he might otherwise have been paid, and this can be considerable. However, the degree of sanction bears no relationship to the degree of negligence displayed. The grossly negligent who has suffered a cut finger loses ten dollars of potential recovery. The barely negligent claimant who is paralyzed for life may lose hundreds of thousands. The arbitrariness of the sanction violates all principles of scientific correction. However, the law in action is more merciful than the formal law, and even negligent claimants make recoveries that might be interpreted by some as rewards for their negligence.

In sum, insurance has in my opinion pretty much drawn the sting from tort law sanctions on the insured defendant, and the law in action has enormously moderated the effect of these sanctions on the claimant. The negligence system without insurance might conceivably be effective as a deterrent, but it would have to be judged grossly unfair because of a lack of proportion between the degree of fault and the degree of punishment. With insurance, I believe it is unreasonable to expect significant deterrent effects from the negligence system.

Mansfield, Book Review
73 Harv. L. Rev. 1243 (1960)

Since the Columbia Study in 1932, a very great deal has been written on the desirability of some sort of scheme for compensating, without regard to fault, the ever-increasing number of victims of automobile accidents. Such a scheme, it has often been pointed out, would simply shift the inevitable cost of motor-vehicle operation from the unfortunate injured minority to the entire class of those who benefit from the activity. Professor Green's short but forceful book [Leon Green, Traffic Victims: Tort Law and Insurance (1958)] . . . is a useful addition to this literature by a recognized authority and spokesman for those who seek immediate and far-reaching change rather than a gradual adjustment of the present system of negligence law and jury trials or no change at all.

As a foundation for his proposals, Professor Green gives us a breathtaking survey of the history of negligence law: its emergence in the early nineteenth century against a background of more or less strict liability, the development of the liability-limiting doctrines of contributory negligence, assumption of risk, and proximate cause, and the partial reappearance in the last part of the century of isolated instances of strict liability and a generally less favorable attitude toward defendants. No one will doubt that an historical inquiry is an important aid to accurate appraisal of our present problems in this area, but juxtaposing such an inquiry to proposals of reform has peculiar dangers. The proposed reforms all too easily appear as the logical outcome of some inexorable historical process whose workings it is only necessary to recognize and accept, a satisfyingly cyclical return to the historical starting point of strict liability, and not the result of a very hard choice, informed by reason and experience, between closely competing considerations. In this regard it is perhaps unwise in debate on this curiously emotional subject (the reasons for so much smoke and heat are not wholly clear) to speak of negligence law and jury trial having "run their course" in automobile accident cases, or to suggest that the courts have lagged behind some sort of ongoing historical process and that the choice whether to proceed in one direction or another is not fully open to us. History illumines but does not solve the problems Professor Green so clearly points to.

The revolutionary character of the change in the early nineteenth century from strict liability to liability based on fault has long been a matter of debate, but surely most would agree that it is overstating the case to say that "the concern of centuries for the injured party was transferred to the offending party, for whom the common law had theretofore shown slight consideration." At the very least there was no conscious change of direction. As Professor Green himself recognizes, it may be correct to think of the development of negligence law in the horse and buggy collision cases and the early railroad cases as involving not so much the abandonment of established standards of liability as the creation of a body of law to meet a new and unique situation to which the old rules spoke no relevant answer. Advances in transportation and industrial development presented the courts with a wholly new subject matter, a range of activities involving risks far more numerous and serious than any theretofore experienced, and for these activities and the distribution of the risks that they entailed the courts set about to fashion an appropriate body of law. It may be an important matter of emphasis in describing these early negligence cases whether to say that now the plaintiff could recover only if he proved a want of ordinary care (implying that earlier he could recover even without such a showing), or, giving the doctrine of negligence a more affirmative role, that the plaintiff could recover if the defendant had failed to exercise ordinary care (implying that he is lucky to recover at all). Both approaches merit consideration in any historical account of the matter.

I confess to being properly startled by Professor Green's description of the nineteenth century as a period of "group welfare" and the twentieth as one bent on the protection of the individual. However, we are given an explanation of the author's inversion of the customary comparison. In the first part of the nineteenth century the paramount interest of the community lay in fostering infant enterprise. To this end it was found advantageous to free enterprise from charges which, under a system of strict liability, might have been so heavy as to retard or altogether prevent a development in which all had a stake, and to cast upon the individual victims of the enterprise the losses that could not be avoided even in the exercise of ordinary care. Thus, a very large measure of freedom of action was the desire not only of the entrepreneur but, happily for him, of the community as well, for the enterprise was "a force in the community." To what extent the community realized on its investment in freedom of action and to what extent the benefits were drained off in strictly private advantage to which no perceptible social gain attached is a question on which the historian might have something to say. In any event, by the opening years of twentieth century the balance had swung over and a securely established industrial economy could well afford to compensate the victims of the risks it created, whether through want of ordinary care or simply as the result of an extremely complex way of life.

Professor Green impressively marshals the reasons for abandoning fault as a basis for recovery in automobile accident cases and substituting a loss-compensation scheme. Indeed, after reading his lectures it is scarcely possible to escape the conviction that some changes in the present system are necessary and that a fairly drastic solution to the problems posed ought to be tried in at least one jurisdiction in this country. In many automobile cases the determination of what happened at all, not to speak of who was at fault, is largely a matter of speculation. Moreover, there is the sheer magnitude of the losses involved and the pressing need for some minimum compensation to the victims of this enormously expensive activity. The need is no less when the defendant is without fault than when he has failed to exercise ordinary care, and a great number of accidents do not in fact result from an absence of care on anyone's part, but are unavoidable by even the most conscientious and skilled drivers. If care is wanting, it is in setting out on the road at all with a lethal instrumentality, but this, it has been determined by a process too fundamental to be reexamined in the courts, is permissible conduct.

In considering whether to abandon fault as a basis of liability, however, it is important to state the doctrine as carefully and sympathetically as possible in order to detect any price that may be involved in its abandonment and so be in a position to determine whether that price ought to be paid.

> The only significance we can accord "liability based on fault" is that it was and is as much a cliché as "absolute liability," "proximate cause," "foreseeability of harm," and many other such terms tossed about so freely by lawyers and judges — and law teachers and law students. It merely means that the law as a basis of liability requires a violation of some legal duty, as for example the failure to exercise reasonable care under the circumstances. . . . But in this case *all* law is based on "fault," and so it is. Morality is deeply embedded in the law, but it is not the only factor that determines liability in tort or elsewhere. In fact it is seldom the dominant factor in any case but is usually associated with more compelling factors.

Surely a better case than this can be made out for "liability based on fault." Admittedly if the phrase simply means that there is liability when under some rule of law there is liability, "fault" adds nothing to understanding. But "liability based on fault" is not simply tautological. The term "fault" has both moral and legal connotations, and through this very ambiguity of meaning standards of moral responsibility enter into and enrich standards of legal responsibility. Of course, there is no simple carry-over of moral standards without consideration of whether they ought to be given legal sanction. Nor are factors having no particular claim to moral significance disregarded in deciding whether liability ought to be imposed; the concept of liability based on fault has not often held the courts back from elaborating rules deemed socially important. But at the same time it must be recognized that in very many instances the concept has aided the courts in apprehending the great legal utility of moral principles and in incorporating these principles into a developing body of tort law; it has provided them with a most serviceable instrument for weighing the freedom of the defendant against the security of the plaintiff in determining when losses should be shifted.

Professor Green does not attribute much importance to notions of moral responsibility in the development of tort law. Courts "not infrequently talked in terms of fault, but in the opinions which established the broad policies of the law of negligence . . . are found more basic considerations." I assume he means not "more basic," but "other" considerations. His view that notions of moral responsibility were not or ought not to have been controlling leads him, it seems to me, into an exaggerated attack, quite beyond the necessities of his proposal for change in the area of automobile accidents, on the whole of what he calls "a comprehensive and bloated system of 'liability based on fault' . . . ." It is difficult enough to decide whether arguments sufficiently weighty have been advanced for abandoning fault in automobile cases without at the same time being faced with the suggestion that the whole of negligence law is fundamentally defective and probably ready for the discard. After all, as Professor Green himself points out, liability based on fault has its merits as a test for the shifting of losses in some situations, and whenever a defendant cannot pass on a loss by insurance or otherwise how many will come forward and say that the test ought to be abandoned?

Even in the area of automobile accidents it is probable that a price will have to be paid for the abandonment of fault, even in the attenuated form in which it is thought now to exist, as the cardinal issue of each case. It may be that there is little sphere for the judgment of ordinary, prudent men to fix blame in these cases, but there is some; it may be that there is little deterrent effect deriving from the fault principle but again there is some, and this even though a driver is secure in the knowledge that if he is determined to have been at fault the insurance company will pay. It is not altogether clear that "insurance against liability will not engender irresponsibility under a compensation system any more than it does at present." Surely it is important to ask whether a formal adjudication of fault, no matter who ultimately satisfies the judgment, is an important auxiliary to the criminal law in condemning reprehensible conduct and impregnating the community with a sense of responsibility and attention to the interests of others that, as far as the driving of automobiles is concerned, we can scarcely afford to do without. Unfortunately, the question cannot be answered by any number of surveys of the present administration of negligence law in jury trials, nor, because of the subtlety and multiplicity of causes at work, even by a period of experimentation with a loss-compensation scheme. Statistics could always plausibly be explained by any number of factors other than the abandonment of fault. The matter is at best one for judgment informed rather vaguely, though not unimportantly, by experience of human conduct and the kinds of considerations likely to affect it.

Professor Green does not suppress the question, but he says that "the means for dealing with the reckless, incompetent, and irresponsible operator are to be found in a criminal proceeding by fine, imprisonment, cancellation of license, and other penalties." That is all well and good, but will the means be used, and used with a comprehensiveness adequate to the problem? And what of ordinary negligence, a significant segment of conduct that ought to be discouraged and yet which, it must be frankly recognized, is most unlikely to be brought within the formal condemnation of the criminal law, much less its actual administration? Professor Ehrenzweig has suggested that the changes proposed by Professor Green "would have to be accompanied by another (psychologically unavoidable) one: the express reservation to court and jury of the true tort claim for criminal (or willful) negligence, the uninsurability of which would not only preserve but increase the much stressed admonitory function of the present law." The "tort fines" recovered in such an action would go to an uncompensated-injury fund and not to the injured party. This arrangement, like Professor Green's, leaves to one side as not of serious concern conduct that does not rise to the level of criminal negligence (why are claims based on criminal or willful negligence the only "true" tort claims?), but it does give additional assurance that there will not be a serious weakening in the "admonitory function" of the law. Surely it is of the utmost moment that there be no such weakening, but rather, looking to the law's total impact, criminal and civil, an increase in its admonitory effect, and that in the area of automobile accidents no scheme be adopted without reasonable assurance that such will be the case. . . .

G. Calabresi, The Costs of Accidents: A Legal and Economic Analysis
5-13 (1970)

. . . Concurrently [with the rise of the no-fault movement], there has been a realization on the part of theoretically inclined writers that the analyses that had seemed to support the trend toward nonfault liability are woefully unsophisticated. Some of these theorists have concluded that the bases of nonfault liability are so weak that fault looks good in comparison. Others have sought instead to develop more satisfactory theoretical bases for what once seemed to be an inexorable trend. As a result of these studies, such phrases as "distribute the risk" and "let the party who benefits from a cost bear it" can no longer be accepted as sufficing to determine who ought to bear accident costs. Such catch phrases of the nonfault trend have become nearly as suspect among scholars as the "justice" of the fault system became fifty years ago. And not surprisingly, in light of this development, there are even those who ask if, after all, the fault system is not indeed the most just.

Despite this state of general uncertainty about the theoretical bases of accident law, plans and suggestions for reform abound, varying as much as their authors both in terms of what they propose and in the degree of theoretical justification they offer. They have, however, one thing in common: they cannot be evaluated properly given the current state of knowledge and analysis of the bases of accident law. A short discussion of a few of the suggested reforms should make this clear. I shall consider five categories of plans: (1) the social insurance and welfare legislation plans; (2) the first-party motorist insurance plans, which include among others the Keeton-O'Connell plan, the Insurance Company of North America proposal, and the report of the Special Committee of the American Insurance Association; (3) the Defense Research Institute approach; (4) the Blum and Kalven "stopgap" plan; and (5) judicial moves toward nonfault liability, characterized by the rapid changes in products liability law.

The most dramatic reform of accident law would abolish the field altogether. Proponents assert that the problem is how to compensate victims adequately and inexpensively and claim this can be best accomplished by generalized social insurance paid by the state out of tax revenues. This, they argue, would effectively eliminate the cost to the victim of insufficient compensation as well as the cost to society of inadequate rehabilitation, obviously desirable goals. The problems arise when one asks who should pay the taxes to fund the program; how much compensation is fair; and whether the plan should be limited to automobile accident victims, or extended to all accident victims, or even to victims of serious illnesses, or become part of a broader negative income tax or income maintenance program. Discussion of any one of these problems reveals the need for more theoretical analysis.

Some proponents suggest that general tax revenues should be the source of the funding; this is inexpensive and held to be fair, as the rich would pay the highest taxes. Others propose that at least part should be raised by direct taxes on the activities that "cause" the accidents; "justice" is marshaled in support of this approach, as is the notion that this is economically correct. The first method is certainly inexpensive, but it fails to deal satisfactorily with the effect a general-tax based compensation system might have on the number of accidents unless it were supplemented by substantial criminal and safety legislation. It also fails to examine when and to what extent such criminal legislation is likely to be effective or desirable in controlling accidents.

The second method appears to deal with the problem of deterring accidents by taxing "accident-causing" activities, but it does not adequately answer the immensely difficult question of which activity "causes" the accident. Is it, for instance, the one in which the victim was engaged or the one in which the injurer was engaged? Nor does it fully examine the question of how specifically we should define the activities or individuals to be taxed. Should pedestrians be treated as a group or should there be subcategories of pedestrians according to age; and why one rather than the other? All these questions depend for their answers on a general theory of accident law, and since such a theory does not exist the plans cannot give fully satisfactory solutions.

The second category of proposals deals specifically with automobile accidents. It encompasses a whole group of admirable plans (there is a new one each month) which have in common an idea derived from their most recent and closely worked out progenitor, the justly celebrated proposal of Robert Keeton and Jeffrey O'Connell.[10] The theme is that, to a greater or lesser extent, fault liability should be removed from automobile accident law and a system of first-party insurance should be substituted in its place. This would require each car owner to protect himself, his family, his passengers, and third parties such as pedestrians (unless they are also car owners and therefore self-insured) from losses due to accidents involving his car.

The differences among these plans are by no means insignificant. For example, some would retain the fault system as an appendage while others would not; some would subtract from the victim's recoveries any benefits due him from collateral sources (such as payments from Blue Cross, or employee wage security plans) while others would let the victim collect his full economic loss from the insured regardless of the existence of such collateral sources; and finally, some would do away with "pain and suffering" recoveries while others would retain them at least partially. These differences raise significant theoretical issues regarding the goals of each plan, but I will not examine them here. Instead I will consider the common denominator of these plans because this will indicate clearly the need for a basic reconsideration of accident law.

Each plan attempts to diminish or eliminate the importance of fault as a criterion for the allocation of accident damages, and each substitutes first-party insurance for the current system, under which the victim collects, if at all, from the party that injures him. Critics such as Walter J. Blum and Harry Kalven, Jr., claim that these plans give no adequate justification for placing accident costs on driving rather than on passengerism or pedestrianism. But whatever one may think of the justification given for placing such costs on driving, which at least has the merit of being in accord with the views of the majority of scholars in the field, it is clear that no sufficient one is given for the almost total shift from third- to first-party insurance. It is claimed that administrative cost savings will accrue. This may well be the case, but it is not the only thing that will occur, and we must ask whether the cost savings are purchased at too high a price or conversely whether other benefits besides administrative cost savings will result from the change.

10. See, generally, R. E. Keeton and J. O'Connell, Basic Protection for the Traffic Victim (Boston, Little, Brown, 1965). . . .

If a person insures himself, his family, and his passengers, the cost of owning a car will depend on the probable number and frailty of his passengers, as well as on how well suited his car is to protect the passengers if an accident occurs. Under the current system, driving costs depend much more on the likelihood of imposing injuries on third parties, such as pedestrians, other drivers, and their passengers. Thus one might expect that adoption of one of these plans would substantially lessen driving costs to the young, who tend to drive alone and who, if injured, are more resilient and less prone to permanent injury, and increase driving costs for middle-aged men with large families. Similarly, insurance would be cheaper for owners of the Juggernaut Eight, which is likely to crush all that comes in contact with it but leave its passengers unhurt, or owners of the Safety Six, which has many expensive devices to protect the riders, and more expensive for owners of the Foreign Fly, which barely scratches what it hits but is likely to collapse on contact with a Juggernaut.

In effect, these plans propose that accident costs be placed not only on driving, but also on certain categories of car ownership. They may well be right, but they certainly give no adequate reason for the decision. Nor can they in the absence of a theory of accident law.

The above plans can be contrasted with the position taken by the Defense Research Institute, an organization dedicated to the worthy purpose of increasing the "Professional Skill and . . . Knowledge of the [Tort] Defense Lawyer." This group is opposed equally to the suggestion that accident victims be compensated out of general tax revenues and to plans like Keeton-O'Connell which place automobile accident costs on driving. Perhaps surprisingly, for a group so dedicated to free enterprise, they make suggestions which call for a plethora of direct government rules and regulations governing who may drive and requiring periodic or spot safety checks on cars. These suggestions are sometimes coupled with attacks on recovery by victims from the faulty injurer's insurance company to the extent that collateral sources are available to them. But as an insurance company association study pointed out, making such collateral sources the primary font of accident recoveries could "lead eventually to a system or systems under which the cost of motoring would be shifted to taxpayers and groups . . . not directly related to motoring." In other words, the Defense Research Institute ends up, perhaps inadvertently, with a system that is perilously close to social insurance paid for out of tax revenues and buttressed by a lot of government safety regulations. One can only assume that it is the unavailability of an adequate theoretical study of the field which has led the Institute to such an improbable result.

Of all the writers in the field, Blum and Kalven have been among the most aware of the frail theoretical underpinnings of most plans. Indeed, at least part of their defense of the fault system can be understood as suggesting simply that no adequate theoretical argument has been offered for any change short of either such radical and politically suspect alterations as social

insurance, or even more fundamental changes such as those implied in negative income tax plans. Recently, however, even they have come up with a plan
they appropriately label a "stopgap."

The plan contemplates the existence of a Guaranteed Benefits system,
now being tried by some insurance companies, under which all victims of
automobile accidents would be offered a settlement of up to $5,000 for
medical expenses, while those who would have a chance to recover under the
fault system would be offered up to $7,500 in addition for all other economic
losses actually suffered, provided they eschew their common law remedies. To
this munificent scheme (which, incidentally, would seem to increase the
current overpayment of minor injuries while hardly helping victims of major
ones, and which is justified, as always, in terms of its administrative cost
savings), Blum and Kalven add that

> *if* it is desired to protect *all* victims one could . . . [similarly compensate] the
> victims who could not recover at common law . . . [by providing that any] . . .
> *additional cost* of [so] extending the compulsory Guaranteed Benefits . . .
> *should be paid for by the state out of general tax revenues.*

Several things should be noticed about Blum and Kalven's plan. First,
they make precisely the opposite decision from Keeton-O'Connell as to
whether those accident costs that are placed on driving should be placed on
drivers on a first- or third-party basis, and opt for a third-party plan. Predict-
ably, they are fully aware of doing this and that they have no special ground
to prefer one to the other; they justify their choice on the simple ground that
it retains the status quo.

Second, they emphasize that their plan is desirable only if we want to
compensate *all* automobile accident victims, not just those who would recover under the fault system. Here too the absence of a theory that would
justify change, or, for that matter, the status quo, is patent.

Finally, they reach the decision that compensation for those who are not
eligible to recover under fault should be limited to the $12,500 of the Guaran-
teed Benefits plan and that the cost of this should be assessed neither as a cost
of driving nor as a cost of the activity in which the victim was engaged, but as
a general cost of living. The $12,500 limit can be explained by their desire to
stay as close to the status quo as possible pending an adequate theory justifying change. Placing the costs of the added protection on the government is
harder to understand, however. This allocation removes it both from the
victim, where it currently lies, and from the motorist, on whom Keeton-
O'Connell would put it, and charges it instead to the taxpayer. Again no
adequate theoretical justification for this "externalization," as economists
would call it, is given. The only justification offered is the remarkable suggestion that allocation to the government will bring into the open the question
of who ought in all fairness to bear accident costs that are currently left on
victims.

Passing over the validity of this justification, the clear fact remains that Blum and Kalven, both when they suggest changes and when they reject them for lack of justification, are asserting the need for a theory of accident law. Indeed, they seem to demand even more; they seem to demand a theory capable of calling forth and structuring empirical research from which alone would come facts that in their judgment would justify compensation plans. I suspect, however, that if we waited for such facts to be adequately proven before we made societal changes, we would rarely if ever depart from the status quo. Still, we do have the right to ask for a theoretical framework that will indicate what facts or political opinions justify what kinds of changes. Only with such a framework can we evaluate the factual premises implied in different systems and, in the absence of hard facts, make good guesses. . . .

Michigan No-Fault Insurance Act
28 Mich. Comp. Laws Ann., Ch. 31 (1980-1981 pocket part)

500.3101 Security for payment of benefits under personal and property protection and residual liability insurance, necessity, form, approval; definitions

Sec. 3101. (1) The owner or registrant of a motor vehicle required to be registered in this state shall maintain security for payment of benefits under personal protection insurance, property protection insurance, and residual liability insurance. Security shall be in effect continuously during the period of registration of the motor vehicle. . . .

500.3105 Personal protection benefits, existence, no fault; definitions, bodily injury, accidental injury

Sec. 3105. (1) Under personal protection insurance an insurer is liable to pay benefits for accidental bodily injury arising out of the ownership, operation, maintenance or use of a motor vehicle as a motor vehicle, subject to the provisions of this chapter.

(2) Personal protection insurance benefits are due under this chapter without regard to fault.

(3) Bodily injury includes death resulting therefrom and damage to or loss of a person's prosthetic devices in connection with the injury.

(4) Bodily injury is accidental as to a person claiming personal protection insurance benefits unless suffered intentionally by the injured person or caused intentionally by the claimant. Even though a person knows that bodily injury is substantially certain to be caused by his act or omission, he does not cause or suffer injury intentionally if he acts or refrains from acting

for the purpose of averting injury to property or to any person including himself.

500.3106 Parked motor vehicles, accidental bodily injury

Sec. 3106. Accidental bodily injury does not arise out of the ownership, operation, maintenance or use of a parked vehicle as a motor vehicle unless any of the following occur:

(a) The vehicle was parked in such a way as to cause unreasonable risk of the bodily injury which occurred.

(b) The injury was a direct result of physical contact with equipment permanently mounted on the vehicle, while the equipment was being operated or used or property being lifted onto or lowered from the vehicle in the loading or unloading process.

(c) The injury was sustained by a person while occupying, entering into or alighting from the vehicle.

500.3107 Personal protection insurance benefits, allowable expenses, work loss

Sec. 3107. Personal protection insurance benefits are payable for the following:

(a) Allowable expenses consisting of all reasonable charges incurred for reasonably necessary products, services and accommodations for an injured person's care, recovery or rehabilitation. Allowable expenses within personal protection insurance coverage shall not include charges for a hospital room in excess of a reasonable and customary charge for semiprivate accommodations except when the injured person requires special or intensive care, or charges for funeral and burial expenses in excess of $1,000.00

(b) Work loss consisting of loss of income from work an injured person would have performed during the first 3 years after the date of the accident if he had not been injured and expenses not exceeding $20.00 per day, reasonably incurred in obtaining ordinary and necessary services in lieu of those that, if he had not been injured, an injured person would have performed during the first 3 years after the date of the accident, not for income but for the benefit of himself or of his dependent. Work loss does not include any loss after the date on which the injured person dies. Because the benefits received from personal protection insurance for loss of income are not taxable income, the benefits payable for such loss of income shall be reduced 15% unless the claimant presents to the insurer in support of his claim reasonable proof of a lower value of the income tax advantage in his case, in which case the lower value shall apply. The benefits payable for work loss sustained in a single 30-day period and the income earned by an injured person for work during the same period together shall not exceed $1,000.00, which maximum shall apply pro rata to any lesser period of work loss. The maximum shall be adjusted annually to reflect changes in the cost of living under rules prescribed by the [state] commissioner [of insurance] but any change in the maximum shall apply only to benefits arising out of accidents occurring subsequent to the date of change in the maximum.

500.3108 Survivors' loss, personal protection benefits, scope, maximum benefits

Sec. 3108. (1) Except as provided in subsection (2), personal protection insurance benefits are payable for a survivor's loss which consists of a loss, after the date on which the deceased died, of contributions of tangible things of economic value, not including services, that dependents of the deceased at the time of the deceased's death would have received for support during their dependency from the deceased if the deceased had not suffered the accidental bodily injury causing death and expenses, not exceeding $20.00 per day, reasonably incurred by these dependents during their dependency and after the date on which the deceased died in obtaining ordinary and necessary services in lieu of those that the deceased would have performed for their benefit if the deceased had not suffered the injury causing death. Except as provided in section (2) the benefits payable for a survivor's loss in connection with the death of a person in a single 30-day period shall not exceed $1,000.00 for accidents occurring before October 1, 1978, and shall not exceed $1,475.00 for accidents occurring on or after October 1, 1978, and is not payable beyond the first three years after the date of the accident.

(2) The maximum payable shall be adjusted annually to reflect changes in the cost of living under rules prescribed by the commissioner. A change in the maximum shall apply only to benefits arising out of accidents occurring subsequent to the date of change in the maximum. The maximum shall apply to the aggregate benefits for all survivors payable under this section on account of the death of any one person.

500.3109 Deductions from personal protection benefits, state or federal benefits; injured person, definition; deductible coverage provisions, personal protection benefits

Sec. 3109. (1) Benefits provided or required to be provided under the laws of any state or the federal government shall be subtracted from the personal protection insurance benefits otherwise payable for the injury.

(2) An injured person is a natural person suffering accidental bodily injury.

(3) An insurer providing personal protection insurance benefits may offer, at appropriately reduced premium rates, a deductible of a specified dollar amount which does not exceed $300.00 per accident. This deductible may be applicable to all or any specified types of personal protection insurance benefits but shall apply only to benefits payable to the person named in the policy, his spouse and any relative of either domiciled in the same

household. Any other deductible provisions require the prior approval of the commissioner. . . .

500.3111 Accidents occurring out of state, personal protection benefits

Sec. 3111. Personal protection insurance benefits are payable for accidental bodily injury suffered in an accident occurring out of this state, if the accident occurs within the United States, its territories and possessions or in Canada, and the person whose injury is the basis of the claim was at the time of the accident a named insured under a personal protection insurance policy, his spouse, a relative of either domiciled in the same household or an occupant of a vehicle involved in the accident whose owner or registrant was insured under a personal protection insurance policy or has provided security approved by the secretary of state under . . . section 3101. . . .

500.3113 Persons not entitled to personal protection benefits

Sec. 3113. A person is not entitled to be paid personal protection insurance benefits for accidental bodily injury if at the time of the accident any of the following circumstances existed:

(a) The person was using a motor vehicle which he had taken unlawfully, unless he reasonably believed that he was entitled to take and use the vehicle.

(b) The person was the owner or registrant of a motor vehicle involved in the accident with respect to which the security required by . . . section 3101 was not in effect.

(c) The person was not a resident of this state, was an occupant of a motor vehicle not registered in this state and was not insured by an insurer which has filed a certification in compliance with [law].

500.3114 Persons entitled to personal protection benefits; insurer providing coverage

Section 3114. (1) Except as provided in subsections [(2) and (3)] . . . a personal protection insurance policy . . . applies to accidental bodily injury to the person named in the policy, the person's spouse, and a relative of either domiciled in the same household if the injury arises from a motor vehicle accident. . . . When personal protection insurance benefits . . . are payable to or for the benefit of an injured person under his or her own policy and would also be payable under the policy of his or her spouse, relative, or relative's spouse, the injured person's insurer shall pay all of the benefits and shall not be entitled to recoupment from the other insurer.

(2) A person suffering accidental bodily injury while an operator or a passenger of a motor vehicle operated in the business of transporting passengers shall receive the personal protection insurance benefits to which the

person is entitled from the insurer of the motor vehicle. This subsection shall not apply to a passenger in the following, unless that passenger is not entitled to personal protection insurance benefits under any other policy:

(a) A school bus, as defined by the department of education, providing transportation not prohibited by law.

(b) A bus operated by a common carrier of passengers certified by the public service commission.

(c) A bus operating under a government sponsored transportation program.

(d) A bus operated by or providing service to a nonprofit organization.

(e) A taxicab insured as prescribed in section 3101 or 3102.

(3) An employee, his or her spouse, or a relative of either domiciled in the same household, who suffers accidental bodily injury while an occupant of a motor vehicle owned or registered by the employer, shall receive personal protection insurance benefits to which the employee is entitled from the insurer of the furnished vehicle. . . .

500.3116 Reimbursement and indemnification among personal protection insurers; tort claims

Sec. 3116. (1) A subtraction from personal protection insurance benefits shall not be made because of the value of a claim in tort based on the same accidental bodily injury.

(2) A subtraction from or reimbursement for personal protection insurance benefits paid or payable under this chapter shall be made only if recovery is realized upon a tort claim arising from an accident occurring outside this state, a tort claim brought within this state against the owner or operator of a motor vehicle with respect to which the security required by section 3101 . . . was not in effect, or a tort claim brought within this state based on intentionally caused harm to persons or property, and shall be made only to the extent that the recovery realized by the claimant is for damages for which the claimant has received or would otherwise be entitled to receive personal protection insurance benefits. A subtraction shall be made only to the extent of the recovery, exclusive of reasonable attorneys' fees and other reasonable expenses incurred in effecting the recovery. If personal protection insurance benefits have already been received, the claimant shall repay to the insurers out of the recovery a sum equal to the benefits received, but not more than the recovery exclusive of reasonable attorneys' fees and other reasonable expenses incurred in effecting the recovery. The insurer shall have a lien on the recovery to this extent. A recovery by an injured person or his or her estate for loss suffered by the person shall not be subtracted in calculating benefits due a dependent after the death and a recovery by a dependent for loss suffered by the dependent after the death shall not be subtracted in calculating benefits due the injured person. . . .

500.3121 Property protection benefits, existence, no fault; definitions,
          property damage, accidental damage; measure of benefits;
          maximum benefits

Sec. 3121. (1) Under property protection insurance an insurer is liable to
pay benefits for accidental damage to tangible property arising out of the
ownership, operation, maintenance or use of a motor vehicle as a motor
vehicle subject to the provisions of this section. . . .

(2) Property protection insurance benefits are due under the conditions
stated in this chapter without regard to fault.

(3) Damage to tangible property consists of physical injury to or destruction of the property and loss of use of the property so injured or destroyed.

(4) Damage to tangible property is accidental, as to a person claiming
property protection insurance benefits, unless it is suffered or caused intentionally by the claimant. Even though a person knows that damage to tangible property is substantially certain to be caused by his act or omission, he
does not cause or suffer such damage intentionally if he acts or refrains from
acting for the purpose of averting injury to any person, including himself, or
for the purpose of averting damage to tangible property. . . .

500.3135 Tort liability for noneconomic loss, existence, extent; tort
          liability from ownership, maintenance, or use of motor vehicle,
          abolishment, exceptions

Sec. 3135. (1) A person remains subject to tort liability for noneconomic
loss caused by his or her ownership, maintenance, or use of a motor vehicle
only if the injured person has suffered death, serious impairment of body
function, or permanent serious disfigurement.

(2) Notwithstanding any other provision of law, tort liability arising from
the ownership, maintenance, or use within this state of a motor vehicle with
respect to which the security required by section 3101 . . . was in effect is
abolished except as to:

(a) Intentionally caused harm to persons or property. Even though a
person knows that harm to persons or property is substantially certain to be
caused by his or her act or omission, the person does not cause or suffer such
harm intentionally if he or she acts or refrains from acting for the purpose of
averting injury to any person, including himself or herself, or for the purpose
of averting damage to tangible property.

(b) Damages for noneconomic loss as provided and limited in subsection
(1).

(c) Damages for allowable expenses, work loss, and survivor's loss as
defined in sections 3107 to 3110 in excess of the daily, monthly, and 3-year
limitations contained in those sections. The party liable for damages is entitled to an exemption reducing his or her liability by the amount of taxes that

would have been payable on account of income the injured person would have received if he or she had not been injured.

(d) Damages up to $400.00 to motor vehicles, to the extent that the damages are not covered by insurance. An action for damages pursuant to this subdivision shall be conducted in compliance with subsection (3).

(3) In an action for damages pursuant to subsection (2)(d):

(a) Damages shall be assessed on the basis of comparative fault, except that damages shall not be assessed in favor of a party who is more than 50% at fault. . . .

(4) Actions under subsection (2)(d) shall be commenced, whenever legally possible, in the small claims division of the district court or the conciliation division of the common pleas court of the city of Detroit or the municipal court. If the defendant or plaintiff removes such an action to a higher court and does not prevail, the judge may assess costs.

(5) A decision of a court made pursuant to subsection (2)(d), shall not be res judicata in any proceeding to determine any other liability arising from the same circumstances as gave rise to the action brought pursuant to subsection (2)(d). . . .

500.3172 Personal protection insurance benefits through assigned claims plan, prerequisites, collection of benefits, reimbursement

Sec. 3172. A person entitled to claim because of accidental bodily injury arising out of the ownership, operation, maintenance or use of a motor vehicle as a motor vehicle in this state may obtain personal protection insurance benefits through an assigned claims plan if no personal protection insurance is applicable to the injury, no personal protection insurance applicable to the injury can be identified, or the only identifiable personal protection insurance applicable to the injury is, because of financial inability of 1 or more insurers to fulfill their obligations, inadequate to provide benefits up to the maximum prescribed. . . .

Note

The Michigan no-fault law, first enacted in 1972 and amended several times since then, is considered the most stringent, and hence purest, of the no-fault laws -- the law closest to the ideal of the no-fault proponents. As one might expect, it has given rise to a number of interpretive questions, which we shall not attempt to examine in this book. For a catalog of these questions see G. T. Sinas, Michigan No-Fault Auto Insurance Decisions (Mich. Trial Lawyers Assn. 1978). See also references and annotations in the 1980-1981 pocket part of 28 Mich. Comp. Laws Ann., ch. 31.

Automobile No-Fault Insurance: A Study by the Special Committee on Automobile Insurance Legislation
9-17, 22-39 (Am. Bar Assn. 1978)

The most common criticism of the fault system is that it is an inadequate and inequitable system of compensation for losses sustained in automobile accidents. But this criticism incorrectly assumes that the purpose of negligence liability is to compensate accident victims and that, therefore, the appropriate criteria for evaluating the system's success are those that are used to evaluate schemes of compensation. Under this view, the fault system is a scheme for insuring automobile accident victims which has been complicated by the injection of a fault criterion for recovery of compensation under the scheme. This ignores the fact that negligence liability in accident cases long predates widespread private insurance, let alone the contemporary interest in social insurance. Negligence liability is rooted in age-old notions of corrective justice, in concepts of moral responsibility, and (according to a newer analysis) in the concept of economic efficiency, which is closely related to the intuitive notion of due care. Negligence liability creates rights against that form of wrongful conduct which consists of carelessly injuring another. Its purpose never was to insure people against mishaps. That idea was rejected in the formative years of the negligence concept.

Insurance became an aspect of fault only because potential injurers bought insurance to protect themselves from the consequences of a legal judgment for negligence. This was insurance for injurers, not for victims. Potential victims could, of course, insure themselves against accident injury, whether caused by careless driving or anything else; but this right existed independently of the fault system. The traditional purpose of the fault system, in short, is to provide remedies for wrongful acts rather than to insure victims of accidents.

To this it may be answered that what society needs in the accident area is not remedies for wrongful conduct but an effective system of compensation. This assumes, however, that there are no social benefits to providing remedies against wrongful conduct in this area, and this assumption, as we shall see, is incorrect. It also assumes incorrectly that the voluntary first-party and voluntary or compulsory third-party insurance that is associated with (and in part motivated by) the fault system is not capable of providing adequate compensation to victims of automobile accidents.

Contrary to widespread belief, universal compensation is not incompatible with the fault system. A fact overlooked by critics of the system is that people who are concerned that they might be injured in an automobile accident in which, for one reason or another, they might not receive adequate compensation through a tort claim, have always been free to take out first-party insurance. Life, disability, accident, collision, and medical insurance policies are widely available at reasonable cost and have the added advantage, compared to a scheme of compensation limited to automobile accidents alone, that they protect the insured against a much broader range of potential mishaps. They also enable the insured to choose the precise amount of coverage that is appropriate to his needs. And the voluntary character of this kind of first-party insurance is a positive feature in a society which values individual freedom of choice.

The combination of tort liability (and liability insurance, which naturally accompanies it) and voluntary first-party insurance constitutes a "system" of sorts, but it is not a system of automobile accident compensation which can be meaningfully compared with workers' compensation or social security or health care plans. The fault principle creates a common-law remedy for certain types of wrongful injury and leaves it to the private insurance market to provide potential accident victims with comprehensive compensation if they want it. If this market is deemed to work inadequately, for one reason or another, that is an argument for reform of the insurance market rather than for abrogation of the fault principle.

Once the fault "system" is viewed in its proper light, not only the criticism of its adequacy as a compensation scheme but also the criticism that it costs too much to operate become largely irrelevant. Of course a judicial determination of negligence and contributory negligence, and a judicial assessment of common-law damages, will seem a cumbersome and costly method of determining entitlement to insurance benefits compared to the methods used in other forms of insurance. The purpose of a tort proceeding is not, however, to determine eligibility for an insurance benefit, but to determine common law rights and liabilities. Since the same method is used to determine these rights and liabilities in automobile accident cases as in other common law cases involving other tortious invasions, breach of contract, property right infringements, and the like, there is no basis for concluding that the procedures used are unduly costly — unless it is proposed to do away with the entire system of private law in this country. . . .

The criticism of the fault system as ineffective in deterring accidents that are due to negligent driving is closely related to the criticism that it is a poor system of insurance. Once it is recognized that liability does deter, it becomes difficult to argue that the tort system is just a scheme for insurance or that invasion of rights committed by the careless driver is not culpable because not deterrable. Stated otherwise, our idea of wrongful conduct is bound up with the idea of deterrability — what is wrongful is not the unavoidable conduct, but the conduct that we can avoid — and that the law gives us incentives to avoid committing wrongful acts through the system of civil and criminal remedies.

Many defenders of the fault system nevertheless concede the criticism that negligence liability does not deter careless behavior, and rejoin that it is the office of the criminal law to deter certain behavior, and of tort law simply to rectify an injury that has already occurred. But this concession is premature. Recent literature which applies economic principle to basic legal doctrines argues that the basic purpose and effect of the common law rules, such as the negligence principle, is to set standards of behavior which deter the commission of socially undesirable (in economic terms, inefficient) acts, such as careless acts harmful to others. The intuitive sense that people do not calculate rationally in matters relating to personal safety, their own or others', has been overthrown in recent empirical studies of the reactions of drivers to compulsory seat-belt laws, of people contemplating "crimes of passion" to changes in the severity of the criminal sanction, and of other conduct in emotional circumstances analogous to that of dangerous driving.[4] Of special relevance is a study showing that liability insurance premium rate increases reduce the incidence of automobile accidents.[5]

This empirical literature is too recent to have been available to the authors of DOT's 1971 report [Department of Transportation, Motor Vehicle Crash Losses and Their Compensation in the United States], in which it was argued that environmental factors, not carelessness — factors such as automobile design, highway conditions, and the age and experience of drivers — are the primary causes of accidents. Yet even without empirical studies, it is obvious that the reasoning of the DOT report is deficient. The decision to drive under adverse highway conditions, to invest in optional safety equipment or purchase a safer car, or to modify one's driving behavior in response to the age and experience of oneself or of other drivers, are all matters of individual choice which can be affected by the rules of liability. Moreover, the very fact that most serious accidents apparently cannot be attributed to driver error, such as driving at excess speed or violating other traffic rules, suggests that deterrence does work. The minimal occurrence of an offense in the presence of a stiff penalty is neither evidence that the offense is unimportant nor that the penalty is ineffective; rather, it is consistent with the hypothesis that the penalty has a significant deterrent effect.

As for the impact of liability insurance on the incentive effects of liability, it is true that insurance blunts the deterrent effect of the negligence principle, but it does not destroy it. Although the relationship between careless driving and liability insurance premiums is not one-to-one, there is a relationship — carelessness will tend to force up one's premiums. Moreover, certain crude insurance classifications, such as those placing young drivers in a high-risk category, are correlated with an increased propensity to drive carelessly. These classifications reflect the insurance industry's experience with different classes of drivers and have the effect of keeping some of the more careless drivers in our society off the road. This effect, documented in a study

4. See, e.g., Sam Peltzman, The Effects of Automobile Safety Regulation, 83 J. Pol. Econ. 677 (1975).
5. Richard W. Grayson, Deterrence in Automobile Liability Insurance (unpublished Ph.D. thesis, U. Chi. Grad. Sch. of Bus., 1971).

referred to earlier,[6] makes the accident rate lower than it otherwise would be. This valuable effect will be lost if the liability principle is abolished.

Once the effect of liability in reducing the accident rate is recognized, the alleged costliness of the tort liability system must be reevaluated. Its costs, while perhaps excessive if the purpose and effect of tort liability are simply to provide insurance against automobile injuries, may well be reasonable if tort liability serves to reduce the accident rate and hence the total losses from accidents. . . .

These conclusions follow without detailed examination of the influential statistical studies which have provided the most powerful ammunition to the critics of the fault principle and the proponents of no-fault. Yet it is at least relevant to note that those studies are also deeply flawed, both conceptually and technically. The most influential statistics are those contained in DOT's multi-volume study of automobile accident reparations. A number of these statistics have been cited repeatedly, and by sheer cumulation have passed into the realm of established truths about automobile insurance and liability. It is difficult to find any advocacy of changes in automobile insurance and accident compensation that does not mention the DOT's findings that:

> Only 45% of all those killed or seriously injured in auto accidents benefited in any way under the tort liability system.

> When the economic loss was small (less than $500), victims recovering under tort received an average of $4^1/_2$ times their economic loss. However, at the other end of the loss spectrum when loss was $25,000 or more, even successful tort claimants averaged a net recovery of only $1/_3$ of their economic loss.

> Final tort settlement took on the average $1/_2$ year longer for seriously injured victims with economic losses of $2,500 or more than it did for persons with small losses.

> Tort liability insurance would appear to cost in the neighborhood of $1.07 in total system expenses to deliver $1.00 in net benefits to victims.

> Motor vehicle accident litigation in the court system was estimated to occupy 17% of the system's available resources.

Every one of these "findings" is seriously misleading, if not demonstrably incorrect. The first, that only 45 percent of those seriously injured in automobile accidents received any benefits under the tort liability system, is meaningless once it is recognized that tort liability is not intended as a system of insurance that can properly be evaluated under a criterion of comprehensiveness. Since not all accidents are the result of culpable fault solely on the part of the injurer, it is not surprising that not all accident victims recover under the tort system. Indeed, if all did, that would be evidence that judges

6. Id.

and juries had converted the tort system into an insurance scheme, contrary to its purposes. This illustrates the dilemma of tort liability, when evaluated as if it were an insurance system: if a low percentage of victims recover, this fact can be used as evidence that liability provides inadequate compensation; but if a high percentage recover, this fact can be used as evidence that liability has been converted into, and hence should be replaced by, explicit insurance.

The 45 percent figure is also misleading in ignoring the degree to which victims of automobile accidents obtain compensation outside of the tort system — from life, collision, disability, accident, medical, and other first-party insurance, and from wage-replacement sources such as sick leave and workers' compensation. When these sources of compensation are included, as DOT acknowledged, of those suffering serious injury or death in automobile accidents, "about 9 out of 10 recovered some losses." This is twice the percentage recovering in tort alone. It suggests that a combination of tort liability and voluntary first-party insurance and other sources of compensation provides compensation for almost all victims of automobile accidents.

The second figure quoted above, relating to the alleged overcompensation of victims who suffer only slight economic loss, is at once the most frequently cited statistic in the DOT studies and the least meaningful. The figure is arrived at by limiting economic loss to lost earnings of individuals aged 18-65 who are in the labor force. Moreover, to be included in the sample a victim had to have sustained "medical costs (excluding hospital) of $500 or more, or two weeks or more of hospitalization, or if working, three weeks or more of missed work, or, if not working, six weeks or more of missed normal activity." Since employed individuals involved in such an accident would normally sustain "economic loss" in excess of $500, the accidents from which the excess compensation statistic was derived are primarily those in which a student, an elderly person, a child, or a housewife was killed or seriously injured. These people, though not employed, suffer real and substantial economic losses arbitrarily excluded (or, in the case of a housewife, arbitrarily limited) by the DOT study. For example, a college student who is permanently disabled suffers a real economic loss measured by his lost future earnings; a disabled housewife suffers a real economic loss measured by her contribution to her family's welfare. That the tort system compensates such accident victims in excess of the paltry measurement of economic loss utilized in the DOT study shows not that the tort system is overly generous with small cases, but that DOT erroneously classified a set of highly costly accidents as trivial by defining "economic loss" incompletely.

The finding that people suffering heavy economic losses tend not to be fully compensated under the tort system ignores the fact that these are the people most capable of voluntarily buying adequate life, medical, disability, and accident insurance. It is within their own power to decide whether to be adequately insured against automobile injury. Moreover, the plight of the high earner is unlikely to be alleviated by any type of no-fault insurance. Like other social insurance schemes (e.g., workers' compensation, social security), no-fault is oriented toward providing minimum rather than maximum benefits; and like the tort system it relies on the high earner to partially protect himself in the voluntary insurance market.

As for the finding that final settlement takes longer in more serious cases, a moment's reflection will suggest that the difference in settlement times is inevitable under any rational system of accident compensation. The stakes are greater for both plaintiff and defendant in a more serious case, so naturally they invest more in establishing or contesting the allegations of the complaint, and this slows the dispute-resolution process. Also, in a more serious case (other than death), the full extent of the injury may not be known for a longer time than in the minor case, and so the suit will not be filed as quickly. In short, the victim of the more serious injury is less an innocent victim of delay than a participant in a more careful and deliberate, and hence more time-consuming, damage-assessment procedure.

One of the most frequently cited statements in the DOT studies is that it costs about $1.07 in administrative expenses for each $1.00 in net benefits delivered to the accident victim. This may seem a high ratio of expense to pay-out — until it is remembered that a major benefit of tort liability which is not counted in the benefits received by victims is the reduction in the accident rate that is brought about by adherence to the standard of care established by the fault system. This effect of tort liability has not been adequately measured, nor its monetary equivalent computed, but to ignore it completely is to give a specious plausibility to DOT's statistical demonstration that the expenses of the system exceed its benefits.

Furthermore, the policy implications of the ratio stressed by DOT are unclear once we look behind the summary figures. According to DOT's own calculations, two-thirds of the $1.07 figure represent the insurance companies' internal administrative expense and, as we shall see elsewhere in this report, those expenses might actually be higher under no-fault. Moreover, some of the litigation expenses which constitute the remaining one-third of the expense of the automobile tort system will reappear under no-fault in the form of litigation over the first-party insurer's obligations to his insured.

This last consideration is also relevant to appraising DOT's estimate that motor vehicle accident litigation consumes 17 percent of the court system's total resources. A shift from third- to first-party insurance will reduce the number of disputes between an accident victim and his injurer's liability insurer but it will increase the number of disputes — some fraction of which will end up in litigation — between victims and their own insurers.

A more fundamental objection is the lack of any standard by which to determine whether 17 percent is really excessive. Automobile accidents are the largest man-made source of injury, death, and property damage in our society — greatly exceeding crimes in this regard, which consume an even greater amount of our judicial resources than accidents. Given the number and severity of automobile accidents, 17 percent may not be an excessive fraction of judicial resources to devote to their adjudication. This becomes

even clearer if we move from percentages to absolute dollar amounts. . . .
[O]ne of DOT's studies estimates total court costs, state and federal, of
automobile accident litigation to be $133.7 million. This is small relative to
the accident costs sustained by the victims of the hundreds of thousands of
automobile accidents that occur every year and which might be even more
numerous were it not for the deterrent effect of the fault system. . . .

Within the past eight years a total of 24 states have enacted no-fault
laws (the law in a 25th state was declared unconstitutional and not re-enacted
in any form), as shown in Table 1. Because the laws vary considerably and are
frequently complex, it is difficult to make generalizations about them or even
to categorize them. A crude categorization can be made, however, by distinguishing between those statutes which significantly limit tort liability and
those which do not, and further by distinguishing between those no-fault laws
that provide very limited benefits and those that provide for more substantial
recovery.

Table 1
State No-Fault Statutes by Effective Dates

Year	# of States	States
1971	1	Massachusetts
1972	5	Delaware, Florida, Oregon, South Dakota, Virginia
1973	7	Connecticut, Hawaii, Maryland, Michigan, Nevada, New Jersey, Texas
1974	7	Arkansas, Colorado, Kansas, New York, Pennsylvania, South Carolina, Utah
1975	3	Georgia, Kentucky, Minnesota
1976	1	North Dakota

In terms of these two variables, the state statutes fall into three basic
categories. In the first category are those laws which provide rather modest
benefits and minimal interference with tort law.[1] These laws either place no
restrictions whatsoever on tort liability, or expressly provide that tort actions
can be maintained and merely require that the judgment be reduced by the
amount of no-fault benefits that have been received. The second category
comprises those states that, while providing only limited no-fault benefits,
restrict tort liability significantly by prohibiting certain tort claims.[2] Finally,
some state statutes both restrict tort liability and provide for extensive no-
fault benefits in its place.[3] . . . To give some idea of the variety of the no-fault
concept as it has been implemented, we shall here indicate briefly the provisions of representative statutes from each of the three categories described

1. Arkansas, Delaware, Maryland, Oregon, South Carolina, South Dakota, Texas, and
Virginia currently have such laws.
2. Colorado, Connecticut, Florida, Georgia, Hawaii, Kansas, Kentucky, Massachusetts,
Minnesota, Nevada, New York, North Dakota, and Utah.
3. Michigan, New Jersey, and Pennsylvania.

above. From the first category, the least tort restrictive, we have chosen Delaware; from the moderately restrictive, Massachusetts; and from the highly restrictive, Michigan.

The Delaware statute provides mandatory first-party personal-injury benefits, regardless of fault, of up to $10,000 per person and $20,000 per accident (if more than one person is injured), for medical expenses, lost earnings, loss of service, and funeral expenses. There is no restriction on bringing a tort suit except that damages cannot be obtained for which no-fault benefits are available.

Massachusetts provides a maximum of $2,000 in no-fault benefits, including medical expenses, lost wages, death, and funeral expenses. No-fault benefits are not available, however, if workers' compensation benefits are available, and benefits for lost wages must be reduced to the extent that the insured receives such benefits from other sources. No tort suit may be brought except in a case where the victim is killed or sustains serious injury (as defined in the statute) or his medical expenses exceed $500.

The Michigan statute provides a complex set of no-fault benefits: medical and hospital expenses without limit; 85 percent of any earnings lost, up to $100 a month for three years; and funeral expenses up to $1,000. No tort suit may be brought for injury arising from an automobile accident except where the injury is intentional, the victim's damages exceed his no-fault entitlement, or there is serious injury (as defined in the statute) or death.

The foregoing descriptions are not exhaustive. The statutes are complex and we have set forth here only the highlights. . . .

. . . [O]ne cannot, simply by reading the words of the statutes, discern the actual operation of no-fault — whether it has made things better, or worse — in the states in which it has been adopted. A further difficulty is that the term "no-fault" does not adequately capture the variety of the state laws which are grouped under it. An extreme no-fault approach would abrogate tort liability and replace it with mandatory first-party insurance. No state has gone that far. The common feature of the no-fault statutes is compulsory first-party insurance. Some of these statutes do not limit tort suits at all. In other states there is some, but often not much, restriction of tort liability.

Thus the term "no-fault" describes a spectrum bounded at one end by compulsory first-party insurance in modest amounts without any limitation of tort rights, and at the other end by the full elimination of tort liability and its replacement by compulsory first-party coverage. Given the variety in the plans it would be misleading to devote too much critical attention to the no-fault "principle" — whatever that is — rather than to specific plans. Hence our primary focus in this chapter will be on the operation of specific state no-fault laws, to the extent that evidence is available with regard to their operation. However, certain contradictions in the no-fault idea that are independent of its particular forms seem worthy of a brief discussion. . . .

The no-fault idea contains inherent contradictions which emerge from a consideration of the criticisms of the fault principle that lie behind the no-fault idea. Those criticisms, it will be recalled, are that the fault system (1) provides incomplete coverage, (2) costs too much to operate, and (3) fails to deter careless driving and the avoidable accidents that result from it. No-fault seeks to meet these criticisms by abrogating or limiting tort liability and substituting first-party insurance. But inescapable dilemmas are created. If coverage is broadened by eliminating the bars to recovery that many victims encounter under the fault system, insurance premiums — and hence the cost of the accident compensation system — must rise unless the average benefit is reduced or administrative costs are drastically slashed. Because most of the expenses of the tort system are the internal administrative expenses of insurance companies which (as we shall see in the next section of this chapter) are not likely to be changed significantly by a switch from third-party to first-party insurance, administrative-cost savings cannot be relied upon to offset the higher pay-out expense caused by broader coverage. Thus, it is not surprising that no-fault proponents recommend reducing the average benefit by abrogation of the collateral-benefits principle and other devices. Yet one of the criticisms of the fault system is that the average recovery, at least in the case of serious accidents, is too low. And there is no credible evidence that it is too high for any class of accidents. Hence, the no-fault principle seems to involve a choice between higher premium costs and even less adequate compensation than under the tort system.

Furthermore, while a principal criticism of the tort system is that it is an inadequate deterrent to careless driving, the no-fault system reduces deterrence by compensating people who would be barred by the fault system because their own carelessness contributed to the accident. To summarize, there is no basis for confidence that no-fault statutes will bring us any closer to the goals of its proponents than the fault system. The actual experience under no-fault, to which we next turn, suggests that, if anything, no-fault has resulted in higher accident rates and higher premium costs in the states which have adopted it.

Most of the few studies that have been made of no-fault in operation are contained in a volume sponsored by the Council on Law-Related Studies (CLRS), entitled No-Fault Automobile Insurance in Action: The Experience in Massachusetts, Florida, Delaware and Michigan, published in 1977.

The most extensive study in this volume is of Massachusetts' no-fault statute, which was the first adopted by any state, becoming effective on January 1, 1971. The study concludes that no-fault works well in Massachusetts, or at least better than the fault system had worked. Even if this conclusion were supported by the researchers' data — and we shall see that it is not — it would have very little relevance to the likely success of no-fault in other states. Massachusetts has long been recognized as atypical in its automobile reparation experience. As one of the researchers noted, Massachusetts' "bodily injury claims frequency (claims per hundred insureds) was traditionally not merely the country's highest, but fully three times the national average." This was the result of the fact that, prior to no-fault, bodily-injury liability insurance had been mandatory in Massachusetts, but collision insurance had not been mandatory. An unusually high percentage of auto accidents in Massachusetts resulted in litigation precisely because drivers involved in minor accidents were alleging minor (and for the most part, nonexistent) personal injuries in the hope of recovering enough money under the other driver's bodily-insurance policy to be able to repair the damage done to their automobile. By forbidding minor tort suits and (a year after the original no-fault statute was passed) by making collision insurance mandatory, Massachusetts' no-fault program succeeded in reducing the number of minor bodily-injury suits. There was an 87 percent reduction in the number of suits filed in the state courts alleging negligent auto injury. The reduction in minor bodily-injury suits is the outstanding achievement of Massachusetts' no-fault law. Whether a similar achievement would follow from the adoption of no-fault in other states may be doubted.

While it reduced the number of minor personal-injury suits filed, the Massachusetts no-fault statute did not reduce court congestion. Because it was the minor suits that were eliminated, and these are normally not tried anyway, the fraction of trials among the automobile suits filed after the no-fault law went into effect rose — in fact, doubled — and the average damages in such suits increased by an even larger percentage. After four years of no-fault, automobile cases were still more than 25 percent of the total civil docket in the superior courts of Massachusetts, which is far above what the national average was before any state adopted a no-fault law.

A disquieting aspect of the Massachusetts experience is that the accident rate may have risen as a result of no-fault. That many careless drivers received compensation under the no-fault law is indicated by the finding that 11.4 percent of all paid no-fault claimants had been driving on the wrong side of the street or had been driving the wrong way on a one-way street when the accident occurred.

Another finding in the Massachusetts study is that a strikingly larger proportion of those who received no-fault benefits were involved in single-vehicle accidents and in rear-end collisions. This may not be simply evidence of the more extensive coverage offered by no-fault, but may also reveal a greater propensity for individuals to become involved in such accidents as a result of no-fault. Also relevant here is the effect of the no-fault property damage insurance (PPI), which was implemented one year after PIP (personal injury no-fault insurance), on rates for property-damage coverage in Massachusetts. In 1975 insurers in Massachusetts demanded a 40 percent increase in aggregate premiums, mainly for property damage coverage. The study also reports that a serious legislative campaign is under way to repeal PPI because of escalating premiums. Although some of the premium escalation may be due to the general presence of inflation, or to increased claim propensity, its magnitude suggests that actual damages incurred — the number and/or severity of accidents — may have increased as a consequence of the law.

For many observers, the "bottom line" of the success of a no-fault statute is the effect on premium rates. Here the evidence gathered in the Massachusetts study is highly adverse to the claims for no-fault's success. While, as expected (because of the special problem in Massachusetts with minor personal injury suits), the rates for bodily-injury insurance in Massachusetts have declined substantially since 1970, the last year prior to no-fault, this reduction has been more than offset by increases in property-damage and comprehensive-insurance rates. For example, according to Representative Eckhardt of Texas, chairman of the House Subcommittee on Consumer Protection and Finance, a total auto insurance package, including bodily injury, property damage, collision, and comprehensive coverage, would have cost a driver in East Boston, Massachusetts $542.24 in 1970. In 1977, after more than six years of no-fault and its purported cost savings, the same coverage would have cost $1,219.00. Thus no-fault "held down" the East Boston driver's insurance bill to an increase of about 125 percent.

The Massachusetts study also revealed a number of problems with no-fault that had not been anticipated. For example, some people who were entitled to no-fault benefits and yet did not try to obtain them stated that they were hesitant to assert claims against their own insurer. (Only about five percent of the nonclaimants gave this as a reason, but even this figure is higher than might be expected and shows that not everyone is better off under no-fault.) Other findings suggest that little good results from offering injured drivers benefits not available under the common law. For example, among the improvements in compensation that the designers of Massachusetts' no-fault scheme sought to effect were compensation for the cost of replacement services (household responsibilities, for example) incurred as a result of an accident, plus a system by which injured victims could receive payments as they incurred losses rather than a single lump-sum payment. The study revealed that the intended recipients of these benefits are, for the most part, indifferent to them. Fewer than one accident victim in thirty actually hired anyone to provide replacement services. Similarly, only one-third of PIP (personal injury protection — the first-party protection mandated by the no-fault law) claimants received more than a single payment.

The Massachusetts study suggests that other hoped-for efficiencies of the no-fault system are unlikely to materialize. For example, a no-fault system is supposed to reduce the ratio of administrative costs to the amount of benefits paid. But the study revealed that more than one-third of PIP claimants received less than $50 in benefits and almost three-quarters of the claims involved payments below $200. No data are presented on the expenses involved in processing a claim, but it is difficult to imagine that any claim can be processed for less than $50 — indeed, for less than $200. A negative cost-benefit ratio seems unavoidable as long as the small claimant is not made to bear the administrative costs of processing the claim; recognition of this problem has led to the use of deductibles in nearly all (other) areas of insurance.

No-fault could have been expected to work better in Massachusetts than in virtually any other state in the union, yet, as we have seen, it cannot be pronounced a success on the basis of empirical study. Although the reported data are insufficient to quantify the Massachusetts program's costs and benefits, it may be doubted whether the benefits in reduced filings of minor cases and quicker payments offset the costs in higher premium rates and, perhaps, higher accident rates.

Yet Massachusetts' experience with no-fault appears triumphantly successful when compared to that of Florida, the second state to adopt a no-fault plan (January 1, 1972). The original plan provided for maximum no-fault benefits of $5,000 (compared to $2,000 under the Massachusetts plan) and barred the filing of a tort suit for losses other than current earnings or medical/funeral expenses unless the victim had more than $1,000 in medical expenses or suffered permanent injury or death.

The CLRS study of the operation of Florida's no-fault program, while conceding problems (including fraud), concluded that Florida's no-fault plan had led to an increase in system efficiency as measured by the ratio of benefits paid to premium charges; however, subsequent and more accurate data have shown that this conclusion was unwarranted.

The study reported that no-fault had led to a reduction in tort litigation in Florida, but the reduction found in the only county for which the researcher could obtain adequate data was only 15 percent, far below the level reported in the Massachusetts study and indeed insignificant when it is considered that the cases eliminated by no-fault are invariably the minor ones. The Florida study found that more benefits were being paid under no-fault — but also that the median time that elapsed from initial claim to settlement for all claimants (both those seeking payment from their own insurer and those seeking payment from a third party) had actually increased from the pre-no-fault level.

Florida's $1,000 tort threshold was evidently perceived by many claimants as a target to shoot for in order that a tort action could be maintained. According to Representative Eckhardt, the Florida insurance department has estimated that as many as 30 percent of all no-fault claims paid in the state were fraudulent to a lesser or greater degree. The threshold also resulted in discrimination against poorer accident victims who sought less costly medical attention. And, of course, it removed any incentive an accident victim might have to minimize his medical expenses.

In response to those problems, the Florida legislature in 1976 amended its no-fault law to change the threshold level of damages that had to be sustained before a tort action could be brought from a dollar figure ($1,000) to a complex verbal formula (loss of a body member; permanent loss of a bodily function; permanent injury other than scarring or disfigurement; a serious nonpermanent injury that has a material bearing on the injured person's ability to resume his or her normal activity and life-style during all or substantially all of the 90-day period after the injury and that is medically or scientifically demonstrable at the end of that period; or death). It may be doubted whether so complicated a formula can be successful in screening out the minor suit.

The key finding of the CLRS study of the Florida no-fault experience was that the ratio of total benefits paid to total premiums charged increased by about 56 percent from the pre-no-fault year of 1971 to the post-no-fault year of 1973. The validity of this analysis today is doubtful. To determine the premium charged, the study estimated that one driver with "typical" characteristics would have paid for bodily injury coverage in the period 1971-1973 if he had purchased the coverage from two specified insurance companies. This was an admittedly rough measure since it could not be assumed that rates rose or fell uniformly for all drivers covered by all insurers. (In fact, the part of the study dealing with Florida's no-fault property damage law, which was in effect for less than two years before being declared unconstitutional, found that rates for property-damage no-fault insurance went up more quickly for prior "good" drivers than for prior "bad" drivers.) The study acknowledged that at least part of the reduction in rates was artificial, since the no-fault law itself had mandated an immediate 15 percent rate reduction.

More is known now about the Florida experience with bodily injury insurance rates under no-fault than was known when the CLRS study was first published in 1975. According to Representative Eckhardt, "The cost of bodily injury insurance has increased markedly in Florida since 1971. Statewide, bodily injury rates are up 84% with some companies reporting increases as high as 210%." The CLRS study's conclusion that the ratio of benefits to premiums has risen can no longer be accepted, since it is premised on the assumption that Florida premium rates went down by 15 percent, while the latest figures show that they rose by more than 80 percent. Unless no-fault benefits have risen by more than 80 percent during this period, the study's efficiency measure shows that no-fault is less efficient than the system it replaced.

Furthermore, there is evidence in the Florida study, not remarked on by its author, that safety deteriorated in Florida after, and conceivably as a result of, the adoption of no-fault. Both personal injury and property damage claims per registered vehicle rose significantly between 1971 and 1973. The rise in personal injury claims of 11 percent between 1971 and 1973 was accompanied by an estimated decline in the frequency of personal injury claims per crash of 14 percent. Combining these figures enables us to estimate an increase in crashes per registered vehicle of about 29 percent (= 111%/86% − 100%). This estimated rise in crashes, combined with a reported large increase in premiums for property damage insurance after the institution of no-fault insurance for property damage and a doubling of the proportion of registered drivers in the assigned risk class, suggests that no-fault insurance in Florida as well as in Massachusetts may have been associated with an increase in crash losses from greater riskiness in drivers.

Michigan's plan for no-fault auto insurance became effective October 1, 1973. It goes the furthest of any state plan in providing benefits on a no-fault basis. . . . The CLRS volume contains a study of the Michigan no-fault experience by the state insurance commissioner. The study shows a modest eight percent decrease in the number of automobile negligence suits filed in the Michigan state courts, a trivial decline if we assume that these are the least complex and time-consuming suits. Evidently, then, even a drastic no-fault law need not result in any noticeable relief from court congestion. No-fault in Michigan has not resulted in any reduction in automobile insurance rates. It is true that the increase from January 1972 to January 1976 was modest (15 percent) compared to the other no-fault states studied, but apparently the increase was controlled only by starving the insurance industry for necessary funds. Insurance companies' ratio of losses incurred to earned premiums rose dramatically and resulted in an actual underwriting loss for the industry in Michigan in 1975.

The Michigan study is fragmentary. The only significant benefit recorded is an increase in benefit payments to victims of single-vehicle accidents, who would be unlikely to recover under traditional tort law. Costs were not systematically examined. There is thus no basis for a conclusion that Michigan's no-fault plan has been a success — let alone so marked a success as to justify its compelled extension to the rest of the nation.

The final state plan examined in a CLRS-sponsored study is that of Delaware. Delaware's no-fault scheme, which became effective January 1, 1972, provides no-fault benefits for medical expense, wage loss, and replacement services up to a limit of $10,000 per person and $20,000 per accident. The distinctive feature of the Delaware plan among those of the states studied under CLRS sponsorship is that it places no restrictions on the right to sue in tort, although in any tort action the plaintiff may not obtain damages to the extent that no-fault compensation is available. The study of the experience in Delaware focused primarily on the no-fault scheme's effect on tort litigation. The study concluded that any decline in tort suits was minimal and that "tort litigation is continuing, substantially unabated by the no-fault legislation." It found that no-fault had had an inconclusive effect on settlement practices and on amounts claimed and received in tort actions. It also reported that auto insurance rates declined an average of 9.4 percent within a year after no-fault went into effect, and that within another year bodily-injury insurance rates further decreased an average of 17 percent and property damage rates an average of 10 percent.

An interesting finding of the Delaware study is the degree to which, as experience with a no-fault system develops, the number of suits on automobile insurance contracts increase. In a first-party auto injury compensation system, such suits, by replacing tort actions, might cancel out the administrative savings resulting from a decline in the number of tort actions filed. In Delaware, in 1973, only seven suits on insurance contracts were filed in New

Castle County Superior Court — less than two percent of the 379 auto tort cases filed in the same court. In 1975, in contrast, 47 cases were filed in which an insured sued his no-fault insurer, or in which a no-fault insurer asserted a subrogation action claim as allowed by Delaware law. This was more than 10 percent of the number of auto tort cases filed in that court (436). . . .

To illuminate the important question of the effect of no-fault on court workloads, we have done our own modest empirical study, comparing the percentage of all civil cases filed in tort-restrictive no-fault states that arise out of motor vehicle personal injuries with the percentage for non-tort-restrictive no-fault states and for non-no-fault states. Recent data are available to enable such comparisons to be made for cases filed in the federal district courts of the various states. Although these figures pertain only to federal district court filings and not to state court filings, comparison is still useful. Federal courts obtain jurisdiction over motor vehicle personal injury suits primarily where there is diversity of citizenship between the parties and the amount in dispute exceeds $10,000. Because of this jurisdictional minimum, it might appear that these suits are by nature too large to be the type sought to be eliminated by a no-fault system and thus that comparisons of the filings of such suits in the federal courts of the states with different types of no-fault plan (or no plan at all) is an invalid measure of the effect of no-fault plans on state court filings. This point, however, is not in the end convincing because once diversity is established "[t]he sum claimed by the plaintiff controls [in determining the amount in controversy] if the claim is apparently made in good faith." The plaintiff can seek whatever amount of damages for pain and suffering he wants (and he will in fact claim a sufficient amount in pain and suffering to reach the jurisdictional threshold if he regards the federal court as a more desirable forum). Hence federal suits can arise from accidents where the "economic" loss is quite small, and can easily be of the type that no-fault plans were designed to eliminate.

According to the 1977 annual report of the Director of the Administrative Office of the U.S. Courts, 4.2 percent of the civil cases commenced in all federal district courts during the first six months of 1977 were motor vehicle personal injury suits. The overall percentage for states having tort-restrictive no-fault plans was 3.9 percent, for states having non-tort-restrictive no-fault plans was 5.3 percent, and for fault states 4.1 percent. Thus, a state which adopted a non-tort-restrictive no-fault plan might expect a trivial increase in relative terms in the number of motor vehicle personal injury suits filed in the state's federal district courts (from 4.1 percent to 5.3 percent), while if the state adopted a tort-restrictive no-fault plan it might expect a trivial decrease in the number of motor vehicle personal injury cases filed (from 4.1 percent of all civil cases filed in federal district court to 3.9 percent). Thus, in a nonlitigious state such as Idaho, which does not have a no-fault plan, and where only 383 civil cases were filed in federal district court in the twelve month period ending June 30, 1977, adoption of a tort-restrictive no-fault plan would probably mean a reduction in the number of motor vehicle suits filed from 16 (the number of motor vehicle tort suits filed in the Idaho Federal District Court in the period studied) to 15 per year.

In short, no-fault plans appear to have only a very small effect on court workloads. The Administrative Office data suggest that other factors play a much more important role in determining the percentage of a district court's caseload that is represented by motor vehicle personal injury cases. This is indicated by the wide differences in this percentage among states having similar policies regarding the fault issue. For example, the percentage of such cases for tort-restrictive no-fault states ranges from a high of 7.0 percent in Pennsylvania to a low of 0.6 percent in Florida. The comparable figures for non-tort-restrictive no-fault states are 11.4 percent in South Carolina and 3.4 percent in Texas. While overall the percentage of motor vehicle suits is lower in tort-restrictive states, it is more than twice as high in the tort-restrictive states of Georgia (8.8 percent), Hawaii (7.6 percent), New Jersey (7.6 percent) and Pennsylvania (7.9 percent) than in the non-tort-restrictive states of Maryland (3.7 percent), Oregon (3.5 percent) and Texas (3.4 percent).

Clearly, if a state has a problem with congested courts, adoption of a tort-restrictive no-fault plan will not cure the situation; it will not even guarantee that the relative number of motor vehicle personal injury cases filed in that state will be less than in a neighboring state which places no restrictions on such suits.

Notes

1. Since the publication of the ABA Special Committee's report, there has been an interesting empirical study of the effect of state no-fault statutes (and hence, implicitly, of the fault system itself) on the automobile accident rate. The study, utilizing statistical techniques to hold constant the effect of other variables on the accident rate besides the legislation, finds that the adoption of no-fault laws raises the accident rate — and the more stringent the law (e.g., Michigan versus Delaware), the greater this effect. See E.M. Landes, Insurance, Liability and Accidents: A Theoretical and Empirical Investigation of the Effect of No-Fault on Accidents (Center for the Study of the Economy and the State, University of Chicago, May 1980). The study finds that states that place relatively moderate restrictions on tort liability experience between two and five percent more fatal accidents as a result, while states with highly restrictive laws experience as many as 10-15 percent more fatal accidents. This result may seem extremely surprising, if only because no-fault laws leave tort liability intact in death cases. However, as Landes points out, if restricting tort liability results in less care in driving, there will be more accidents, some fraction of which result in death. For other empirical evidence on the operation of no fault, see All-Industry Research Advisory Comm., Automobile Injuries and Their Compensation in the United States (1979).

2. Federal no-fault automobile legislation similar to the Michigan statute has been proposed. The proposal is summarized and criticized in the ABA
Special Committee's report, chs. 7-8.

O'Connell & Beck, An Update of the Surveys on the Operation of No-Fault Auto Laws
1979 Ins. L.J. 129

Two years ago, the senior author of this article reported on various
surveys on the operation of no-fault auto insurance statutes in the United
States.[1]

Since then, other surveys and studies have been published, and we herein
undertake to update that earlier effort, based on at least the bulk of the
intervening works.

Then, as now, a central concern of the no-fault debate was no-fault's
effect on insurance rates. In this connection, a problem with which the
insurance industry has been confronted under no-fault is discussed in the
1977 report of the U.S. Department of Transportation (DOT) entitled State
No-Fault Automobile Insurance Experience, 1971-1977.

> When faced with large or unlimited exposures beyond their individual
> prident risk-taking abilities, insurance companies typically reinsure all or a
> portion of the risk with another insurer (usually a specialty insurer known as a
> "reinsurer") and cede him a portion of the premium received. Under insured
> tort liability, where financial responsibility or compulsory insurance laws re-
> quired only relatively low minimum insurance coverage limits, small companies
> could choose whether to insure a large exposure and reinsure or to reject the
> risk. Under no-fault, the unlimited exposures become mandatory in three
> States [for medical losses in Michigan, New Jersey, and Pennsylvania] and small
> companies had to accept them or drop out of the business. Reinsurers, them-
> selves uncertain of how unlimited no-fault claims might develop understand-
> ably tended to price their reinsurance conservatively. Small insurers, with
> relatively small capital positions and unable to spread the risk across a large
> block of business, found themselves, in their opinion, competitively disadvan-
> taged vis-à-vis the larger auto insurance companies. The States are now grap-
> pling with this problem. One of the solutions advanced is to pool all exposures
> about a certain limit and pay benefits out of a central fund.

This type of problem, as well as that of premium pricing, is only to be
expected as the insurance industry gradually adjusts from a tort to a no-fault

---

1. O'Connell, "Operation of No-Fault Auto Laws: A Survey of Surveys," 56 Nebraska Law
Review 23 (1977); reprinted in 650 Insurance Law Journal 152 (March 1977). [This article is
recommended as a sympathetic review of some of the same studies discussed critically in the
American Bar Association's committee report on no fault, supra. — Ed.]

system. These problems, however, are merely symptomatic of transition and are not to be regarded as permanent obstacles to the implementation of a smoothly operating no-fault insurance system.

On this subject of costs, a 1978 report by the Michigan Insurance Bureau notes the effect of inflation in wiping out possible premium decreases stemming from no-fault:

> During the past five years Michigan and the rest of the country have seen price levels rise at a rate higher than in recent history. From 1972 to 1977 the cost of goods and services, as measured by the Consumers Price Index, rose 45% Unfortunately many of the factors affecting the cost of automobile insurance, such as the value of cars, the cost of medical care, and the cost of automobile repair and parts, have had increases much above the increase in overall price levels. Inflation has wiped out the hopes of some that the introduction of no-fault auto insurance in Michigan would result in lower premium rates.

Still on the subject of costs, the U.S. Department of Transportation study of states' no-fault experience points out that only a small part of the average motorist's insurance coverage applies to bodily injury. The remaining coverages (such as collision, physical damage, comprehensive, and towing) are not affected by the switch from a tort to a no-fault system covering only bodily injury. For a typical package of coverages including 25/50 bodily injury (BI) liability, $10,000 property damage liability, $1,000 medical payment, 10/20 bodily injury uninsured motorists, basic personal injury no-fault protection, full coverage comprehensive, and $100 deductible collision, the typical bodily injury portion of the total insurance premium is only about 25 per cent. From the perspective of a motorist with this coverage, an increase in the total insurance premium has great psychological and fiscal impact; the (relatively minor) portion of the premium attributable to personal injury protection which may have decreased is almost invisible. Thus, a report to the New Jersey Legislature on New Jersey's no-fault experience indicates that although premiums there generally have increased, the average cost for personal injury coverage actually decreased by 5.5 percent, from $74.29 in 1972 (the year before no-fault was enacted) to $70.18 in 1977.

The Department of Transportation survey studied premium rate changes from 1971 to 1977 in the 14 "modified" no-fault states, as well as in New York, Michigan (states with more ambitious no-fault laws), and in representative states without no-fault laws. The Department published the rate information obtained from two major insurance companies writing insurance in these states. The study concludes that:

> — In current dollars, premiums rose significantly between 1971 and 1976 in virtually all cases, rural and urban, fault and no-fault.
> — In constant dollars (i.e., adjusted for inflation), most premiums exhibited decreases, for both rural and urban, and for fault and no-fault states.

— Even after adjusting for inflation, premiums in certain urban areas exhibited very sharp rises. . . . Interestingly . . . this phenomenon was not restricted to no-fault states. . . .

— When adjusted for inflation, rates in Michigan (the state whose plan most resembles that called for in the original DOT Auto Insurance Report) either held steady or dropped.

A recent study published in the Rutgers Law Review evaluated the cost-benefit performances of the varieties of state no-fault laws. The Study examined the extent to which these laws meet the goals of (1) providing coverage to victims who would not have been covered under tort liability laws, (2) distributing benefits to correspond with the severity of economic loss sustained, and (3) keeping bodily injury (BI) premiums (as distinguished from property damage premiums) "at or below the level they would have reached had no-fault not been enacted." The Study used as a control the non-no-fault states in order to compare the level of BI premiums in fault and no-fault states for factor (3) above, and, in addition, divided the no-fault states into add-on, modified low benefit, modified high benefit, and "pure" no-fault statutes in order to determine relative cost-benefit levels within the group of no-fault states. The Study used rate data for capital cities provided by the State Farm Insurance Company for the five-year period between December 31, 1971-January 1, 1977. Both mean and median rates were included for BI premiums, which basically include BI liability, medical payments, uninsured motorist, and, in no-fault states, no-fault coverage — often referred to as personal injury protection (PIP). BI premiums in fault states increased 22 percent (both mean and median) during the period studied. The Study attributed the increases to higher BI liability costs induced by inflation.

The data for states with add-on no-fault plans indicated a 48 per cent mean and 49.5 per cent median increase in total BI premiums. The Study attributed this to the failure to reduce BI liability costs while at the same time providing no-fault benefits. The reason for this failure to decrease BI liability costs is the absence of any "threshold" restriction on tort suits for pain and suffering. "[N]early all states which have imposed such restrictions have reduced or maintained pre-no-fault liability premium levels, and all have kept liability costs far below the control group [non-no-fault states] averages." The Study concluded that the no-fault benefits provided by add-on plans have been provided at "significant additional cost," and that this type of no-fault plan is thus unsuccessful in providing benefits at traditional tort insurance premium levels.

The Study divided data from modified no-fault states according to the level of benefits provided. Connecticut, Florida, Georgia, Hawaii, Kansas, Kentucky, Massachusetts, Minnesota, Nevada, North Dakota, and Utah were classified as low benefit. "[A]ll low benefit states except Minnesota provide PIP [no-fault] medical and wage loss coverage totaling less than

$15,000. High benefit plans have comparable dollar thresholds but seek to provide far more extensive benefits." The results of the Study show that "while total BI premiums have generally increased in [such] low benefit states, the mean and median [premium] increases have been smaller than those experienced by the control group." The mean increase in total BI for low benefit states was 14 per cent, the median 18 per cent. The Study found considerable variation in rate levels among low benefit states despite roughly similar tort thresholds. Over half the low benefit states included in the Study experienced reductions in their BI liability rates over the five-year test period. None of the low benefit states showed an increase in BI liability rates as great as the control group's mean or median. As one would expect, "[t]his suggests that dollar thresholds have reduced the number of trivial tort claims, producing savings in nuisance overpayments and adversarial procedures which are reflected in liability premiums." The Study concluded that Florida, Minnesota, and Utah — the low benefit states which experienced total BI premium increases in excess of the control group averages — had tort thresholds which failed to check liability costs. Both Florida and Minnesota have recently adopted more restrictive tort thresholds. The Study found no apparent explanation for the varying effectiveness of similar dollar thresholds, but concluded that "an effective threshold is necessary to facilitate economical PIP [no-fault]." The Study found that, as a group, modified no-fault states provided total BI coverage at slightly lower costs than the cost of such coverage in fault states.

In high benefit states — Colorado, New Jersey, New York, and Pennsylvania — total BI premium levels increased by a mean of 15 per cent and a median of 13 per cent. "Surprisingly," says the Rutgers Study, "the State Farm data do not show a statistically significant difference between average premium changes for total BI in low benefit and high benefit modified states. Both groups have experienced increases somewhat smaller than the control group averages." This similarity between low and high benefit states was unexpected because, in theory, the higher the benefits the higher should be the tort threshold to contain costs.

In an attempt to explain the unexpected similarity in low and high benefit states' total BI costs, the Study conducted a further breakdown of total BI into its components. This analysis showed that BI liability rates decreased by 10 per cent (mean) and 12 per cent (median) in the high benefit states, as compared to mean and median decreases of only 1 per cent and 2.5 per cent in low benefit states and an increase of about 27 per cent in fault states.

"This divergence in liability rates, considered with the non-divergence of the *total* BI data, indicates that but for high benefit states' surprising liability savings, they would have, consistent with expectations, shown larger total BI increases than low benefit states. Thus the apparent similarity in total BI cost is inconclusive, based as it is upon an improbable dissimilarity in the performance of near-identical thresholds."

As to why BI liability rates were unusually low in high benefit states, the Study surmised that one reason might be that BI premiums in New Jersey, New York and Pennsylvania, all high benefit states, were being kept artificially low by tight state rate regulation.

The Rutgers Study found that in Michigan, designated "pure" no-fault, an 11 per cent decrease in total BI premiums indicated by State Farm data was substantiated by data from other sources. The Michigan data showed a 53 per cent decrease in BI liability premiums and an 87 per cent decrease in the number of BI liability claims filed.

"Together, reductions in premiums and third-party [tort] claims are, powerful evidence of the efficacy of Michigan's verbal threshold [barring tort claims]. Furthermore, the fact that liability premium decreases have more than offset the added cost of [no-fault benefits] ... suggests that the cost tradeoff envisioned by no-fault proponents is not only a viable concept, but can be implemented effectively for even the most generous [no-fault benefit] ... packages."

The 1978 study by the Michigan Insurance Bureau indicates that no-fault has reduced by 31 per cent the number of automobile negligence suits filed. Liability payments in the first year after an accident have decreased from about $20 million under the tort system to about $2 million under Michigan's no-fault verbal threshold. The Michigan Report states that insurance companies in that state are apprehensive of "erosion" of the strict threshold, and have established large reserves to deal with losses which may be thrust upon them if the Michigan courts permit such an erosion. The Report notes:

"If court decisions do erode the threshold ... the rate of payment of losses will increase drastically, and the costs to policyholders will also rise significantly as more payments are made to less seriously injured individuals. Such a development would break the promise of no-fault and betray the public's expressed desires to control the awards for pain and suffering losses in return for more adequate compensation for economic losses."

The Report compared the rates of increase (reflecting inflation) of various price indices with that of Michigan car insurance premiums and found that "all of the major price indices affecting the price of no-fault [including those for medical care, used cars, and crash parts] are rising faster than automobile insurance prices," except for auto repairs. The Report concludes that "increases in Michigan automobile rates would have occurred even if no-fault had not been adopted."

But, as indicated in the prior article, simple premium aggregates are not by any means the only way of measuring costs. An arguably better measure is the *value* of the insurance purchased.

The New Jersey Legislative Study Commission, examining that state's experience with no-fault, commented that unlimited medical benefits under New Jersey's no-fault law

. . . have resulted in insurers paying for an extraordinary range of services in certain catastrophic cases. Some examples may be cited to illustrate the benefits which some New Jersey residents have received as a result of this unlimited coverage. In one case a young man became a quadraplegic as a result of an automobile accident. As he had no one to care for him, he would normally have been placed in a nursing home, where the kind of care he needed would have been available. The insurer, however, contacted his parents, who lived in England, and they agreed to come to the United States to care for him. The insurer brought them from England, placed a $10,000 down payment on a mobile home for them, and found the father a job. The insurer continued to pay the medical bills for the young man, who has received better and less costly care than if he had been placed in a nursing home or extended care facility. . . .

In New Jersey, although no-fault benefits are provided in unlimited amounts for medical loss, only up to $100 a week for a year, or a maximum of $5,200, is provided for wage loss. In addition, tort claims are preserved for almost anyone — including anyone whose medical expenses exceed only $200. And yet the annual cost in 1977 of all those no-fault benefits for the average car owner, as reported by the New Jersey Legislative Study Commission, was $40.92 versus $70.18 for the $15,000 of coverage for BI liability claims that is preserved under the new law. In other words, tort liability coverage of bodily injury — with low benefits and many impediments to payments — costs almost twice the huge coverage readily payable under no-fault. One can see how easy it would be to further limit tort liability claims and use the money saved to greatly increase no-fault wage loss coverage.

In connection with the arguably improved value per insurance dollar under no-fault, the 1978 Michigan Insurance Bureau Report analyzed the performance of that state's no-fault law in relation to no-fault's promise that payment of first-party no-fault benefits would be adequate to pay all economic loss. The Report judged the success of no-fault by studying whether no-fault compensated victims for their economic loss at a higher level than the tort system. "The Insurance Bureau study . . . showed that real payments [that is, adjusted for the cost of living] for economic loss for the first three full years of no-fault were about 65% higher than for the three years immediately prior to no-fault." The Report attributed this jump in benefits to two factors: under no-fault, previously uncompensable victims (such as victims in one-car accidents) are now being paid; and victims are now receiving the full value of their economic losses (such as medical and rehabilitation services, lost wages up to $19,355 per year, replacement household services, and survivors' benefits). Under the tort system, "recovery was usually limited to the [often low] liability limits which the [other driver] who caused the accident carried. Most individuals carried only $20,000 liability which does not even begin to cover the damages of the most seriously injured individuals."

As to the costs of high no-fault benefits, according to the Michigan Report,

... [A] $100,000 ceiling [on Michigan's no-fault benefits] since the inception of no-fault would have saved only about $6 per car per year, based on claim reserves of the state's six largest insurers. One large insurer estimates the cost of paying claims in excess of $100,000 as no more than the cost of insuring against the theft of CB radios. Providing protection against the catastrophic loss represents the essence of insurance. To attempt to place the burden of catastrophic losses on the individuals suffering the loss, when its average cost is only a few dollars[,] is inconsistent with the provision of insurance.

On the other hand, the recent study by the U.S. Department of Transportation explains actuarial confusion over the determination of the cost of no-fault systems:

... the "cost" of the product that the insurance company sells is, from its perspective, not finally determinable until every claim arising in a given period is paid. Many claims, ... especially those involving serious injuries, may not be finally settled for years or even decades. ... Insurance companies attempt to deal with this uncertainty by establishing loss reserves, i.e., estimated set asides of funds in amounts they believe may be needed to meet the future loss costs of a claimant as the losses develop over time. While insurance actuaries have a number of sophisticated analytical tools to help them establish these loss reserves, judgment does play a large role. In the case of a relatively unfamiliar situation such as no-fault, judgment becomes particularly important in determining this perception of "cost," especially from the viewpoint of the insurance industry.

Professor Alan Widiss of the University of Iowa Law School conducted a study of closed claims in Massachusetts. Fourteen insurance companies, representing a major share of the automobile liability insurance market in Massachusetts, provided information from all files closed by those companies during October 1972. The study was based upon 2,340 no-fault claims which were closed during the period of the survey. In two-thirds of the claim files, some payment had been made. Most of the remaining one-third were files which had been opened upon report of an accident and closed when no claim was made. The results of this survey was compared with those of a similar survey conducted by the U.S. Department of Transportation in 1970, prior to the effective date of Massachusett's no-fault law. Professor Widiss noted that:

... [T]here are several instances when claimants in a subgroup — such as the age group 16-20 years — were compensated under the [no-fault] coverage in about the proportions that they were represented among the DOT liability claim files that were closed without payment. This result seems to validate what would be reasonably expected of a no-fault coverage — specifically that no-fault coverage provides compensation for claimants who were or would have been precluded from receiving reparation under the fault system.

Professor Widiss found that over 20 per cent of the no-fault claims were paid as a result of one-car accidents. These injuries would most likely have gone uncompensated under the fault-based system since there was by definition no other driver to sue for damages in such cases. By comparison, only 2.9 per cent of the claims due to one-car accidents were paid under the pre-no-fault law, according to the DOT study. The Massachusetts study also reveals that bicyclists, who under the DOT study of tort claims had comprised only 0.03 per cent of all claimants receiving compensation, represented 3.6 per cent of no-fault claims paid. Professor Widiss concluded that, "[f]ault considerations again may be significant in regard to such claims. . . . [B]icyclists may . . . constitute a group of persons who, when injured in automobile accidents, were often precluded from recovering and who are now afforded compensation under [the no-fault] coverage."

The 1977 Department of Transportation study published data released by State Farm Insurance comparing the number of pre-no-fault (or tort) claims paid with post-no-fault claims paid for 13 "modified" no-fault states and Michigan. The DOT Study concluded from these figures that "the huge jumps in the frequency of paid claims, even in the face of such countervailing forces as the lower accident rates caused by the 1974 gas shortage, can only be explained by the conversion from third-party tort liability systems to first-party no-fault systems in these States." Thus, in Colorado, for 1972 and 1973, the two years immediately preceding the gas shortage, 9.2 and 7.8 claims (respectively) were paid per 1,000 insured cars, whereas for 1974 and 1975, 13.5 and 12.9 no-fault claims were paid per 1,000 insured cars. These last figures increase when bodily injury (tort) claims paid during 1974 and 1975 are included, yielding a total of 15.8 claims paid for 1974, and 14.6 for 1975. In Michigan, where no-fault became effective October 1, 1973, the figures for the two years immediately preceding no-fault are 12.7 and 13.5 claims paid per 1,000 cars insured, while the no-fault benefits paid for 1973, 1974, and 1975 are 17.1, 14.7, and 14.4, respectively. The DOT study notes in particular two states whose no-fault laws became effective January 1, 1974, at the height of the gas shortage:

> Due in part to the shortage, Kansas had a decline of 0.6 percent in the number of reported motor vehicle accidents which resulted in bodily injury in 1974 compared to the 1971-1973 average for such accidents, and Utah experienced a decline of 8.9 percent. Despite these declines in the accident rate, the 1974 PIP [no-fault] paid claim frequency for State Farm in Kansas was 11.4 compared to the 1971-1973 pre-no-fault average BI paid claim frequency of 6.8. The comparable figures for Utah were 12.2 for PIP and 9.5 for [pre-no-fault] BI.

The DOT study later points out that the shift from third-party to first-party claims indicated by the paid claims frequency data leads to the conclusion that cost efficiency has improved under no-fault. All the states studied show sharp decreases in the number of bodily injury tort claim frequencies after the inception of no-fault. According to the Department of Transportation study, attorneys' fees and other litigation expenses cost $1.084 billion out of a total system expense for the automobile liability industry of $3.768 billion. When the public costs of providing courts are included, the amount rises to $1.218 billion, or nearly one-third of the total system expense. By shifting from third-party to first-party claims, thus eliminating much litigation, it is reasonable to assume that litigation expense will also have diminished. The DOT study affirms that, although "there has been no quantification of the effects of this shift [from third-party to first-party claims] on the administrative costs of the auto insurance systems" in the no-fault states surveyed for paid claim frequencies, "the major shift to first-party benefits . . . for the no-fault states has undoubtedly significantly improved the cost efficiency of their auto insurance systems; the major unanswered question is the extent of this improvement."

The 1978 Michigan Insurance Bureau study similarly found more compensation for genuine losses and for serious victims under no-fault. Under the fault system, payments for pain and suffering are most often made to the less seriously injured — often really as "bribes" to get rid of the "nuisance" value of smaller claims. But under Michigan's no-fault law, much more of the insurance dollar is being paid for genuine dollar losses and, given the fact that no-fault law eliminates smaller tort claims, what is paid for pain and suffering goes to more seriously injured victims (who do, after all, suffer the most pain from accidents).

The Michigan Report indicates that, for the two years prior to no-fault, about 45 per cent of payments to victims was for economic loss and 55 per cent was for noneconomic loss. By contrast, for the three complete years studied which no-fault has been operating, about 63 per cent of payments were to compensate for economic loss, as opposed to 37 per cent for noneconomic loss. "This represents an increase of up to 20 per cent in the proportion of loss dollars going to pay for actual economic loss of accident victims rather than for pain and suffering," with more equitable distribution of benefits since, as stated above, only the most seriously injured victims receive payments for pain and suffering under no-fault.

As to the aim of prompt payment under no-fault, the Massachusetts survey by Professor Widiss discloses some striking figures regarding timeliness of payment under no-fault as opposed to tort: The time lapse between receipt by the insurance company of documentation "sufficient for payment of medical expenses" and the first no-fault medical payment received by the victim was between four and seven days in over 50 per cent of the cases. Eighty per cent received the first payment within a month, and 97.9 per cent within 180 days. The time lapse between the date of accident and date of receipt of first no-fault payment was necessarily longer, dependent as it is upon the filing of claims and supporting documents by claimants. Even here, 63.3 per cent of the claimants received the first no-fault payment within 90 days and 84.8 per cent within 180 days. Under the tort system, according to the U.S. Department of Transportation, only 40.5 per cent of claims were settled and paid within 90 days of the accident and 57.6 per cent within 180 days. Reports to the Department of Transportation from the insurance departments of Colorado, Connecticut, Michigan, and New Jersey show comparable statistics, with Michigan's Insurance Bureau reporting that "almost all auto accident claims are settled within 30 days."

The Rutgers Law Review study cites a report by the Colorado Division of Insurance to the effect that 90 per cent of no-fault claims are handled within six months. A similar report by the New York Superintendent of Insurance indicated that the average no-fault claimant in that state received initial payment within three months of the accident.

The 1978 Michigan Report states that in Wayne County in 1968, prior to no-fault, the average period between the time a tort suit was filed and the time it was settled was 18 months, and many cases were delayed up to four years. Michigan no-fault requires that all no-fault benefits be paid within 30 days after the insurer receives reasonable proof of loss. If payment is withheld after the 30-day period, the balance due collects interest at 12 per cent. The Report shows the efficacy of this type of incentive to prompt payment; "[a]ll Michigan policyholders are receiving [no-fault] benefit payments without undue delay, and virtually all claims are being paid within the 30-day time limit."

Statistics compiled by the Michigan Insurance Bureau and published in the U.S. Department of Transportation's recent survey show that the number of auto negligence cases filed in the Michigan Circuit Court increased by 16 percent in 1972, the year just prior to the effective date of Michigan's no-fault law. Between 1973 and June 1976, the number of auto negligence cases filed had decreased by nearly 20 per cent. Although the oil crisis seems to have accounted for a decrease in the overall number of automobile accidents during this period, the accident rate decreased less drastically than did the number of auto negligence cases filed. Some of the cases filed during this period represented accidents which occurred prior to the effective date of no-fault, so the decrease in suits filed under no-fault is probably even more marked than appears from the Bureau's figures.

The 1978 Michigan Insurance Bureau Report also contains the results of public opinion surveys regarding public attitudes to various individual aspects of no-fault and regarding no-fault in general. The results show that the public favors, by a 62 per cent to 23 per cent margin, the idea providing full medical and rehabilitation benefits to all accident victims. The public also favors, by 79 per cent to 10 per cent, the concept of curtailing rights to pain and suffering in order to provide more adequate medical and wage loss benefits. Furthermore, 53 per cent to 18 per cent said they would relinquish their own rights to damages for pain and suffering in exchange for prompt and complete payment of medical bills and lost wages. Finally, 65 per cent to 26 per cent favored coordination of no-fault benefits for the same economic loss. The Report concluded that, "[t]he responses ... show that people do not

support the tort system as an effective means of providing accident reparations and that no-fault is clearly preferred."

It is thus somewhat surprising to discover that, in response to questions
regarding attitudes to no-fault in general, only 17 per cent of those polled
said that Michigan no-fault is a "good system." Those who said it was a
"poor system" included 55 per cent of those polled. The Report stated that
when these responses were analyzed, it became clear that almost two-thirds
of those giving a "poor" rating identified for reasons for that rating as being
due to problems that plague the entire automobile insurance system and
are not directly related to fault versus no-fault systems. Another 38 per cent
indicated that the basis of their dissatisfaction lay in problems related to
car damage, not to the aspects of the law pertaining to injury to persons.
"Of the . . . categories of problems identified, only the collision problems
are directly related to no-fault. The other problems either were due to
misunderstandings or general factors independent of no-fault." When the
Insurance Bureau evaluated consumer needs in conjunction with the actual
performance of Michigan's no-fault law, the conclusion drawn was that
Michigan no-fault is successful in "meeting the real needs of the
people." . . .

Notes

1. Professor O'Connell has been one of the most vigorous advocates of
doing away with the fault system — for all accidents. For the most recent
comprehensive expression of his views, see J. O'Connell, The Lawsuit Lottery
(1979).

2. In the debate over no fault, the principal issues have been compensation, deterrence, and cost of insurance. Could it be argued that however these
issues (which are empirical) were resolved, justice would require, or at least
provide an argument in favor of, retaining the tort system, at least where the
injurer is guilty of negligence? This issue has surfaced occasionally in the
debate, for example in Coleman, Justice and the Argument of No-Fault, 3
Soc. Theory & Practice 161 (1975). His views are discussed and the issue
explored in the following excerpt from Posner, The Concept of Corrective
Justice in Recent Theories of Tort Law, 10 J. Legal Stud. 187, 197-199, 202-
203 (1981):

> Defending no-fault automobile accident compensation plans against argu-
> ments based on corrective justice notions, Coleman argues that the victim of an
> accident in which the injurer was at fault is entitled to compensation and
> receives it under a no-fault system, but the injurer is not required as a matter of
> justice to be the source of the compensation because he does not gain by his
> wrongful act, as he would if we were speaking of a theft rather than an acci-

dent.[43] Both propositions — that the victim is compensated, and that the wrongdoer does not gain — can be questioned. Take the second first. The injurer avoids the costs of taking care. This cost saving is a gain to him; if his conduct (driving too fast, or whatever) is wrongful, it is a wrongful gain. Negligence under the Hand formula is a failure to take cost-justified precautions, and this failure involves a cost saving to the injurer which is a wrongful gain to him. Coleman has made not only a mistake in economics but a mistake about Aristotle, who used "gain" and "loss" to describe the relation between injurer and victim even when the term "gain" was (he thought) not quite appropriate, as in the case of a wounding.[44]

And is the victim really compensated? He receives the insurance proceeds, and let us assume they are sufficient to make him whole; but he paid for the insurance, so he just receives what is his. Potential victims as a class are clearly harmed by people who cause accidents; accident insurance premiums will be higher the higher the accident rate, and there will be no compensation by the wrongdoers for these higher premiums. Therefore, no-fault automobile accident compensation plans, which amount to eliminating liability and compelling potential victims to insure (at their own cost) against being hurt in automobile accidents, would appear to violate corrective justice because they do not redress injuries caused by wrongdoing.[45] . . .

. . . Suppose the advocates of no-fault automobile accident compensation plans are correct that a combination of criminal penalties for dangerous driving and compulsory accident insurance for potential victims would be a more efficient method of accident control, considering all relevant social costs — the costs of accidents, the costs of accident avoidance, and the costs of administering the accident-control system itself — than the present tort system. If the criminal penalties deterred all negligent driving, there would be no victims of wrongful conduct and so no problem with the abolition of liability. But not all negligent injuries would be deterred, so some victims of wrongful injury would go uncompensated. Would the no-fault system therefore violate corrective justice? Not necessarily. The concept of ex ante compensation [see note on corrective justice in Chapter 7] . . . is . . . relevant. If the no-fault system is really cheaper, potential victims (who are also drivers) may prefer to buy accident insurance and forgo their tort rights in exchange for not having to buy liability insurance.

But there is a simpler route to the conclusion that a no-fault plan would not necessarily violate the concept of corrective justice. If there are good reasons, grounded in considerations of social utility, for abolishing the wrong of negligently injuring another, then the failure to compensate for such an injury is

43. "But in the case of accidental torts there is, in general, no gain on the wrongdoer's behalf that needs to be eliminated. That his conduct is wrongful supports the right of the victim to recompense, nothing more." Coleman, Justice and the Argument for No-Fault.

44. . . . To be sure, as Coleman has pointed out to me, the gain in the negligence case is not triggered by the loss — it would be the same if the accident had not occurred — but I do not see what difference that makes so far as the wrongfulness of the injury is concerned. We would say that a robber who shot his victim injured him wrongfully, though it was no part of his plan to shoot him and he did so only because the victim resisted.

45. This assumes, of course, that negligence is wrongful. Aristotle would not have thought so, but, as Coleman and I both believe, Aristotle's idea of what constitutes wrongful conduct can be severed from his idea of corrective justice. . . .

not a failure to compensate for *wrongful* injury. To repeat an earlier point [see id.], corrective justice is a procedural principle; the meaning of wrongful conduct must be sought elsewhere.

Schwartz & Komesar, Damages and Deterrence: An Economic View of Medical Malpractice
298 New Eng. J. Med. 1282 (1978)

Attacks on the malpractice system are widespread and intense. According to some critics, too many claims are brought, and excessive damages are awarded. Others decry the lawyers' contingency fee as an inducement to unwarranted suits, or assert that the system penalizes physicians randomly. These and other criticisms have led to demands for major reform — even to proposals that the tort system be replaced wholly or in part by other methods for dealing with medical injury. Curiously enough, the perceived failings and proposed correctives are rarely subjected to critical scrutiny; rather, they are taken as self evident.

These critiques of the existing system rest largely on an assumption that the primary or sole purpose of malpractice law is to compensate injured patients. But it can be argued, on the basis of modern economic analysis, that this rationale is unduly narrow: findings of negligence are seen not only as redressing past wrongs but also as giving providers an incentive to avoid future careless injuries. Viewed in this way, the malpractice system and its problems dramatically change character.

As early as 1881, Justice Holmes, in a classic treatise on the subject, observed that compensation should not be viewed as the rationale of negligence law. Because individuals could, if they wished, insure themselves against accidents, he could see little reason for a government-operated system of compensation. More recently, critics of the compensation rationale have pointed out that patients could be indemnified against medical accidents through insurance programs, private or social, at a much lower administrative cost than that exacted by tort proceedings. Indeed, the legal apparatus required to determine negligence and place blame is so expensive that only about 35 cents of every dollar in malpractice premiums is paid to successful claimants; by contrast, 80 cents of every premium dollar reaches patients with health insurance.

Even if negligence litigation were not expensive, as a means primarily to compensate the innocent injured, it would have puzzling features: two different people may sustain an identical injury and be equally innocent of its cause, and yet their prospects for receiving damages may be entirely different. Eligibility for compensation is determined by the behavior of the person responsible for the injury; so if negligence is present in one case and not in the other, one person will be compensated, and the other will not.

The negligence system makes a great deal more sense if it is understood primarily as a means to deter careless behavior rather than to compensate its victims. By finding fault and assessing damages against the negligent provider, the system sends all providers a signal that discourages future carelessness and reduces further damages.

The concept of negligence is fundamental to malpractice law, but the usual definitions of negligence, even in law books, suffer from vagueness. Legal formulations, such as "conduct which involves an unreasonably great risk of causing damage" or "conduct which falls below the standard established by law for the protection of others against unreasonably great risk of harm," are intuitively appealing. But such definitions only substitute, by implication, a term like "unreasonable conduct" for "negligence"; they do not specify what "unreasonable" means.

Some 30 years ago, the distinguished jurist Learned Hand formulated an explicit definition of negligence, which has now become a textbook definition. Negligence occurs, he stated, whenever it would cost less to prevent a mishap than to pay for the damages predicted to result from it. More explicitly, the cost of preventing a mishap (C) must be less than the probability that it will occur (P) multiplied by the loss suffered when it occurs (L). Restating the rule in symbols: negligence occurs whenever $C < P \times L$. The product ($P \times L$) is usually called "expected loss" or "expected damages." . . .

The Learned Hand Rule has a rather obvious corollary, which some people find difficult to accept: there are accidents that, from society's point of view, are not worth avoiding. The cost of prevention far exceeds the expected loss; so the accident should be allowed to occur. . . .

For the malpractice system to work as an efficient deterrent to negligent behavior, physicians must encounter an expected loss ($P \times L$) sufficient to make them fully aware of their deficiencies, but not substantially above that level. If awards do, in fact, exceed the losses suffered by claimants, and if there are too many successful claims we have a "malpractice problem" much as the critics represent it.

The theoretical aim of the tort system is to set the value of an award equal to the loss suffered. Such an award has three components in a malpractice judgment: medical expenses, both past and future; lost earnings, past and future; and compensation for pain and suffering.

It is a widespread belief that damages being awarded by the American courts are excessive when judged by these criteria. Criticism of high damages appears to be based, in part, on the attitude that pain and suffering are not legitimate losses for which compensation is warranted. But someone whose injury affects his life-style — say, the ability to participate in recreation or the ability to have children — is paying a price that is properly included in a damages award.

The highest, and therefore the most conspicuous, awards — those in excess of $50,000 — have the largest element of compensation for pain and suffering. Such awards occur almost exclusively when a catastrophic injury, such as paralysis or severe brain damage, has resulted from negligence. In such circumstances, the effect on life-style is enormous, and a jury properly assesses the loss as a real injury that can only be compensated monetarily. In these terms, even the largest awards do not seem excessive.

The average payment in the award range of less than $50,000 was substantially below medical expenses and lost earnings — typically in the range of one third to two thirds of such losses. Indeed, in the aggregate, awards in 1974 were slightly below medical expenses and lost earnings.

Many more incidents of malpractice occur, it appears, than result in a claim for damages. Records of patients discharged from two hospitals during 1972 revealed a large number of severe injuries resulting from malpractice; of these, only one in every 15 led to malpractice claims. The same study also suggested that many more incidents of malpractice had actually occurred than could be established from the records (this finding will hardly surprise physicians familiar with hospitals' record-keeping practices).

The conclusion that many incidents never lead to a claim is bolstered by the observation that 40 per cent of the file entries held by insurance companies consist of mishaps reported by a physician but never pursued by the patient. There is, moreover, a large pool of malpractice incidents in which the decision to carry out a procedure, rather than a bad outcome, is a form of negligence. Unnecessary surgical procedures, most often hysterectomies and tonsillectomies, probably comprise the bulk of these instances. Numerous as they are, unnecessary operations rarely lead to malpractice claims and have not been included in the analysis of incidents versus claims.

Since 1972, the number of malpractice claims has risen by nearly 50 per cent. Even after estimates are adjusted to account for this change, at most only one out of every six or seven incidents can be expected to result in a claim. A recent study in California supports this estimate: of malpractice incidents detected in hospital records, no more than one sixth eventuated in a claim. This conclusion is based on the calculation that there were approximately 24,000 instances of malpractice in California hospitals during 1974, but that no more than 4,000 of the injured filed claims.

The fraction (detected from the record) of malpractice incidents manifested in claims against the provider is thus quite small, probably below 20 per cent. Given the degree of uncertainty in the data, we calculate, however, that the ratio of claims to incidents could be as high as 0.3 or less than 0.1. In any case, the number of suits, even though it is burgeoning, remains far below the theoretical level required as a full signal of the expected loss (P × L) resulting from negligence. On the other hand, from society's point of view, some of the suits required to convey the full message may actually not be "worth" bringing. . . .

A court's failure to recognize negligent behavior has the effect of reducing the expected loss and thus permits physicians to set their investment in mishap avoidance below the ideal level. At the same time, the malpractice system as a whole is made more expensive because the proceeding raises administrative costs but yields no benefit.

When non-negligent physicians are penalized, the result is also costly. Physicians, realizing that such errors occur, are induced to practice inappropriately "defensive medicine" — i.e., to provide medically unjustified care to reduce the probability of a malpractice suit. The availability of third-party payment permits a physician to use diagnostic tests and hospitalization without restraint from the patient or cost to himself, and thus to demonstrate a level of care so painstaking that neither a patient nor a jury would be likely to make the error of calling him negligent. But this immunity is bought at a cost to society far in excess of anticipated benefits. The excesses of defensive medicine will be discouraged only if providers of health care can be encouraged to compete with each other. When a provider, such as a prepaid health plan, lowers its expenditures on defensive medicine and then passes the savings on to its members, it can attract patients away from the more wasteful, and thus more expensive, providers.

Any system is liable to error, the costs of which must be subtracted from the profits of the system as a whole. In cases of negligence, there are two incentives to avoid mistaken judgments: the economic loss sustained by society and the personal injuries suffered by a plaintiff or defendant.

Even if the signal were perfect — every incident of malpractice leading to a proper claim, and every award equal to the loss suffered by a patient — under existing conditions it would fail to elicit the appropriate response from physicians. Malpractice insurance, as it is currently administered, virtually insulates the negligent physician from the damages award and, thus, from the malpractice signal.

The reason is simple: the malpractice premiums of individual physicians are rarely influenced by their record of claims, settlements and verdicts. Rather, premiums are usually set for an entire specialty group in a given region. Thus, the physician with a record of frequent negligence bears no larger a share of the burden than his colleagues with excellent records. No individual physician has more than a slight pecuniary incentive to reduce the expected losses resulting from his own behavior.

Under the prevailing system of group rating, we can imagine a physician who could avoid an unexpected loss of $1,000 by spending $100. And yet, if his malpractice premiums are set for a group of 100 physicians, his own premium will rise, as a result of the mishap, by only $10 (and so will that of 99 other physicians). The individual physician is thus assessed only one tenth of what it would have cost him to prevent the injury. In reality, the physician may not lose even the $10; for in most cases all physicians in a given group can pass on nearly all of the cost of their rising premiums, as increased fees, to third-party payers. Thus, the burden of higher malpractice premiums falls largely on the patient in the form of a higher health-insurance premium.

As a rule, the system of group rating successfully interferes with transmission of the signal, but there is one partial exception. Part-time practitioners of a specialty must pay the full premium, even though only a fraction of their income derives from it. To the extent that a part-time practitioner — say, an otolaryngologist doing some plastic surgery — is incompetent, he is successfully weeded out by the group rating. In this situation, the malpractice system still has a deterrent effect, as was demonstrated by a recent study of California physicians who have been relinquishing part-time activity and reclassifying themselves exclusively into their primary area of competence. Of course, the effect is clumsy, in that it also eliminates part-time specialists who are competent but cannot or will not pay the full specialty premium. Group rating is then an exceedingly insensitive method of identifying the negligent physician.

Malpractice insurance, on the other hand, has important social value, and our comments should not be taken as an argument for abolishing insurance protection. Because insurance spreads risks, it protects the physician against the financial catastrophe that could result from even a single large finding against him, and also against erroneous findings of negligence. A balance must therefore be struck between the risk-spreading value of insurance and the need for experience rating as a means of sending the deterrent signal to the physician.

The lack of individual experience rating in malpractice premiums has, in the past, been economically acceptable to both the insurance industry and the medical profession. For the industry, the cost of identifying individual bad risks has probably not been worth the potential savings. Now, as malpractice litigation comes to involve ever larger amounts of money, the interests of both the industry and the profession may shift toward a system of experience rating.

If a physician were rated by his individual experience, his premium would reflect, to at least some degree, the risk that he poses to the insurer. Moreover, given the procedures employed by health-insurance companies, such physicians would probably not be able to raise fees much above those prevailing in the community. Thus, physicians who pose substantially more risk than others would themselves have to absorb much of the extra burden of premium costs.

Experience rating of physicians is, of course, justifiable only if suits are not brought randomly or capriciously. It has been argued that "good" physicians are sued as often as the "bad." In support of this contention, the belief is expressed that doctors with board certification are sued as often as those who are less well trained. Even if this statement should prove correct, it is not evidence that negligence is inaccurately found. Many factors could lead well trained specialists to perform below their presumptive level of competence. Some well trained physicians may take on too many patients and invest less time per case than is appropriate. Others may assume responsibilities in areas for which they are not trained or experienced. Moreover, the thesis that suits are brought randomly is not supported by a recent study of 8,000 physicians in the Los Angeles area. In a four-year period, 46 physicians (0.6 per cent of the 8,000) accounted for 10 percent of all claims and 30 per cent of all payments made by the insurance plan. The average number of suits against the 46 doctors was $1^{1}/_{2}$ per year. Analysis indicates that doctors against whom multiple suits are brought do, indeed, represent a higher-risk population than their colleagues.

Virtually the only penalty currently paid by the negligent physician is the value of his time spent in defending a suit and the costs of his embarassment. In the absence of experience-rated premiums, these factors may be the only effective component of the signal and may serve some useful purpose. But because the costs cannot be purposely set, they are not likely to equal the damage assessment that the physician should experience if resources are to be efficiently allocated. "Time and embarassment" costs may be either larger or smaller than the optimum.

According to a popular line of reasoning, lawyers are encouraged to bring malpractice suits that lack merit because they are paid a percentage, usually one third, of the damages awarded; if they were paid a flat fee for service they would not be so indiscriminate. Even if it is true that too many frivolous suits are brought, this analysis of the contingency-fee system would be incorrect.

The lawyer who is paid a contingency fee is compensated only if he succeeds in obtaining either a settlement out of court or an award from a jury. He is not likely to invest time and several thousand dollars in out-of-pocket expenses on a case with little prospect of success. Under the system of contingency fees, lawyers thus have the incentive to filter out capricious suits, which otherwise would overload the courts, harass physicians and produce no social benefits.

Payment by contingency fee not only encourages the lawyer to turn away baseless claims but permits him to accept clients lacking the funds to pay a fee for service. The contingency fee offers "a key to the courthouse door" to some persons with valid claims that would otherwise be lost to the system. Without contingency fees, the deterrent signal to the physician would be reduced.

Why, then, if contingency fees are such an incentive to careful selection of cases, are 80 per cent of claims that reach trial ultimately resolved in the physician's favor? During periods of rapidly changing technology, like the present one, we must expect that individual doctors and lawyers cannot always be certain of correct medical practice. Litigation can serve to establish proper standards and thus to provide important information about the changing limits of malpractice. The suits providing this information may well be appropriately brought, even if the accused physician is exonerated.

Fee-for-service payments to lawyers would be likely to have perverse effects on the malpractice system because lawyers would actually have an incentive to encourage suits, regardless of their merits. Responsibility for screening suits would then devolve on the client himself, who is unlikely to be adequately informed about prospects for success. The number of suits might be reduced, but not because the frivolous ones had been eliminated. Rather, those who simply could not afford to pay for litigation would be discouraged.

Dissatisfaction with malpractice proceedings has produced various suggestions for changing the system, such as ceilings on the size of awards and a shift to fee-for-service payment of lawyers — changes that might well have undesirable effects. Also advocated is a system of arbitration whereby a panel of experts would reach a finding through less formal means than a full-fledged jury trial. With this system, the gains in efficiency might be offset by substantial losses: the protection against bias and influence that a broadly based, rotating jury provides and the accuracy attained by complete and careful presentations in court.

The negligence standard might be abandoned altogether, and another form of liability substituted for it. One approach, for example, would establish a system of negotiations between patient and physician, who would agree, in advance, to a given investment in mishap avoidance. This "contractarian" approach, as it is called, neglects the basic problem that necessitated regulation of medical care, in the form of malpractice law, to begin with: the consumer of medical services, more than the consumer of most goods and services, lacks the information and sophistication needed for bargaining. It is precisely this market failure that created the need for regulation of health services, whether in the form of licensing or litigation.

At another extreme, and currently receiving the widest attention, is a proposal to make the physician automatically responsible for many types of mishap, regardless of fault. The no-fault alternative deserves some scrutiny because it may prove to be a problematic "solution" to existing problems.

Under most of the proposed no-fault programs, the physician would be held liable for any bad outcome associated with a particular "compensable event" — any complication of a blood transfusion, for example — and would be insured accordingly. Such no-fault liability would remove from litigation a number of events in which bad outcomes are usually, but by no means exclusively, the results of negligence. In such cases, the costs and unpleasantness of malpractice proceedings could be avoided, and, proponents argue, a net saving relative to current expenditures would be achieved.

It is not clear how great the real savings under a no-fault system would be, because a no-fault system could hardly eliminate disputes and litigation. As with workmen's compensation (another form of no-fault insurance), disagreements might arise over whether a particular outcome — say, hepatitis — was in fact the result of a compensable event, such as a blood transfusion, or was the untoward effect of a drug concomitantly administered and known occasionally to cause liver damage. Litigation would be inevitable. The combined cost of such litigation, and of payments to patients who were injured but not as a result of negligence, could well offset the overall saving that a no-fault system might otherwise achieve.

In the design of a no-fault system, the most serious question must be: Who will pay the damages? If the individual physician's premiums do not reflect the costs of compensable events attributed to him, he will not be deterred from negligence. To achieve deterrence, the individual physician must be rated by his experience. But the use of individual experience ratings for no-fault insurance premiums could be expected to have some distinctly perverse effects. The practice of "defensive medicine" based on third-party resources would be encouraged because the physician would be liable for any bad outcome and would thus gain maximum protection from highly redundant safeguards. The savings would go directly to the physician; the costs would be borne by the patients.

Perhaps more seriously, physicians would be deterred from undertaking risky procedures, even when such procedures were, on medical grounds, most appropriate and should, for the patient's sake, be ventured. The cost of a bad outcome from the procedure would be borne solely by the physician, and in this case, the patient would probably be deprived of an opportunity for proper care. Skilled physicians, to whom difficult and high-risk patients are referred, would be especially penalized. In principle, a complex schedule of premiums could offset this tendency by comparing liability payments with the risk profile of a given doctor's practice. In reality, such a scheme would be difficult to implement and open to abuse.

If, on the other hand, experience ratings were abandoned, the physician would have little or no economic incentive to prevent mishaps, and a rise in the number of bad outcomes — compensable events — could reasonably be predicted. (Not only would premiums fail to reflect negligence, but time and embarrassment costs would have disappeared.) An increased frequency of bad outcomes would also raise the costs of a no-fault system above currently predicted levels.

The no-fault alternative does not a priori appear to offer noteworthy advantages over the present system. And even if it could be implemented for some selected group of events, the malpractice system would still be needed to deal with the very large number of cases that could not feasibly be dealt with under a no-fault system. The prospect of two systems, both of them complex and fraught with problems, is not an attractive one. . . .

Notes

1. Concern with tort liability for medical malpractice has been voiced primarily by physicians and their insurers, reflecting steep increases in medical malpractice insurance rates. Between 1966 and 1972, those rates rose fivefold for physicians, and more than that for surgeons. See Reder, Medical Malpractice: An Economist's View, 1976 Am. Bar Foundation Research J. 511, 513 (table 1). (What developments in the law discussed elsewhere in this book might explain this rise?) Since 1972, malpractice insurance rates have

continued to rise, and although the increase has been moderated by the passage in many states of legislation limiting damage awards in malpractice suits and sometimes (as we have seen in previous chapters) abrogating specific liability doctrines (e.g., strict liability for serum hepatitis), malpractice insurance rates more than doubled between 1974 and 1978 — and the fraction of doctors with no insurance tripled during this period. See Statistical Abstract of the U.S. 113 (U.S. Dept. of Commerce) (table 175).

2. Reder, supra at 560, summarizes the results of his economic study of medical malpractice as follows:

> 1. The sharp increases in malpractice premiums demanded by insurers in 1975 were foreseen and the reaction of the medical profession was premeditated. Because of their strategic position, medical organizations have had substantial success in exerting political pressure to reduce the malpractice liability of doctors and hospitals and the fee schedules of plaintiffs' lawyers engaged in malpractice litigation.
>
> 2. Economic theory offers no criterion for deciding whether victims of any kind of injury are compensated adequately. However, a commonsense judgment would be that compensation should depend only upon the extent of loss and not upon the circumstances under which the injury occurred or the identity of the victim. Data exist in the records of insurance companies that would enable an investigator to ascertain the extent to which victims of medical malpractice are compensated better, or worse, than victims of injuries causing equal loss but arising under different circumstances; however, as yet, these data have not been systematically collected or analyzed. As a result, we are unable to say whether victims of malpractice are compensated better or worse than victims of other types of injuries.
>
> 3. Though solid data are lacking for the years since 1972, it is clear that premiums for medical malpractice insurance have been rising faster, at least since 1960, than either the consumer price index or (even) its medical care component. The cause of this rise cannot be attributed to any appreciable degree to deterioration of the quality of medical care, though measurements of quality cannot be made easily and none is available. As nearly as can be ascertained at present, the factors that have exerted the greatest upward pressure upon malpractice premium rates have been (i) rising per capita earning power, which results in greater loss of earnings per injury, and (ii) a legal climate that has been increasingly favorable to malpractice plaintiffs.
>
> 4. Economic theory suggests that it is better for the distribution of risk of iatrogenic injury to be determined by individual agreement between doctors and patients than by legal prescription. The advantage of individual agreement over legal prescription lies in the ability to "tailor" the terms of individual contracts to the particular desires of the parties. The disadvantage is the large "transaction cost" of drawing up agreements that cover the whole range of possible contingencies. To overcome this cost, standard contract forms would have to be used, and the provisions of such forms would be a matter of legislative and judicial concern.
>
> Legislatures and courts might permit malpractice liability to be determined by contract, provided that (i) the less informed parties, the patients, had

sufficient counsel to protect their interests, and (ii) the contracts did not entail lower standards of liability and, by implication, inferior medical care for patients who pay lower fees and presumably have less wealth. These two provisions would greatly limit, though not necessarily eliminate, variation in the terms of contractually determined malpractice liability that courts and legislatures might permit.

5. The cost of adjudicating malpractice claims absorbs more than half of the total amount paid claimants. This cost represents primarily the value of lawyers' time required for both prosecuting and defending claims. The value of an hour of lawyers' time in malpractice work is determined by what a lawyer of comparable skill and experience could earn in other branches of the legal profession.

The amount of attorney time required to recover a dollar for a given injury depends upon the mechanics of the legal process. These mechanics are such as to make large recoveries attainable only as part of a negotiation process that involves substantial risk of going to trial in the face of a probability of about .7 of obtaining a zero recovery after trial. Consequently the large attorney rewards that result from contingent fees in successful cases must serve as an offset to numerous and costly failures.

The scant empirical evidence available does not suggest that, after allowing for the cost of failures to obtain recovery, plaintiffs' malpractice attorneys earn more than a competitive return per hour. Consequently, any legislatively imposed limit upon plaintiffs' attorneys' fees, whether imposed directly through a schedule of maximum fees permitted or indirectly by a limit upon gross recovery permitted under specified circumstances, will reduce the amount of attorney time invested in prosecuting malpractice claims.

6. The prevalent method of compensating plaintiff attorneys in malpractice litigation is by contingent fee. The reason this method of payment is so widely used is the great advantage plaintiffs' attorneys have, relative to their clients, in financing a lawsuit. Prohibiting contingent fees would, therefore, reduce the ability of plaintiffs to finance prosecution of their claims and thereby reduce the expected recovery from a given malpractice event.

7. The distribution of the cost of malpractice settlements as between patients and doctors depends upon the relative elasticities of the supply and demand curves for medical services. The elasticity of demand is well below unity, but we have no reliable estimates of supply elasticity. The supply elasticity depends critically upon (i) the willingness of medical schools to vary admission standards in order to maintain a desired growth rate in the number of doctors, and (ii) the responsiveness of immigration policy to anticipated variations in the growth rate in the number of native-born doctors. Virtually nothing is known about the empirical magnitude either of (i) or (ii).

An increase in the cost of settling malpractice claims will tend to cause a change in quality of medical service toward a style of care less likely to generate malpractice claims. This tendency will operate on both the supply and demand sides of the market. The induced change in quality will partially offset whatever increase in price of medical service would otherwise have occurred. However, as little can be said about the empirical magnitudes involved, confident statements about the distribution of the burden of increased malpractice premiums are not warranted.

See also Reder, An Economic Analysis of Medical Malpractice, 5 J. Legal Stud. 267 (1976).

3. Notice how, in the debate over medical malpractice, unlike the debate over automobile accidents, the deterrent effect of tort liability is conceded (though alleged to be perverse) under the rubric of "defensive medicine."

4. Extending the no-fault principle to medical malpractice and products liability is advocated in J. O'Connell, The Lawsuit Lottery, chs. 9-10 (1979). An earlier version of his proposal is discussed in the next, and concluding, excerpt.

Posner, A Comment on No-Fault Insurance for All Accidents
13 Osgoode Hall L.J. 471 (1975)

O'Connell's insensitivity (if I may speak bluntly) to the basic policy issues involved in the debate over no-fault insurance is illustrated by the way in which he moves from no liability to strict liability apparently without awareness that these are significantly different principles. In the automobile-accident context no-fault insurance has meant abrogating tort liability and compelling the victim to buy accident insurance. O'Connell rejects such an approach for non-automobile accidents as too costly and proposes instead that manufacturers be permitted to elect to be strictly liable for accidents caused by their products, but at a reduced schedule of damages. The analogy is worker's compensation, not no-fault insurance. But I suspect that to Professor O'Connell worker's compensation, no liability, and strict liability are pretty much the same thing since they all do away with the fault principle which for him is the principal goal of reform.

I shall attempt here, perhaps too briefly, to disentangle what seem to me to be the major policy questions in the legal control of two types of personal injury that O'Connell discusses — injury resulting from a malfunctioning product and injury induced by medical treatment.

These are both areas where the fault principle is firmly embedded and where, while it would be easy to understand what would be meant by a proposal to substitute no liability, the very meaning of "strict liability" is a puzzle. Although we speak of strict liability for product accidents, the term is a misnomer. Liability is limited to defective products and the determination whether a product is defective resembles the usual negligence determination. To be sure, the manufacturer's liability includes defective components supplied by other manufacturers in circumstances where his failure to discover the defect cannot be judged blameworthy; but this aspect of strict liability has its counterpart in respondeat superior in the ordinary negligence context.

What would it mean to say that a manufacturer should be strictly liable for the consequences of accidents resulting from the use of his *non*defective product? If A hits B with a baseball bat, would the manufacturer of the bat be liable for B's injury? Would he be liable if A (nonnegligently) dropped the bat on his own toe? Suppose a manufacturer of tires guaranteed that his tires would not blow out in normal use for 20,000 miles: would he, under O'Connell's proposal, be liable for an accident that occurred after 100,000 miles of normal use, or after 15,000 miles of driving at high speeds over ungraded roads? I assume the answer in all of these cases is "no." But that makes me wonder what exactly Professor O'Connell is proposing. A similar puzzle would arise with respect to a proposal to impose strict liability for medical mishaps. Suppose the proper treatment for some ailment involves a drug that has harmful side effects. Is the physician liable for those side effects? That seems an absurd result. But if he is not liable I do not see what meaning can be assigned the notion of strict liability for injuries arising from medical treatment.

Passing these difficulties, I come to what to me are the fundamental questions that must be answered in designing a system of legal control of personal injuries: what are the likely effects on the safety, and the prices, of products and of medical treatment if manufacturers and health-care providers are made strictly liable for injuries resulting from product use or medical care? At first glance it might appear obvious that enlarging the liability of a seller will induce him to increase the safety of his product, but there are two reasons for doubting that this is necessarily true. First, if the alternative to strict liability is some form of negligence liability and if negligence, roughly speaking, means failure to take cost-justified precautions, why should the imposition of strict liability induce the seller to take additional precautions that cost less than the savings in reduced accident liability? Strict liability will not induce him to take additional precautions — precautions that are by definition not cost-justified to him — since if the savings in reduced liability are smaller than the costs of averting that liability, he is better off accepting the increased liability and forgoing the additional precautions. This assumes, to be sure, that sellers of products and of medical services are rational calculators of their self-interest. I find the assumption quite plausible, as does O'Connell. Certainly the usual arguments made against treating the average automobile driver as nicely calculating the costs and benefits of alternative levels of safety lose much of their force when applied to manufacturers, hospitals, and physicians.

Second, the products and medical-treatment contexts differ from the automobile-accident context in that there is a preexisting seller-buyer relationship between injurer and victim. The seller of a potentially dangerous product can be viewed as selling a combination of two products, one of which has a negative value to the consumer. There is the product itself, but tied to it is the danger of a mishap resulting from its use. The maximum price that the consumer will pay for the product is the sum of the values of these two goods (one a bad). Clearly, the safer the product, other things being equal, the higher the price for the package that the seller can command.

This suggests that the optimum level of product safety will be supplied without any intervention by the legal system, save perhaps to prevent misleading claims relating to product safety. Suppose that the use value of a widget is $1 and the expected accident cost of using the product is one cent.[1] Then the most the consumer will pay for a widget is 99 cents. Suppose that the sort of accident to which widgets are prone occurs and that the consumer sustains an accident that costs him $10,000. Has he cause to complain to the widget producer? He does not. He was compensated for bearing the risk of an accident by being permitted to purchase widgets for 99 cents instead of $1. His situation is the same as that of the person who goes to a baseball game and thereby assumes the risk of being beaned. Presumably if there were no such risk the price of a baseball ticket would be (infinitesimally) higher.

Now suppose that widget producers are made strictly liable for any accidents to consumers using their product. In effect, the widget producer is being forced to sell a new package, consisting of (1) the use value of a widget, (2) the expected accident cost, and (3) an insurance policy against that accident. The value of the new package is $1. But the cost to the consumer has not changed. The higher price simply buys an insurance policy that he would otherwise have had to pay for out of his own pocket. The output of widgets will not be changed, nor will the safety incentives of the widget industry be altered.

This analysis suggests that the choice of the rule of liability is less important in a sales context (including the sale of medical care) than in accidents between persons not in a sales relationship. But it may not be wholly unimportant. There is a rather technical objection to strict liability in the sales context, which I have discussed elsewhere and will not try to go into here; it has to do with differential attitudes toward risk.[2] There is also an objection to no liability. In order for consumers to be able to choose that mixture of use value and danger that maximizes their satisfactions, they have to know something about the relative dangers of competing products. But because product accidents are (happily) extraordinarily infrequent, most consumers have only the vaguest idea of the relative dangers. The producer who has a safer product therefore cannot rely on the consumer to discover its greater safety on his own. The usual method by which producers draw attention to nonobvious improvements in their products is by advertising. But the producer who advertises a safer product runs the risk of alerting the consumer to a danger of which he may have been unaware; after all, saf*er* implies

1. The expected accident cost is the product of the likelihood of an accident's occurring and the cost of an accident if it does occur. A consumer having an aversion to risk would demand greater compensation for bearing this risk than the expected accident cost, and a risk-preferring consumer would be willing to accept less. Thus the example in the text assumes a risk-neutral consumer.

2. Strict liability, assuming that disclaimers of liability are prohibited, in effect forces the producer to insure the consumer against an accident. A risk preferrer, however, prefers the risk of an accident to the certainty of insurance and he is made worse off by a compulsory insurance scheme.

dangerous. Safety advertising is thus a double-edged sword and this may limit not only the amount of such advertising but the incentive to market safer products. Strict liability eliminates this problem by making the consumer's knowledge of product safety irrelevant. Though the consumer has absolutely no knowledge of product danger, strict liability will induce the producer to compare the costs and benefits of possible safety improvements and to introduce those that are cost-justified — those, that is, that will reduce his net liability costs.

A similar problem exists in the medical area, compounded by the great uncertainties that surround many forms of medical treatment and the prohibition against advertising by physicians. While in theory one could dispense with malpractice liability and permit doctors and patients in effect to negotiate the desired standard of care, the incompleteness of the customer's knowledge and the absence of effective channels by which competing health-care providers might communicate the requisite information to the customer may argue for imposing liability for failure to follow standard methods of treatment.

O'Connell would evidently prefer no liability in both the products and medical-care contexts if society would accept the price tag for compulsory accident insurance covering the two areas. But if the foregoing analysis is correct no liability would reduce the incentives to take precautions and would increase the social loss from defective products and improper medical treatment. His proposal for permitting injurers in these areas to limit their liability to what he calls "out-of-pocket" expenses works in the same direction. He seems to think that if strict liability would make an injurer liable in twice as many cases as would negligence liability, but the extent of his liability in each case was halved, nothing would have changed but the distribution of compensation among accident victims. This is incorrect. As suggested earlier, imposing strict liability may not result in any reduction in the total number of accidents. But halving the cost of every accident for which the injurer would be liable under a negligence system will cause him to revise downward the benefits to him of preventing each accident, and with the benefits of precautions now lower, he will take fewer precautions and there will be more accidents. . . .

TABLE OF CASES